CONAN
OMNIBUS

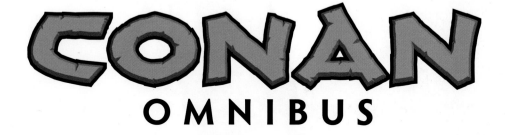

GARY NORD   DAVE STEWART

CONAN OMNIBUS

BIRTH OF THE LEGEND

SCRIPTS
KURT BUSIEK

ART
CARY NORD
GREG RUTH
THOMAS YEATES
TOM MANDRAKE

COLORS
DAVE STEWART
GREG RUTH

LETTERING
RICHARD STARKINGS AND
COMICRAFT'S ALBERT DESCHESNE

COVER ART
JOSEPH MICHAEL LINSNER

CREATOR OF CONAN
ROBERT E. HOWARD

Dark Horse Books

PUBLISHER **MIKE RICHARDSON**   SERIES EDITORS **SCOTT ALLIE** ◎ **MATT DRYER**

SERIES ASSISTANT EDITORS **JEREMY BARLOW** ◎ **MATT DRYER** ◎ **RYAN JORGENSEN** ◎ **DAVE MARSHALL**

COLLECTION EDITOR **AARON WALKER**   COLLECTION ASSISTANT EDITOR **RACHEL ROBERTS**

DESIGNER **DAVID NESTELLE**   DIGITAL ART TECHNICIAN **ADAM PRUETT**

Special thanks to Joakim Zetterberg and Fredrik Malmberg at Conan Properties.

This volume collects issues #0–#15, #23, #32, #45, and #46 of the Dark Horse Comics monthly *Conan* series.

Published by Dark Horse Books
A division of Dark Horse Comics, Inc.
10956 SE Main Street
Milwaukie, OR 97222

DarkHorse.com

Library of Congress Cataloging-in-Publication Data

Names: Busiek, Kurt, author. | Nord, Cary, artist. | Ruth, Greg, artist. |
Yeates, Thomas, artist. | Mandrake, Tom, 1956- artist. | Stewart, Dave,
colorist. | Starkings, Richard, letterer. | Linsner, Joseph Michael, 1968-
artist. | Howard, Robert E. (Robert Ervin), 1906-1936, creator. |
Comicraft (Firm), letterer.
Title: Conan omnibus. Volume 1, Birth of the legend / scripts, Kurt Busiek ;
art, Cary Nord, Greg Ruth, Thomas Yeates, Tom Mandrake ; colors, Dave
Stewart, Greg Ruth ; lettering, Richard Starkings and ComiCraft ; cover
art, Joseph Michael Linsner ; creator of Conan, Robert E. Howard.
Other titles: Birth of the legend
Description: First edition. | Milwaukie, OR : Dark Horse Books, 2016. |
"Contains Conan Volume 0 (Born on the Battlefield), Volume 1 (The Frost
Giants Daughter) and Volume 2 (The God in the Bowl)"
Identifiers: LCCN 2016030332 | ISBN 9781506702827 (paperback)
Subjects: LCSH: Comic books, strips, etc. | BISAC: COMICS & GRAPHIC NOVELS /
Fantasy. | FICTION / Fantasy / General.
Classification: LCC PN6728.C65 B9 2016 | DDC 741.5/973--dc23
LC record available at https://lccn.loc.gov/2016030332

International Licensing: (503) 905-2377
To find a comics shop in your area, call the
Comic Shop Locator Service toll-free at 1-888-266-4226.

First edition: December 2016
ISBN 978-1-50670-282-7

1 3 5 7 9 10 8 6 4 2
Printed in China

PROLOGUE

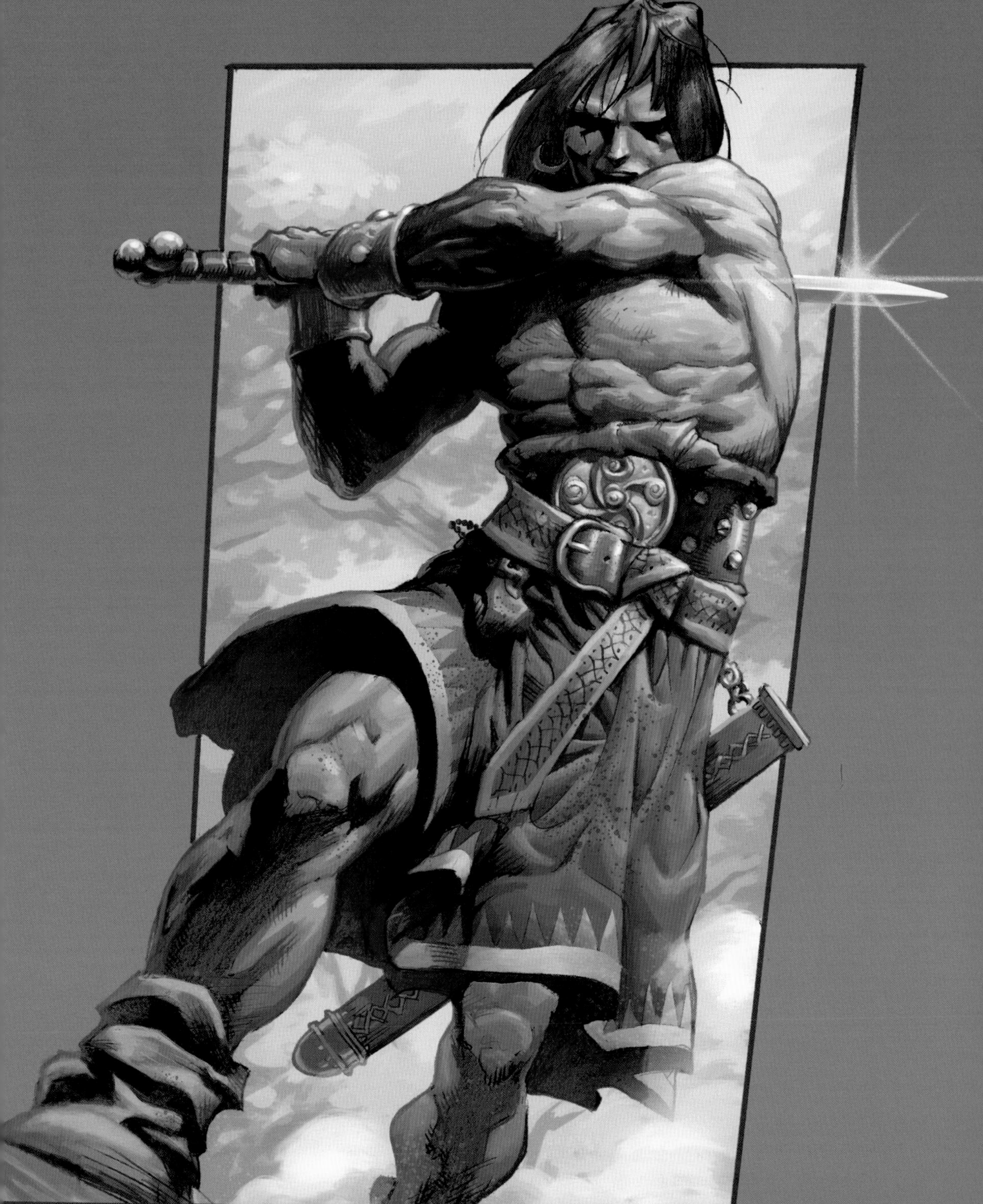

Illustration by **CARY NORD** and **DAVE STEWART**

THE LEGEND

SCRIPT
KURT BUSIEK

ART
CARY NORD

COLORS
DAVE STEWART

LETTERING
RICHARD STARKINGS
AND **COMICRAFT**

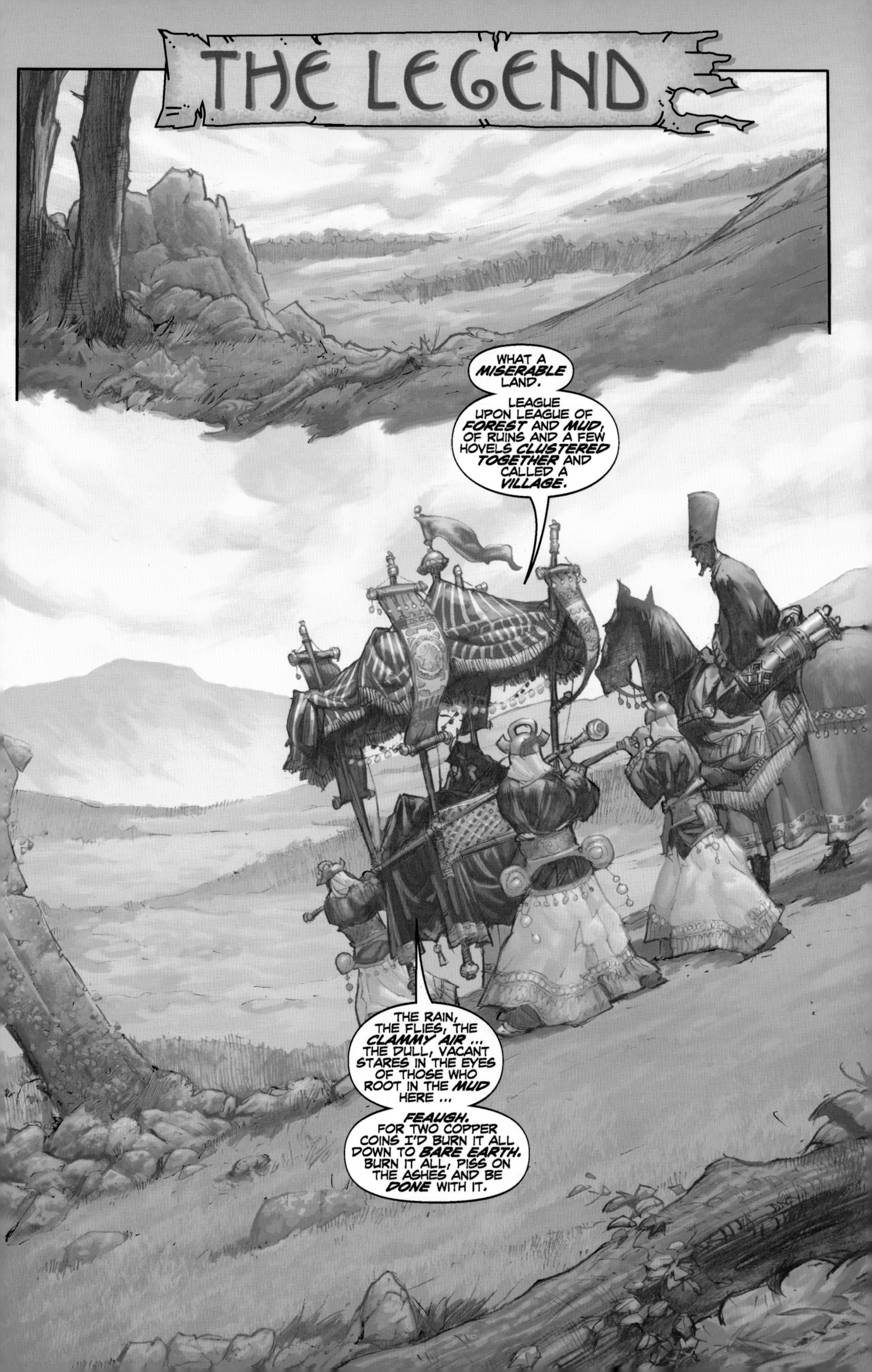
THE LEGEND
WHAT A MISERABLE LAND.
LEAGUE UPON LEAGUE OF FOREST AND MUD, OF RUINS AND A FEW HOVELS CLUSTERED TOGETHER AND CALLED A VILLAGE.
THE RAIN, THE FLIES, THE CLAMMY AIR ... THE DULL, VACANT STARES IN THE EYES OF THOSE WHO ROOT IN THE MUD HERE ...
FEAUGH. FOR TWO COPPER COINS I'D BURN IT ALL DOWN TO BARE EARTH. BURN IT ALL, PISS ON THE ASHES AND BE DONE WITH IT.

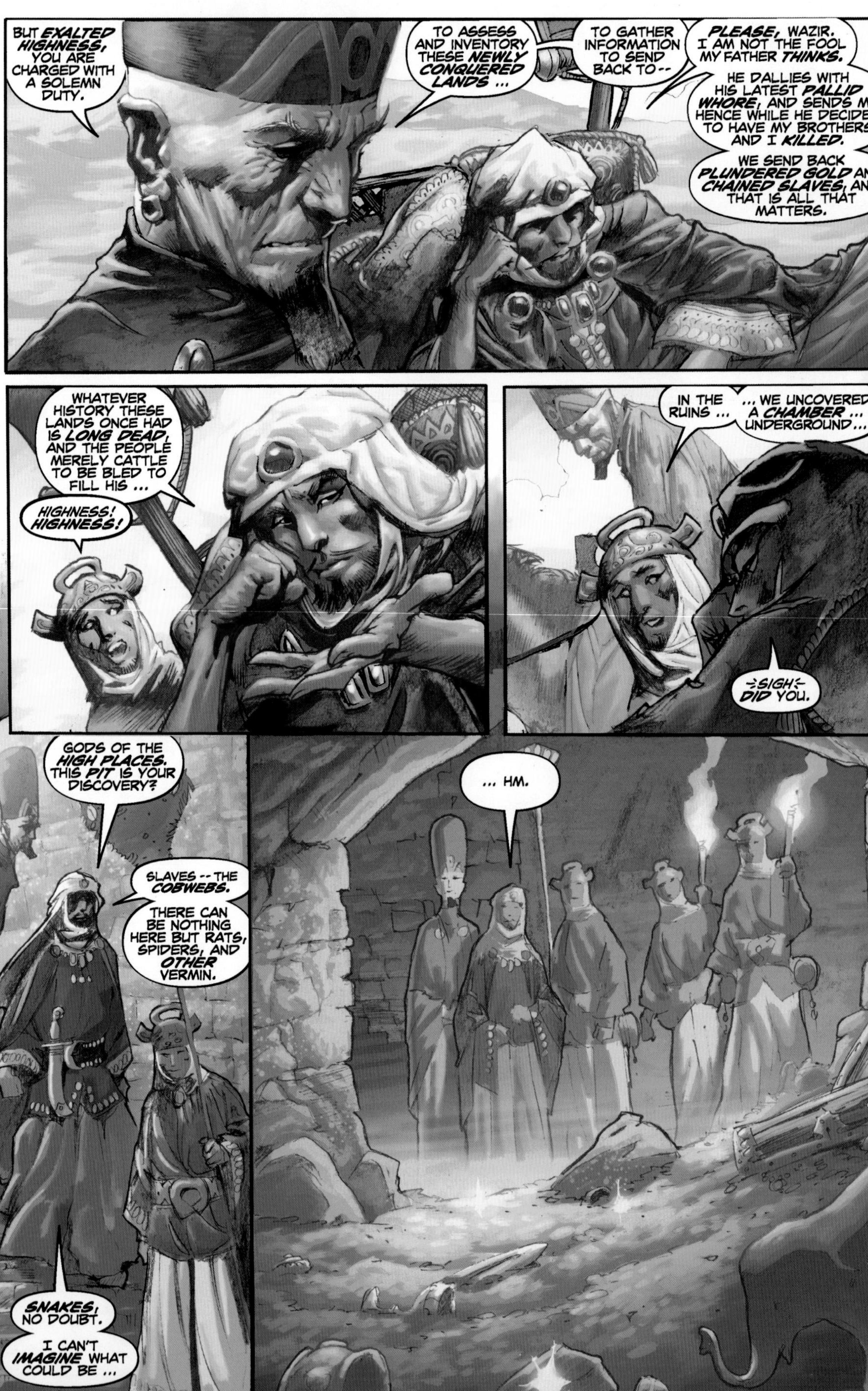
BUT EXALTED HIGHNESS, YOU ARE CHARGED WITH A SOLEMN DUTY.
TO ASSESS AND INVENTORY THESE NEWLY CONQUERED LANDS ...
TO GATHER INFORMATION TO SEND BACK TO --
PLEASE, WAZIR. I AM NOT THE FOOL MY FATHER THINKS.
HE DALLIES WITH HIS LATEST PALLID WHORE, AND SENDS ME HENCE WHILE HE DECIDES TO HAVE MY BROTHERS AND I KILLED.
WE SEND BACK PLUNDERED GOLD AND CHAINED SLAVES, AND THAT IS ALL THAT MATTERS.
WHATEVER HISTORY THESE LANDS ONCE HAD IS LONG DEAD, AND THE PEOPLE MERELY CATTLE TO BE BLED TO FILL HIS ...
HIGHNESS! HIGHNESS!
IN THE RUINS ...
... WE UNCOVERED A CHAMBER ... UNDERGROUND ...
-SIGH- DID YOU.
GODS OF THE HIGH PLACES. THIS PIT IS YOUR DISCOVERY?
SLAVES -- THE COBWEBS.
THERE CAN BE NOTHING HERE BUT RATS, SPIDERS, AND OTHER VERMIN.
SNAKES, NO DOUBT.
I CAN'T IMAGINE WHAT COULD BE ...
... HM.

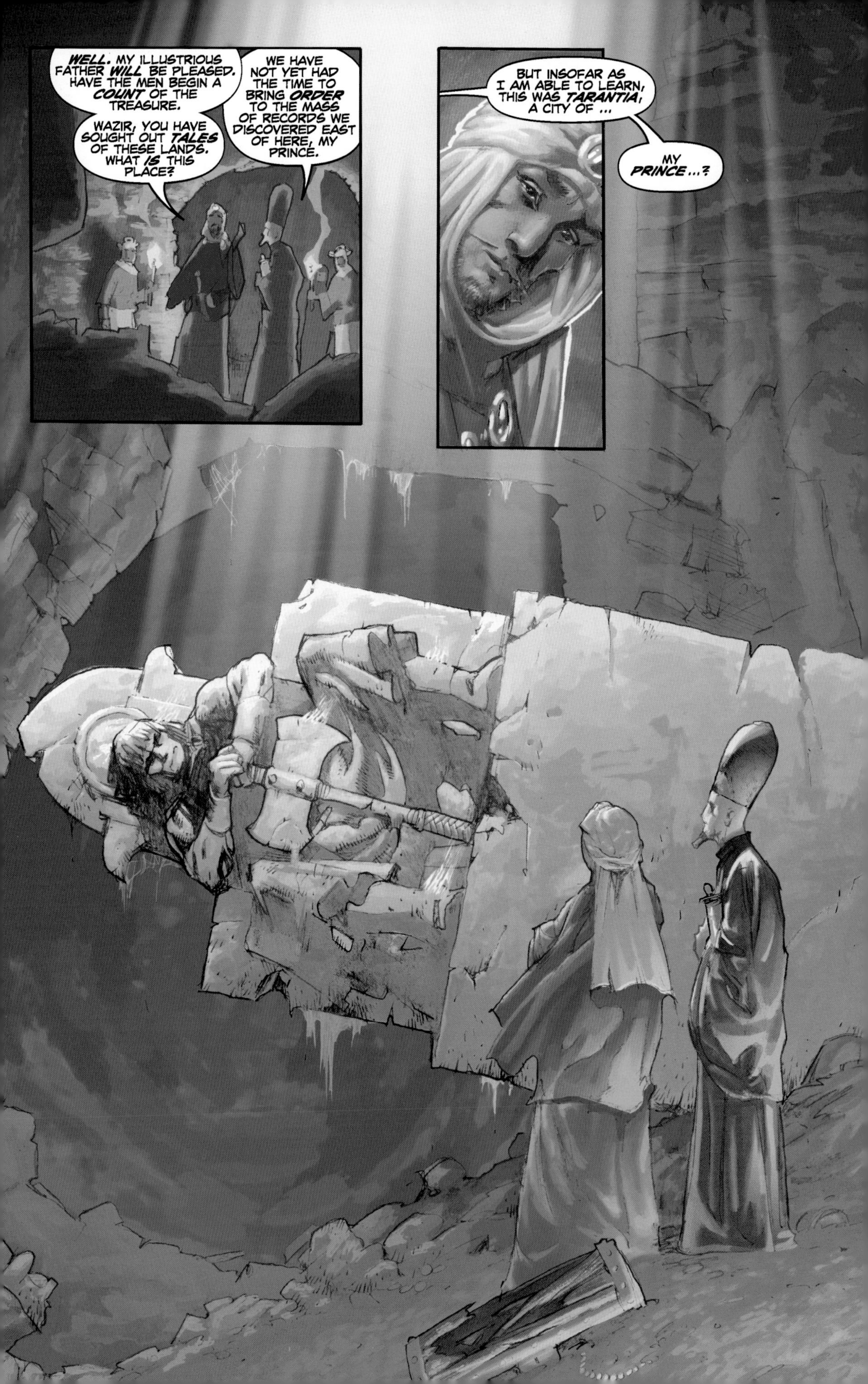
WELL. MY ILLUSTRIOUS FATHER WILL BE PLEASED. HAVE THE MEN BEGIN A COUNT OF THE TREASURE.
WAZIR, YOU HAVE SOUGHT OUT TALES OF THESE LANDS. WHAT IS THIS PLACE?
WE HAVE NOT YET HAD THE TIME TO BRING ORDER TO THE MASS OF RECORDS WE DISCOVERED EAST OF HERE, MY PRINCE.
BUT INSOFAR AS I AM ABLE TO LEARN, THIS WAS TARANTIA, A CITY OF ...
MY PRINCE ...?

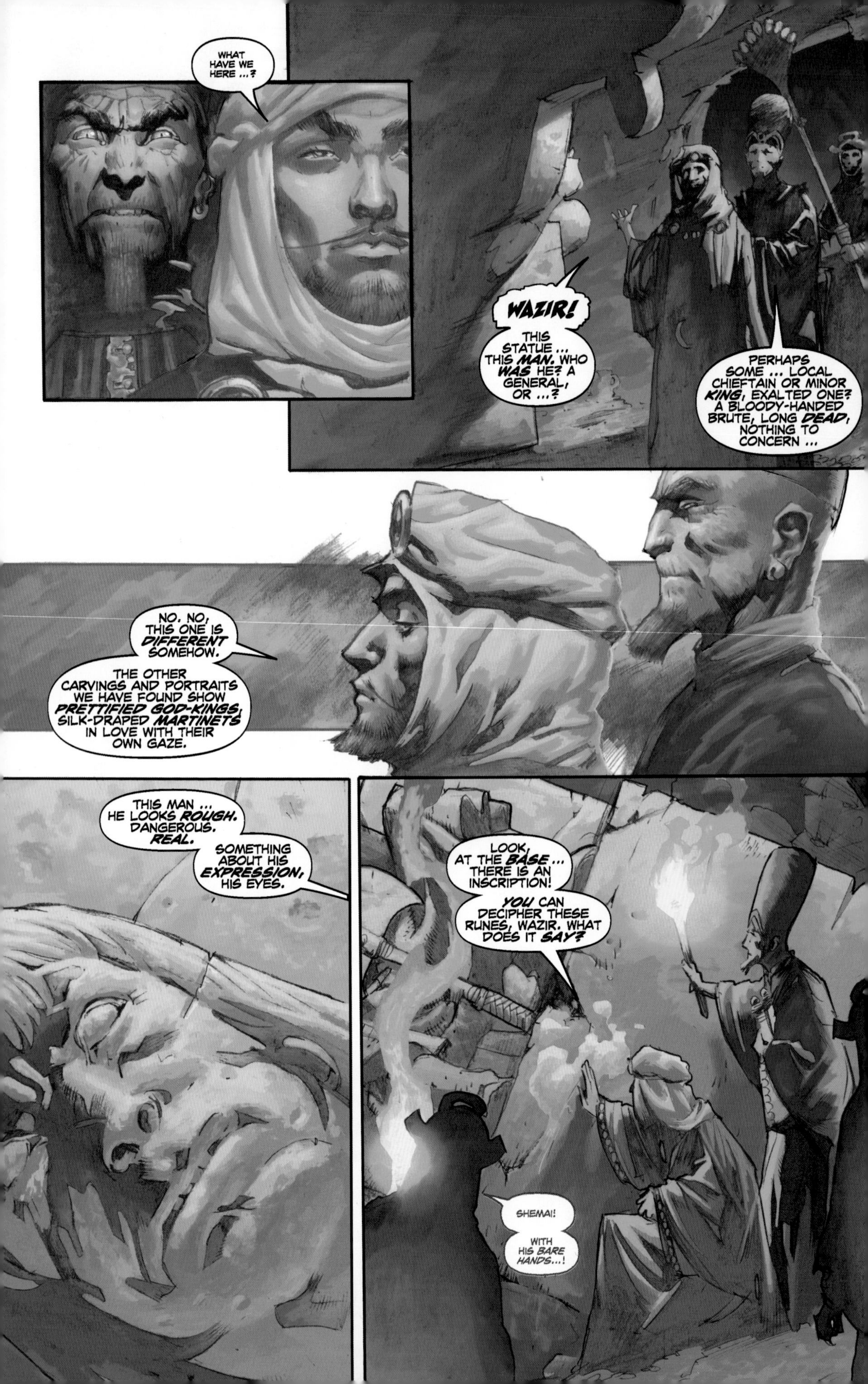

WHAT HAVE WE HERE ...?
WAZIR!
THIS STATUE ... THIS MAN. WHO WAS HE? A GENERAL, OR ...?
PERHAPS SOME ... LOCAL CHIEFTAIN OR MINOR KING, EXALTED ONE? A BLOODY-HANDED BRUTE, LONG DEAD, NOTHING TO CONCERN ...
NO. NO, THIS ONE IS DIFFERENT SOMEHOW.
THE OTHER CARVINGS AND PORTRAITS WE HAVE FOUND SHOW PRETTIFIED GOD-KINGS, SILK-DRAPED MARTINETS IN LOVE WITH THEIR OWN GAZE.
THIS MAN ... HE LOOKS ROUGH. DANGEROUS. REAL.
SOMETHING ABOUT HIS EXPRESSION, HIS EYES.
LOOK, AT THE BASE ... THERE IS AN INSCRIPTION!
YOU CAN DECIPHER THESE RUNES, WAZIR. WHAT DOES IT SAY?
SHEMAI!
WITH HIS BARE HANDS ...!

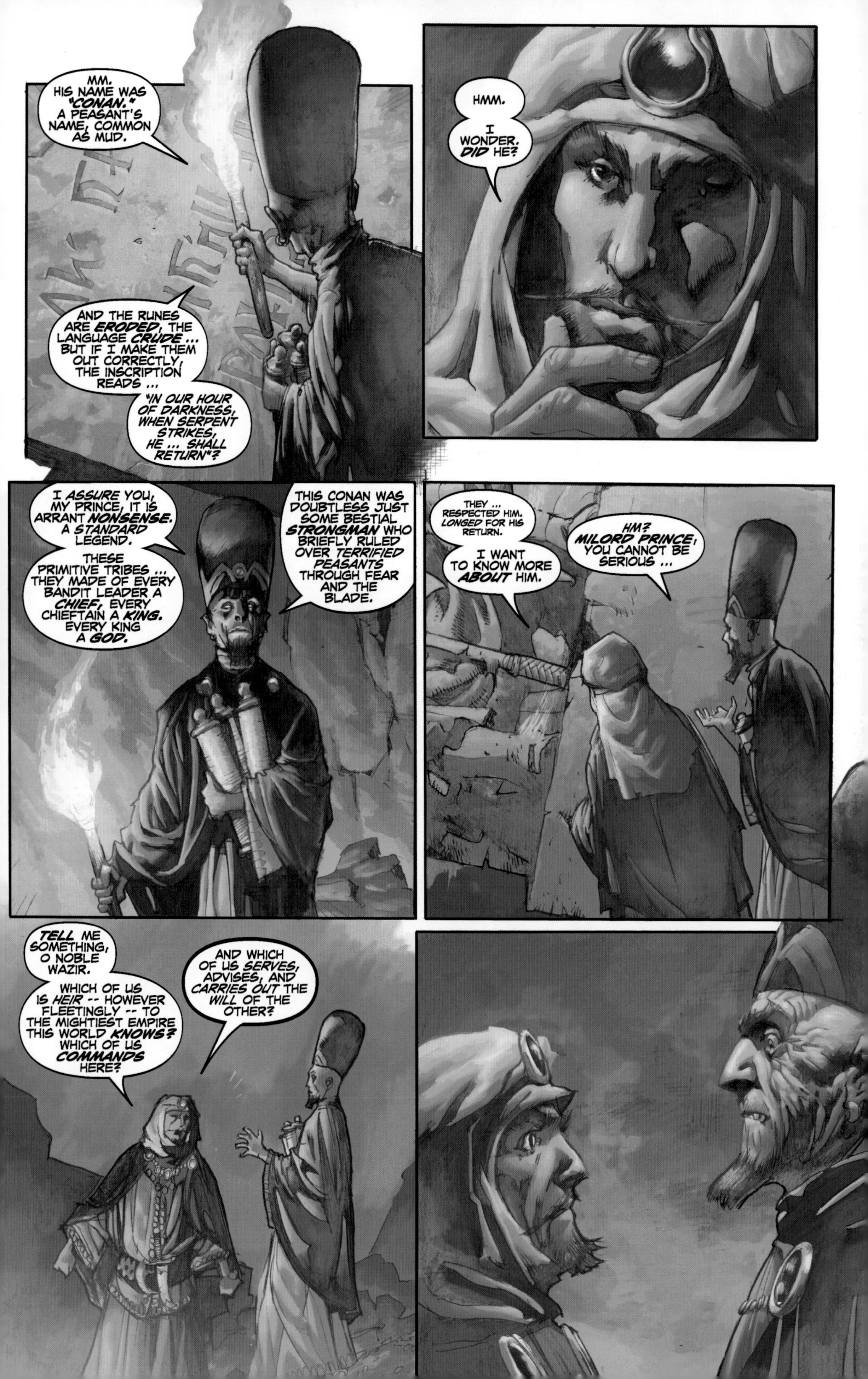
MM. HIS NAME WAS "CONAN." A PEASANT'S NAME, COMMON AS MUD.
AND THE RUNES ARE ERODED, THE LANGUAGE CRUDE ... BUT IF I MAKE THEM OUT CORRECTLY, THE INSCRIPTION READS ...
"IN OUR HOUR OF DARKNESS, WHEN SERPENT STRIKES, HE ... SHALL RETURN"?
HMM.
I WONDER. DID HE?
I ASSURE YOU, MY PRINCE, IT IS ARRANT NONSENSE. A STANDARD LEGEND.
THESE PRIMITIVE TRIBES ... THEY MADE OF EVERY BANDIT LEADER A CHIEF, EVERY CHIEFTAIN A KING. EVERY KING A GOD.
THIS CONAN WAS DOUBTLESS JUST SOME BESTIAL STRONGMAN WHO BRIEFLY RULED OVER TERRIFIED PEASANTS THROUGH FEAR AND THE BLADE.
THEY ... RESPECTED HIM. LONGED FOR HIS RETURN.
I WANT TO KNOW MORE ABOUT HIM.
HM? MILORD PRINCE, YOU CANNOT BE SERIOUS ...
TELL ME SOMETHING, O NOBLE WAZIR.
WHICH OF US IS HEIR -- HOWEVER FLEETINGLY -- TO THE MIGHTIEST EMPIRE THIS WORLD KNOWS? WHICH OF US COMMANDS HERE?
AND WHICH OF US SERVES, ADVISES, AND CARRIES OUT THE WILL OF THE OTHER?

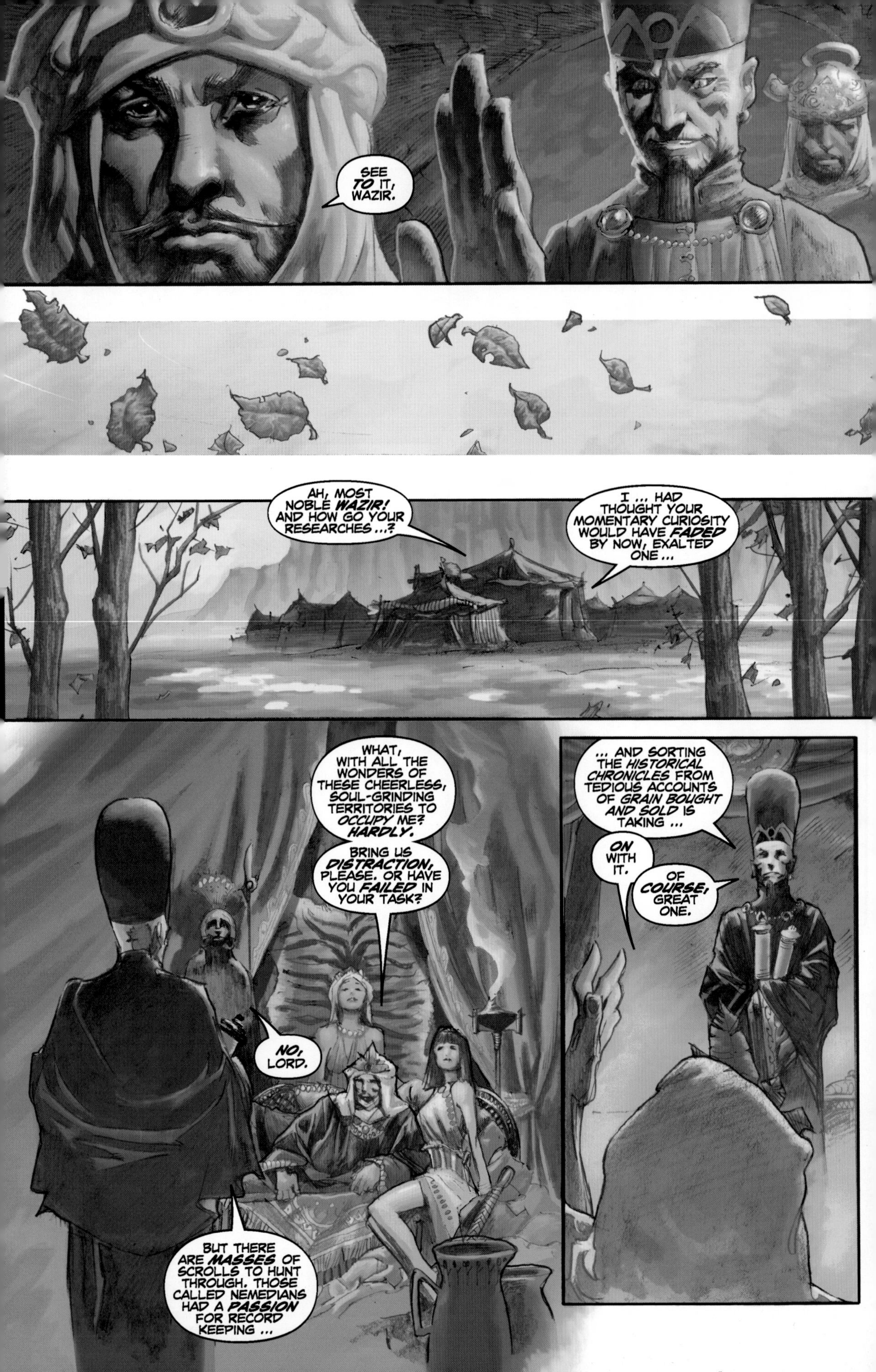
SEE *TO* IT, WAZIR.
AH, MOST NOBLE *WAZIR!* AND HOW GO YOUR RESEARCHES ...?
I ... HAD THOUGHT YOUR MOMENTARY CURIOSITY WOULD HAVE *FADED* BY NOW, EXALTED ONE ...
WHAT, WITH ALL THE WONDERS OF THESE CHEERLESS, SOUL-GRINDING TERRITORIES TO *OCCUPY* ME? *HARDLY.*
BRING US *DISTRACTION,* PLEASE. OR HAVE YOU *FAILED* IN YOUR TASK?
NO, LORD.
BUT THERE ARE *MASSES* OF SCROLLS TO HUNT THROUGH. THOSE CALLED NEMEDIANS HAD A *PASSION* FOR RECORD KEEPING ...
... AND SORTING THE *HISTORICAL CHRONICLES* FROM TEDIOUS ACCOUNTS OF *GRAIN BOUGHT AND SOLD* IS TAKING ...
ON WITH IT.
OF *COURSE,* GREAT ONE.

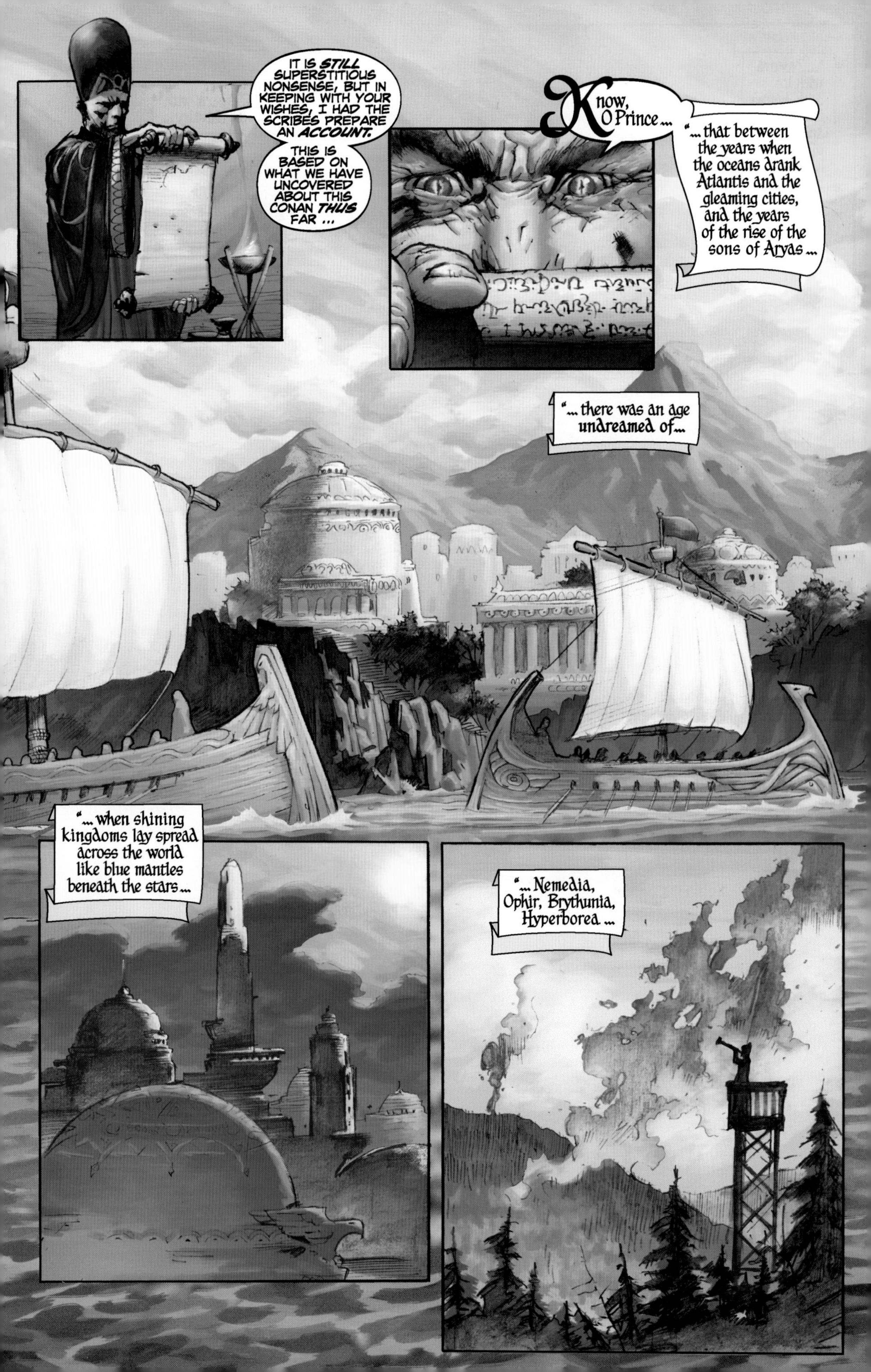

IT IS STILL SUPERSTITIOUS NONSENSE, BUT IN KEEPING WITH YOUR WISHES, I HAD THE SCRIBES PREPARE AN ACCOUNT.
THIS IS BASED ON WHAT WE HAVE UNCOVERED ABOUT THIS CONAN THUS FAR ...
Know, O Prince ...
"... that between the years when the oceans drank Atlantis and the gleaming cities, and the years of the rise of the sons of Aryas ...
"... there was an age undreamed of...
"... when shining kingdoms lay spread across the world like blue mantles beneath the stars ...
"... Nemedia, Ophir, Brythunia, Hyperborea ...

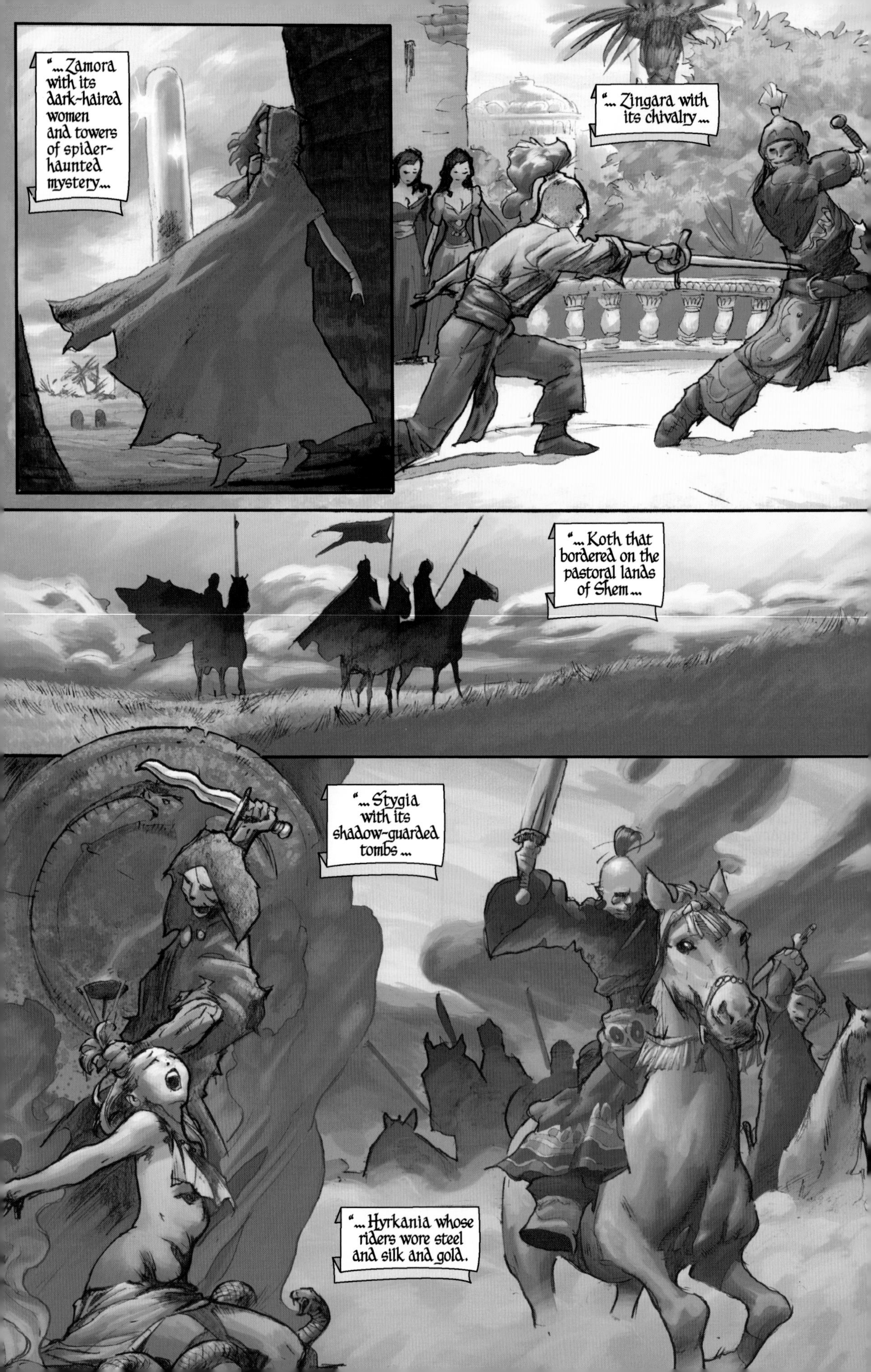
"... Zamora with its dark-haired women and towers of spider-haunted mystery...
"... Zingara with its chivalry ...
"... Koth that bordered on the pastoral lands of Shem ...
"... Stygia with its shadow-guarded tombs ...
"... Hyrkania whose riders wore steel and silk and gold.

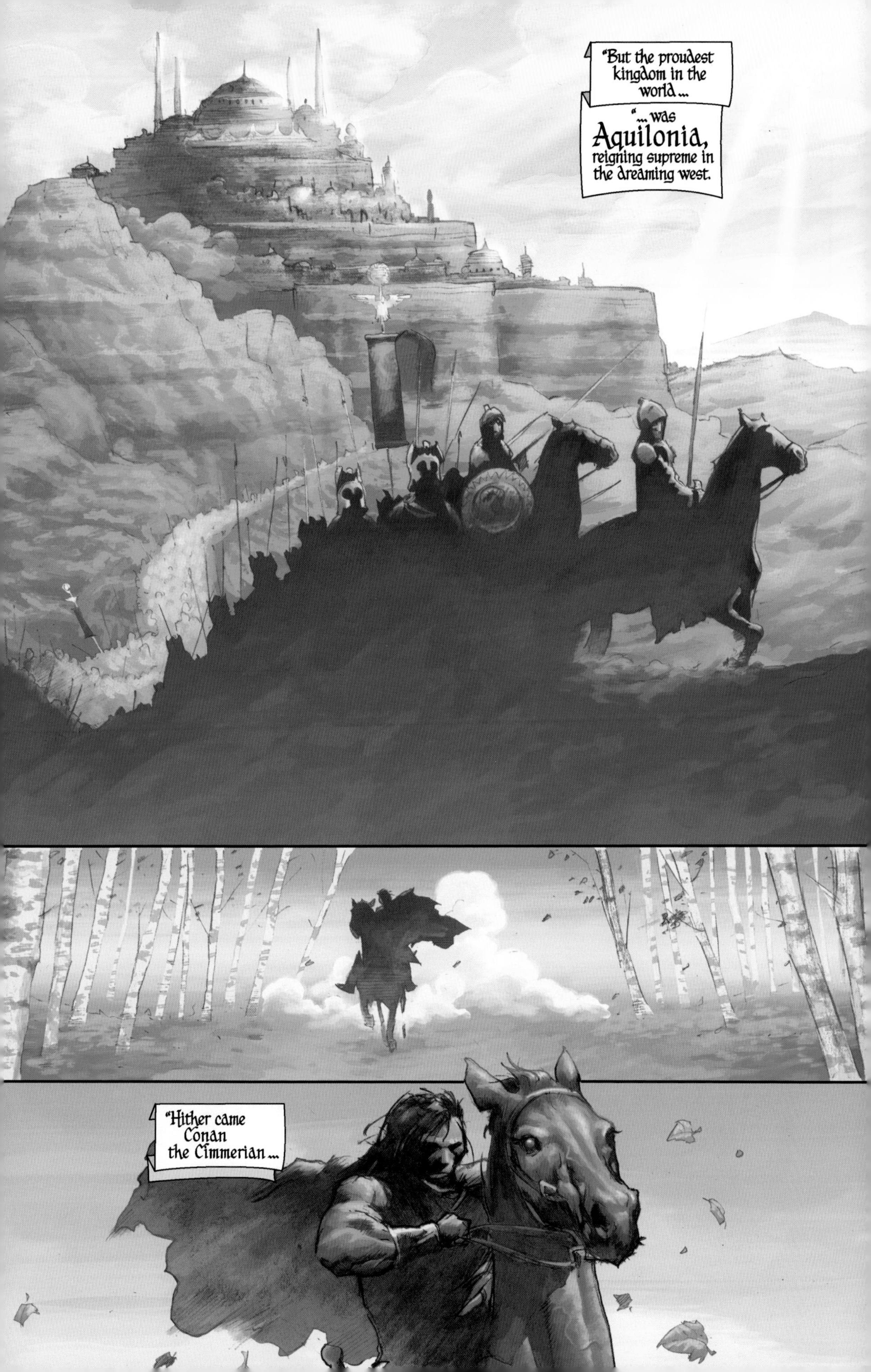
"But the proudest kingdom in the world...
"... was Aquilonia, reigning supreme in the dreaming west.
"Hither came Conan the Cimmerian...

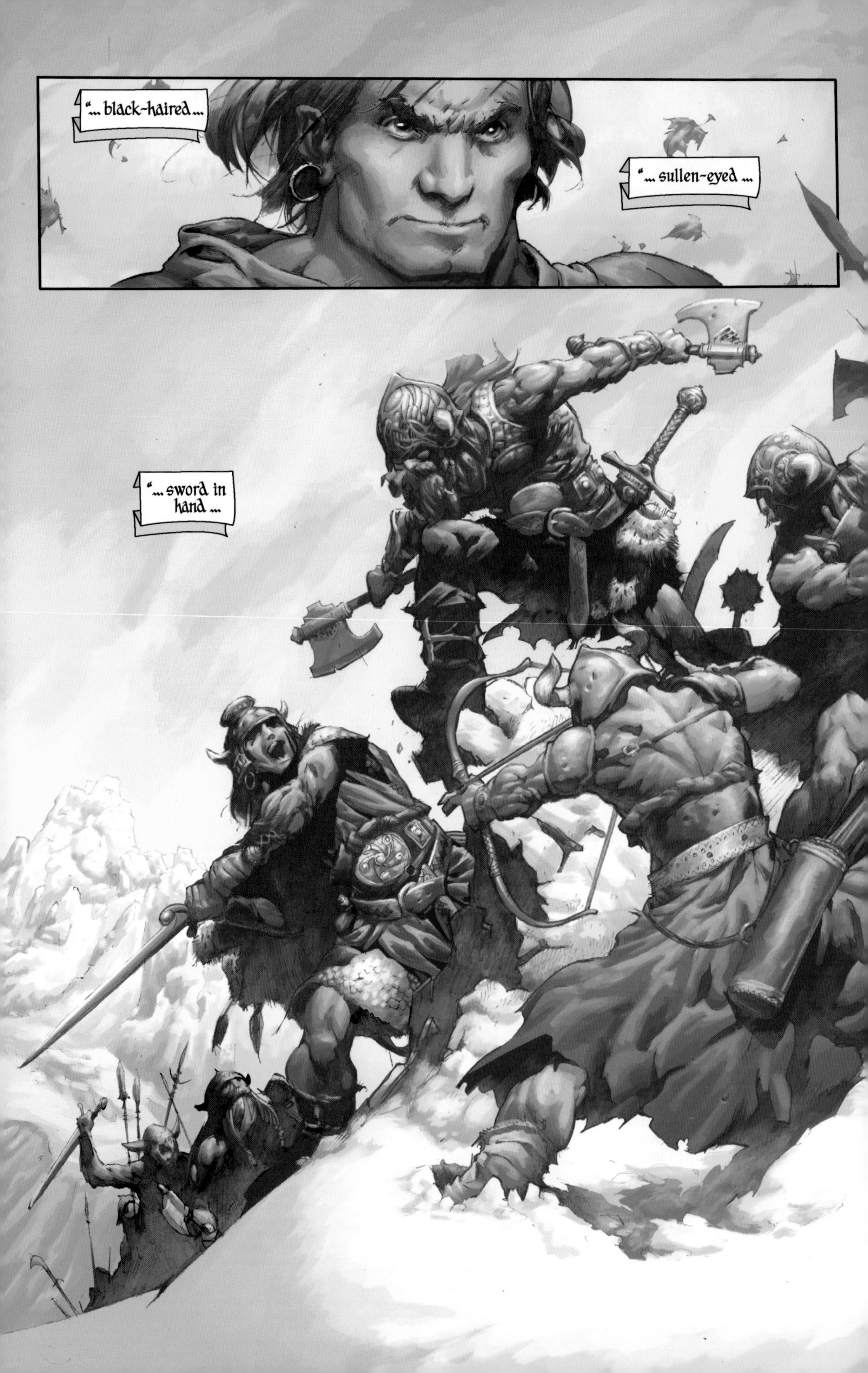
"... black-haired ...
"... sullen-eyed ...
"... sword in hand ...

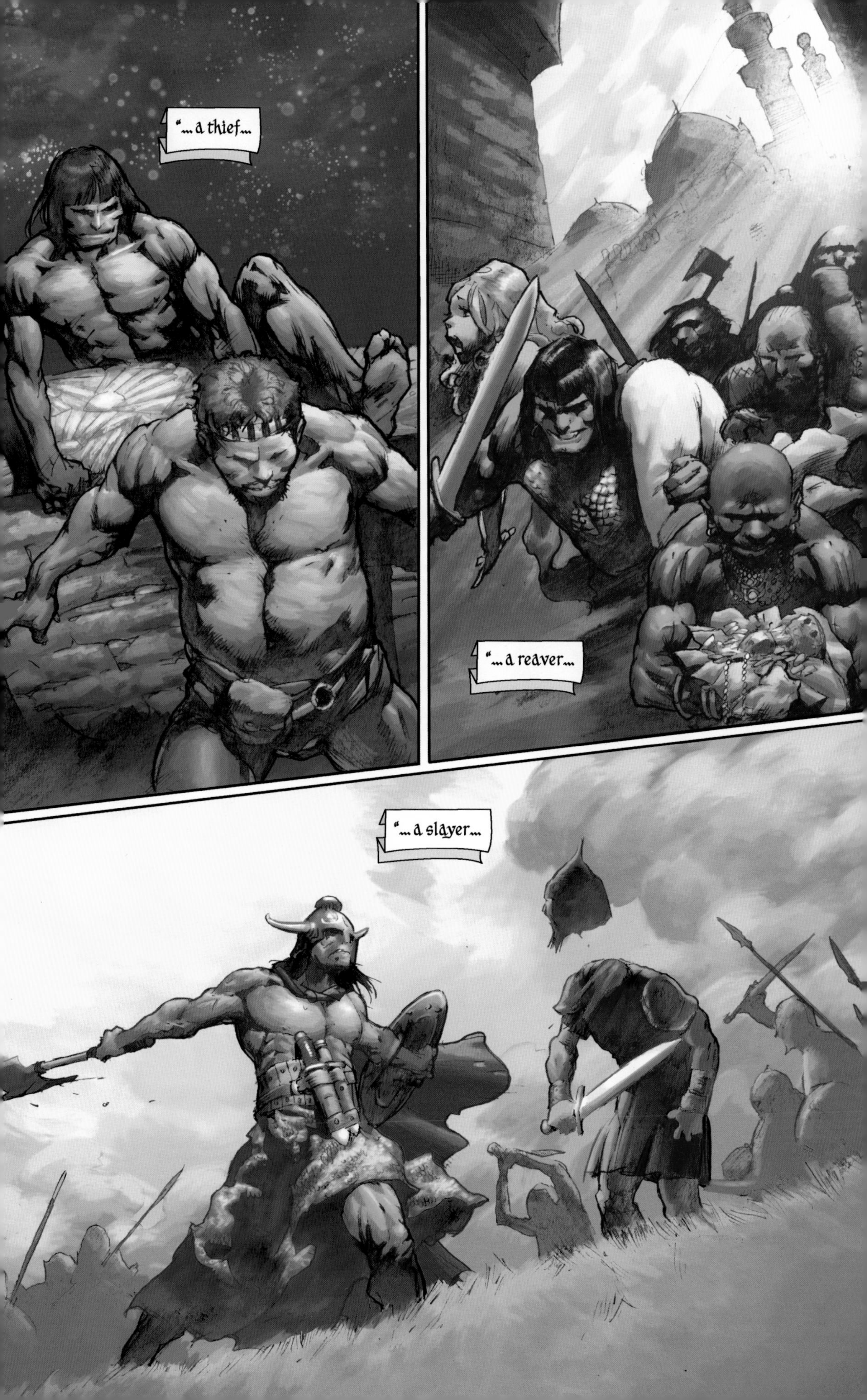
"... a thief...
"... a reaver...
"... a slayer...

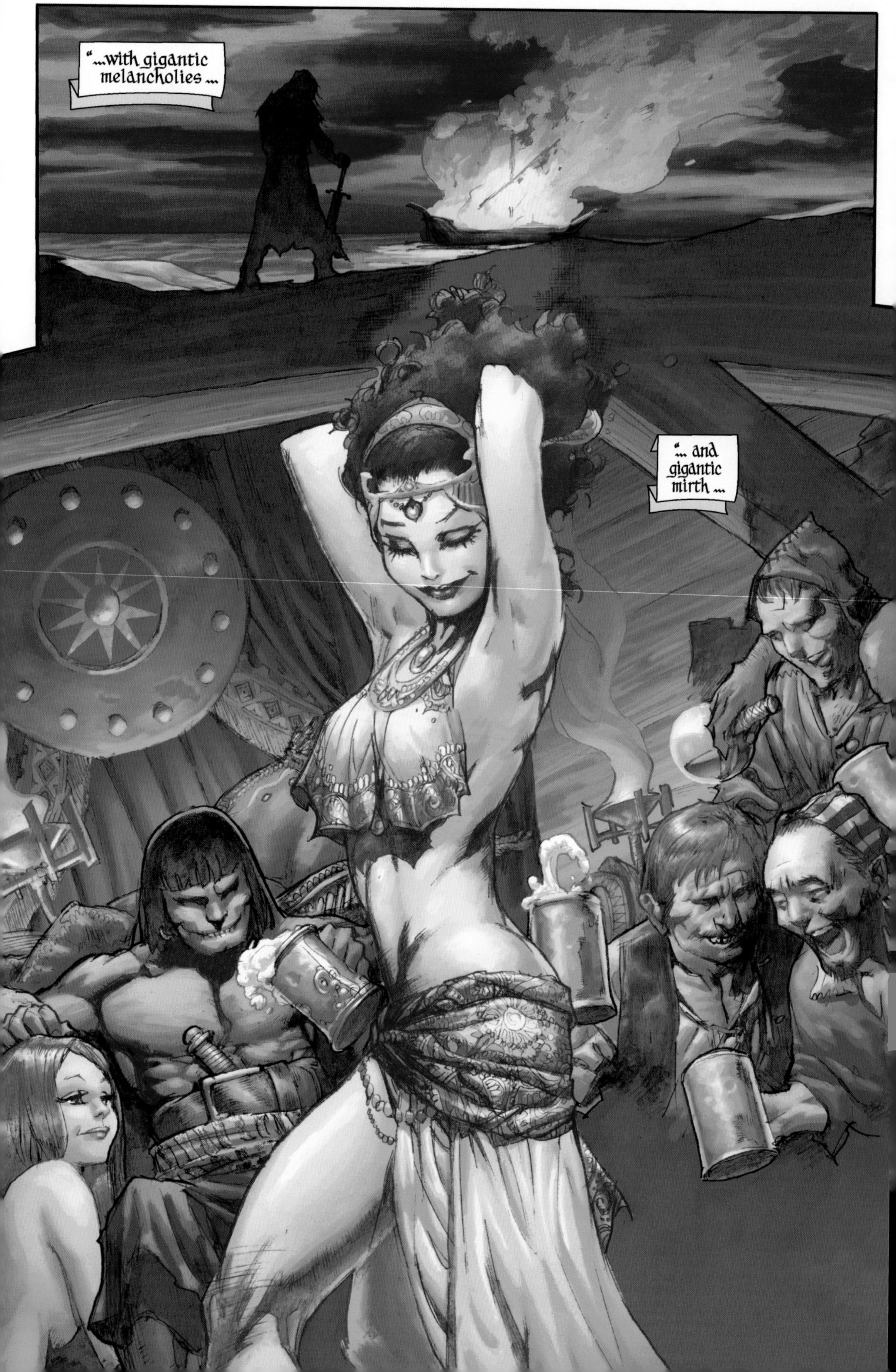
"...with gigantic melancholies...
"... and gigantic mirth...

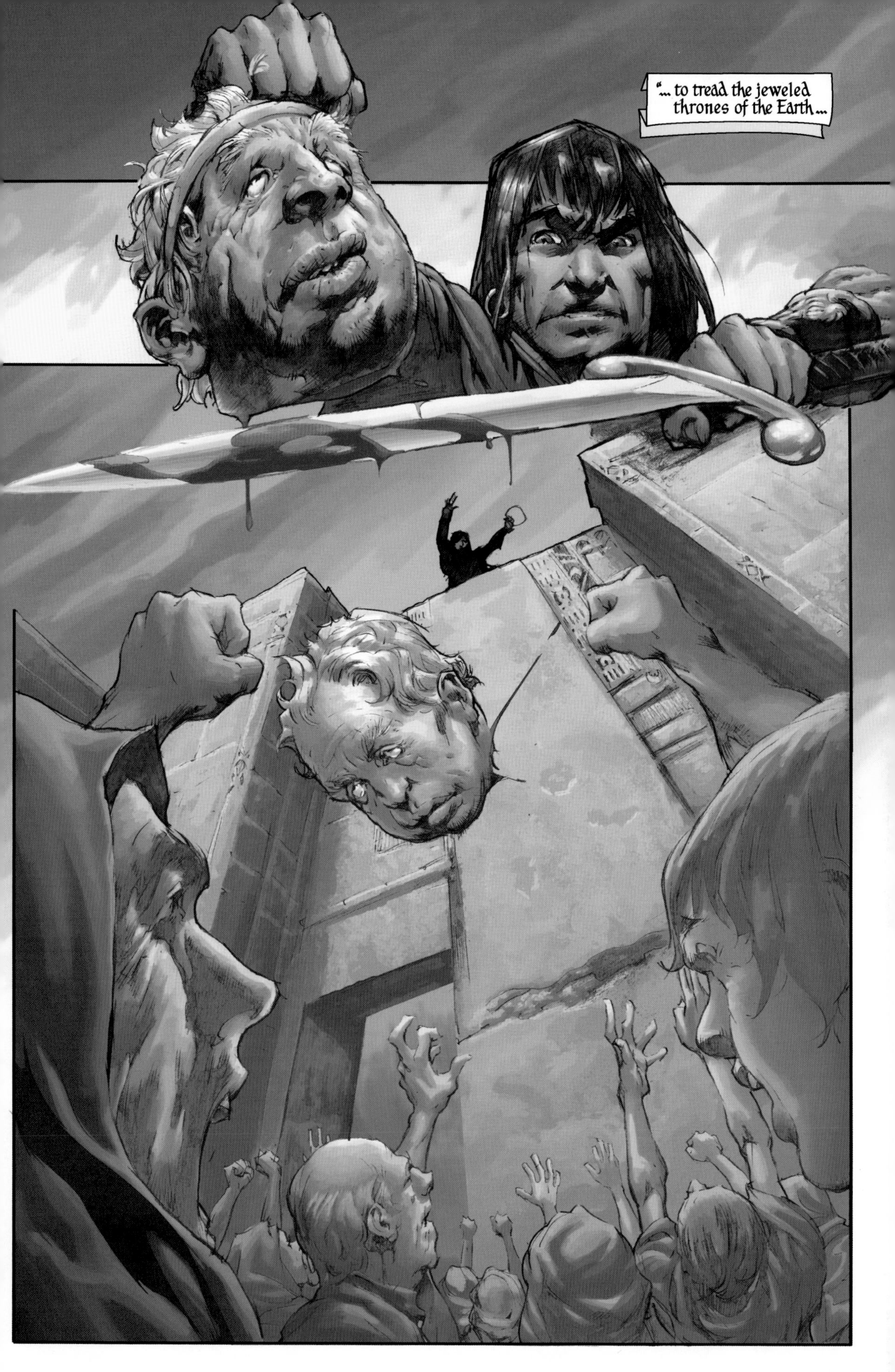
"... to tread the jeweled thrones of the Earth...

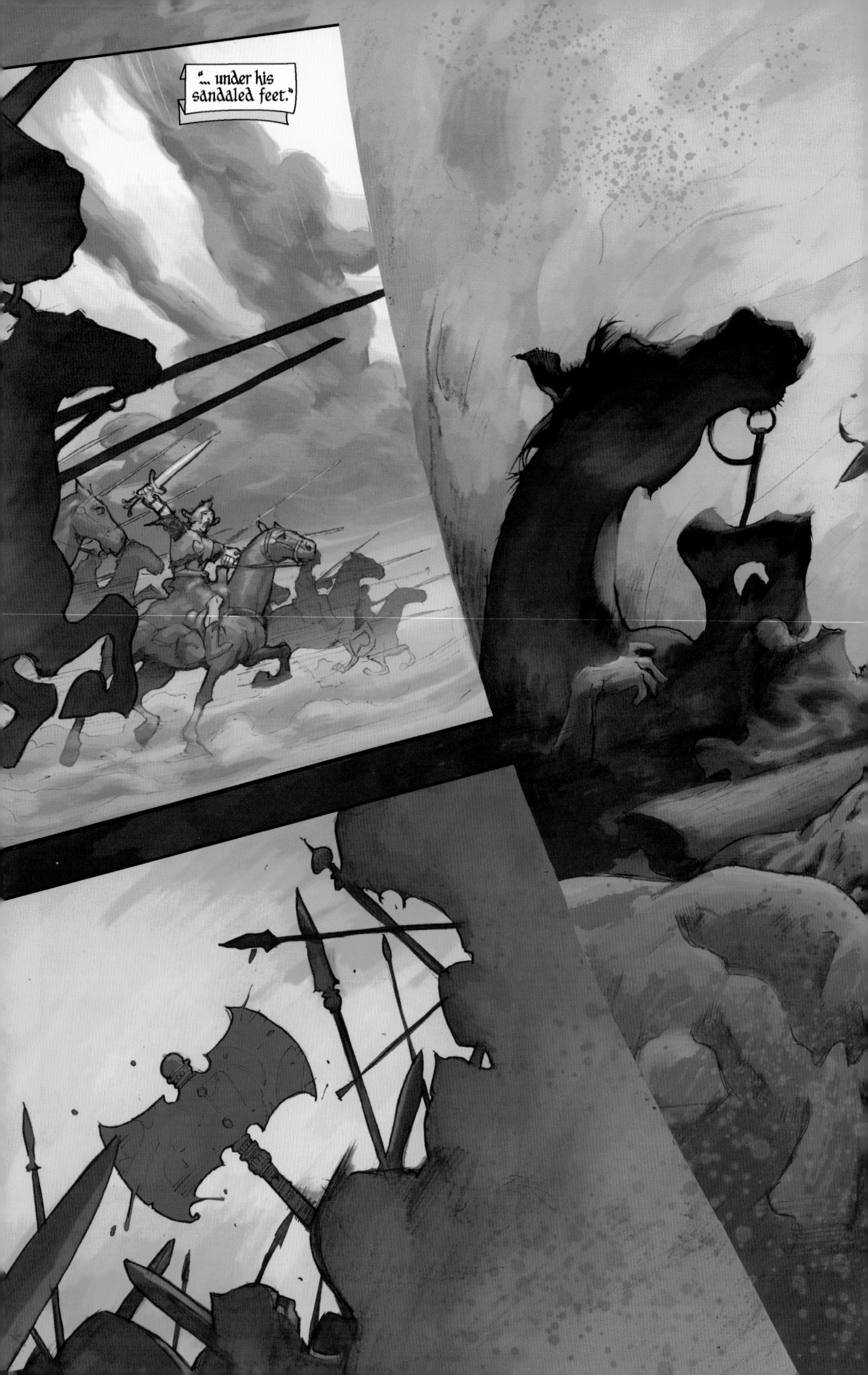
"... under his sandaled feet."

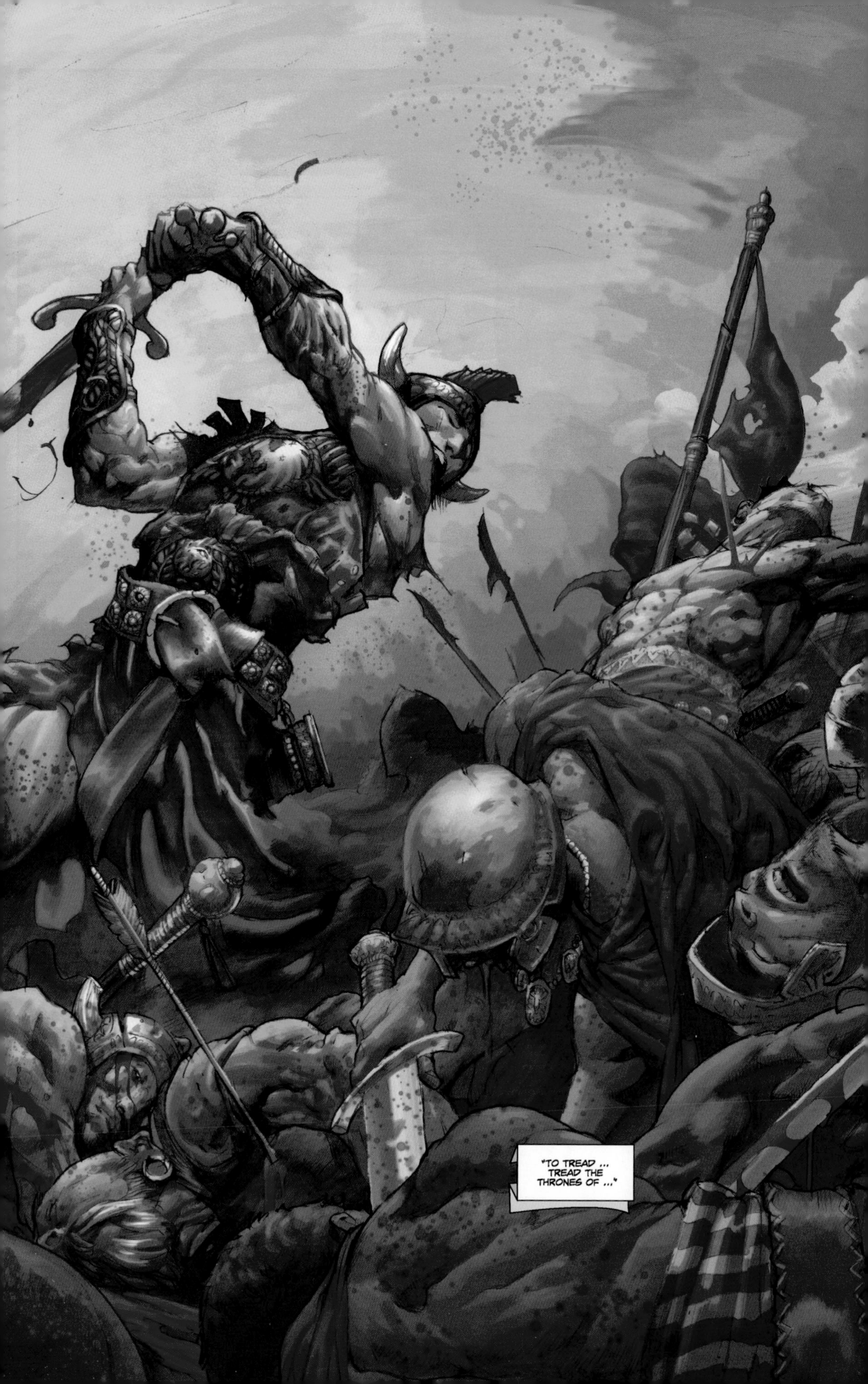
"TO TREAD ... TREAD THE THRONES OF ..."

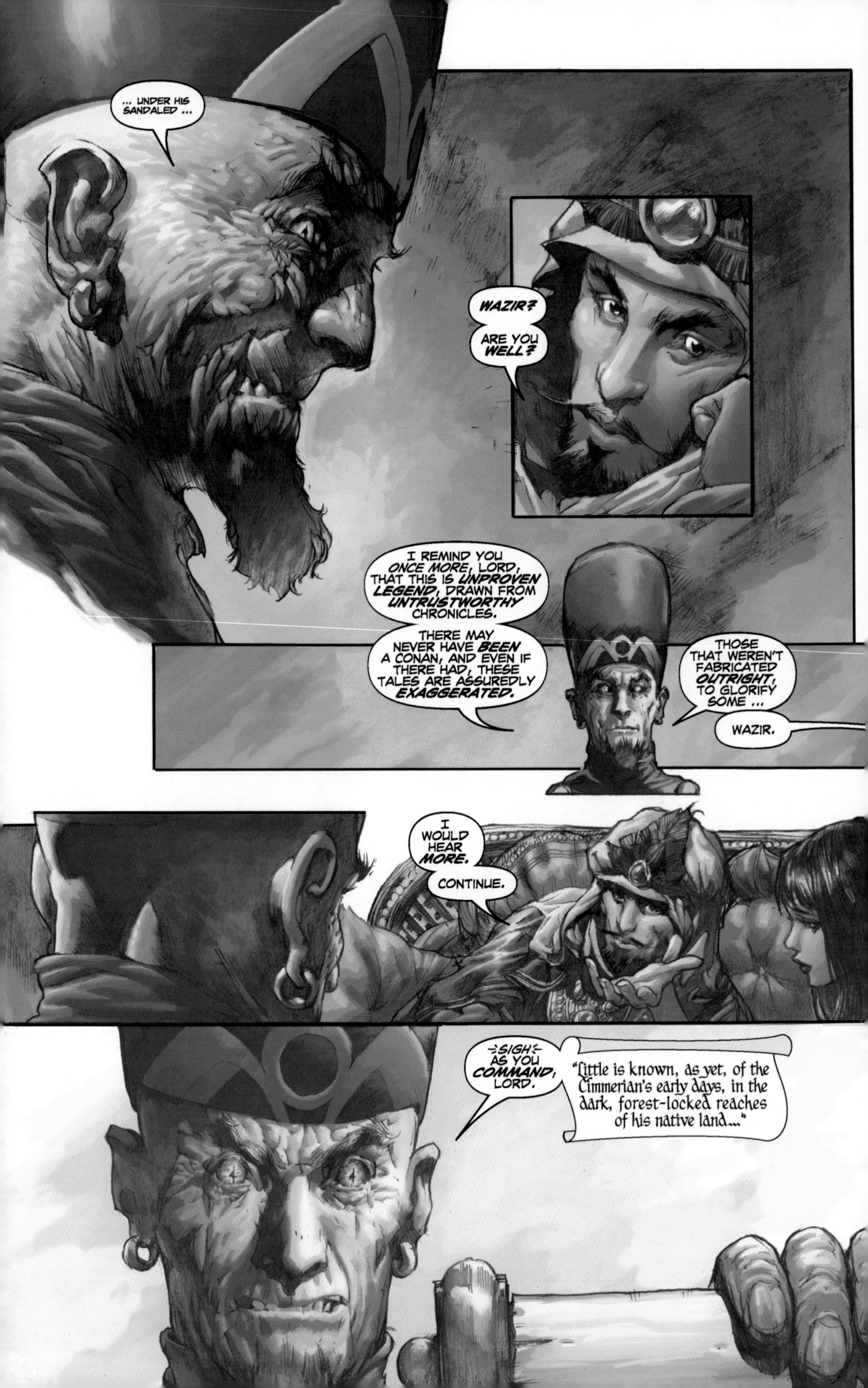
... UNDER HIS SANDALED ...
WAZIR?
ARE YOU WELL?
I REMIND YOU ONCE MORE, LORD, THAT THIS IS UNPROVEN LEGEND, DRAWN FROM UNTRUSTWORTHY CHRONICLES.
THERE MAY NEVER HAVE BEEN A CONAN, AND EVEN IF THERE HAD, THESE TALES ARE ASSUREDLY EXAGGERATED.
THOSE THAT WEREN'T FABRICATED OUTRIGHT, TO GLORIFY SOME ...
WAZIR.
I WOULD HEAR MORE.
CONTINUE.
-SIGH- AS YOU COMMAND, LORD.
"Little is known, as yet, of the Cimmerian's early days, in the dark, forest-locked reaches of his native land..."

PART ONE

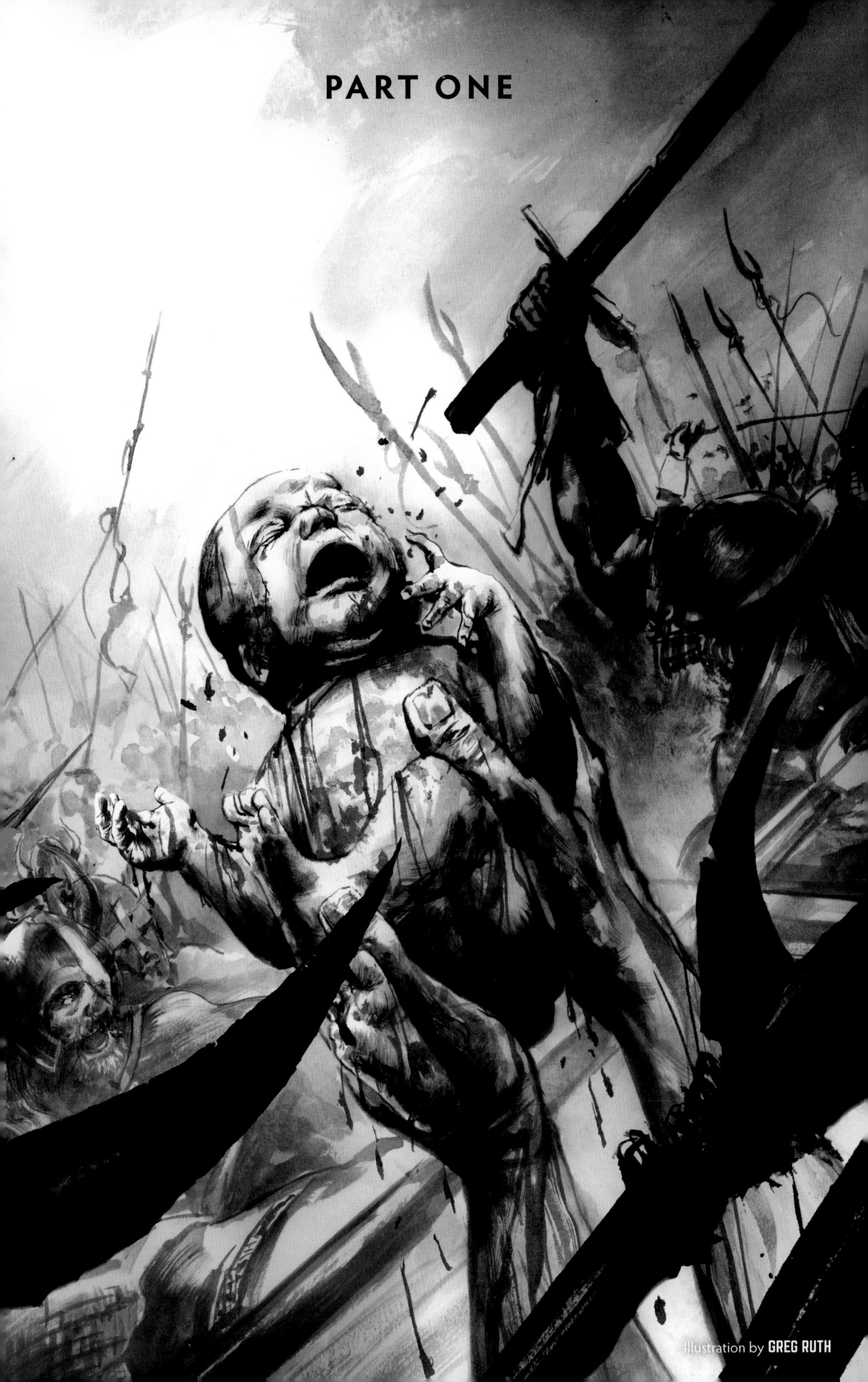

Illustration by **GREG RUTH**

BORN ON THE BATTLEFIELD

SCRIPTS
KURT BUSIEK

ART
GREG RUTH

LETTERING
RICHARD STARKINGS AND
COMICRAFT'S ALBERT DESCHESNE

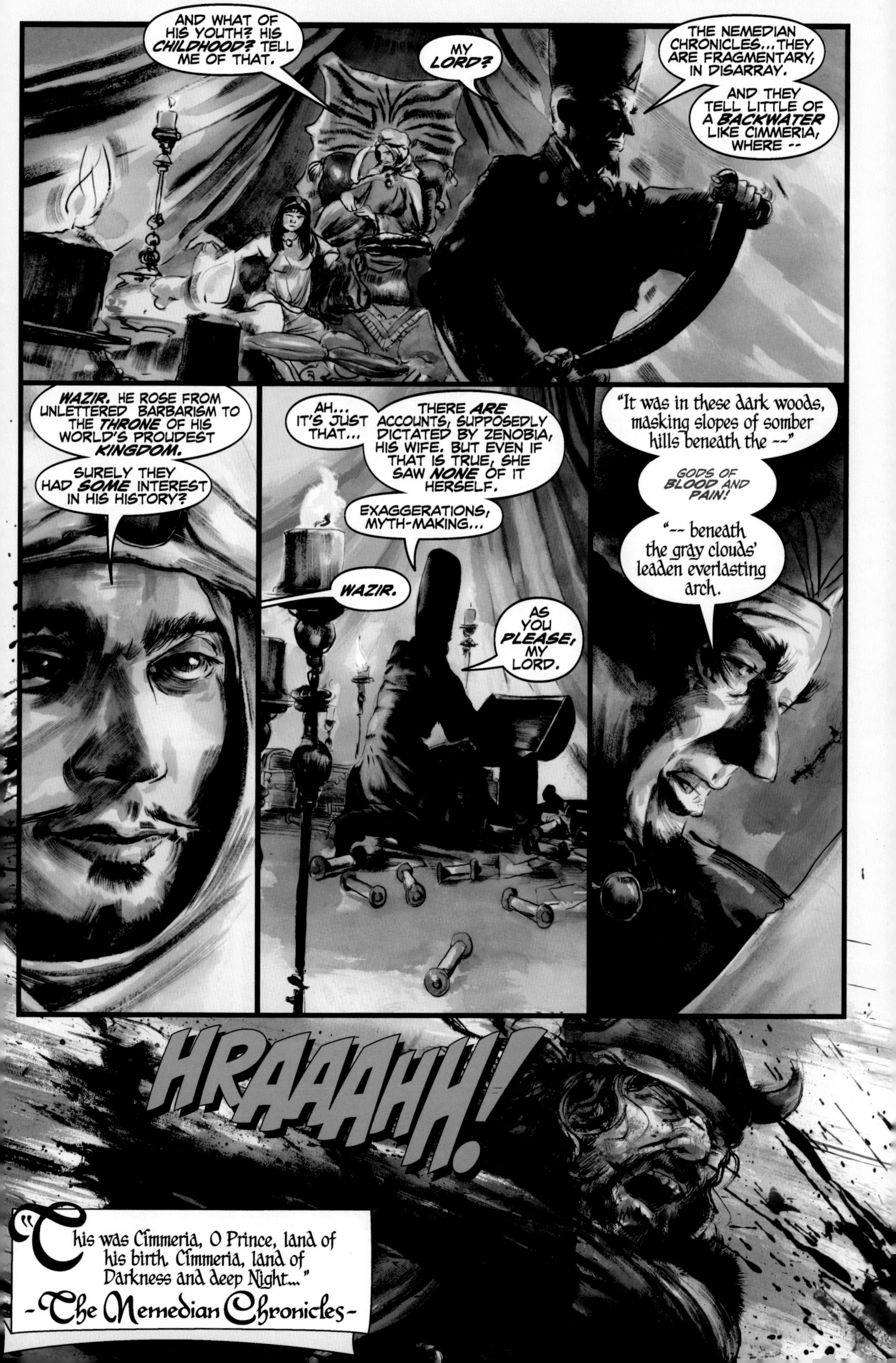
AND WHAT OF HIS YOUTH? HIS CHILDHOOD? TELL ME OF THAT.
MY LORD?
THE NEMEDIAN CHRONICLES... THEY ARE FRAGMENTARY, IN DISARRAY.
AND THEY TELL LITTLE OF A BACKWATER LIKE CIMMERIA, WHERE --
WAZIR. HE ROSE FROM UNLETTERED BARBARISM TO THE THRONE OF HIS WORLD'S PROUDEST KINGDOM.
SURELY THEY HAD SOME INTEREST IN HIS HISTORY?
AH... IT'S JUST THAT...
THERE ARE ACCOUNTS, SUPPOSEDLY DICTATED BY ZENOBIA, HIS WIFE. BUT EVEN IF THAT IS TRUE, SHE SAW NONE OF IT HERSELF.
EXAGGERATIONS, MYTH-MAKING...
WAZIR.
AS YOU PLEASE, MY LORD.
"It was in these dark woods, masking slopes of somber hills beneath the --"
GODS OF BLOOD AND PAIN!
"-- beneath the gray clouds' leaden everlasting arch.
HRAAAHH!
"This was Cimmeria, O Prince, land of his birth. Cimmeria, land of Darkness and deep Night..."
-The Nemedian Chronicles-

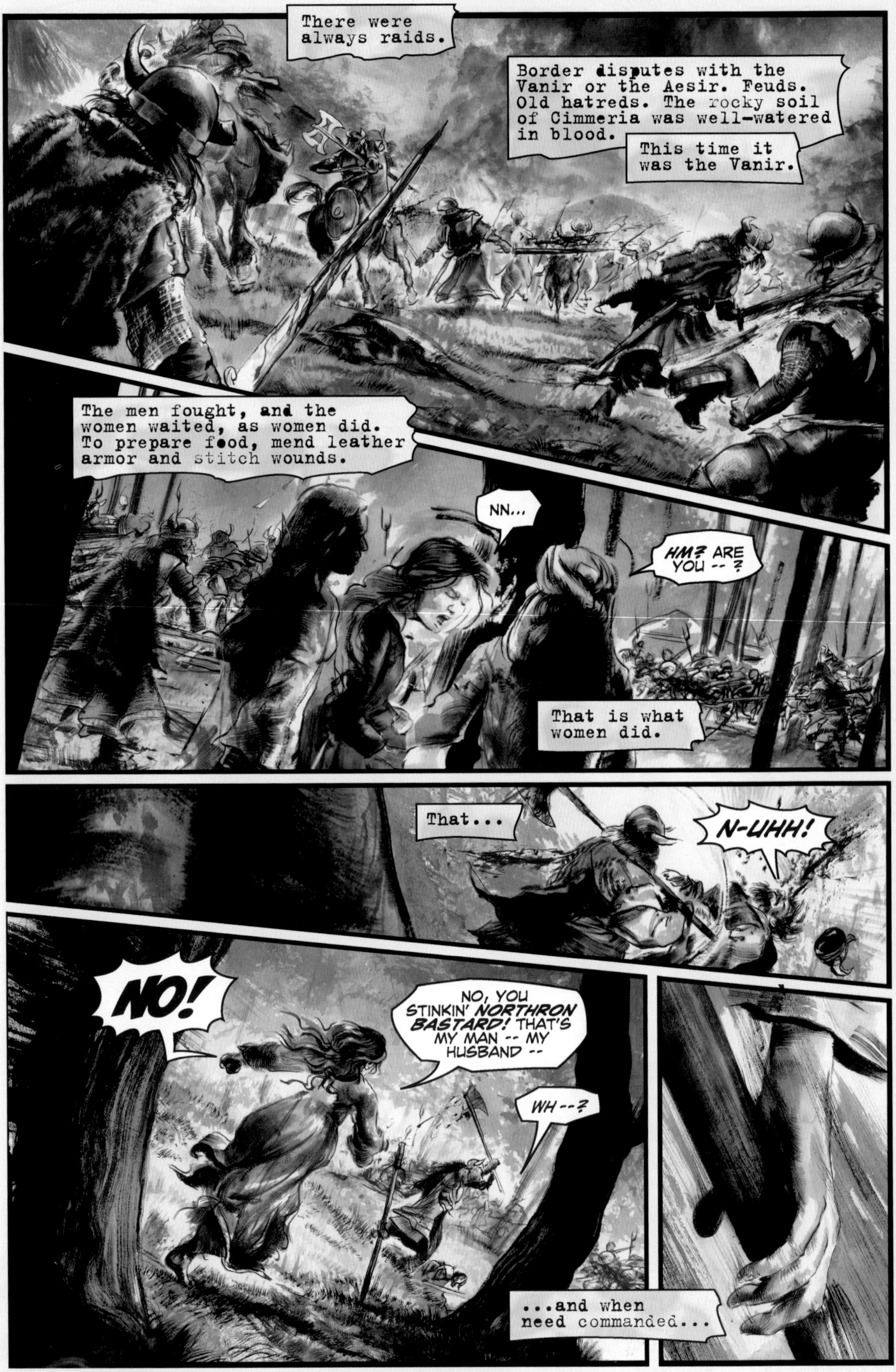
There were always raids.
Border disputes with the Vanir or the Aesir. Feuds. Old hatreds. The rocky soil of Cimmeria was well-watered in blood.
This time it was the Vanir.
The men fought, and the women waited, as women did. To prepare food, mend leather armor and stitch wounds.
NN...
HM? ARE YOU -- ?
That is what women did.
That...
N-UHH!
NO!
NO, YOU STINKIN' NORTHRON BASTARD! THAT'S MY MAN -- MY HUSBAND --
WH -- ?
...and when need commanded...

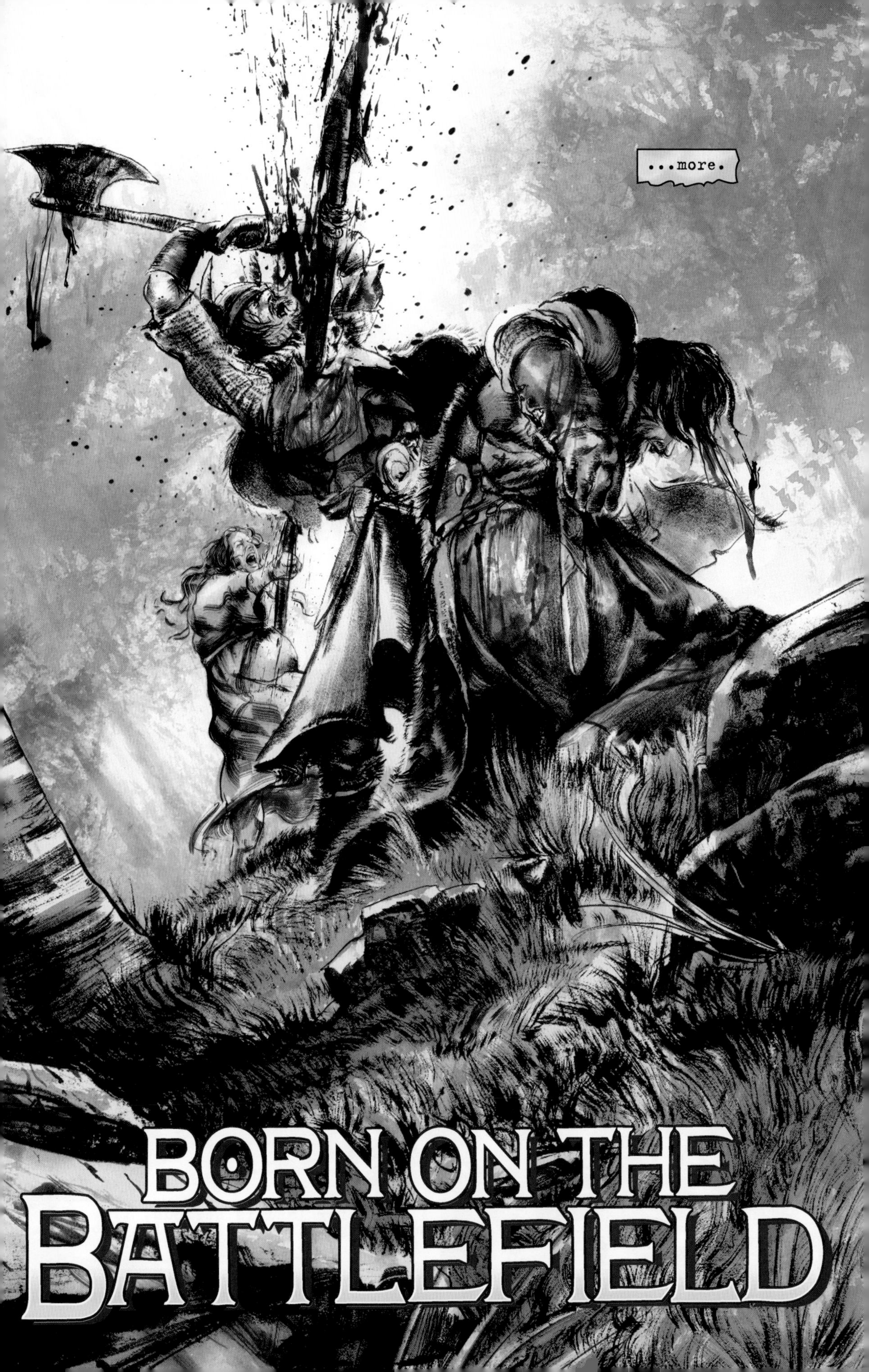
...more.
BORN ON THE BATTLEFIELD

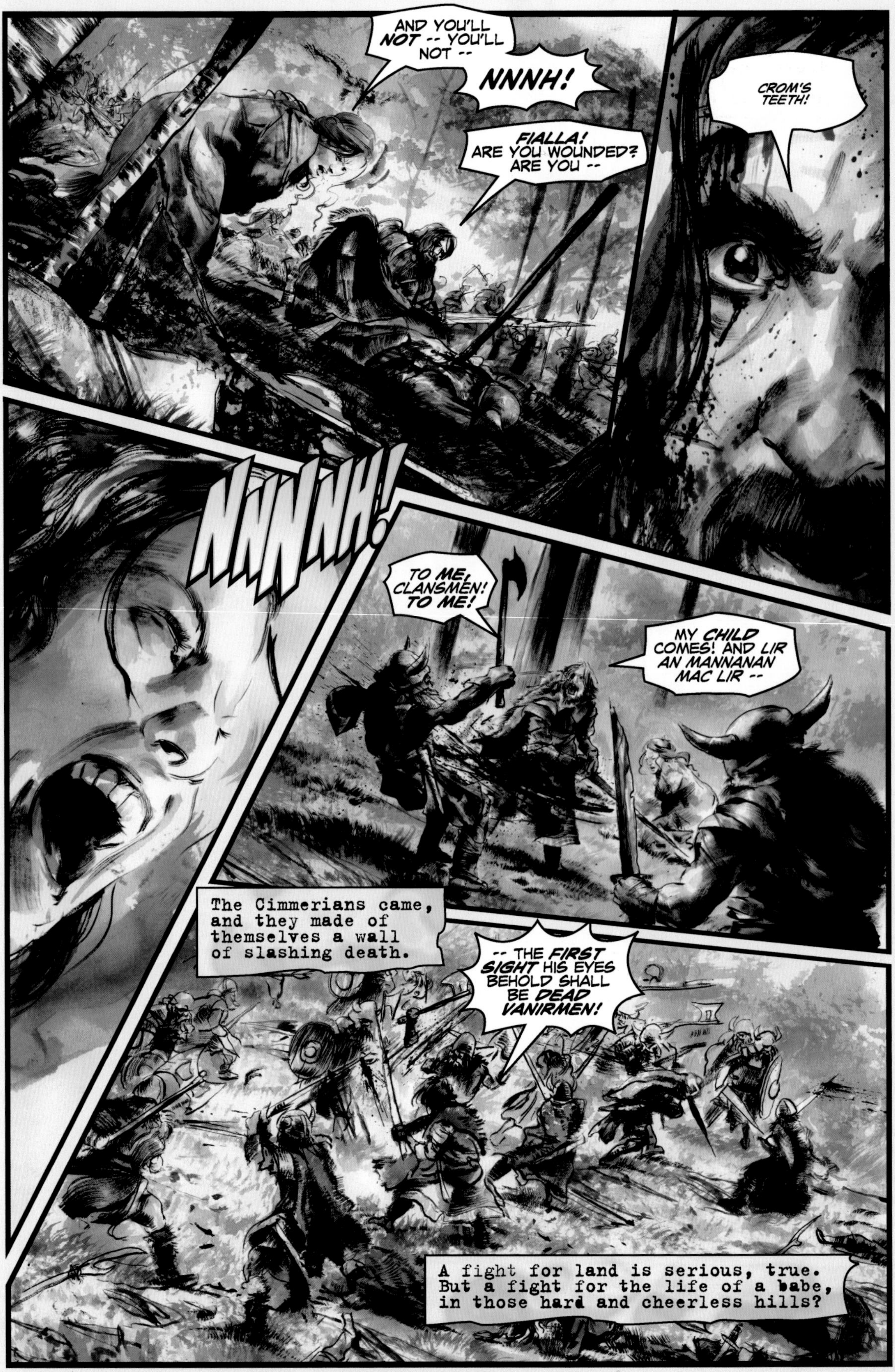
AND YOU'LL NOT -- YOU'LL NOT --
NNNH!
FIALLA! ARE YOU WOUNDED? ARE YOU --
CROM'S TEETH!
NNNNH!
TO ME, CLANSMEN! TO ME!
MY CHILD COMES! AND LIR AN MANNANAN MAC LIR --
The Cimmerians came, and they made of themselves a wall of slashing death.
-- THE FIRST SIGHT HIS EYES BEHOLD SHALL BE DEAD VANIRMEN!
A fight for land is serious, true. But a fight for the life of a babe, in those hard and cheerless hills?

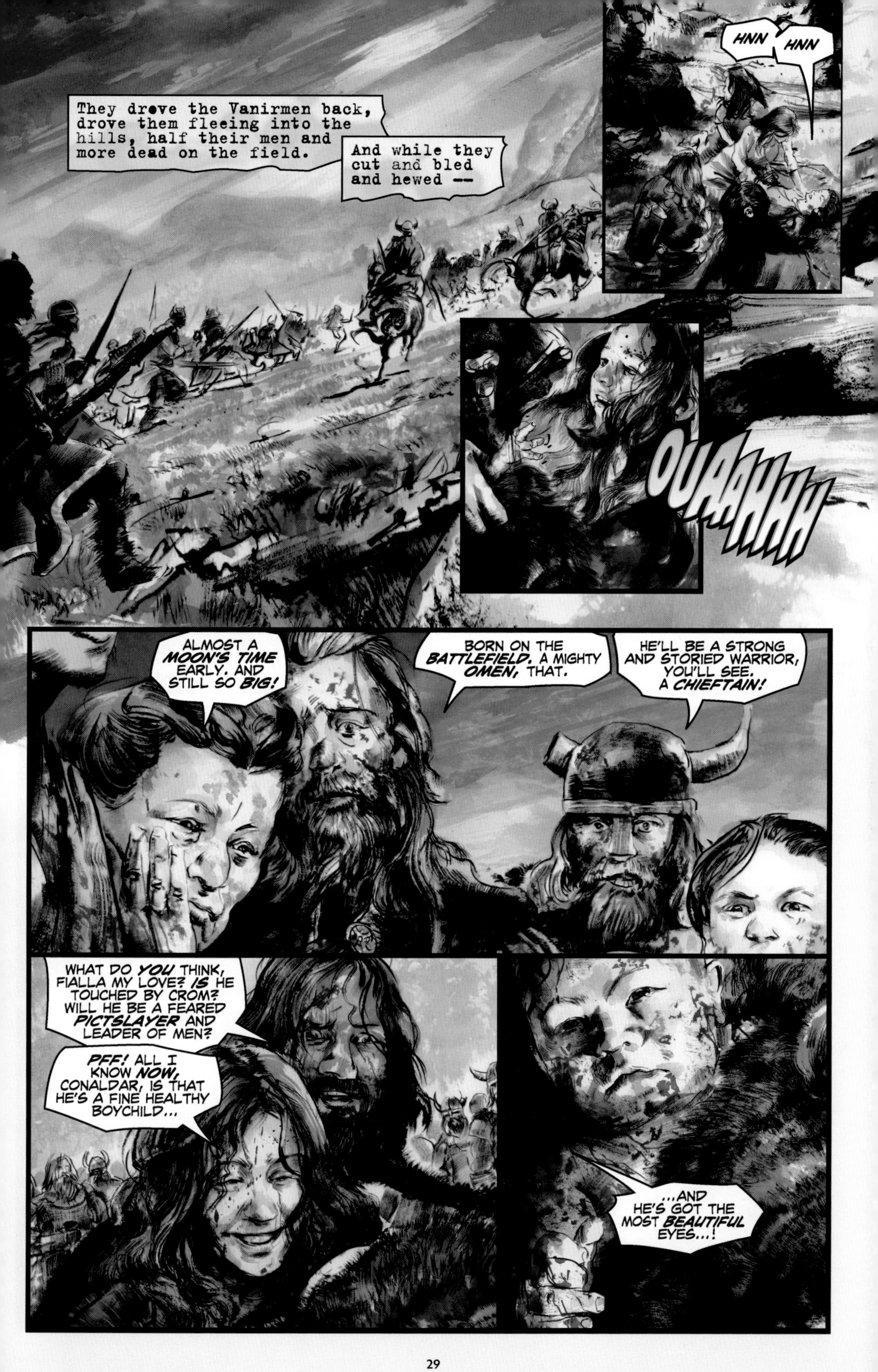
They drove the Vanirmen back, drove them fleeing into the hills, half their men and more dead on the field.
And while they cut and bled and hewed --
HNN
HNN
OUAAHHH
ALMOST A MOON'S TIME EARLY. AND STILL SO BIG!
BORN ON THE BATTLEFIELD. A MIGHTY OMEN, THAT.
HE'LL BE A STRONG AND STORIED WARRIOR, YOU'LL SEE. A CHIEFTAIN!
WHAT DO YOU THINK, FIALLA MY LOVE? IS HE TOUCHED BY CROM? WILL HE BE A FEARED PICTSLAYER AND LEADER OF MEN?
PFF! ALL I KNOW NOW, CONALDAR, IS THAT HE'S A FINE HEALTHY BOYCHILD...
...AND HE'S GOT THE MOST BEAUTIFUL EYES...!

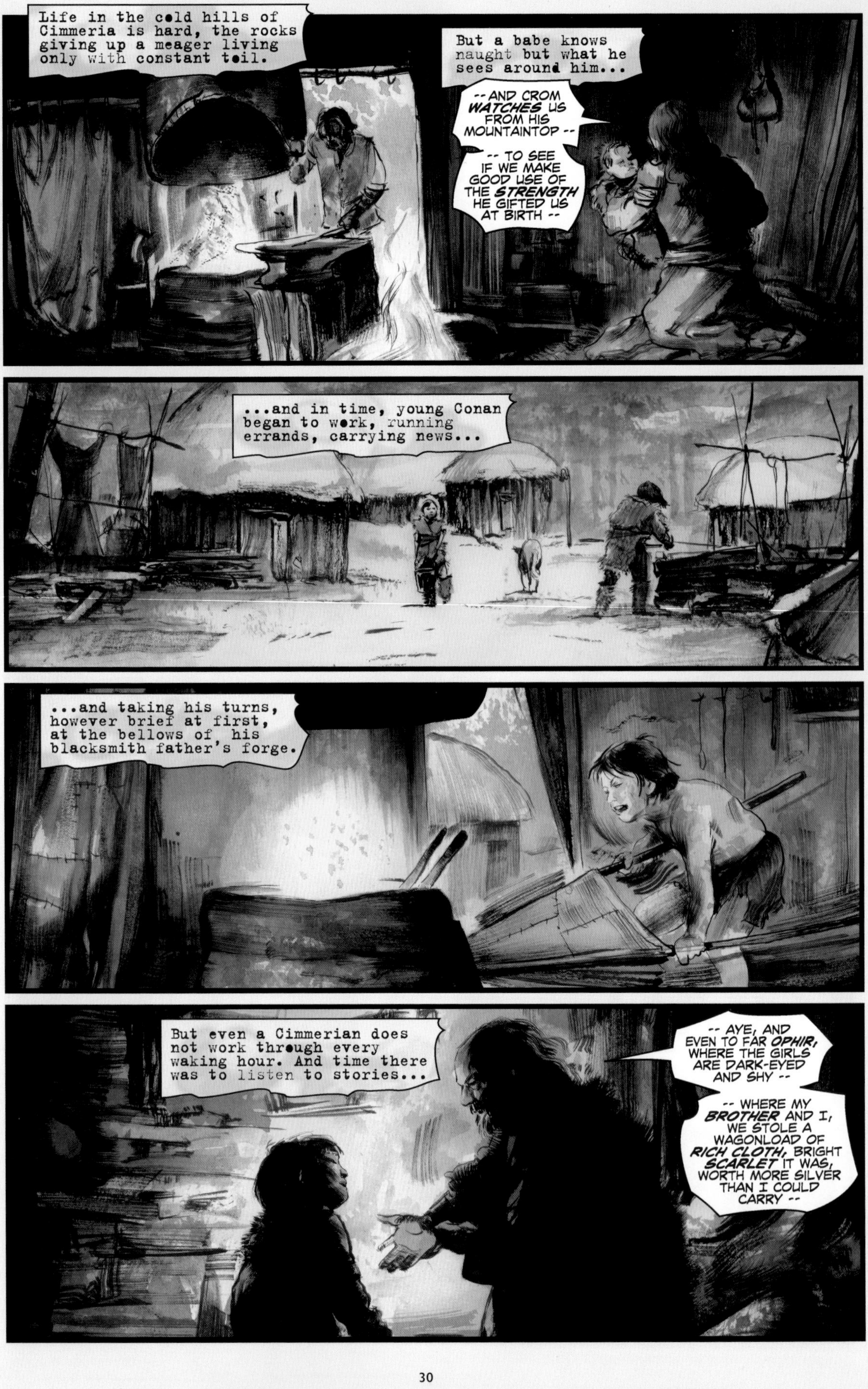

Life in the cold hills of Cimmeria is hard, the rocks giving up a meager living only with constant toil.
But a babe knows naught but what he sees around him...
-- AND CROM WATCHES US FROM HIS MOUNTAINTOP --
-- TO SEE IF WE MAKE GOOD USE OF THE STRENGTH HE GIFTED US AT BIRTH --
...and in time, young Conan began to work, running errands, carrying news...
...and taking his turns, however brief at first, at the bellows of his blacksmith father's forge.
But even a Cimmerian does not work through every waking hour. And time there was to listen to stories...
-- AYE, AND EVEN TO FAR OPHIR, WHERE THE GIRLS ARE DARK-EYED AND SHY --
-- WHERE MY BROTHER AND I, WE STOLE A WAGONLOAD OF RICH CLOTH, BRIGHT SCARLET IT WAS, WORTH MORE SILVER THAN I COULD CARRY --

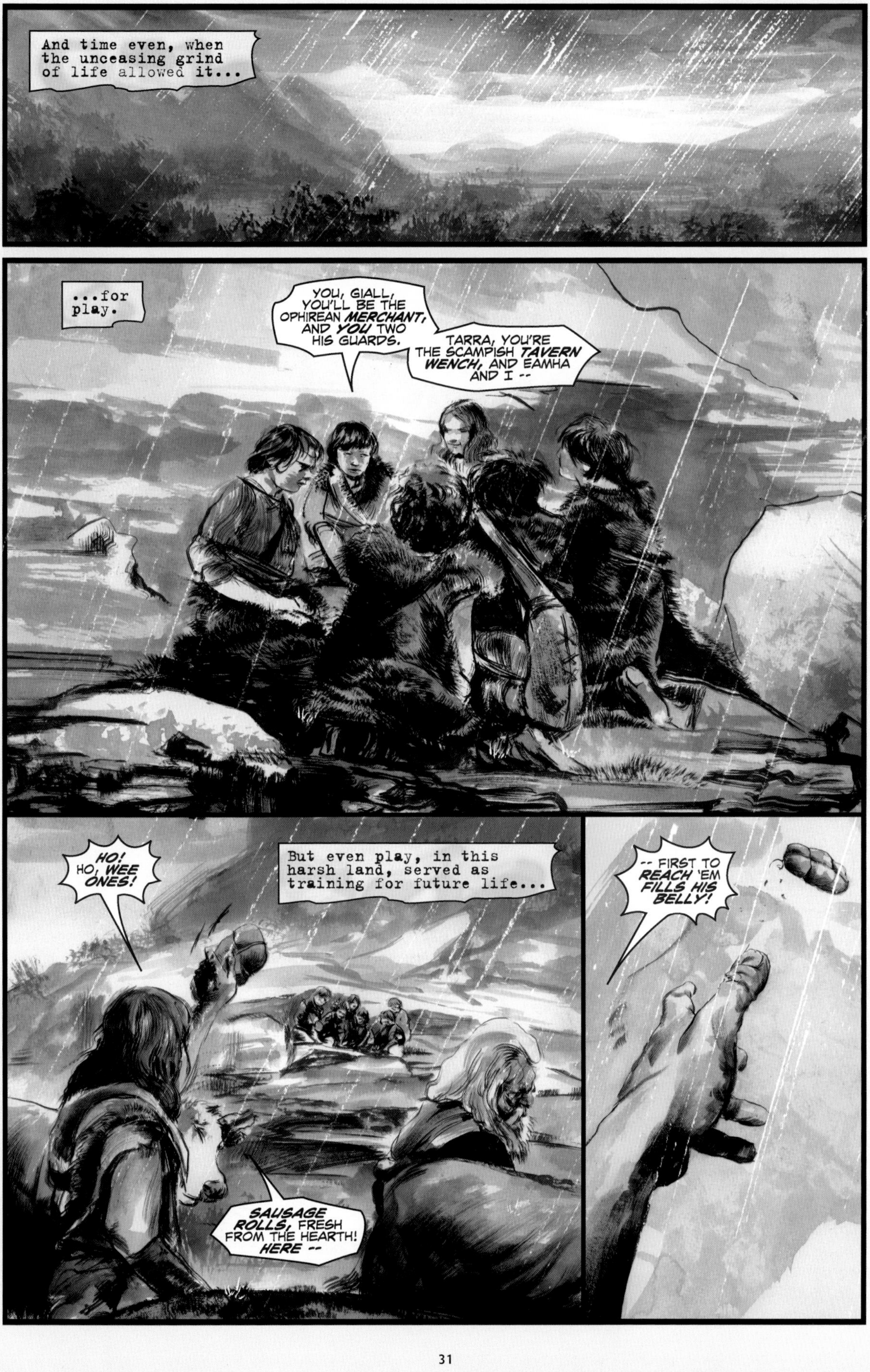
And time even, when the unceasing grind of life allowed it...
...for play.
YOU, GIALL, YOU'LL BE THE OPHIREAN MERCHANT, AND YOU TWO HIS GUARDS.
TARRA, YOU'RE THE SCAMPISH TAVERN WENCH, AND EAMHA AND I --
HO! HO, WEE ONES!
But even play, in this harsh land, served as training for future life...
SAUSAGE ROLLS, FRESH FROM THE HEARTH! HERE --
-- FIRST TO REACH 'EM FILLS HIS BELLY!

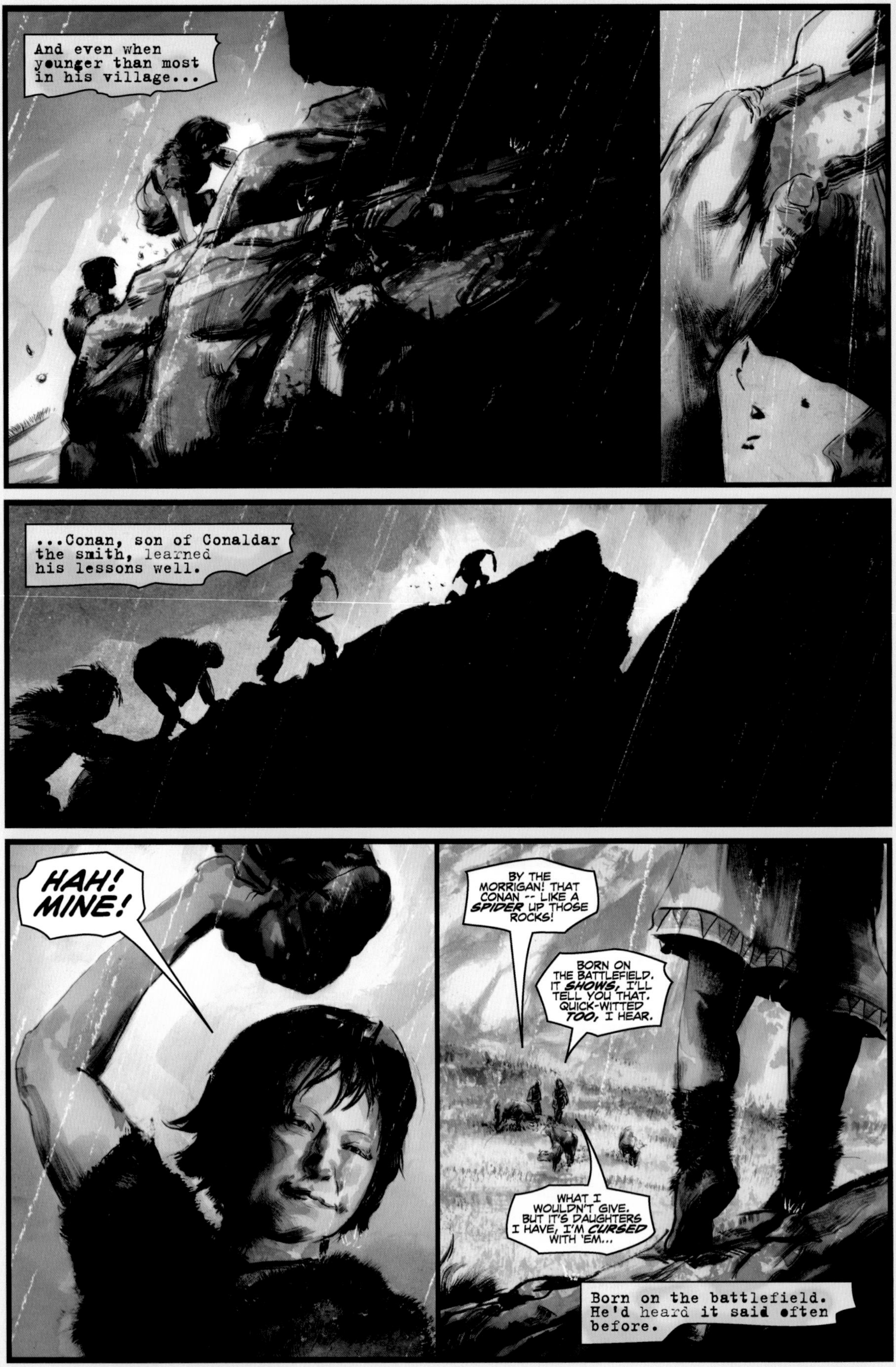

And even when younger than most in his village...
...Conan, son of Conaldar the smith, learned his lessons well.
HAH! MINE!
BY THE MORRIGAN! THAT CONAN -- LIKE A SPIDER UP THOSE ROCKS!
BORN ON THE BATTLEFIELD. IT SHOWS, I'LL TELL YOU THAT. QUICK-WITTED TOO, I HEAR.
WHAT I WOULDN'T GIVE. BUT IT'S DAUGHTERS I HAVE, I'M CURSED WITH 'EM...
Born on the battlefield. He'd heard it said often before.

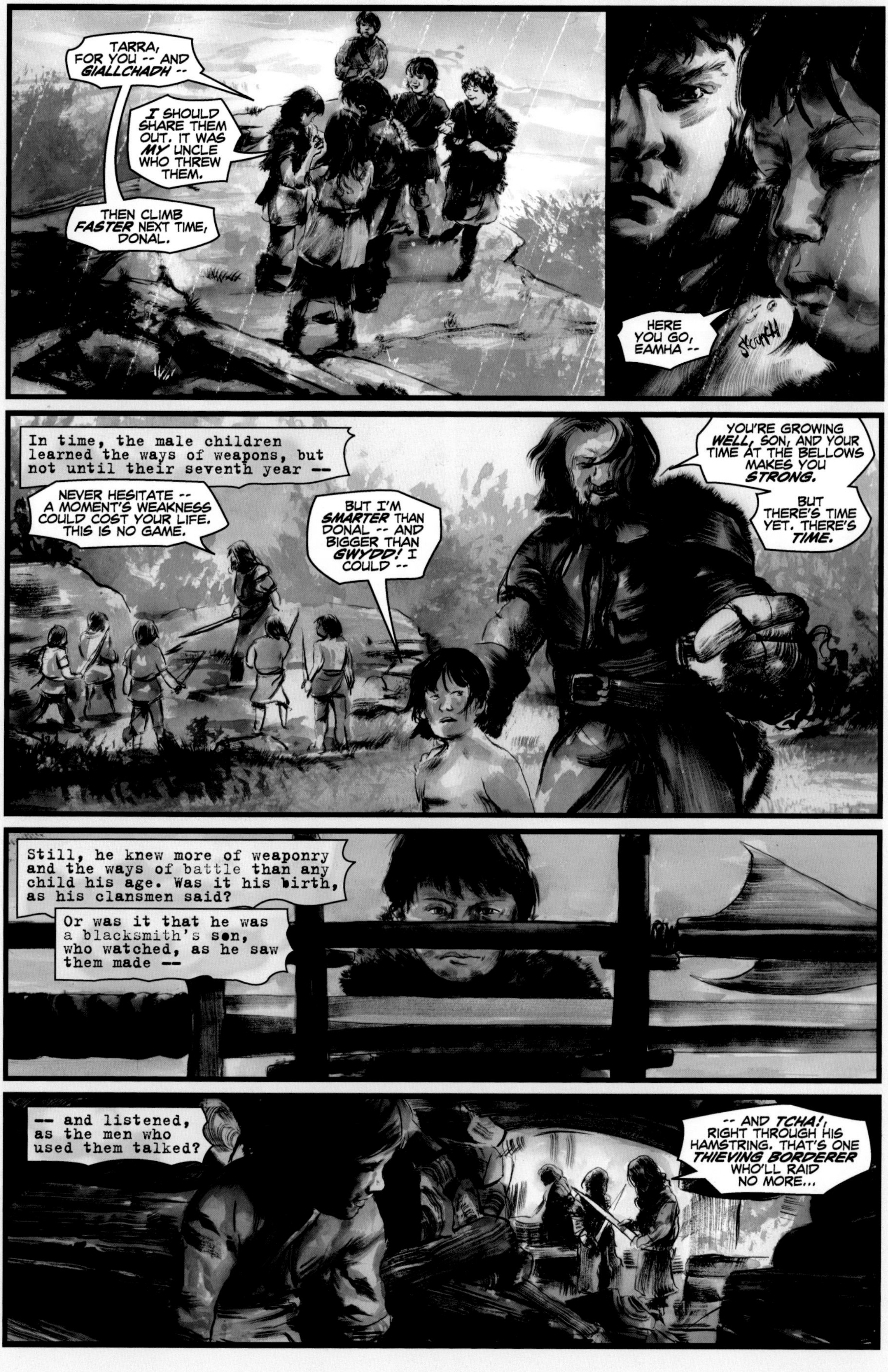
TARRA, FOR YOU -- AND GIALLCHADH --
I SHOULD SHARE THEM OUT. IT WAS MY UNCLE WHO THREW THEM.
THEN CLIMB FASTER NEXT TIME, DONAL.
HERE YOU GO, EAMHA --
In time, the male children learned the ways of weapons, but not until their seventh year --
NEVER HESITATE -- A MOMENT'S WEAKNESS COULD COST YOUR LIFE. THIS IS NO GAME.
BUT I'M SMARTER THAN DONAL -- AND BIGGER THAN GWYDD! I COULD --
YOU'RE GROWING WELL, SON, AND YOUR TIME AT THE BELLOWS MAKES YOU STRONG.
BUT THERE'S TIME YET. THERE'S TIME.
Still, he knew more of weaponry and the ways of battle than any child his age. Was it his birth, as his clansmen said?
Or was it that he was a blacksmith's son, who watched, as he saw them made --
-- and listened, as the men who used them talked?
-- AND TCHA! RIGHT THROUGH HIS HAMSTRING. THAT'S ONE THIEVING BORDERER WHO'LL RAID NO MORE...

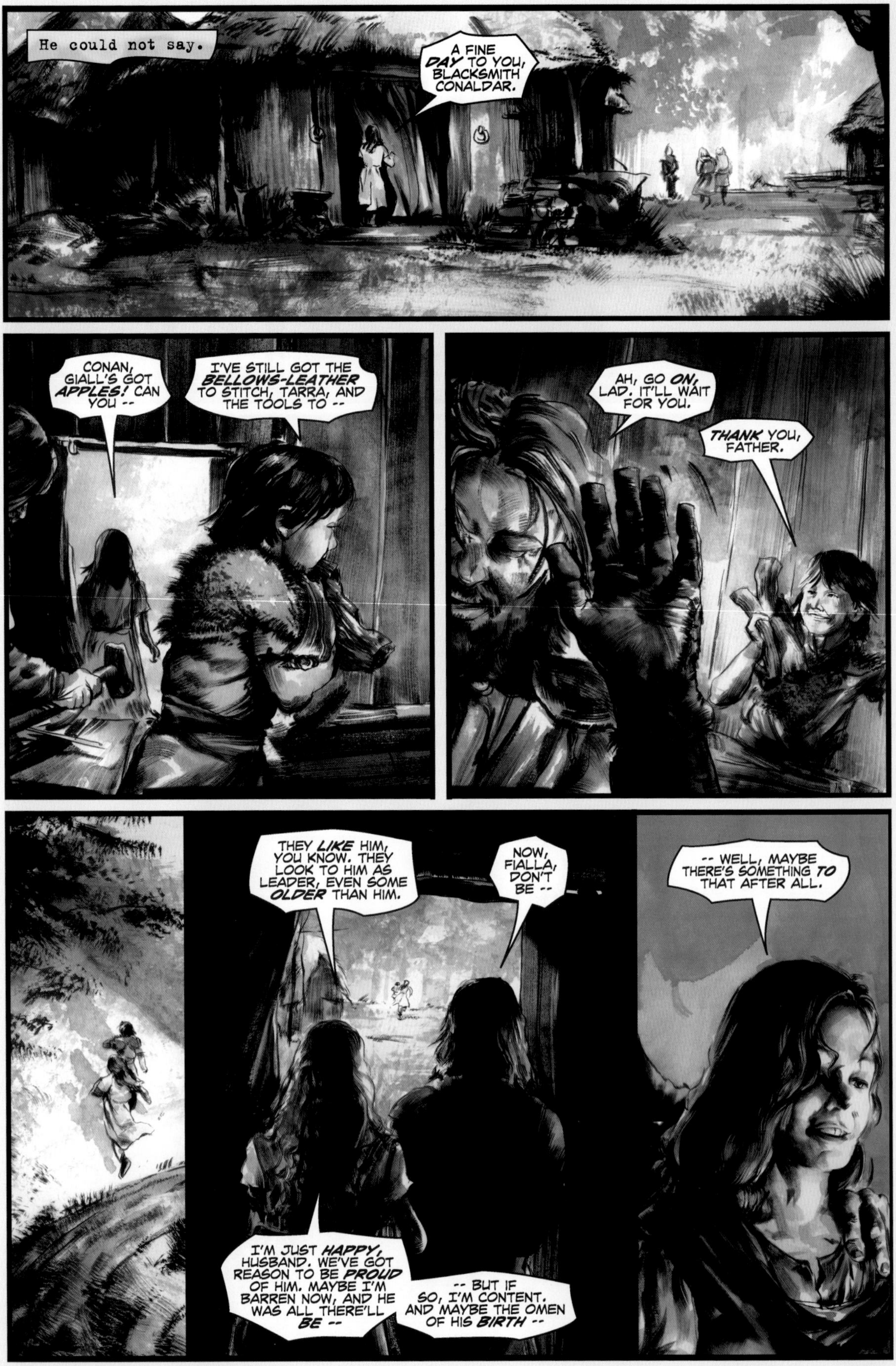
He could not say.
A FINE DAY TO YOU, BLACKSMITH CONALDAR.
CONAN, GIALL'S GOT APPLES! CAN YOU --
I'VE STILL GOT THE BELLOWS-LEATHER TO STITCH, TARRA, AND THE TOOLS TO --
AH, GO ON, LAD. IT'LL WAIT FOR YOU.
THANK YOU, FATHER.
THEY LIKE HIM, YOU KNOW. THEY LOOK TO HIM AS LEADER, EVEN SOME OLDER THAN HIM.
NOW, FIALLA, DON'T BE --
I'M JUST HAPPY, HUSBAND. WE'VE GOT REASON TO BE PROUD OF HIM. MAYBE I'M BARREN NOW, AND HE WAS ALL THERE'LL BE --
-- BUT IF SO, I'M CONTENT. AND MAYBE THE OMEN OF HIS BIRTH --
-- WELL, MAYBE THERE'S SOMETHING TO THAT AFTER ALL.

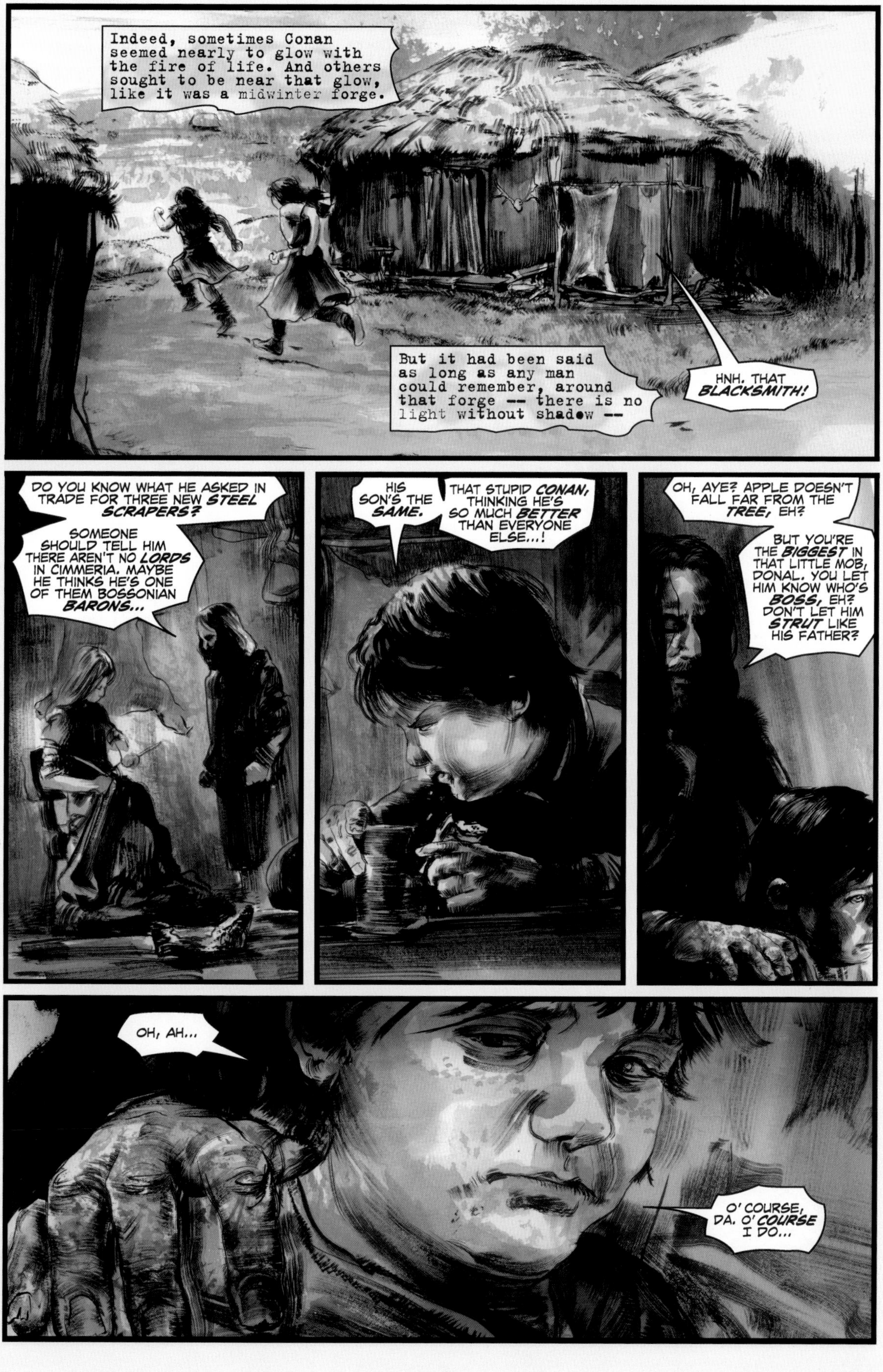

Indeed, sometimes Conan seemed nearly to glow with the fire of life. And others sought to be near that glow, like it was a midwinter forge.
But it had been said as long as any man could remember, around that forge -- there is no light without shadow --
HNH. THAT BLACKSMITH!
DO YOU KNOW WHAT HE ASKED IN TRADE FOR THREE NEW STEEL SCRAPERS?
SOMEONE SHOULD TELL HIM THERE AREN'T NO LORDS IN CIMMERIA. MAYBE HE THINKS HE'S ONE OF THEM BOSSONIAN BARONS...
HIS SON'S THE SAME.
THAT STUPID CONAN, THINKING HE'S SO MUCH BETTER THAN EVERYONE ELSE...!
OH, AYE? APPLE DOESN'T FALL FAR FROM THE TREE, EH?
BUT YOU'RE THE BIGGEST IN THAT LITTLE MOB, DONAL. YOU LET HIM KNOW WHO'S BOSS, EH? DON'T LET HIM STRUT LIKE HIS FATHER?
OH, AH...
O' COURSE, DA. O' COURSE I DO...

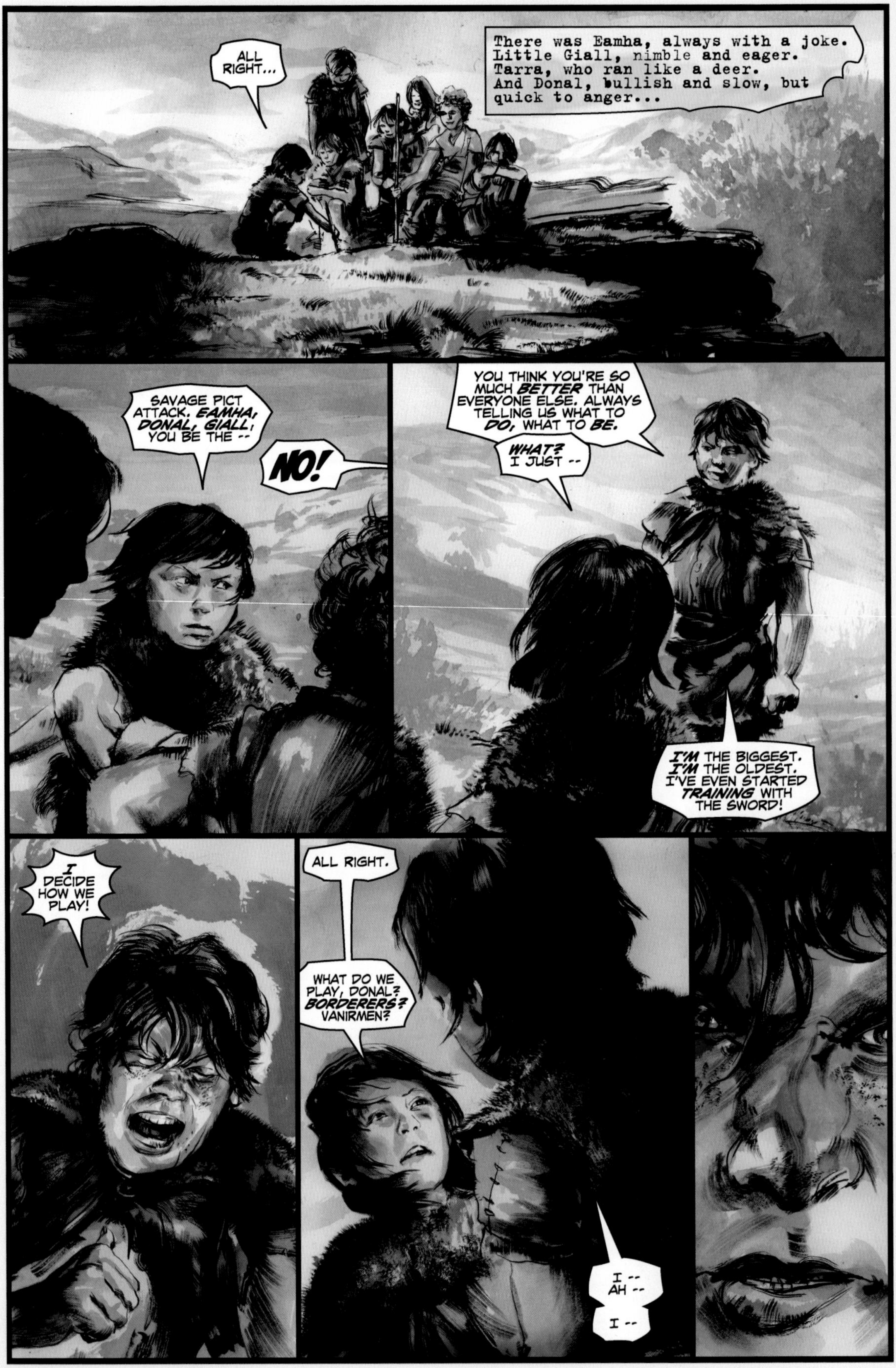
ALL RIGHT...
There was Eamha, always with a joke. Little Giall, nimble and eager. Tarra, who ran like a deer. And Donal, bullish and slow, but quick to anger...
SAVAGE PICT ATTACK. EAMHA, DONAL, GIALL, YOU BE THE --
NO!
YOU THINK YOU'RE SO MUCH BETTER THAN EVERYONE ELSE. ALWAYS TELLING US WHAT TO DO, WHAT TO BE.
WHAT? I JUST --
I'M THE BIGGEST. I'M THE OLDEST. I'VE EVEN STARTED TRAINING WITH THE SWORD!
I DECIDE HOW WE PLAY!
ALL RIGHT.
WHAT DO WE PLAY, DONAL? BORDERERS? VANIRMEN?
I -- AH --
I --

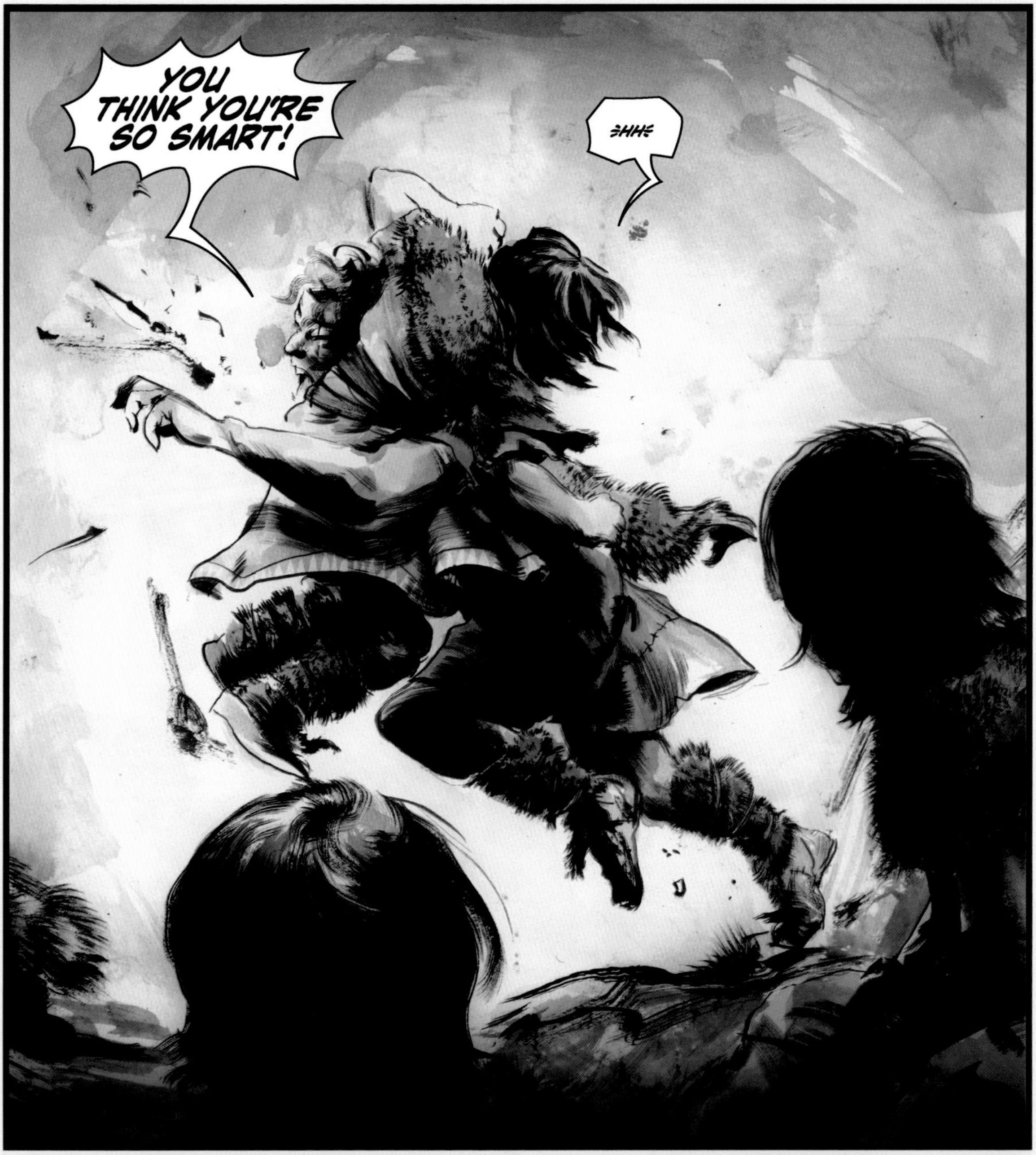
YOU THINK YOU'RE SO SMART!
HHH

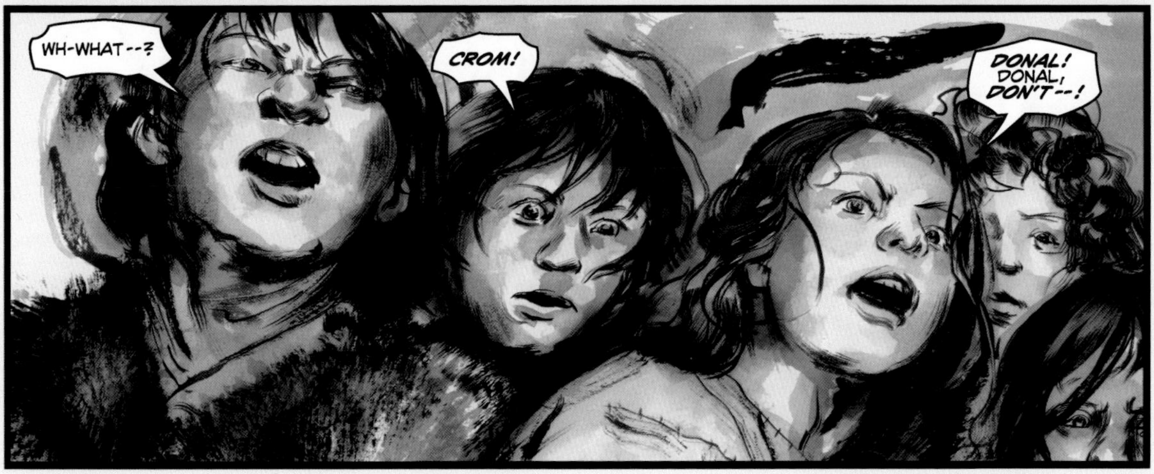
WH-WHAT--?
CROM!
DONAL! DONAL, DON'T--!

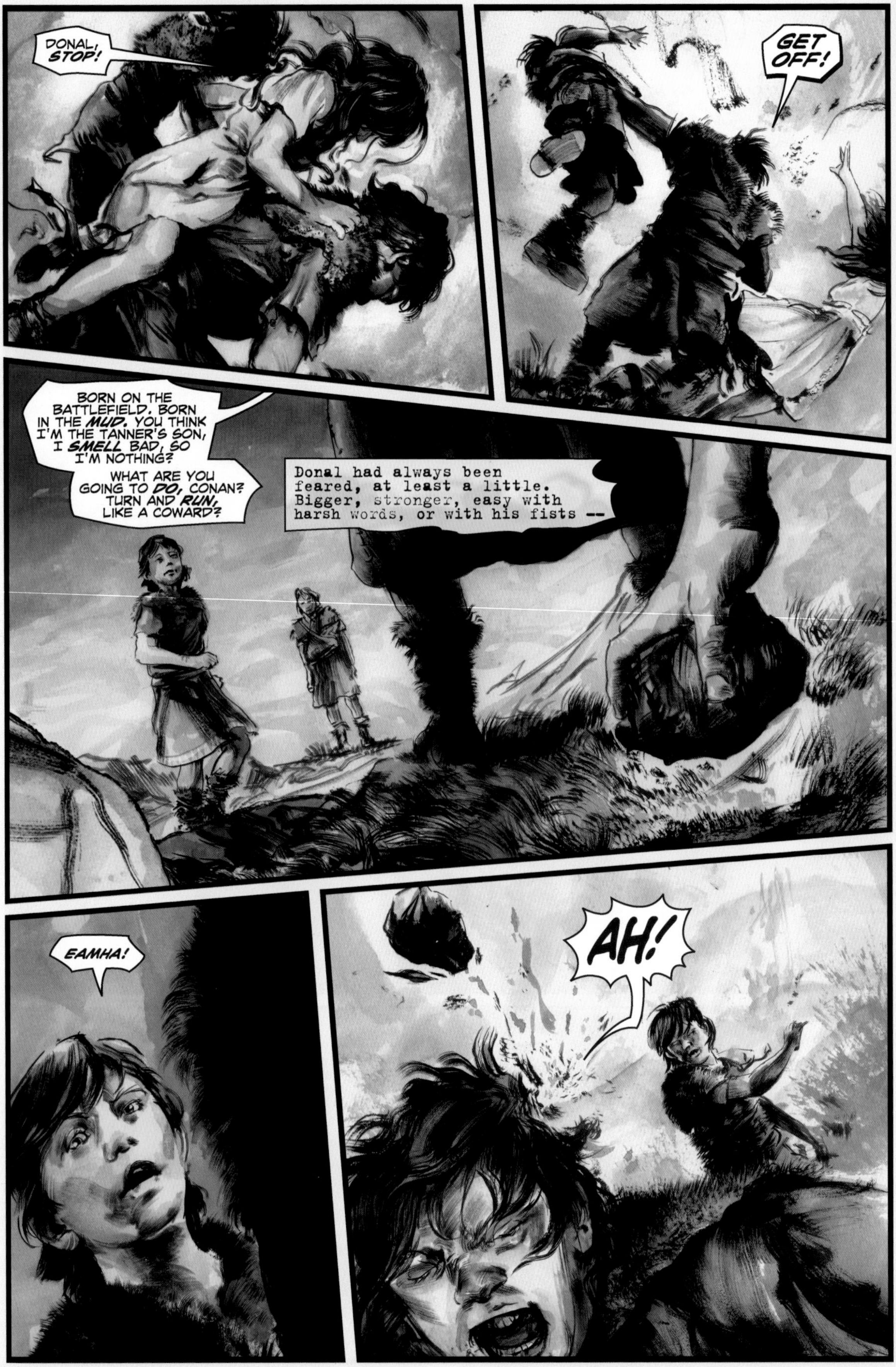

DONAL, STOP!
GET OFF!
BORN ON THE BATTLEFIELD. BORN IN THE MUD. YOU THINK I'M THE TANNER'S SON, I SMELL BAD, SO I'M NOTHING?
WHAT ARE YOU GOING TO DO, CONAN? TURN AND RUN, LIKE A COWARD?
Donal had always been feared, at least a little. Bigger, stronger, easy with harsh words, or with his fists --
EAMHA!
AH!

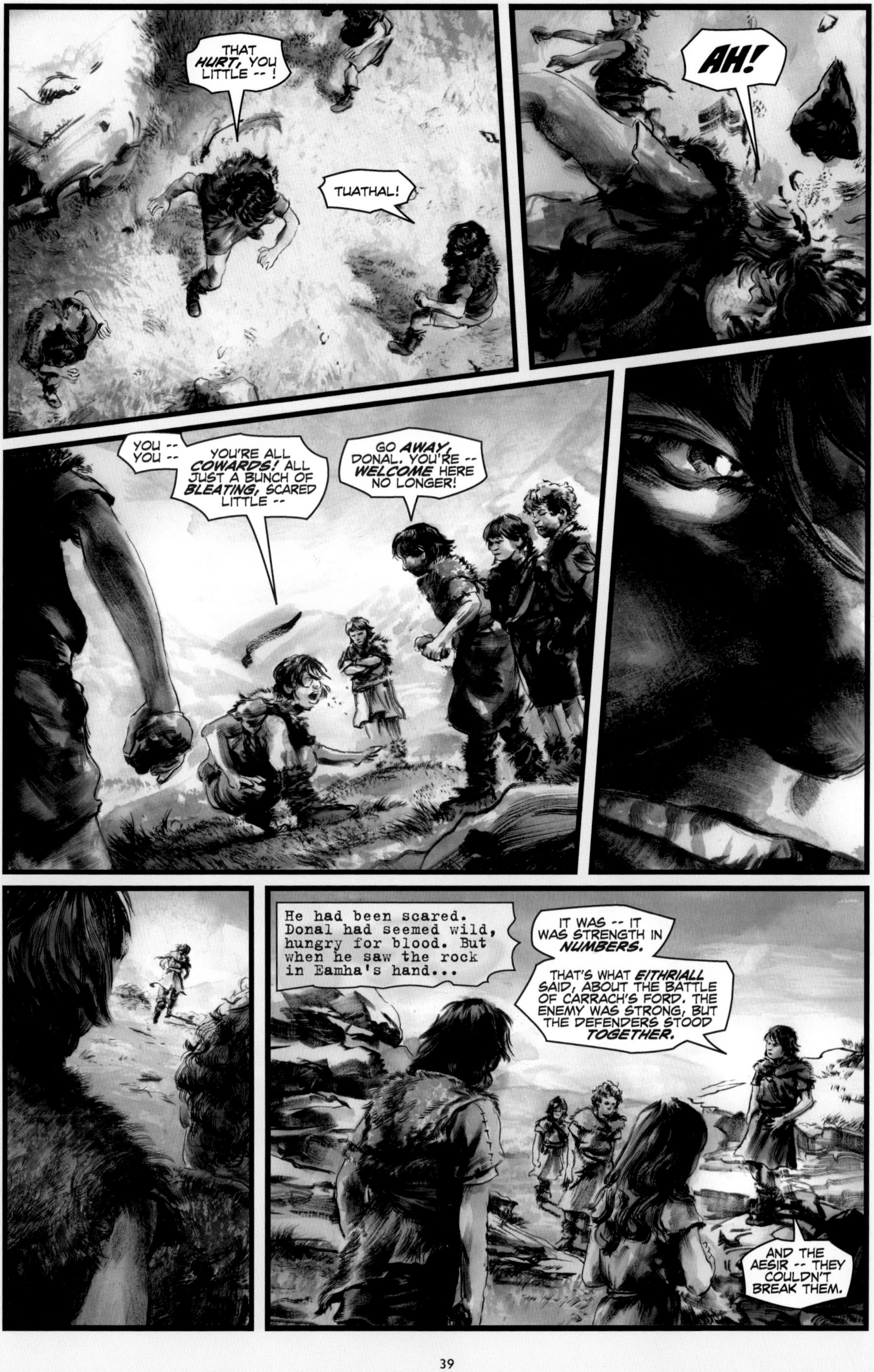
THAT HURT, YOU LITTLE -- !
TUATHAL!
AH!
YOU -- YOU --
YOU'RE ALL COWARDS! ALL JUST A BUNCH OF BLEATING, SCARED LITTLE --
GO AWAY, DONAL. YOU'RE -- WELCOME HERE NO LONGER!
He had been scared. Donal had seemed wild, hungry for blood. But when he saw the rock in Eamha's hand...
IT WAS -- IT WAS STRENGTH IN NUMBERS.
THAT'S WHAT EITHRIALL SAID, ABOUT THE BATTLE OF CARRACH'S FORD. THE ENEMY WAS STRONG, BUT THE DEFENDERS STOOD TOGETHER.
AND THE AESIR -- THEY COULDN'T BREAK THEM.

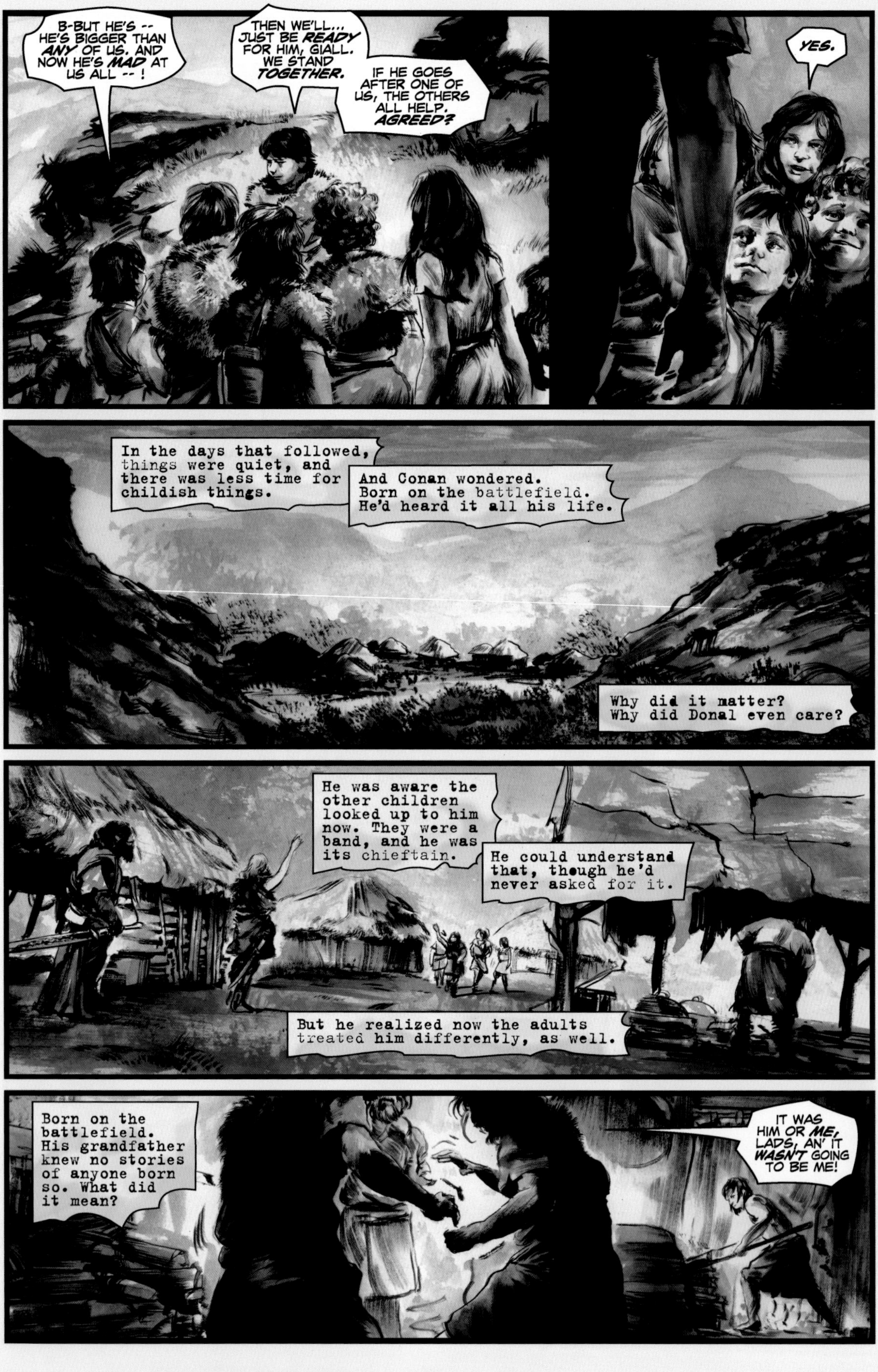
B-BUT HE'S -- HE'S BIGGER THAN ANY OF US. AND NOW HE'S MAD AT US ALL -- !
THEN WE'LL... JUST BE READY FOR HIM, GIALL. WE STAND TOGETHER.
IF HE GOES AFTER ONE OF US, THE OTHERS ALL HELP. AGREED?
YES.
In the days that followed, things were quiet, and there was less time for childish things.
And Conan wondered. Born on the battlefield. He'd heard it all his life.
Why did it matter? Why did Donal even care?
He was aware the other children looked up to him now. They were a band, and he was its chieftain.
He could understand that, though he'd never asked for it.
But he realized now the adults treated him differently, as well.
Born on the battlefield. His grandfather knew no stories of anyone born so. What did it mean?
IT WAS HIM OR ME, LADS, AN' IT WASN'T GOING TO BE ME!

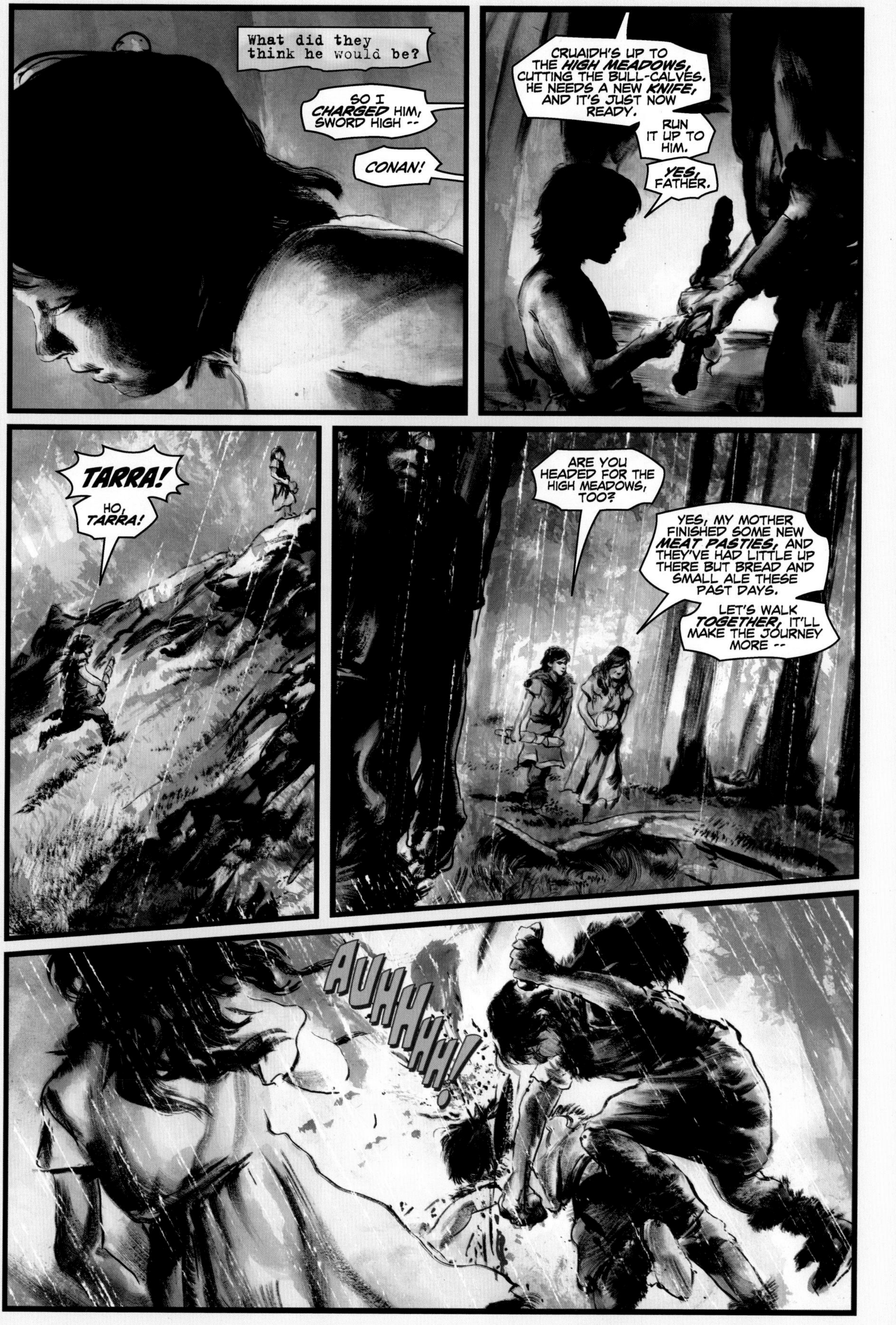
What did they think he would be?
SO I CHARGED HIM, SWORD HIGH --
CONAN!
CRUAIDH'S UP TO THE HIGH MEADOWS, CUTTING THE BULL-CALVES. HE NEEDS A NEW KNIFE, AND IT'S JUST NOW READY.
RUN IT UP TO HIM.
YES, FATHER.
TARRA!
HO, TARRA!
ARE YOU HEADED FOR THE HIGH MEADOWS, TOO?
YES, MY MOTHER FINISHED SOME NEW MEAT PASTIES, AND THEY'VE HAD LITTLE UP THERE BUT BREAD AND SMALL ALE THESE PAST DAYS.
LET'S WALK TOGETHER, IT'LL MAKE THE JOURNEY MORE --
AUHHHH!

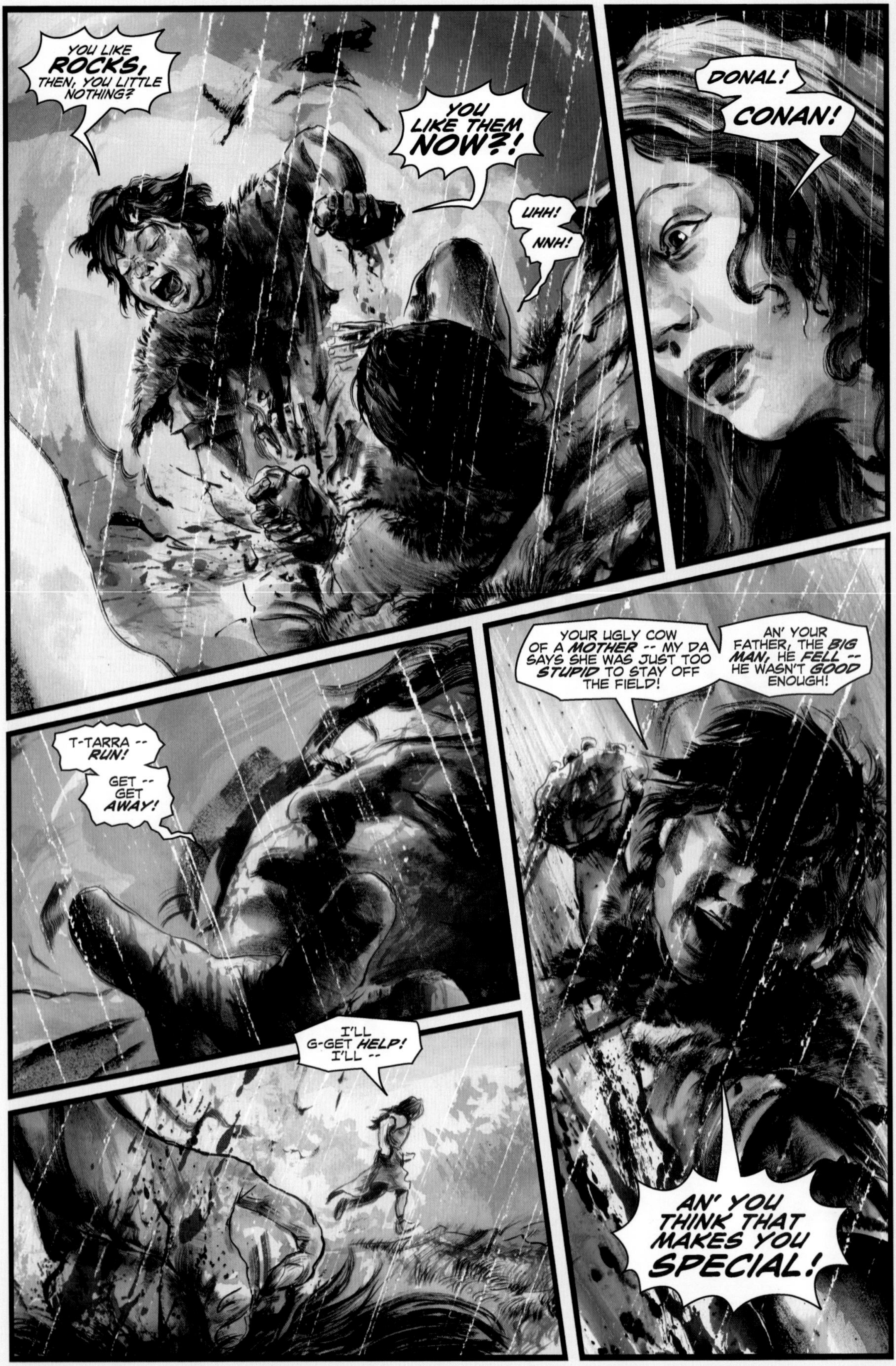
YOU LIKE ROCKS, THEN, YOU LITTLE NOTHING?
YOU LIKE THEM NOW?!
UHH!
NNH!
DONAL!
CONAN!
T-TARRA -- RUN!
GET -- GET AWAY!
YOUR UGLY COW OF A MOTHER -- MY DA SAYS SHE WAS JUST TOO STUPID TO STAY OFF THE FIELD!
AN' YOUR FATHER, THE BIG MAN, HE FELL -- HE WASN'T GOOD ENOUGH!
I'LL G-GET HELP! I'LL --
AN' YOU THINK THAT MAKES YOU SPECIAL!

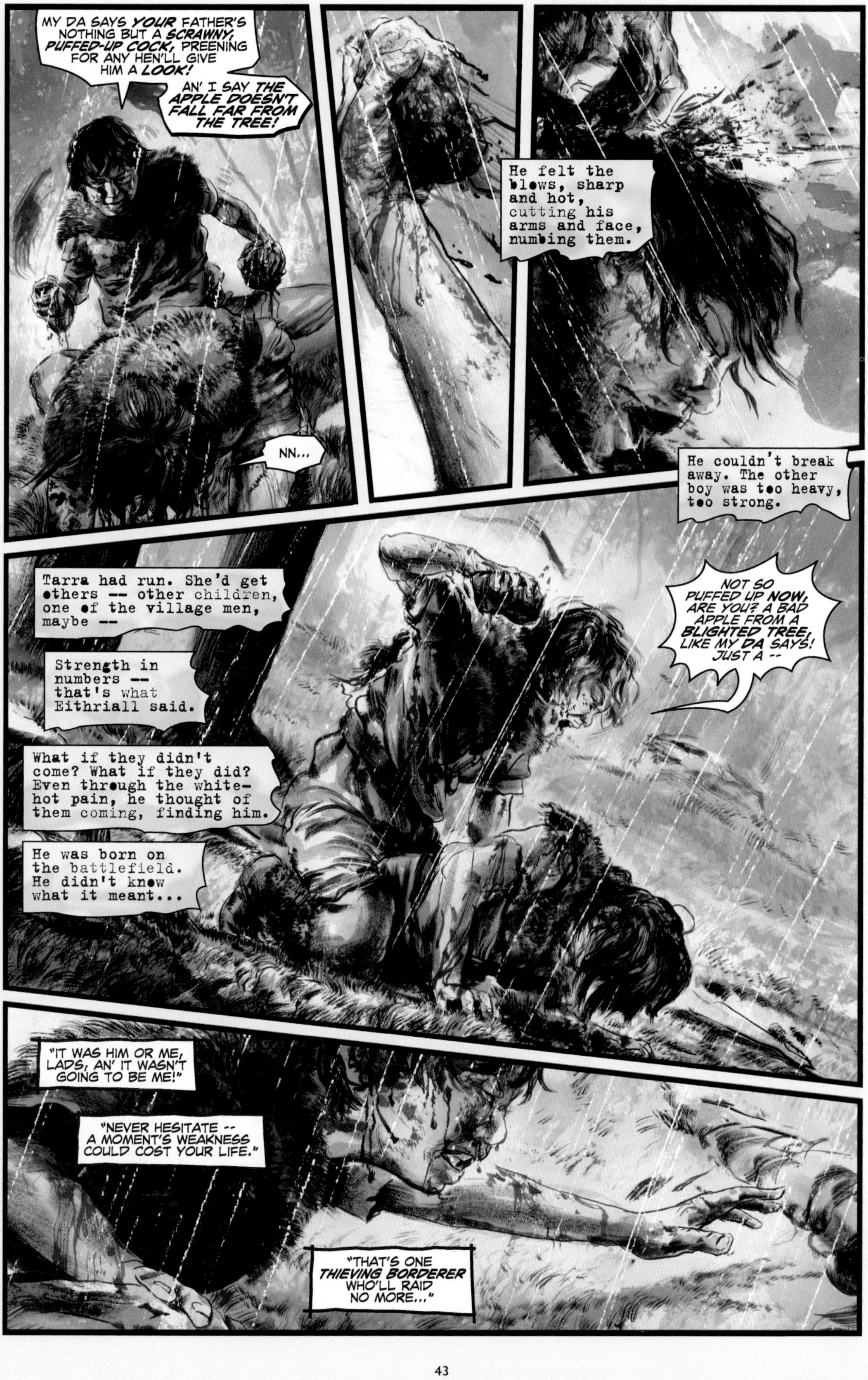
MY DA SAYS YOUR FATHER'S NOTHING BUT A SCRAWNY, PUFFED-UP COCK, PREENING FOR ANY HEN'LL GIVE HIM A LOOK!
AN' I SAY THE APPLE DOESN'T FALL FAR FROM THE TREE!
NN...
He felt the blows, sharp and hot, cutting his arms and face, numbing them.
He couldn't break away. The other boy was too heavy, too strong.
Tarra had run. She'd get others -- other children, one of the village men, maybe --
Strength in numbers -- that's what Eithriall said.
What if they didn't come? What if they did? Even through the white-hot pain, he thought of them coming, finding him.
He was born on the battlefield. He didn't know what it meant...
NOT SO PUFFED UP NOW, ARE YOU? A BAD APPLE FROM A BLIGHTED TREE, LIKE MY DA SAYS! JUST A --
"IT WAS HIM OR ME, LADS, AN' IT WASN'T GOING TO BE ME!"
"NEVER HESITATE -- A MOMENT'S WEAKNESS COULD COST YOUR LIFE."
"THAT'S ONE THIEVING BORDERER WHO'LL RAID NO MORE..."

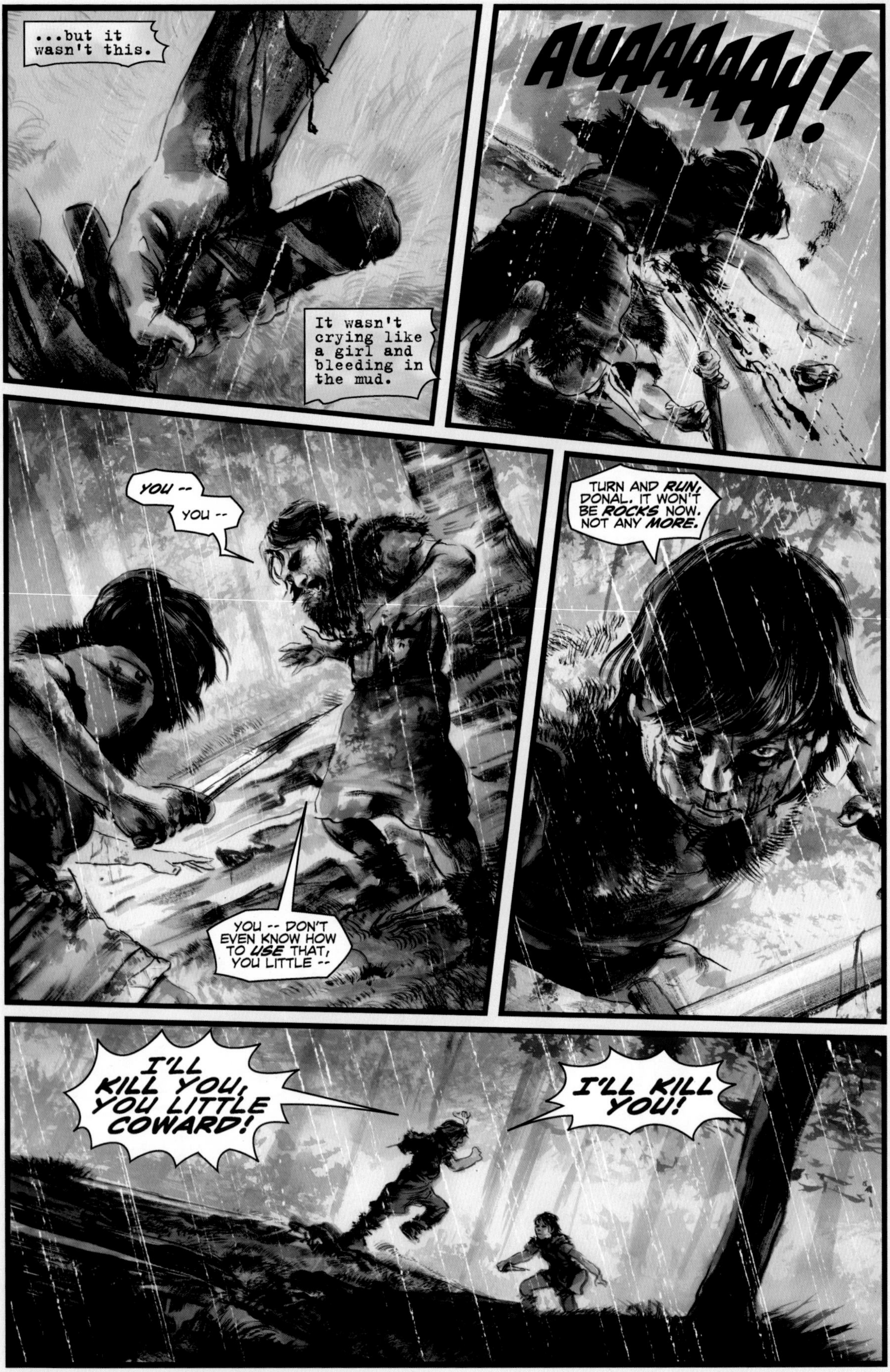

...but it wasn't this.
It wasn't crying like a girl and bleeding in the mud.
AUAAAAAAH!
YOU --
YOU --
YOU -- DON'T EVEN KNOW HOW TO USE THAT, YOU LITTLE --
TURN AND RUN, DONAL. IT WON'T BE ROCKS NOW. NOT ANY MORE.
I'LL KILL YOU, YOU LITTLE COWARD!
I'LL KILL YOU!

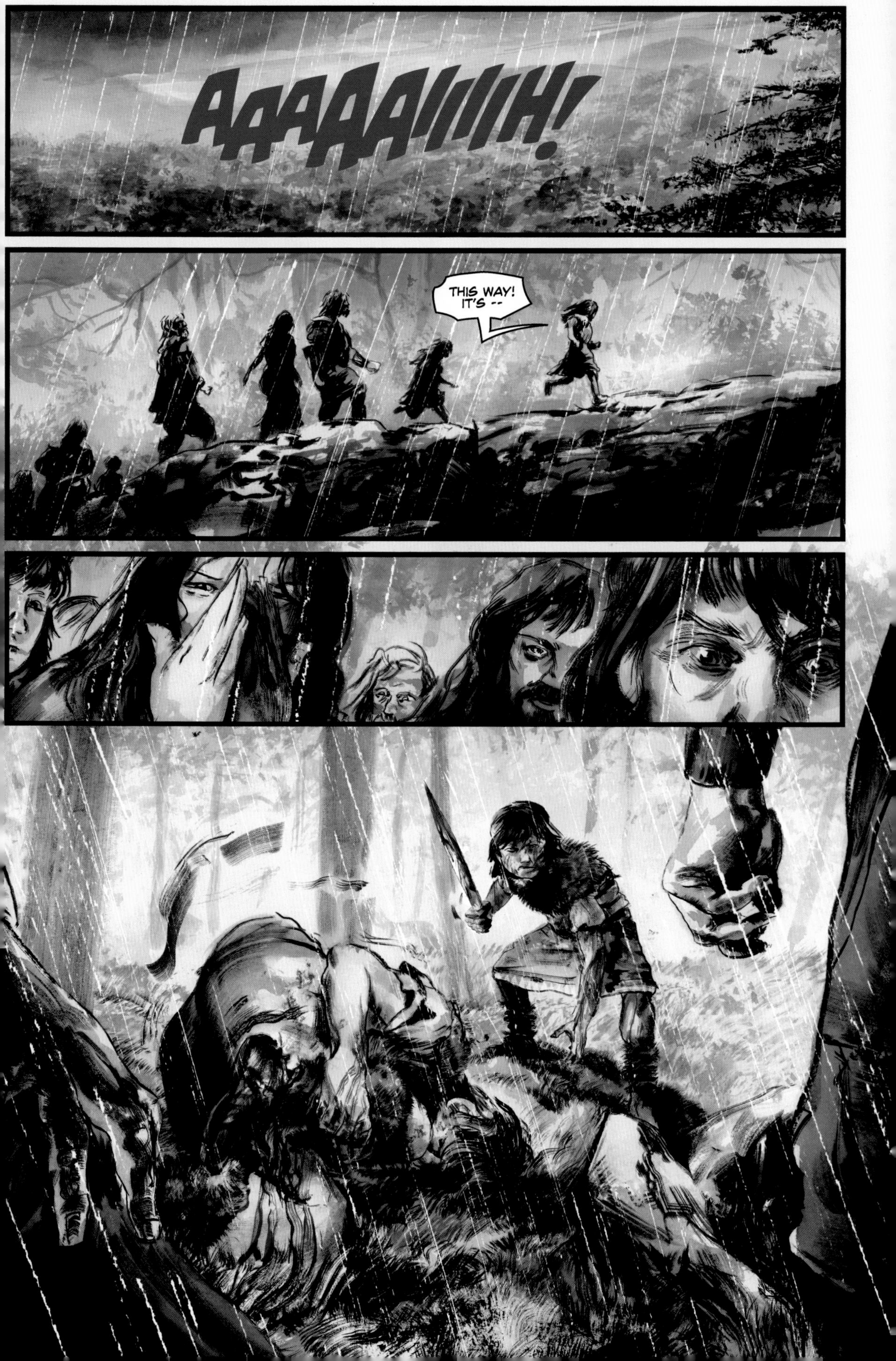
AAAAAIIIIH!
THIS WAY! IT'S --

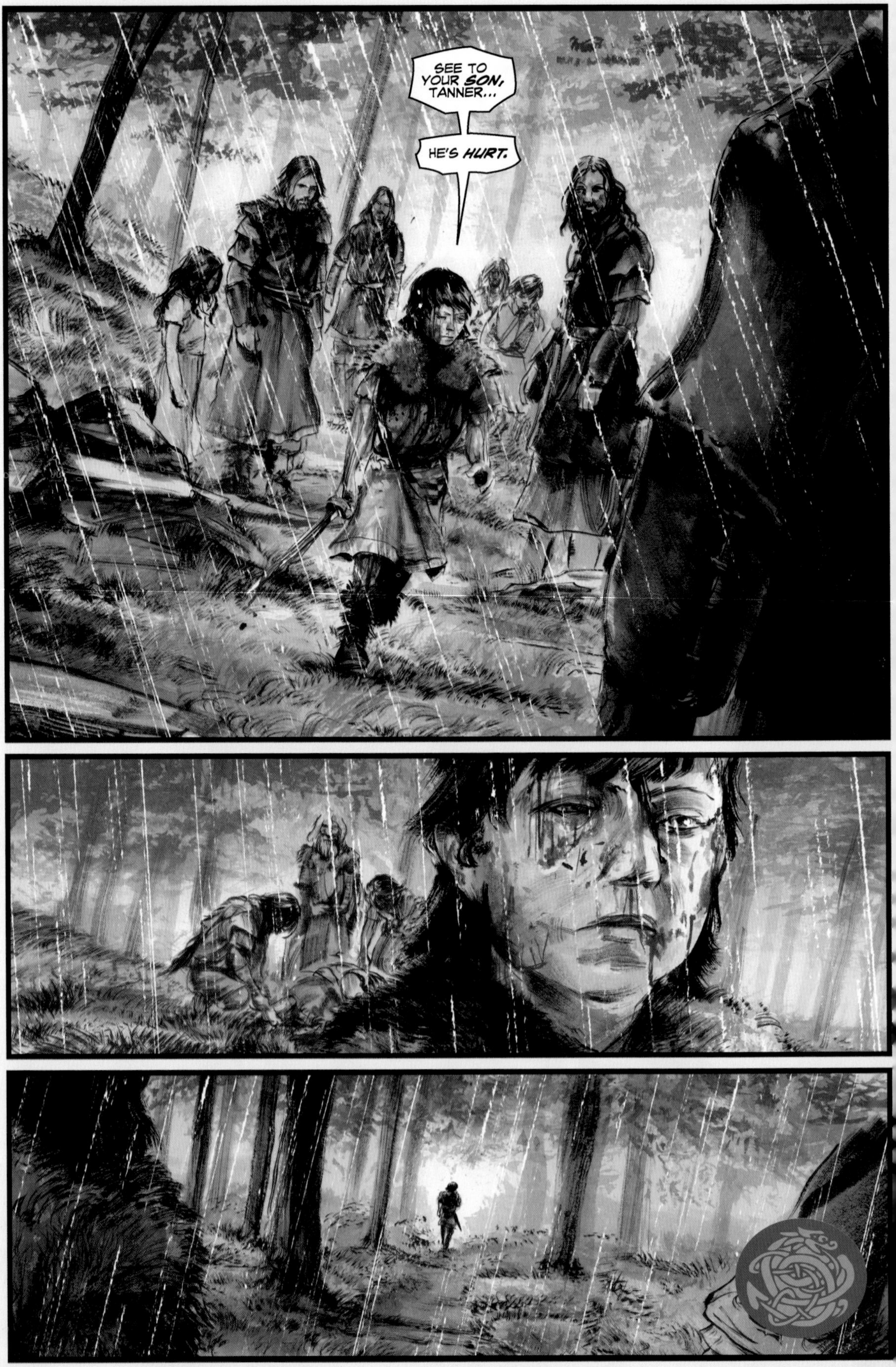
SEE TO YOUR SON, TANNER...
HE'S HURT.

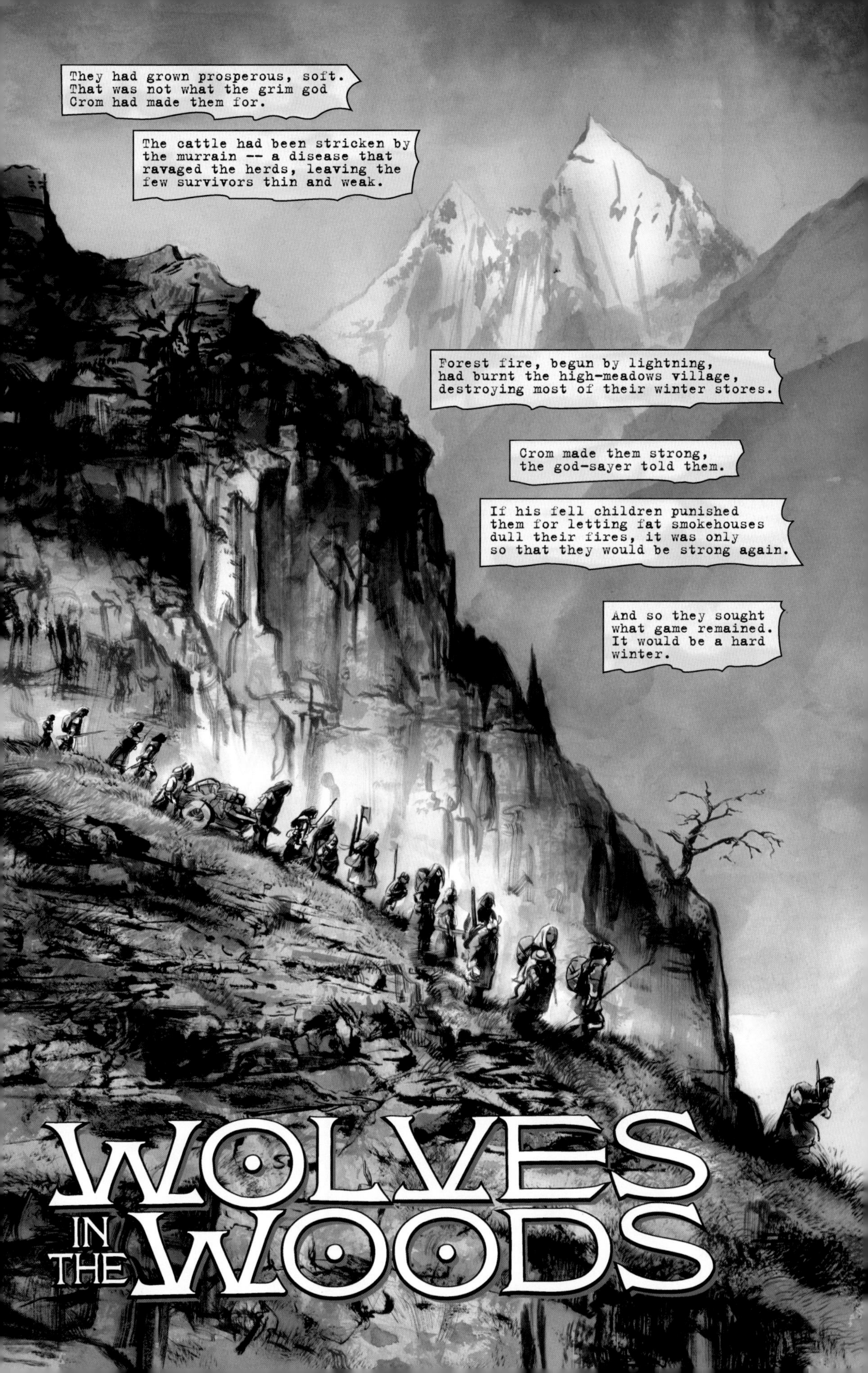
They had grown prosperous, soft. That was not what the grim god Crom had made them for.
The cattle had been stricken by the murrain -- a disease that ravaged the herds, leaving the few survivors thin and weak.
Forest fire, begun by lightning, had burnt the high-meadows village, destroying most of their winter stores.
Crom made them strong, the god-sayer told them.
If his fell children punished them for letting fat smokehouses dull their fires, it was only so that they would be strong again.
And so they sought what game remained. It would be a hard winter.
WOLVES IN THE WOODS

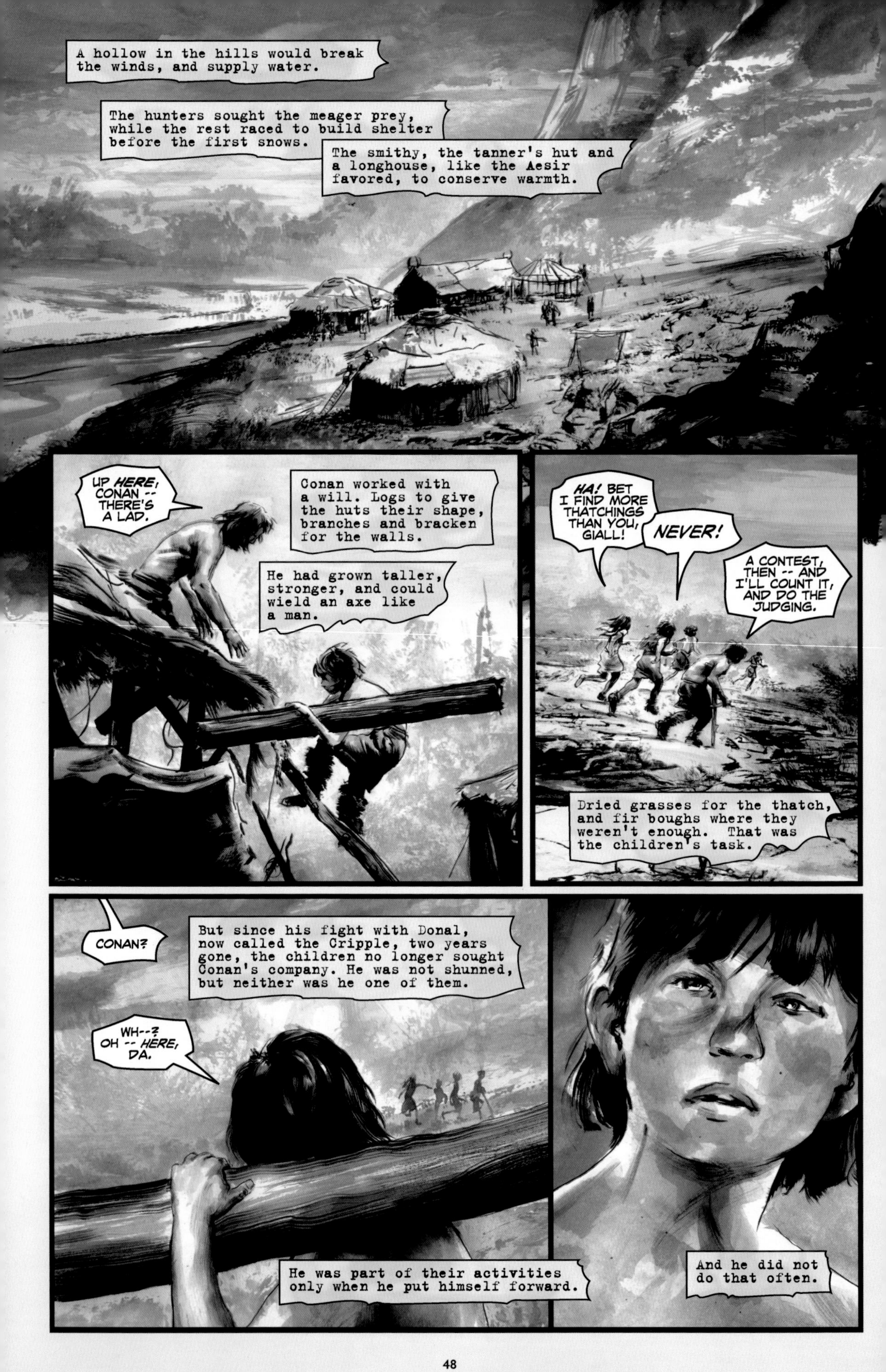
A hollow in the hills would break the winds, and supply water.
The hunters sought the meager prey, while the rest raced to build shelter before the first snows.
The smithy, the tanner's hut and a longhouse, like the Aesir favored, to conserve warmth.
UP HERE, CONAN -- THERE'S A LAD.
Conan worked with a will. Logs to give the huts their shape, branches and bracken for the walls.
He had grown taller, stronger, and could wield an axe like a man.
HA! BET I FIND MORE THATCHINGS THAN YOU, GIALL!
NEVER!
A CONTEST, THEN -- AND I'LL COUNT IT, AND DO THE JUDGING.
Dried grasses for the thatch, and fir boughs where they weren't enough. That was the children's task.
CONAN?
But since his fight with Donal, now called the Cripple, two years gone, the children no longer sought Conan's company. He was not shunned, but neither was he one of them.
WH--? OH -- HERE, DA.
He was part of their activities only when he put himself forward.
And he did not do that often.

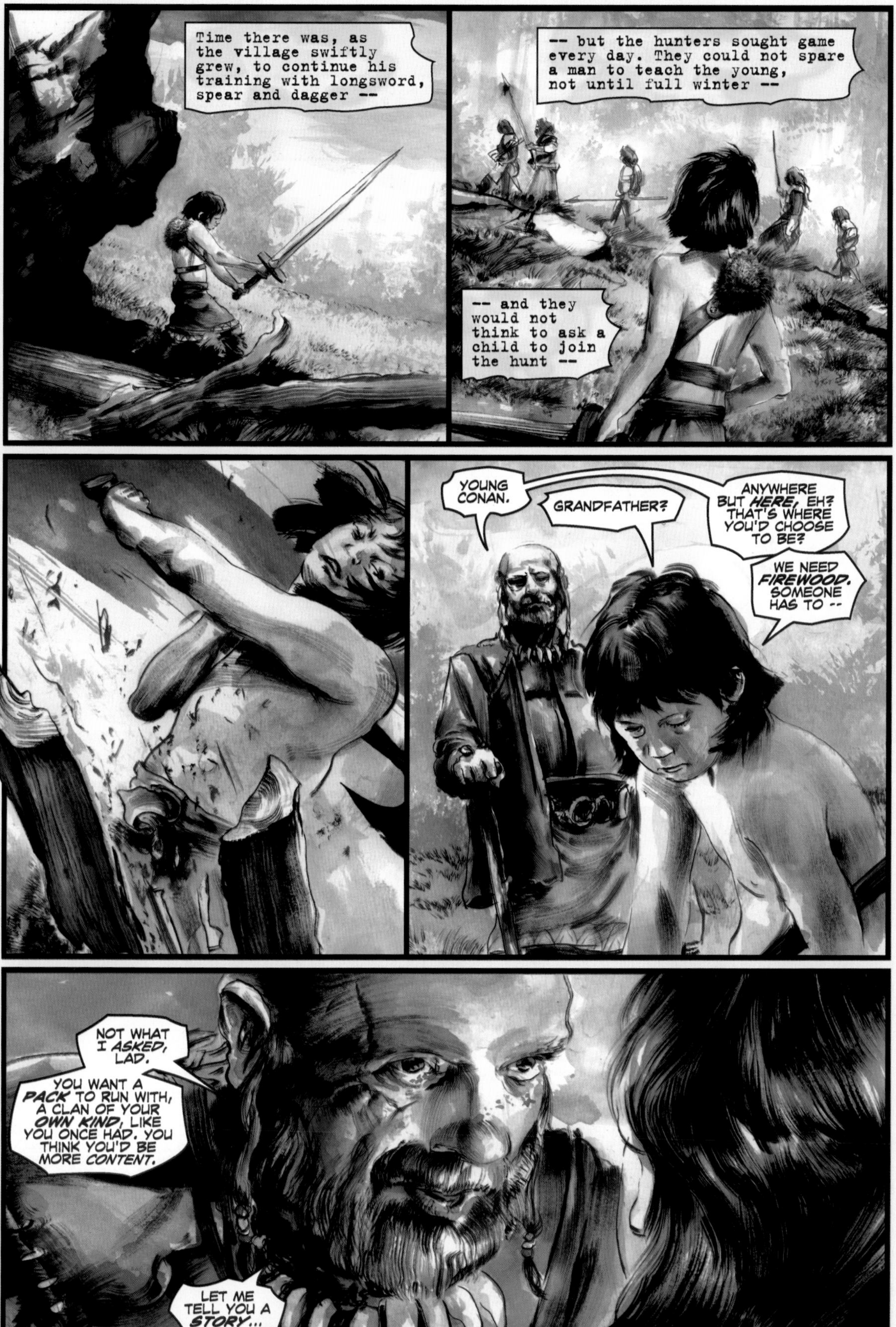
Time there was, as the village swiftly grew, to continue his training with longsword, spear and dagger --
-- but the hunters sought game every day. They could not spare a man to teach the young, not until full winter --
-- and they would not think to ask a child to join the hunt --
YOUNG CONAN.
GRANDFATHER?
ANYWHERE BUT HERE, EH? THAT'S WHERE YOU'D CHOOSE TO BE?
WE NEED FIREWOOD. SOMEONE HAS TO --
NOT WHAT I ASKED, LAD.
YOU WANT A PACK TO RUN WITH, A CLAN OF YOUR OWN KIND, LIKE YOU ONCE HAD. YOU THINK YOU'D BE MORE CONTENT.
LET ME TELL YOU A STORY...

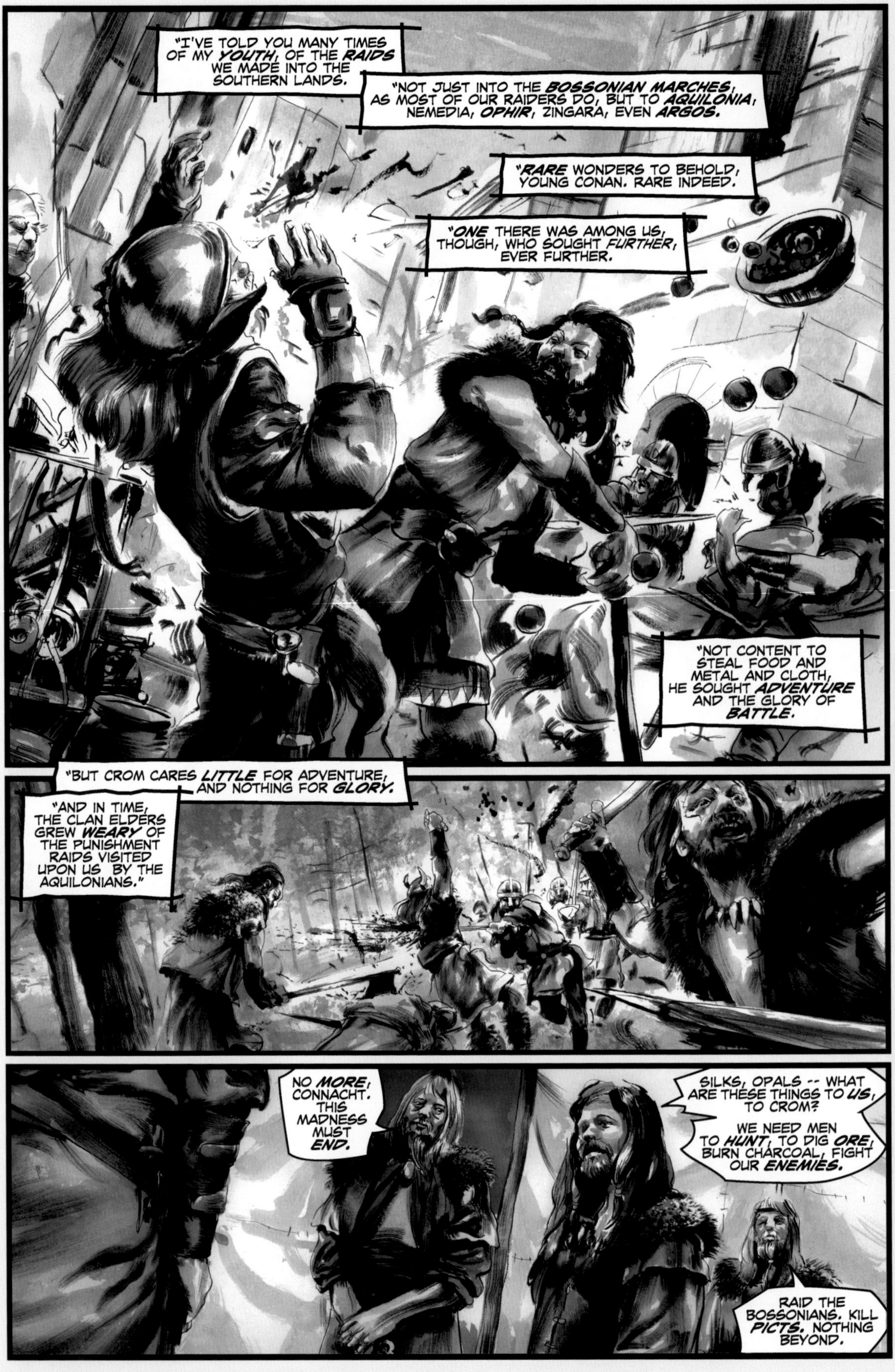
"I'VE TOLD YOU MANY TIMES OF MY YOUTH, OF THE RAIDS WE MADE INTO THE SOUTHERN LANDS.
"NOT JUST INTO THE BOSSONIAN MARCHES, AS MOST OF OUR RAIDERS DO, BUT TO AQUILONIA, NEMEDIA, OPHIR, ZINGARA, EVEN ARGOS.
"RARE WONDERS TO BEHOLD, YOUNG CONAN. RARE INDEED.
"ONE THERE WAS AMONG US, THOUGH, WHO SOUGHT FURTHER, EVER FURTHER.
"NOT CONTENT TO STEAL FOOD AND METAL AND CLOTH, HE SOUGHT ADVENTURE AND THE GLORY OF BATTLE.
"BUT CROM CARES LITTLE FOR ADVENTURE, AND NOTHING FOR GLORY.
"AND IN TIME, THE CLAN ELDERS GREW WEARY OF THE PUNISHMENT RAIDS VISITED UPON US BY THE AQUILONIANS."
NO MORE, CONNACHT. THIS MADNESS MUST END.
SILKS, OPALS -- WHAT ARE THESE THINGS TO US, TO CROM?
WE NEED MEN TO HUNT, TO DIG ORE, BURN CHARCOAL, FIGHT OUR ENEMIES.
RAID THE BOSSONIANS. KILL PICTS. NOTHING BEYOND.

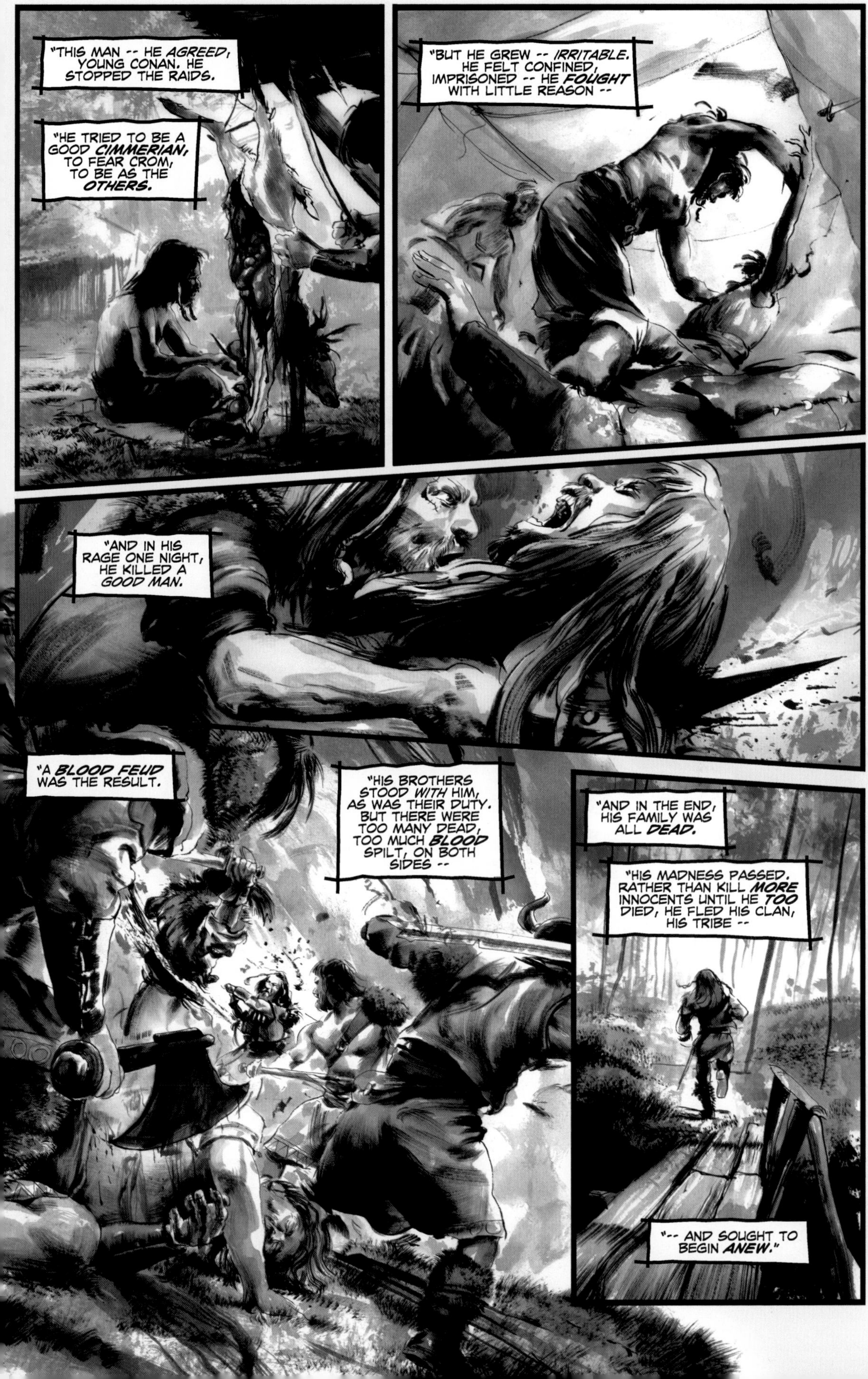
"THIS MAN -- HE *AGREED*, YOUNG CONAN. HE STOPPED THE RAIDS.
"HE TRIED TO BE A GOOD *CIMMERIAN*, TO FEAR CROM, TO BE AS THE *OTHERS*.
"BUT HE GREW -- *IRRITABLE*. HE FELT CONFINED, IMPRISONED -- HE *FOUGHT* WITH LITTLE REASON --
"AND IN HIS RAGE ONE NIGHT, HE KILLED A *GOOD MAN*.
"A *BLOOD FEUD* WAS THE RESULT.
"HIS BROTHERS STOOD *WITH* HIM, AS WAS THEIR DUTY. BUT THERE WERE TOO MANY DEAD, TOO MUCH *BLOOD* SPILT, ON BOTH SIDES --
"AND IN THE END, HIS FAMILY WAS ALL *DEAD*.
"HIS MADNESS PASSED. RATHER THAN KILL *MORE* INNOCENTS UNTIL HE *TOO* DIED, HE FLED HIS CLAN, HIS TRIBE --
"-- AND SOUGHT TO BEGIN *ANEW*."

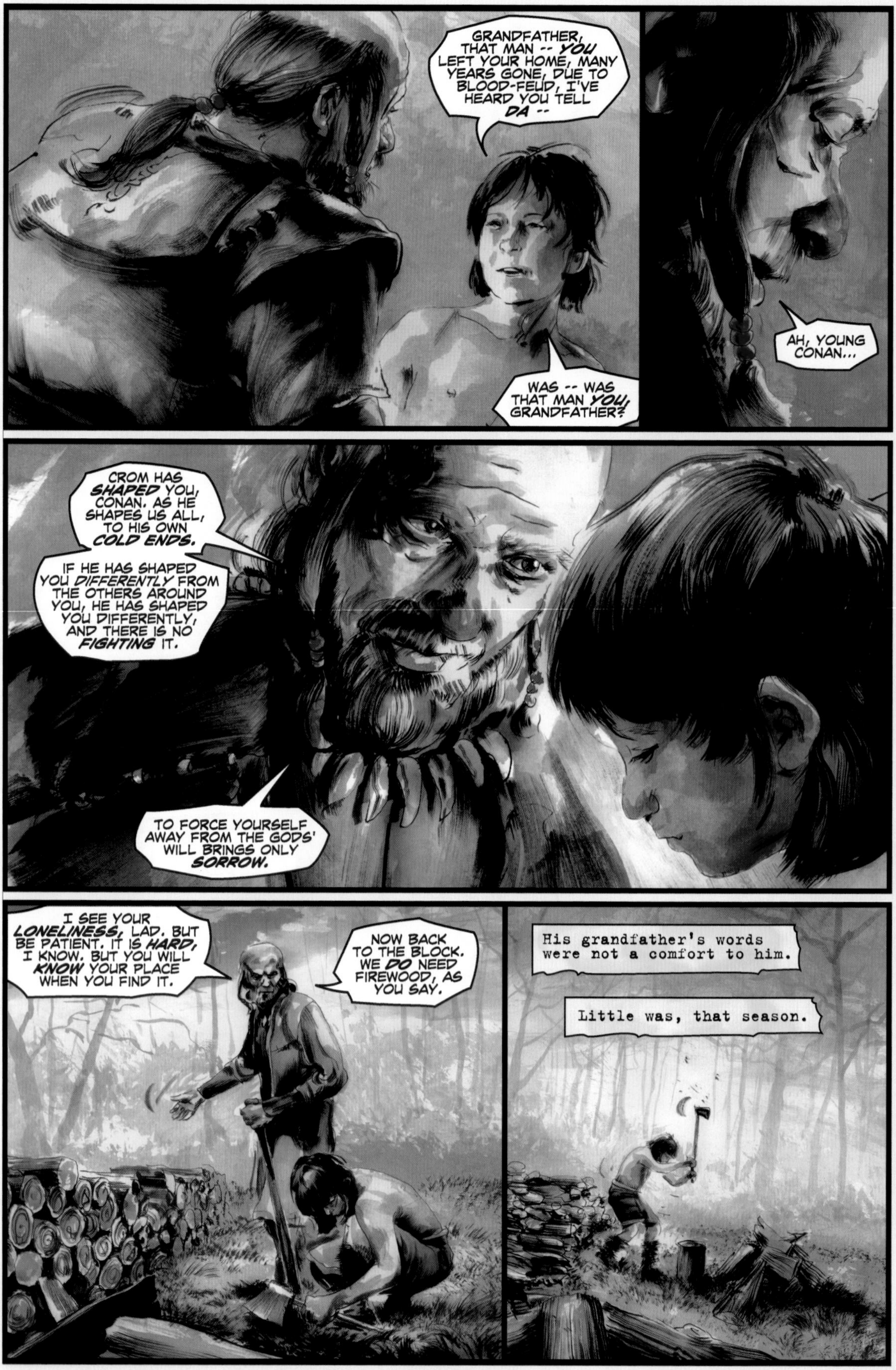
GRANDFATHER, THAT MAN -- YOU LEFT YOUR HOME, MANY YEARS GONE, DUE TO BLOOD-FEUD, I'VE HEARD YOU TELL DA --
WAS -- WAS THAT MAN YOU, GRANDFATHER?
AH, YOUNG CONAN...
CROM HAS SHAPED YOU, CONAN. AS HE SHAPES US ALL, TO HIS OWN COLD ENDS.
IF HE HAS SHAPED YOU DIFFERENTLY FROM THE OTHERS AROUND YOU, HE HAS SHAPED YOU DIFFERENTLY, AND THERE IS NO FIGHTING IT.
TO FORCE YOURSELF AWAY FROM THE GODS' WILL BRINGS ONLY SORROW.
I SEE YOUR LONELINESS, LAD. BUT BE PATIENT. IT IS HARD, I KNOW. BUT YOU WILL KNOW YOUR PLACE WHEN YOU FIND IT.
NOW BACK TO THE BLOCK. WE DO NEED FIREWOOD, AS YOU SAY.
His grandfather's words were not a comfort to him.
Little was, that season.

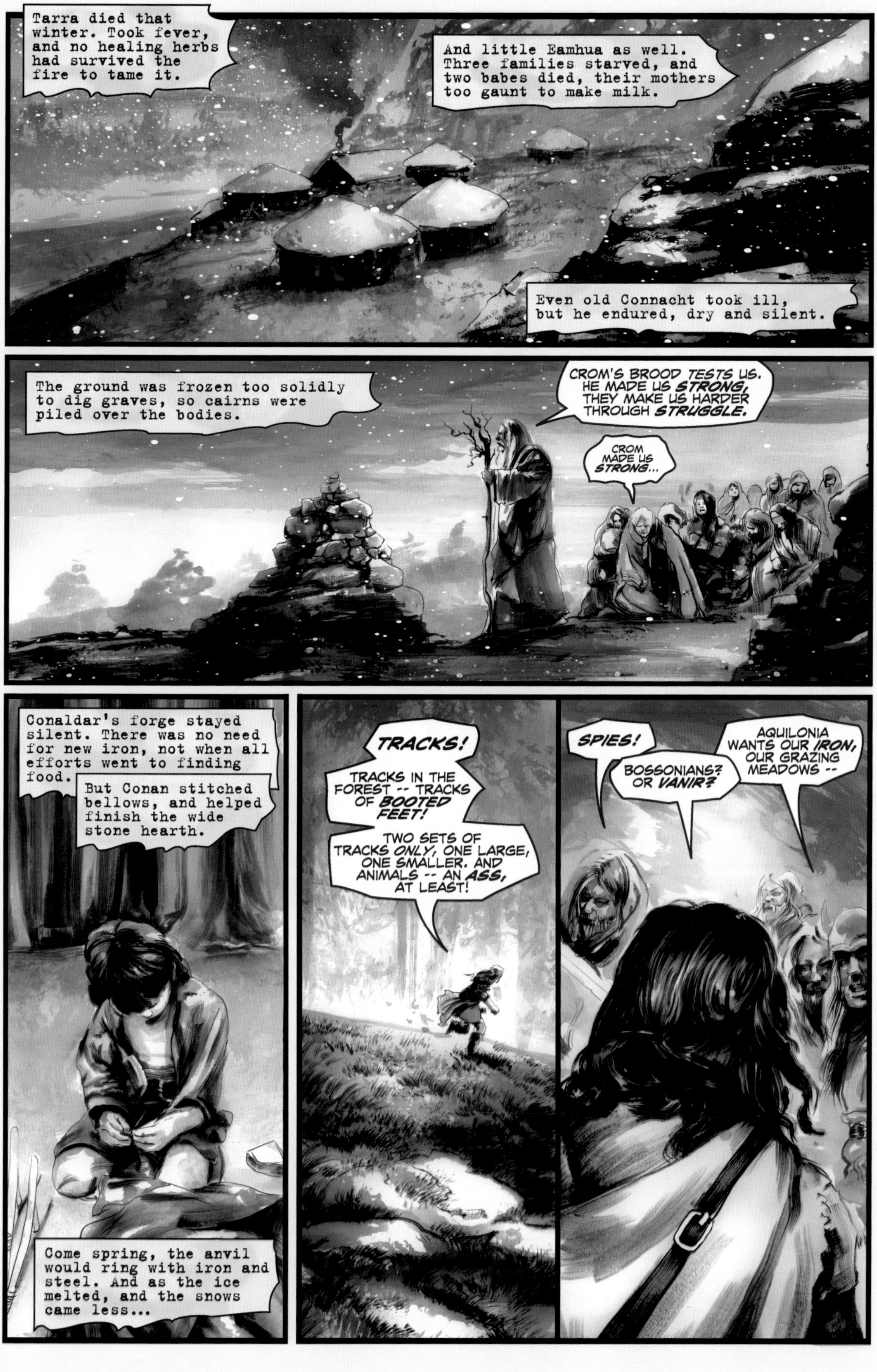

Tarra died that winter. Took fever, and no healing herbs had survived the fire to tame it.
And little Eamhua as well. Three families starved, and two babes died, their mothers too gaunt to make milk.
Even old Connacht took ill, but he endured, dry and silent.
The ground was frozen too solidly to dig graves, so cairns were piled over the bodies.
CROM'S BROOD TESTS US. HE MADE US STRONG, THEY MAKE US HARDER THROUGH STRUGGLE.
CROM MADE US STRONG...
Conaldar's forge stayed silent. There was no need for new iron, not when all efforts went to finding food.
But Conan stitched bellows, and helped finish the wide stone hearth.
Come spring, the anvil would ring with iron and steel. And as the ice melted, and the snows came less...
TRACKS!
TRACKS IN THE FOREST -- TRACKS OF BOOTED FEET!
TWO SETS OF TRACKS ONLY, ONE LARGE, ONE SMALLER. AND ANIMALS -- AN ASS, AT LEAST!
SPIES!
BOSSONIANS? OR VANIR?
AQUILONIA WANTS OUR IRON, OUR GRAZING MEADOWS --

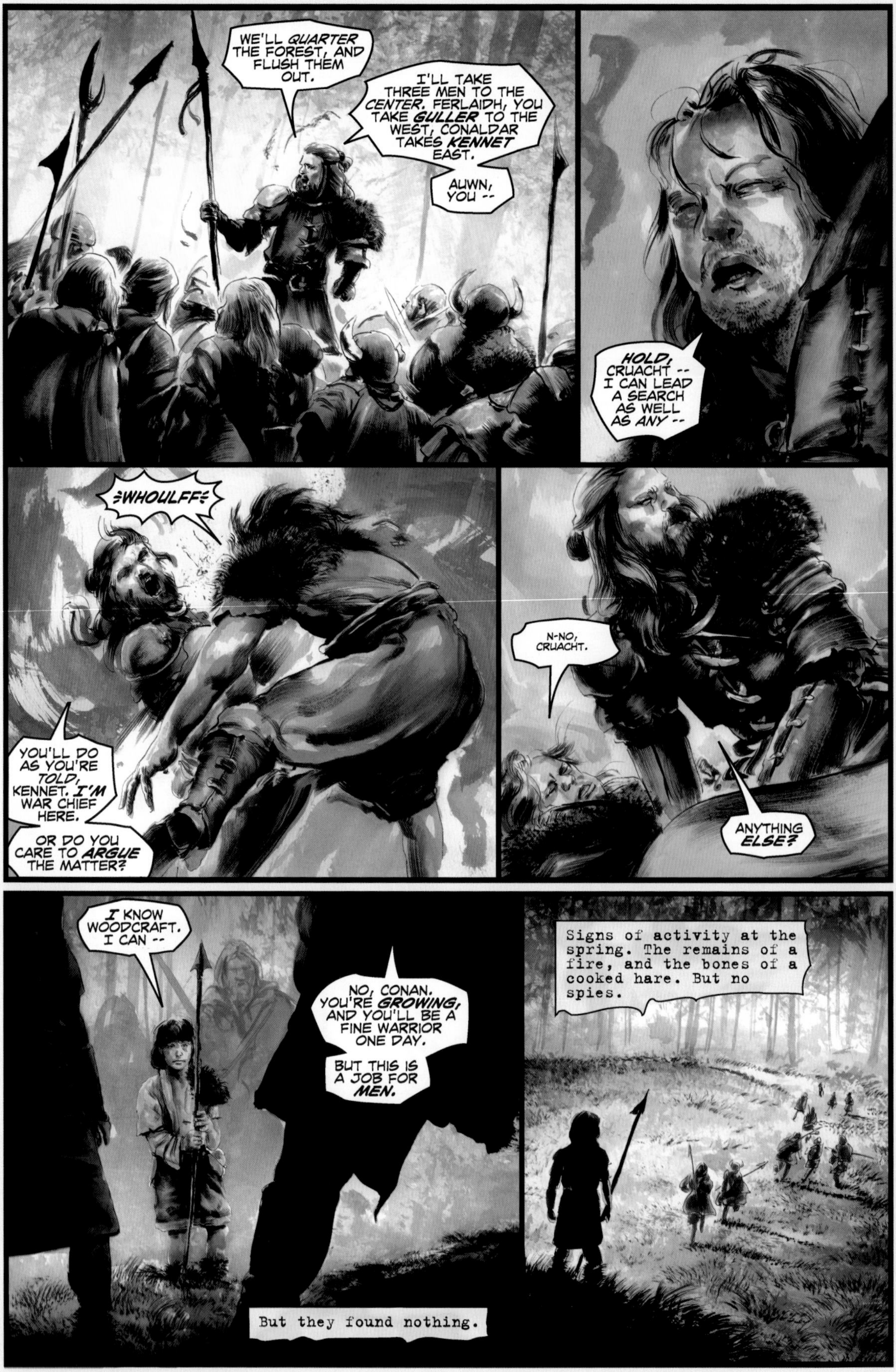
WE'LL QUARTER THE FOREST, AND FLUSH THEM OUT.
I'LL TAKE THREE MEN TO THE CENTER. FERLAIDH, YOU TAKE GULLER TO THE WEST, CONALDAR TAKES KENNET EAST.
AUWN, YOU --
HOLD, CRUACHT -- I CAN LEAD A SEARCH AS WELL AS ANY --
WHOULFF
YOU'LL DO AS YOU'RE TOLD, KENNET. I'M WAR CHIEF HERE.
OR DO YOU CARE TO ARGUE THE MATTER?
N-NO, CRUACHT.
ANYTHING ELSE?
I KNOW WOODCRAFT. I CAN --
NO, CONAN. YOU'RE GROWING, AND YOU'LL BE A FINE WARRIOR ONE DAY.
BUT THIS IS A JOB FOR MEN.
But they found nothing.
Signs of activity at the spring. The remains of a fire, and the bones of a cooked hare. But no spies.

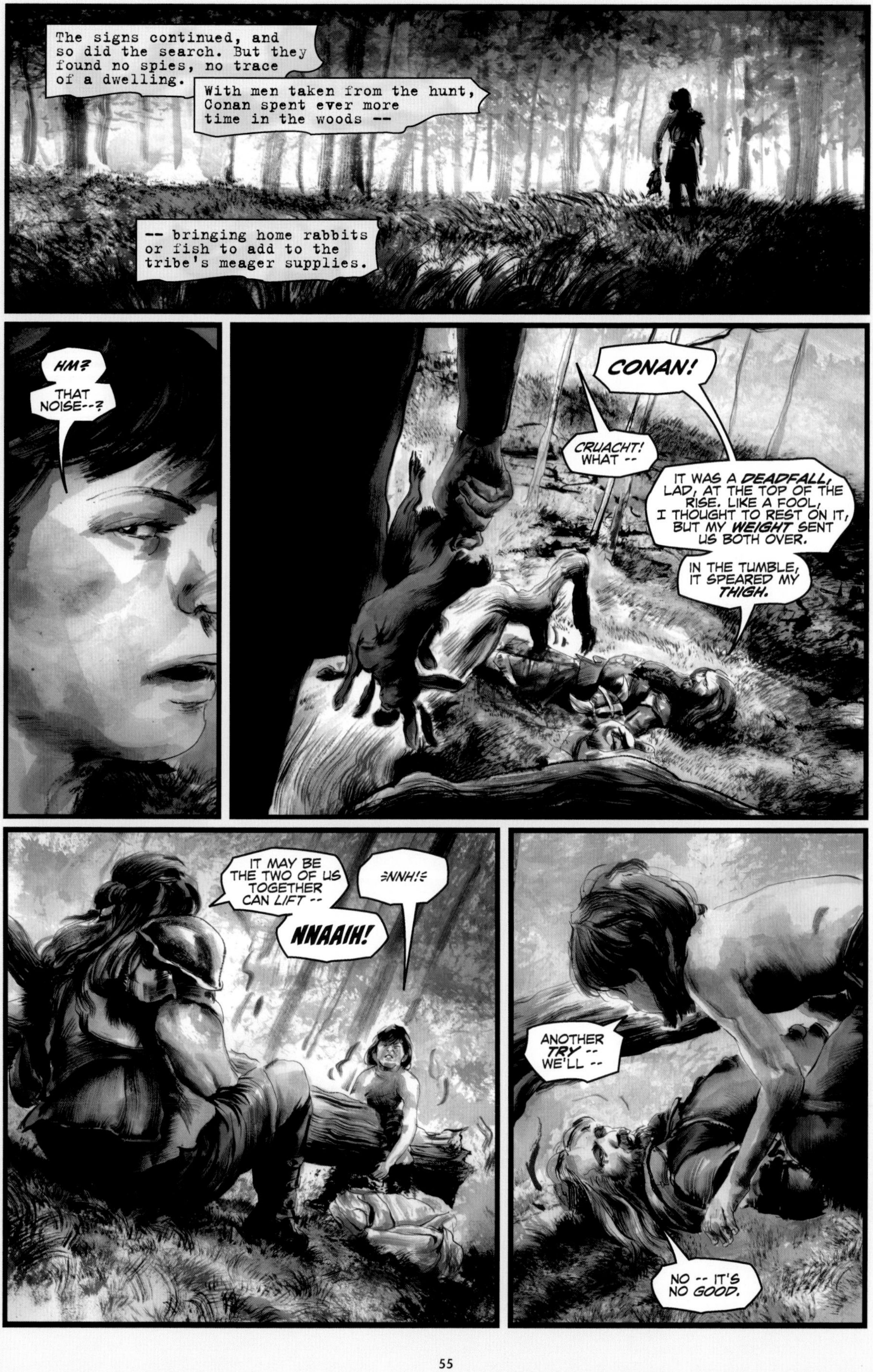
The signs continued, and so did the search. But they found no spies, no trace of a dwelling.
With men taken from the hunt, Conan spent ever more time in the woods --
-- bringing home rabbits or fish to add to the tribe's meager supplies.
HM? THAT NOISE--?
CONAN!
CRUACHT! WHAT --
IT WAS A DEADFALL, LAD, AT THE TOP OF THE RISE. LIKE A FOOL, I THOUGHT TO REST ON IT, BUT MY WEIGHT SENT US BOTH OVER.
IN THE TUMBLE, IT SPEARED MY THIGH.
IT MAY BE THE TWO OF US TOGETHER CAN LIFT --
NNH!
NNAAIH!
ANOTHER TRY -- WE'LL --
NO -- IT'S NO GOOD.

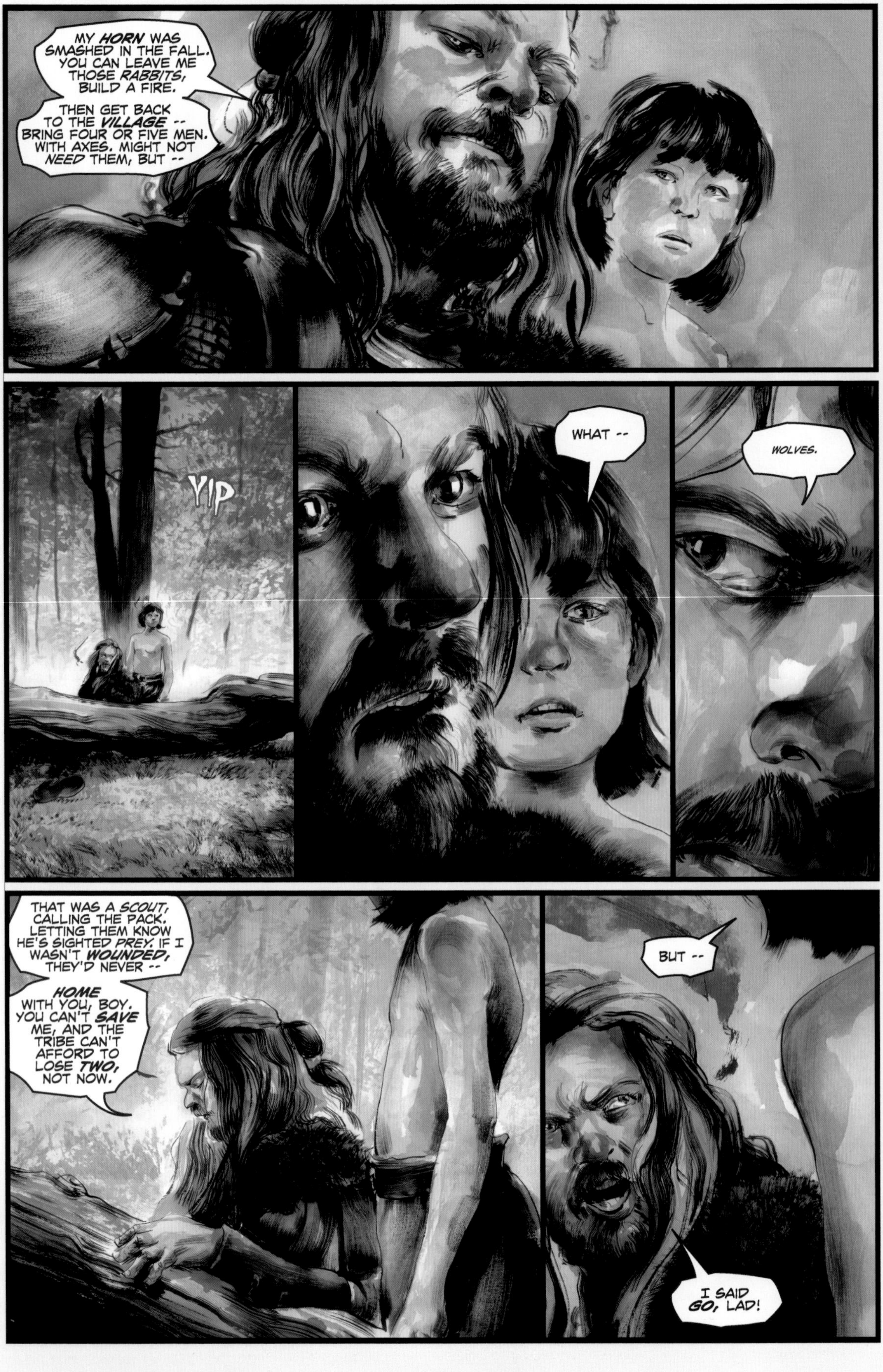

MY HORN WAS SMASHED IN THE FALL. YOU CAN LEAVE ME THOSE RABBITS, BUILD A FIRE.
THEN GET BACK TO THE VILLAGE -- BRING FOUR OR FIVE MEN. WITH AXES. MIGHT NOT NEED THEM, BUT --
YIP
WHAT --
WOLVES.
THAT WAS A SCOUT, CALLING THE PACK. LETTING THEM KNOW HE'S SIGHTED PREY. IF I WASN'T WOUNDED, THEY'D NEVER --
HOME WITH YOU, BOY. YOU CAN'T SAVE ME, AND THE TRIBE CAN'T AFFORD TO LOSE TWO, NOT NOW.
BUT --
I SAID GO, LAD!

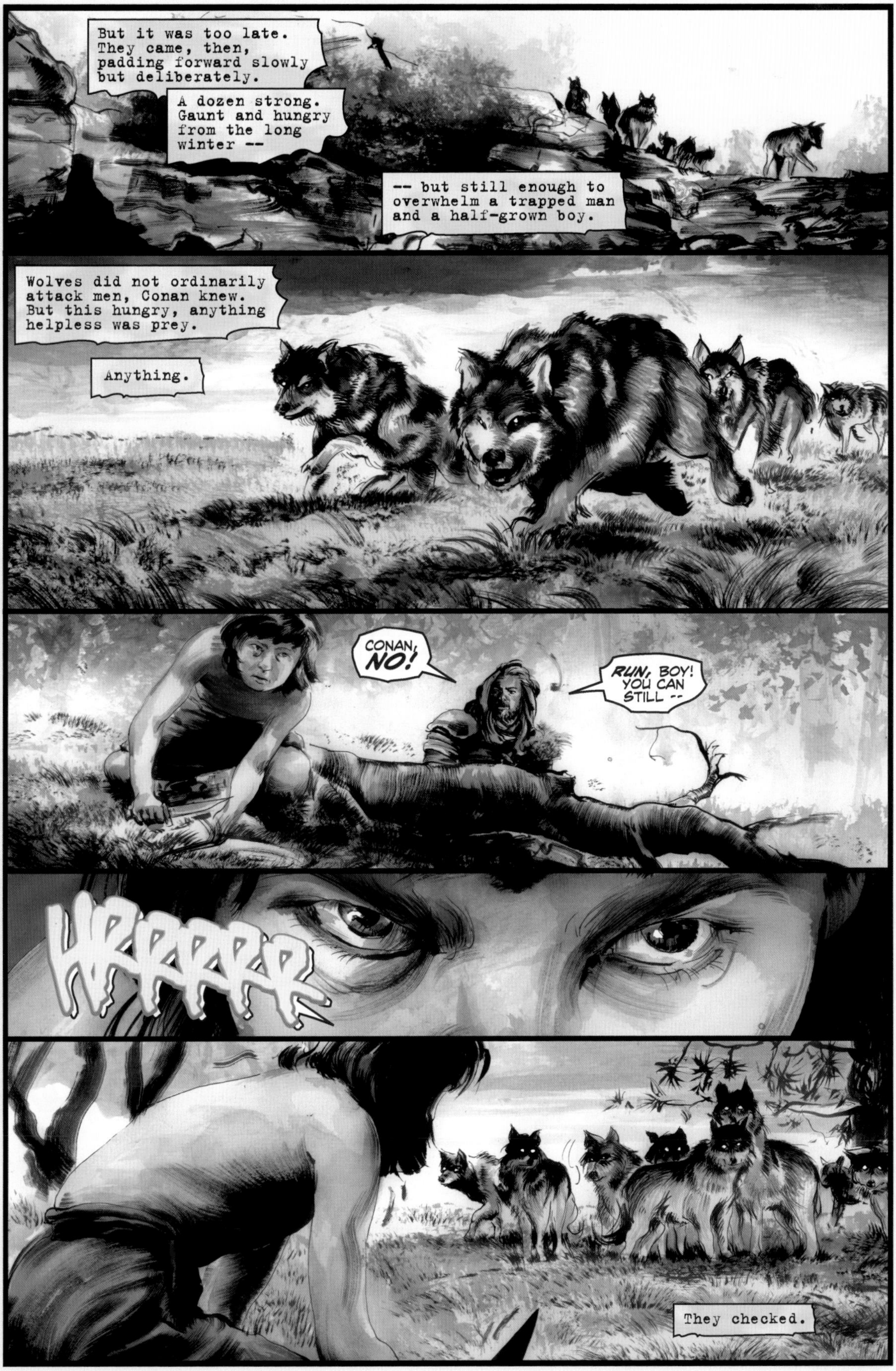
But it was too late. They came, then, padding forward slowly but deliberately.
A dozen strong. Gaunt and hungry from the long winter --
-- but still enough to overwhelm a trapped man and a half-grown boy.
Wolves did not ordinarily attack men, Conan knew. But this hungry, anything helpless was prey.
Anything.
CONAN, NO!
RUN, BOY! YOU CAN STILL --
HRRRRR
They checked.

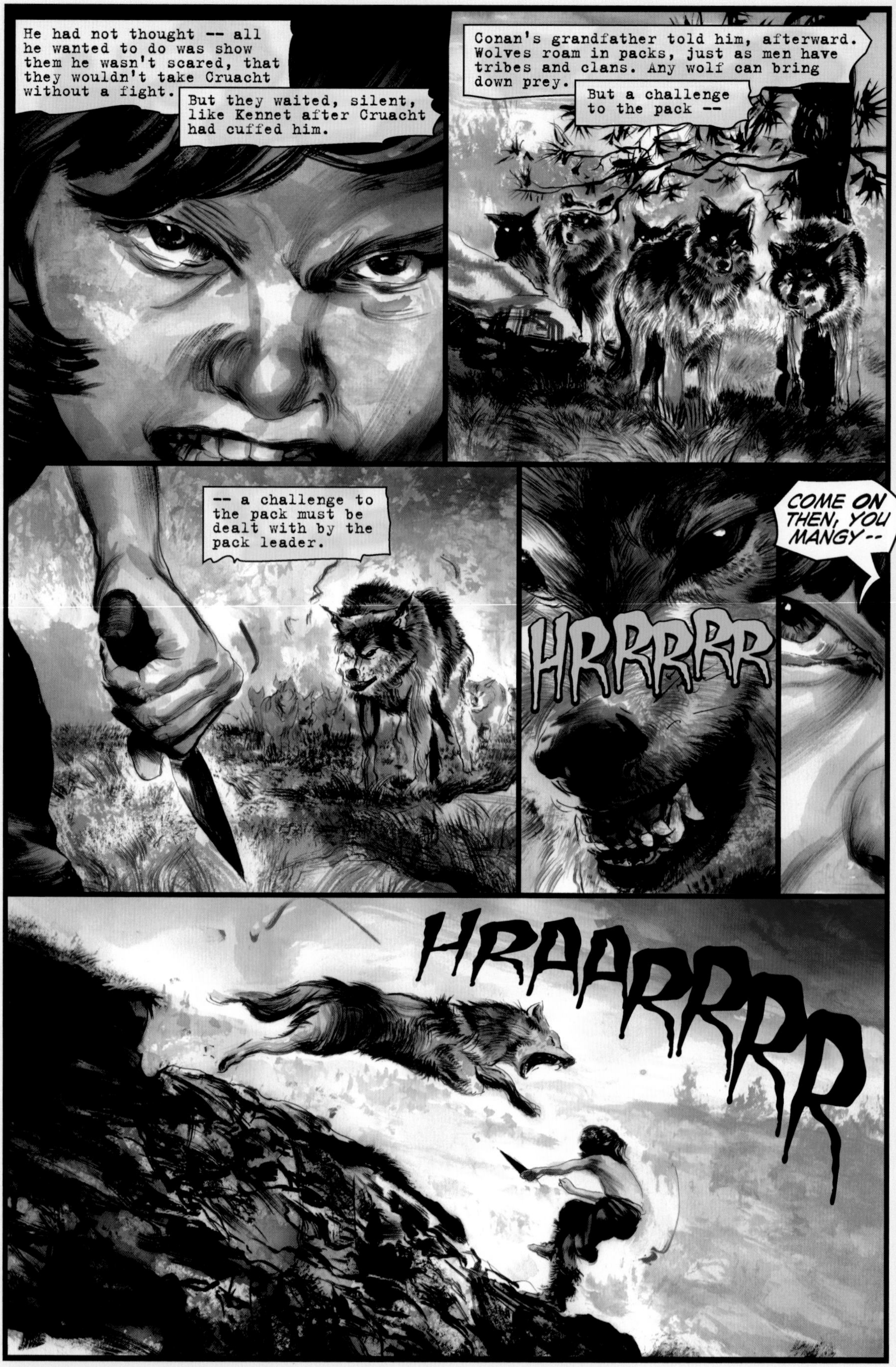
He had not thought -- all he wanted to do was show them he wasn't scared, that they wouldn't take Cruacht without a fight.
But they waited, silent, like Kennet after Cruacht had cuffed him.
Conan's grandfather told him, afterward. Wolves roam in packs, just as men have tribes and clans. Any wolf can bring down prey.
But a challenge to the pack --
-- a challenge to the pack must be dealt with by the pack leader.
HRRRRR
COME ON THEN, YOU MANGY --
HRAARRRRR

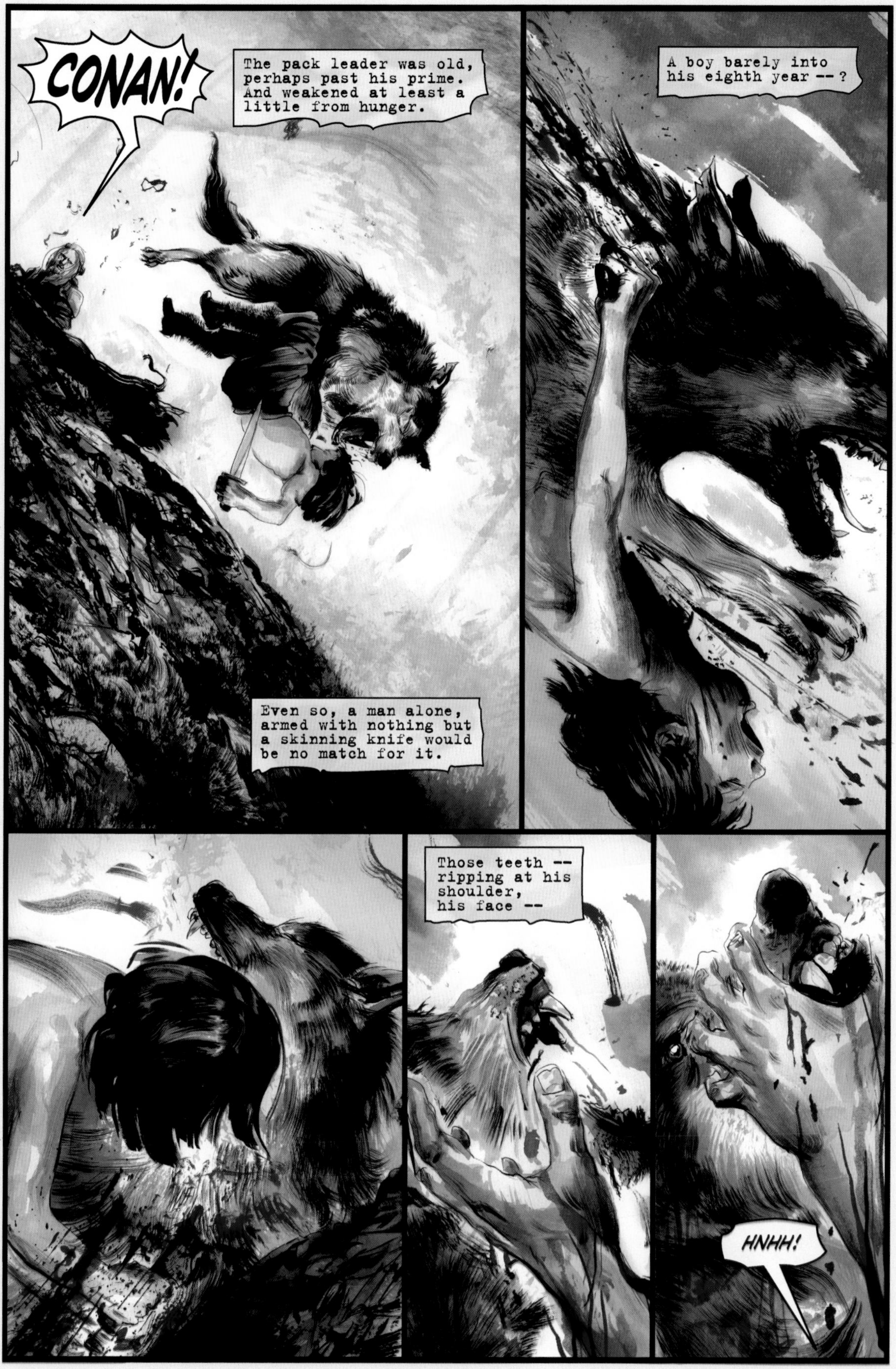

CONAN!
The pack leader was old, perhaps past his prime. And weakened at least a little from hunger.
Even so, a man alone, armed with nothing but a skinning knife would be no match for it.
A boy barely into his eighth year -- ?
Those teeth -- ripping at his shoulder, his face --
HNHH!

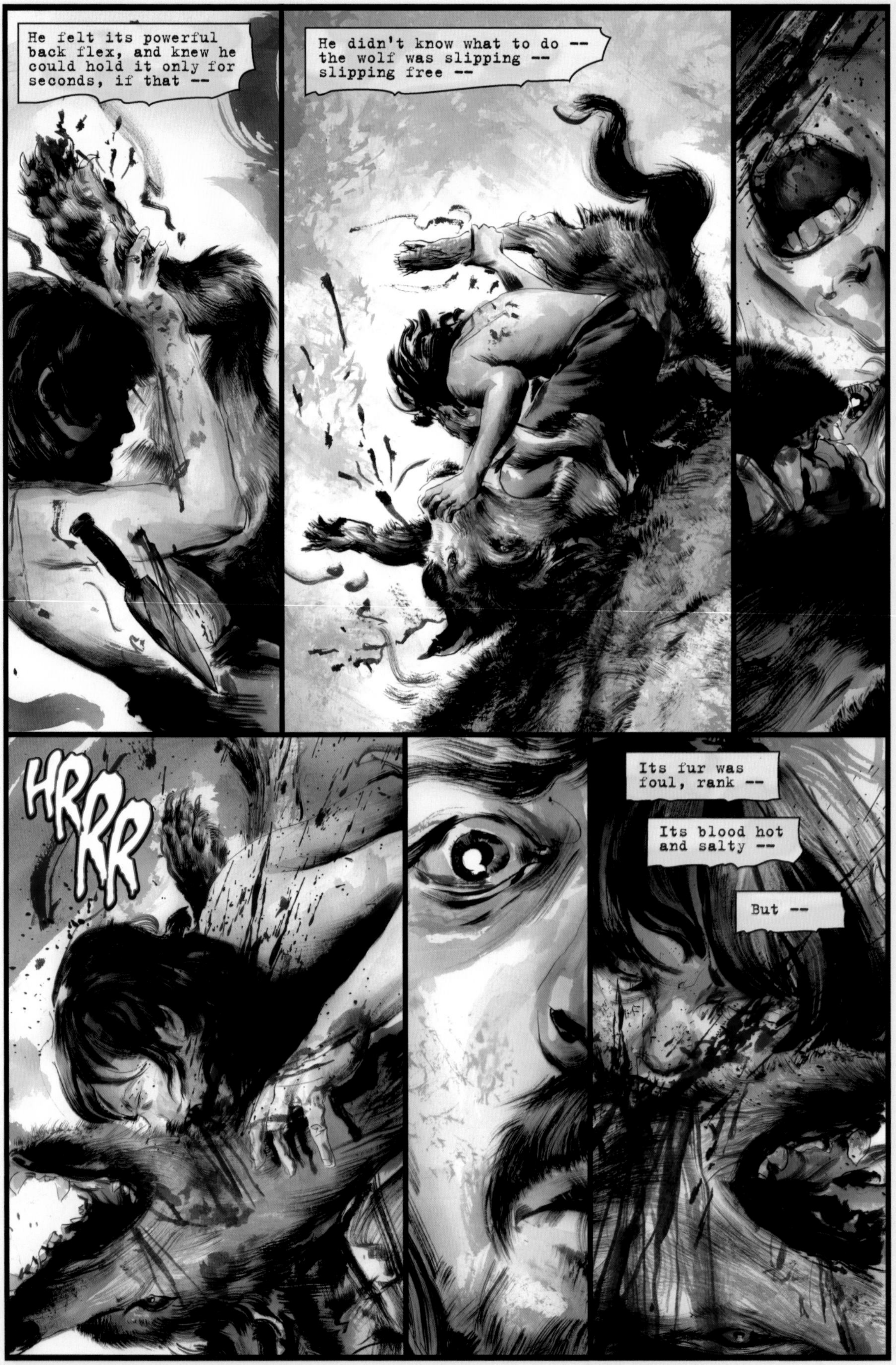
He felt its powerful back flex, and knew he could hold it only for seconds, if that --
He didn't know what to do -- the wolf was slipping -- slipping free --
HRRR
Its fur was foul, rank --
Its blood hot and salty --
But --

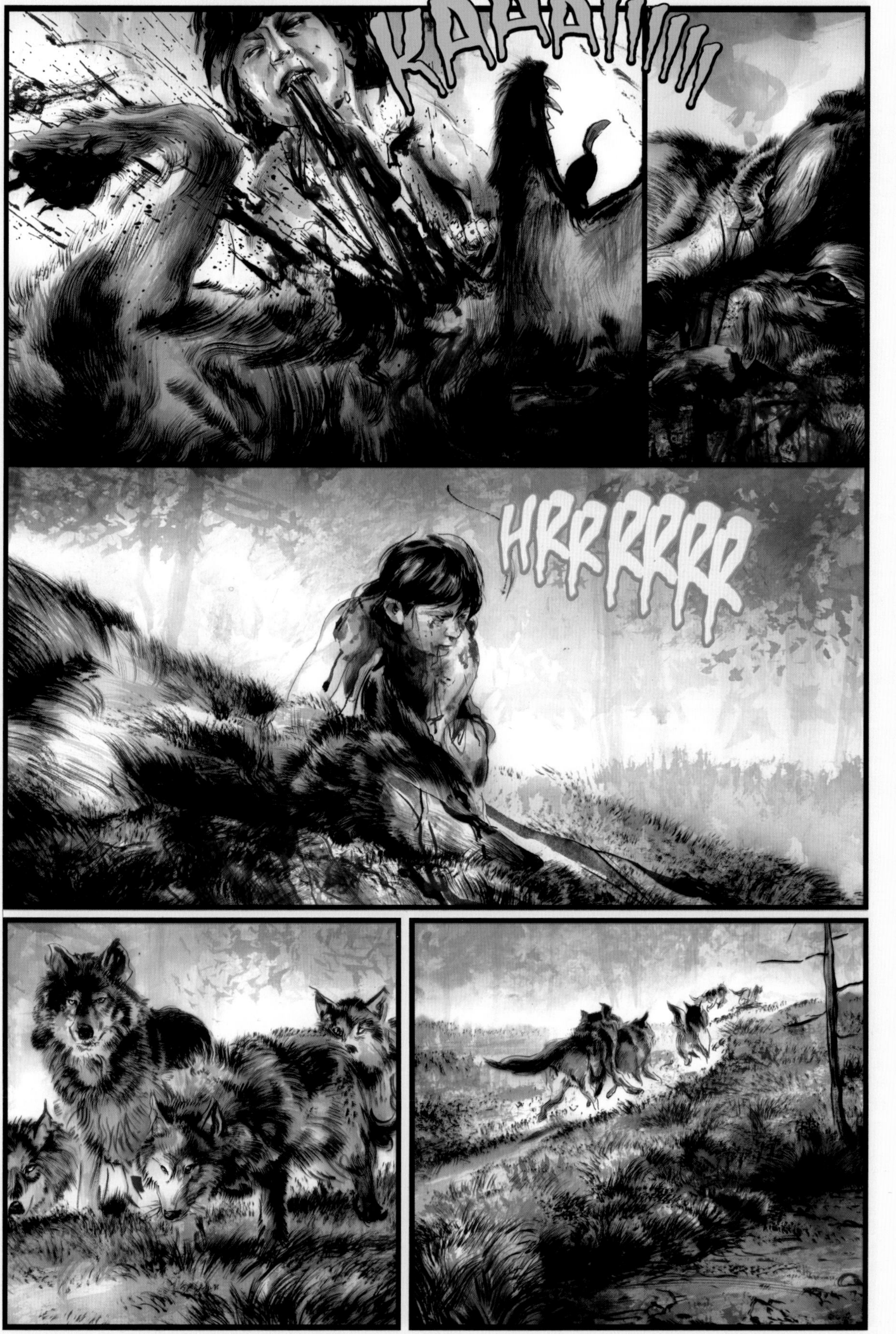
KAAAIIIIII
HRRRRRR

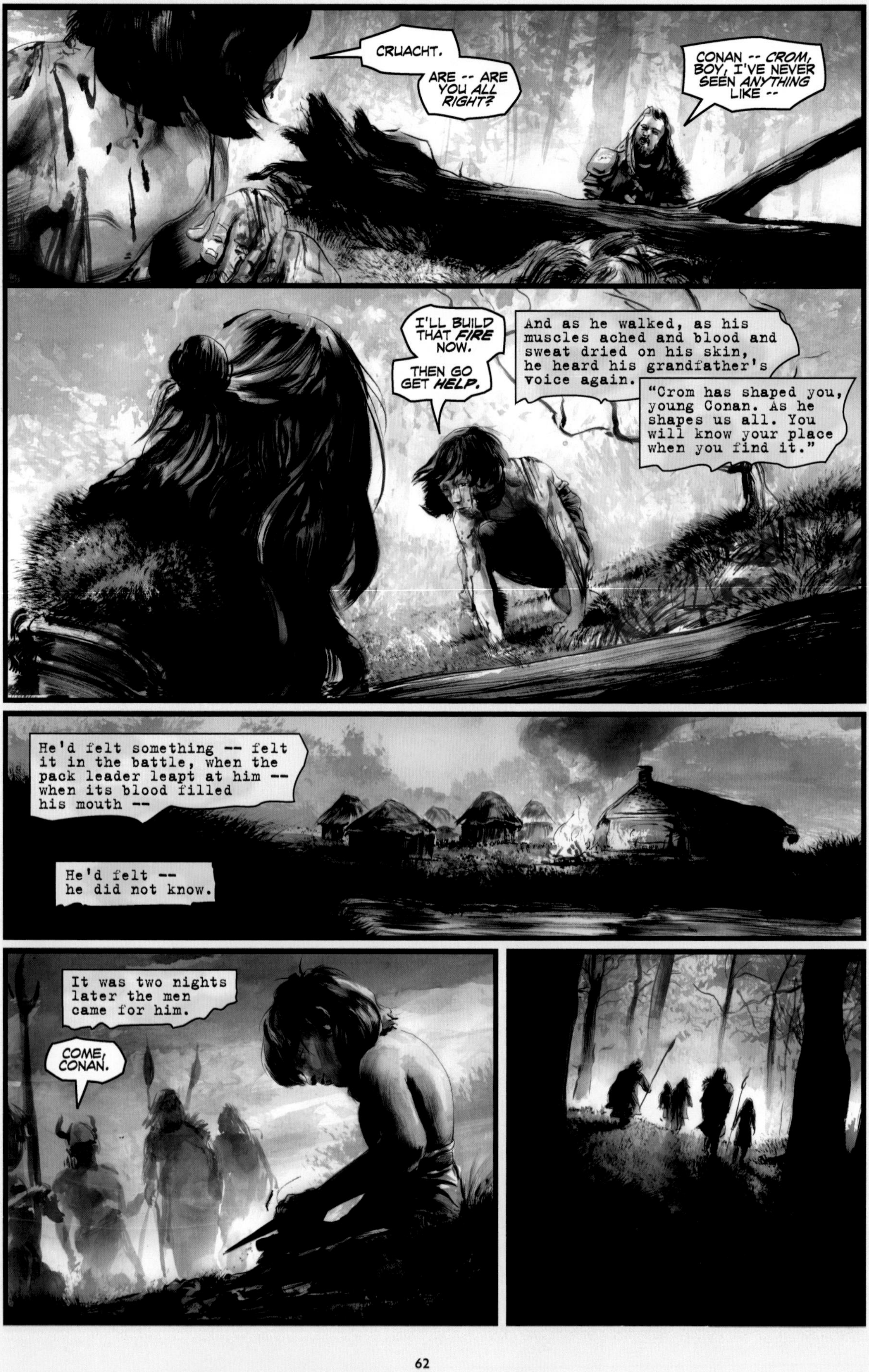
CRUACHT.
ARE -- ARE YOU ALL RIGHT?
CONAN -- CROM, BOY, I'VE NEVER SEEN ANYTHING LIKE --
I'LL BUILD THAT FIRE NOW.
THEN GO GET HELP.
And as he walked, as his muscles ached and blood and sweat dried on his skin, he heard his grandfather's voice again.
"Crom has shaped you, young Conan. As he shapes us all. You will know your place when you find it."
He'd felt something -- felt it in the battle, when the pack leader leapt at him -- when its blood filled his mouth --
He'd felt -- he did not know.
It was two nights later the men came for him.
COME, CONAN.

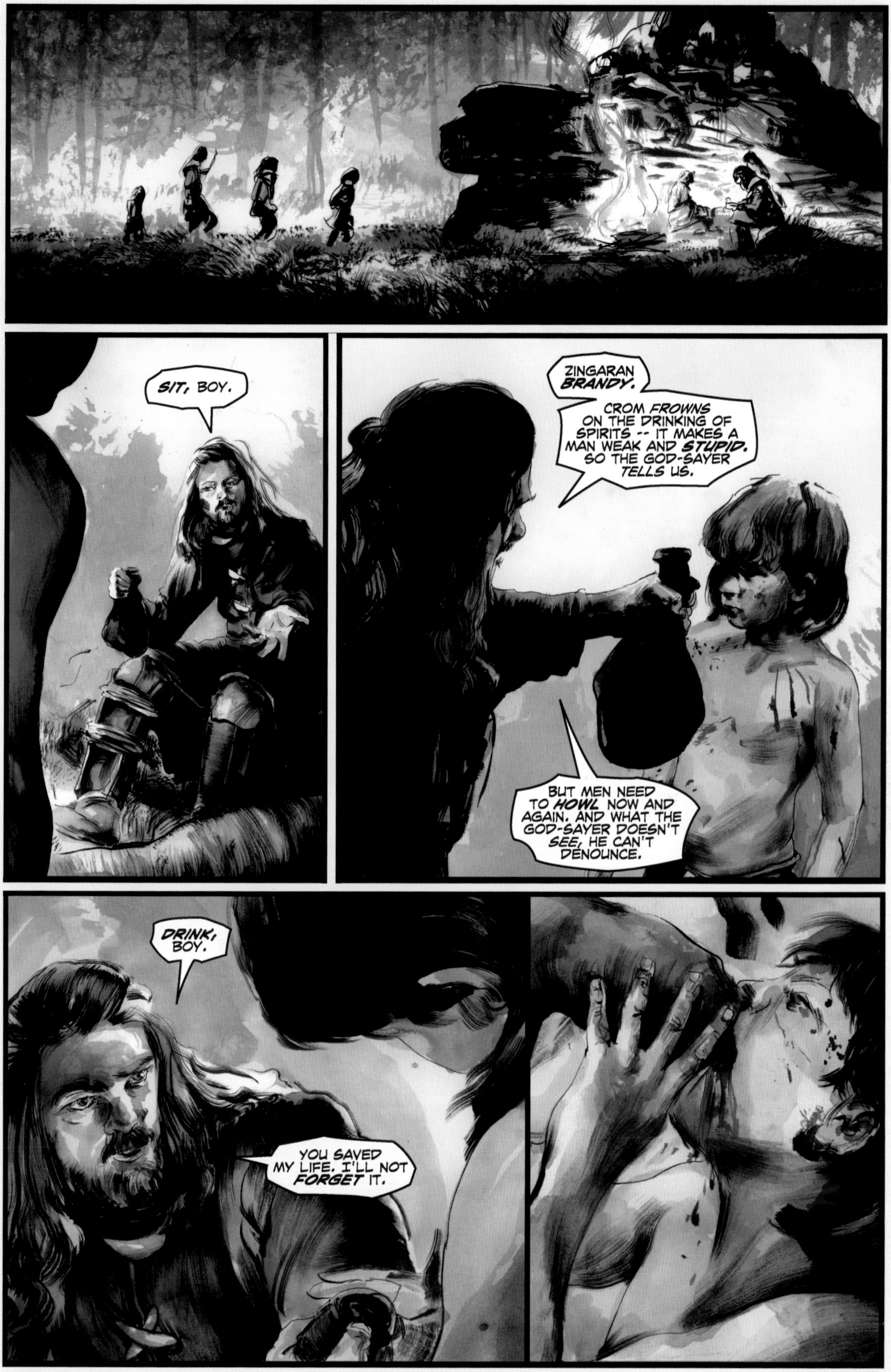
SIT, BOY.
ZINGARAN BRANDY.
CROM FROWNS ON THE DRINKING OF SPIRITS -- IT MAKES A MAN WEAK AND STUPID. SO THE GOD-SAYER TELLS US.
BUT MEN NEED TO HOWL NOW AND AGAIN. AND WHAT THE GOD-SAYER DOESN'T SEE, HE CAN'T DENOUNCE.
DRINK, BOY.
YOU SAVED MY LIFE. I'LL NOT FORGET IT.

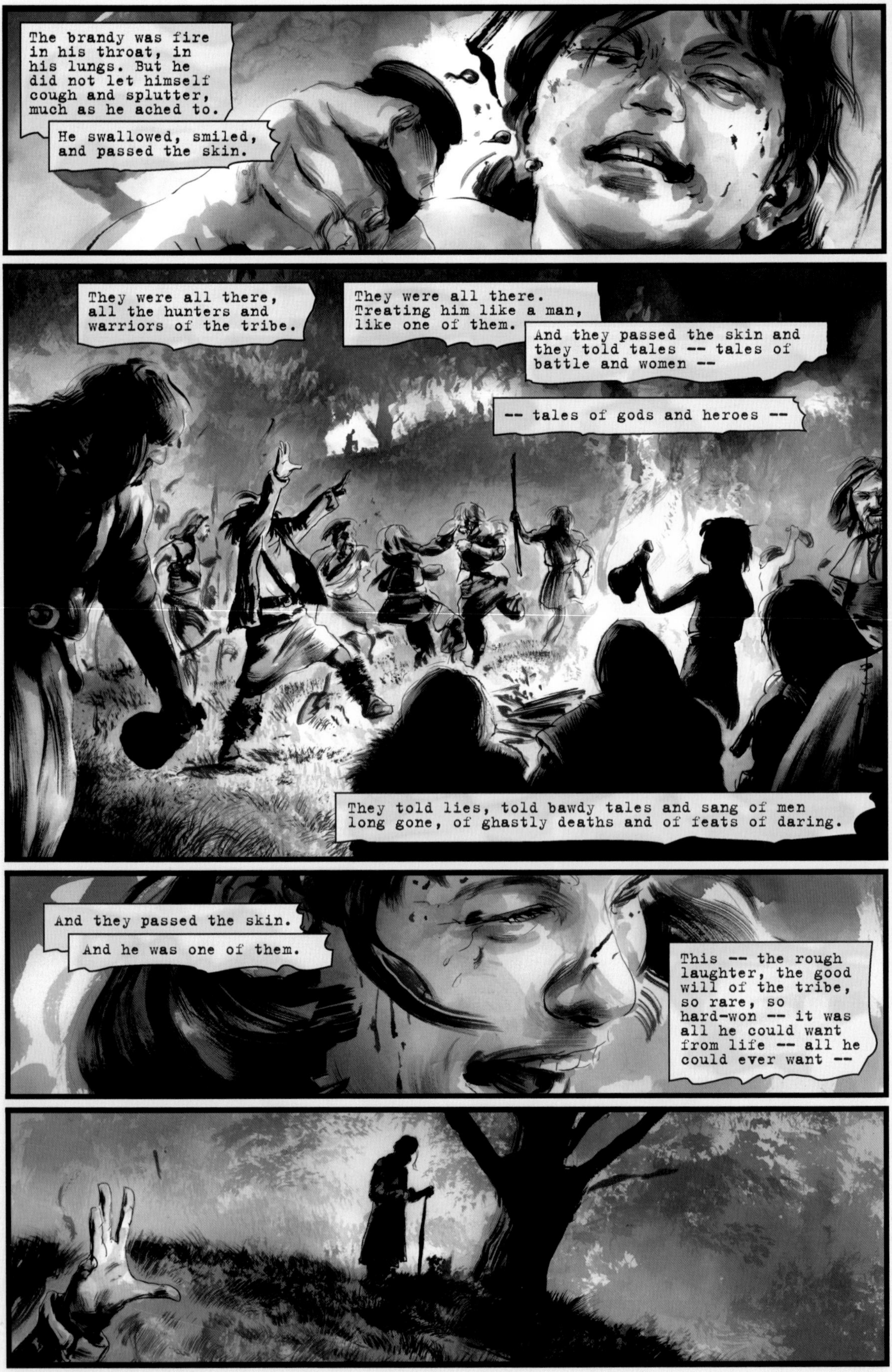
The brandy was fire in his throat, in his lungs. But he did not let himself cough and splutter, much as he ached to.
He swallowed, smiled, and passed the skin.
They were all there, all the hunters and warriors of the tribe.
They were all there. Treating him like a man, like one of them.
And they passed the skin and they told tales -- tales of battle and women --
-- tales of gods and heroes --
They told lies, told bawdy tales and sang of men long gone, of ghastly deaths and of feats of daring.
And they passed the skin.
And he was one of them.
This -- the rough laughter, the good will of the tribe, so rare, so hard-won -- it was all he could want from life -- all he could ever want --

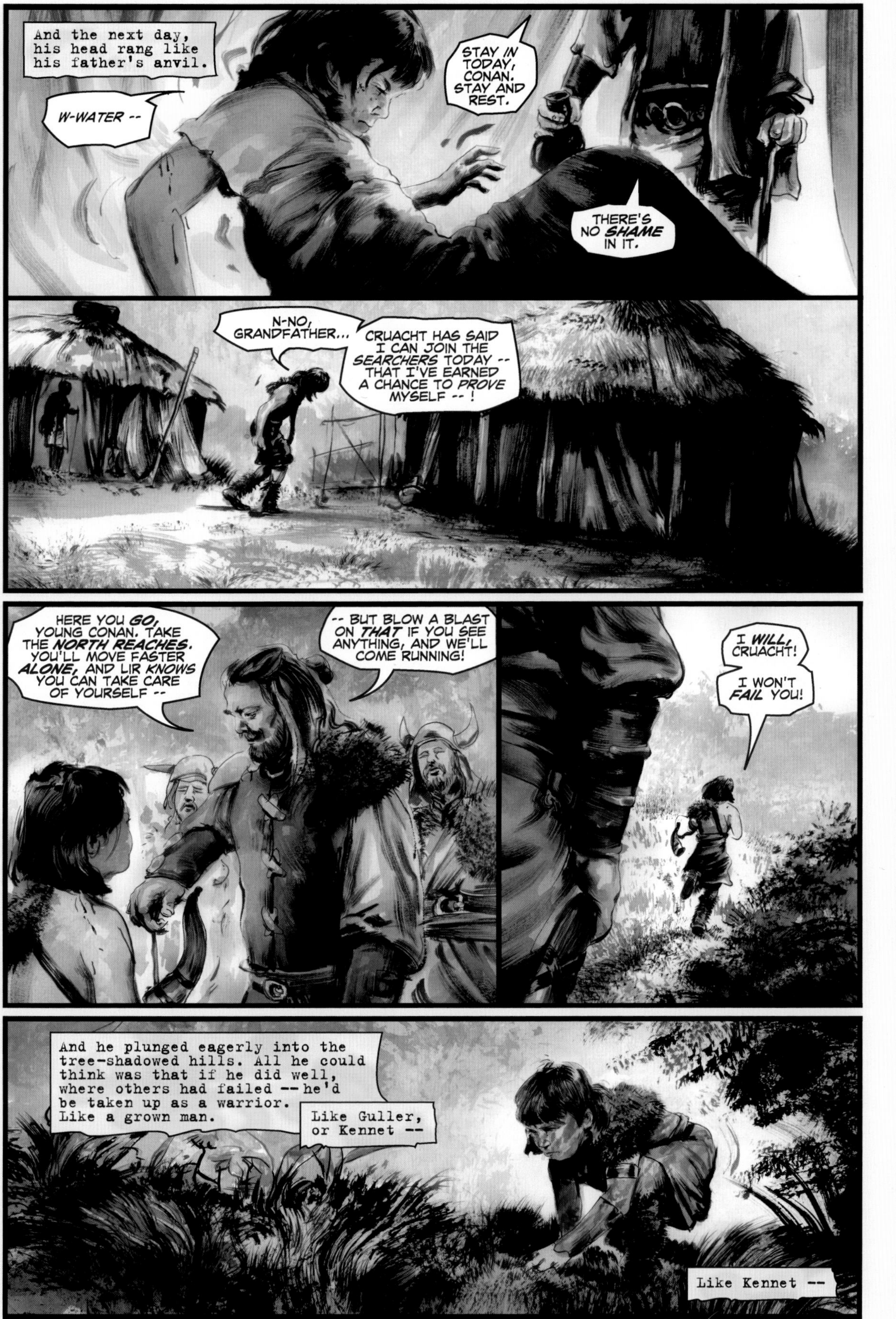
And the next day, his head rang like his father's anvil.
W-WATER --
STAY IN TODAY, CONAN. STAY AND REST.
THERE'S NO SHAME IN IT.
N-NO, GRANDFATHER...
CRUACHT HAS SAID I CAN JOIN THE SEARCHERS TODAY -- THAT I'VE EARNED A CHANCE TO PROVE MYSELF -- !
HERE YOU GO, YOUNG CONAN. TAKE THE NORTH REACHES. YOU'LL MOVE FASTER ALONE, AND LIR KNOWS YOU CAN TAKE CARE OF YOURSELF --
-- BUT BLOW A BLAST ON THAT IF YOU SEE ANYTHING, AND WE'LL COME RUNNING!
I WILL, CRUACHT!
I WON'T FAIL YOU!
And he plunged eagerly into the tree-shadowed hills. All he could think was that if he did well, where others had failed -- he'd be taken up as a warrior. Like a grown man.
Like Guller, or Kennet --
Like Kennet --

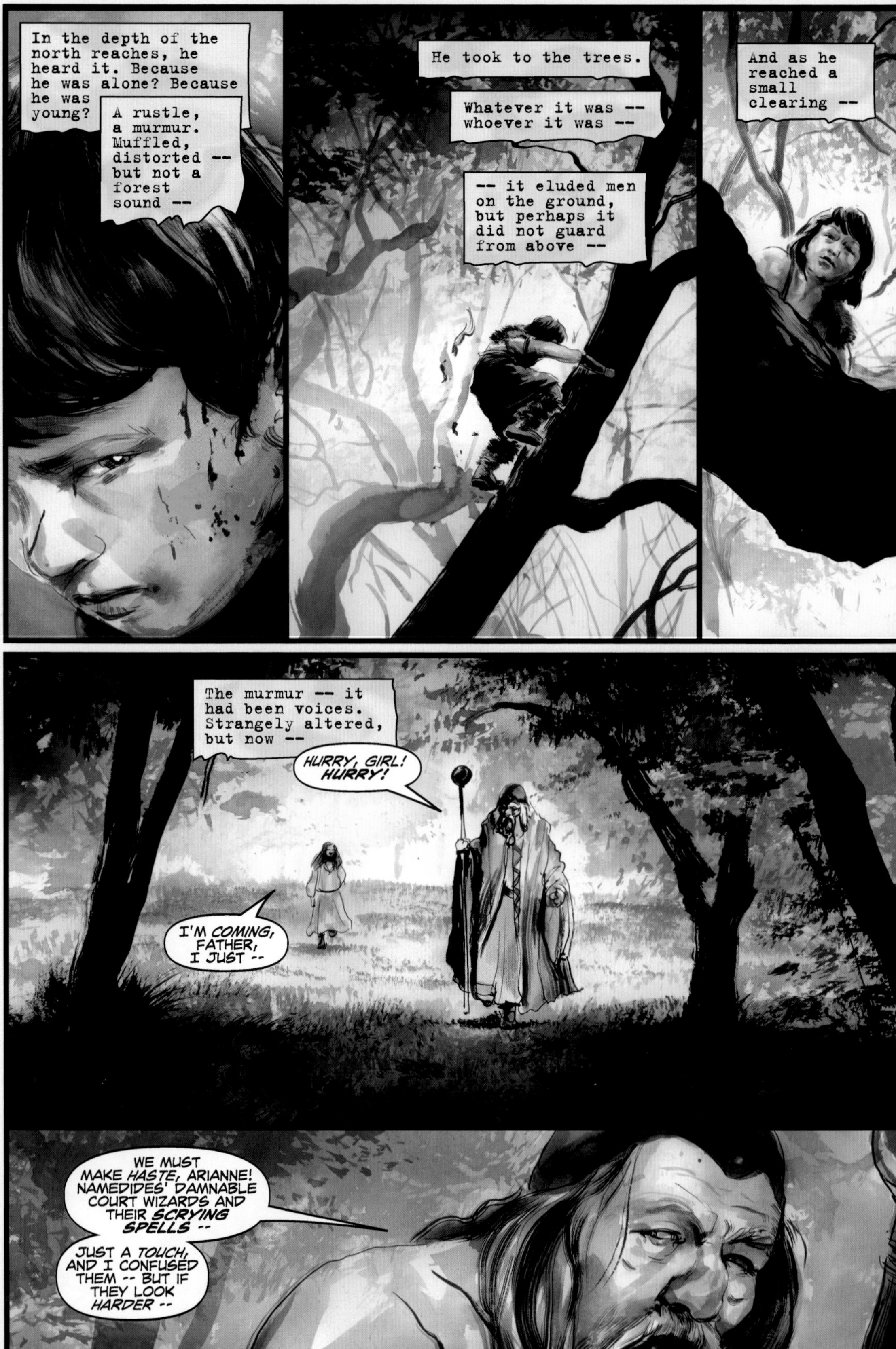
In the depth of the north reaches, he heard it. Because he was alone? Because he was young?
A rustle, a murmur. Muffled, distorted -- but not a forest sound --
He took to the trees.
Whatever it was -- whoever it was --
-- it eluded men on the ground, but perhaps it did not guard from above --
And as he reached a small clearing --
The murmur -- it had been voices. Strangely altered, but now --
HURRY, GIRL! HURRY!
I'M COMING, FATHER, I JUST --
WE MUST MAKE HASTE, ARIANNE! NAMEDIDES' DAMNABLE COURT WIZARDS AND THEIR SCRYING SPELLS --
JUST A TOUCH, AND I CONFUSED THEM -- BUT IF THEY LOOK HARDER --

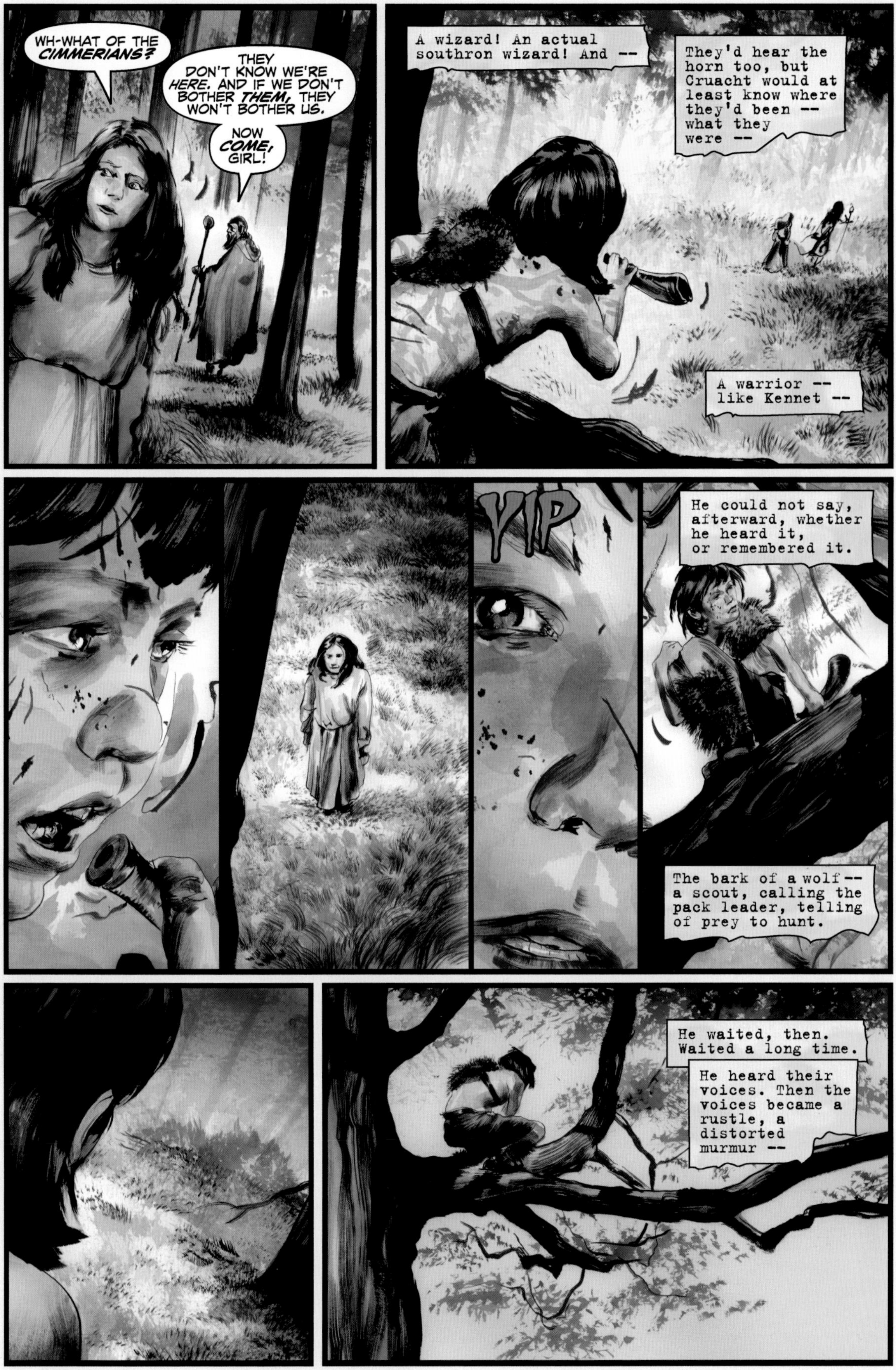
WH-WHAT OF THE *CIMMERIANS?*
THEY DON'T KNOW WE'RE *HERE*. AND IF WE DON'T BOTHER *THEM,* THEY WON'T BOTHER US.
NOW *COME,* GIRL!
A wizard! An actual southron wizard! And --
They'd hear the horn too, but Cruacht would at least know where they'd been -- what they were --
A warrior -- like Kennet --
VIP
He could not say, afterward, whether he heard it, or remembered it.
The bark of a wolf -- a scout, calling the pack leader, telling of prey to hunt.
He waited, then. Waited a long time.
He heard their voices. Then the voices became a rustle, a distorted murmur --

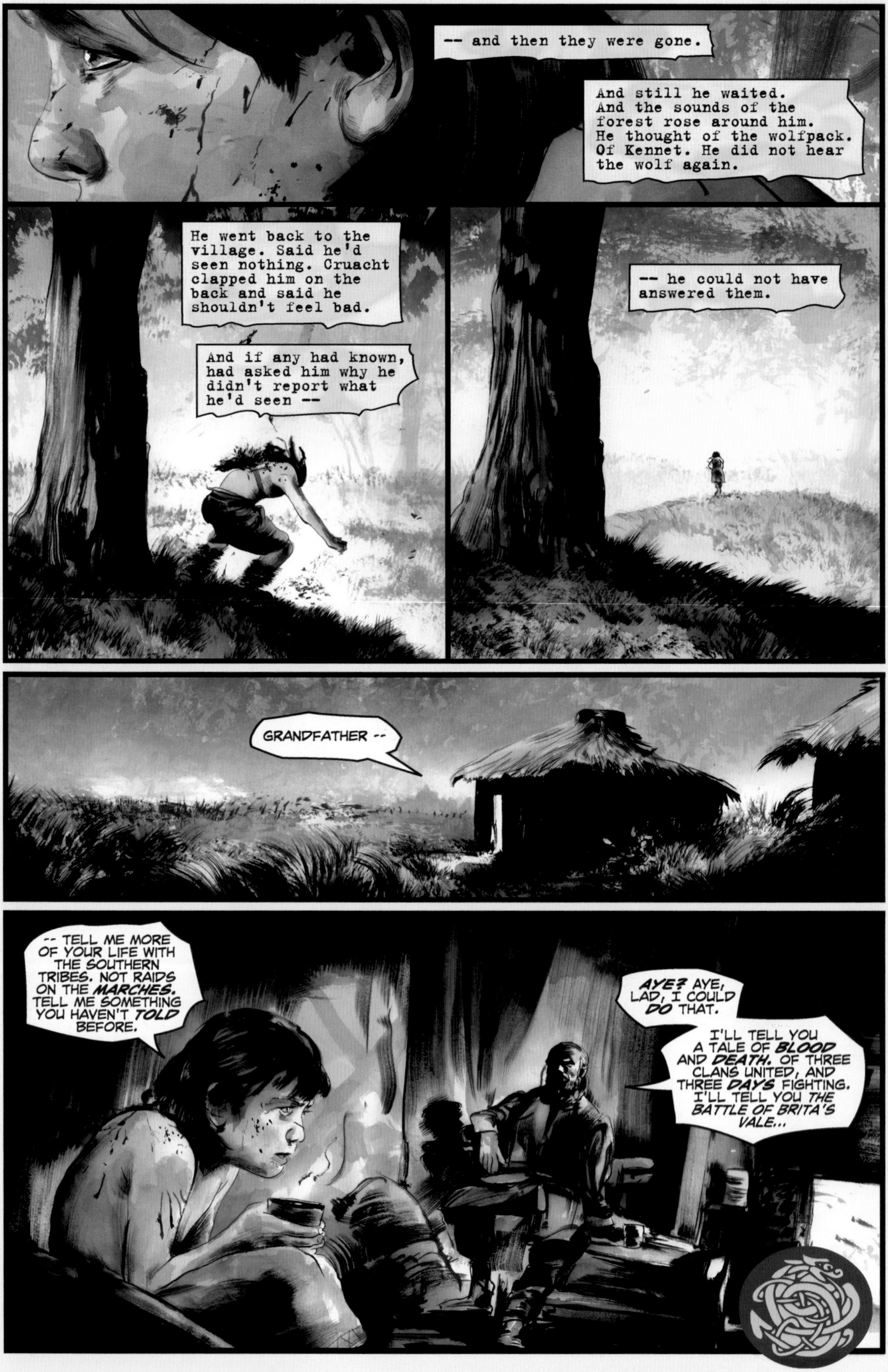

-- and then they were gone.
And still he waited. And the sounds of the forest rose around him. He thought of the wolfpack. Of Kennet. He did not hear the wolf again.
He went back to the village. Said he'd seen nothing. Cruacht clapped him on the back and said he shouldn't feel bad.
And if any had known, had asked him why he didn't report what he'd seen --
-- he could not have answered them.
GRANDFATHER --
-- TELL ME MORE OF YOUR LIFE WITH THE SOUTHERN TRIBES. NOT RAIDS ON THE MARCHES. TELL ME SOMETHING YOU HAVEN'T TOLD BEFORE.
AYE? AYE, LAD, I COULD DO THAT.
I'LL TELL YOU A TALE OF BLOOD AND DEATH. OF THREE CLANS UNITED, AND THREE DAYS FIGHTING. I'LL TELL YOU THE BATTLE OF BRITA'S VALE...

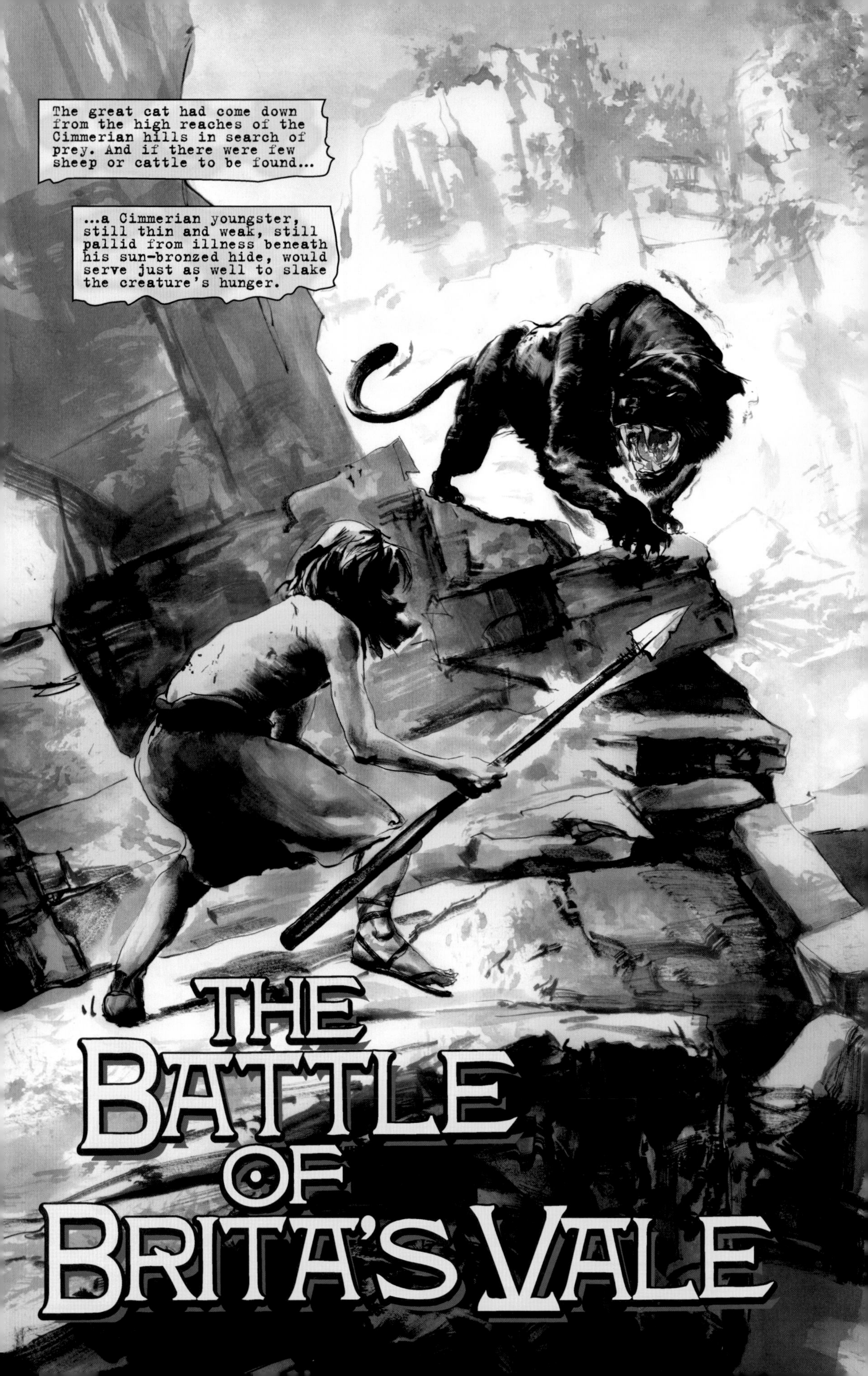
The great cat had come down from the high reaches of the Cimmerian hills in search of prey. And if there were few sheep or cattle to be found...
...a Cimmerian youngster, still thin and weak, still pallid from illness beneath his sun-bronzed hide, would serve just as well to slake the creature's hunger.
THE BATTLE OF BRITA'S VALE

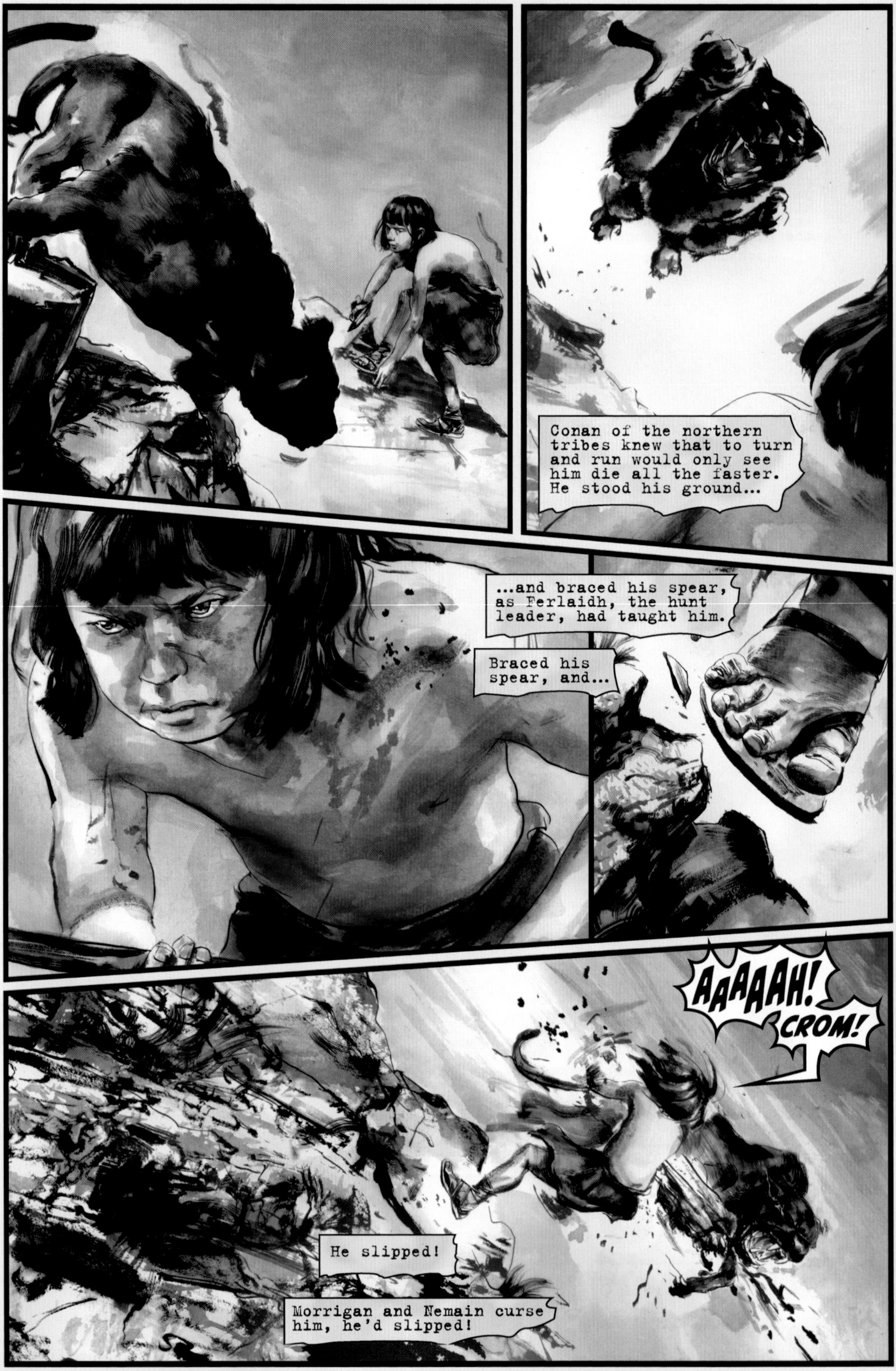
Conan of the northern tribes knew that to turn and run would only see him die all the faster. He stood his ground...
...and braced his spear, as Ferlaidh, the hunt leader, had taught him.
Braced his spear, and...
AAAAAH! CROM!
He slipped!
Morrigan and Nemain curse him, he'd slipped!

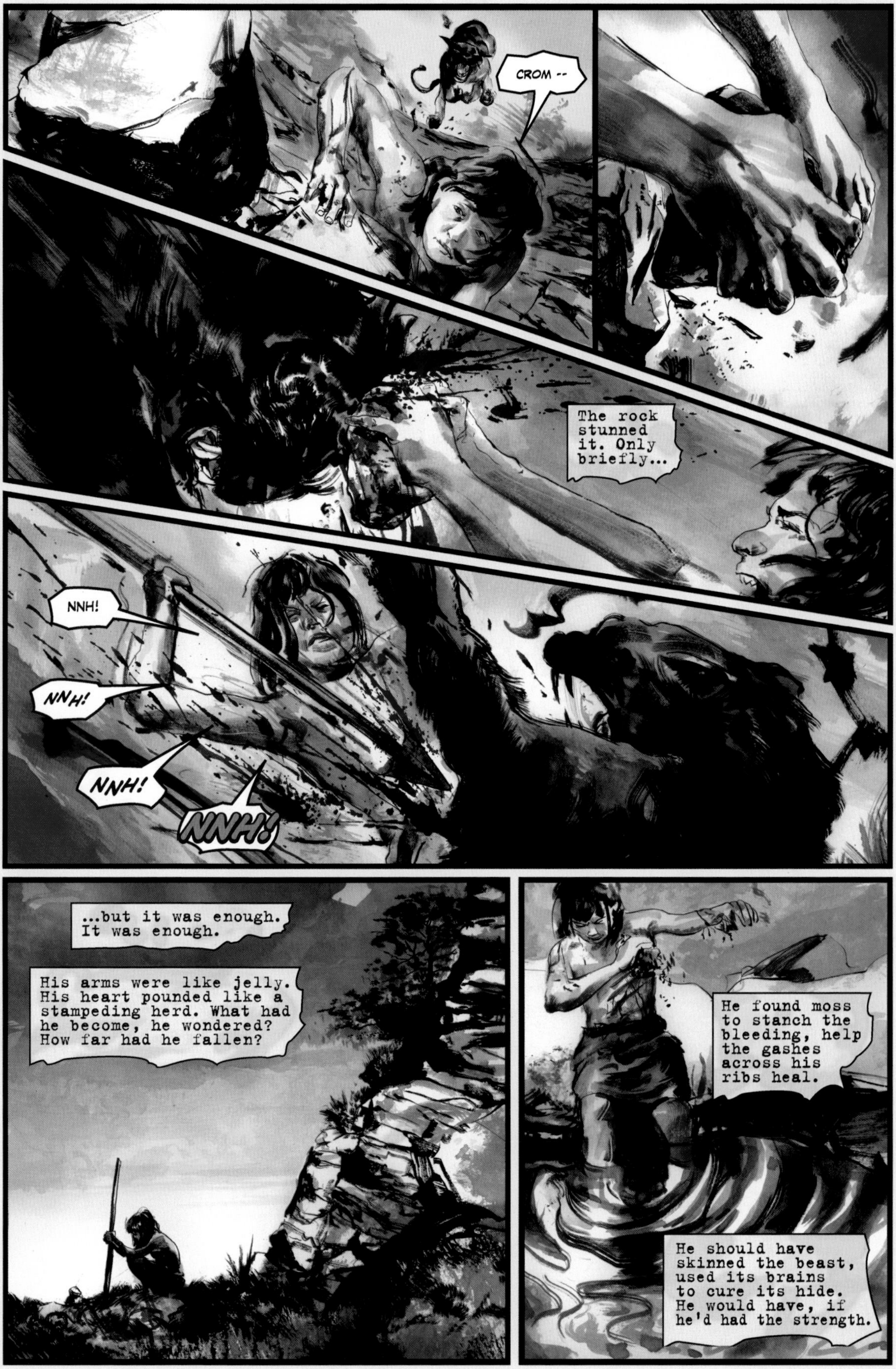
CROM --
The rock stunned it. Only briefly...
NNH!
NNH!
NNH!
NNH!
...but it was enough. It was enough.
His arms were like jelly. His heart pounded like a stampeding herd. What had he become, he wondered? How far had he fallen?
He found moss to stanch the bleeding, help the gashes across his ribs heal.
He should have skinned the beast, used its brains to cure its hide. He would have, if he'd had the strength.

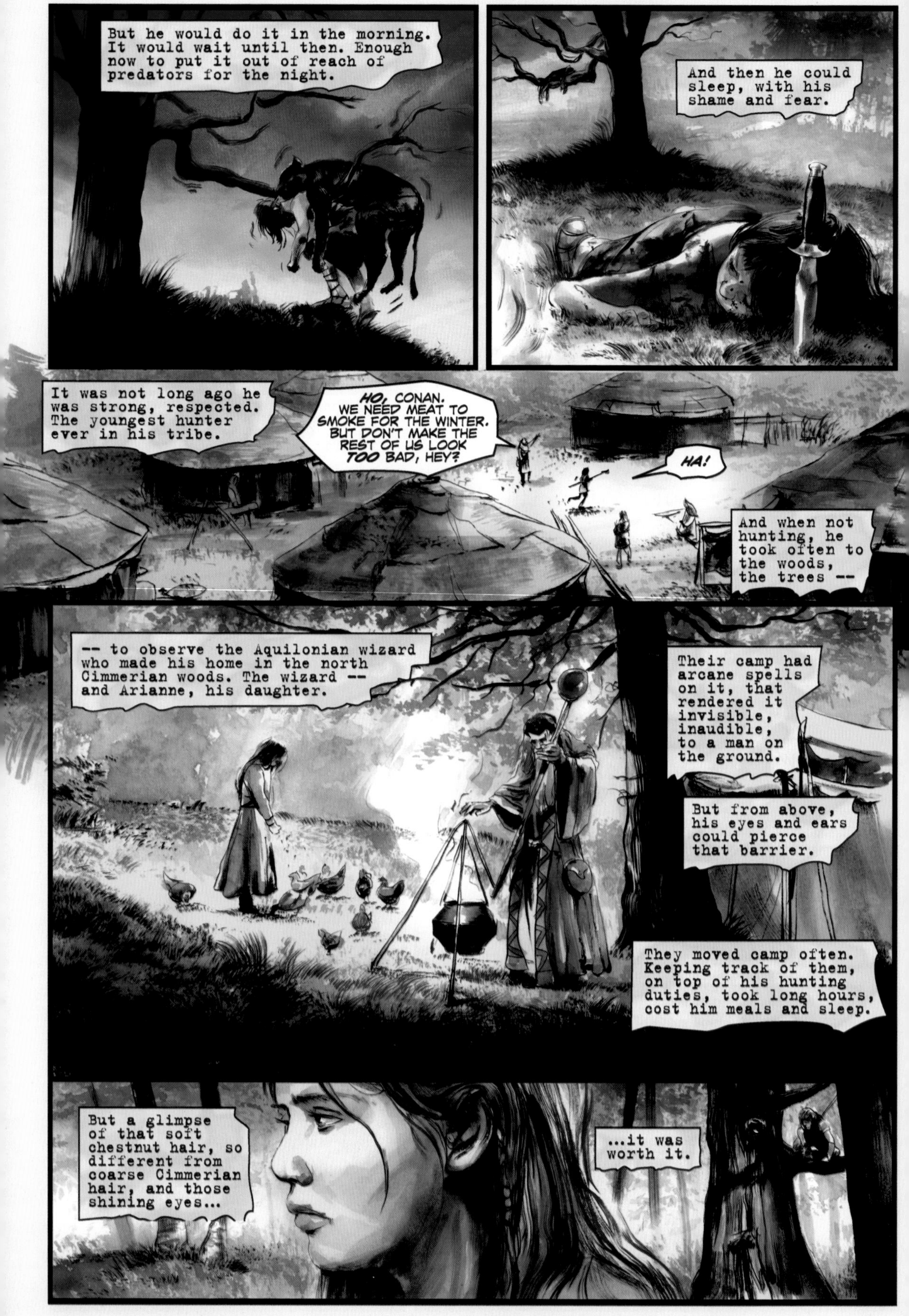

But he would do it in the morning. It would wait until then. Enough now to put it out of reach of predators for the night.
And then he could sleep, with his shame and fear.
It was not long ago he was strong, respected. The youngest hunter ever in his tribe.
HO, CONAN. WE NEED MEAT TO SMOKE FOR THE WINTER. BUT DON'T MAKE THE REST OF US LOOK TOO BAD, HEY?
HA!
And when not hunting, he took often to the woods, the trees --
-- to observe the Aquilonian wizard who made his home in the north Cimmerian woods. The wizard -- and Arianne, his daughter.
Their camp had arcane spells on it, that rendered it invisible, inaudible, to a man on the ground.
But from above, his eyes and ears could pierce that barrier.
They moved camp often. Keeping track of them, on top of his hunting duties, took long hours, cost him meals and sleep.
But a glimpse of that soft chestnut hair, so different from coarse Cimmerian hair, and those shining eyes...
...it was worth it.

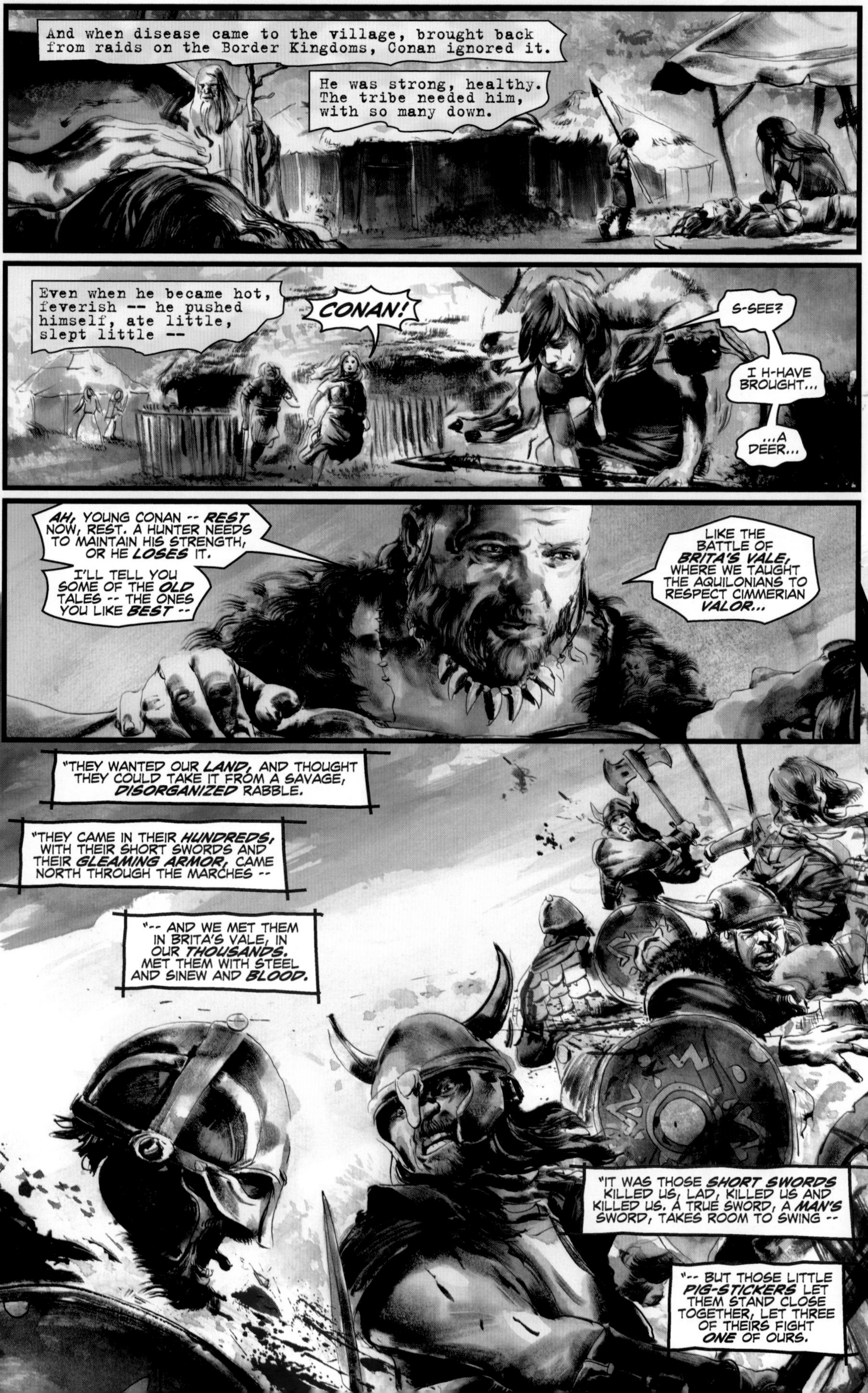

And when disease came to the village, brought back from raids on the Border Kingdoms, Conan ignored it.
He was strong, healthy. The tribe needed him, with so many down.
Even when he became hot, feverish -- he pushed himself, ate little, slept little --
CONAN!
S-SEE?
I H-HAVE BROUGHT...
...A DEER...
AH, YOUNG CONAN -- REST NOW, REST. A HUNTER NEEDS TO MAINTAIN HIS STRENGTH, OR HE LOSES IT.
I'LL TELL YOU SOME OF THE OLD TALES -- THE ONES YOU LIKE BEST --
LIKE THE BATTLE OF BRITA'S VALE, WHERE WE TAUGHT THE AQUILONIANS TO RESPECT CIMMERIAN VALOR...
"THEY WANTED OUR LAND, AND THOUGHT THEY COULD TAKE IT FROM A SAVAGE, DISORGANIZED RABBLE.
"THEY CAME IN THEIR HUNDREDS, WITH THEIR SHORT SWORDS AND THEIR GLEAMING ARMOR, CAME NORTH THROUGH THE MARCHES --
"-- AND WE MET THEM IN BRITA'S VALE, IN OUR THOUSANDS. MET THEM WITH STEEL AND SINEW AND BLOOD.
"IT WAS THOSE SHORT SWORDS KILLED US, LAD, KILLED US AND KILLED US. A TRUE SWORD, A MAN'S SWORD, TAKES ROOM TO SWING --
"-- BUT THOSE LITTLE PIG-STICKERS LET THEM STAND CLOSE TOGETHER, LET THREE OF THEIRS FIGHT ONE OF OURS.

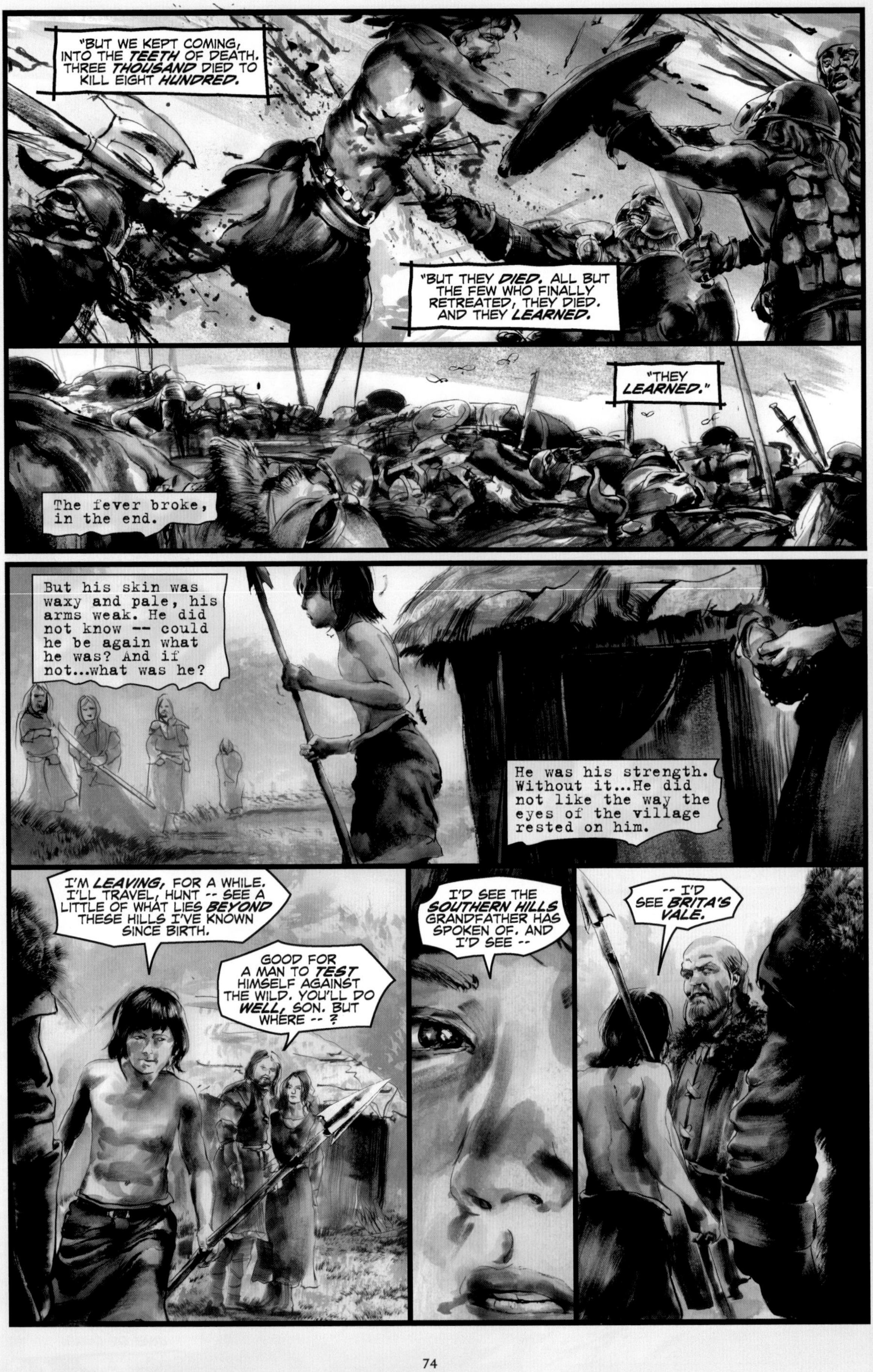
"BUT WE KEPT COMING, INTO THE TEETH OF DEATH. THREE THOUSAND DIED TO KILL EIGHT HUNDRED.
"BUT THEY DIED. ALL BUT THE FEW WHO FINALLY RETREATED, THEY DIED. AND THEY LEARNED.
"THEY LEARNED."
The fever broke, in the end.
But his skin was waxy and pale, his arms weak. He did not know -- could he be again what he was? And if not...what was he?
He was his strength. Without it...He did not like the way the eyes of the village rested on him.
I'M LEAVING, FOR A WHILE. I'LL TRAVEL, HUNT -- SEE A LITTLE OF WHAT LIES BEYOND THESE HILLS I'VE KNOWN SINCE BIRTH.
GOOD FOR A MAN TO TEST HIMSELF AGAINST THE WILD. YOU'LL DO WELL, SON. BUT WHERE -- ?
I'D SEE THE SOUTHERN HILLS GRANDFATHER HAS SPOKEN OF. AND I'D SEE --
-- I'D SEE BRITA'S VALE.

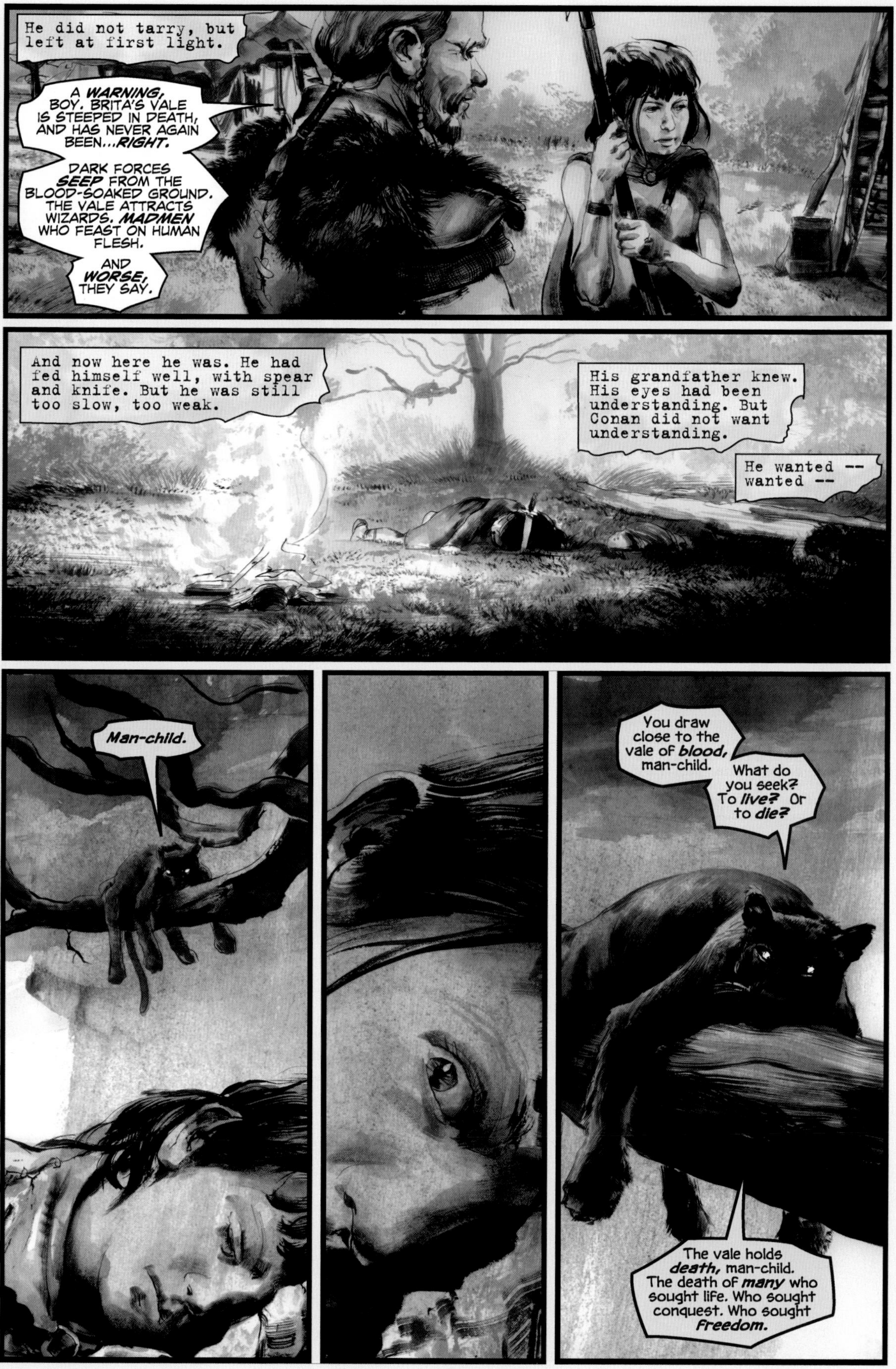

He did not tarry, but left at first light.
A WARNING, BOY. BRITA'S VALE IS STEEPED IN DEATH, AND HAS NEVER AGAIN BEEN... RIGHT.
DARK FORCES SEEP FROM THE BLOOD-SOAKED GROUND. THE VALE ATTRACTS WIZARDS. MADMEN WHO FEAST ON HUMAN FLESH.
AND WORSE, THEY SAY.
And now here he was. He had fed himself well, with spear and knife. But he was still too slow, too weak.
His grandfather knew. His eyes had been understanding. But Conan did not want understanding.
He wanted -- wanted --
Man-child.
You draw close to the vale of blood, man-child.
What do you seek? To live? Or to die?
The vale holds death, man-child. The death of many who sought life. Who sought conquest. Who sought Freedom.

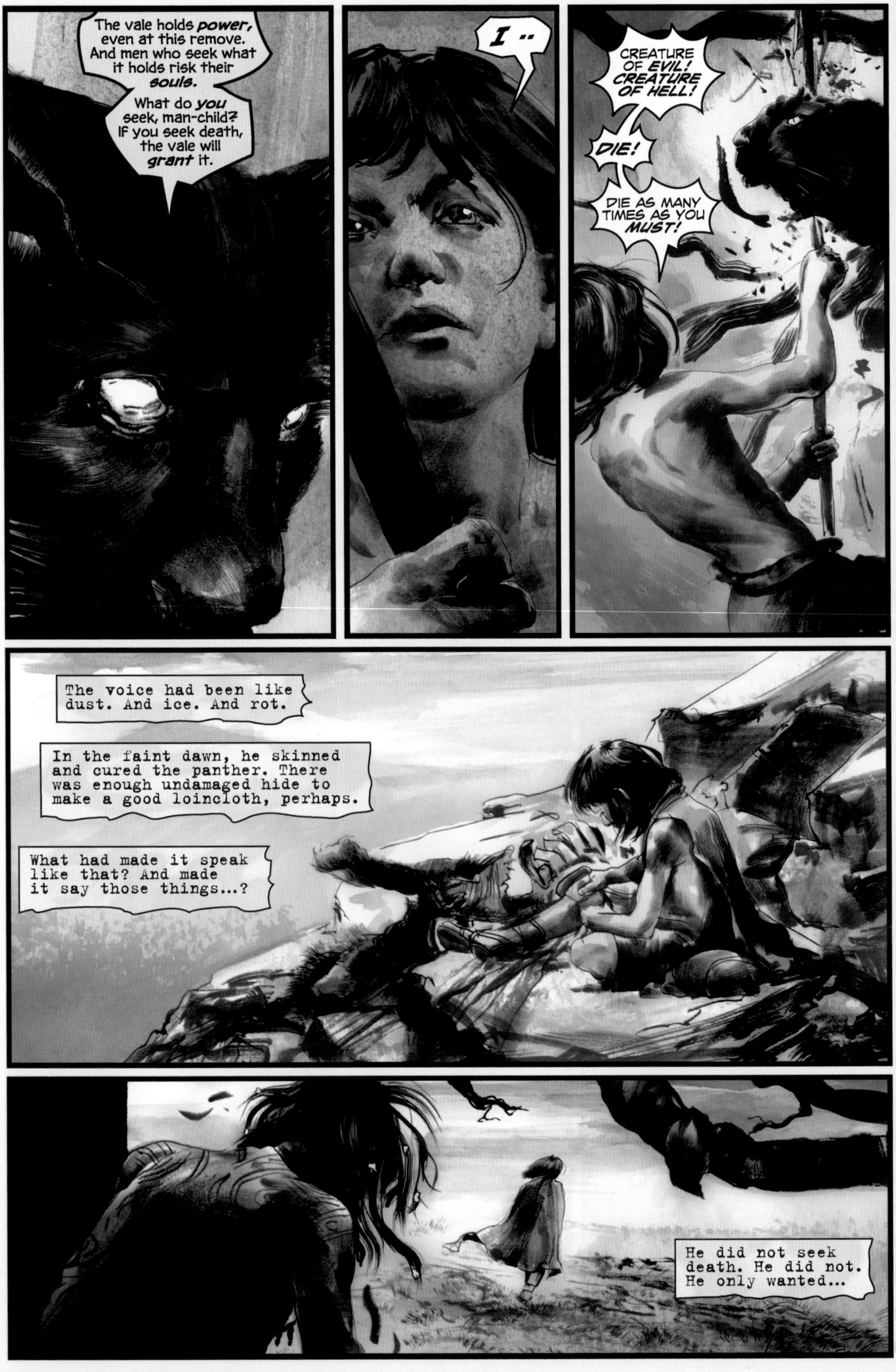
The vale holds *power,* even at this remove. And men who seek what it holds risk their *souls.*
What do *you* seek, man-child? If you seek death, the vale will *grant* it.
I ..
CREATURE OF *EVIL! CREATURE OF HELL!*
DIE!
DIE AS MANY TIMES AS YOU *MUST!*
The voice had been like dust. And ice. And rot.
In the faint dawn, he skinned and cured the panther. There was enough undamaged hide to make a good loincloth, perhaps.
What had made it speak like that? And made it say those things...?
He did not seek death. He did not. He only wanted...

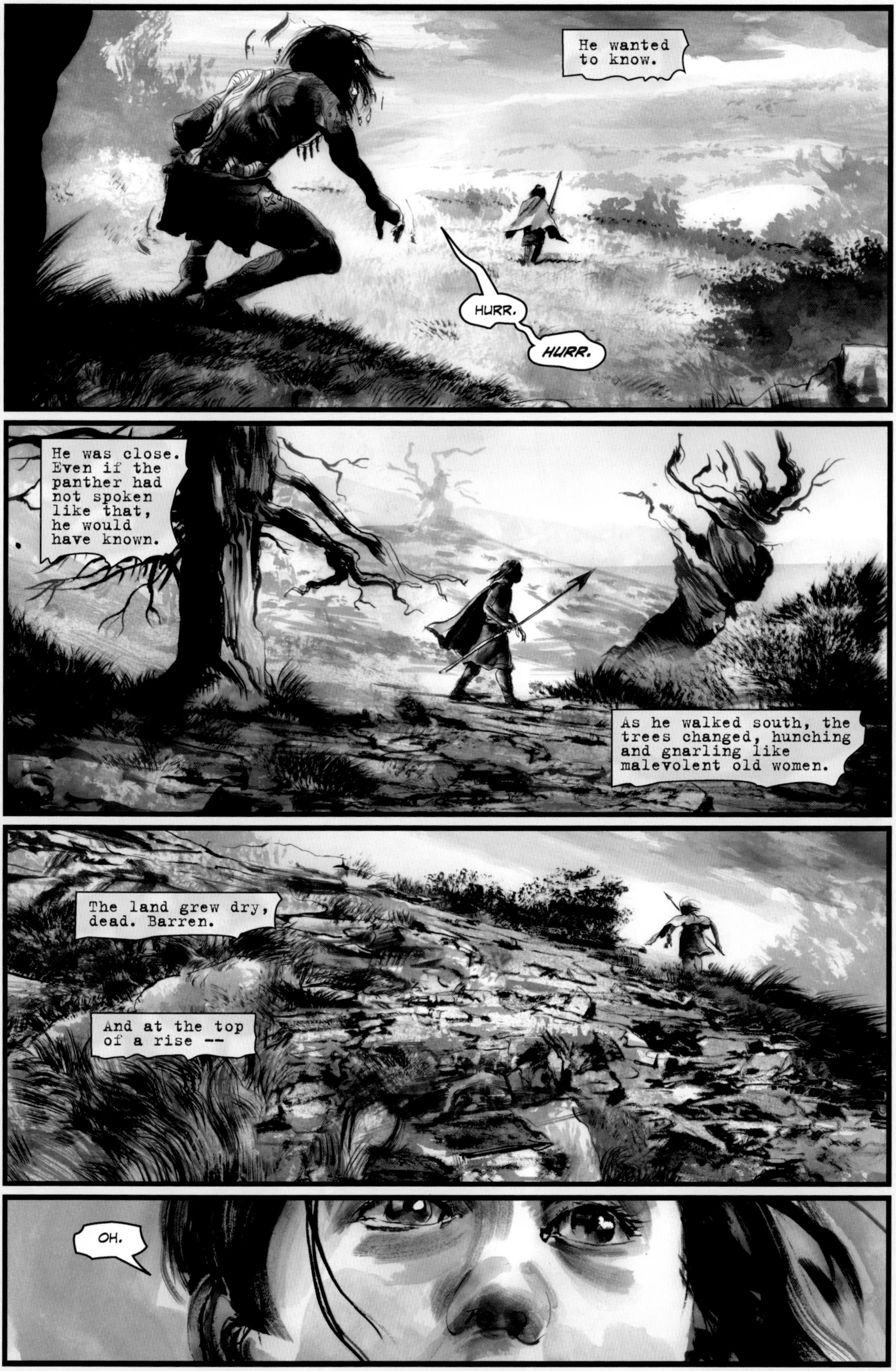
He wanted to know.
HURR.
HURR.
He was close. Even if the panther had not spoken like that, he would have known.
As he walked south, the trees changed, hunching and gnarling like malevolent old women.
The land grew dry, dead. Barren.
And at the top of a rise --
OH.

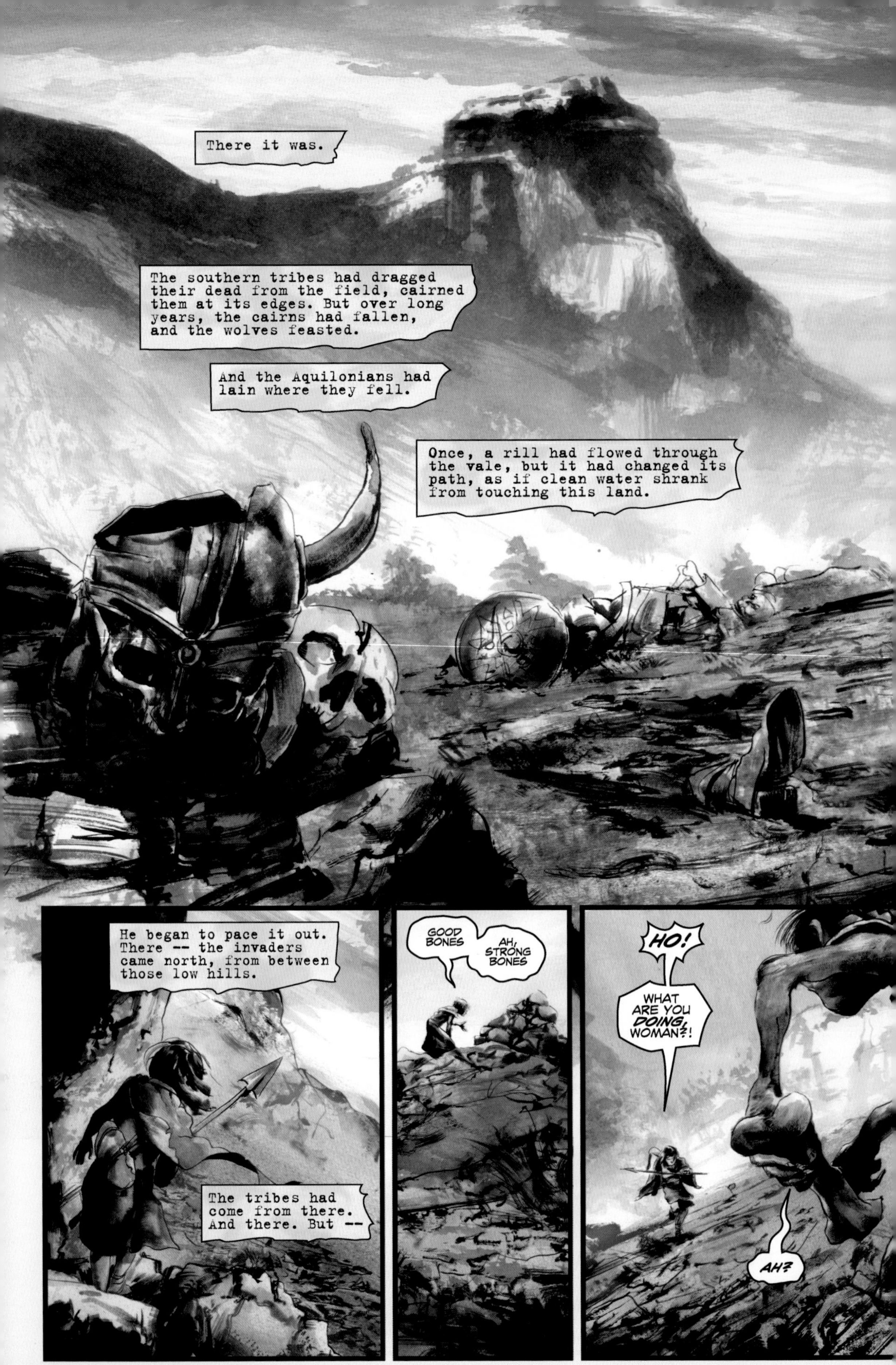
There it was.
The southern tribes had dragged their dead from the field, cairned them at its edges. But over long years, the cairns had fallen, and the wolves feasted.
And the Aquilonians had lain where they fell.
Once, a rill had flowed through the vale, but it had changed its path, as if clean water shrank from touching this land.
He began to pace it out. There -- the invaders came north, from between those low hills.
The tribes had come from there. And there. But --
GOOD BONES
AH, STRONG BONES
HO!
WHAT ARE YOU DOING, WOMAN?!
AH?

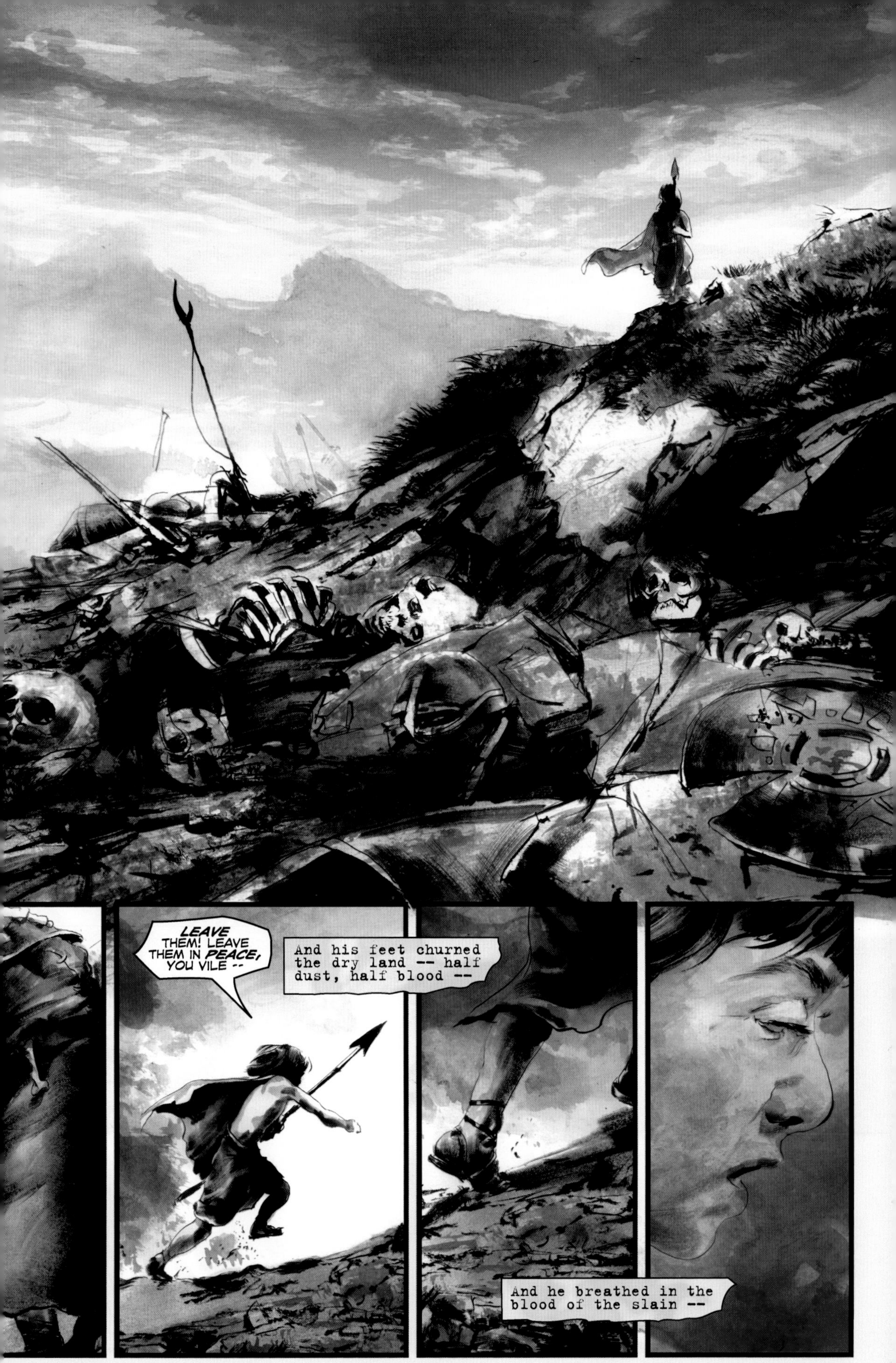
LEAVE THEM! LEAVE THEM IN PEACE, YOU VILE --
And his feet churned the dry land -- half dust, half blood --
And he breathed in the blood of the slain --

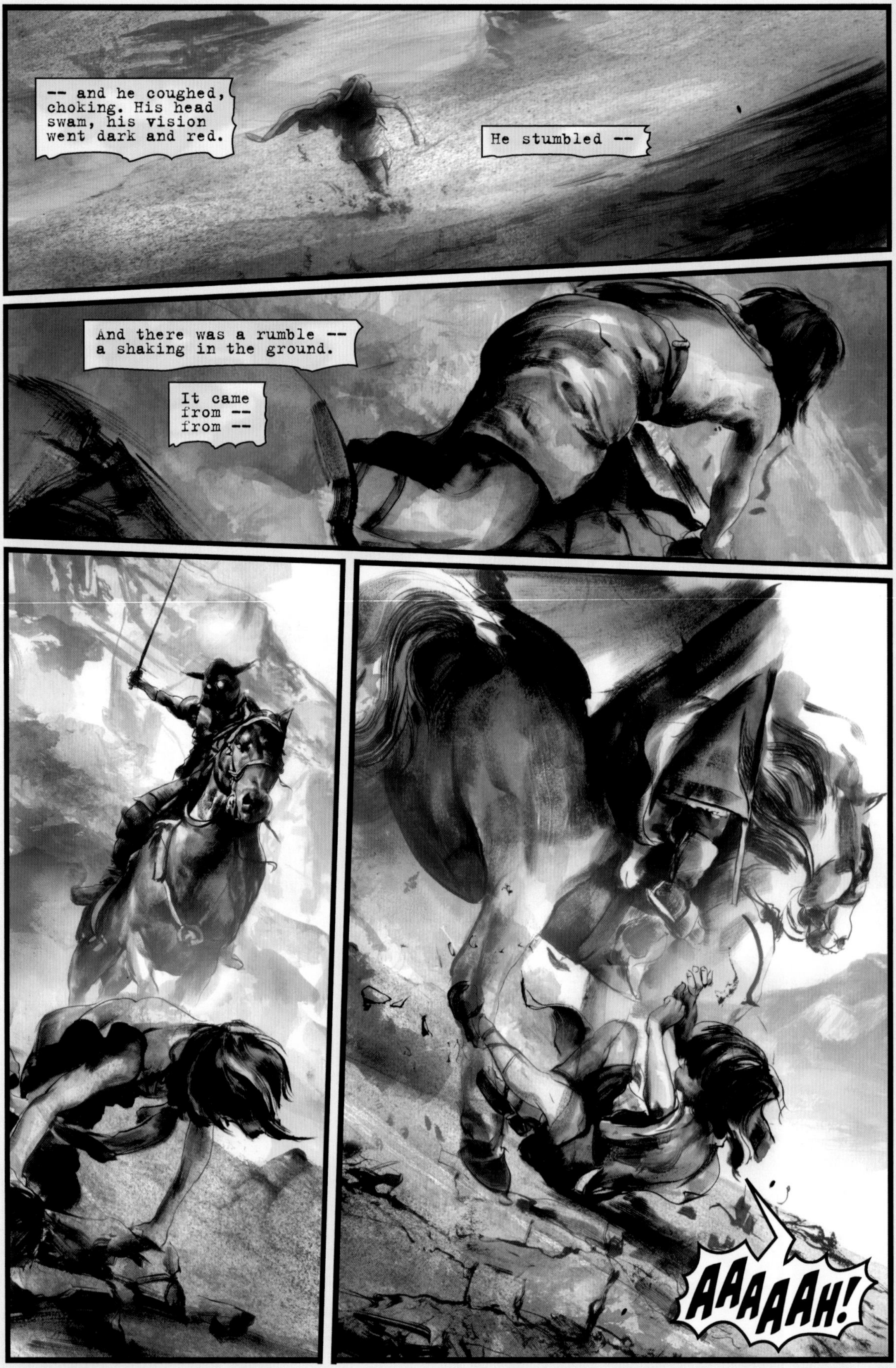
-- and he coughed, choking. His head swam, his vision went dark and red.
He stumbled --
And there was a rumble -- a shaking in the ground.
It came from -- from --
AAAAAH!

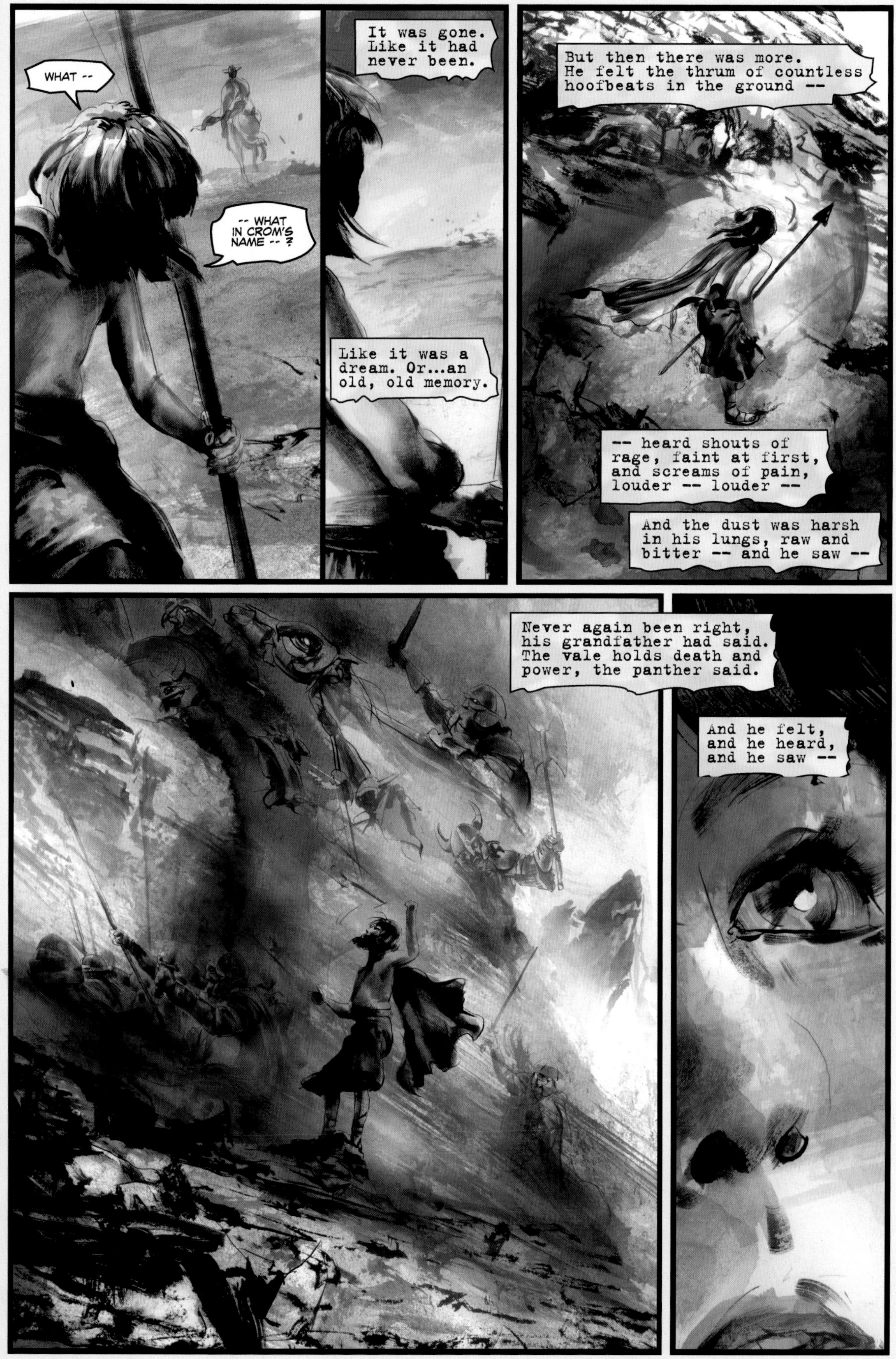
WHAT --
-- WHAT IN CROM'S NAME -- ?
It was gone. Like it had never been.
Like it was a dream. Or...an old, old memory.
But then there was more. He felt the thrum of countless hoofbeats in the ground --
-- heard shouts of rage, faint at first, and screams of pain, louder -- louder --
And the dust was harsh in his lungs, raw and bitter -- and he saw --
Never again been right, his grandfather had said. The vale holds death and power, the panther said.
And he felt, and he heard, and he saw --

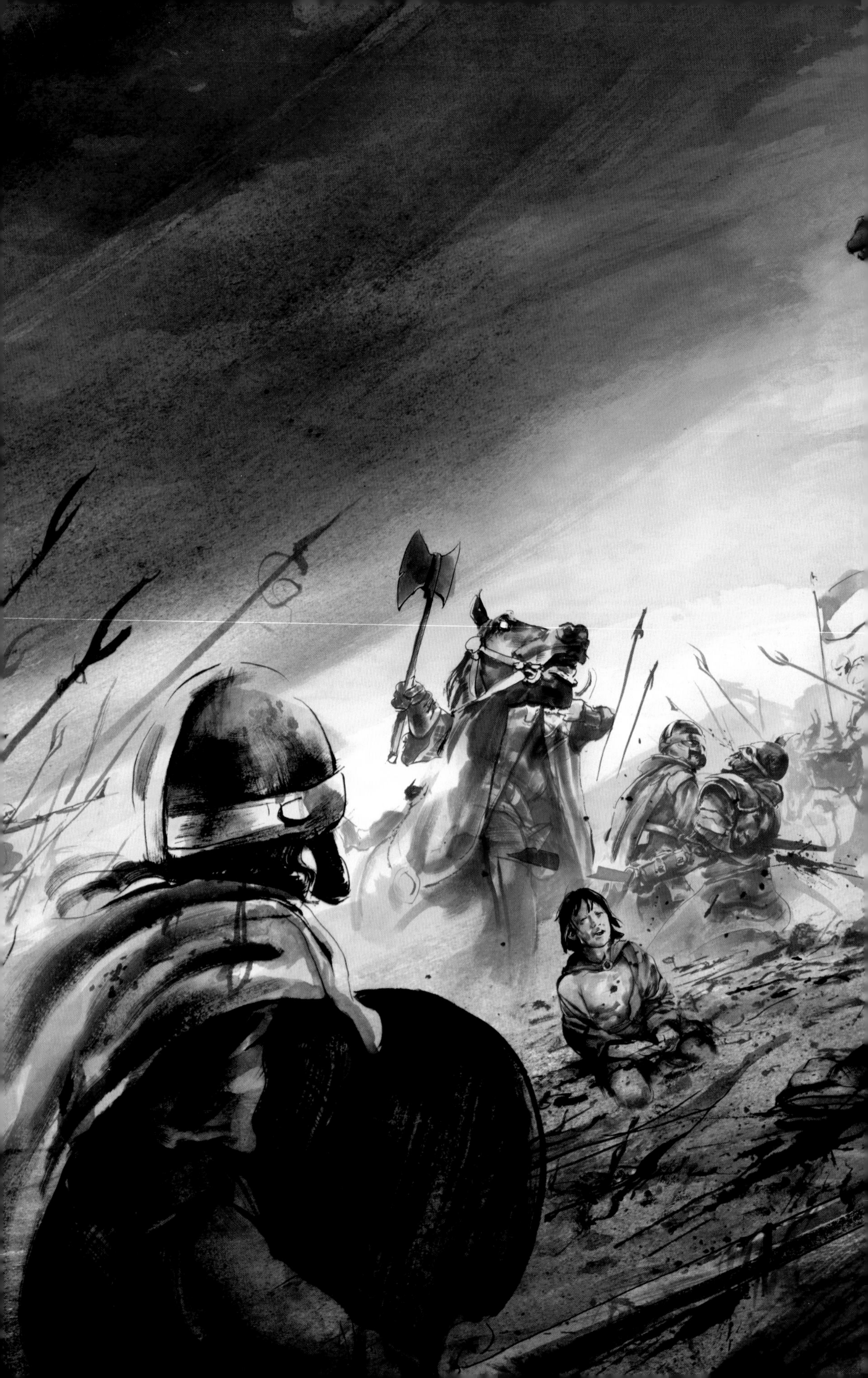

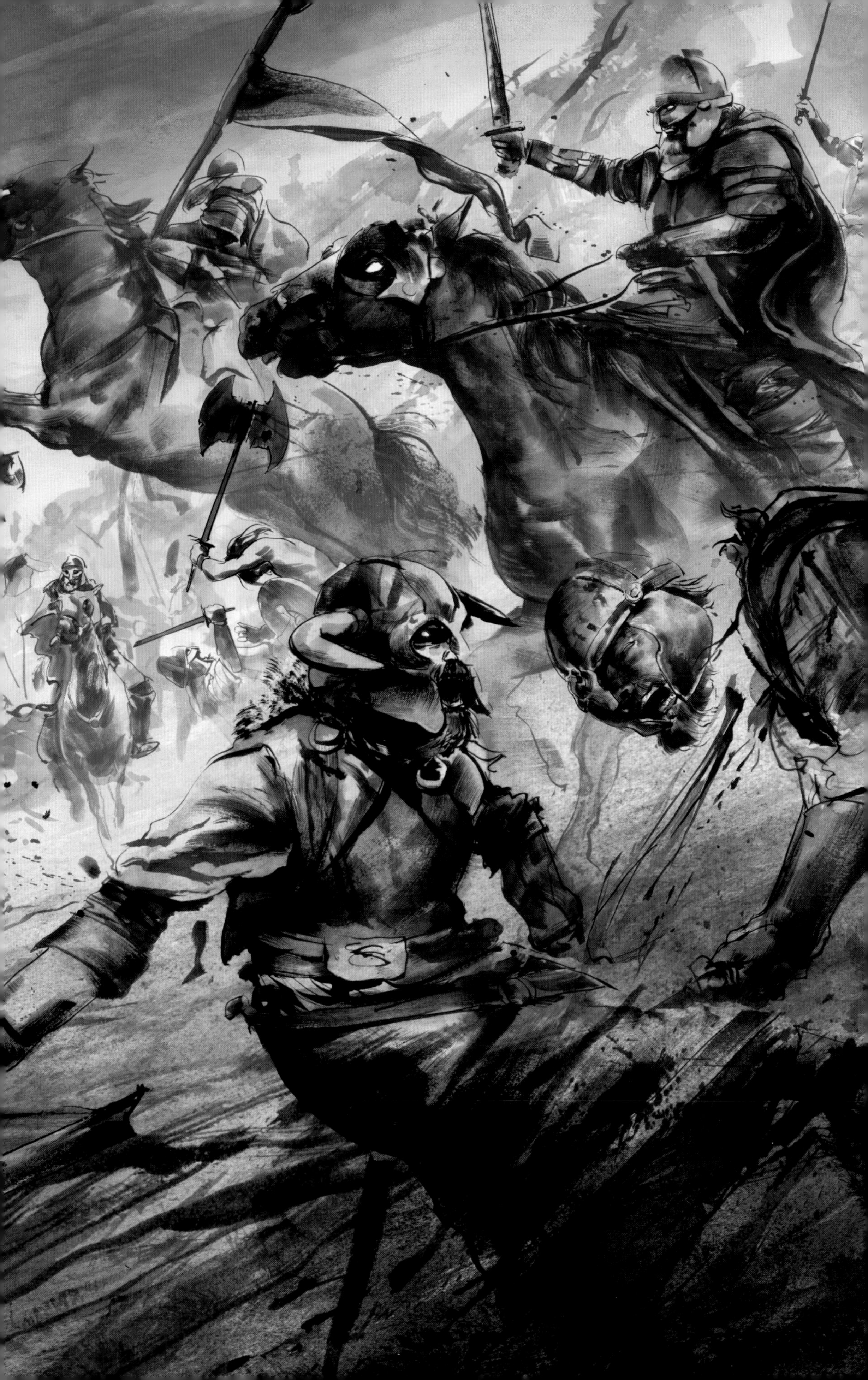

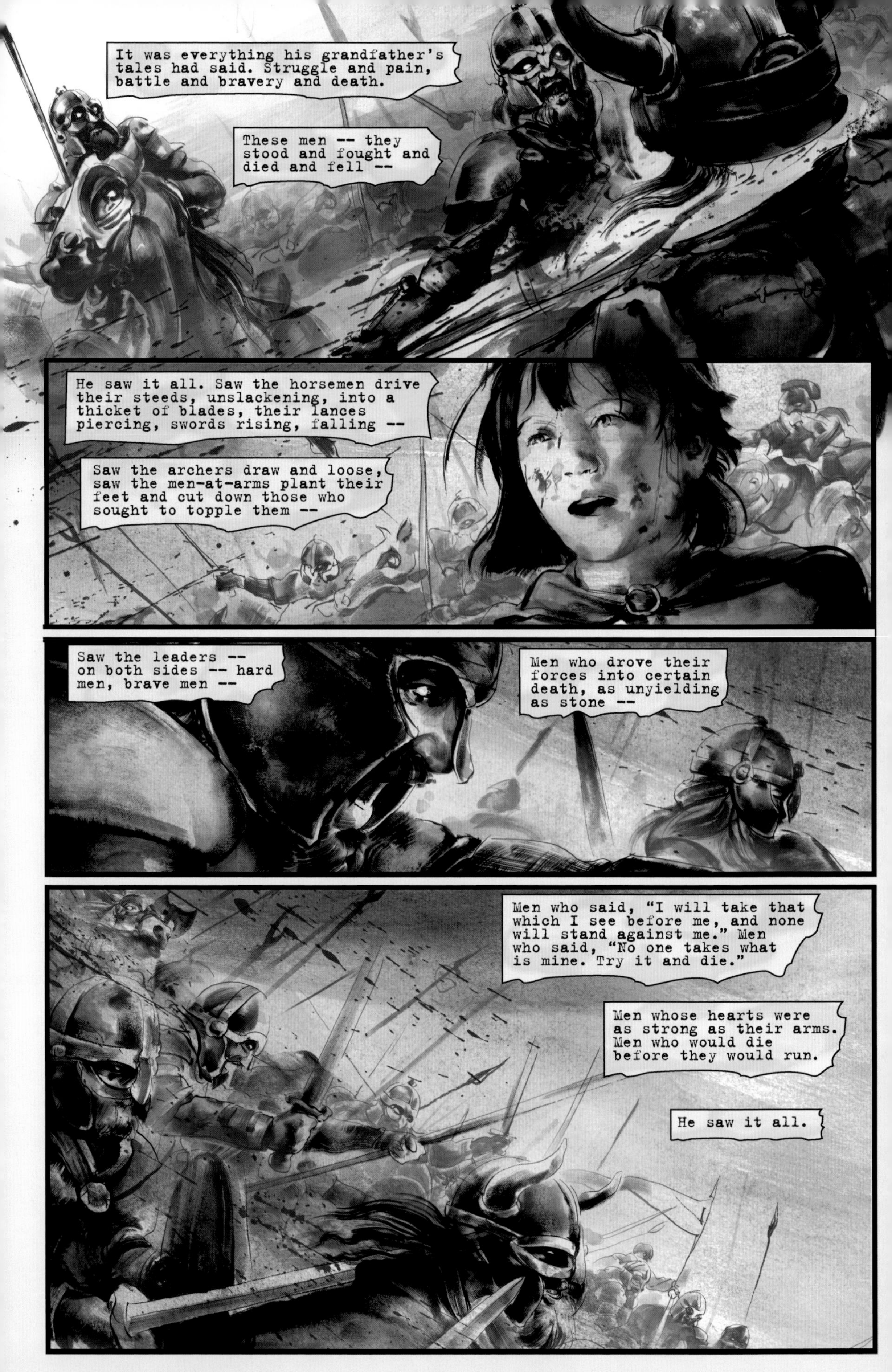
It was everything his grandfather's tales had said. Struggle and pain, battle and bravery and death.
These men -- they stood and fought and died and fell --
He saw it all. Saw the horsemen drive their steeds, unslackening, into a thicket of blades, their lances piercing, swords rising, falling --
Saw the archers draw and loose, saw the men-at-arms plant their feet and cut down those who sought to topple them --
Saw the leaders -- on both sides -- hard men, brave men --
Men who drove their forces into certain death, as unyielding as stone --
Men who said, "I will take that which I see before me, and none will stand against me." Men who said, "No one takes what is mine. Try it and die."
Men whose hearts were as strong as their arms. Men who would die before they would run.
He saw it all.

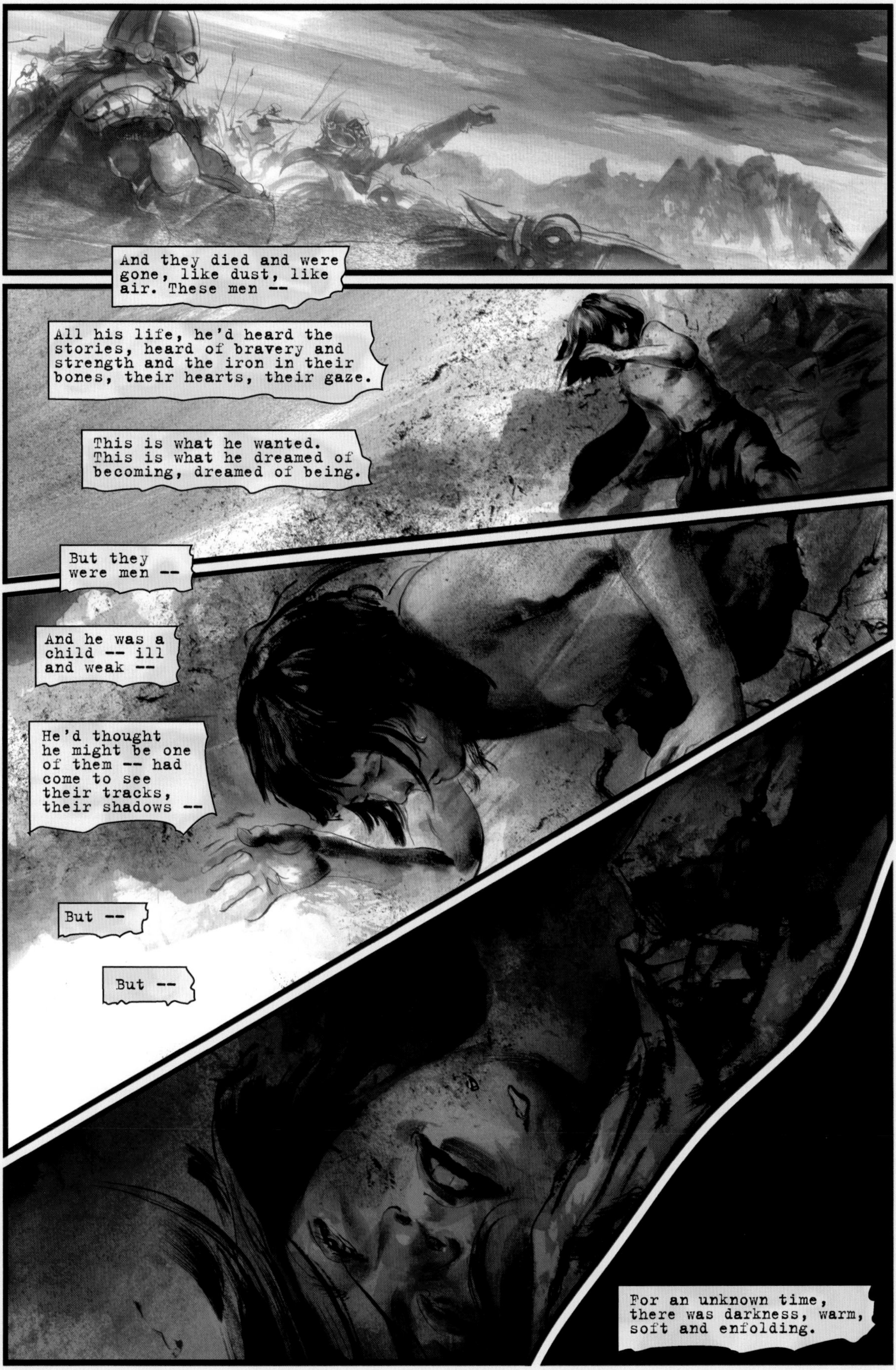
And they died and were gone, like dust, like air. These men --
All his life, he'd heard the stories, heard of bravery and strength and the iron in their bones, their hearts, their gaze.
This is what he wanted. This is what he dreamed of becoming, dreamed of being.
But they were men --
And he was a child -- ill and weak --
He'd thought he might be one of them -- had come to see their tracks, their shadows --
But --
But --
For an unknown time, there was darkness, warm, soft and enfolding.

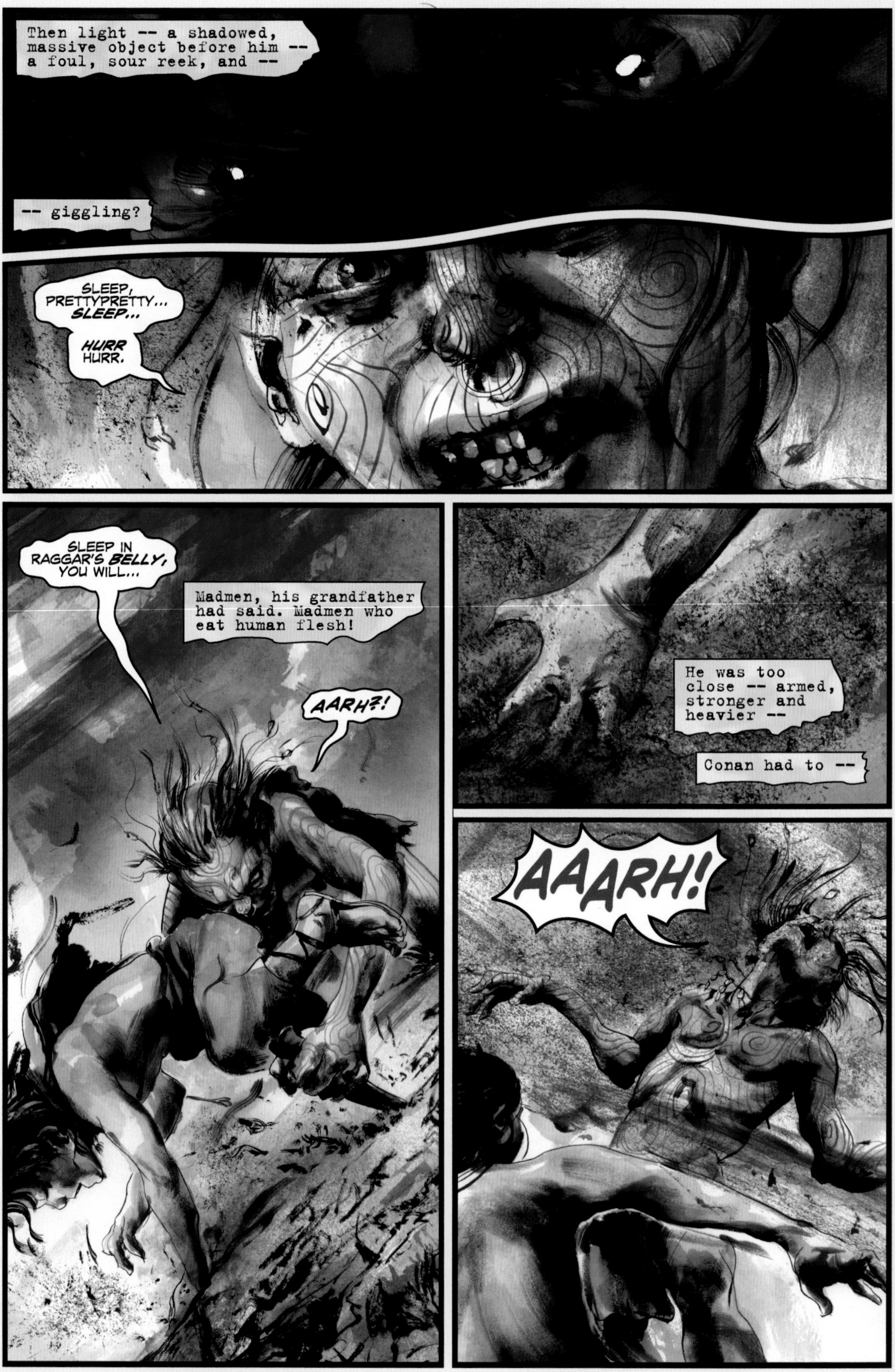
Then light -- a shadowed, massive object before him -- a foul, sour reek, and --
-- giggling?
SLEEP, PRETTYPRETTY... SLEEP...
HURR HURR.
SLEEP IN RAGGAR'S BELLY, YOU WILL...
Madmen, his grandfather had said. Madmen who eat human flesh!
AARH?!
He was too close -- armed, stronger and heavier --
Conan had to --
AAARH!

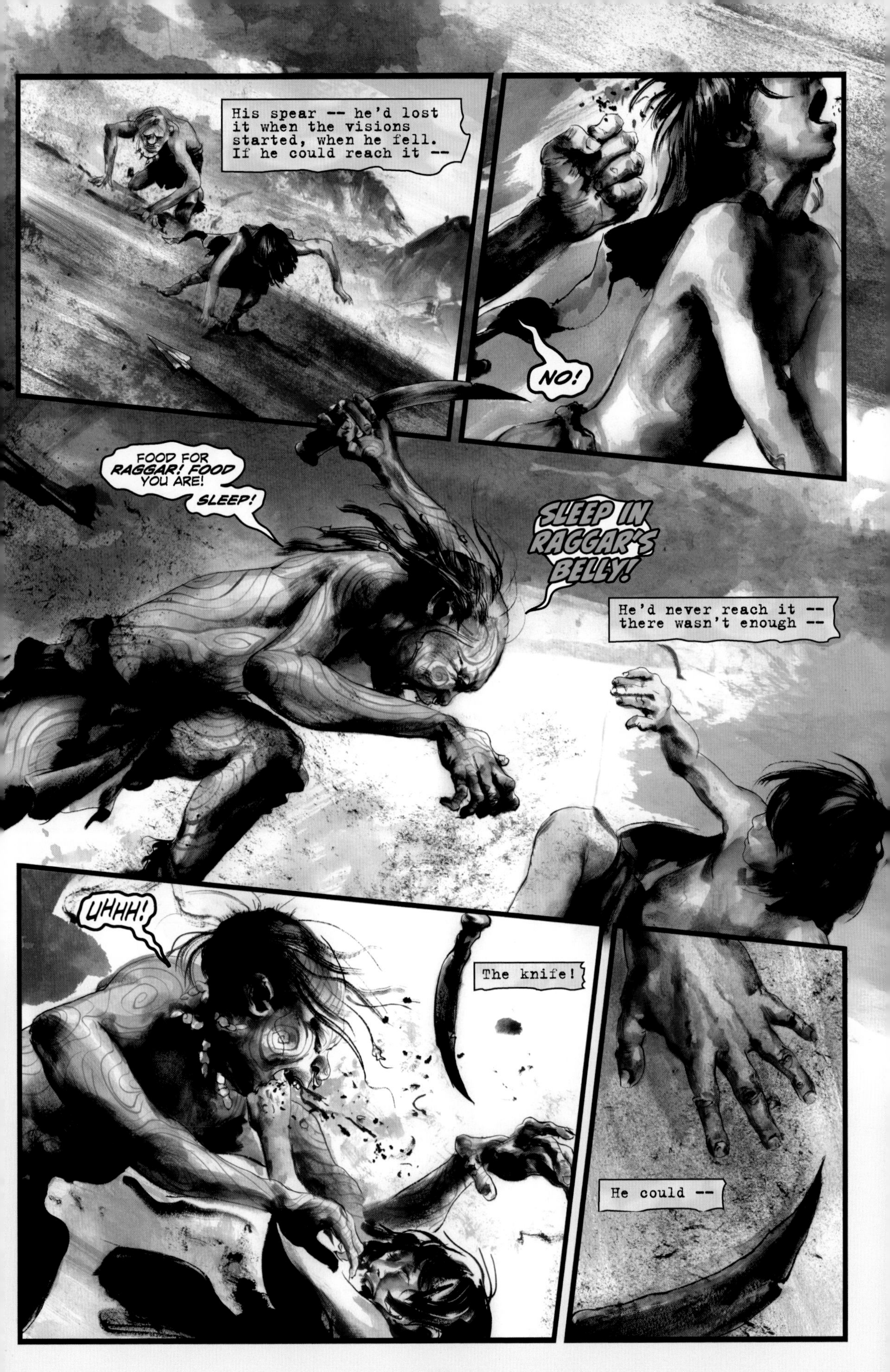
His spear -- he'd lost it when the visions started, when he fell. If he could reach it --
NO!
FOOD FOR RAGGAR! FOOD YOU ARE!
SLEEP!
SLEEP IN RAGGAR'S BELLY!
He'd never reach it -- there wasn't enough --
UHHH!
The knife!
He could --

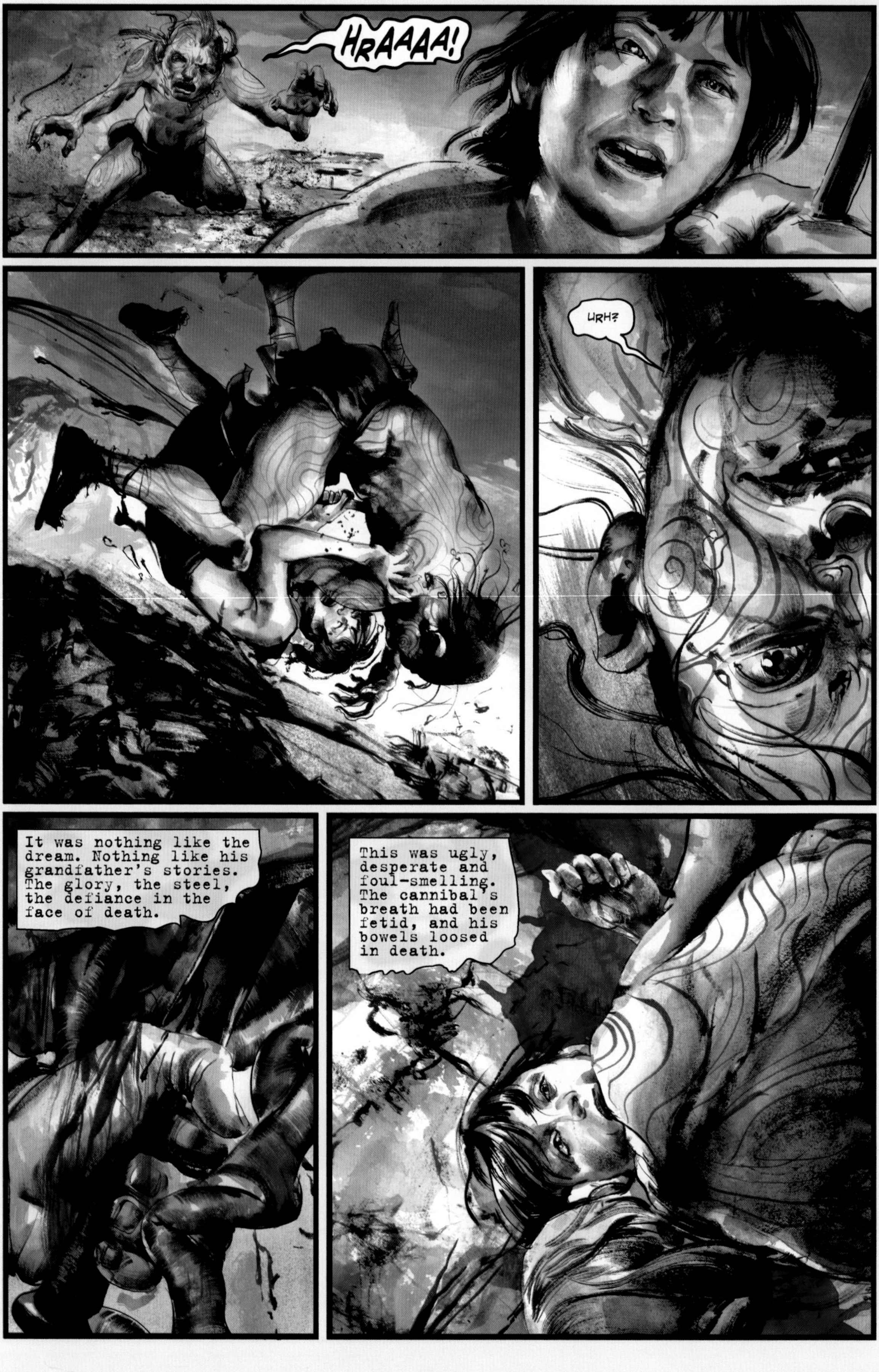
HRAAAA!
URH?
It was nothing like the dream. Nothing like his grandfather's stories. The glory, the steel, the defiance in the face of death.
This was ugly, desperate and foul-smelling. The cannibal's breath had been fetid, and his bowels loosed in death.

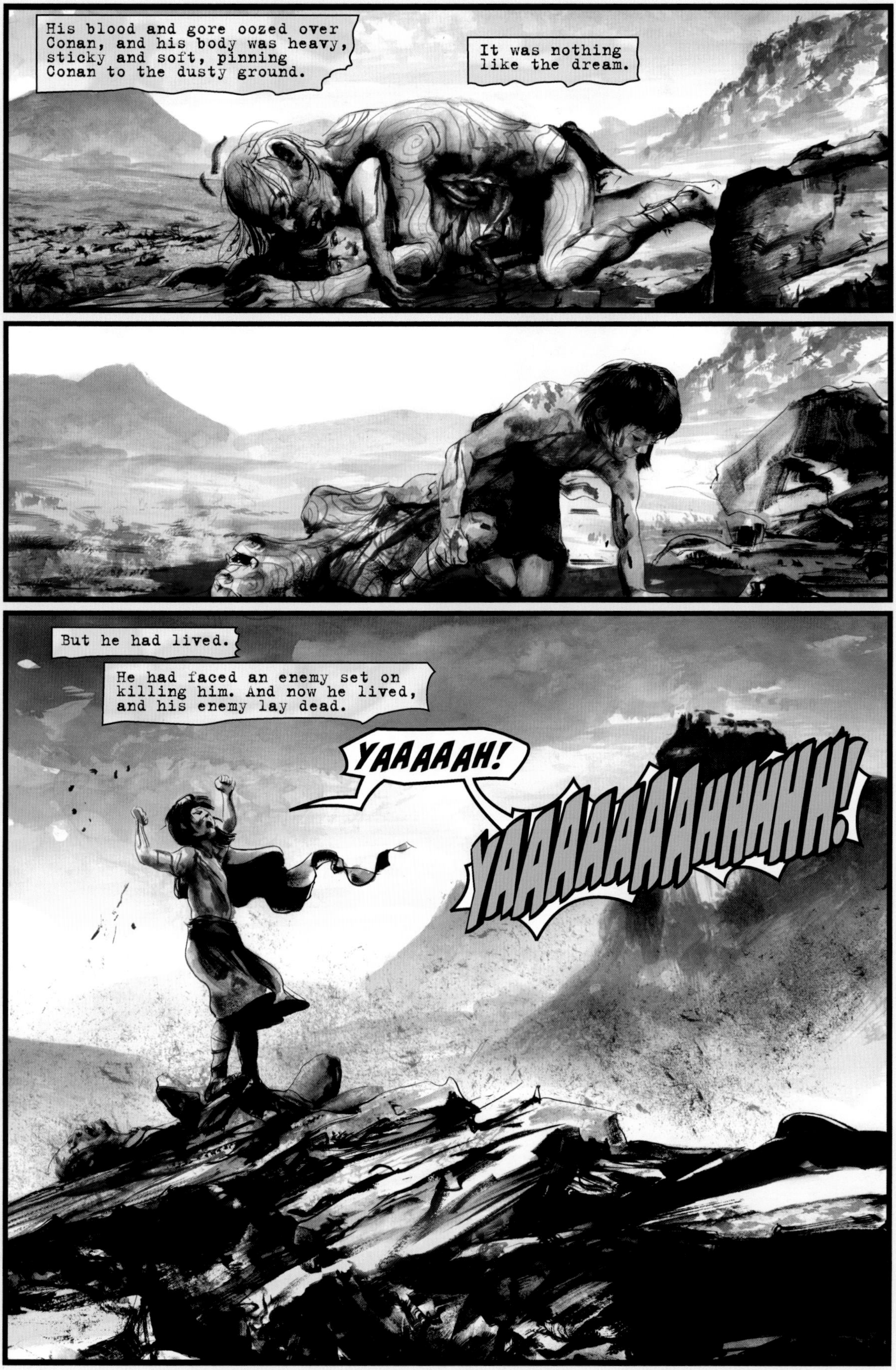
His blood and gore oozed over Conan, and his body was heavy, sticky and soft, pinning Conan to the dusty ground.
It was nothing like the dream.
But he had lived.
He had faced an enemy set on killing him. And now he lived, and his enemy lay dead.
YAAAAAH!
YAAAAAAAHHHHH!

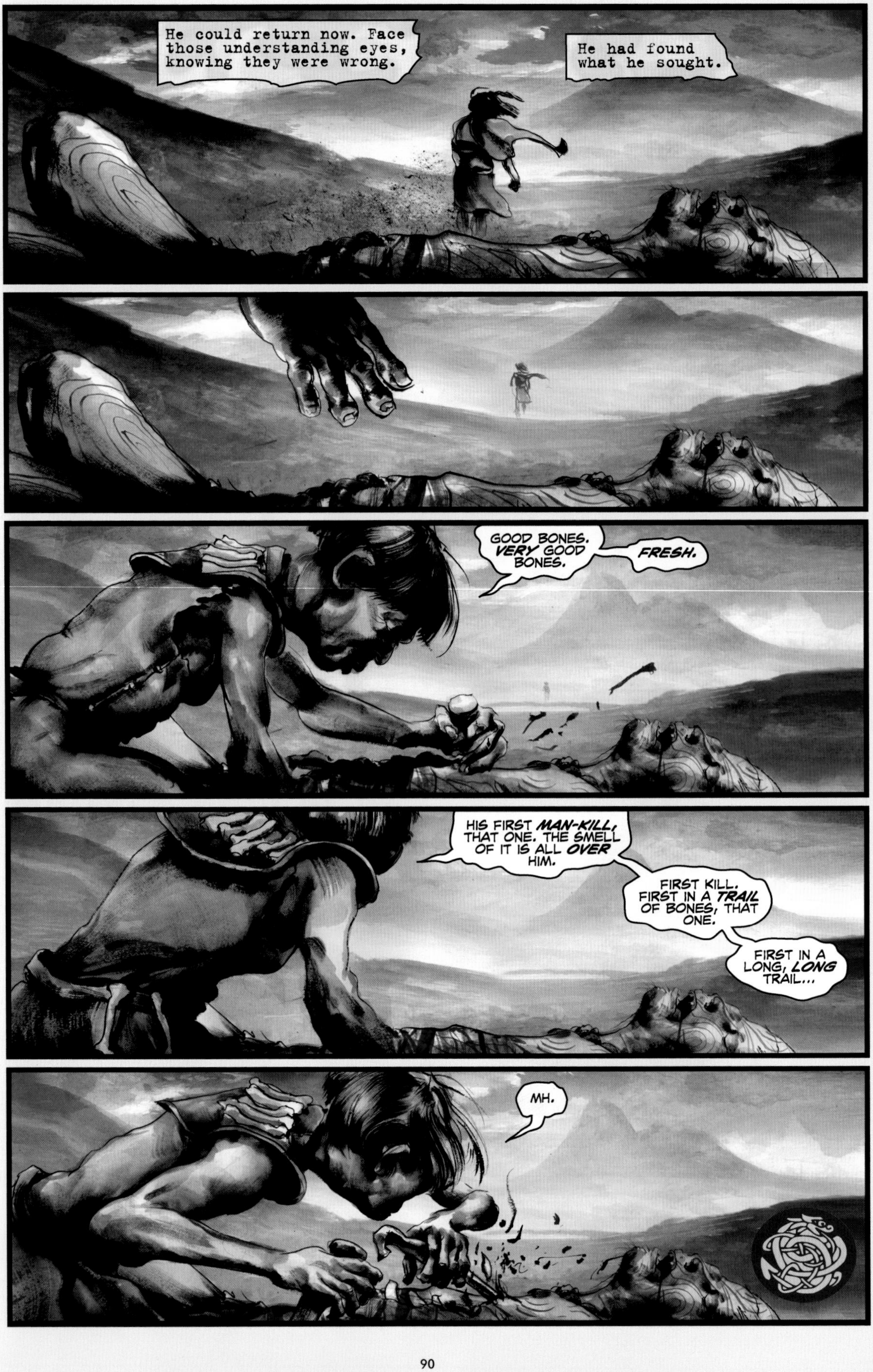
He could return now. Face those understanding eyes, knowing they were wrong.
He had found what he sought.
GOOD BONES. VERY GOOD BONES.
FRESH.
HIS FIRST MAN-KILL, THAT ONE. THE SMELL OF IT IS ALL OVER HIM.
FIRST KILL. FIRST IN A TRAIL OF BONES, THAT ONE.
FIRST IN A LONG, LONG TRAIL...
MH.

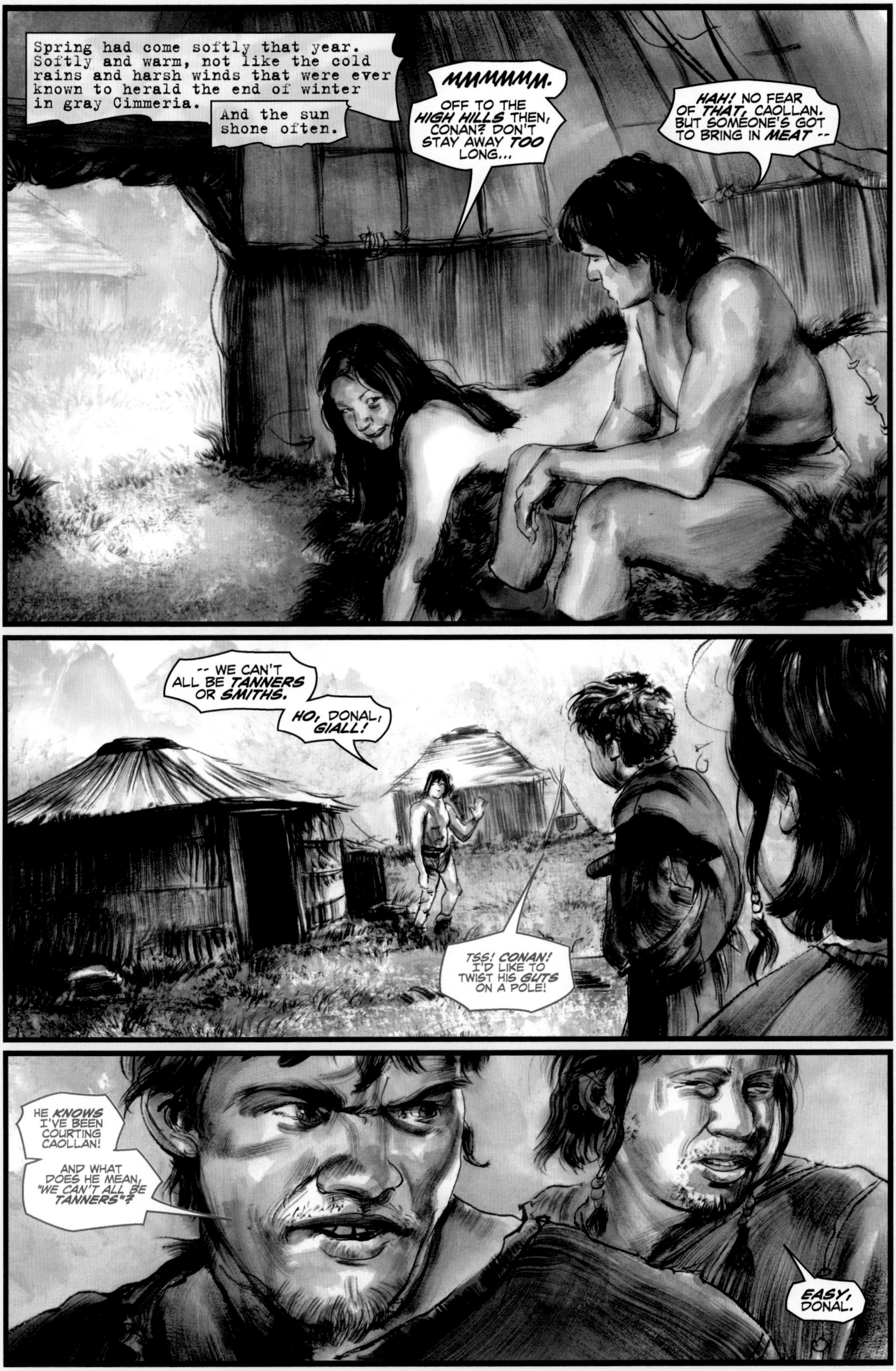
Spring had come softly that year. Softly and warm, not like the cold rains and harsh winds that were ever known to herald the end of winter in gray Cimmeria.
And the sun shone often.
MMMMMM.
OFF TO THE HIGH HILLS THEN, CONAN? DON'T STAY AWAY TOO LONG...
HAH! NO FEAR OF THAT, CAOLLAN. BUT SOMEONE'S GOT TO BRING IN MEAT --
-- WE CAN'T ALL BE TANNERS OR SMITHS.
HO, DONAL, GIALL!
TSS! CONAN! I'D LIKE TO TWIST HIS GUTS ON A POLE!
HE KNOWS I'VE BEEN COURTING CAOLLAN!
AND WHAT DOES HE MEAN, "WE CAN'T ALL BE TANNERS"?
EASY, DONAL.

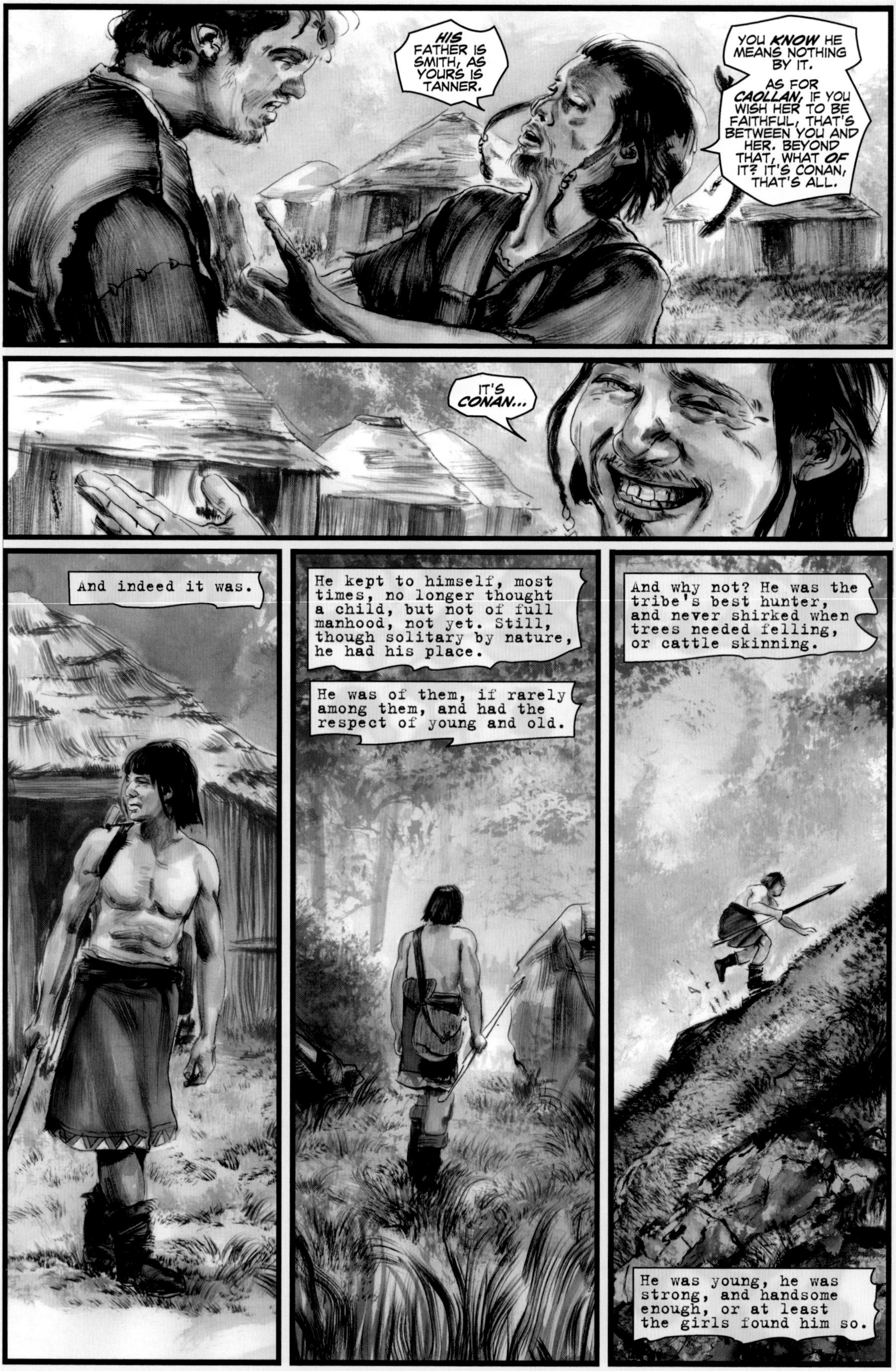
HIS FATHER IS SMITH, AS YOURS IS TANNER.
YOU KNOW HE MEANS NOTHING BY IT.
AS FOR CAOLLAN, IF YOU WISH HER TO BE FAITHFUL, THAT'S BETWEEN YOU AND HER. BEYOND THAT, WHAT OF IT? IT'S CONAN, THAT'S ALL.
IT'S CONAN...
And indeed it was.
He kept to himself, most times, no longer thought a child, but not of full manhood, not yet. Still, though solitary by nature, he had his place.
He was of them, if rarely among them, and had the respect of young and old.
And why not? He was the tribe's best hunter, and never shirked when trees needed felling, or cattle skinning.
He was young, he was strong, and handsome enough, or at least the girls found him so.

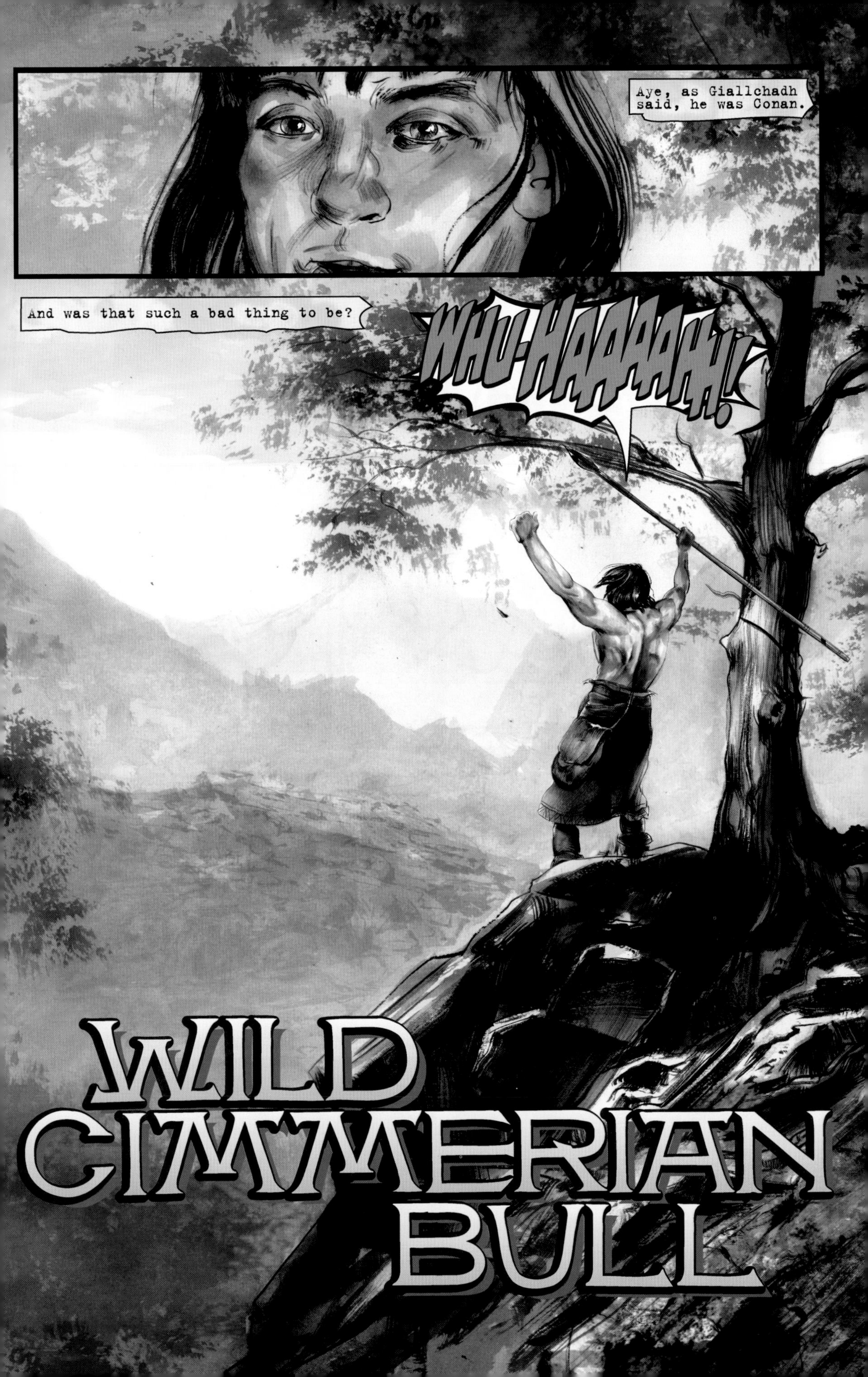
Aye, as Giallchadh said, he was Conan.
And was that such a bad thing to be?
WHU-HAAAAHH!
WILD CIMMERIAN BULL

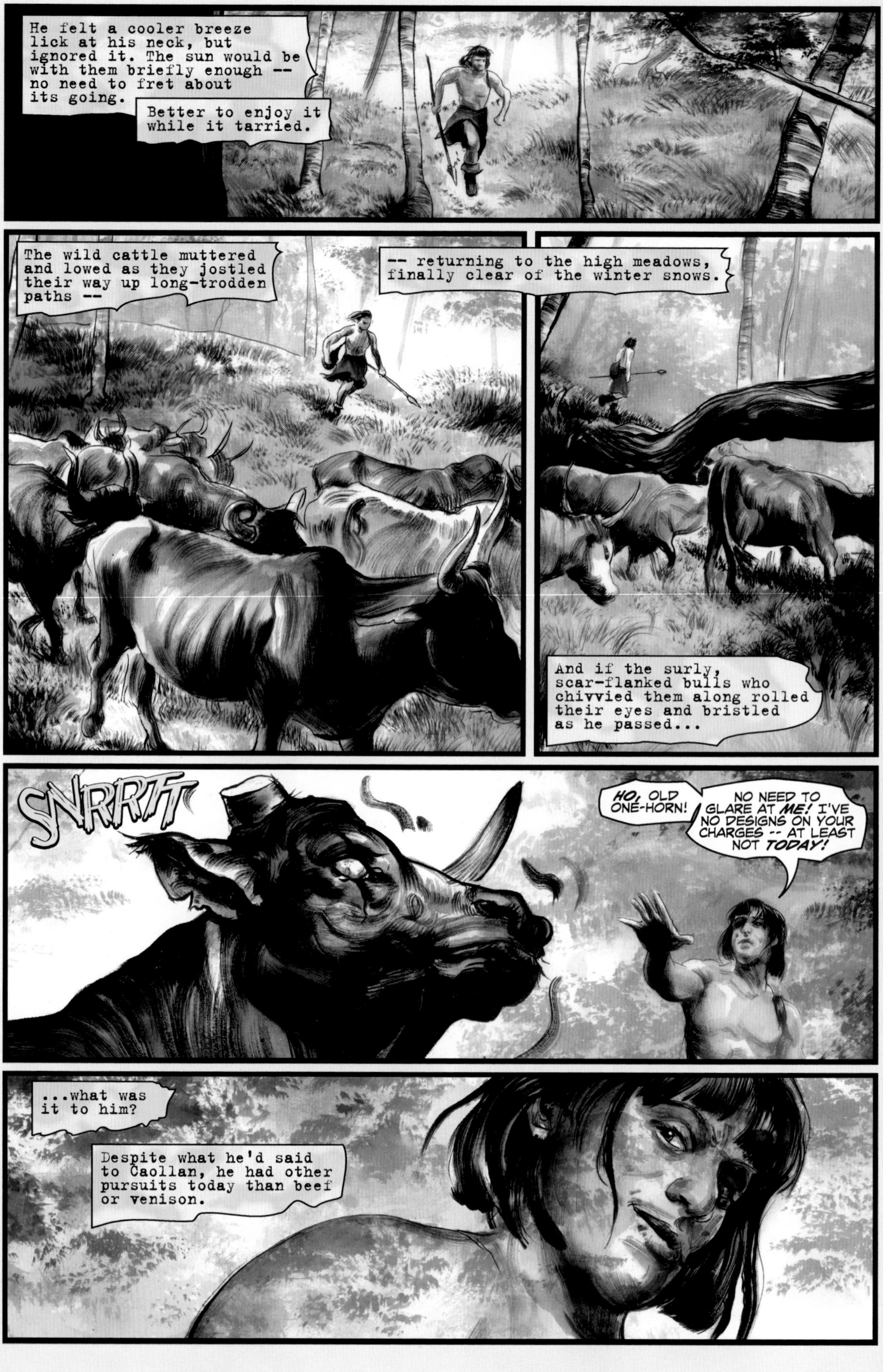
He felt a cooler breeze lick at his neck, but ignored it. The sun would be with them briefly enough -- no need to fret about its going.
Better to enjoy it while it tarried.
The wild cattle muttered and lowed as they jostled their way up long-trodden paths --
-- returning to the high meadows, finally clear of the winter snows.
And if the surly, scar-flanked bulls who chivvied them along rolled their eyes and bristled as he passed...
SNRRFT
HO, OLD ONE-HORN!
NO NEED TO GLARE AT ME! I'VE NO DESIGNS ON YOUR CHARGES -- AT LEAST NOT TODAY!
...what was it to him?
Despite what he'd said to Caollan, he had other pursuits today than beef or venison.

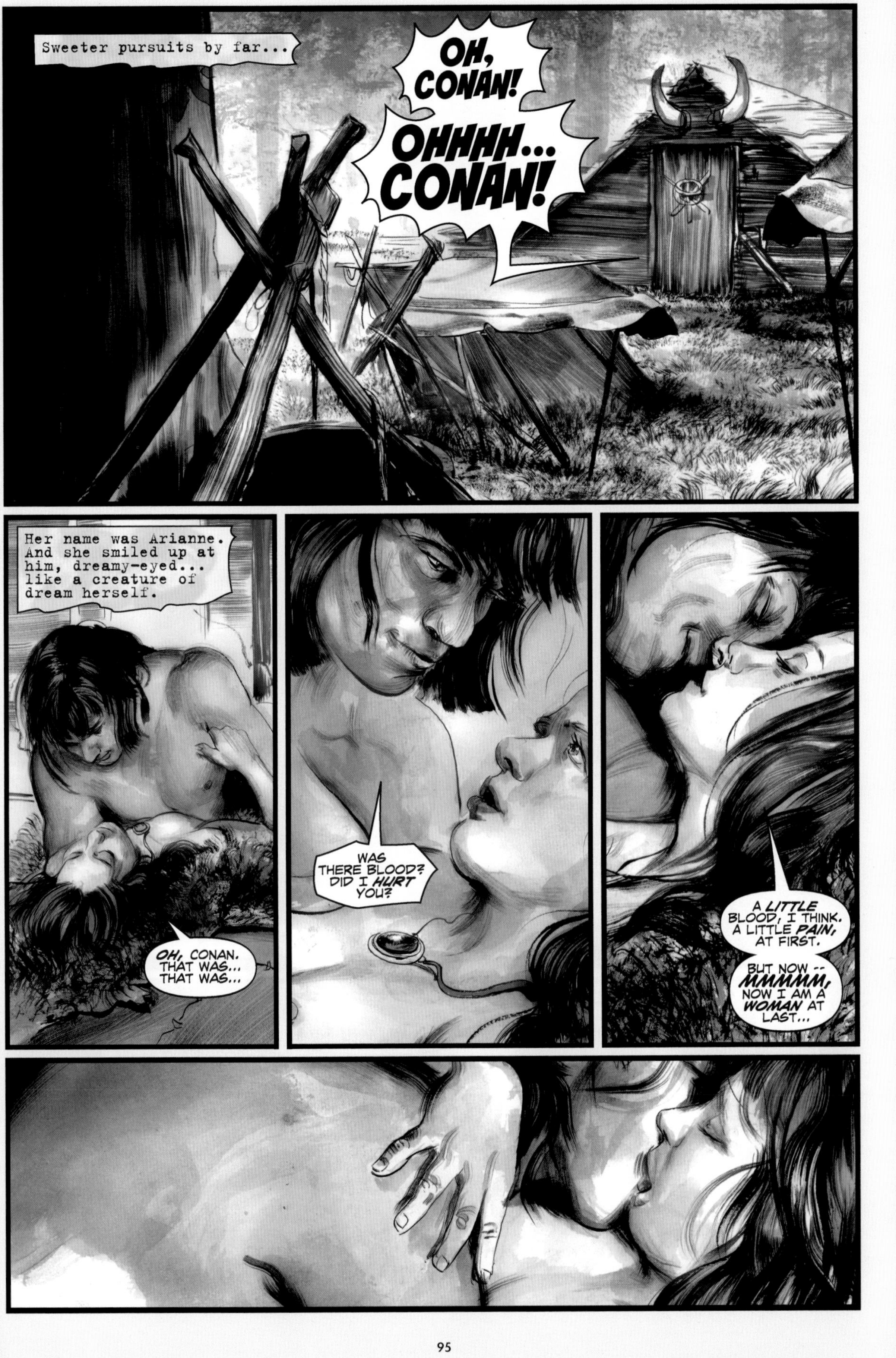

Sweeter pursuits by far...
OH, CONAN!
OHHHH... CONAN!
Her name was Arianne. And she smiled up at him, dreamy-eyed... like a creature of dream herself.
OH, CONAN. THAT WAS... THAT WAS...
WAS THERE BLOOD? DID I HURT YOU?
A LITTLE BLOOD, I THINK. A LITTLE PAIN, AT FIRST.
BUT NOW -- MMMMM, NOW I AM A WOMAN AT LAST...

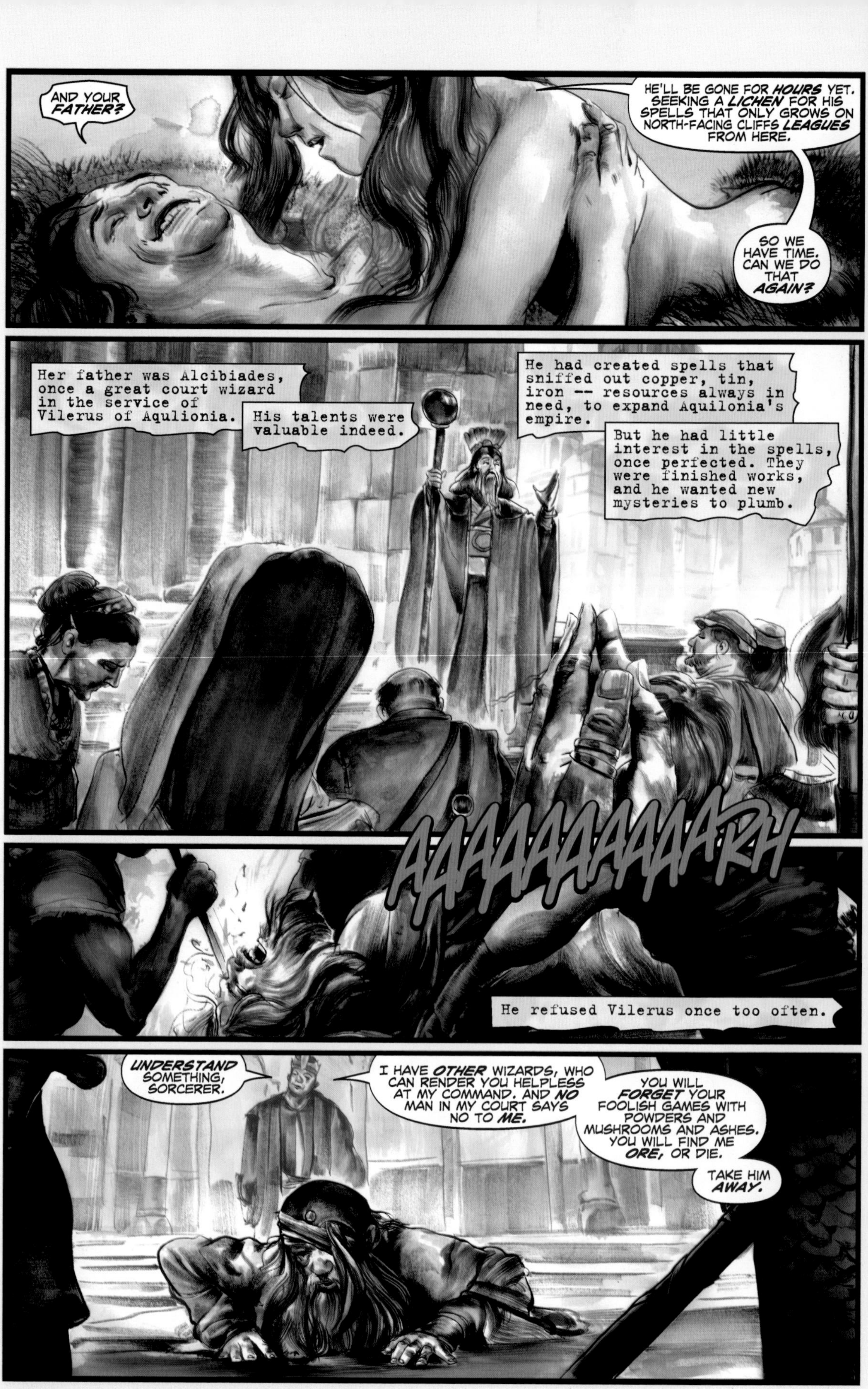
AND YOUR FATHER?
HE'LL BE GONE FOR HOURS YET. SEEKING A LICHEN FOR HIS SPELLS THAT ONLY GROWS ON NORTH-FACING CLIFFS LEAGUES FROM HERE.
SO WE HAVE TIME. CAN WE DO THAT AGAIN?
Her father was Alcibiades, once a great court wizard in the service of Vilerus of Aqulionia.
His talents were valuable indeed.
He had created spells that sniffed out copper, tin, iron -- resources always in need, to expand Aquilonia's empire.
But he had little interest in the spells, once perfected. They were finished works, and he wanted new mysteries to plumb.
AAAAAAAAAARH
He refused Vilerus once too often.
UNDERSTAND SOMETHING, SORCERER.
I HAVE OTHER WIZARDS, WHO CAN RENDER YOU HELPLESS AT MY COMMAND. AND NO MAN IN MY COURT SAYS NO TO ME.
YOU WILL FORGET YOUR FOOLISH GAMES WITH POWDERS AND MUSHROOMS AND ASHES. YOU WILL FIND ME ORE, OR DIE.
TAKE HIM AWAY.

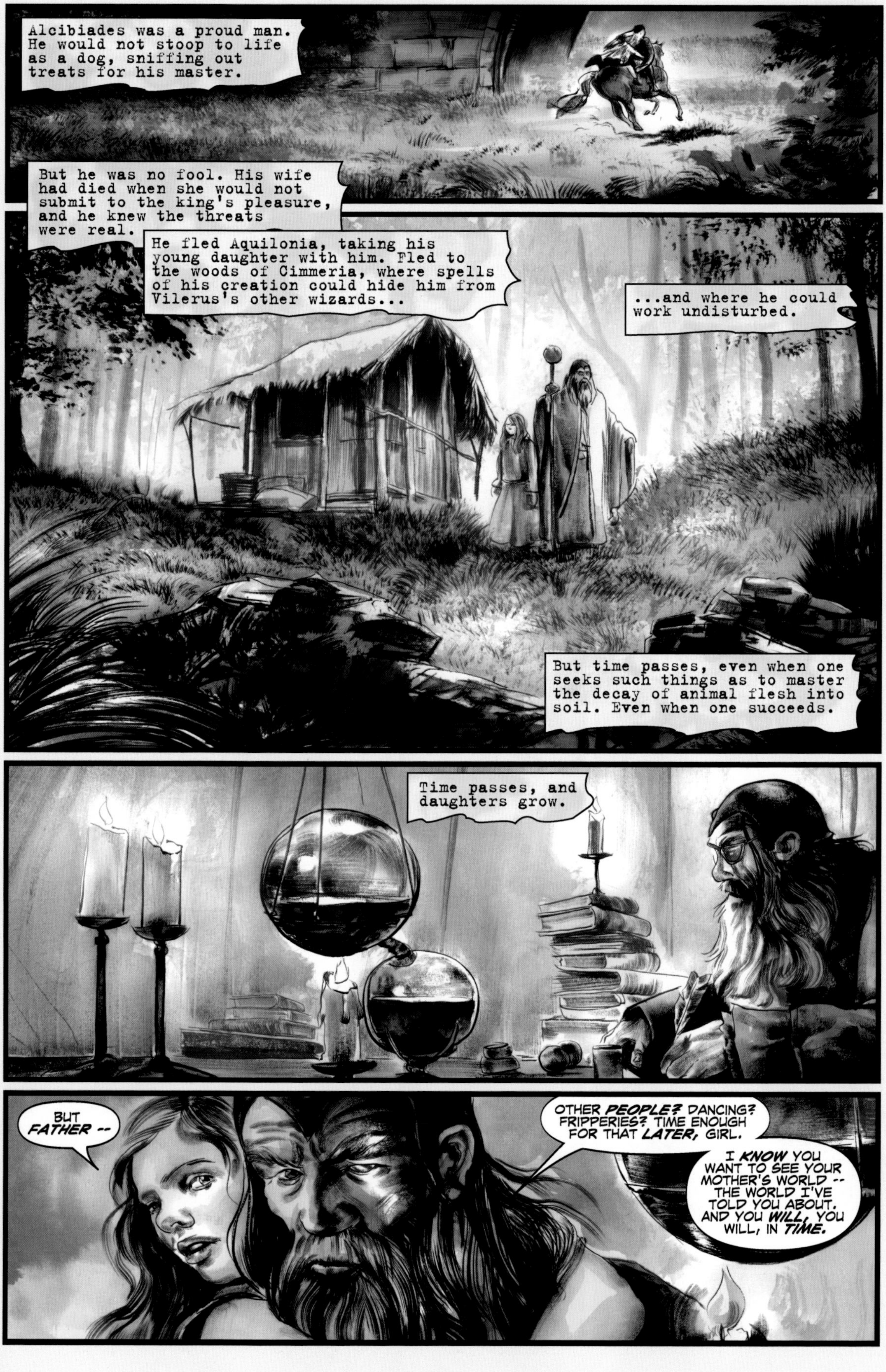
Alcibiades was a proud man. He would not stoop to life as a dog, sniffing out treats for his master.
But he was no fool. His wife had died when she would not submit to the king's pleasure, and he knew the threats were real.
He fled Aquilonia, taking his young daughter with him. Fled to the woods of Cimmeria, where spells of his creation could hide him from Vilerus's other wizards...
...and where he could work undisturbed.
But time passes, even when one seeks such things as to master the decay of animal flesh into soil. Even when one succeeds.
Time passes, and daughters grow.
BUT FATHER --
OTHER PEOPLE? DANCING? FRIPPERIES? TIME ENOUGH FOR THAT LATER, GIRL.
I KNOW YOU WANT TO SEE YOUR MOTHER'S WORLD -- THE WORLD I'VE TOLD YOU ABOUT. AND YOU WILL, YOU WILL, IN TIME.

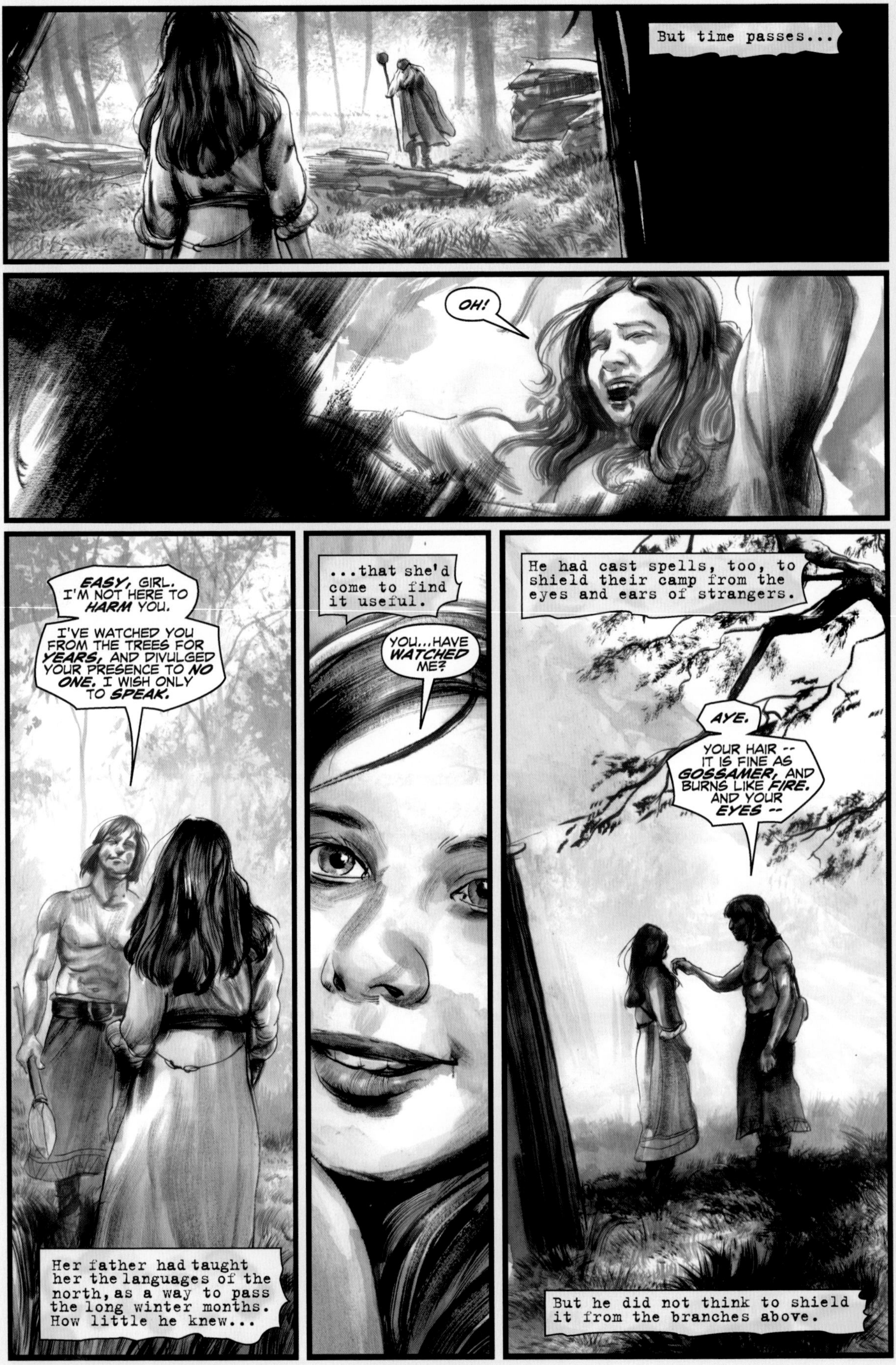
But time passes...
OH!
EASY, GIRL. I'M NOT HERE TO HARM YOU.
I'VE WATCHED YOU FROM THE TREES FOR YEARS, AND DIVULGED YOUR PRESENCE TO NO ONE. I WISH ONLY TO SPEAK.
Her father had taught her the languages of the north, as a way to pass the long winter months. How little he knew...
...that she'd come to find it useful.
YOU...HAVE WATCHED ME?
He had cast spells, too, to shield their camp from the eyes and ears of strangers.
AYE.
YOUR HAIR -- IT IS FINE AS GOSSAMER, AND BURNS LIKE FIRE. AND YOUR EYES --
But he did not think to shield it from the branches above.

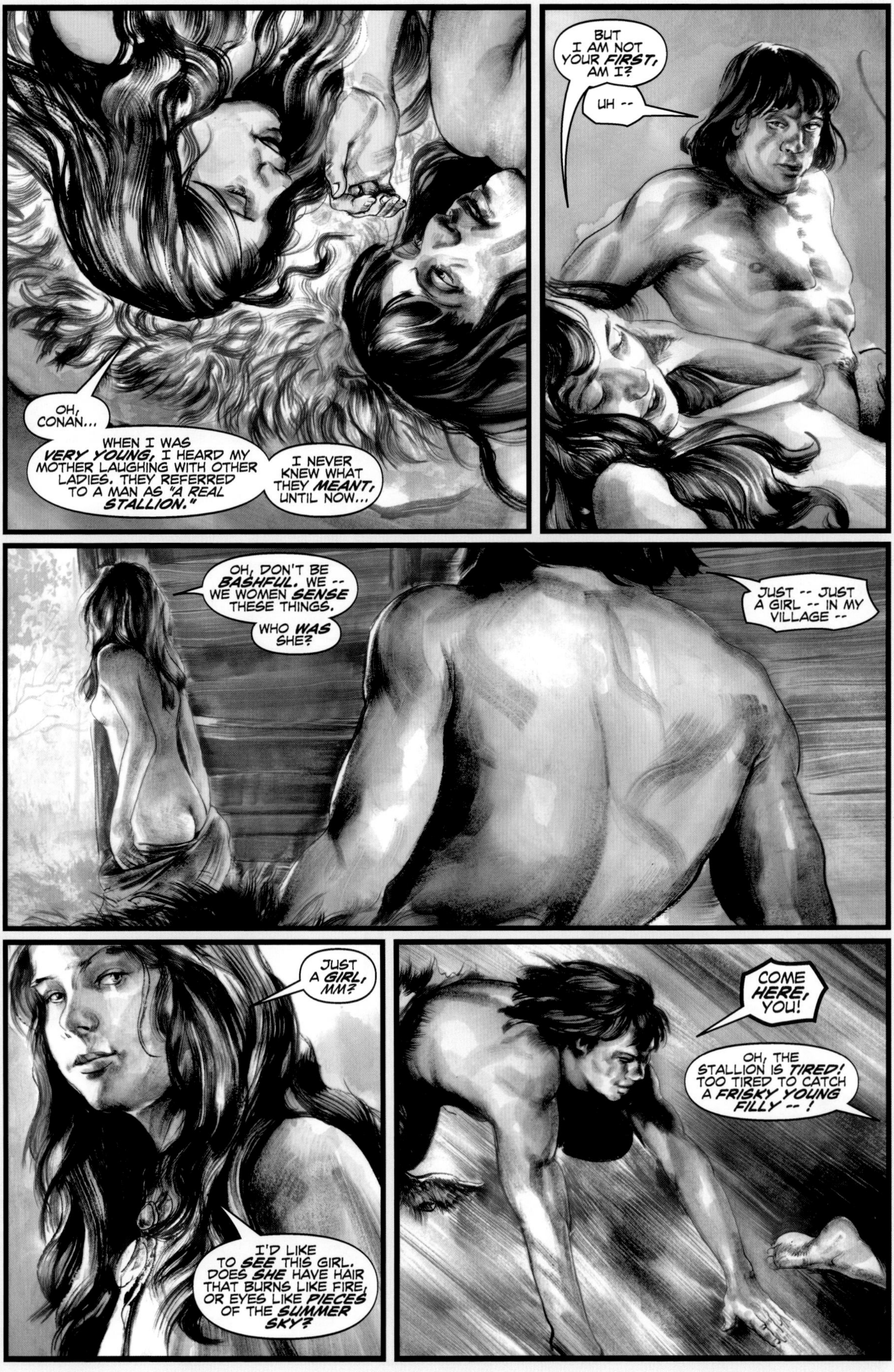
OH, CONAN...
WHEN I WAS VERY YOUNG, I HEARD MY MOTHER LAUGHING WITH OTHER LADIES. THEY REFERRED TO A MAN AS "A REAL STALLION."
I NEVER KNEW WHAT THEY MEANT, UNTIL NOW...
BUT I AM NOT YOUR FIRST, AM I?
UH --
OH, DON'T BE BASHFUL. WE -- WE WOMEN SENSE THESE THINGS.
WHO WAS SHE?
JUST -- JUST A GIRL -- IN MY VILLAGE --
JUST A GIRL, MM?
I'D LIKE TO SEE THIS GIRL. DOES SHE HAVE HAIR THAT BURNS LIKE FIRE, OR EYES LIKE PIECES OF THE SUMMER SKY?
COME HERE, YOU!
OH, THE STALLION IS TIRED! TOO TIRED TO CATCH A FRISKY YOUNG FILLY -- !

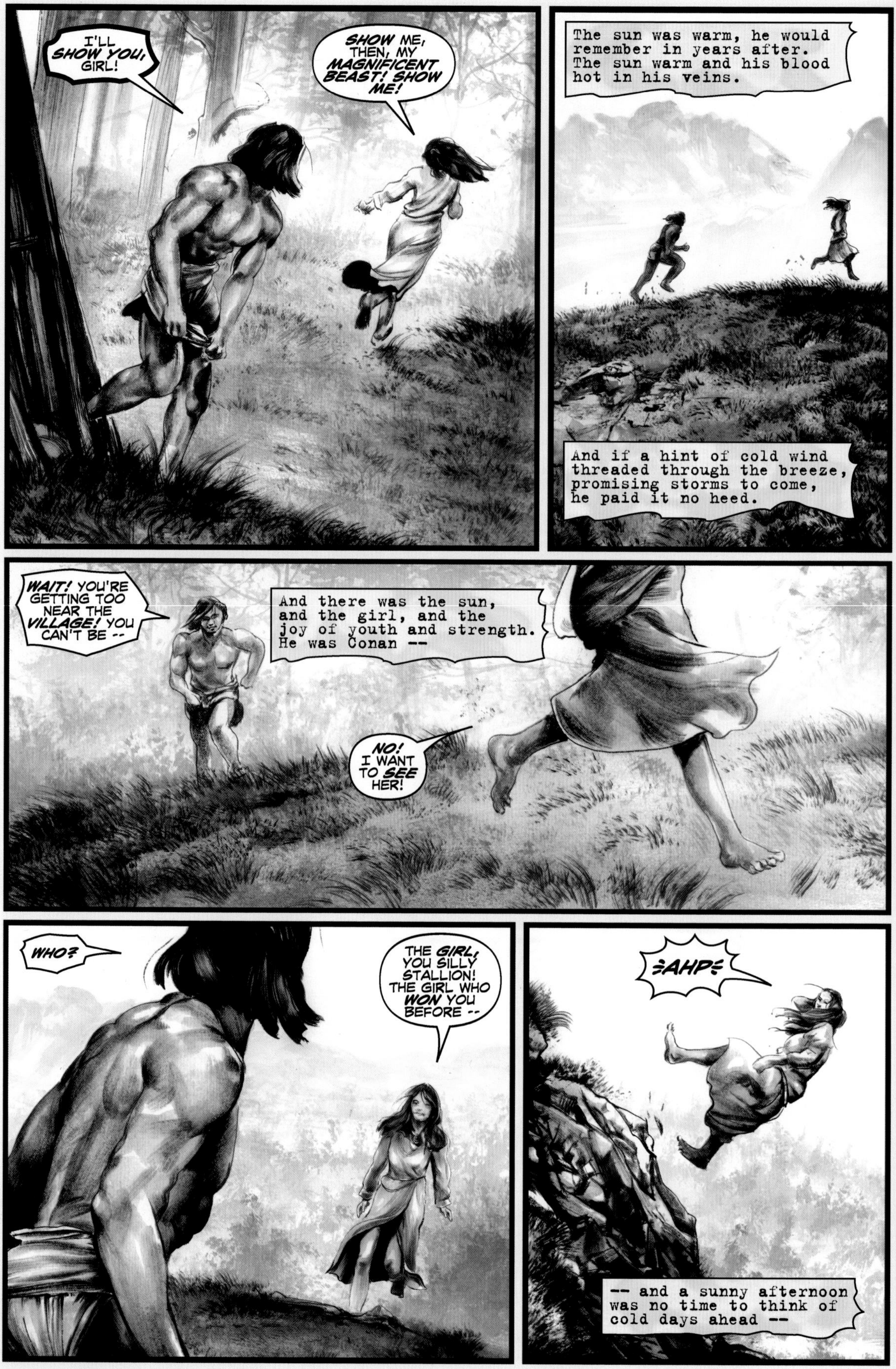
I'LL SHOW YOU, GIRL!
SHOW ME, THEN, MY MAGNIFICENT BEAST! SHOW ME!
The sun was warm, he would remember in years after. The sun warm and his blood hot in his veins.
And if a hint of cold wind threaded through the breeze, promising storms to come, he paid it no heed.
WAIT! YOU'RE GETTING TOO NEAR THE VILLAGE! YOU CAN'T BE --
And there was the sun, and the girl, and the joy of youth and strength. He was Conan --
NO! I WANT TO SEE HER!
WHO?
THE GIRL, YOU SILLY STALLION! THE GIRL WHO WON YOU BEFORE --
AHP
-- and a sunny afternoon was no time to think of cold days ahead --

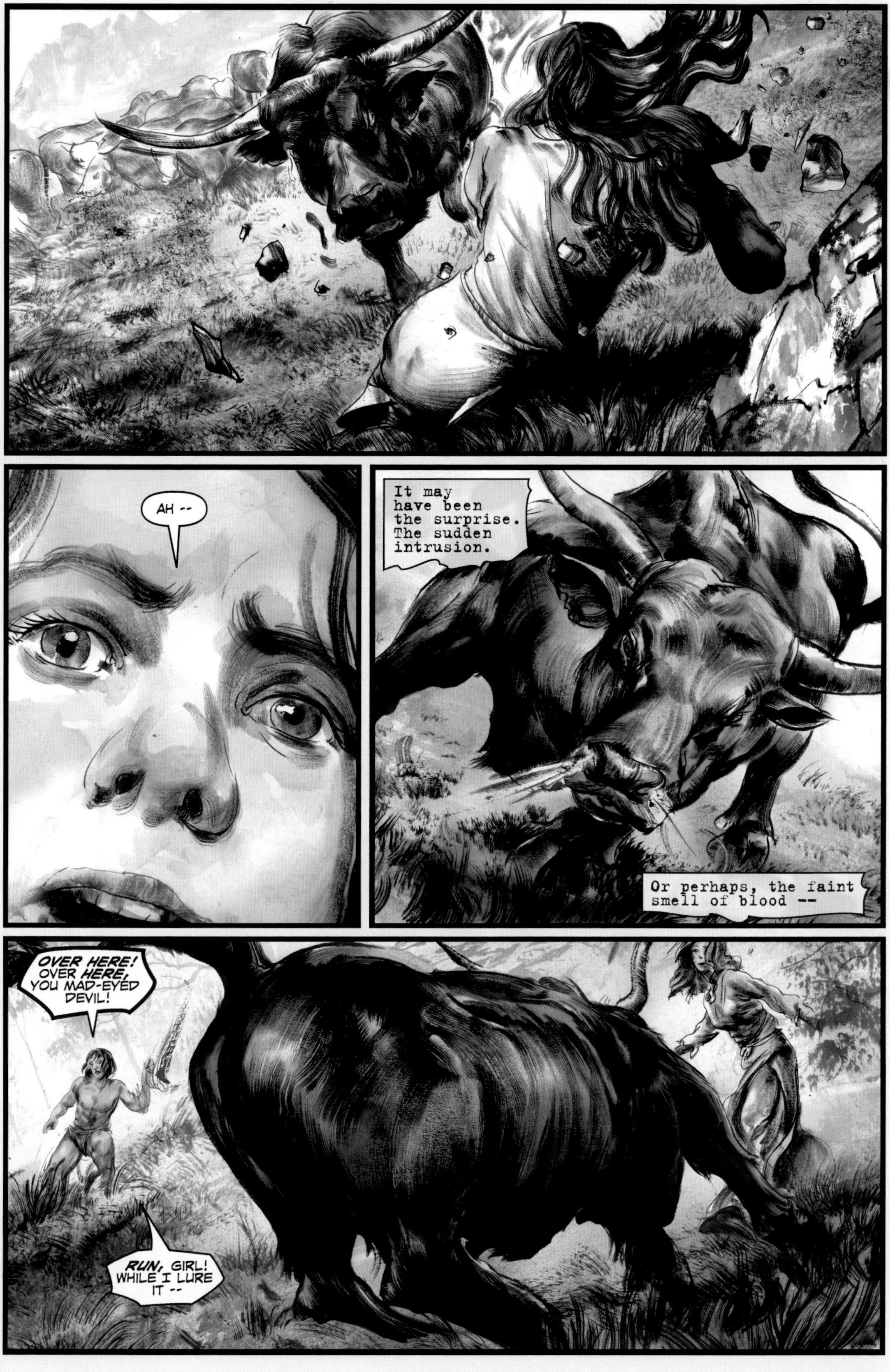
AH --
It may have been the surprise. The sudden intrusion.
Or perhaps, the faint smell of blood --
OVER HERE! OVER HERE, YOU MAD-EYED DEVIL!
RUN, GIRL! WHILE I LURE IT --

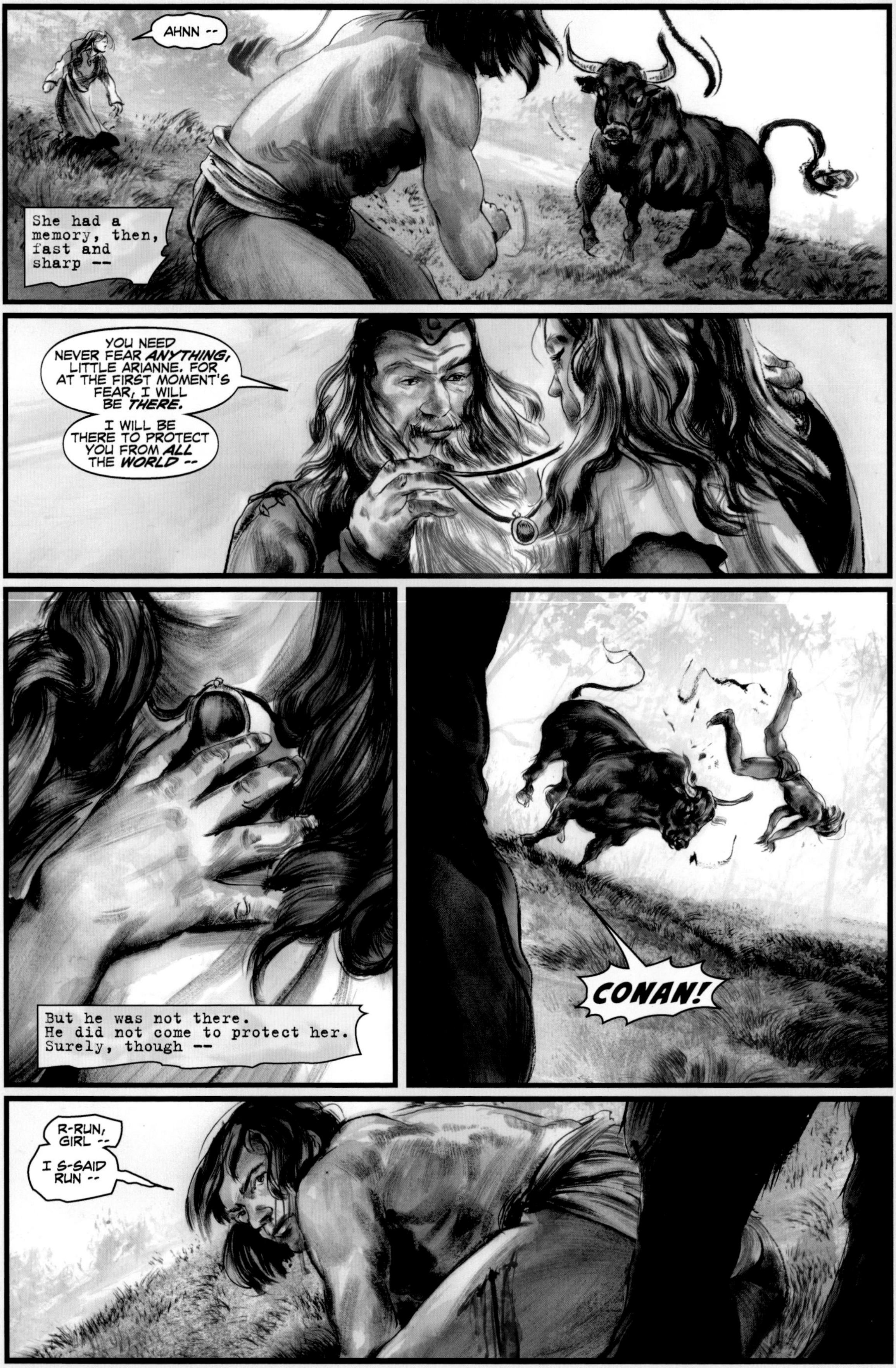
AHNN --
She had a memory, then, fast and sharp --
YOU NEED NEVER FEAR ANYTHING, LITTLE ARIANNE. FOR AT THE FIRST MOMENT'S FEAR, I WILL BE THERE.
I WILL BE THERE TO PROTECT YOU FROM ALL THE WORLD --
But he was not there. He did not come to protect her. Surely, though --
CONAN!
R-RUN, GIRL --
I S-SAID RUN --

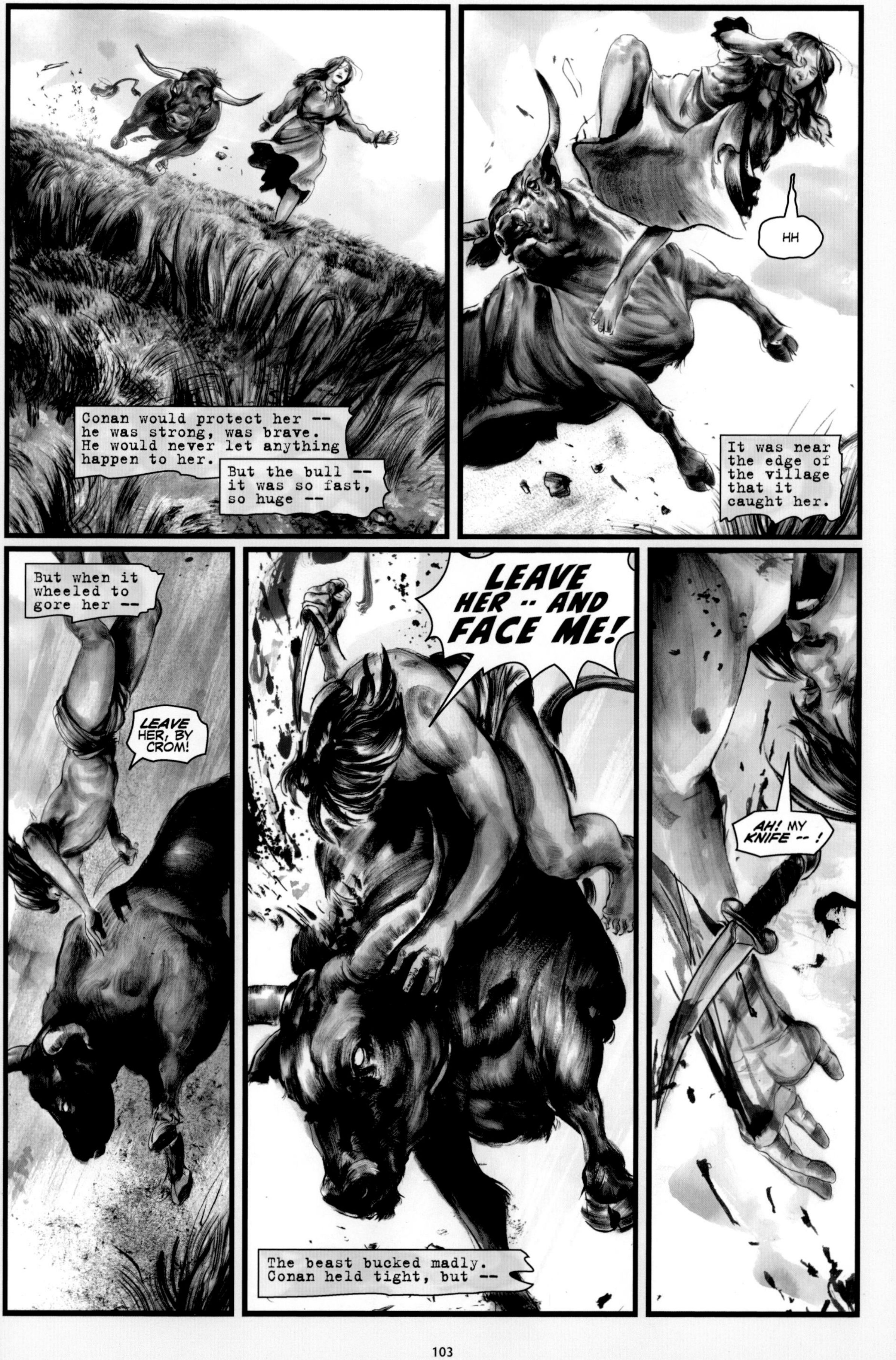

Conan would protect her -- he was strong, was brave. He would never let anything happen to her.
But the bull -- it was so fast, so huge --
HH
It was near the edge of the village that it caught her.
But when it wheeled to gore her --
LEAVE HER, BY CROM!
LEAVE HER -- AND FACE ME!
The beast bucked madly. Conan held tight, but --
AH! MY KNIFE -- !

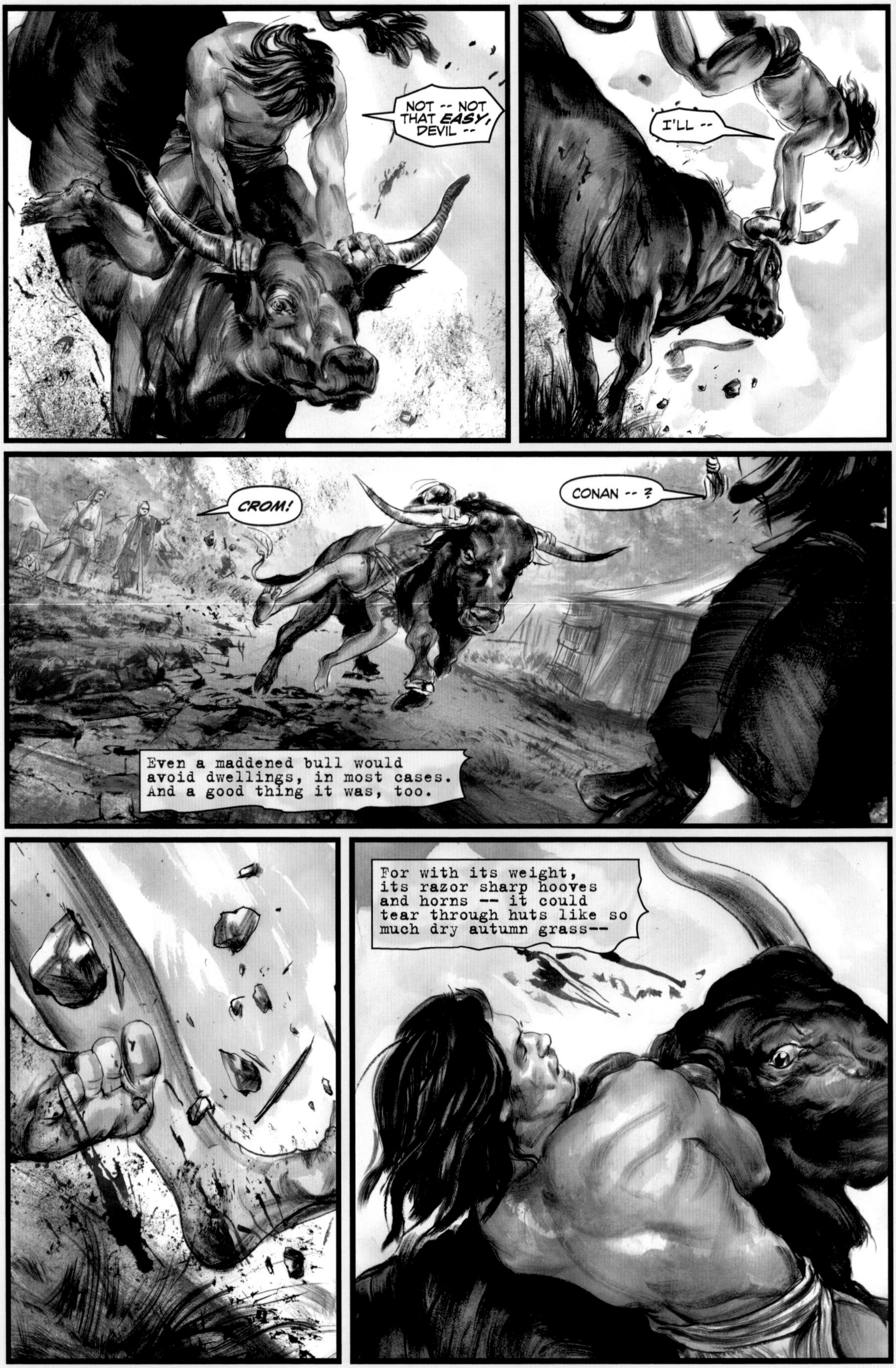
NOT -- NOT THAT EASY, DEVIL --
I'LL --
CROM!
CONAN -- ?
Even a maddened bull would avoid dwellings, in most cases. And a good thing it was, too.
For with its weight, its razor sharp hooves and horns -- it could tear through huts like so much dry autumn grass--

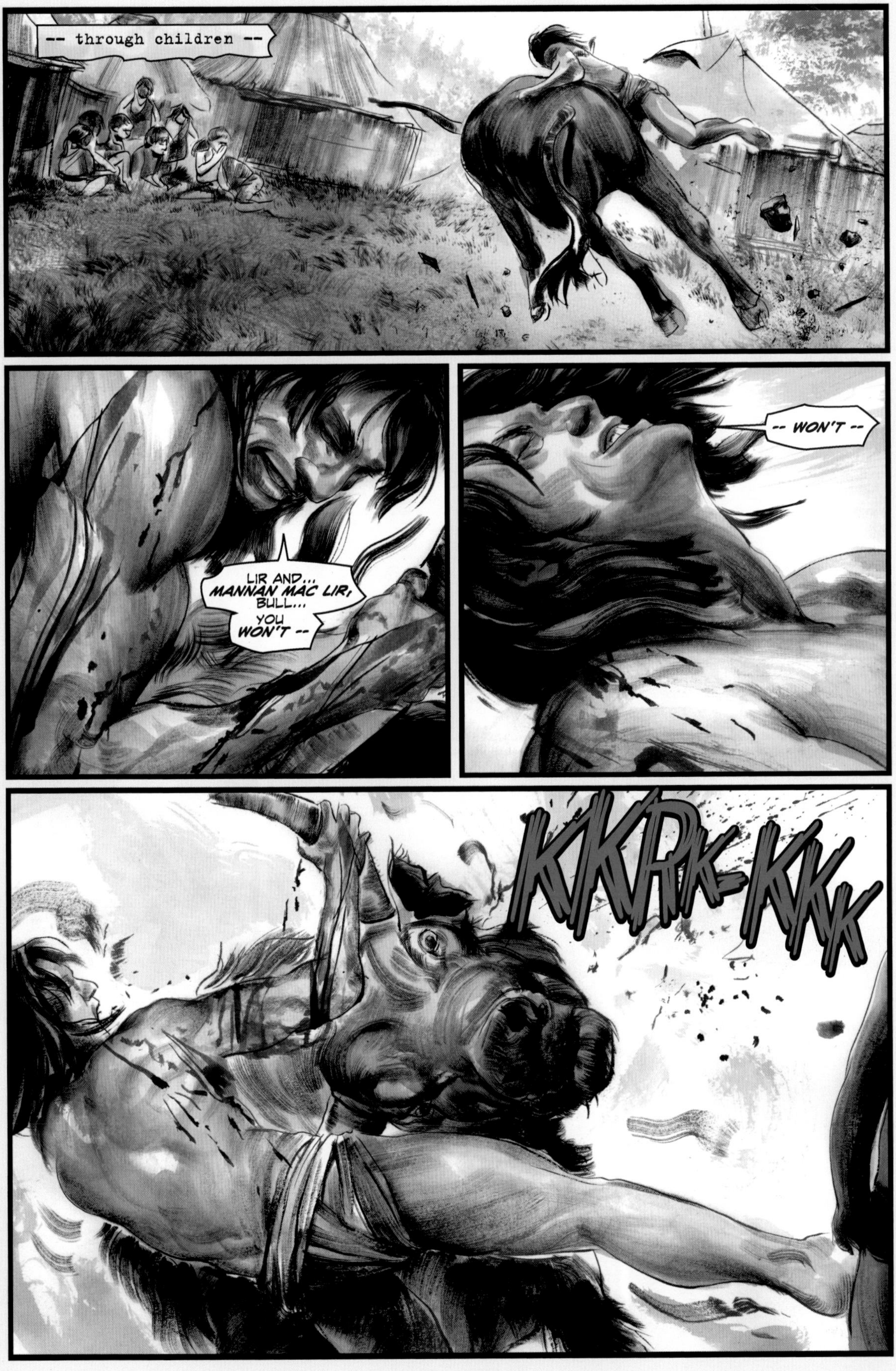
-- through children --
LIR AND... MANNAN MAC LIR, BULL... YOU WON'T --
-- WON'T --
KKRK-KKK

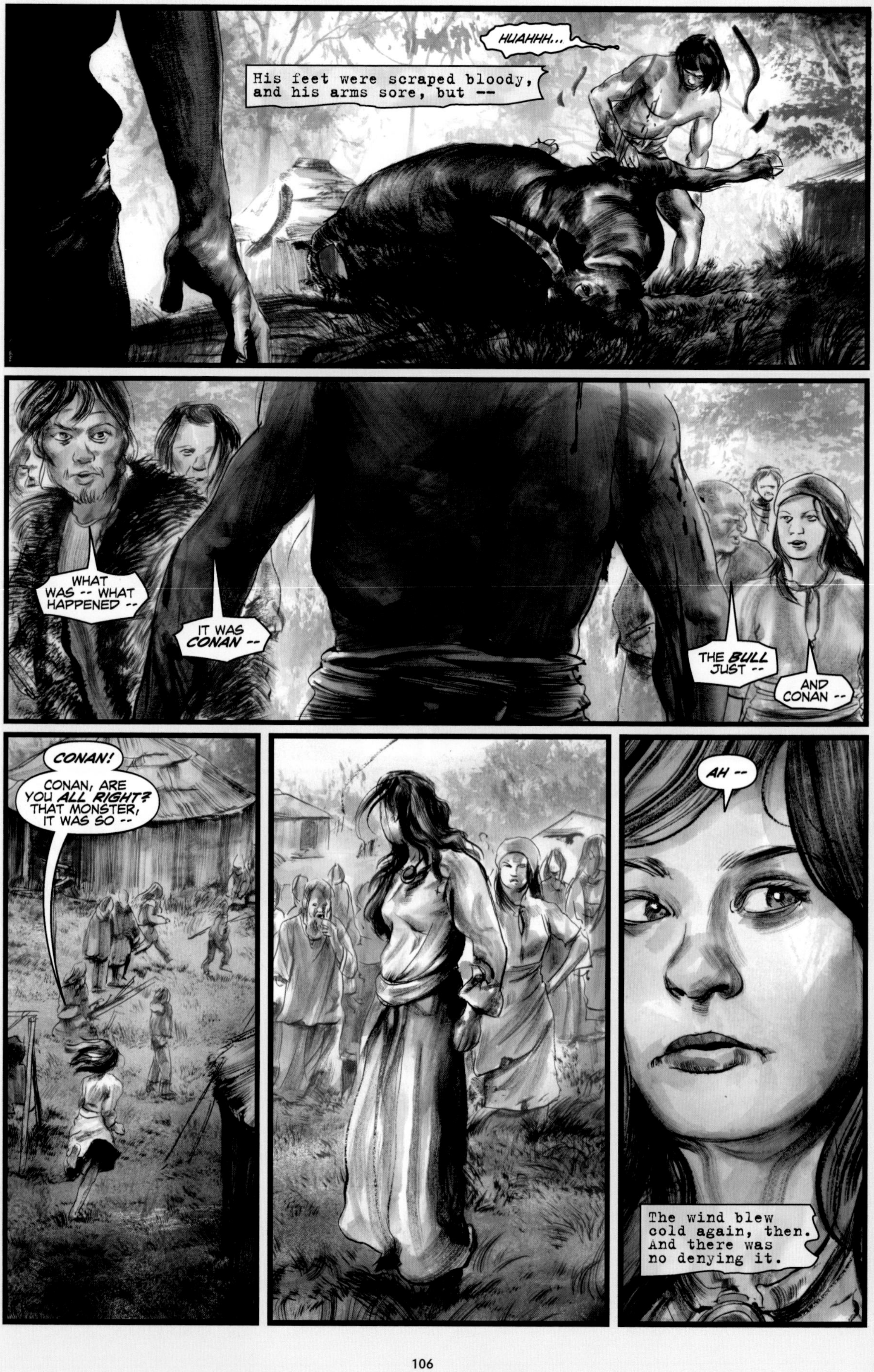

HUAHHH...
His feet were scraped bloody, and his arms sore, but --
WHAT WAS -- WHAT HAPPENED --
IT WAS CONAN --
THE BULL JUST --
AND CONAN --
CONAN!
CONAN, ARE YOU ALL RIGHT? THAT MONSTER, IT WAS SO --
AH --
The wind blew cold again, then. And there was no denying it.

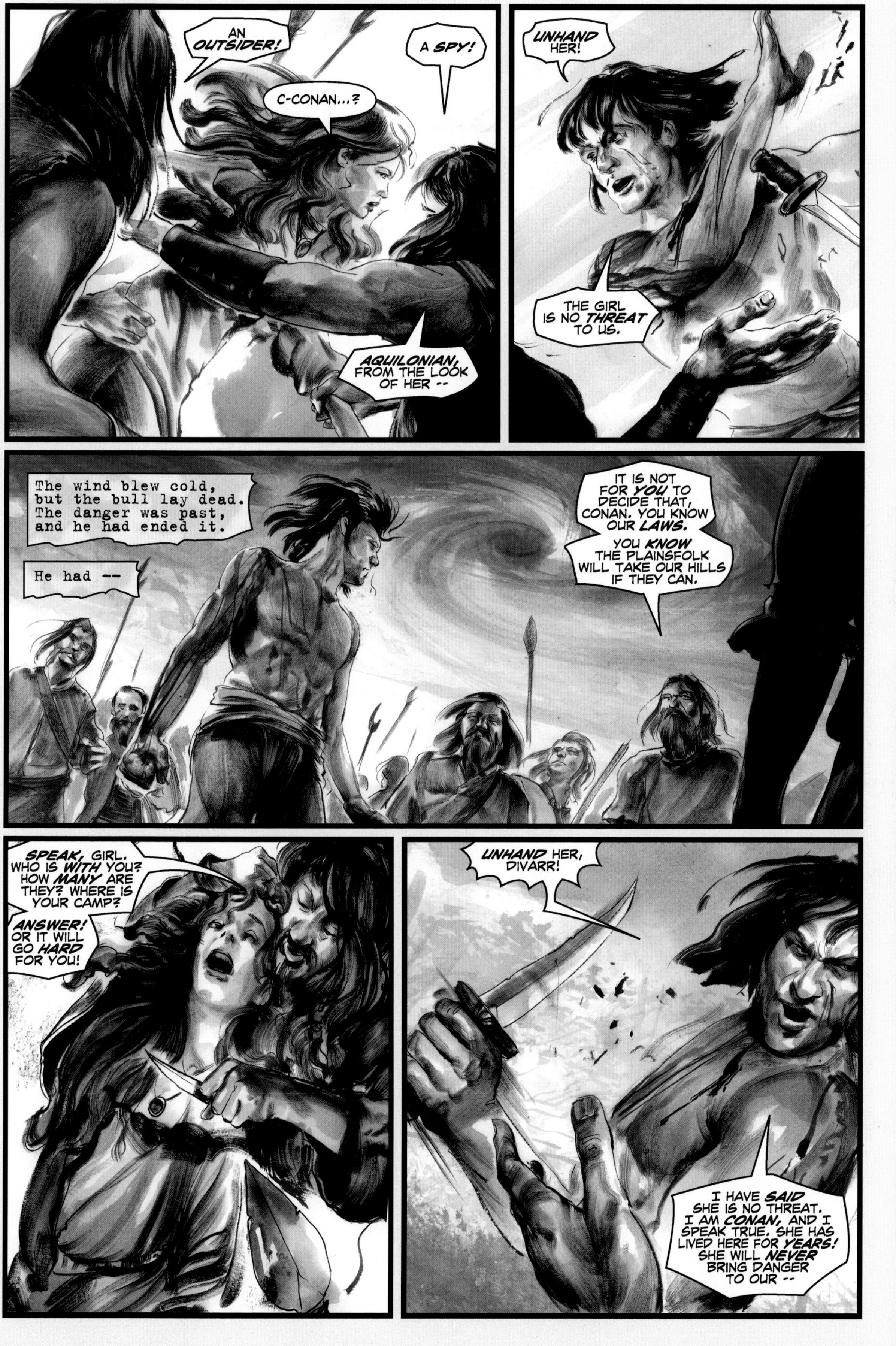
AN OUTSIDER!
A SPY!
C-CONAN...?
AQUILONIAN, FROM THE LOOK OF HER --
UNHAND HER!
THE GIRL IS NO THREAT TO US.
The wind blew cold, but the bull lay dead. The danger was past, and he had ended it.
He had --
IT IS NOT FOR YOU TO DECIDE THAT, CONAN. YOU KNOW OUR LAWS.
YOU KNOW THE PLAINSFOLK WILL TAKE OUR HILLS IF THEY CAN.
SPEAK, GIRL. WHO IS WITH YOU? HOW MANY ARE THEY? WHERE IS YOUR CAMP?
ANSWER! OR IT WILL GO HARD FOR YOU!
UNHAND HER, DIVARR!
I HAVE SAID SHE IS NO THREAT. I AM CONAN, AND I SPEAK TRUE. SHE HAS LIVED HERE FOR YEARS! SHE WILL NEVER BRING DANGER TO OUR --

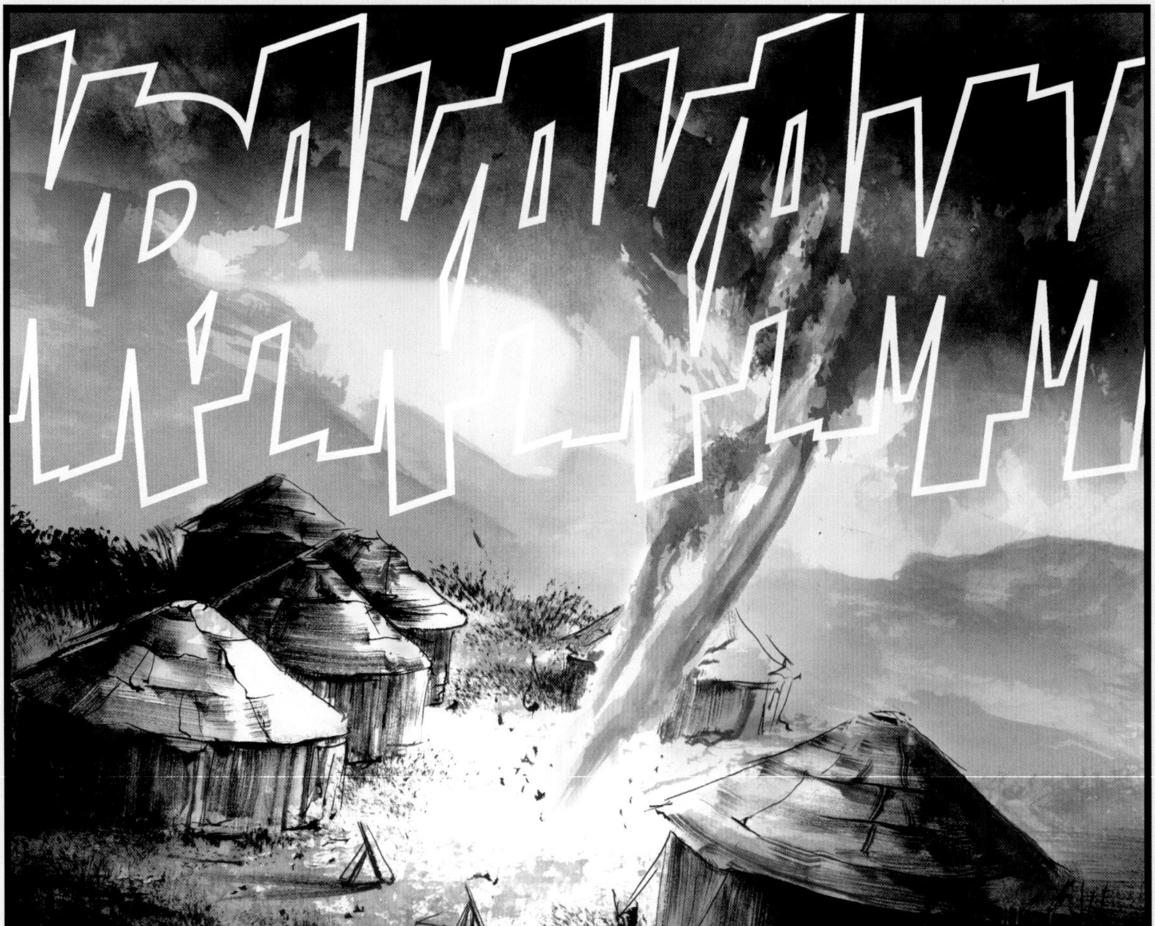

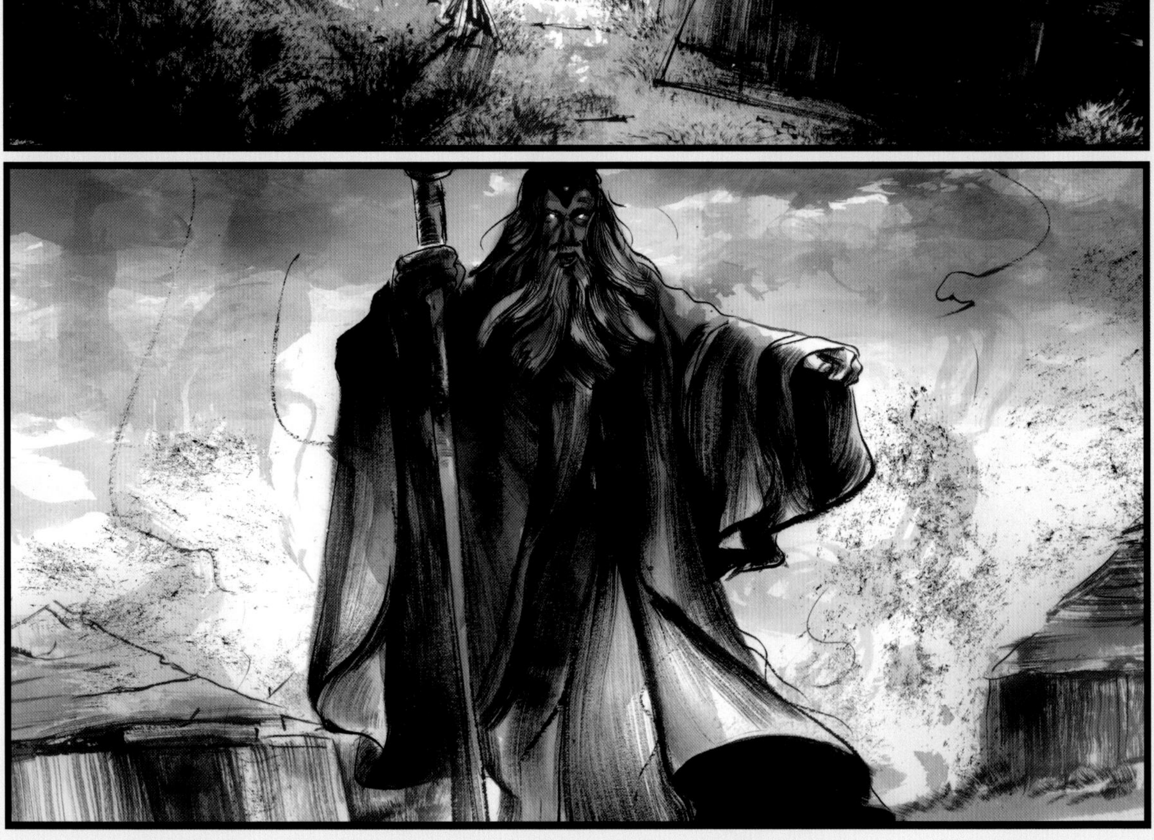

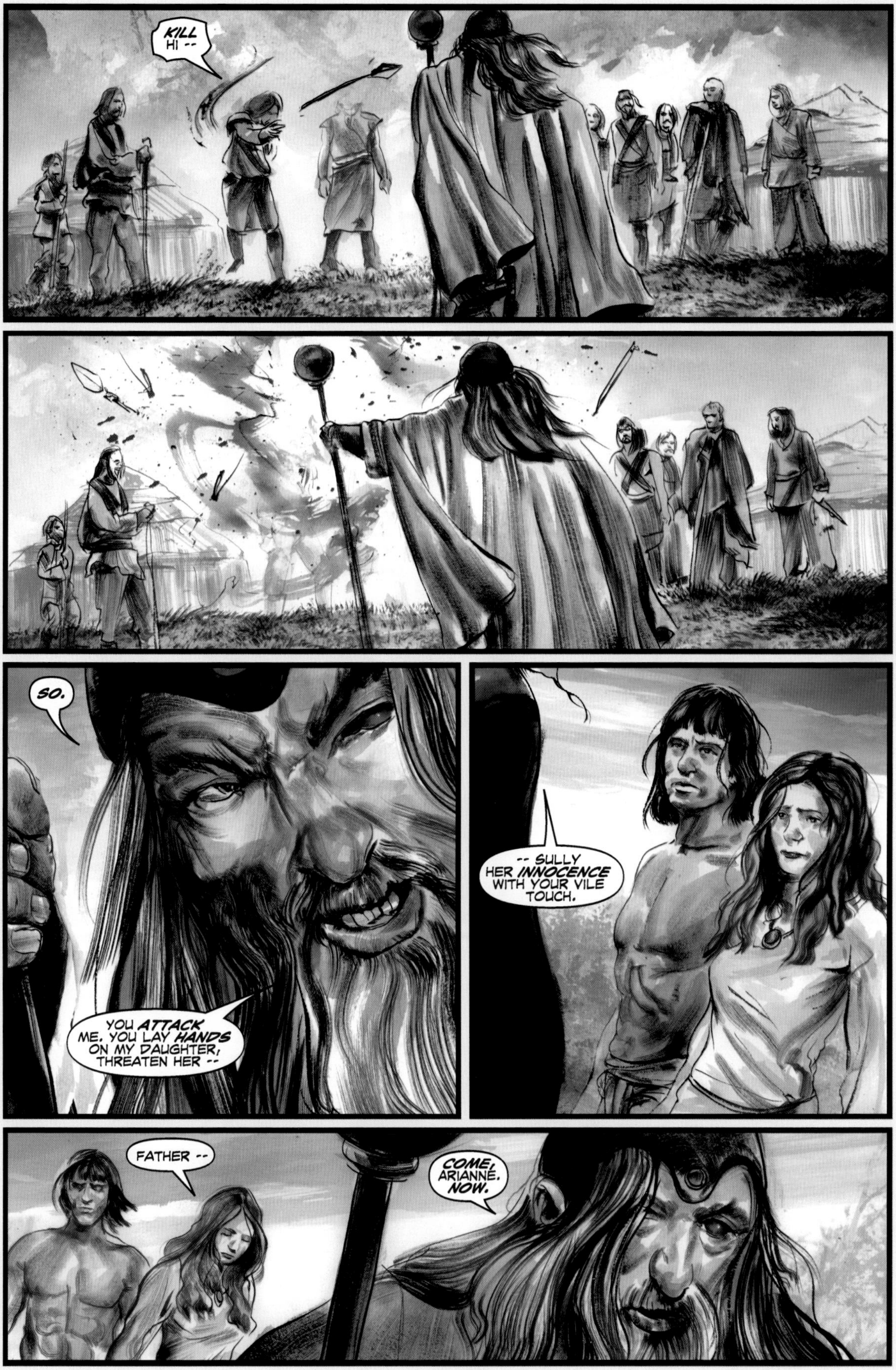
KILL HI --
SO.
YOU ATTACK ME. YOU LAY HANDS ON MY DAUGHTER, THREATEN HER --
-- SULLY HER INNOCENCE WITH YOUR VILE TOUCH.
FATHER --
COME, ARIANNE. NOW.

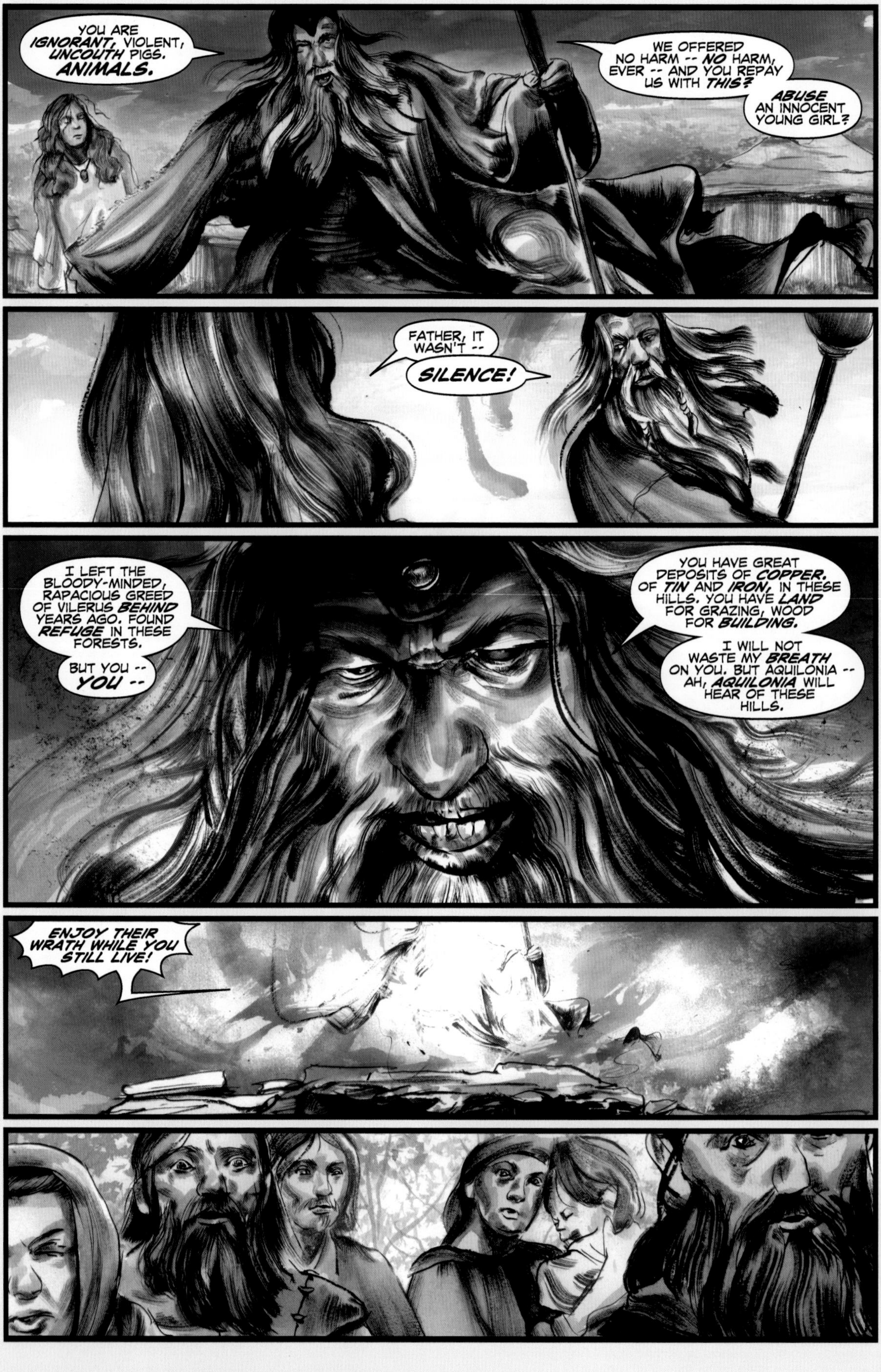
YOU ARE IGNORANT, VIOLENT, UNCOUTH PIGS. ANIMALS.
WE OFFERED NO HARM -- NO HARM, EVER -- AND YOU REPAY US WITH THIS?
ABUSE AN INNOCENT YOUNG GIRL?
FATHER, IT WASN'T --
SILENCE!
I LEFT THE BLOODY-MINDED, RAPACIOUS GREED OF VILERUS BEHIND YEARS AGO. FOUND REFUGE IN THESE FORESTS.
BUT YOU -- YOU --
YOU HAVE GREAT DEPOSITS OF COPPER, OF TIN AND IRON, IN THESE HILLS. YOU HAVE LAND FOR GRAZING, WOOD FOR BUILDING.
I WILL NOT WASTE MY BREATH ON YOU. BUT AQUILONIA -- AH, AQUILONIA WILL HEAR OF THESE HILLS.
ENJOY THEIR WRATH WHILE YOU STILL LIVE!

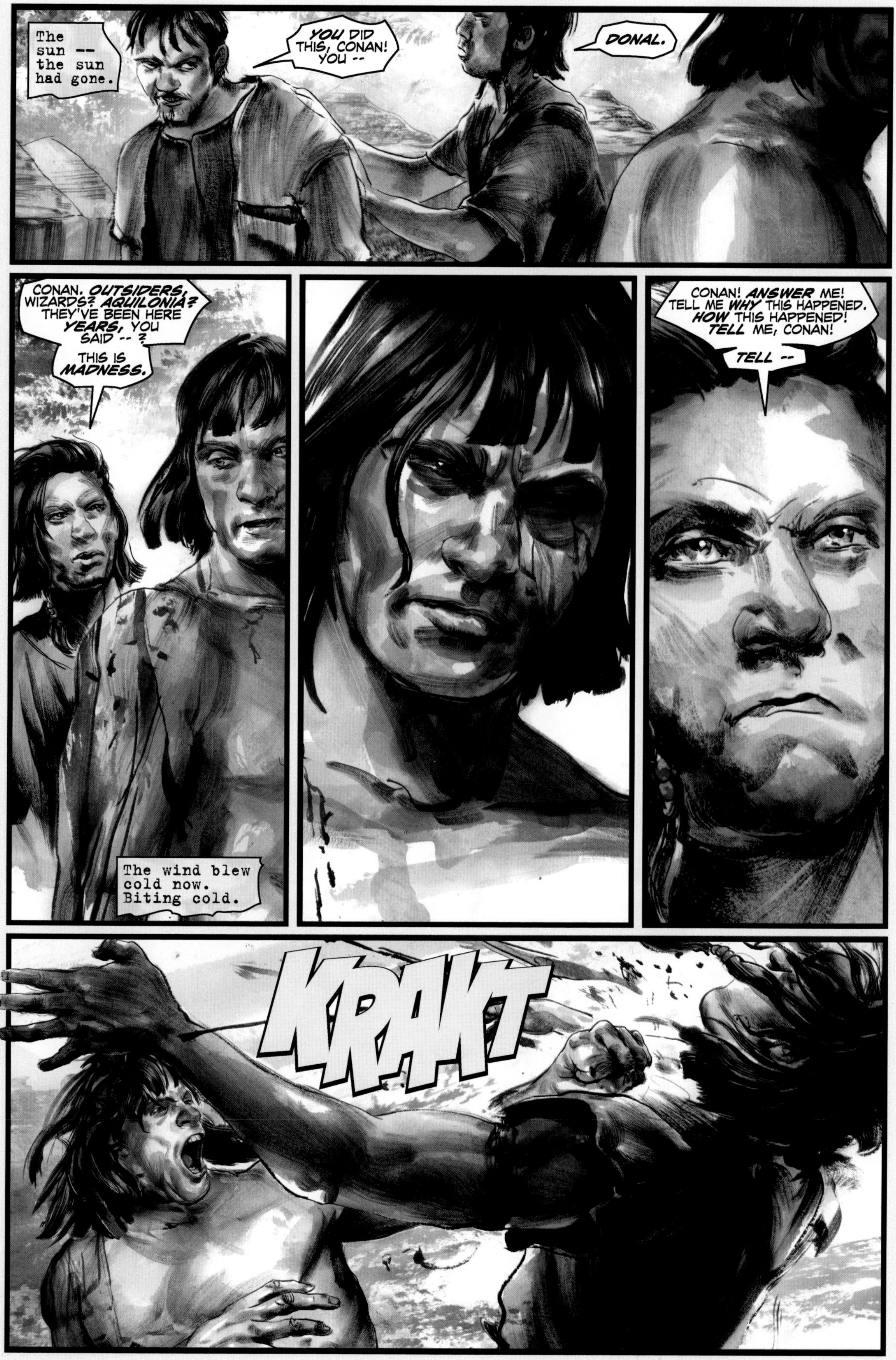
The sun -- the sun had gone.
YOU DID THIS, CONAN! YOU --
DONAL.
CONAN. OUTSIDERS, WIZARDS? AQUILONIA? THEY'VE BEEN HERE YEARS, YOU SAID -- ?
THIS IS MADNESS.
The wind blew cold now. Biting cold.
CONAN! ANSWER ME! TELL ME WHY THIS HAPPENED. HOW THIS HAPPENED! TELL ME, CONAN!
TELL --
KRAKT

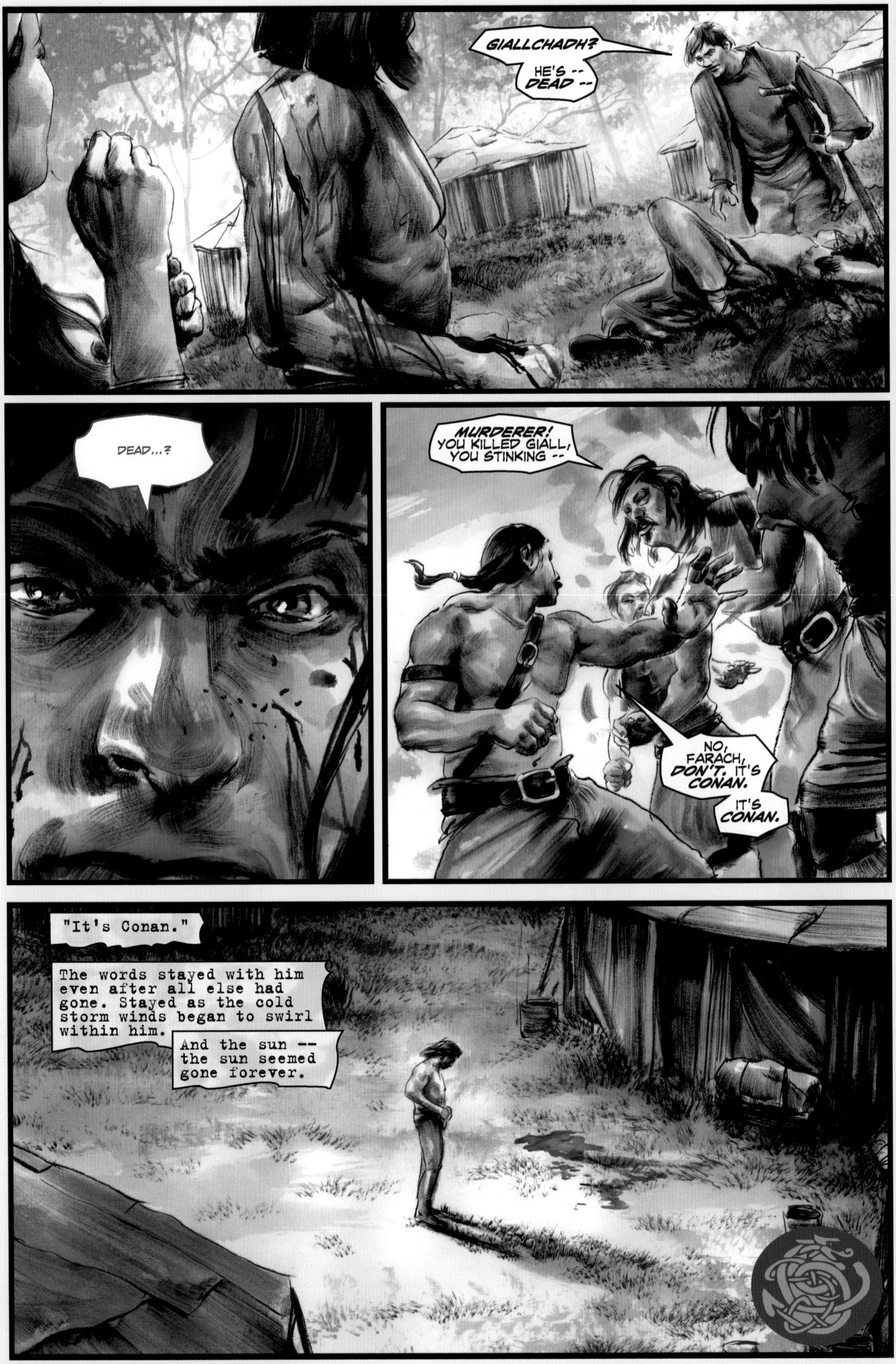
GIALLCHADH?
HE'S -- DEAD --
DEAD...?
MURDERER! YOU KILLED GIALL, YOU STINKING --
NO, FARACH, DON'T. IT'S CONAN.
IT'S CONAN.
"It's Conan."
The words stayed with him even after all else had gone. Stayed as the cold storm winds began to swirl within him.
And the sun -- the sun seemed gone forever.

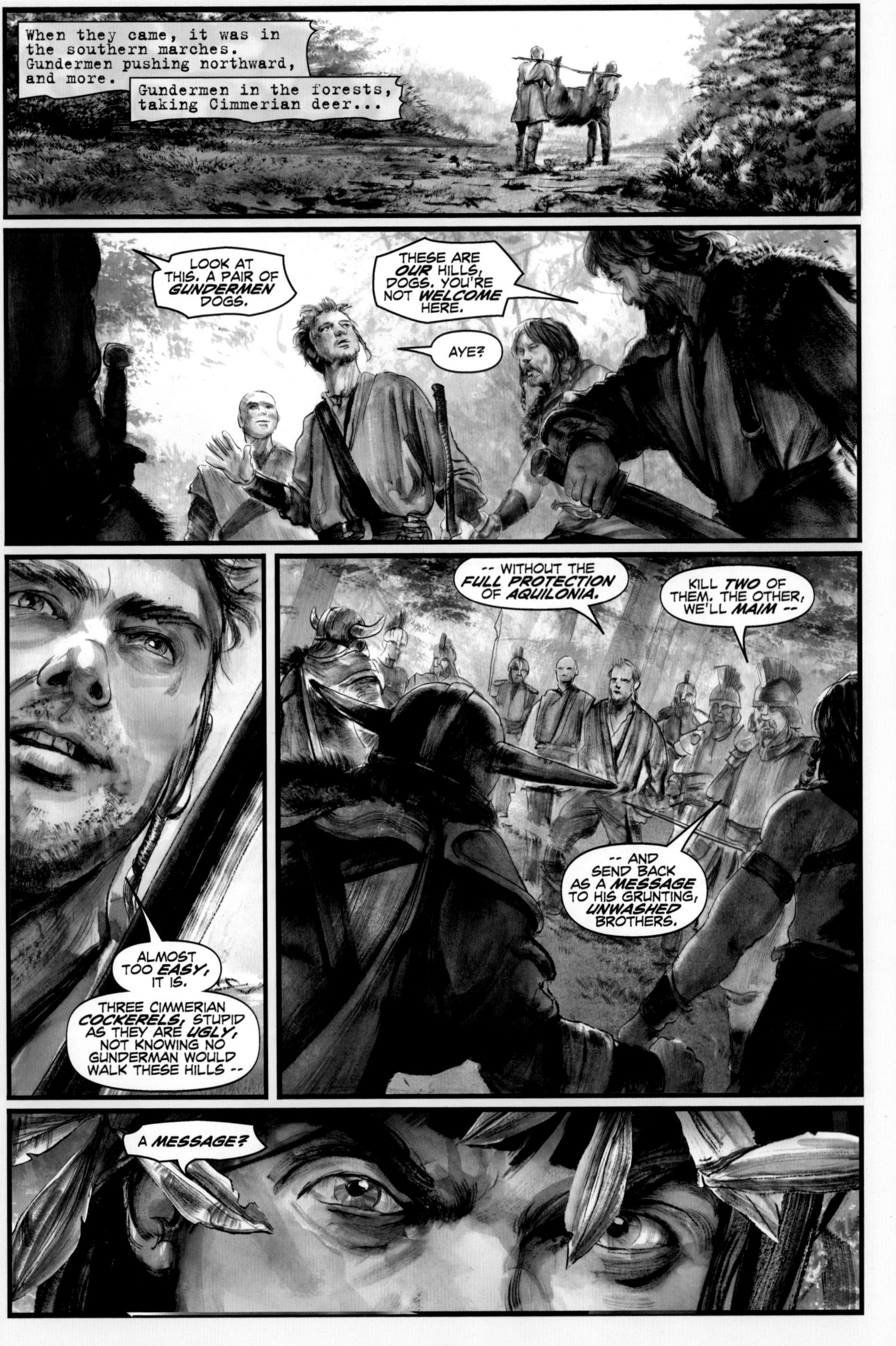

When they came, it was in the southern marches. Gundermen pushing northward, and more.
Gundermen in the forests, taking Cimmerian deer...
LOOK AT THIS. A PAIR OF GUNDERMEN DOGS.
THESE ARE OUR HILLS, DOGS. YOU'RE NOT WELCOME HERE.
AYE?
ALMOST TOO EASY, IT IS.
THREE CIMMERIAN COCKERELS, STUPID AS THEY ARE UGLY, NOT KNOWING NO GUNDERMAN WOULD WALK THESE HILLS --
-- WITHOUT THE FULL PROTECTION OF AQUILONIA.
KILL TWO OF THEM. THE OTHER, WE'LL MAIM --
-- AND SEND BACK AS A MESSAGE TO HIS GRUNTING, UNWASHED BROTHERS.
A MESSAGE?

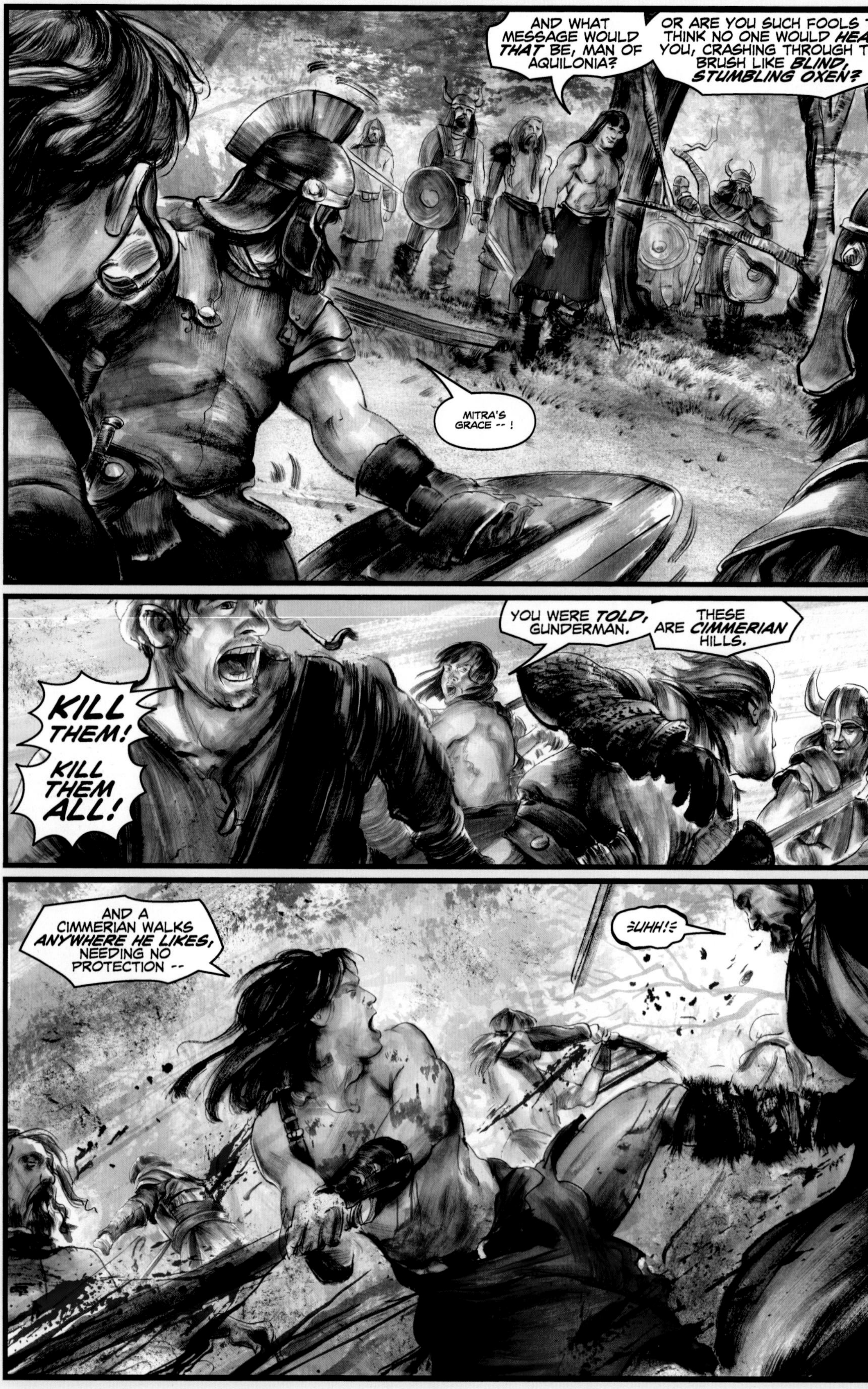
AND WHAT MESSAGE WOULD THAT BE, MAN OF AQUILONIA?
OR ARE YOU SUCH FOOLS TO THINK NO ONE WOULD HEAR YOU, CRASHING THROUGH THE BRUSH LIKE BLIND, STUMBLING OXEN?
MITRA'S GRACE -- !
KILL THEM! KILL THEM ALL!
YOU WERE TOLD, GUNDERMAN.
THESE ARE CIMMERIAN HILLS.
AND A CIMMERIAN WALKS ANYWHERE HE LIKES, NEEDING NO PROTECTION --
UHH!

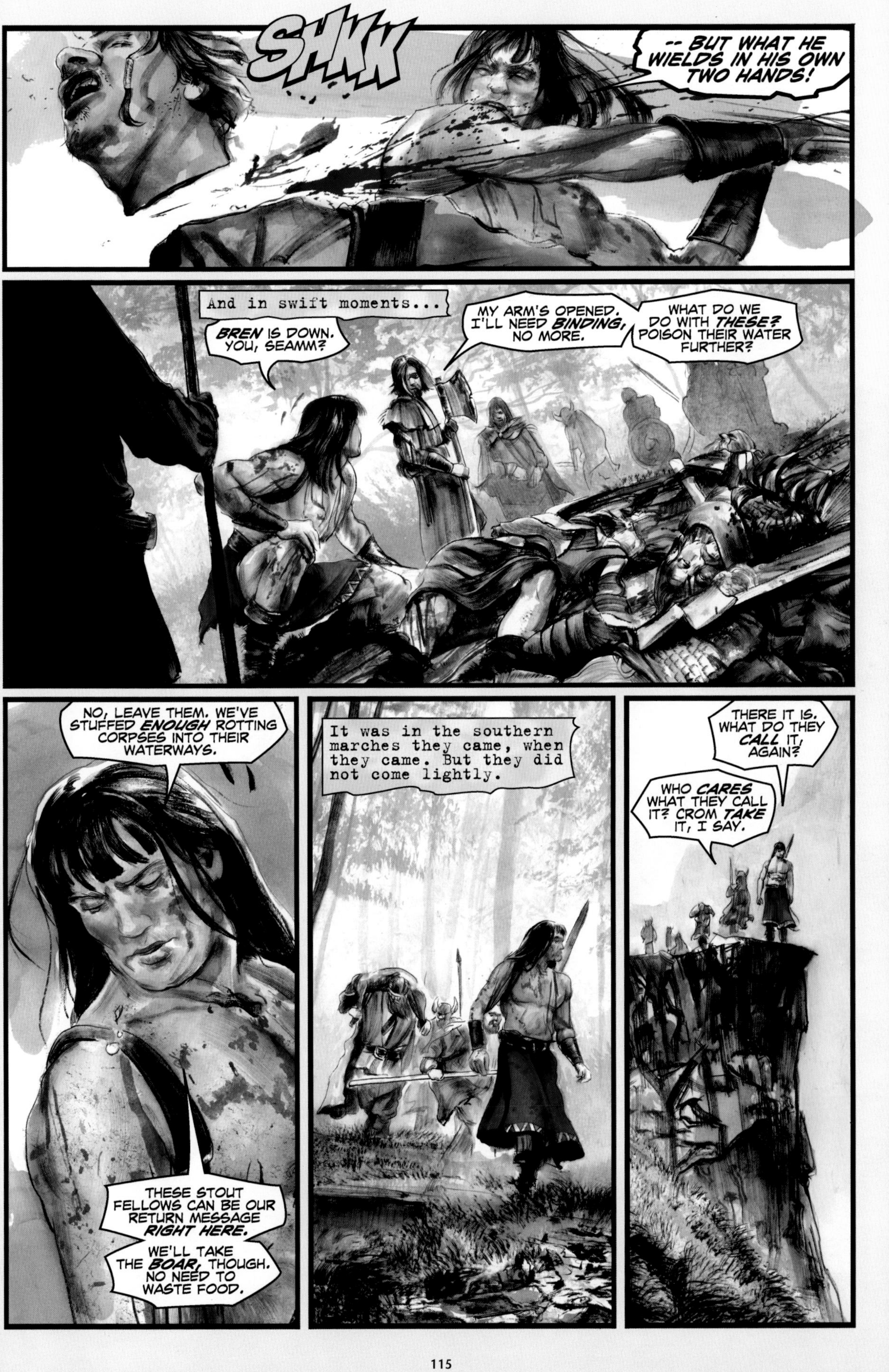
SHKK
-- BUT WHAT HE WIELDS IN HIS OWN TWO HANDS!
And in swift moments...
BREN IS DOWN. YOU, SEAMM?
MY ARM'S OPENED. I'LL NEED BINDING, NO MORE.
WHAT DO WE DO WITH THESE? POISON THEIR WATER FURTHER?
NO, LEAVE THEM. WE'VE STUFFED ENOUGH ROTTING CORPSES INTO THEIR WATERWAYS.
THESE STOUT FELLOWS CAN BE OUR RETURN MESSAGE RIGHT HERE.
WE'LL TAKE THE BOAR, THOUGH. NO NEED TO WASTE FOOD.
It was in the southern marches they came, when they came. But they did not come lightly.
THERE IT IS. WHAT DO THEY CALL IT, AGAIN?
WHO CARES WHAT THEY CALL IT? CROM TAKE IT, I SAY.

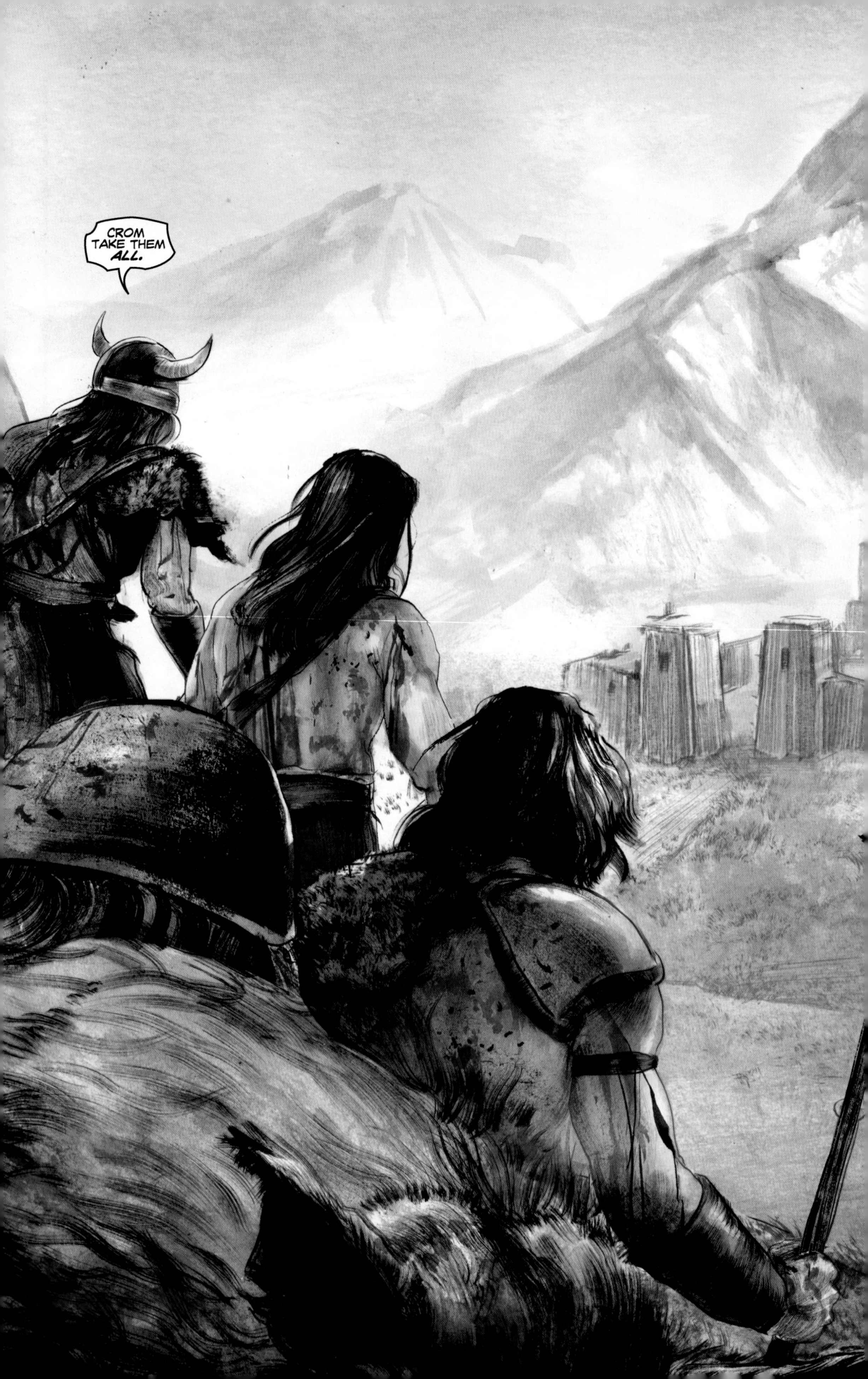
CROM TAKE THEM ALL.

VENARIUM

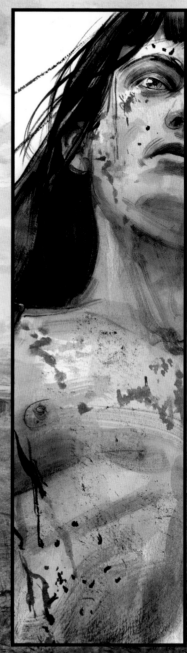

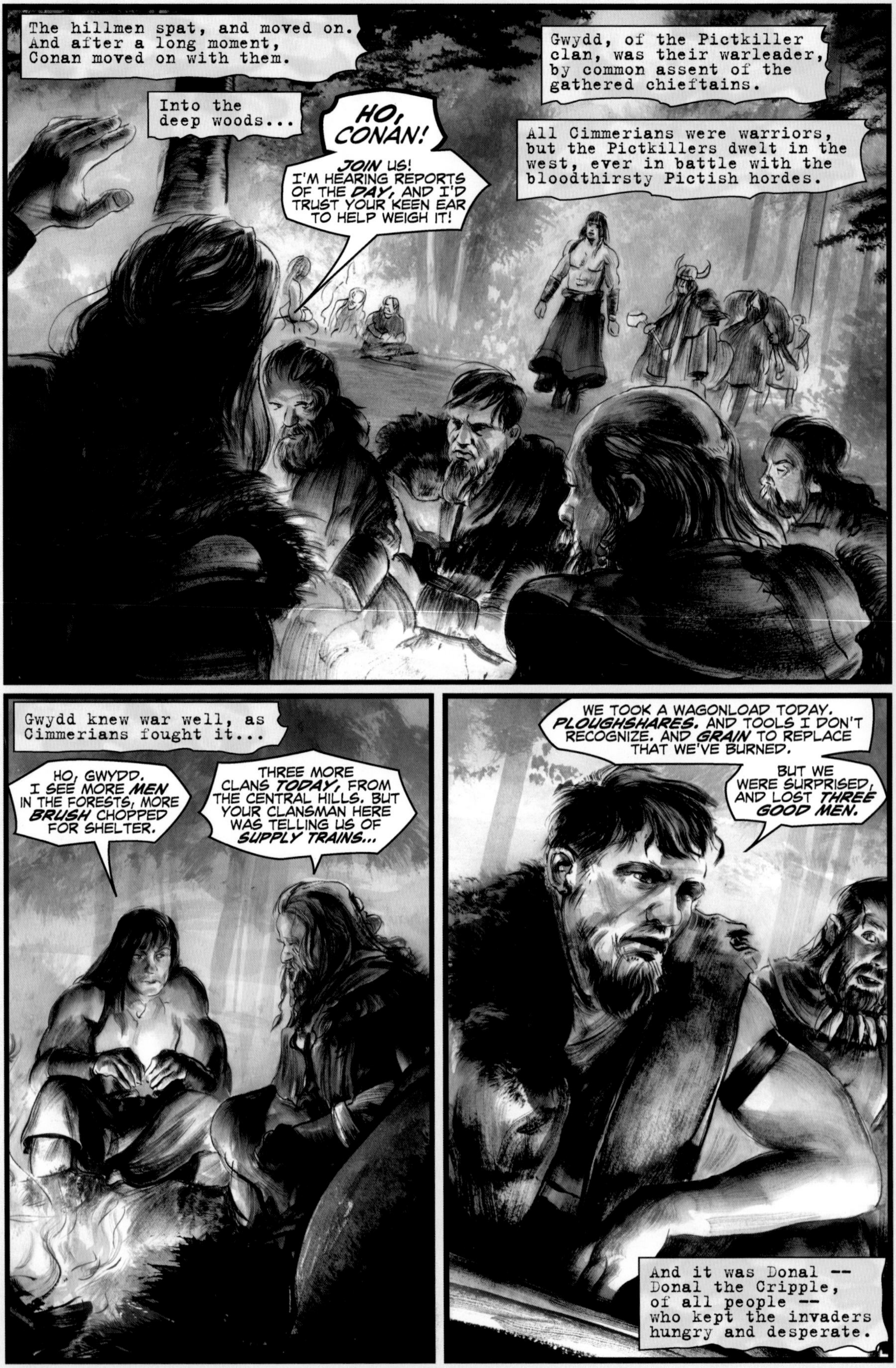
The hillmen spat, and moved on. And after a long moment, Conan moved on with them.
Into the deep woods...
HO, CONAN!
JOIN US! I'M HEARING REPORTS OF THE DAY, AND I'D TRUST YOUR KEEN EAR TO HELP WEIGH IT!
Gwydd, of the Pictkiller clan, was their warleader, by common assent of the gathered chieftains.
All Cimmerians were warriors, but the Pictkillers dwelt in the west, ever in battle with the bloodthirsty Pictish hordes.
Gwydd knew war well, as Cimmerians fought it...
HO, GWYDD. I SEE MORE MEN IN THE FORESTS, MORE BRUSH CHOPPED FOR SHELTER.
THREE MORE CLANS TODAY, FROM THE CENTRAL HILLS. BUT YOUR CLANSMAN HERE WAS TELLING US OF SUPPLY TRAINS...
WE TOOK A WAGONLOAD TODAY. PLOUGHSHARES. AND TOOLS I DON'T RECOGNIZE. AND GRAIN TO REPLACE THAT WE'VE BURNED.
BUT WE WERE SURPRISED, AND LOST THREE GOOD MEN.
And it was Donal -- Donal the Cripple, of all people -- who kept the invaders hungry and desperate.

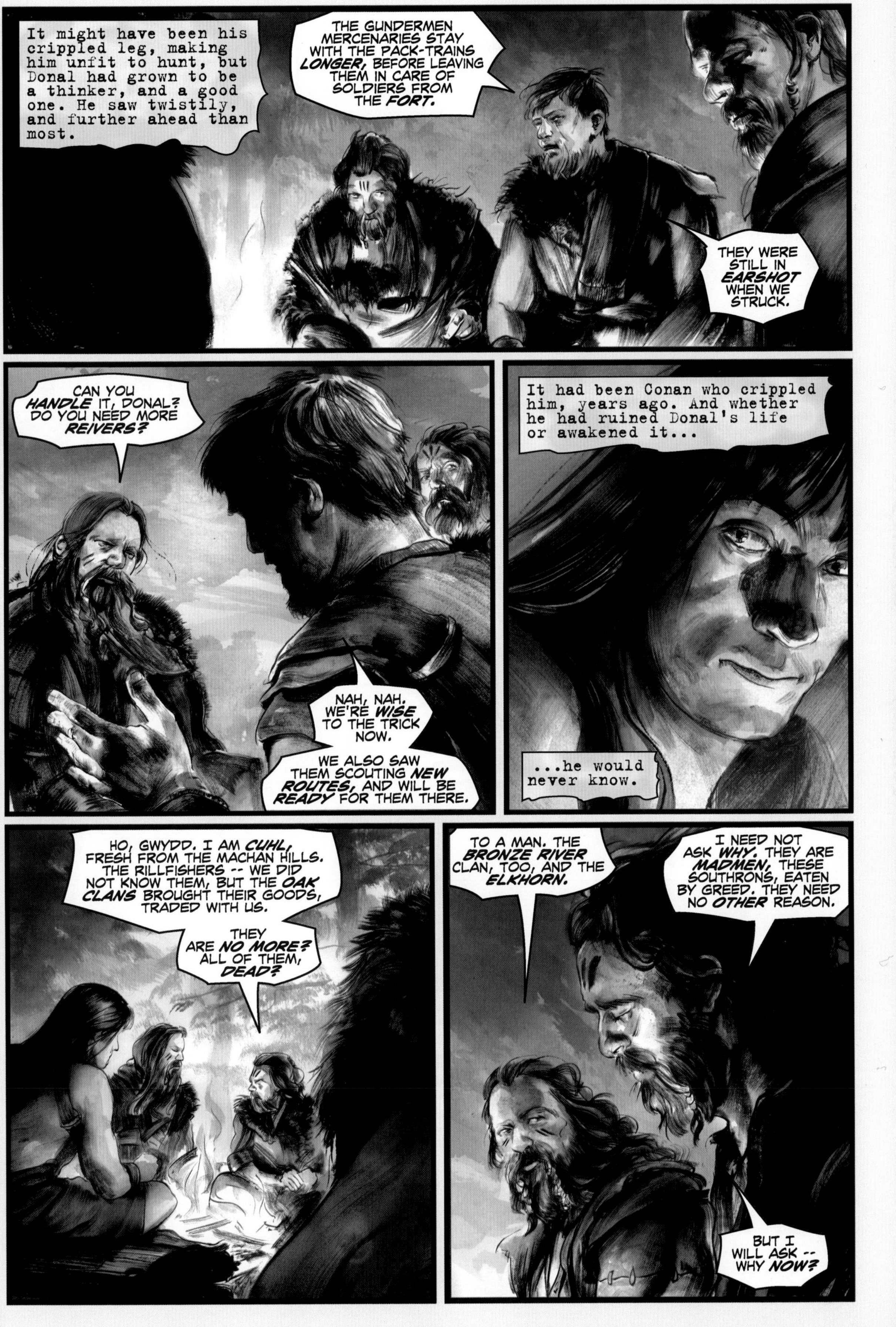
It might have been his crippled leg, making him unfit to hunt, but Donal had grown to be a thinker, and a good one. He saw twistily, and further ahead than most.
THE GUNDERMEN MERCENARIES STAY WITH THE PACK-TRAINS LONGER, BEFORE LEAVING THEM IN CARE OF SOLDIERS FROM THE FORT.
THEY WERE STILL IN EARSHOT WHEN WE STRUCK.
CAN YOU HANDLE IT, DONAL? DO YOU NEED MORE REIVERS?
NAH, NAH. WE'RE WISE TO THE TRICK NOW.
WE ALSO SAW THEM SCOUTING NEW ROUTES, AND WILL BE READY FOR THEM THERE.
It had been Conan who crippled him, years ago. And whether he had ruined Donal's life or awakened it...
...he would never know.
HO, GWYDD. I AM CUHL, FRESH FROM THE MACHAN HILLS. THE RILLFISHERS -- WE DID NOT KNOW THEM, BUT THE OAK CLANS BROUGHT THEIR GOODS, TRADED WITH US.
THEY ARE NO MORE? ALL OF THEM, DEAD?
TO A MAN. THE BRONZE RIVER CLAN, TOO, AND THE ELKHORN.
I NEED NOT ASK WHY. THEY ARE MADMEN, THESE SOUTHRONS, EATEN BY GREED. THEY NEED NO OTHER REASON.
BUT I WILL ASK -- WHY NOW?

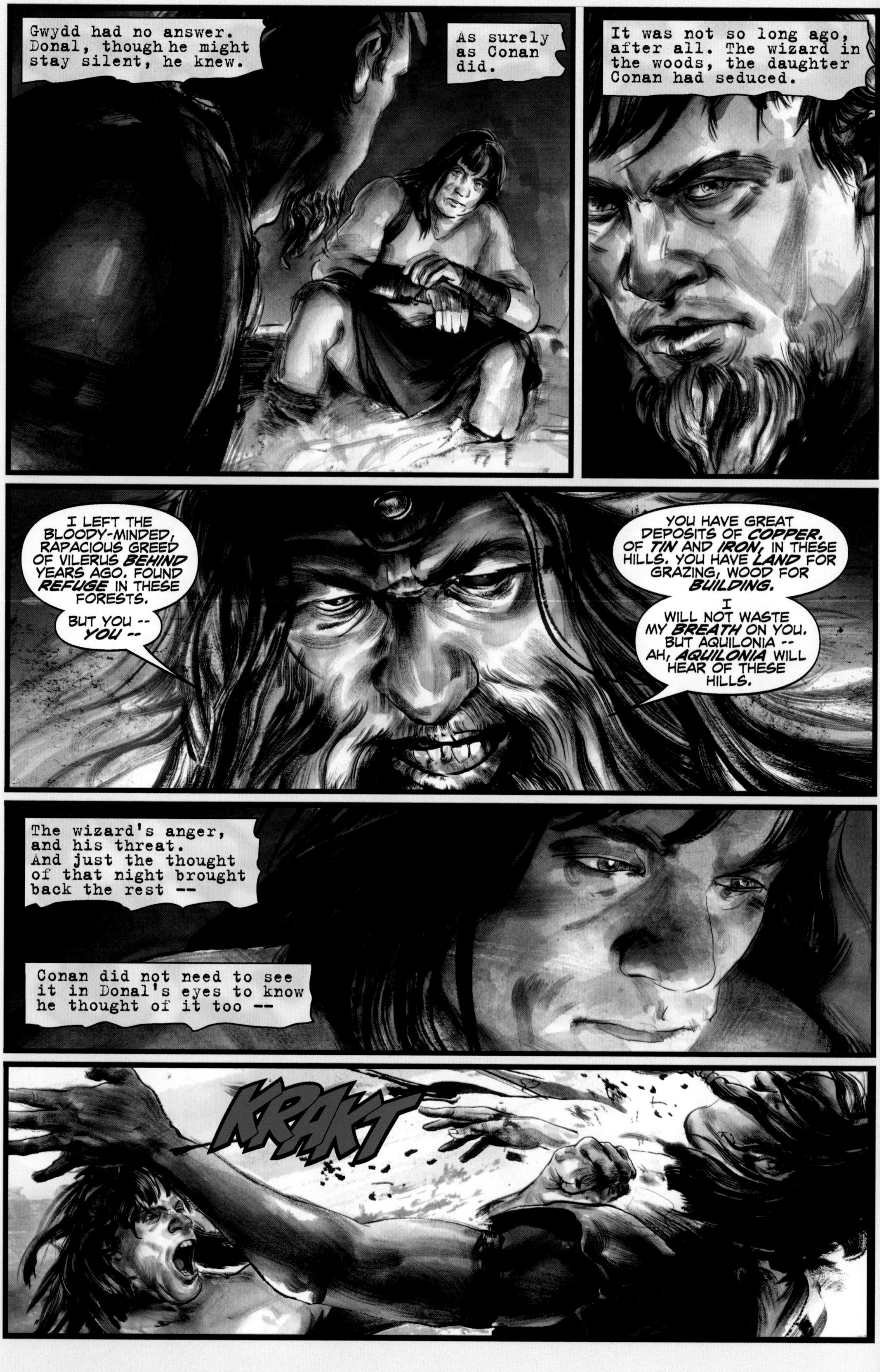
Gwydd had no answer. Donal, though he might stay silent, he knew.
As surely as Conan did.
It was not so long ago, after all. The wizard in the woods, the daughter Conan had seduced.
I LEFT THE BLOODY-MINDED, RAPACIOUS GREED OF VILERUS *BEHIND* YEARS AGO. FOUND *REFUGE* IN THESE FORESTS.
BUT YOU -- *YOU* --
YOU HAVE GREAT DEPOSITS OF *COPPER*. OF *TIN* AND *IRON*, IN THESE HILLS. YOU HAVE *LAND* FOR GRAZING, WOOD FOR *BUILDING*.
I WILL NOT WASTE MY *BREATH* ON YOU. BUT AQUILONIA -- AH, *AQUILONIA* WILL HEAR OF THESE HILLS.
The wizard's anger, and his threat. And just the thought of that night brought back the rest --
Conan did not need to see it in Donal's eyes to know he thought of it too --
KRAKT

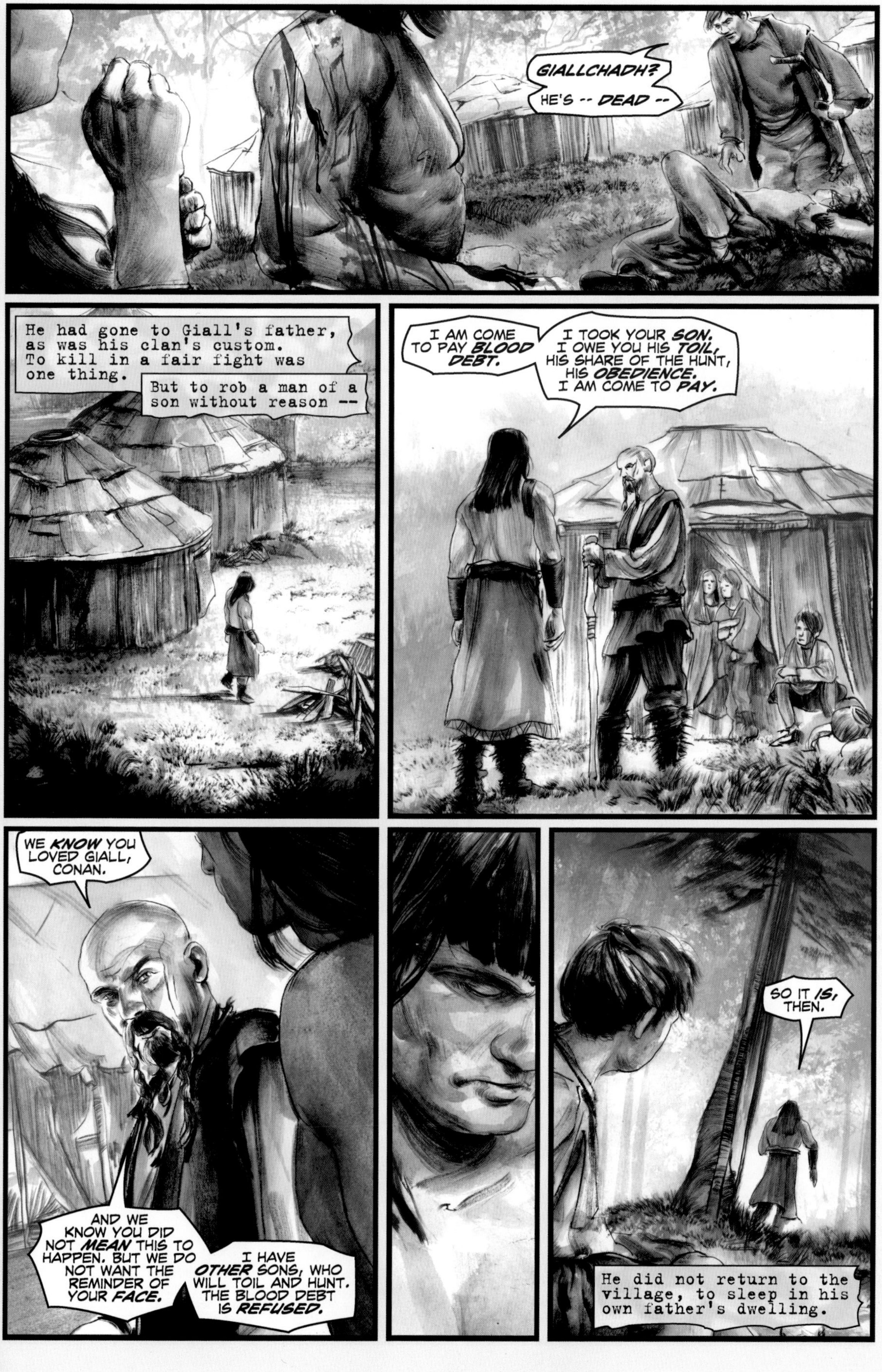
GIALLCHADH?
HE'S -- DEAD --
He had gone to Giall's father, as was his clan's custom. To kill in a fair fight was one thing.
But to rob a man of a son without reason --
I AM COME TO PAY BLOOD DEBT.
I TOOK YOUR SON. I OWE YOU HIS TOIL, HIS SHARE OF THE HUNT, HIS OBEDIENCE. I AM COME TO PAY.
WE KNOW YOU LOVED GIALL, CONAN.
AND WE KNOW YOU DID NOT MEAN THIS TO HAPPEN. BUT WE DO NOT WANT THE REMINDER OF YOUR FACE.
I HAVE OTHER SONS, WHO WILL TOIL AND HUNT. THE BLOOD DEBT IS REFUSED.
SO IT IS, THEN.
He did not return to the village, to sleep in his own father's dwelling.

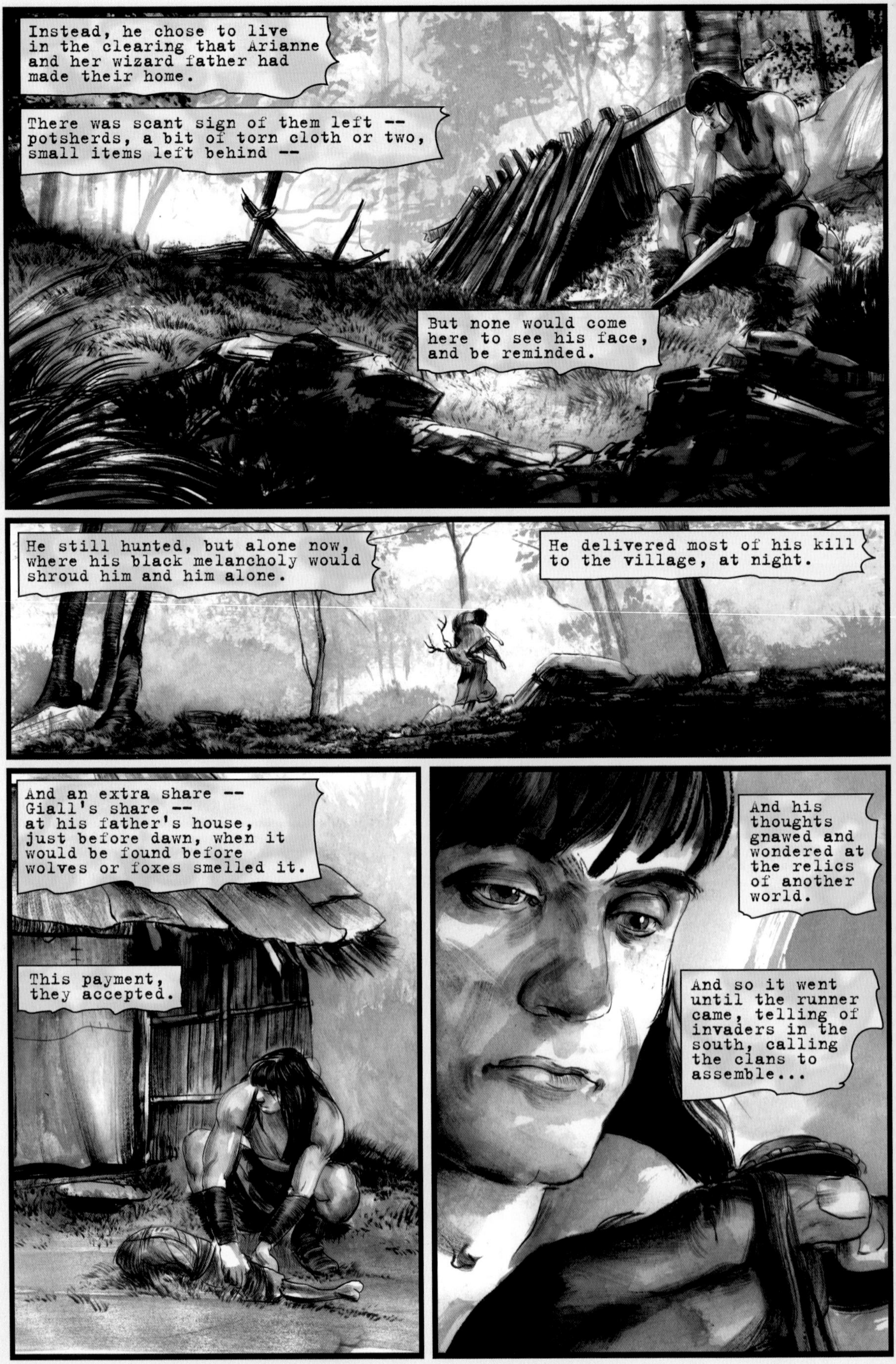
Instead, he chose to live in the clearing that Arianne and her wizard father had made their home.
There was scant sign of them left -- potsherds, a bit of torn cloth or two, small items left behind --
But none would come here to see his face, and be reminded.
He still hunted, but alone now, where his black melancholy would shroud him and him alone.
He delivered most of his kill to the village, at night.
And an extra share -- Giall's share -- at his father's house, just before dawn, when it would be found before wolves or foxes smelled it.
This payment, they accepted.
And his thoughts gnawed and wondered at the relics of another world.
And so it went until the runner came, telling of invaders in the south, calling the clans to assemble...

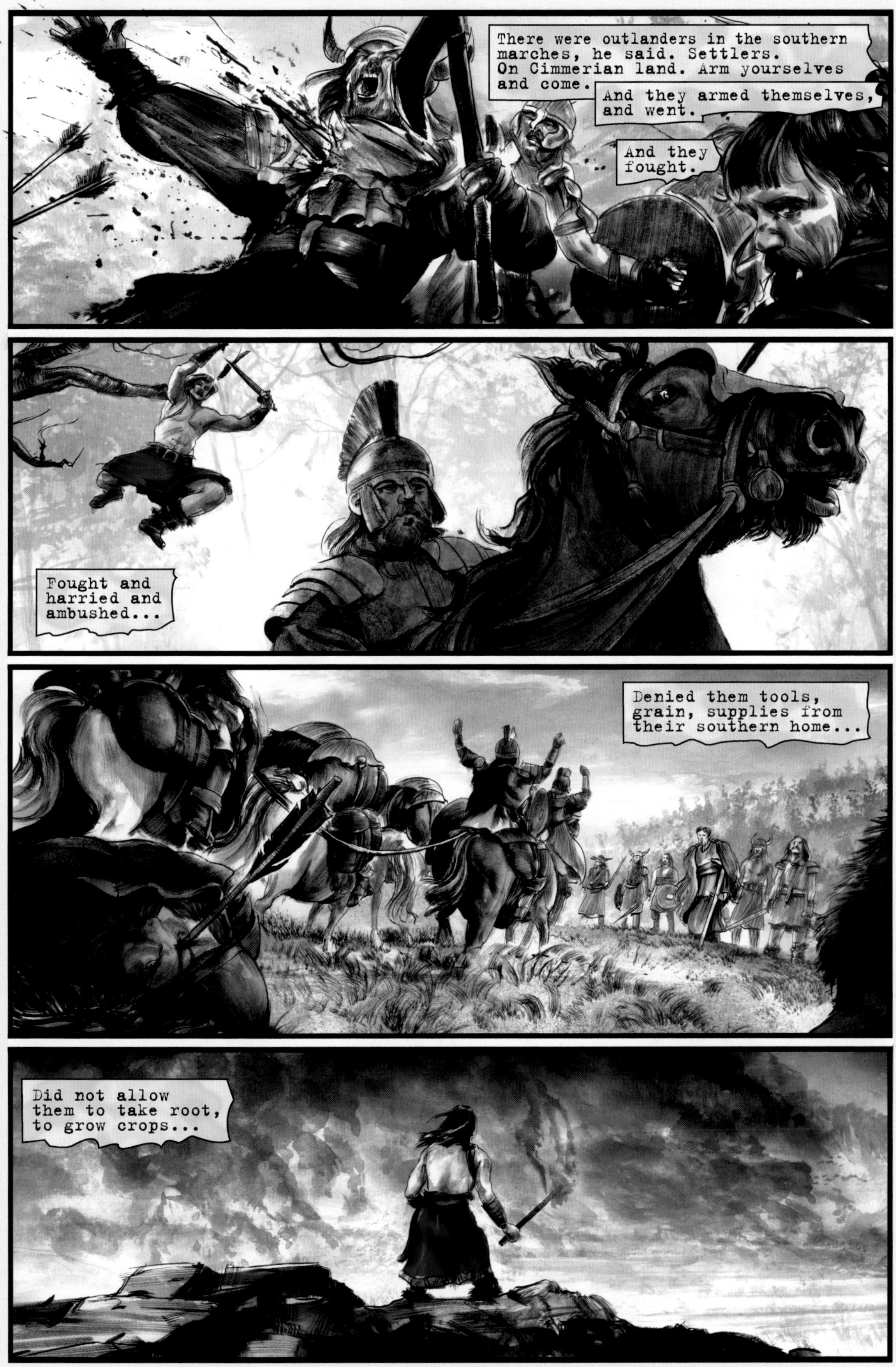
There were outlanders in the southern marches, he said. Settlers. On Cimmerian land. Arm yourselves and come.
And they armed themselves, and went.
And they fought.
Fought and harried and ambushed...
Denied them tools, grain, supplies from their southern home...
Did not allow them to take root, to grow crops...

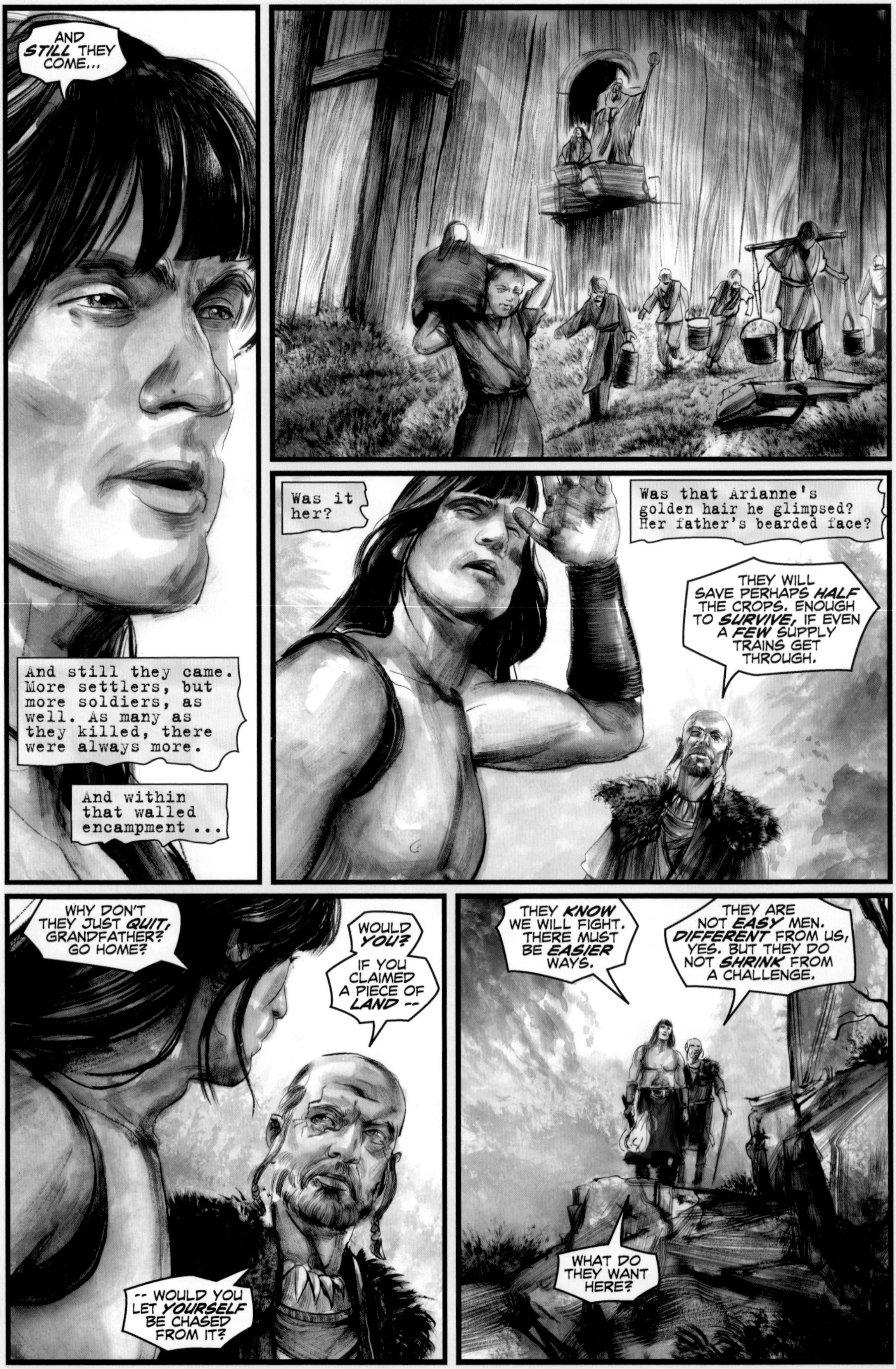
AND STILL THEY COME...
And still they came. More settlers, but more soldiers, as well. As many as they killed, there were always more.
And within that walled encampment ...
Was it her?
Was that Arianne's golden hair he glimpsed? Her father's bearded face?
THEY WILL SAVE PERHAPS HALF THE CROPS. ENOUGH TO SURVIVE, IF EVEN A FEW SUPPLY TRAINS GET THROUGH.
WHY DON'T THEY JUST QUIT, GRANDFATHER? GO HOME?
WOULD YOU?
IF YOU CLAIMED A PIECE OF LAND --
-- WOULD YOU LET YOURSELF BE CHASED FROM IT?
THEY KNOW WE WILL FIGHT. THERE MUST BE EASIER WAYS.
THEY ARE NOT EASY MEN. DIFFERENT FROM US, YES. BUT THEY DO NOT SHRINK FROM A CHALLENGE.
WHAT DO THEY WANT HERE?

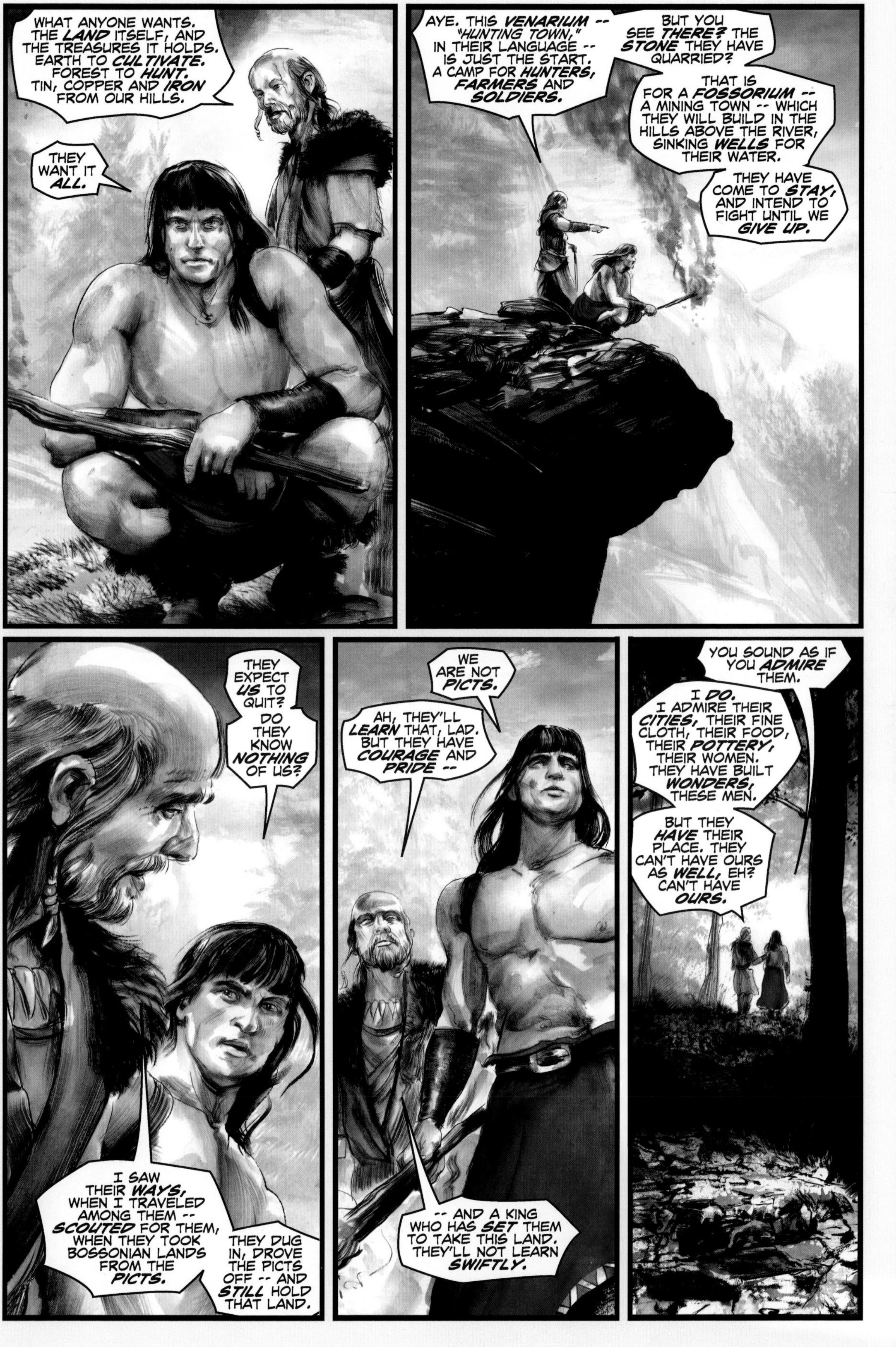
WHAT ANYONE WANTS. THE LAND ITSELF, AND THE TREASURES IT HOLDS. EARTH TO CULTIVATE. FOREST TO HUNT. TIN, COPPER AND IRON FROM OUR HILLS.
THEY WANT IT ALL.
AYE. THIS VENARIUM -- "HUNTING TOWN," IN THEIR LANGUAGE -- IS JUST THE START. A CAMP FOR HUNTERS, FARMERS AND SOLDIERS.
BUT YOU SEE THERE? THE STONE THEY HAVE QUARRIED?
THAT IS FOR A FOSSORIUM -- A MINING TOWN -- WHICH THEY WILL BUILD IN THE HILLS ABOVE THE RIVER, SINKING WELLS FOR THEIR WATER.
THEY HAVE COME TO STAY, AND INTEND TO FIGHT UNTIL WE GIVE UP.
THEY EXPECT US TO QUIT?
DO THEY KNOW NOTHING OF US?
I SAW THEIR WAYS, WHEN I TRAVELED AMONG THEM -- SCOUTED FOR THEM, WHEN THEY TOOK BOSSONIAN LANDS FROM THE PICTS.
THEY DUG IN, DROVE THE PICTS OFF -- AND STILL HOLD THAT LAND.
WE ARE NOT PICTS.
AH, THEY'LL LEARN THAT, LAD. BUT THEY HAVE COURAGE AND PRIDE --
-- AND A KING WHO HAS SET THEM TO TAKE THIS LAND. THEY'LL NOT LEARN SWIFTLY.
YOU SOUND AS IF YOU ADMIRE THEM.
I DO. I ADMIRE THEIR CITIES, THEIR FINE CLOTH, THEIR FOOD, THEIR POTTERY, THEIR WOMEN. THEY HAVE BUILT WONDERS, THESE MEN.
BUT THEY HAVE THEIR PLACE. THEY CAN'T HAVE OURS AS WELL, EH? CAN'T HAVE OURS.

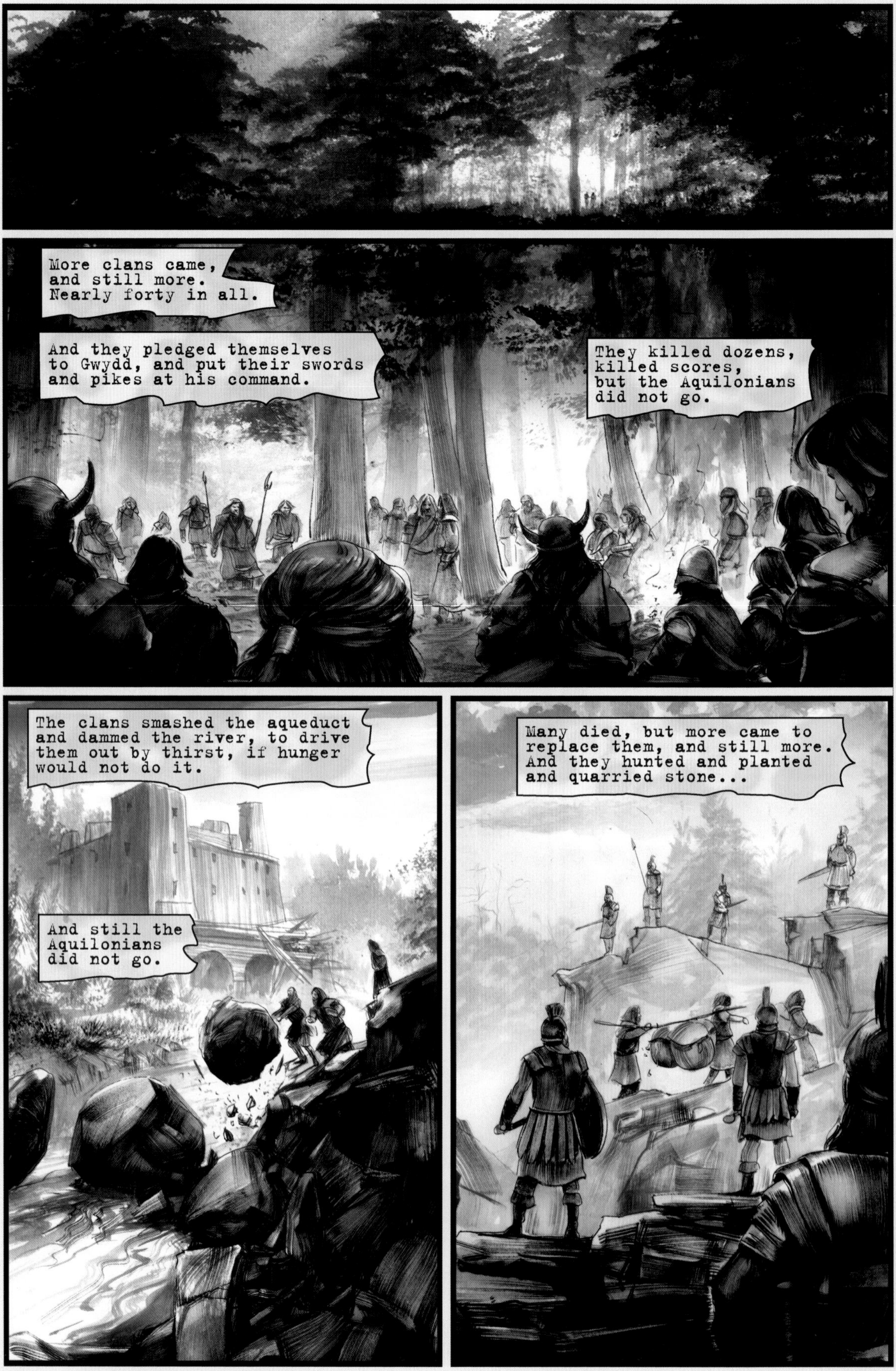

More clans came, and still more. Nearly forty in all.
And they pledged themselves to Gwydd, and put their swords and pikes at his command.
They killed dozens, killed scores, but the Aquilonians did not go.
The clans smashed the aqueduct and dammed the river, to drive them out by thirst, if hunger would not do it.
And still the Aquilonians did not go.
Many died, but more came to replace them, and still more. And they hunted and planted and quarried stone...

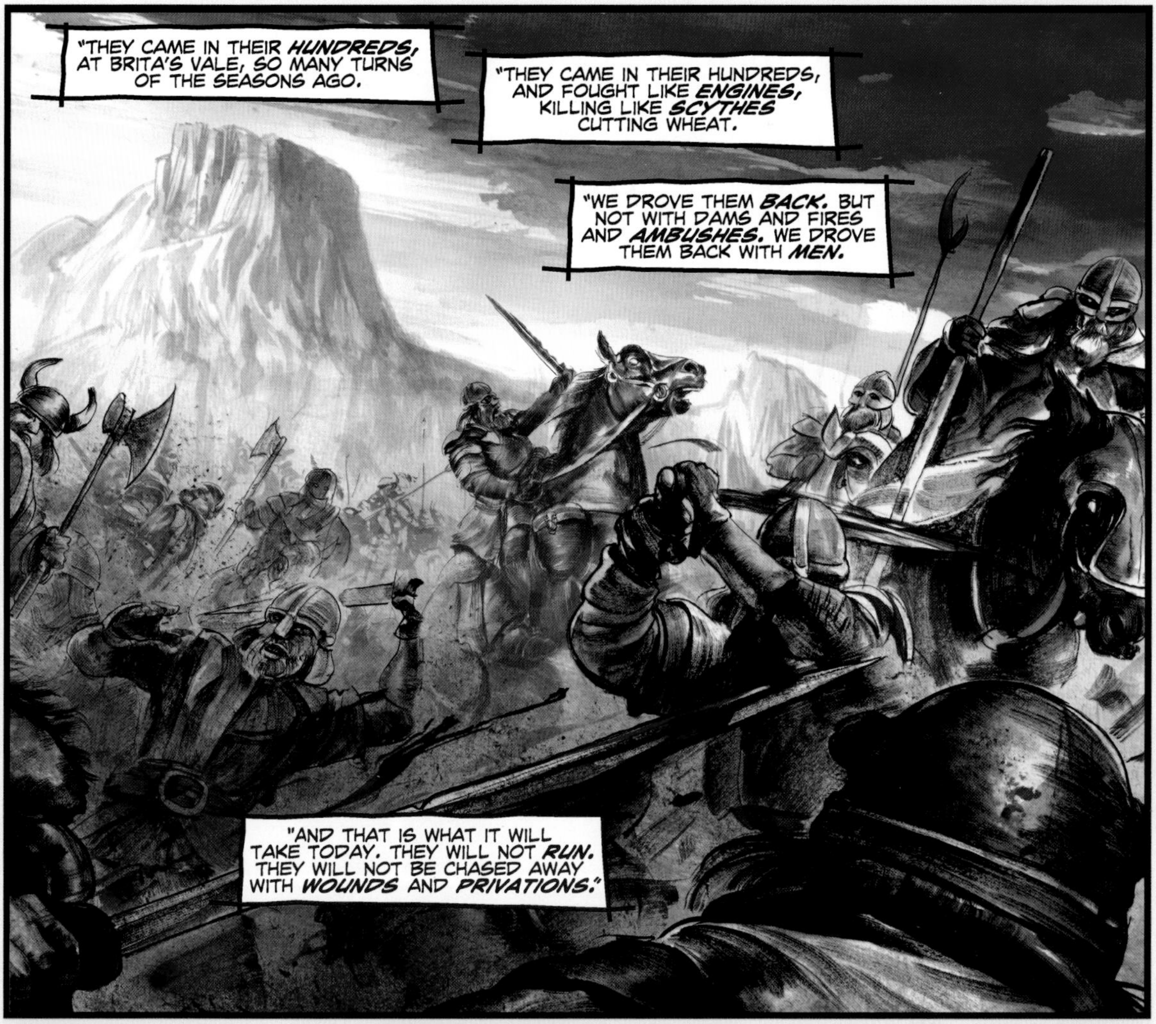
"THEY CAME IN THEIR HUNDREDS, AT BRITA'S VALE, SO MANY TURNS OF THE SEASONS AGO.
"THEY CAME IN THEIR HUNDREDS, AND FOUGHT LIKE ENGINES, KILLING LIKE SCYTHES CUTTING WHEAT.
"WE DROVE THEM BACK. BUT NOT WITH DAMS AND FIRES AND AMBUSHES. WE DROVE THEM BACK WITH MEN.
"AND THAT IS WHAT IT WILL TAKE TODAY. THEY WILL NOT RUN. THEY WILL NOT BE CHASED AWAY WITH WOUNDS AND PRIVATIONS."

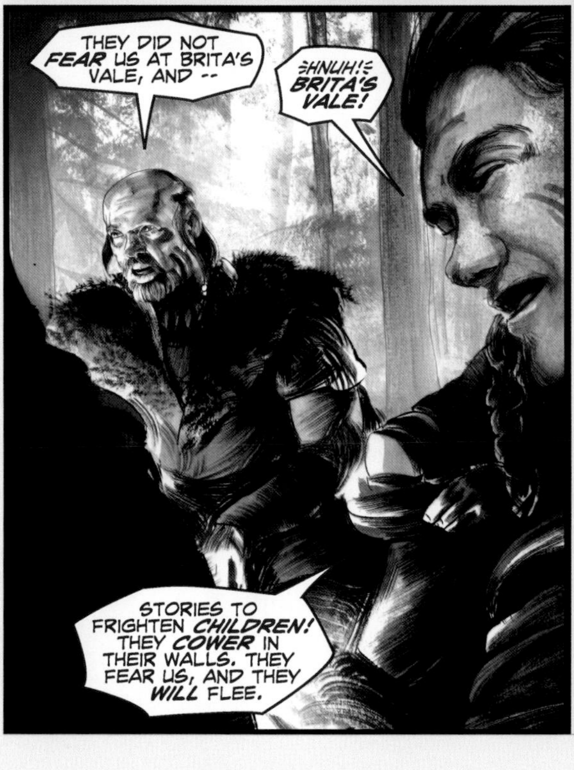
THEY DID NOT FEAR US AT BRITA'S VALE, AND --
HNUH! BRITA'S VALE!
STORIES TO FRIGHTEN CHILDREN! THEY COWER IN THEIR WALLS. THEY FEAR US, AND THEY WILL FLEE.

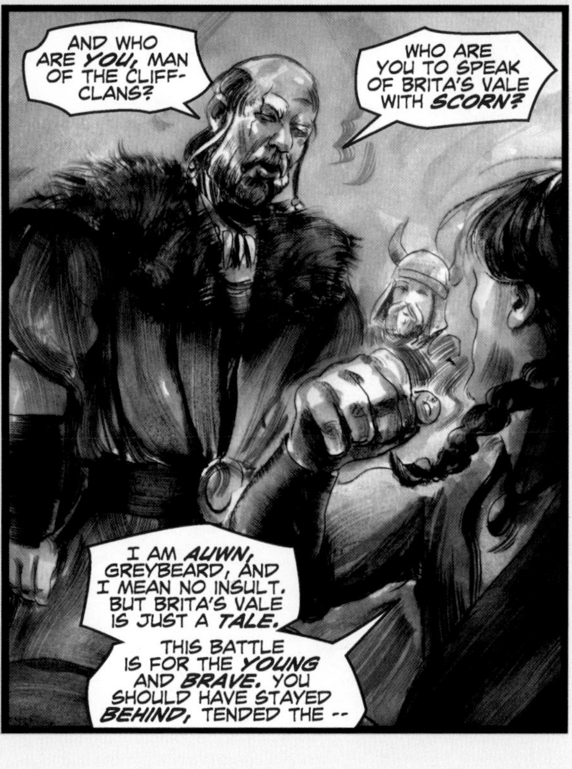
AND WHO ARE YOU, MAN OF THE CLIFF-CLANS?
WHO ARE YOU TO SPEAK OF BRITA'S VALE WITH SCORN?
I AM AUWN, GREYBEARD, AND I MEAN NO INSULT. BUT BRITA'S VALE IS JUST A TALE.
THIS BATTLE IS FOR THE YOUNG AND BRAVE. YOU SHOULD HAVE STAYED BEHIND, TENDED THE --

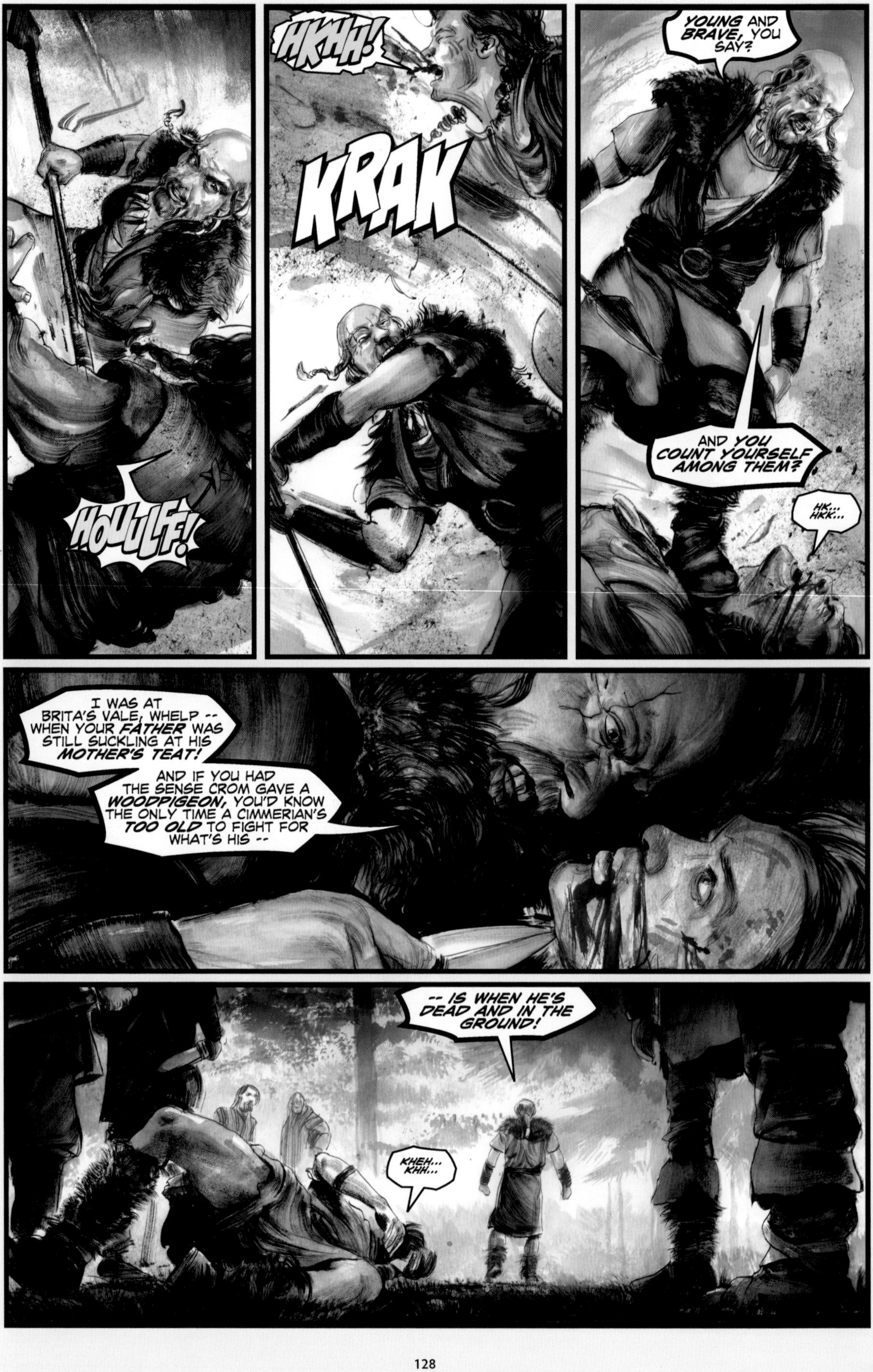
HOUULFF!
HKHH!
KRAK
YOUNG AND BRAVE, YOU SAY?
AND YOU COUNT YOURSELF AMONG THEM?
HK... HKK...
I WAS AT BRITA'S VALE, WHELP -- WHEN YOUR FATHER WAS STILL SUCKLING AT HIS MOTHER'S TEAT!
AND IF YOU HAD THE SENSE CROM GAVE A WOODPIGEON, YOU'D KNOW THE ONLY TIME A CIMMERIAN'S TOO OLD TO FIGHT FOR WHAT'S HIS --
-- IS WHEN HE'S DEAD AND IN THE GROUND!
KHEH... KHH...

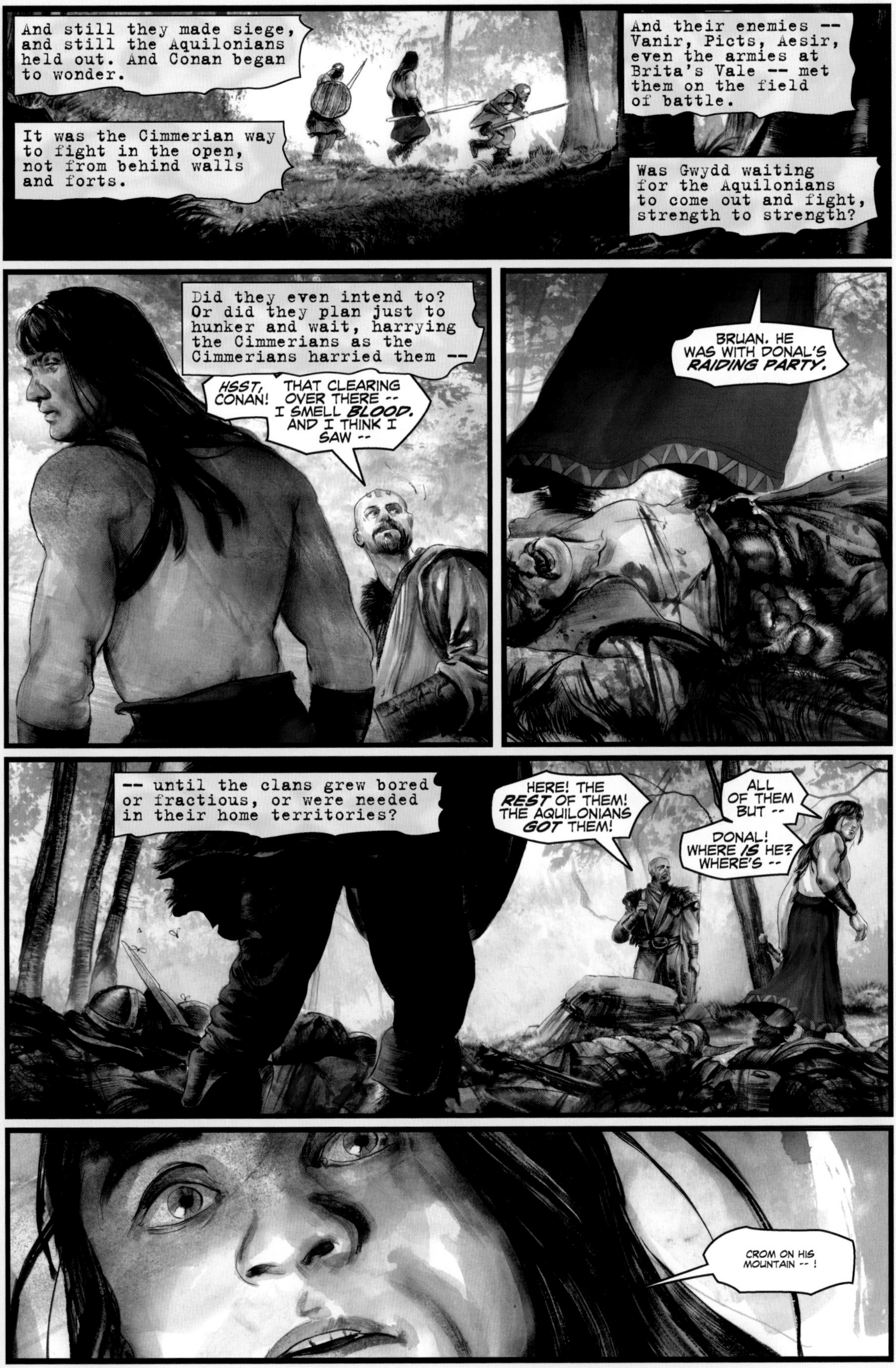

And still they made siege, and still the Aquilonians held out. And Conan began to wonder.
It was the Cimmerian way to fight in the open, not from behind walls and forts.
And their enemies -- Vanir, Picts, Aesir, even the armies at Brita's Vale -- met them on the field of battle.
Was Gwydd waiting for the Aquilonians to come out and fight, strength to strength?
Did they even intend to? Or did they plan just to hunker and wait, harrying the Cimmerians as the Cimmerians harried them --
HSST, CONAN!
THAT CLEARING OVER THERE -- I SMELL BLOOD. AND I THINK I SAW --
BRUAN. HE WAS WITH DONAL'S RAIDING PARTY.
-- until the clans grew bored or fractious, or were needed in their home territories?
HERE! THE REST OF THEM! THE AQUILONIANS GOT THEM!
ALL OF THEM BUT --
DONAL! WHERE IS HE? WHERE'S --
CROM ON HIS MOUNTAIN -- !

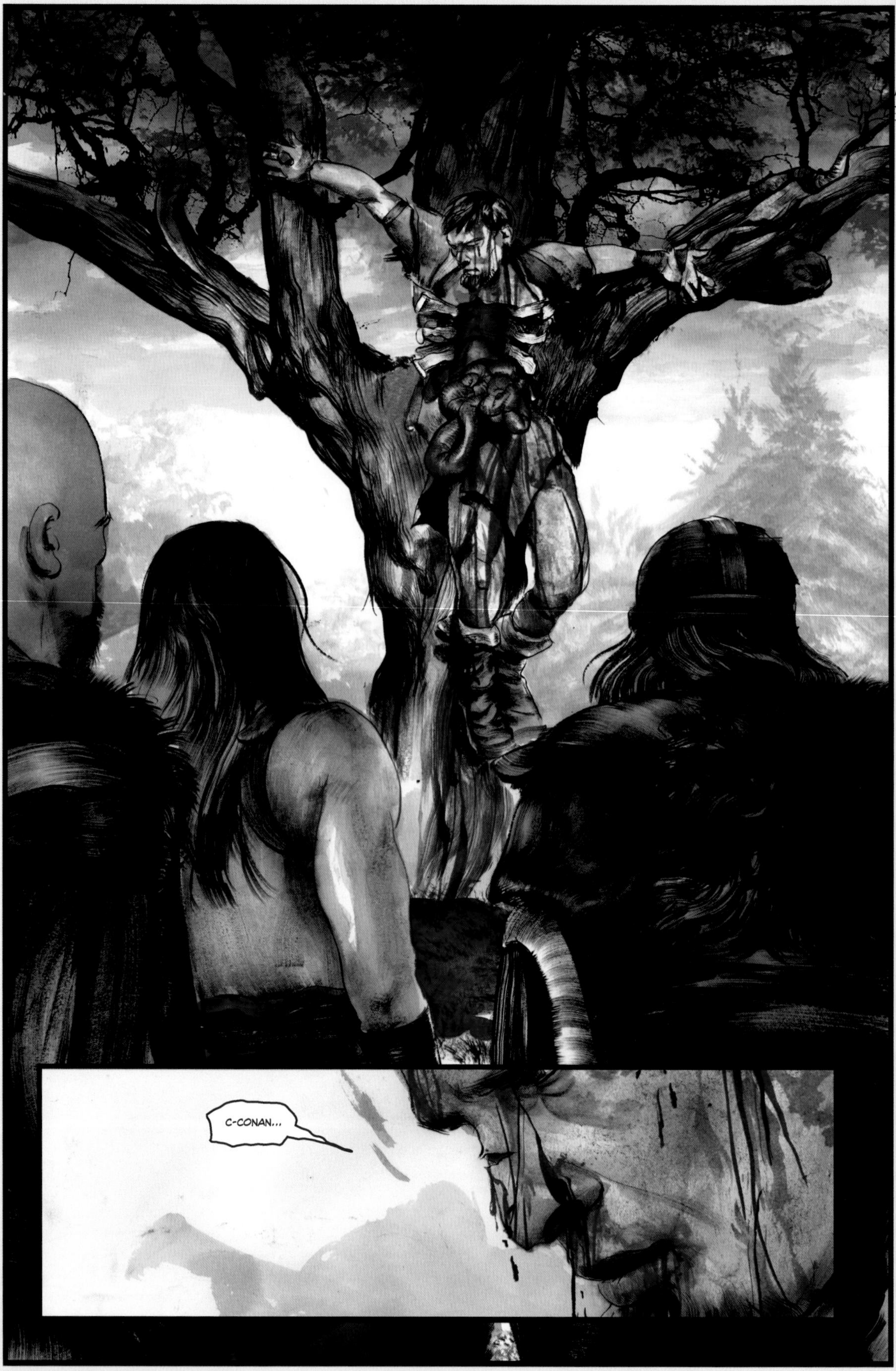
C-CONAN...

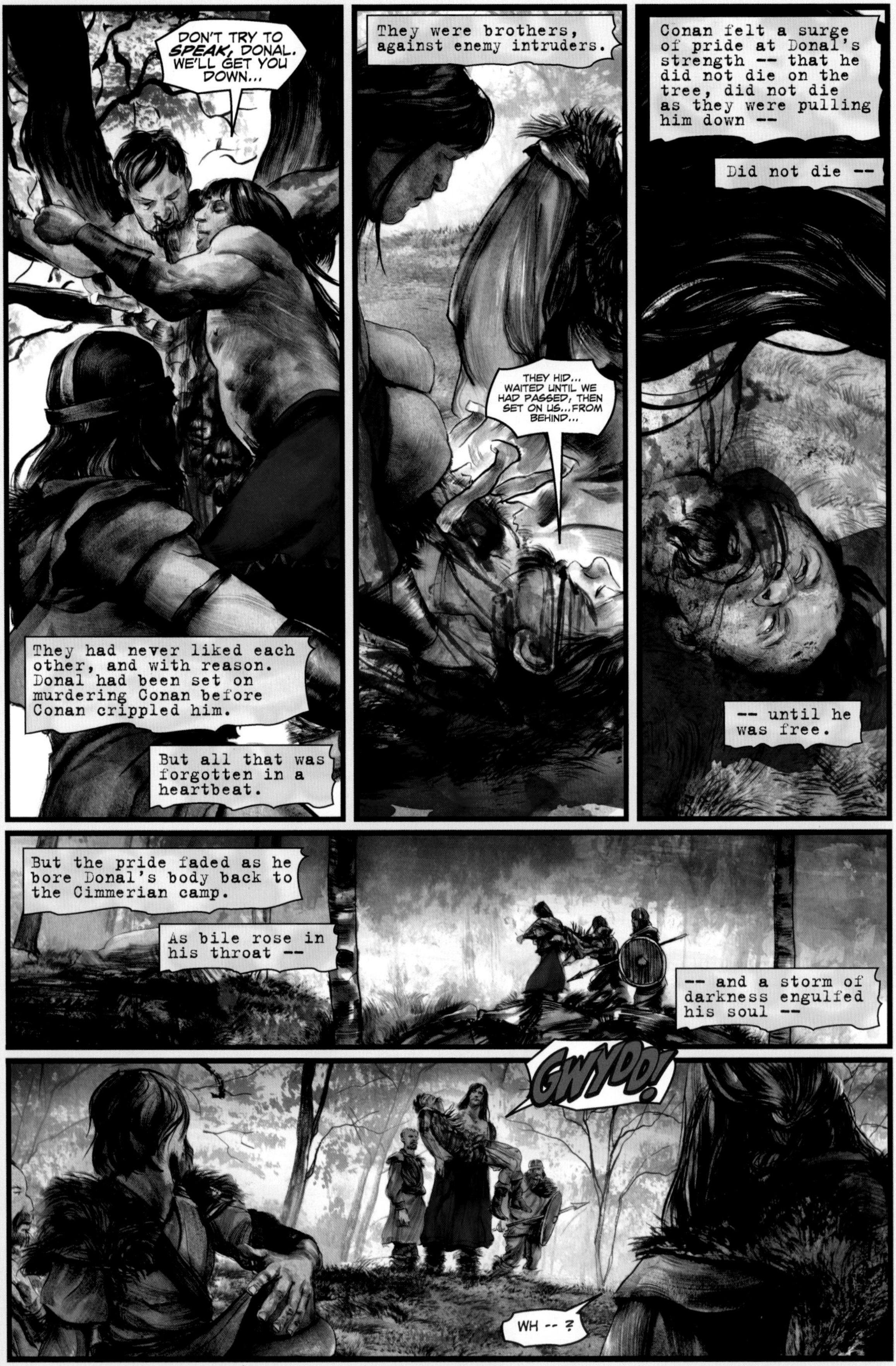
DON'T TRY TO SPEAK, DONAL. WE'LL GET YOU DOWN...
They had never liked each other, and with reason. Donal had been set on murdering Conan before Conan crippled him.
But all that was forgotten in a heartbeat.
They were brothers, against enemy intruders.
THEY HID... WAITED UNTIL WE HAD PASSED, THEN SET ON US...FROM BEHIND...
Conan felt a surge of pride at Donal's strength -- that he did not die on the tree, did not die as they were pulling him down --
Did not die --
-- until he was free.
But the pride faded as he bore Donal's body back to the Cimmerian camp.
As bile rose in his throat --
-- and a storm of darkness engulfed his soul --
GWYDD!
WH -- ?

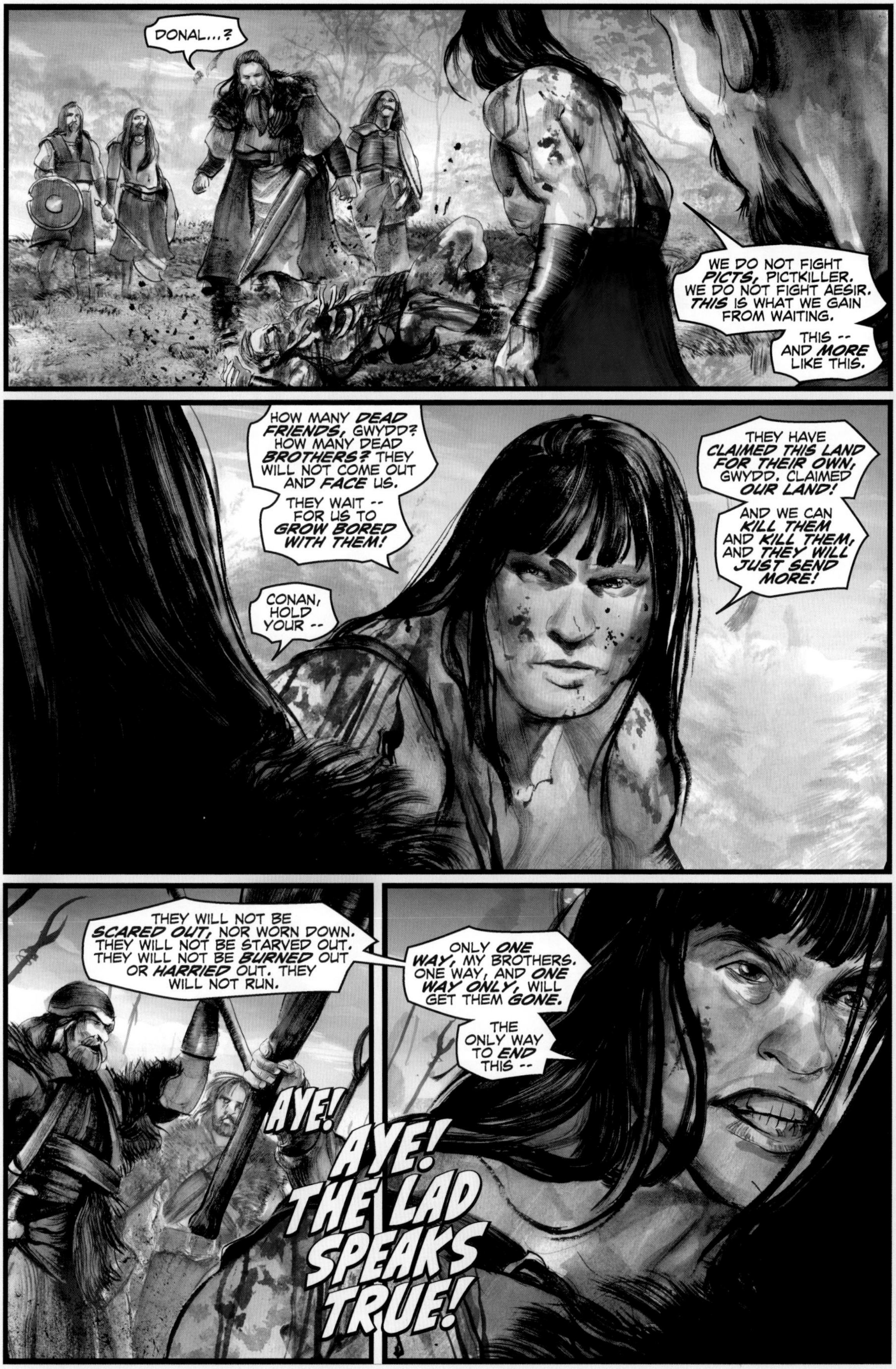
DONAL...?
WE DO NOT FIGHT PICTS, PICTKILLER. WE DO NOT FIGHT AESIR. THIS IS WHAT WE GAIN FROM WAITING.
THIS -- AND MORE LIKE THIS.
HOW MANY DEAD FRIENDS, GWYDD? HOW MANY DEAD BROTHERS? THEY WILL NOT COME OUT AND FACE US.
THEY WAIT -- FOR US TO GROW BORED WITH THEM!
CONAN, HOLD YOUR --
THEY HAVE CLAIMED THIS LAND FOR THEIR OWN, GWYDD. CLAIMED OUR LAND!
AND WE CAN KILL THEM AND KILL THEM, AND THEY WILL JUST SEND MORE!
THEY WILL NOT BE SCARED OUT, NOR WORN DOWN. THEY WILL NOT BE STARVED OUT. THEY WILL NOT BE BURNED OUT OR HARRIED OUT. THEY WILL NOT RUN.
ONLY ONE WAY, MY BROTHERS. ONE WAY, AND ONE WAY ONLY, WILL GET THEM GONE.
THE ONLY WAY TO END THIS --
AYE!
AYE! THE LAD SPEAKS TRUE!

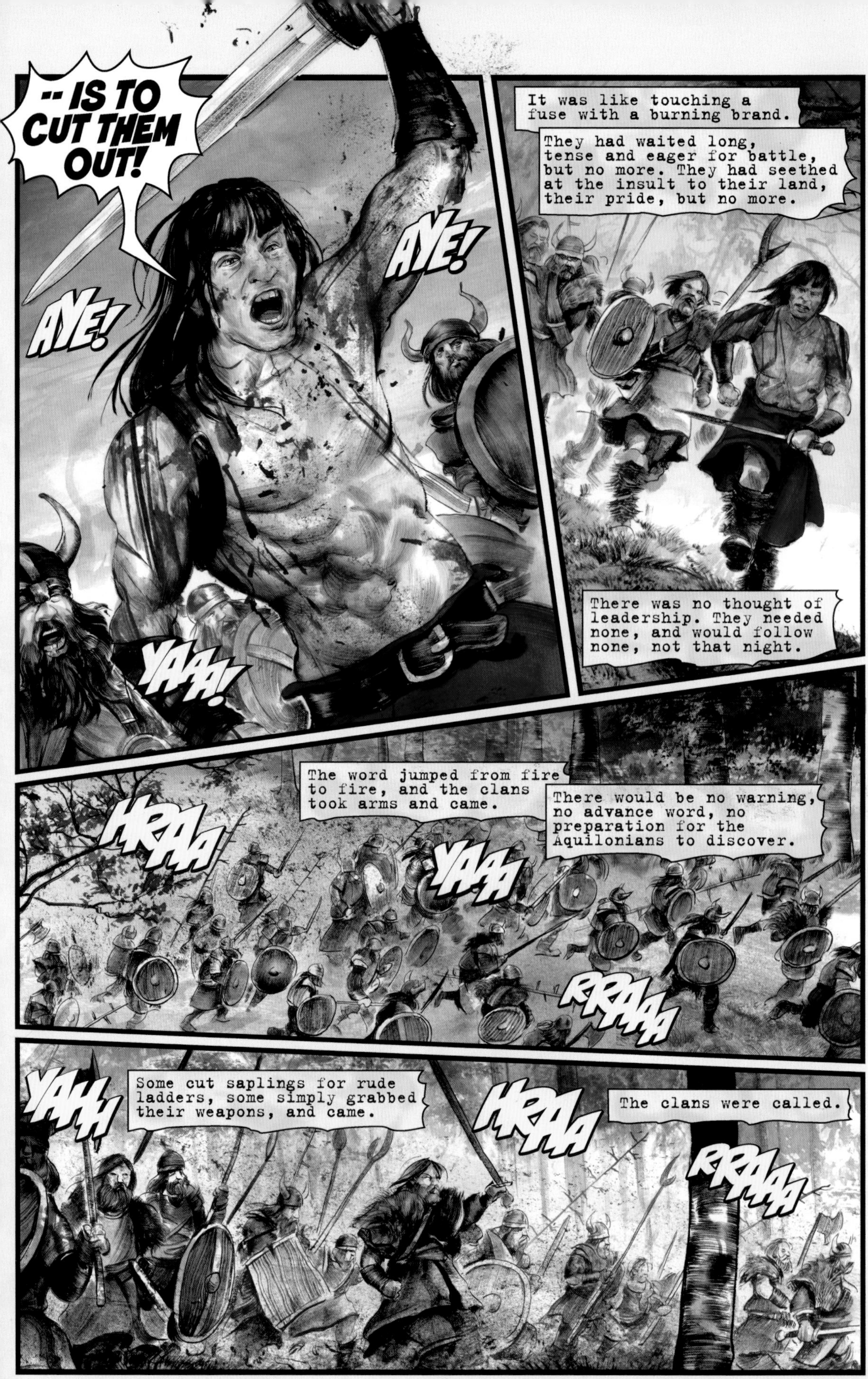
-- IS TO CUT THEM OUT!
AYE!
AYE!
YAAA!
It was like touching a fuse with a burning brand.
They had waited long, tense and eager for battle, but no more. They had seethed at the insult to their land, their pride, but no more.
There was no thought of leadership. They needed none, and would follow none, not that night.
The word jumped from fire to fire, and the clans took arms and came.
There would be no warning, no advance word, no preparation for the Aquilonians to discover.
HRAAA
YAAA
RRAAAA
YAHH
Some cut saplings for rude ladders, some simply grabbed their weapons, and came.
HRAAA
The clans were called.
RRAAAA

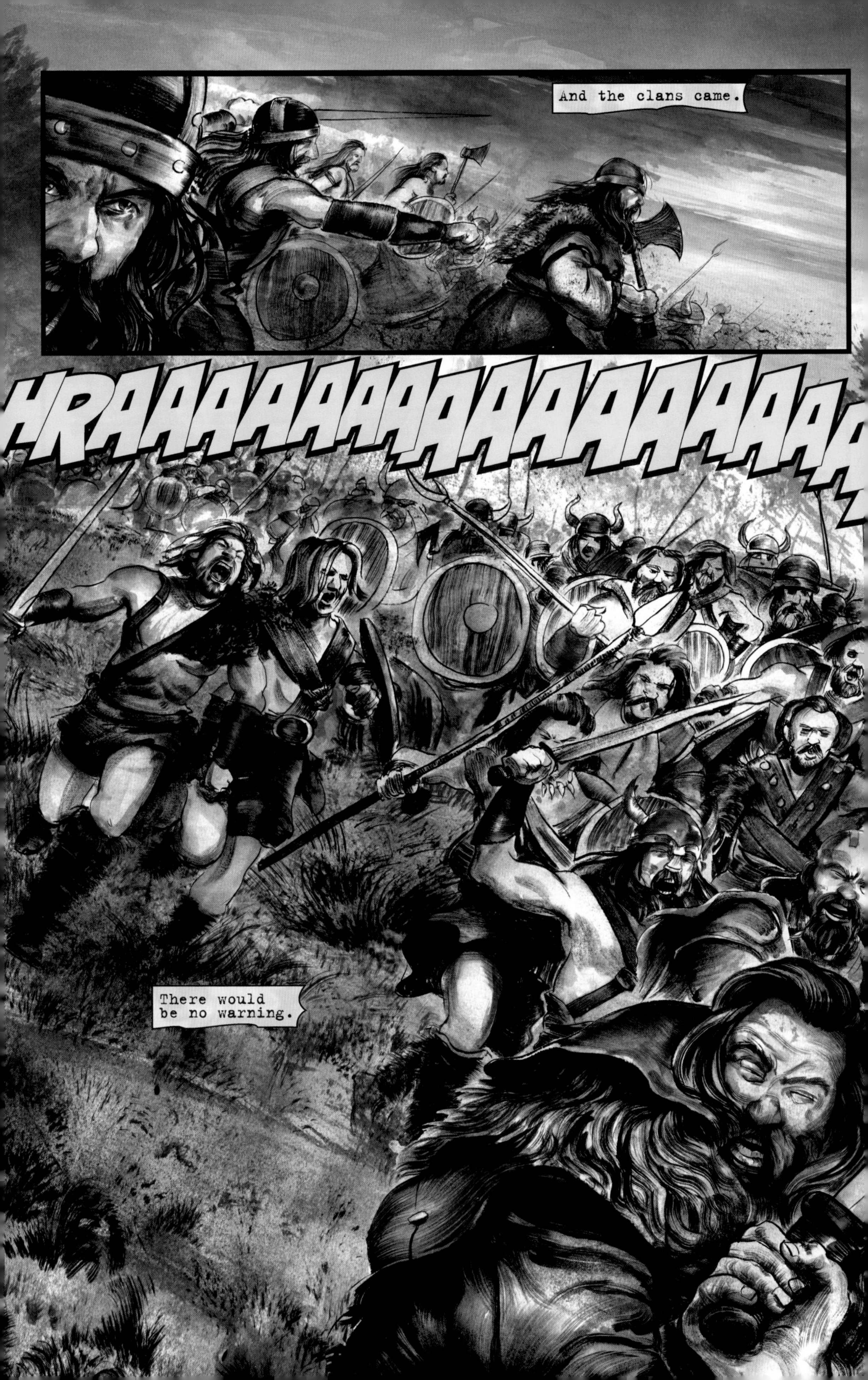
And the clans came.
HRAAAAAAAAAAAAAAAAA
There would be no warning.

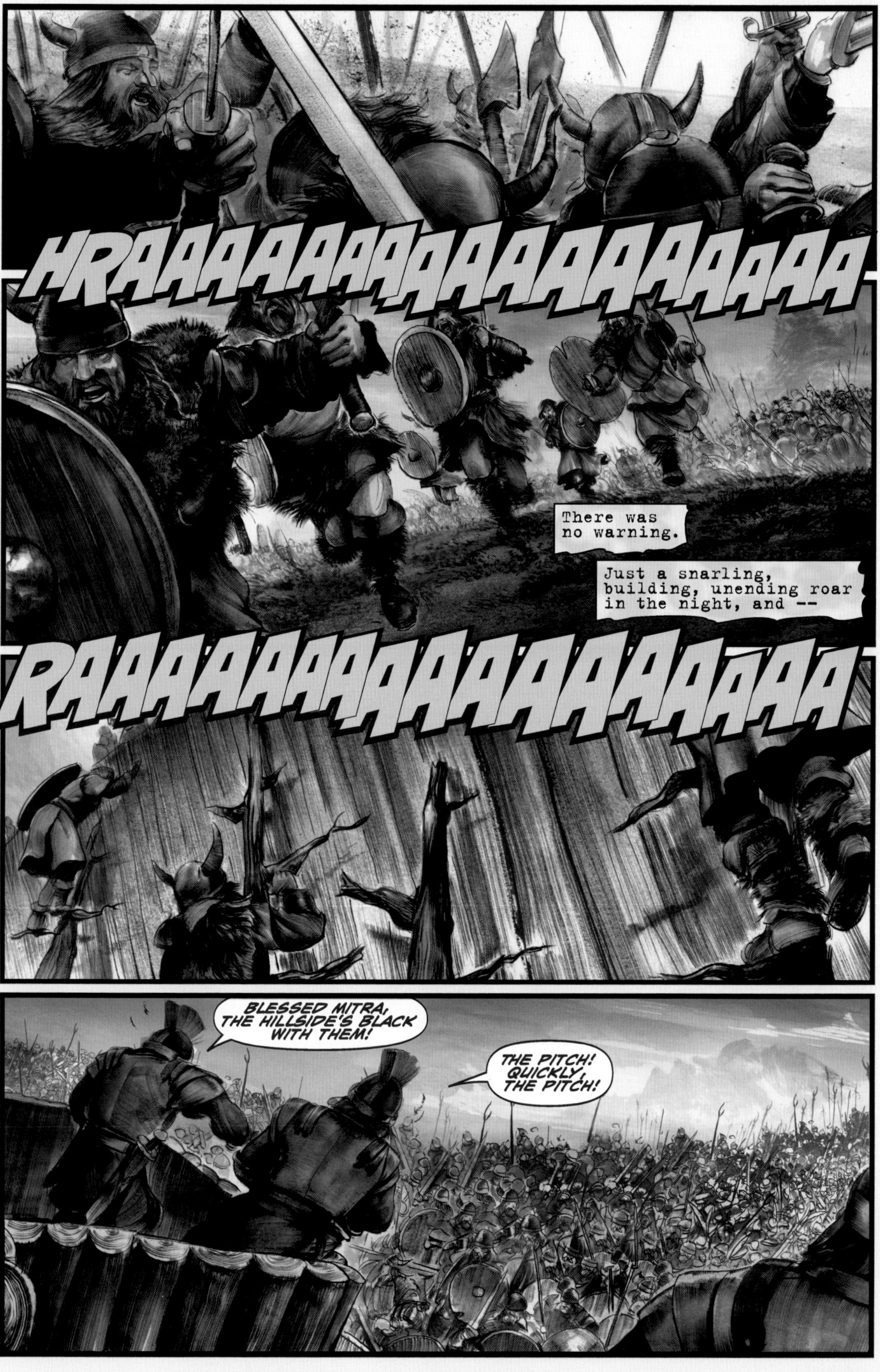
HRAAAAAAAAAAAAAAAAA
There was no warning.
Just a snarling, building, unending roar in the night, and --
RAAAAAAAAAAAAAAAAAA
BLESSED MITRA, THE HILLSIDE'S BLACK WITH THEM!
THE PITCH! QUICKLY, THE PITCH!

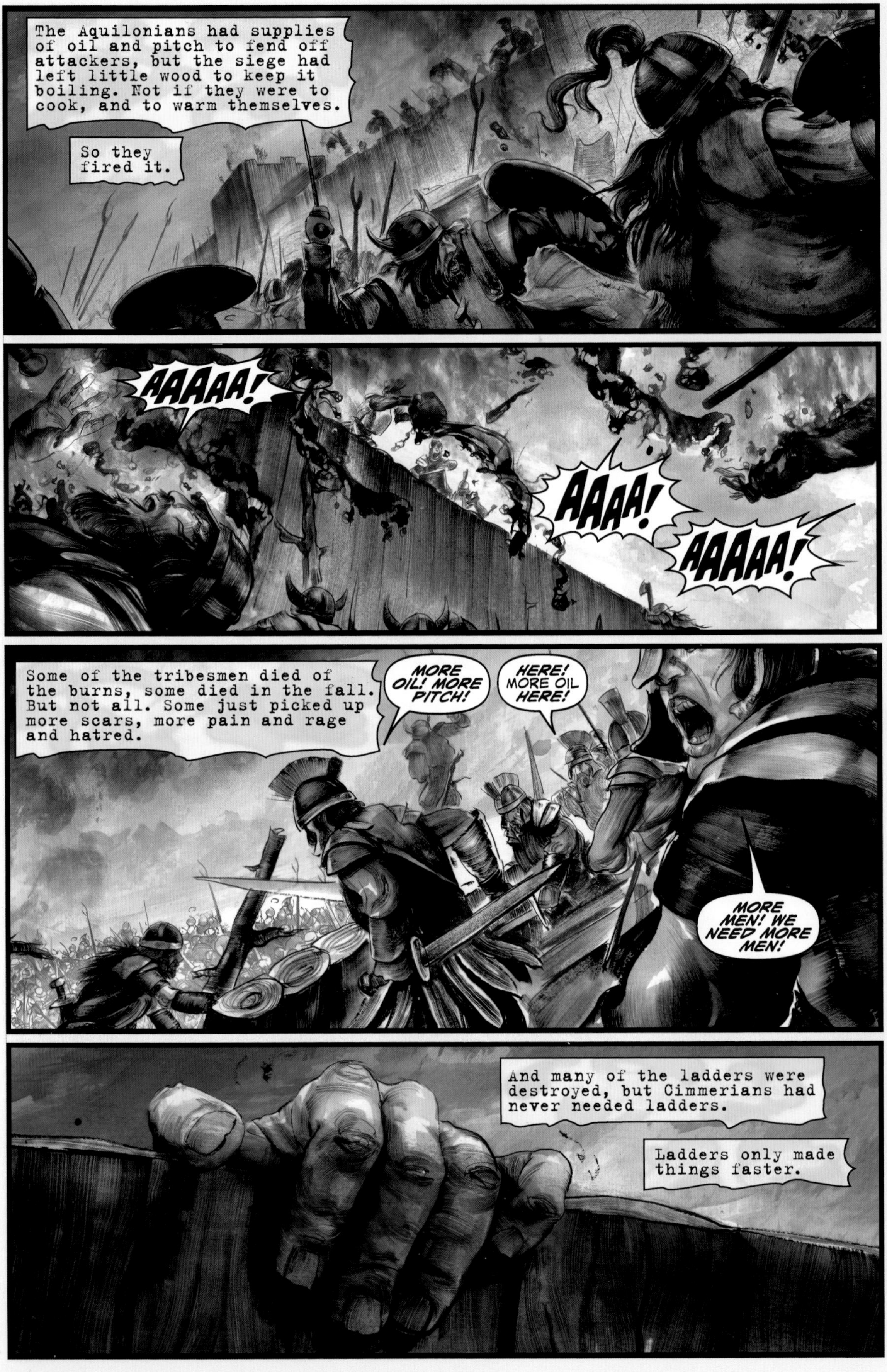
The Aquilonians had supplies of oil and pitch to fend off attackers, but the siege had left little wood to keep it boiling. Not if they were to cook, and to warm themselves.
So they fired it.
AAAAA!
AAAA!
AAAAA!
Some of the tribesmen died of the burns, some died in the fall. But not all. Some just picked up more scars, more pain and rage and hatred.
MORE OIL! MORE PITCH!
HERE! MORE OIL HERE!
MORE MEN! WE NEED MORE MEN!
And many of the ladders were destroyed, but Cimmerians had never needed ladders.
Ladders only made things faster.

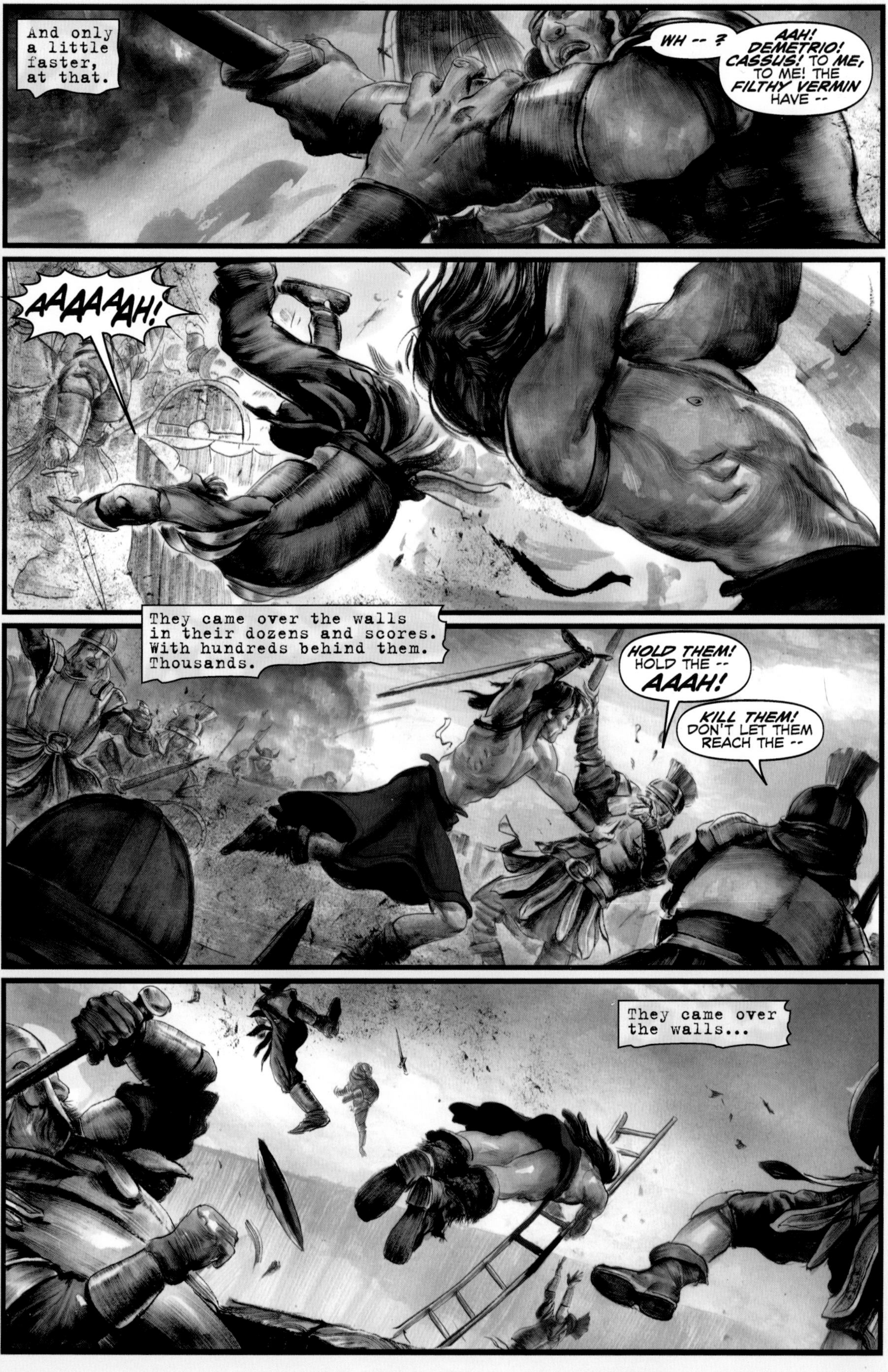
And only a little faster, at that.
WH -- ?
AAH! DEMETRIO! CASSUS! TO ME, TO ME! THE FILTHY VERMIN HAVE --
AAAAAAH!
They came over the walls in their dozens and scores. With hundreds behind them. Thousands.
HOLD THEM! HOLD THE -- AAAH!
KILL THEM! DON'T LET THEM REACH THE --
They came over the walls...

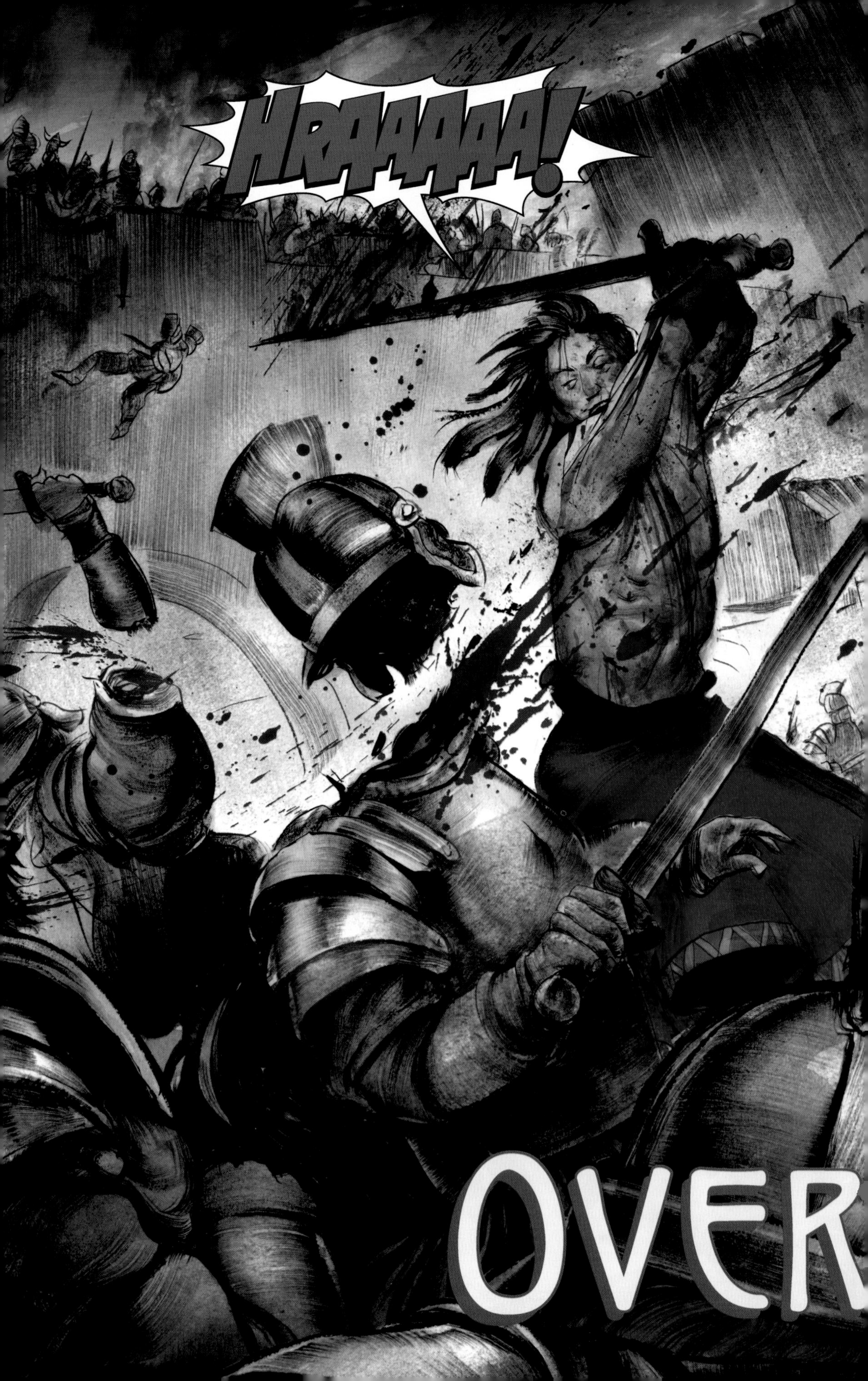
HRAAAAAA!
OVER

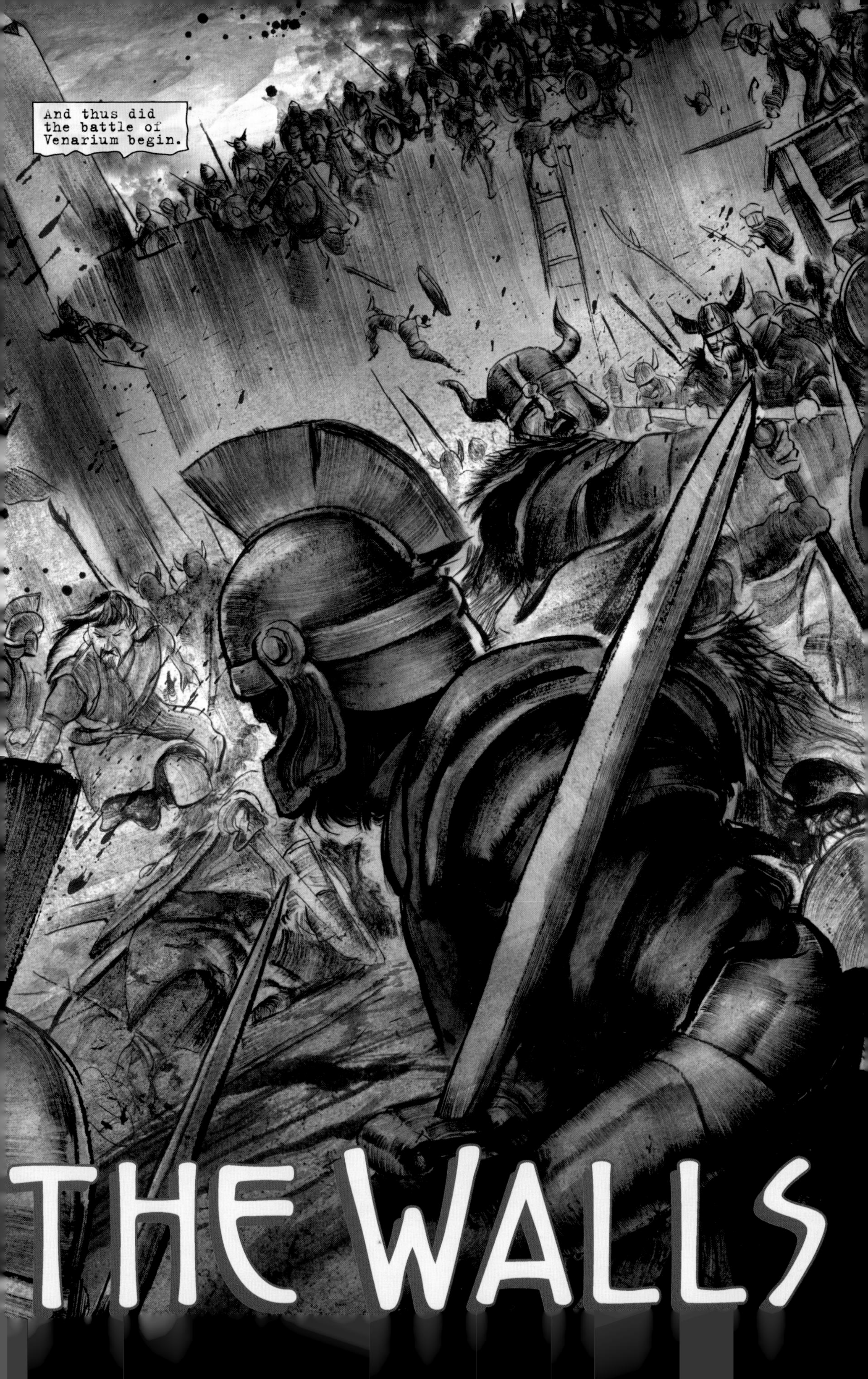
And thus did the battle of Venarium begin.
THE WALLS

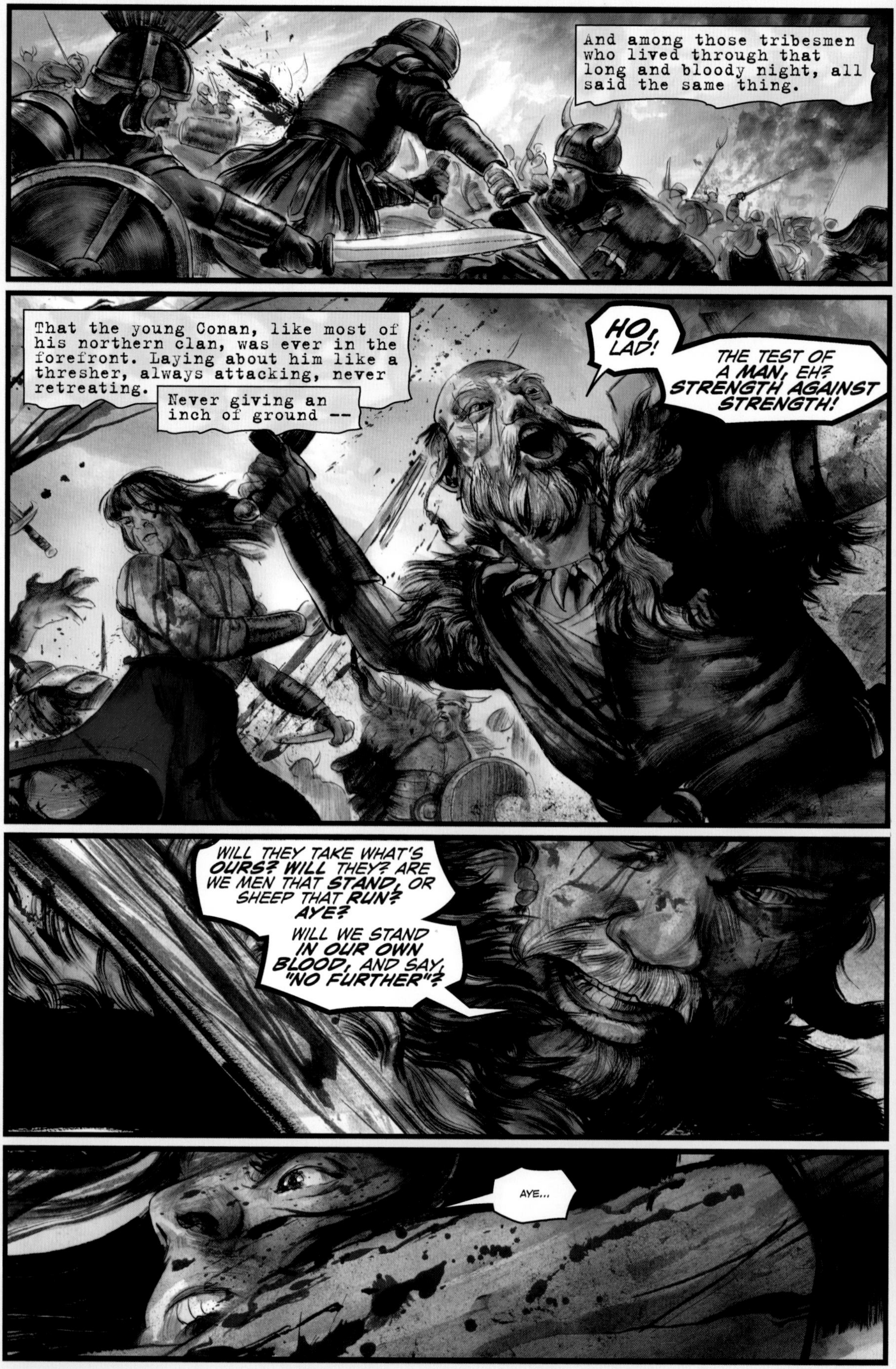

And among those tribesmen who lived through that long and bloody night, all said the same thing.
That the young Conan, like most of his northern clan, was ever in the forefront. Laying about him like a thresher, always attacking, never retreating.
Never giving an inch of ground --
HO, LAD!
THE TEST OF A MAN, EH? STRENGTH AGAINST STRENGTH!
WILL THEY TAKE WHAT'S OURS? WILL THEY? ARE WE MEN THAT STAND, OR SHEEP THAT RUN? AYE?
WILL WE STAND IN OUR OWN BLOOD, AND SAY, "NO FURTHER"?
AYE...

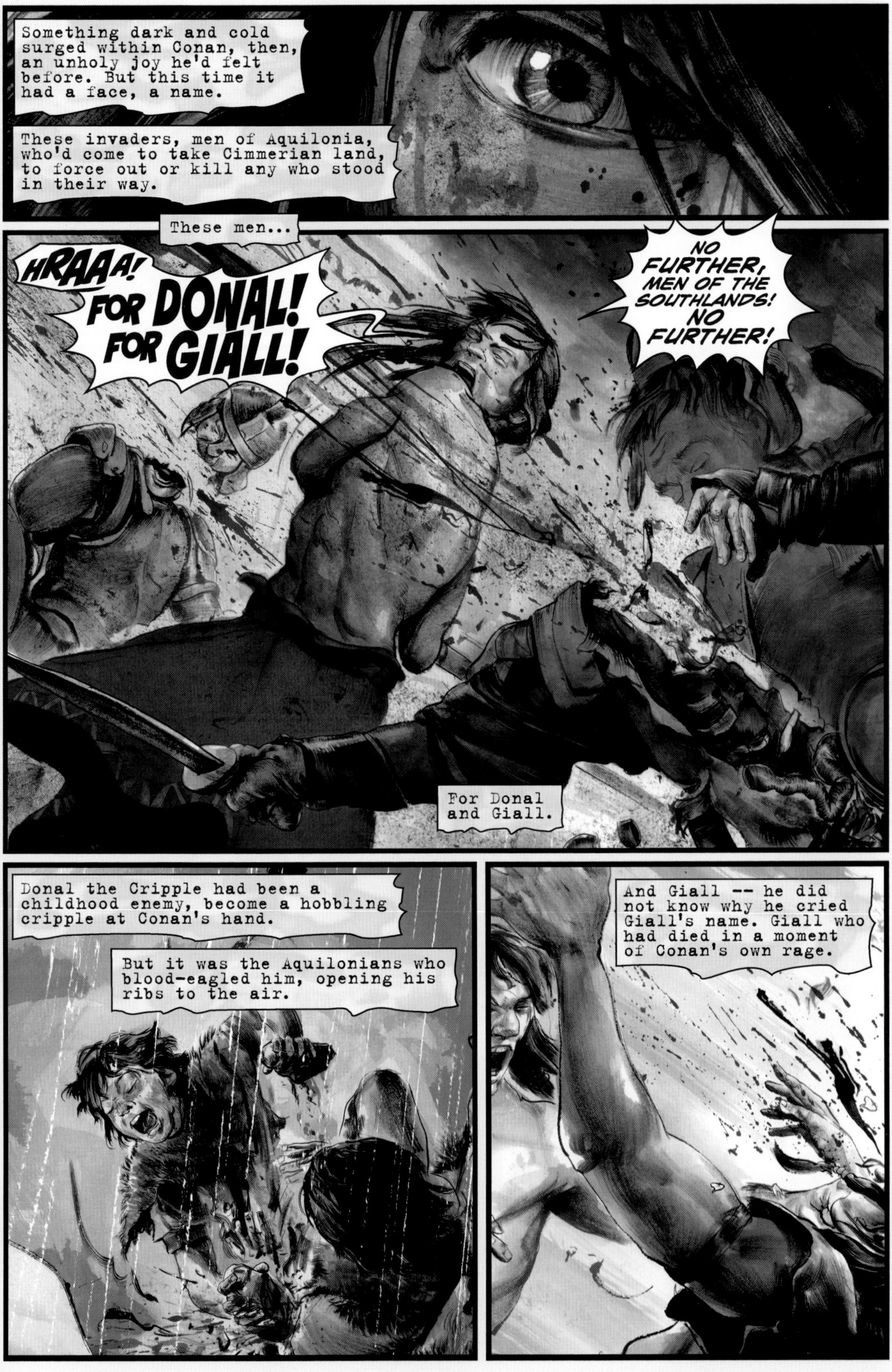
Something dark and cold surged within Conan, then, an unholy joy he'd felt before. But this time it had a face, a name.
These invaders, men of Aquilonia, who'd come to take Cimmerian land, to force out or kill any who stood in their way.
These men...
HRAAA! FOR DONAL! FOR GIALL!
NO FURTHER, MEN OF THE SOUTHLANDS! NO FURTHER!
For Donal and Giall.
Donal the Cripple had been a childhood enemy, become a hobbling cripple at Conan's hand.
But it was the Aquilonians who blood-eagled him, opening his ribs to the air.
And Giall -- he did not know why he cried Giall's name. Giall who had died in a moment of Conan's own rage.

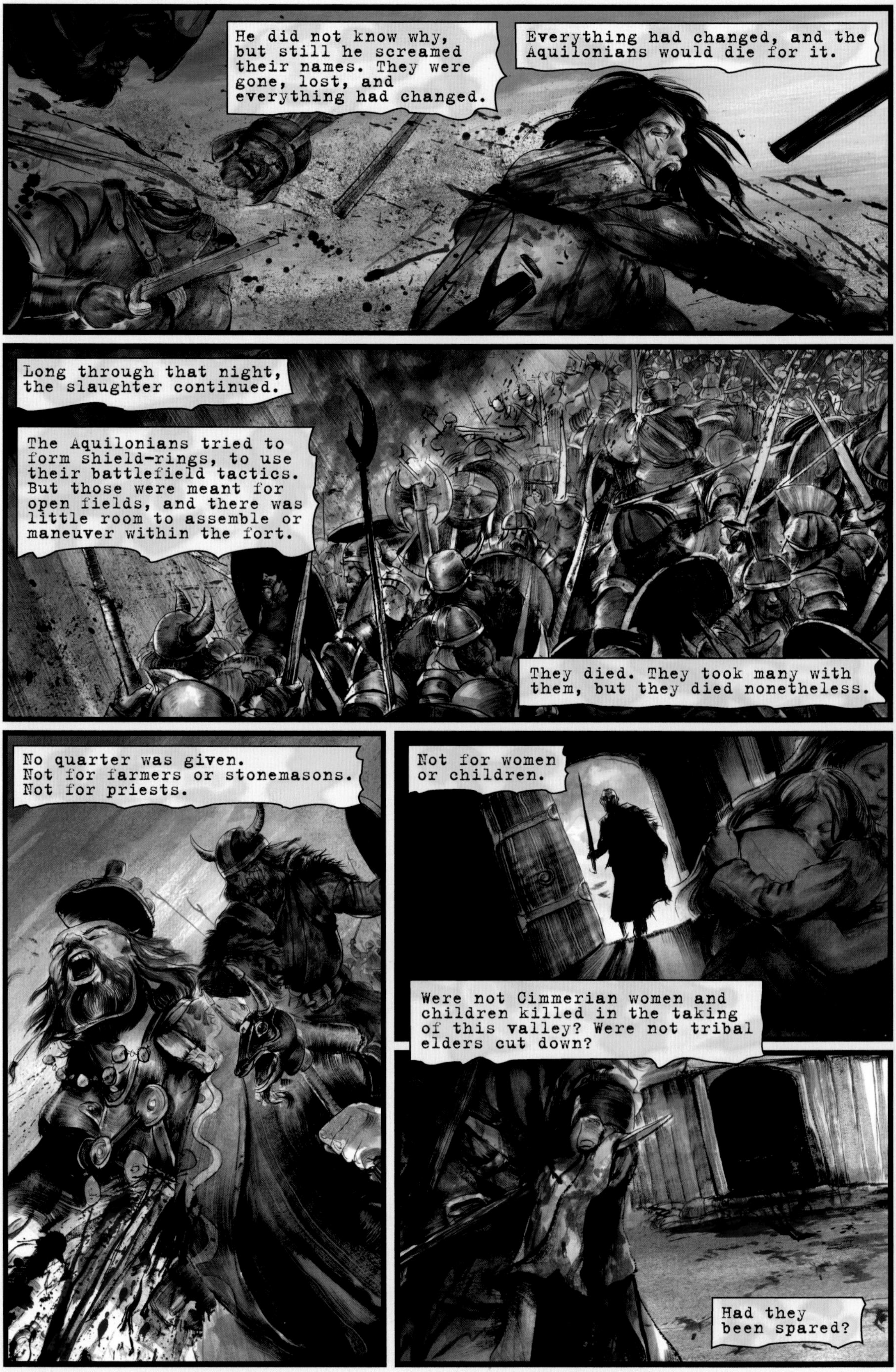
He did not know why, but still he screamed their names. They were gone, lost, and everything had changed.
Everything had changed, and the Aquilonians would die for it.
Long through that night, the slaughter continued.
The Aquilonians tried to form shield-rings, to use their battlefield tactics. But those were meant for open fields, and there was little room to assemble or maneuver within the fort.
They died. They took many with them, but they died nonetheless.
No quarter was given. Not for farmers or stonemasons. Not for priests.
Not for women or children.
Were not Cimmerian women and children killed in the taking of this valley? Were not tribal elders cut down?
Had they been spared?

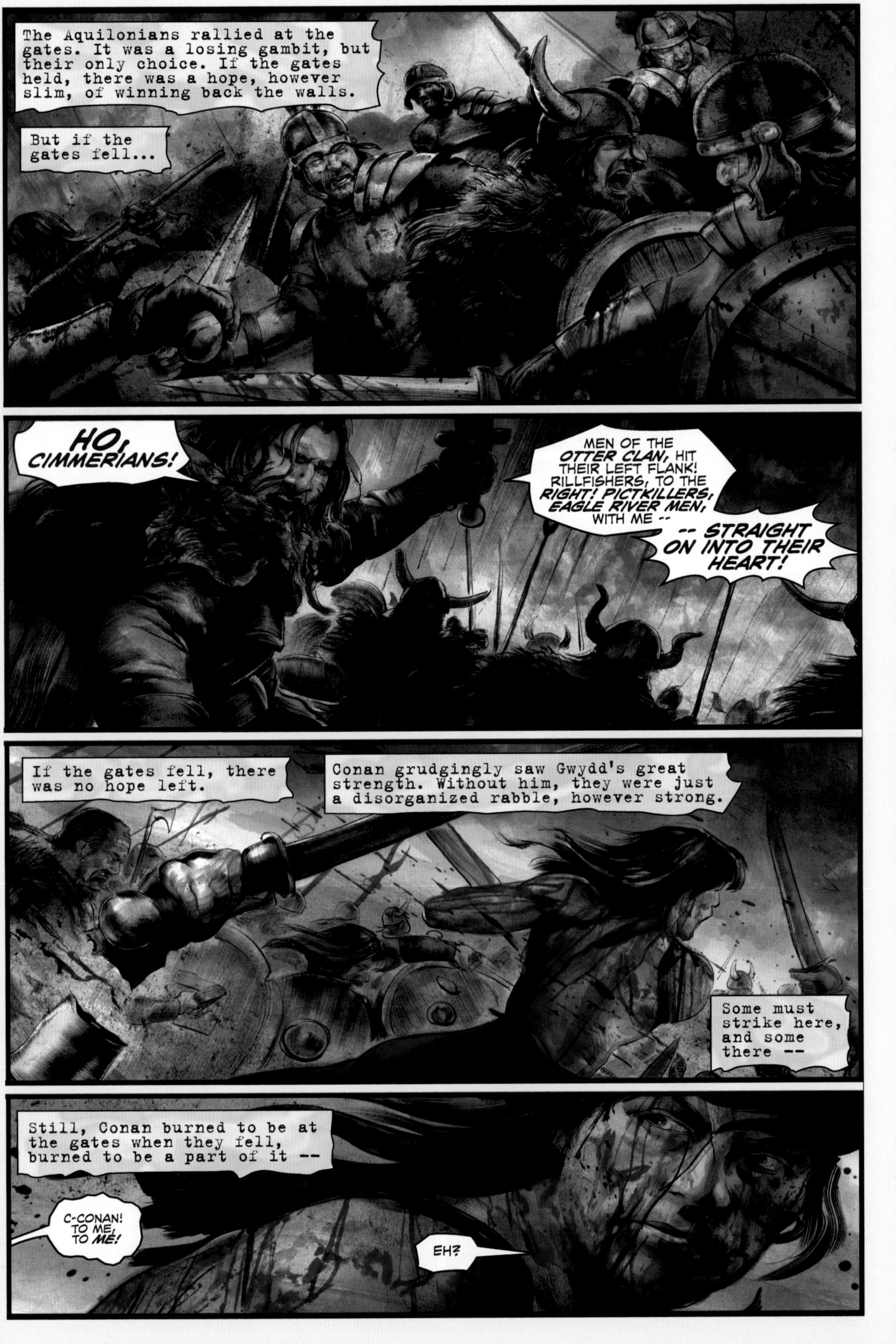
The Aquilonians rallied at the gates. It was a losing gambit, but their only choice. If the gates held, there was a hope, however slim, of winning back the walls.
But if the gates fell...
HO, CIMMERIANS!
MEN OF THE OTTER CLAN, HIT THEIR LEFT FLANK! RILLFISHERS, TO THE RIGHT! PICTKILLERS, EAGLE RIVER MEN, WITH ME --
-- STRAIGHT ON INTO THEIR HEART!
If the gates fell, there was no hope left.
Conan grudgingly saw Gwydd's great strength. Without him, they were just a disorganized rabble, however strong.
Some must strike here, and some there --
Still, Conan burned to be at the gates when they fell, burned to be a part of it --
C-CONAN! TO ME, TO ME!
EH?

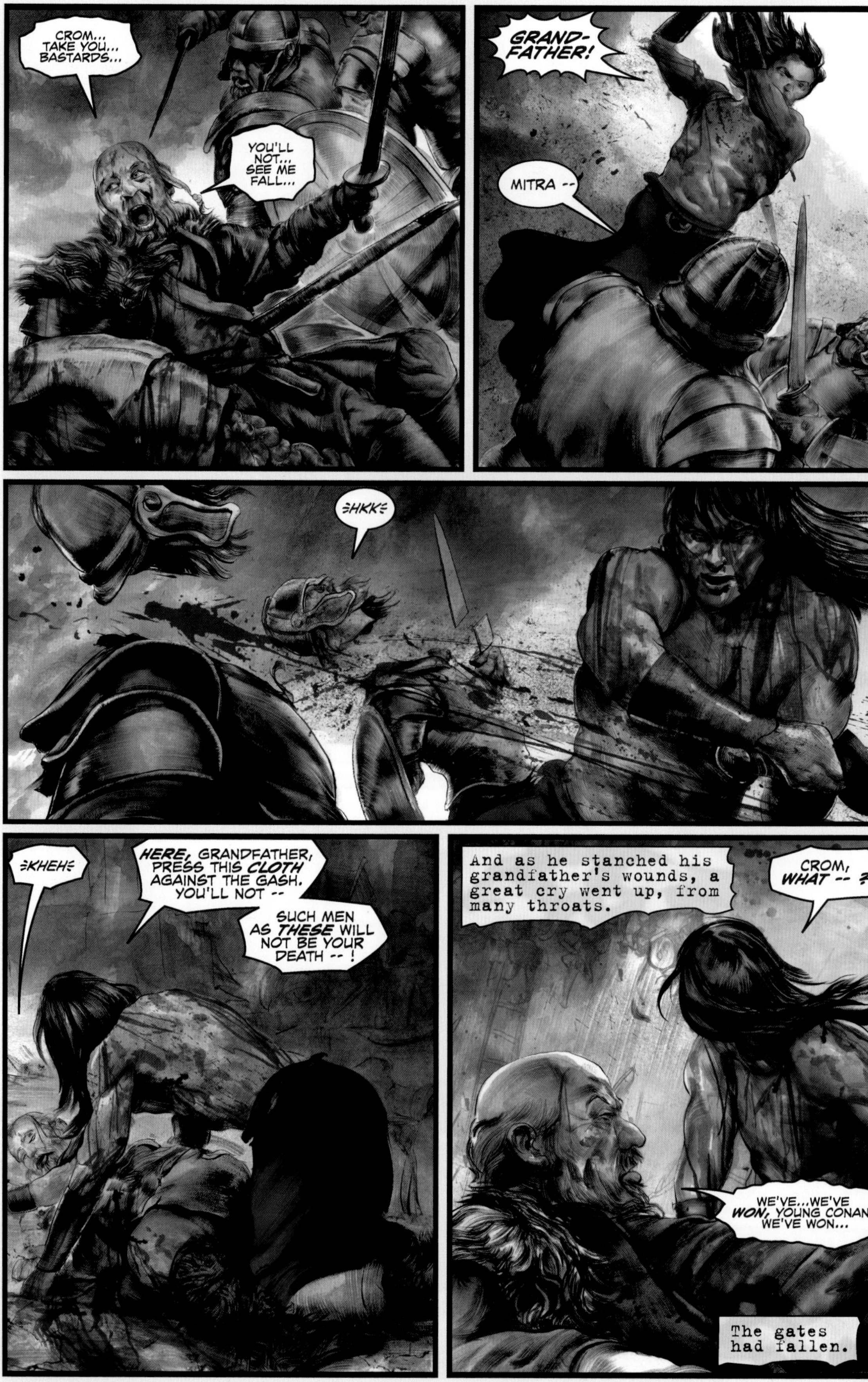
CROM... TAKE YOU... BASTARDS...
YOU'LL NOT... SEE ME FALL...
GRAND-FATHER!
MITRA --
HKK
KHEH
HERE, GRANDFATHER, PRESS THIS CLOTH AGAINST THE GASH. YOU'LL NOT --
SUCH MEN AS THESE WILL NOT BE YOUR DEATH -- !
And as he stanched his grandfather's wounds, a great cry went up, from many throats.
CROM, WHAT -- ?
WE'VE...WE'VE WON, YOUNG CONAN. WE'VE WON...
The gates had fallen.

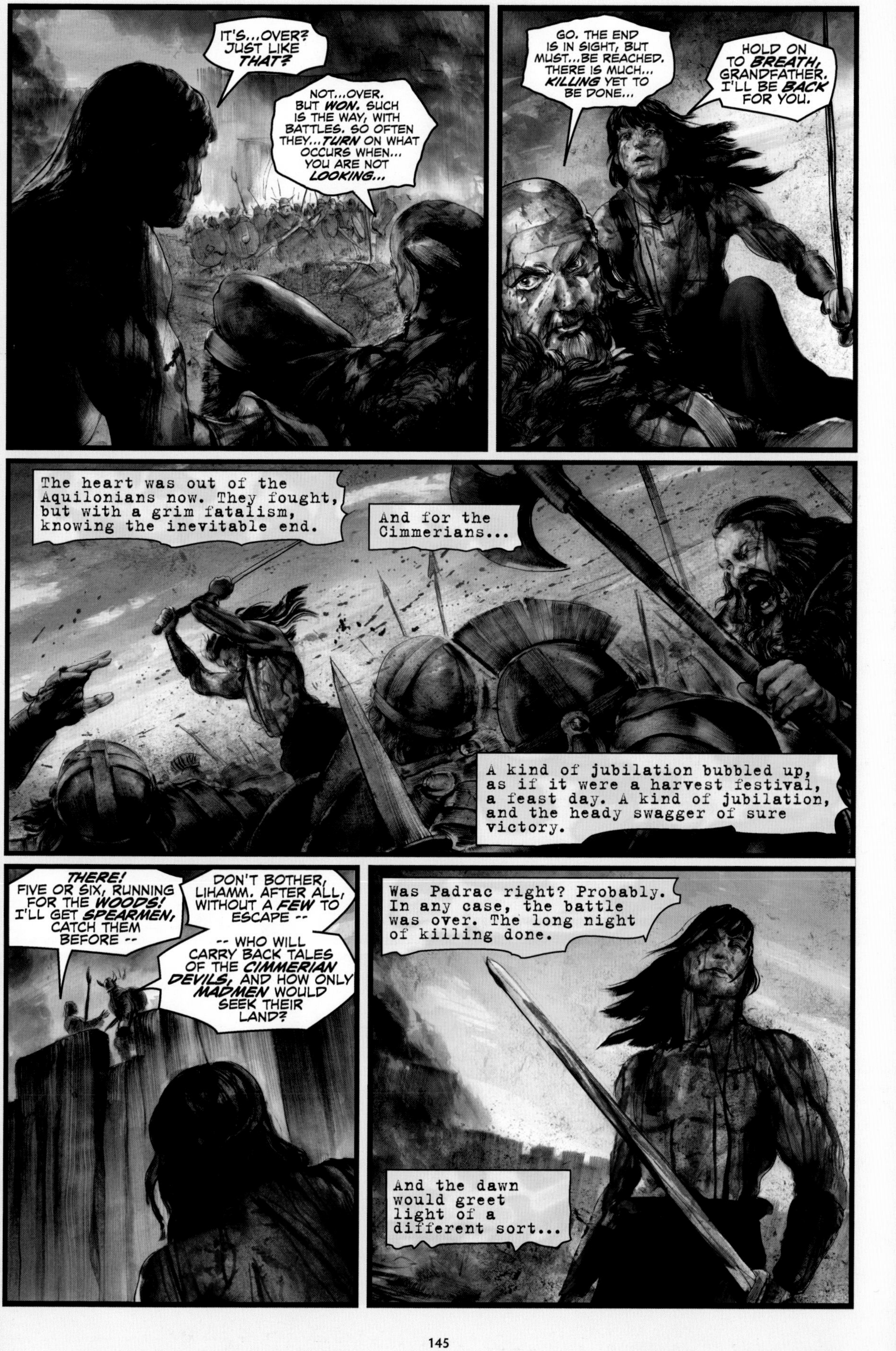
IT'S...OVER? JUST LIKE *THAT?*
NOT...OVER. BUT *WON.* SUCH IS THE WAY, WITH BATTLES. SO OFTEN THEY...*TURN* ON WHAT OCCURS WHEN... YOU ARE NOT *LOOKING...*
GO. THE END IS IN SIGHT, BUT MUST...BE REACHED. THERE IS MUCH... *KILLING* YET TO BE DONE...
HOLD ON TO *BREATH,* GRANDFATHER. I'LL BE *BACK* FOR YOU.
The heart was out of the Aquilonians now. They fought, but with a grim fatalism, knowing the inevitable end.
And for the Cimmerians...
A kind of jubilation bubbled up, as if it were a harvest festival, a feast day. A kind of jubilation, and the heady swagger of sure victory.
THERE! FIVE OR SIX, RUNNING FOR THE *WOODS!* I'LL GET *SPEARMEN,* CATCH THEM BEFORE --
DON'T BOTHER, LIHAMM. AFTER ALL, WITHOUT A *FEW* TO ESCAPE --
-- WHO WILL CARRY BACK TALES OF THE *CIMMERIAN DEVILS,* AND HOW ONLY *MADMEN* WOULD SEEK THEIR LAND?
Was Padrac right? Probably. In any case, the battle was over. The long night of killing done.
And the dawn would greet light of a different sort...

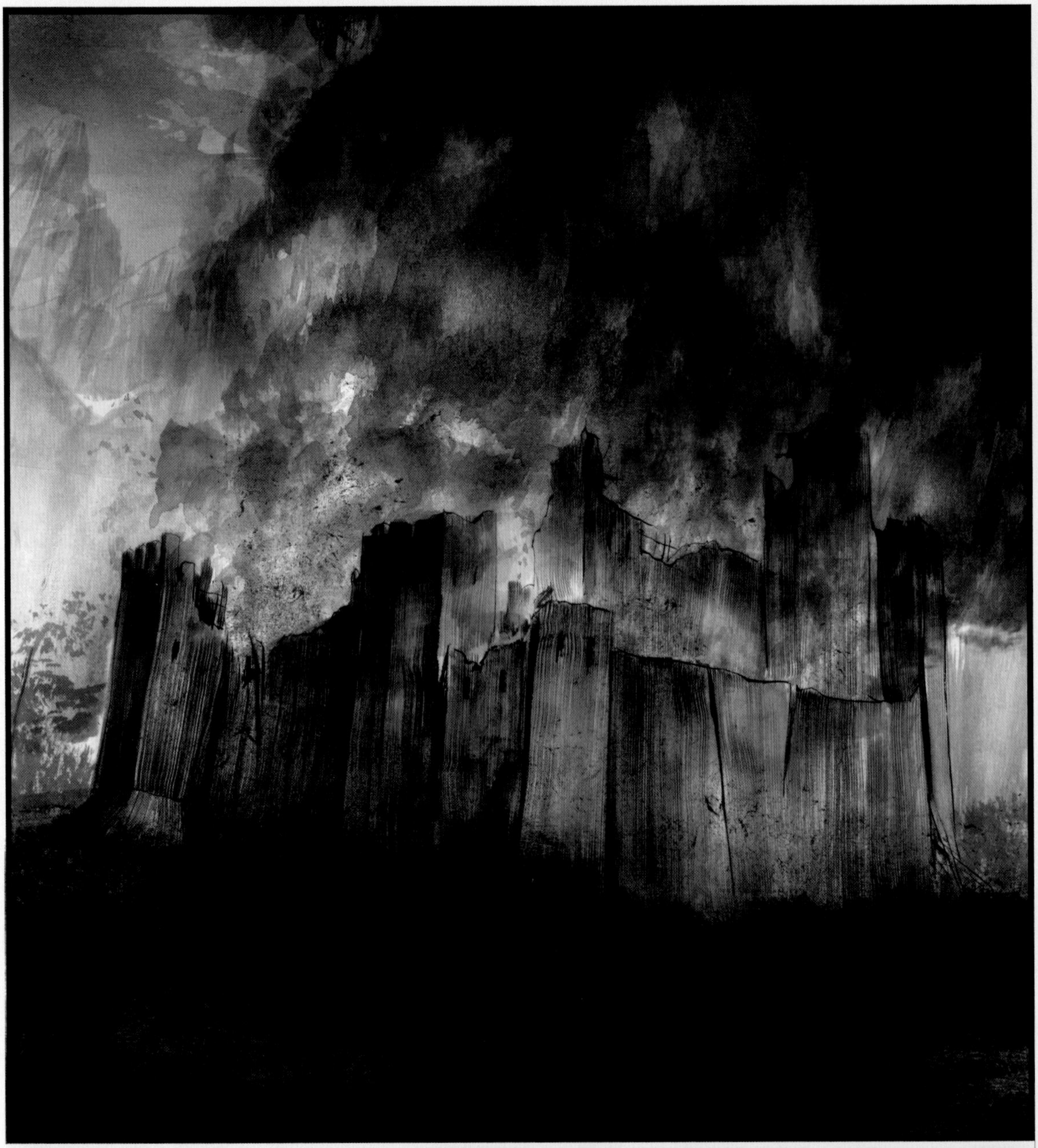

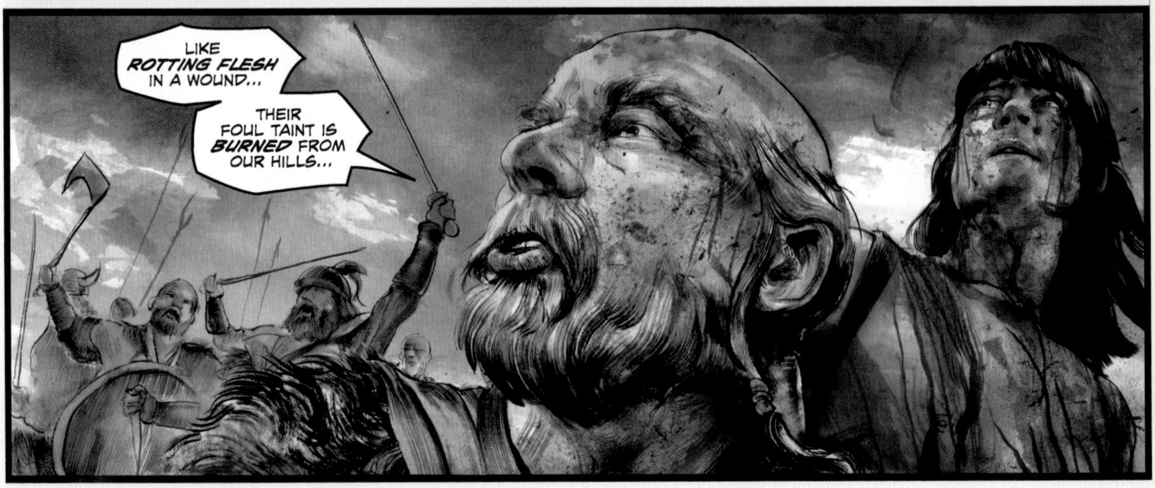
LIKE ROTTING FLESH IN A WOUND...
THEIR FOUL TAINT IS BURNED FROM OUR HILLS...

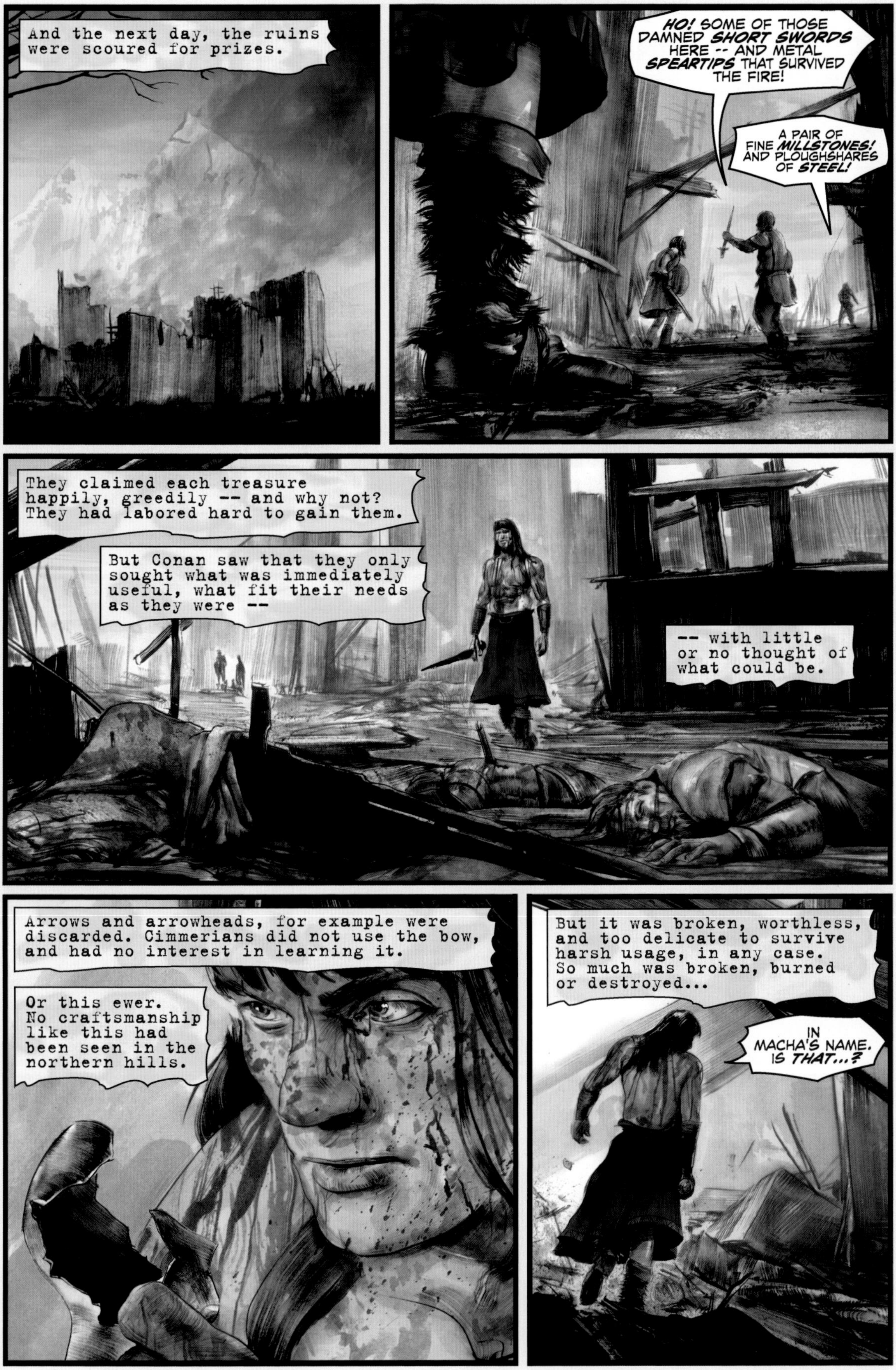
And the next day, the ruins were scoured for prizes.
HO! SOME OF THOSE DAMNED SHORT SWORDS HERE -- AND METAL SPEARTIPS THAT SURVIVED THE FIRE!
A PAIR OF FINE MILLSTONES! AND PLOUGHSHARES OF STEEL!
They claimed each treasure happily, greedily -- and why not? They had labored hard to gain them.
But Conan saw that they only sought what was immediately useful, what fit their needs as they were --
-- with little or no thought of what could be.
Arrows and arrowheads, for example were discarded. Cimmerians did not use the bow, and had no interest in learning it.
Or this ewer. No craftsmanship like this had been seen in the northern hills.
But it was broken, worthless, and too delicate to survive harsh usage, in any case. So much was broken, burned or destroyed...
IN MACHA'S NAME. IS THAT...?

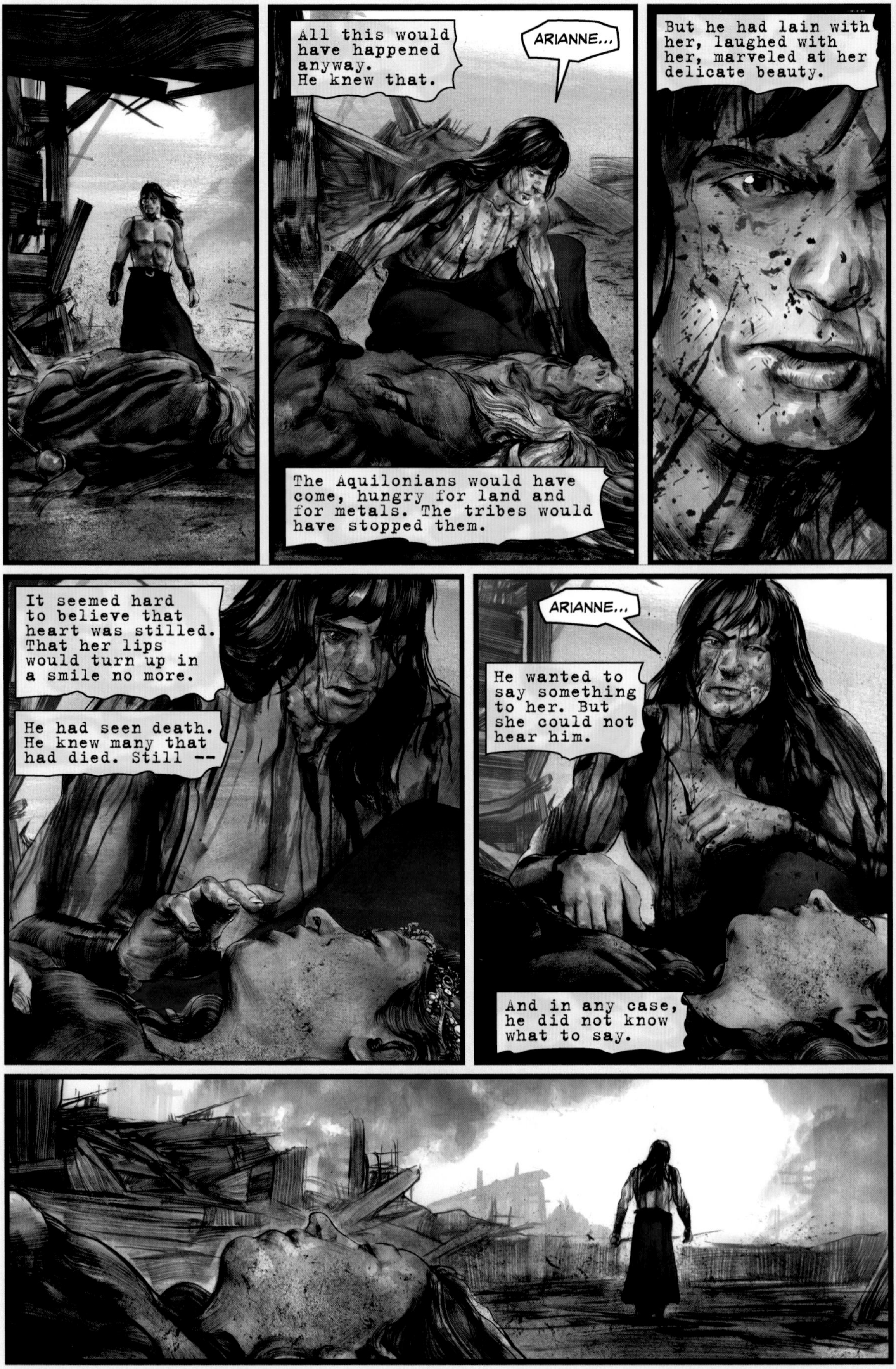
All this would have happened anyway. He knew that.
ARIANNE...
The Aquilonians would have come, hungry for land and for metals. The tribes would have stopped them.
But he had lain with her, laughed with her, marveled at her delicate beauty.
It seemed hard to believe that heart was stilled. That her lips would turn up in a smile no more.
He had seen death. He knew many that had died. Still --
ARIANNE...
He wanted to say something to her. But she could not hear him.
And in any case, he did not know what to say.

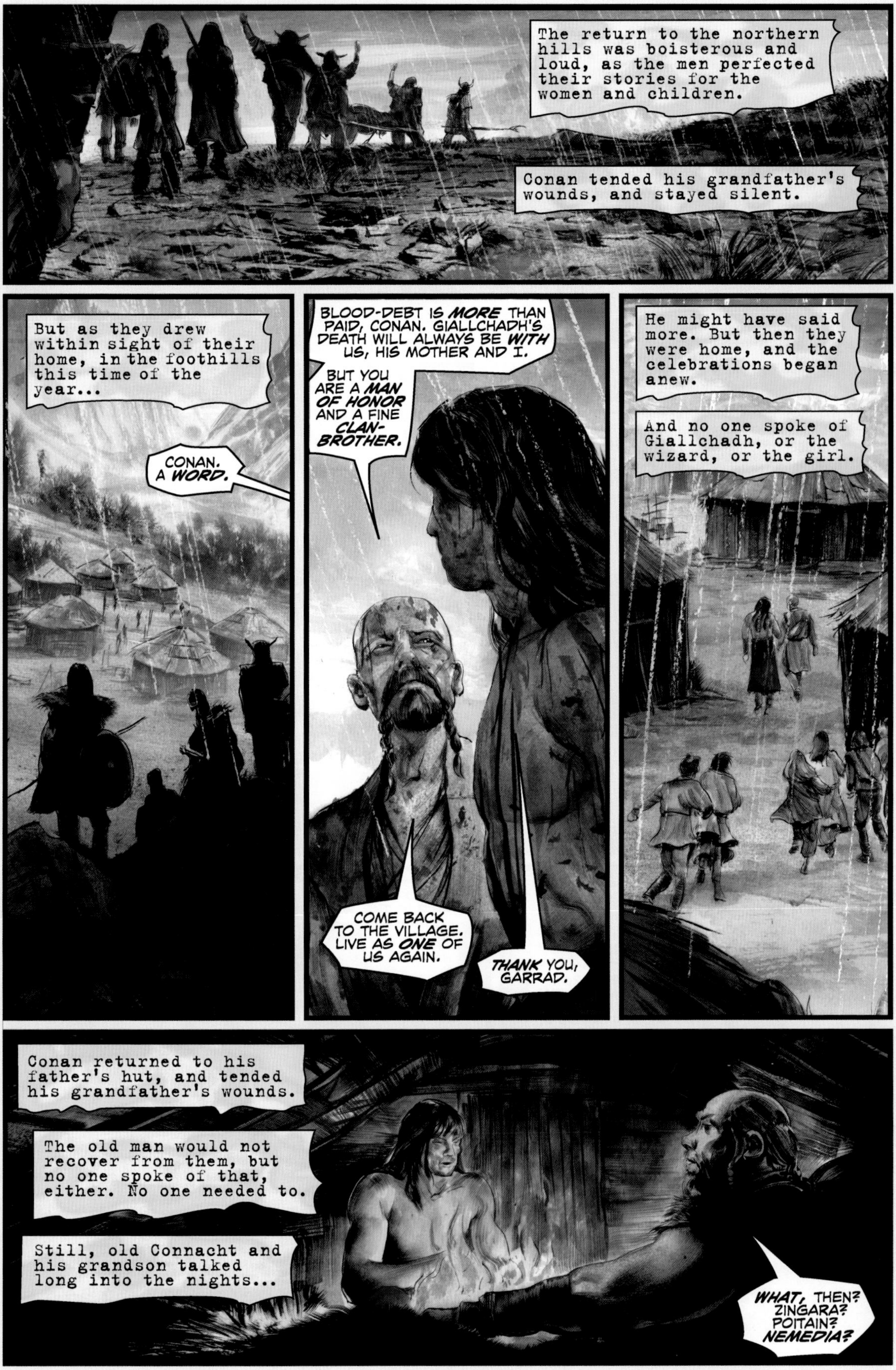
The return to the northern hills was boisterous and loud, as the men perfected their stories for the women and children.
Conan tended his grandfather's wounds, and stayed silent.
But as they drew within sight of their home, in the foothills this time of the year...
CONAN. A *WORD.*
BLOOD-DEBT IS *MORE* THAN PAID, CONAN. GIALLCHADH'S DEATH WILL ALWAYS BE *WITH* US, HIS MOTHER AND I.
BUT YOU ARE A *MAN OF HONOR* AND A FINE *CLAN-BROTHER.*
COME BACK TO THE VILLAGE. LIVE AS *ONE* OF US AGAIN.
THANK YOU, GARRAD.
He might have said more. But then they were home, and the celebrations began anew.
And no one spoke of Giallchadh, or the wizard, or the girl.
Conan returned to his father's hut, and tended his grandfather's wounds.
The old man would not recover from them, but no one spoke of that, either. No one needed to.
Still, old Connacht and his grandson talked long into the nights...
WHAT, THEN? ZINGARA? POITAIN? *NEMEDIA?*

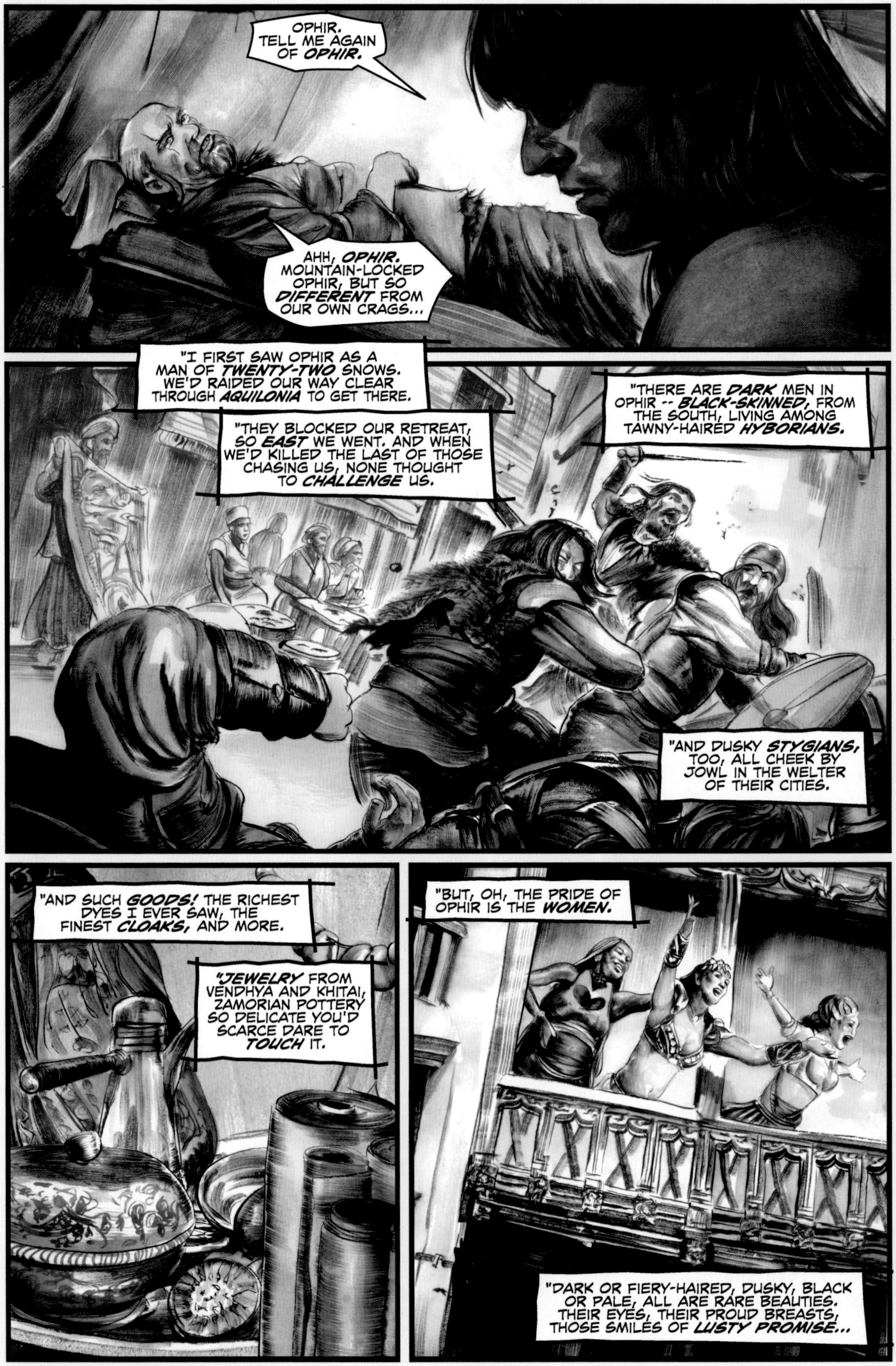
OPHIR. TELL ME AGAIN OF OPHIR.
AHH, OPHIR. MOUNTAIN-LOCKED OPHIR, BUT SO DIFFERENT FROM OUR OWN CRAGS...
"I FIRST SAW OPHIR AS A MAN OF TWENTY-TWO SNOWS. WE'D RAIDED OUR WAY CLEAR THROUGH AQUILONIA TO GET THERE.
"THEY BLOCKED OUR RETREAT, SO EAST WE WENT. AND WHEN WE'D KILLED THE LAST OF THOSE CHASING US, NONE THOUGHT TO CHALLENGE US.
"THERE ARE DARK MEN IN OPHIR -- BLACK-SKINNED, FROM THE SOUTH, LIVING AMONG TAWNY-HAIRED HYBORIANS.
"AND DUSKY STYGIANS, TOO, ALL CHEEK BY JOWL IN THE WELTER OF THEIR CITIES.
"AND SUCH GOODS! THE RICHEST DYES I EVER SAW, THE FINEST CLOAKS, AND MORE.
"JEWELRY FROM VENDHYA AND KHITAI, ZAMORIAN POTTERY SO DELICATE YOU'D SCARCE DARE TO TOUCH IT.
"BUT, OH, THE PRIDE OF OPHIR IS THE WOMEN.
"DARK OR FIERY-HAIRED, DUSKY, BLACK OR PALE, ALL ARE RARE BEAUTIES. THEIR EYES, THEIR PROUD BREASTS, THOSE SMILES OF LUSTY PROMISE...

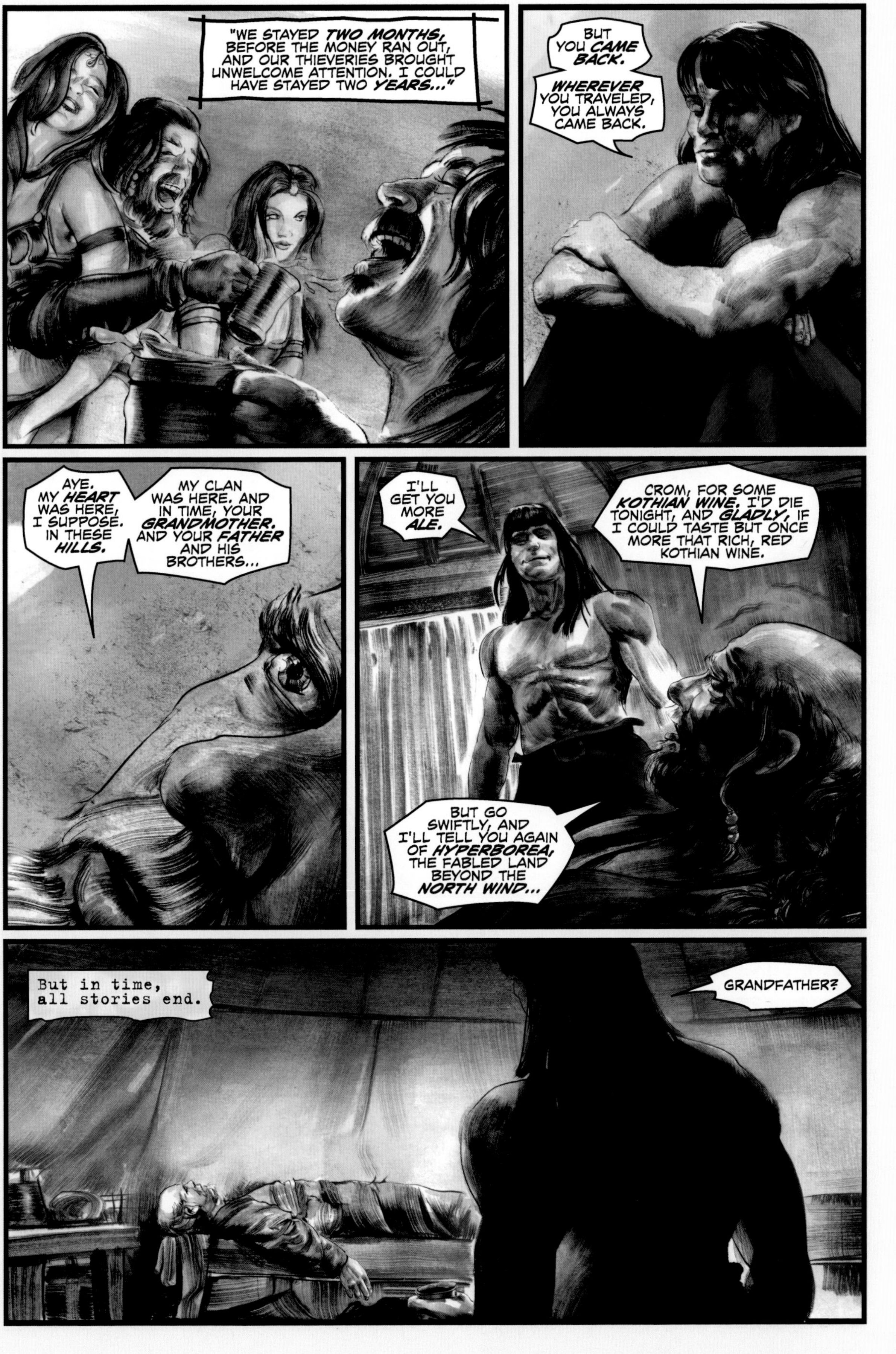
"WE STAYED TWO MONTHS, BEFORE THE MONEY RAN OUT, AND OUR THIEVERIES BROUGHT UNWELCOME ATTENTION. I COULD HAVE STAYED TWO YEARS..."
BUT YOU CAME BACK.
WHEREVER YOU TRAVELED, YOU ALWAYS CAME BACK.
AYE. MY HEART WAS HERE, I SUPPOSE. IN THESE HILLS.
MY CLAN WAS HERE. AND IN TIME, YOUR GRANDMOTHER. AND YOUR FATHER AND HIS BROTHERS...
I'LL GET YOU MORE ALE.
CROM, FOR SOME KOTHIAN WINE, I'D DIE TONIGHT, AND GLADLY, IF I COULD TASTE BUT ONCE MORE THAT RICH, RED KOTHIAN WINE.
BUT GO SWIFTLY, AND I'LL TELL YOU AGAIN OF HYPERBOREA, THE FABLED LAND BEYOND THE NORTH WIND...
But in time, all stories end.
GRANDFATHER?

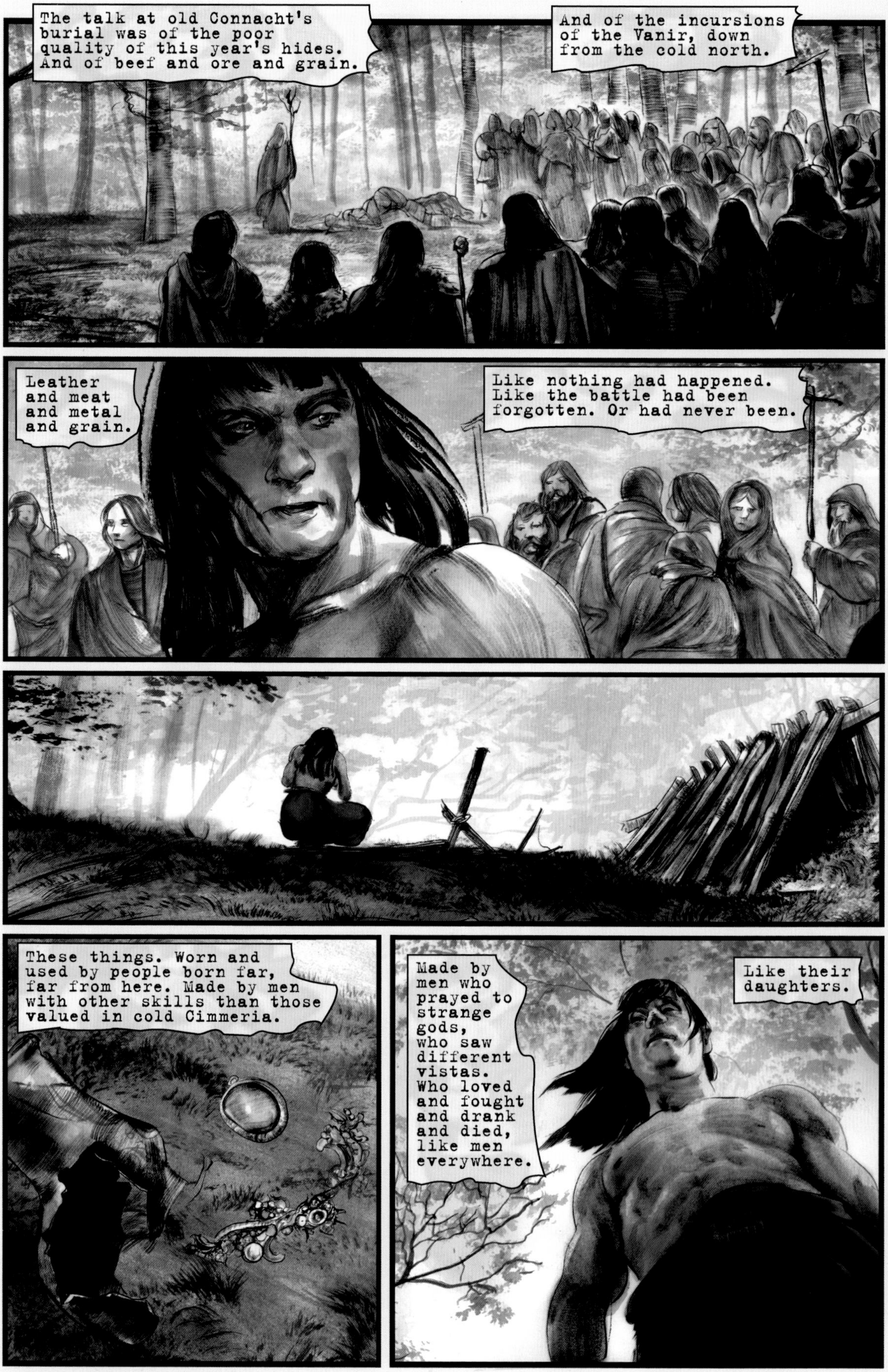
The talk at old Connacht's burial was of the poor quality of this year's hides. And of beef and ore and grain.
And of the incursions of the Vanir, down from the cold north.
Leather and meat and metal and grain.
Like nothing had happened. Like the battle had been forgotten. Or had never been.
These things. Worn and used by people born far, far from here. Made by men with other skills than those valued in cold Cimmeria.
Made by men who prayed to strange gods, who saw different vistas. Who loved and fought and drank and died, like men everywhere.
Like their daughters.

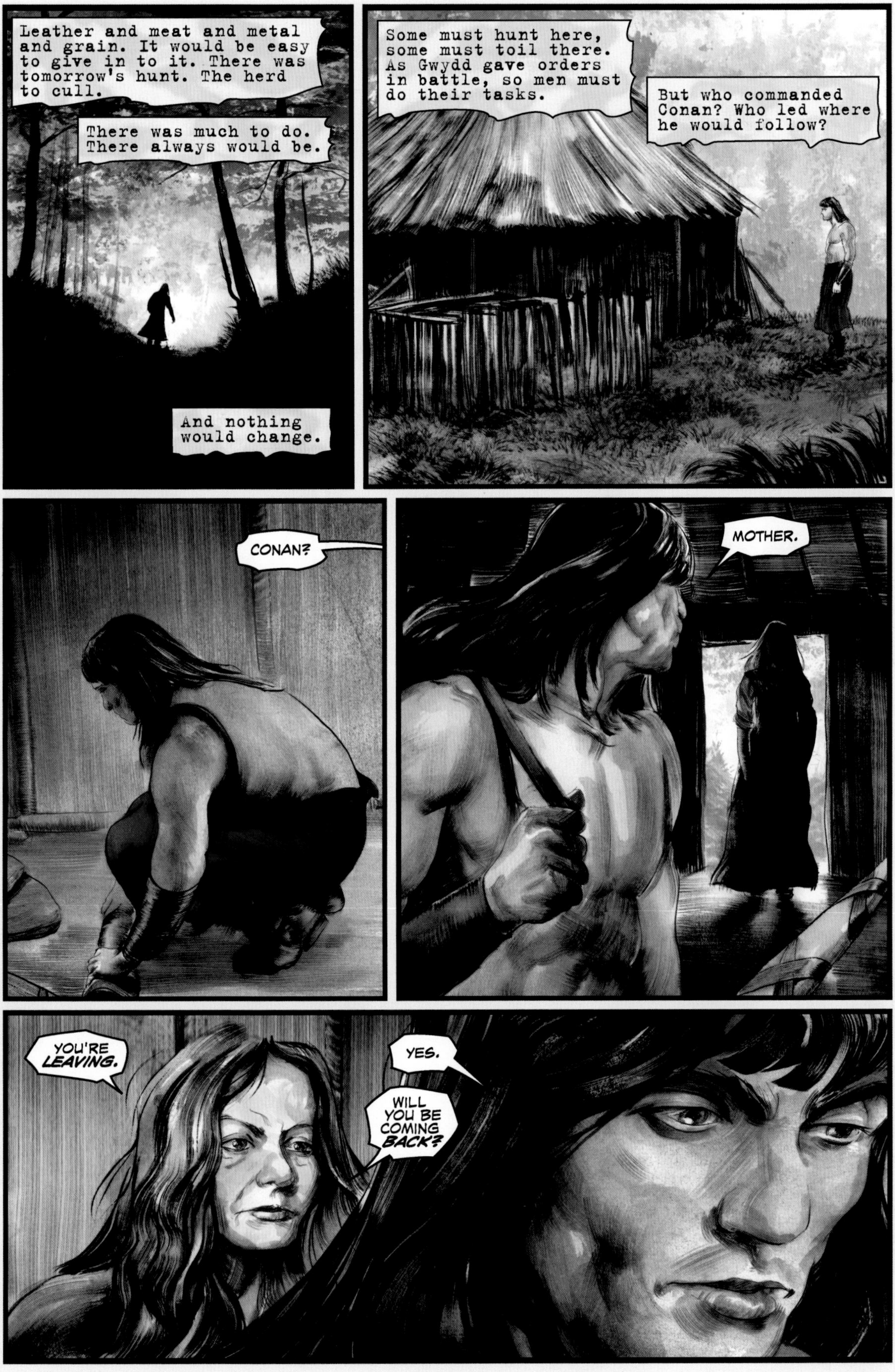
Leather and meat and metal and grain. It would be easy to give in to it. There was tomorrow's hunt. The herd to cull.
There was much to do. There always would be.
And nothing would change.
Some must hunt here, some must toil there. As Gwydd gave orders in battle, so men must do their tasks.
But who commanded Conan? Who led where he would follow?
CONAN?
MOTHER.
YOU'RE *LEAVING.*
YES.
WILL YOU BE COMING *BACK?*

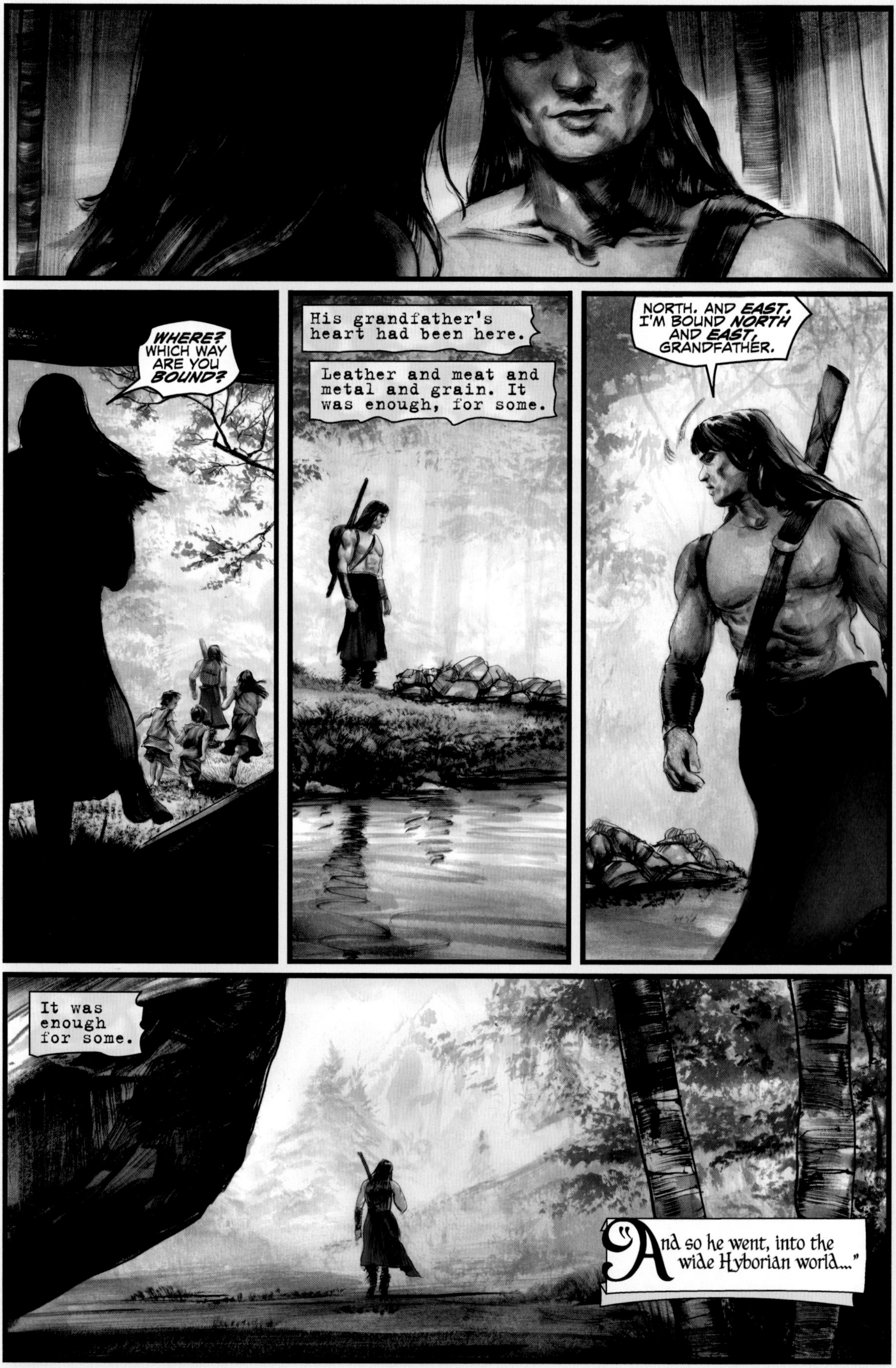
WHERE? WHICH WAY ARE YOU BOUND?
His grandfather's heart had been here.
Leather and meat and metal and grain. It was enough, for some.
NORTH. AND EAST. I'M BOUND NORTH AND EAST, GRANDFATHER.
It was enough for some.
"And so he went, into the wide Hyborian world..."

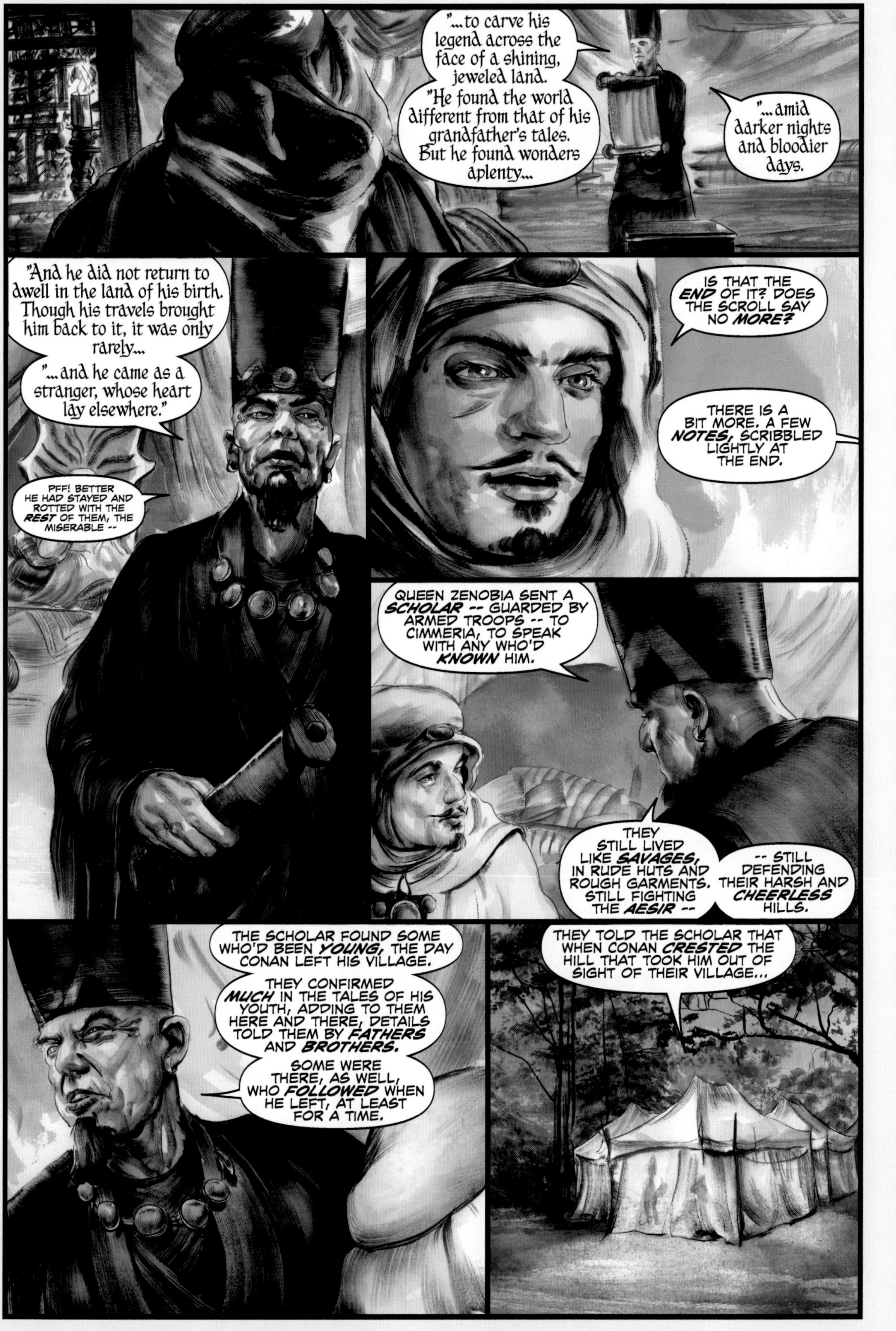
"...to carve his legend across the face of a shining, jeweled land.
"He found the world different from that of his grandfather's tales. But he found wonders aplenty...
"...amid darker nights and bloodier days.
"And he did not return to dwell in the land of his birth. Though his travels brought him back to it, it was only rarely...
"...and he came as a stranger, whose heart lay elsewhere."
PFF! BETTER HE HAD STAYED AND ROTTED WITH THE REST OF THEM, THE MISERABLE --
IS THAT THE END OF IT? DOES THE SCROLL SAY NO MORE?
THERE IS A BIT MORE. A FEW NOTES, SCRIBBLED LIGHTLY AT THE END.
QUEEN ZENOBIA SENT A SCHOLAR -- GUARDED BY ARMED TROOPS -- TO CIMMERIA, TO SPEAK WITH ANY WHO'D KNOWN HIM.
THEY STILL LIVED LIKE SAVAGES, IN RUDE HUTS AND ROUGH GARMENTS. STILL FIGHTING THE AESIR --
-- STILL DEFENDING THEIR HARSH AND CHEERLESS HILLS.
THE SCHOLAR FOUND SOME WHO'D BEEN YOUNG, THE DAY CONAN LEFT HIS VILLAGE.
THEY CONFIRMED MUCH IN THE TALES OF HIS YOUTH, ADDING TO THEM HERE AND THERE, DETAILS TOLD THEM BY FATHERS AND BROTHERS.
SOME WERE THERE, AS WELL, WHO FOLLOWED WHEN HE LEFT, AT LEAST FOR A TIME.
THEY TOLD THE SCHOLAR THAT WHEN CONAN CRESTED THE HILL THAT TOOK HIM OUT OF SIGHT OF THEIR VILLAGE...

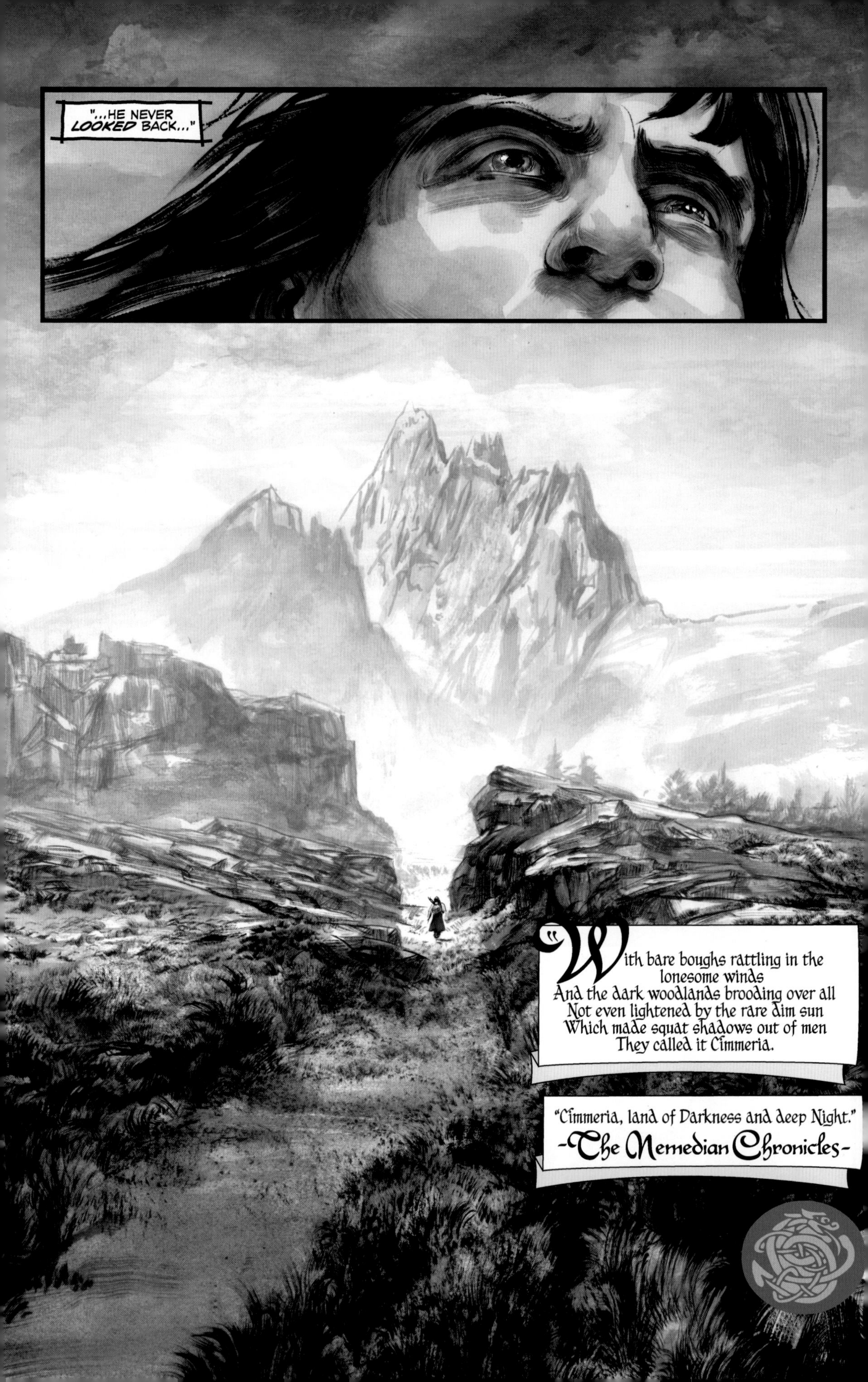
"...HE NEVER LOOKED BACK..."
"With bare boughs rattling in the lonesome winds
And the dark woodlands brooding over all
Not even lightened by the rare dim sun
Which made squat shadows out of men
They called it Cimmeria.
"Cimmeria, land of Darkness and deep Night."
-The Nemedian Chronicles-

PART TWO

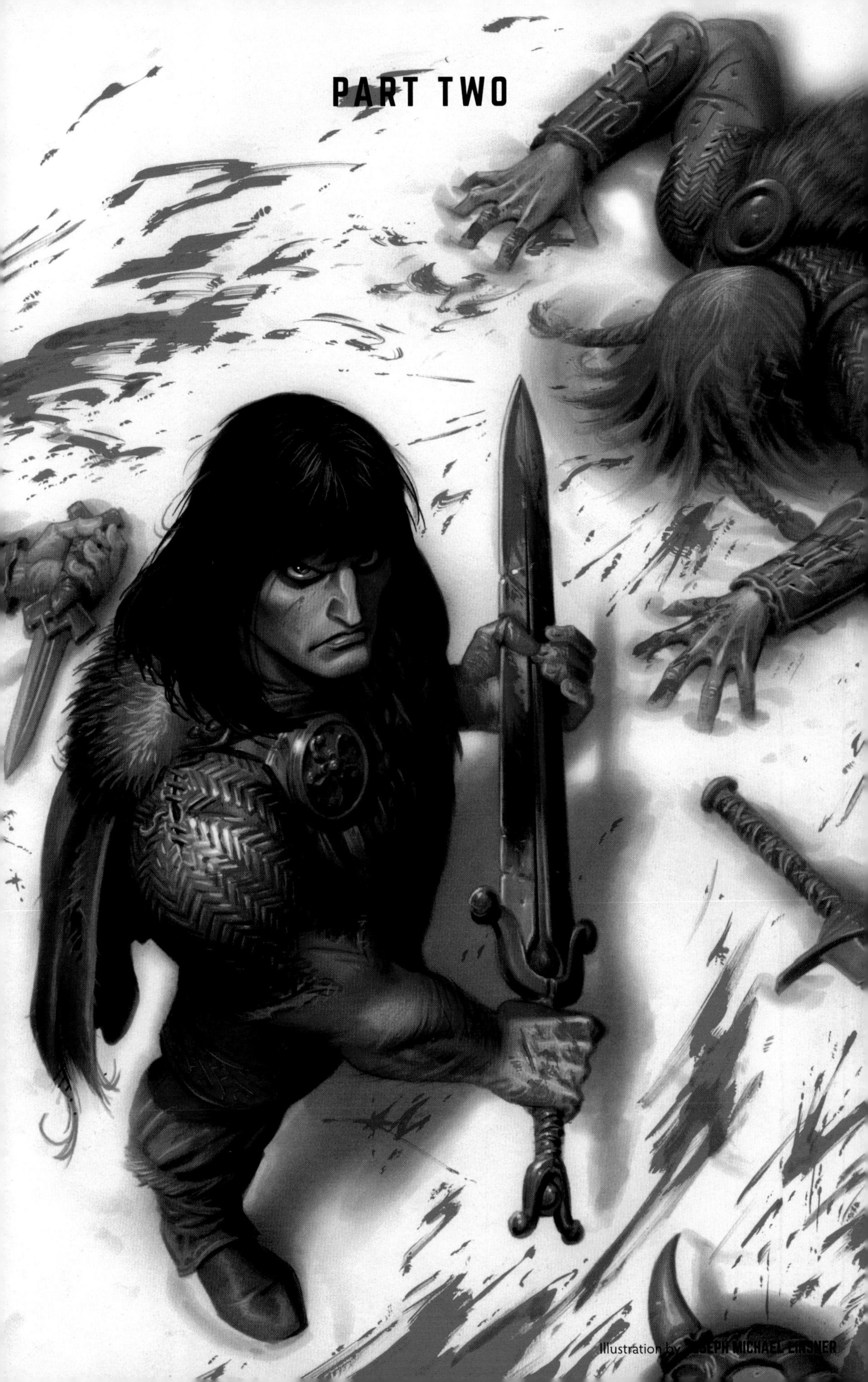

Illustration by JOSEPH MICHAEL LINSNER

THE FROST-GIANT'S DAUGHTER AND OTHER STORIES

SCRIPTS
KURT BUSIEK

ART
CARY NORD
THOMAS YEATES

COLORS
DAVE STEWART

LETTERING
RICHARD STARKINGS
AND **COMICRAFT**

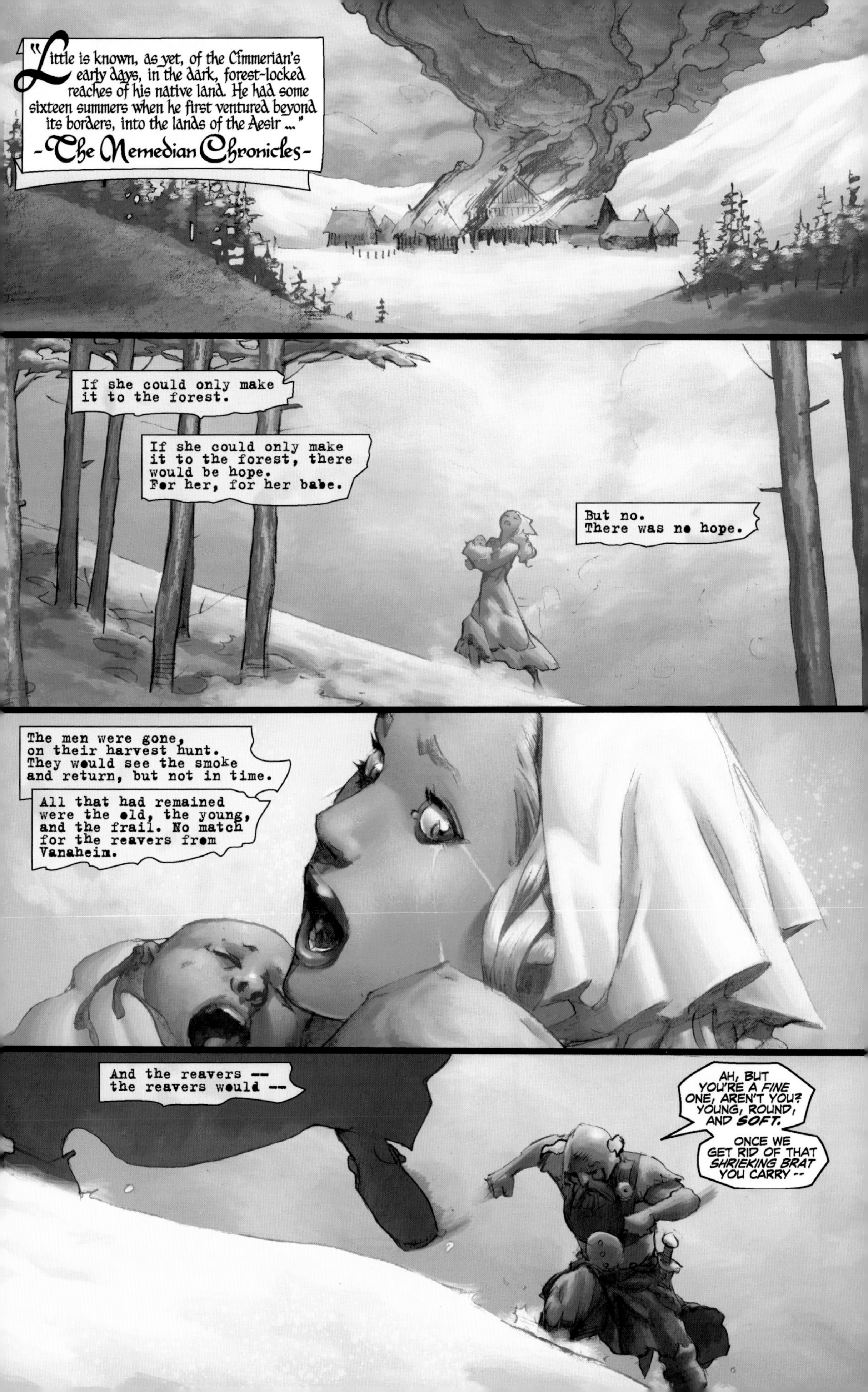
"Little is known, as yet, of the Cimmerian's early days, in the dark, forest-locked reaches of his native land. He had some sixteen summers when he first ventured beyond its borders, into the lands of the Aesir ..."
-The Nemedian Chronicles-
If she could only make it to the forest.
If she could only make it to the forest, there would be hope. For her, for her babe.
But no. There was no hope.
The men were gone, on their harvest hunt. They would see the smoke and return, but not in time.
All that had remained were the old, the young, and the frail. No match for the reavers from Vanaheim.
And the reavers -- the reavers would --
AH, BUT YOU'RE A FINE ONE, AREN'T YOU? YOUNG, ROUND, AND SOFT.
ONCE WE GET RID OF THAT SHRIEKING BRAT YOU CARRY --

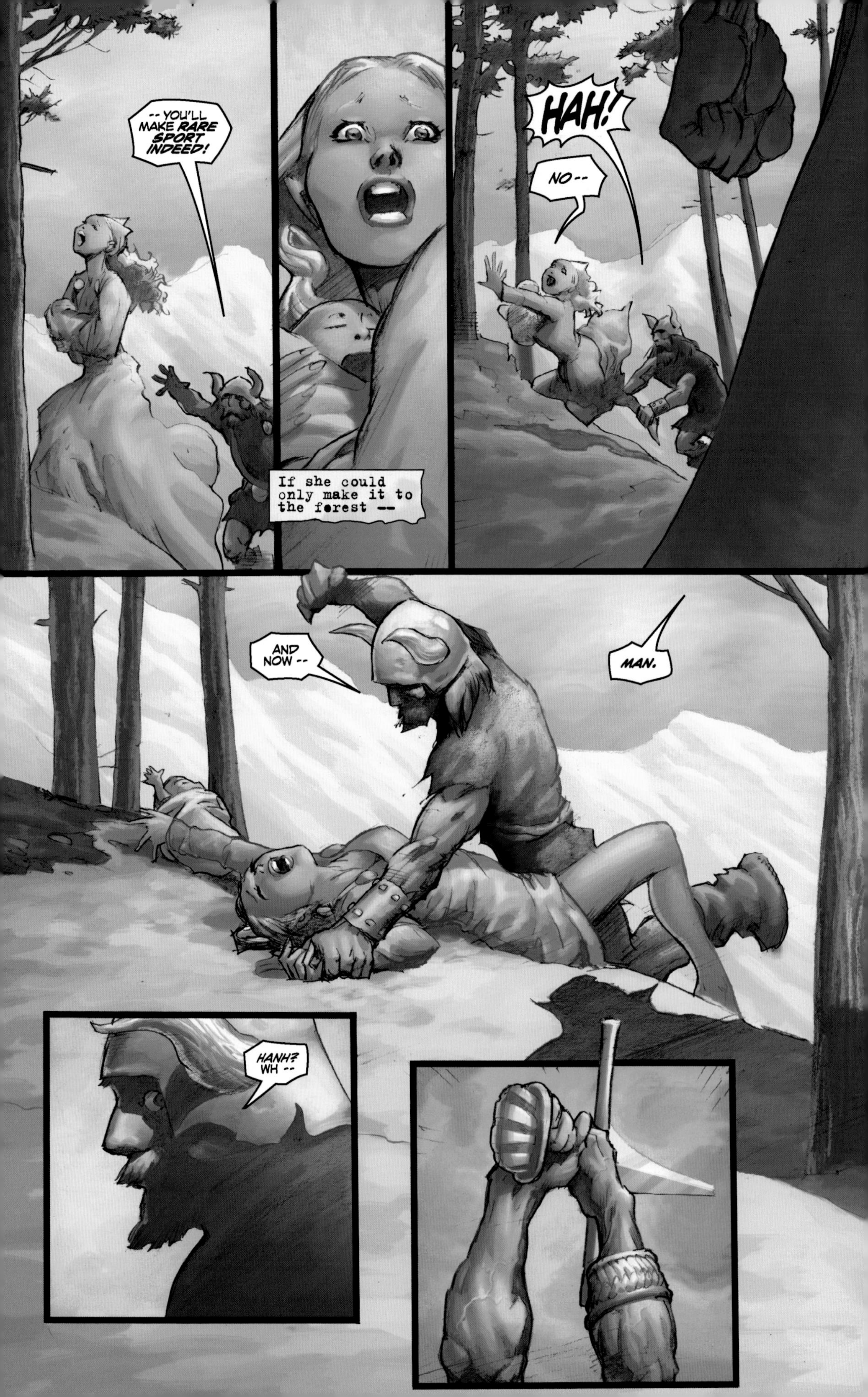
-- YOU'LL MAKE RARE SPORT INDEED!
If she could only make it to the forest --
HAH!
NO --
AND NOW --
MAN.
HANH? WH --

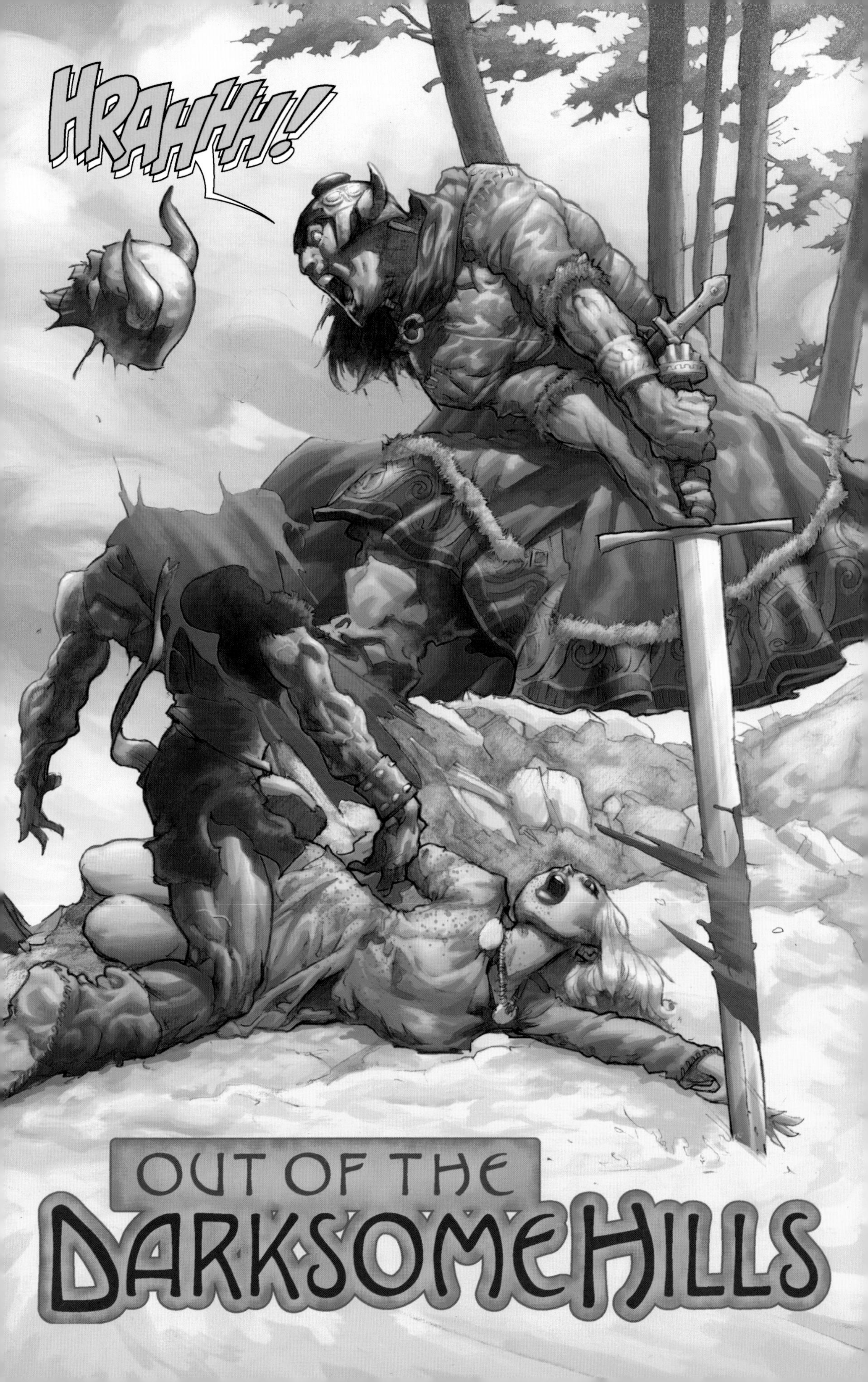
HRAHHH!
OUT OF THE
DARKSOME HILLS

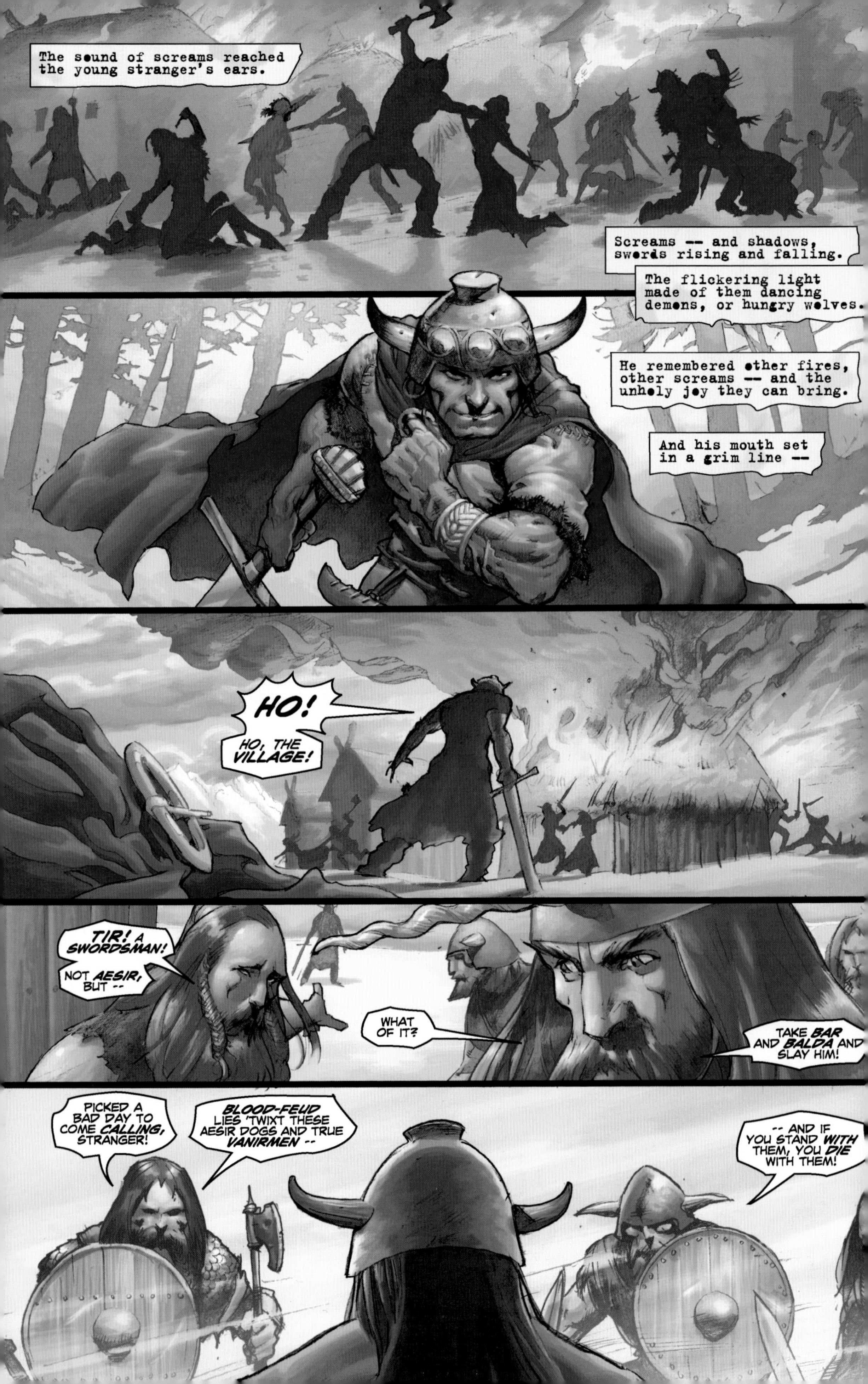
The sound of screams reached the young stranger's ears.
Screams -- and shadows, swords rising and falling.
The flickering light made of them dancing demons, or hungry wolves.
He remembered other fires, other screams -- and the unholy joy they can bring.
And his mouth set in a grim line --
HO!
HO, THE VILLAGE!
TIR! A SWORDSMAN!
NOT AESIR, BUT --
WHAT OF IT?
TAKE BAR AND BALDA AND SLAY HIM!
PICKED A BAD DAY TO COME CALLING, STRANGER!
BLOOD-FEUD LIES 'TWIXT THESE AESIR DOGS AND TRUE VANIRMEN --
-- AND IF YOU STAND WITH THEM, YOU DIE WITH THEM!

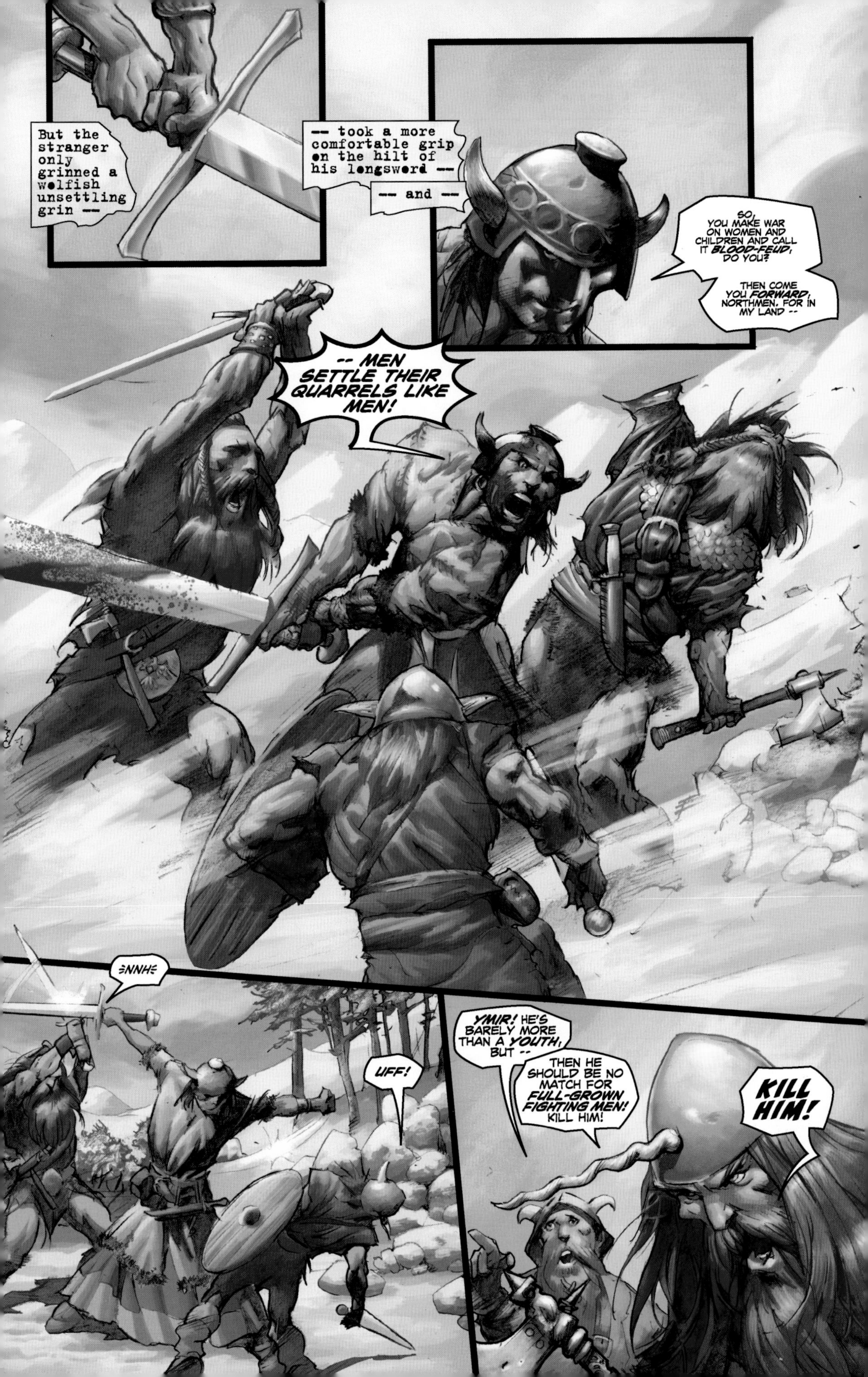

But the stranger only grinned a wolfish unsettling grin --
-- took a more comfortable grip on the hilt of his longsword --
-- and --
SO, YOU MAKE WAR ON WOMEN AND CHILDREN AND CALL IT BLOOD-FEUD, DO YOU?
THEN COME YOU FORWARD, NORTHMEN, FOR IN MY LAND --
-- MEN SETTLE THEIR QUARRELS LIKE MEN!
NNH
UFF!
YMIR! HE'S BARELY MORE THAN A YOUTH, BUT --
THEN HE SHOULD BE NO MATCH FOR FULL-GROWN FIGHTING MEN! KILL HIM!
KILL HIM!

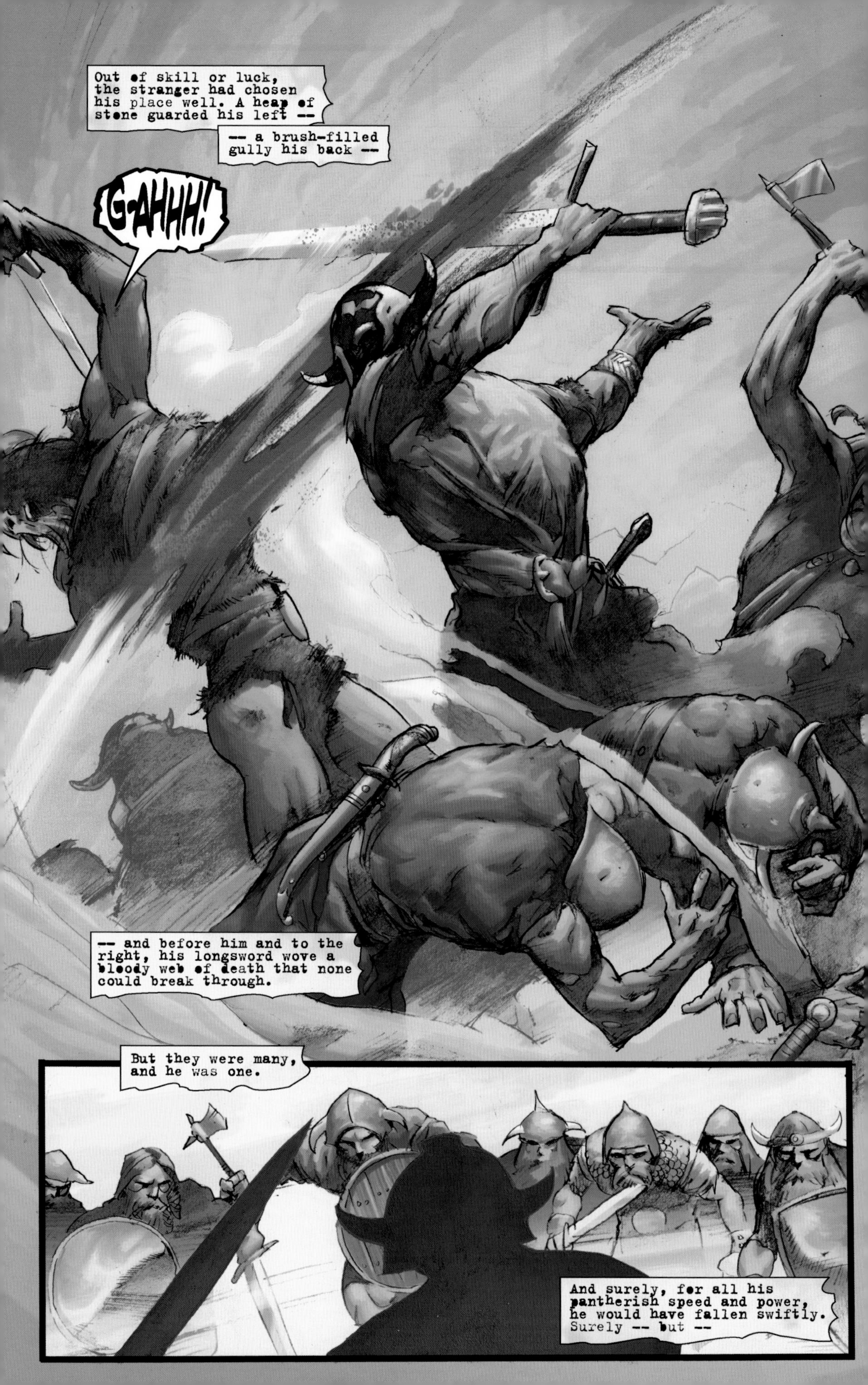
Out of skill or luck, the stranger had chosen his place well. A heap of stone guarded his left --
-- a brush-filled gully his back --
G-AHHH!
-- and before him and to the right, his longsword wove a bloody web of death that none could break through.
But they were many, and he was one.
And surely, for all his pantherish speed and power, he would have fallen swiftly. Surely -- but --

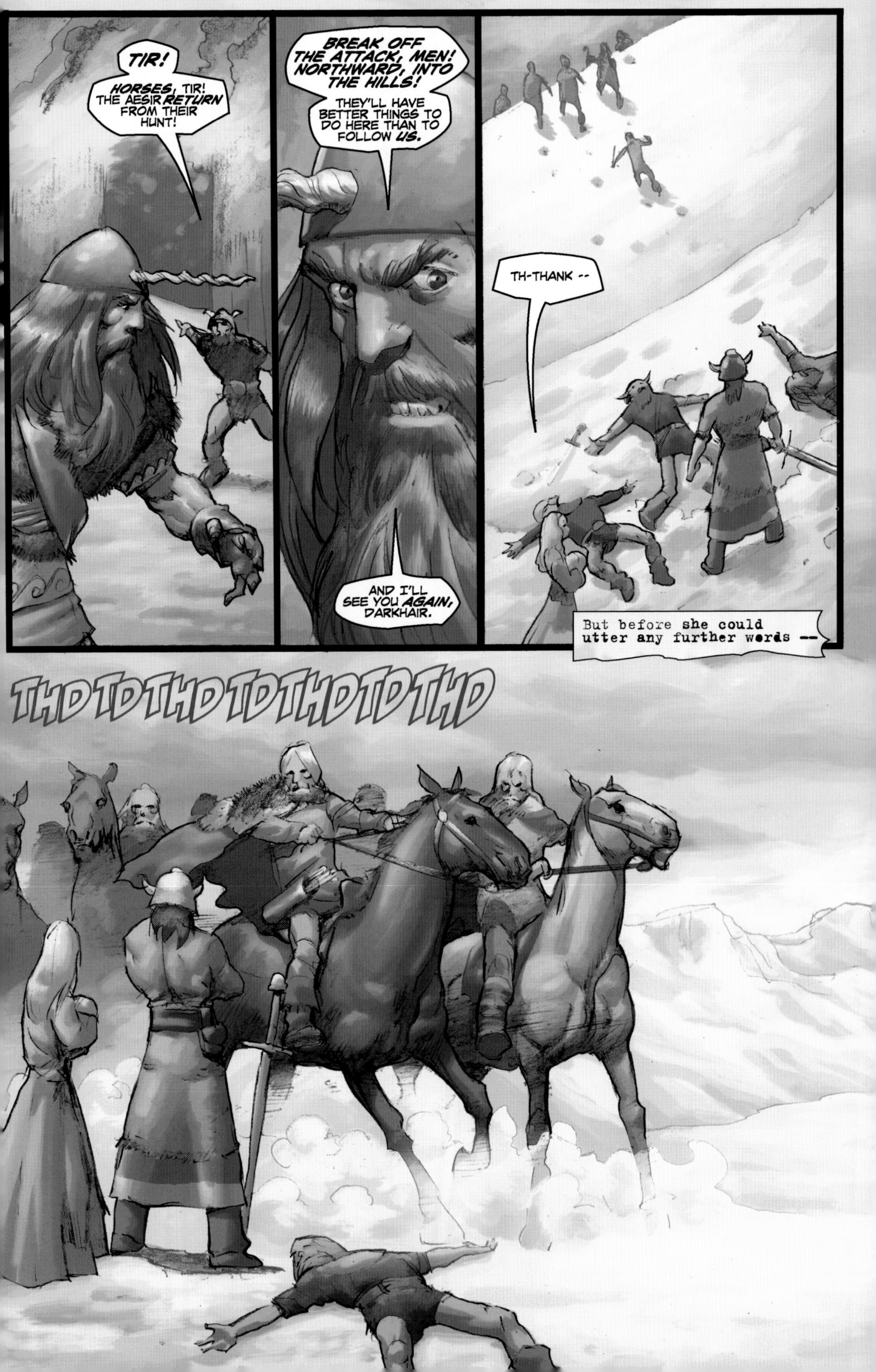
TIR!
HORSES, TIR! THE AESIR RETURN FROM THEIR HUNT!
BREAK OFF THE ATTACK, MEN! NORTHWARD, INTO THE HILLS!
THEY'LL HAVE BETTER THINGS TO DO HERE THAN TO FOLLOW US.
AND I'LL SEE YOU AGAIN, DARKHAIR.
TH-THANK --
But before she could utter any further words --
THDTDTHDTDTHDTDTHD

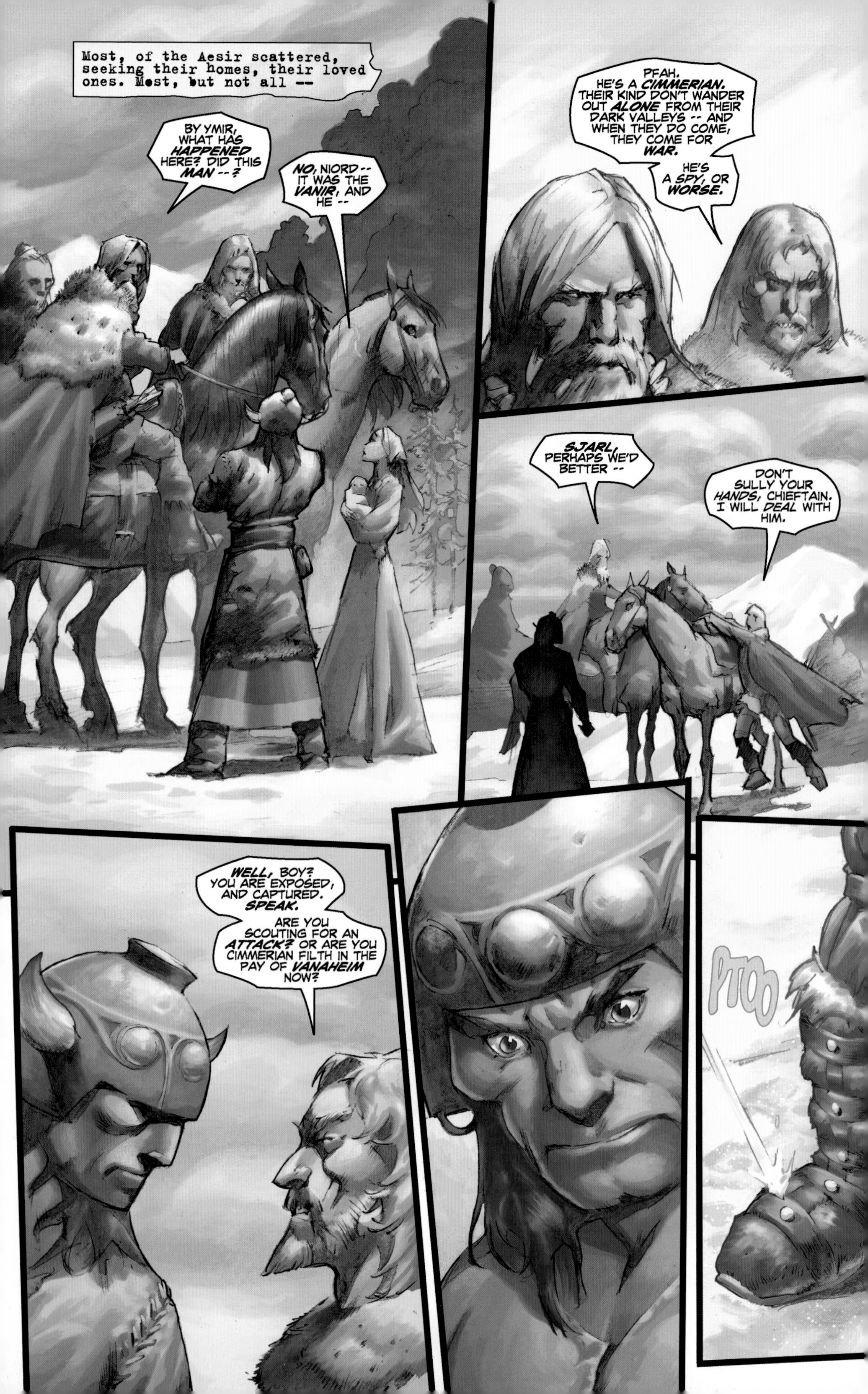
Most, of the Aesir scattered, seeking their homes, their loved ones. Most, but not all --
BY YMIR, WHAT HAS HAPPENED HERE? DID THIS MAN -- ?
NO, NIORD -- IT WAS THE VANIR, AND HE --
PFAH. HE'S A CIMMERIAN. THEIR KIND DON'T WANDER OUT ALONE FROM THEIR DARK VALLEYS -- AND WHEN THEY DO COME, THEY COME FOR WAR.
HE'S A SPY, OR WORSE.
SJARL, PERHAPS WE'D BETTER --
DON'T SULLY YOUR HANDS, CHIEFTAIN. I WILL DEAL WITH HIM.
WELL, BOY? YOU ARE EXPOSED, AND CAPTURED. SPEAK.
ARE YOU SCOUTING FOR AN ATTACK? OR ARE YOU CIMMERIAN FILTH IN THE PAY OF VANAHEIM NOW?
PTOO

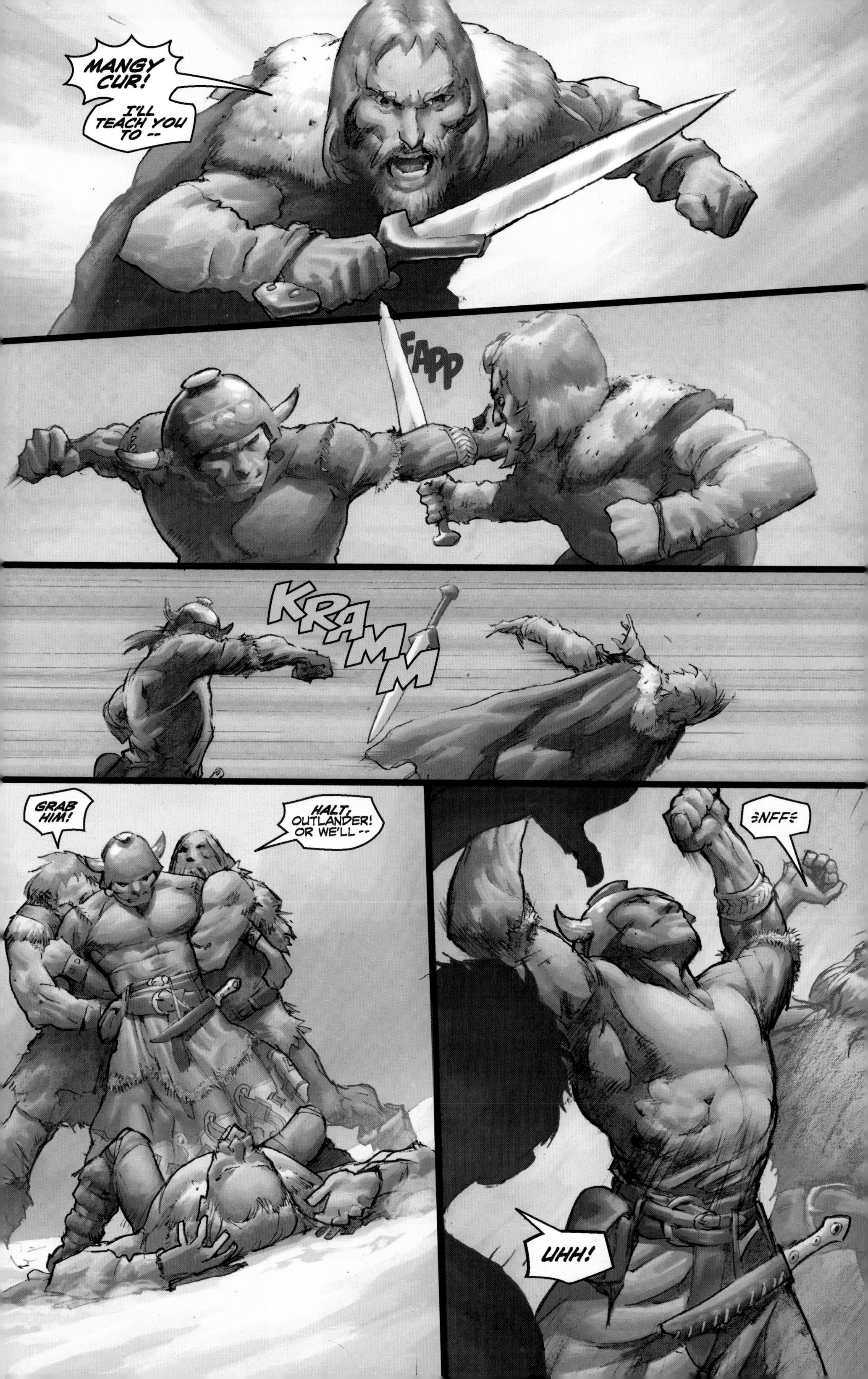
MANGY CUR!
I'LL TEACH YOU TO --
FAPP
KRAMMM
GRAB HIM!
HALT, OUTLANDER! OR WE'LL --
NFF
UHH!

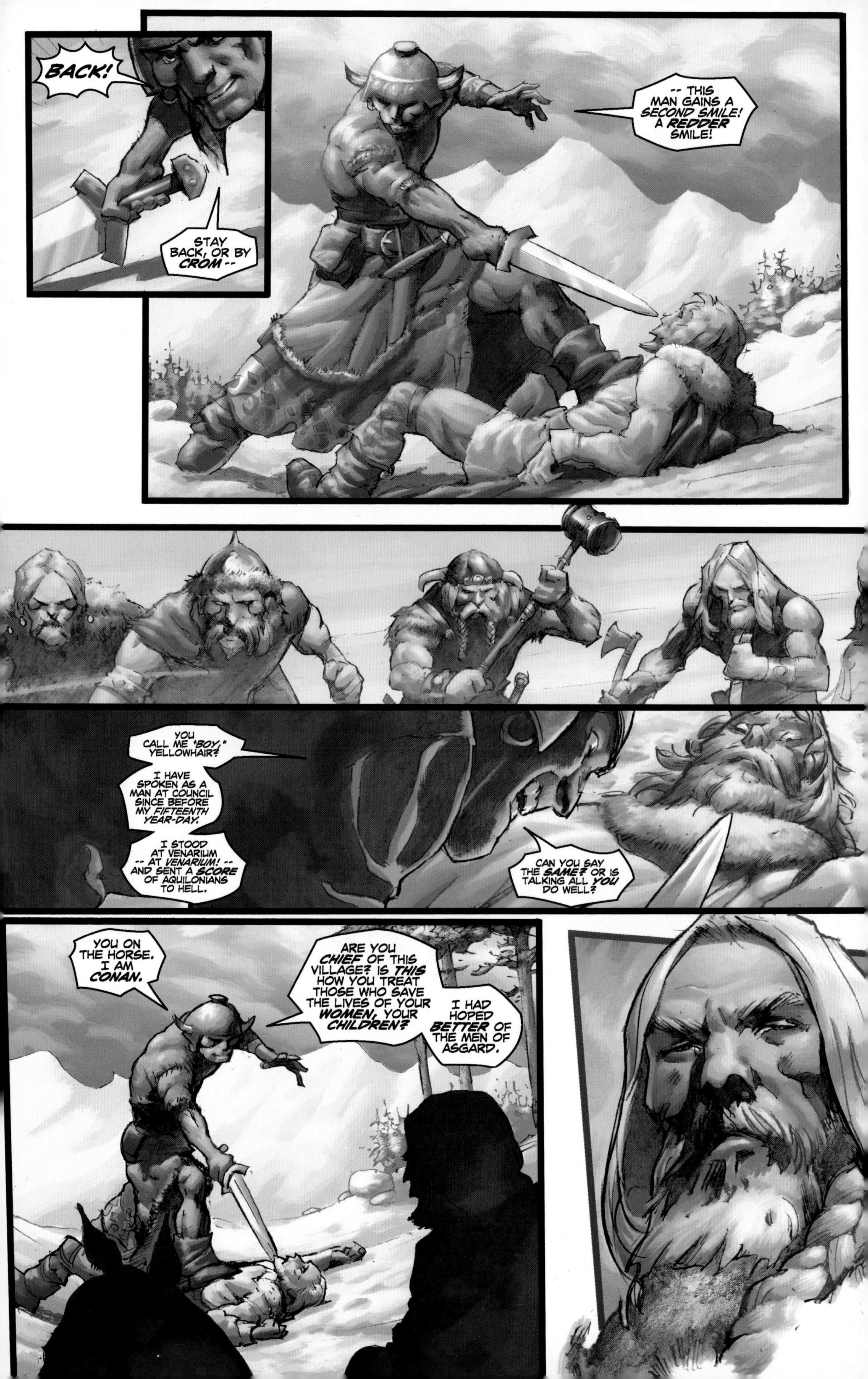
BACK!
STAY BACK, OR BY CROM --
-- THIS MAN GAINS A SECOND SMILE! A REDDER SMILE!
YOU CALL ME "BOY," YELLOWHAIR?
I HAVE SPOKEN AS A MAN AT COUNCIL SINCE BEFORE MY FIFTEENTH YEAR-DAY.
I STOOD AT VENARIUM -- AT VENARIUM! -- AND SENT A SCORE OF AQUILONIANS TO HELL.
CAN YOU SAY THE SAME? OR IS TALKING ALL YOU DO WELL?
YOU ON THE HORSE. I AM CONAN.
ARE YOU CHIEF OF THIS VILLAGE? IS THIS HOW YOU TREAT THOSE WHO SAVE THE LIVES OF YOUR WOMEN, YOUR CHILDREN?
I HAD HOPED BETTER OF THE MEN OF ASGARD.

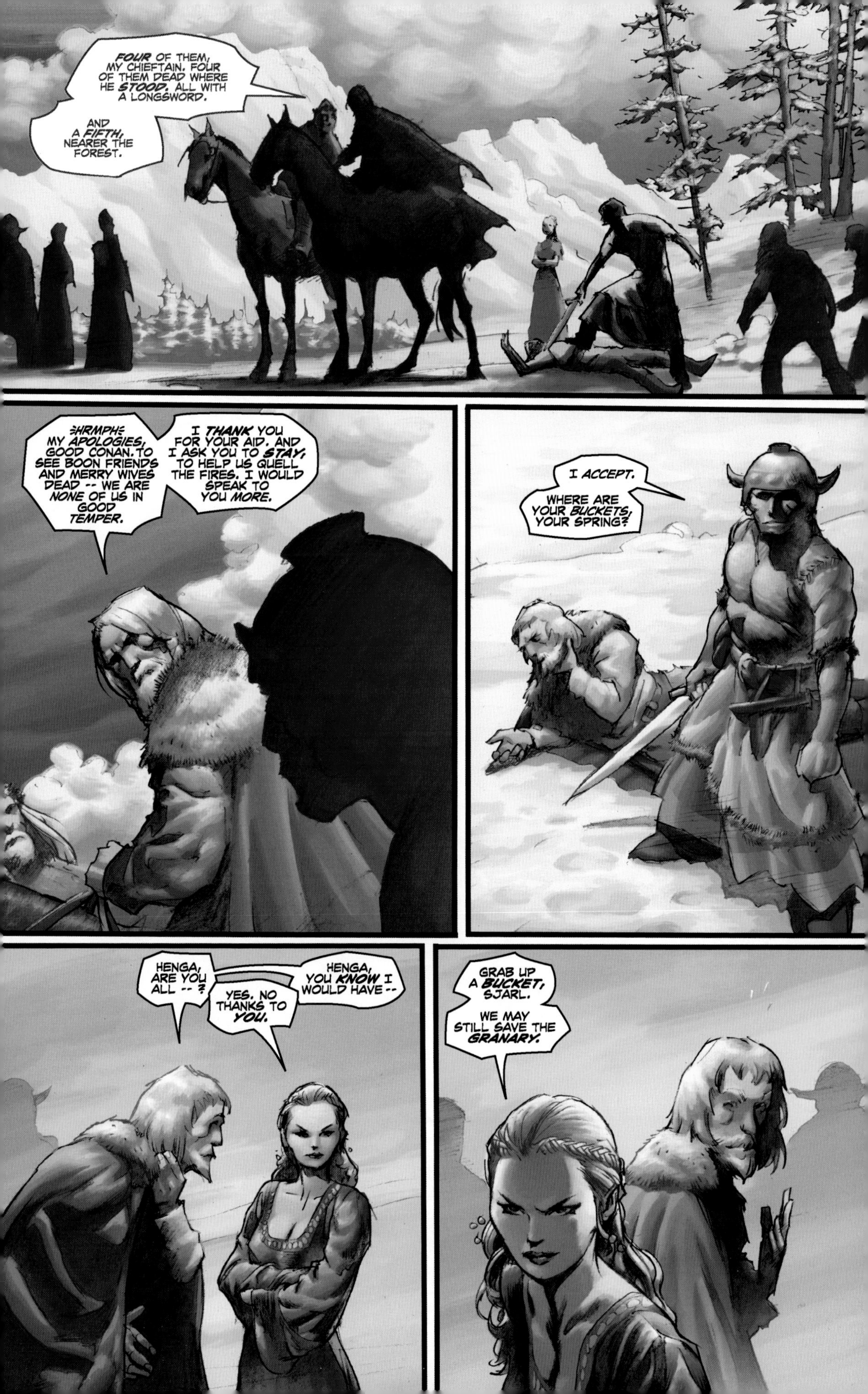

FOUR OF THEM, MY CHIEFTAIN. FOUR OF THEM DEAD WHERE HE STOOD. ALL WITH A LONGSWORD.
AND A FIFTH, NEARER THE FOREST.
HRMPH
MY APOLOGIES, GOOD CONAN. TO SEE BOON FRIENDS AND MERRY WIVES DEAD -- WE ARE NONE OF US IN GOOD TEMPER.
I THANK YOU FOR YOUR AID. AND I ASK YOU TO STAY; TO HELP US QUELL THE FIRES. I WOULD SPEAK TO YOU MORE.
I ACCEPT.
WHERE ARE YOUR BUCKETS, YOUR SPRING?
HENGA, ARE YOU ALL -- ?
YES. NO THANKS TO YOU.
HENGA, YOU KNOW I WOULD HAVE --
GRAB UP A BUCKET, SJARL.
WE MAY STILL SAVE THE GRANARY.

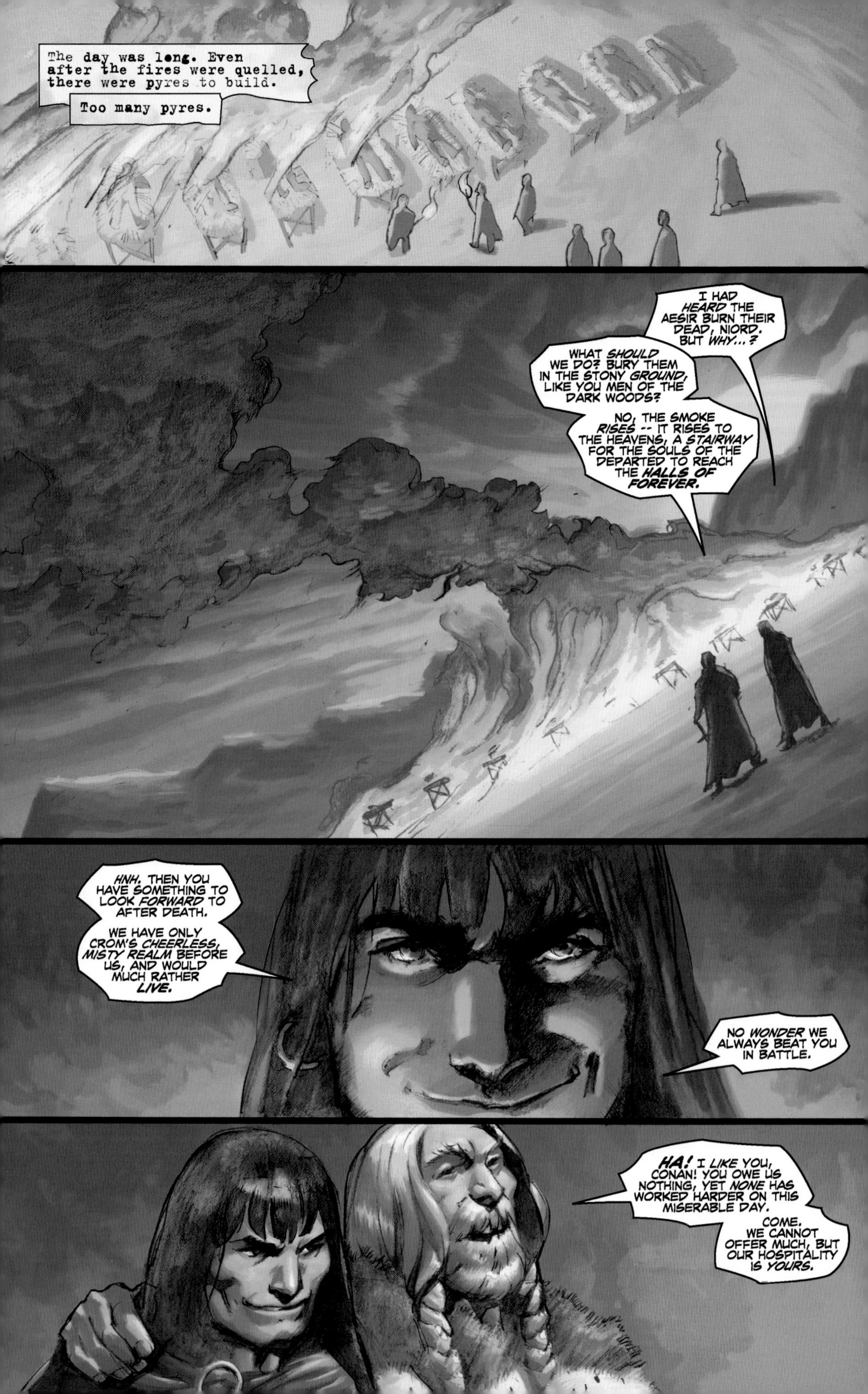
The day was long. Even after the fires were quelled, there were pyres to build.
Too many pyres.
I HAD HEARD THE AESIR BURN THEIR DEAD, NIORD. BUT WHY...?
WHAT SHOULD WE DO? BURY THEM IN THE STONY GROUND, LIKE YOU MEN OF THE DARK WOODS?
NO, THE SMOKE RISES -- IT RISES TO THE HEAVENS, A STAIRWAY FOR THE SOULS OF THE DEPARTED TO REACH THE HALLS OF FOREVER.
HNH. THEN YOU HAVE SOMETHING TO LOOK FORWARD TO AFTER DEATH.
WE HAVE ONLY CROM'S CHEERLESS, MISTY REALM BEFORE US, AND WOULD MUCH RATHER LIVE.
NO WONDER WE ALWAYS BEAT YOU IN BATTLE.
HA! I LIKE YOU, CONAN! YOU OWE US NOTHING, YET NONE HAS WORKED HARDER ON THIS MISERABLE DAY.
COME. WE CANNOT OFFER MUCH, BUT OUR HOSPITALITY IS YOURS.

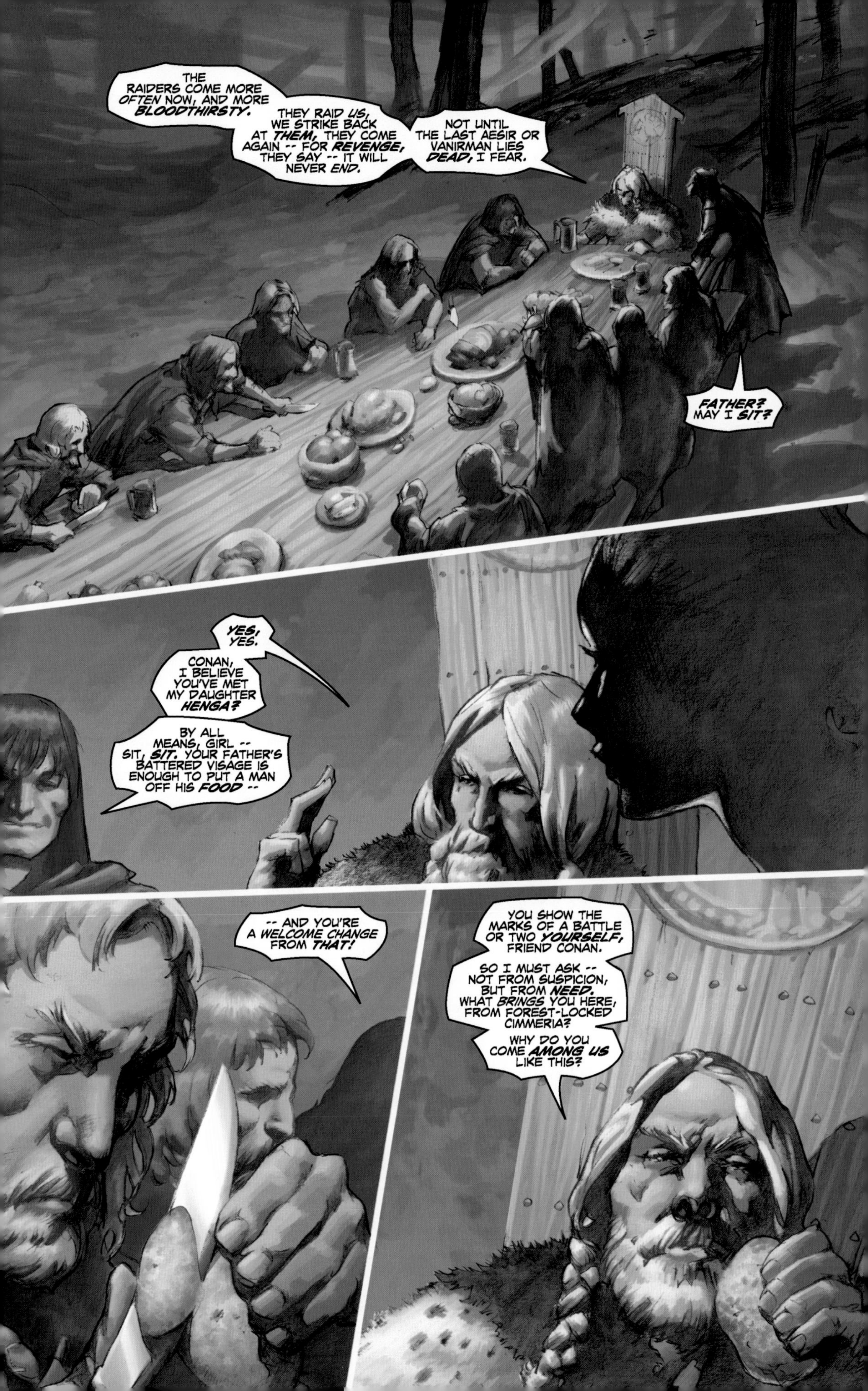
THE RAIDERS COME MORE OFTEN NOW, AND MORE BLOODTHIRSTY.
THEY RAID US, WE STRIKE BACK AT THEM, THEY COME AGAIN -- FOR REVENGE, THEY SAY -- IT WILL NEVER END.
NOT UNTIL THE LAST AESIR OR VANIRMAN LIES DEAD, I FEAR.
FATHER? MAY I SIT?
YES, YES.
CONAN, I BELIEVE YOU'VE MET MY DAUGHTER HENGA?
BY ALL MEANS, GIRL -- SIT, SIT. YOUR FATHER'S BATTERED VISAGE IS ENOUGH TO PUT A MAN OFF HIS FOOD --
-- AND YOU'RE A WELCOME CHANGE FROM THAT!
YOU SHOW THE MARKS OF A BATTLE OR TWO YOURSELF, FRIEND CONAN.
SO I MUST ASK -- NOT FROM SUSPICION, BUT FROM NEED. WHAT BRINGS YOU HERE, FROM FOREST-LOCKED CIMMERIA?
WHY DO YOU COME AMONG US LIKE THIS?

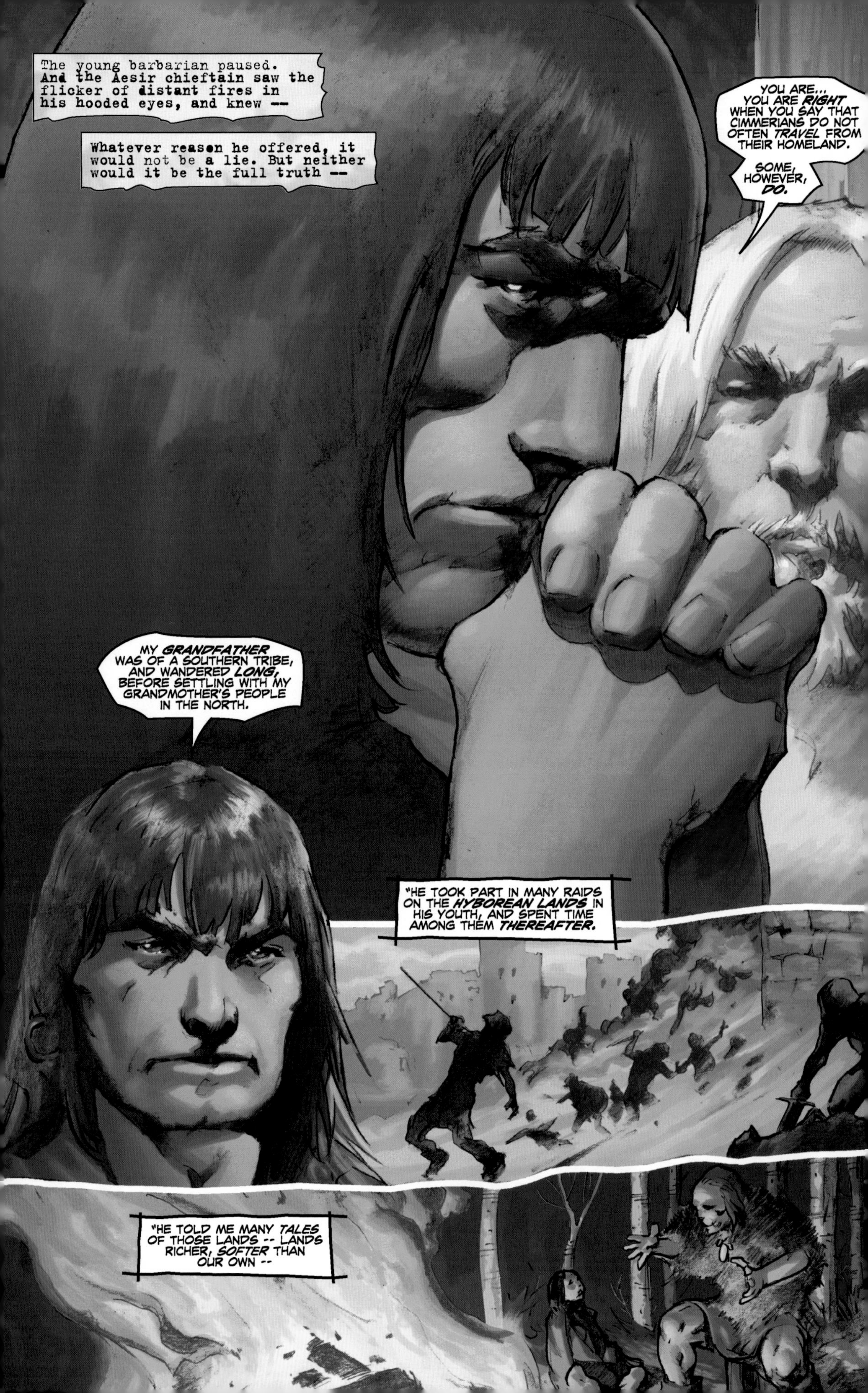

The young barbarian paused. And the Aesir chieftain saw the flicker of distant fires in his hooded eyes, and knew --
Whatever reason he offered, it would not be a lie. But neither would it be the full truth --
YOU ARE... YOU ARE RIGHT WHEN YOU SAY THAT CIMMERIANS DO NOT OFTEN TRAVEL FROM THEIR HOMELAND.
SOME, HOWEVER, DO.
MY GRANDFATHER WAS OF A SOUTHERN TRIBE, AND WANDERED LONG, BEFORE SETTLING WITH MY GRANDMOTHER'S PEOPLE IN THE NORTH.
"HE TOOK PART IN MANY RAIDS ON THE HYBOREAN LANDS IN HIS YOUTH, AND SPENT TIME AMONG THEM THEREAFTER.
"HE TOLD ME MANY TALES OF THOSE LANDS -- LANDS RICHER, SOFTER THAN OUR OWN --

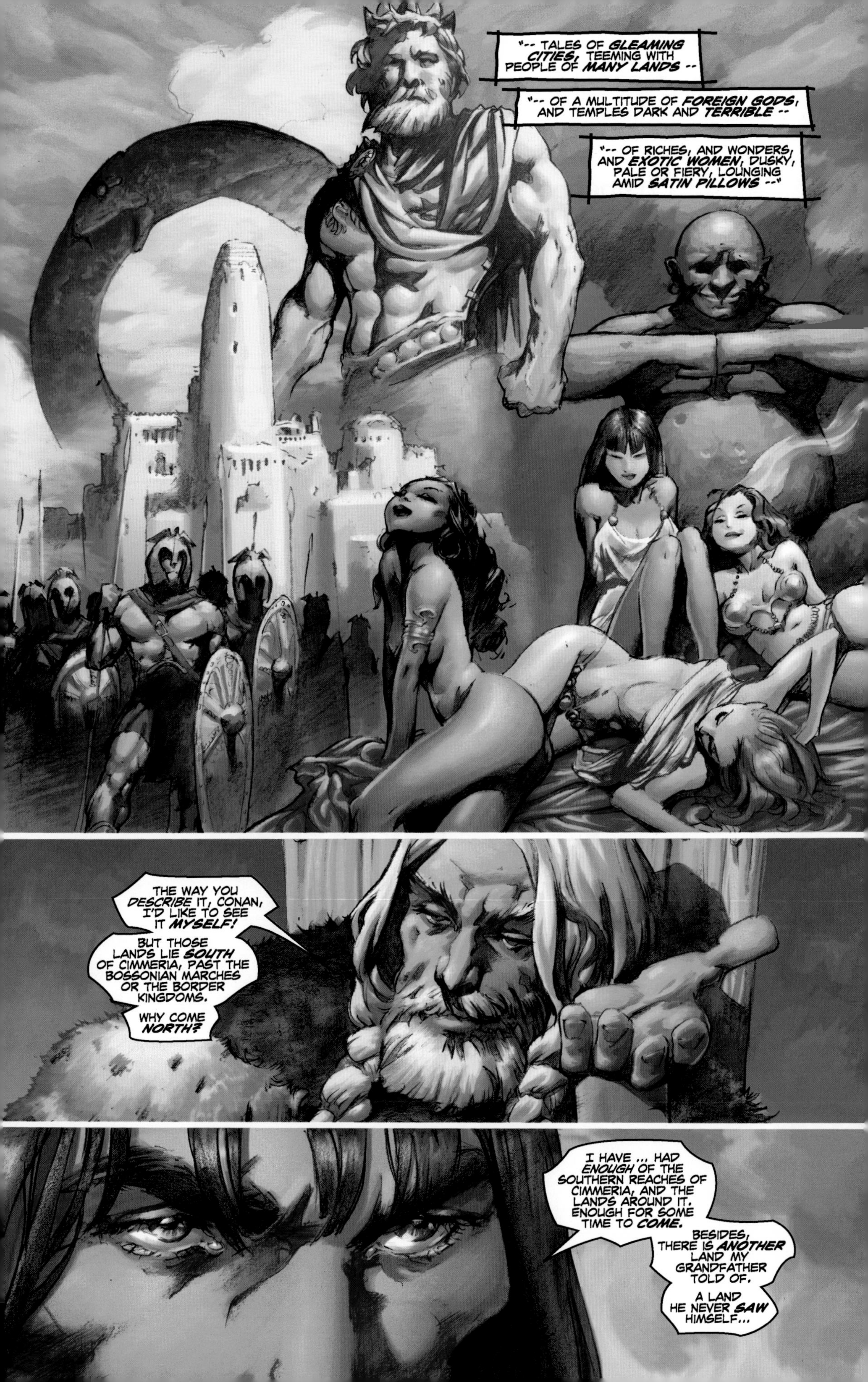
"-- TALES OF GLEAMING CITIES, TEEMING WITH PEOPLE OF MANY LANDS --
"-- OF A MULTITUDE OF FOREIGN GODS, AND TEMPLES DARK AND TERRIBLE --
"-- OF RICHES, AND WONDERS, AND EXOTIC WOMEN, DUSKY, PALE OR FIERY, LOUNGING AMID SATIN PILLOWS --"
THE WAY YOU DESCRIBE IT, CONAN, I'D LIKE TO SEE IT MYSELF!
BUT THOSE LANDS LIE SOUTH OF CIMMERIA, PAST THE BOSSONIAN MARCHES OR THE BORDER KINGDOMS.
WHY COME NORTH?
I HAVE ... HAD ENOUGH OF THE SOUTHERN REACHES OF CIMMERIA, AND THE LANDS AROUND IT. ENOUGH FOR SOME TIME TO COME.
BESIDES, THERE IS ANOTHER LAND MY GRANDFATHER TOLD OF.
A LAND HE NEVER SAW HIMSELF...

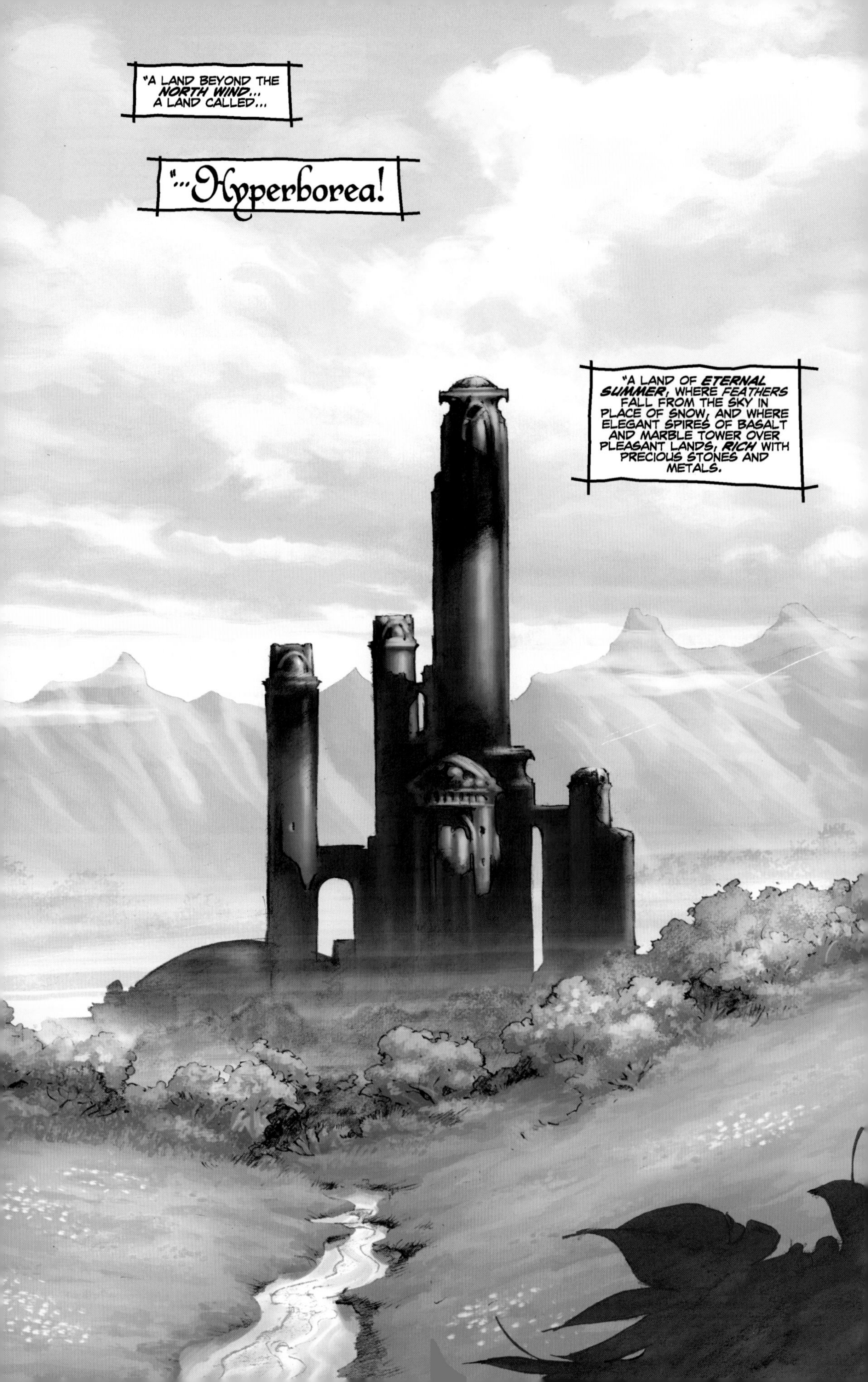
"A LAND BEYOND THE NORTH WIND... A LAND CALLED...
"...Hyperborea!
"A LAND OF ETERNAL SUMMER, WHERE FEATHERS FALL FROM THE SKY IN PLACE OF SNOW, AND WHERE ELEGANT SPIRES OF BASALT AND MARBLE TOWER OVER PLEASANT LANDS, RICH WITH PRECIOUS STONES AND METALS.

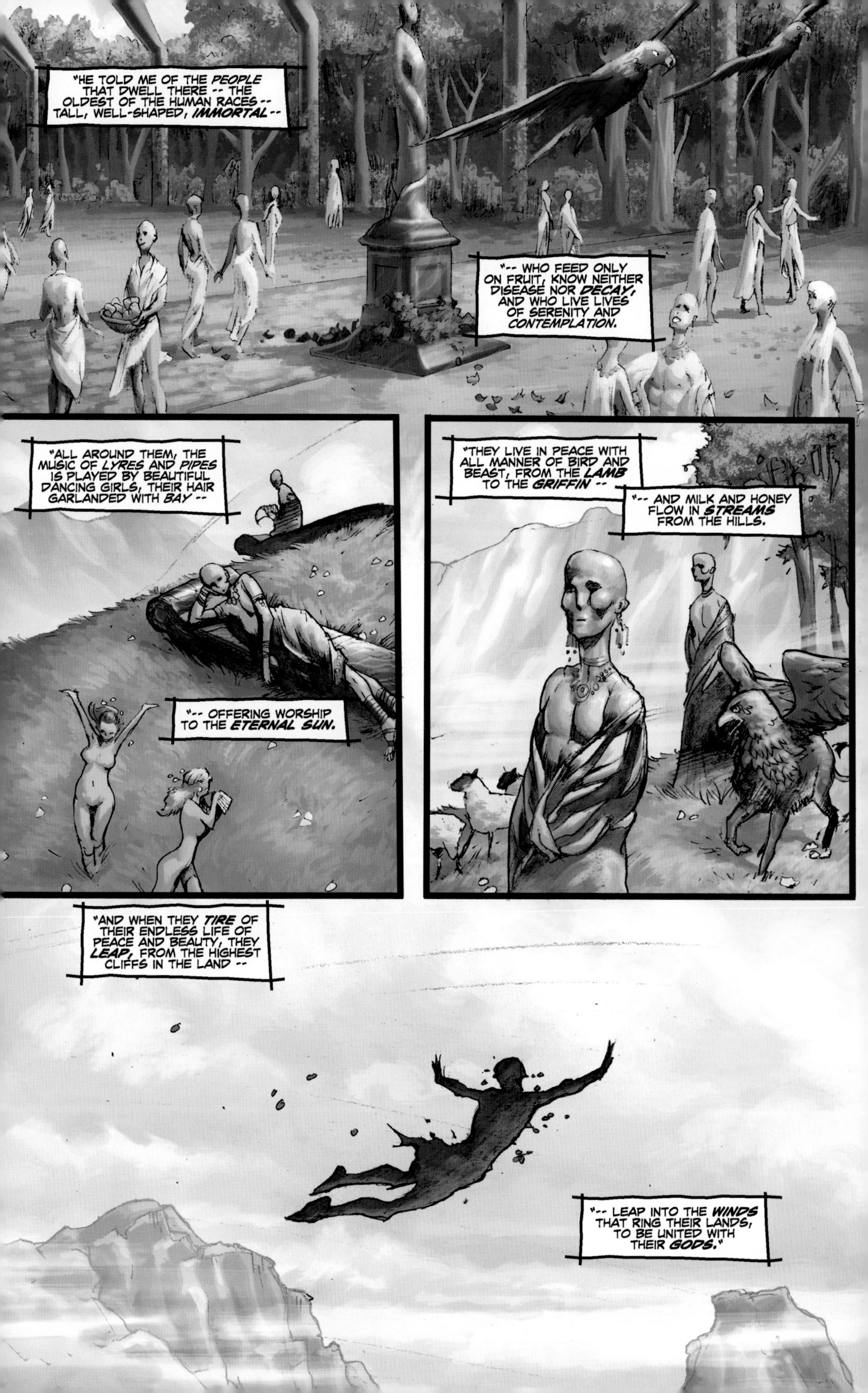
"HE TOLD ME OF THE PEOPLE THAT DWELL THERE -- THE OLDEST OF THE HUMAN RACES -- TALL, WELL-SHAPED, IMMORTAL --
"-- WHO FEED ONLY ON FRUIT, KNOW NEITHER DISEASE NOR DECAY, AND WHO LIVE LIVES OF SERENITY AND CONTEMPLATION.
"ALL AROUND THEM, THE MUSIC OF LYRES AND PIPES IS PLAYED BY BEAUTIFUL DANCING GIRLS, THEIR HAIR GARLANDED WITH BAY --
"-- OFFERING WORSHIP TO THE ETERNAL SUN.
"THEY LIVE IN PEACE WITH ALL MANNER OF BIRD AND BEAST, FROM THE LAMB TO THE GRIFFIN --
"-- AND MILK AND HONEY FLOW IN STREAMS FROM THE HILLS.
"AND WHEN THEY TIRE OF THEIR ENDLESS LIFE OF PEACE AND BEAUTY, THEY LEAP, FROM THE HIGHEST CLIFFS IN THE LAND --
"-- LEAP INTO THE WINDS THAT RING THEIR LANDS, TO BE UNITED WITH THEIR GODS."

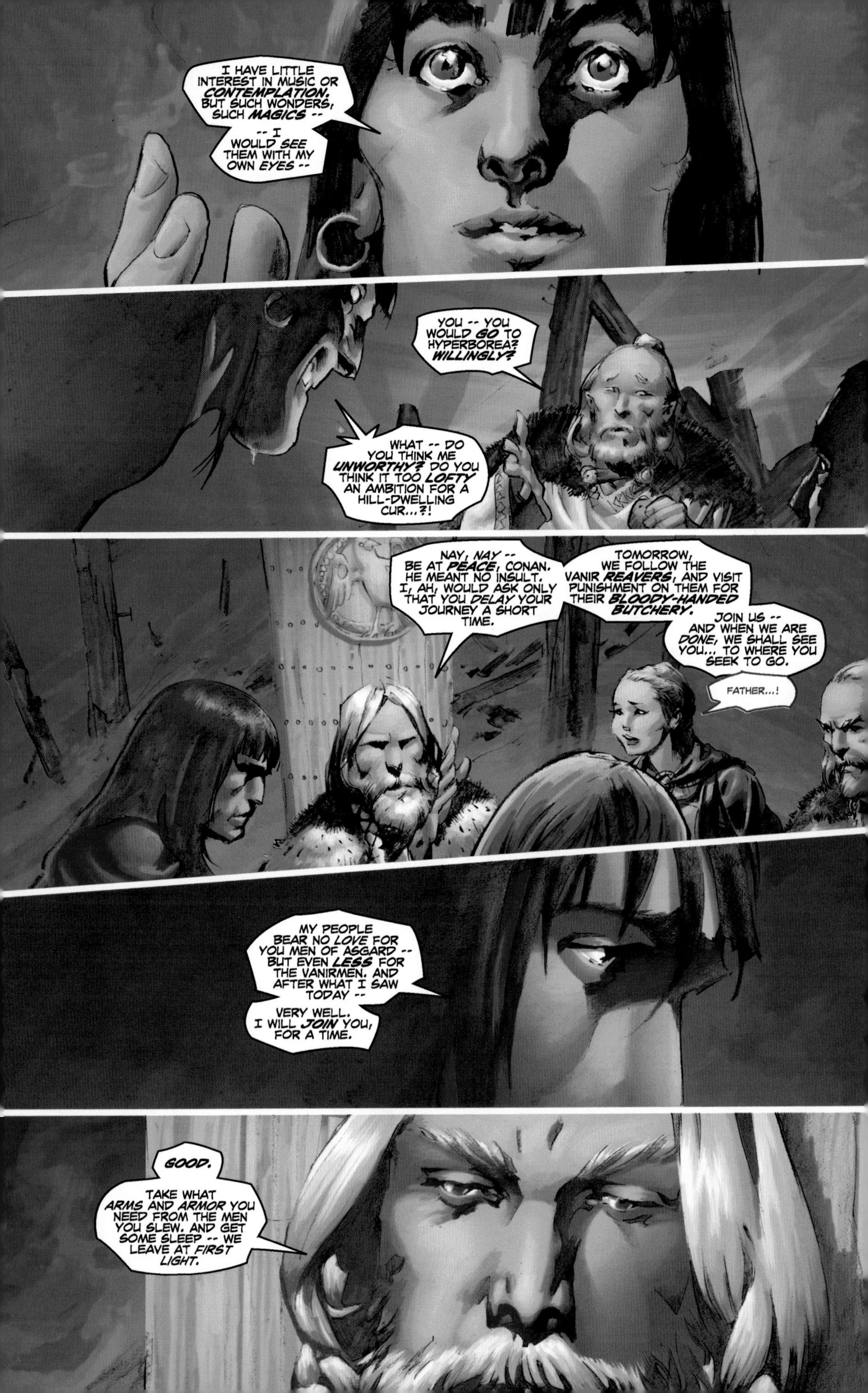
I HAVE LITTLE INTEREST IN MUSIC OR CONTEMPLATION. BUT SUCH WONDERS, SUCH MAGICS --
-- I WOULD SEE THEM WITH MY OWN EYES --
YOU -- YOU WOULD GO TO HYPERBOREA? WILLINGLY?
WHAT -- DO YOU THINK ME UNWORTHY? DO YOU THINK IT TOO LOFTY AN AMBITION FOR A HILL-DWELLING CUR...?!
NAY, NAY -- BE AT PEACE, CONAN. HE MEANT NO INSULT. I, AH, WOULD ASK ONLY THAT YOU DELAY YOUR JOURNEY A SHORT TIME.
TOMORROW, WE FOLLOW THE VANIR REAVERS, AND VISIT PUNISHMENT ON THEM FOR THEIR BLOODY-HANDED BUTCHERY.
JOIN US -- AND WHEN WE ARE DONE, WE SHALL SEE YOU... TO WHERE YOU SEEK TO GO.
FATHER...!
MY PEOPLE BEAR NO LOVE FOR YOU MEN OF ASGARD -- BUT EVEN LESS FOR THE VANIRMEN. AND AFTER WHAT I SAW TODAY --
VERY WELL. I WILL JOIN YOU, FOR A TIME.
GOOD.
TAKE WHAT ARMS AND ARMOR YOU NEED FROM THE MEN YOU SLEW. AND GET SOME SLEEP -- WE LEAVE AT FIRST LIGHT.

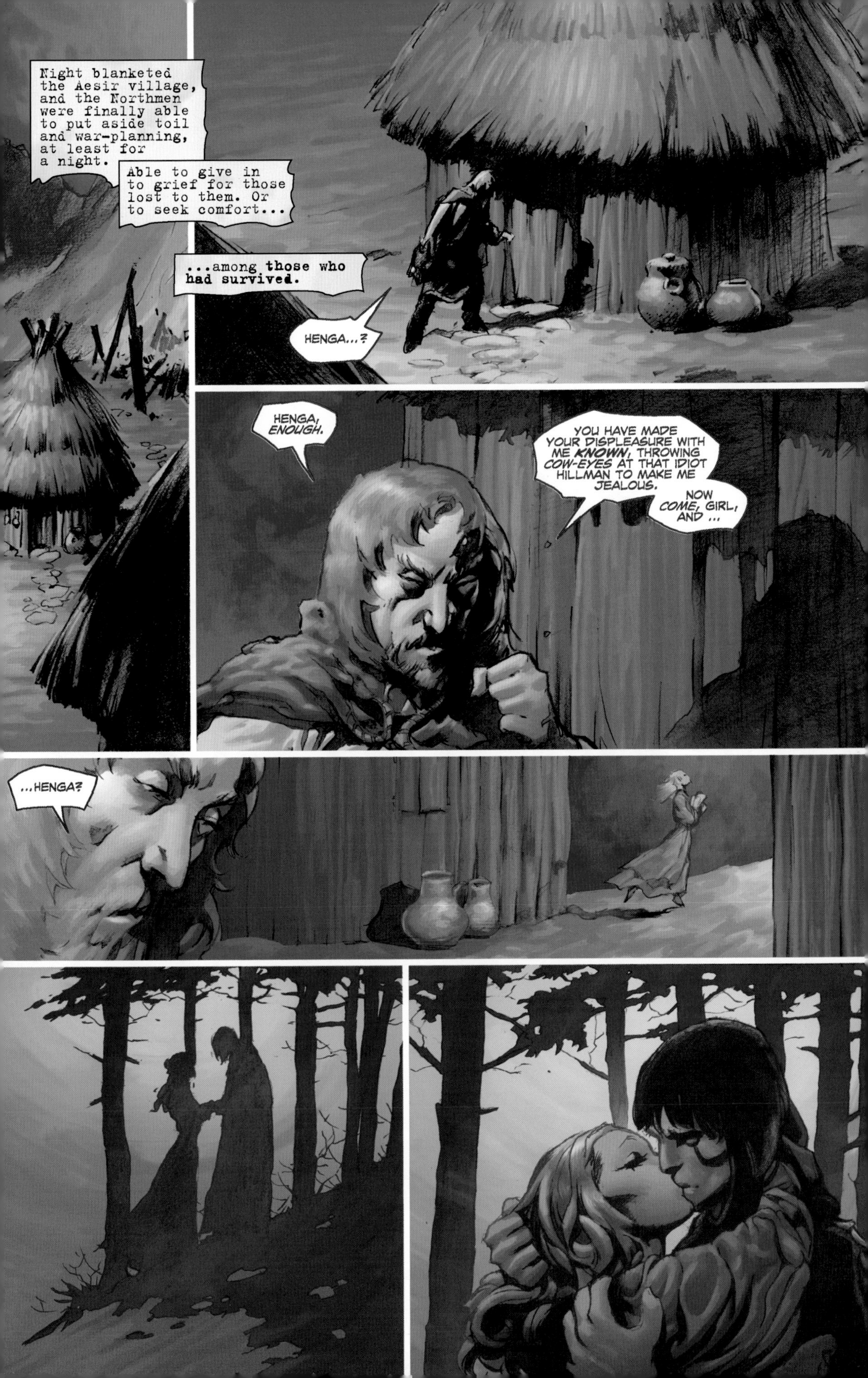
Night blanketed the Aesir village, and the Northmen were finally able to put aside toil and war-planning, at least for a night.
Able to give in to grief for those lost to them. Or to seek comfort...
...among those who had survived.
HENGA...?
HENGA, ENOUGH.
YOU HAVE MADE YOUR DISPLEASURE WITH ME KNOWN, THROWING COW-EYES AT THAT IDIOT HILLMAN TO MAKE ME JEALOUS.
NOW COME, GIRL, AND ...
...HENGA?

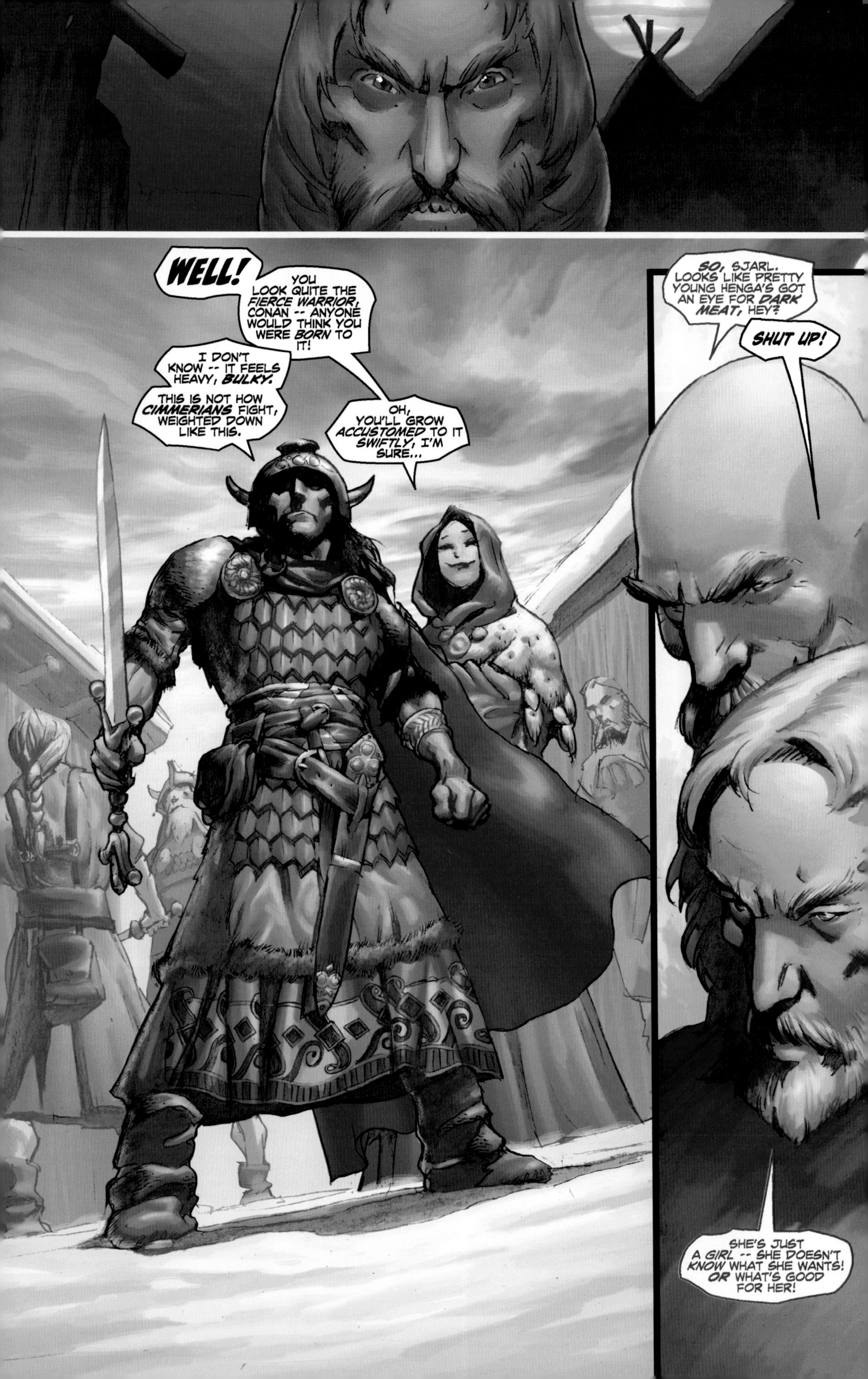
WELL!
YOU LOOK QUITE THE FIERCE WARRIOR, CONAN -- ANYONE WOULD THINK YOU WERE BORN TO IT!
I DON'T KNOW -- IT FEELS HEAVY, BULKY.
THIS IS NOT HOW CIMMERIANS FIGHT, WEIGHTED DOWN LIKE THIS.
OH, YOU'LL GROW ACCUSTOMED TO IT SWIFTLY, I'M SURE...
SO, SJARL. LOOKS LIKE PRETTY YOUNG HENGA'S GOT AN EYE FOR DARK MEAT, HEY?
SHUT UP!
SHE'S JUST A GIRL -- SHE DOESN'T KNOW WHAT SHE WANTS! OR WHAT'S GOOD FOR HER!

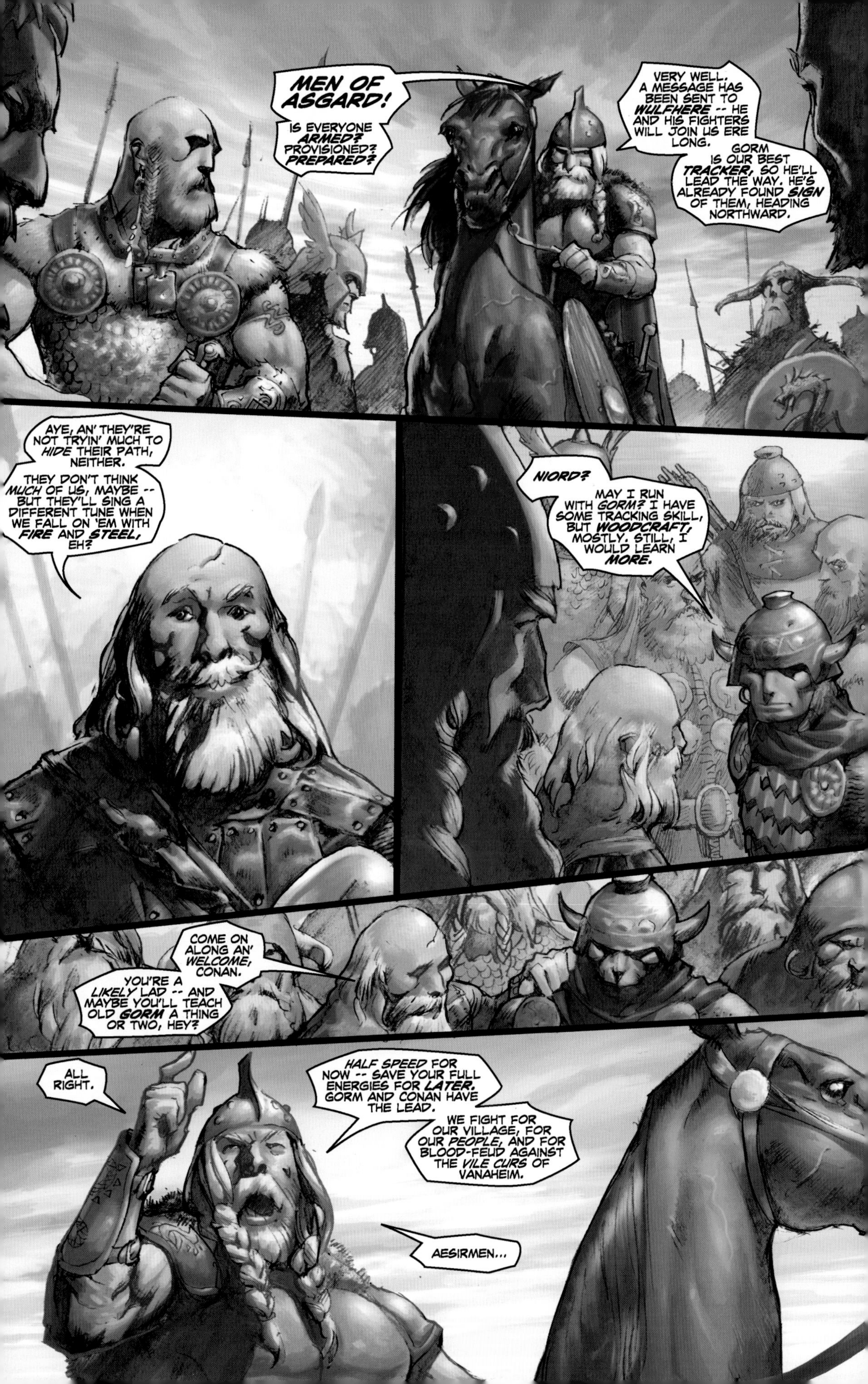

MEN OF ASGARD!
IS EVERYONE ARMED? PROVISIONED? PREPARED?
VERY WELL. A MESSAGE HAS BEEN SENT TO WULFHERE -- HE AND HIS FIGHTERS WILL JOIN US ERE LONG.
GORM IS OUR BEST TRACKER, SO HE'LL LEAD THE WAY. HE'S ALREADY FOUND SIGN OF THEM, HEADING NORTHWARD.
AYE, AN' THEY'RE NOT TRYIN' MUCH TO HIDE THEIR PATH, NEITHER.
THEY DON'T THINK MUCH OF US, MAYBE -- BUT THEY'LL SING A DIFFERENT TUNE WHEN WE FALL ON 'EM WITH FIRE AND STEEL, EH?
NIORD?
MAY I RUN WITH GORM? I HAVE SOME TRACKING SKILL, BUT WOODCRAFT, MOSTLY. STILL, I WOULD LEARN MORE.
COME ON ALONG AN' WELCOME, CONAN.
YOU'RE A LIKELY LAD -- AND MAYBE YOU'LL TEACH OLD GORM A THING OR TWO, HEY?
ALL RIGHT.
HALF SPEED FOR NOW -- SAVE YOUR FULL ENERGIES FOR LATER. GORM AND CONAN HAVE THE LEAD.
WE FIGHT FOR OUR VILLAGE, FOR OUR PEOPLE, AND FOR BLOOD-FEUD AGAINST THE VILE CURS OF VANAHEIM.
AESIRMEN...

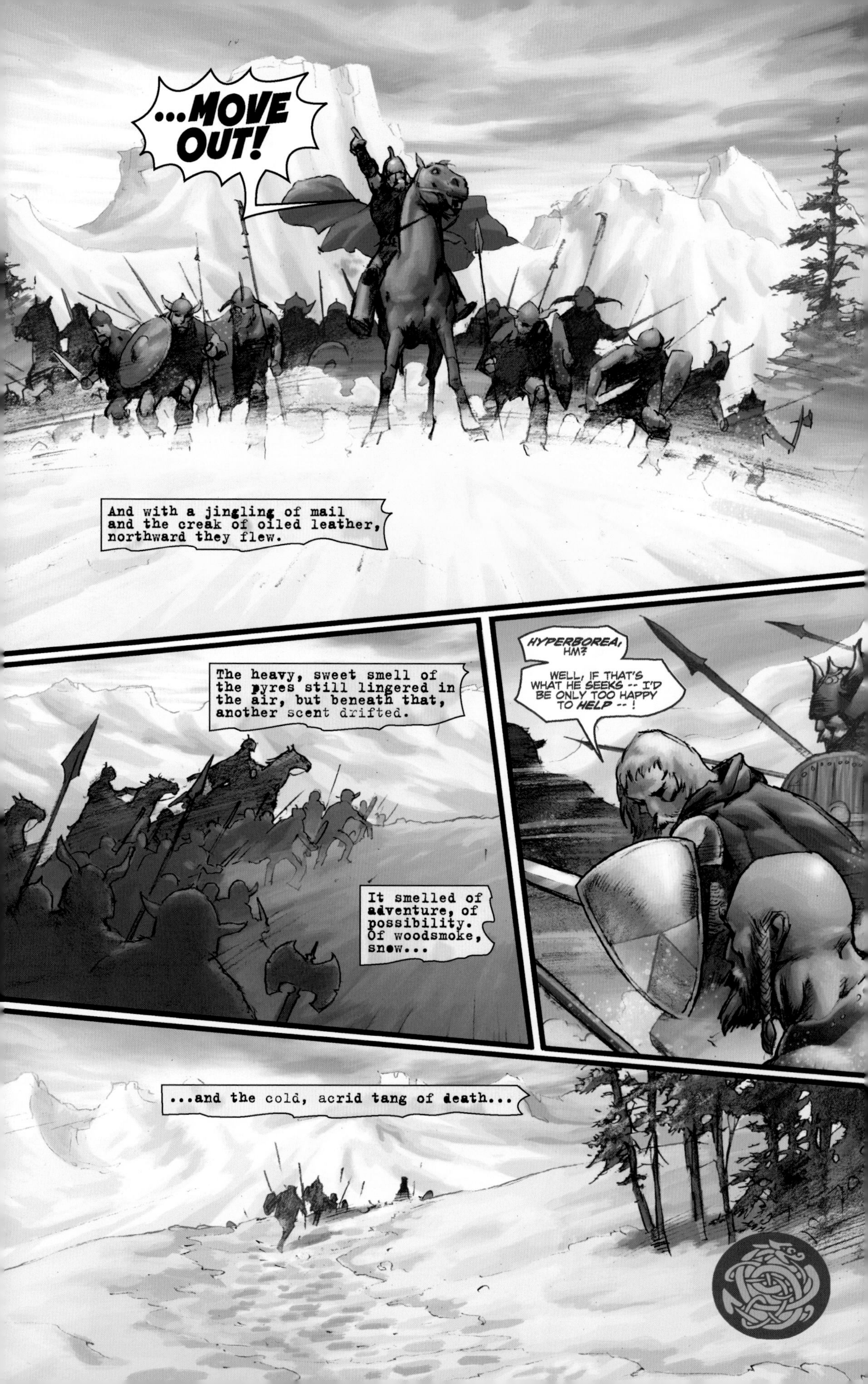
...MOVE OUT!
And with a jingling of mail and the creak of oiled leather, northward they flew.
The heavy, sweet smell of the pyres still lingered in the air, but beneath that, another scent drifted.
It smelled of adventure, of possibility. Of woodsmoke, snow...
HYPERBOREA, HM?
WELL, IF THAT'S WHAT HE SEEKS -- I'D BE ONLY TOO HAPPY TO HELP -- !
...and the cold, acrid tang of death...

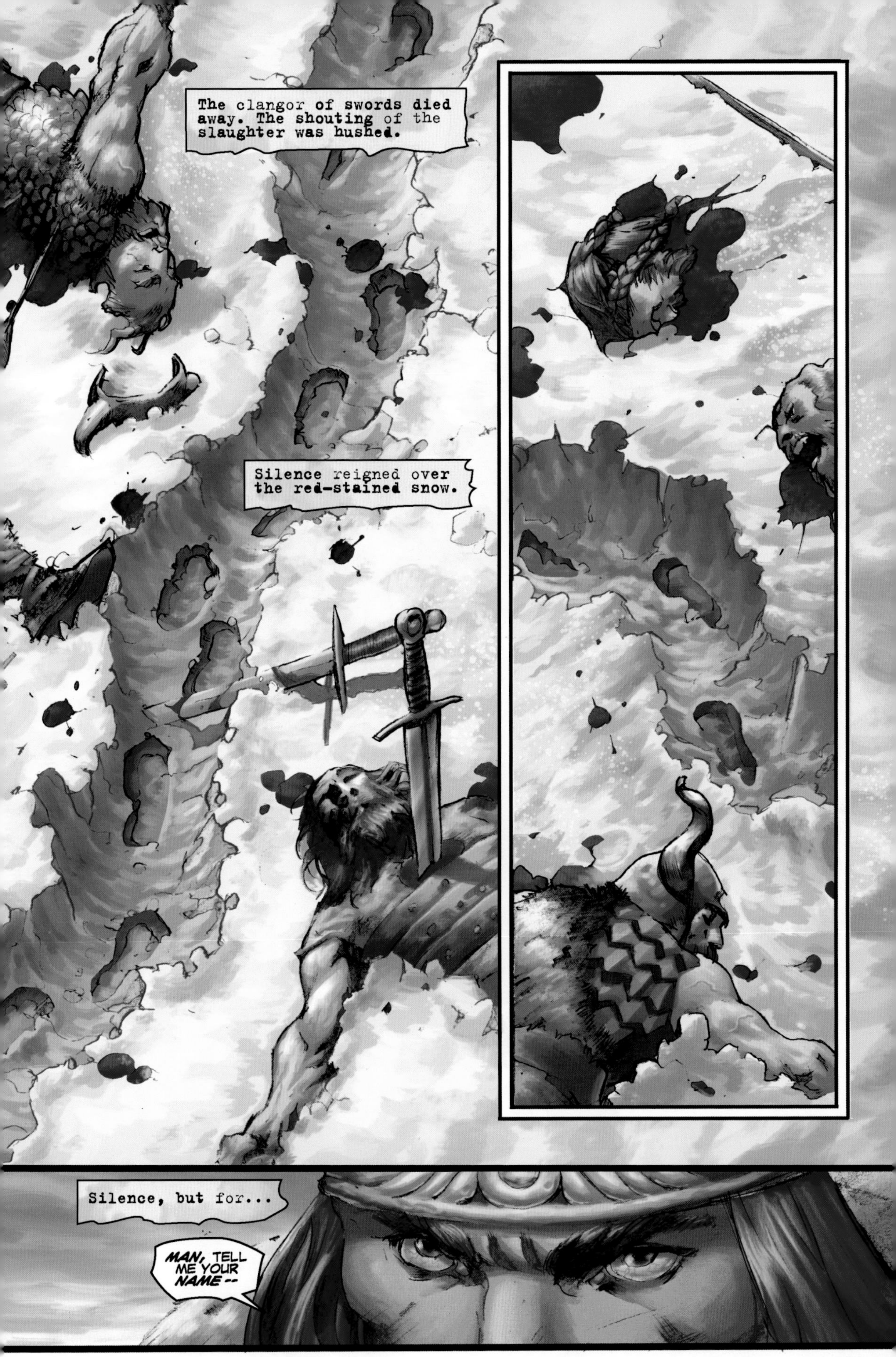
The clangor of swords died away. The shouting of the slaughter was hushed.
Silence reigned over the red-stained snow.
Silence, but for...
MAN, TELL ME YOUR NAME --

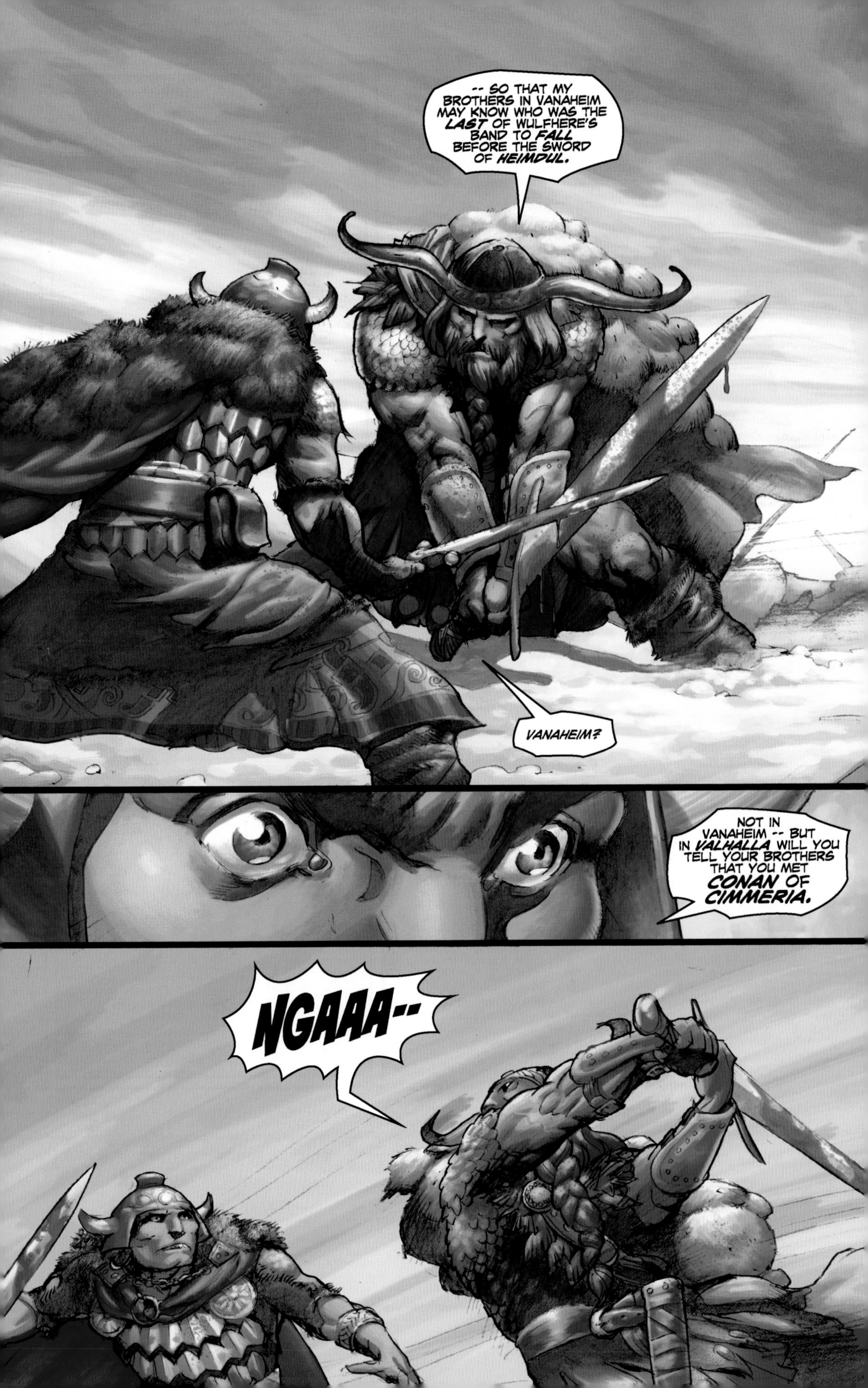
-- SO THAT MY BROTHERS IN VANAHEIM MAY KNOW WHO WAS THE LAST OF WULFHERE'S BAND TO FALL BEFORE THE SWORD OF HEIMDUL.
VANAHEIM?
NOT IN VANAHEIM -- BUT IN VALHALLA WILL YOU TELL YOUR BROTHERS THAT YOU MET CONAN OF CIMMERIA.
NGAAA--

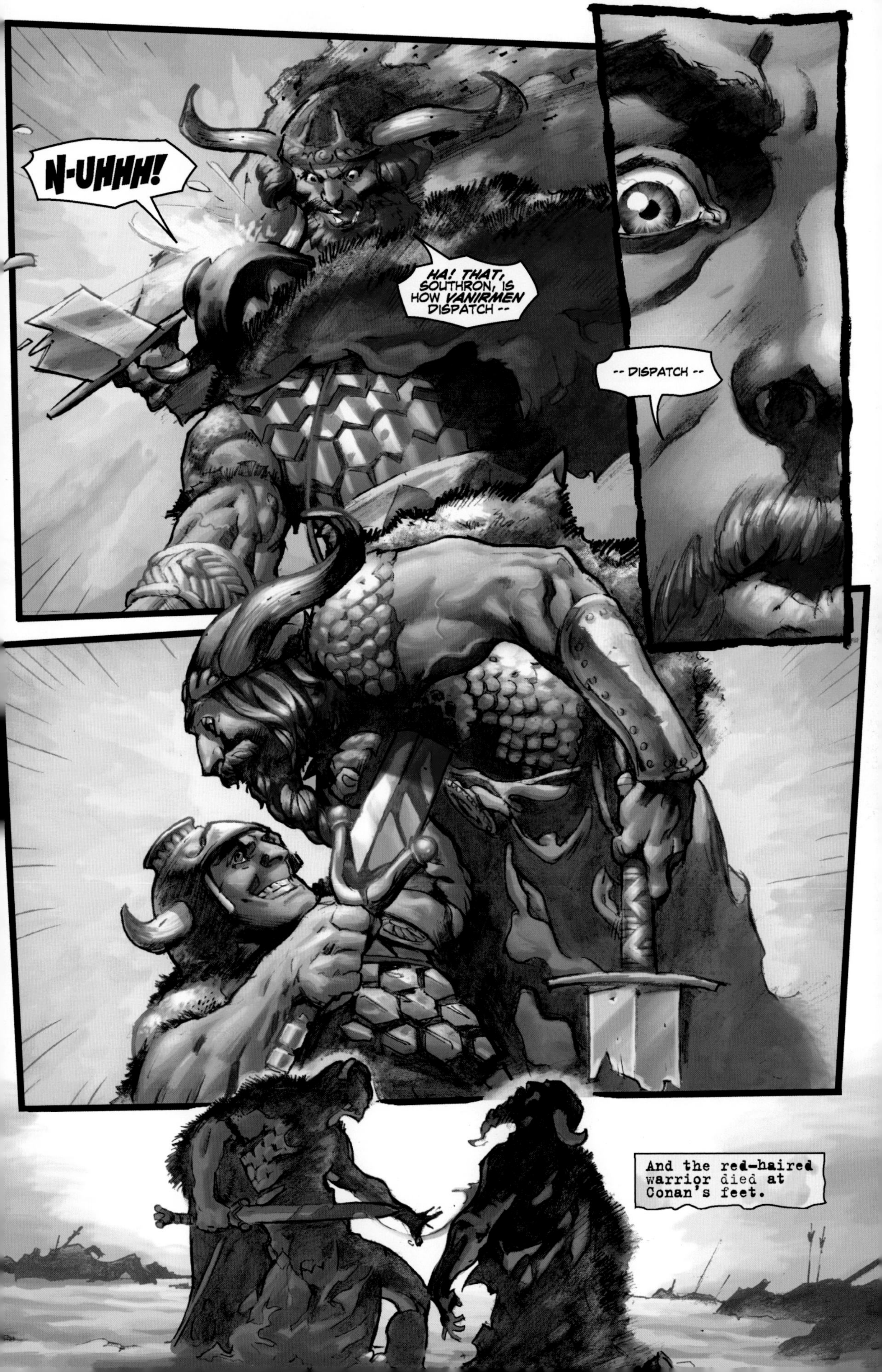
N-UHHH!
HA! THAT, SOUTHRON, IS HOW VANIRMEN DISPATCH --
-- DISPATCH --
And the red-haired warrior died at Conan's feet.

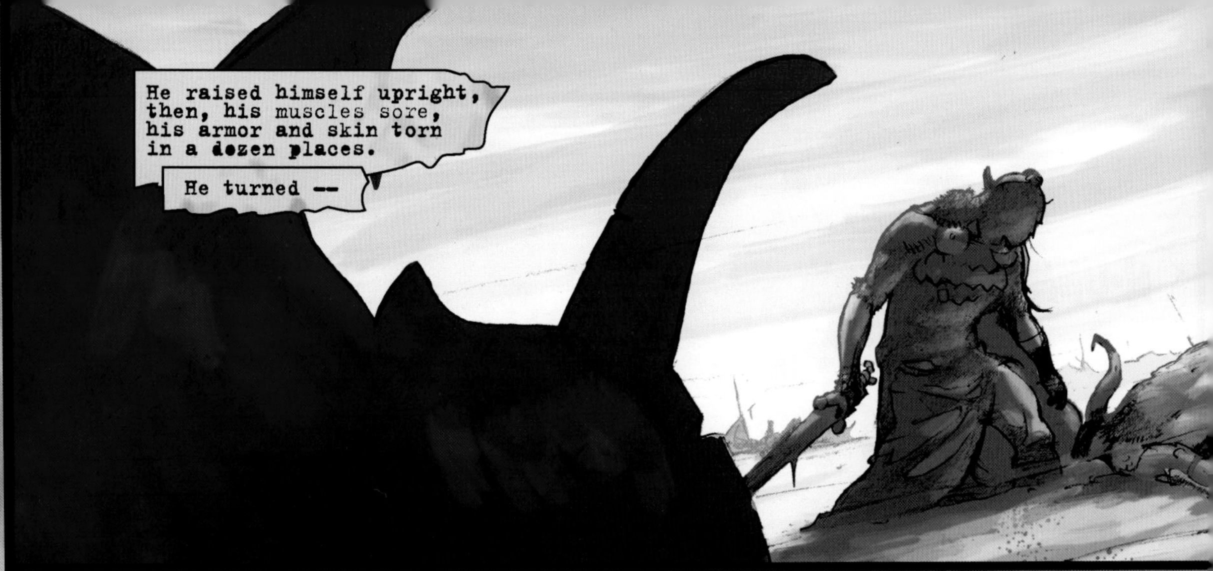
He raised himself upright, then, his muscles sore, his armor and skin torn in a dozen places.
He turned --
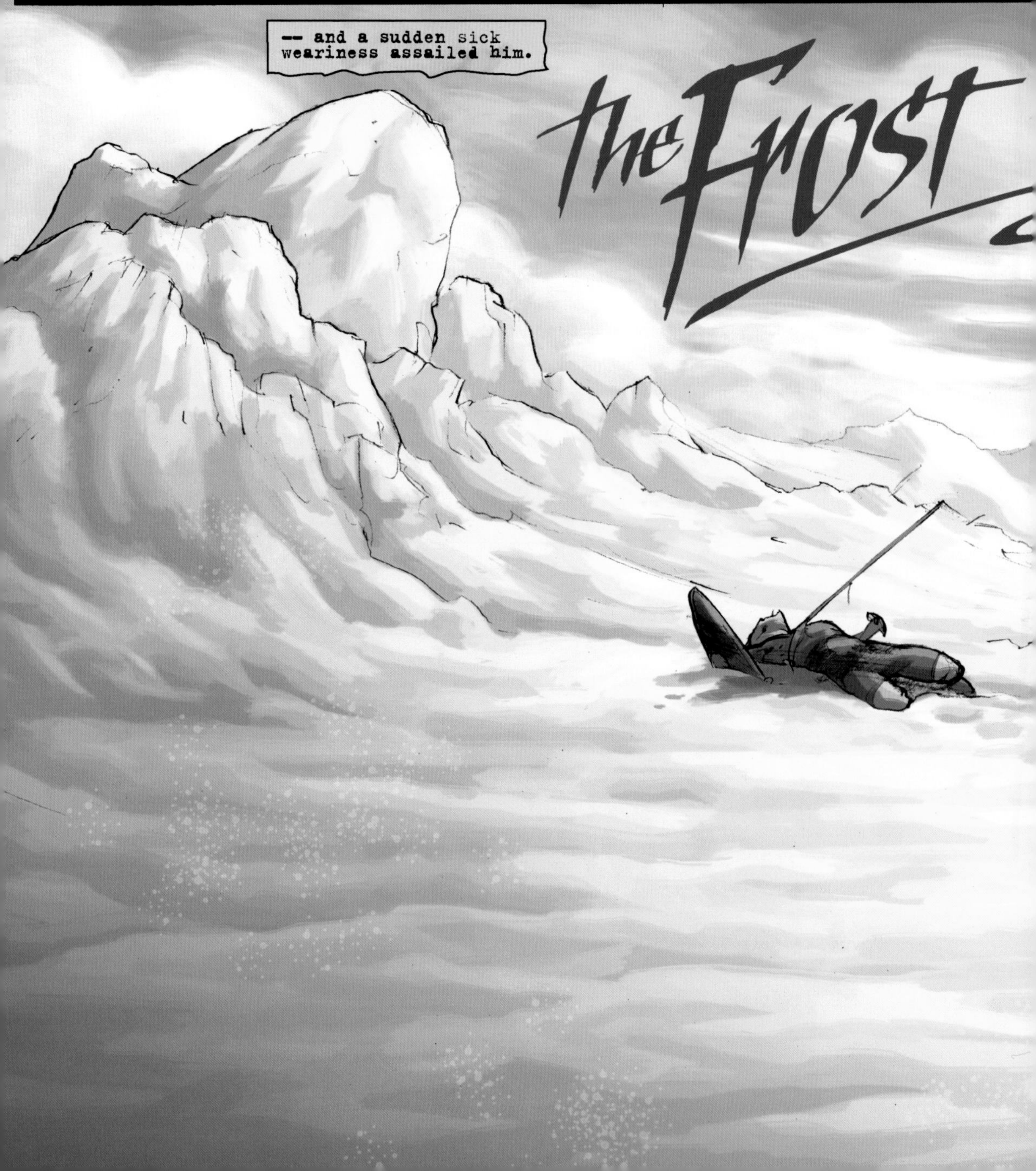
-- and a sudden sick weariness assailed him.
the Frost

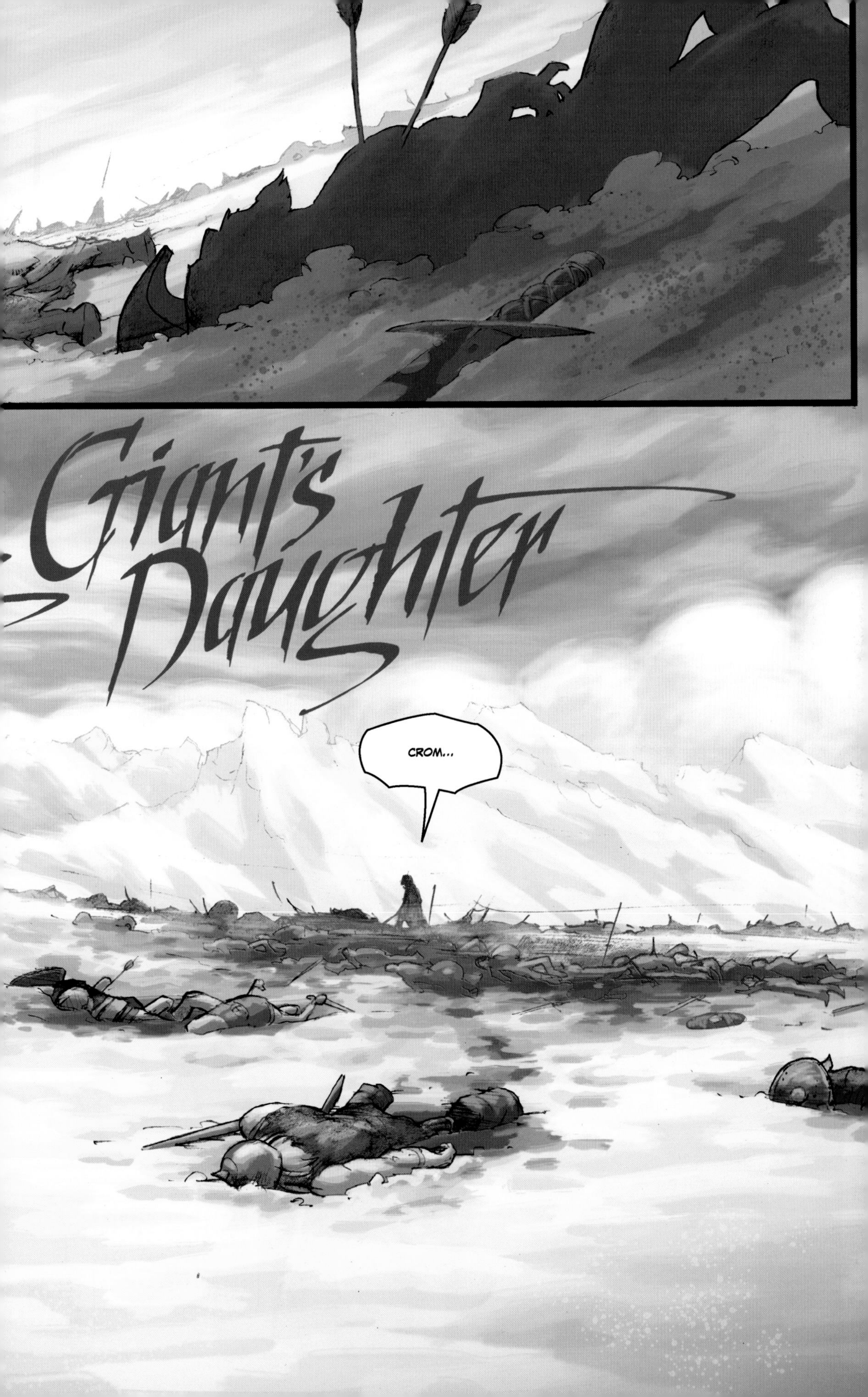
Giant's Daughter
CROM...

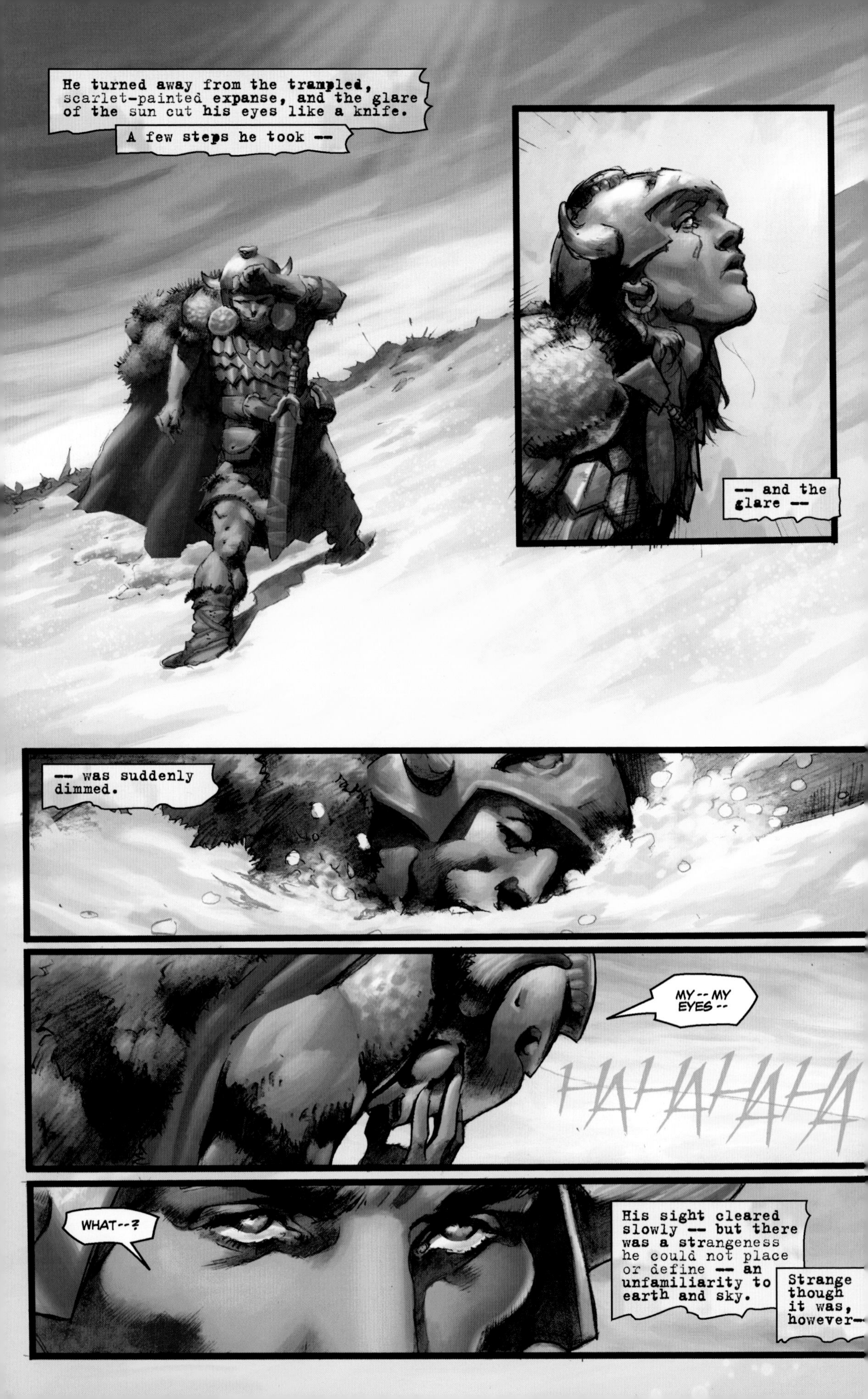
He turned away from the trampled, scarlet-painted expanse, and the glare of the sun cut his eyes like a knife.
A few steps he took --
-- and the glare --
-- was suddenly dimmed.
MY -- MY EYES --
HAHAHAHA
WHAT --?
His sight cleared slowly -- but there was a strangeness he could not place or define -- an unfamiliarity to earth and sky.
Strange though it was, however--

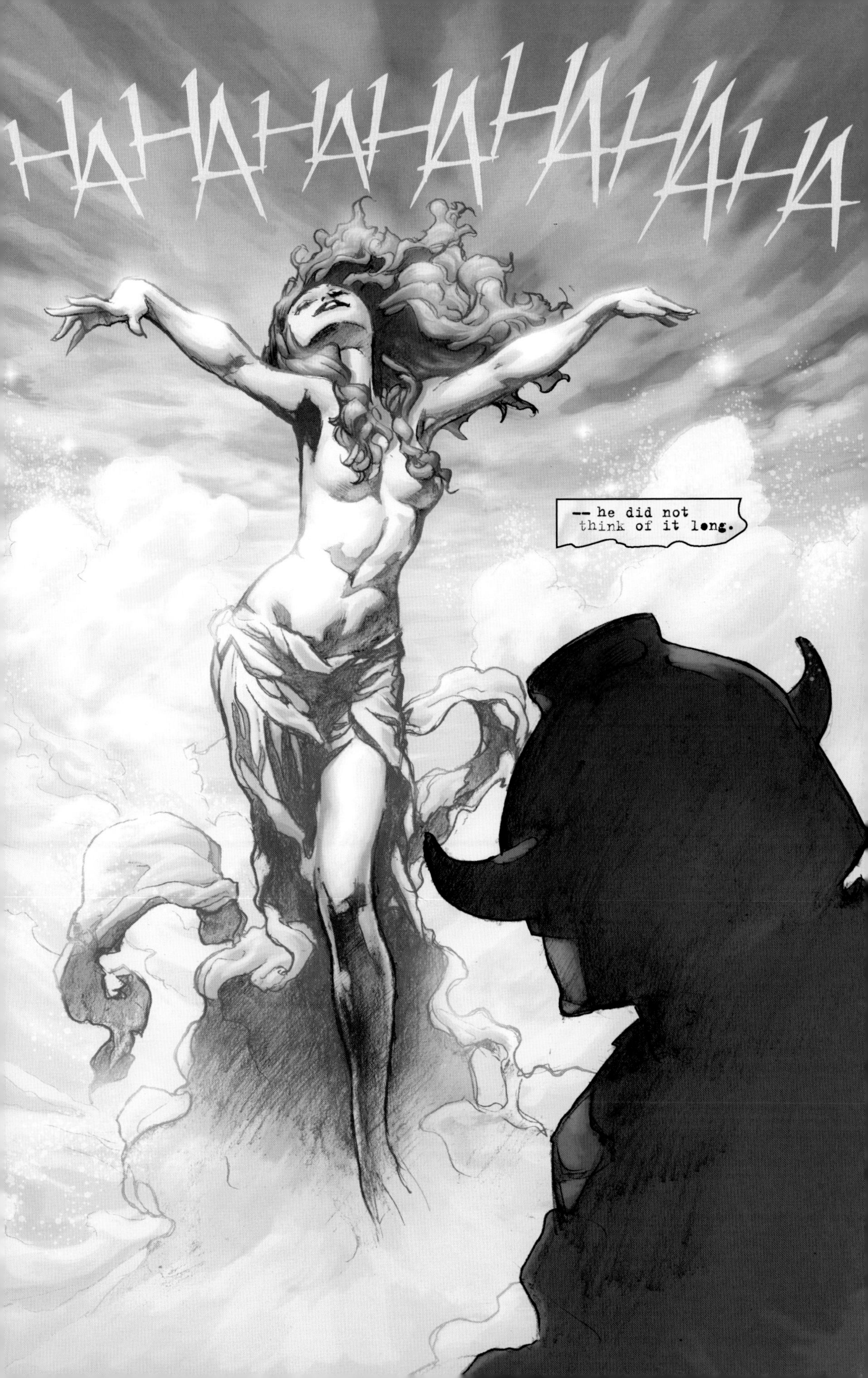
HAHAHAHAHAHAHAHA
-- he did not think of it long.

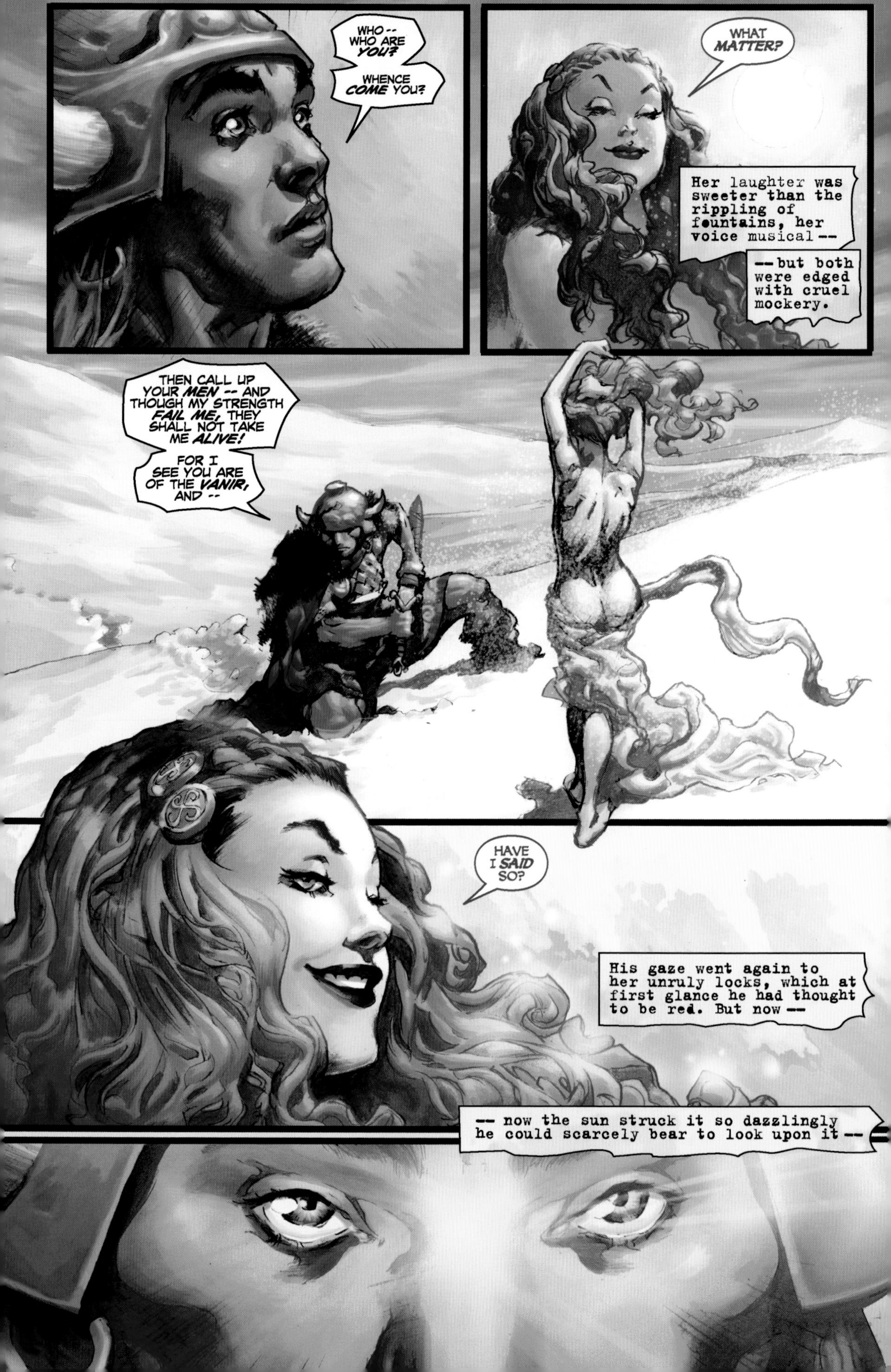

WHO -- WHO ARE YOU?
WHENCE COME YOU?
WHAT MATTER?
Her laughter was sweeter than the rippling of fountains, her voice musical --
-- but both were edged with cruel mockery.
THEN CALL UP YOUR MEN -- AND THOUGH MY STRENGTH FAIL ME, THEY SHALL NOT TAKE ME ALIVE!
FOR I SEE YOU ARE OF THE VANIR, AND --
HAVE I SAID SO?
His gaze went again to her unruly locks, which at first glance he had thought to be red. But now --
-- now the sun struck it so dazzlingly he could scarcely bear to look upon it --

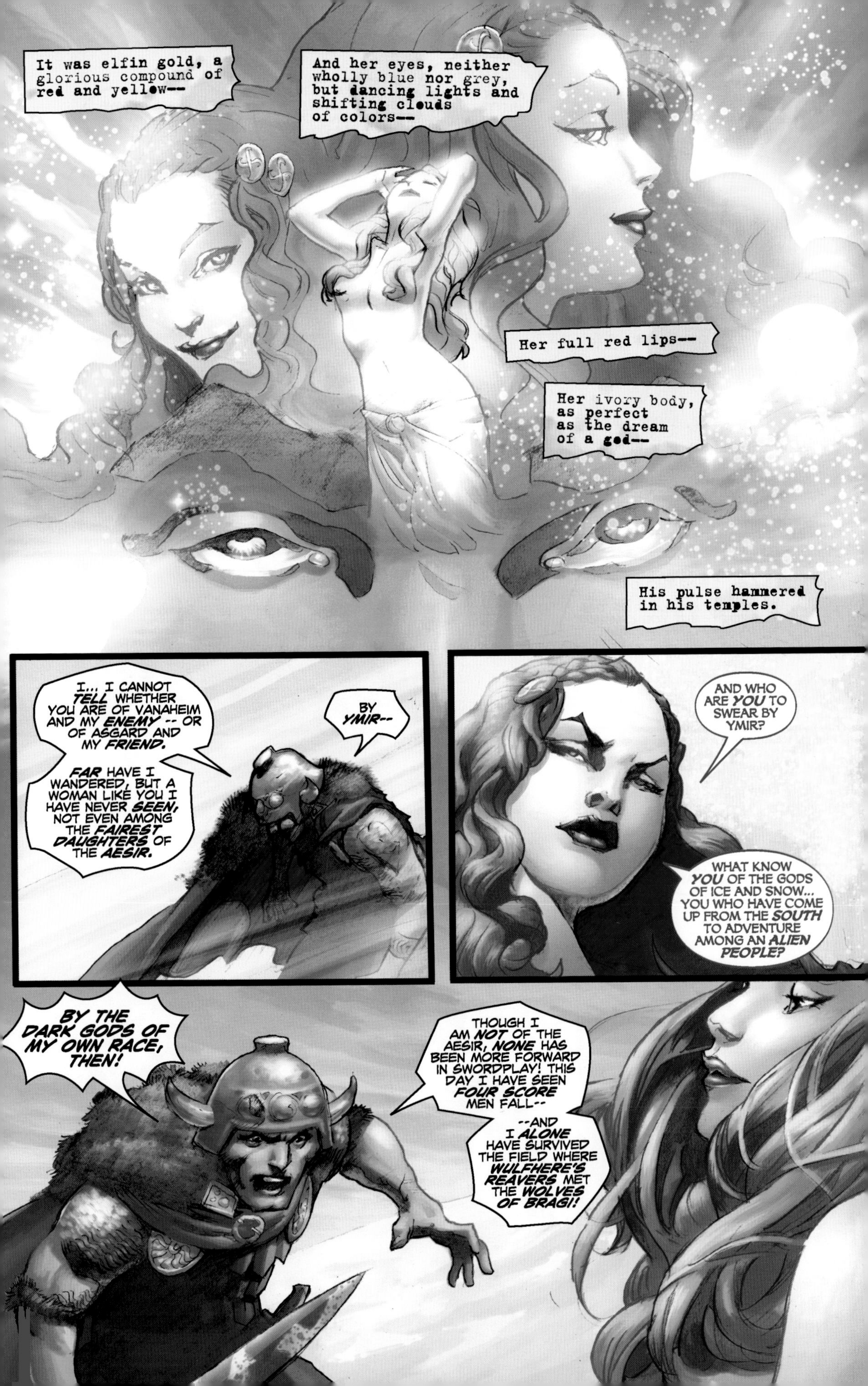
It was elfin gold, a glorious compound of red and yellow--
And her eyes, neither wholly blue nor grey, but dancing lights and shifting clouds of colors--
Her full red lips--
Her ivory body, as perfect as the dream of a god--
His pulse hammered in his temples.
I... I CANNOT TELL WHETHER YOU ARE OF VANAHEIM AND MY ENEMY -- OR OF ASGARD AND MY FRIEND.
FAR HAVE I WANDERED, BUT A WOMAN LIKE YOU I HAVE NEVER SEEN, NOT EVEN AMONG THE FAIREST DAUGHTERS OF THE AESIR.
BY YMIR--
AND WHO ARE YOU TO SWEAR BY YMIR?
WHAT KNOW YOU OF THE GODS OF ICE AND SNOW... YOU WHO HAVE COME UP FROM THE SOUTH TO ADVENTURE AMONG AN ALIEN PEOPLE?
BY THE DARK GODS OF MY OWN RACE, THEN!
THOUGH I AM NOT OF THE AESIR, NONE HAS BEEN MORE FORWARD IN SWORDPLAY! THIS DAY I HAVE SEEN FOUR SCORE MEN FALL--
--AND I ALONE HAVE SURVIVED THE FIELD WHERE WULFHERE'S REAVERS MET THE WOLVES OF BRAGI!

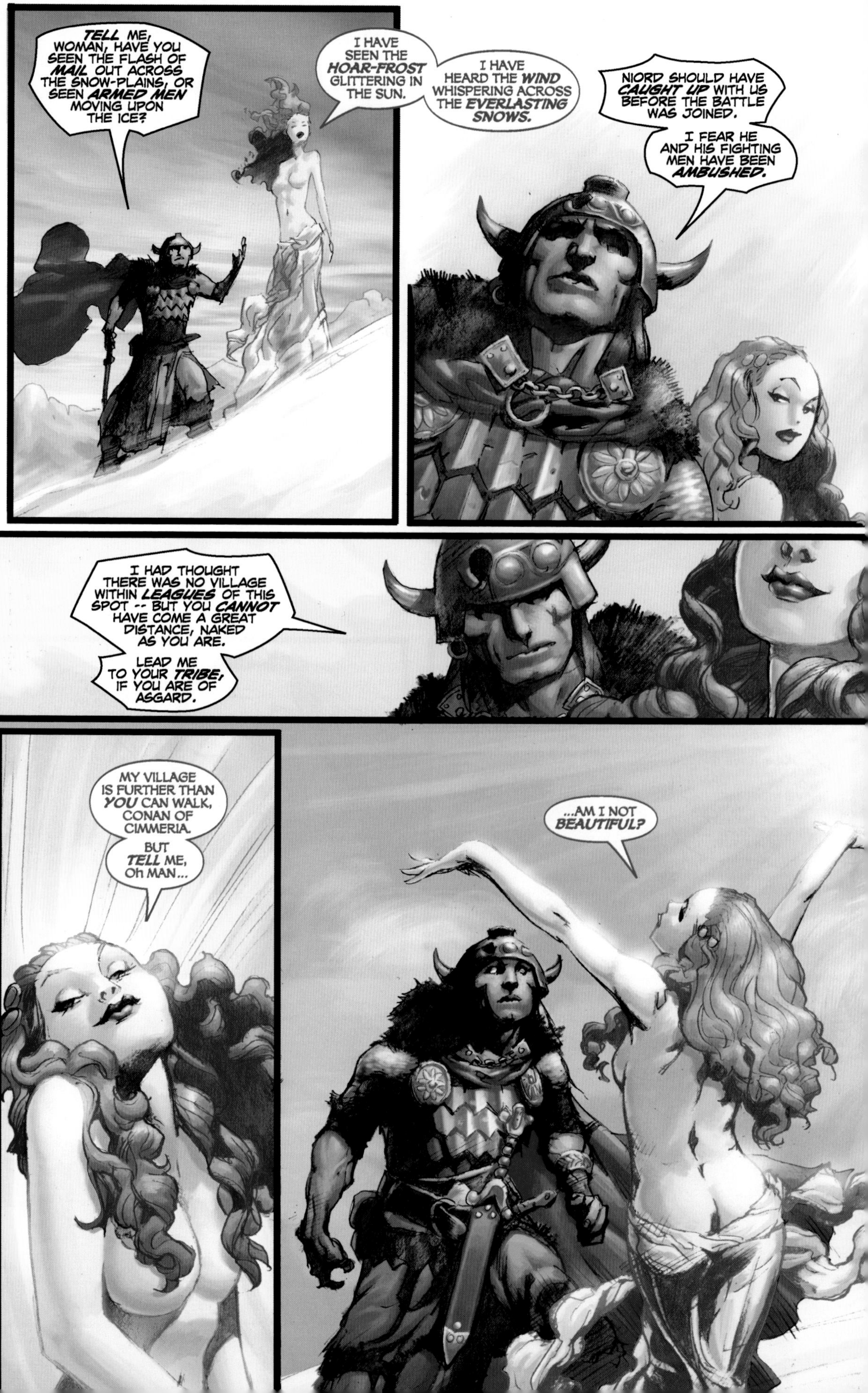
TELL ME, WOMAN, HAVE YOU SEEN THE FLASH OF MAIL OUT ACROSS THE SNOW-PLAINS, OR SEEN ARMED MEN MOVING UPON THE ICE?
I HAVE SEEN THE HOAR-FROST GLITTERING IN THE SUN.
I HAVE HEARD THE WIND WHISPERING ACROSS THE EVERLASTING SNOWS.
NIORD SHOULD HAVE CAUGHT UP WITH US BEFORE THE BATTLE WAS JOINED.
I FEAR HE AND HIS FIGHTING MEN HAVE BEEN AMBUSHED.
I HAD THOUGHT THERE WAS NO VILLAGE WITHIN LEAGUES OF THIS SPOT -- BUT YOU CANNOT HAVE COME A GREAT DISTANCE, NAKED AS YOU ARE.
LEAD ME TO YOUR TRIBE, IF YOU ARE OF ASGARD.
MY VILLAGE IS FURTHER THAN YOU CAN WALK, CONAN OF CIMMERIA.
BUT TELL ME, Oh MAN...
...AM I NOT BEAUTIFUL?

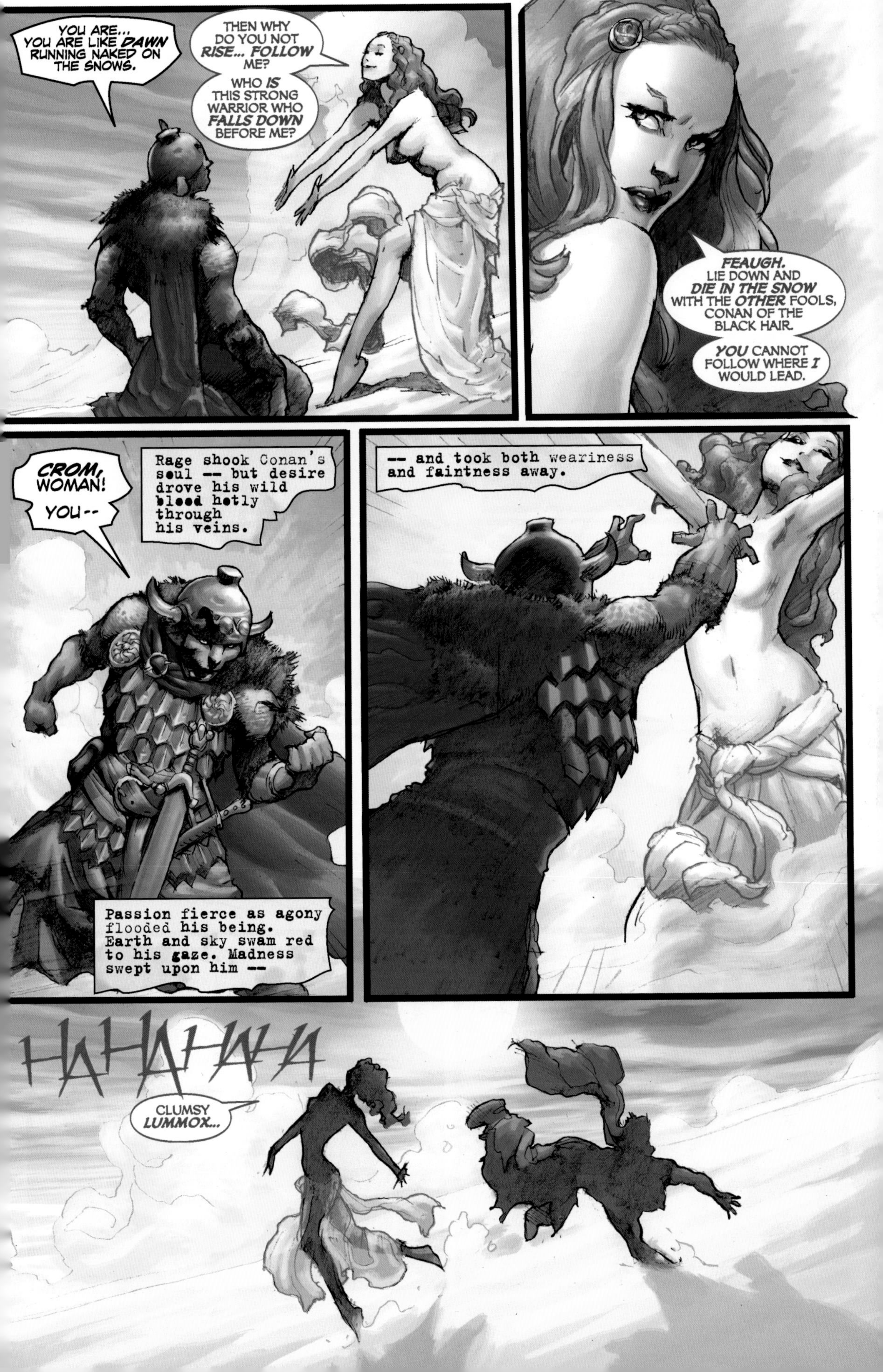
YOU ARE... YOU ARE LIKE DAWN RUNNING NAKED ON THE SNOWS.
THEN WHY DO YOU NOT RISE... FOLLOW ME?
WHO IS THIS STRONG WARRIOR WHO FALLS DOWN BEFORE ME?
FEAUGH. LIE DOWN AND DIE IN THE SNOW WITH THE OTHER FOOLS, CONAN OF THE BLACK HAIR.
YOU CANNOT FOLLOW WHERE I WOULD LEAD.
CROM, WOMAN!
YOU--
Rage shook Conan's soul -- but desire drove his wild blood hotly through his veins.
Passion fierce as agony flooded his being. Earth and sky swam red to his gaze. Madness swept upon him --
-- and took both weariness and faintness away.
HAHAHAHA
CLUMSY LUMMOX...

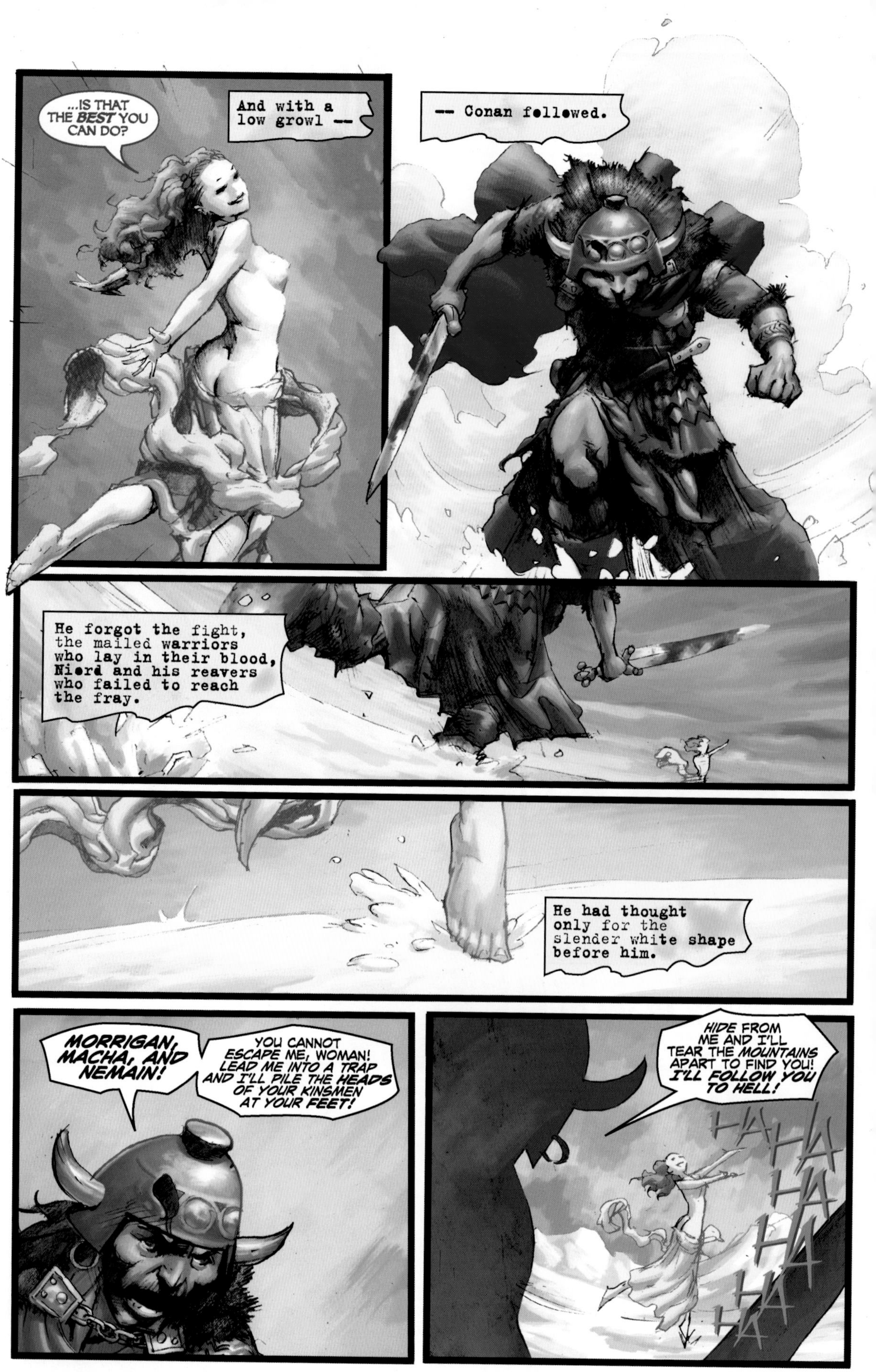

...IS THAT THE *BEST* YOU CAN DO?
And with a low growl --
-- Conan followed.
He forgot the fight, the mailed warriors who lay in their blood, Niord and his reavers who failed to reach the fray.
He had thought only for the slender white shape before him.
MORRIGAN, MACHA, AND NEMAIN!
YOU CANNOT ESCAPE ME, WOMAN! LEAD ME INTO A TRAP AND I'LL PILE THE HEADS OF YOUR KINSMEN AT YOUR FEET!
HIDE FROM ME AND I'LL TEAR THE MOUNTAINS APART TO FIND YOU! I'LL FOLLOW YOU TO HELL!
HA HA HA HA HA HA HA

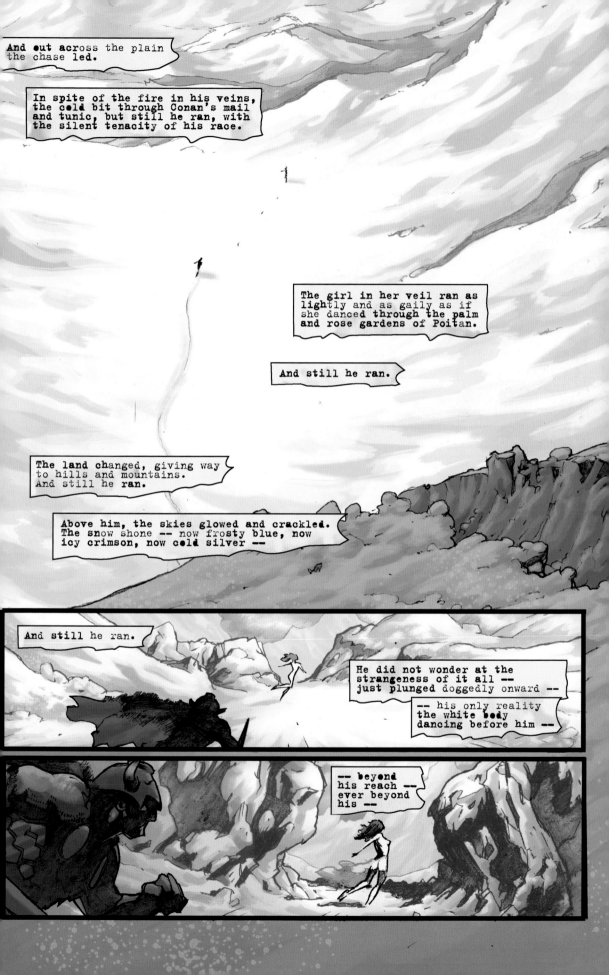

And out across the plain the chase led.

In spite of the fire in his veins, the cold bit through Conan's mail and tunic, but still he ran, with the silent tenacity of his race.

The girl in her veil ran as lightly and as gaily as if she danced through the palm and rose gardens of Poitan.

And still he ran.

The land changed, giving way to hills and mountains. And still he ran.

Above him, the skies glowed and crackled. The snow shone -- now frosty blue, now icy crimson, now cold silver --

And still he ran.

He did not wonder at the strangeness of it all -- just plunged doggedly onward --

-- his only reality the white body dancing before him --

-- beyond his reach -- ever beyond his --

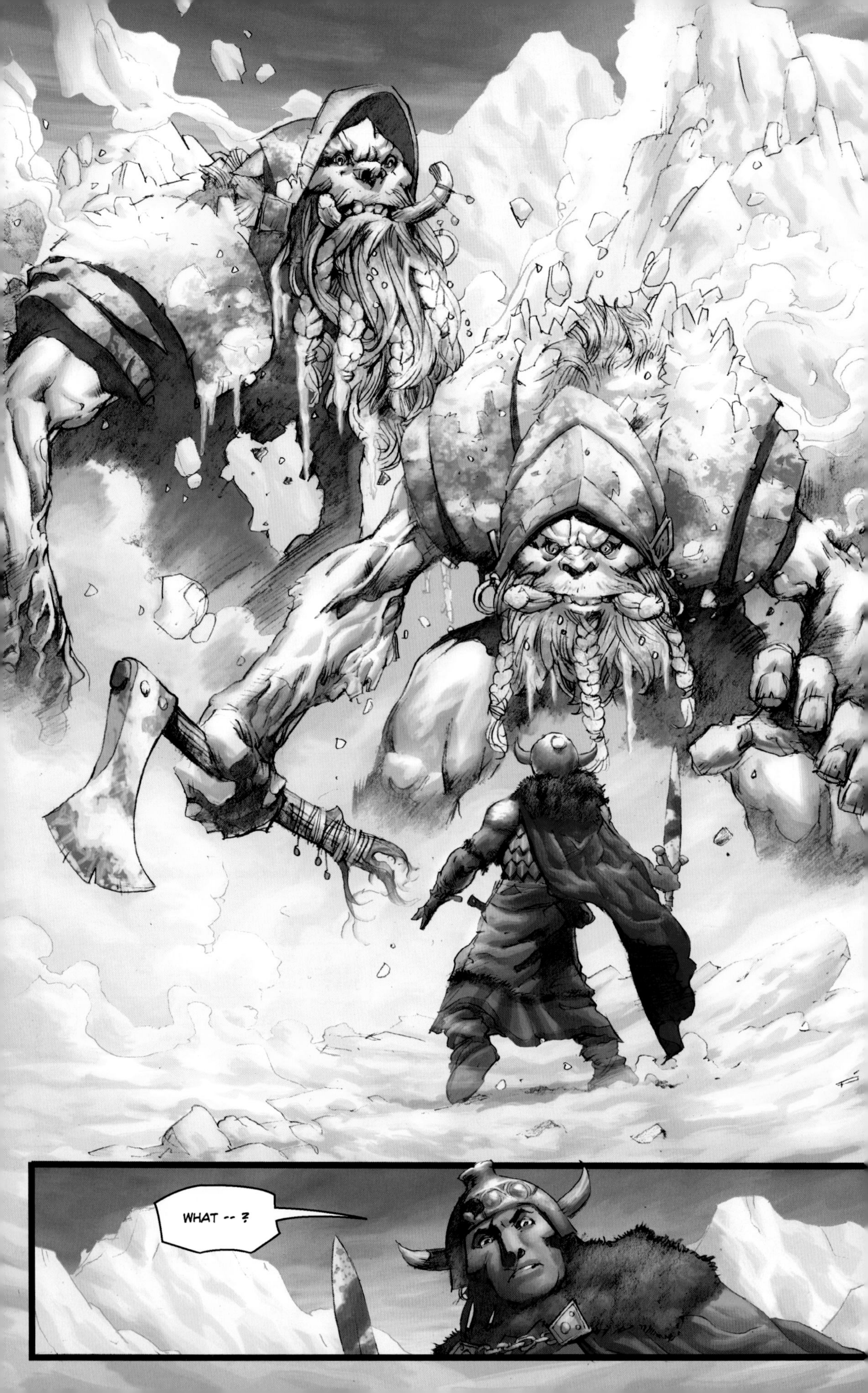
WHAT -- ?

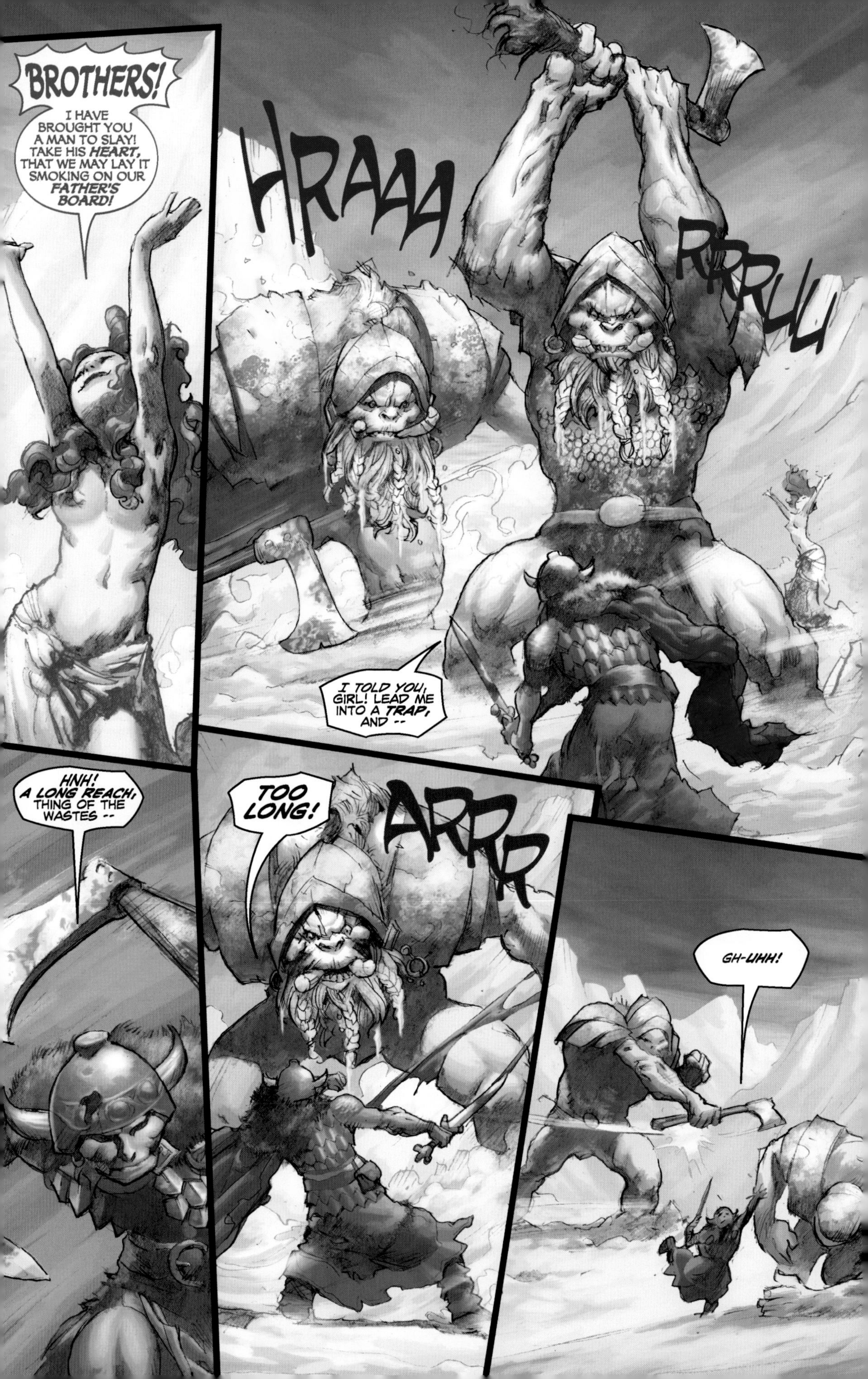
BROTHERS!
I HAVE BROUGHT YOU A MAN TO SLAY! TAKE HIS HEART, THAT WE MAY LAY IT SMOKING ON OUR FATHER'S BOARD!
HRAAAA
RRRUU
I TOLD YOU, GIRL! LEAD ME INTO A TRAP, AND --
HNH! A LONG REACH, THING OF THE WASTES --
TOO LONG!
ARRR
GH-UHH!

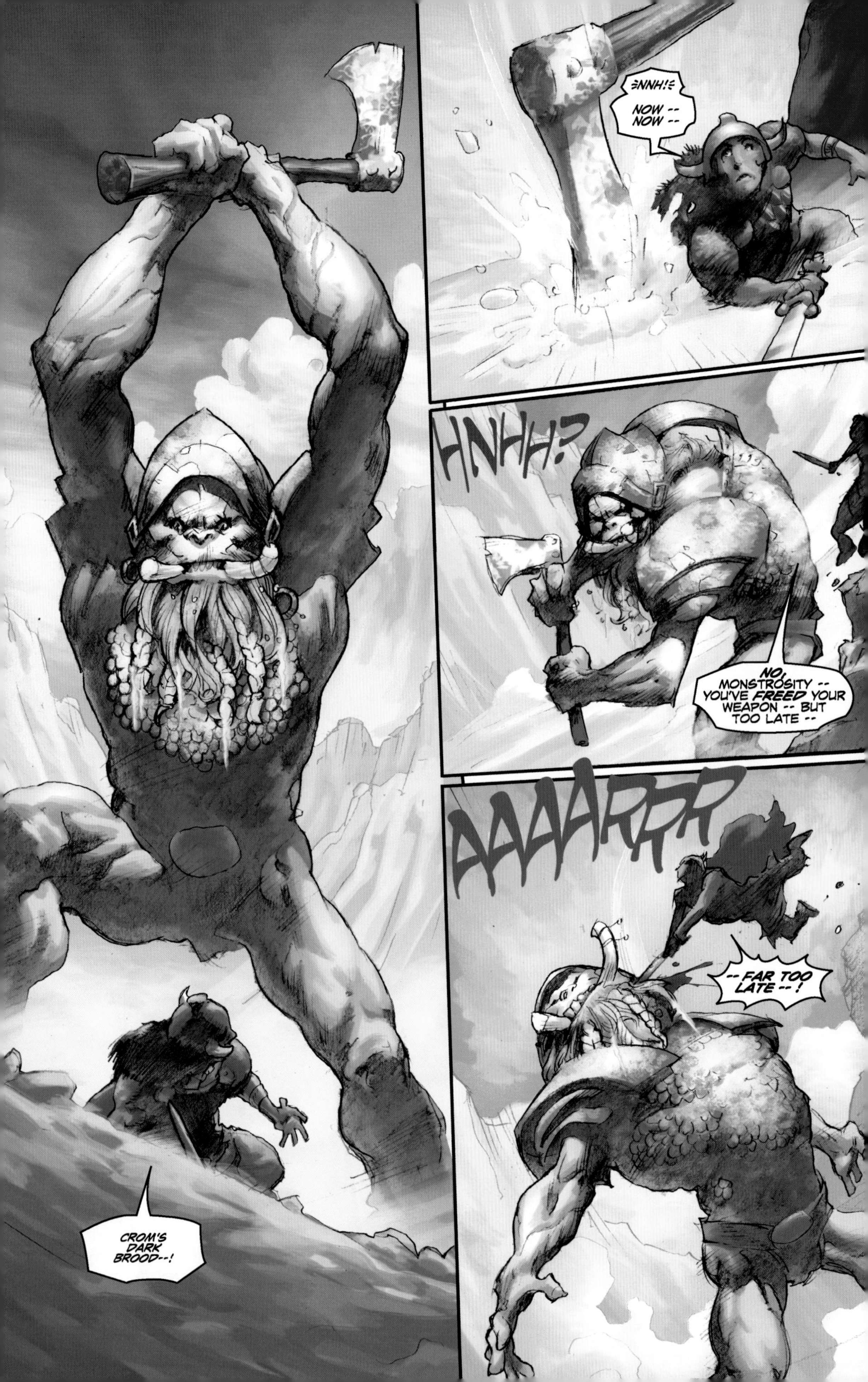

CROM'S DARK BROOD--!
ŊNNH!Ŋ
NOW -- NOW --
HNHH?
NO, MONSTROSITY -- YOU'VE FREED YOUR WEAPON -- BUT TOO LATE --
AAAARRR
-- FAR TOO LATE -- !

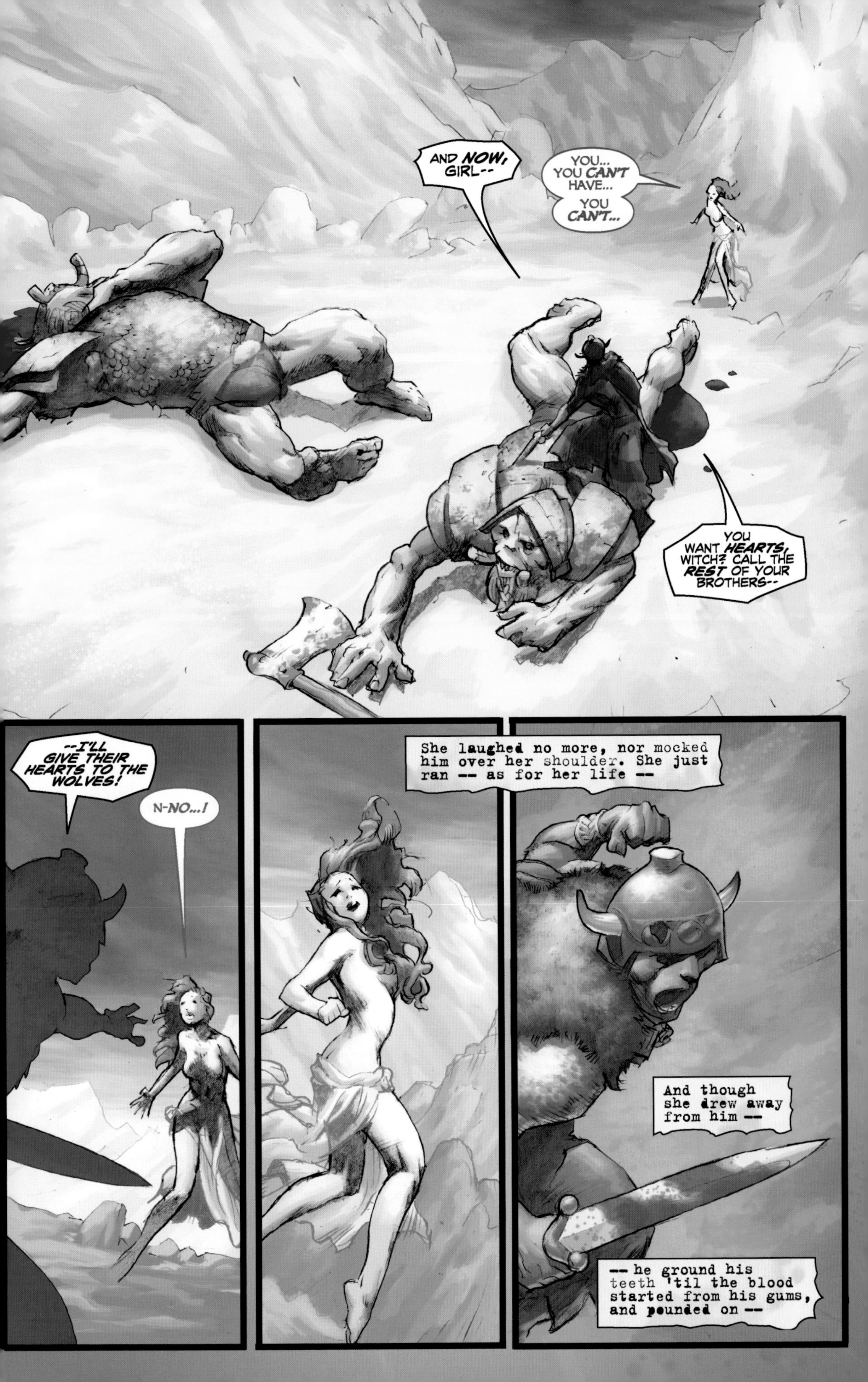
AND NOW, GIRL--
YOU... YOU CAN'T HAVE... YOU CAN'T...
YOU WANT HEARTS, WITCH? CALL THE REST OF YOUR BROTHERS--
--I'LL GIVE THEIR HEARTS TO THE WOLVES!
N-NO...!
She laughed no more, nor mocked him over her shoulder. She just ran -- as for her life --
And though she drew away from him --
-- he ground his teeth 'til the blood started from his gums, and pounded on --

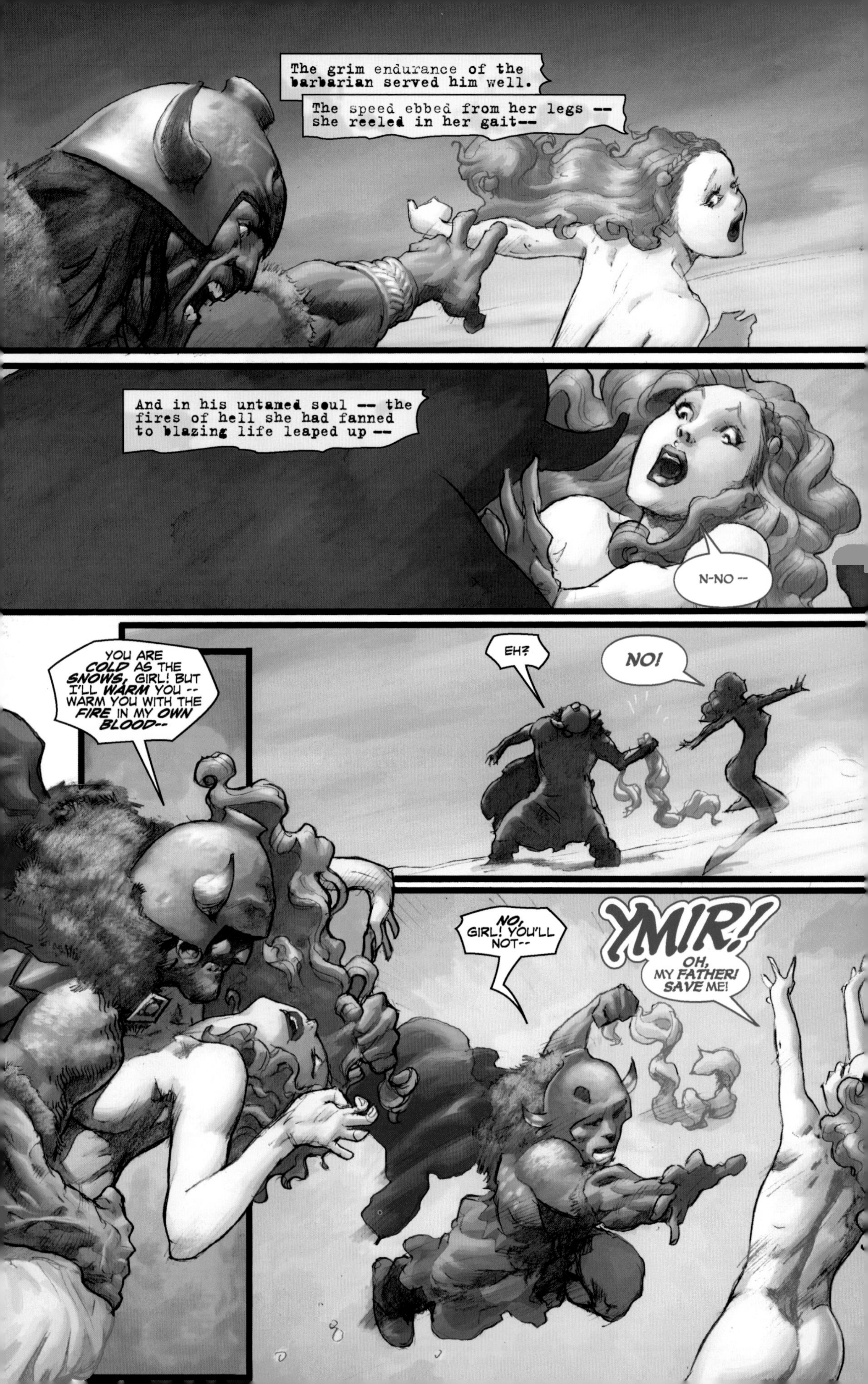
The grim endurance of the barbarian served him well.
The speed ebbed from her legs -- she reeled in her gait--
And in his untamed soul -- the fires of hell she had fanned to blazing life leaped up --
N-NO --
YOU ARE COLD AS THE SNOWS, GIRL! BUT I'LL WARM YOU -- WARM YOU WITH THE FIRE IN MY OWN BLOOD--
EH?
NO!
NO, GIRL! YOU'LL NOT--
YMIR!
OH, MY FATHER! SAVE ME!

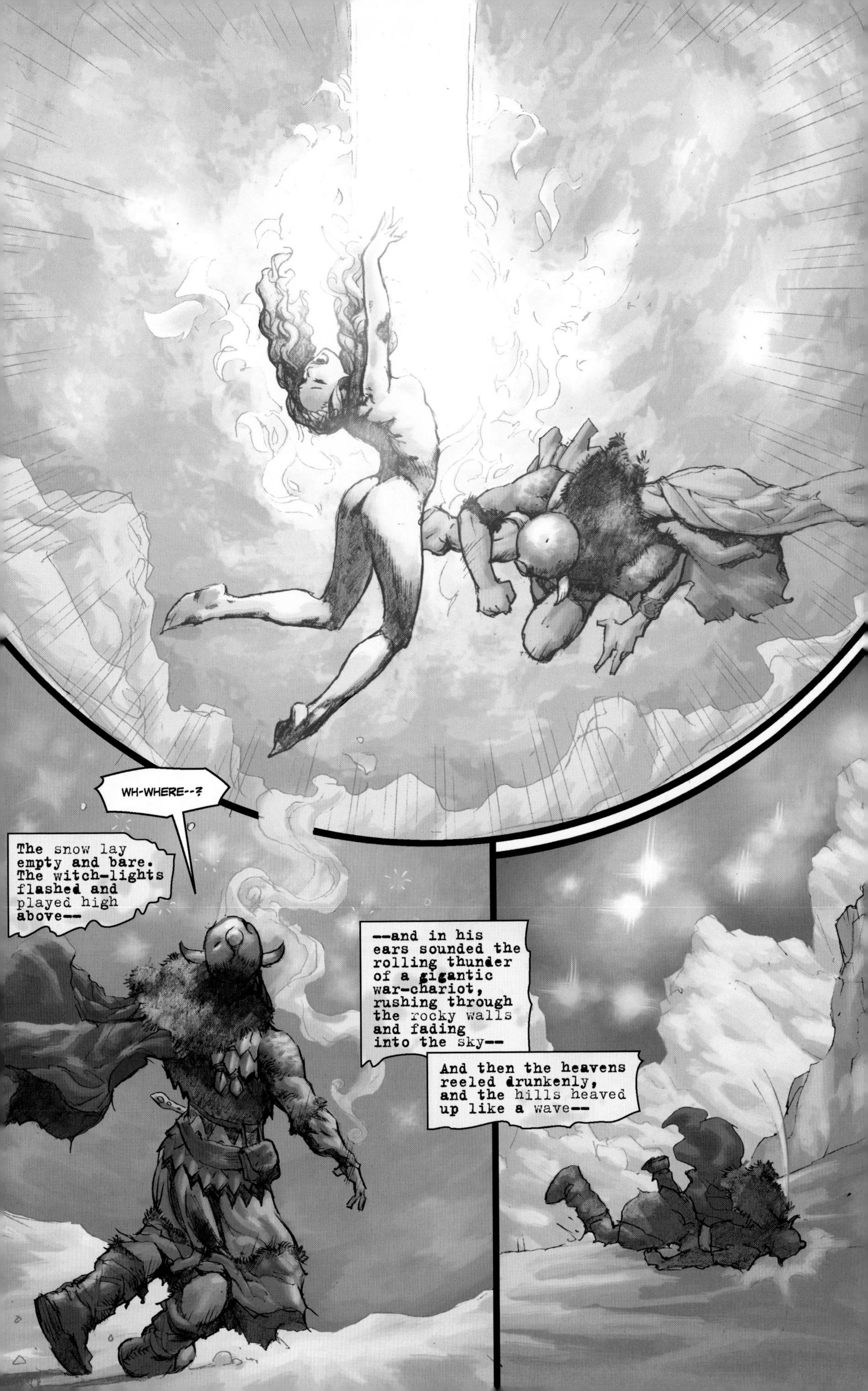
WH-WHERE--?
The snow lay empty and bare. The witch-lights flashed and played high above--
--and in his ears sounded the rolling thunder of a gigantic war-chariot, rushing through the rocky walls and fading into the sky--
And then the heavens reeled drunkenly, and the hills heaved up like a wave--

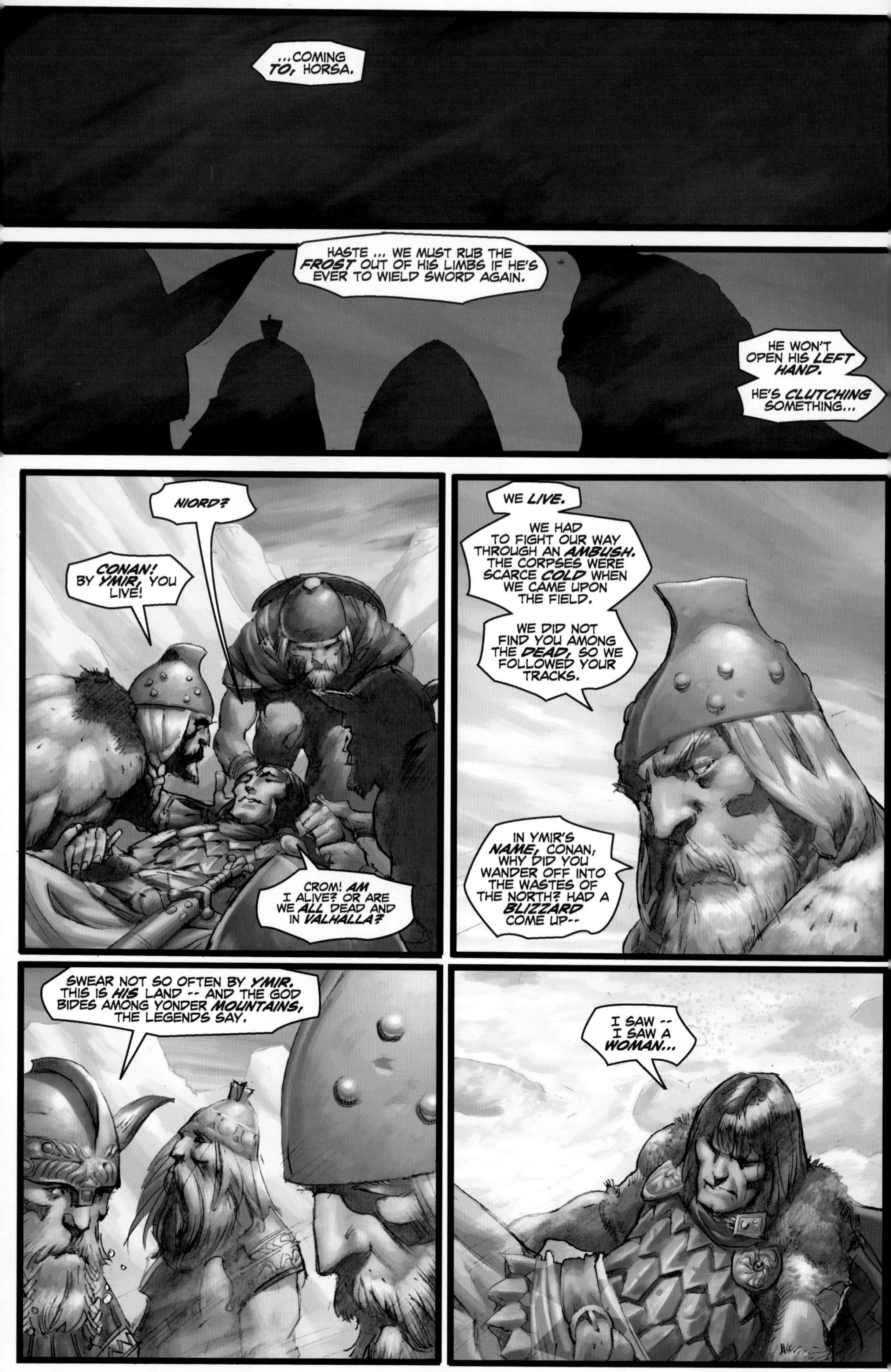

...COMING TO, HORSA.
HASTE ... WE MUST RUB THE FROST OUT OF HIS LIMBS IF HE'S EVER TO WIELD SWORD AGAIN.
HE WON'T OPEN HIS LEFT HAND.
HE'S CLUTCHING SOMETHING...
NIORD?
BY CONAN! BY YMIR, YOU LIVE!
CROM! AM I ALIVE? OR ARE WE ALL DEAD AND IN VALHALLA?
WE LIVE.
WE HAD TO FIGHT OUR WAY THROUGH AN AMBUSH. THE CORPSES WERE SCARCE COLD WHEN WE CAME UPON THE FIELD.
WE DID NOT FIND YOU AMONG THE DEAD, SO WE FOLLOWED YOUR TRACKS.
IN YMIR'S NAME, CONAN, WHY DID YOU WANDER OFF INTO THE WASTES OF THE NORTH? HAD A BLIZZARD COME UP--
SWEAR NOT SO OFTEN BY YMIR. THIS IS HIS LAND -- AND THE GOD BIDES AMONG YONDER MOUNTAINS, THE LEGENDS SAY.
I SAW -- I SAW A WOMAN...

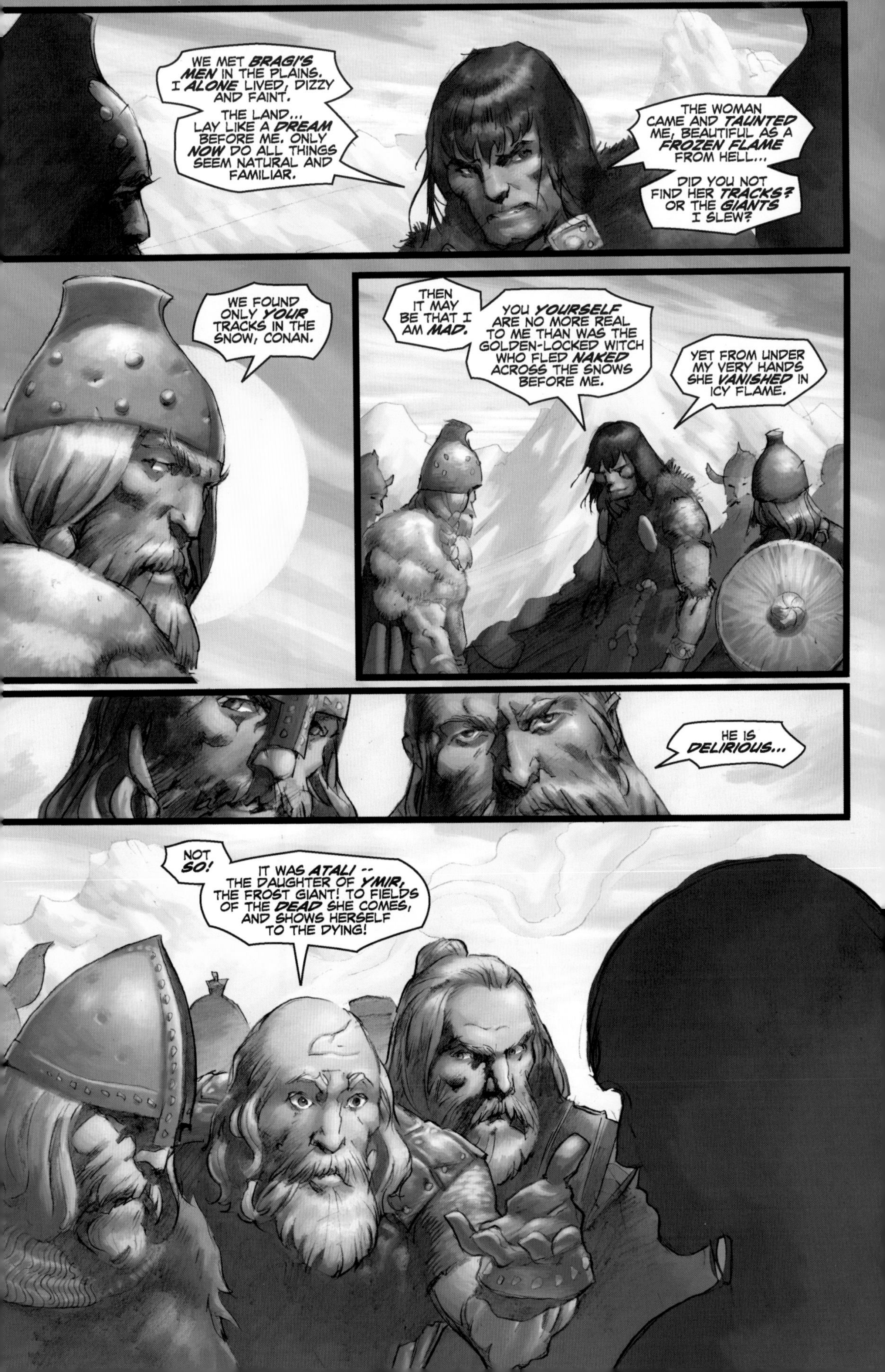
WE MET BRAGI'S MEN IN THE PLAINS. I ALONE LIVED, DIZZY AND FAINT.
THE LAND... LAY LIKE A DREAM BEFORE ME. ONLY NOW DO ALL THINGS SEEM NATURAL AND FAMILIAR.
THE WOMAN CAME AND TAUNTED ME, BEAUTIFUL AS A FROZEN FLAME FROM HELL...
DID YOU NOT FIND HER TRACKS? OR THE GIANTS I SLEW?
WE FOUND ONLY YOUR TRACKS IN THE SNOW, CONAN.
THEN IT MAY BE THAT I AM MAD.
YOU YOURSELF ARE NO MORE REAL TO ME THAN WAS THE GOLDEN-LOCKED WITCH WHO FLED NAKED ACROSS THE SNOWS BEFORE ME.
YET FROM UNDER MY VERY HANDS SHE VANISHED IN ICY FLAME.
HE IS DELIRIOUS...
NOT SO!
IT WAS ATALI -- THE DAUGHTER OF YMIR, THE FROST GIANT! TO FIELDS OF THE DEAD SHE COMES, AND SHOWS HERSELF TO THE DYING!

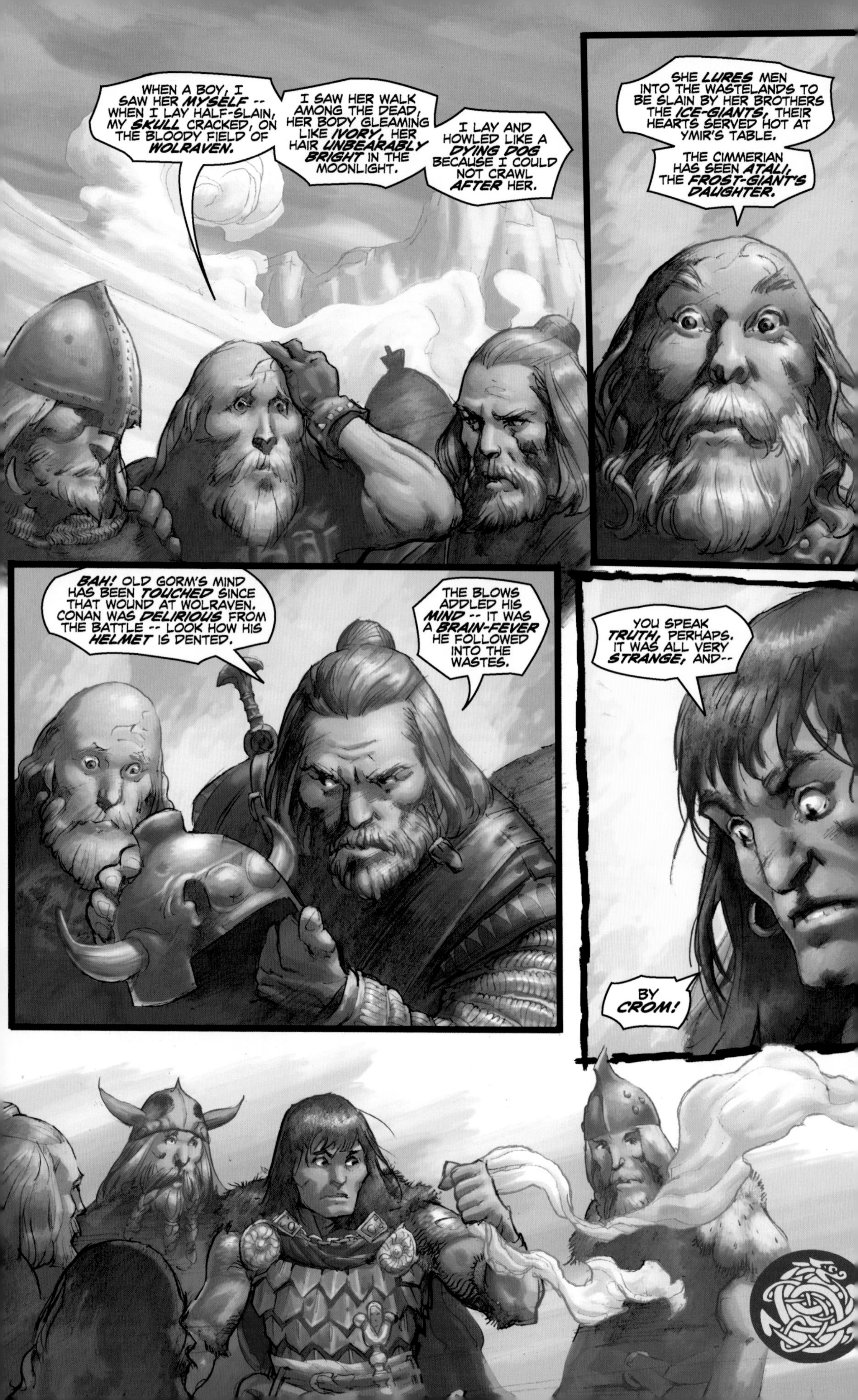
WHEN A BOY, I SAW HER MYSELF -- WHEN I LAY HALF-SLAIN, MY SKULL CRACKED, ON THE BLOODY FIELD OF WOLRAVEN.
I SAW HER WALK AMONG THE DEAD, HER BODY GLEAMING LIKE IVORY, HER HAIR UNBEARABLY BRIGHT IN THE MOONLIGHT.
I LAY AND HOWLED LIKE A DYING DOG BECAUSE I COULD NOT CRAWL AFTER HER.
SHE LURES MEN INTO THE WASTELANDS TO BE SLAIN BY HER BROTHERS THE ICE-GIANTS, THEIR HEARTS SERVED HOT AT YMIR'S TABLE.
THE CIMMERIAN HAS SEEN ATALI, THE FROST-GIANT'S DAUGHTER.
BAH! OLD GORM'S MIND HAS BEEN TOUCHED SINCE THAT WOUND AT WOLRAVEN. CONAN WAS DELIRIOUS FROM THE BATTLE -- LOOK HOW HIS HELMET IS DENTED.
THE BLOWS ADDLED HIS MIND -- IT WAS A BRAIN-FEVER HE FOLLOWED INTO THE WASTES.
YOU SPEAK TRUTH, PERHAPS. IT WAS ALL VERY STRANGE, AND--
BY CROM!

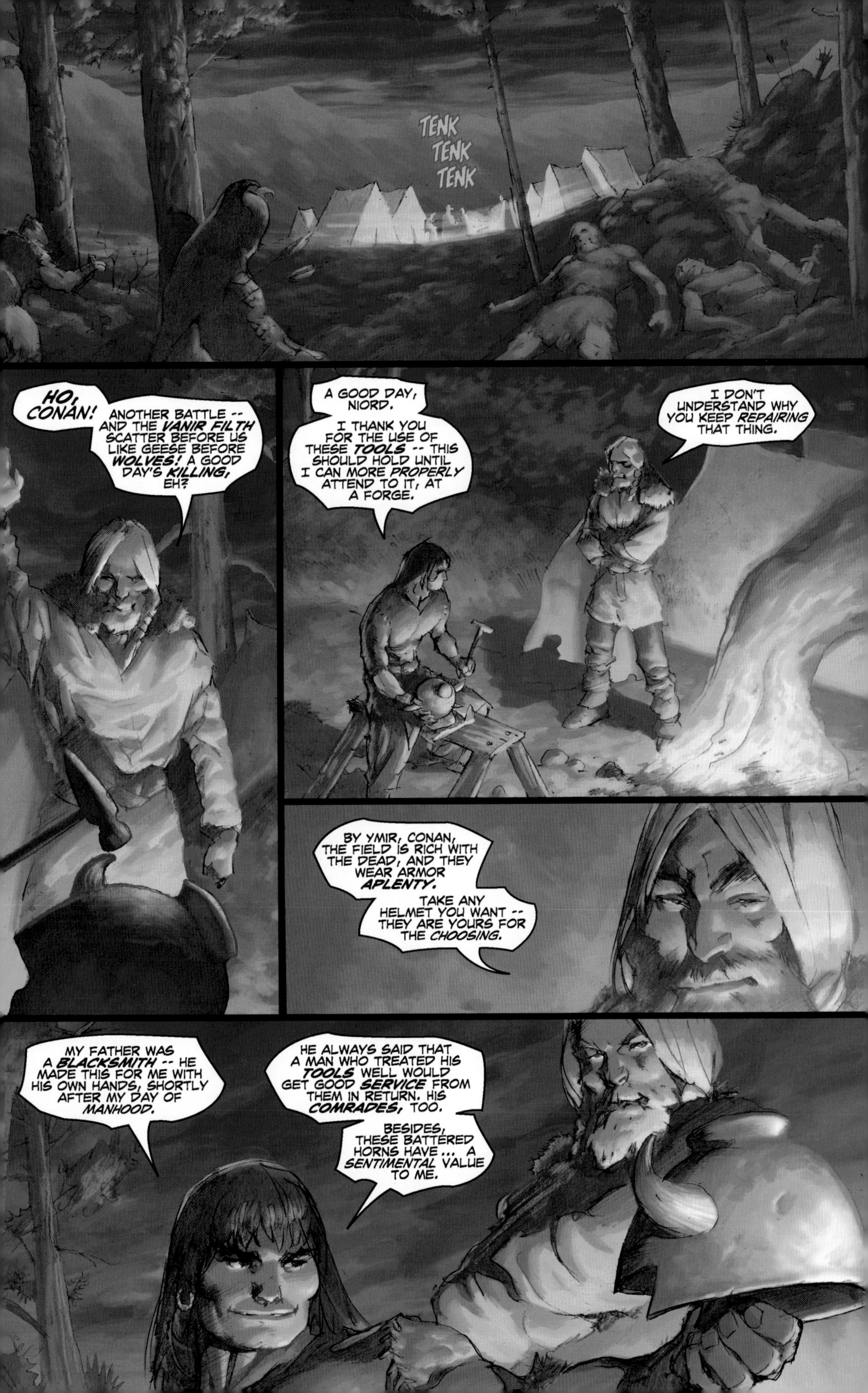
TENK TENK TENK
HO, CONAN!
ANOTHER BATTLE -- AND THE VANIR FILTH SCATTER BEFORE US LIKE GEESE BEFORE WOLVES! A GOOD DAY'S KILLING, EH?
A GOOD DAY, NIORD.
I THANK YOU FOR THE USE OF THESE TOOLS -- THIS SHOULD HOLD UNTIL I CAN MORE PROPERLY ATTEND TO IT, AT A FORGE.
I DON'T UNDERSTAND WHY YOU KEEP REPAIRING THAT THING.
BY YMIR, CONAN, THE FIELD IS RICH WITH THE DEAD, AND THEY WEAR ARMOR APLENTY.
TAKE ANY HELMET YOU WANT -- THEY ARE YOURS FOR THE CHOOSING.
MY FATHER WAS A BLACKSMITH -- HE MADE THIS FOR ME WITH HIS OWN HANDS, SHORTLY AFTER MY DAY OF MANHOOD.
HE ALWAYS SAID THAT A MAN WHO TREATED HIS TOOLS WELL WOULD GET GOOD SERVICE FROM THEM IN RETURN. HIS COMRADES, TOO.
BESIDES, THESE BATTERED HORNS HAVE... A SENTIMENTAL VALUE TO ME.

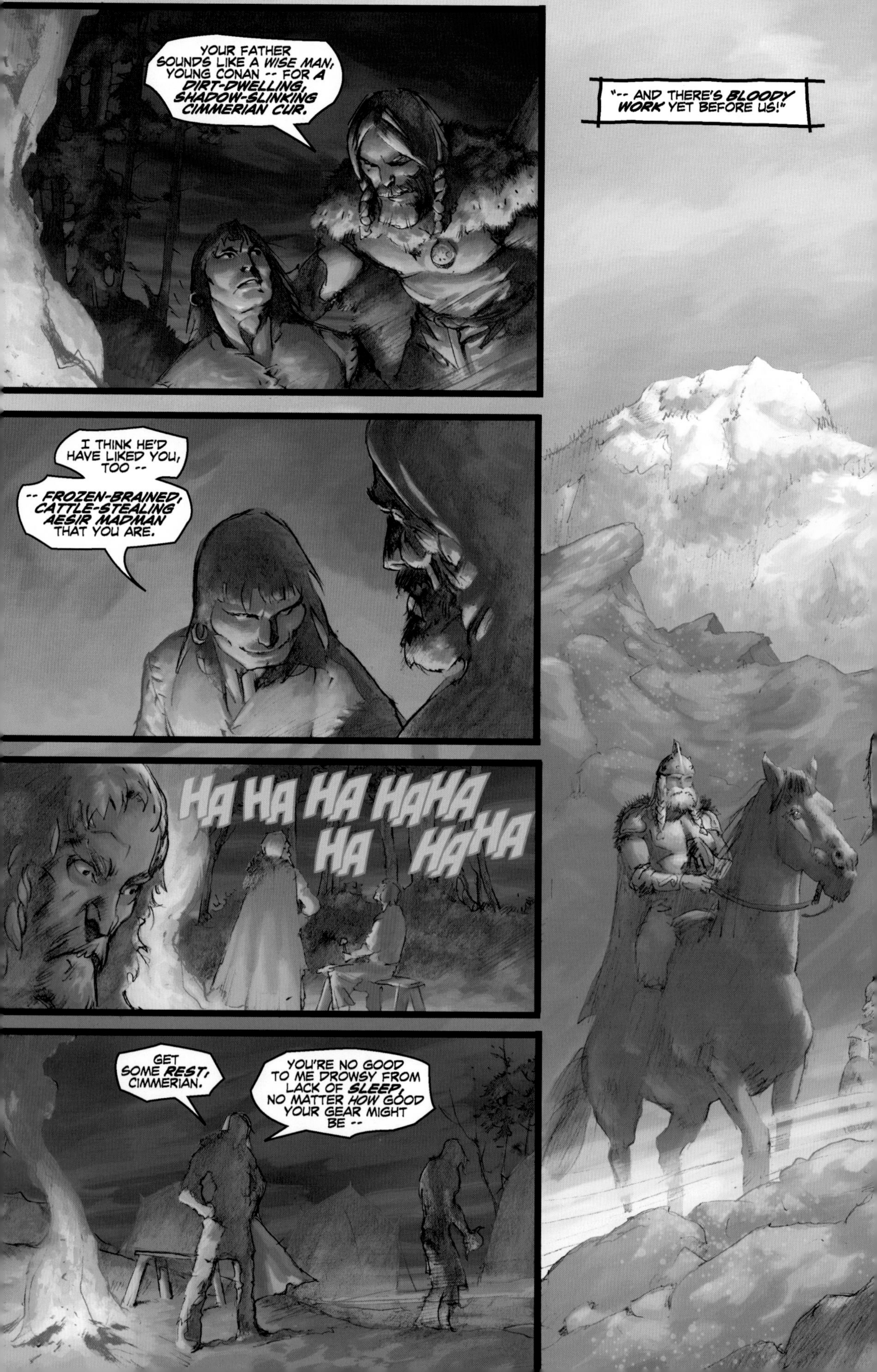

YOUR FATHER SOUNDS LIKE A WISE MAN, YOUNG CONAN -- FOR A DIRT-DWELLING, SHADOW-SLINKING CIMMERIAN CUR.
I THINK HE'D HAVE LIKED YOU, TOO --
-- FROZEN-BRAINED, CATTLE-STEALING AESIR MADMAN THAT YOU ARE.
HA HA HA HAHA HA HAHA
GET SOME REST, CIMMERIAN.
YOU'RE NO GOOD TO ME DROWSY FROM LACK OF SLEEP, NO MATTER HOW GOOD YOUR GEAR MIGHT BE --
"-- AND THERE'S BLOODY WORK YET BEFORE US!"

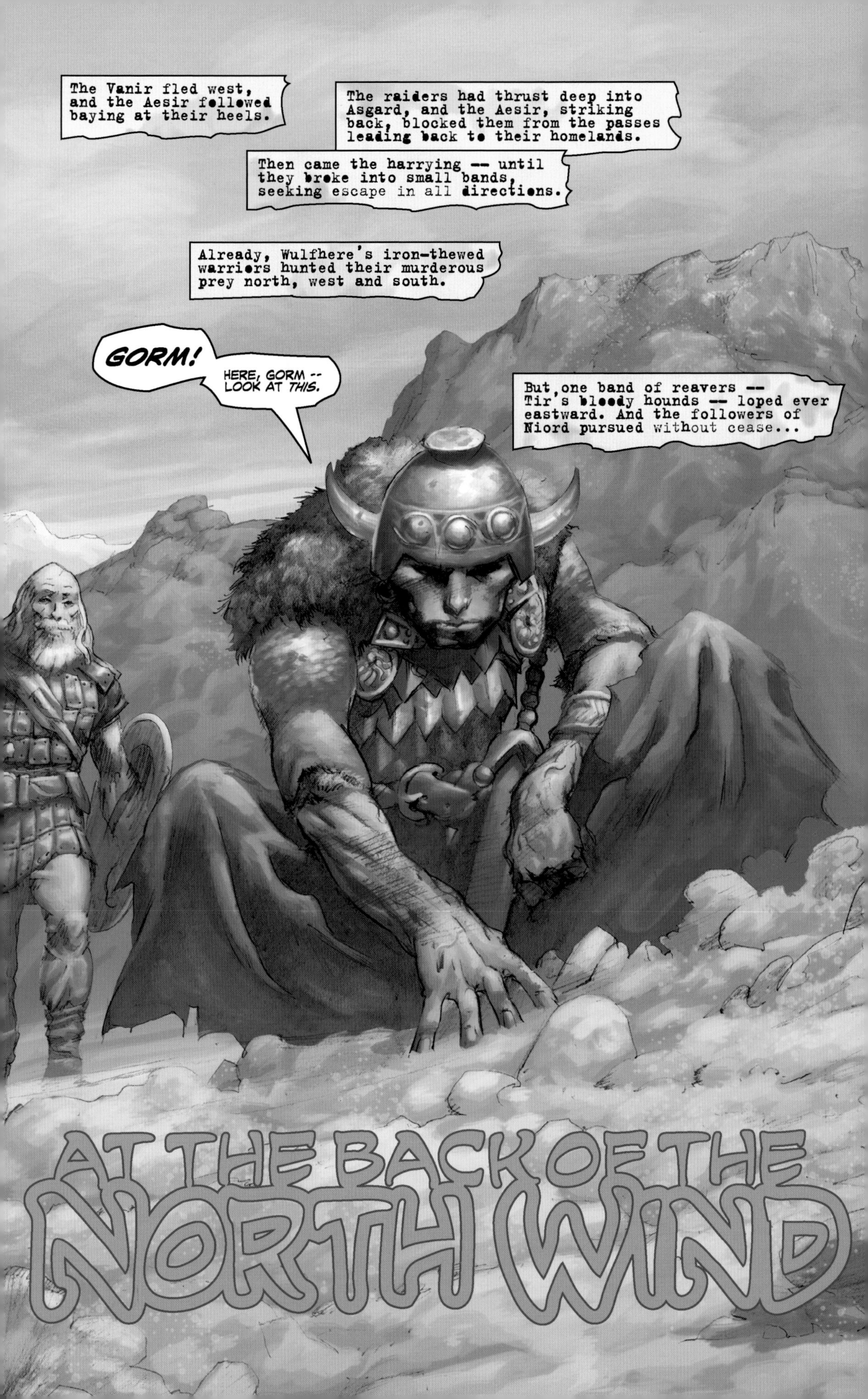
The Vanir fled west, and the Aesir followed baying at their heels.
The raiders had thrust deep into Asgard, and the Aesir, striking back, blocked them from the passes leading back to their homelands.
Then came the harrying -- until they broke into small bands, seeking escape in all directions.
Already, Wulfhere's iron-thewed warriors hunted their murderous prey north, west and south.
GORM!
HERE, GORM -- LOOK AT THIS.
But, one band of reavers -- Tir's bloody hounds -- loped ever eastward. And the followers of Niord pursued without cease...
AT THE BACK OF THE NORTH WIND

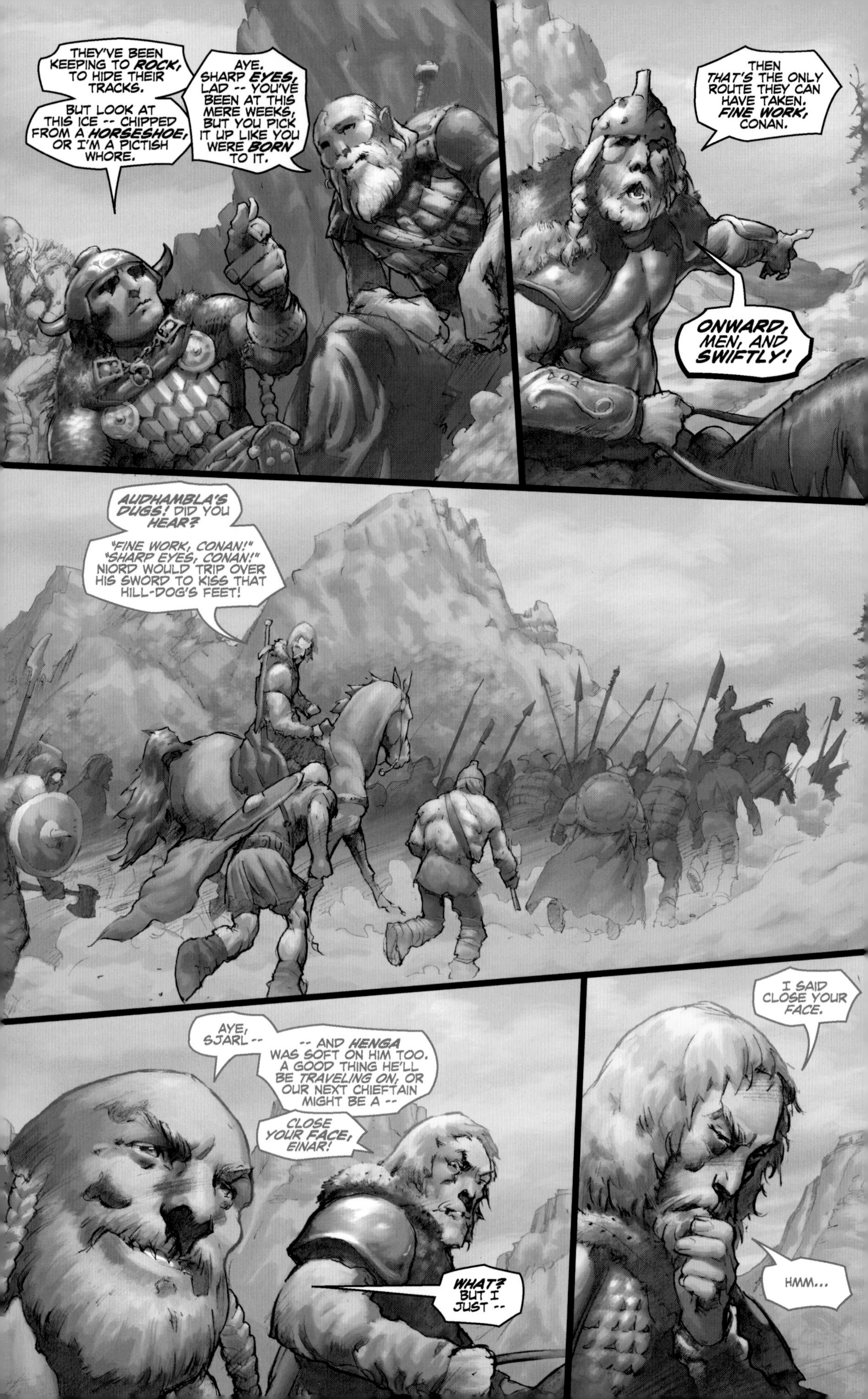
THEY'VE BEEN KEEPING TO ROCK, TO HIDE THEIR TRACKS.
BUT LOOK AT THIS ICE -- CHIPPED FROM A HORSESHOE, OR I'M A PICTISH WHORE.
AYE. SHARP EYES, LAD -- YOU'VE BEEN AT THIS MERE WEEKS, BUT YOU PICK IT UP LIKE YOU WERE BORN TO IT.
THEN THAT'S THE ONLY ROUTE THEY CAN HAVE TAKEN. FINE WORK, CONAN.
ONWARD, MEN, AND SWIFTLY!
AUDHAMBLA'S DUGS! DID YOU HEAR?
"FINE WORK, CONAN!" "SHARP EYES, CONAN!" NIORD WOULD TRIP OVER HIS SWORD TO KISS THAT HILL-DOG'S FEET!
AYE, SJARL --
-- AND HENGA WAS SOFT ON HIM TOO. A GOOD THING HE'LL BE TRAVELING ON, OR OUR NEXT CHIEFTAIN MIGHT BE A --
CLOSE YOUR FACE, EINAR!
WHAT? BUT I JUST --
I SAID CLOSE YOUR FACE.
HMM...

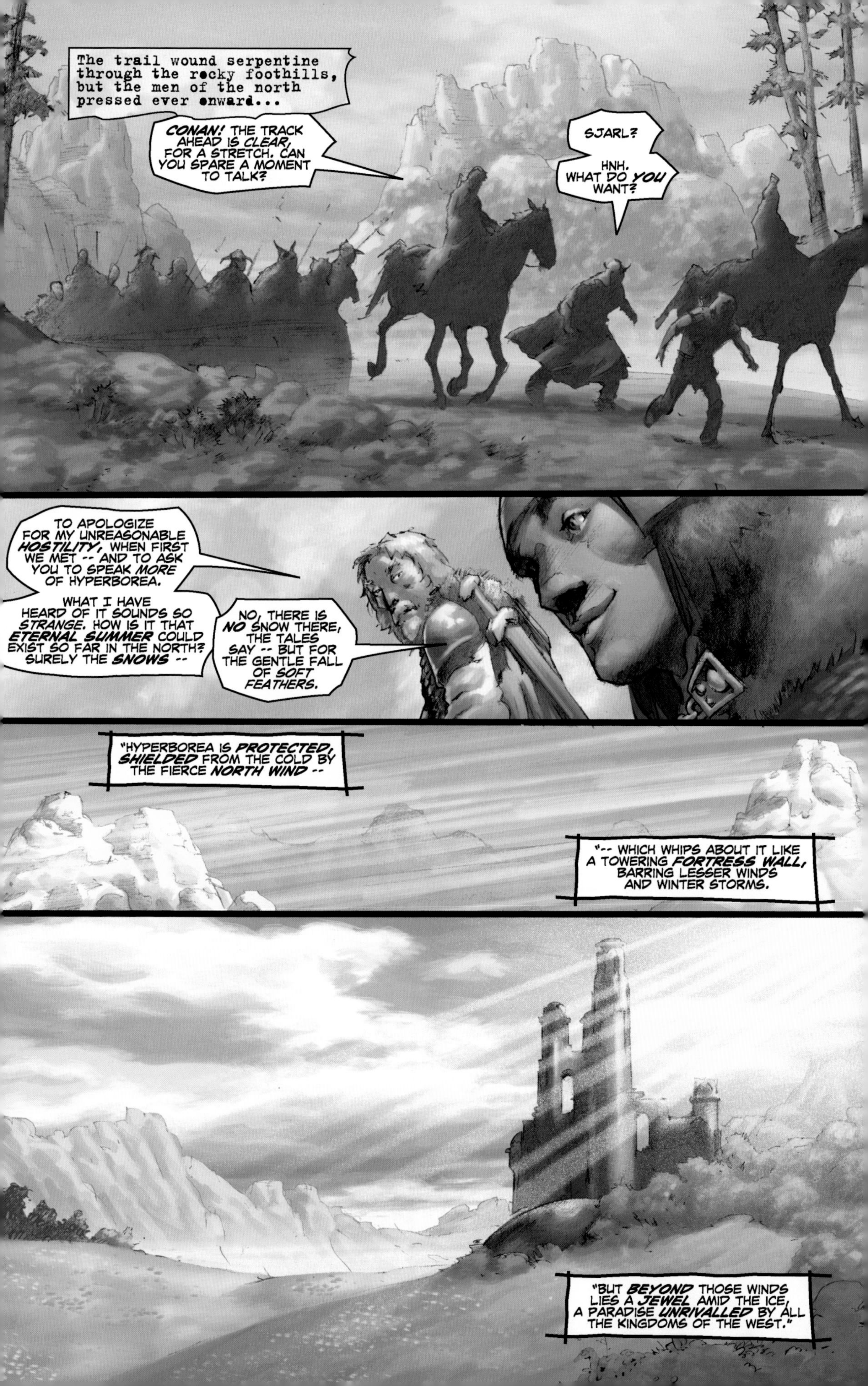
The trail wound serpentine through the rocky foothills, but the men of the north pressed ever onward...
CONAN! THE TRACK AHEAD IS CLEAR, FOR A STRETCH. CAN YOU SPARE A MOMENT TO TALK?
SJARL?
HNH. WHAT DO YOU WANT?
TO APOLOGIZE FOR MY UNREASONABLE HOSTILITY, WHEN FIRST WE MET -- AND TO ASK YOU TO SPEAK MORE OF HYPERBOREA.
WHAT I HAVE HEARD OF IT SOUNDS SO STRANGE. HOW IS IT THAT ETERNAL SUMMER COULD EXIST SO FAR IN THE NORTH? SURELY THE SNOWS --
NO, THERE IS NO SNOW THERE, THE TALES SAY -- BUT FOR THE GENTLE FALL OF SOFT FEATHERS.
"HYPERBOREA IS PROTECTED, SHIELDED FROM THE COLD BY THE FIERCE NORTH WIND --
"-- WHICH WHIPS ABOUT IT LIKE A TOWERING FORTRESS WALL, BARRING LESSER WINDS AND WINTER STORMS.
"BUT BEYOND THOSE WINDS LIES A JEWEL AMID THE ICE, A PARADISE UNRIVALLED BY ALL THE KINGDOMS OF THE WEST."

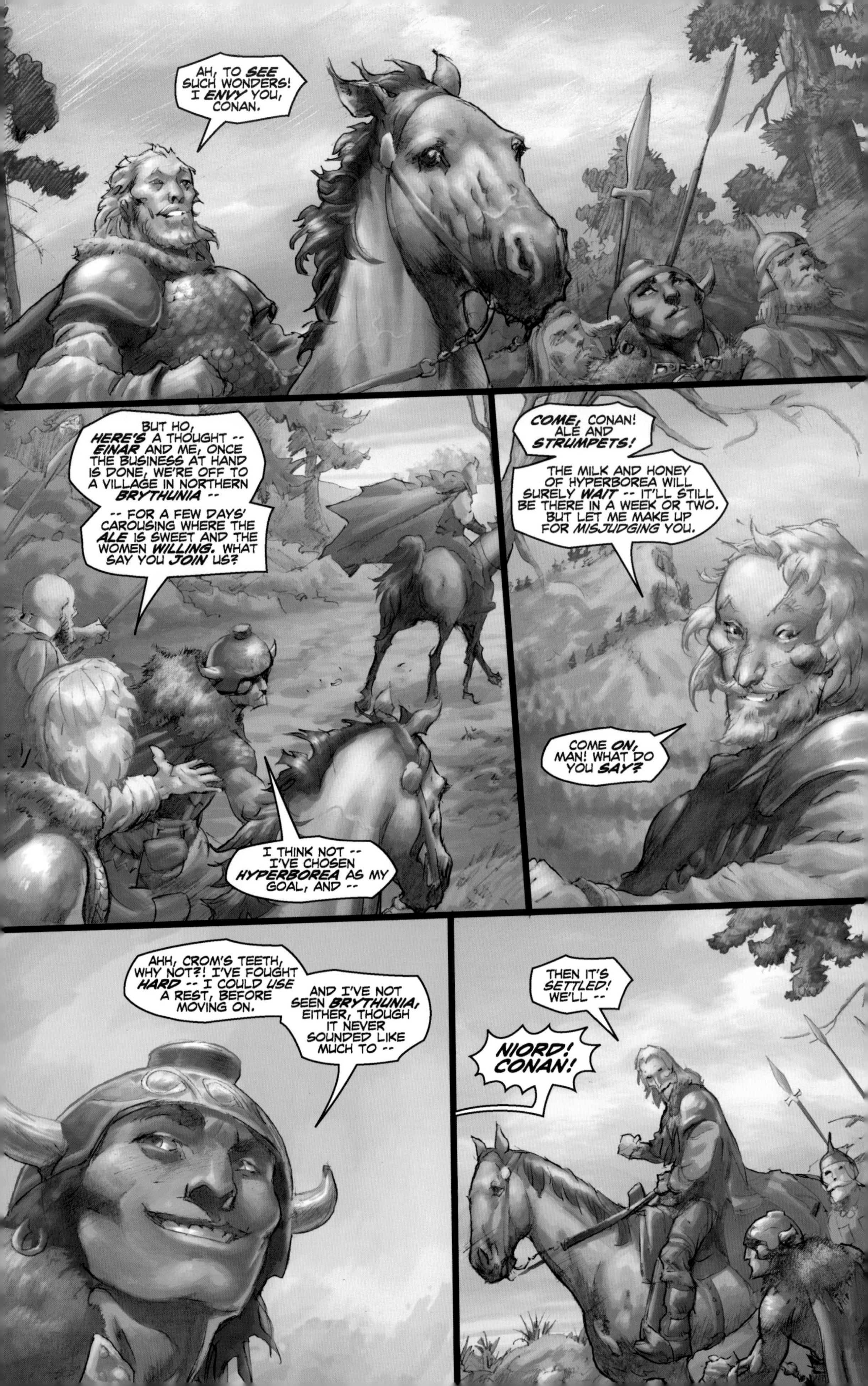
AH, TO SEE SUCH WONDERS! I ENVY YOU, CONAN.
BUT HO, HERE'S A THOUGHT -- EINAR AND ME, ONCE THE BUSINESS AT HAND IS DONE, WE'RE OFF TO A VILLAGE IN NORTHERN BRYTHUNIA --
-- FOR A FEW DAYS' CAROUSING WHERE THE ALE IS SWEET AND THE WOMEN WILLING. WHAT SAY YOU JOIN US?
I THINK NOT -- I'VE CHOSEN HYPERBOREA AS MY GOAL, AND --
COME, CONAN! ALE AND STRUMPETS!
THE MILK AND HONEY OF HYPERBOREA WILL SURELY WAIT -- IT'LL STILL BE THERE IN A WEEK OR TWO. BUT LET ME MAKE UP FOR MISJUDGING YOU.
COME ON, MAN! WHAT DO YOU SAY?
AHH, CROM'S TEETH, WHY NOT?! I'VE FOUGHT HARD -- I COULD USE A REST, BEFORE MOVING ON.
AND I'VE NOT SEEN BRYTHUNIA, EITHER, THOUGH IT NEVER SOUNDED LIKE MUCH TO --
THEN IT'S SETTLED! WE'LL --
NIORD! CONAN!

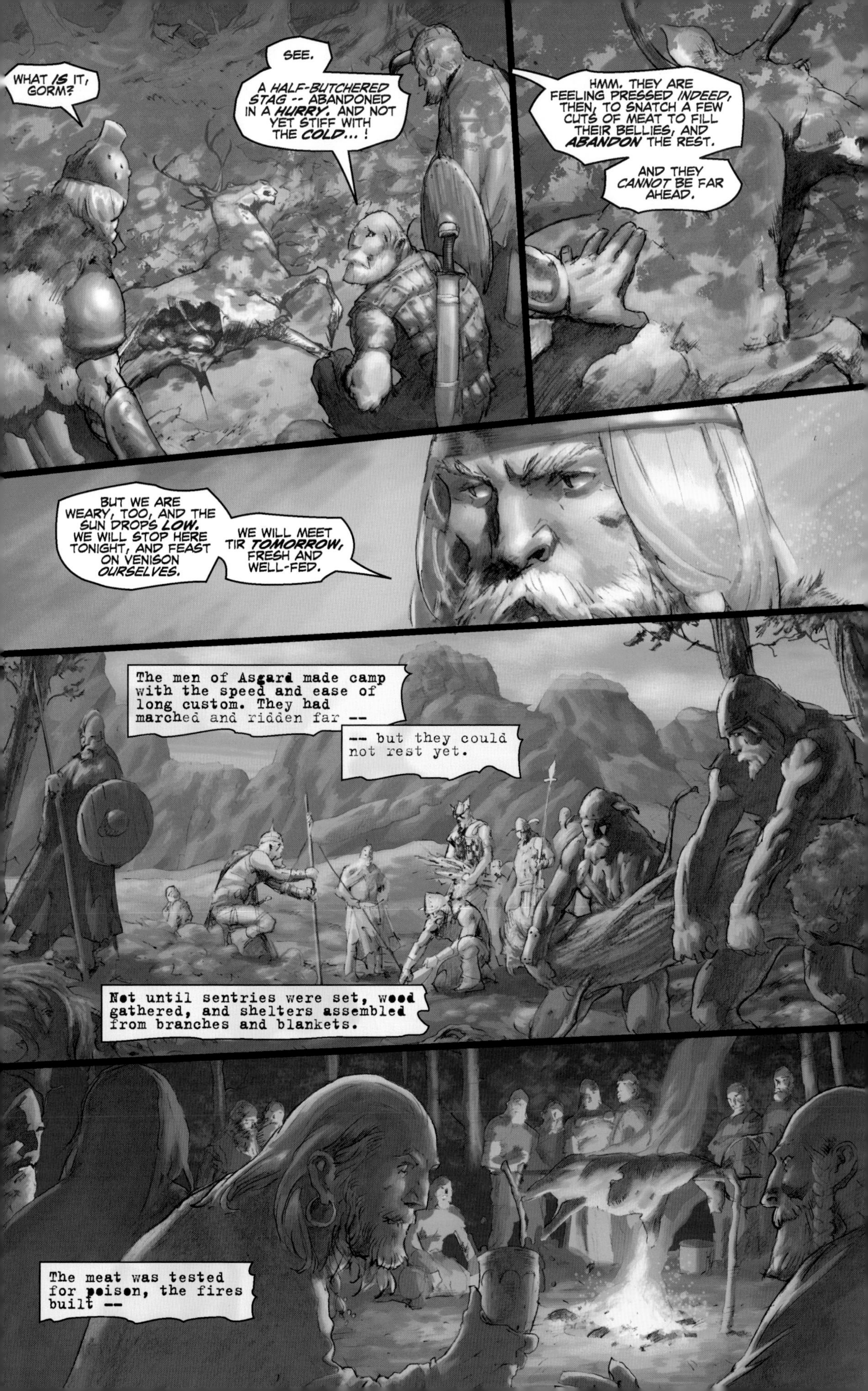
WHAT *IS* IT, GORM?
SEE.
A *HALF-BUTCHERED STAG* -- ABANDONED IN A *HURRY.* AND NOT YET STIFF WITH THE *COLD*... !
HMM. THEY ARE FEELING PRESSED *INDEED,* THEN, TO SNATCH A FEW CUTS OF MEAT TO FILL THEIR BELLIES, AND ***ABANDON*** THE REST.
AND THEY *CANNOT* BE FAR AHEAD.
BUT WE ARE WEARY, TOO, AND THE SUN DROPS ***LOW.*** WE WILL STOP HERE TONIGHT, AND FEAST ON VENISON *OURSELVES.*
WE WILL MEET TIR ***TOMORROW,*** FRESH AND WELL-FED.
The men of Asgard made camp with the speed and ease of long custom. They had marched and ridden far --
-- but they could not rest yet.
Not until sentries were set, wood gathered, and shelters assembled from branches and blankets.
The meat was tested for poison, the fires built --

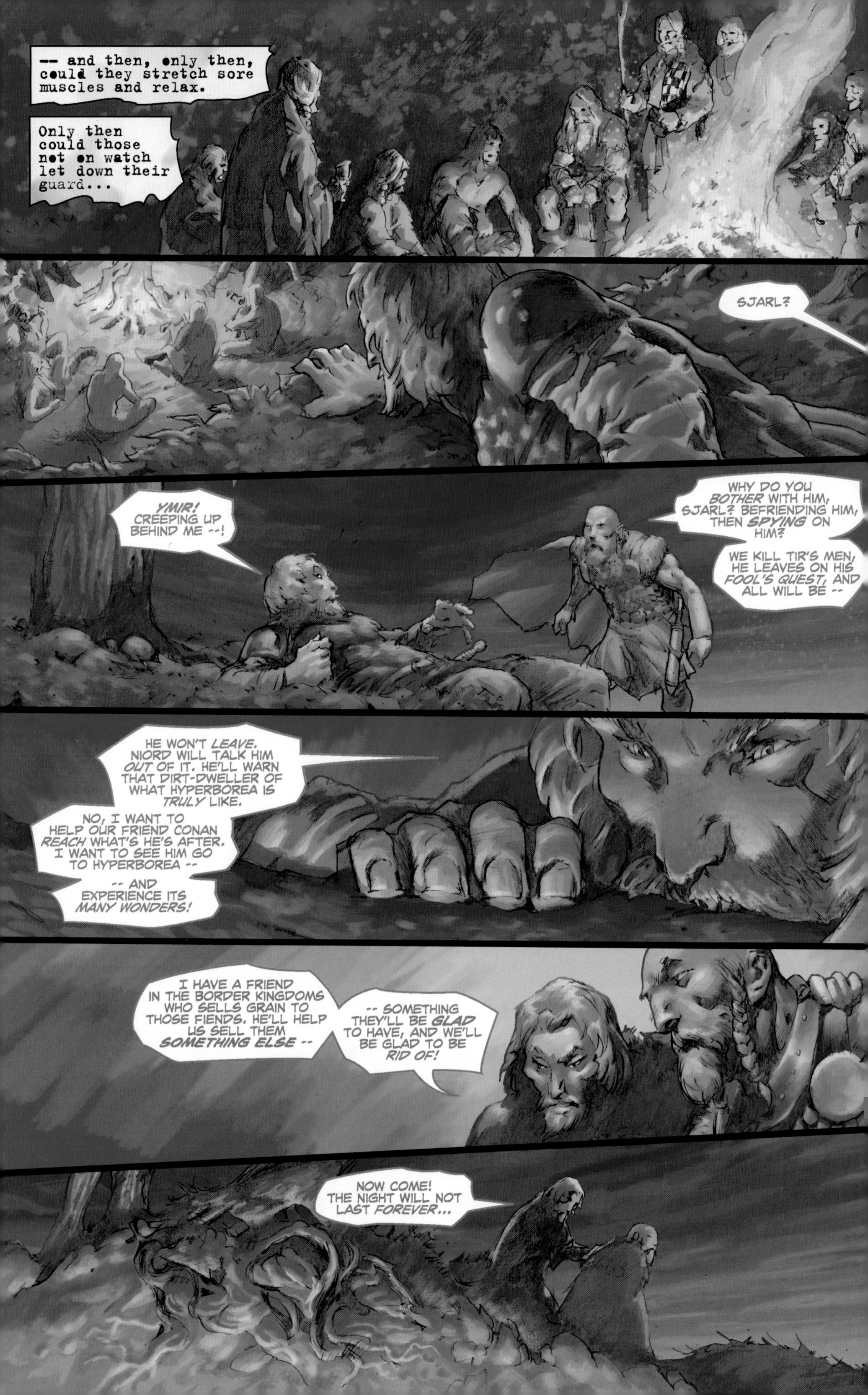

-- and then, only then, could they stretch sore muscles and relax.
Only then could those not on watch let down their guard...
SJARL?
YMIR! CREEPING UP BEHIND ME --!
WHY DO YOU BOTHER WITH HIM, SJARL? BEFRIENDING HIM, THEN SPYING ON HIM?
WE KILL TIR'S MEN, HE LEAVES ON HIS FOOL'S QUEST, AND ALL WILL BE --
HE WON'T LEAVE. NIORD WILL TALK HIM OUT OF IT. HE'LL WARN THAT DIRT-DWELLER OF WHAT HYPERBOREA IS TRULY LIKE.
NO, I WANT TO HELP OUR FRIEND CONAN REACH WHAT'S HE'S AFTER. I WANT TO SEE HIM GO TO HYPERBOREA --
-- AND EXPERIENCE ITS MANY WONDERS!
I HAVE A FRIEND IN THE BORDER KINGDOMS WHO SELLS GRAIN TO THOSE FIENDS. HE'LL HELP US SELL THEM SOMETHING ELSE --
-- SOMETHING THEY'LL BE GLAD TO HAVE, AND WE'LL BE GLAD TO BE RID OF!
NOW COME! THE NIGHT WILL NOT LAST FOREVER...

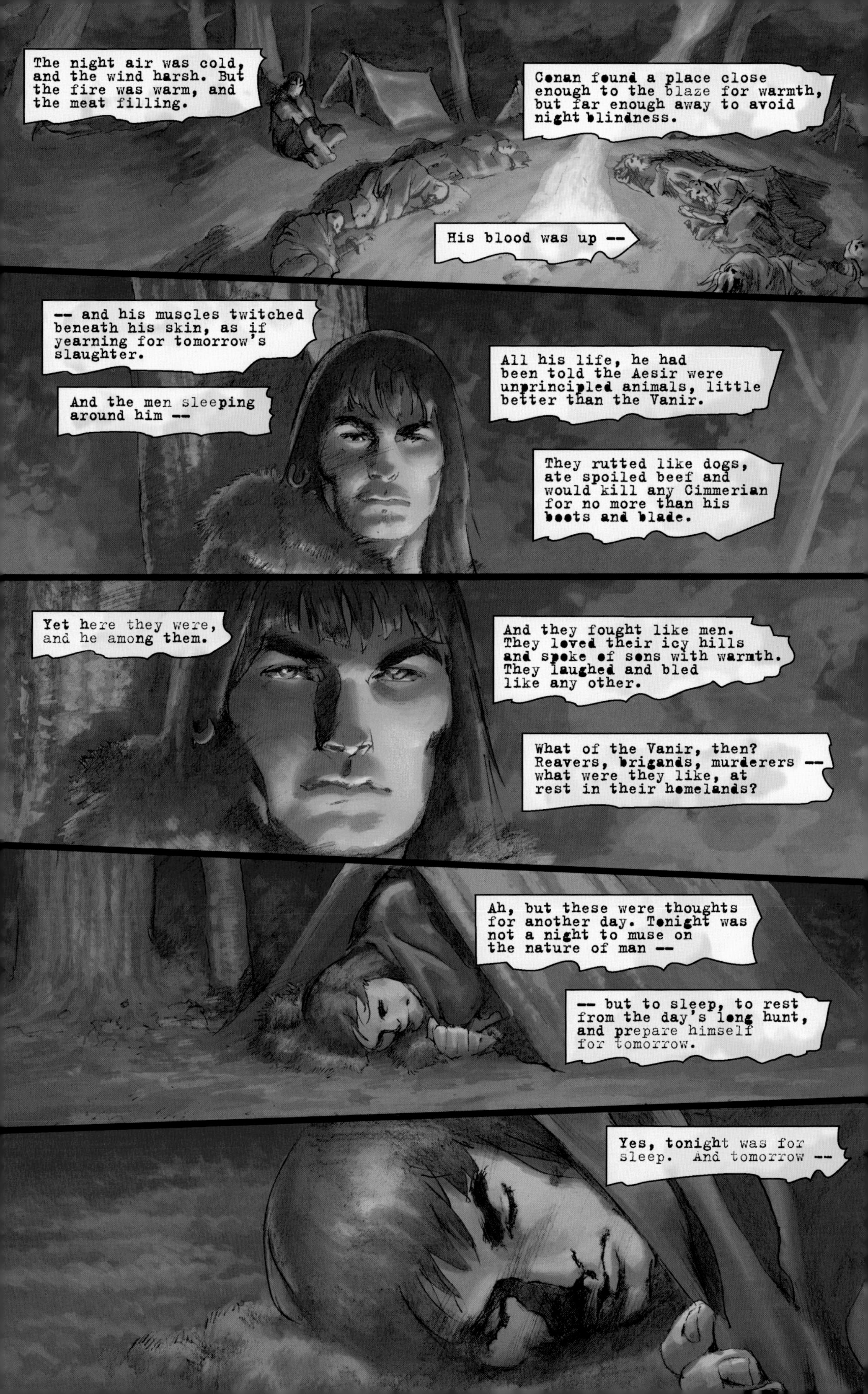

The night air was cold, and the wind harsh. But the fire was warm, and the meat filling.
Conan found a place close enough to the blaze for warmth, but far enough away to avoid night blindness.
His blood was up --
-- and his muscles twitched beneath his skin, as if yearning for tomorrow's slaughter.
And the men sleeping around him --
All his life, he had been told the Aesir were unprincipled animals, little better than the Vanir.
They rutted like dogs, ate spoiled beef and would kill any Cimmerian for no more than his boots and blade.
Yet here they were, and he among them.
And they fought like men. They loved their icy hills and spoke of sons with warmth. They laughed and bled like any other.
What of the Vanir, then? Reavers, brigands, murderers -- what were they like, at rest in their homelands?
Ah, but these were thoughts for another day. Tonight was not a night to muse on the nature of man --
-- but to sleep, to rest from the day's long hunt, and prepare himself for tomorrow.
Yes, tonight was for sleep. And tomorrow --

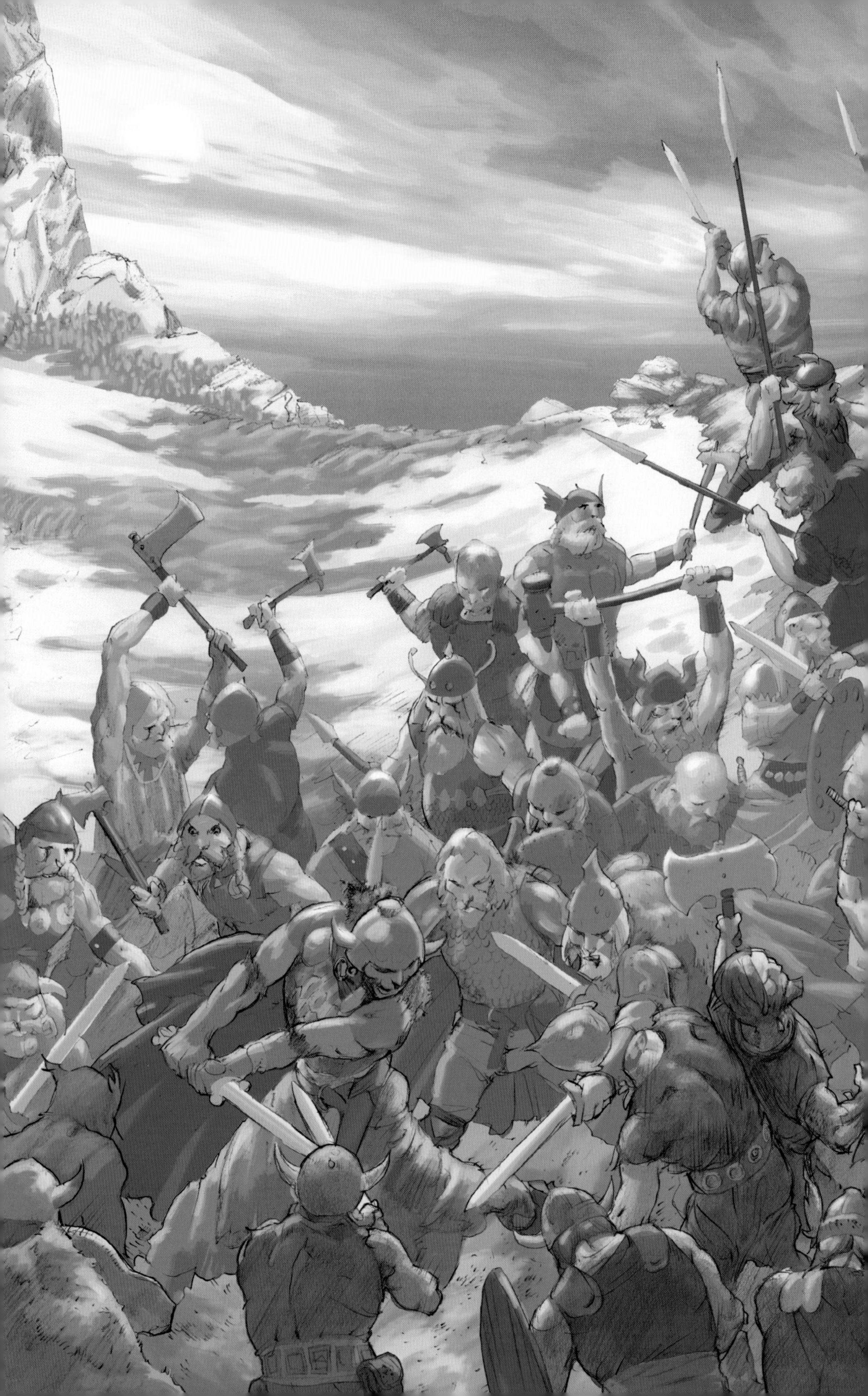

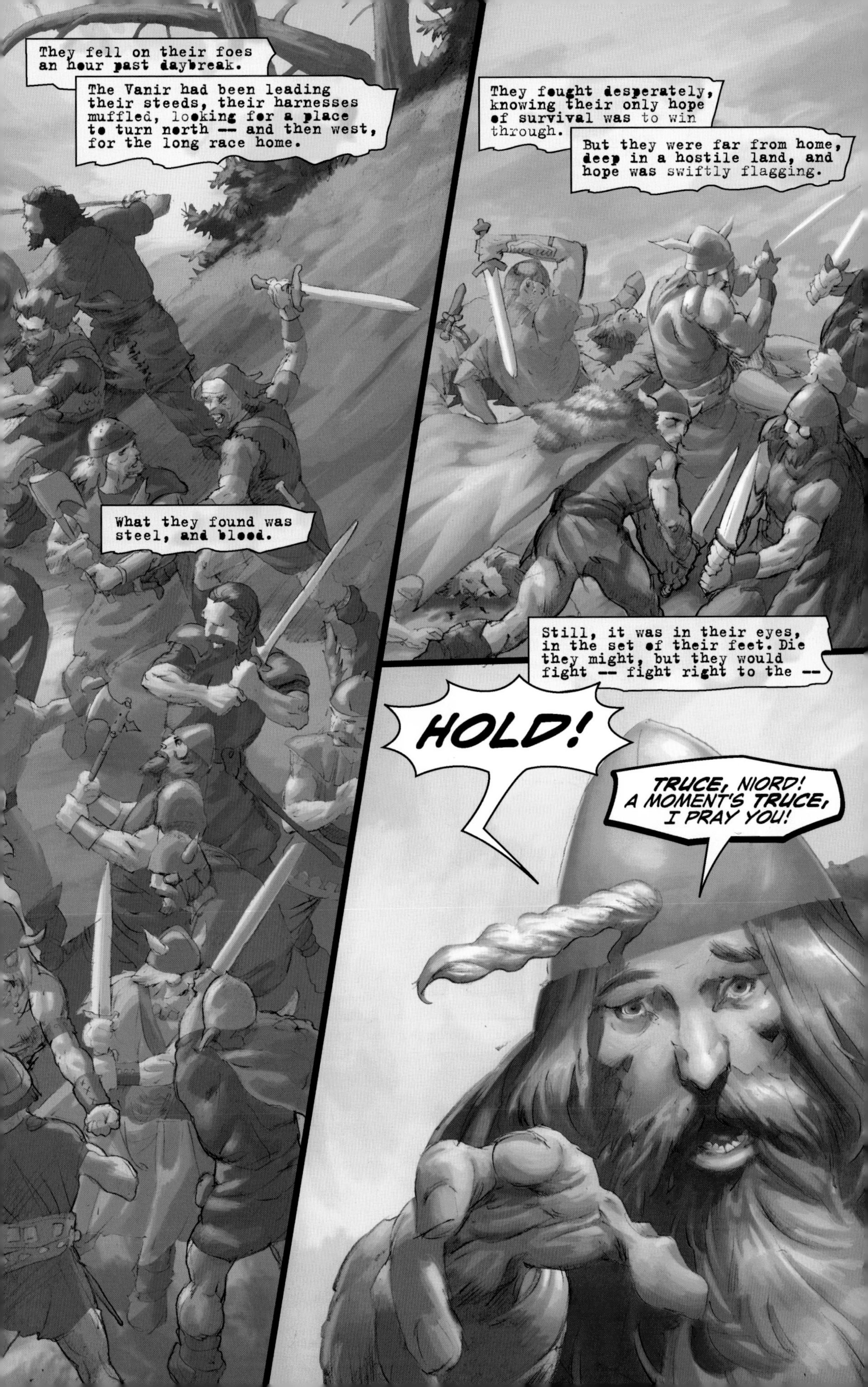
They fell on their foes an hour past daybreak.
The Vanir had been leading their steeds, their harnesses muffled, looking for a place to turn north -- and then west, for the long race home.
What they found was steel, and blood.
They fought desperately, knowing their only hope of survival was to win through.
But they were far from home, deep in a hostile land, and hope was swiftly flagging.
Still, it was in their eyes, in the set of their feet. Die they might, but they would fight -- fight right to the --
HOLD!
TRUCE, NIORD! A MOMENT'S TRUCE, I PRAY YOU!

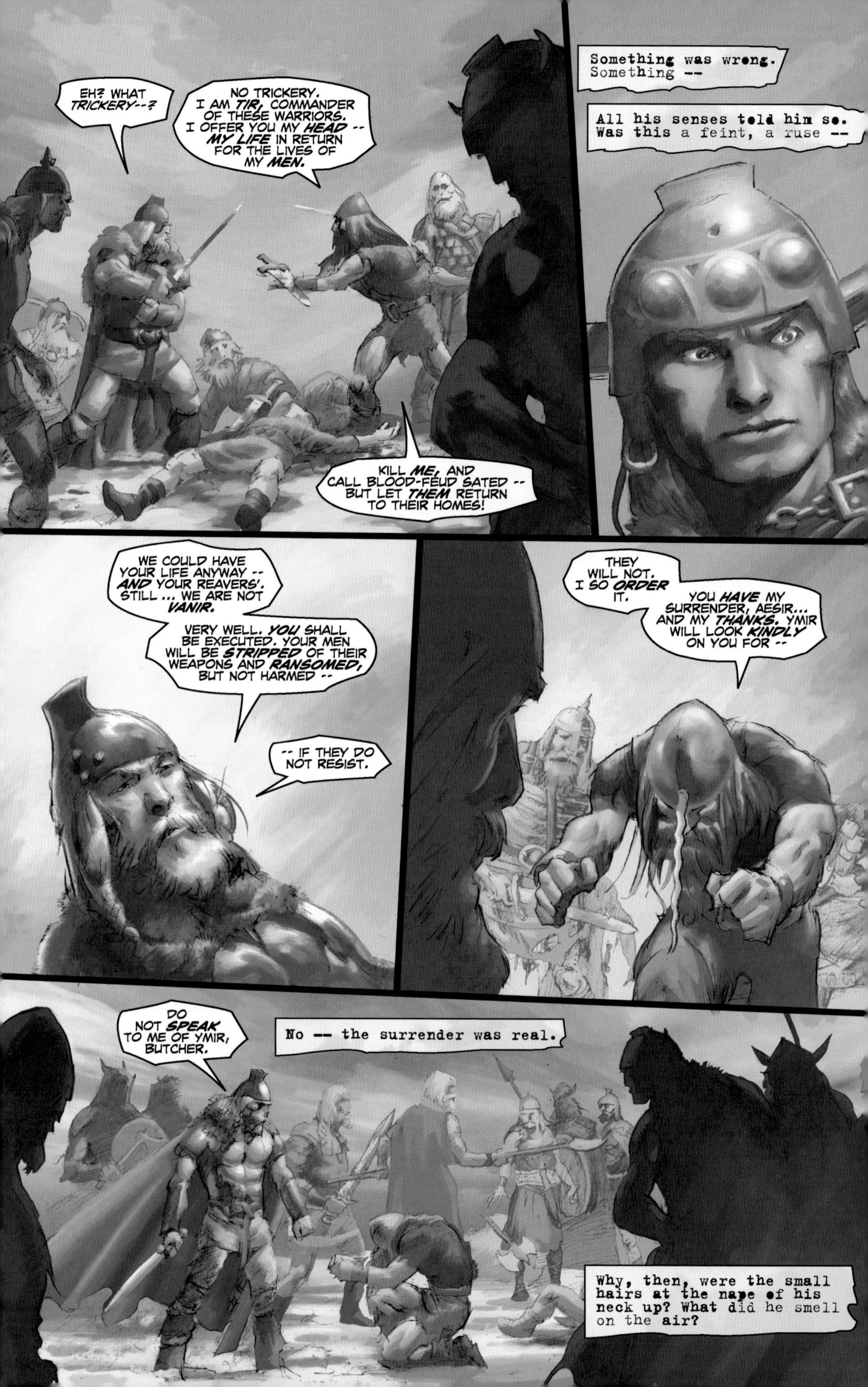
EH? WHAT TRICKERY--?
NO TRICKERY. I AM TIR, COMMANDER OF THESE WARRIORS. I OFFER YOU MY HEAD -- MY LIFE IN RETURN FOR THE LIVES OF MY MEN.
KILL ME, AND CALL BLOOD-FEUD SATED -- BUT LET THEM RETURN TO THEIR HOMES!
Something was wrong. Something --
All his senses told him so. Was this a feint, a ruse --
WE COULD HAVE YOUR LIFE ANYWAY -- AND YOUR REAVERS'. STILL ... WE ARE NOT VANIR.
VERY WELL. YOU SHALL BE EXECUTED. YOUR MEN WILL BE STRIPPED OF THEIR WEAPONS AND RANSOMED, BUT NOT HARMED --
-- IF THEY DO NOT RESIST.
THEY WILL NOT. I SO ORDER IT.
YOU HAVE MY SURRENDER, AESIR... AND MY THANKS. YMIR WILL LOOK KINDLY ON YOU FOR --
DO NOT SPEAK TO ME OF YMIR, BUTCHER.
No -- the surrender was real.
Why, then, were the small hairs at the nape of his neck up? What did he smell on the air?

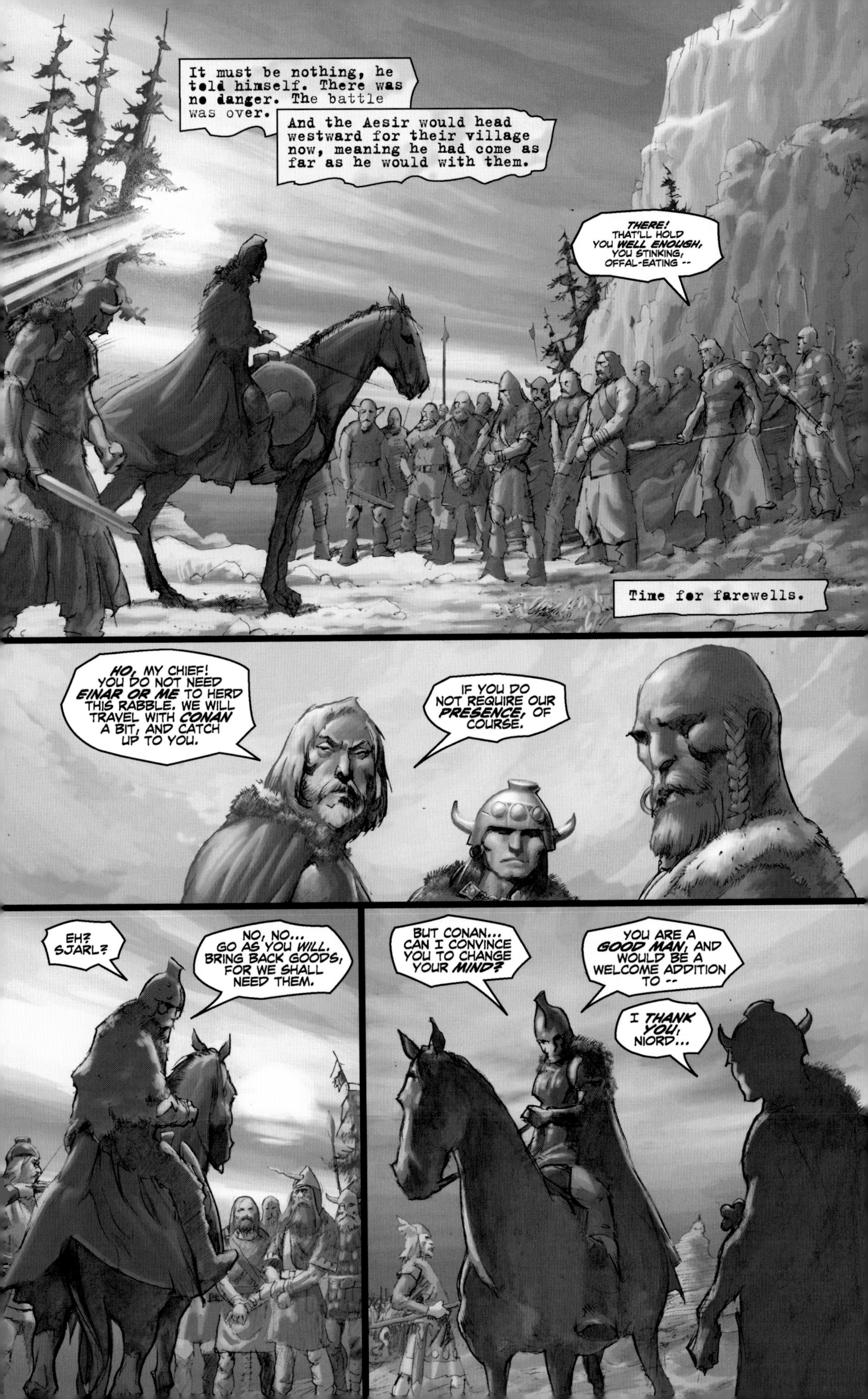
It must be nothing, he told himself. There was no danger. The battle was over.
And the Aesir would head westward for their village now, meaning he had come as far as he would with them.
THERE! THAT'LL HOLD YOU WELL ENOUGH, YOU STINKING, OFFAL-EATING --
Time for farewells.
HO, MY CHIEF! YOU DO NOT NEED EINAR OR ME TO HERD THIS RABBLE. WE WILL TRAVEL WITH CONAN A BIT, AND CATCH UP TO YOU.
IF YOU DO NOT REQUIRE OUR PRESENCE, OF COURSE.
EH? SJARL?
NO, NO... GO AS YOU WILL. BRING BACK GOODS, FOR WE SHALL NEED THEM.
BUT CONAN... CAN I CONVINCE YOU TO CHANGE YOUR MIND?
YOU ARE A GOOD MAN, AND WOULD BE A WELCOME ADDITION TO --
I THANK YOU, NIORD...

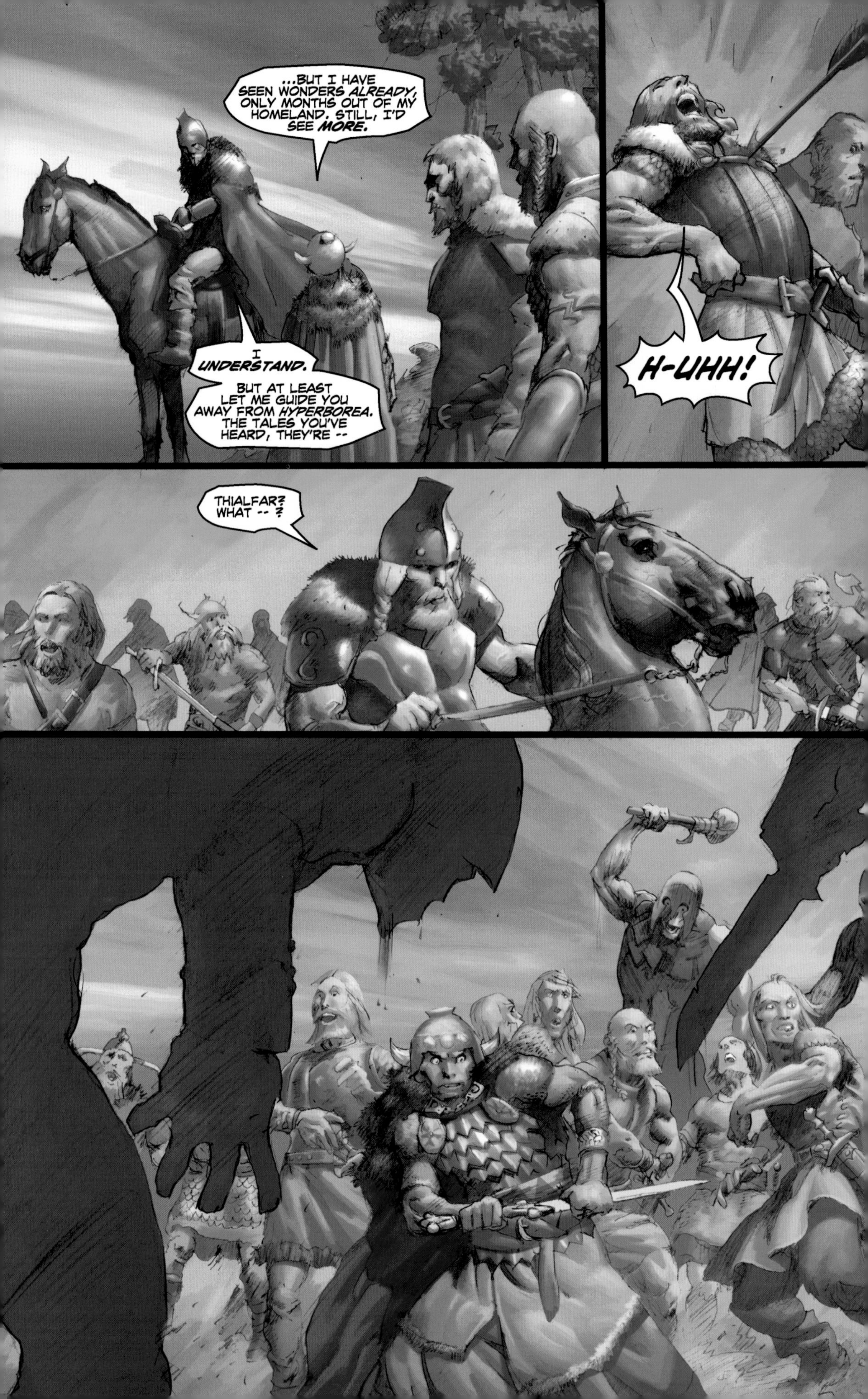
...BUT I HAVE SEEN WONDERS ALREADY, ONLY MONTHS OUT OF MY HOMELAND. STILL, I'D SEE MORE.
I UNDERSTAND.
BUT AT LEAST LET ME GUIDE YOU AWAY FROM HYPERBOREA. THE TALES YOU'VE HEARD, THEY'RE --
H-UHH!
THIALFAR? WHAT -- ?

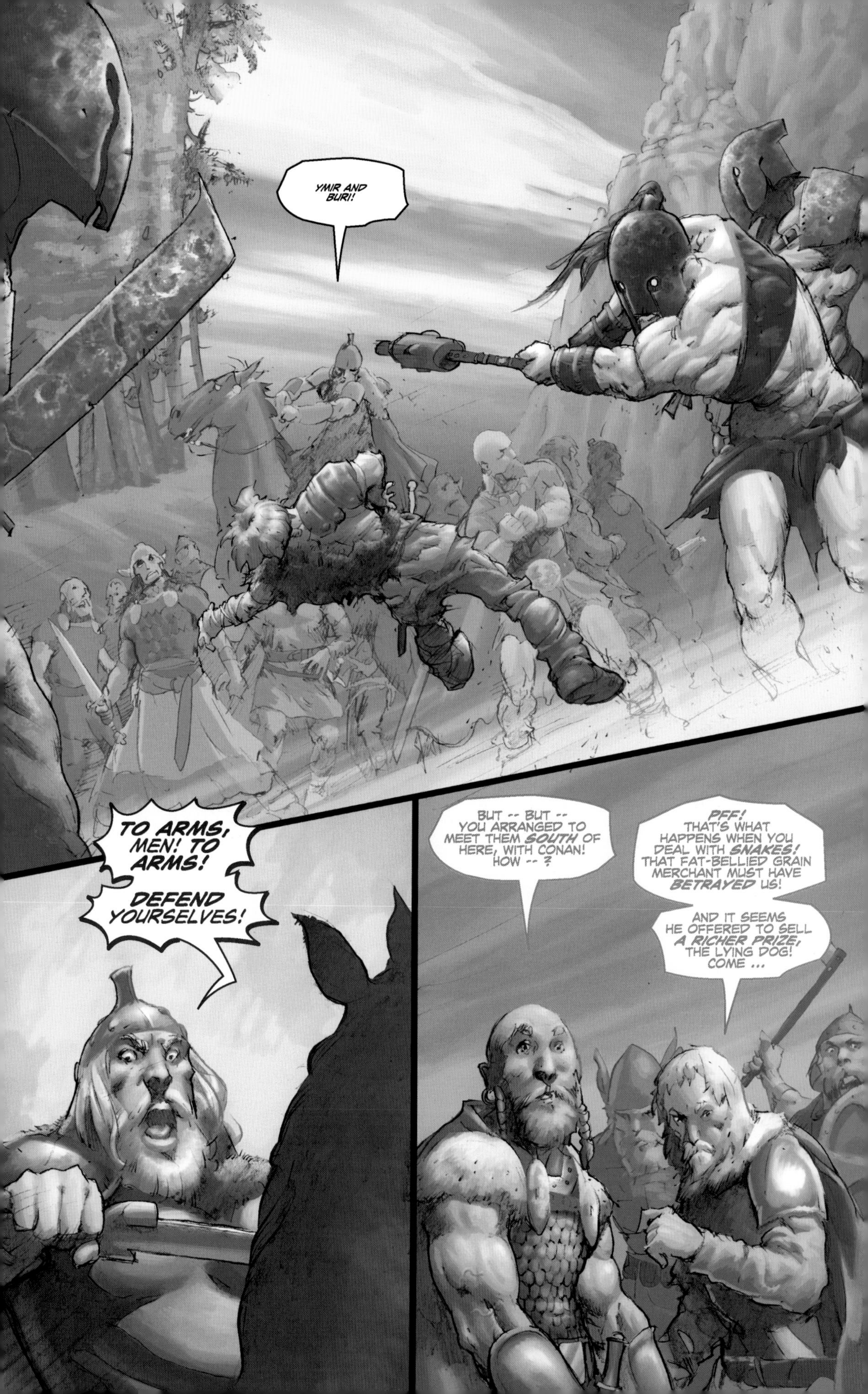
YMIR AND BURI!
TO ARMS, MEN! TO ARMS!
DEFEND YOURSELVES!
BUT -- BUT -- YOU ARRANGED TO MEET THEM SOUTH OF HERE, WITH CONAN! HOW -- ?
PFF! THAT'S WHAT HAPPENS WHEN YOU DEAL WITH SNAKES! THAT FAT-BELLIED GRAIN MERCHANT MUST HAVE BETRAYED US!
AND IT SEEMS HE OFFERED TO SELL A RICHER PRIZE, THE LYING DOG! COME ...

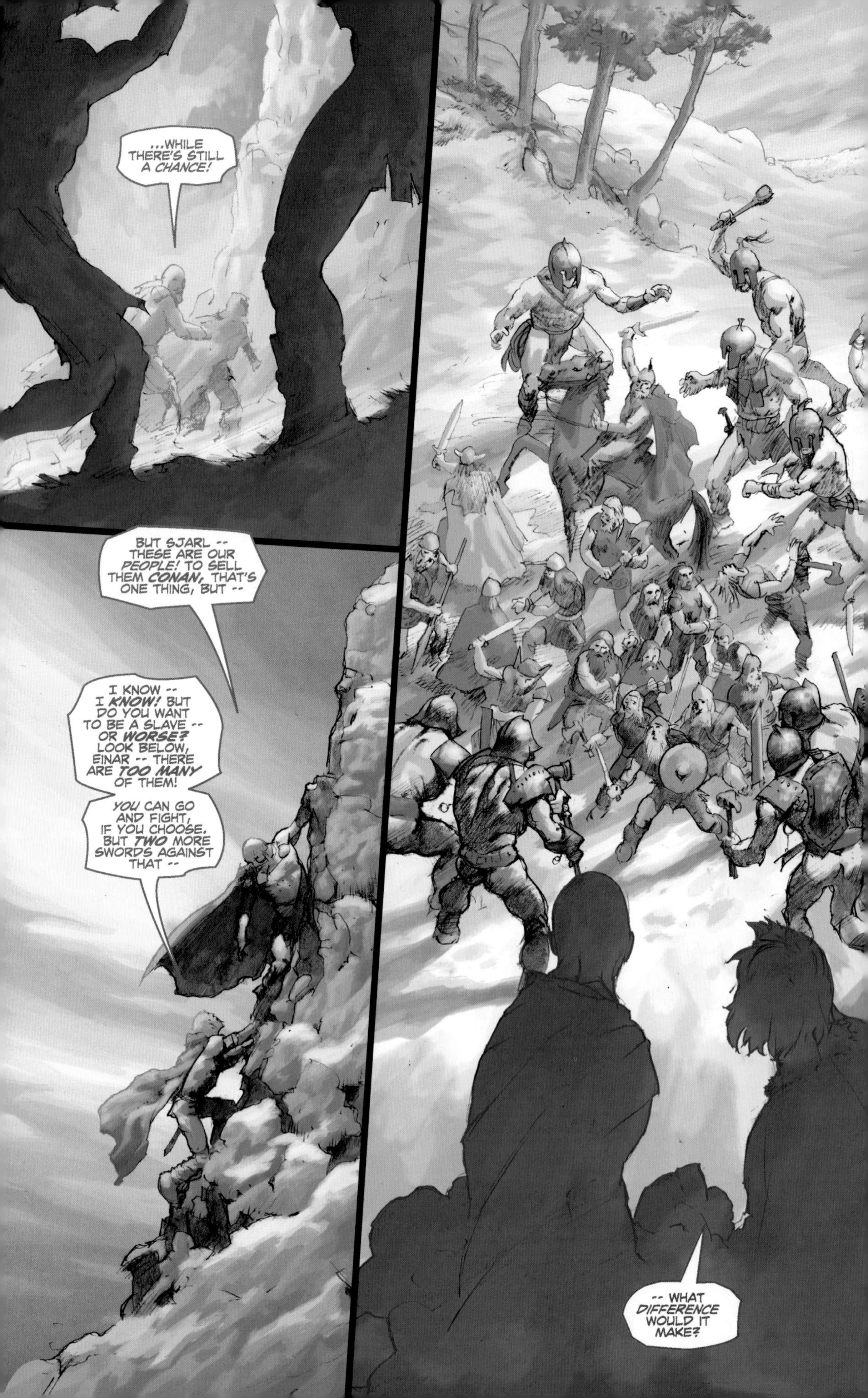
...WHILE THERE'S STILL A *CHANCE!*
BUT SJARL -- THESE ARE OUR *PEOPLE!* TO SELL THEM **CONAN**, THAT'S ONE THING, BUT --
I KNOW -- I ***KNOW!*** BUT DO YOU WANT TO BE A SLAVE -- OR ***WORSE?*** LOOK BELOW, EINAR -- THERE ARE ***TOO MANY*** OF THEM!
YOU CAN GO AND FIGHT, IF YOU CHOOSE. BUT ***TWO*** MORE SWORDS AGAINST THAT --
-- WHAT *DIFFERENCE* WOULD IT MAKE?

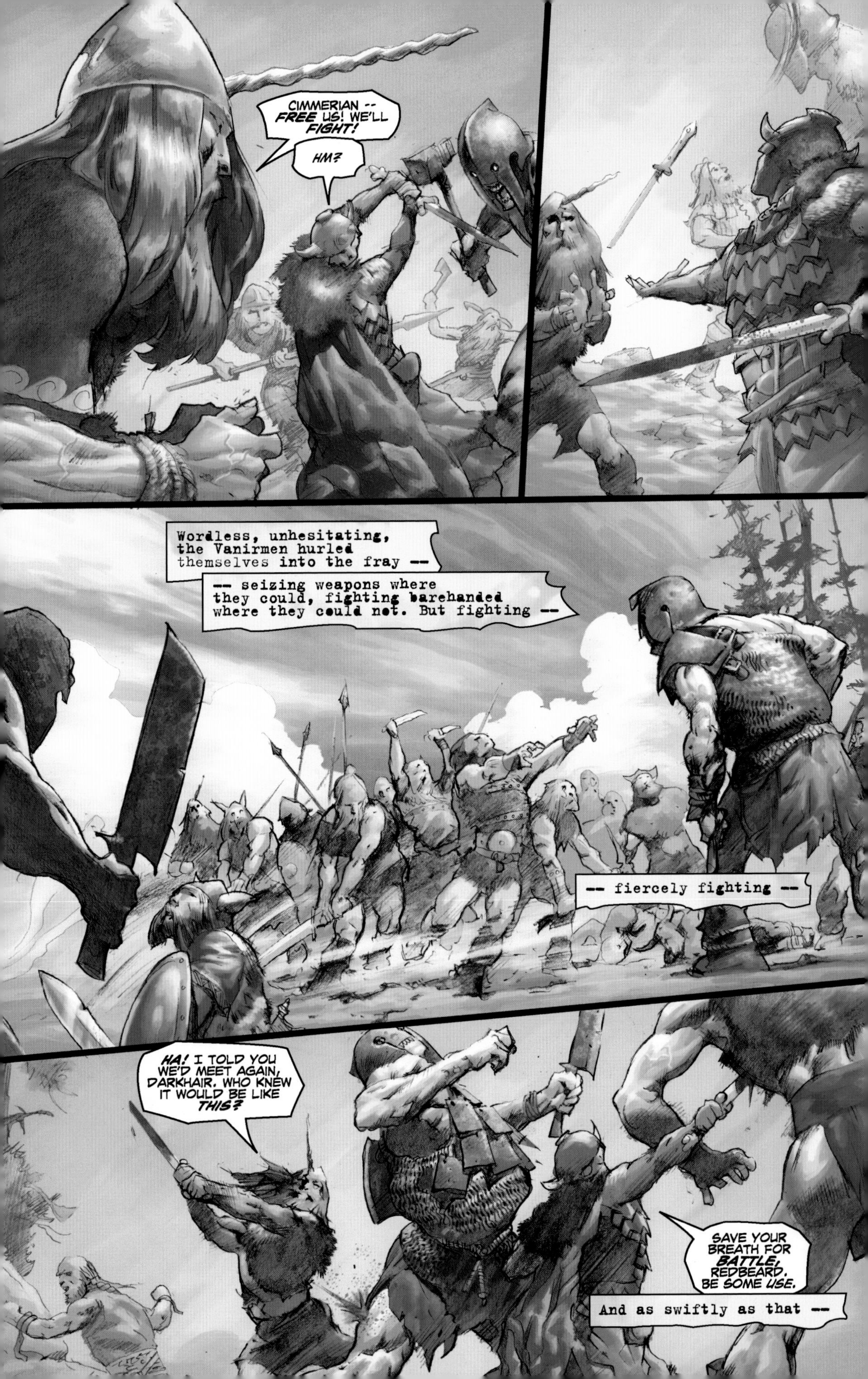
CIMMERIAN -- FREE US! WE'LL FIGHT!
HM?
Wordless, unhesitating, the Vanirmen hurled themselves into the fray --
-- seizing weapons where they could, fighting barehanded where they could not. But fighting --
-- fiercely fighting --
HA! I TOLD YOU WE'D MEET AGAIN, DARKHAIR. WHO KNEW IT WOULD BE LIKE THIS?
SAVE YOUR BREATH FOR BATTLE, REDBEARD. BE SOME USE.
And as swiftly as that --

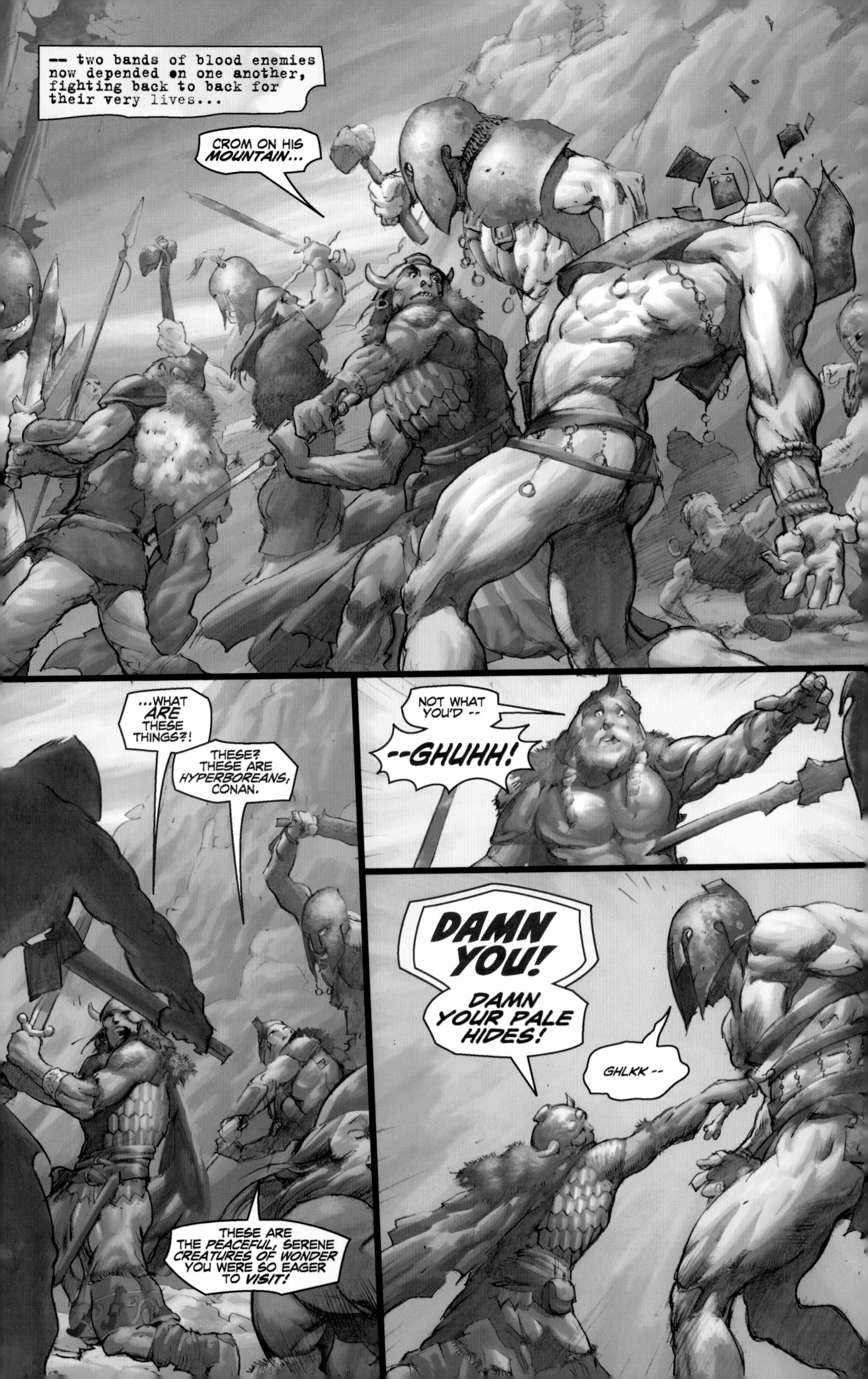
-- two bands of blood enemies now depended on one another, fighting back to back for their very lives...
CROM ON HIS MOUNTAIN...
...WHAT ARE THESE THINGS?!
THESE? THESE ARE HYPERBOREANS, CONAN.
THESE ARE THE PEACEFUL, SERENE CREATURES OF WONDER YOU WERE SO EAGER TO VISIT!
NOT WHAT YOU'D --
--GHUHH!
DAMN YOU! DAMN YOUR PALE HIDES!
GHLKK --

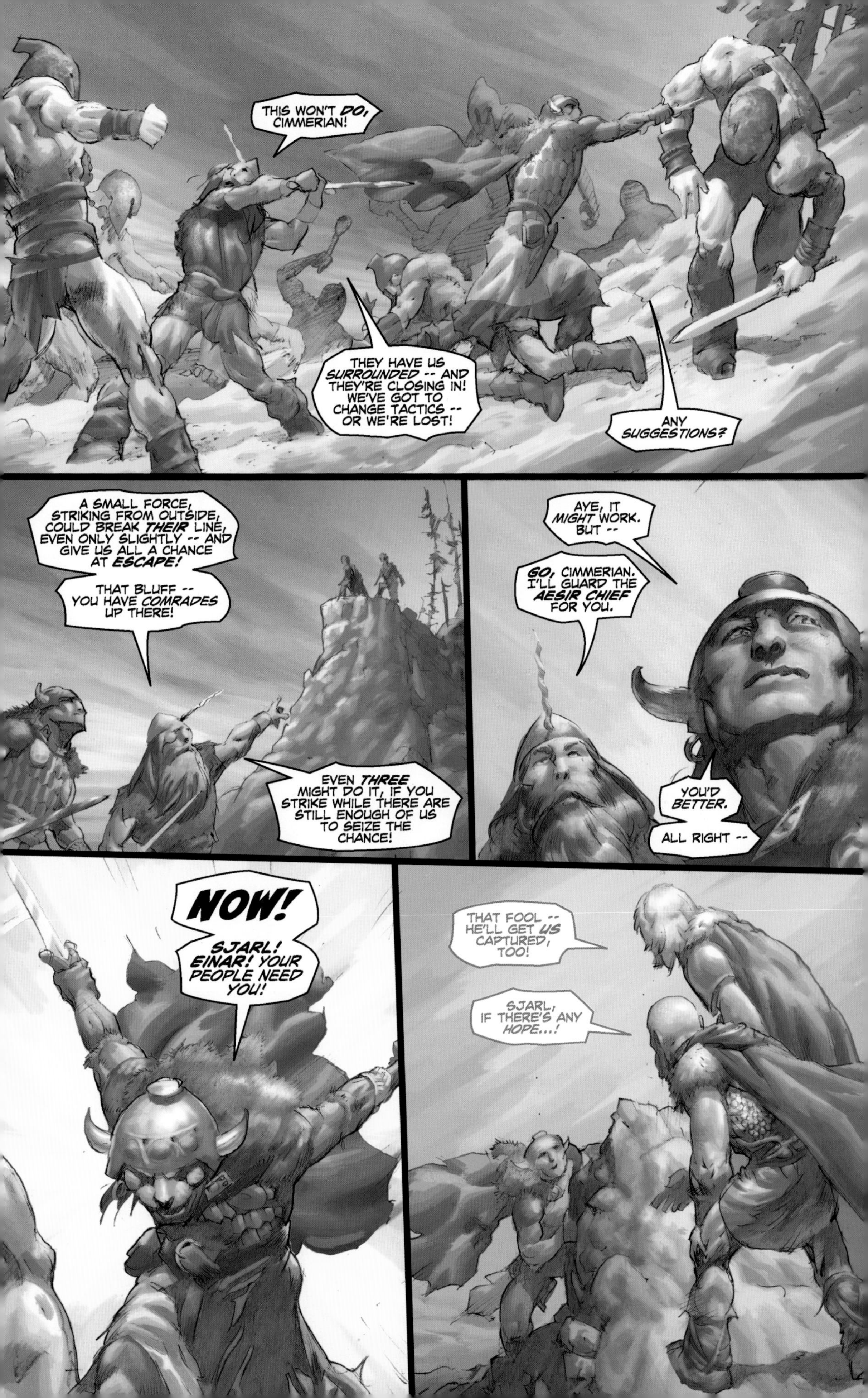
THIS WON'T DO, CIMMERIAN!
THEY HAVE US SURROUNDED -- AND THEY'RE CLOSING IN! WE'VE GOT TO CHANGE TACTICS -- OR WE'RE LOST!
ANY SUGGESTIONS?
A SMALL FORCE, STRIKING FROM OUTSIDE, COULD BREAK THEIR LINE, EVEN ONLY SLIGHTLY -- AND GIVE US ALL A CHANCE AT ESCAPE!
THAT BLUFF -- YOU HAVE COMRADES UP THERE!
EVEN THREE MIGHT DO IT, IF YOU STRIKE WHILE THERE ARE STILL ENOUGH OF US TO SEIZE THE CHANCE!
AYE, IT MIGHT WORK. BUT --
GO, CIMMERIAN. I'LL GUARD THE AESIR CHIEF FOR YOU.
YOU'D BETTER.
ALL RIGHT --
NOW!
SJARL! EINAR! YOUR PEOPLE NEED YOU!
THAT FOOL -- HE'LL GET US CAPTURED, TOO!
SJARL, IF THERE'S ANY HOPE...!

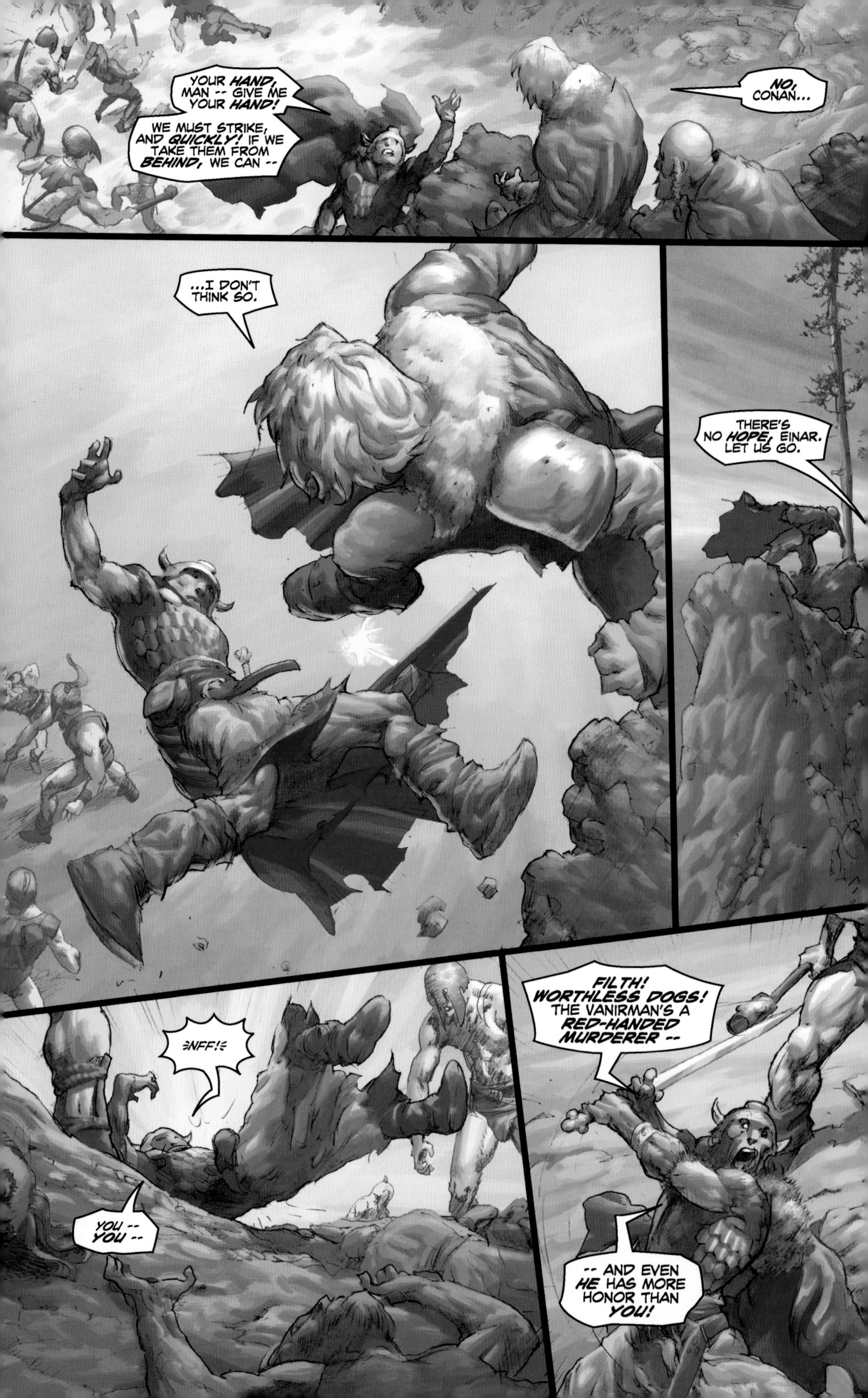
YOUR HAND, MAN -- GIVE ME YOUR HAND!
WE MUST STRIKE, AND QUICKLY! IF WE TAKE THEM FROM BEHIND, WE CAN --
NO, CONAN...
...I DON'T THINK SO.
THERE'S NO HOPE, EINAR. LET US GO.
NFF!
YOU -- YOU --
FILTH! WORTHLESS DOGS! THE VANIRMAN'S A RED-HANDED MURDERER --
-- AND EVEN HE HAS MORE HONOR THAN YOU!

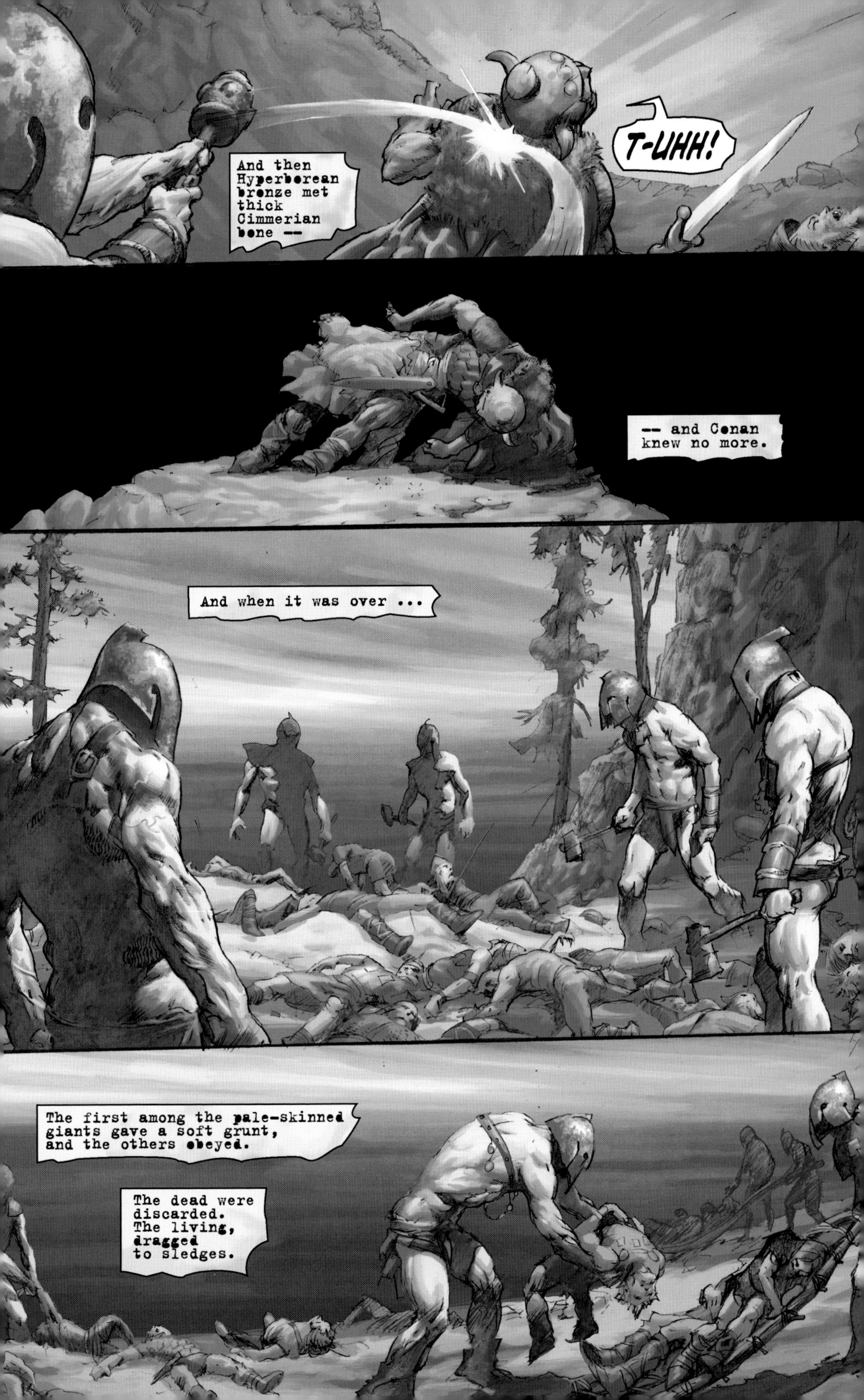
And then Hyperborean bronze met thick Cimmerian bone --
T-UHH!
-- and Conan knew no more.
And when it was over ...
The first among the pale-skinned giants gave a soft grunt, and the others obeyed.
The dead were discarded. The living, dragged to sledges.

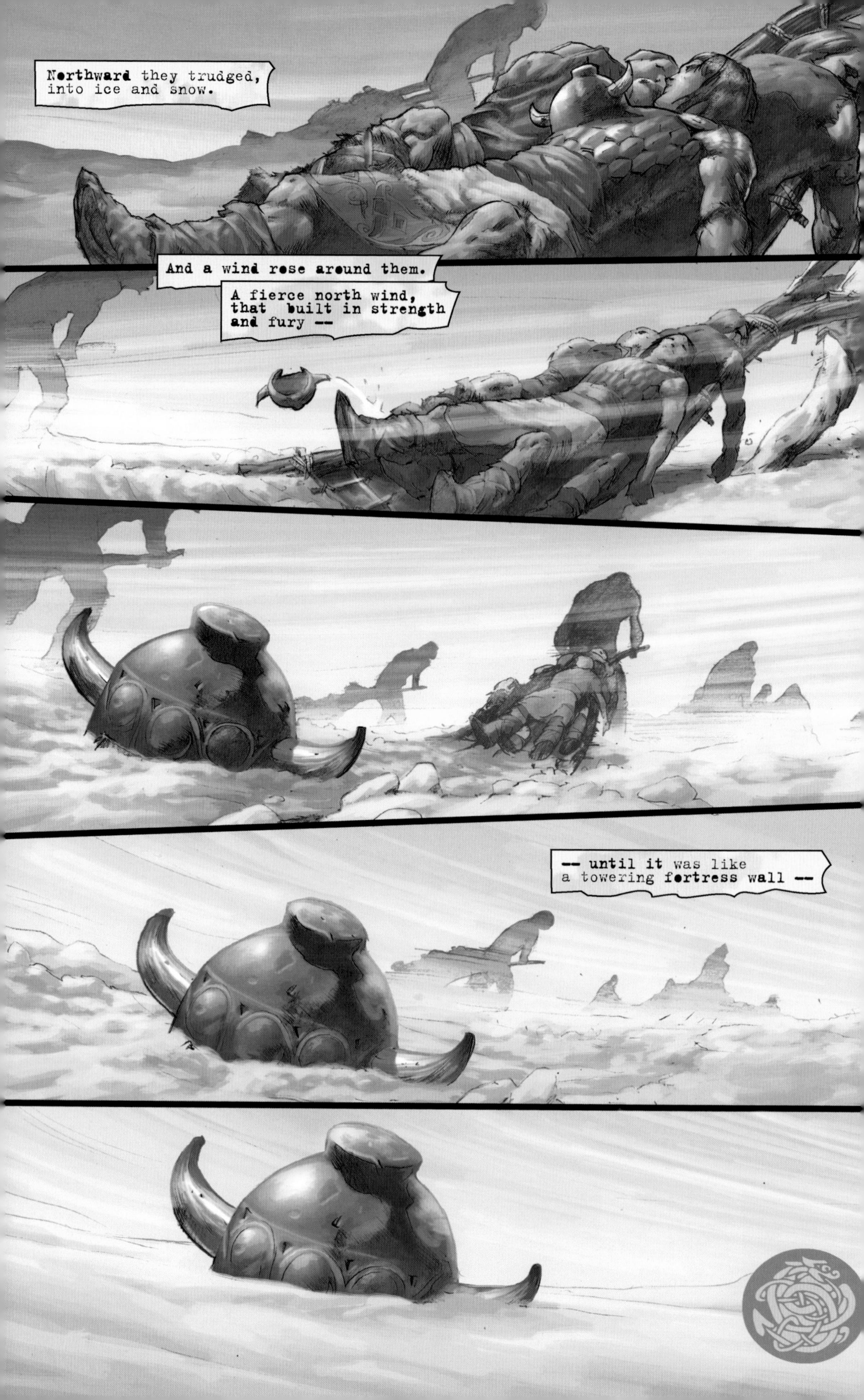
Northward they trudged, into ice and snow.
And a wind rose around them.
A fierce north wind, that built in strength and fury --
-- until it was like a towering fortress wall --

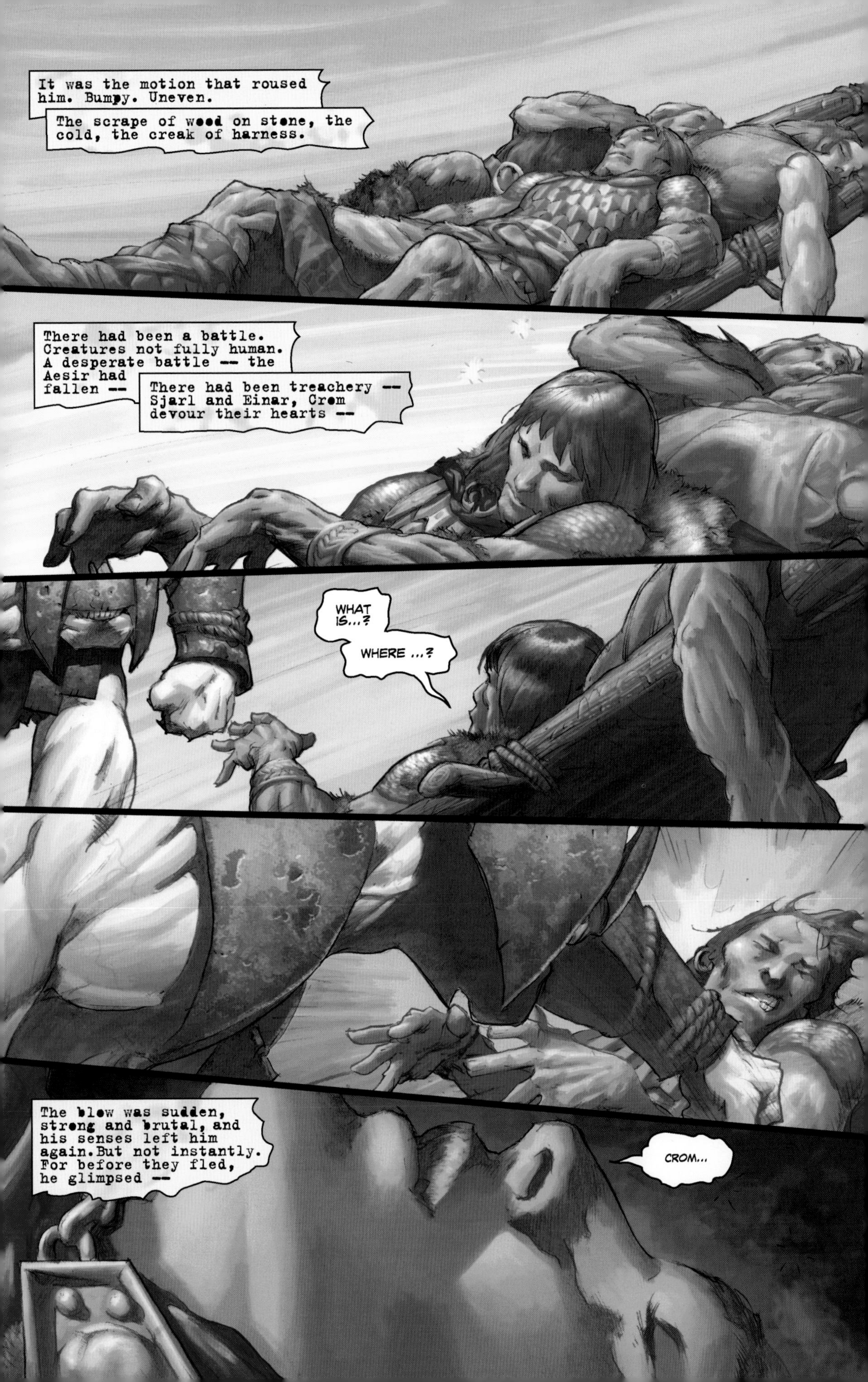
It was the motion that roused him. Bumpy. Uneven.
The scrape of wood on stone, the cold, the creak of harness.
There had been a battle. Creatures not fully human. A desperate battle -- the Aesir had fallen --
There had been treachery -- Sjarl and Einar, Crom devour their hearts --
WHAT IS...?
WHERE ...?
The blow was sudden, strong and brutal, and his senses left him again. But not instantly. For before they fled, he glimpsed --
CROM...

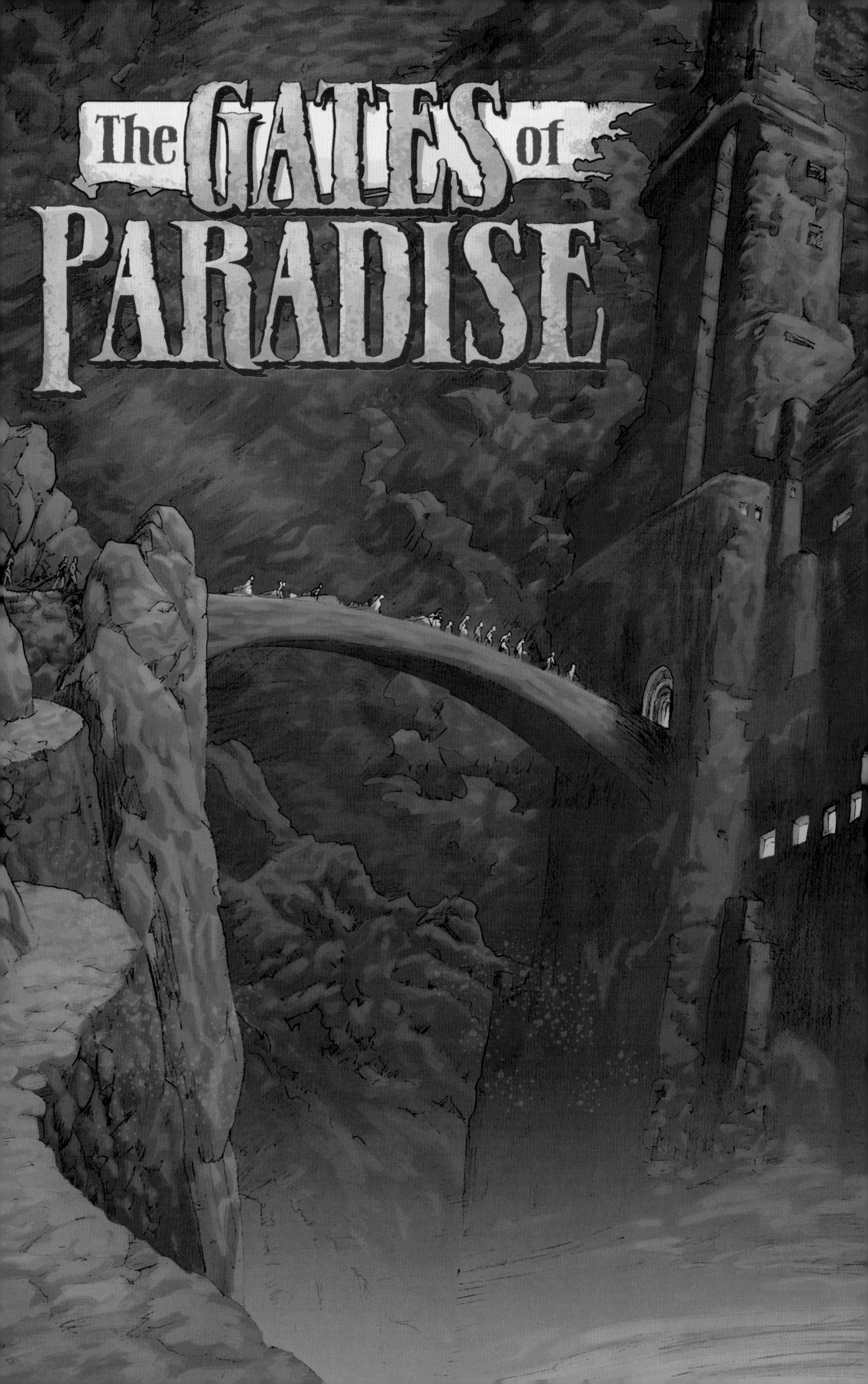
The GATES of
PARADISE

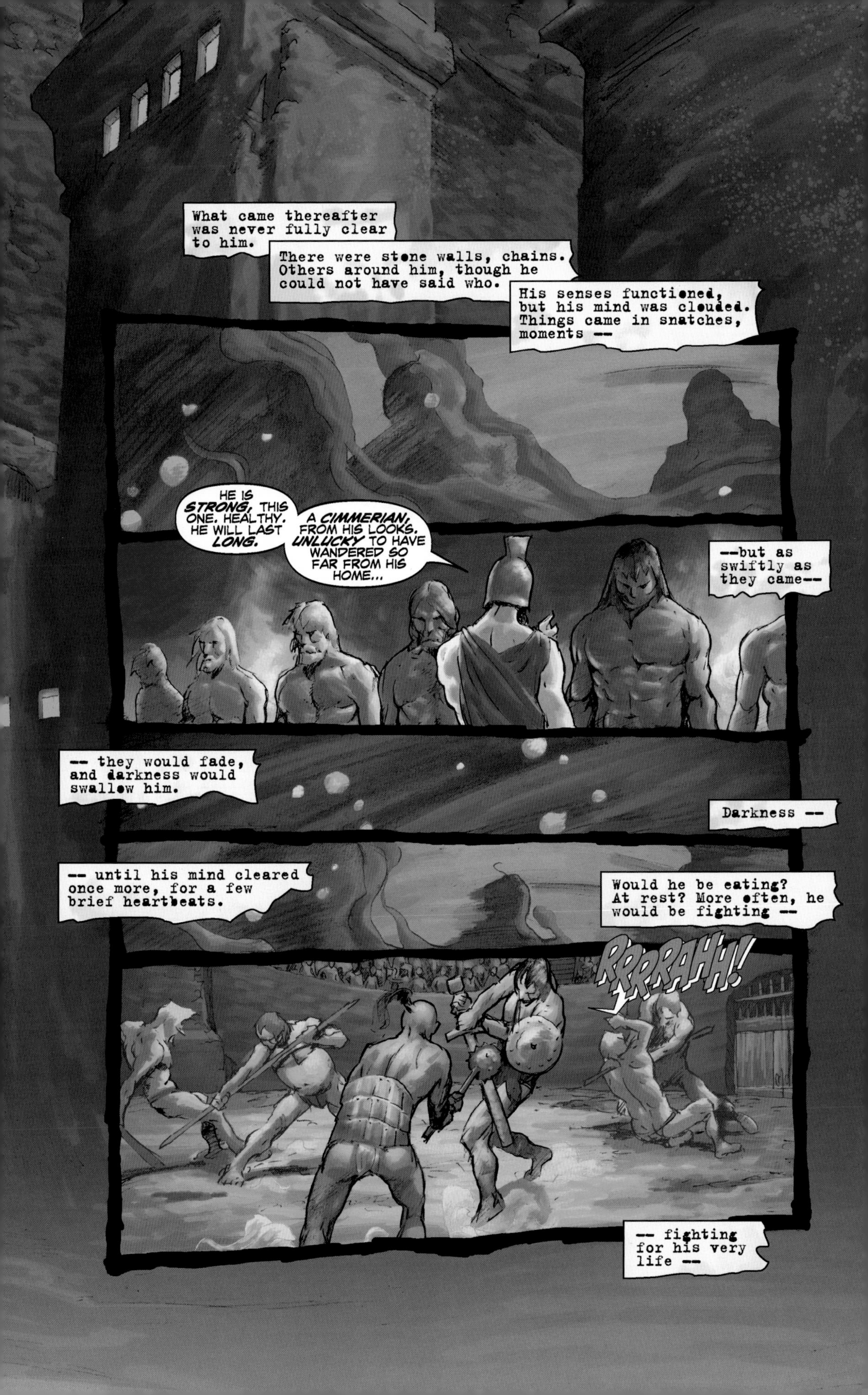

What came thereafter was never fully clear to him.
There were stone walls, chains. Others around him, though he could not have said who.
His senses functioned, but his mind was clouded. Things came in snatches, moments --
HE IS STRONG, THIS ONE. HEALTHY. HE WILL LAST LONG.
A CIMMERIAN, FROM HIS LOOKS. UNLUCKY TO HAVE WANDERED SO FAR FROM HIS HOME...
--but as swiftly as they came--
-- they would fade, and darkness would swallow him.
Darkness --
-- until his mind cleared once more, for a few brief heartbeats.
Would he be eating? At rest? More often, he would be fighting --
RRRRAHH!
-- fighting for his very life --

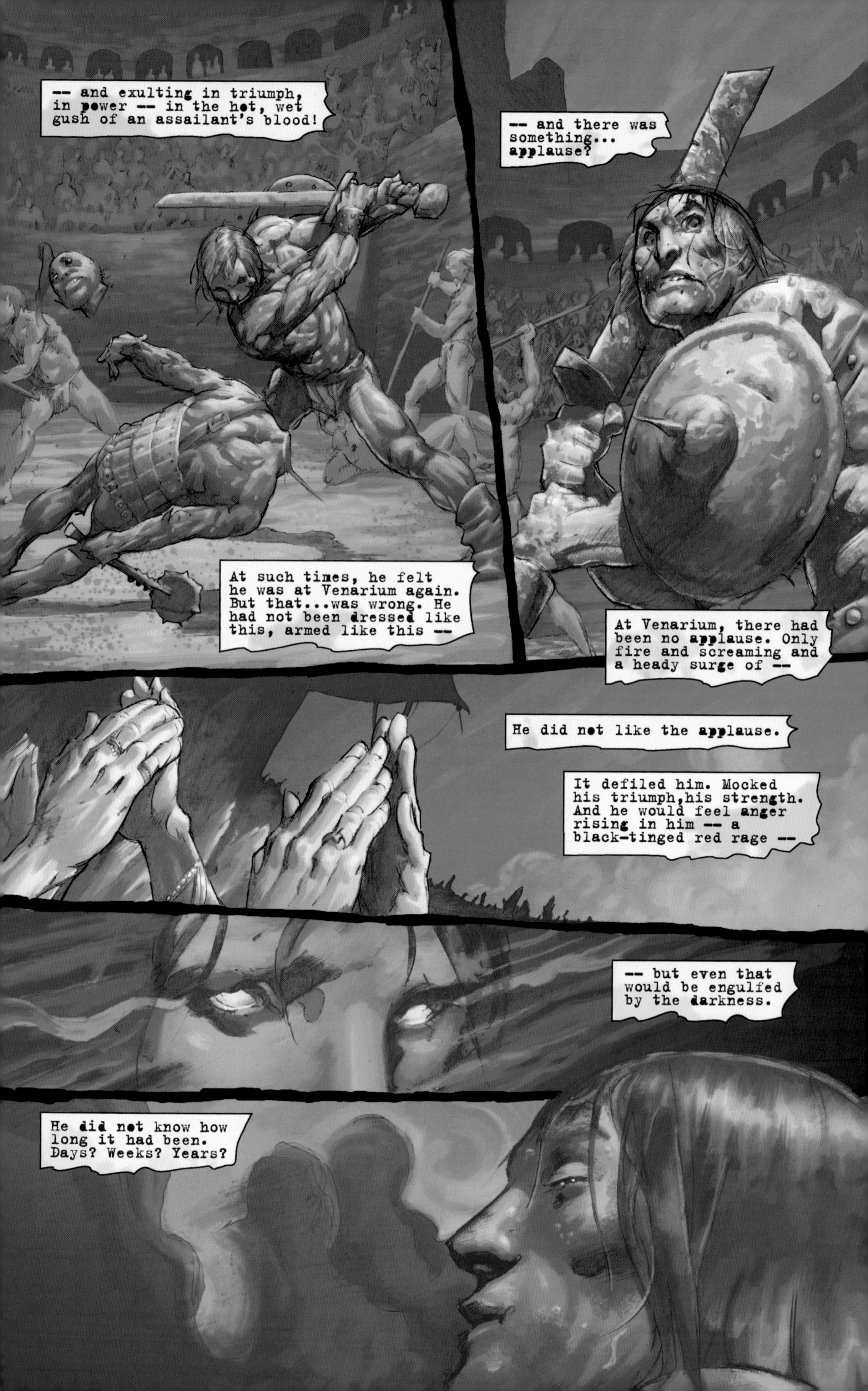
-- and exulting in triumph, in power -- in the hot, wet gush of an assailant's blood!
-- and there was something... applause?
At such times, he felt he was at Venarium again. But that...was wrong. He had not been dressed like this, armed like this --
At Venarium, there had been no applause. Only fire and screaming and a heady surge of --
He did not like the applause.
It defiled him. Mocked his triumph,his strength. And he would feel anger rising in him -- a black-tinged red rage --
-- but even that would be engulfed by the darkness.
He did not know how long it had been. Days? Weeks? Years?

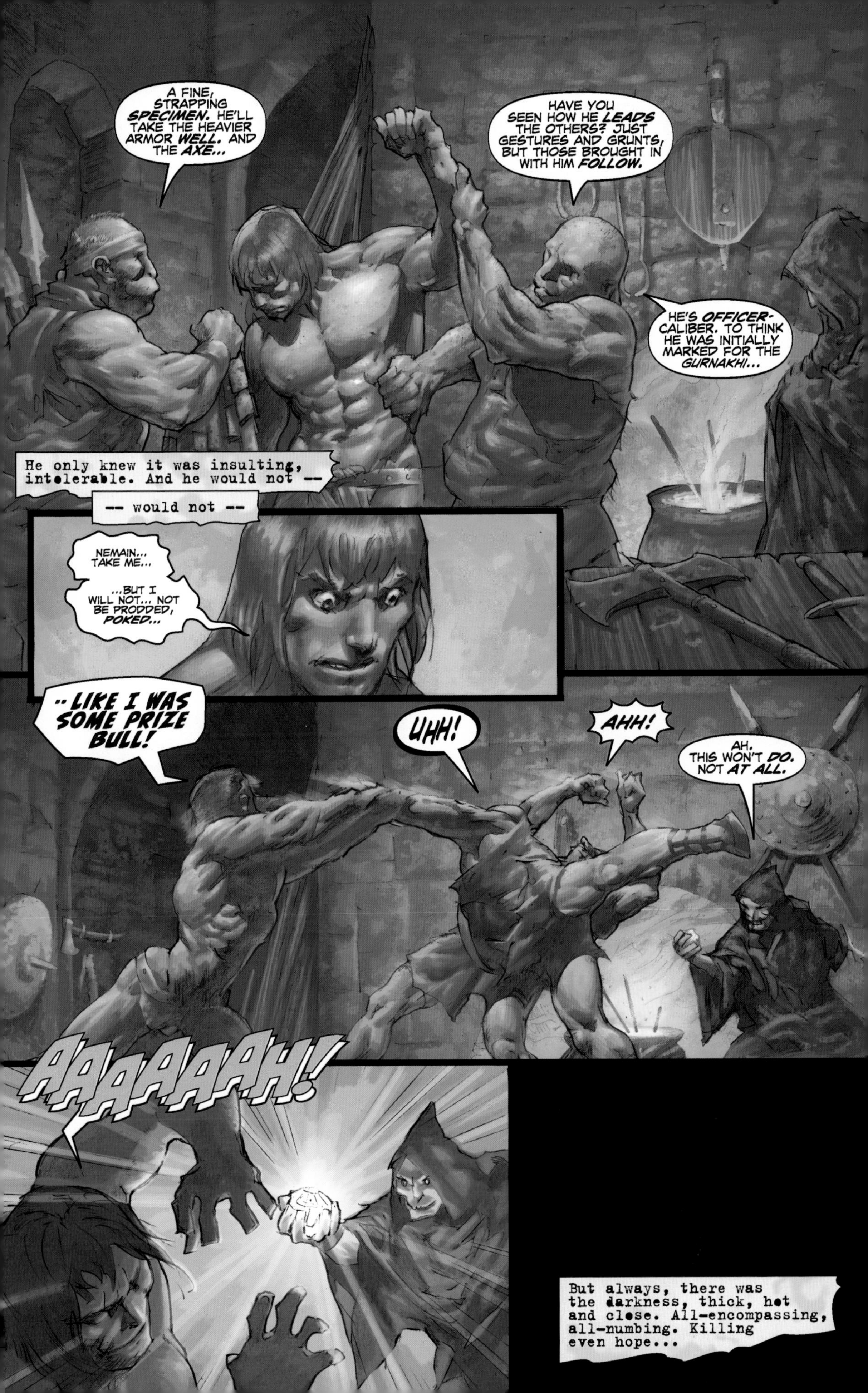
A FINE, STRAPPING SPECIMEN. HE'LL TAKE THE HEAVIER ARMOR WELL. AND THE AXE...
HAVE YOU SEEN HOW HE LEADS THE OTHERS? JUST GESTURES AND GRUNTS, BUT THOSE BROUGHT IN WITH HIM FOLLOW.
HE'S OFFICER-CALIBER. TO THINK HE WAS INITIALLY MARKED FOR THE GURNAKHI...
He only knew it was insulting, intolerable. And he would not --
-- would not --
NEMAIN... TAKE ME...
...BUT I WILL NOT... NOT BE PRODDED, POKED...
..LIKE I WAS SOME PRIZE BULL!
UHH!
AHH!
AH. THIS WON'T DO. NOT AT ALL.
AAAAAAAH!
But always, there was the darkness, thick, hot and close. All-encompassing, all-numbing. Killing even hope...

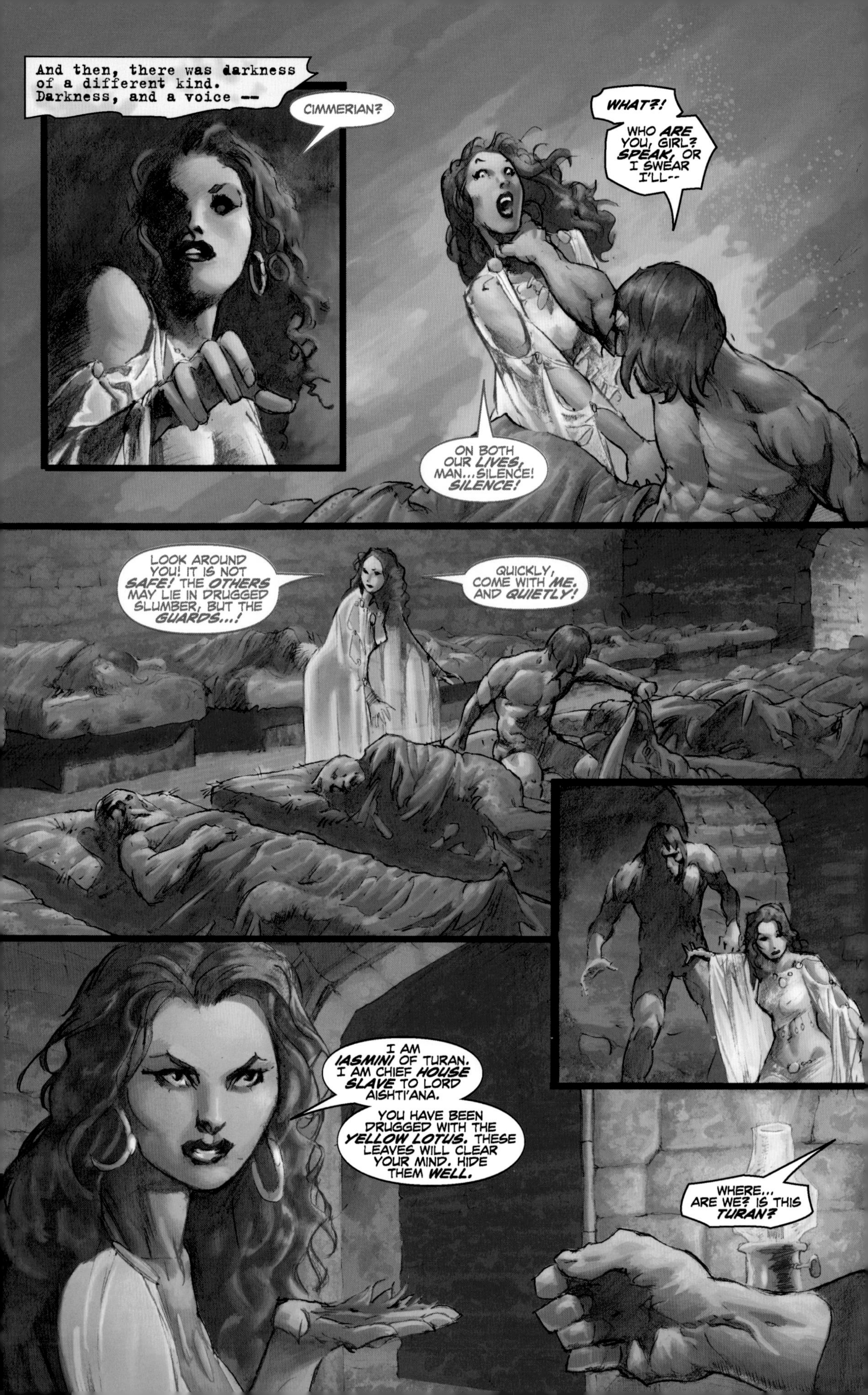
And then, there was darkness of a different kind. Darkness, and a voice --
CIMMERIAN?
WHAT?!
WHO ARE YOU, GIRL? SPEAK, OR I SWEAR I'LL--
ON BOTH OUR LIVES, MAN...SILENCE! SILENCE!
LOOK AROUND YOU! IT IS NOT SAFE! THE OTHERS MAY LIE IN DRUGGED SLUMBER, BUT THE GUARDS...!
QUICKLY, COME WITH ME. AND QUIETLY!
I AM IASMINI OF TURAN. I AM CHIEF HOUSE SLAVE TO LORD AISHTI'ANA.
YOU HAVE BEEN DRUGGED WITH THE YELLOW LOTUS. THESE LEAVES WILL CLEAR YOUR MIND. HIDE THEM WELL.
WHERE... ARE WE? IS THIS TURAN?

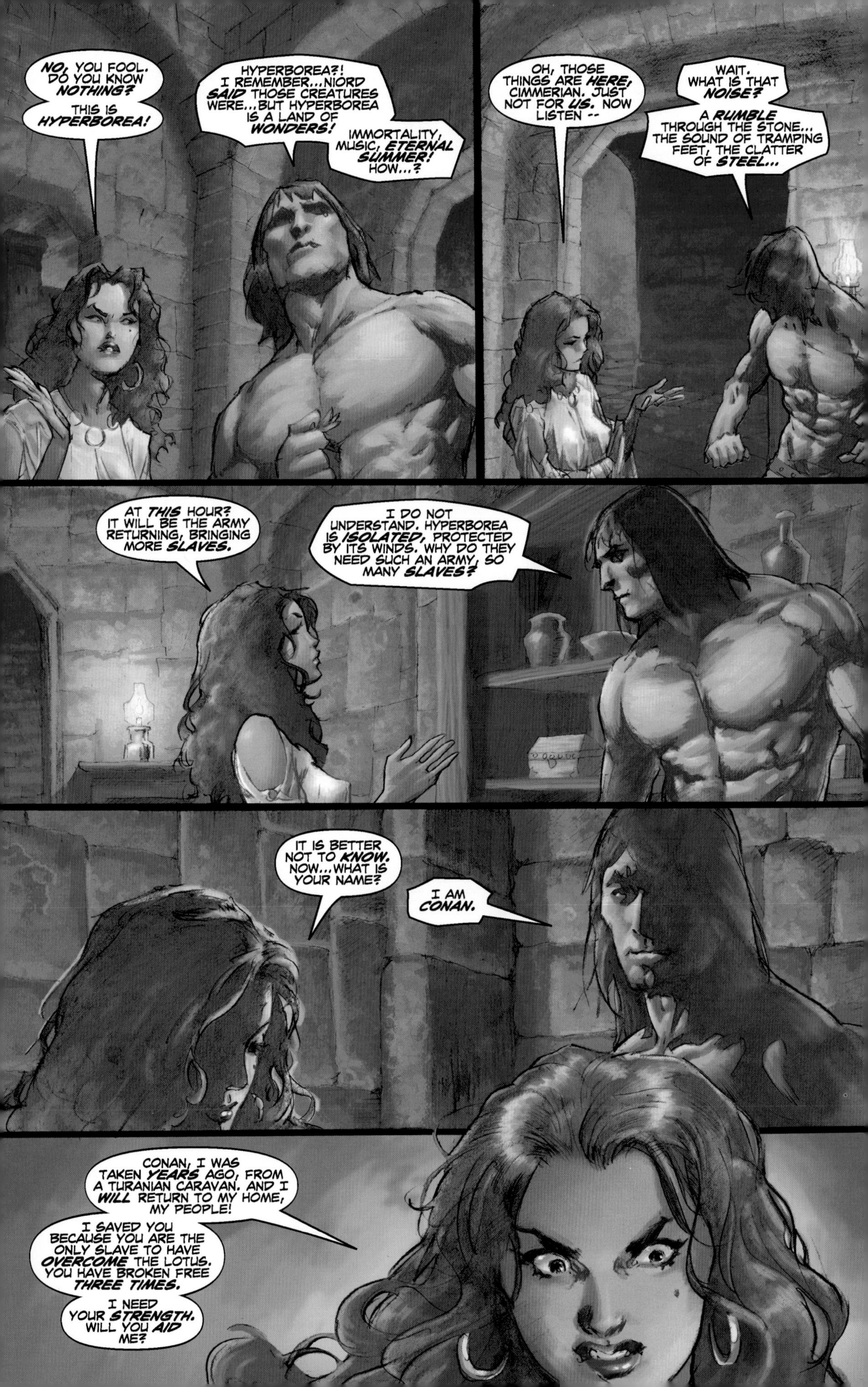
NO, YOU FOOL. DO YOU KNOW NOTHING?
THIS IS HYPERBOREA!
HYPERBOREA?! I REMEMBER...NIORD SAID THOSE CREATURES WERE...BUT HYPERBOREA IS A LAND OF WONDERS!
IMMORTALITY, MUSIC, ETERNAL SUMMER! HOW...?
OH, THOSE THINGS ARE HERE, CIMMERIAN. JUST NOT FOR US. NOW LISTEN --
WAIT. WHAT IS THAT NOISE?
A RUMBLE THROUGH THE STONE... THE SOUND OF TRAMPING FEET, THE CLATTER OF STEEL...
AT THIS HOUR? IT WILL BE THE ARMY RETURNING, BRINGING MORE SLAVES.
I DO NOT UNDERSTAND. HYPERBOREA IS ISOLATED, PROTECTED BY ITS WINDS. WHY DO THEY NEED SUCH AN ARMY, SO MANY SLAVES?
IT IS BETTER NOT TO KNOW. NOW...WHAT IS YOUR NAME?
I AM CONAN.
CONAN, I WAS TAKEN YEARS AGO, FROM A TURANIAN CARAVAN. AND I WILL RETURN TO MY HOME, MY PEOPLE!
I SAVED YOU BECAUSE YOU ARE THE ONLY SLAVE TO HAVE OVERCOME THE LOTUS. YOU HAVE BROKEN FREE THREE TIMES.
I NEED YOUR STRENGTH. WILL YOU AID ME?

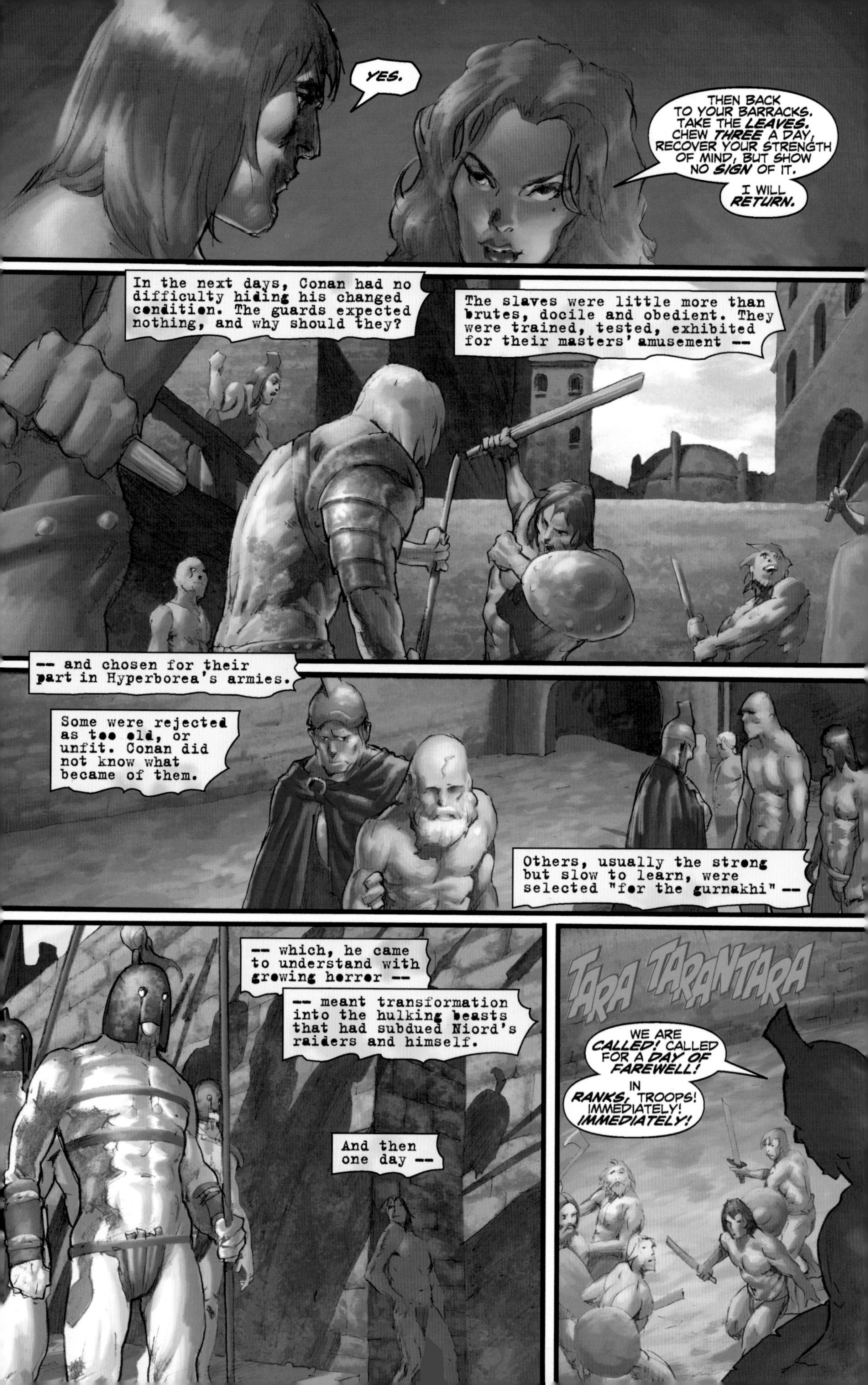
YES.
THEN BACK TO YOUR BARRACKS. TAKE THE LEAVES. CHEW THREE A DAY, RECOVER YOUR STRENGTH OF MIND, BUT SHOW NO SIGN OF IT.
I WILL RETURN.
In the next days, Conan had no difficulty hiding his changed condition. The guards expected nothing, and why should they?
The slaves were little more than brutes, docile and obedient. They were trained, tested, exhibited for their masters' amusement --
-- and chosen for their part in Hyperborea's armies.
Some were rejected as too old, or unfit. Conan did not know what became of them.
Others, usually the strong but slow to learn, were selected "for the gurnakhi" --
-- which, he came to understand with growing horror --
-- meant transformation into the hulking beasts that had subdued Niord's raiders and himself.
And then one day --
TARA TARANTARA
WE ARE CALLED! CALLED FOR A DAY OF FAREWELL!
IN RANKS, TROOPS! IMMEDIATELY! IMMEDIATELY!

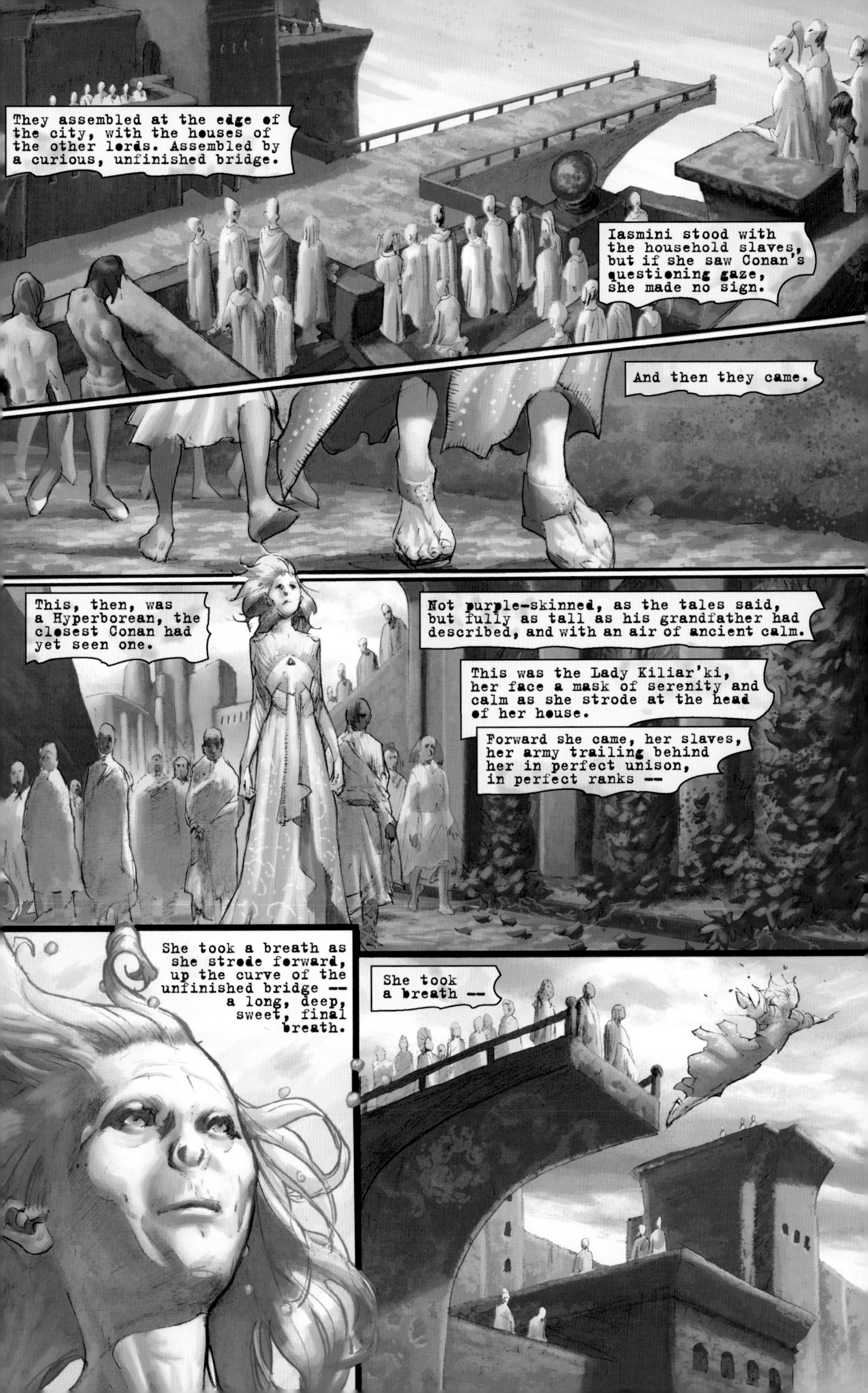
They assembled at the edge of the city, with the houses of the other lords. Assembled by a curious, unfinished bridge.
Iasmini stood with the household slaves, but if she saw Conan's questioning gaze, she made no sign.
And then they came.
This, then, was a Hyperborean, the closest Conan had yet seen one.
Not purple-skinned, as the tales said, but fully as tall as his grandfather had described, and with an air of ancient calm.
This was the Lady Kiliar'ki, her face a mask of serenity and calm as she strode at the head of her house.
Forward she came, her slaves, her army trailing behind her in perfect unison, in perfect ranks --
She took a breath as she strode forward, up the curve of the unfinished bridge -- a long, deep, sweet, final breath.
She took a breath --

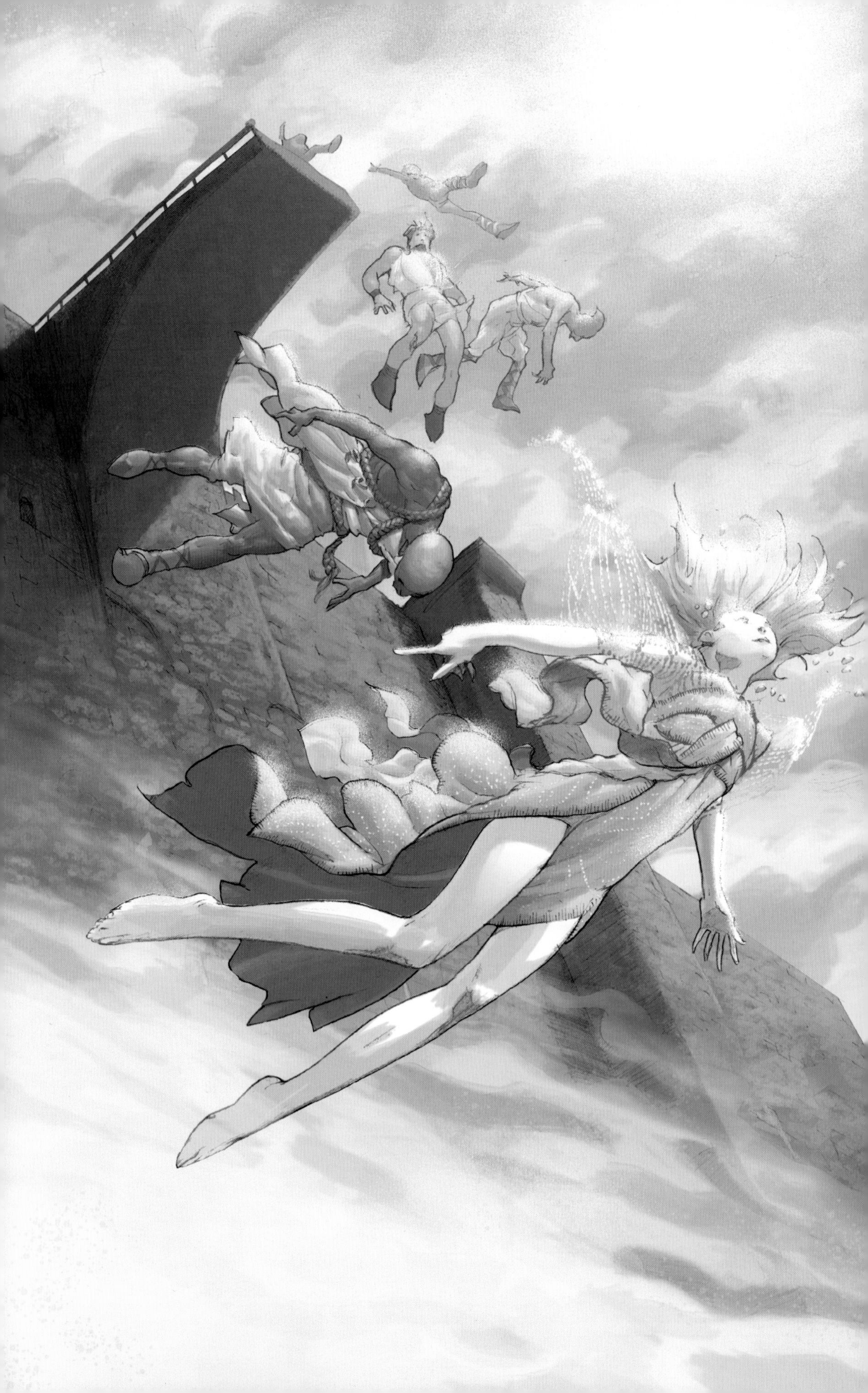

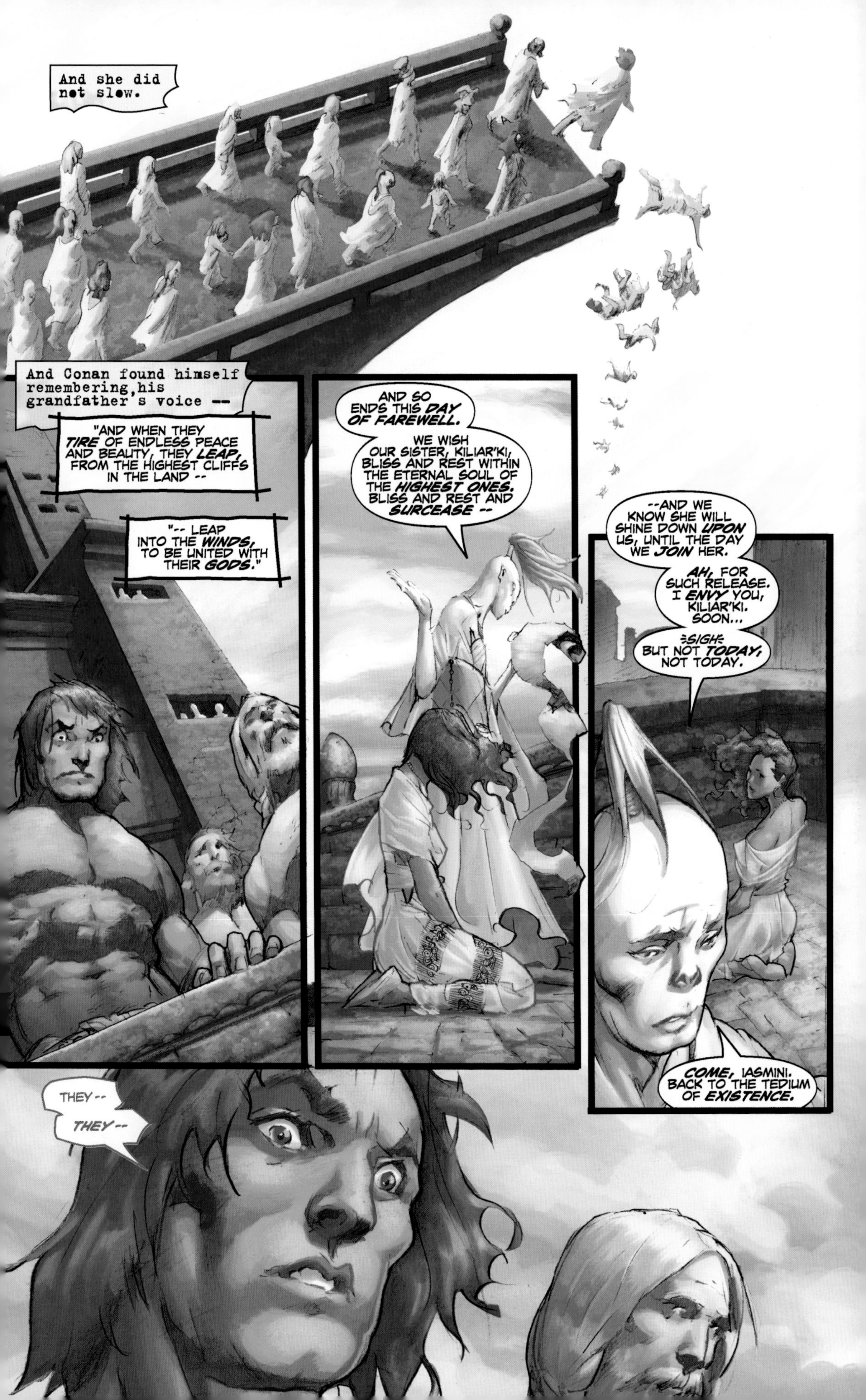
And she did not slow.
And Conan found himself remembering, his grandfather's voice --
"AND WHEN THEY TIRE OF ENDLESS PEACE AND BEAUTY, THEY LEAP, FROM THE HIGHEST CLIFFS IN THE LAND --
"-- LEAP INTO THE WINDS, TO BE UNITED WITH THEIR GODS."
AND SO ENDS THIS DAY OF FAREWELL.
WE WISH OUR SISTER, KILIAR'KI, BLISS AND REST WITHIN THE ETERNAL SOUL OF THE HIGHEST ONES. BLISS AND REST AND SURCEASE --
--AND WE KNOW SHE WILL SHINE DOWN UPON US, UNTIL THE DAY WE JOIN HER.
AH, FOR SUCH RELEASE. I ENVY YOU, KILIAR'KI. SOON...
=SIGH= BUT NOT TODAY, NOT TODAY.
COME, IASMINI. BACK TO THE TEDIUM OF EXISTENCE.
THEY --
THEY --

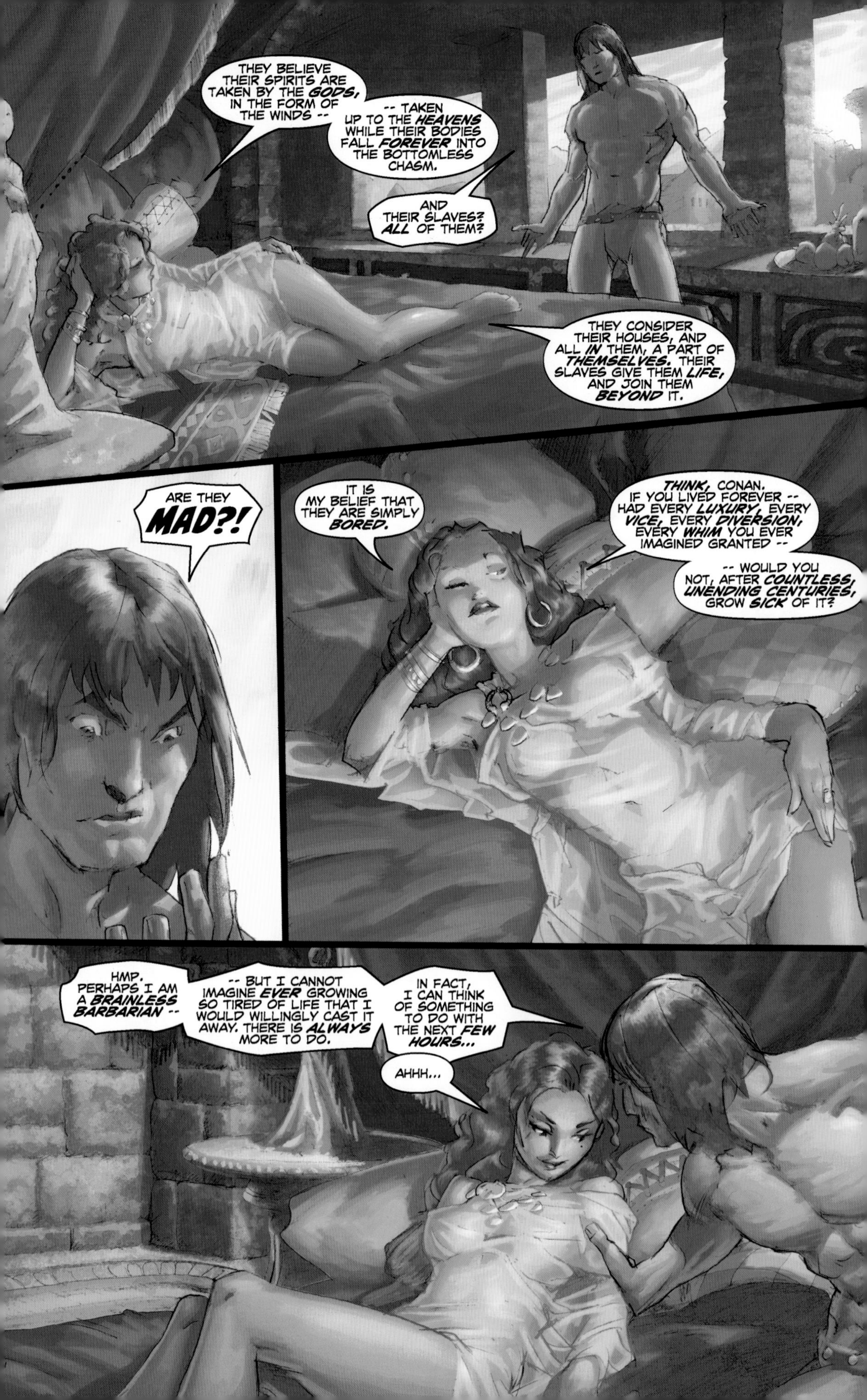
THEY BELIEVE THEIR SPIRITS ARE TAKEN BY THE GODS, IN THE FORM OF THE WINDS --
-- TAKEN UP TO THE HEAVENS WHILE THEIR BODIES FALL FOREVER INTO THE BOTTOMLESS CHASM.
AND THEIR SLAVES? ALL OF THEM?
THEY CONSIDER THEIR HOUSES, AND ALL IN THEM, A PART OF THEMSELVES. THEIR SLAVES GIVE THEM LIFE, AND JOIN THEM BEYOND IT.
ARE THEY MAD?!
IT IS MY BELIEF THAT THEY ARE SIMPLY BORED.
THINK, CONAN. IF YOU LIVED FOREVER -- HAD EVERY LUXURY, EVERY VICE, EVERY DIVERSION, EVERY WHIM YOU EVER IMAGINED GRANTED --
-- WOULD YOU NOT, AFTER COUNTLESS, UNENDING CENTURIES, GROW SICK OF IT?
HMP. PERHAPS I AM A BRAINLESS BARBARIAN --
-- BUT I CANNOT IMAGINE EVER GROWING SO TIRED OF LIFE THAT I WOULD WILLINGLY CAST IT AWAY. THERE IS ALWAYS MORE TO DO.
IN FACT, I CAN THINK OF SOMETHING TO DO WITH THE NEXT FEW HOURS...
AHHH...

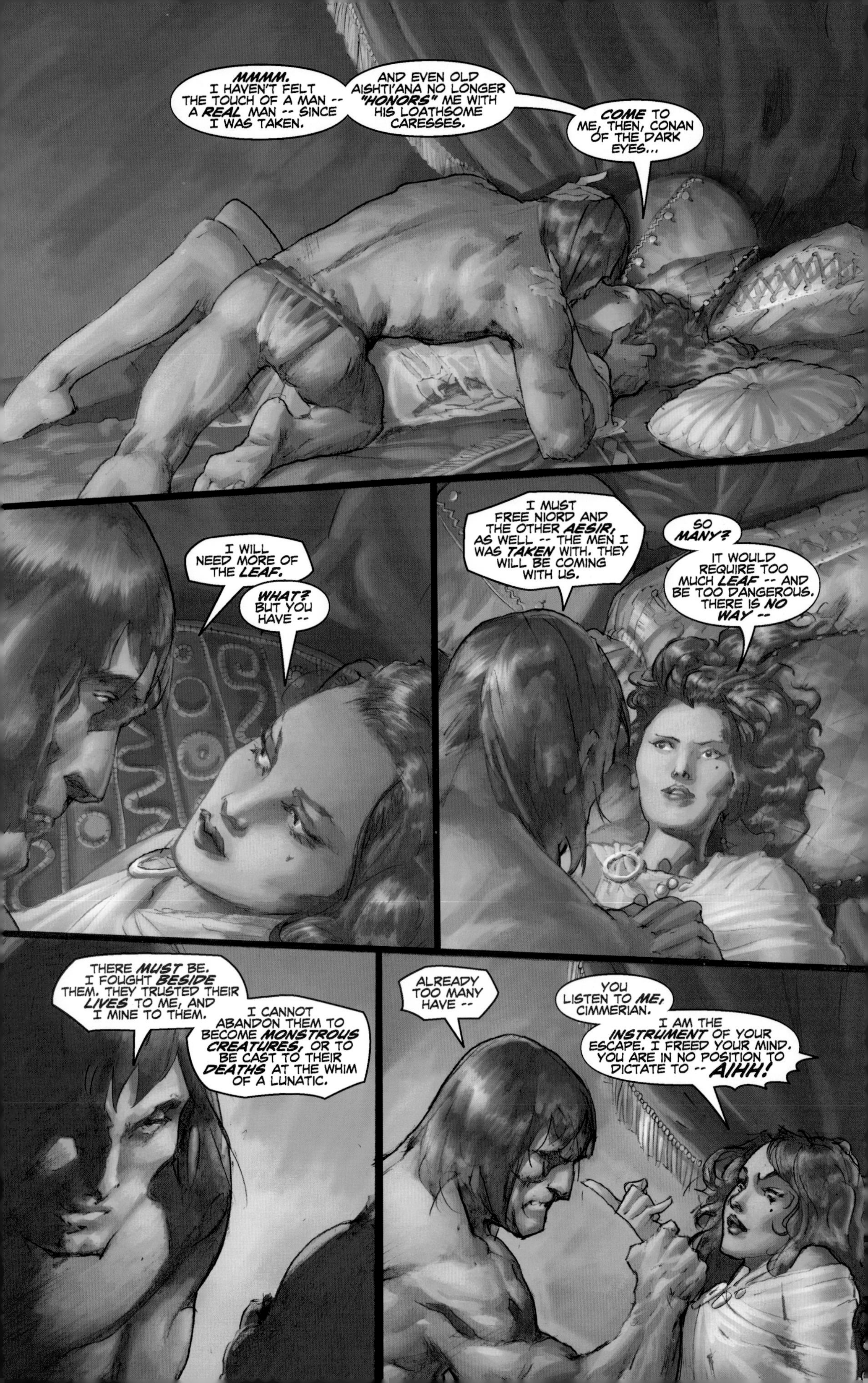
MMMM. I HAVEN'T FELT THE TOUCH OF A MAN -- A REAL MAN -- SINCE I WAS TAKEN.
AND EVEN OLD AISHTI'ANA NO LONGER "HONORS" ME WITH HIS LOATHSOME CARESSES.
COME TO ME, THEN, CONAN OF THE DARK EYES...
I WILL NEED MORE OF THE LEAF.
WHAT? BUT YOU HAVE --
I MUST FREE NIORD AND THE OTHER AESIR, AS WELL -- THE MEN I WAS TAKEN WITH. THEY WILL BE COMING WITH US.
SO MANY?
IT WOULD REQUIRE TOO MUCH LEAF -- AND BE TOO DANGEROUS. THERE IS NO WAY --
THERE MUST BE. I FOUGHT BESIDE THEM. THEY TRUSTED THEIR LIVES TO ME, AND I MINE TO THEM.
I CANNOT ABANDON THEM TO BECOME MONSTROUS CREATURES, OR TO BE CAST TO THEIR DEATHS AT THE WHIM OF A LUNATIC.
ALREADY TOO MANY HAVE --
YOU LISTEN TO ME, CIMMERIAN.
I AM THE INSTRUMENT OF YOUR ESCAPE. I FREED YOUR MIND. YOU ARE IN NO POSITION TO DICTATE TO -- AIHH!

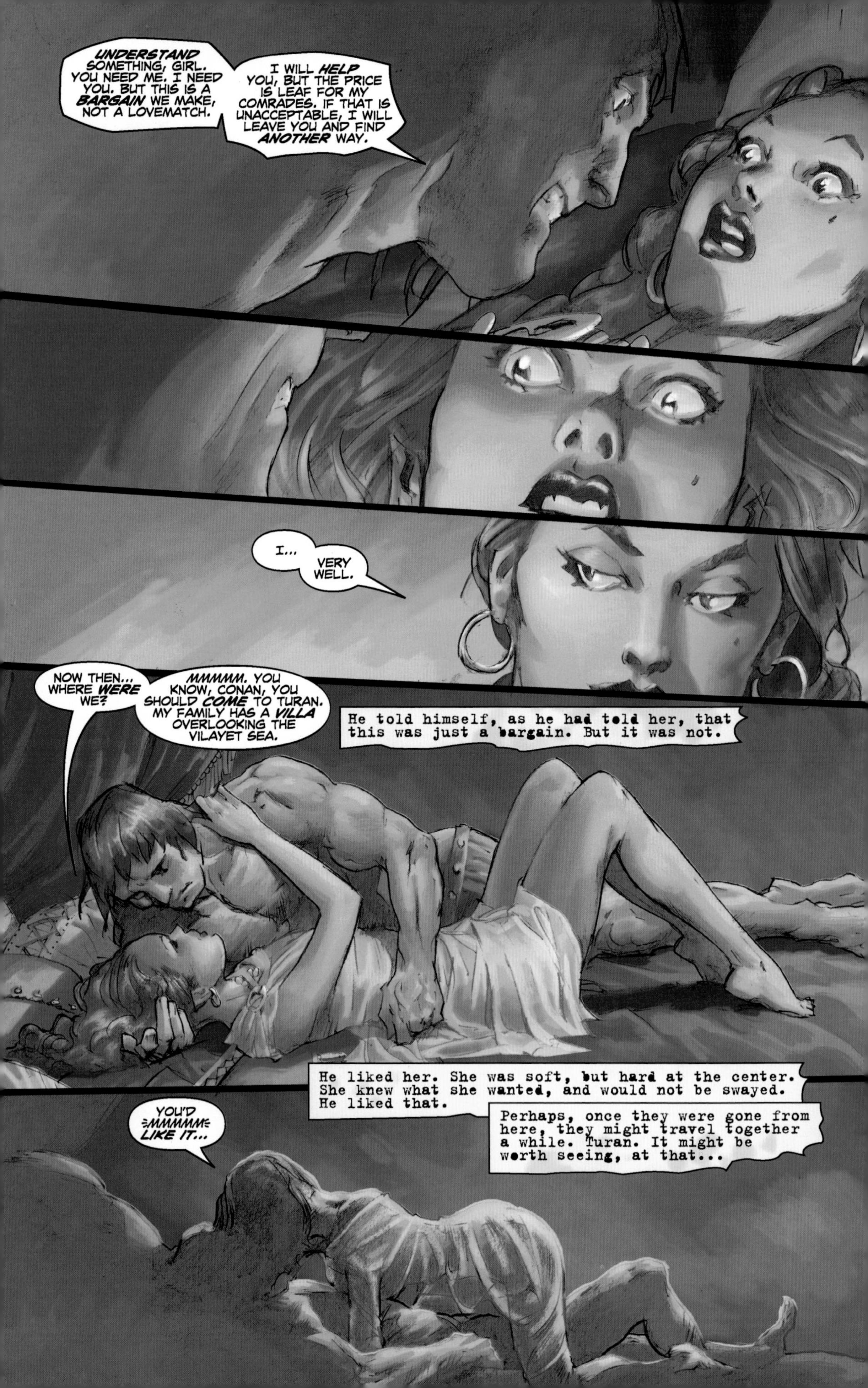
UNDERSTAND SOMETHING, GIRL. YOU NEED ME. I NEED YOU. BUT THIS IS A BARGAIN WE MAKE, NOT A LOVEMATCH.
I WILL HELP YOU, BUT THE PRICE IS LEAF FOR MY COMRADES. IF THAT IS UNACCEPTABLE, I WILL LEAVE YOU AND FIND ANOTHER WAY.
I... VERY WELL.
NOW THEN... WHERE WERE WE?
MMMMM. YOU KNOW, CONAN, YOU SHOULD COME TO TURAN. MY FAMILY HAS A VILLA OVERLOOKING THE VILAYET SEA.
He told himself, as he had told her, that this was just a bargain. But it was not.
He liked her. She was soft, but hard at the center. She knew what she wanted, and would not be swayed. He liked that.
YOU'D =MMMMM= LIKE IT...
Perhaps, once they were gone from here, they might travel together a while. Turan. It might be worth seeing, at that...

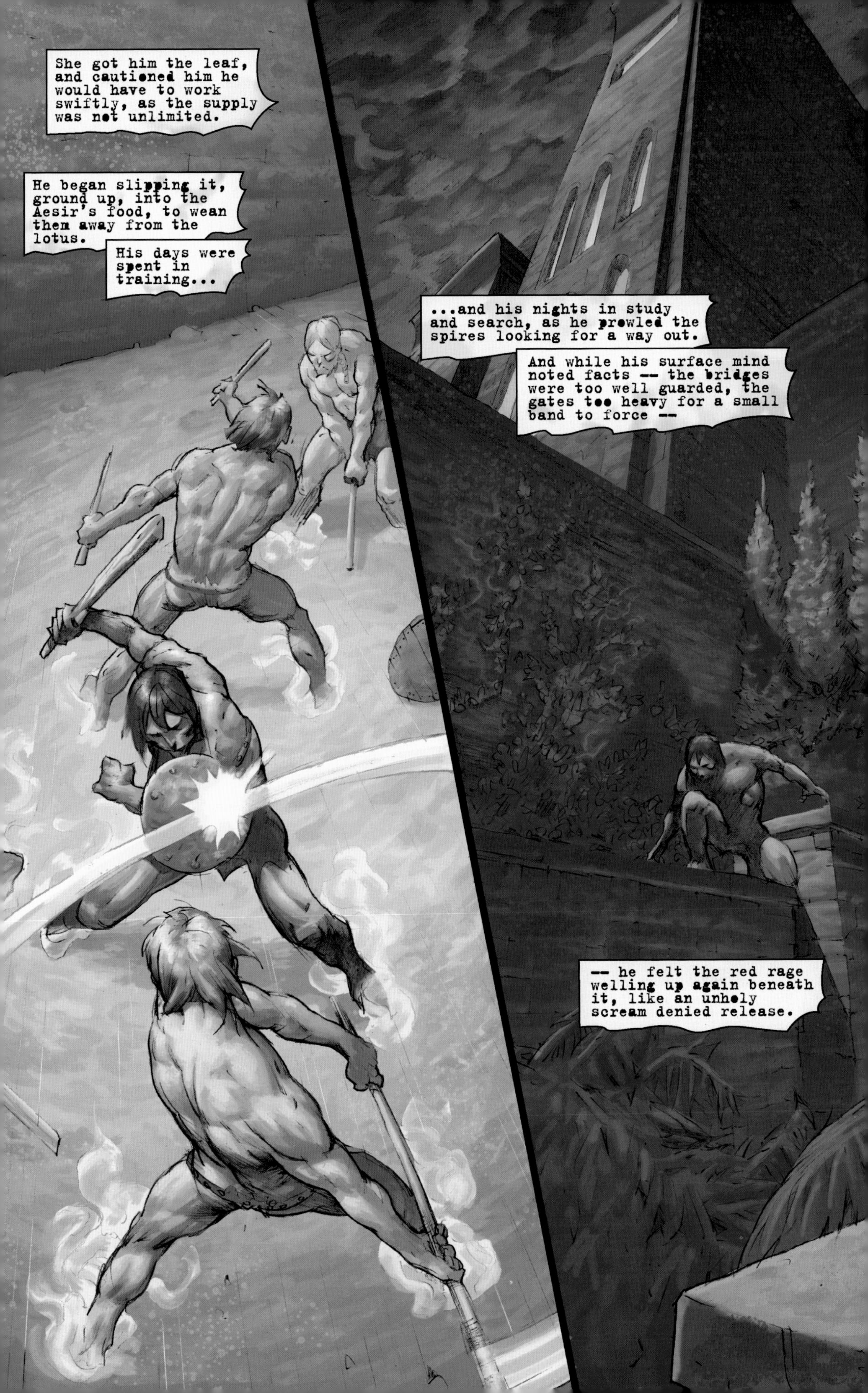
She got him the leaf, and cautioned him he would have to work swiftly, as the supply was not unlimited.
He began slipping it, ground up, into the Aesir's food, to wean them away from the lotus.
His days were spent in training...
...and his nights in study and search, as he prowled the spires looking for a way out.
And while his surface mind noted facts -- the bridges were too well guarded, the gates too heavy for a small band to force --
-- he felt the red rage welling up again beneath it, like an unholy scream denied release.

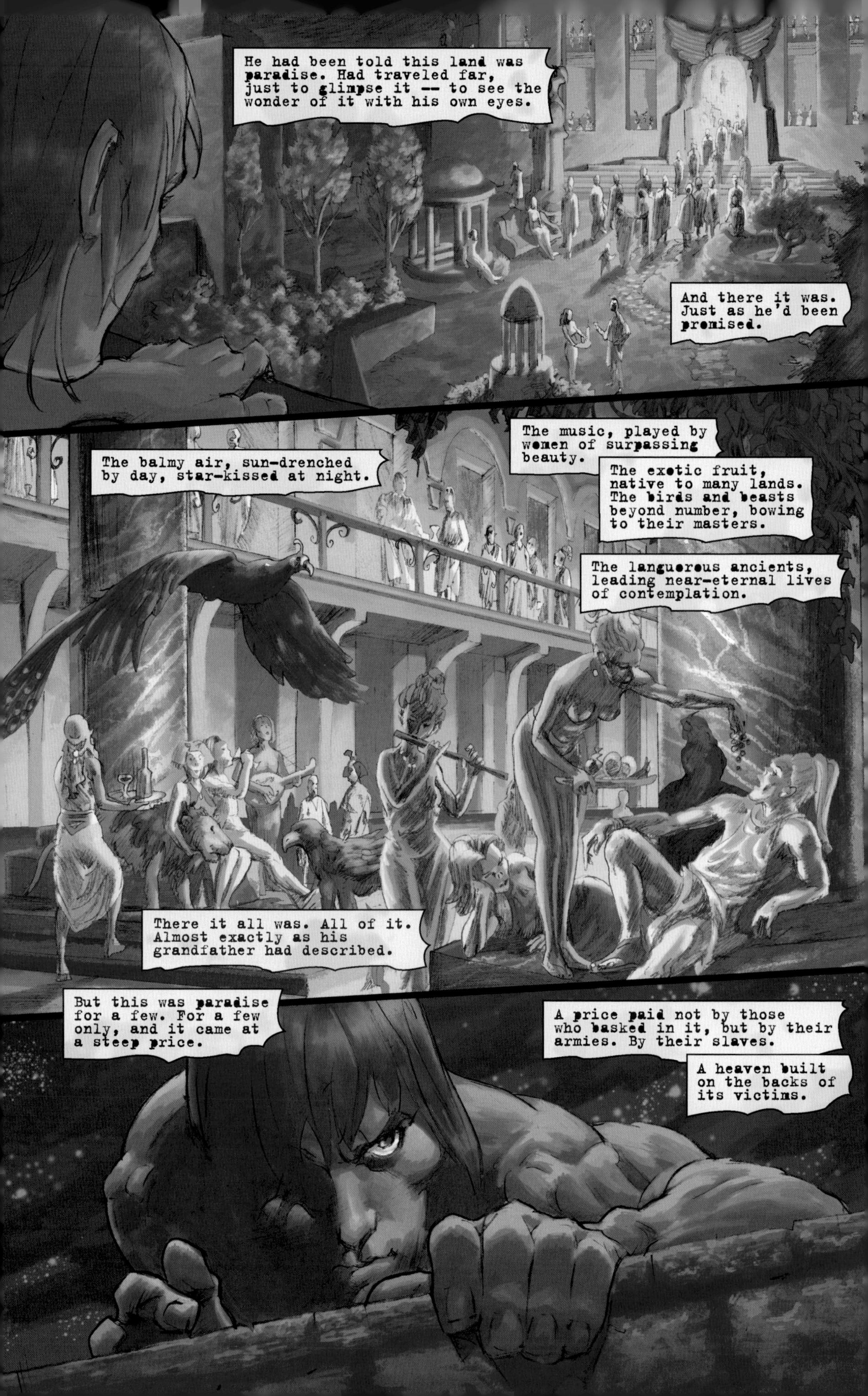
He had been told this land was paradise. Had traveled far, just to glimpse it -- to see the wonder of it with his own eyes.
And there it was. Just as he'd been promised.
The balmy air, sun-drenched by day, star-kissed at night.
The music, played by women of surpassing beauty.
The exotic fruit, native to many lands. The birds and beasts beyond number, bowing to their masters.
The languorous ancients, leading near-eternal lives of contemplation.
There it all was. All of it. Almost exactly as his grandfather had described.
But this was paradise for a few. For a few only, and it came at a steep price.
A price paid not by those who basked in it, but by their armies. By their slaves.
A heaven built on the backs of its victims.

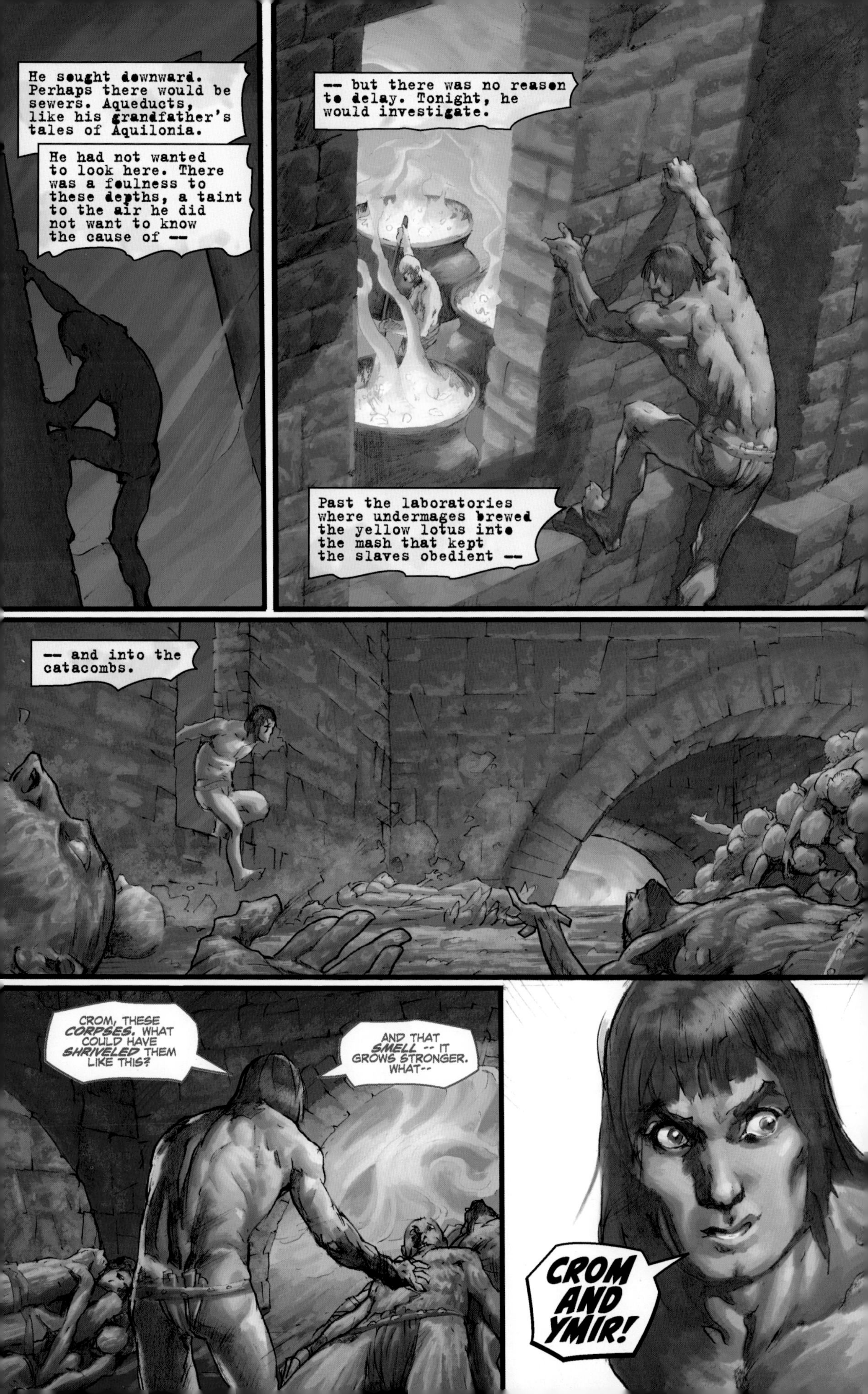

He sought downward. Perhaps there would be sewers. Aqueducts, like his grandfather's tales of Aquilonia.
He had not wanted to look here. There was a foulness to these depths, a taint to the air he did not want to know the cause of --
-- but there was no reason to delay. Tonight, he would investigate.
Past the laboratories where undermages brewed the yellow lotus into the mash that kept the slaves obedient --
-- and into the catacombs.
CROM, THESE CORPSES. WHAT COULD HAVE SHRIVELED THEM LIKE THIS?
AND THAT SMELL -- IT GROWS STRONGER. WHAT--
CROM AND YMIR!

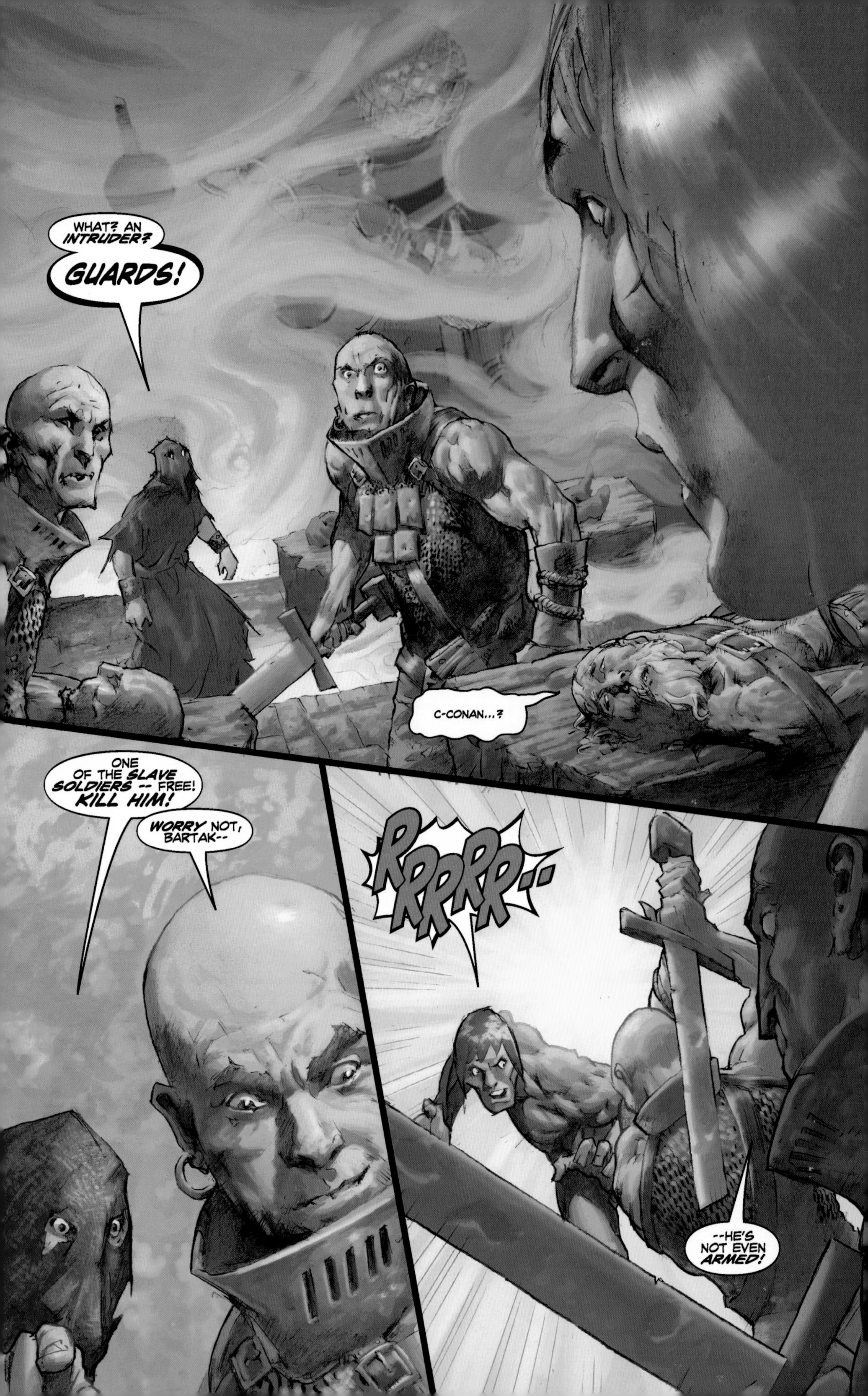
WHAT? AN INTRUDER?
GUARDS!
C-CONAN...?
ONE OF THE SLAVE SOLDIERS -- FREE! KILL HIM!
WORRY NOT, BARTAK--
RRRRR--
--HE'S NOT EVEN ARMED!

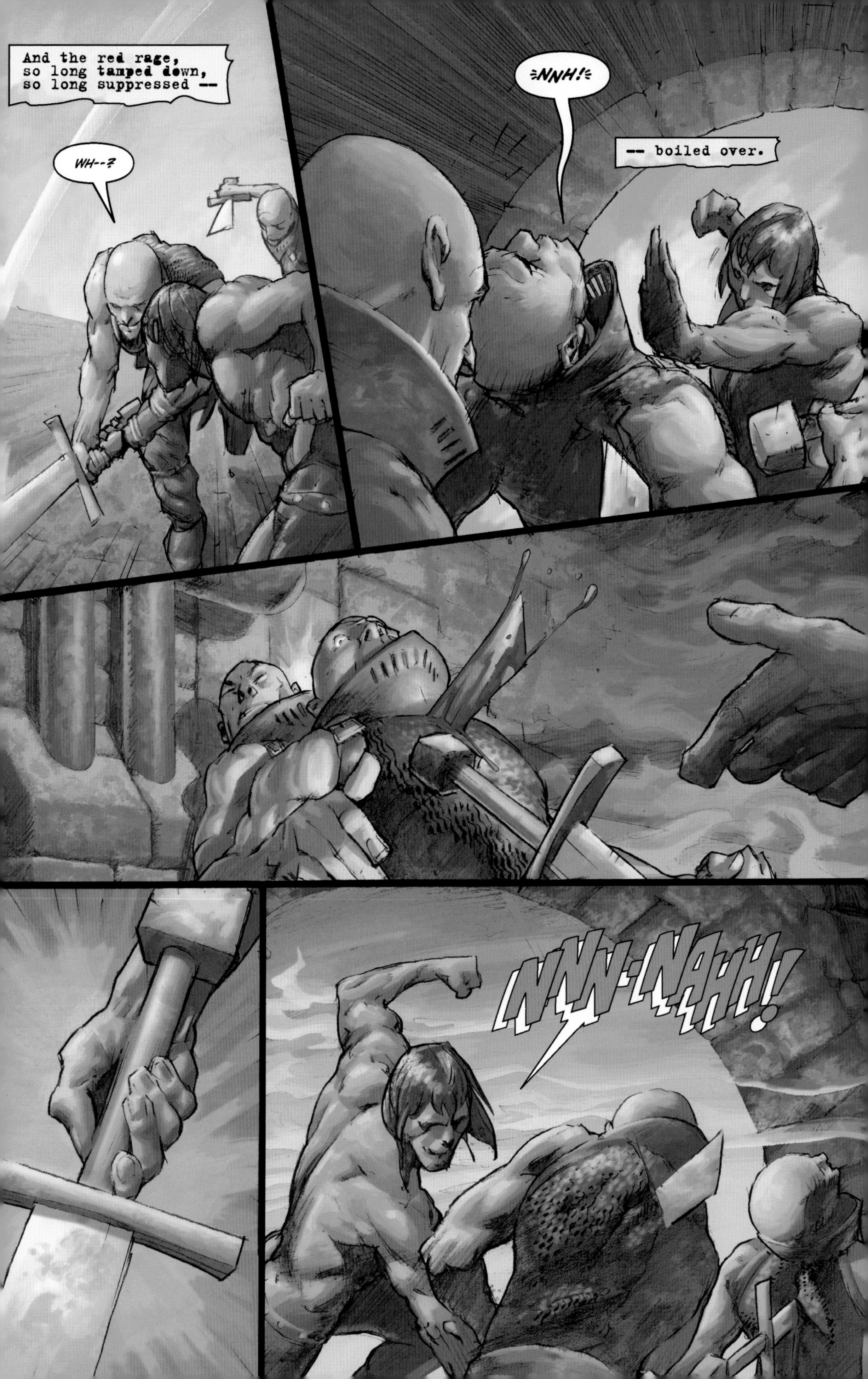

And the red rage, so long tamped down, so long suppressed --
WH--?
NNH!
-- boiled over.
NNN-NAHH!

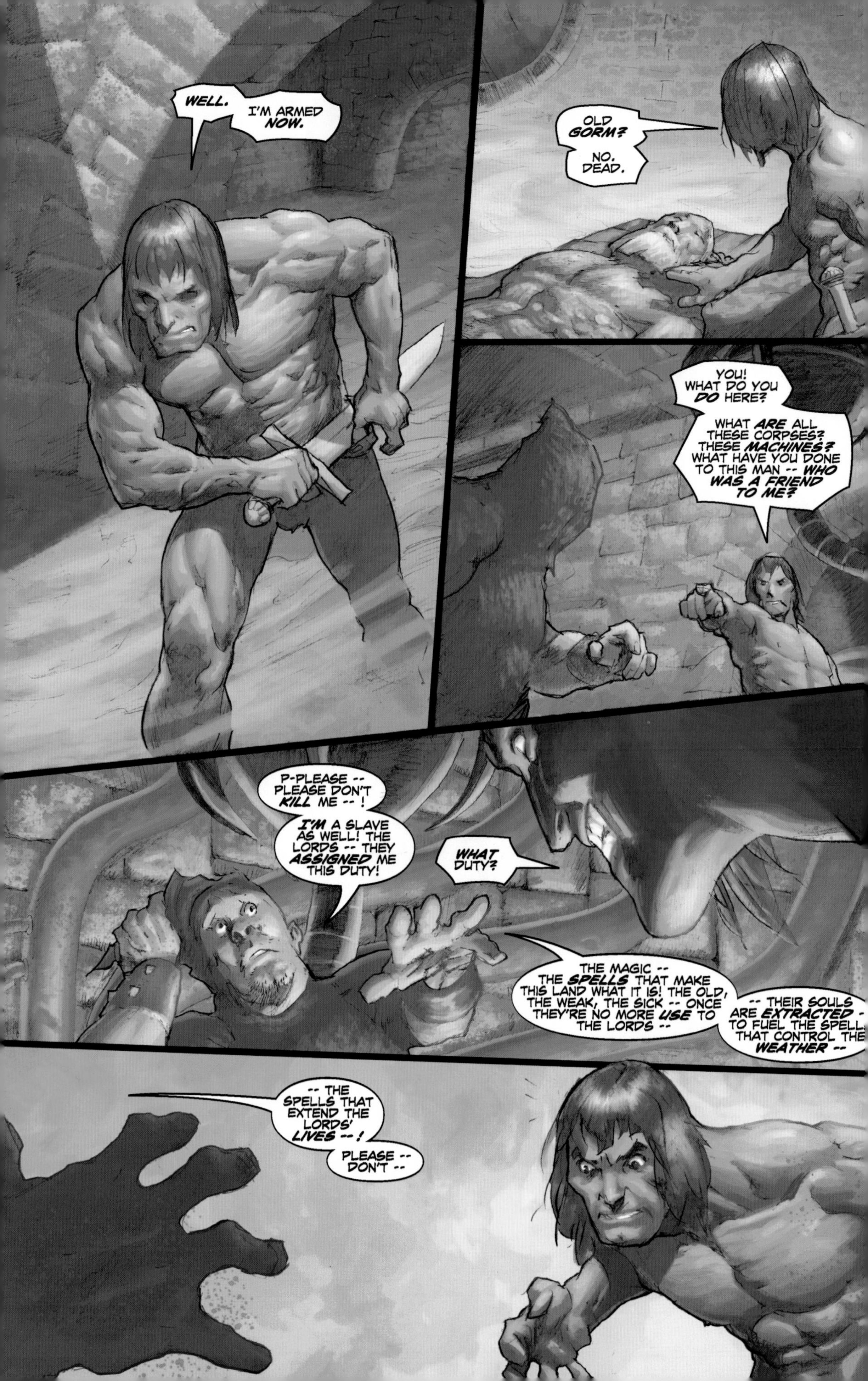
WELL.
I'M ARMED NOW.
OLD GORM?
NO. DEAD.
YOU! WHAT DO YOU DO HERE?
WHAT ARE ALL THESE CORPSES? THESE MACHINES? WHAT HAVE YOU DONE TO THIS MAN -- WHO WAS A FRIEND TO ME?
P-PLEASE -- PLEASE DON'T KILL ME -- !
I'M A SLAVE AS WELL! THE LORDS -- THEY ASSIGNED ME THIS DUTY!
WHAT DUTY?
THE MAGIC -- THE SPELLS THAT MAKE THIS LAND WHAT IT IS! THE OLD, THE WEAK, THE SICK -- ONCE THEY'RE NO MORE USE TO THE LORDS --
-- THEIR SOULS ARE EXTRACTED -- TO FUEL THE SPELL THAT CONTROL THE WEATHER --
-- THE SPELLS THAT EXTEND THE LORDS' LIVES -- !
PLEASE -- DON'T --

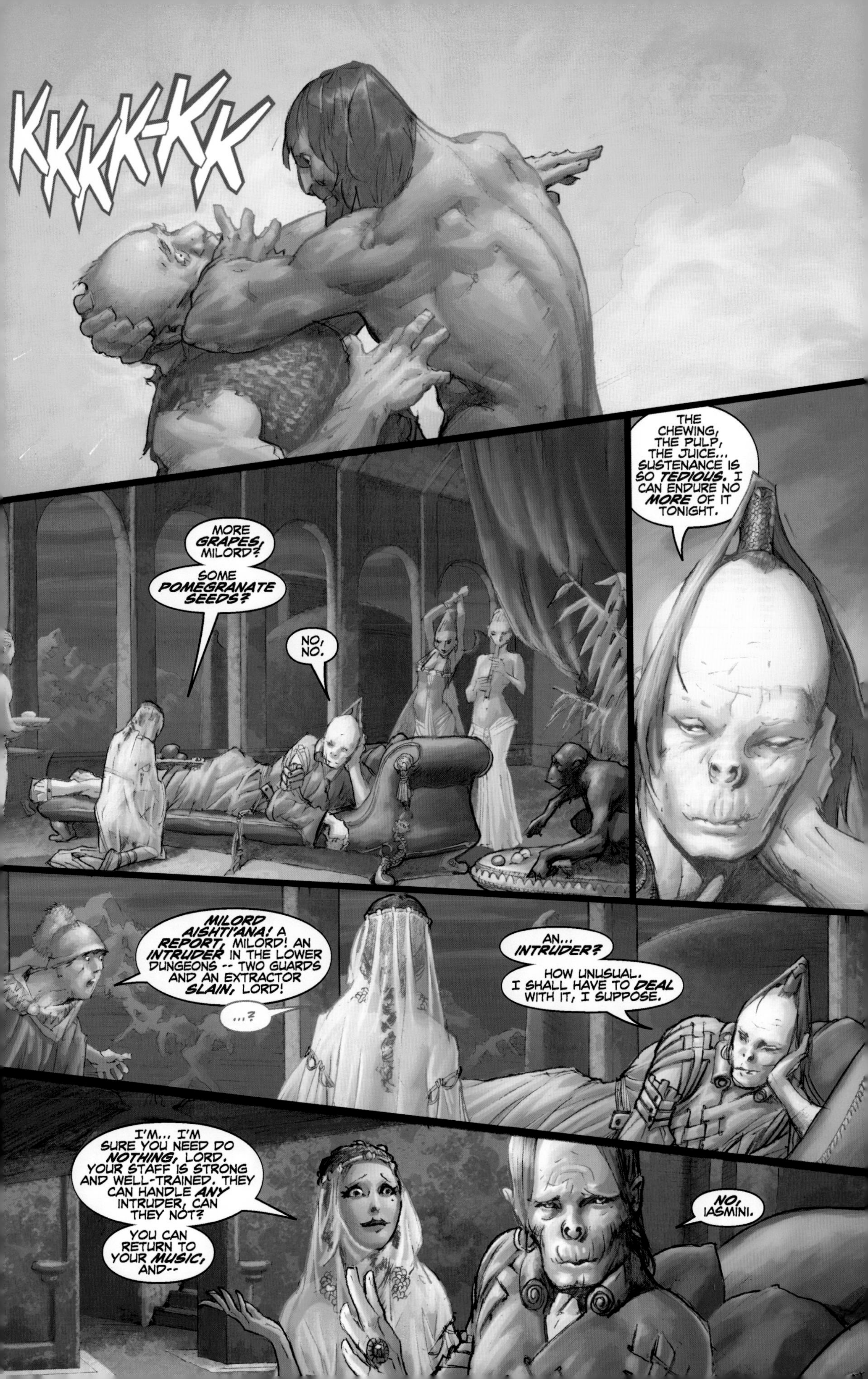
KKKK-KK
THE CHEWING, THE PULP, THE JUICE... SUSTENANCE IS SO TEDIOUS. I CAN ENDURE NO MORE OF IT TONIGHT.
MORE GRAPES, MILORD?
SOME POMEGRANATE SEEDS?
NO, NO.
MILORD AISHTI'ANA! A REPORT, MILORD! AN INTRUDER IN THE LOWER DUNGEONS -- TWO GUARDS AND AN EXTRACTOR SLAIN, LORD!
...?
AN... INTRUDER?
HOW UNUSUAL. I SHALL HAVE TO DEAL WITH IT, I SUPPOSE.
I'M... I'M SURE YOU NEED DO NOTHING, LORD. YOUR STAFF IS STRONG AND WELL-TRAINED. THEY CAN HANDLE ANY INTRUDER, CAN THEY NOT?
YOU CAN RETURN TO YOUR MUSIC, AND--
NO, IASMINI.

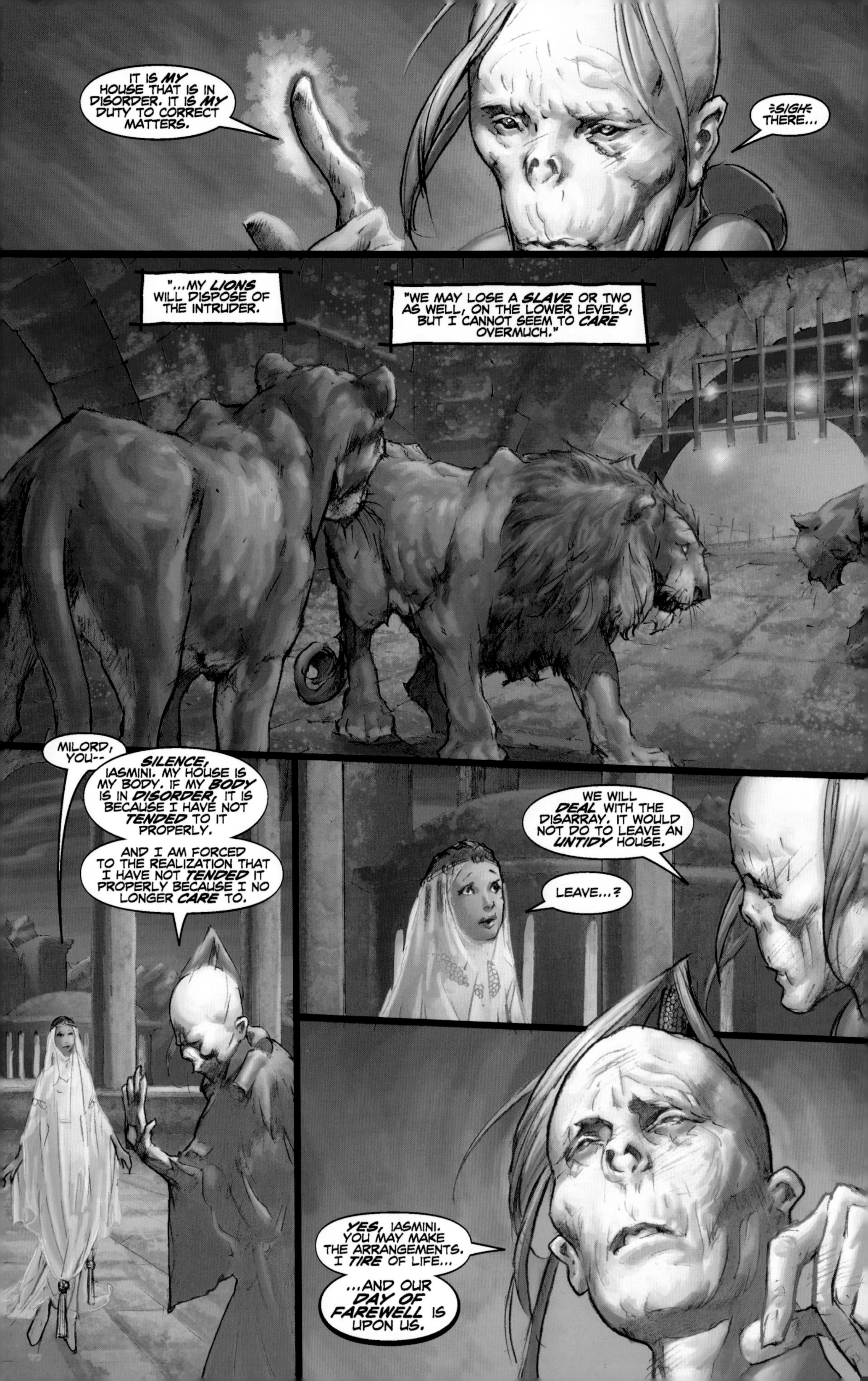
IT IS MY HOUSE THAT IS IN DISORDER. IT IS MY DUTY TO CORRECT MATTERS.
SIGH THERE...
"...MY LIONS WILL DISPOSE OF THE INTRUDER.
"WE MAY LOSE A SLAVE OR TWO AS WELL, ON THE LOWER LEVELS, BUT I CANNOT SEEM TO CARE OVERMUCH."
MILORD, YOU--
SILENCE, IASMINI. MY HOUSE IS MY BODY. IF MY BODY IS IN DISORDER, IT IS BECAUSE I HAVE NOT TENDED TO IT PROPERLY.
AND I AM FORCED TO THE REALIZATION THAT I HAVE NOT TENDED IT PROPERLY BECAUSE I NO LONGER CARE TO.
WE WILL DEAL WITH THE DISARRAY. IT WOULD NOT DO TO LEAVE AN UNTIDY HOUSE.
LEAVE...?
YES, IASMINI. YOU MAY MAKE THE ARRANGEMENTS. I TIRE OF LIFE...
...AND OUR DAY OF FAREWELL IS UPON US.

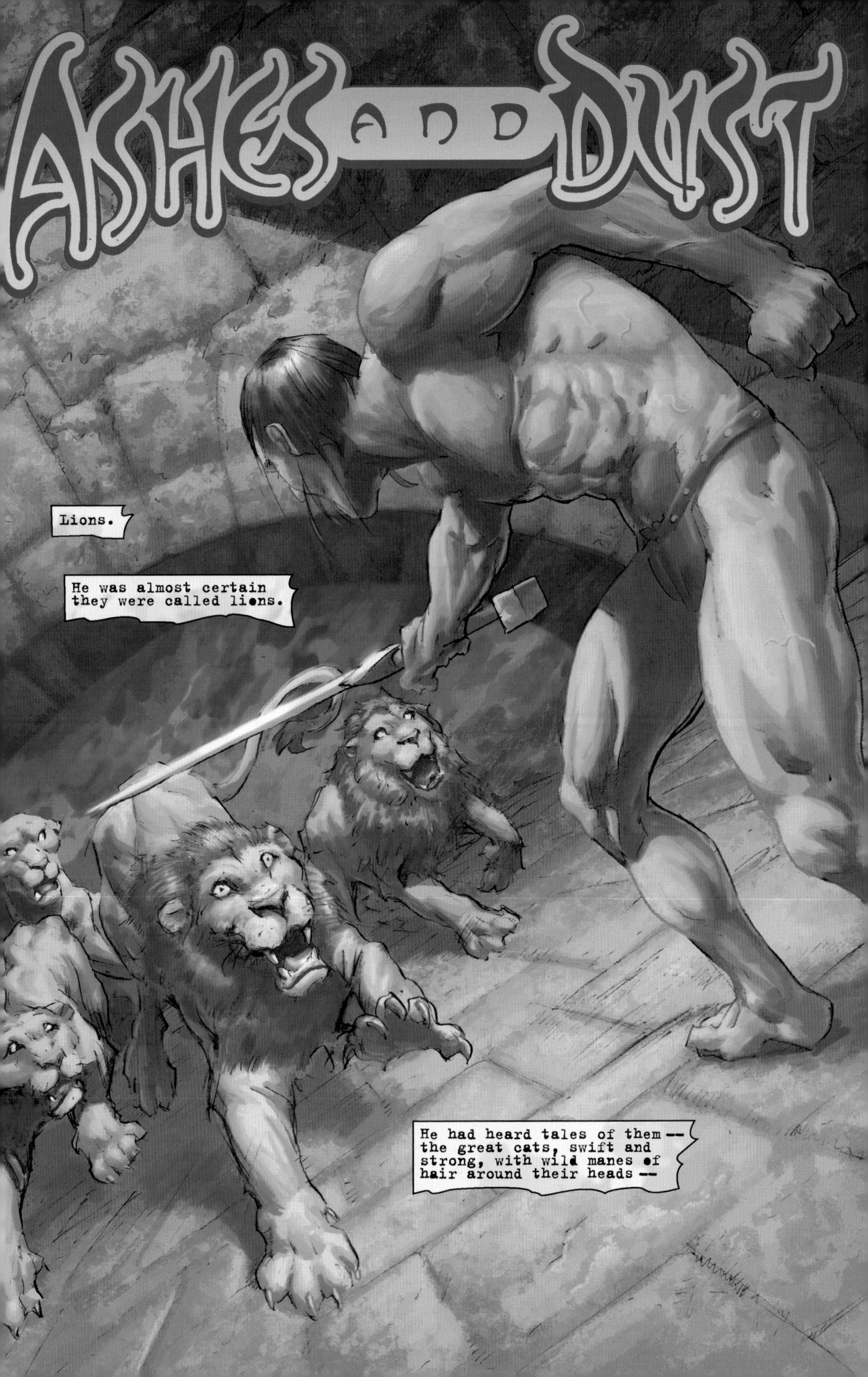
ASHES AND DUST
Lions.
He was almost certain they were called lions.
He had heard tales of them -- the great cats, swift and strong, with wild manes of hair around their heads --

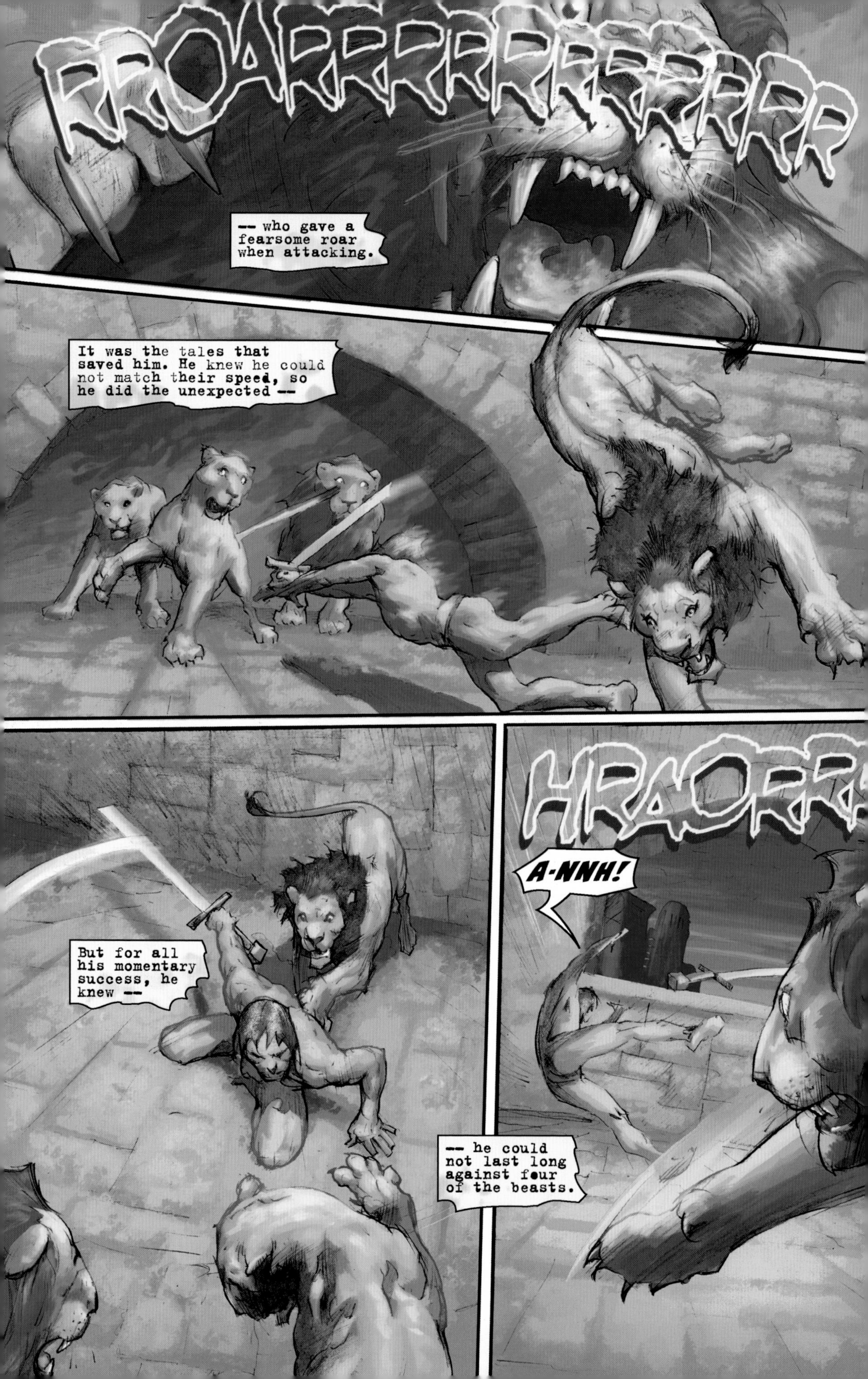
RROARRRRRRRRRRRR
-- who gave a fearsome roar when attacking.
It was the tales that saved him. He knew he could not match their speed, so he did the unexpected --
But for all his momentary success, he knew --
HRAORR
A-NNH!
-- he could not last long against four of the beasts.

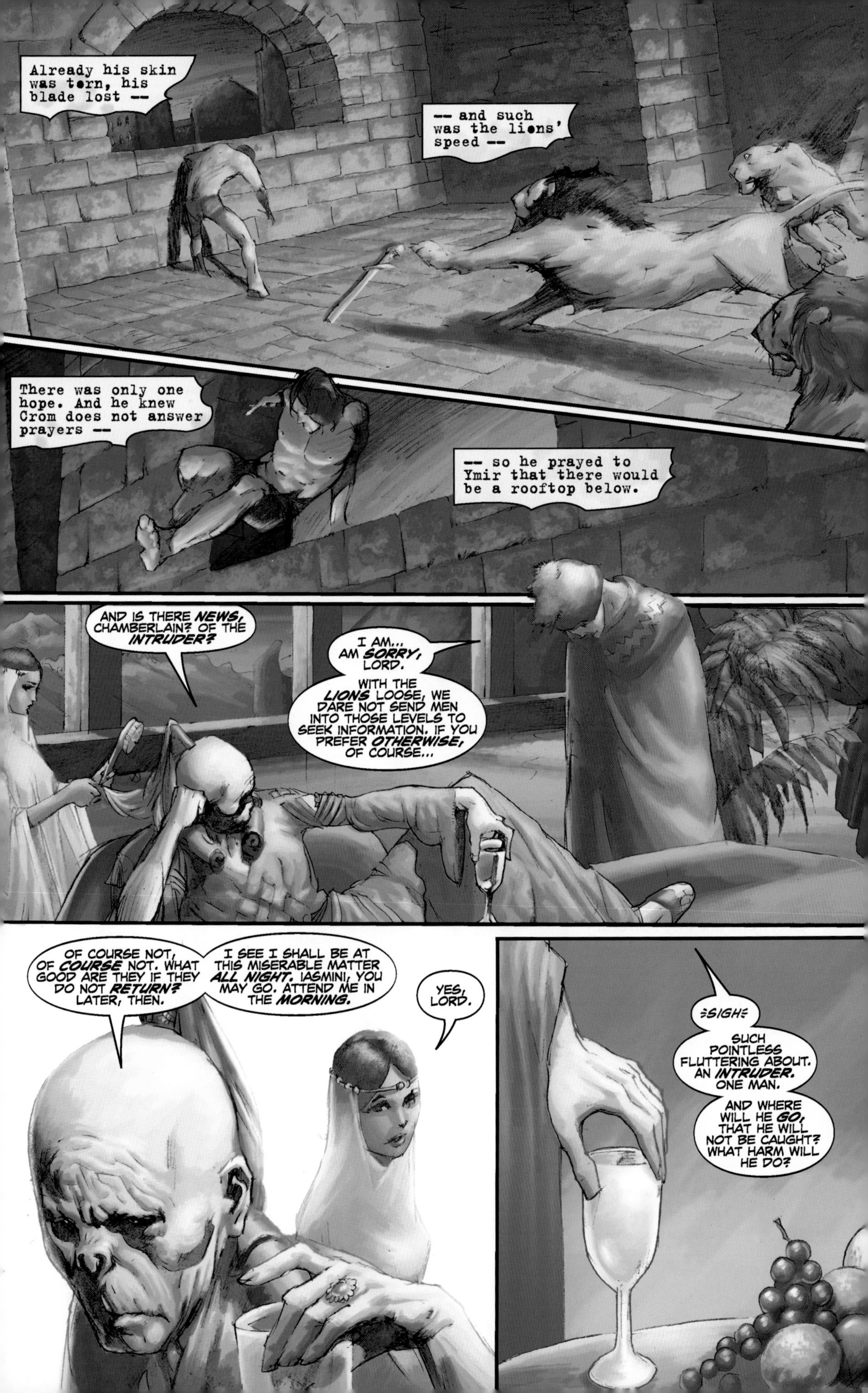
Already his skin was torn, his blade lost --
-- and such was the lions' speed --
There was only one hope. And he knew Crom does not answer prayers --
-- so he prayed to Ymir that there would be a rooftop below.
AND IS THERE NEWS, CHAMBERLAIN? OF THE INTRUDER?
I AM... AM SORRY, LORD.
WITH THE LIONS LOOSE, WE DARE NOT SEND MEN INTO THOSE LEVELS TO SEEK INFORMATION. IF YOU PREFER OTHERWISE, OF COURSE...
OF COURSE NOT, OF COURSE NOT. WHAT GOOD ARE THEY IF THEY DO NOT RETURN? LATER, THEN.
I SEE I SHALL BE AT THIS MISERABLE MATTER ALL NIGHT. IASMINI, YOU MAY GO. ATTEND ME IN THE MORNING.
YES, LORD.
SIGH
SUCH POINTLESS FLUTTERING ABOUT. AN INTRUDER. ONE MAN.
AND WHERE WILL HE GO, THAT HE WILL NOT BE CAUGHT? WHAT HARM WILL HE DO?

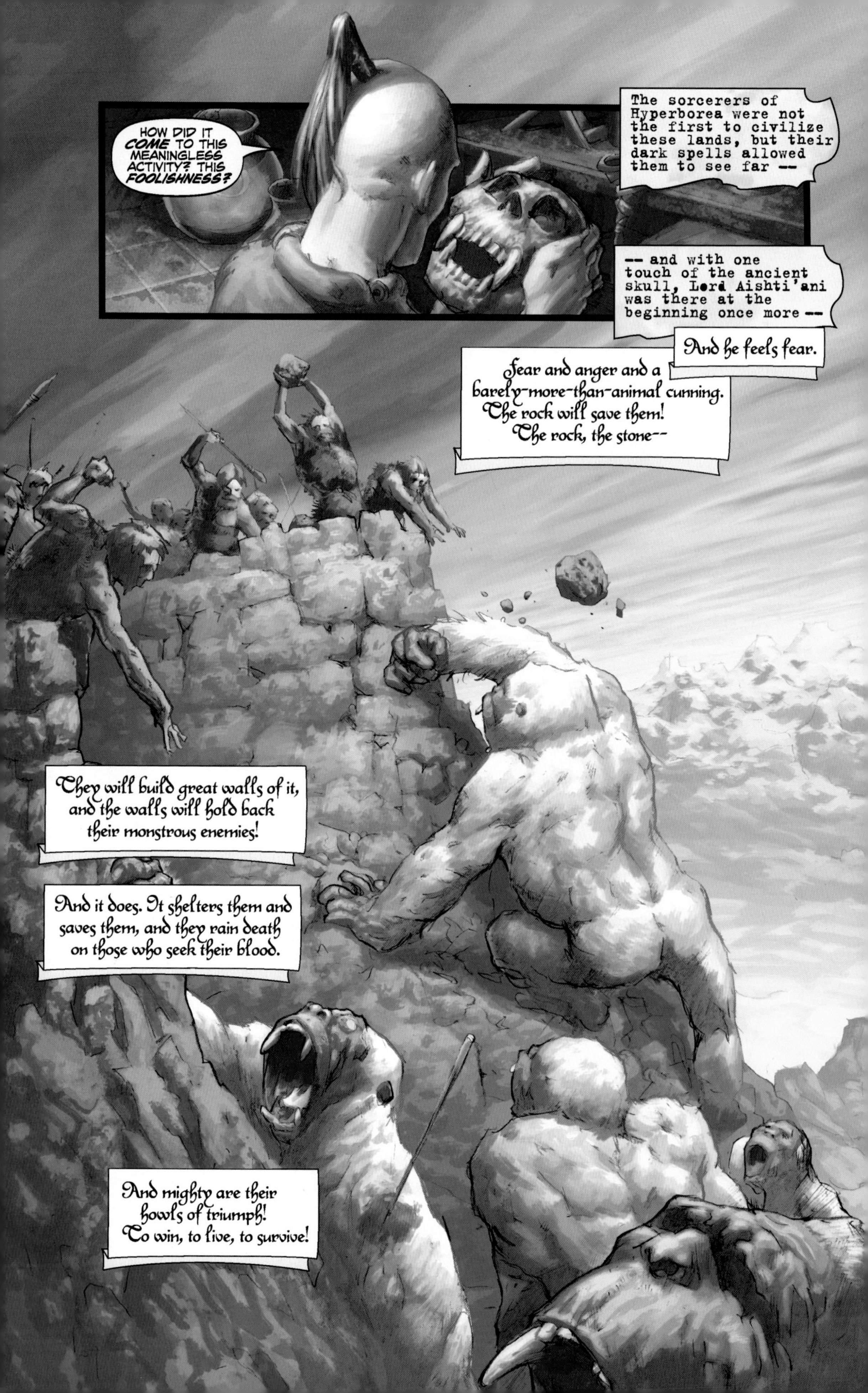

HOW DID IT COME TO THIS MEANINGLESS ACTIVITY? THIS FOOLISHNESS?
The sorcerers of Hyperborea were not the first to civilize these lands, but their dark spells allowed them to see far --
-- and with one touch of the ancient skull, Lord Aishti'ani was there at the beginning once more --
And he feels fear.
Fear and anger and a barely-more-than-animal cunning. The rock will save them! The rock, the stone--
They will build great walls of it, and the walls will hold back their monstrous enemies!
And it does. It shelters them and saves them, and they rain death on those who seek their blood.
And mighty are their howls of triumph! To win, to live, to survive!

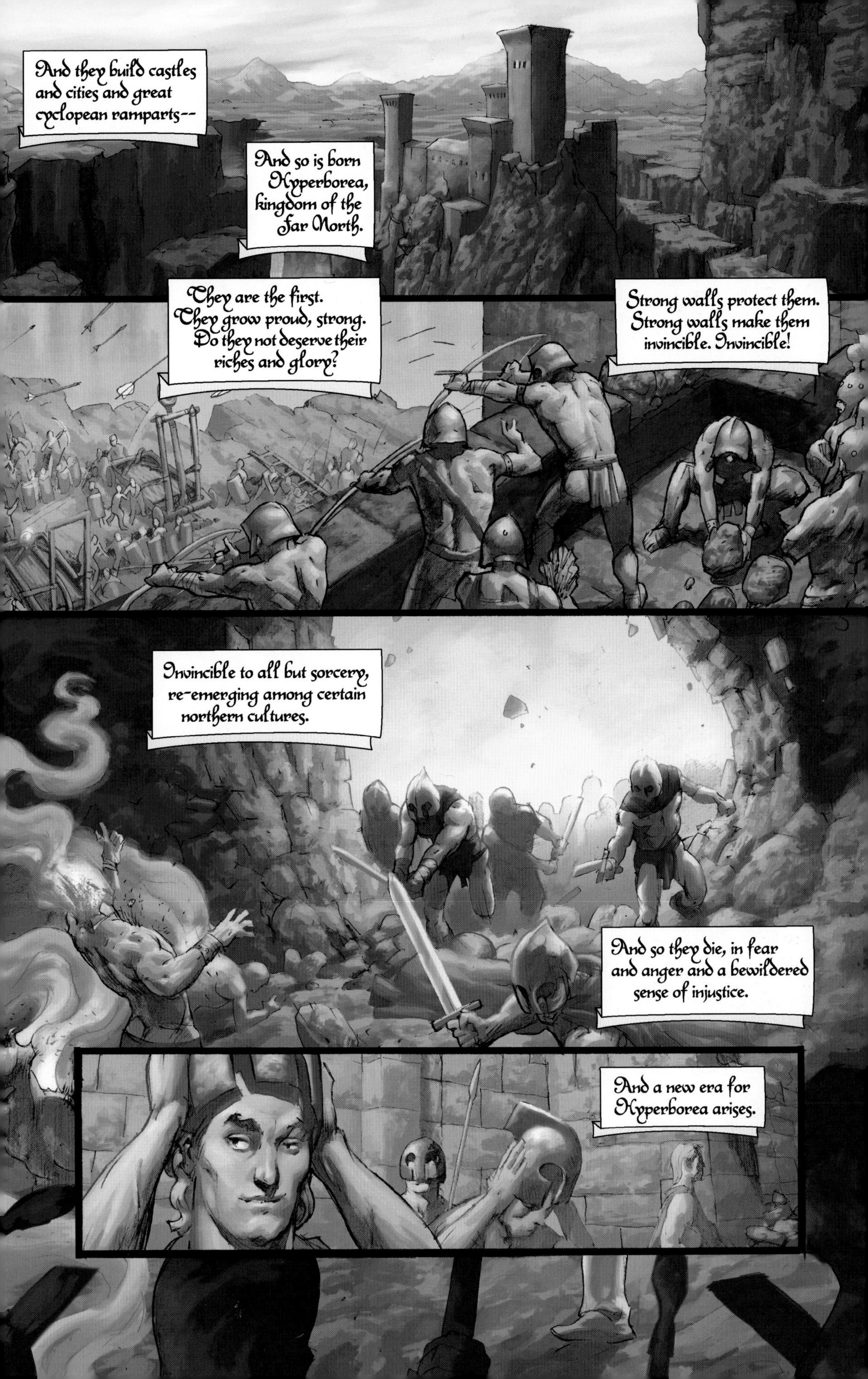

And they build castles and cities and great cyclopean ramparts--
And so is born Hyperborea, kingdom of the far North.
They are the first. They grow proud, strong. Do they not deserve their riches and glory?
Strong walls protect them. Strong walls make them invincible. Invincible!
Invincible to all but sorcery, re-emerging among certain northern cultures.
And so they die, in fear and anger and a bewildered sense of injustice.
And a new era for Hyperborea arises.

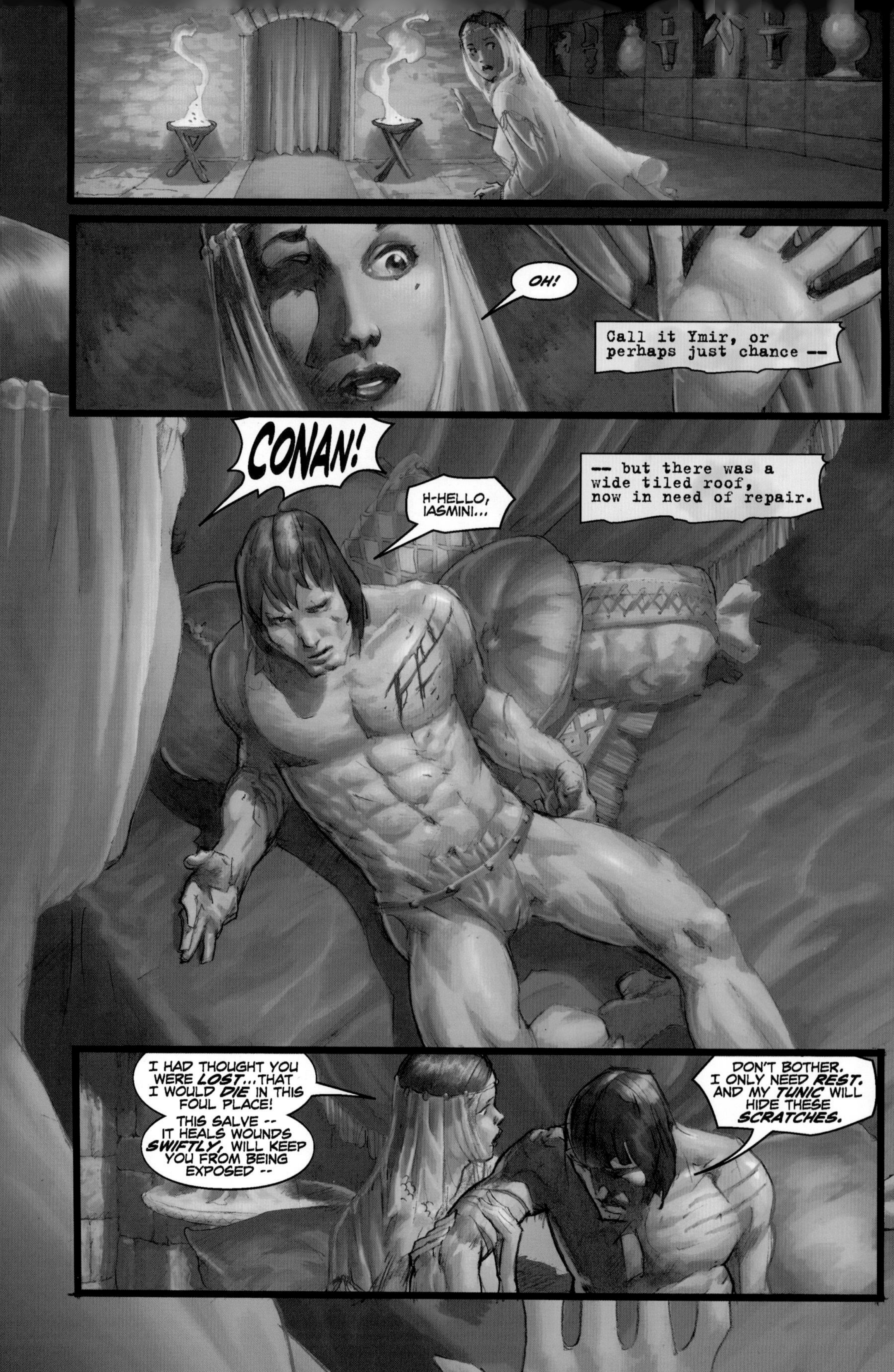
OH!
Call it Ymir, or perhaps just chance --
CONAN!
H-HELLO, IASMINI...
-- but there was a wide tiled roof, now in need of repair.
I HAD THOUGHT YOU WERE LOST...THAT I WOULD DIE IN THIS FOUL PLACE!
THIS SALVE -- IT HEALS WOUNDS SWIFTLY, WILL KEEP YOU FROM BEING EXPOSED --
DON'T BOTHER. I ONLY NEED REST. AND MY TUNIC WILL HIDE THESE SCRATCHES.

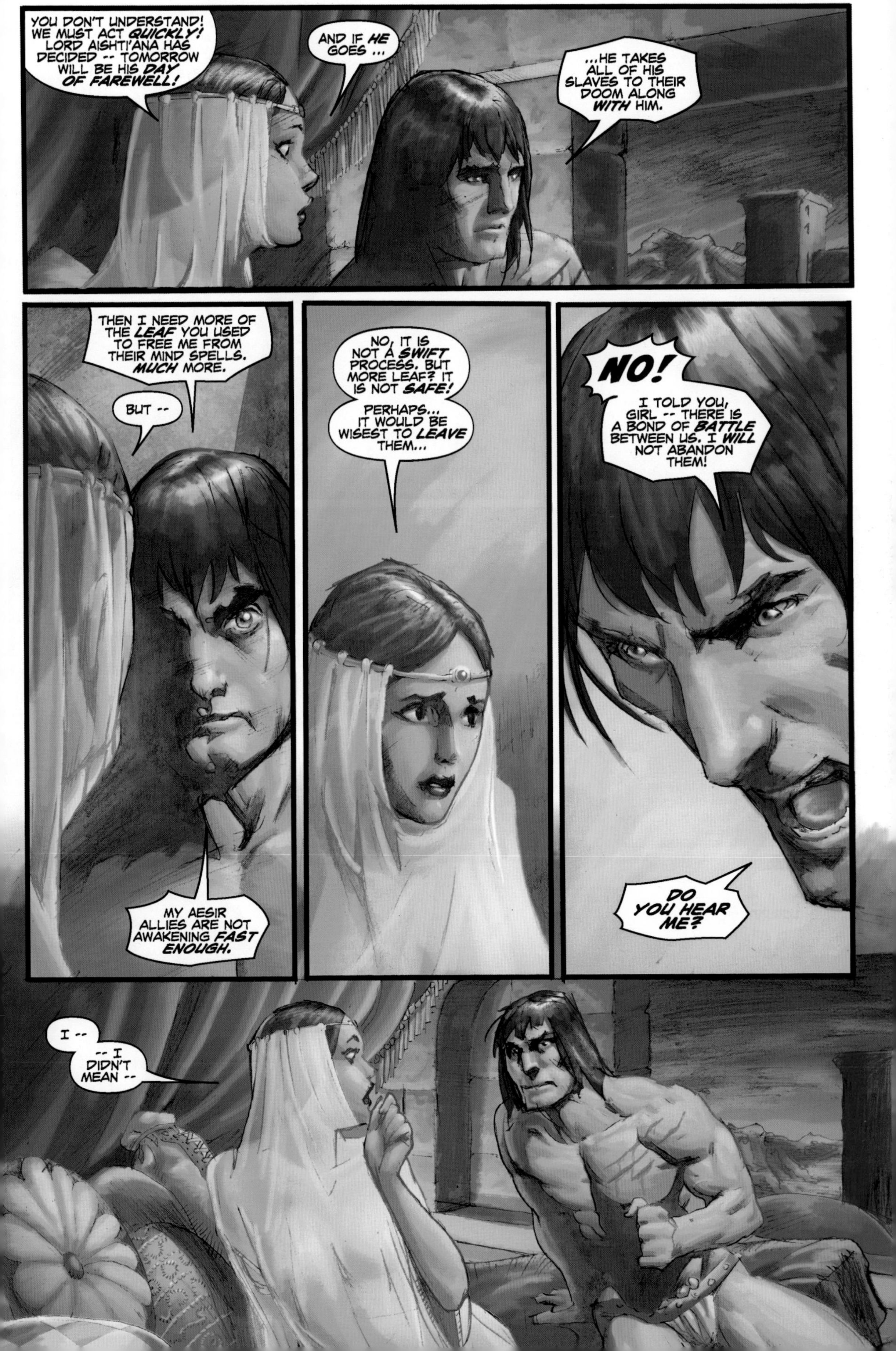
YOU DON'T UNDERSTAND! WE MUST ACT QUICKLY! LORD AISHTI'ANA HAS DECIDED -- TOMORROW WILL BE HIS DAY OF FAREWELL!
AND IF HE GOES ...
...HE TAKES ALL OF HIS SLAVES TO THEIR DOOM ALONG WITH HIM.
THEN I NEED MORE OF THE LEAF YOU USED TO FREE ME FROM THEIR MIND SPELLS. MUCH MORE.
BUT --
MY AESIR ALLIES ARE NOT AWAKENING FAST ENOUGH.
NO, IT IS NOT A SWIFT PROCESS. BUT MORE LEAF? IT IS NOT SAFE!
PERHAPS... IT WOULD BE WISEST TO LEAVE THEM...
NO!
I TOLD YOU, GIRL -- THERE IS A BOND OF BATTLE BETWEEN US. I WILL NOT ABANDON THEM!
DO YOU HEAR ME?
I --
-- I DIDN'T MEAN --

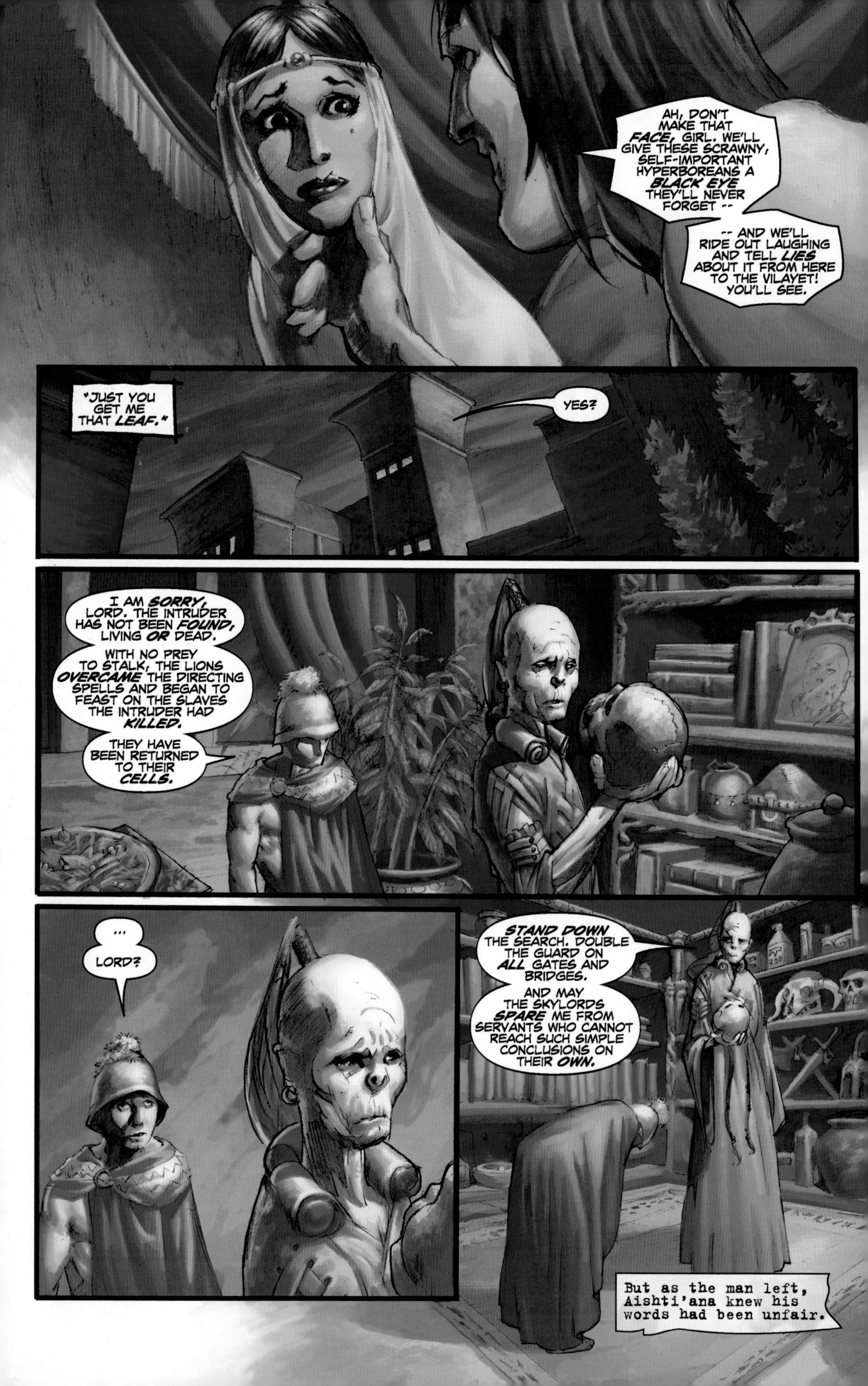
AH, DON'T MAKE THAT FACE, GIRL. WE'LL GIVE THESE SCRAWNY, SELF-IMPORTANT HYPERBOREANS A BLACK EYE THEY'LL NEVER FORGET --
-- AND WE'LL RIDE OUT LAUGHING AND TELL LIES ABOUT IT FROM HERE TO THE VILAYET! YOU'LL SEE.
"JUST YOU GET ME THAT LEAF."
YES?
I AM SORRY, LORD. THE INTRUDER HAS NOT BEEN FOUND, LIVING OR DEAD.
WITH NO PREY TO STALK, THE LIONS OVERCAME THE DIRECTING SPELLS AND BEGAN TO FEAST ON THE SLAVES THE INTRUDER HAD KILLED.
THEY HAVE BEEN RETURNED TO THEIR CELLS.
...
LORD?
STAND DOWN THE SEARCH. DOUBLE THE GUARD ON ALL GATES AND BRIDGES.
AND MAY THE SKYLORDS SPARE ME FROM SERVANTS WHO CANNOT REACH SUCH SIMPLE CONCLUSIONS ON THEIR OWN.
But as the man left, Aishti'ana knew his words had been unfair.

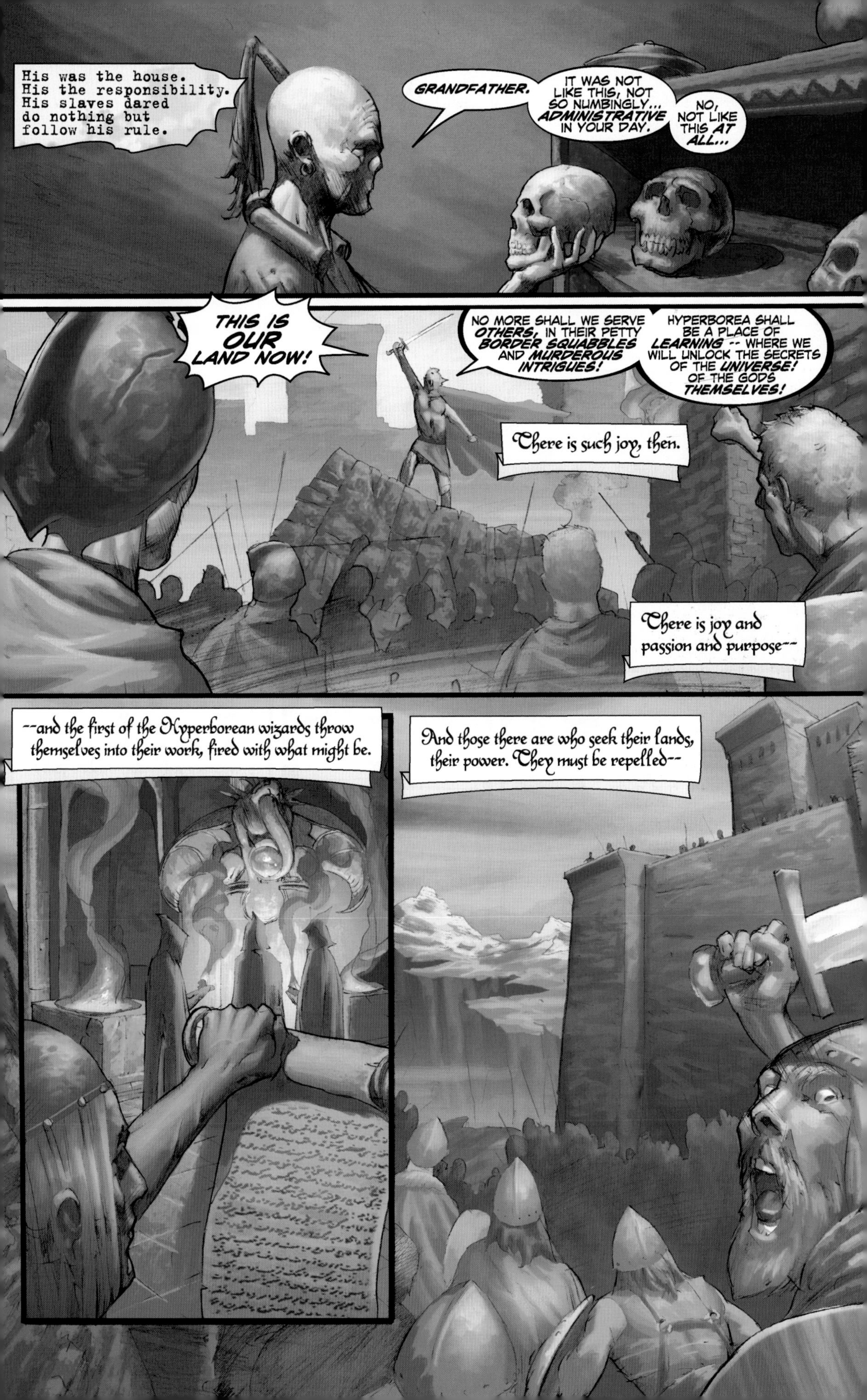
His was the house. His the responsibility. His slaves dared do nothing but follow his rule.
GRANDFATHER.
IT WAS NOT LIKE THIS, NOT SO NUMBINGLY... ADMINISTRATIVE IN YOUR DAY.
NO, NOT LIKE THIS AT ALL...
THIS IS OUR LAND NOW!
NO MORE SHALL WE SERVE OTHERS, IN THEIR PETTY BORDER SQUABBLES AND MURDEROUS INTRIGUES!
HYPERBOREA SHALL BE A PLACE OF LEARNING -- WHERE WE WILL UNLOCK THE SECRETS OF THE UNIVERSE! OF THE GODS THEMSELVES!
There is such joy, then.
There is joy and passion and purpose--
--and the first of the Hyperborean wizards throw themselves into their work, fired with what might be.
And those there are who seek their lands, their power. They must be repelled--

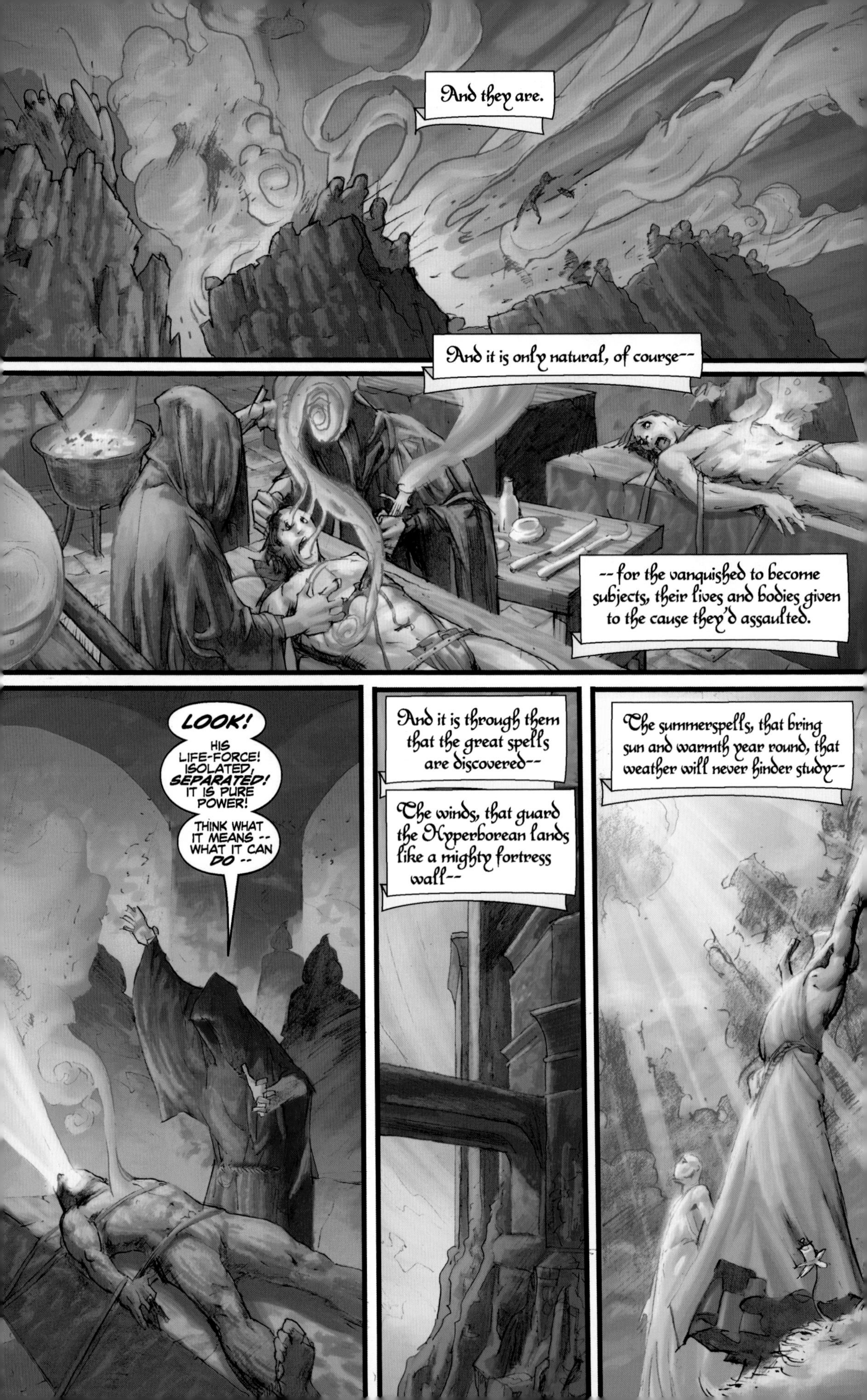
And they are.
And it is only natural, of course--
--for the vanquished to become subjects, their lives and bodies given to the cause they'd assaulted.
LOOK!
HIS LIFE-FORCE! ISOLATED, SEPARATED! IT IS PURE POWER!
THINK WHAT IT MEANS -- WHAT IT CAN DO --
And it is through them that the great spells are discovered--
The winds, that guard the Hyperborean lands like a mighty fortress wall--
The summerspells, that bring sun and warmth year round, that weather will never hinder study--

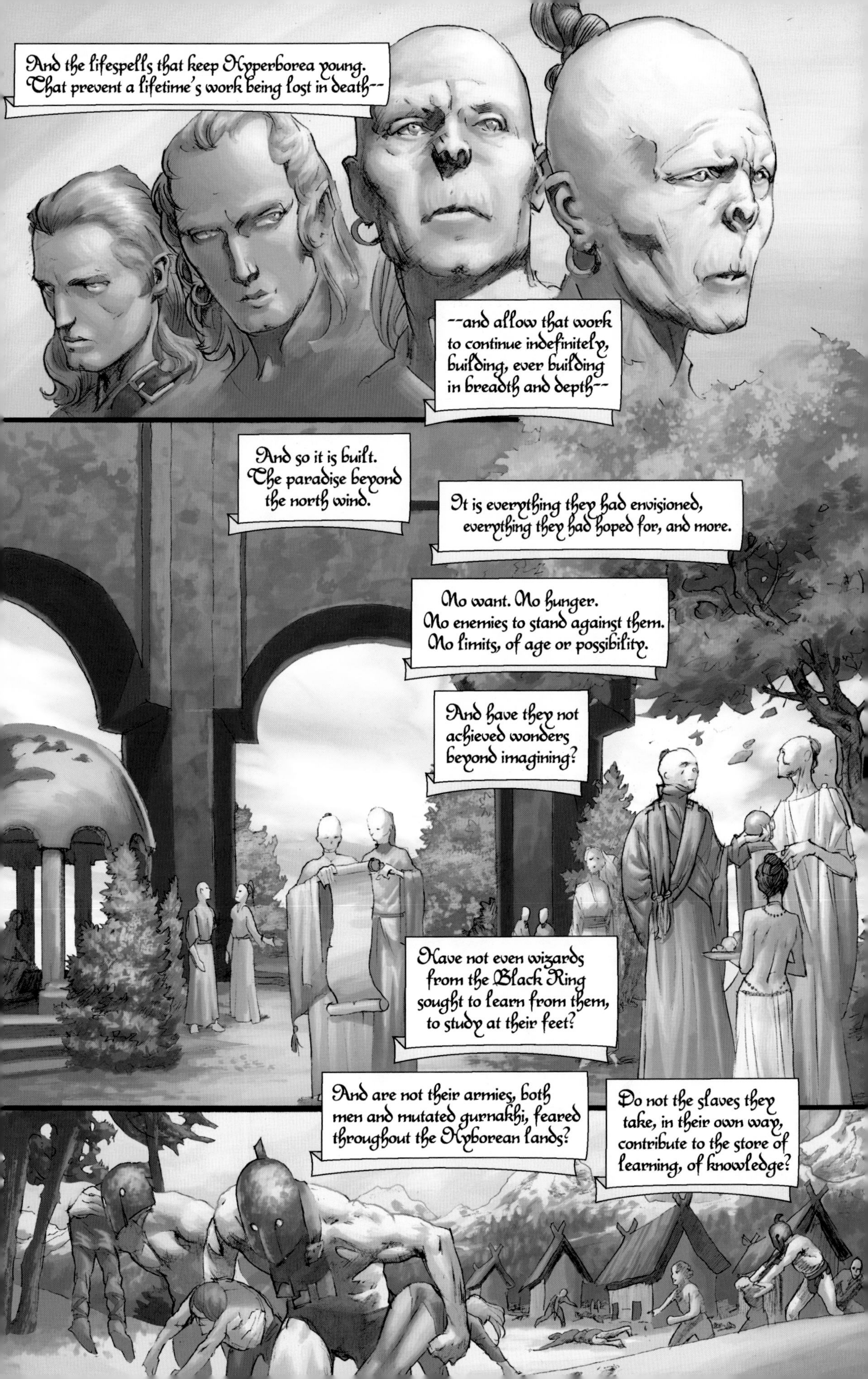
And the lifespells that keep Hyperborea young. That prevent a lifetime's work being lost in death--
--and allow that work to continue indefinitely, building, ever building in breadth and depth--
And so it is built. The paradise beyond the north wind.
It is everything they had envisioned, everything they had hoped for, and more.
No want. No hunger. No enemies to stand against them. No limits, of age or possibility.
And have they not achieved wonders beyond imagining?
Have not even wizards from the Black Ring sought to learn from them, to study at their feet?
And are not their armies, both men and mutated gurnakhi, feared throughout the Hyborean lands?
Do not the slaves they take, in their own way, contribute to the store of learning, of knowledge?

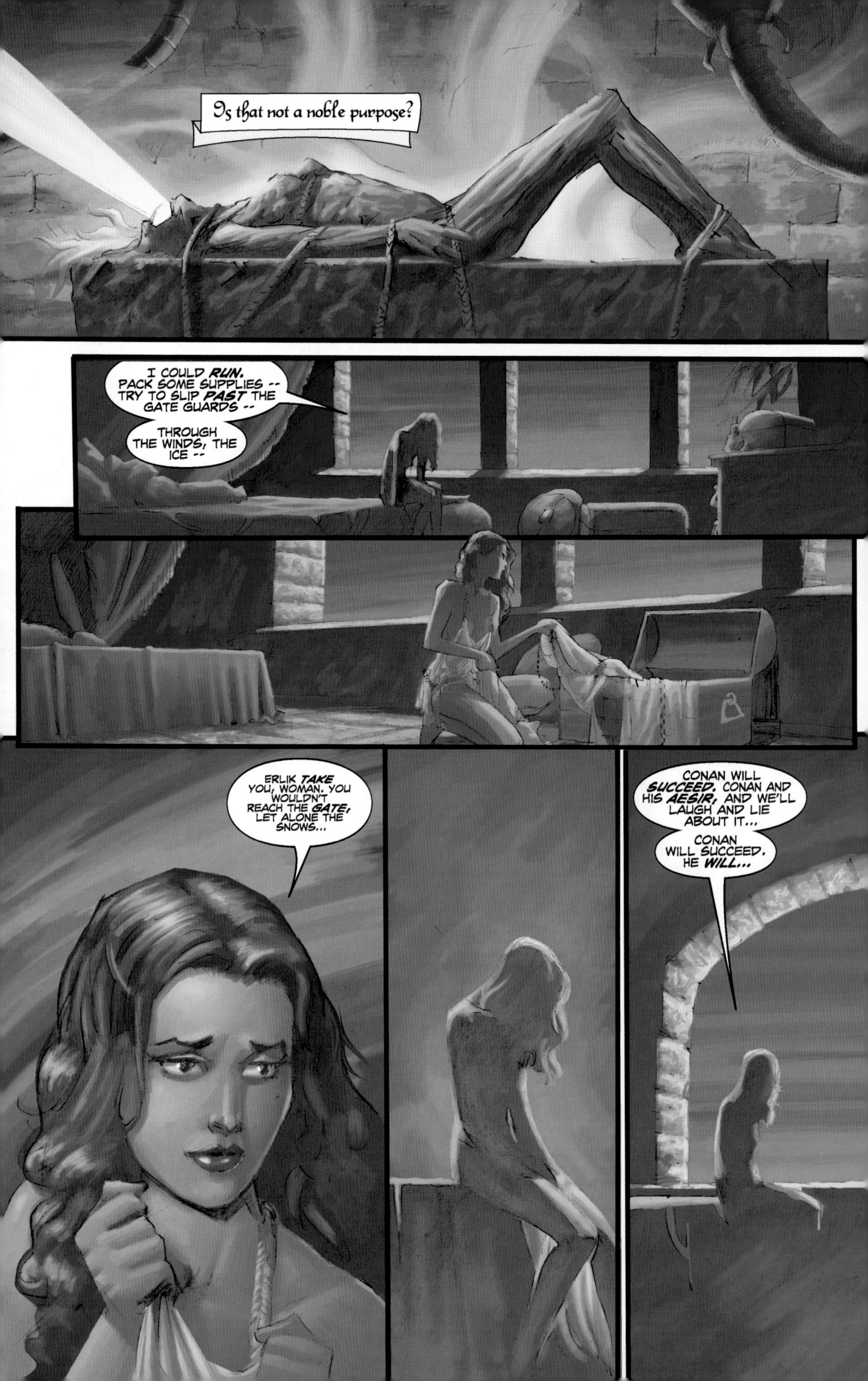
Is that not a noble purpose?
I COULD RUN. PACK SOME SUPPLIES -- TRY TO SLIP PAST THE GATE GUARDS --
THROUGH THE WINDS, THE ICE --
ERLIK TAKE YOU, WOMAN. YOU WOULDN'T REACH THE GATE, LET ALONE THE SNOWS...
CONAN WILL SUCCEED. CONAN AND HIS AESIR, AND WE'LL LAUGH AND LIE ABOUT IT...
CONAN WILL SUCCEED. HE WILL...

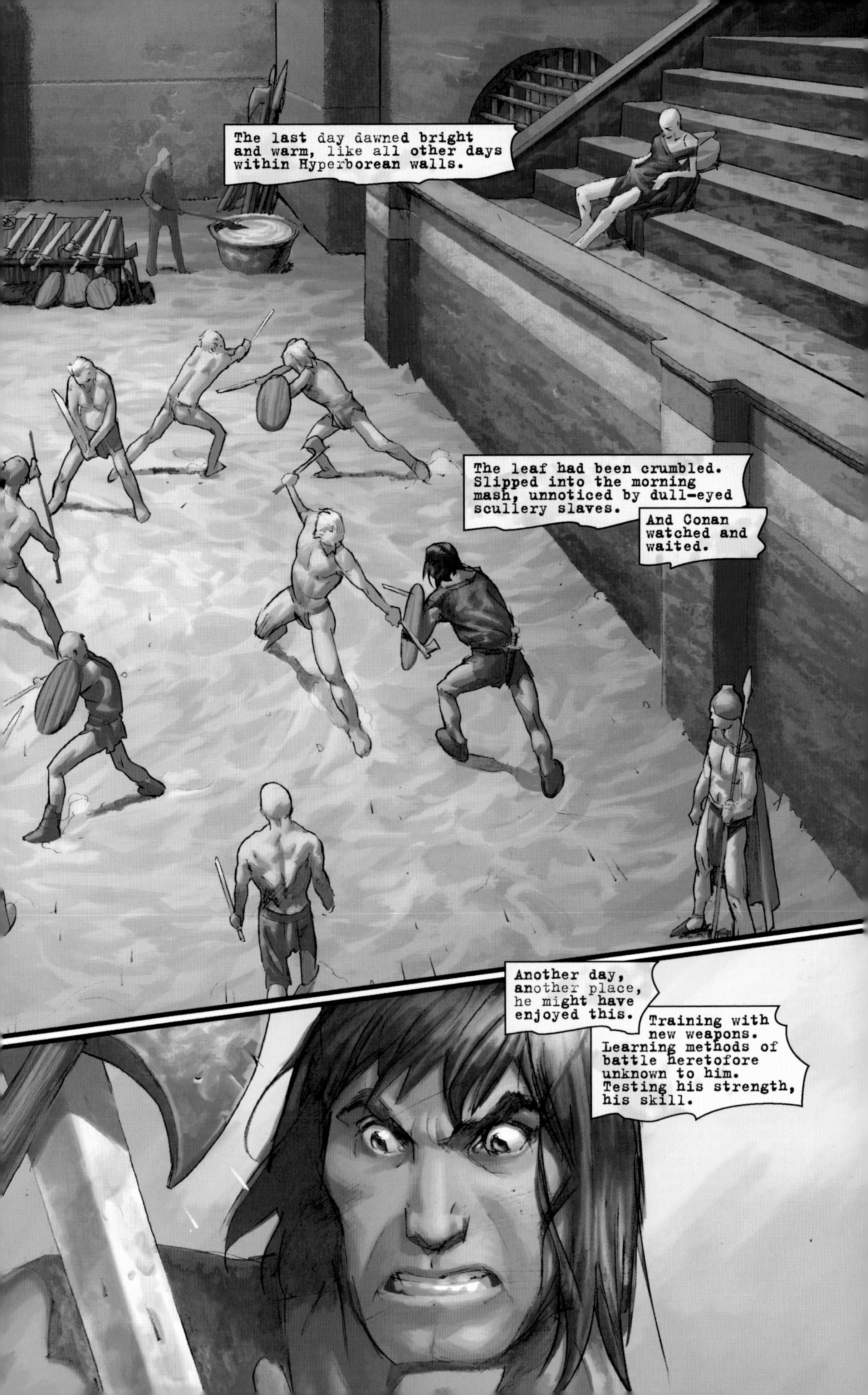
The last day dawned bright and warm, like all other days within Hyperborean walls.
The leaf had been crumbled. Slipped into the morning mash, unnoticed by dull-eyed scullery slaves.
And Conan watched and waited.
Another day, another place, he might have enjoyed this.
Training with new weapons. Learning methods of battle heretofore unknown to him. Testing his strength, his skill.

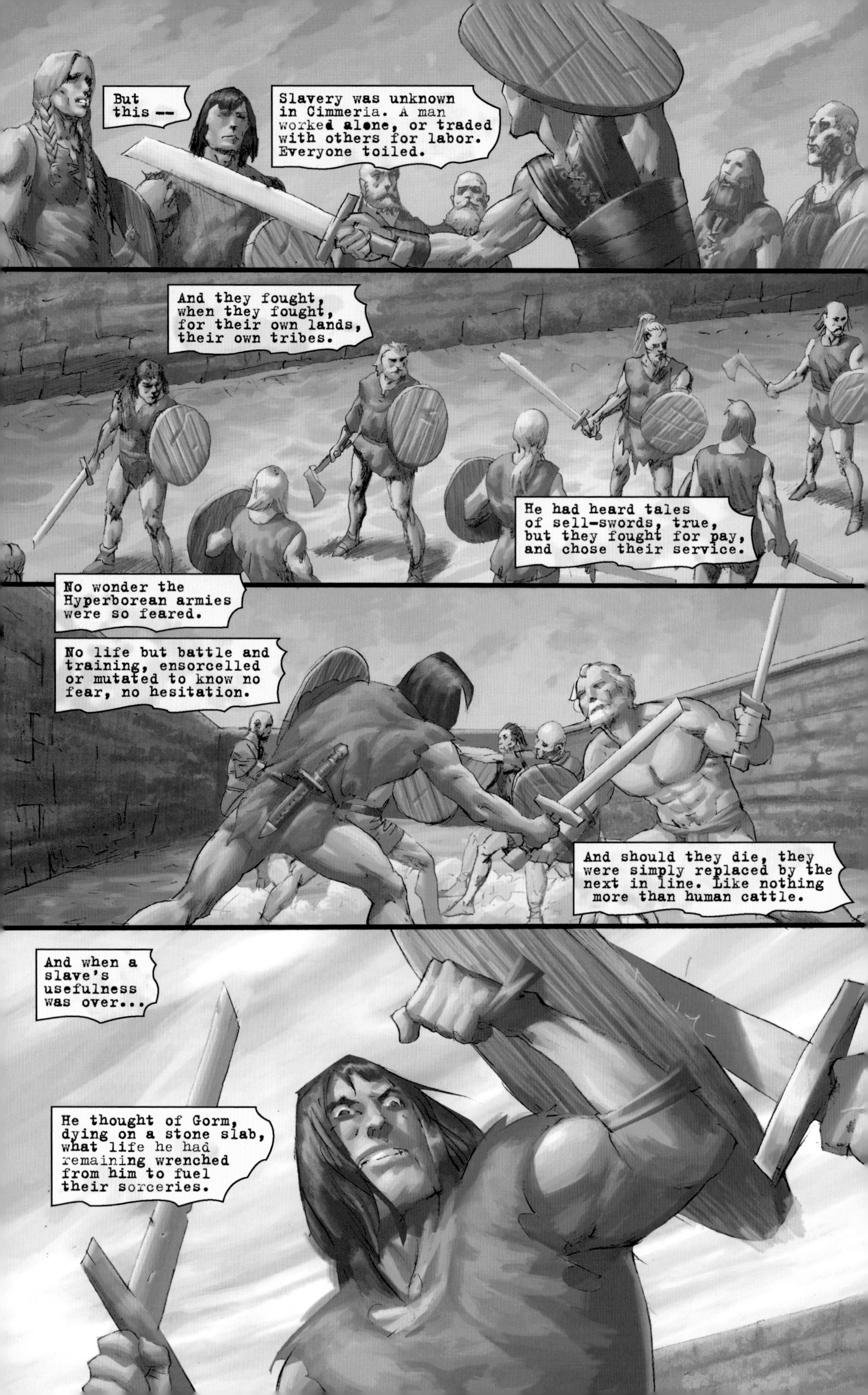
But this --
Slavery was unknown in Cimmeria. A man worked alone, or traded with others for labor. Everyone toiled.
And they fought, when they fought, for their own lands, their own tribes.
He had heard tales of sell-swords, true, but they fought for pay, and chose their service.
No wonder the Hyperborean armies were so feared.
No life but battle and training, ensorcelled or mutated to know no fear, no hesitation.
And should they die, they were simply replaced by the next in line. Like nothing more than human cattle.
And when a slave's usefulness was over...
He thought of Gorm, dying on a stone slab, what life he had remaining wrenched from him to fuel their sorceries.

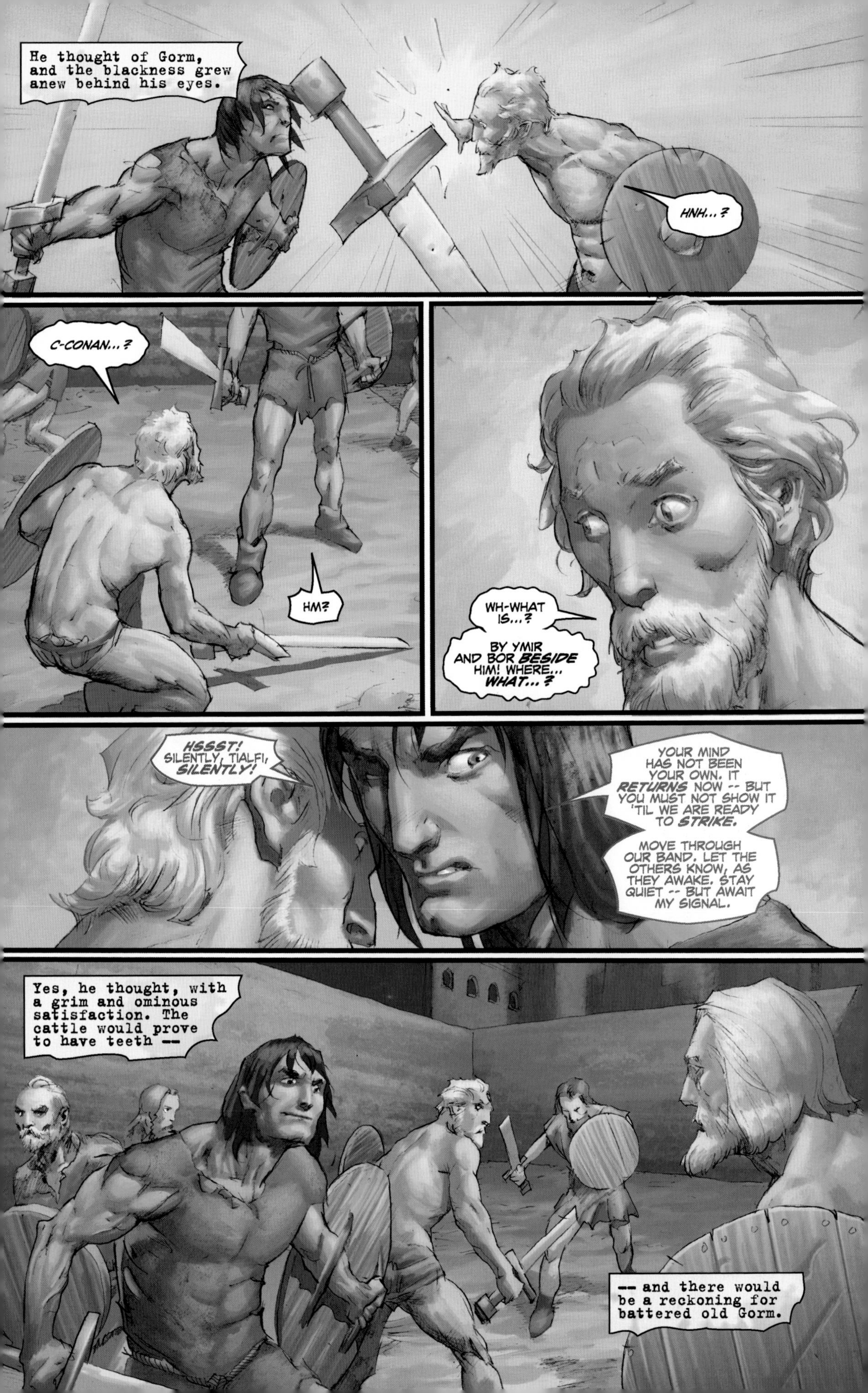
He thought of Gorm, and the blackness grew anew behind his eyes.
HNH...?
C-CONAN...?
HM?
WH-WHAT IS...?
BY YMIR AND BOR BESIDE HIM! WHERE... WHAT...?
HSSST! SILENTLY, TIALFI, SILENTLY!
YOUR MIND HAS NOT BEEN YOUR OWN. IT RETURNS NOW -- BUT YOU MUST NOT SHOW IT 'TIL WE ARE READY TO STRIKE.
MOVE THROUGH OUR BAND. LET THE OTHERS KNOW, AS THEY AWAKE. STAY QUIET -- BUT AWAIT MY SIGNAL.
Yes, he thought, with a grim and ominous satisfaction. The cattle would prove to have teeth --
-- and there would be a reckoning for battered old Gorm.

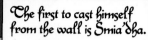

The first to cast himself
from the wall is Smia'dha.

He simply puts down his quill,
strides to the ramparts and
flings himself into space.

It is surprising how little
shock there is at the act.

His leap is debated, discussed
and analyzed, like a piece
of data to be studied.

An aberration, they say.
A lapse in rigor.
But it is said with a
certain wistfulness --
an envy --

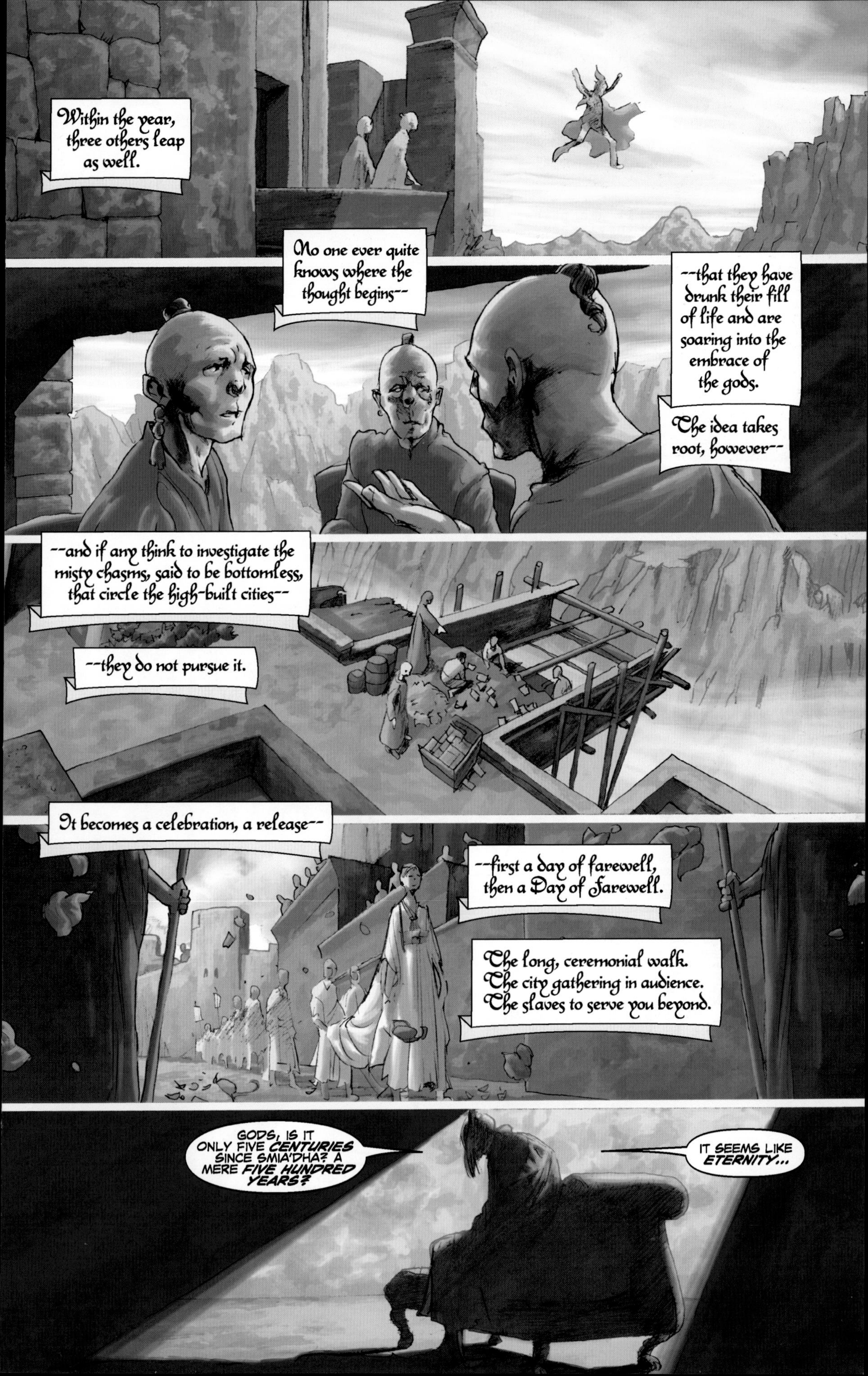
Within the year, three others leap as well.
No one ever quite knows where the thought begins--
--that they have drunk their fill of life and are soaring into the embrace of the gods.
The idea takes root, however--
--and if any think to investigate the misty chasms, said to be bottomless, that circle the high-built cities--
--they do not pursue it.
It becomes a celebration, a release--
--first a day of farewell, then a Day of Farewell.
The long, ceremonial walk.
The city gathering in audience.
The slaves to serve you beyond.
GODS, IS IT ONLY FIVE CENTURIES SINCE SMIA'DHA? A MERE FIVE HUNDRED YEARS?
IT SEEMS LIKE ETERNITY...

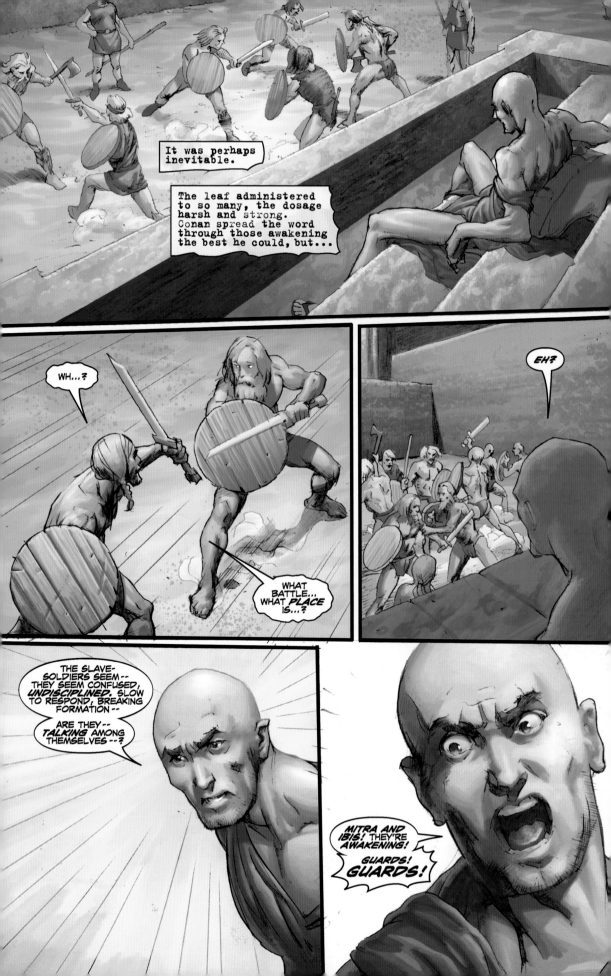

It was perhaps inevitable.

The leaf administered to so many, the dosage harsh and strong. Conan spread the word through those awakening the best he could, but...

WH...?

WHAT BATTLE... WHAT *PLACE* IS...?

EH?

THE SLAVE-SOLDIERS SEEM-- THEY SEEM CONFUSED, *UNDISCIPLINED,* SLOW TO RESPOND, BREAKING FORMATION --

ARE THEY -- *TALKING* AMONG THEMSELVES --?

MITRA AND IBIS! THEY'RE AWAKENING!

GUARDS! GUARDS!

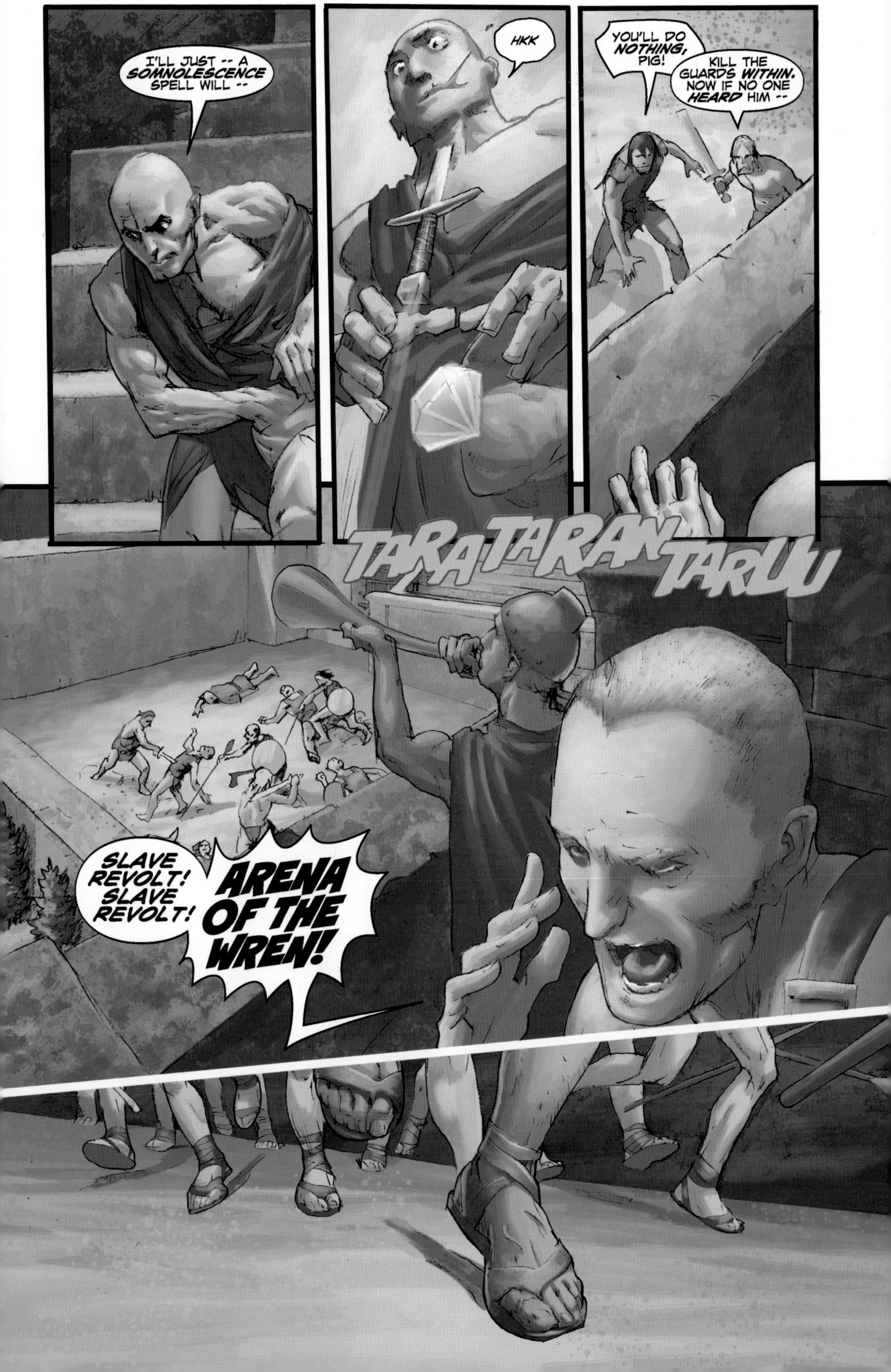
I'LL JUST -- A SOMNOLESCENCE SPELL WILL --
HKK
YOU'LL DO NOTHING, PIG!
KILL THE GUARDS WITHIN. NOW IF NO ONE HEARD HIM --
TARA TARAN TARUU
SLAVE REVOLT! SLAVE REVOLT!
ARENA OF THE WREN!

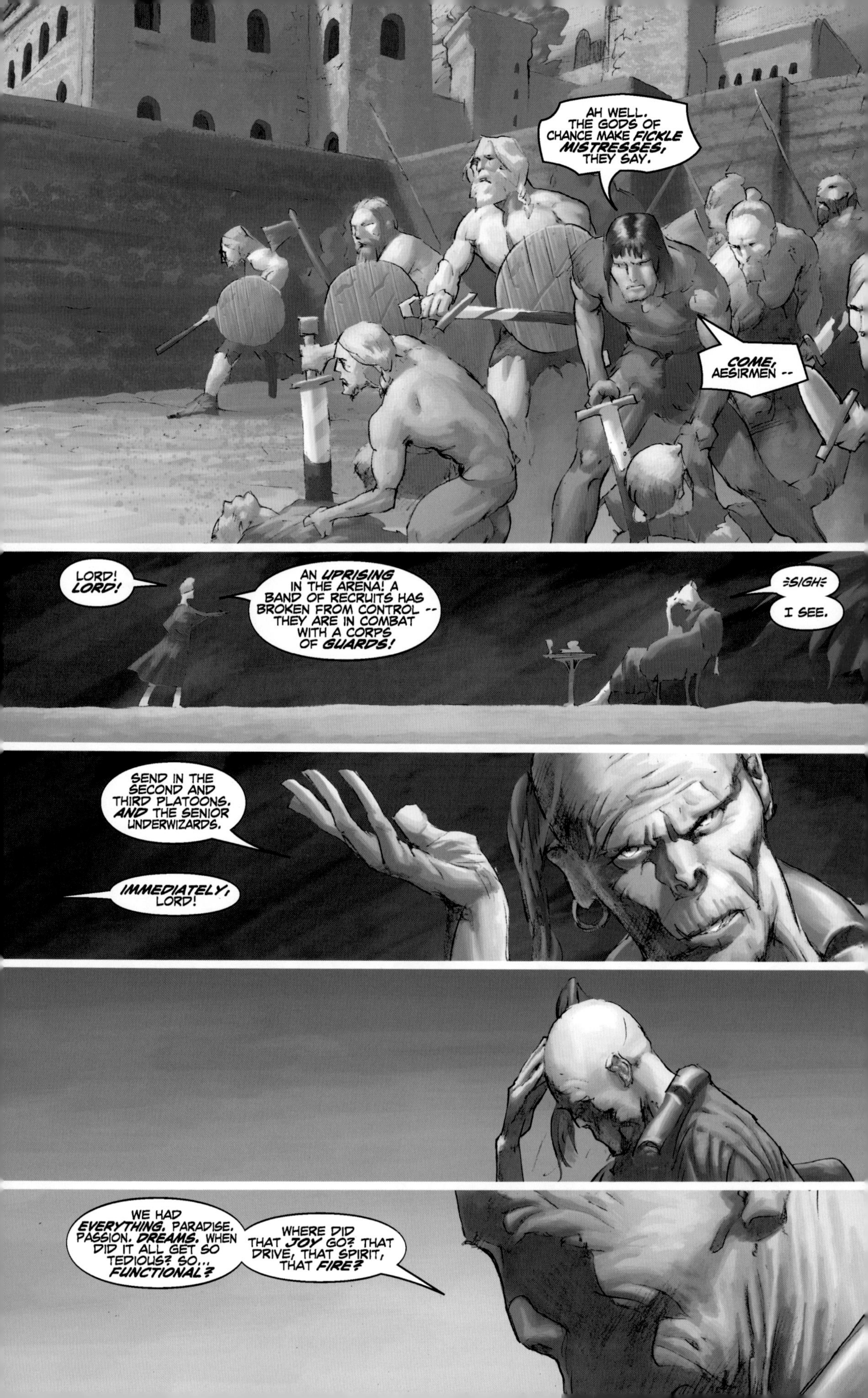
AH WELL. THE GODS OF CHANCE MAKE FICKLE MISTRESSES, THEY SAY.
COME, AESIRMEN --
LORD! LORD!
AN UPRISING IN THE ARENA! A BAND OF RECRUITS HAS BROKEN FROM CONTROL -- THEY ARE IN COMBAT WITH A CORPS OF GUARDS!
SIGH
I SEE.
SEND IN THE SECOND AND THIRD PLATOONS. AND THE SENIOR UNDERWIZARDS.
IMMEDIATELY, LORD!
WE HAD EVERYTHING. PARADISE. PASSION. DREAMS. WHEN DID IT ALL GET SO TEDIOUS? SO... FUNCTIONAL?
WHERE DID THAT JOY GO? THAT DRIVE, THAT SPIRIT, THAT FIRE?

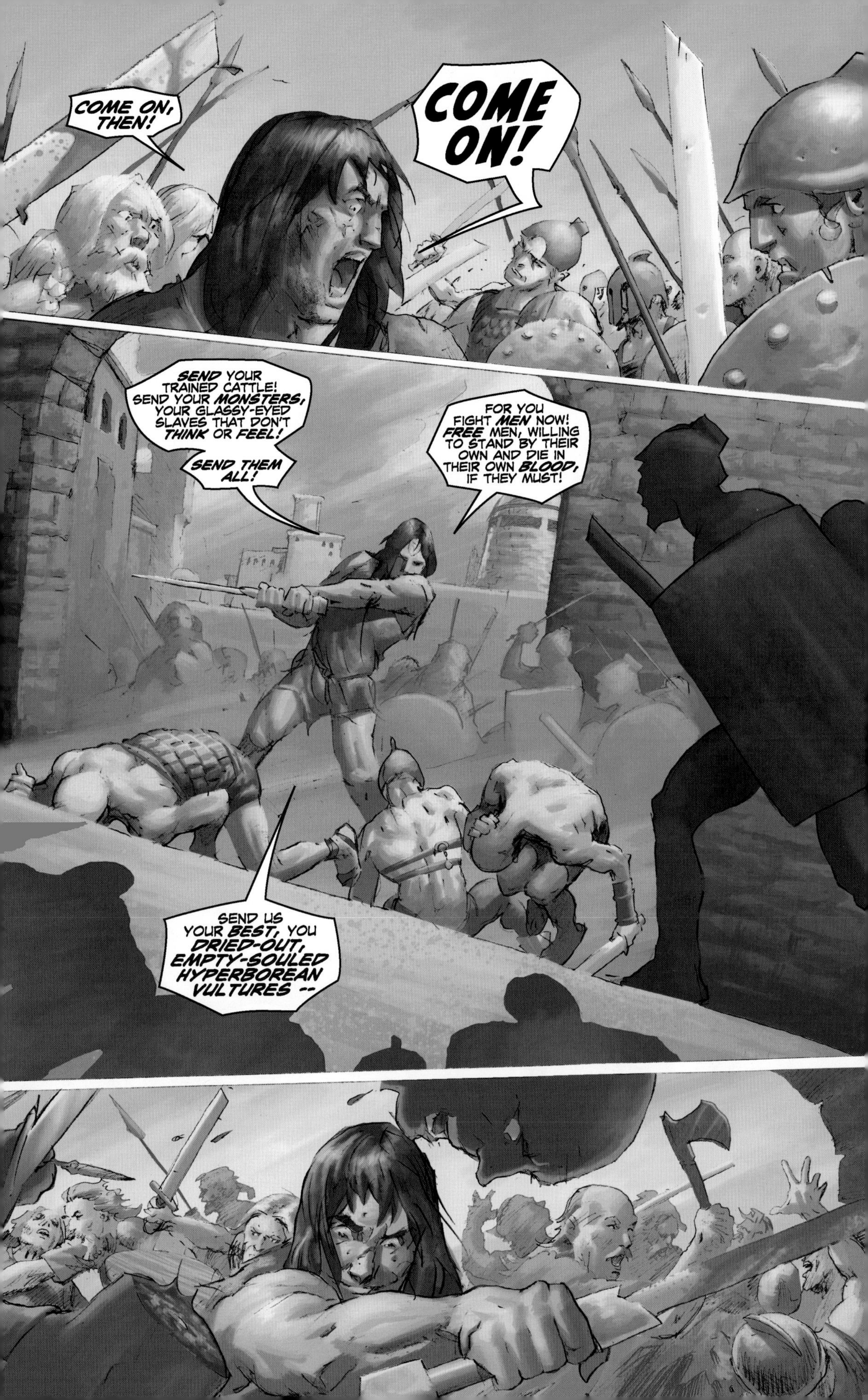
COME ON, THEN!
COME ON!
SEND YOUR TRAINED CATTLE! SEND YOUR MONSTERS, YOUR GLASSY-EYED SLAVES THAT DON'T THINK OR FEEL!
SEND THEM ALL!
FOR YOU FIGHT MEN NOW! FREE MEN, WILLING TO STAND BY THEIR OWN AND DIE IN THEIR OWN BLOOD, IF THEY MUST!
SEND US YOUR BEST, YOU DRIED-OUT, EMPTY-SOULED HYPERBOREAN VULTURES --

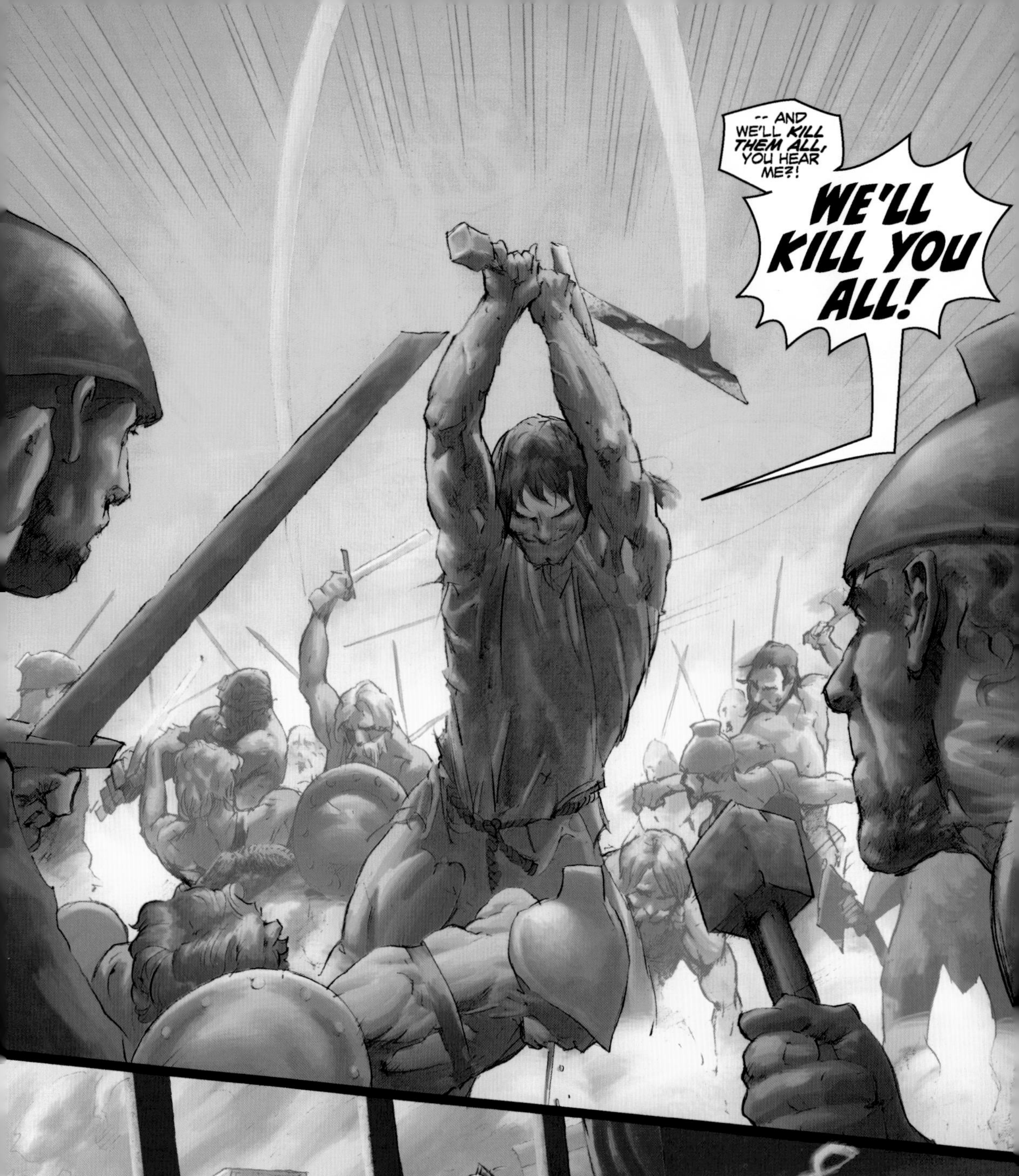
-- AND WE'LL *KILL THEM ALL*, YOU HEAR ME?!
WE'LL KILL YOU ALL!
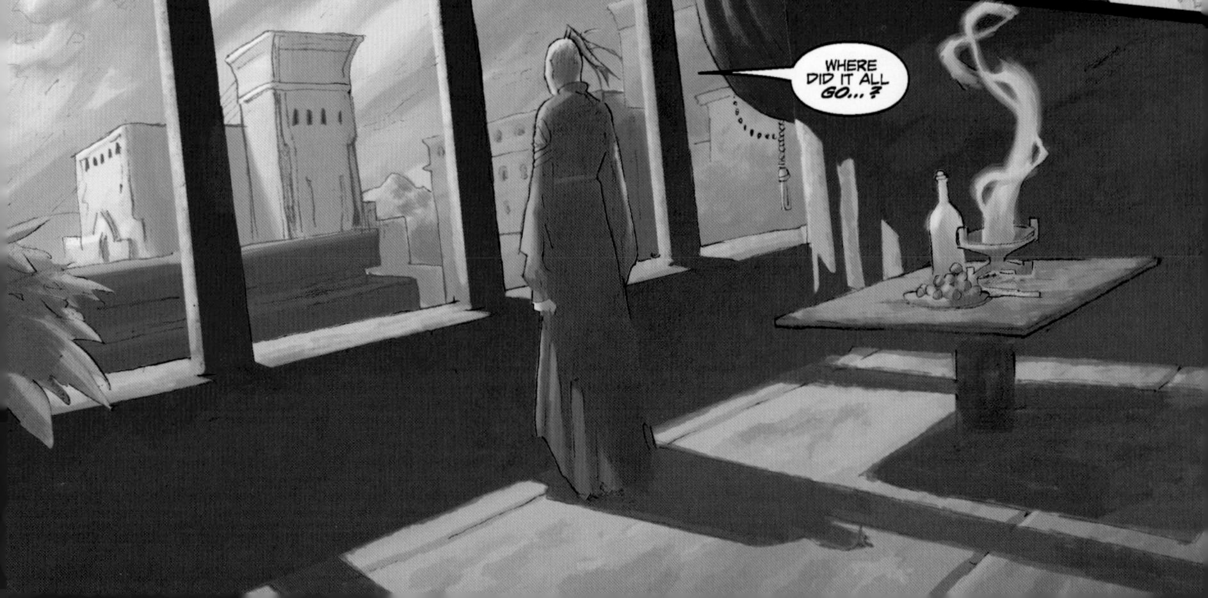
WHERE DID IT ALL *GO*...?

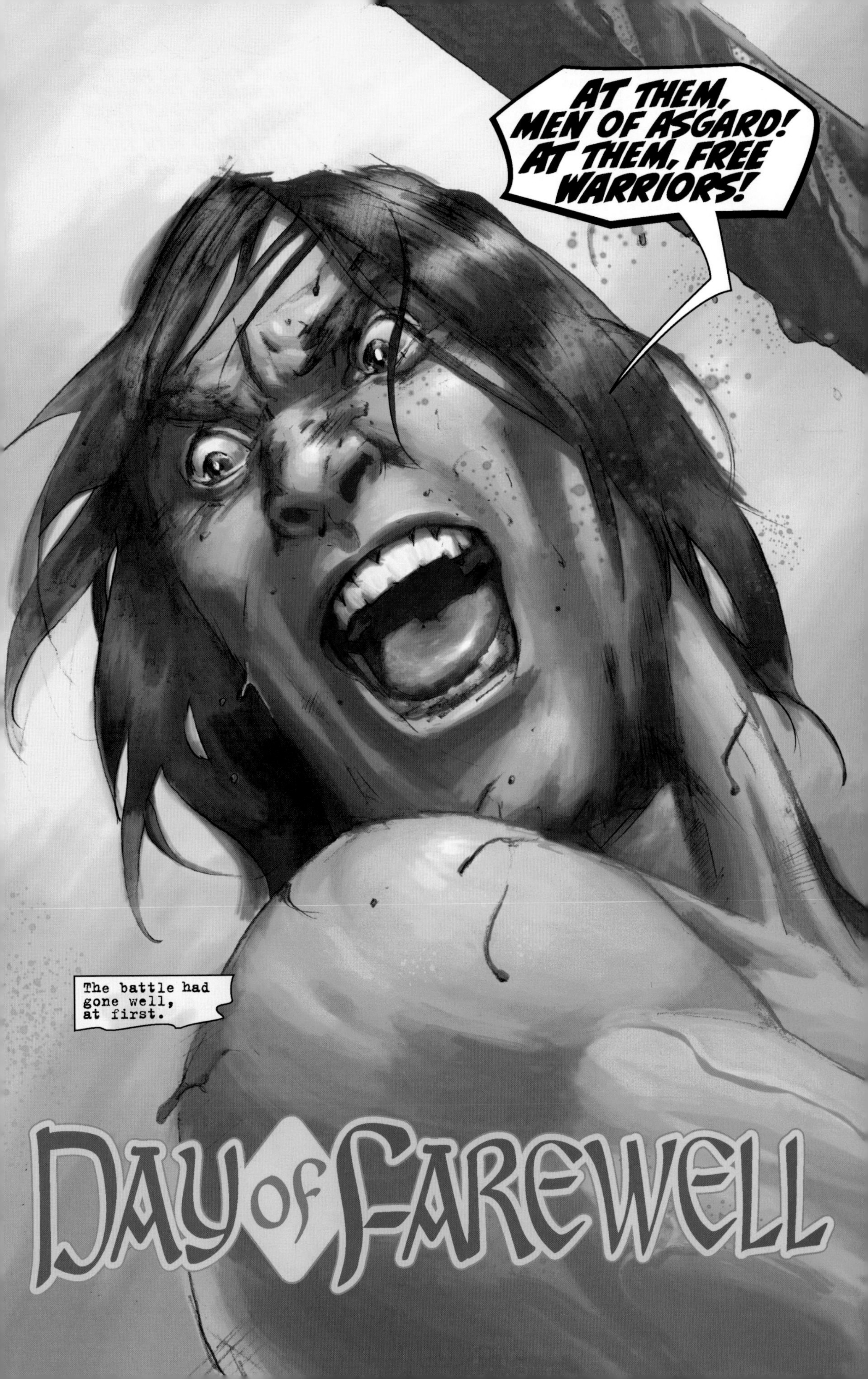
AT THEM, MEN OF ASGARD! AT THEM, FREE WARRIORS!
The battle had gone well, at first.
DAY OF FAREWELL

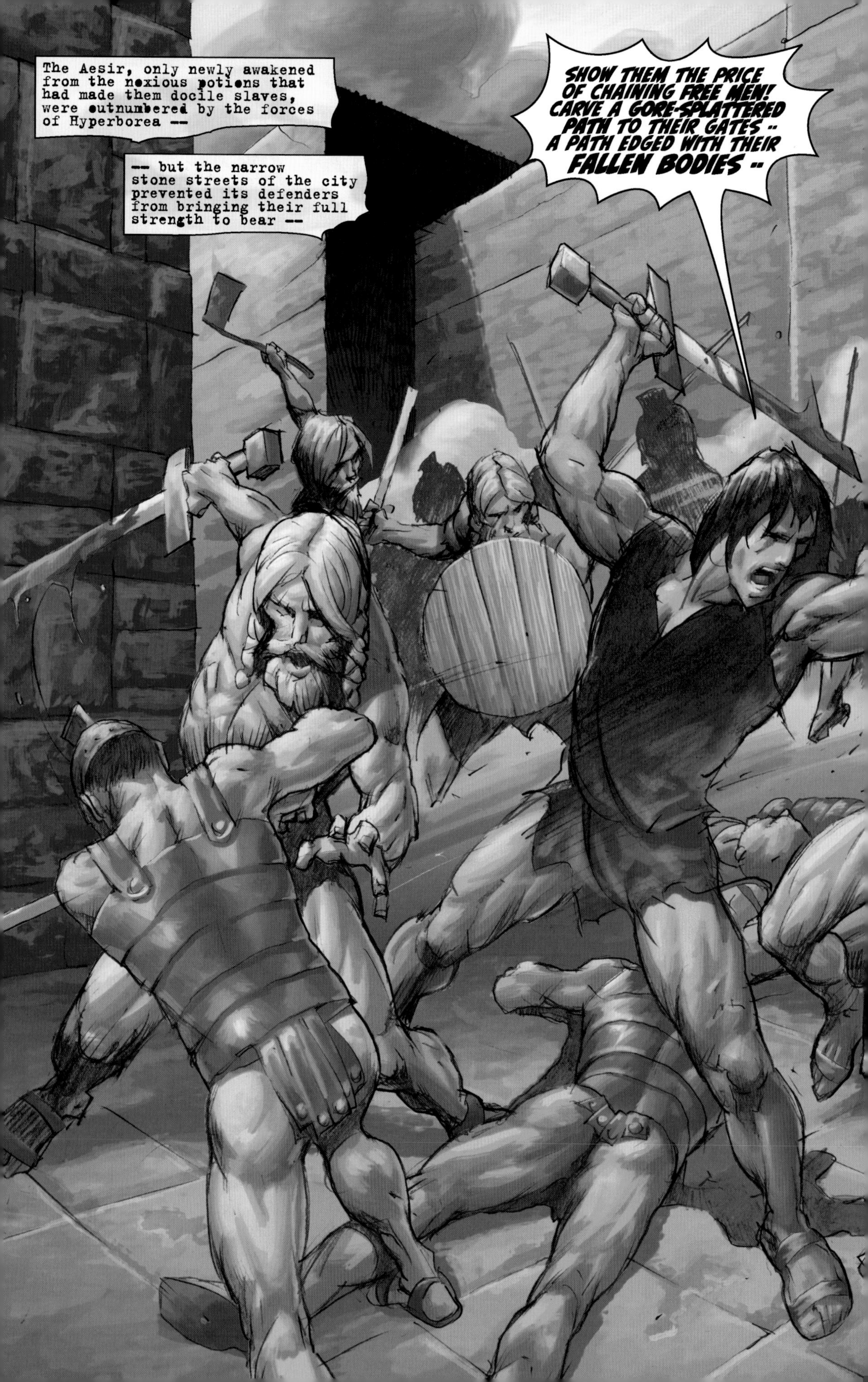
The Aesir, only newly awakened from the noxious potions that had made them docile slaves, were outnumbered by the forces of Hyperborea --
-- but the narrow stone streets of the city prevented its defenders from bringing their full strength to bear --
SHOW THEM THE PRICE OF CHAINING FREE MEN! CARVE A GORE-SPLATTERED PATH TO THEIR GATES -- A PATH EDGED WITH THEIR FALLEN BODIES --

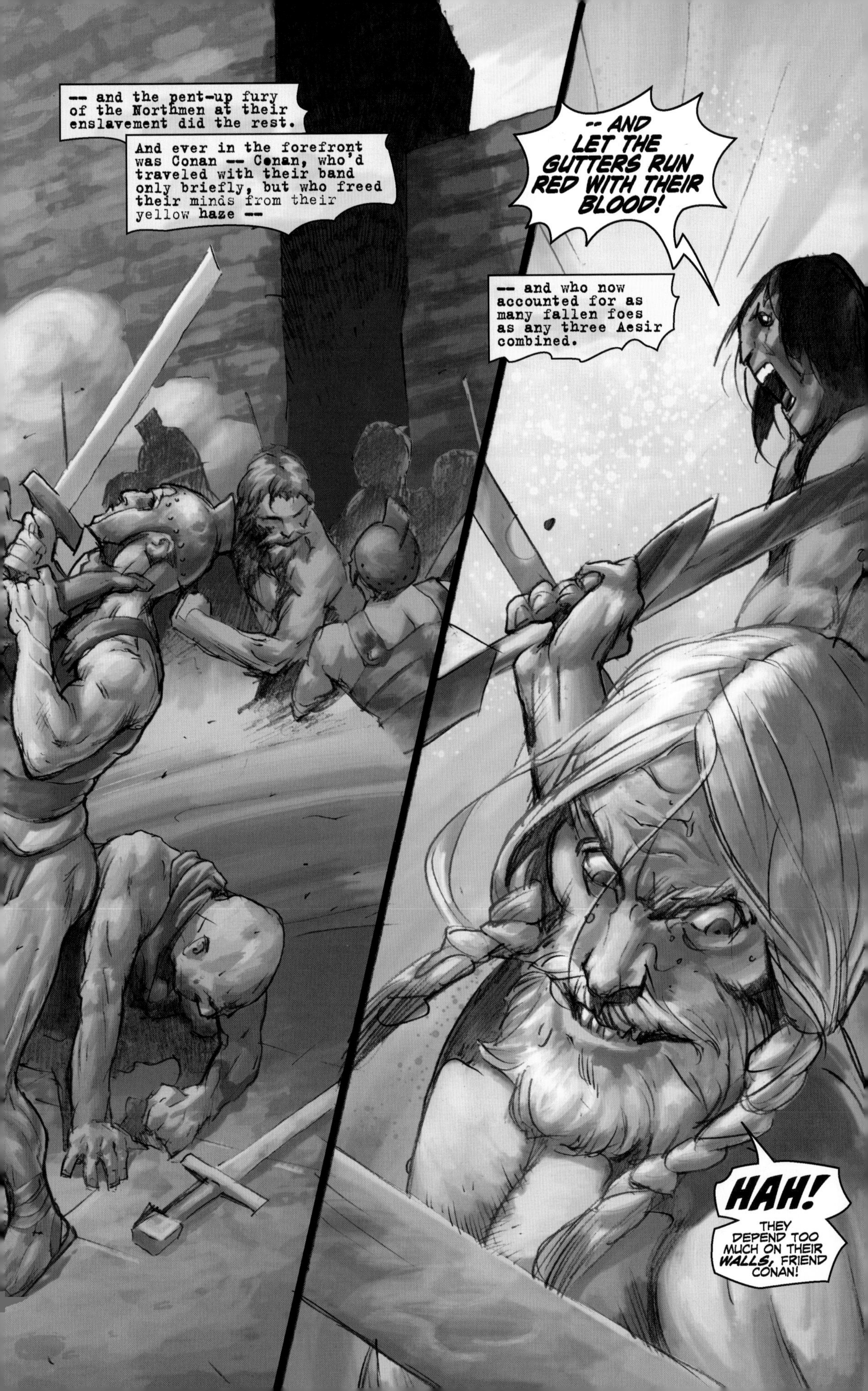
-- and the pent-up fury of the Northmen at their enslavement did the rest.
And ever in the forefront was Conan -- Conan, who'd traveled with their band only briefly, but who freed their minds from their yellow haze --
-- AND LET THE GUTTERS RUN RED WITH THEIR BLOOD!
-- and who now accounted for as many fallen foes as any three Aesir combined.
HAH!
THEY DEPEND TOO MUCH ON THEIR WALLS, FRIEND CONAN!

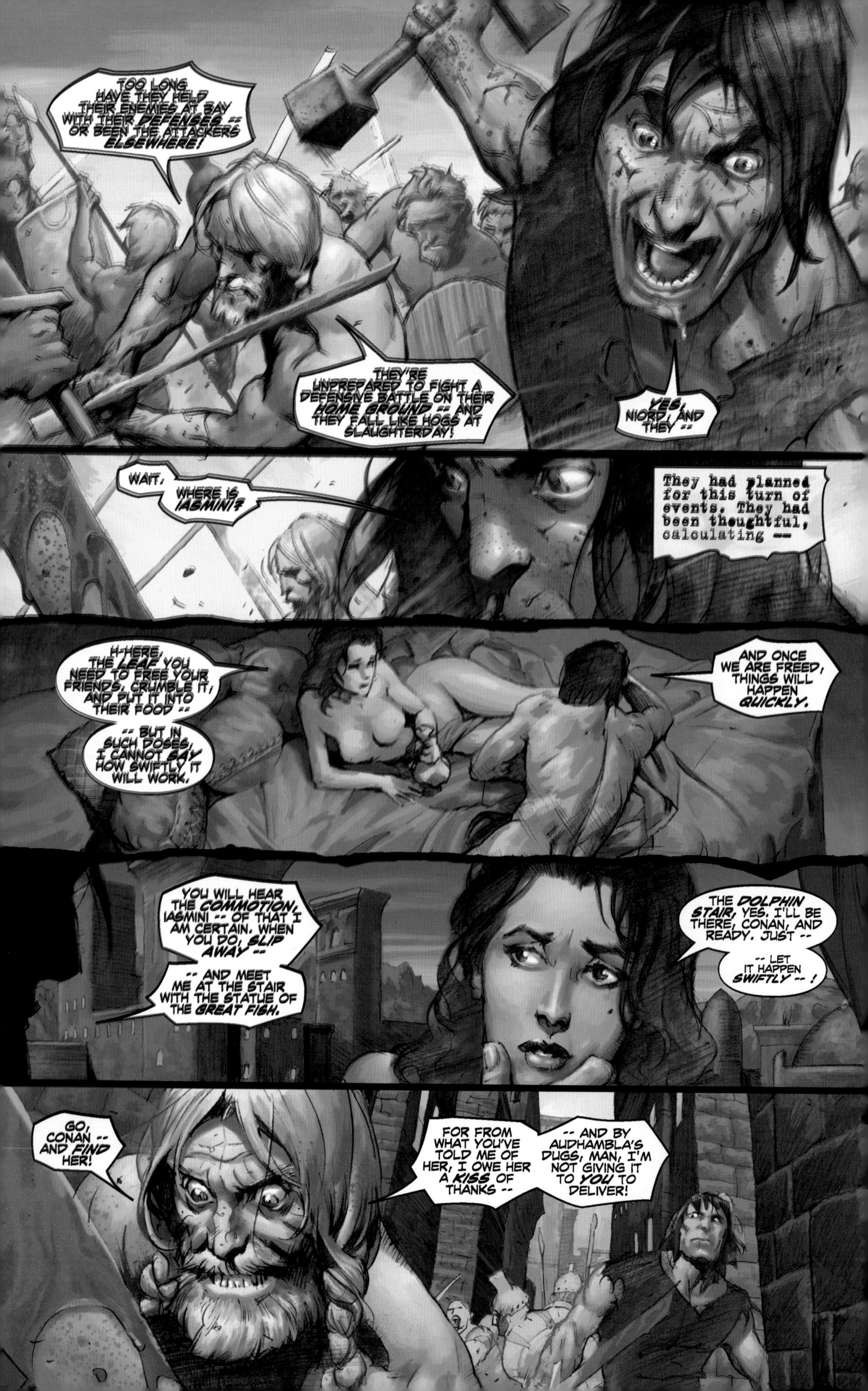
TOO LONG HAVE THEY HELD THEIR ENEMIES AT BAY WITH THEIR DEFENSES -- OR BEEN THE ATTACKERS ELSEWHERE!
THEY'RE UNPREPARED TO FIGHT A DEFENSIVE BATTLE ON THEIR HOME GROUND -- AND THEY FALL LIKE HOGS AT SLAUGHTERDAY!
YES, NIORD, AND THEY --
WAIT.
WHERE IS IASMINI?
They had planned for this turn of events. They had been thoughtful, calculating --
H-HERE, THE LEAF YOU NEED TO FREE YOUR FRIENDS. CRUMBLE IT, AND PUT IT INTO THEIR FOOD --
-- BUT IN SUCH DOSES, I CANNOT SAY HOW SWIFTLY IT WILL WORK.
AND ONCE WE ARE FREED, THINGS WILL HAPPEN QUICKLY.
YOU WILL HEAR THE COMMOTION, IASMINI -- OF THAT I AM CERTAIN. WHEN YOU DO, SLIP AWAY --
-- AND MEET ME AT THE STAIR WITH THE STATUE OF THE GREAT FISH.
THE DOLPHIN STAIR, YES. I'LL BE THERE, CONAN, AND READY. JUST --
-- LET IT HAPPEN SWIFTLY -- !
GO, CONAN -- AND FIND HER!
FOR FROM WHAT YOU'VE TOLD ME OF HER, I OWE HER A KISS OF THANKS --
-- AND BY AUDHAMBLA'S DUGS, MAN, I'M NOT GIVING IT TO YOU TO DELIVER!

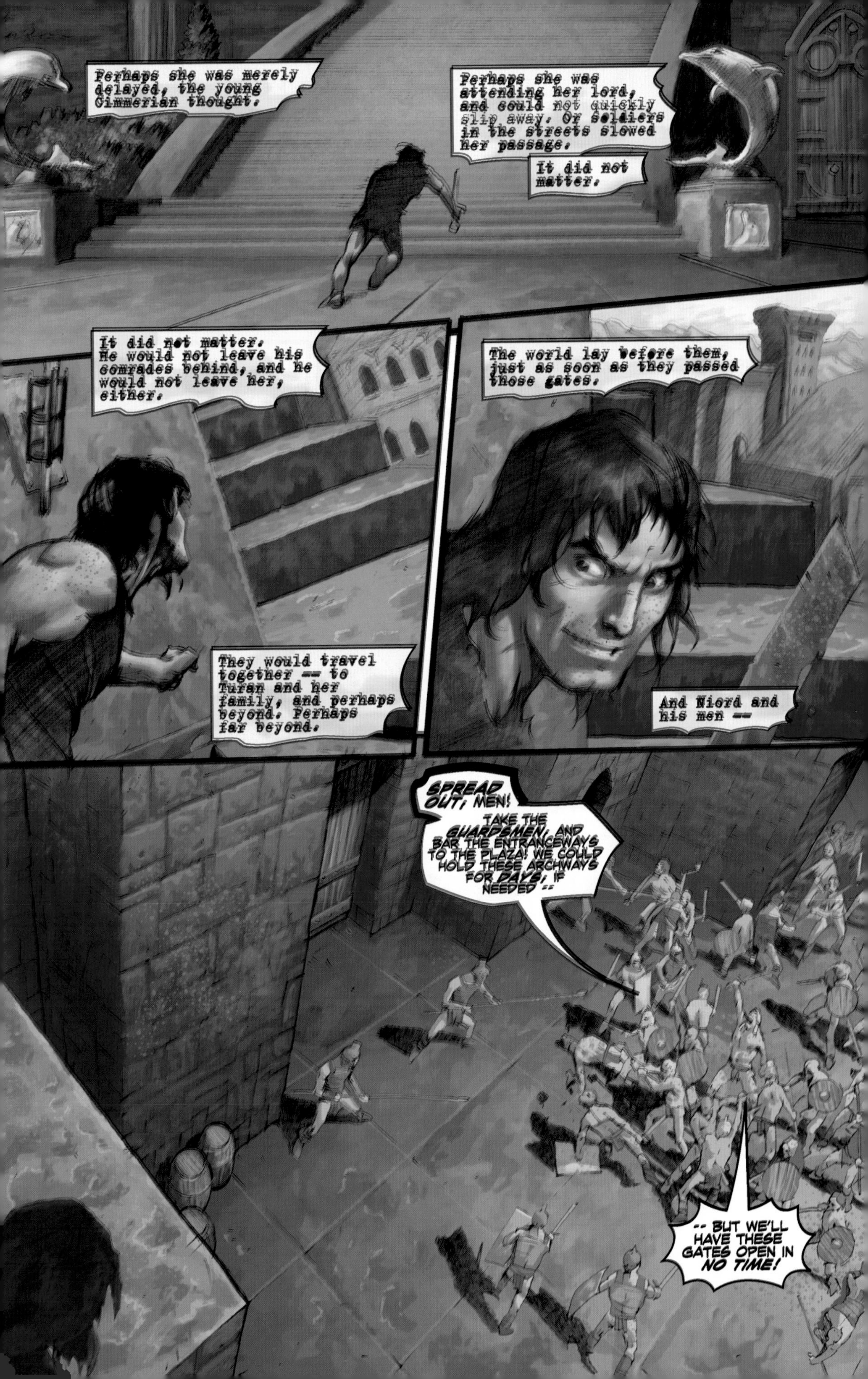

Perhaps she was merely delayed, the young Cimmerian thought.
Perhaps she was attending her lord, and could not quickly slip away. Or soldiers in the streets slowed her passage.
It did not matter.
It did not matter. He would not leave his comrades behind, and he would not leave her, either.
They would travel together -- to Turan and her family, and perhaps beyond. Perhaps far beyond.
The world lay before them, just as soon as they passed those gates.
And Niord and his men --
SPREAD OUT, MEN!
TAKE THE GUARDSMEN, AND BAR THE ENTRANCEWAYS TO THE PLAZA! WE COULD HOLD THESE ARCHWAYS FOR DAYS, IF NEEDED --
-- BUT WE'LL HAVE THESE GATES OPEN IN NO TIME!

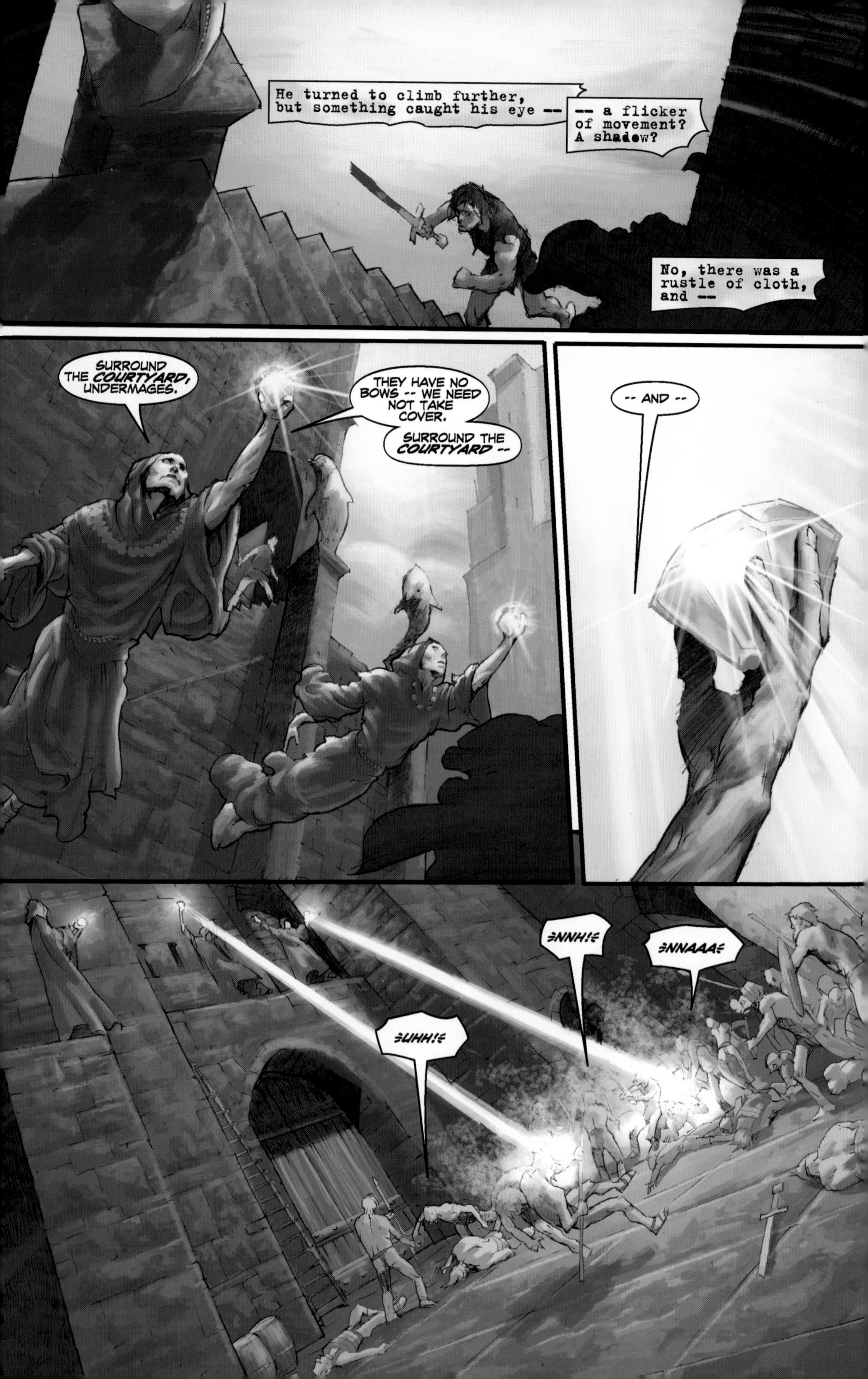
He turned to climb further, but something caught his eye --
-- a flicker of movement? A shadow?
No, there was a rustle of cloth, and --
SURROUND THE COURTYARD, UNDERMAGES.
THEY HAVE NO BOWS -- WE NEED NOT TAKE COVER.
SURROUND THE COURTYARD --
-- AND --
NNH!
NNAAA
UHH!

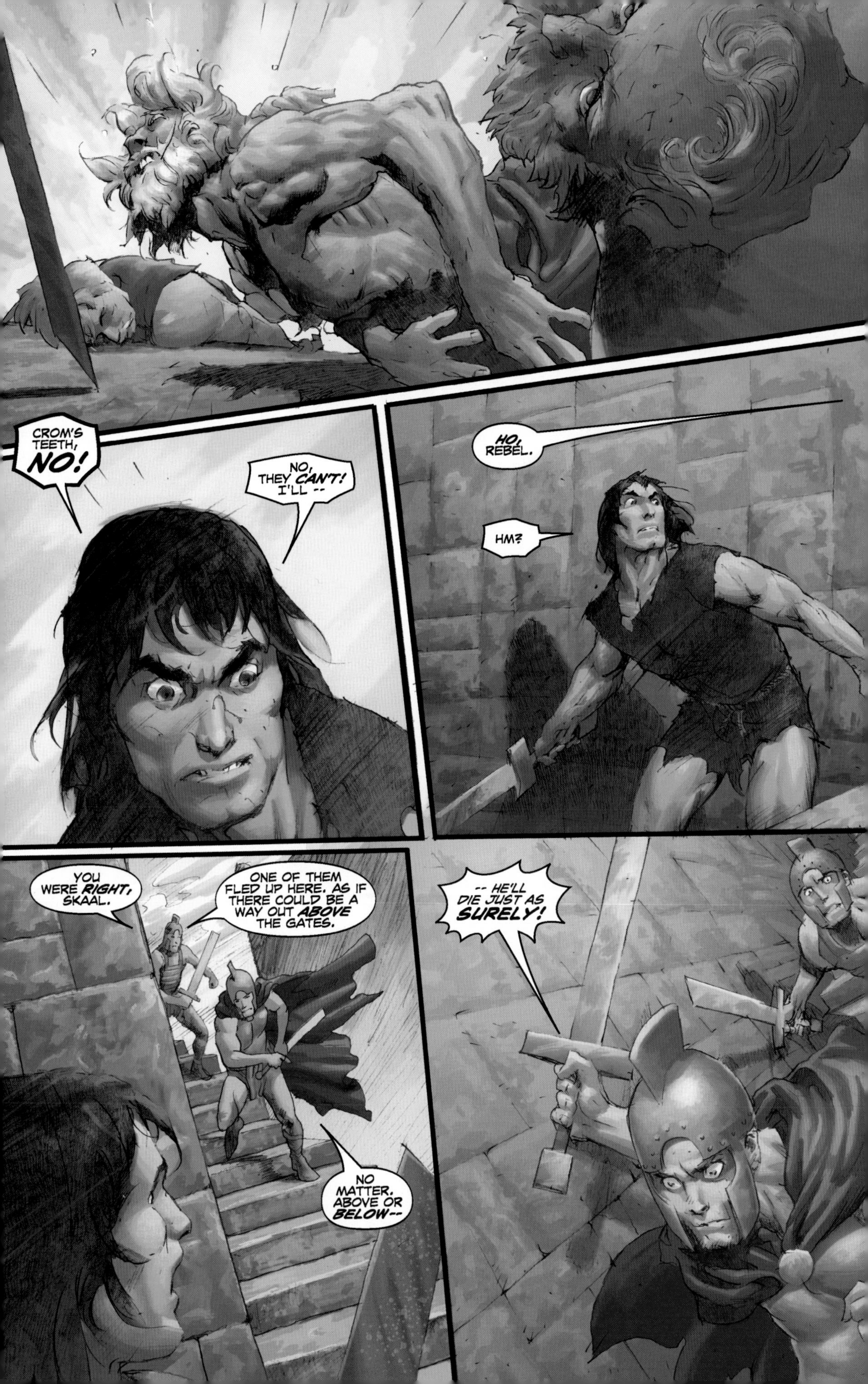
CROM'S TEETH, NO!
NO, THEY CAN'T! I'LL --
HO, REBEL.
HM?
YOU WERE RIGHT, SKAAL.
ONE OF THEM FLED UP HERE. AS IF THERE COULD BE A WAY OUT ABOVE THE GATES.
NO MATTER. ABOVE OR BELOW--
-- HE'LL DIE JUST AS SURELY!

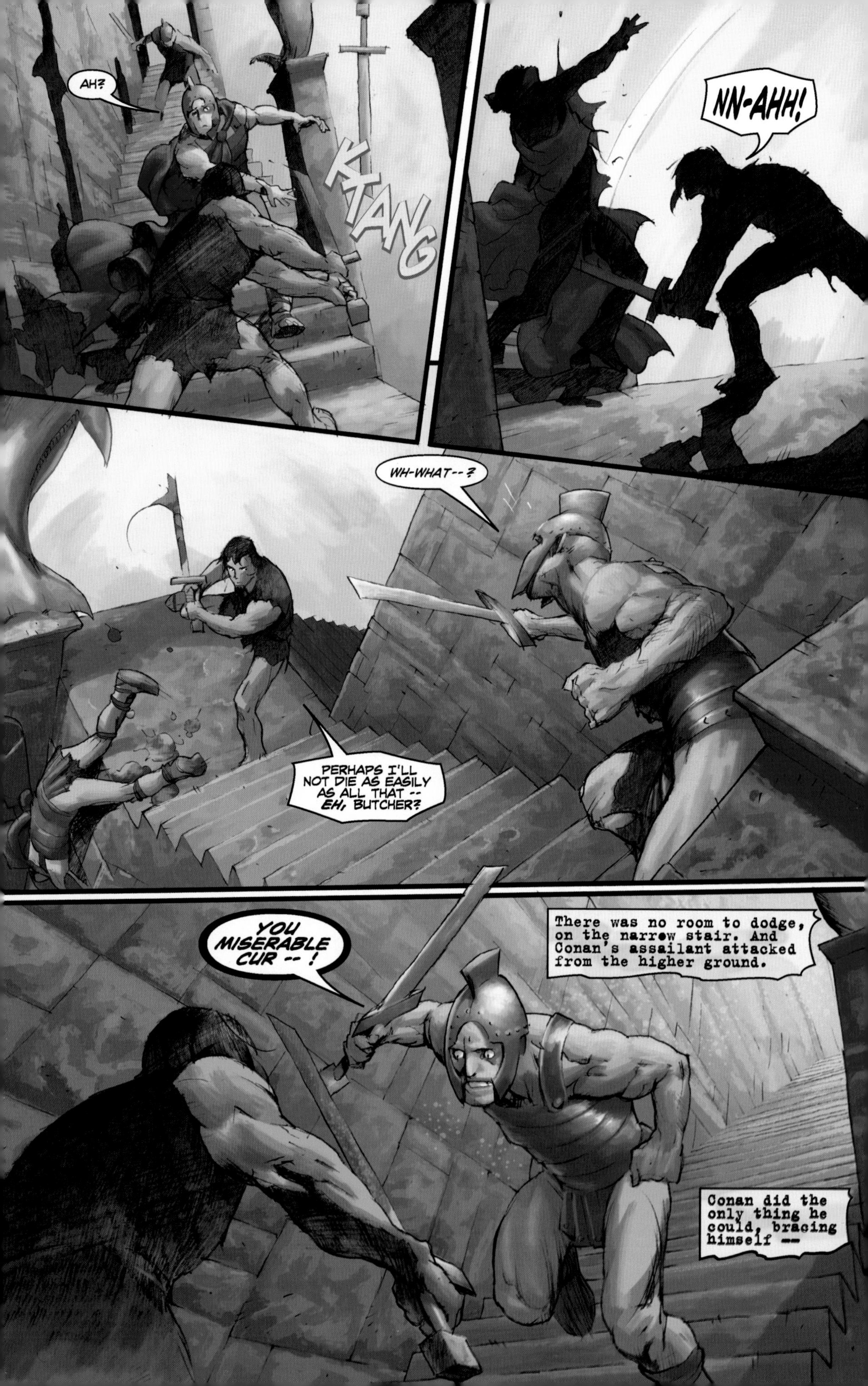
AH?
KTANG
NN-AHH!
WH-WHAT-- ?
PERHAPS I'LL NOT DIE AS EASILY AS ALL THAT -- EH, BUTCHER?
YOU MISERABLE CUR -- !
There was no room to dodge, on the narrow stair. And Conan's assailant attacked from the higher ground.
Conan did the only thing he could, bracing himself --

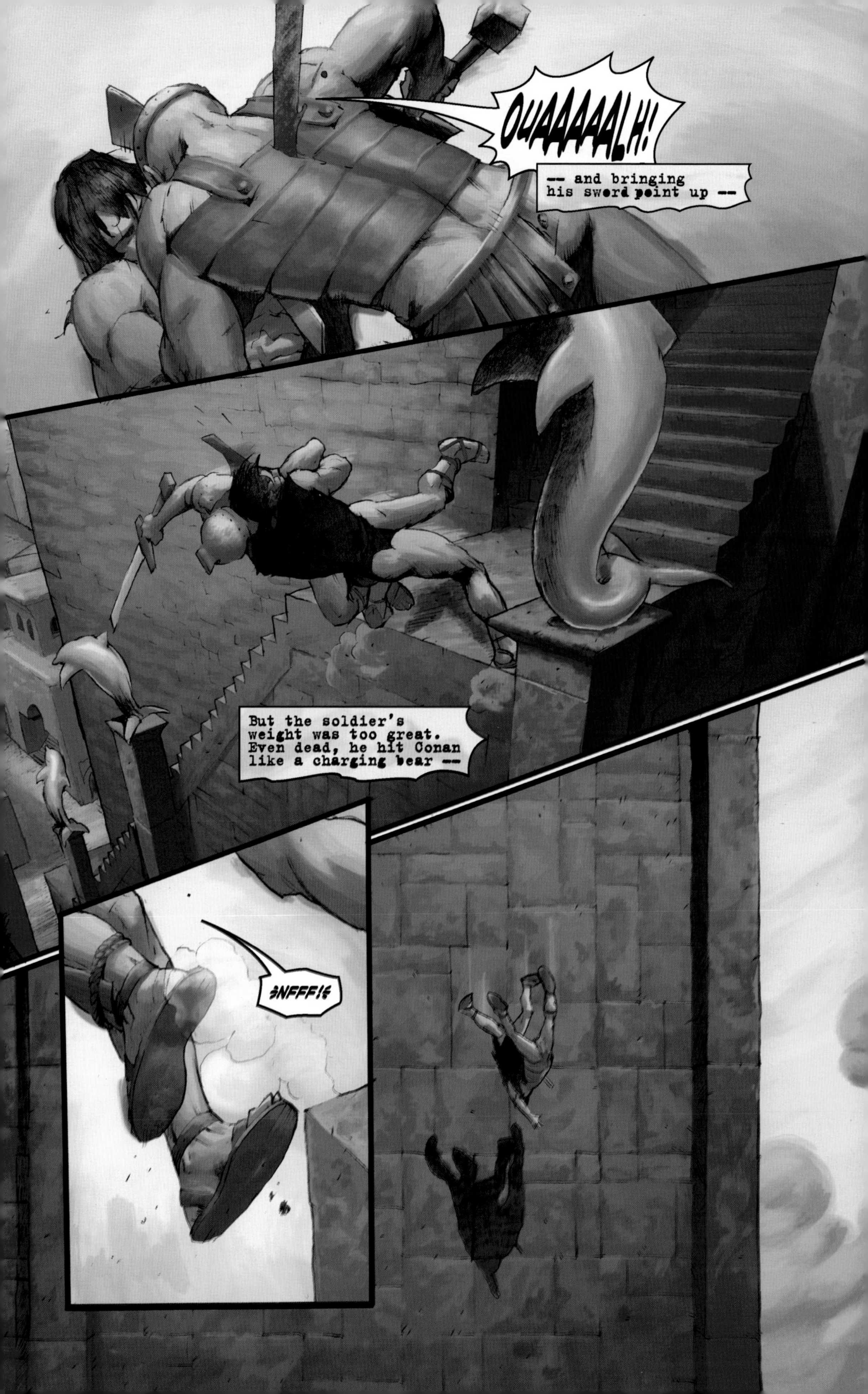

OUAAAAAALH!
—— and bringing his sword point up ——
But the soldier's weight was too great. Even dead, he hit Conan like a charging bear ——
SNFFF!!

-- and darkness swallowed the world.

How long he lay as one dead, he did not know.

But in time, sense returned --

None had found him.

The two soldiers who'd attacked -- they had both died, and no one else must have seen. There was no one to raise an alarm.

Something had awakened him. Some sound, or movement. He did not know what it had been.

Iasmini -- Iasmini, Niord, and the others. Where were they?

TARATARANTARA

WHAT?

IASMINI!! NIORD!

Horns! It was the call to assemble! That was what had awakened him!

The call for one of their damned Days of Farewell!

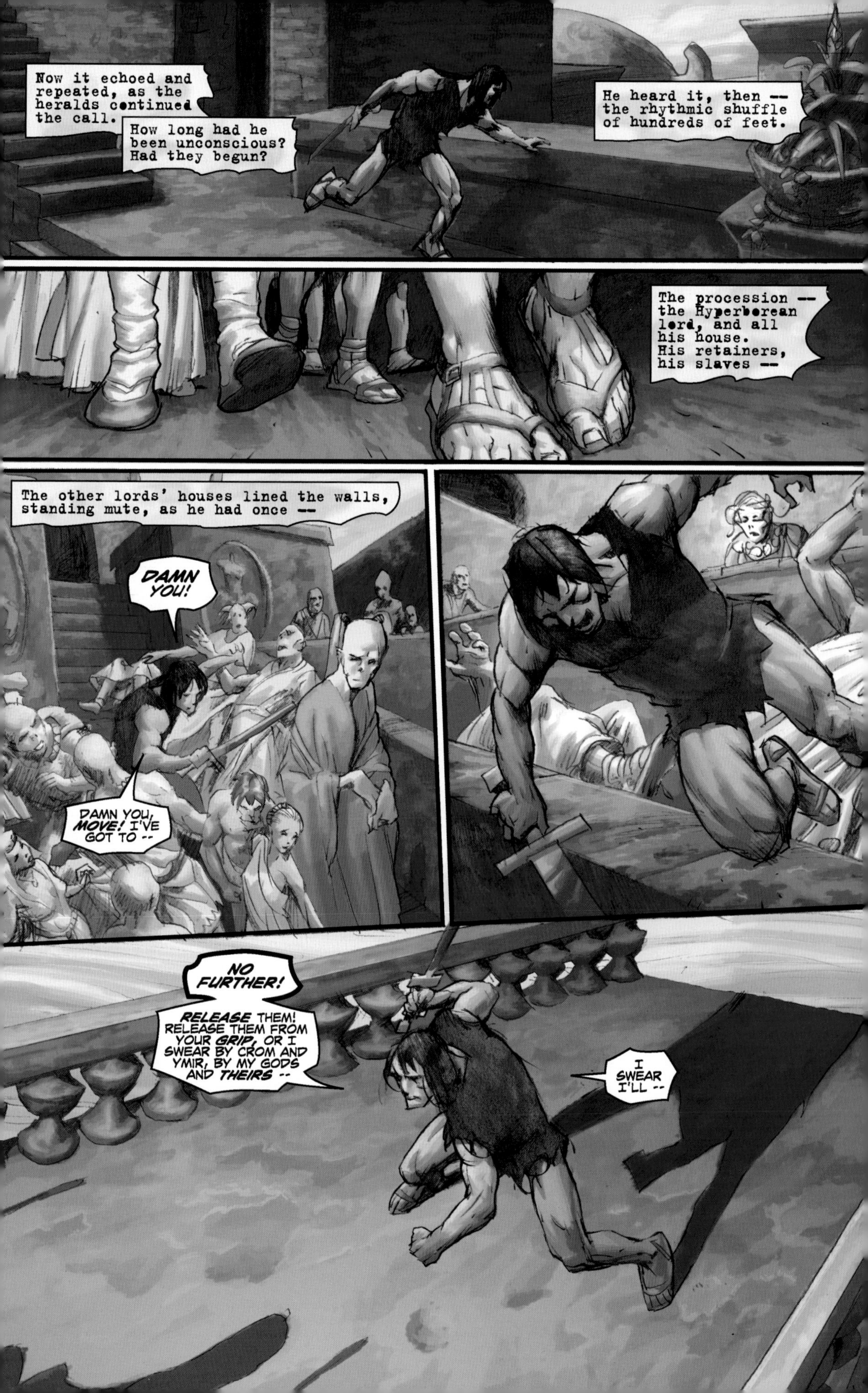

Now it echoed and repeated, as the heralds continued the call.
How long had he been unconscious? Had they begun?
He heard it, then -- the rhythmic shuffle of hundreds of feet.
The procession -- the Hyperborean lord, and all his house. His retainers, his slaves --
The other lords' houses lined the walls, standing mute, as he had once --
DAMN YOU!
DAMN YOU, MOVE! I'VE GOT TO --
NO FURTHER!
RELEASE THEM! RELEASE THEM FROM YOUR GRIP, OR I SWEAR BY CROM AND YMIR, BY MY GODS AND THEIRS --
I SWEAR I'LL --

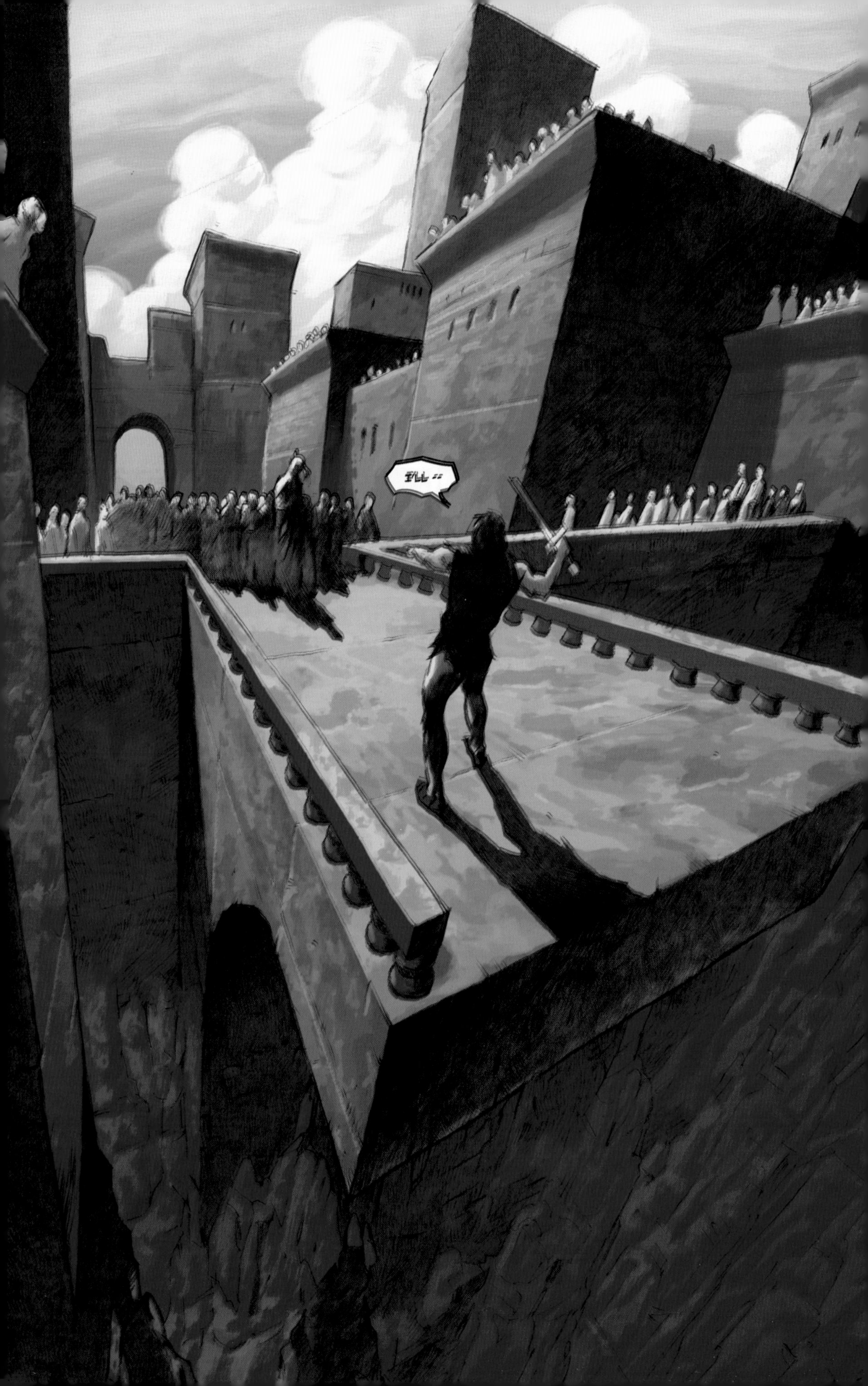
I'LL --

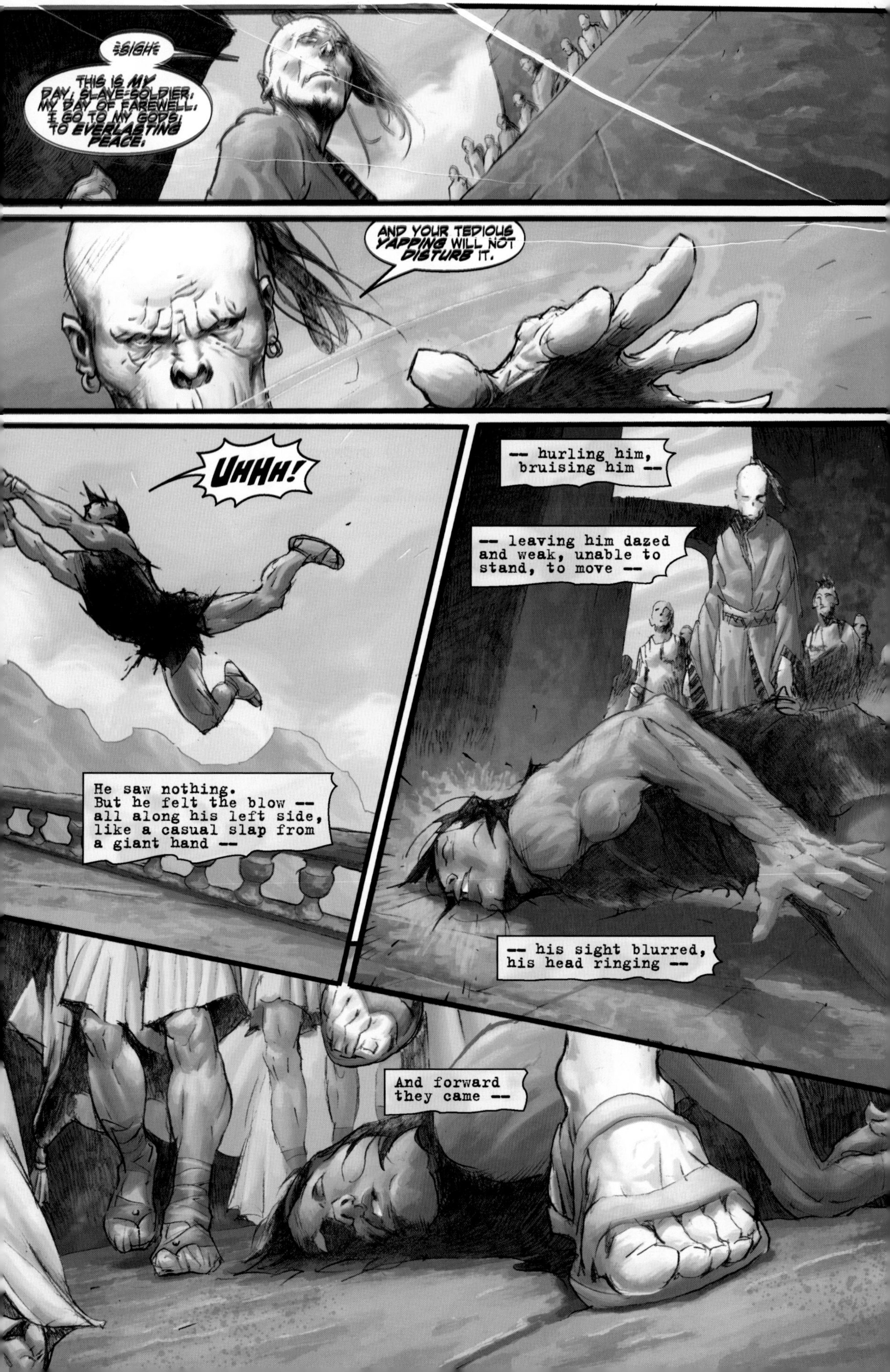

SIGH
THIS IS MY DAY, SLAVE-SOLDIER. MY DAY OF FAREWELL. I GO TO MY GODS, TO EVERLASTING PEACE.
AND YOUR TEDIOUS YAPPING WILL NOT DISTURB IT.
UHHH!
He saw nothing. But he felt the blow -- all along his left side, like a casual slap from a giant hand --
-- hurling him, bruising him --
-- leaving him dazed and weak, unable to stand, to move --
-- his sight blurred, his head ringing --
And forward they came --

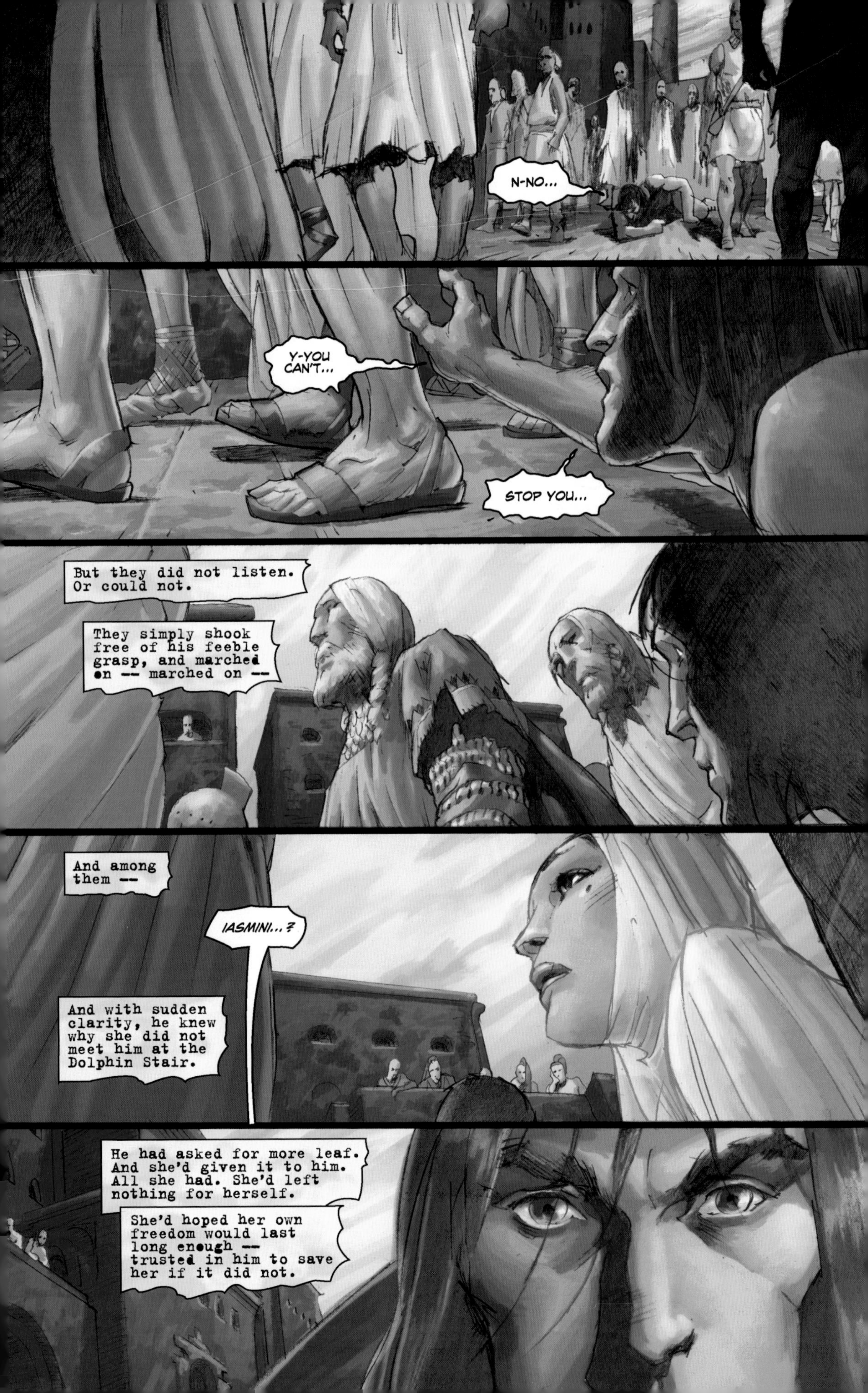
N-NO...
Y-YOU CAN'T...
STOP YOU...
But they did not listen. Or could not.
They simply shook free of his feeble grasp, and marched on -- marched on --
And among them --
IASMINI...?
And with sudden clarity, he knew why she did not meet him at the Dolphin Stair.
He had asked for more leaf. And she'd given it to him. All she had. She'd left nothing for herself.
She'd hoped her own freedom would last long enough -- trusted in him to save her if it did not.

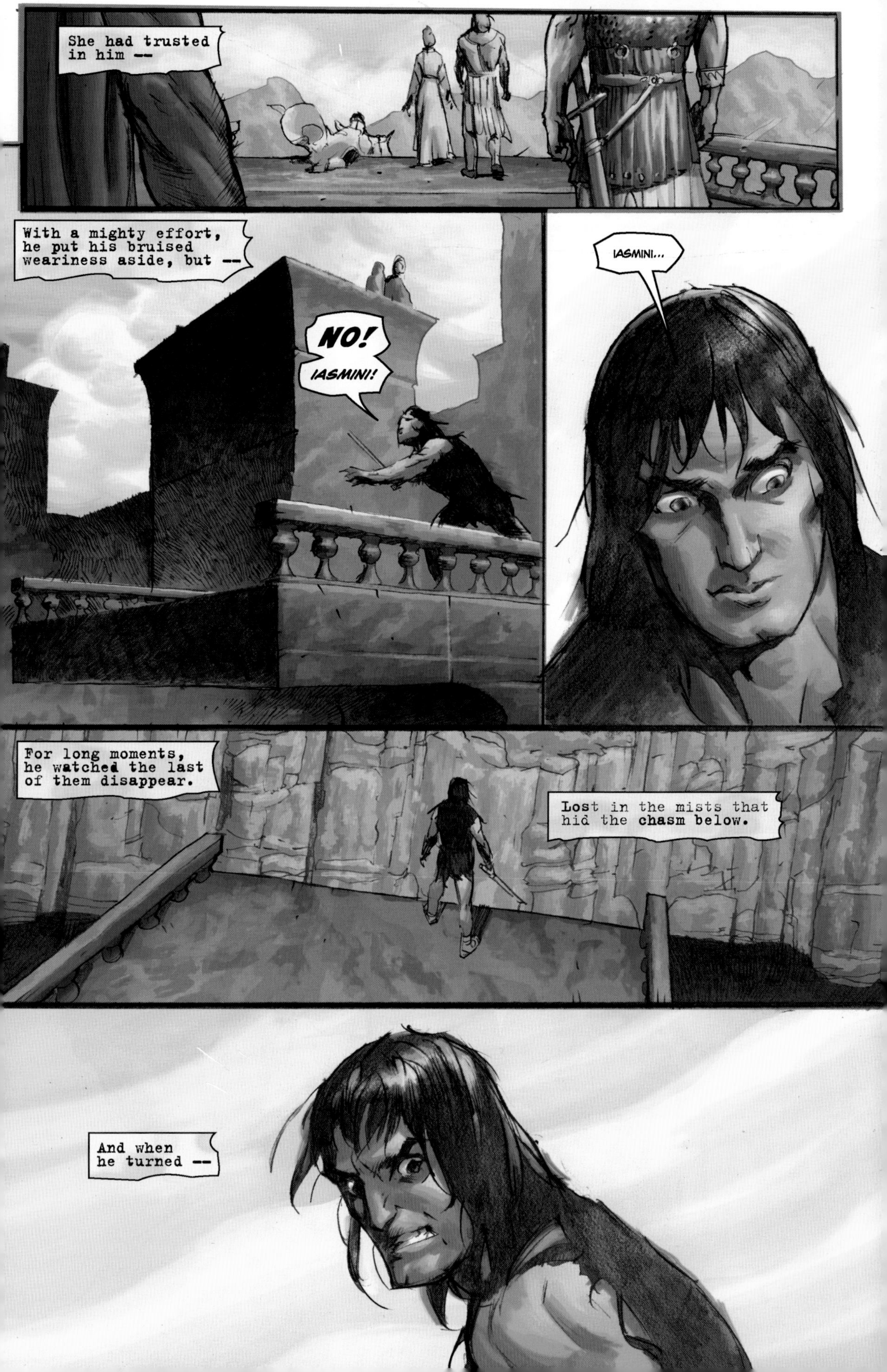
She had trusted in him --
With a mighty effort, he put his bruised weariness aside, but --
NO!
IASMINI!
IASMINI...
For long moments, he watched the last of them disappear.
Lost in the mists that hid the chasm below.
And when he turned --

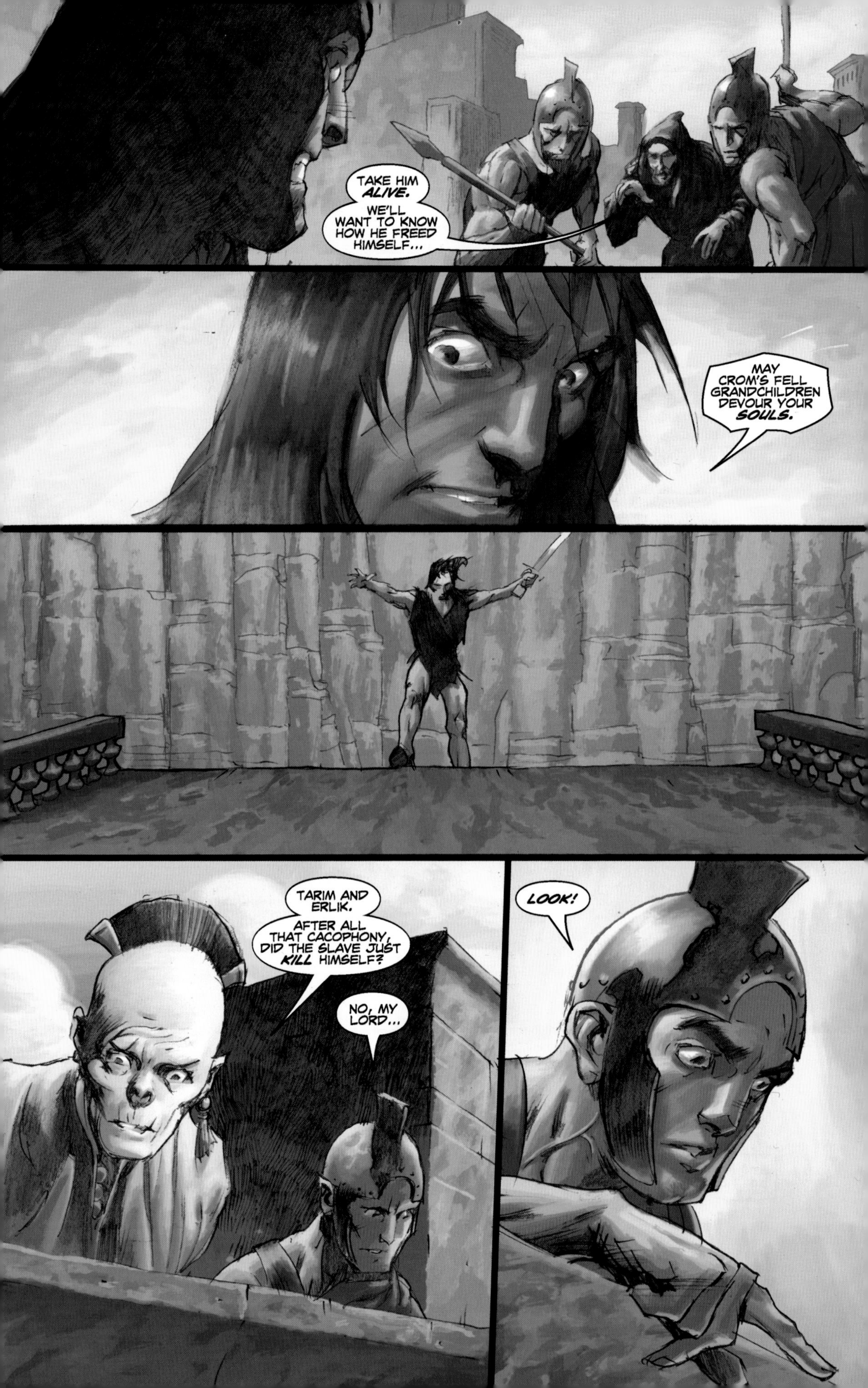
TAKE HIM ALIVE.
WE'LL WANT TO KNOW HOW HE FREED HIMSELF...
MAY CROM'S FELL GRANDCHILDREN DEVOUR YOUR SOULS.
TARIM AND ERLIK.
AFTER ALL THAT CACOPHONY, DID THE SLAVE JUST KILL HIMSELF?
NO, MY LORD...
LOOK!

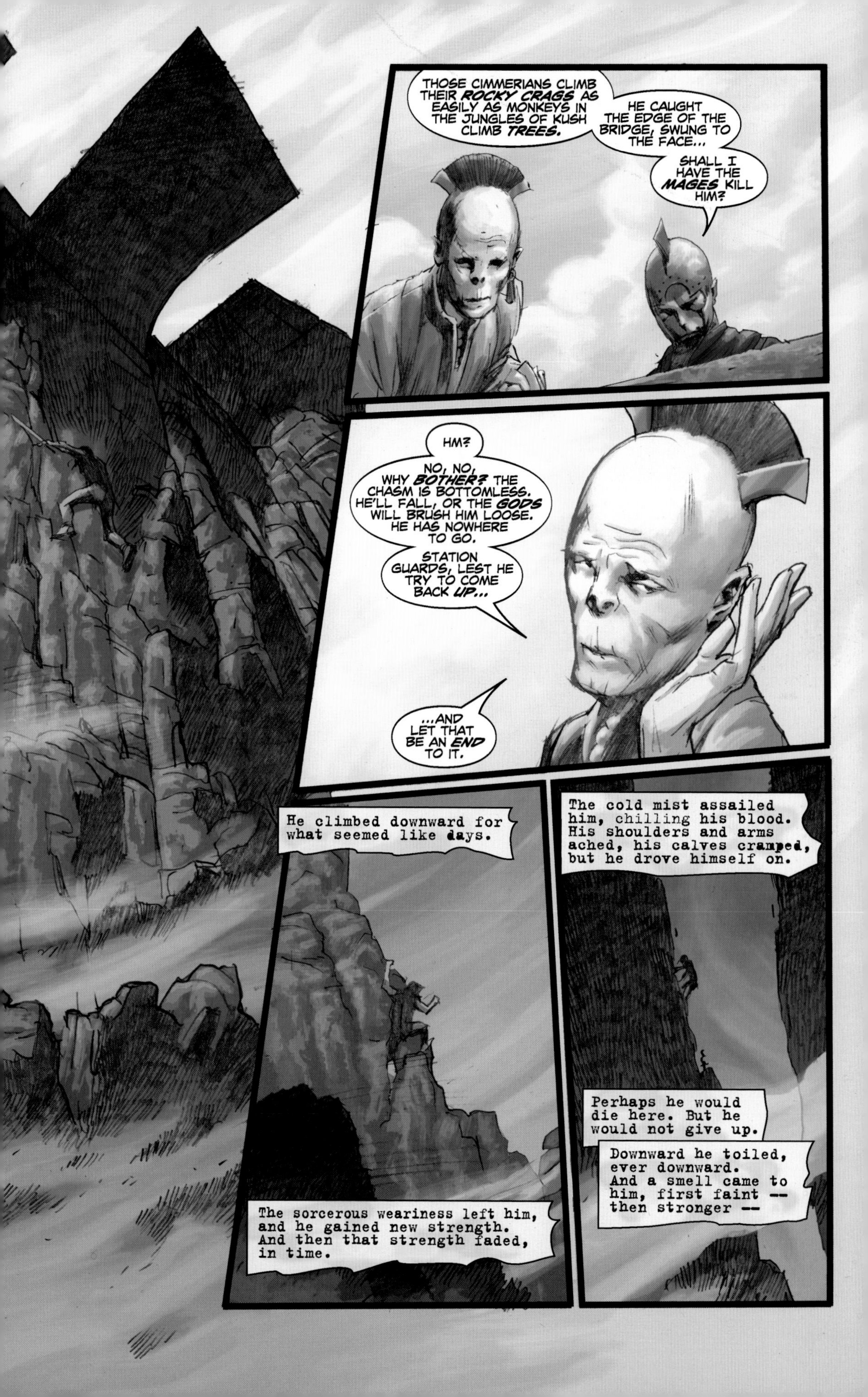
THOSE CIMMERIANS CLIMB THEIR ROCKY CRAGS AS EASILY AS MONKEYS IN THE JUNGLES OF KUSH CLIMB TREES.
HE CAUGHT THE EDGE OF THE BRIDGE, SWUNG TO THE FACE...
SHALL I HAVE THE MAGES KILL HIM?
HM?
NO, NO, WHY BOTHER? THE CHASM IS BOTTOMLESS. HE'LL FALL, OR THE GODS WILL BRUSH HIM LOOSE. HE HAS NOWHERE TO GO.
STATION GUARDS, LEST HE TRY TO COME BACK UP...
...AND LET THAT BE AN END TO IT.
He climbed downward for what seemed like days.
The sorcerous weariness left him, and he gained new strength. And then that strength faded, in time.
The cold mist assailed him, chilling his blood. His shoulders and arms ached, his calves cramped, but he drove himself on.
Perhaps he would die here. But he would not give up.
Downward he toiled, ever downward. And a smell came to him, first faint -- then stronger --

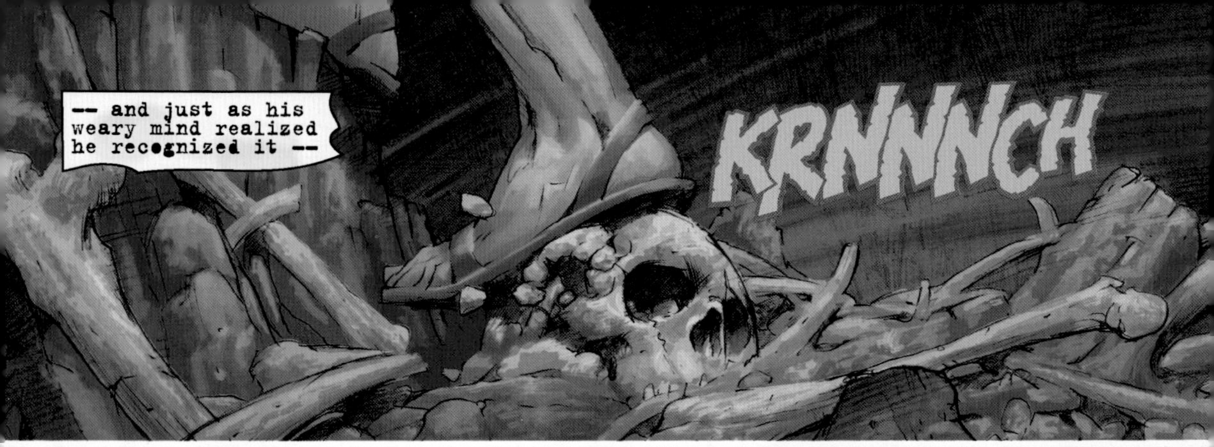
-- and just as his weary mind realized he recognized it --
KRNNNCH

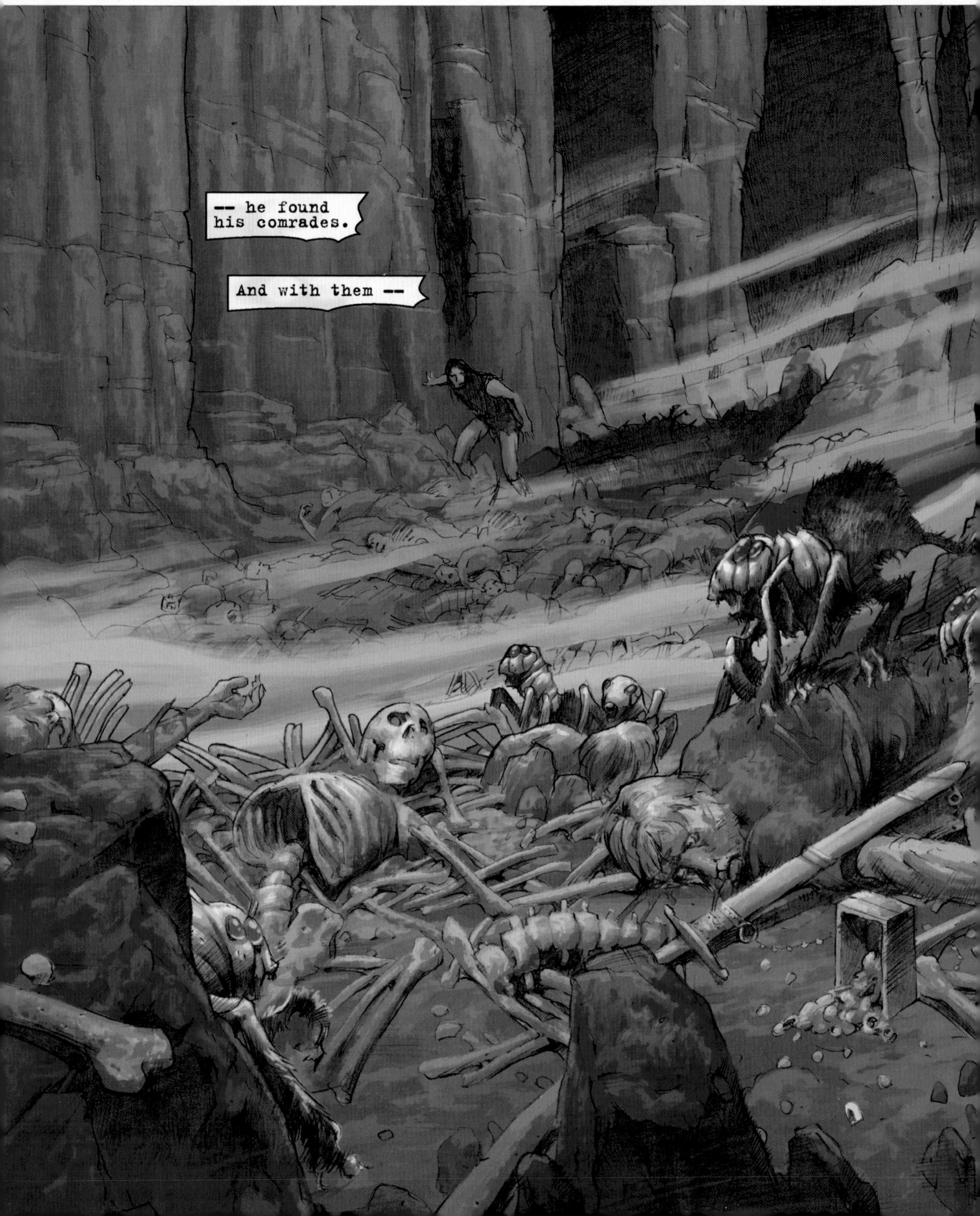
-- he found his comrades.
And with them --

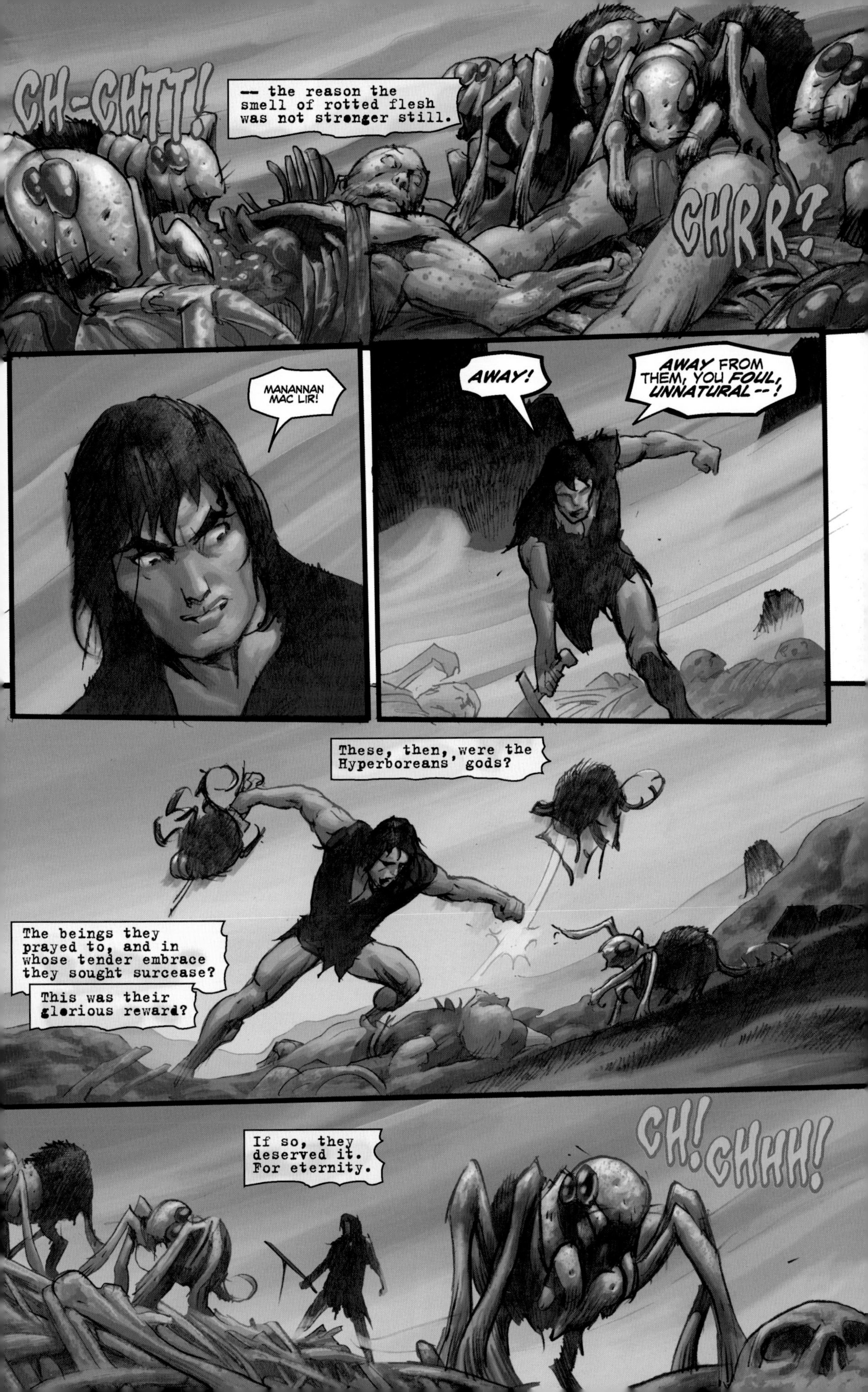
CH-CHTT!
-- the reason the smell of rotted flesh was not stronger still.
CHRR?
MANANNAN MAC LIR!
AWAY!
AWAY FROM THEM, YOU FOUL, UNNATURAL --!
These, then, were the Hyperboreans' gods?
The beings they prayed to, and in whose tender embrace they sought surcease?
This was their glorious reward?
If so, they deserved it. For eternity.
CH! CHHH!

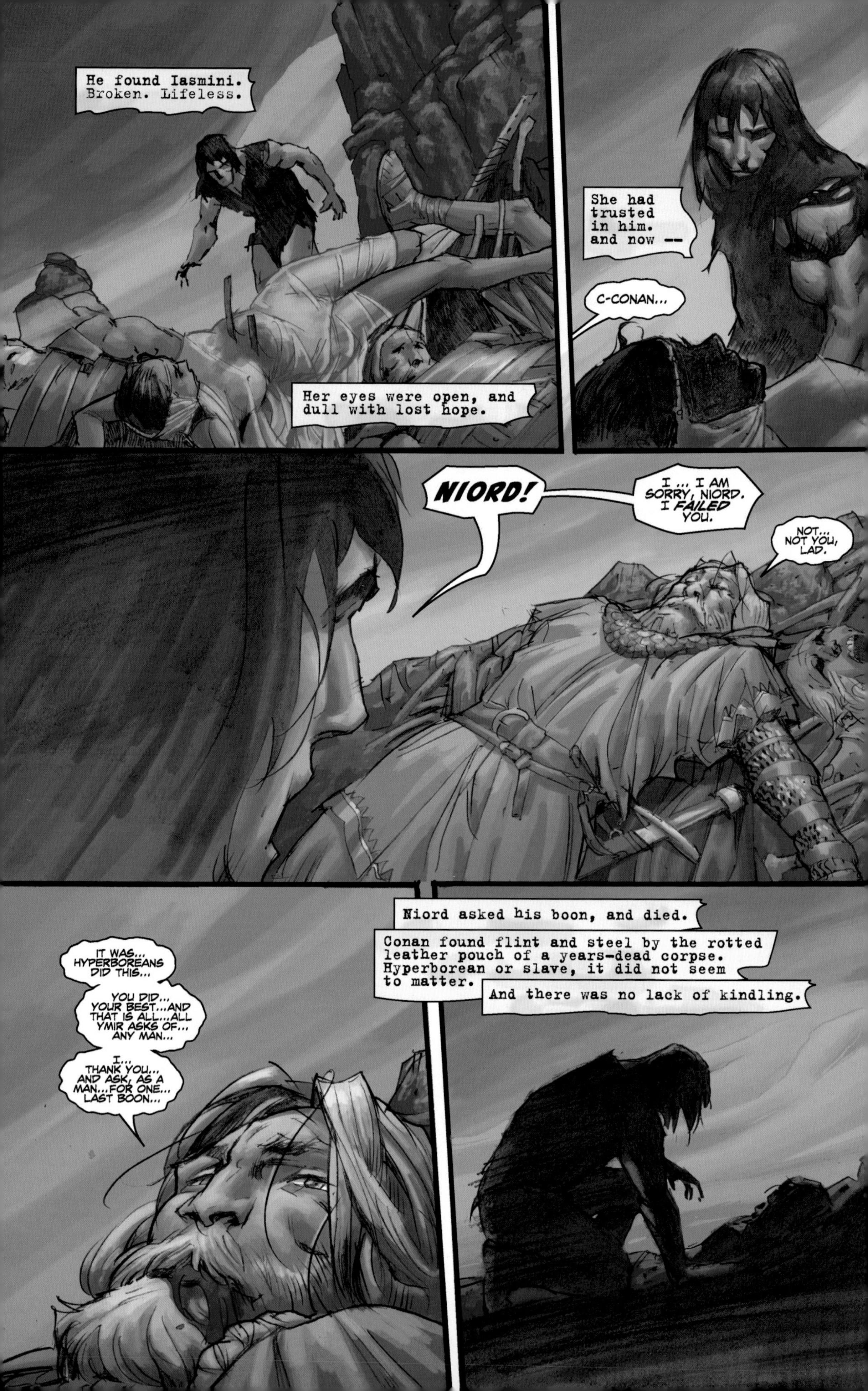
He found Iasmini. Broken. Lifeless.
Her eyes were open, and dull with lost hope.
She had trusted in him. and now --
C-CONAN...
NIORD!
I ... I AM SORRY, NIORD. I FAILED YOU.
NOT... NOT YOU, LAD.
IT WAS... HYPERBOREANS DID THIS...
YOU DID... YOUR BEST...AND THAT IS ALL...ALL YMIR ASKS OF... ANY MAN...
I... THANK YOU... AND ASK, AS A MAN...FOR ONE... LAST BOON...
Niord asked his boon, and died.
Conan found flint and steel by the rotted leather pouch of a years-dead corpse. Hyperborean or slave, it did not seem to matter.
And there was no lack of kindling.

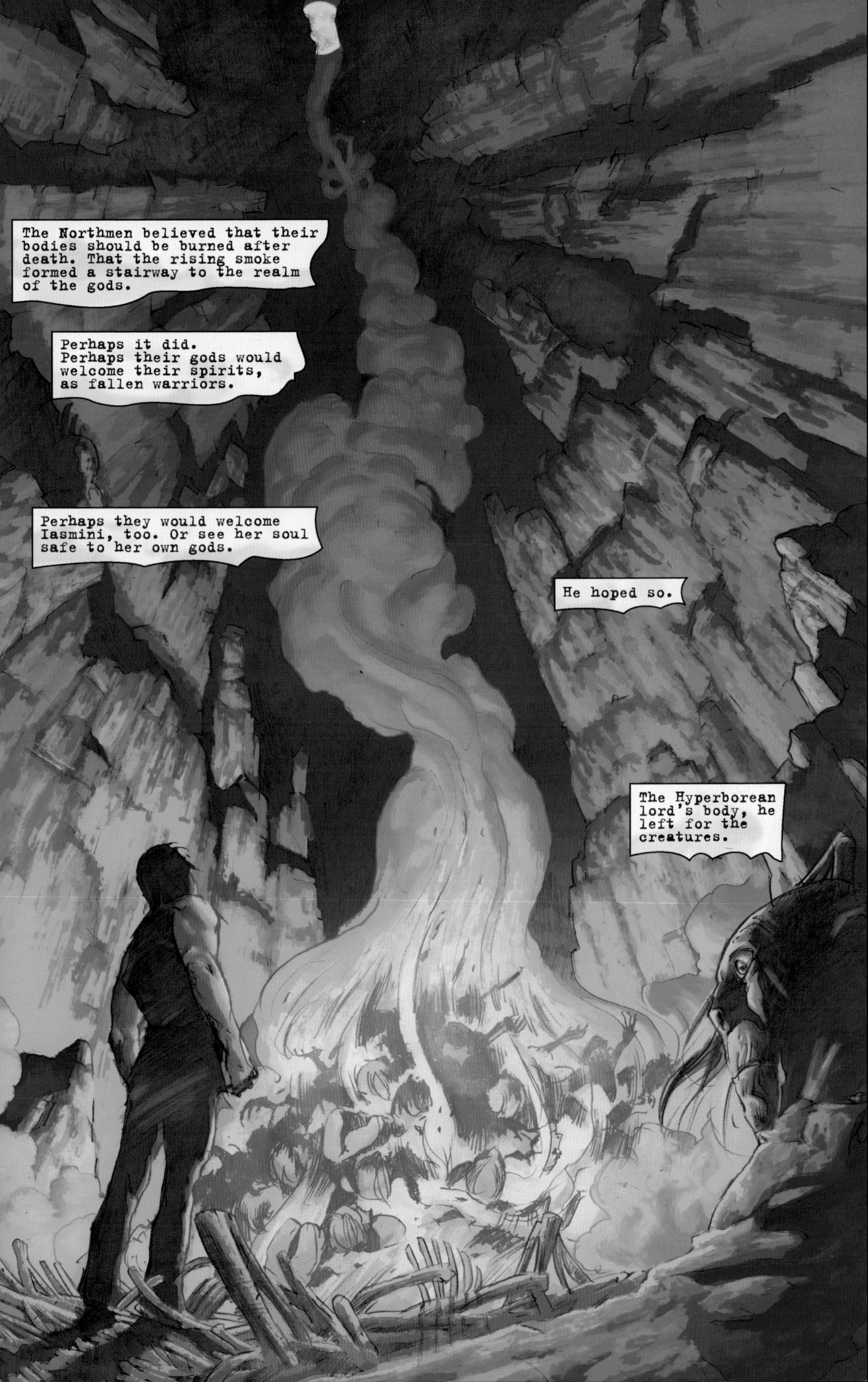
The Northmen believed that their bodies should be burned after death. That the rising smoke formed a stairway to the realm of the gods.
Perhaps it did. Perhaps their gods would welcome their spirits, as fallen warriors.
Perhaps they would welcome Iasmini, too. Or see her soul safe to her own gods.
He hoped so.
The Hyperborean lord's body, he left for the creatures.

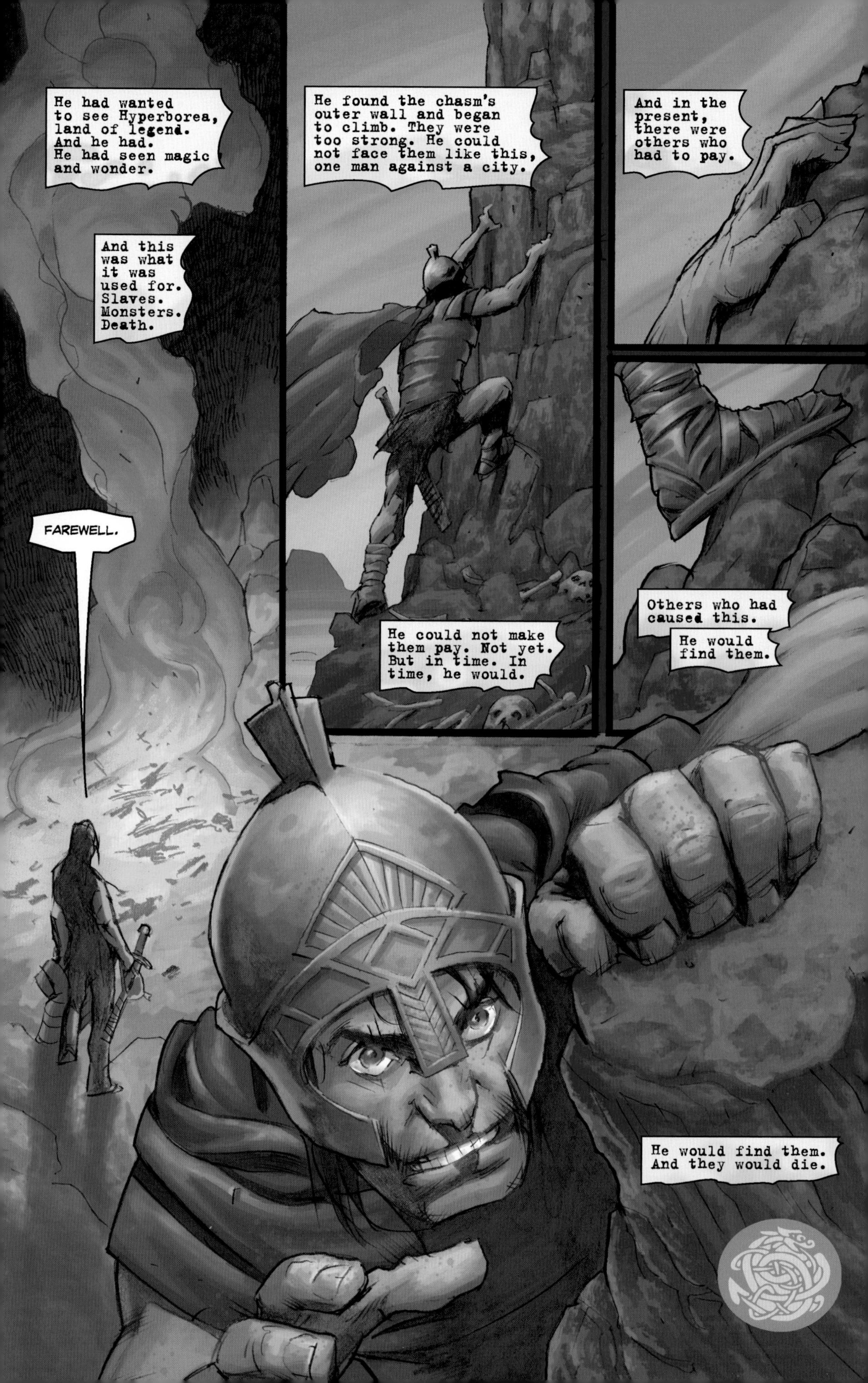
He had wanted to see Hyperborea, land of legend. And he had. He had seen magic and wonder.
And this was what it was used for. Slaves. Monsters. Death.
FAREWELL.
He found the chasm's outer wall and began to climb. They were too strong. He could not face them like this, one man against a city.
He could not make them pay. Not yet. But in time. In time, he would.
And in the present, there were others who had to pay.
Others who had caused this.
He would find them.
He would find them. And they would die.

BLOOD for BLOOD

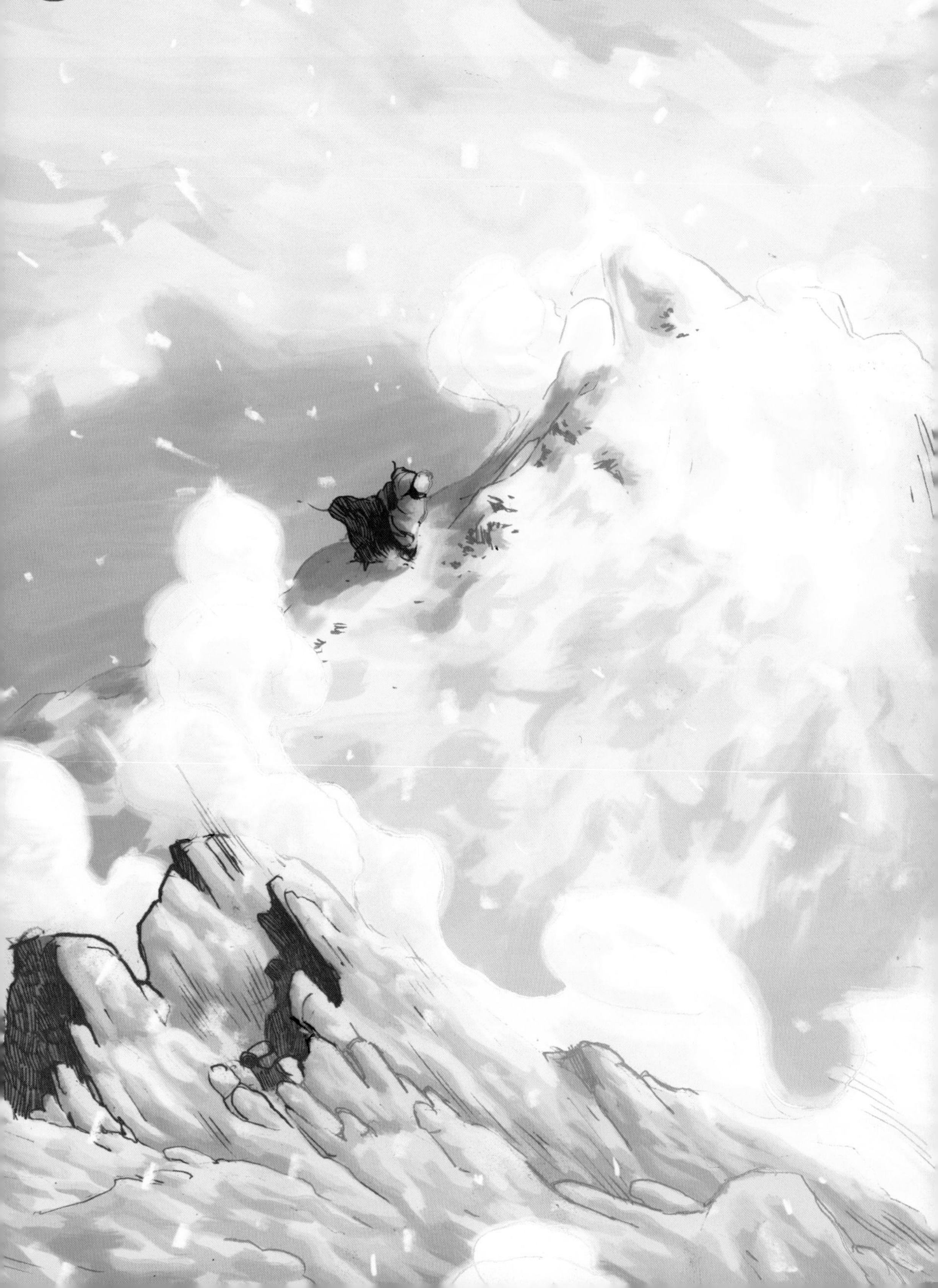

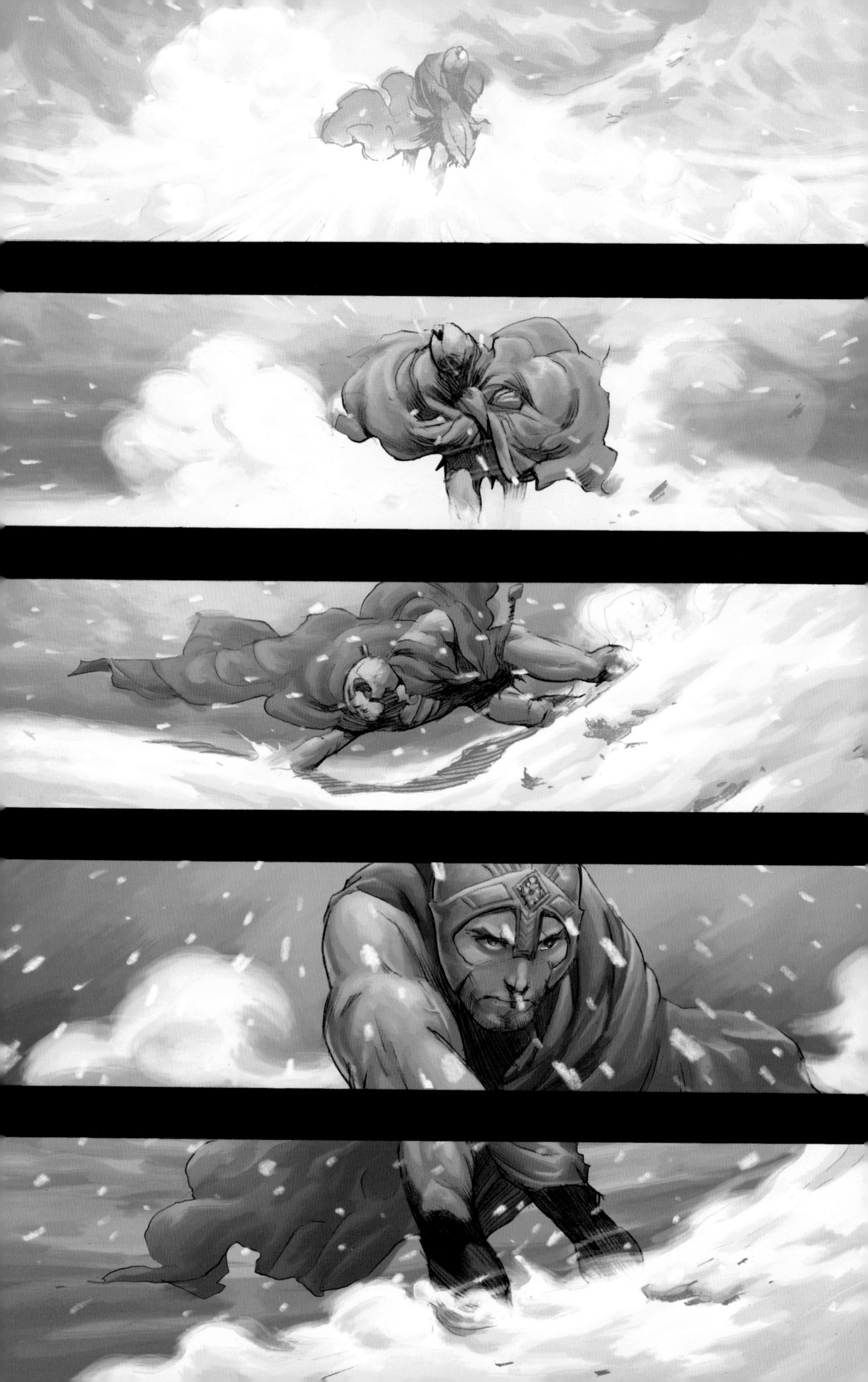

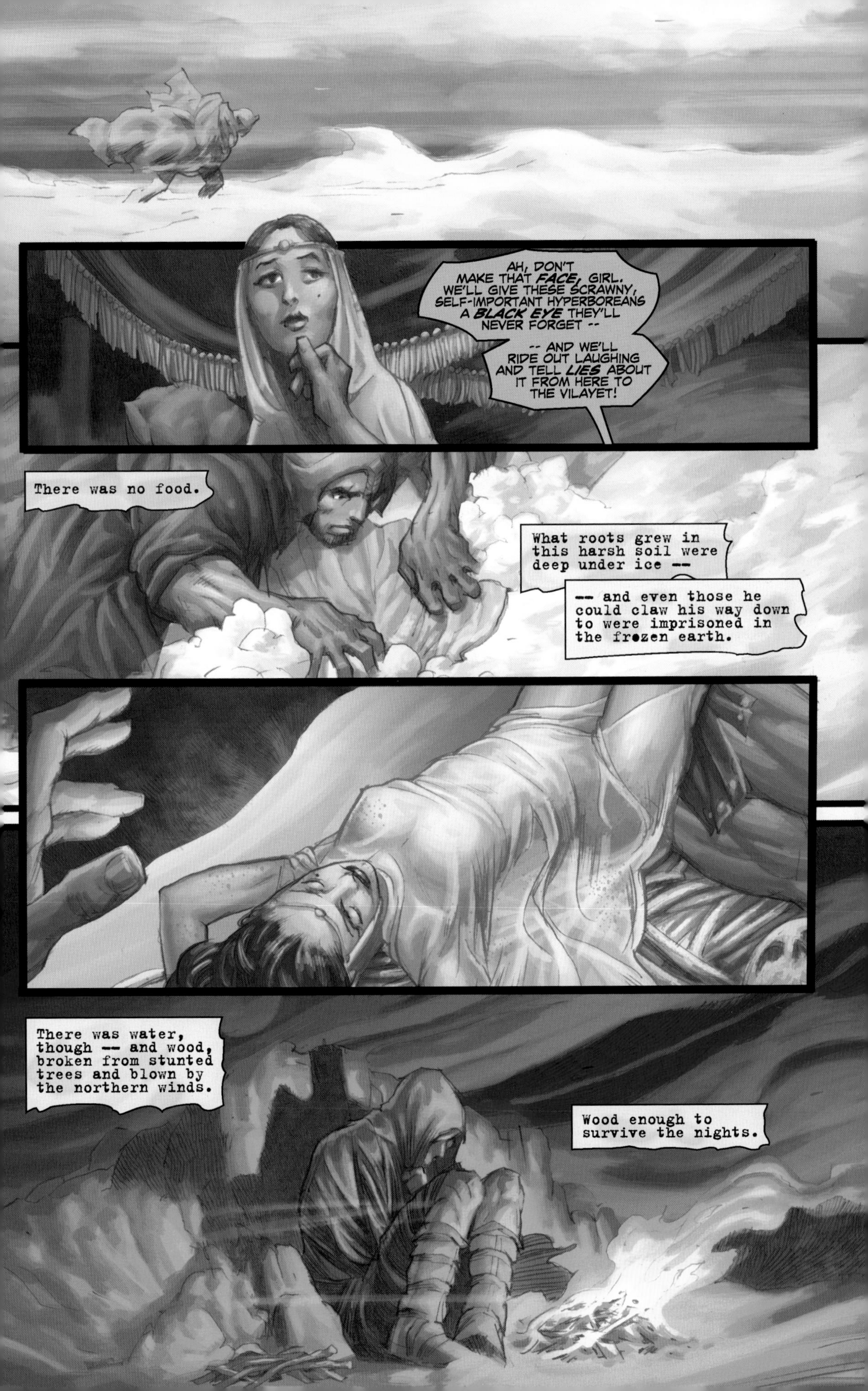
AH, DON'T MAKE THAT *FACE,* GIRL. WE'LL GIVE THESE SCRAWNY, SELF-IMPORTANT HYPERBOREANS A *BLACK EYE* THEY'LL NEVER FORGET --
-- AND WE'LL RIDE OUT LAUGHING AND TELL *LIES* ABOUT IT FROM HERE TO THE VILAYET!
There was no food.
What roots grew in this harsh soil were deep under ice --
-- and even those he could claw his way down to were imprisoned in the frozen earth.
There was water, though -- and wood, broken from stunted trees and blown by the northern winds.
Wood enough to survive the nights.

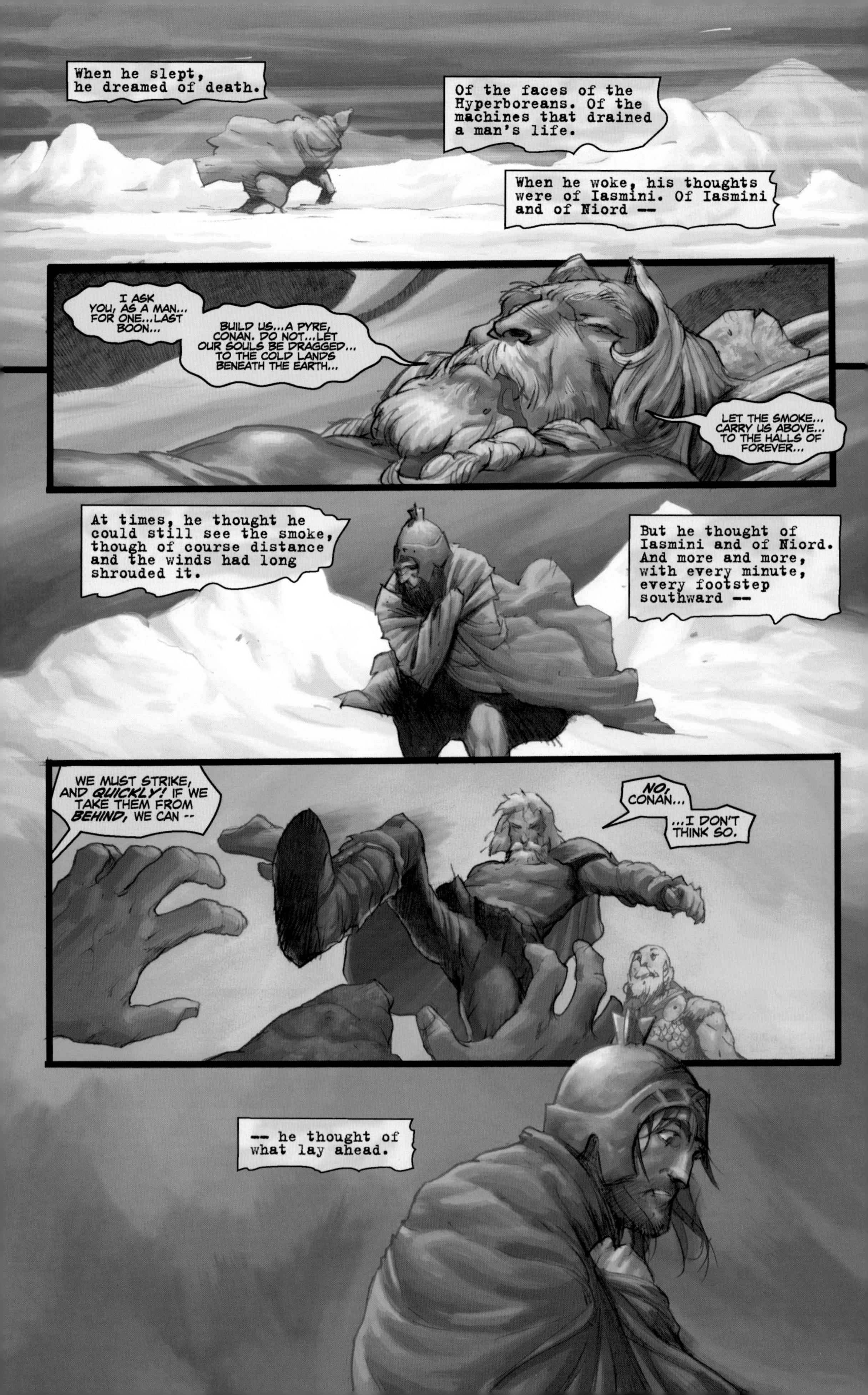
When he slept, he dreamed of death.
Of the faces of the Hyperboreans. Of the machines that drained a man's life.
When he woke, his thoughts were of Iasmini. Of Iasmini and of Niord --
I ASK YOU, AS A MAN... FOR ONE...LAST BOON...
BUILD US...A PYRE, CONAN. DO NOT...LET OUR SOULS BE DRAGGED... TO THE COLD LANDS BENEATH THE EARTH...
LET THE SMOKE... CARRY US ABOVE... TO THE HALLS OF FOREVER...
At times, he thought he could still see the smoke, though of course distance and the winds had long shrouded it.
But he thought of Iasmini and of Niord. And more and more, with every minute, every footstep southward --
WE MUST STRIKE, AND QUICKLY! IF WE TAKE THEM FROM BEHIND, WE CAN --
NO, CONAN...
...I DON'T THINK SO.
-- he thought of what lay ahead.

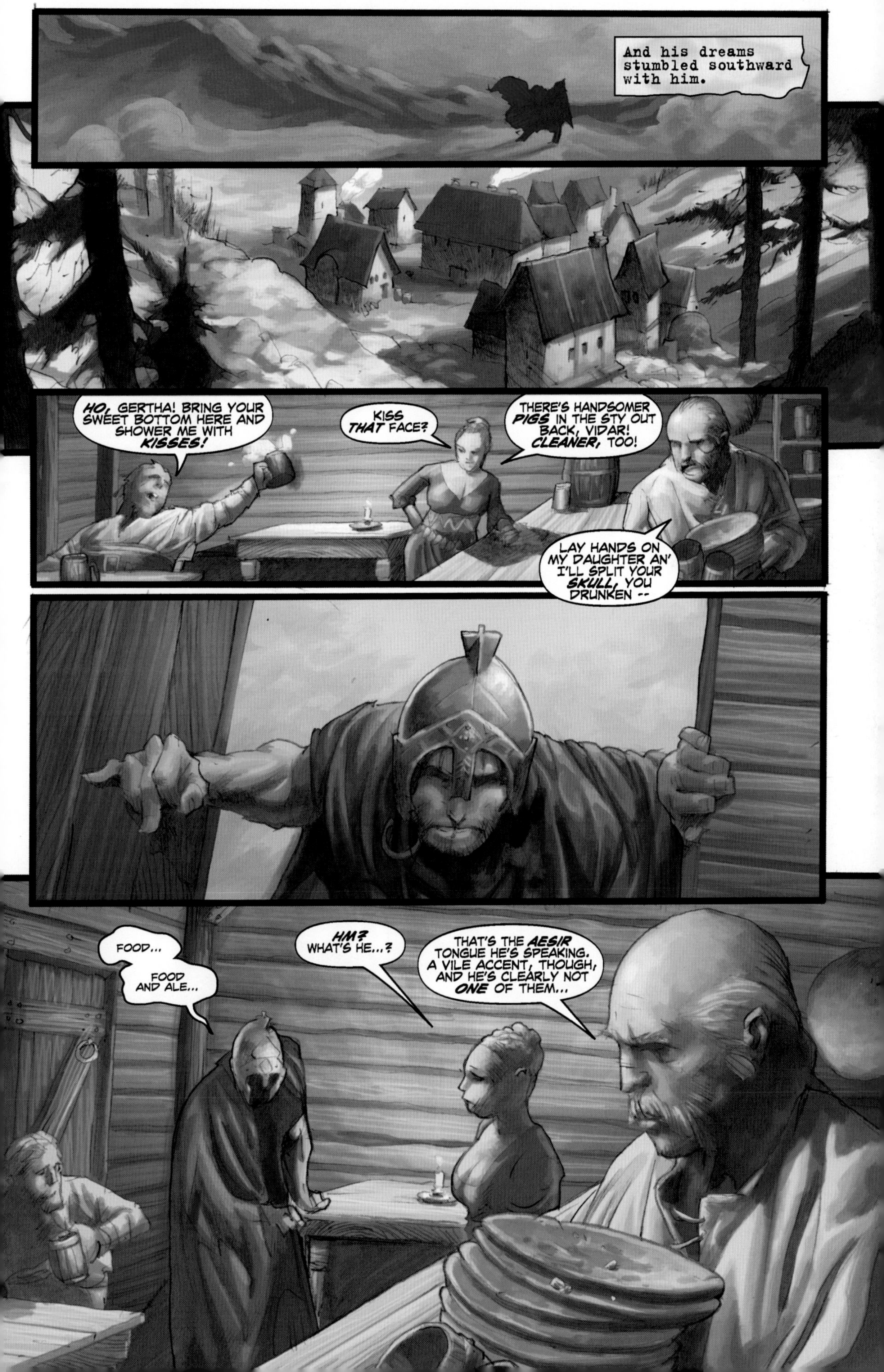
And his dreams stumbled southward with him.
HO, GERTHA! BRING YOUR SWEET BOTTOM HERE AND SHOWER ME WITH KISSES!
KISS THAT FACE?
THERE'S HANDSOMER PIGS IN THE STY OUT BACK, VIDAR! CLEANER, TOO!
LAY HANDS ON MY DAUGHTER AN' I'LL SPLIT YOUR SKULL, YOU DRUNKEN --
FOOD...
FOOD AND ALE...
HM? WHAT'S HE...?
THAT'S THE AESIR TONGUE HE'S SPEAKING. A VILE ACCENT, THOUGH, AND HE'S CLEARLY NOT ONE OF THEM...

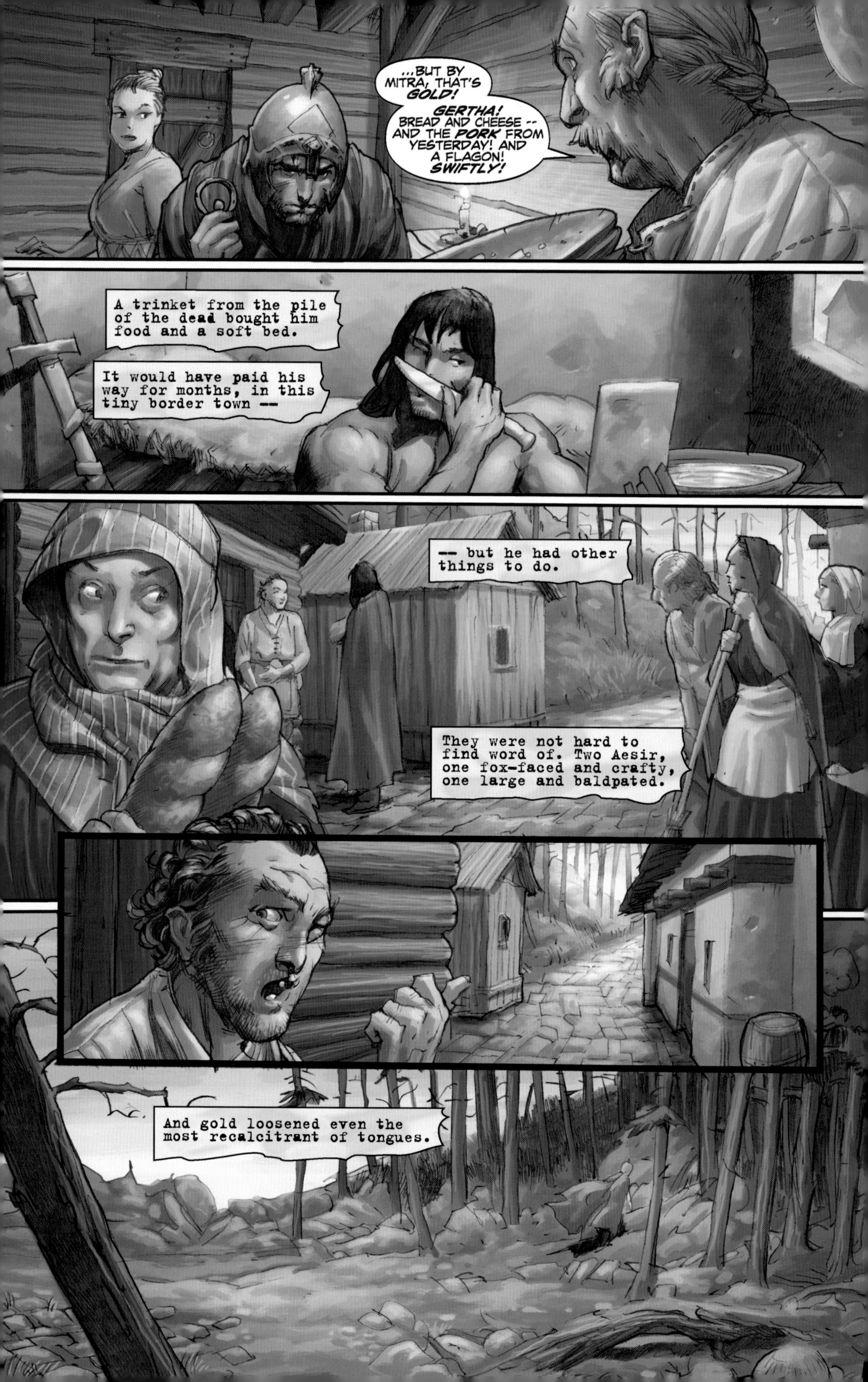
...BUT BY MITRA, THAT'S GOLD!
GERTHA! BREAD AND CHEESE -- AND THE PORK FROM YESTERDAY! AND A FLAGON! SWIFTLY!
A trinket from the pile of the dead bought him food and a soft bed.
It would have paid his way for months, in this tiny border town --
-- but he had other things to do.
They were not hard to find word of. Two Aesir, one fox-faced and crafty, one large and baldpated.
And gold loosened even the most recalcitrant of tongues.

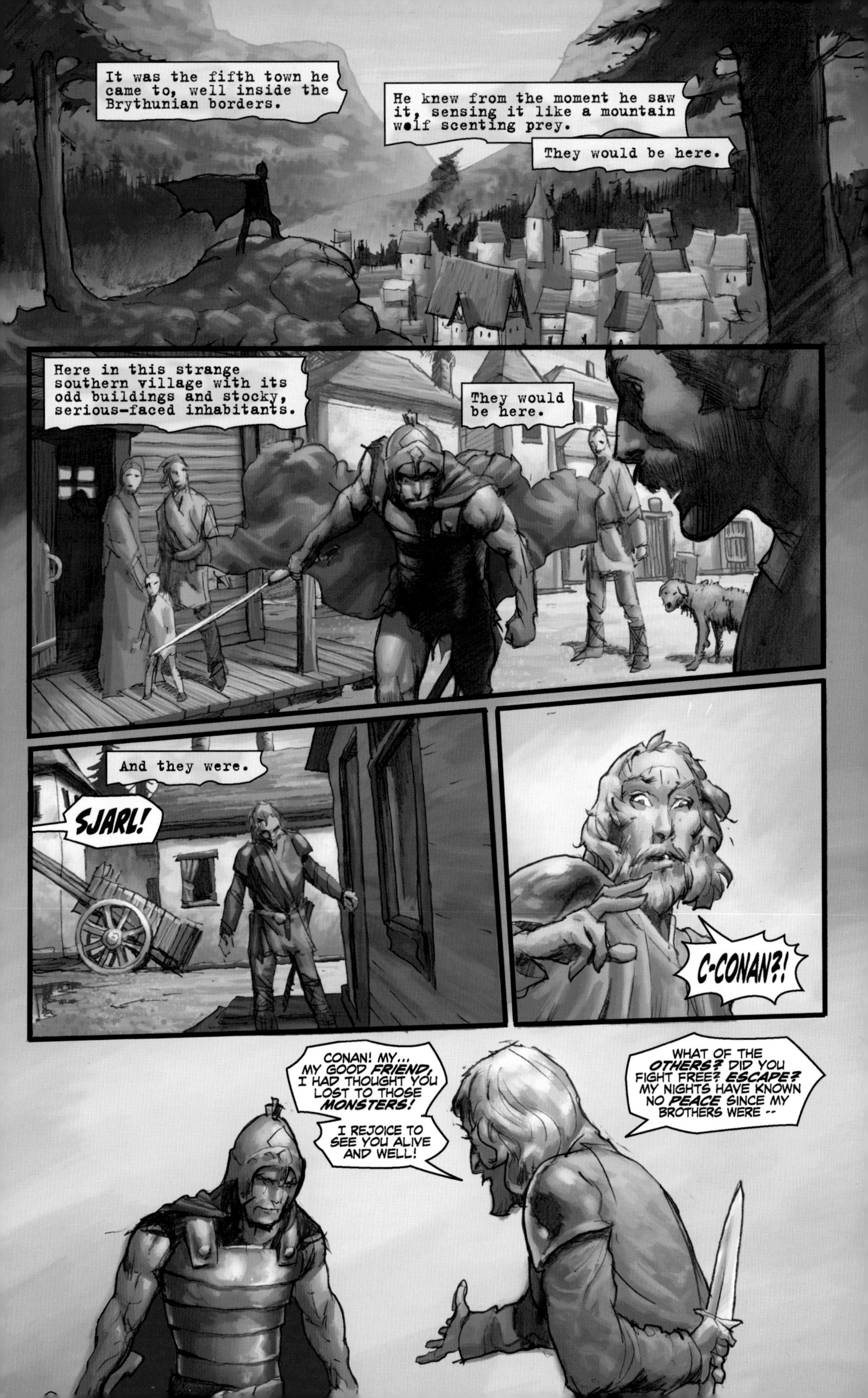
It was the fifth town he came to, well inside the Brythunian borders.
He knew from the moment he saw it, sensing it like a mountain wolf scenting prey.
They would be here.
Here in this strange southern village with its odd buildings and stocky, serious-faced inhabitants.
They would be here.
And they were.
SJARL!
C-CONAN?!
CONAN! MY... MY GOOD FRIEND, I HAD THOUGHT YOU LOST TO THOSE MONSTERS!
I REJOICE TO SEE YOU ALIVE AND WELL!
WHAT OF THE OTHERS? DID YOU FIGHT FREE? ESCAPE? MY NIGHTS HAVE KNOWN NO PEACE SINCE MY BROTHERS WERE --

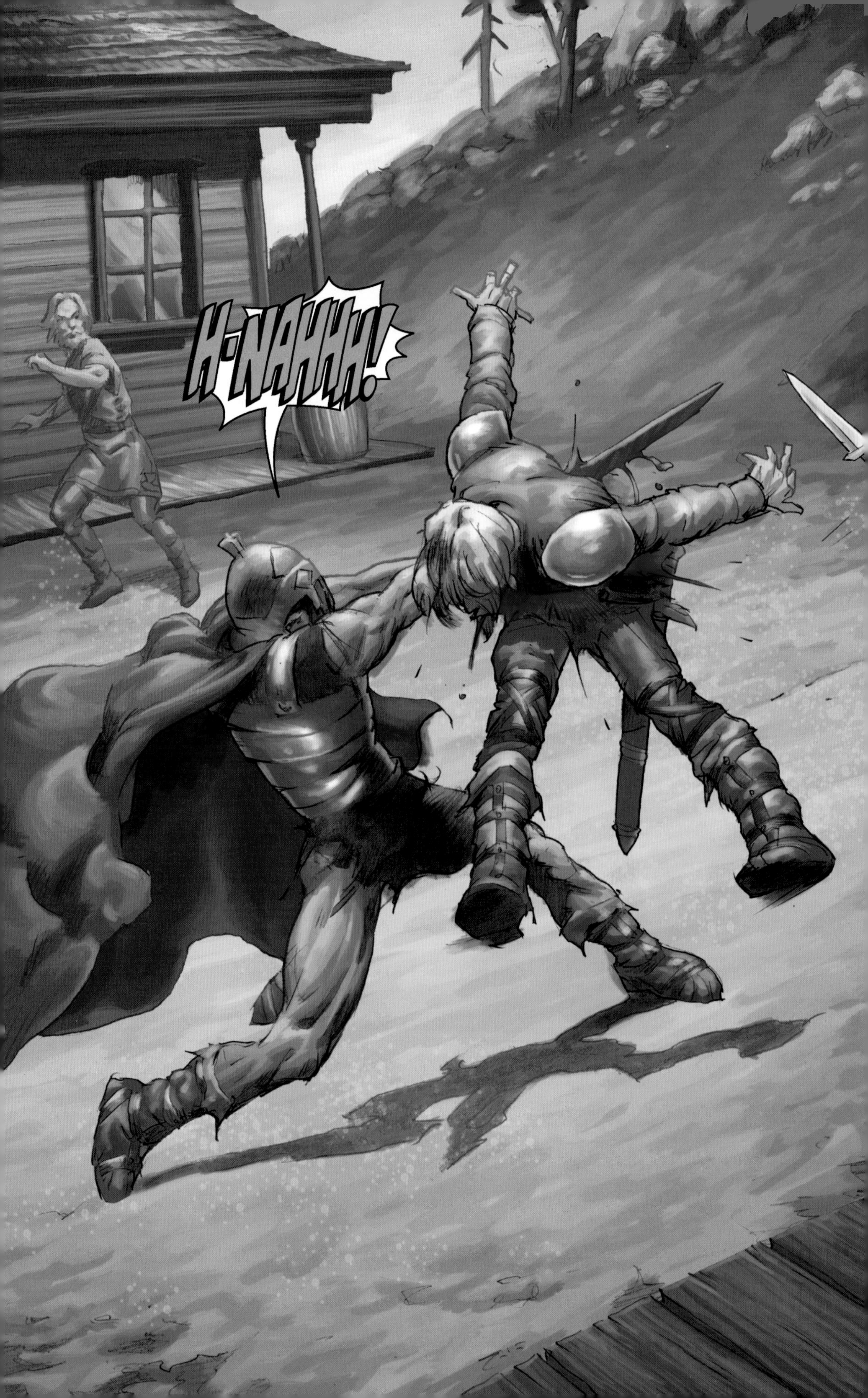
H-NAHHH!

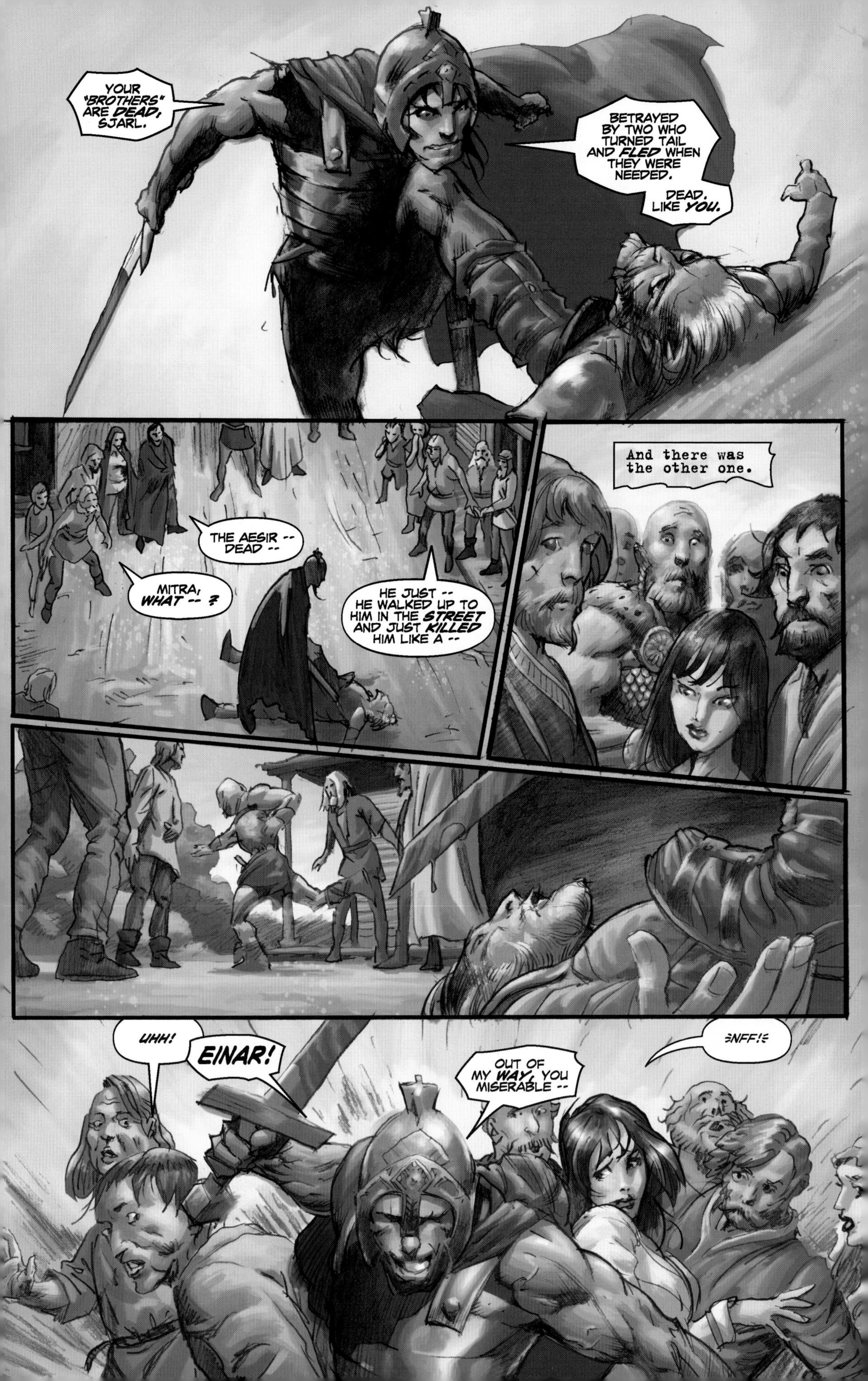
YOUR "BROTHERS" ARE DEAD, SJARL.
BETRAYED BY TWO WHO TURNED TAIL AND FLED WHEN THEY WERE NEEDED.
DEAD. LIKE YOU.
THE AESIR -- DEAD --
MITRA, WHAT -- ?
HE JUST -- HE WALKED UP TO HIM IN THE STREET AND JUST KILLED HIM LIKE A --
And there was the other one.
UHH!
EINAR!
OUT OF MY WAY, YOU MISERABLE --
NFF!

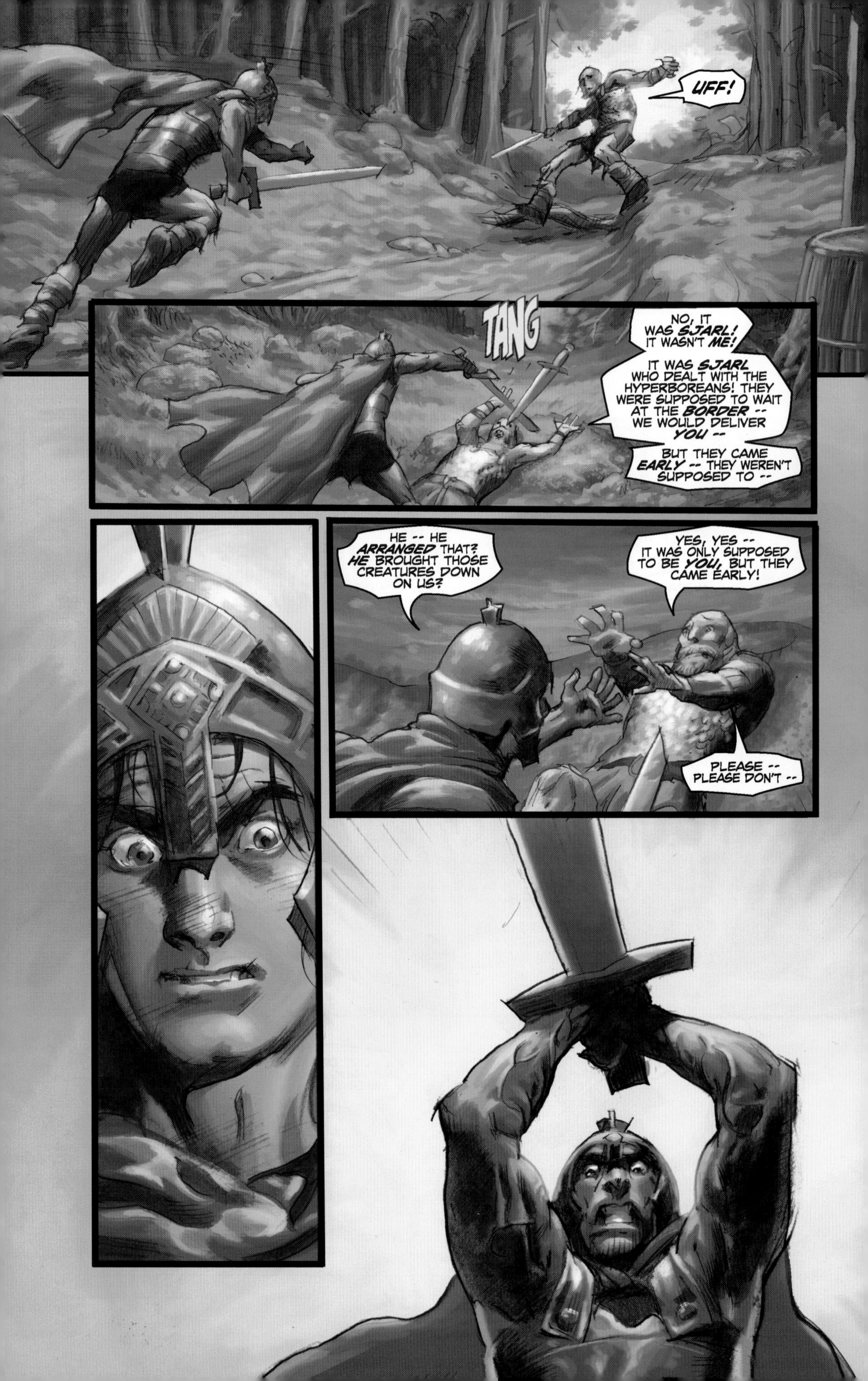
UFF!
TANG
NO, IT WAS SJARL! IT WASN'T ME!
IT WAS SJARL WHO DEALT WITH THE HYPERBOREANS! THEY WERE SUPPOSED TO WAIT AT THE BORDER -- WE WOULD DELIVER YOU --
BUT THEY CAME EARLY -- THEY WEREN'T SUPPOSED TO --
HE -- HE ARRANGED THAT? HE BROUGHT THOSE CREATURES DOWN ON US?
YES, YES -- IT WAS ONLY SUPPOSED TO BE YOU, BUT THEY CAME EARLY!
PLEASE -- PLEASE DON'T --

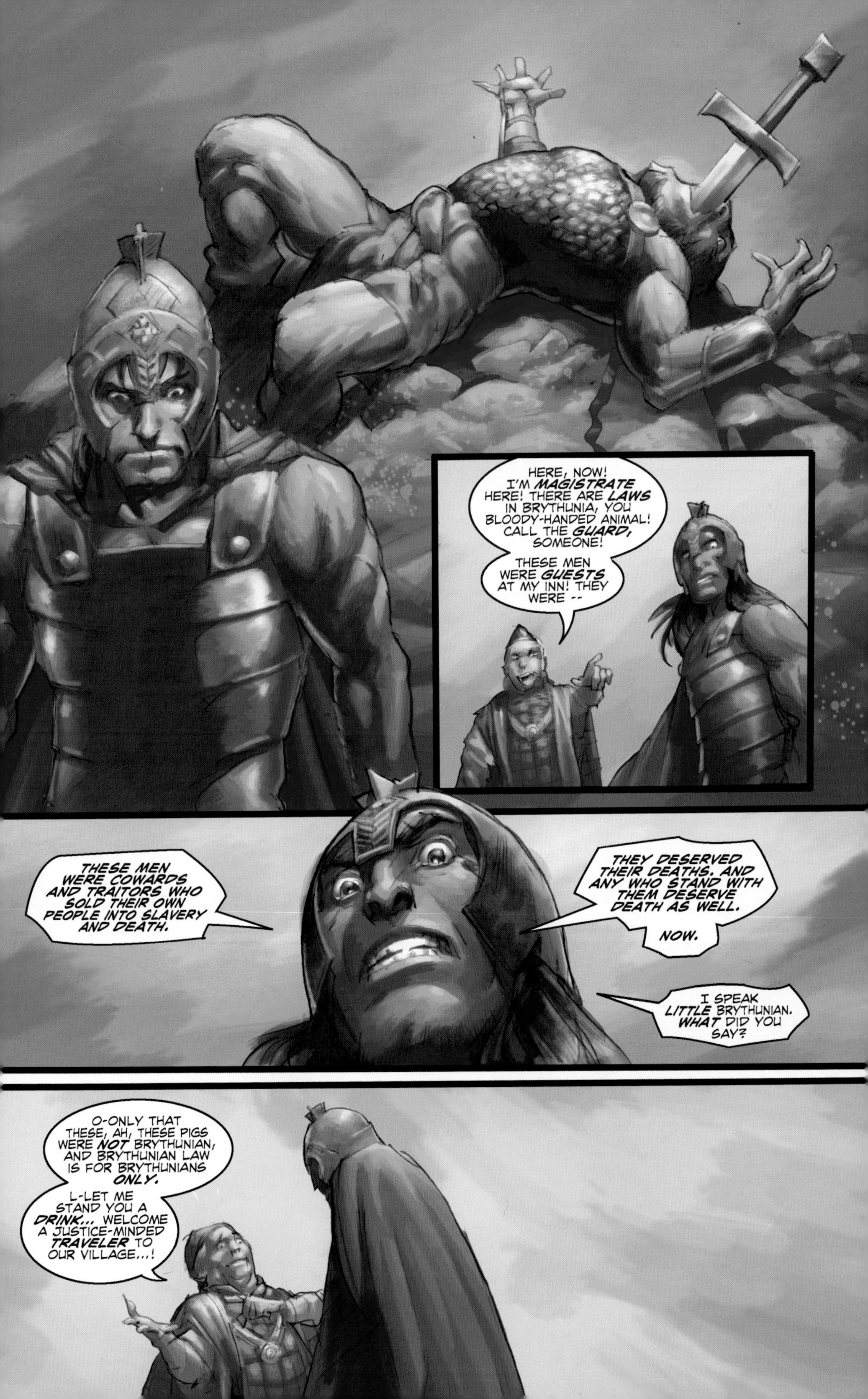
HERE, NOW! I'M MAGISTRATE HERE! THERE ARE LAWS IN BRYTHUNIA, YOU BLOODY-HANDED ANIMAL! CALL THE GUARD, SOMEONE!
THESE MEN WERE GUESTS AT MY INN! THEY WERE --
THESE MEN WERE COWARDS AND TRAITORS WHO SOLD THEIR OWN PEOPLE INTO SLAVERY AND DEATH.
THEY DESERVED THEIR DEATHS. AND ANY WHO STAND WITH THEM DESERVE DEATH AS WELL.
NOW.
I SPEAK LITTLE BRYTHUNIAN. WHAT DID YOU SAY?
O-ONLY THAT THESE, AH, THESE PIGS WERE NOT BRYTHUNIAN, AND BRYTHUNIAN LAW IS FOR BRYTHUNIANS ONLY.
L-LET ME STAND YOU A DRINK... WELCOME A JUSTICE-MINDED TRAVELER TO OUR VILLAGE...!

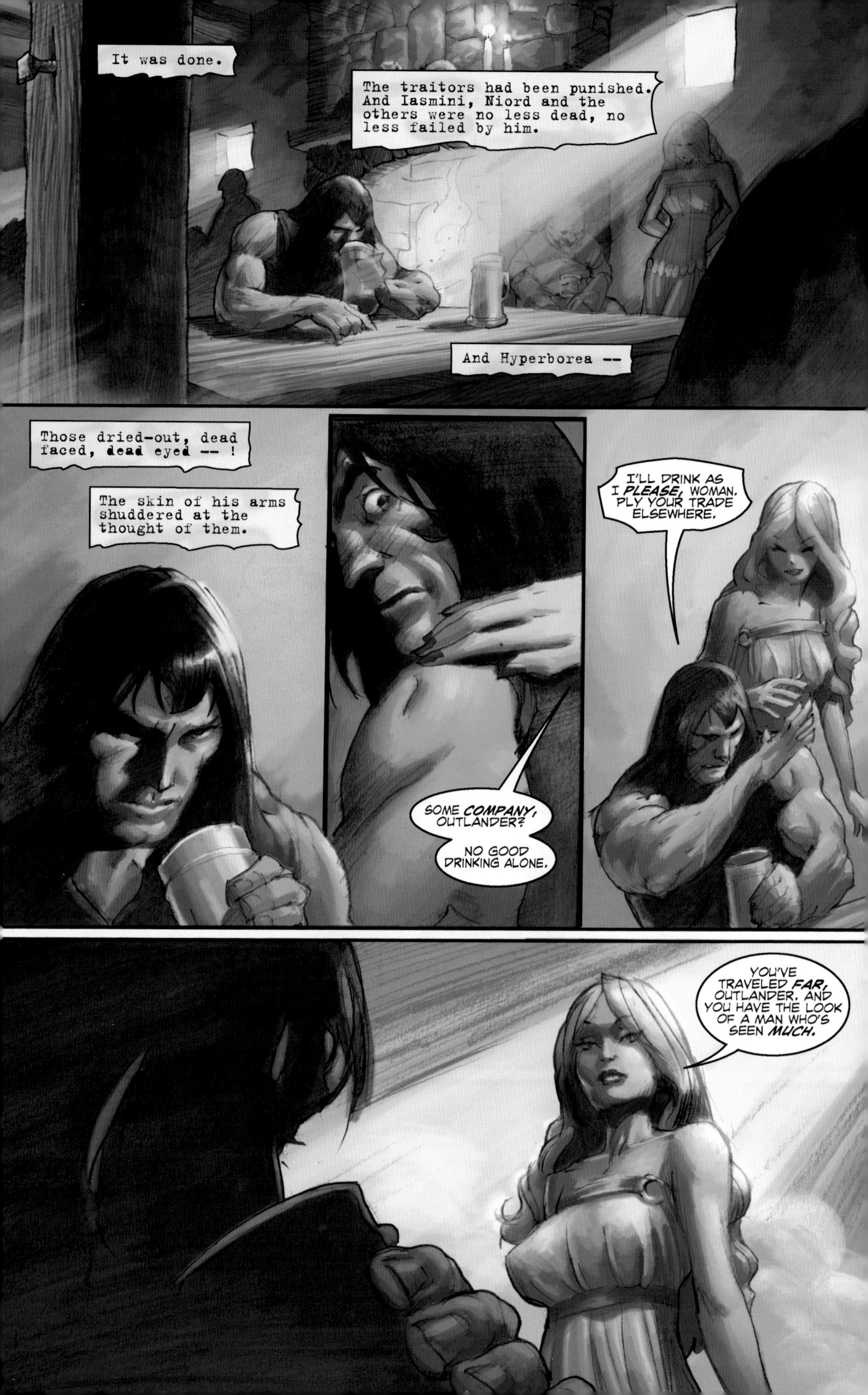
It was done.
The traitors had been punished. And Iasmini, Niord and the others were no less dead, no less failed by him.
And Hyperborea --
Those dried-out, dead faced, dead eyed -- !
The skin of his arms shuddered at the thought of them.
SOME COMPANY, OUTLANDER?
NO GOOD DRINKING ALONE.
I'LL DRINK AS I PLEASE, WOMAN. PLY YOUR TRADE ELSEWHERE.
YOU'VE TRAVELED FAR, OUTLANDER. AND YOU HAVE THE LOOK OF A MAN WHO'S SEEN MUCH.

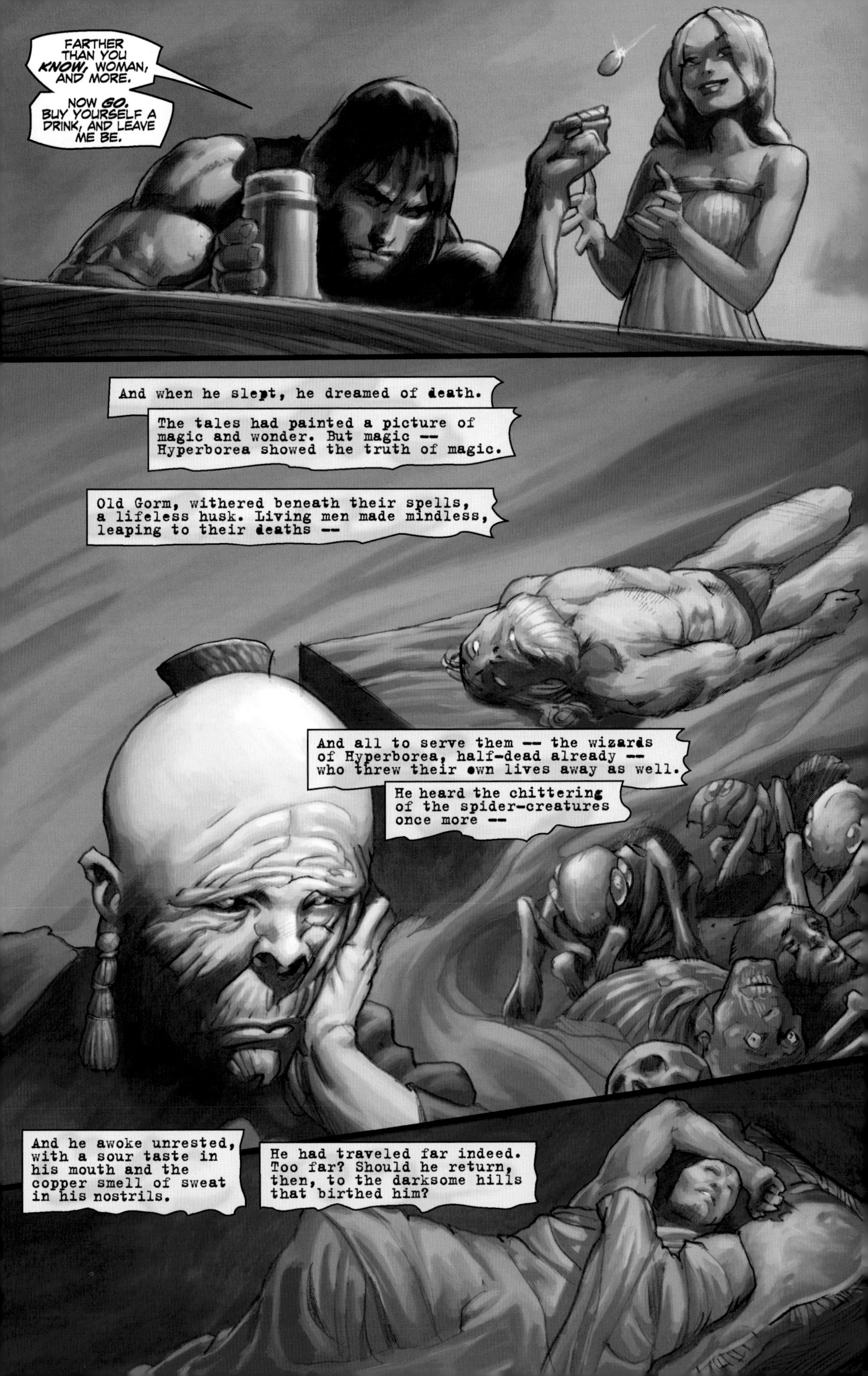
FARTHER THAN YOU KNOW, WOMAN, AND MORE.
NOW GO. BUY YOURSELF A DRINK, AND LEAVE ME BE.
And when he slept, he dreamed of death.
The tales had painted a picture of magic and wonder. But magic -- Hyperborea showed the truth of magic.
Old Gorm, withered beneath their spells, a lifeless husk. Living men made mindless, leaping to their deaths --
And all to serve them -- the wizards of Hyperborea, half-dead already -- who threw their own lives away as well.
He heard the chittering of the spider-creatures once more --
And he awoke unrested, with a sour taste in his mouth and the copper smell of sweat in his nostrils.
He had traveled far indeed. Too far? Should he return, then, to the darksome hills that birthed him?

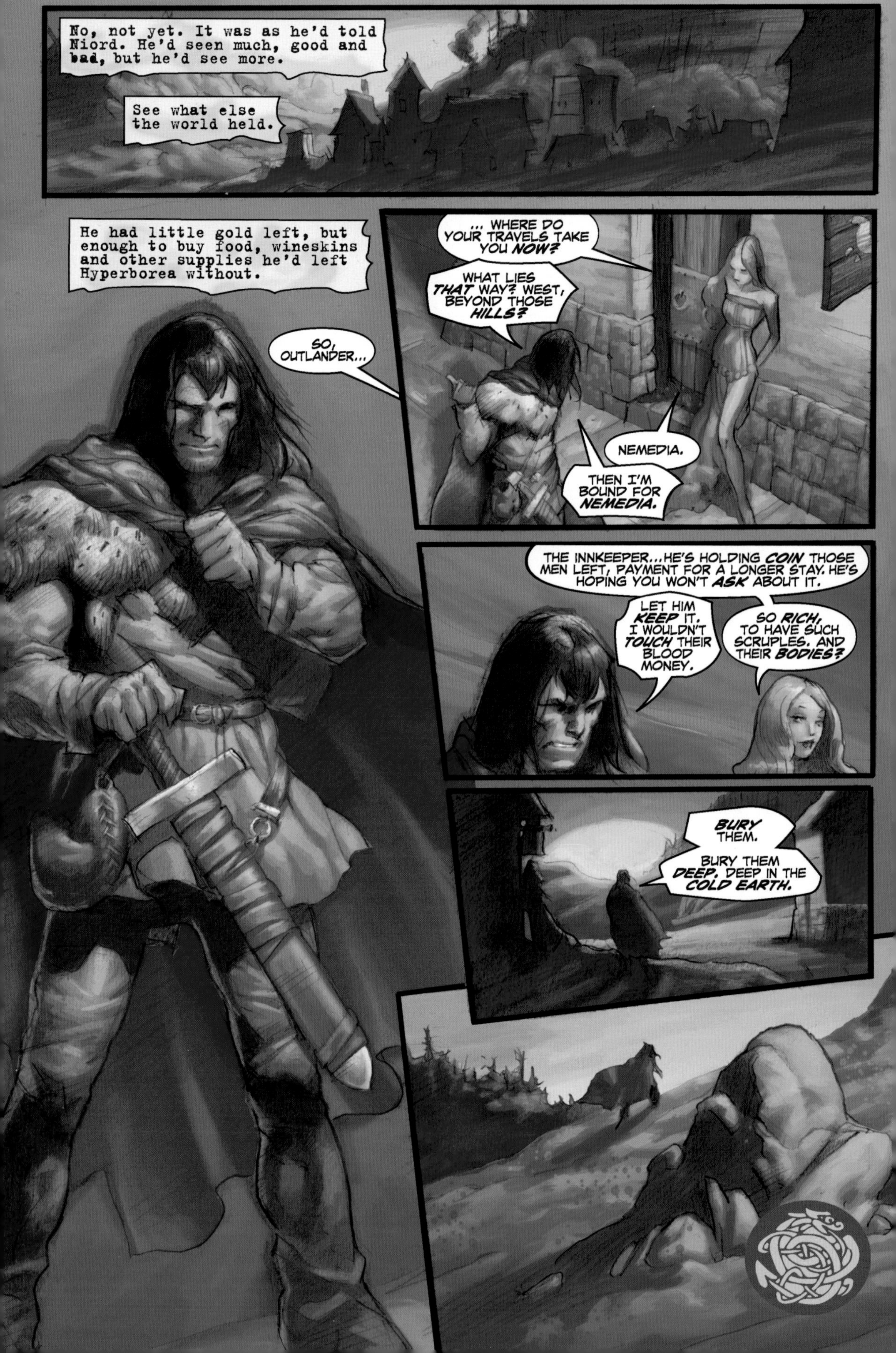

No, not yet. It was as he'd told Niord. He'd seen much, good and bad, but he'd see more.
See what else the world held.
He had little gold left, but enough to buy food, wineskins and other supplies he'd left Hyperborea without.
SO, OUTLANDER...
... WHERE DO YOUR TRAVELS TAKE YOU NOW?
WHAT LIES THAT WAY? WEST, BEYOND THOSE HILLS?
NEMEDIA.
THEN I'M BOUND FOR NEMEDIA.
THE INNKEEPER...HE'S HOLDING COIN THOSE MEN LEFT, PAYMENT FOR A LONGER STAY. HE'S HOPING YOU WON'T ASK ABOUT IT.
LET HIM KEEP IT. I WOULDN'T TOUCH THEIR BLOOD MONEY.
SO RICH, TO HAVE SUCH SCRUPLES. AND THEIR BODIES?
BURY THEM.
BURY THEM DEEP. DEEP IN THE COLD EARTH.

PART THREE

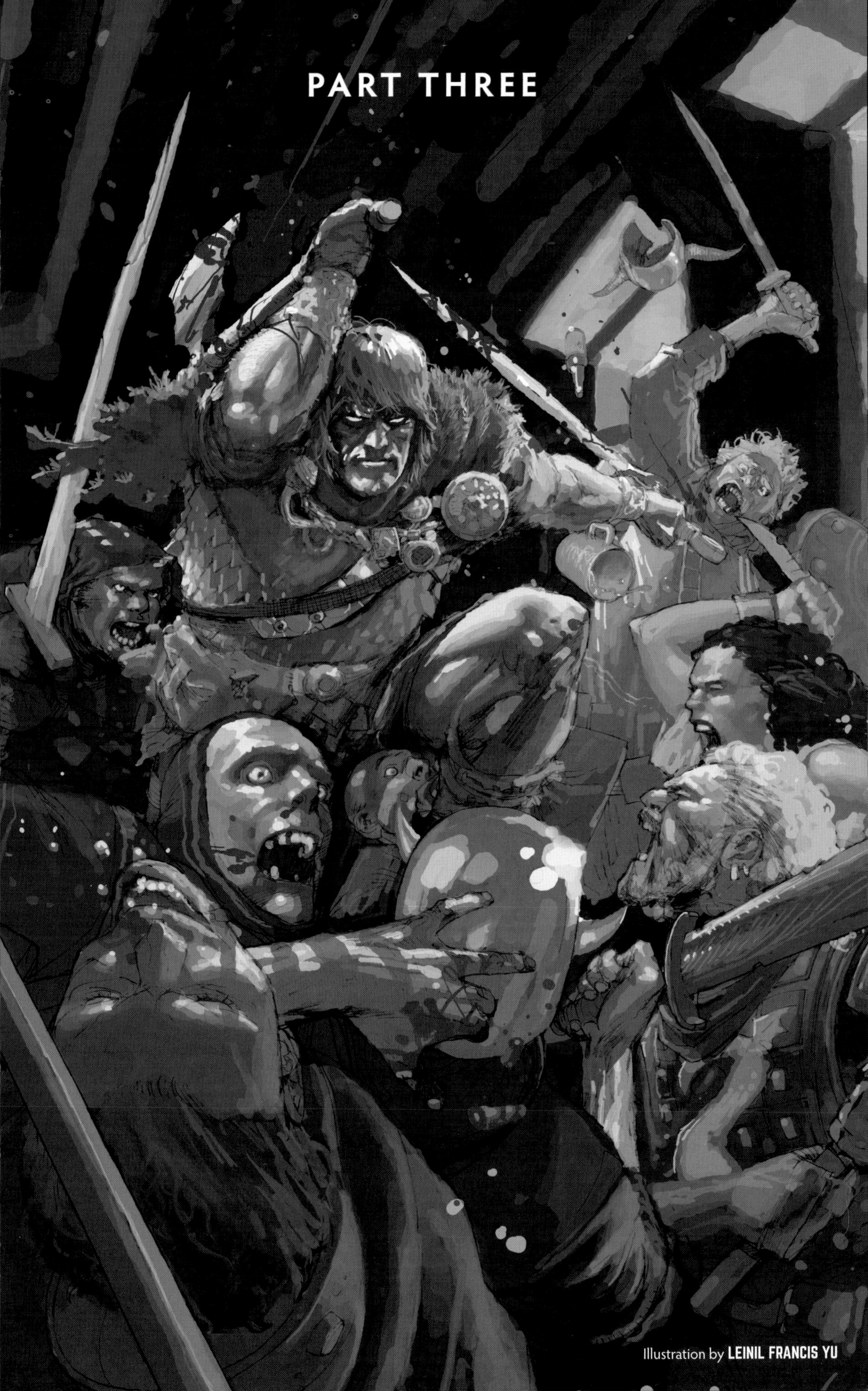

Illustration by **LEINIL FRANCIS YU**

THE GOD IN THE BOWL AND OTHER STORIES

SCRIPTS
KURT BUSIEK

ART
CARY NORD
THOMAS YEATES
TOM MANDRAKE

COLORS
DAVE STEWART

LETTERING
RICHARD STARKINGS
AND **COMICRAFT**

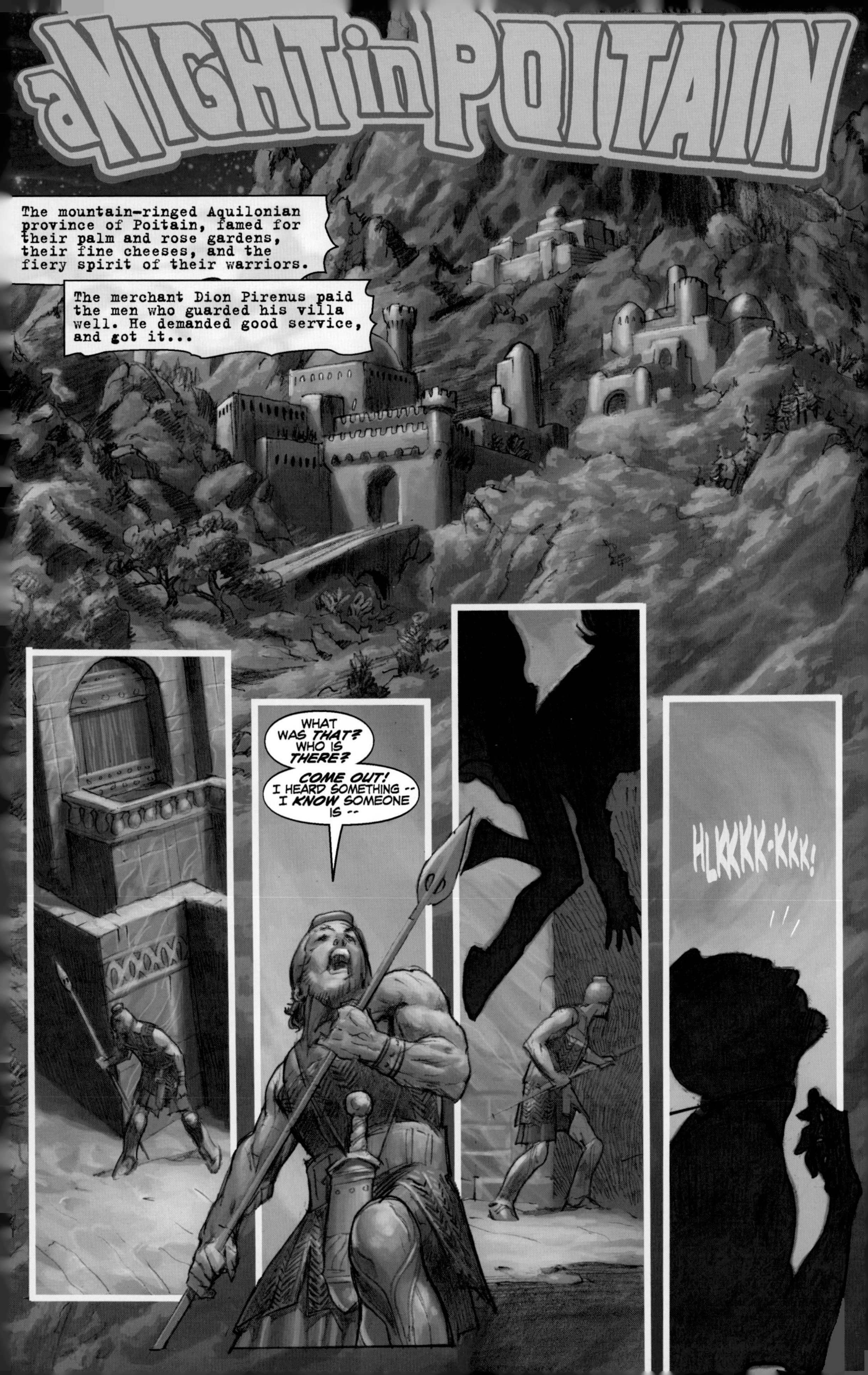

a NIGHT in POITAIN
The mountain-ringed Aquilonian province of Poitain, famed for their palm and rose gardens, their fine cheeses, and the fiery spirit of their warriors.
The merchant Dion Pirenus paid the men who guarded his villa well. He demanded good service, and got it...
WHAT WAS THAT? WHO IS THERE?
COME OUT! I HEARD SOMETHING -- I KNOW SOMEONE IS --
HLKKKK-KKK!

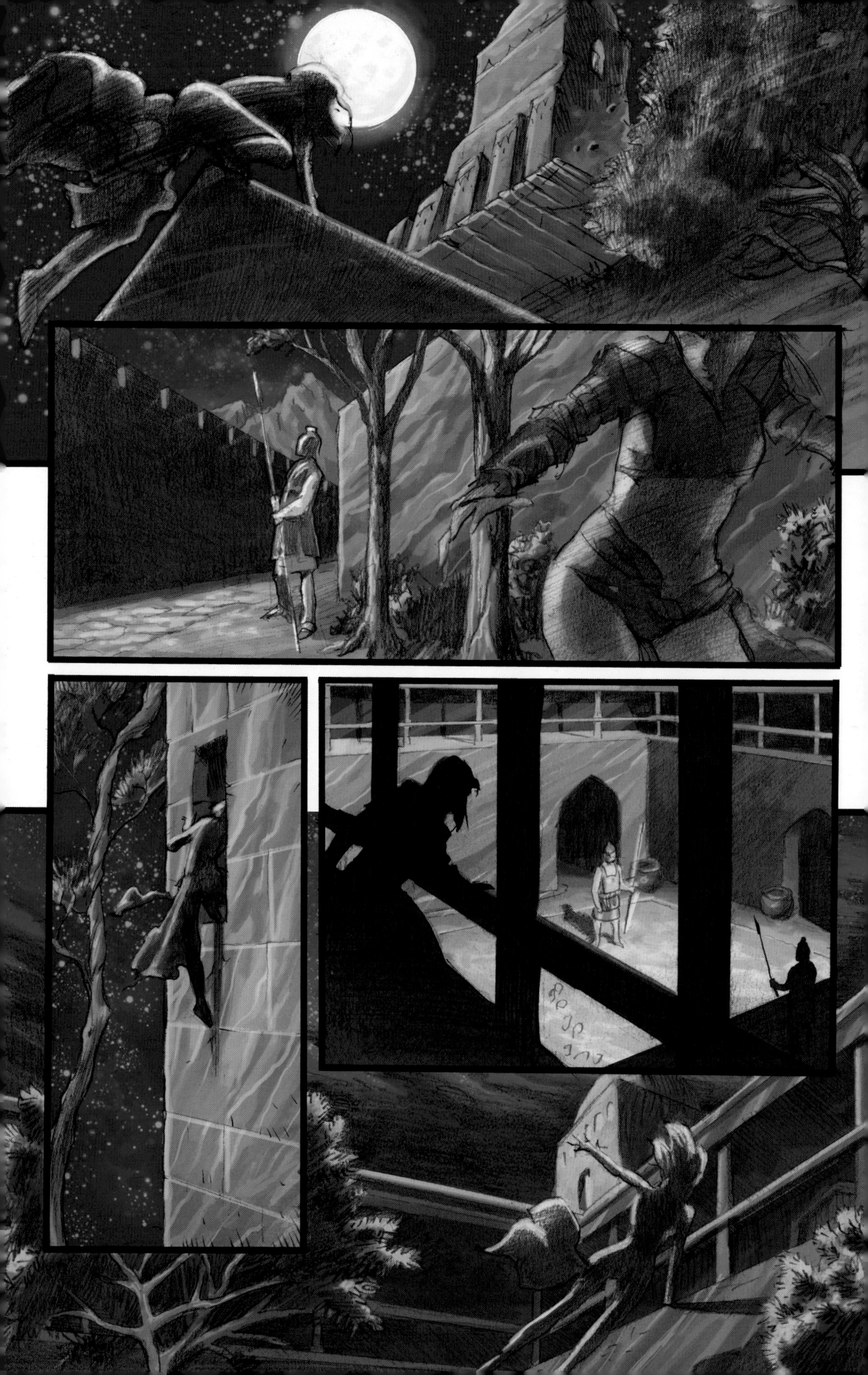

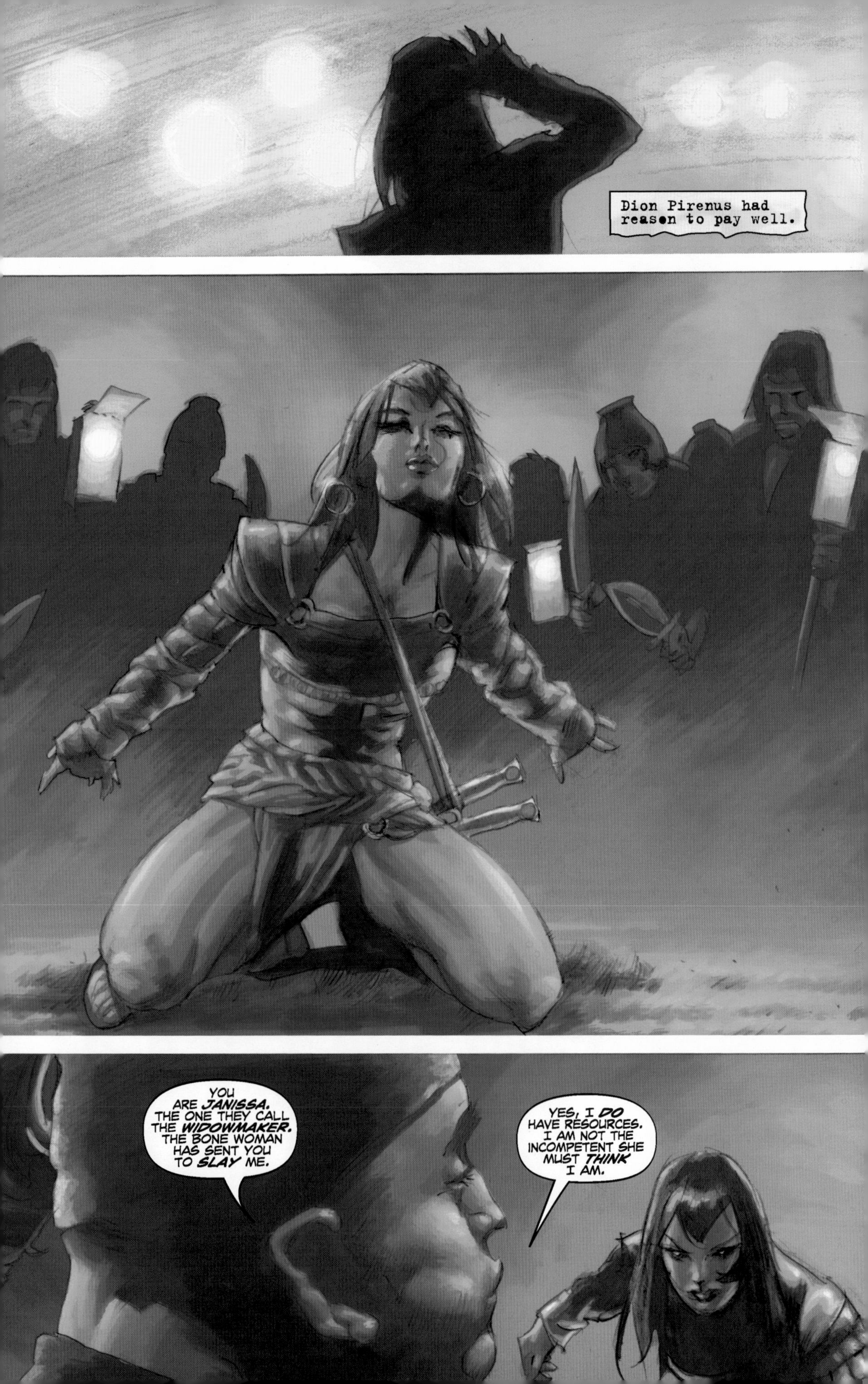

Dion Pirenus had reason to pay well.
YOU ARE JANISSA. THE ONE THEY CALL THE WIDOWMAKER. THE BONE WOMAN HAS SENT YOU TO SLAY ME.
YES, I DO HAVE RESOURCES. I AM NOT THE INCOMPETENT SHE MUST THINK I AM.

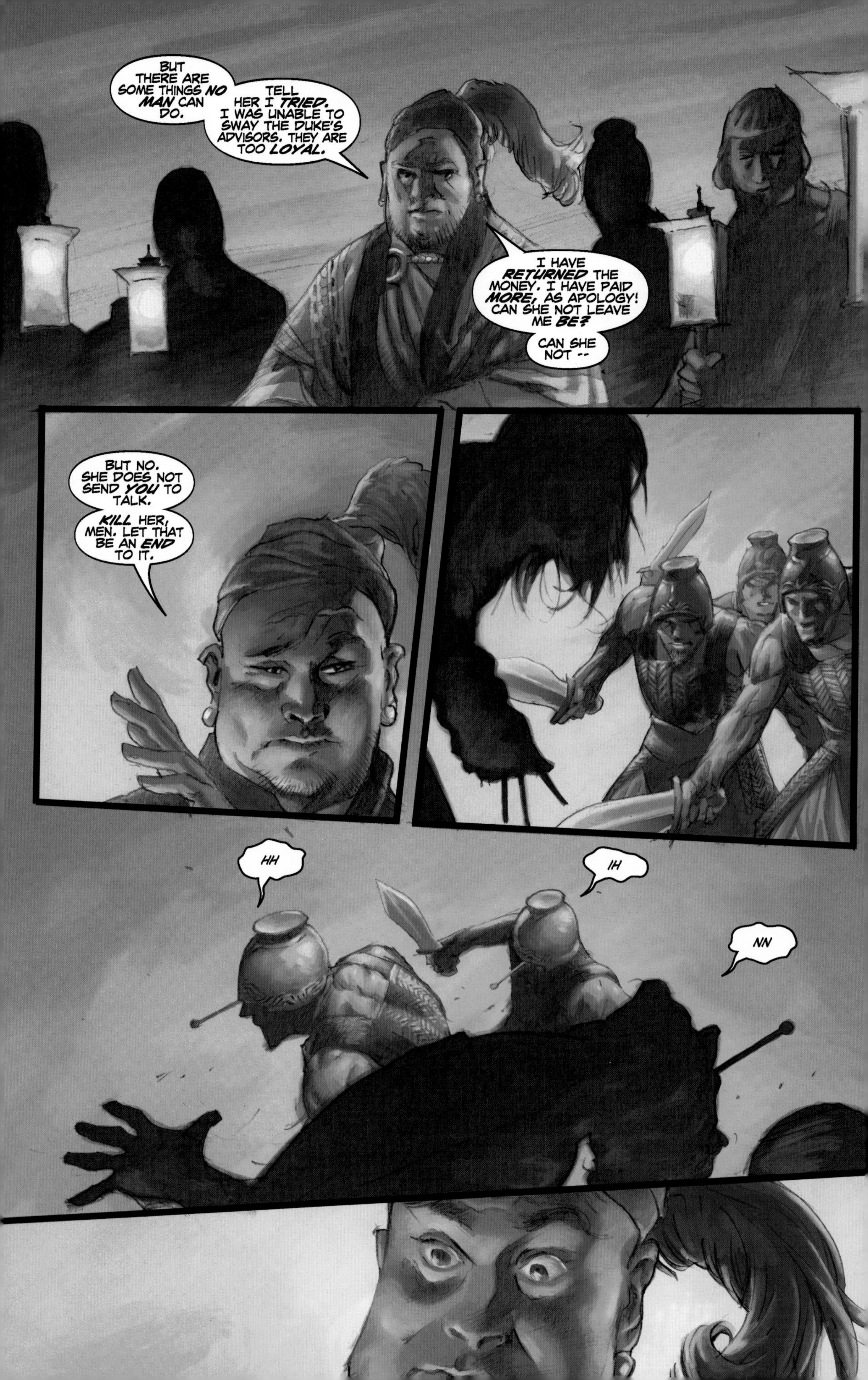
BUT THERE ARE SOME THINGS NO MAN CAN DO.
TELL HER I TRIED. I WAS UNABLE TO SWAY THE DUKE'S ADVISORS. THEY ARE TOO LOYAL.
I HAVE RETURNED THE MONEY. I HAVE PAID MORE, AS APOLOGY! CAN SHE NOT LEAVE ME BE?
CAN SHE NOT --
BUT NO. SHE DOES NOT SEND YOU TO TALK.
KILL HER, MEN. LET THAT BE AN END TO IT.
HH
IH
NN

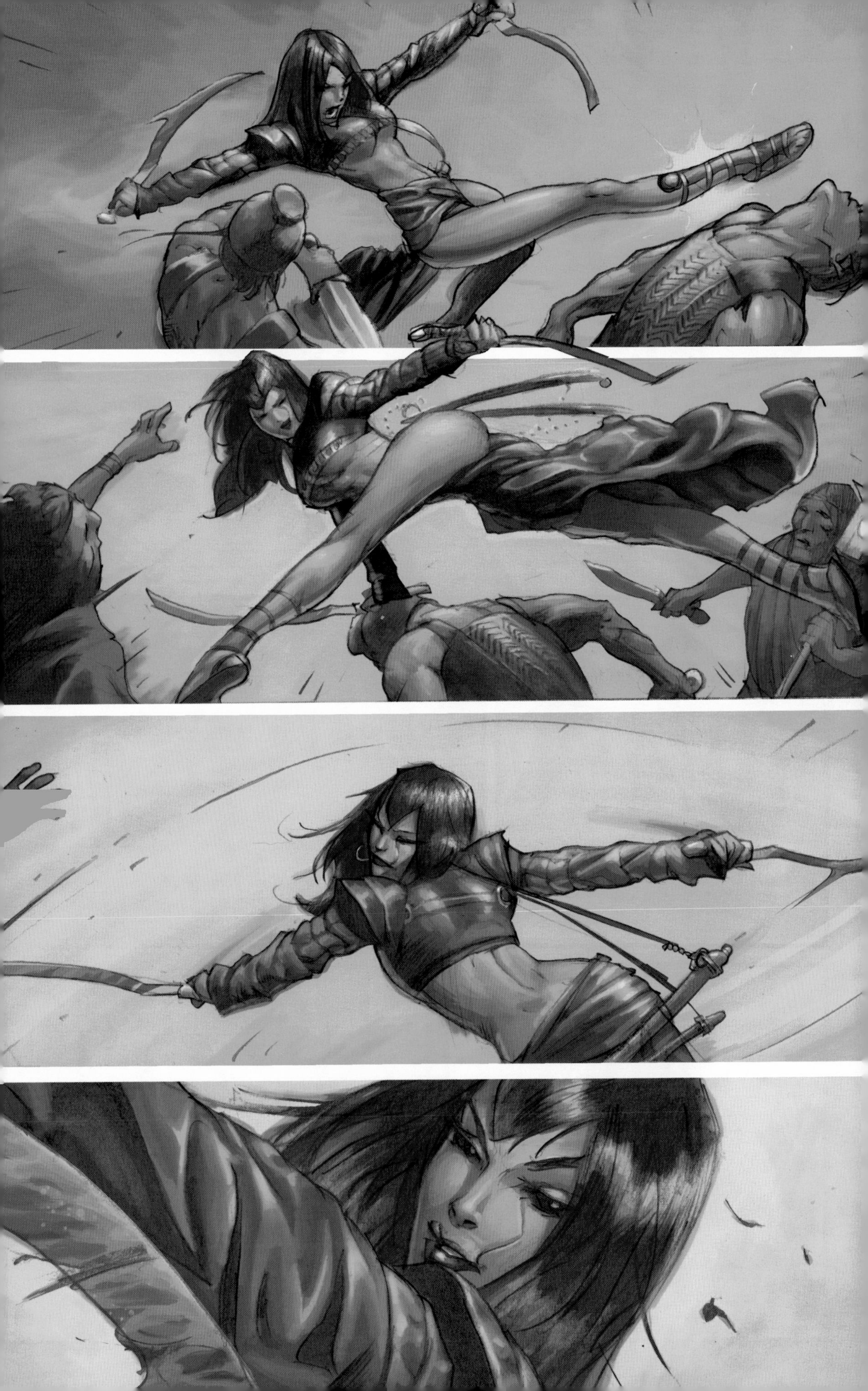

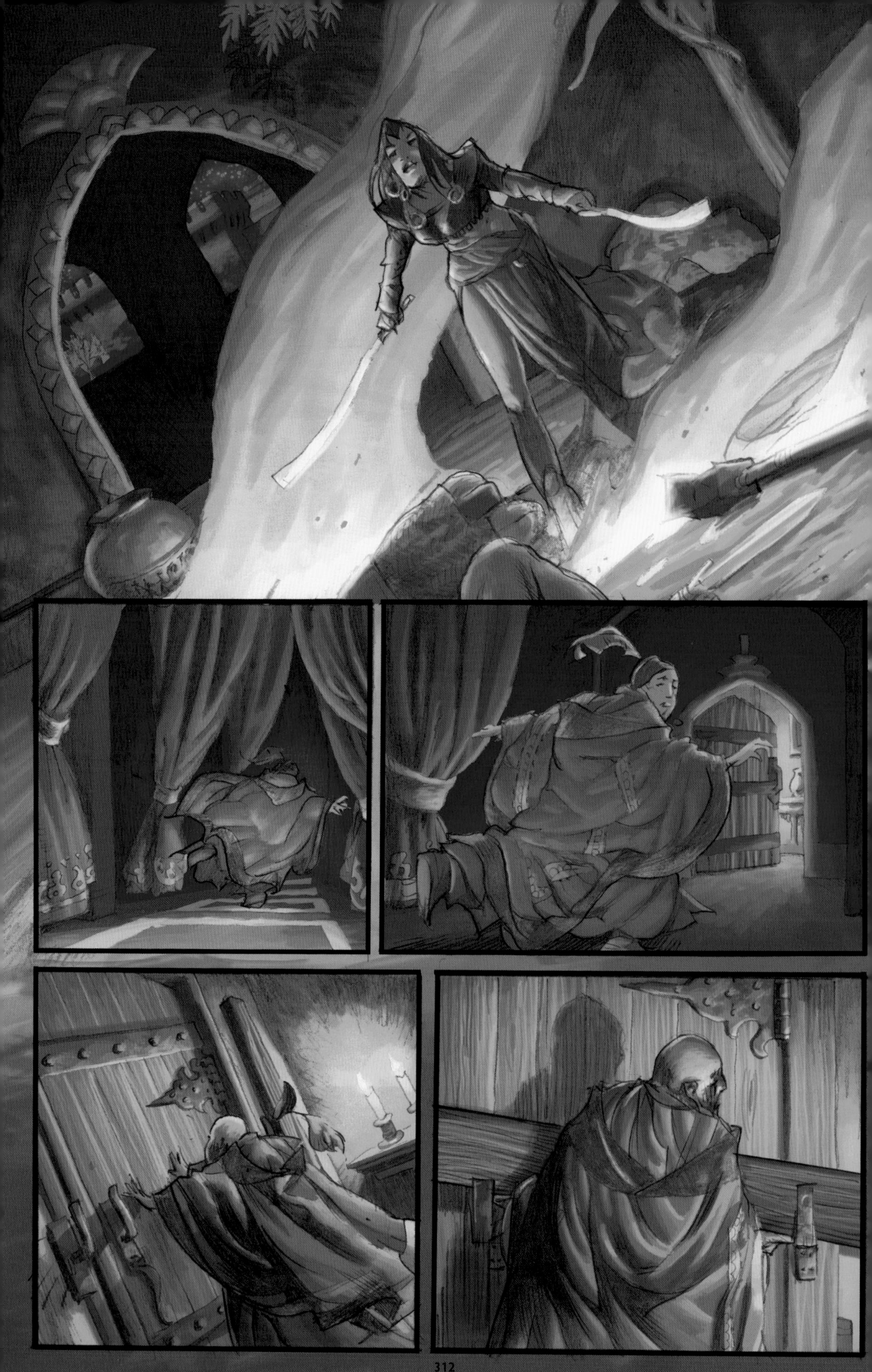

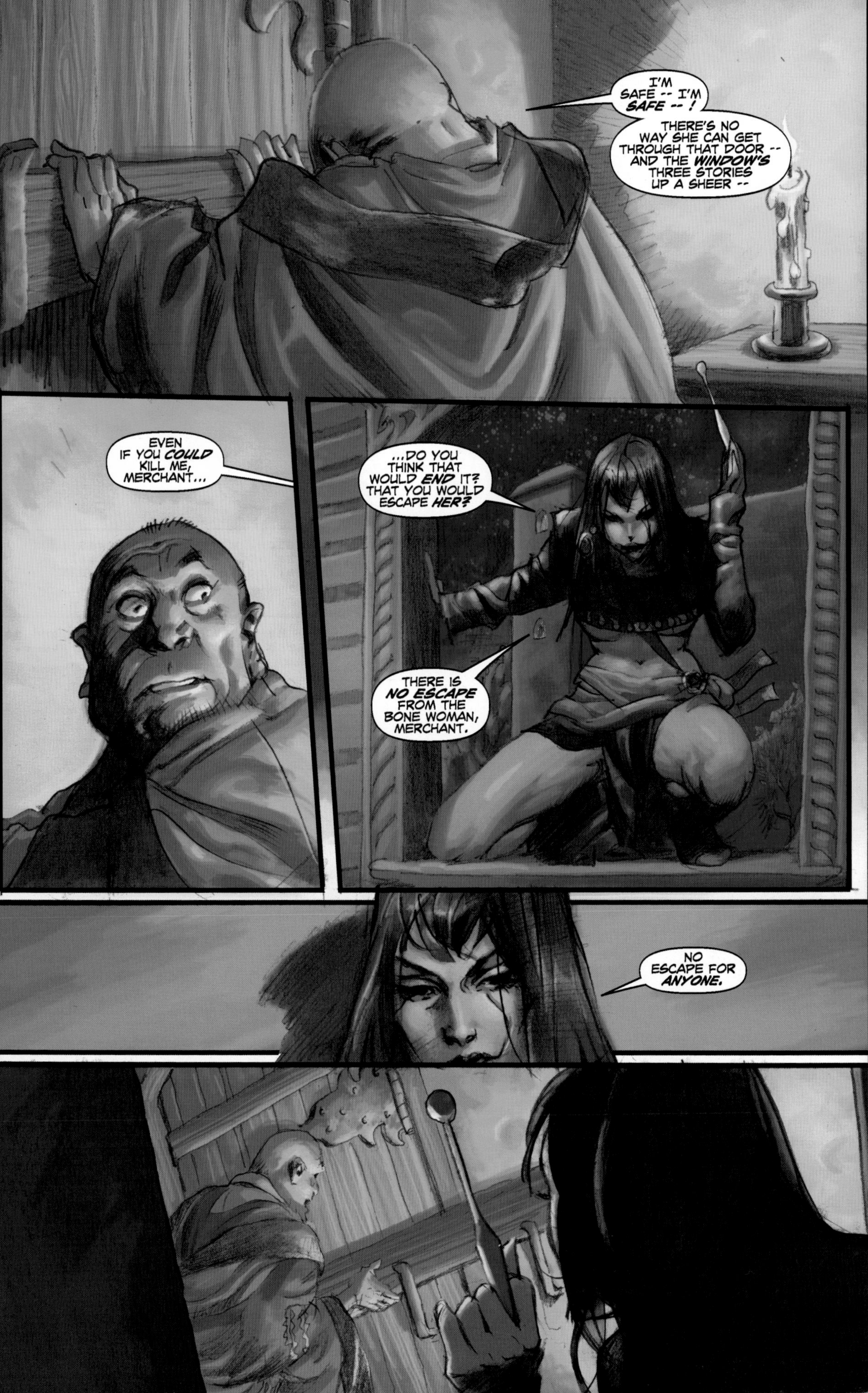
I'M SAFE -- I'M SAFE -- !
THERE'S NO WAY SHE CAN GET THROUGH THAT DOOR -- AND THE WINDOW'S THREE STORIES UP A SHEER --
EVEN IF YOU COULD KILL ME, MERCHANT...
...DO YOU THINK THAT WOULD END IT? THAT YOU WOULD ESCAPE HER?
THERE IS NO ESCAPE FROM THE BONE WOMAN, MERCHANT.
NO ESCAPE FOR ANYONE.

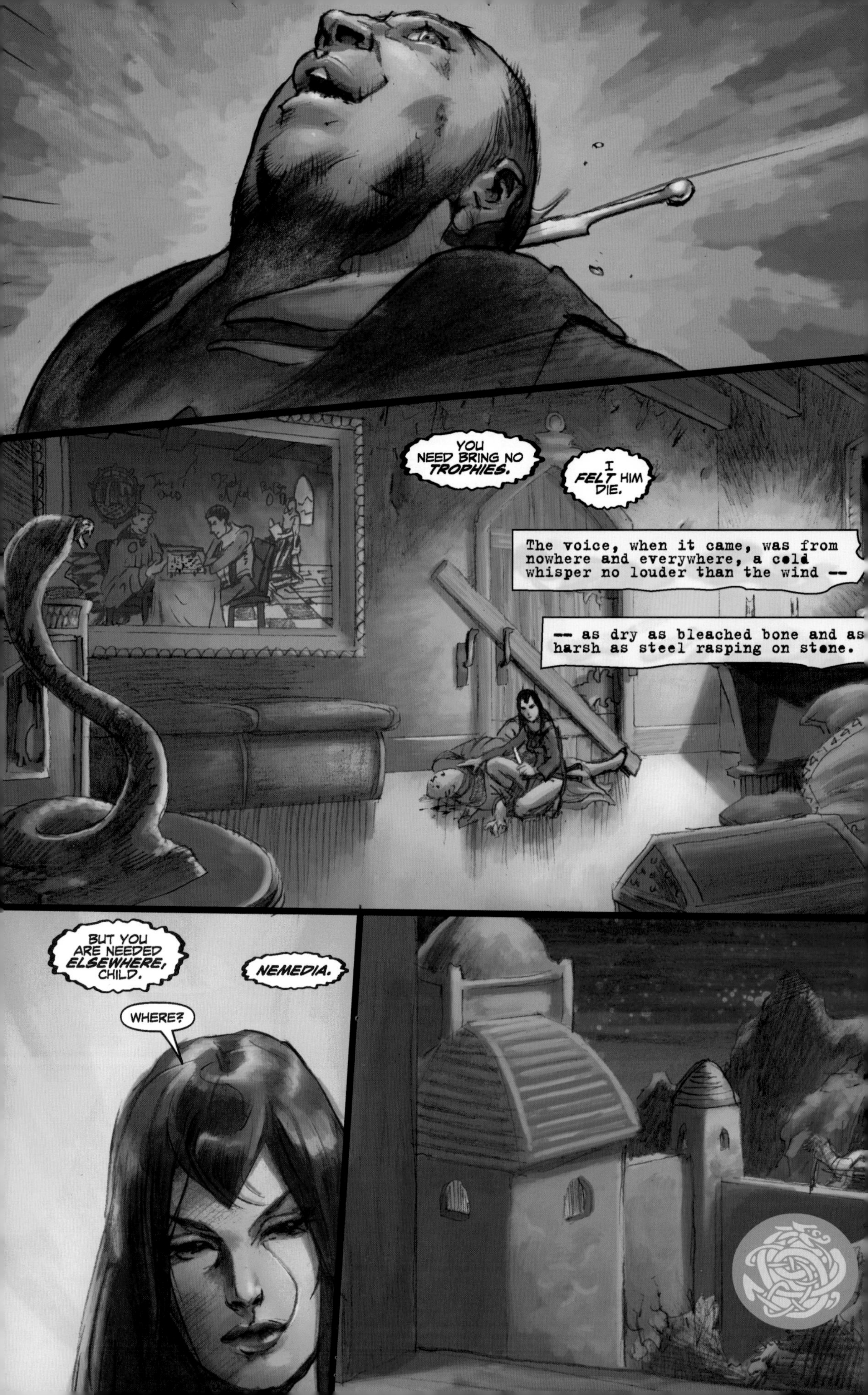
YOU NEED BRING NO TROPHIES.
I FELT HIM DIE.
The voice, when it came, was from nowhere and everywhere, a cold whisper no louder than the wind --
-- as dry as bleached bone and as harsh as steel rasping on stone.
BUT YOU ARE NEEDED ELSEWHERE, CHILD.
WHERE?
NEMEDIA.

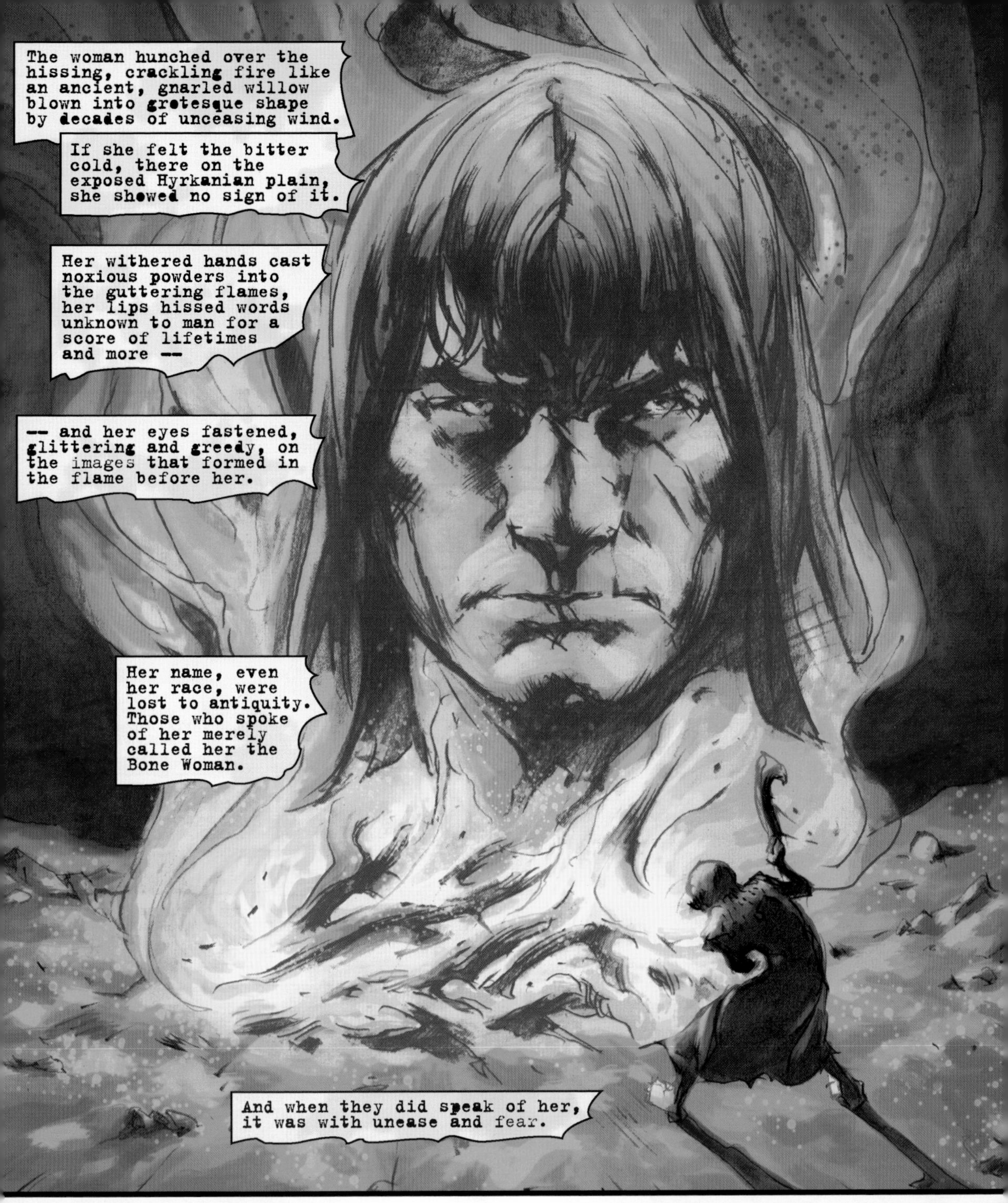
The woman hunched over the hissing, crackling fire like an ancient, gnarled willow blown into grotesque shape by decades of unceasing wind.
If she felt the bitter cold, there on the exposed Hyrkanian plain, she showed no sign of it.
Her withered hands cast noxious powders into the guttering flames, her lips hissed words unknown to man for a score of lifetimes and more --
-- and her eyes fastened, glittering and greedy, on the images that formed in the flame before her.
Her name, even her race, were lost to antiquity. Those who spoke of her merely called her the Bone Woman.
And when they did speak of her, it was with unease and fear.

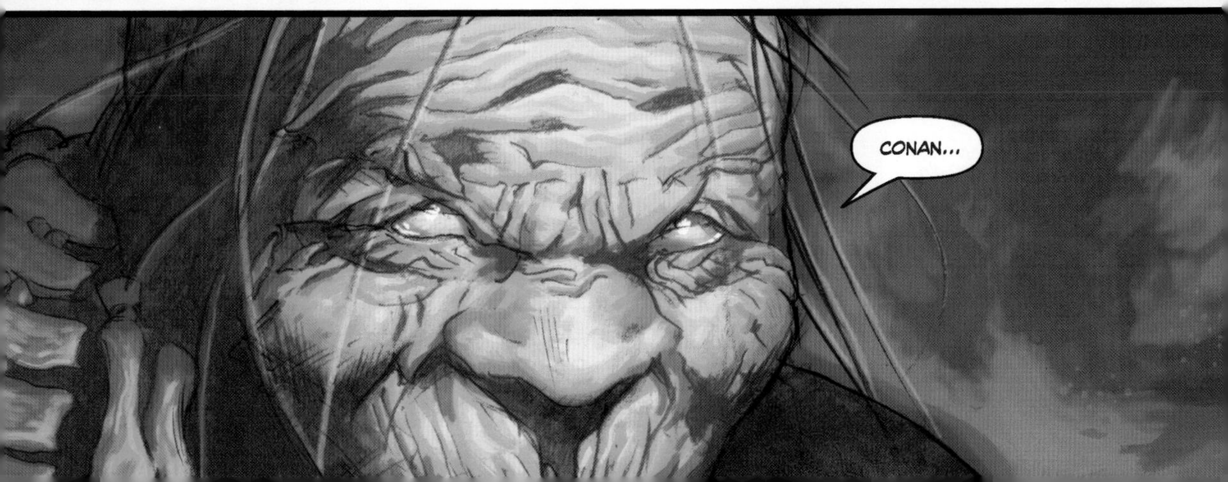
CONAN...

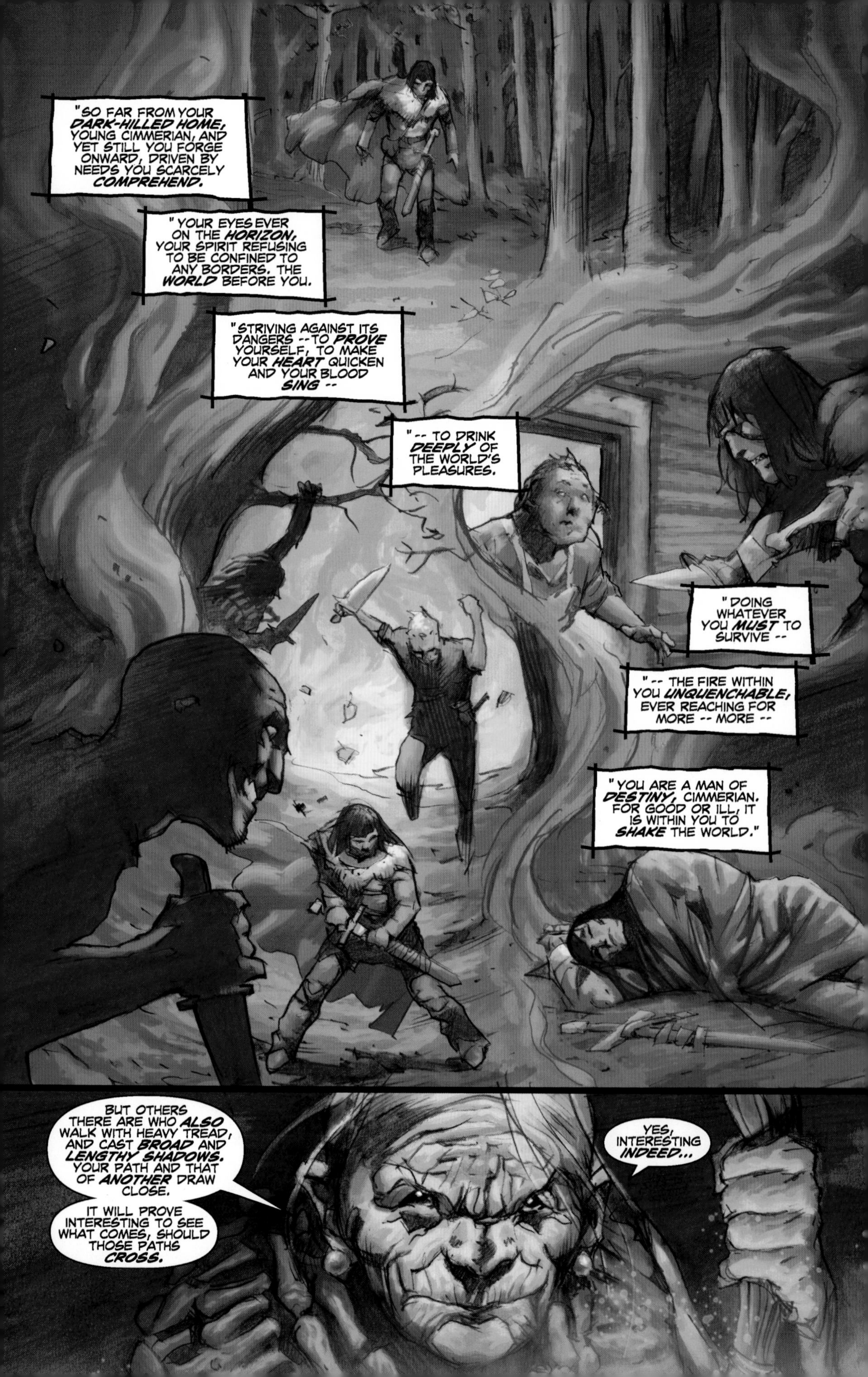
"SO FAR FROM YOUR DARK-HILLED HOME, YOUNG CIMMERIAN, AND YET STILL YOU FORGE ONWARD, DRIVEN BY NEEDS YOU SCARCELY COMPREHEND.
"YOUR EYES EVER ON THE HORIZON, YOUR SPIRIT REFUSING TO BE CONFINED TO ANY BORDERS. THE WORLD BEFORE YOU.
"STRIVING AGAINST ITS DANGERS --TO PROVE YOURSELF, TO MAKE YOUR HEART QUICKEN AND YOUR BLOOD SING --
"-- TO DRINK DEEPLY OF THE WORLD'S PLEASURES.
"DOING WHATEVER YOU MUST TO SURVIVE --
"-- THE FIRE WITHIN YOU UNQUENCHABLE, EVER REACHING FOR MORE -- MORE --
"YOU ARE A MAN OF DESTINY, CIMMERIAN. FOR GOOD OR ILL, IT IS WITHIN YOU TO SHAKE THE WORLD."
BUT OTHERS THERE ARE WHO ALSO WALK WITH HEAVY TREAD, AND CAST BROAD AND LENGTHY SHADOWS. YOUR PATH AND THAT OF ANOTHER DRAW CLOSE.
IT WILL PROVE INTERESTING TO SEE WHAT COMES, SHOULD THOSE PATHS CROSS.
YES, INTERESTING INDEED...

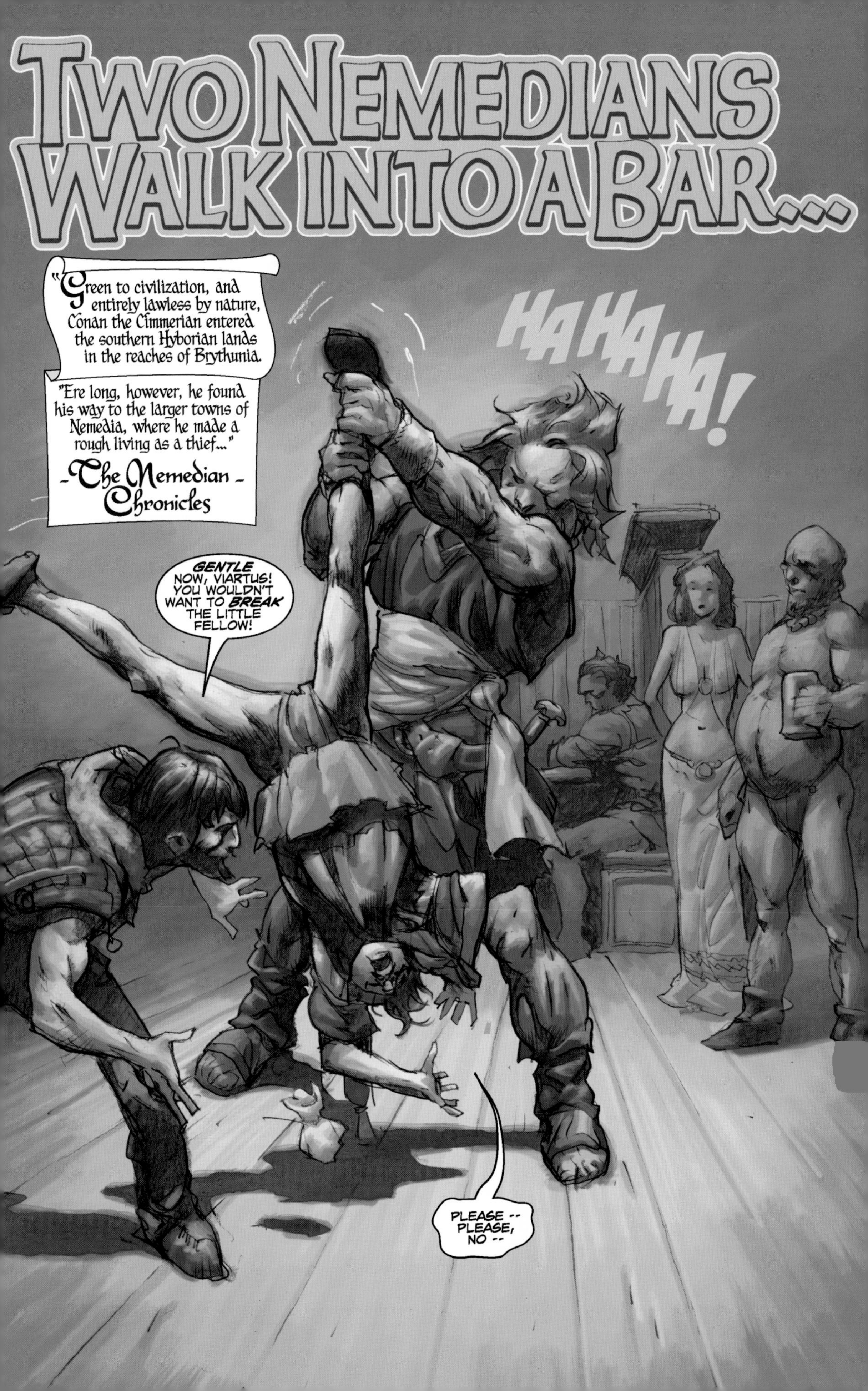
TWO NEMEDIANS WALK INTO A BAR...
"Green to civilization, and entirely lawless by nature, Conan the Cimmerian entered the southern Hyborian lands in the reaches of Brythunia.
"Ere long, however, he found his way to the larger towns of Nemedia, where he made a rough living as a thief..."
-The Nemedian Chronicles-
HA HA HA HA!
GENTLE NOW, VIARTUS! YOU WOULDN'T WANT TO BREAK THE LITTLE FELLOW!
PLEASE -- PLEASE, NO --

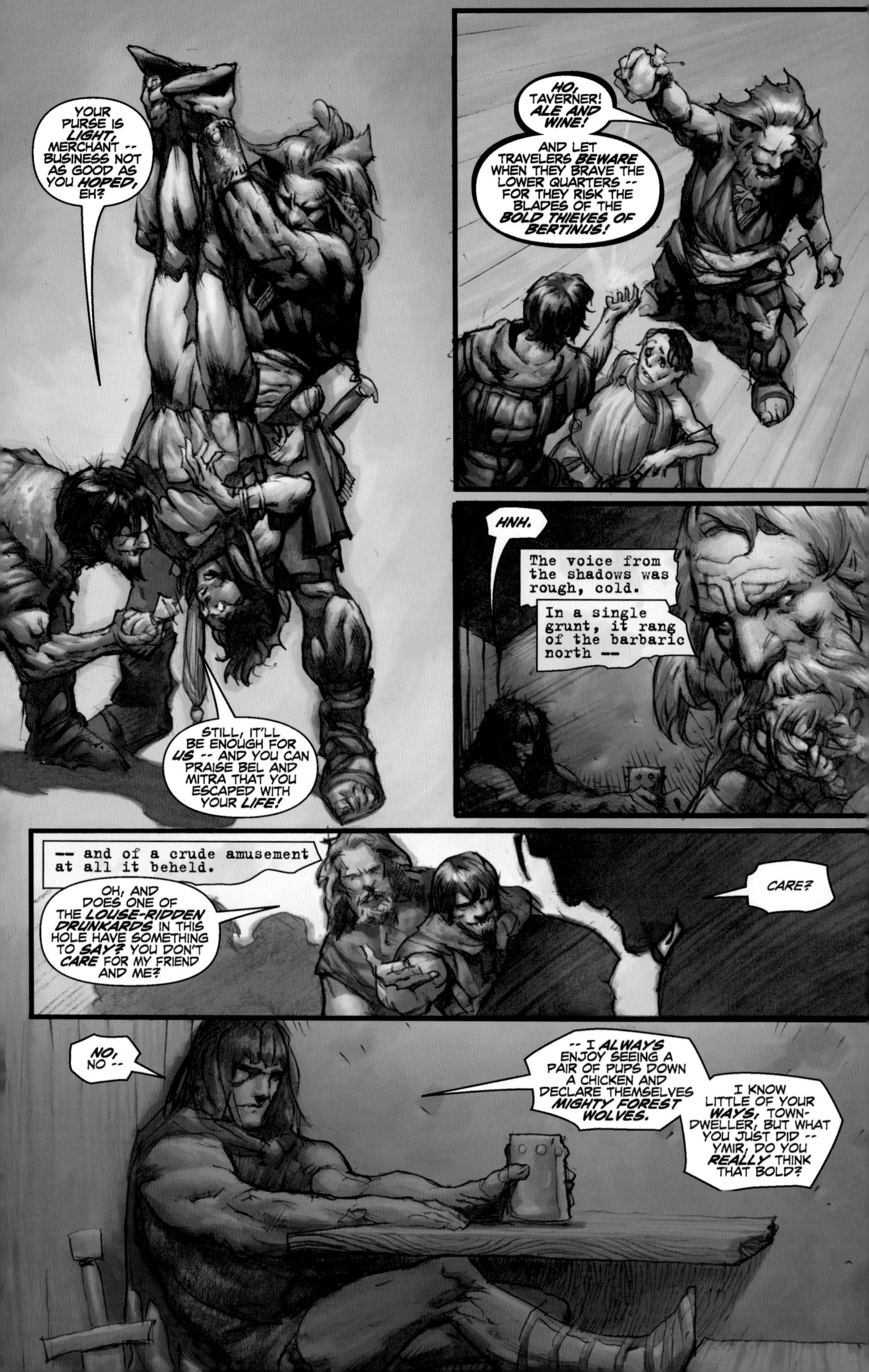
YOUR PURSE IS LIGHT, MERCHANT -- BUSINESS NOT AS GOOD AS YOU HOPED, EH?
STILL, IT'LL BE ENOUGH FOR US -- AND YOU CAN PRAISE BEL AND MITRA THAT YOU ESCAPED WITH YOUR LIFE!
HO, TAVERNER! ALE AND WINE!
AND LET TRAVELERS BEWARE WHEN THEY BRAVE THE LOWER QUARTERS -- FOR THEY RISK THE BLADES OF THE BOLD THIEVES OF BERTINUS!
HNH.
The voice from the shadows was rough, cold.
In a single grunt, it rang of the barbaric north --
-- and of a crude amusement at all it beheld.
OH, AND DOES ONE OF THE LOUSE-RIDDEN DRUNKARDS IN THIS HOLE HAVE SOMETHING TO SAY? YOU DON'T CARE FOR MY FRIEND AND ME?
CARE?
NO, NO --
-- I ALWAYS ENJOY SEEING A PAIR OF PUPS DOWN A CHICKEN AND DECLARE THEMSELVES MIGHTY FOREST WOLVES.
I KNOW LITTLE OF YOUR WAYS, TOWN-DWELLER, BUT WHAT YOU JUST DID -- YMIR, DO YOU REALLY THINK THAT BOLD?

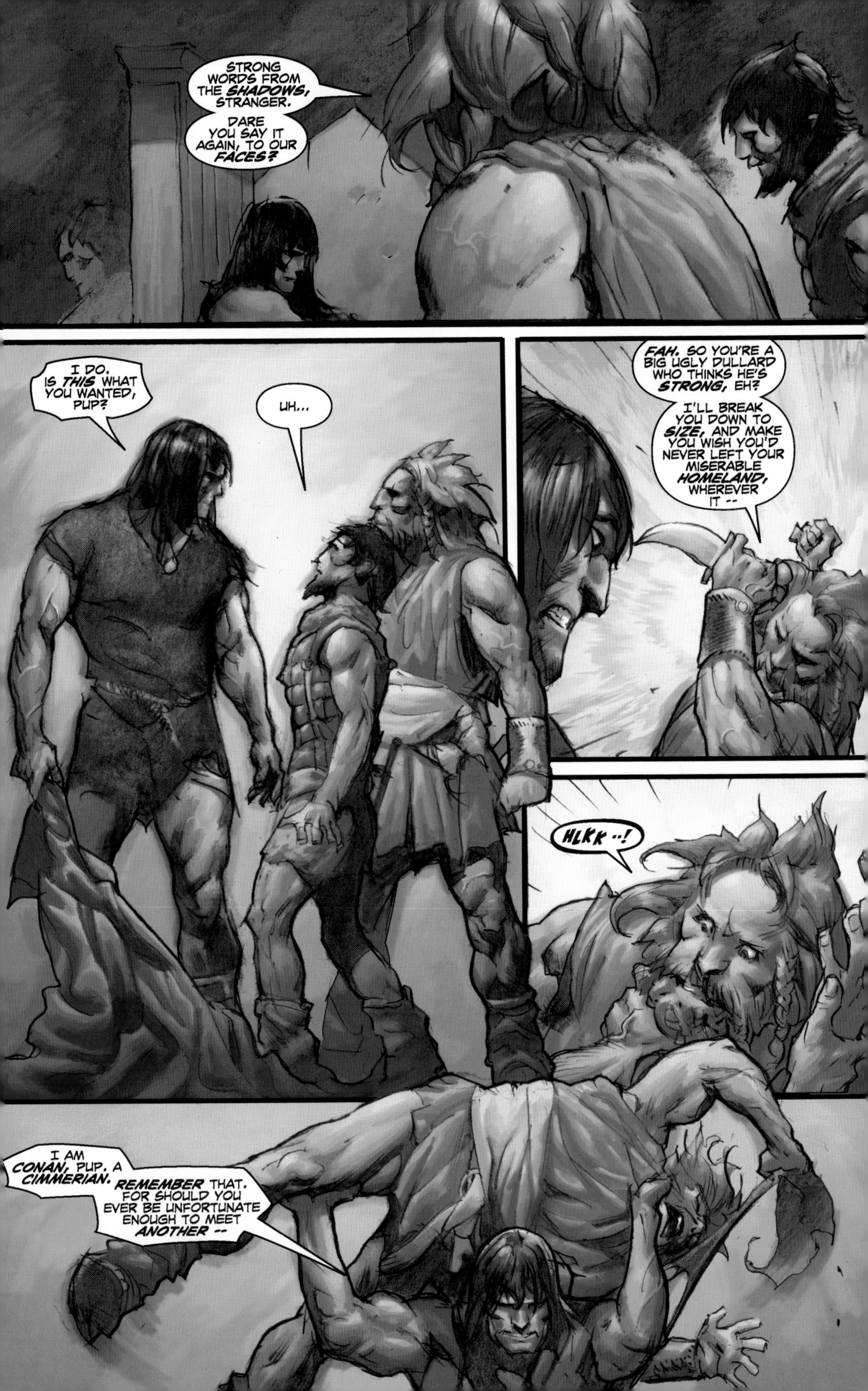

STRONG WORDS FROM THE SHADOWS, STRANGER.
DARE YOU SAY IT AGAIN, TO OUR FACES?
I DO. IS THIS WHAT YOU WANTED, PUP?
UH...
FAH. SO YOU'RE A BIG UGLY DULLARD WHO THINKS HE'S STRONG, EH?
I'LL BREAK YOU DOWN TO SIZE, AND MAKE YOU WISH YOU'D NEVER LEFT YOUR MISERABLE HOMELAND, WHEREVER IT --
HLKK --!
I AM CONAN, PUP. A CIMMERIAN.
REMEMBER THAT. FOR SHOULD YOU EVER BE UNFORTUNATE ENOUGH TO MEET ANOTHER --

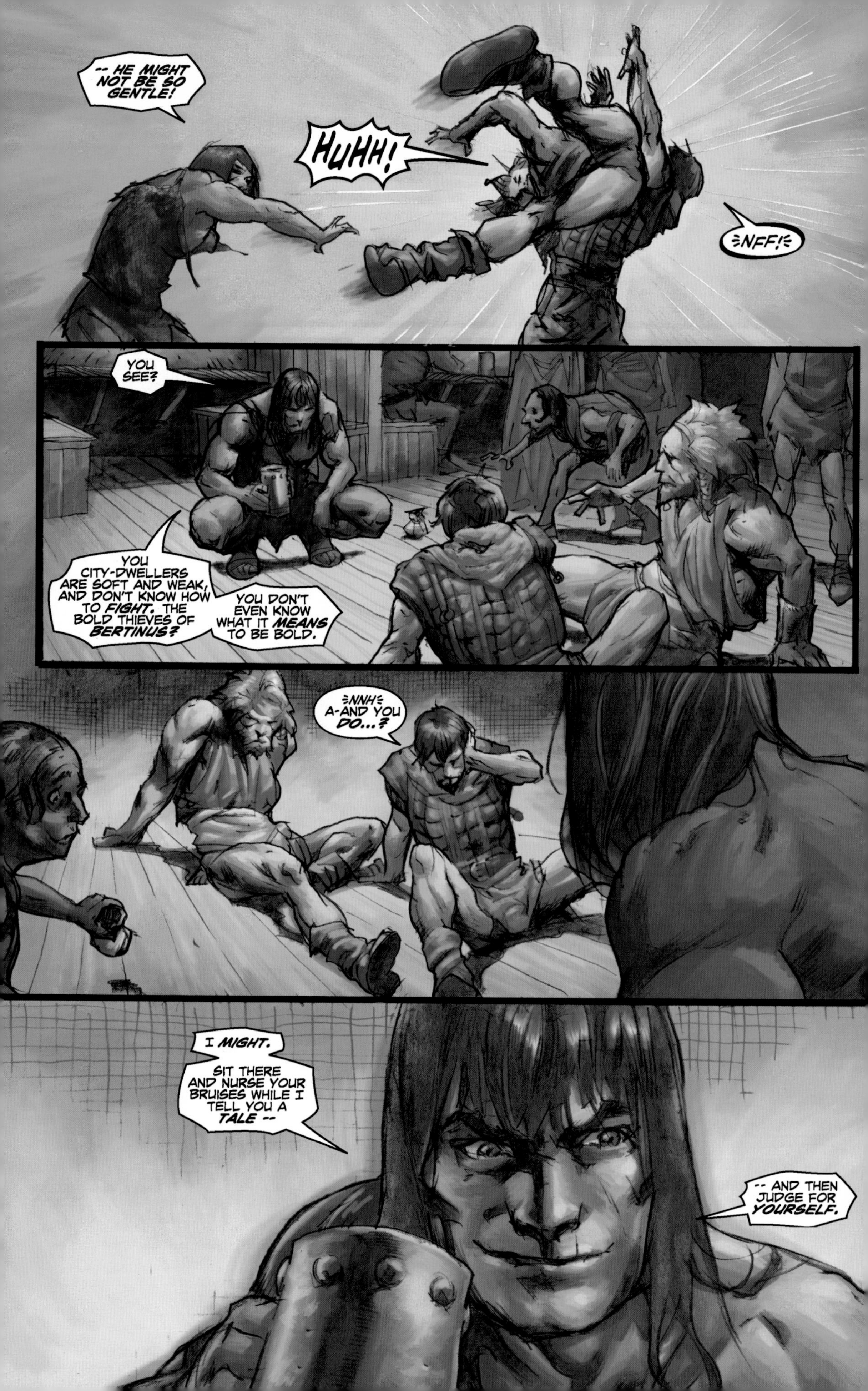
-- HE MIGHT NOT BE SO GENTLE!
HUHH!
NFF!
YOU SEE?
YOU CITY-DWELLERS ARE SOFT AND WEAK, AND DON'T KNOW HOW TO FIGHT. THE BOLD THIEVES OF BERTINUS?
YOU DON'T EVEN KNOW WHAT IT MEANS TO BE BOLD.
NNH A-AND YOU DO...?
I MIGHT.
SIT THERE AND NURSE YOUR BRUISES WHILE I TELL YOU A TALE --
-- AND THEN JUDGE FOR YOURSELF.

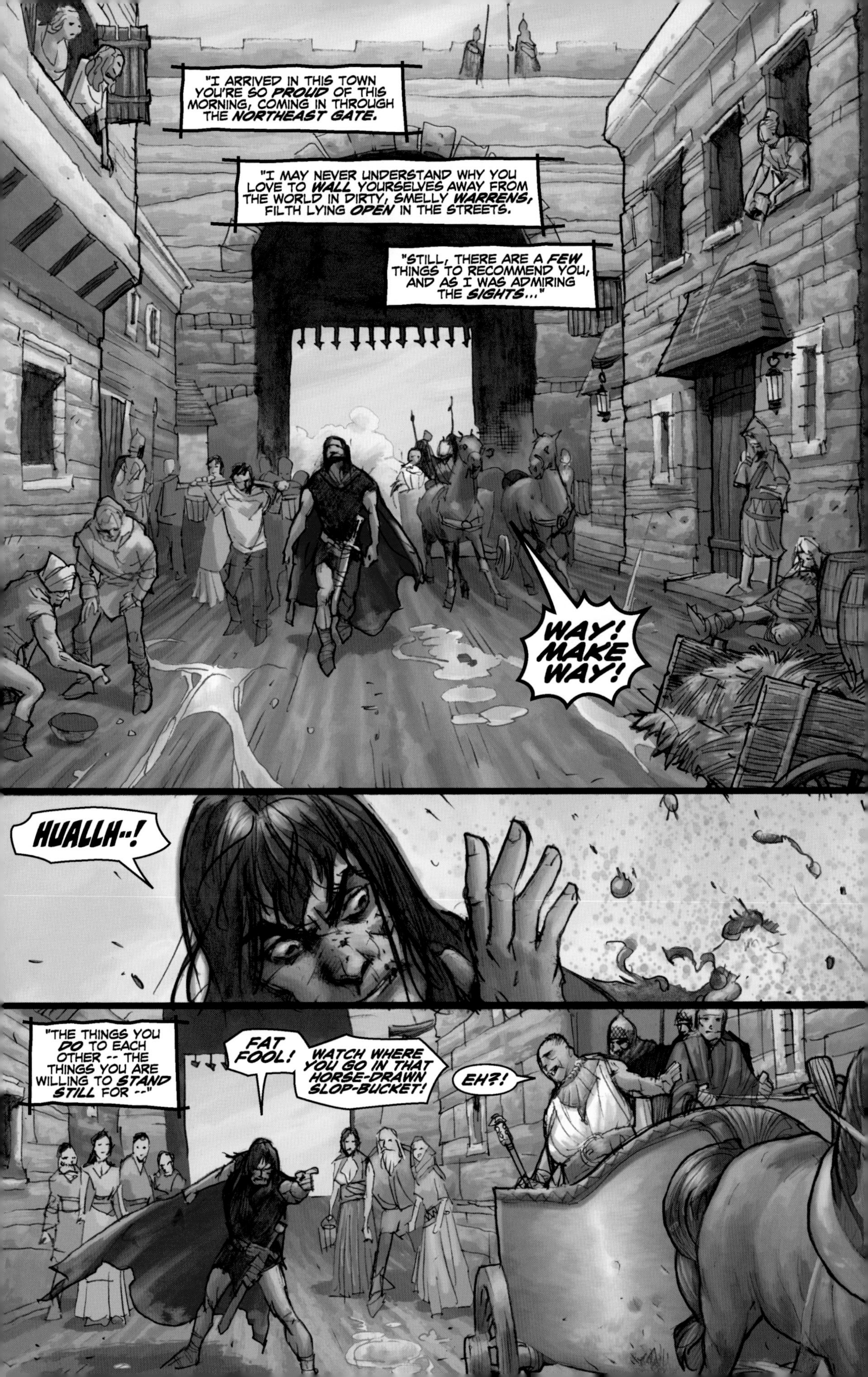
"I ARRIVED IN THIS TOWN YOU'RE SO PROUD OF THIS MORNING, COMING IN THROUGH THE NORTHEAST GATE.
"I MAY NEVER UNDERSTAND WHY YOU LOVE TO WALL YOURSELVES AWAY FROM THE WORLD IN DIRTY, SMELLY WARRENS, FILTH LYING OPEN IN THE STREETS.
"STILL, THERE ARE A FEW THINGS TO RECOMMEND YOU, AND AS I WAS ADMIRING THE SIGHTS..."
WAY! MAKE WAY!
HUALLH--!
"THE THINGS YOU DO TO EACH OTHER -- THE THINGS YOU ARE WILLING TO STAND STILL FOR --"
FAT FOOL!
WATCH WHERE YOU GO IN THAT HORSE-DRAWN SLOP-BUCKET!
EH?!

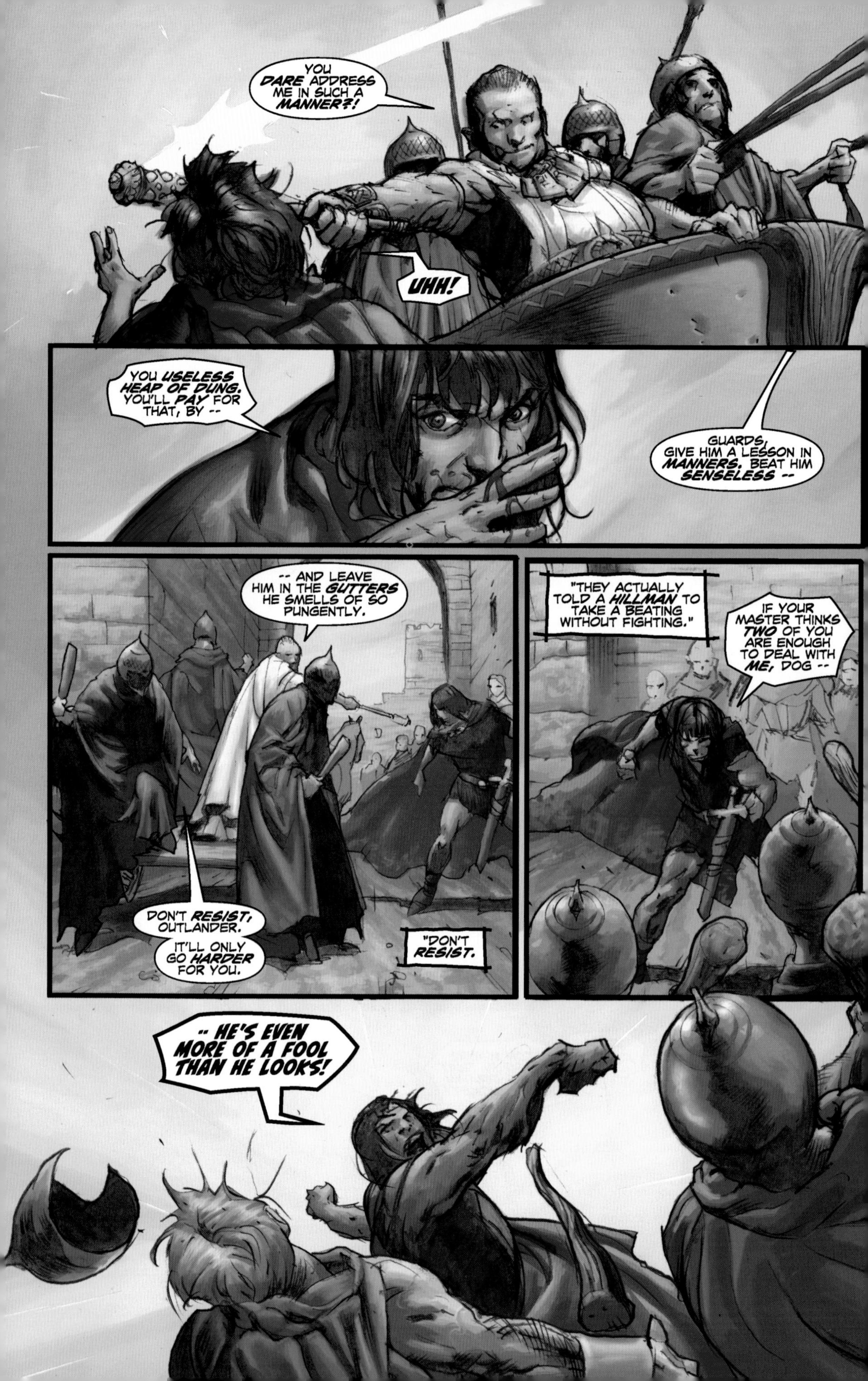
YOU DARE ADDRESS ME IN SUCH A MANNER?!
UHH!
YOU USELESS HEAP OF DUNG. YOU'LL PAY FOR THAT, BY --
GUARDS, GIVE HIM A LESSON IN MANNERS. BEAT HIM SENSELESS --
-- AND LEAVE HIM IN THE GUTTERS HE SMELLS OF SO PUNGENTLY.
DON'T RESIST, OUTLANDER.
IT'LL ONLY GO HARDER FOR YOU.
"DON'T RESIST.
"THEY ACTUALLY TOLD A HILLMAN TO TAKE A BEATING WITHOUT FIGHTING."
IF YOUR MASTER THINKS TWO OF YOU ARE ENOUGH TO DEAL WITH ME, DOG --
-- HE'S EVEN MORE OF A FOOL THAN HE LOOKS!

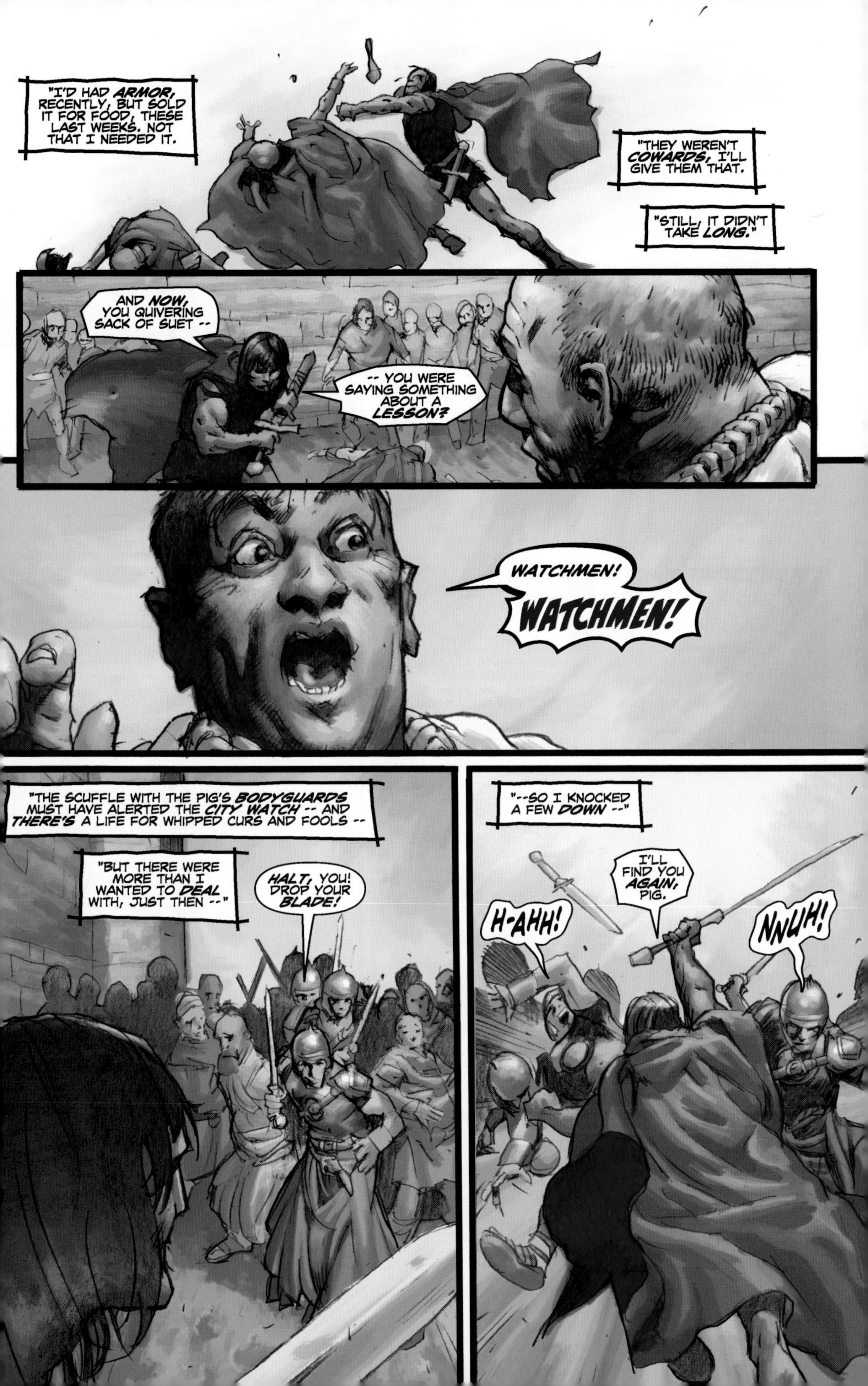
"I'D HAD ARMOR, RECENTLY, BUT SOLD IT FOR FOOD, THESE LAST WEEKS. NOT THAT I NEEDED IT.
"THEY WEREN'T COWARDS, I'LL GIVE THEM THAT.
"STILL, IT DIDN'T TAKE LONG."
AND NOW, YOU QUIVERING SACK OF SUET --
-- YOU WERE SAYING SOMETHING ABOUT A LESSON?
WATCHMEN!
WATCHMEN!
"THE SCUFFLE WITH THE PIG'S BODYGUARDS MUST HAVE ALERTED THE CITY WATCH -- AND THERE'S A LIFE FOR WHIPPED CURS AND FOOLS --
"BUT THERE WERE MORE THAN I WANTED TO DEAL WITH, JUST THEN --"
HALT, YOU! DROP YOUR BLADE!
"--SO I KNOCKED A FEW DOWN --"
I'LL FIND YOU AGAIN, PIG.
H-AHH!
NNUH!

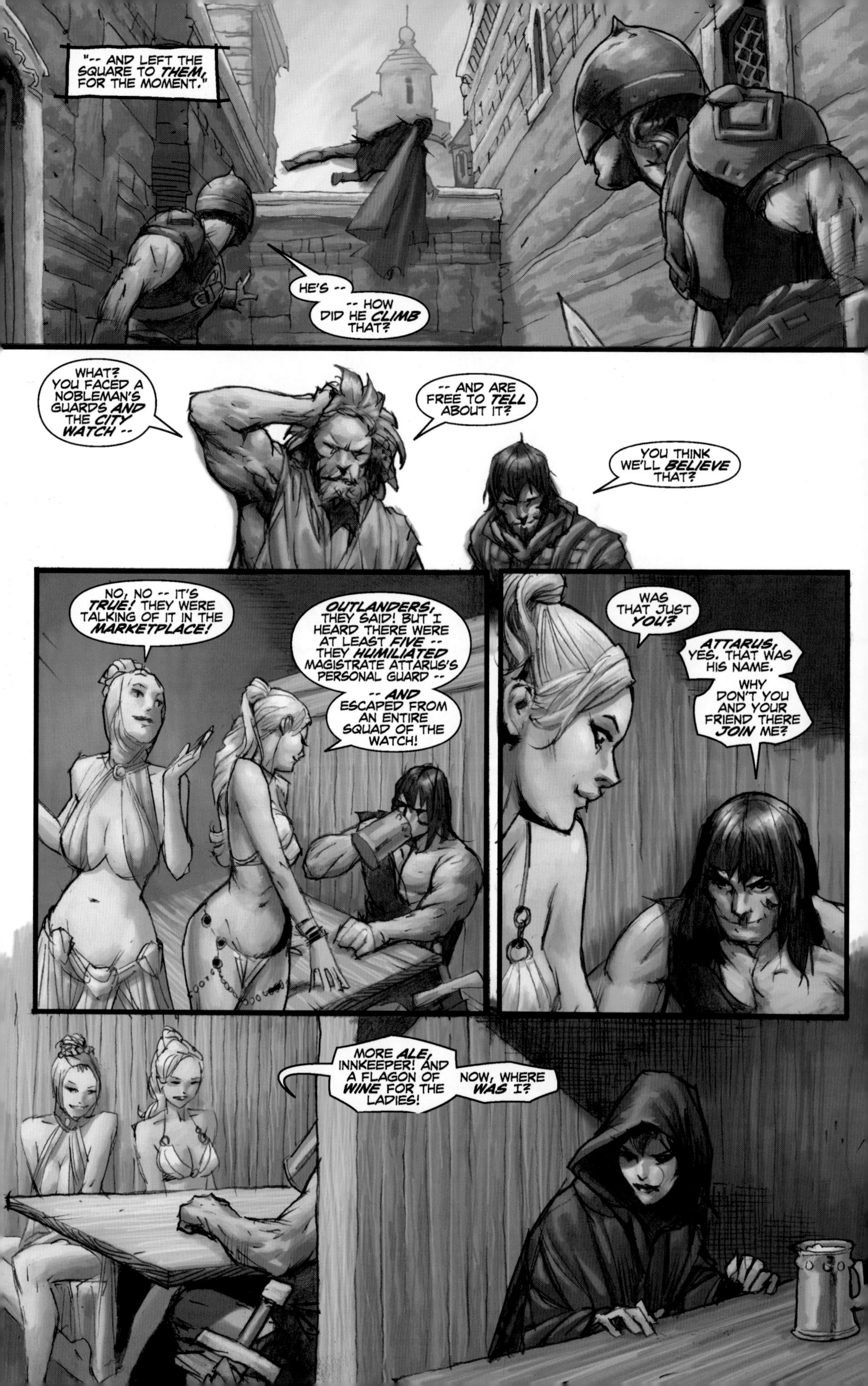
"-- AND LEFT THE SQUARE TO *THEM*, FOR THE MOMENT."
HE'S --
-- HOW DID HE *CLIMB* THAT?
WHAT? YOU FACED A NOBLEMAN'S GUARDS *AND* THE *CITY WATCH* --
-- AND ARE FREE TO *TELL* ABOUT IT?
YOU THINK WE'LL *BELIEVE* THAT?
NO, NO -- IT'S *TRUE!* THEY WERE TALKING OF IT IN THE *MARKETPLACE!*
OUTLANDERS, THEY SAID! BUT I HEARD THERE WERE AT LEAST *FIVE* -- THEY *HUMILIATED* MAGISTRATE ATTARUS'S PERSONAL GUARD --
-- *AND* ESCAPED FROM AN ENTIRE SQUAD OF THE WATCH!
WAS THAT JUST *YOU?*
ATTARUS, YES. THAT WAS HIS NAME.
WHY DON'T YOU AND YOUR FRIEND THERE *JOIN* ME?
MORE *ALE,* INNKEEPER! AND A FLAGON OF *WINE* FOR THE LADIES!
NOW, WHERE *WAS* I?

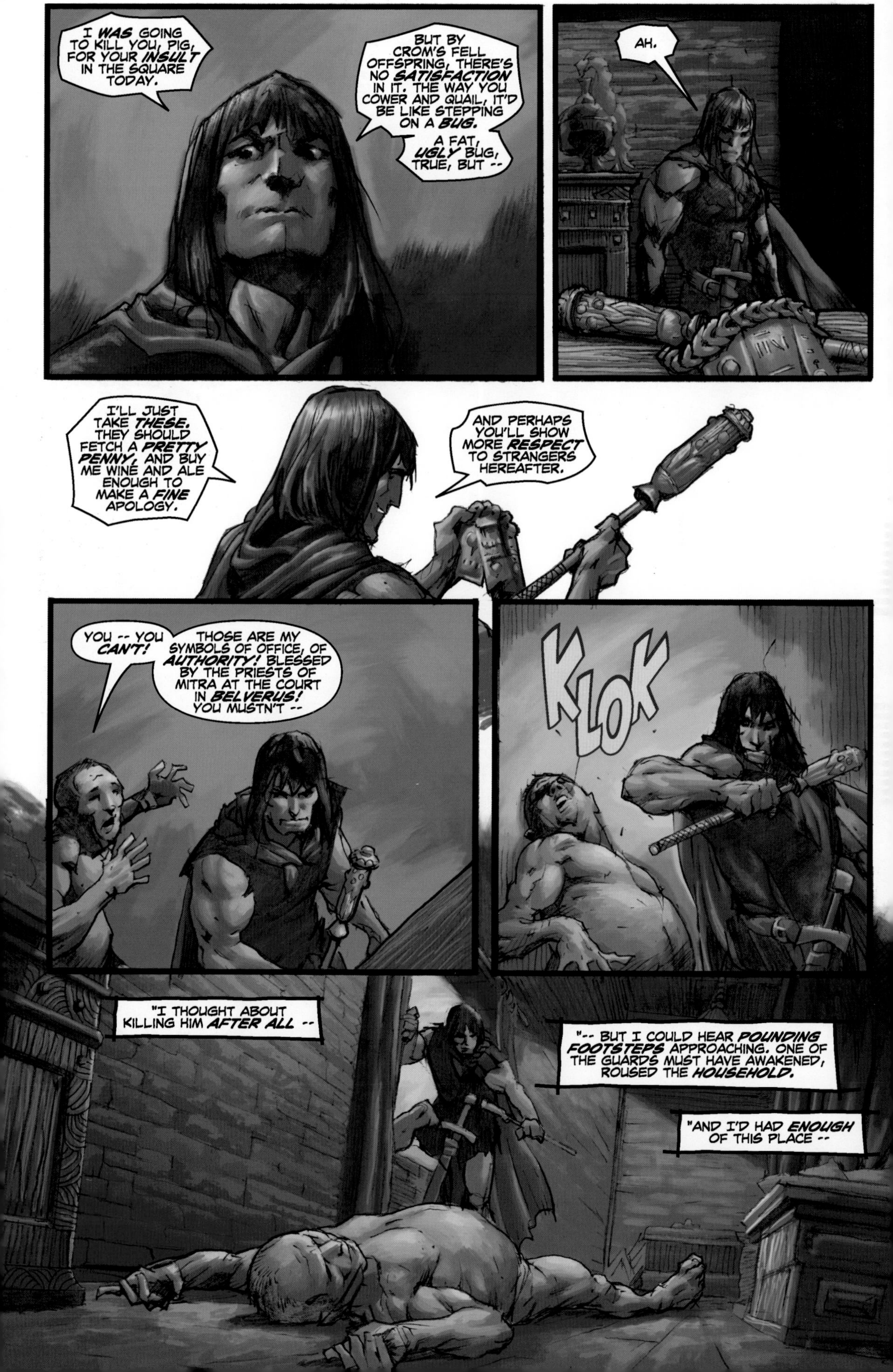
I WAS GOING TO KILL YOU, PIG, FOR YOUR INSULT IN THE SQUARE TODAY.
BUT BY CROM'S FELL OFFSPRING, THERE'S NO SATISFACTION IN IT. THE WAY YOU COWER AND QUAIL, IT'D BE LIKE STEPPING ON A BUG.
A FAT, UGLY BUG, TRUE, BUT --
AH.
I'LL JUST TAKE THESE. THEY SHOULD FETCH A PRETTY PENNY, AND BUY ME WINE AND ALE ENOUGH TO MAKE A FINE APOLOGY.
AND PERHAPS YOU'LL SHOW MORE RESPECT TO STRANGERS HEREAFTER.
YOU -- YOU CAN'T!
THOSE ARE MY SYMBOLS OF OFFICE, OF AUTHORITY! BLESSED BY THE PRIESTS OF MITRA AT THE COURT IN BELVERUS! YOU MUSTN'T --
KLOK
"I THOUGHT ABOUT KILLING HIM AFTER ALL --
"-- BUT I COULD HEAR POUNDING FOOTSTEPS APPROACHING. ONE OF THE GUARDS MUST HAVE AWAKENED, ROUSED THE HOUSEHOLD.
"AND I'D HAD ENOUGH OF THIS PLACE --

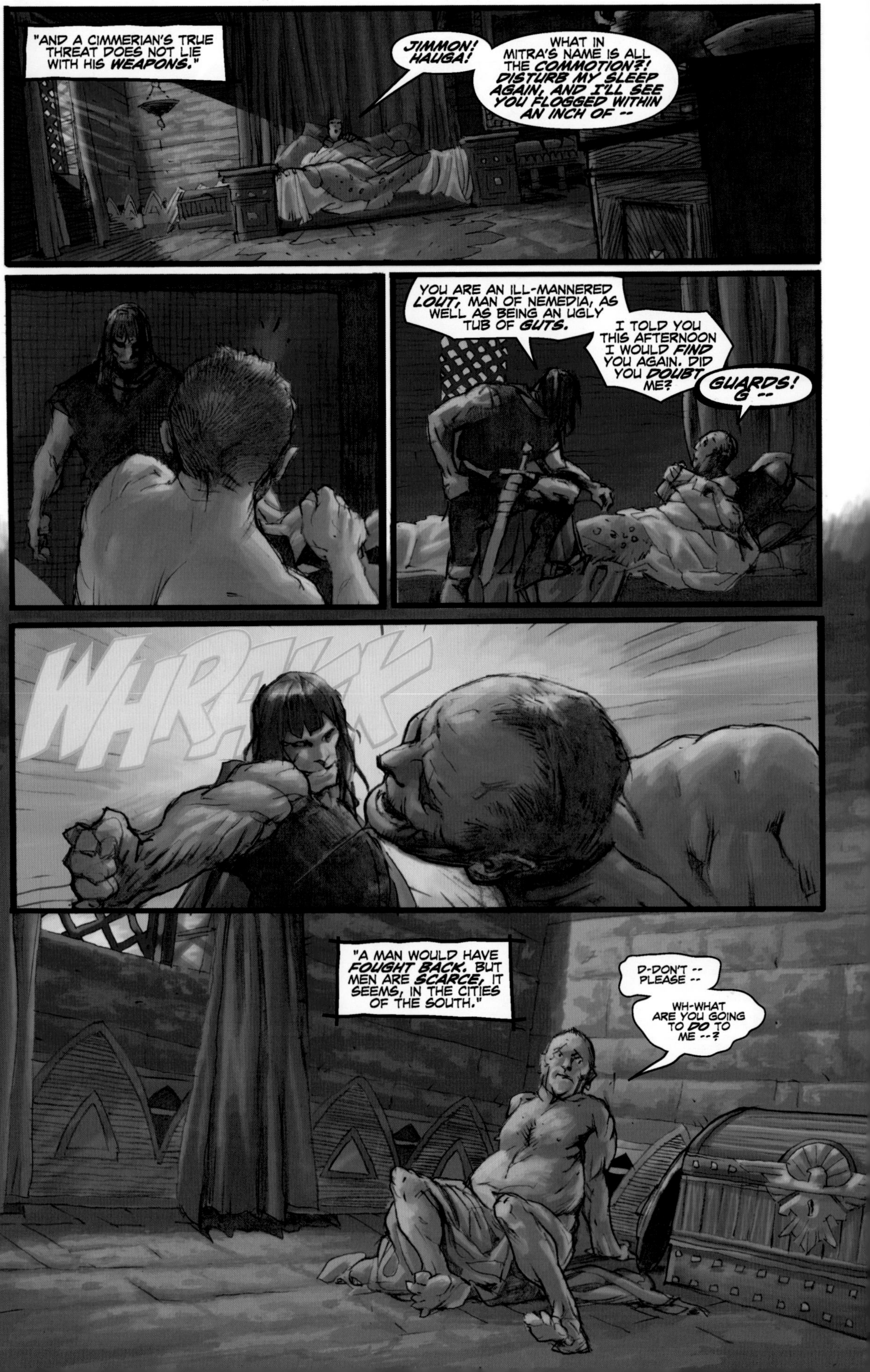
"AND A CIMMERIAN'S TRUE THREAT DOES NOT LIE WITH HIS *WEAPONS.*"
JIMMON! HAUGA!
WHAT IN MITRA'S NAME IS ALL THE *COMMOTION?! DISTURB MY SLEEP AGAIN, AND I'LL SEE YOU FLOGGED WITHIN AN INCH OF --*
YOU ARE AN ILL-MANNERED *LOUT,* MAN OF NEMEDIA, AS WELL AS BEING AN UGLY TUB OF *GUTS.*
I TOLD YOU THIS AFTERNOON I WOULD *FIND* YOU AGAIN. DID YOU *DOUBT* ME?
GUARDS! G --
WHRAKK
"A MAN WOULD HAVE *FOUGHT BACK.* BUT MEN ARE *SCARCE,* IT SEEMS, IN THE CITIES OF THE SOUTH."
D-DON'T -- PLEASE --
WH-WHAT ARE YOU GOING TO *DO* TO ME --?

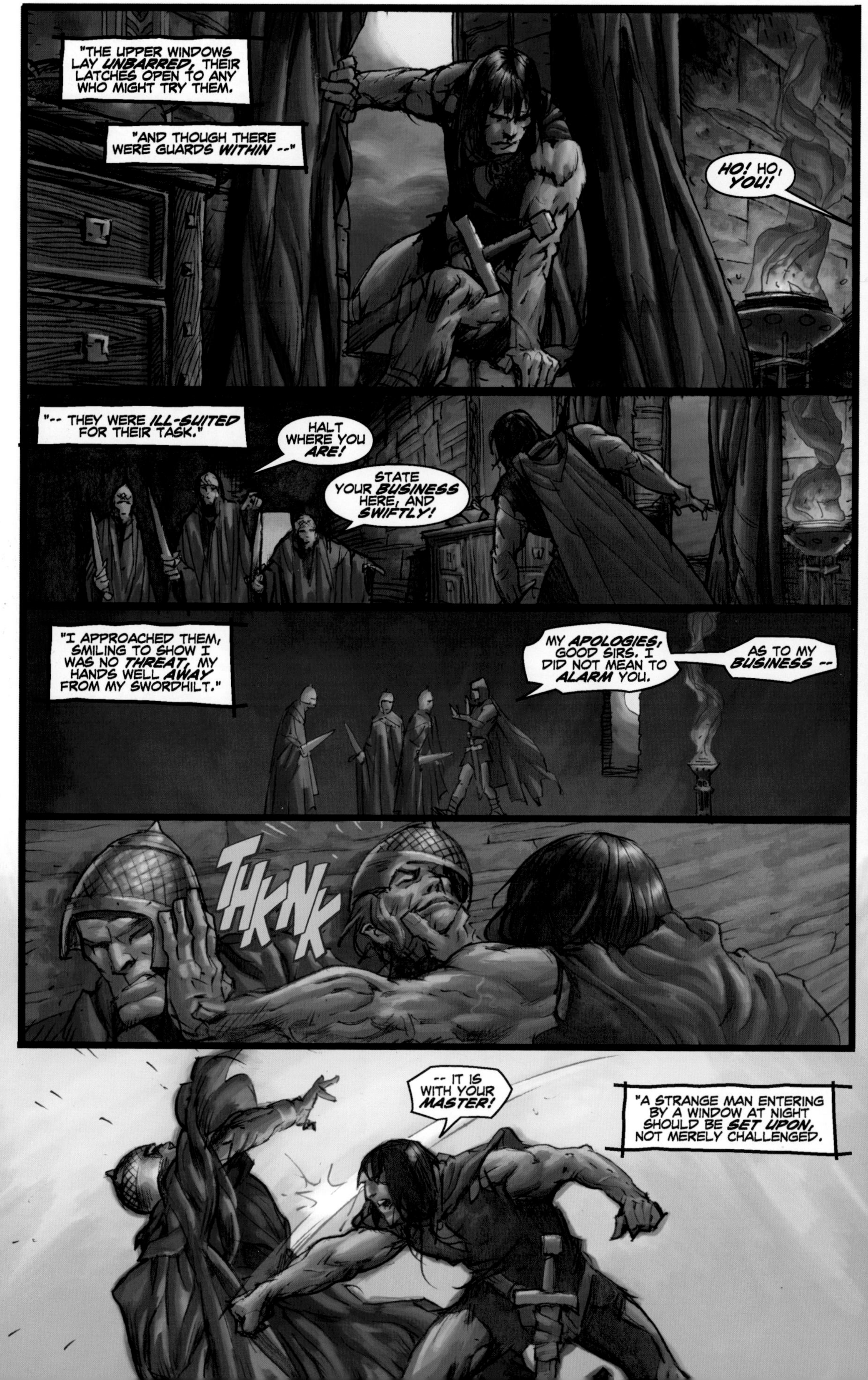
"THE UPPER WINDOWS LAY UNBARRED, THEIR LATCHES OPEN TO ANY WHO MIGHT TRY THEM.
"AND THOUGH THERE WERE GUARDS WITHIN --"
HO! HO, YOU!
"-- THEY WERE ILL-SUITED FOR THEIR TASK."
HALT WHERE YOU ARE!
STATE YOUR BUSINESS HERE, AND SWIFTLY!
"I APPROACHED THEM, SMILING TO SHOW I WAS NO THREAT, MY HANDS WELL AWAY FROM MY SWORDHILT."
MY APOLOGIES, GOOD SIRS. I DID NOT MEAN TO ALARM YOU.
AS TO MY BUSINESS --
THKNK
-- IT IS WITH YOUR MASTER!
"A STRANGE MAN ENTERING BY A WINDOW AT NIGHT SHOULD BE SET UPON, NOT MERELY CHALLENGED.

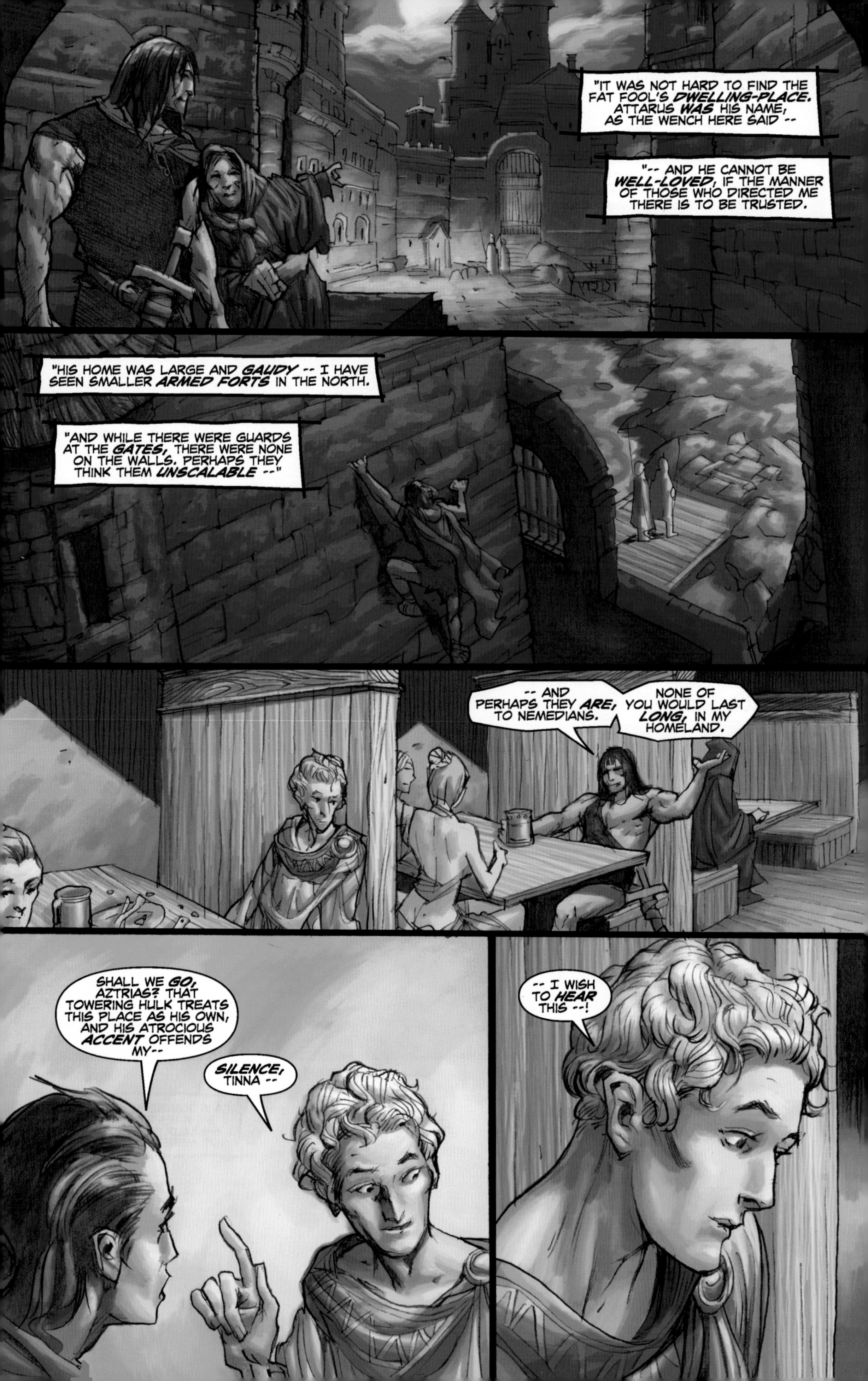
"IT WAS NOT HARD TO FIND THE FAT FOOL'S DWELLING-PLACE. ATTARUS WAS HIS NAME, AS THE WENCH HERE SAID --
"-- AND HE CANNOT BE WELL-LOVED, IF THE MANNER OF THOSE WHO DIRECTED ME THERE IS TO BE TRUSTED.
"HIS HOME WAS LARGE AND GAUDY -- I HAVE SEEN SMALLER ARMED FORTS IN THE NORTH.
"AND WHILE THERE WERE GUARDS AT THE GATES, THERE WERE NONE ON THE WALLS. PERHAPS THEY THINK THEM UNSCALABLE --"
-- AND PERHAPS THEY ARE, TO NEMEDIANS.
NONE OF YOU WOULD LAST LONG, IN MY HOMELAND.
SHALL WE GO, AZTRIAS? THAT TOWERING HULK TREATS THIS PLACE AS HIS OWN, AND HIS ATROCIOUS ACCENT OFFENDS MY--
SILENCE, TINNA --
-- I WISH TO HEAR THIS --!

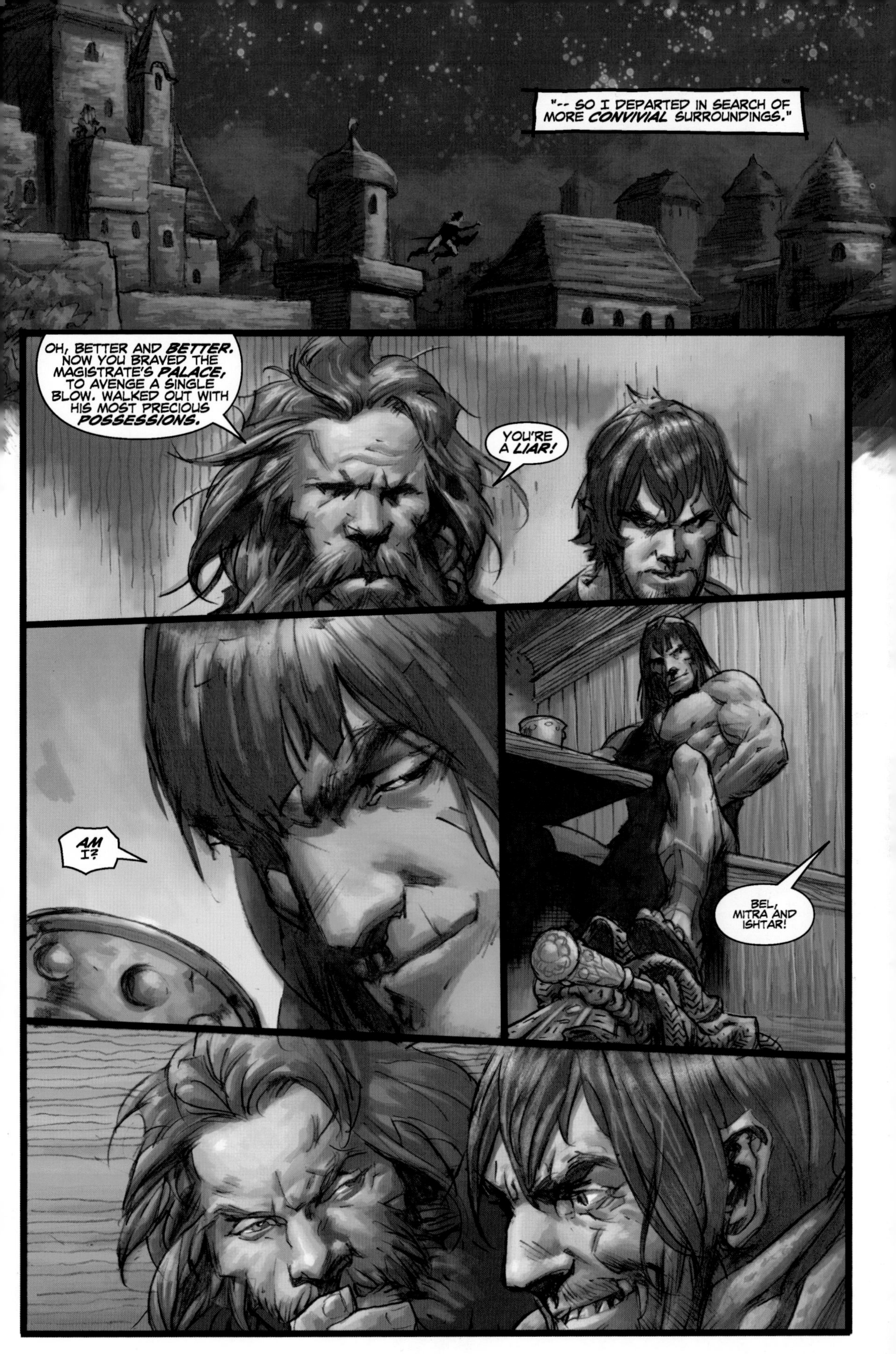
"-- SO I DEPARTED IN SEARCH OF MORE CONVIVIAL SURROUNDINGS."
OH, BETTER AND BETTER. NOW YOU BRAVED THE MAGISTRATE'S PALACE, TO AVENGE A SINGLE BLOW. WALKED OUT WITH HIS MOST PRECIOUS POSSESSIONS.
YOU'RE A LIAR!
AM I?
BEL, MITRA AND ISHTAR!

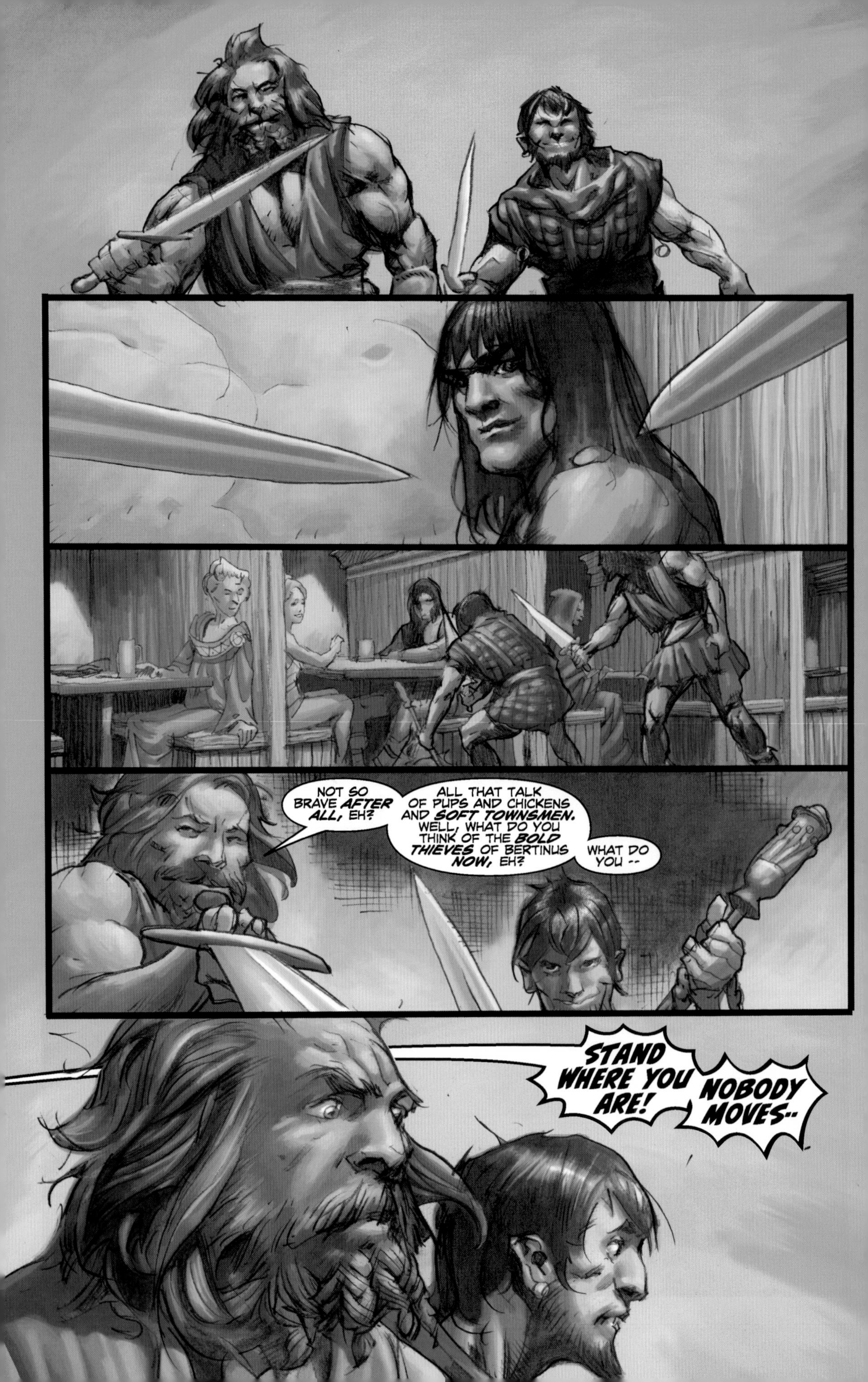

NOT SO BRAVE AFTER ALL, EH?
ALL THAT TALK OF PUPS AND CHICKENS AND SOFT TOWNSMEN. WELL, WHAT DO YOU THINK OF THE BOLD THIEVES OF BERTINUS NOW, EH?
WHAT DO YOU --
STAND WHERE YOU ARE!
NOBODY MOVES--

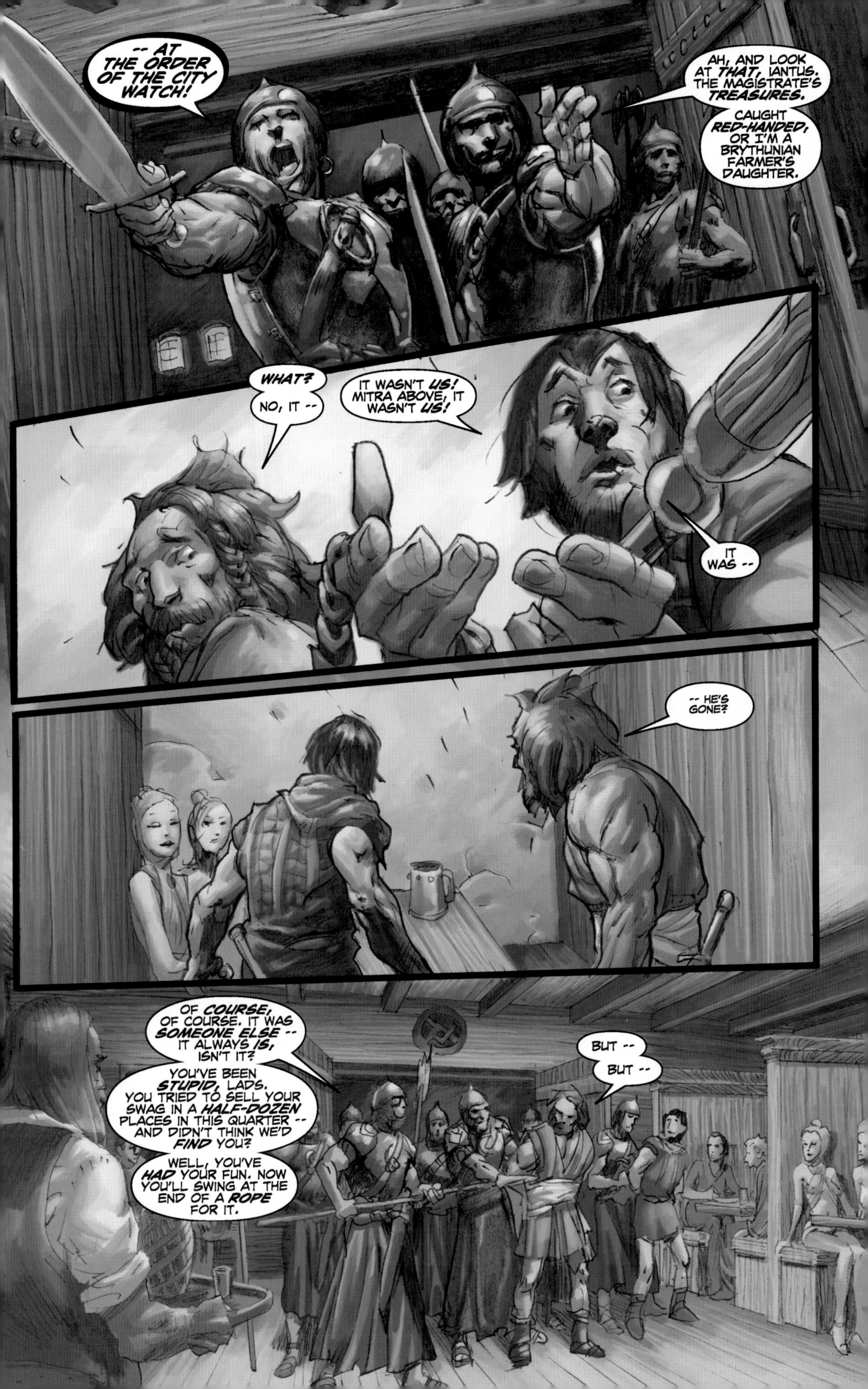
-- AT THE ORDER OF THE CITY WATCH!
AH, AND LOOK AT THAT, IANTUS. THE MAGISTRATE'S TREASURES.
CAUGHT RED-HANDED, OR I'M A BRYTHUNIAN FARMER'S DAUGHTER.
WHAT?
NO, IT --
IT WASN'T US! MITRA ABOVE, IT WASN'T US!
IT WAS --
-- HE'S GONE?
OF COURSE, OF COURSE. IT WAS SOMEONE ELSE -- IT ALWAYS IS, ISN'T IT?
YOU'VE BEEN STUPID, LADS. YOU TRIED TO SELL YOUR SWAG IN A HALF-DOZEN PLACES IN THIS QUARTER -- AND DIDN'T THINK WE'D FIND YOU?
WELL, YOU'VE HAD YOUR FUN. NOW YOU'LL SWING AT THE END OF A ROPE FOR IT.
BUT --
BUT --

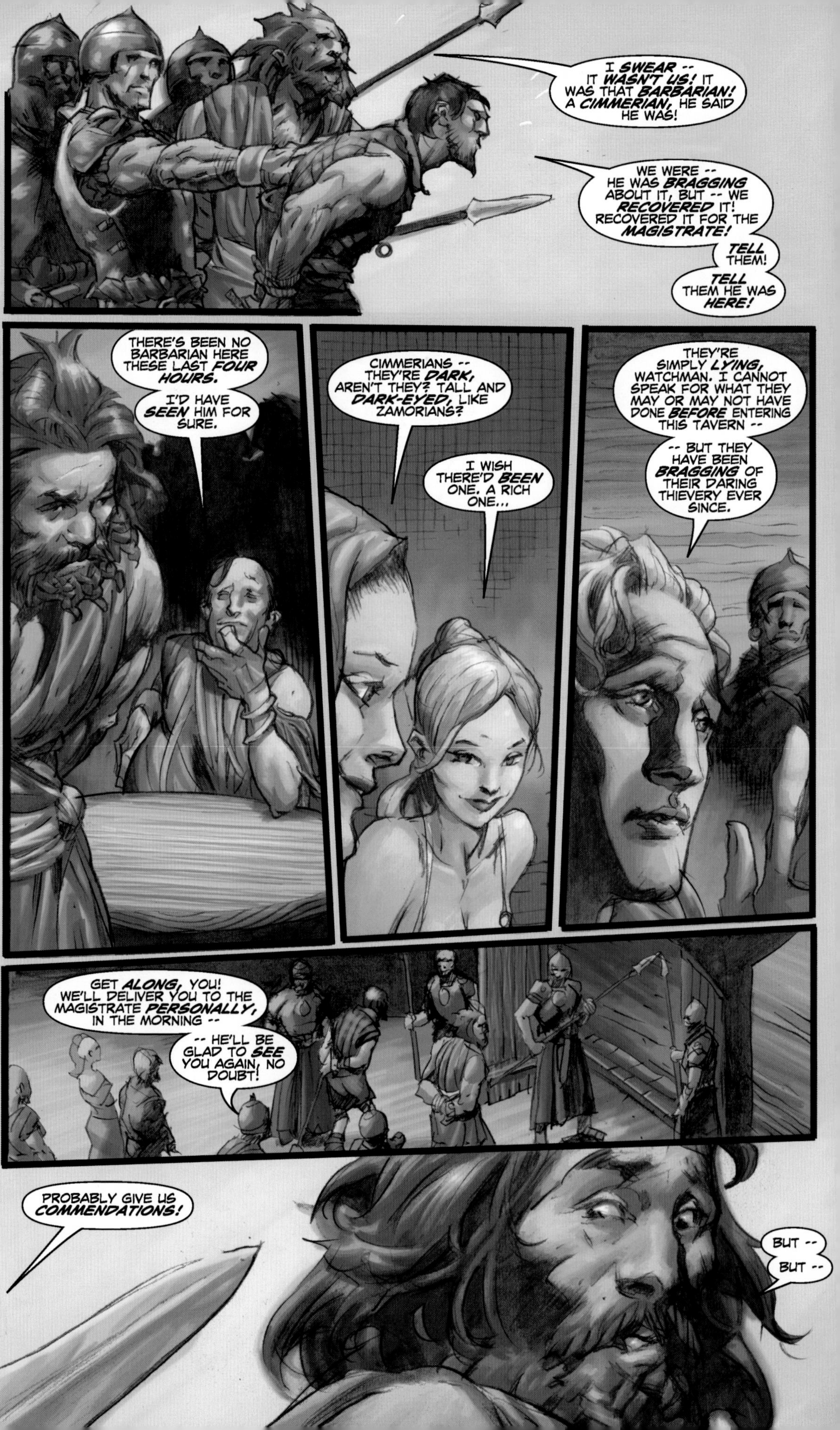
I SWEAR -- IT WASN'T US! IT WAS THAT BARBARIAN! A CIMMERIAN, HE SAID HE WAS!
WE WERE -- HE WAS BRAGGING ABOUT IT, BUT -- WE RECOVERED IT! RECOVERED IT FOR THE MAGISTRATE!
TELL THEM!
TELL THEM HE WAS HERE!
THERE'S BEEN NO BARBARIAN HERE THESE LAST FOUR HOURS.
I'D HAVE SEEN HIM FOR SURE.
CIMMERIANS -- THEY'RE DARK, AREN'T THEY? TALL AND DARK-EYED, LIKE ZAMORIANS?
I WISH THERE'D BEEN ONE. A RICH ONE...
THEY'RE SIMPLY LYING, WATCHMAN. I CANNOT SPEAK FOR WHAT THEY MAY OR MAY NOT HAVE DONE BEFORE ENTERING THIS TAVERN --
-- BUT THEY HAVE BEEN BRAGGING OF THEIR DARING THIEVERY EVER SINCE.
GET ALONG, YOU! WE'LL DELIVER YOU TO THE MAGISTRATE PERSONALLY, IN THE MORNING --
-- HE'LL BE GLAD TO SEE YOU AGAIN, NO DOUBT!
PROBABLY GIVE US COMMENDATIONS!
BUT --
BUT --

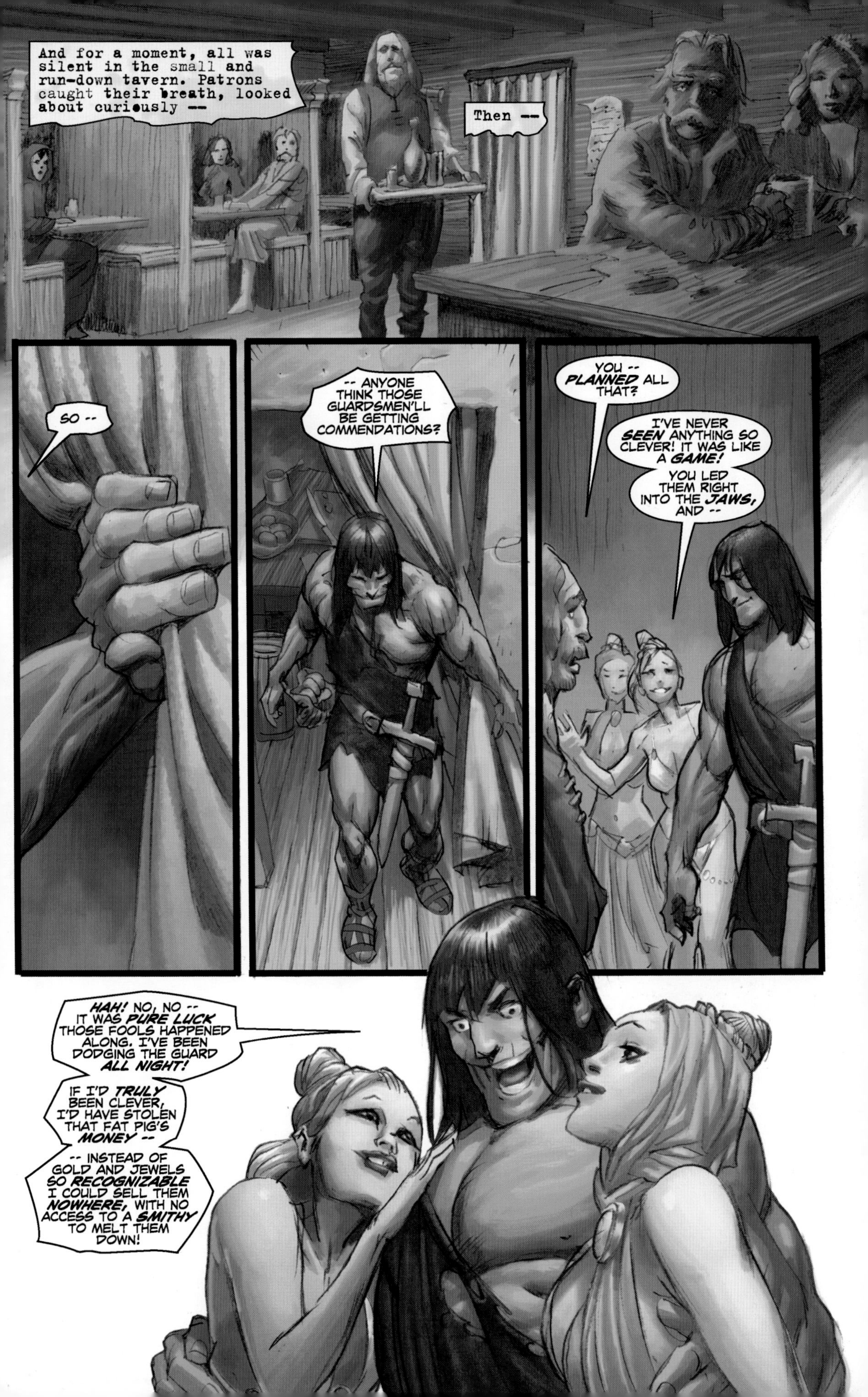
And for a moment, all was silent in the small and run-down tavern. Patrons caught their breath, looked about curiously --
Then --
SO --
-- ANYONE THINK THOSE GUARDSMEN'LL BE GETTING COMMENDATIONS?
YOU -- PLANNED ALL THAT?
I'VE NEVER SEEN ANYTHING SO CLEVER! IT WAS LIKE A GAME!
YOU LED THEM RIGHT INTO THE JAWS, AND --
HAH! NO, NO -- IT WAS PURE LUCK THOSE FOOLS HAPPENED ALONG. I'VE BEEN DODGING THE GUARD ALL NIGHT!
IF I'D TRULY BEEN CLEVER, I'D HAVE STOLEN THAT FAT PIG'S MONEY --
-- INSTEAD OF GOLD AND JEWELS SO RECOGNIZABLE I COULD SELL THEM NOWHERE, WITH NO ACCESS TO A SMITHY TO MELT THEM DOWN!

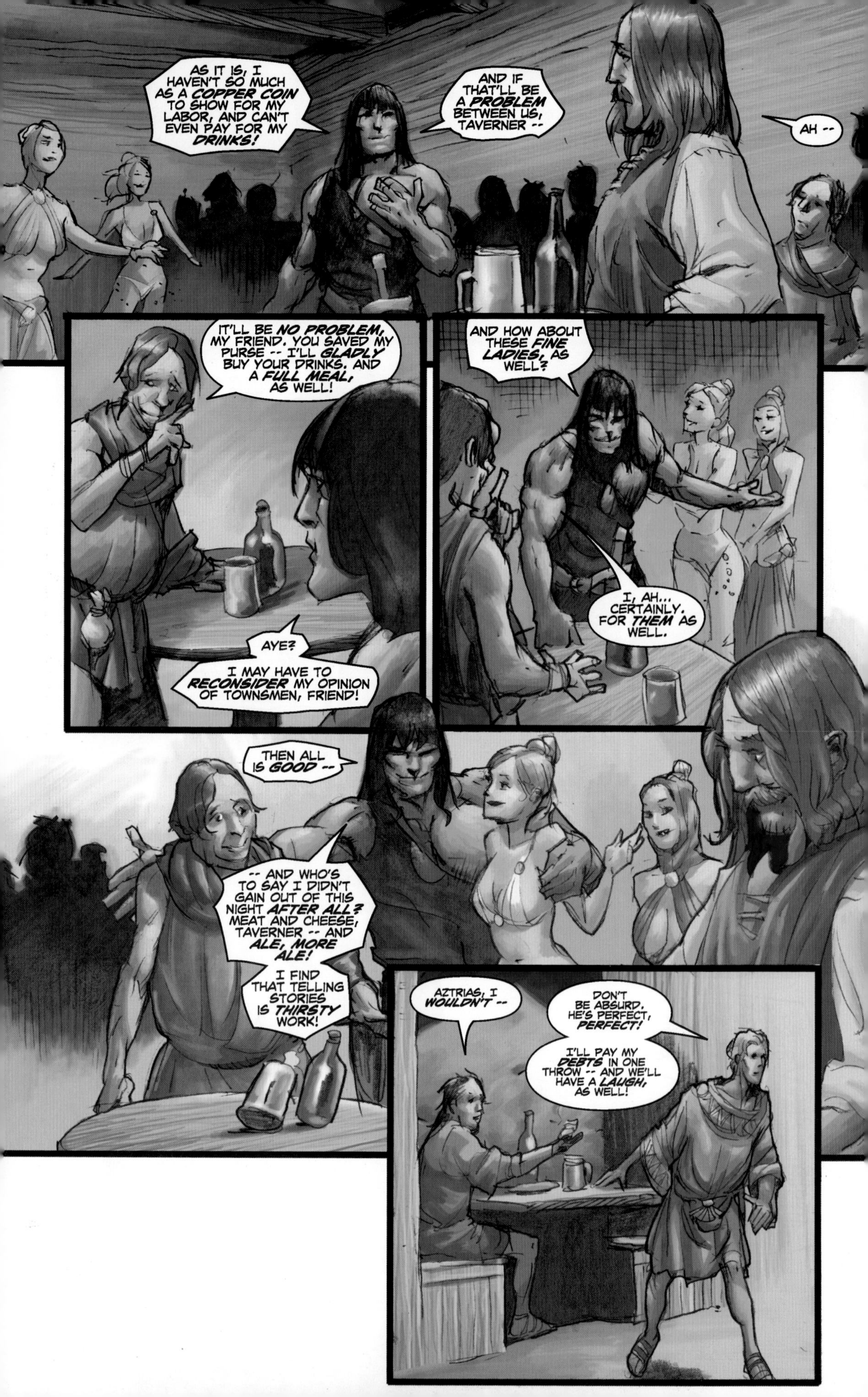
AS IT IS, I HAVEN'T SO MUCH AS A COPPER COIN TO SHOW FOR MY LABOR, AND CAN'T EVEN PAY FOR MY DRINKS!
AND IF THAT'LL BE A PROBLEM BETWEEN US, TAVERNER --
AH --
IT'LL BE NO PROBLEM, MY FRIEND. YOU SAVED MY PURSE -- I'LL GLADLY BUY YOUR DRINKS. AND A FULL MEAL, AS WELL!
AYE?
I MAY HAVE TO RECONSIDER MY OPINION OF TOWNSMEN, FRIEND!
AND HOW ABOUT THESE FINE LADIES, AS WELL?
I, AH... CERTAINLY. FOR THEM AS WELL.
THEN ALL IS GOOD --
-- AND WHO'S TO SAY I DIDN'T GAIN OUT OF THIS NIGHT AFTER ALL? MEAT AND CHEESE, TAVERNER -- AND ALE, MORE ALE!
I FIND THAT TELLING STORIES IS THIRSTY WORK!
AZTRIAS, I WOULDN'T --
DON'T BE ABSURD. HE'S PERFECT, PERFECT!
I'LL PAY MY DEBTS IN ONE THROW -- AND WE'LL HAVE A LAUGH, AS WELL!

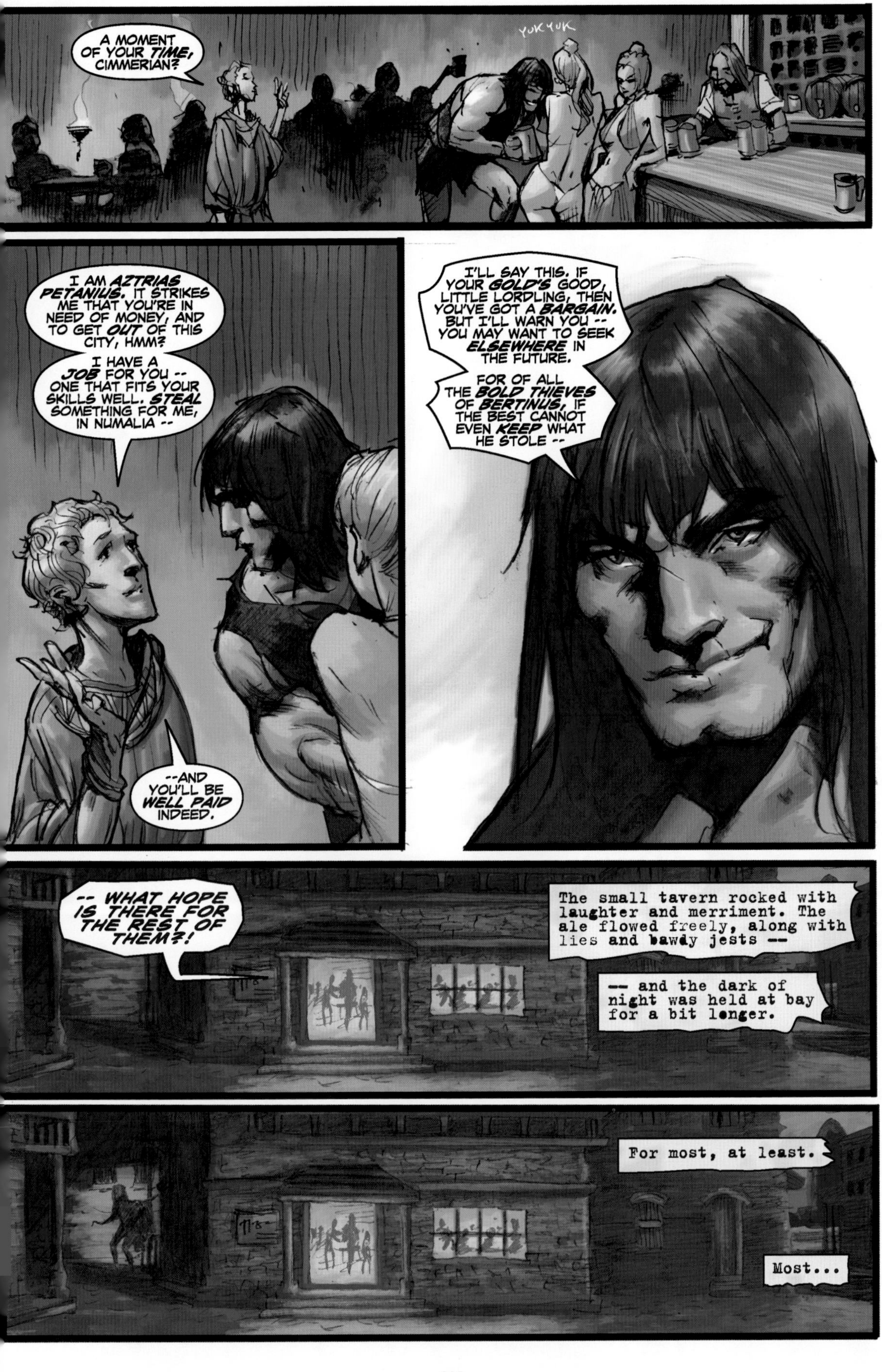
A MOMENT OF YOUR TIME, CIMMERIAN?
YUK YUK
I AM AZTRIAS PETANIUS. IT STRIKES ME THAT YOU'RE IN NEED OF MONEY, AND TO GET OUT OF THIS CITY, HMM?
I HAVE A JOB FOR YOU -- ONE THAT FITS YOUR SKILLS WELL. STEAL SOMETHING FOR ME, IN NUMALIA --
--AND YOU'LL BE WELL PAID INDEED.
I'LL SAY THIS. IF YOUR GOLD'S GOOD, LITTLE LORDLING, THEN YOU'VE GOT A BARGAIN. BUT I'LL WARN YOU -- YOU MAY WANT TO SEEK ELSEWHERE IN THE FUTURE.
FOR OF ALL THE BOLD THIEVES OF BERTINUS, IF THE BEST CANNOT EVEN KEEP WHAT HE STOLE --
-- WHAT HOPE IS THERE FOR THE REST OF THEM?!
The small tavern rocked with laughter and merriment. The ale flowed freely, along with lies and bawdy jests --
-- and the dark of night was held at bay for a bit longer.
For most, at least.
Most...

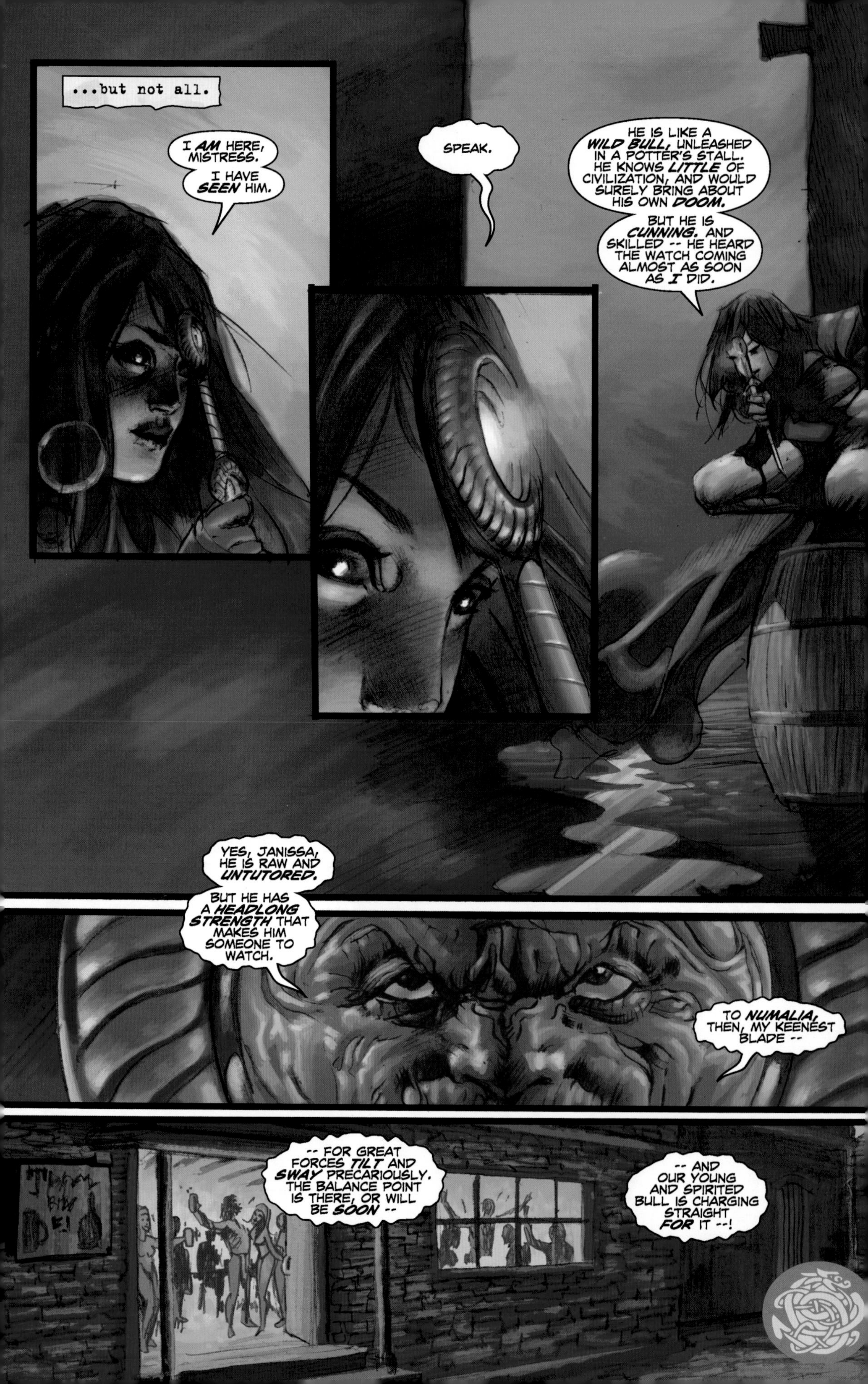

...but not all.
I AM HERE, MISTRESS. I HAVE SEEN HIM.
SPEAK.
HE IS LIKE A WILD BULL, UNLEASHED IN A POTTER'S STALL. HE KNOWS LITTLE OF CIVILIZATION, AND WOULD SURELY BRING ABOUT HIS OWN DOOM.
BUT HE IS CUNNING. AND SKILLED -- HE HEARD THE WATCH COMING ALMOST AS SOON AS I DID.
YES, JANISSA, HE IS RAW AND UNTUTORED.
BUT HE HAS A HEADLONG STRENGTH THAT MAKES HIM SOMEONE TO WATCH.
TO NUMALIA, THEN, MY KEENEST BLADE --
-- FOR GREAT FORCES TILT AND SWAY PRECARIOUSLY. THE BALANCE POINT IS THERE, OR WILL BE SOON --
-- AND OUR YOUNG AND SPIRITED BULL IS CHARGING STRAIGHT FOR IT --!

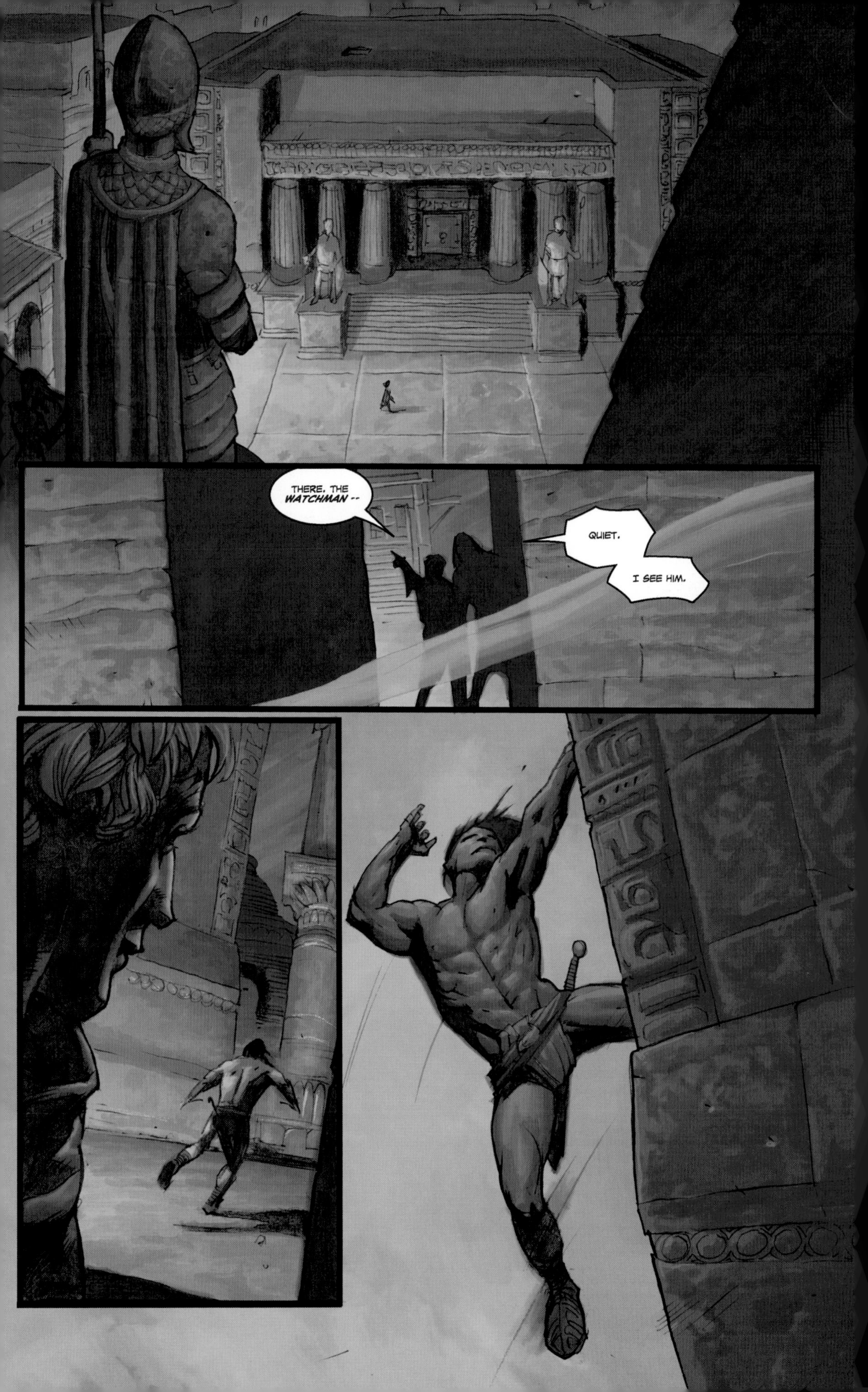
THERE. THE *WATCHMAN --*
QUIET.
I SEE HIM.

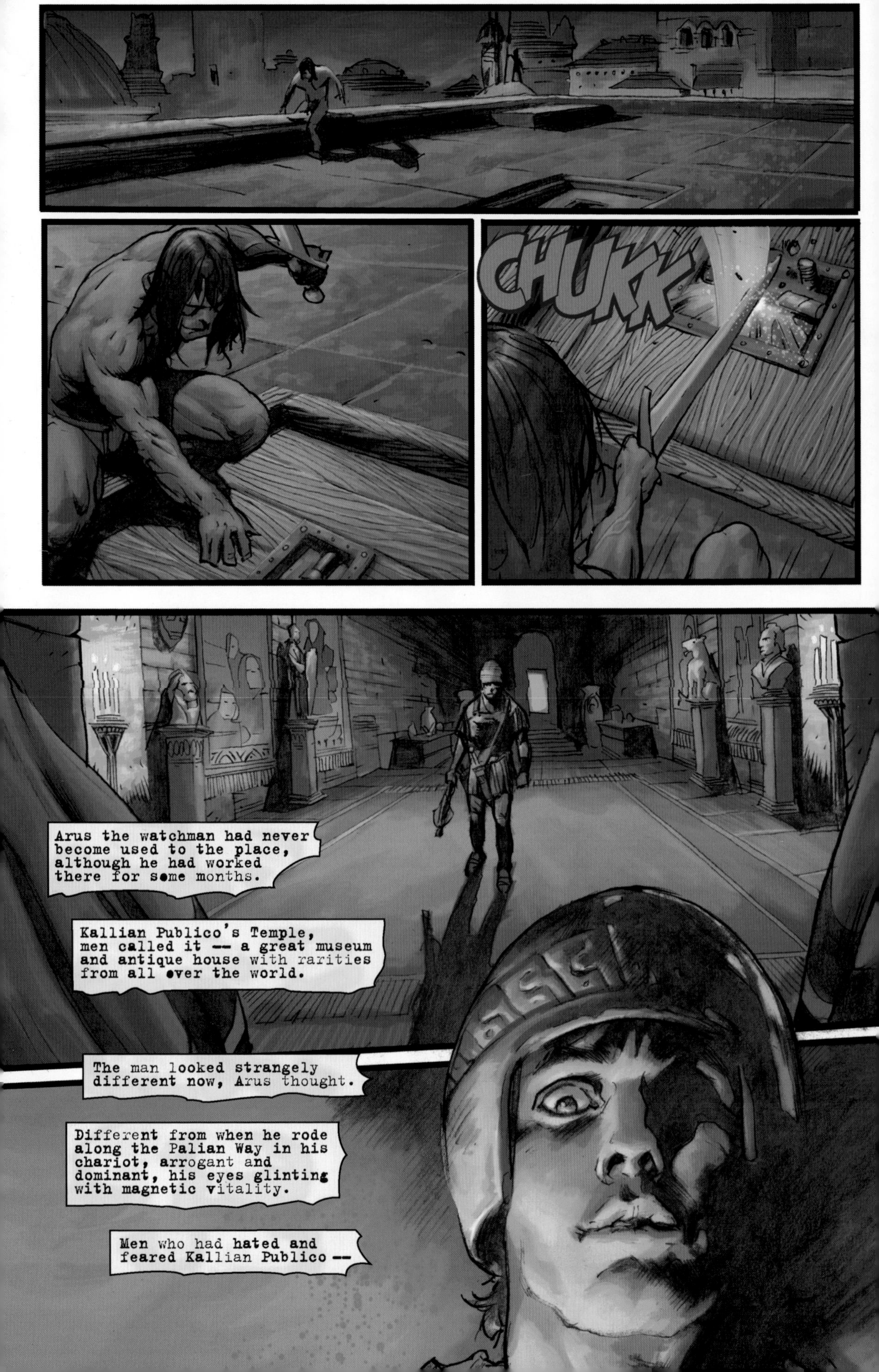
CHUKK
Arus the watchman had never become used to the place, although he had worked there for some months.
Kallian Publico's Temple, men called it -- a great museum and antique house with rarities from all over the world.
The man looked strangely different now, Arus thought.
Different from when he rode along the Palian Way in his chariot, arrogant and dominant, his eyes glinting with magnetic vitality.
Men who had hated and feared Kallian Publico --

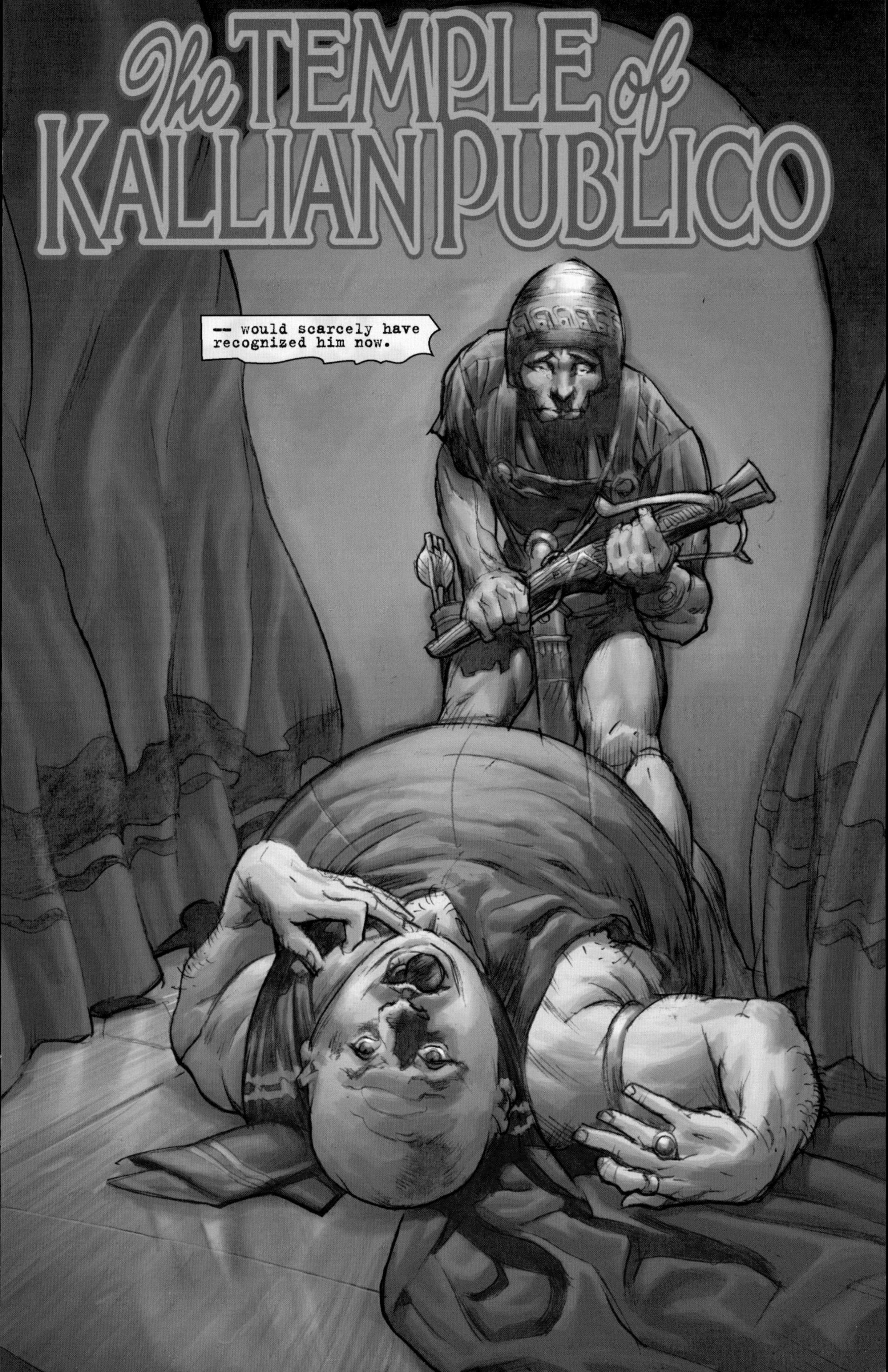
The TEMPLE of KALLIAN PUBLICO
-- would scarcely have recognized him now.

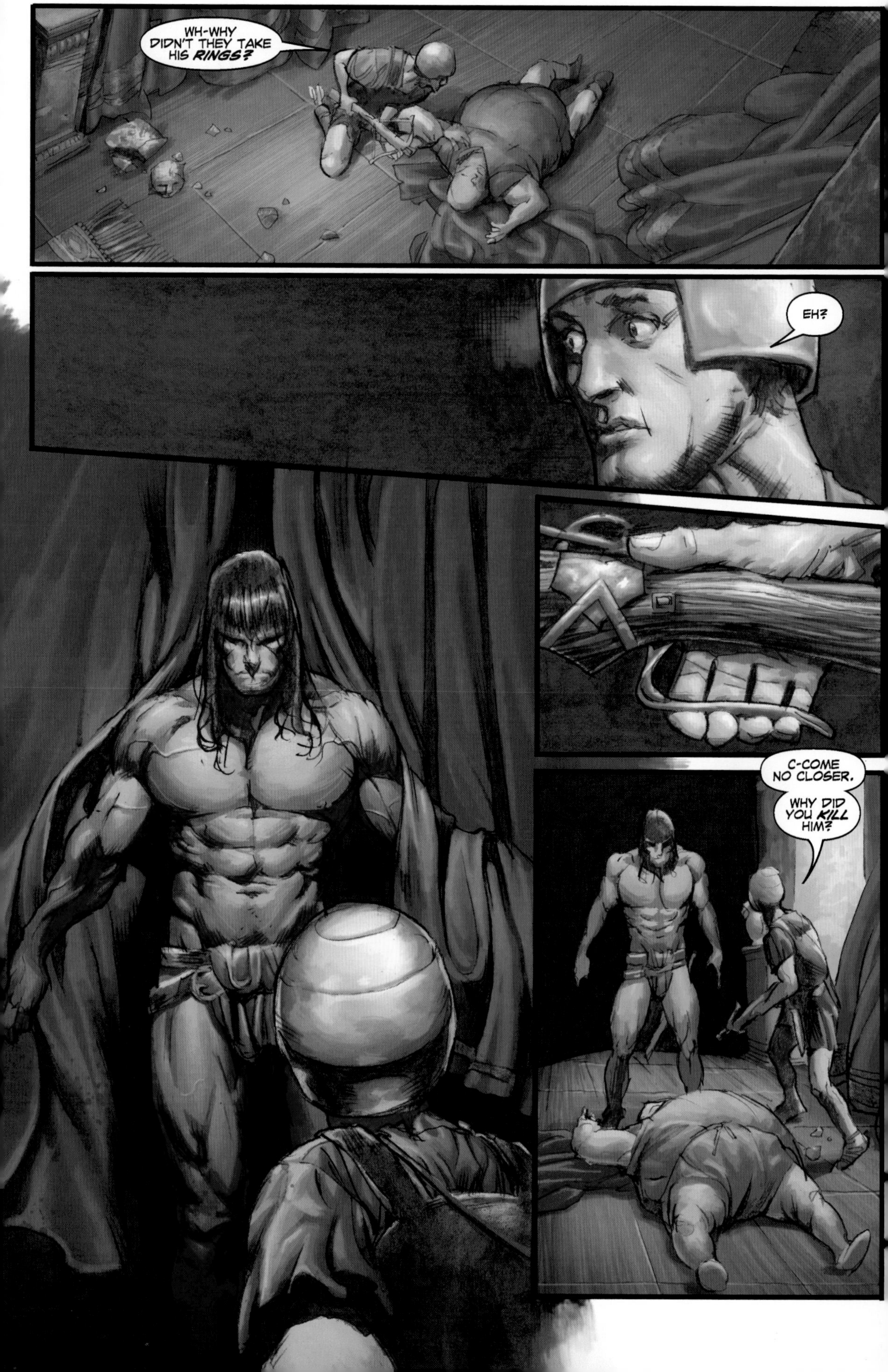
WH-WHY DIDN'T THEY TAKE HIS RINGS?
EH?
C-COME NO CLOSER.
WHY DID YOU KILL HIM?

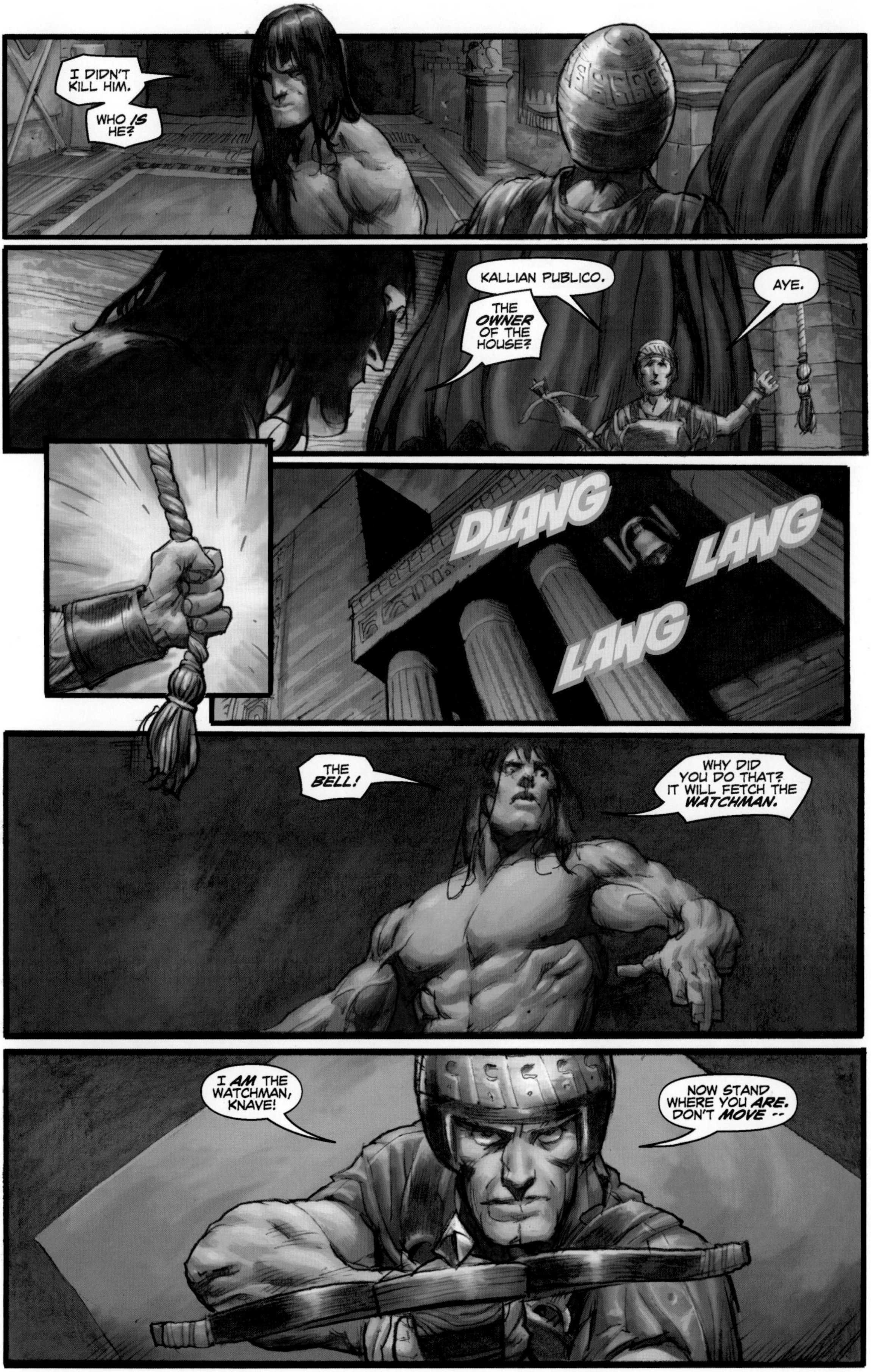
I DIDN'T KILL HIM.
WHO *IS* HE?
KALLIAN PUBLICO.
THE *OWNER* OF THE HOUSE?
AYE.
DLANG
LANG
LANG
THE *BELL!*
WHY DID YOU DO THAT? IT WILL FETCH THE *WATCHMAN.*
I *AM* THE WATCHMAN, KNAVE!
NOW STAND WHERE YOU *ARE.* DON'T *MOVE* --

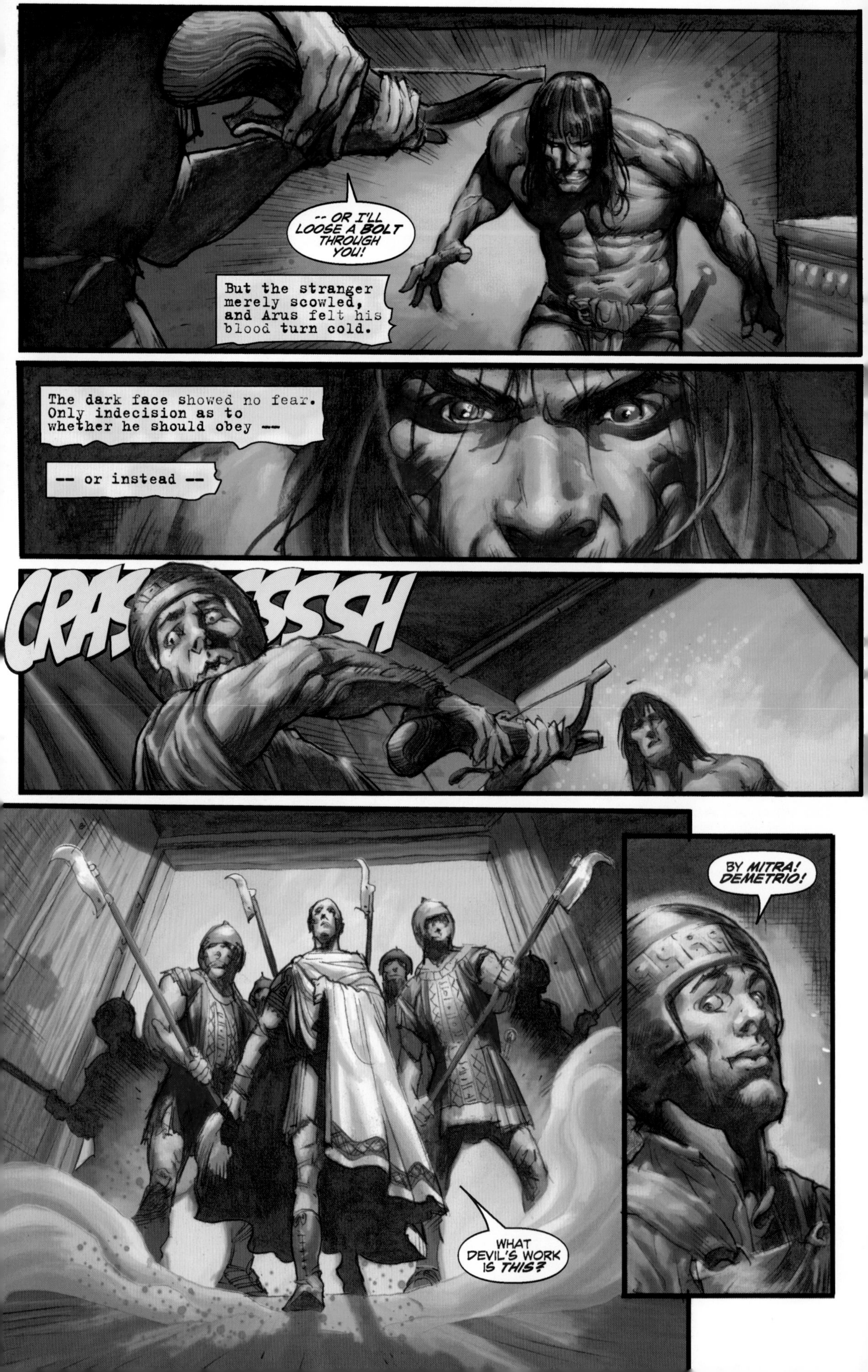
-- OR I'LL LOOSE A BOLT THROUGH YOU!
But the stranger merely scowled, and Arus felt his blood turn cold.
The dark face showed no fear. Only indecision as to whether he should obey --
-- or instead --
CRASSSSSH
BY MITRA! DEMETRIO!
WHAT DEVIL'S WORK IS THIS?

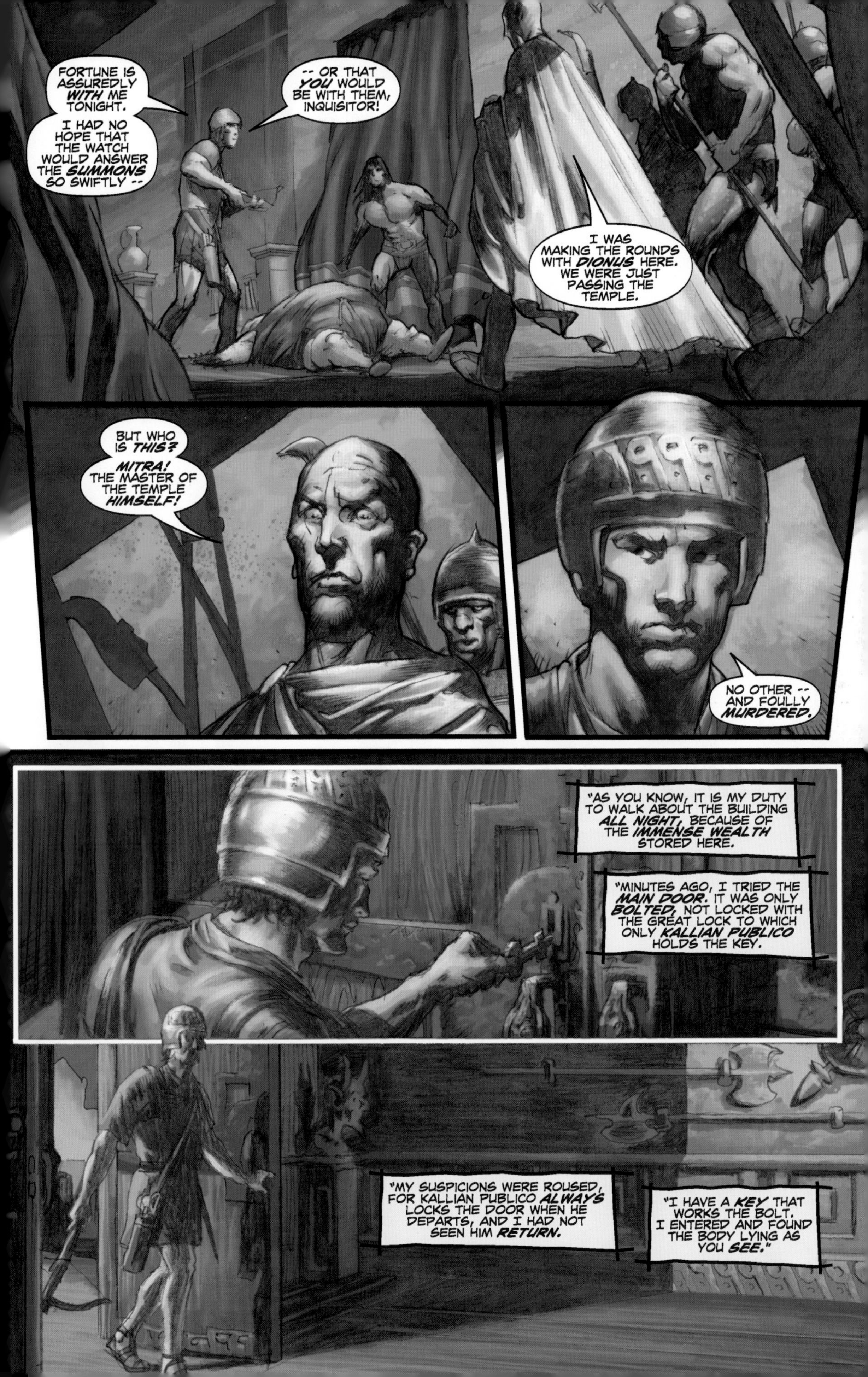

FORTUNE IS ASSUREDLY WITH ME TONIGHT.
I HAD NO HOPE THAT THE WATCH WOULD ANSWER THE SUMMONS SO SWIFTLY --
-- OR THAT YOU WOULD BE WITH THEM, INQUISITOR!
I WAS MAKING THE ROUNDS WITH DIONUS HERE. WE WERE JUST PASSING THE TEMPLE.
BUT WHO IS THIS? MITRA! THE MASTER OF THE TEMPLE HIMSELF!
NO OTHER -- AND FOULLY MURDERED.
"AS YOU KNOW, IT IS MY DUTY TO WALK ABOUT THE BUILDING ALL NIGHT, BECAUSE OF THE IMMENSE WEALTH STORED HERE.
"MINUTES AGO, I TRIED THE MAIN DOOR. IT WAS ONLY BOLTED, NOT LOCKED WITH THE GREAT LOCK TO WHICH ONLY KALLIAN PUBLICO HOLDS THE KEY.
"MY SUSPICIONS WERE ROUSED, FOR KALLIAN PUBLICO ALWAYS LOCKS THE DOOR WHEN HE DEPARTS, AND I HAD NOT SEEN HIM RETURN.
"I HAVE A KEY THAT WORKS THE BOLT. I ENTERED AND FOUND THE BODY LYING AS YOU SEE."

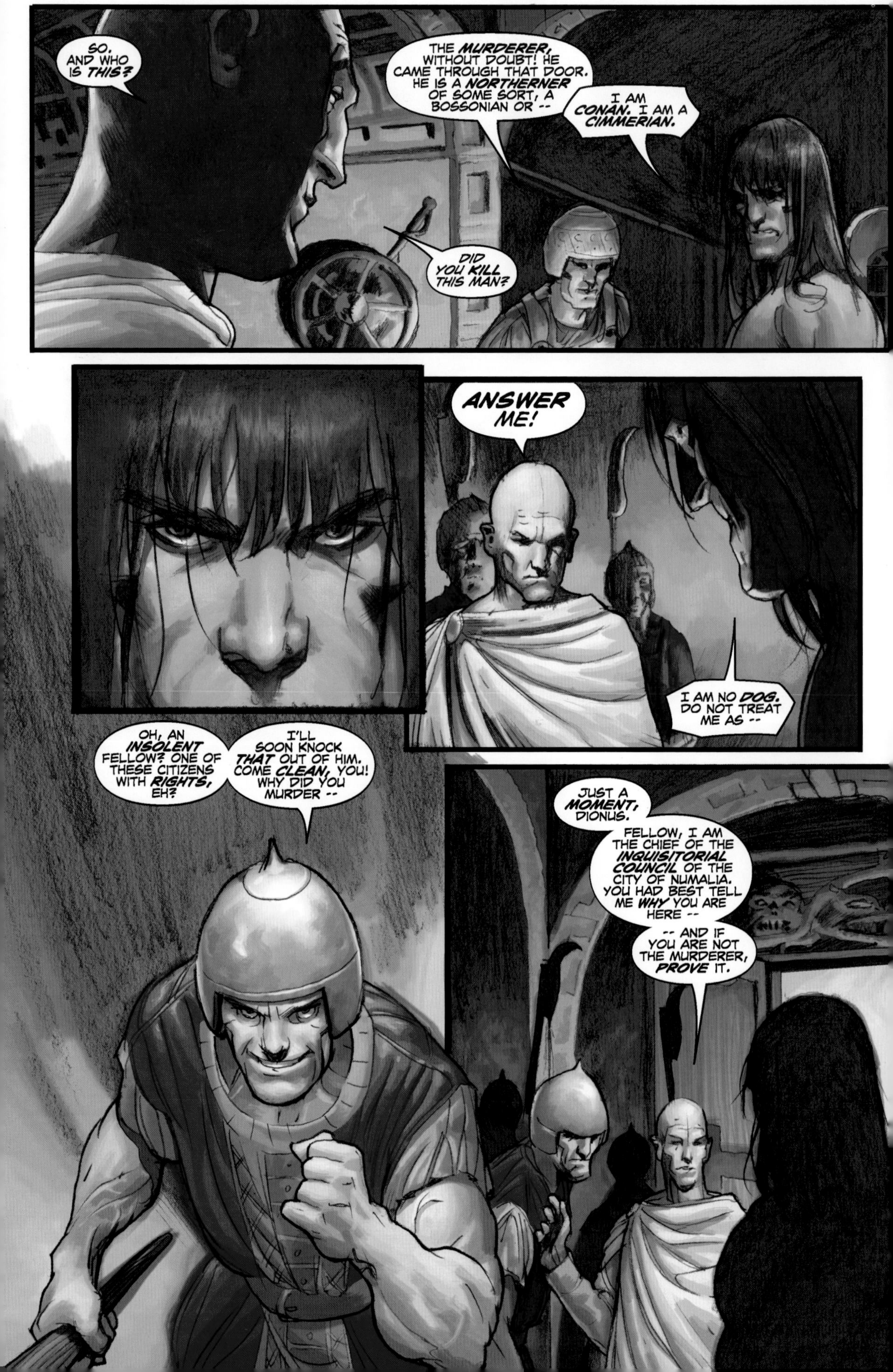
SO. AND WHO IS THIS?
THE MURDERER, WITHOUT DOUBT! HE CAME THROUGH THAT DOOR. HE IS A NORTHERNER OF SOME SORT, A BOSSONIAN OR --
I AM CONAN. I AM A CIMMERIAN.
DID YOU KILL THIS MAN?
ANSWER ME!
I AM NO DOG. DO NOT TREAT ME AS --
OH, AN INSOLENT FELLOW? ONE OF THESE CITIZENS WITH RIGHTS, EH?
I'LL SOON KNOCK THAT OUT OF HIM. COME CLEAN, YOU! WHY DID YOU MURDER --
JUST A MOMENT, DIONUS.
FELLOW, I AM THE CHIEF OF THE INQUISITORIAL COUNCIL OF THE CITY OF NUMALIA. YOU HAD BEST TELL ME WHY YOU ARE HERE --
-- AND IF YOU ARE NOT THE MURDERER, PROVE IT.

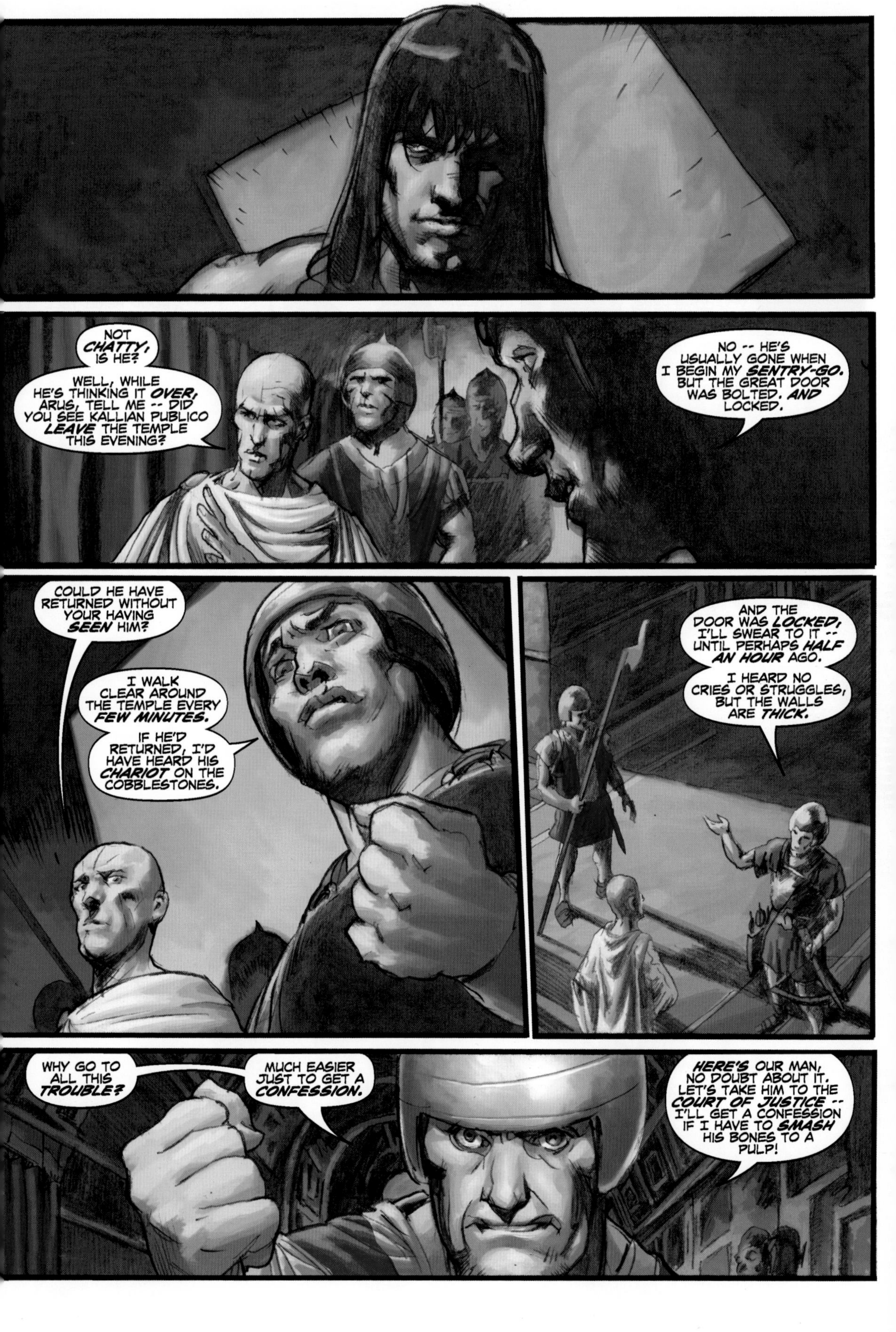
NOT CHATTY, IS HE?
WELL, WHILE HE'S THINKING IT OVER, ARUS, TELL ME -- DID YOU SEE KALLIAN PUBLICO LEAVE THE TEMPLE THIS EVENING?
NO -- HE'S USUALLY GONE WHEN I BEGIN MY SENTRY-GO. BUT THE GREAT DOOR WAS BOLTED. AND LOCKED.
COULD HE HAVE RETURNED WITHOUT YOUR HAVING SEEN HIM?
I WALK CLEAR AROUND THE TEMPLE EVERY FEW MINUTES.
IF HE'D RETURNED, I'D HAVE HEARD HIS CHARIOT ON THE COBBLESTONES.
AND THE DOOR WAS LOCKED, I'LL SWEAR TO IT -- UNTIL PERHAPS HALF AN HOUR AGO.
I HEARD NO CRIES OR STRUGGLES, BUT THE WALLS ARE THICK.
WHY GO TO ALL THIS TROUBLE?
MUCH EASIER JUST TO GET A CONFESSION.
HERE'S OUR MAN, NO DOUBT ABOUT IT. LET'S TAKE HIM TO THE COURT OF JUSTICE -- I'LL GET A CONFESSION IF I HAVE TO SMASH HIS BONES TO A PULP!

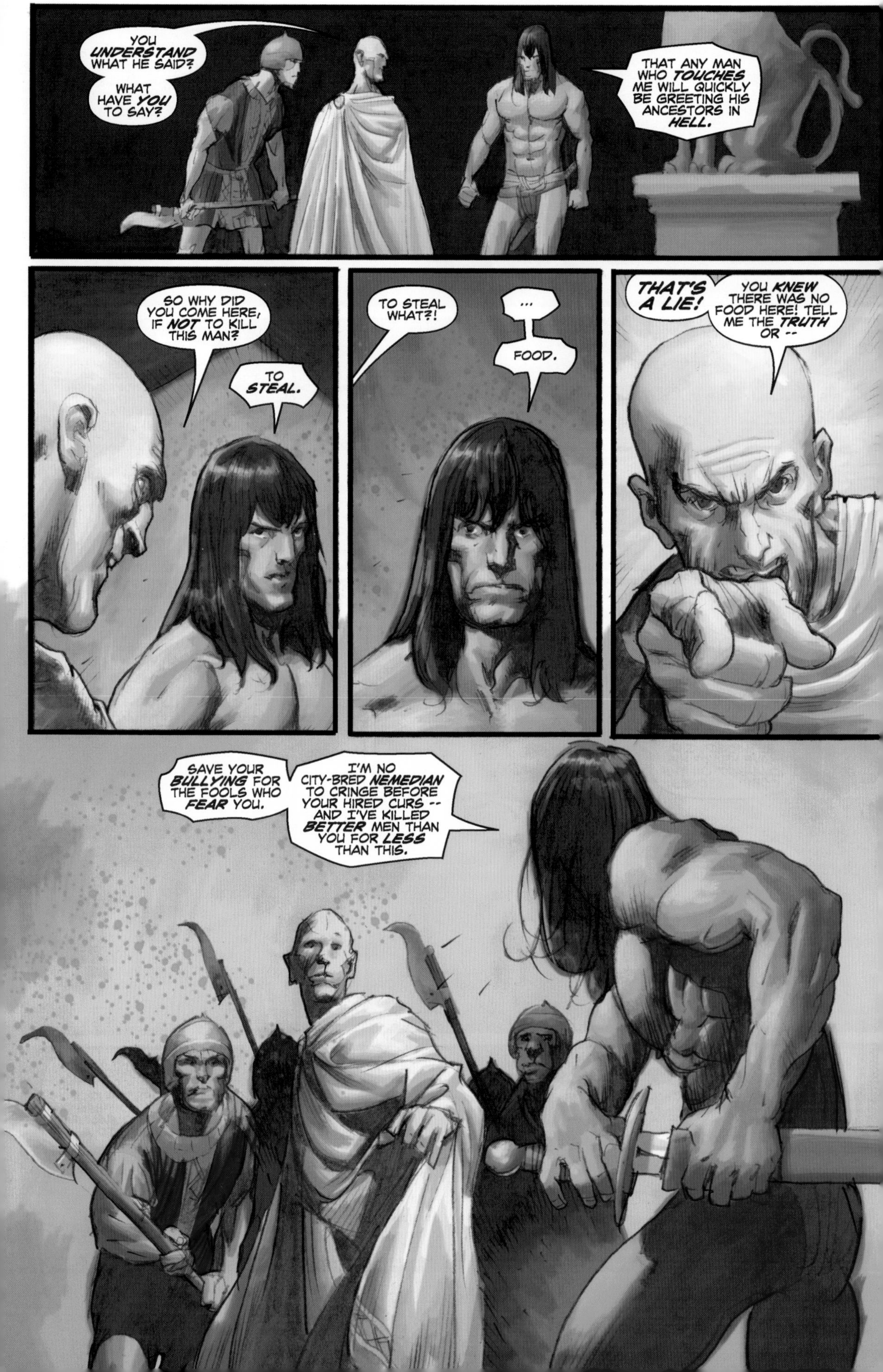

YOU UNDERSTAND WHAT HE SAID?
WHAT HAVE YOU TO SAY?
THAT ANY MAN WHO TOUCHES ME WILL QUICKLY BE GREETING HIS ANCESTORS IN HELL.
SO WHY DID YOU COME HERE, IF NOT TO KILL THIS MAN?
TO STEAL.
TO STEAL WHAT?!
...
FOOD.
THAT'S A LIE!
YOU KNEW THERE WAS NO FOOD HERE! TELL ME THE TRUTH OR --
SAVE YOUR BULLYING FOR THE FOOLS WHO FEAR YOU.
I'M NO CITY-BRED NEMEDIAN TO CRINGE BEFORE YOUR HIRED CURS -- AND I'VE KILLED BETTER MEN THAN YOU FOR LESS THAN THIS.

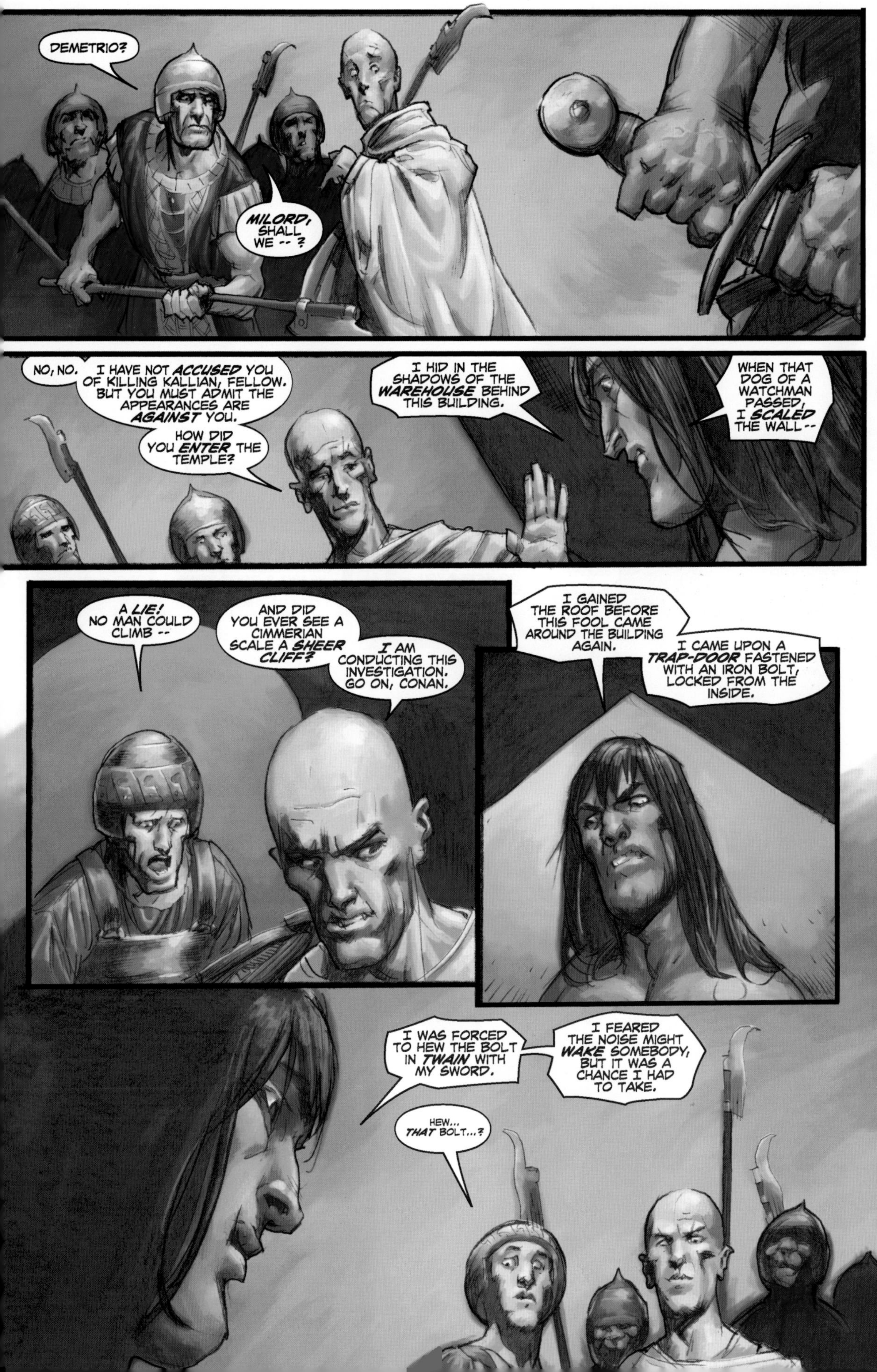
DEMETRIO?
MILORD, SHALL WE -- ?
NO, NO.
I HAVE NOT ACCUSED YOU OF KILLING KALLIAN, FELLOW. BUT YOU MUST ADMIT THE APPEARANCES ARE AGAINST YOU.
HOW DID YOU ENTER THE TEMPLE?
I HID IN THE SHADOWS OF THE WAREHOUSE BEHIND THIS BUILDING.
WHEN THAT DOG OF A WATCHMAN PASSED, I SCALED THE WALL --
A LIE! NO MAN COULD CLIMB --
AND DID YOU EVER SEE A CIMMERIAN SCALE A SHEER CLIFF?
I AM CONDUCTING THIS INVESTIGATION. GO ON, CONAN.
I GAINED THE ROOF BEFORE THIS FOOL CAME AROUND THE BUILDING AGAIN.
I CAME UPON A TRAP-DOOR FASTENED WITH AN IRON BOLT, LOCKED FROM THE INSIDE.
I WAS FORCED TO HEW THE BOLT IN TWAIN WITH MY SWORD.
I FEARED THE NOISE MIGHT WAKE SOMEBODY, BUT IT WAS A CHANCE I HAD TO TAKE.
HEW... THAT BOLT...?

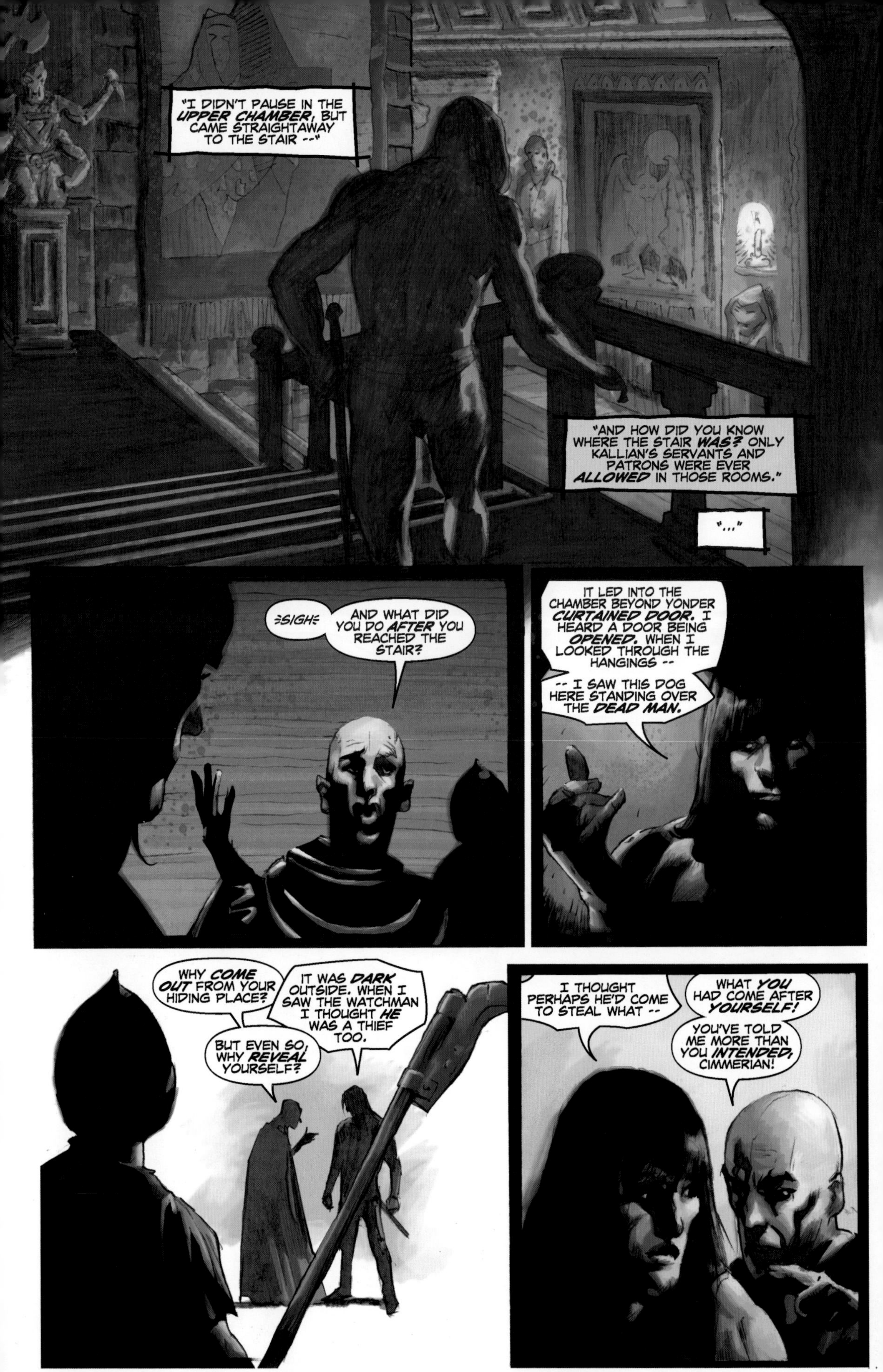
"I DIDN'T PAUSE IN THE UPPER CHAMBER, BUT CAME STRAIGHTAWAY TO THE STAIR --"
"AND HOW DID YOU KNOW WHERE THE STAIR WAS? ONLY KALLIAN'S SERVANTS AND PATRONS WERE EVER ALLOWED IN THOSE ROOMS."
"..."
SIGH
AND WHAT DID YOU DO AFTER YOU REACHED THE STAIR?
IT LED INTO THE CHAMBER BEYOND YONDER CURTAINED DOOR. I HEARD A DOOR BEING OPENED. WHEN I LOOKED THROUGH THE HANGINGS --
-- I SAW THIS DOG HERE STANDING OVER THE DEAD MAN.
WHY COME OUT FROM YOUR HIDING PLACE?
IT WAS DARK OUTSIDE. WHEN I SAW THE WATCHMAN I THOUGHT HE WAS A THIEF TOO.
BUT EVEN SO, WHY REVEAL YOURSELF?
I THOUGHT PERHAPS HE'D COME TO STEAL WHAT --
WHAT YOU HAD COME AFTER YOURSELF!
YOU'VE TOLD ME MORE THAN YOU INTENDED, CIMMERIAN!

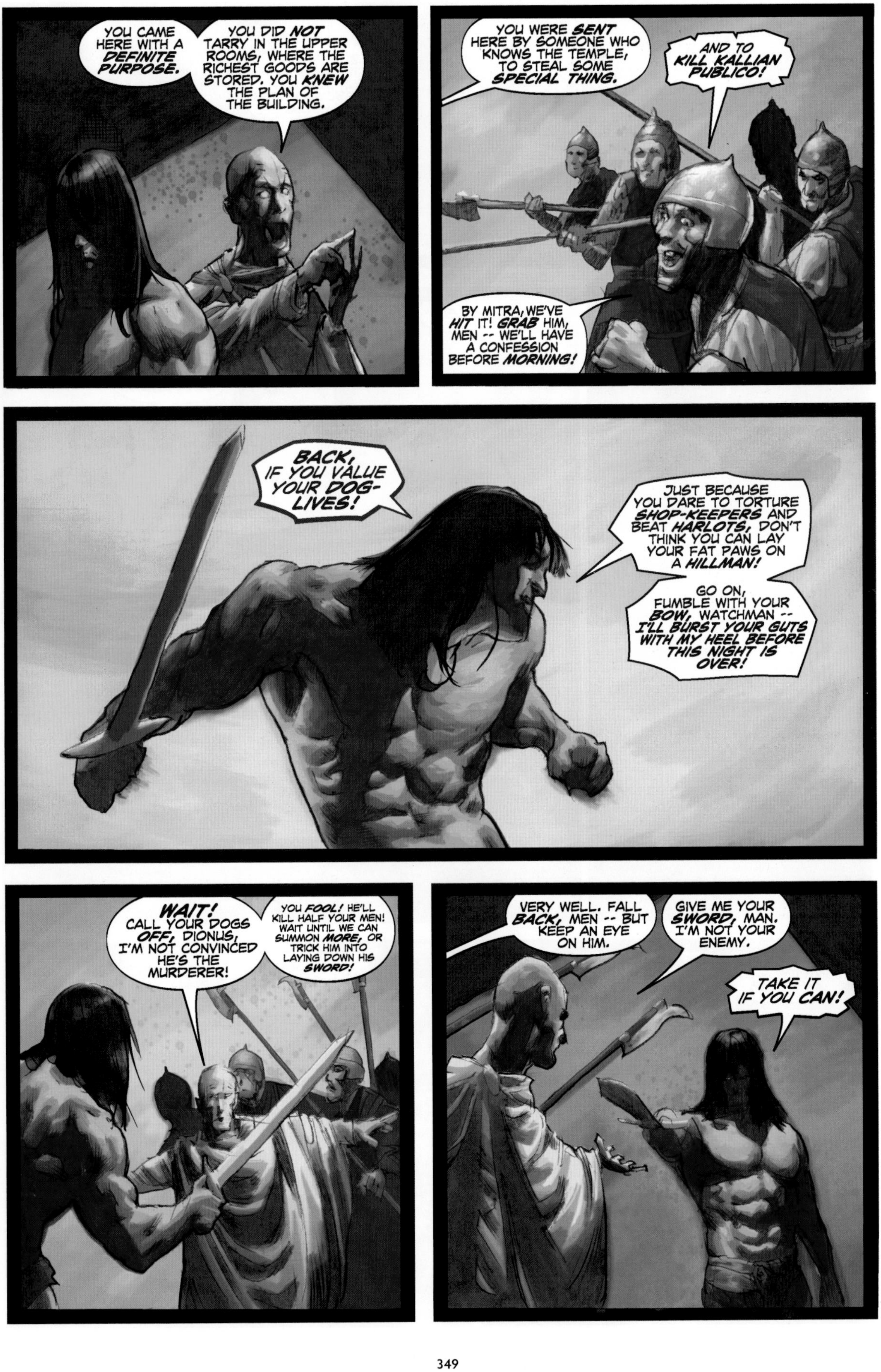
YOU CAME HERE WITH A DEFINITE PURPOSE.
YOU DID NOT TARRY IN THE UPPER ROOMS, WHERE THE RICHEST GOODS ARE STORED. YOU KNEW THE PLAN OF THE BUILDING.
YOU WERE SENT HERE BY SOMEONE WHO KNOWS THE TEMPLE, TO STEAL SOME SPECIAL THING.
AND TO KILL KALLIAN PUBLICO!
BY MITRA, WE'VE HIT IT! GRAB HIM, MEN -- WE'LL HAVE A CONFESSION BEFORE MORNING!
BACK, IF YOU VALUE YOUR DOG-LIVES!
JUST BECAUSE YOU DARE TO TORTURE SHOP-KEEPERS AND BEAT HARLOTS, DON'T THINK YOU CAN LAY YOUR FAT PAWS ON A HILLMAN!
GO ON, FUMBLE WITH YOUR BOW, WATCHMAN -- I'LL BURST YOUR GUTS WITH MY HEEL BEFORE THIS NIGHT IS OVER!
WAIT! CALL YOUR DOGS OFF, DIONUS, I'M NOT CONVINCED HE'S THE MURDERER!
YOU FOOL! HE'LL KILL HALF YOUR MEN! WAIT UNTIL WE CAN SUMMON MORE, OR TRICK HIM INTO LAYING DOWN HIS SWORD!
VERY WELL. FALL BACK, MEN -- BUT KEEP AN EYE ON HIM.
GIVE ME YOUR SWORD, MAN. I'M NOT YOUR ENEMY.
TAKE IT IF YOU CAN!

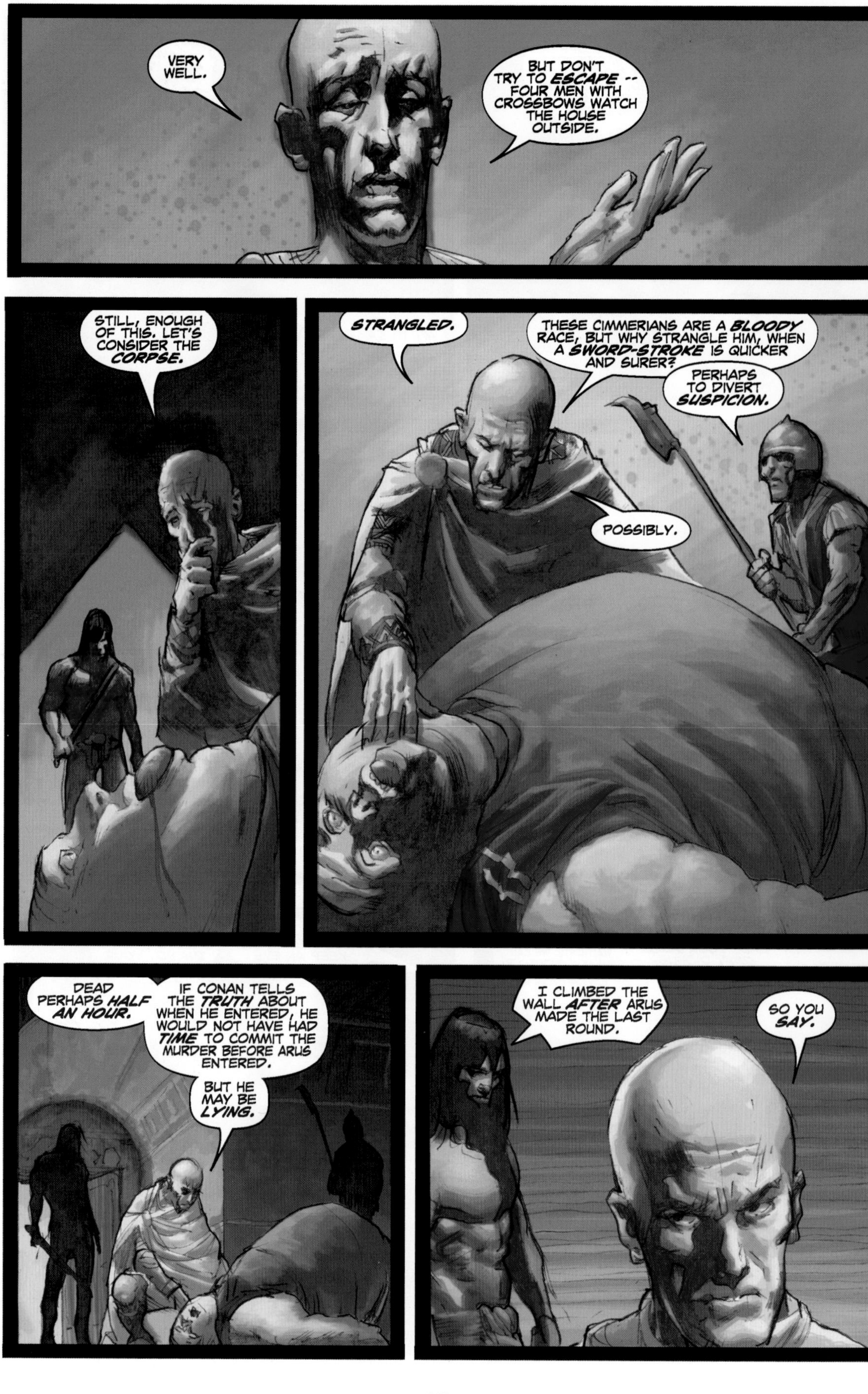
VERY WELL.
BUT DON'T TRY TO ESCAPE -- FOUR MEN WITH CROSSBOWS WATCH THE HOUSE OUTSIDE.
STILL, ENOUGH OF THIS. LET'S CONSIDER THE CORPSE.
STRANGLED.
THESE CIMMERIANS ARE A BLOODY RACE, BUT WHY STRANGLE HIM, WHEN A SWORD-STROKE IS QUICKER AND SURER?
PERHAPS TO DIVERT SUSPICION.
POSSIBLY.
DEAD PERHAPS HALF AN HOUR.
IF CONAN TELLS THE TRUTH ABOUT WHEN HE ENTERED, HE WOULD NOT HAVE HAD TIME TO COMMIT THE MURDER BEFORE ARUS ENTERED.
BUT HE MAY BE LYING.
I CLIMBED THE WALL AFTER ARUS MADE THE LAST ROUND.
SO YOU SAY.

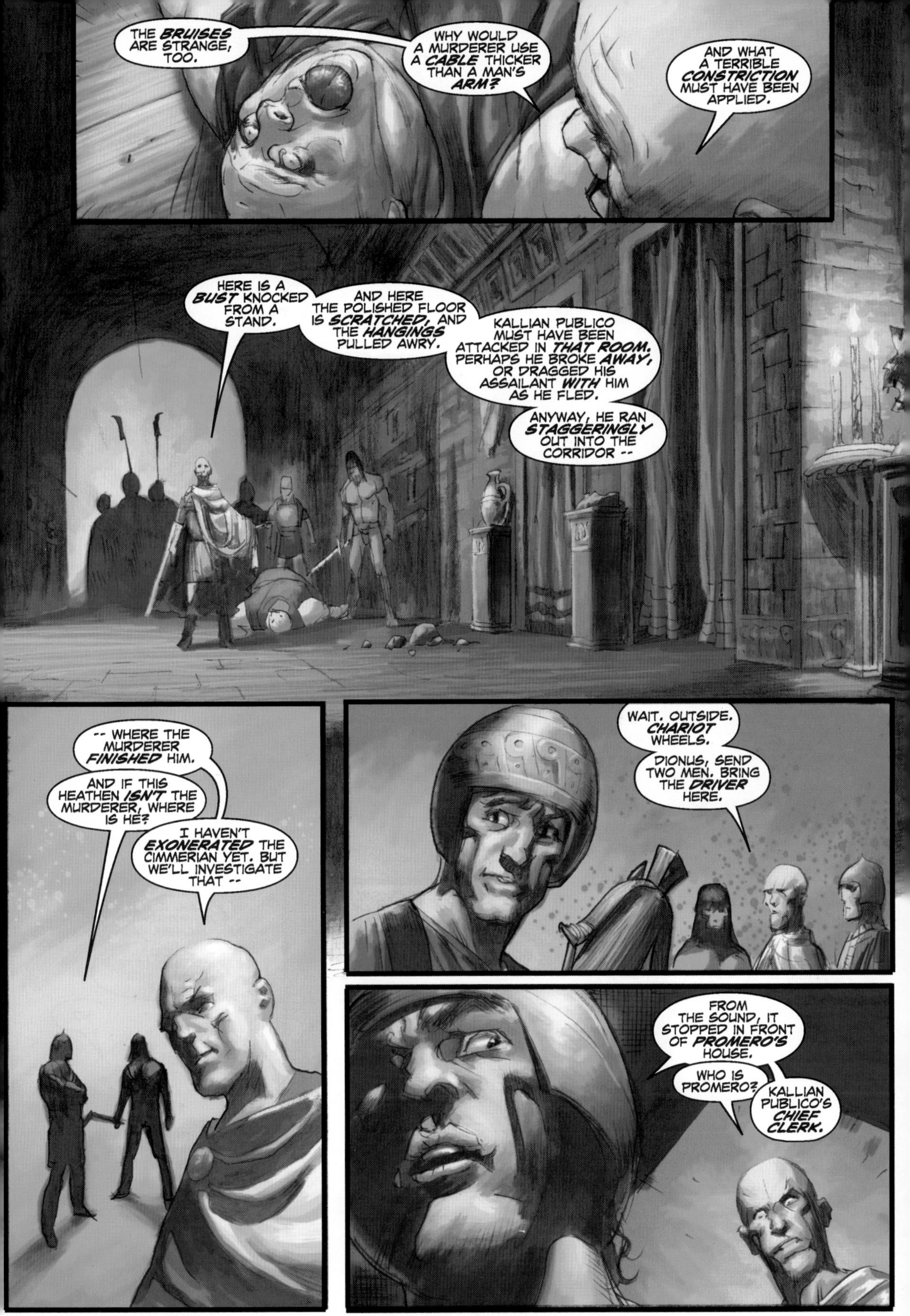
THE BRUISES ARE STRANGE, TOO.
WHY WOULD A MURDERER USE A CABLE THICKER THAN A MAN'S ARM?
AND WHAT A TERRIBLE CONSTRICTION MUST HAVE BEEN APPLIED.
HERE IS A BUST KNOCKED FROM A STAND.
AND HERE THE POLISHED FLOOR IS SCRATCHED, AND THE HANGINGS PULLED AWRY.
KALLIAN PUBLICO MUST HAVE BEEN ATTACKED IN THAT ROOM. PERHAPS HE BROKE AWAY, OR DRAGGED HIS ASSAILANT WITH HIM AS HE FLED.
ANYWAY, HE RAN STAGGERINGLY OUT INTO THE CORRIDOR --
-- WHERE THE MURDERER FINISHED HIM.
AND IF THIS HEATHEN ISN'T THE MURDERER, WHERE IS HE?
I HAVEN'T EXONERATED THE CIMMERIAN YET. BUT WE'LL INVESTIGATE THAT --
WAIT. OUTSIDE. CHARIOT WHEELS.
DIONUS, SEND TWO MEN. BRING THE DRIVER HERE.
FROM THE SOUND, IT STOPPED IN FRONT OF PROMERO'S HOUSE.
WHO IS PROMERO?
KALLIAN PUBLICO'S CHIEF CLERK.

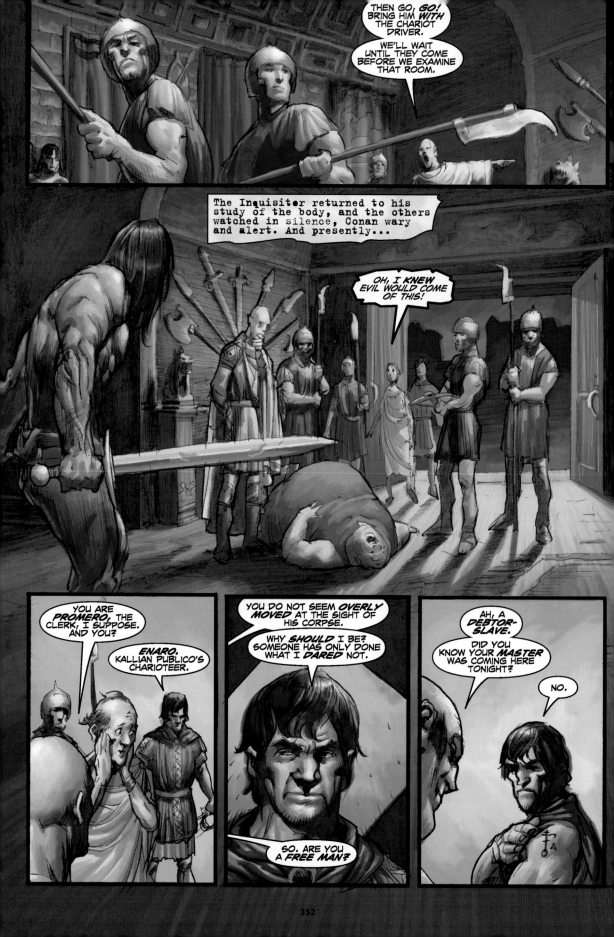

THEN GO, *GO!* BRING HIM *WITH* THE CHARIOT DRIVER.

WE'LL WAIT UNTIL THEY COME BEFORE WE EXAMINE THAT ROOM.

The Inquisitor returned to his study of the body, and the others watched in silence, Conan wary and alert. And presently...

OH, I KNEW EVIL WOULD COME OF THIS!

YOU ARE *PROMERO,* THE CLERK, I SUPPOSE. AND YOU?

ENARO. KALLIAN PUBLICO'S CHARIOTEER.

YOU DO NOT SEEM *OVERLY MOVED* AT THE SIGHT OF HIS CORPSE.

WHY *SHOULD* I BE? SOMEONE HAS ONLY DONE WHAT I *DARED* NOT.

SO. ARE YOU A *FREE MAN?*

AH, A *DEBTOR-SLAVE.*

DID YOU KNOW YOUR *MASTER* WAS COMING HERE TONIGHT?

NO.

352

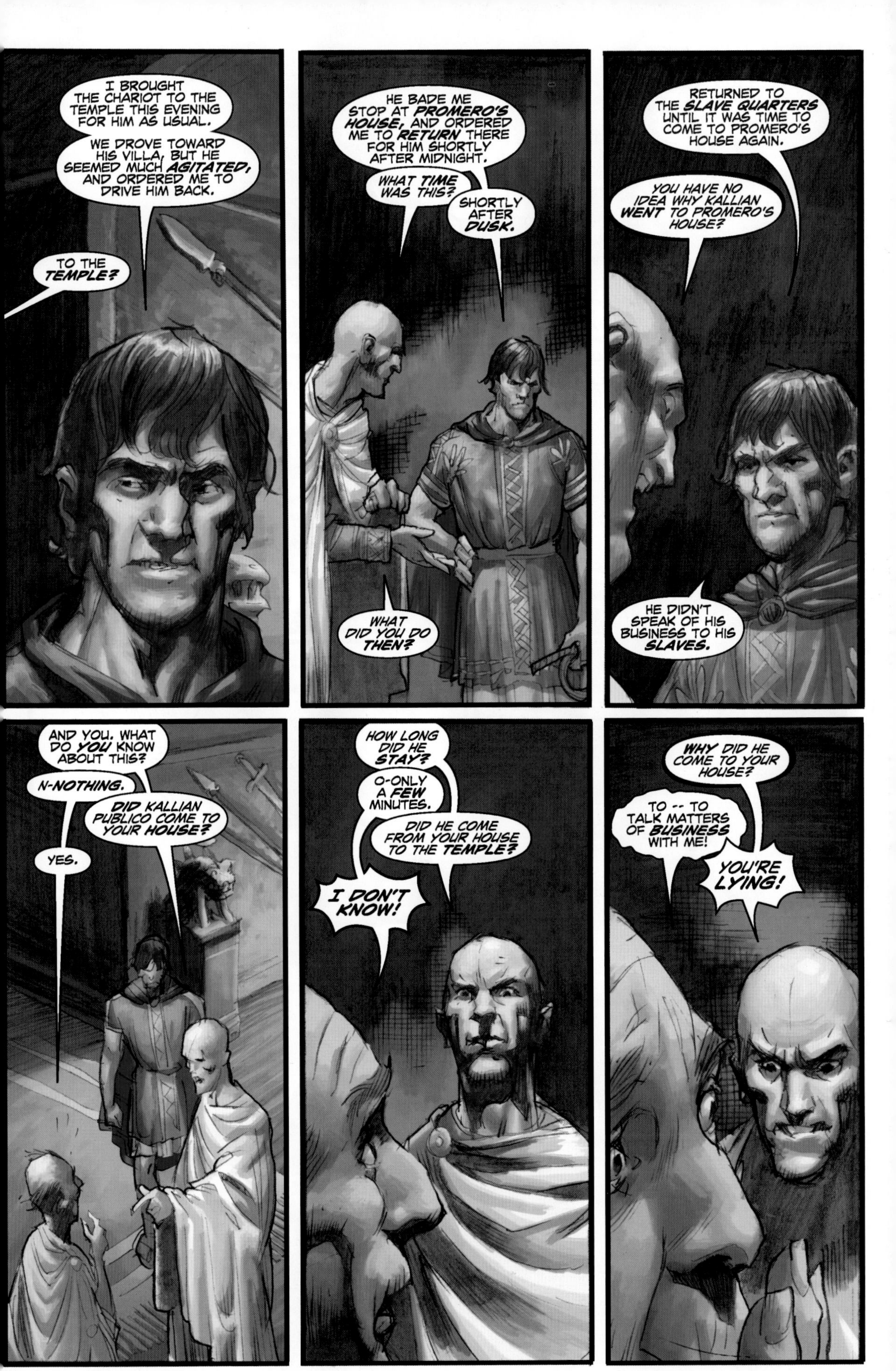
I BROUGHT THE CHARIOT TO THE TEMPLE THIS EVENING FOR HIM AS USUAL.
WE DROVE TOWARD HIS VILLA, BUT HE SEEMED MUCH AGITATED, AND ORDERED ME TO DRIVE HIM BACK.
TO THE TEMPLE?
HE BADE ME STOP AT PROMERO'S HOUSE, AND ORDERED ME TO RETURN THERE FOR HIM SHORTLY AFTER MIDNIGHT.
WHAT TIME WAS THIS?
SHORTLY AFTER DUSK.
WHAT DID YOU DO THEN?
RETURNED TO THE SLAVE QUARTERS UNTIL IT WAS TIME TO COME TO PROMERO'S HOUSE AGAIN.
YOU HAVE NO IDEA WHY KALLIAN WENT TO PROMERO'S HOUSE?
HE DIDN'T SPEAK OF HIS BUSINESS TO HIS SLAVES.
AND YOU. WHAT DO YOU KNOW ABOUT THIS?
N-NOTHING.
DID KALLIAN PUBLICO COME TO YOUR HOUSE?
YES.
HOW LONG DID HE STAY?
O-ONLY A FEW MINUTES.
DID HE COME FROM YOUR HOUSE TO THE TEMPLE?
I DON'T KNOW!
WHY DID HE COME TO YOUR HOUSE?
TO -- TO TALK MATTERS OF BUSINESS WITH ME!
YOU'RE LYING!

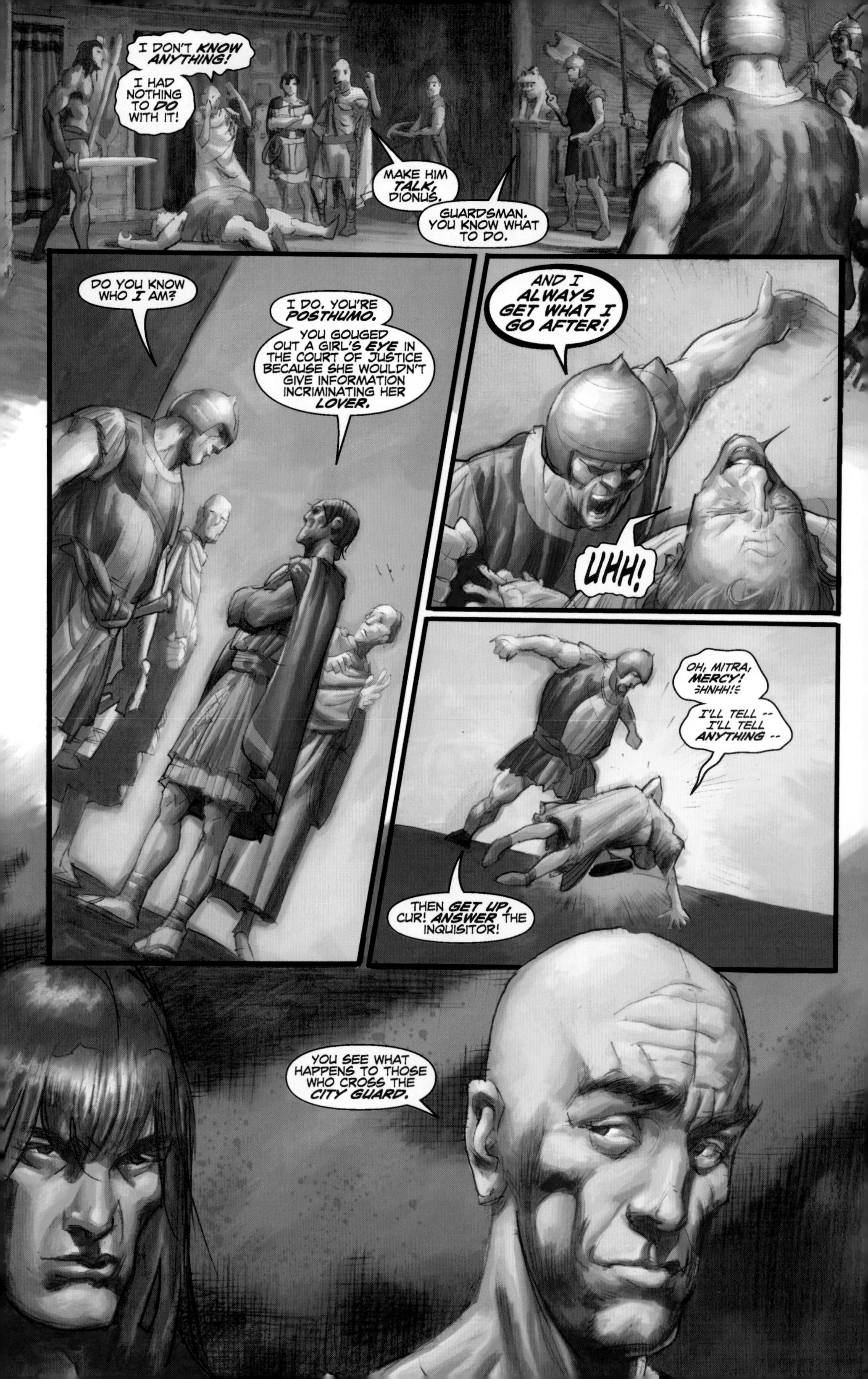
I DON'T KNOW ANYTHING!
I HAD NOTHING TO DO WITH IT!
MAKE HIM TALK, DIONUS.
GUARDSMAN. YOU KNOW WHAT TO DO.
DO YOU KNOW WHO I AM?
I DO. YOU'RE POSTHUMO.
YOU GOUGED OUT A GIRL'S EYE IN THE COURT OF JUSTICE BECAUSE SHE WOULDN'T GIVE INFORMATION INCRIMINATING HER LOVER.
AND I ALWAYS GET WHAT I GO AFTER!
UHH!
OH, MITRA, MERCY!
I'LL TELL -- I'LL TELL ANYTHING --
THEN GET UP, CUR! ANSWER THE INQUISITOR!
YOU SEE WHAT HAPPENS TO THOSE WHO CROSS THE CITY GUARD.

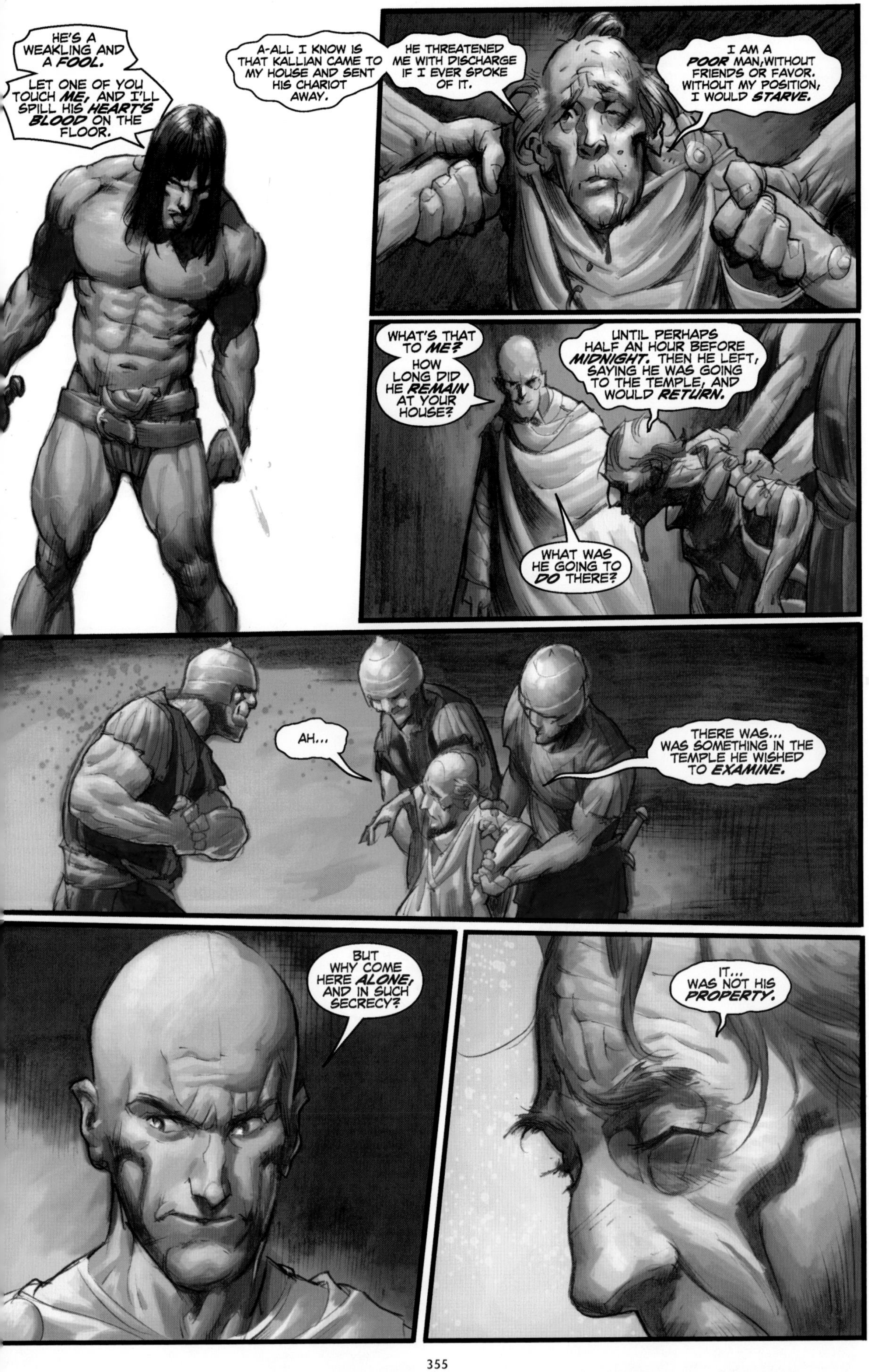
HE'S A WEAKLING AND A FOOL.
LET ONE OF YOU TOUCH ME, AND I'LL SPILL HIS HEART'S BLOOD ON THE FLOOR.
A-ALL I KNOW IS THAT KALLIAN CAME TO MY HOUSE AND SENT HIS CHARIOT AWAY.
HE THREATENED ME WITH DISCHARGE IF I EVER SPOKE OF IT.
I AM A POOR MAN, WITHOUT FRIENDS OR FAVOR. WITHOUT MY POSITION, I WOULD STARVE.
WHAT'S THAT TO ME?
HOW LONG DID HE REMAIN AT YOUR HOUSE?
UNTIL PERHAPS HALF AN HOUR BEFORE MIDNIGHT. THEN HE LEFT, SAYING HE WAS GOING TO THE TEMPLE, AND WOULD RETURN.
WHAT WAS HE GOING TO DO THERE?
AH...
THERE WAS... WAS SOMETHING IN THE TEMPLE HE WISHED TO EXAMINE.
BUT WHY COME HERE ALONE, AND IN SUCH SECRECY?
IT... WAS NOT HIS PROPERTY.

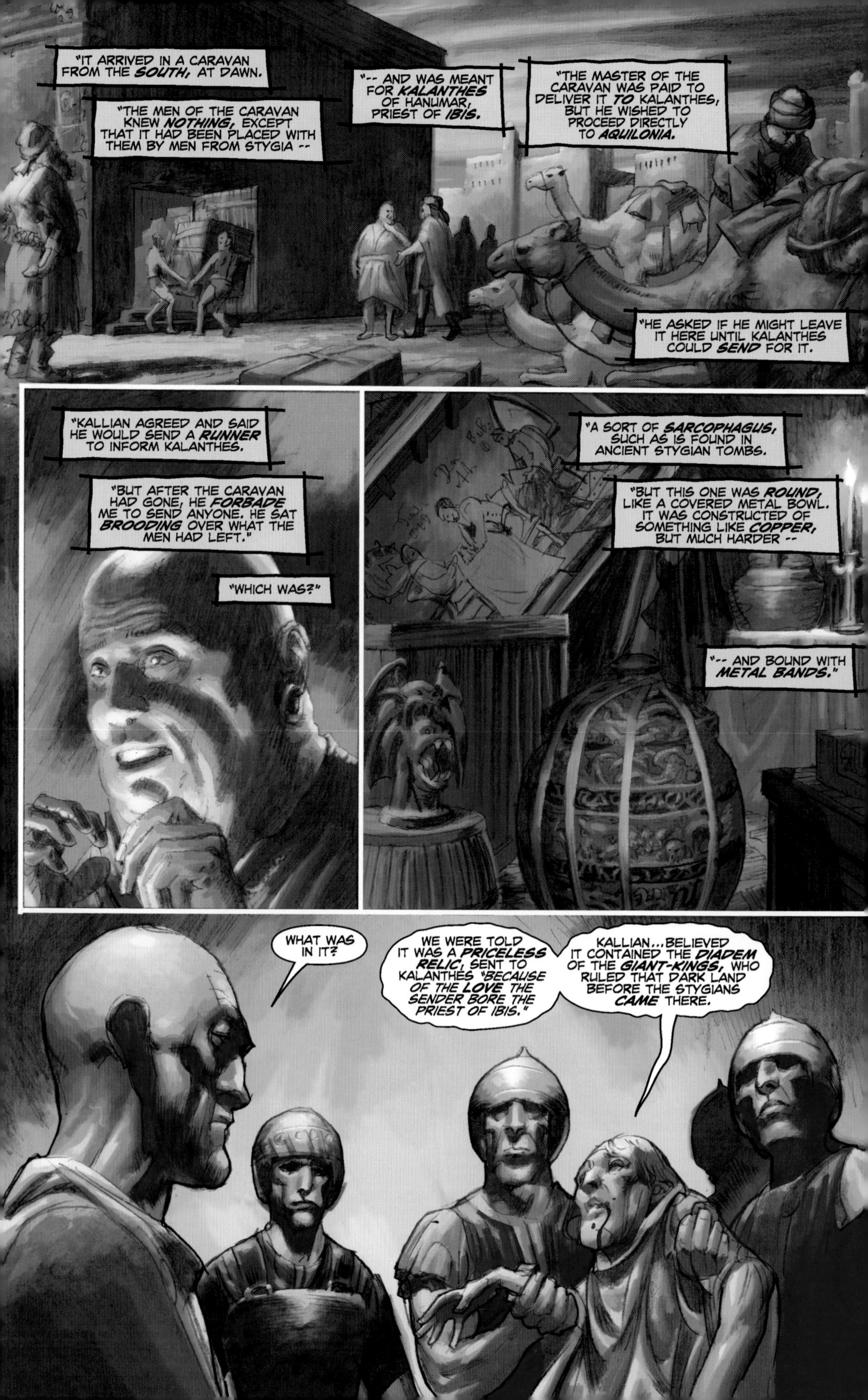
"IT ARRIVED IN A CARAVAN FROM THE SOUTH, AT DAWN.
"THE MEN OF THE CARAVAN KNEW NOTHING, EXCEPT THAT IT HAD BEEN PLACED WITH THEM BY MEN FROM STYGIA --
"-- AND WAS MEANT FOR KALANTHES OF HANUMAR, PRIEST OF IBIS.
"THE MASTER OF THE CARAVAN WAS PAID TO DELIVER IT TO KALANTHES, BUT HE WISHED TO PROCEED DIRECTLY TO AQUILONIA.
"HE ASKED IF HE MIGHT LEAVE IT HERE UNTIL KALANTHES COULD SEND FOR IT.
"KALLIAN AGREED AND SAID HE WOULD SEND A RUNNER TO INFORM KALANTHES.
"BUT AFTER THE CARAVAN HAD GONE, HE FORBADE ME TO SEND ANYONE. HE SAT BROODING OVER WHAT THE MEN HAD LEFT."
"WHICH WAS?"
"A SORT OF SARCOPHAGUS, SUCH AS IS FOUND IN ANCIENT STYGIAN TOMBS.
"BUT THIS ONE WAS ROUND, LIKE A COVERED METAL BOWL. IT WAS CONSTRUCTED OF SOMETHING LIKE COPPER, BUT MUCH HARDER --
"-- AND BOUND WITH METAL BANDS."
WHAT WAS IN IT?
WE WERE TOLD IT WAS A PRICELESS RELIC, SENT TO KALANTHES "BECAUSE OF THE LOVE THE SENDER BORE THE PRIEST OF IBIS."
KALLIAN...BELIEVED IT CONTAINED THE DIADEM OF THE GIANT-KINGS, WHO RULED THAT DARK LAND BEFORE THE STYGIANS CAME THERE.

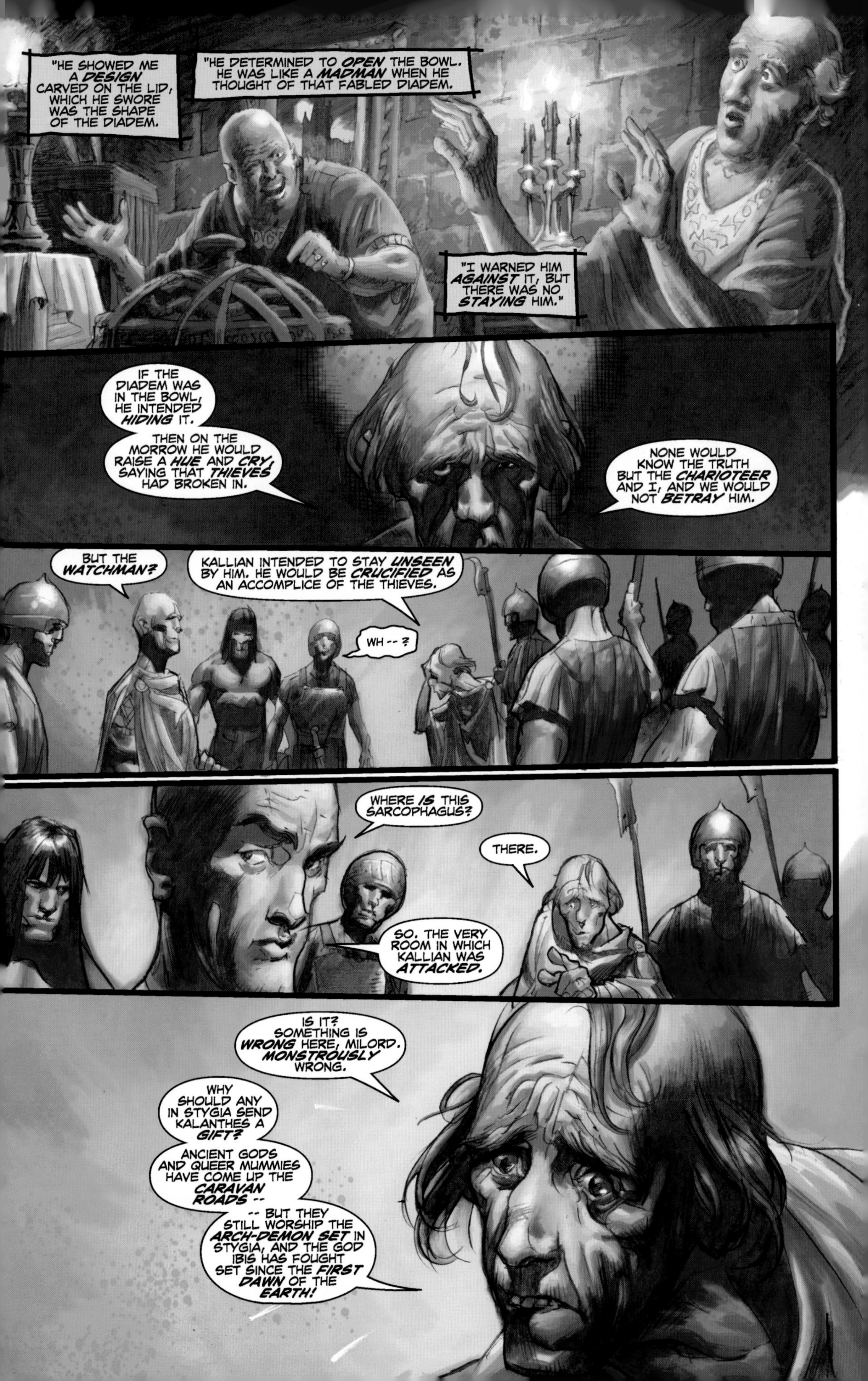
"HE SHOWED ME A DESIGN CARVED ON THE LID, WHICH HE SWORE WAS THE SHAPE OF THE DIADEM.
"HE DETERMINED TO OPEN THE BOWL. HE WAS LIKE A MADMAN WHEN HE THOUGHT OF THAT FABLED DIADEM.
"I WARNED HIM AGAINST IT, BUT THERE WAS NO STAYING HIM."
IF THE DIADEM WAS IN THE BOWL, HE INTENDED HIDING IT.
THEN ON THE MORROW HE WOULD RAISE A HUE AND CRY, SAYING THAT THIEVES HAD BROKEN IN.
NONE WOULD KNOW THE TRUTH BUT THE CHARIOTEER AND I, AND WE WOULD NOT BETRAY HIM.
BUT THE WATCHMAN?
KALLIAN INTENDED TO STAY UNSEEN BY HIM. HE WOULD BE CRUCIFIED AS AN ACCOMPLICE OF THE THIEVES.
WH -- ?
WHERE IS THIS SARCOPHAGUS?
THERE.
SO. THE VERY ROOM IN WHICH KALLIAN WAS ATTACKED.
IS IT? SOMETHING IS WRONG HERE, MILORD. MONSTROUSLY WRONG.
WHY SHOULD ANY IN STYGIA SEND KALANTHES A GIFT?
ANCIENT GODS AND QUEER MUMMIES HAVE COME UP THE CARAVAN ROADS --
-- BUT THEY STILL WORSHIP THE ARCH-DEMON SET IN STYGIA, AND THE GOD IBIS HAS FOUGHT SET SINCE THE FIRST DAWN OF THE EARTH!

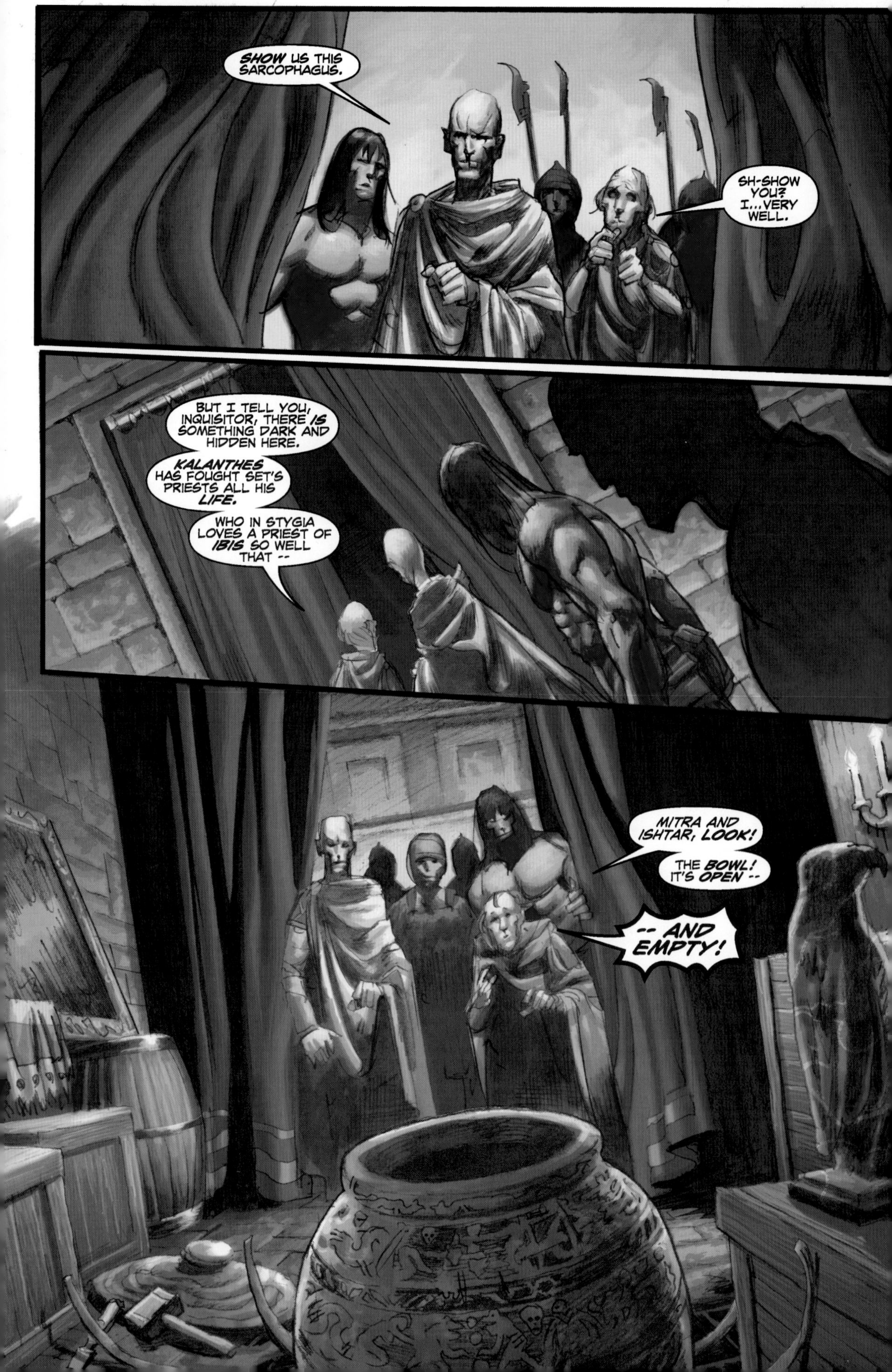
SHOW US THIS SARCOPHAGUS.
SH-SHOW YOU? I...VERY WELL.
BUT I TELL YOU, INQUISITOR, THERE IS SOMETHING DARK AND HIDDEN HERE.
KALANTHES HAS FOUGHT SET'S PRIESTS ALL HIS LIFE.
WHO IN STYGIA LOVES A PRIEST OF IBIS SO WELL THAT --
MITRA AND ISHTAR, LOOK!
THE BOWL! IT'S OPEN --
-- AND EMPTY!

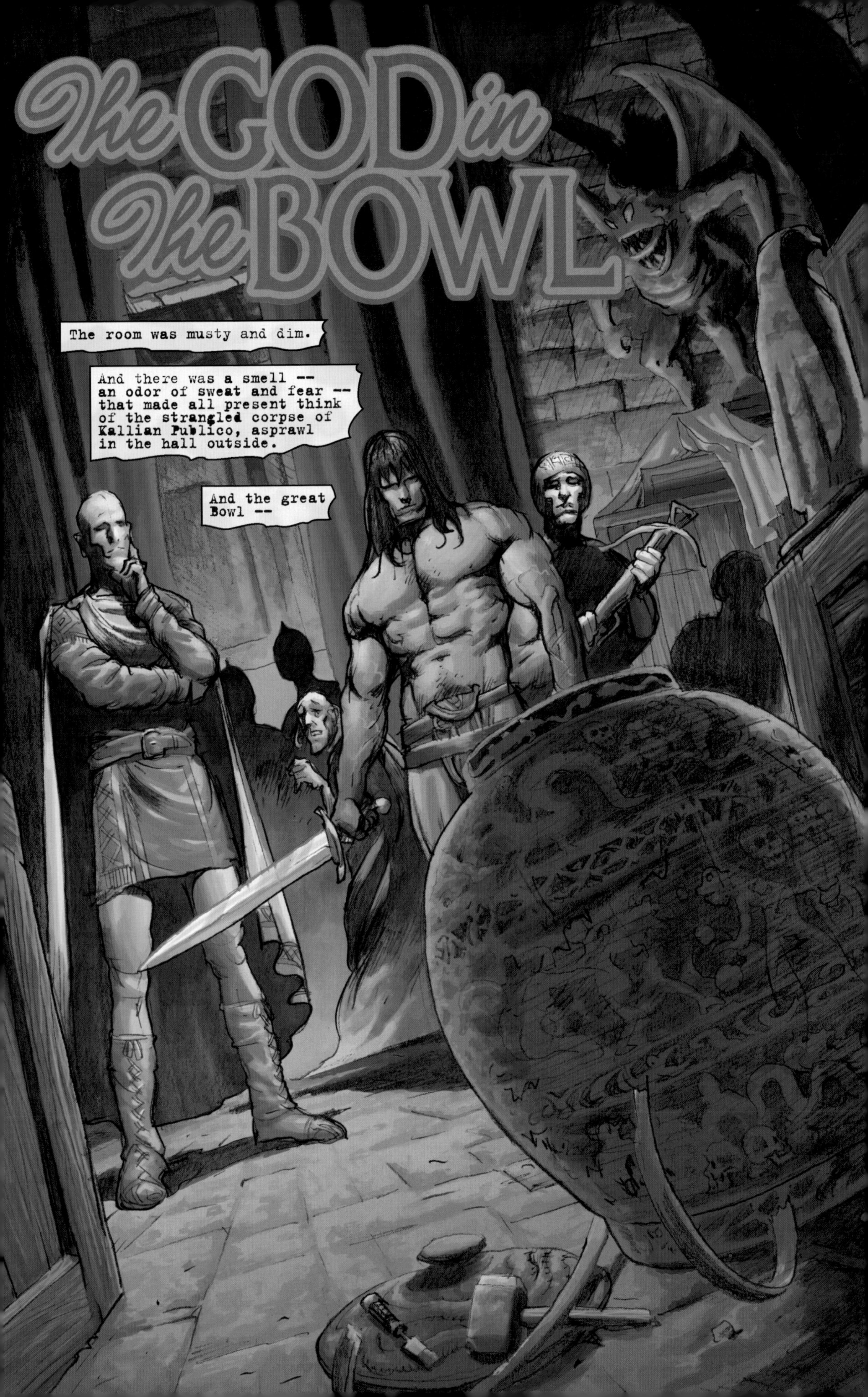
The GOD in the BOWL
The room was musty and dim.
And there was a smell -- an odor of sweat and fear -- that made all present think of the strangled corpse of Kallian Publico, asprawl in the hall outside.
And the great Bowl --

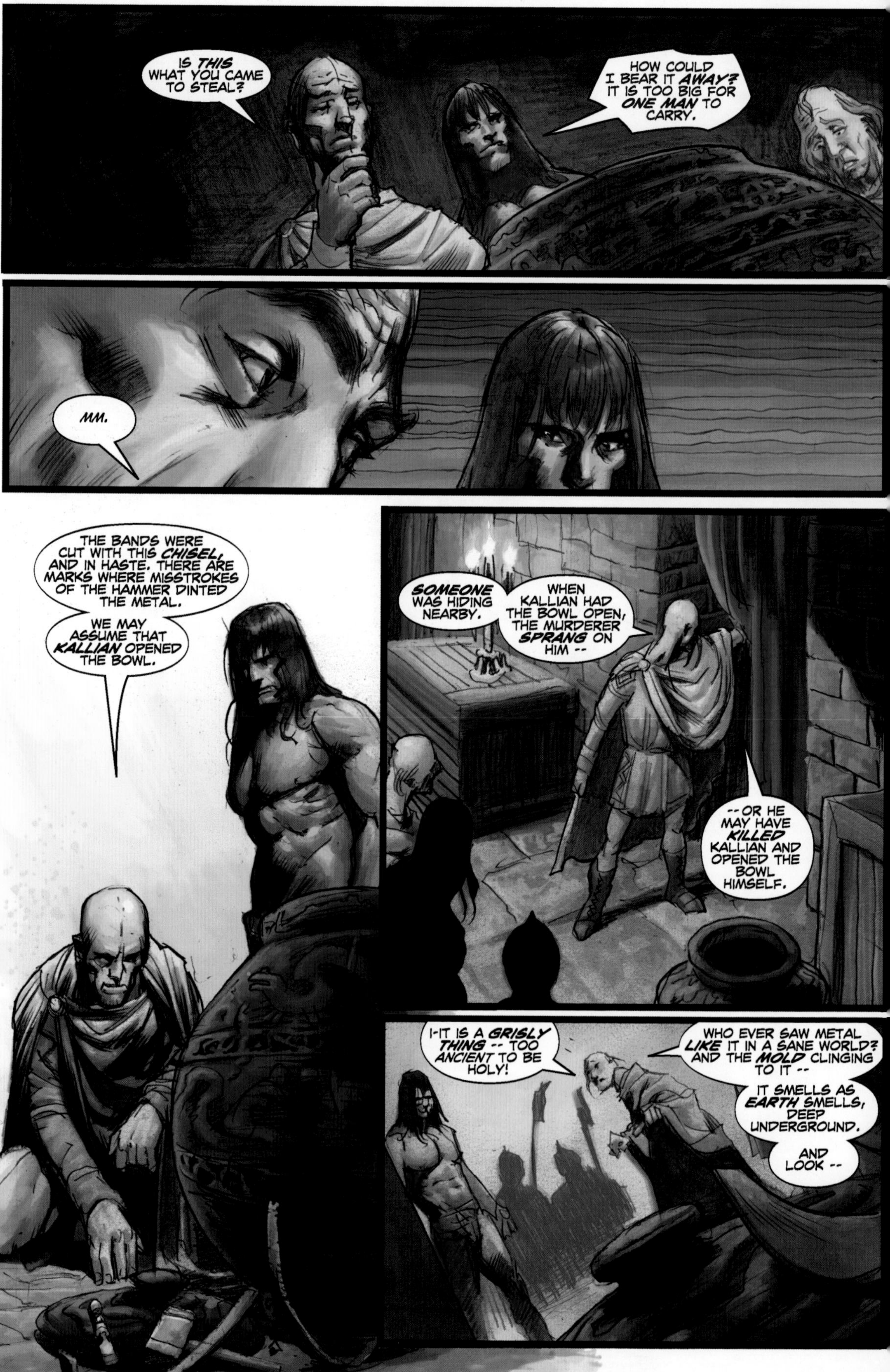
IS THIS WHAT YOU CAME TO STEAL?
HOW COULD I BEAR IT AWAY? IT IS TOO BIG FOR ONE MAN TO CARRY.
MM.
THE BANDS WERE CUT WITH THIS CHISEL, AND IN HASTE. THERE ARE MARKS WHERE MISSTROKES OF THE HAMMER DINTED THE METAL.
WE MAY ASSUME THAT KALLIAN OPENED THE BOWL.
SOMEONE WAS HIDING NEARBY.
WHEN KALLIAN HAD THE BOWL OPEN, THE MURDERER SPRANG ON HIM --
-- OR HE MAY HAVE KILLED KALLIAN AND OPENED THE BOWL HIMSELF.
I-IT IS A GRISLY THING -- TOO ANCIENT TO BE HOLY!
WHO EVER SAW METAL LIKE IT IN A SANE WORLD? AND THE MOLD CLINGING TO IT --
IT SMELLS AS EARTH SMELLS, DEEP UNDERGROUND.
AND LOOK --

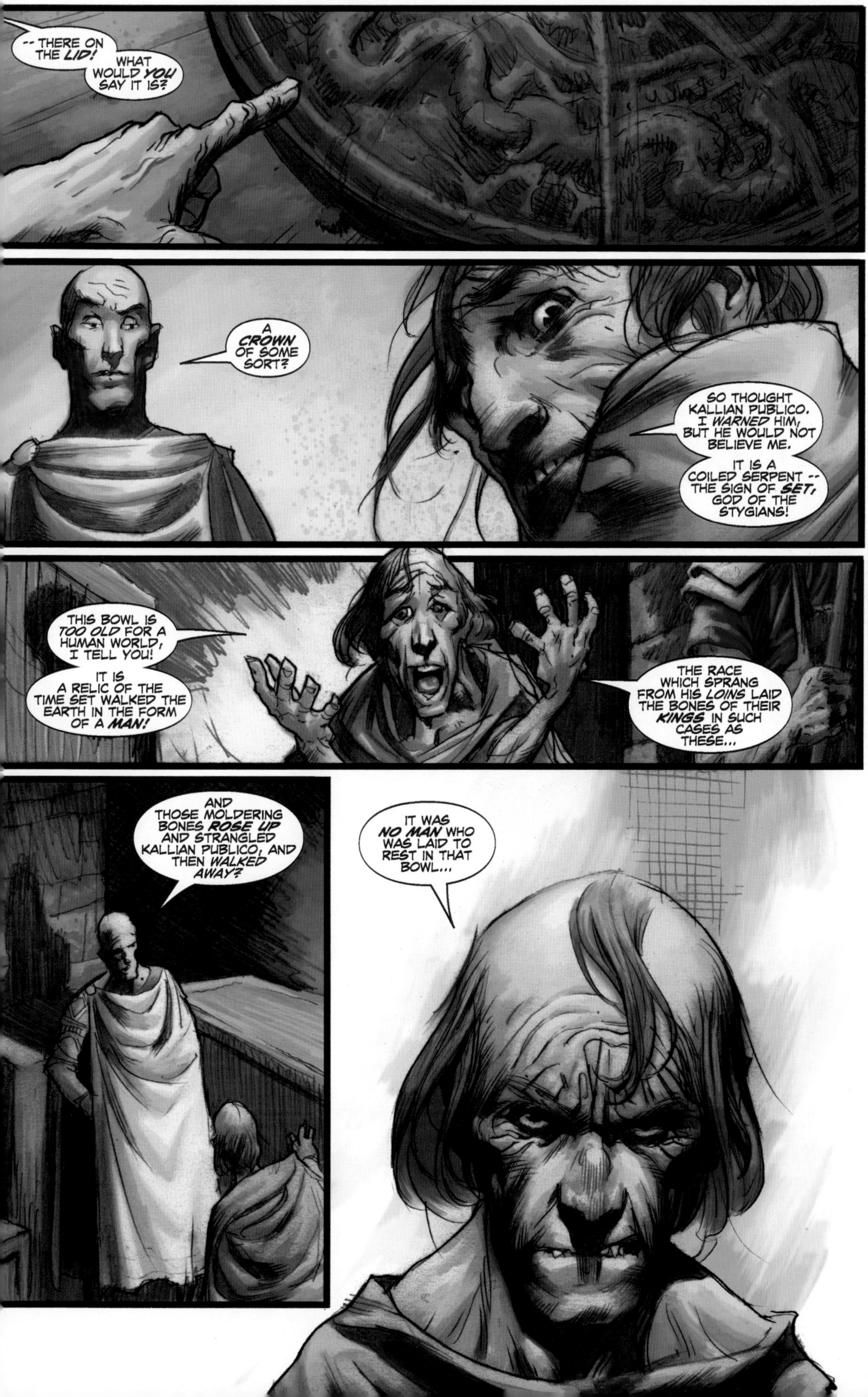
-- THERE ON THE LID! WHAT WOULD YOU SAY IT IS?
A CROWN OF SOME SORT?
SO THOUGHT KALLIAN PUBLICO. I WARNED HIM, BUT HE WOULD NOT BELIEVE ME.
IT IS A COILED SERPENT -- THE SIGN OF SET, GOD OF THE STYGIANS!
THIS BOWL IS TOO OLD FOR A HUMAN WORLD, I TELL YOU!
IT IS A RELIC OF THE TIME SET WALKED THE EARTH IN THE FORM OF A MAN!
THE RACE WHICH SPRANG FROM HIS LOINS LAID THE BONES OF THEIR KINGS IN SUCH CASES AS THESE...
AND THOSE MOLDERING BONES ROSE UP AND STRANGLED KALLIAN PUBLICO, AND THEN WALKED AWAY?
IT WAS NO MAN WHO WAS LAID TO REST IN THAT BOWL...

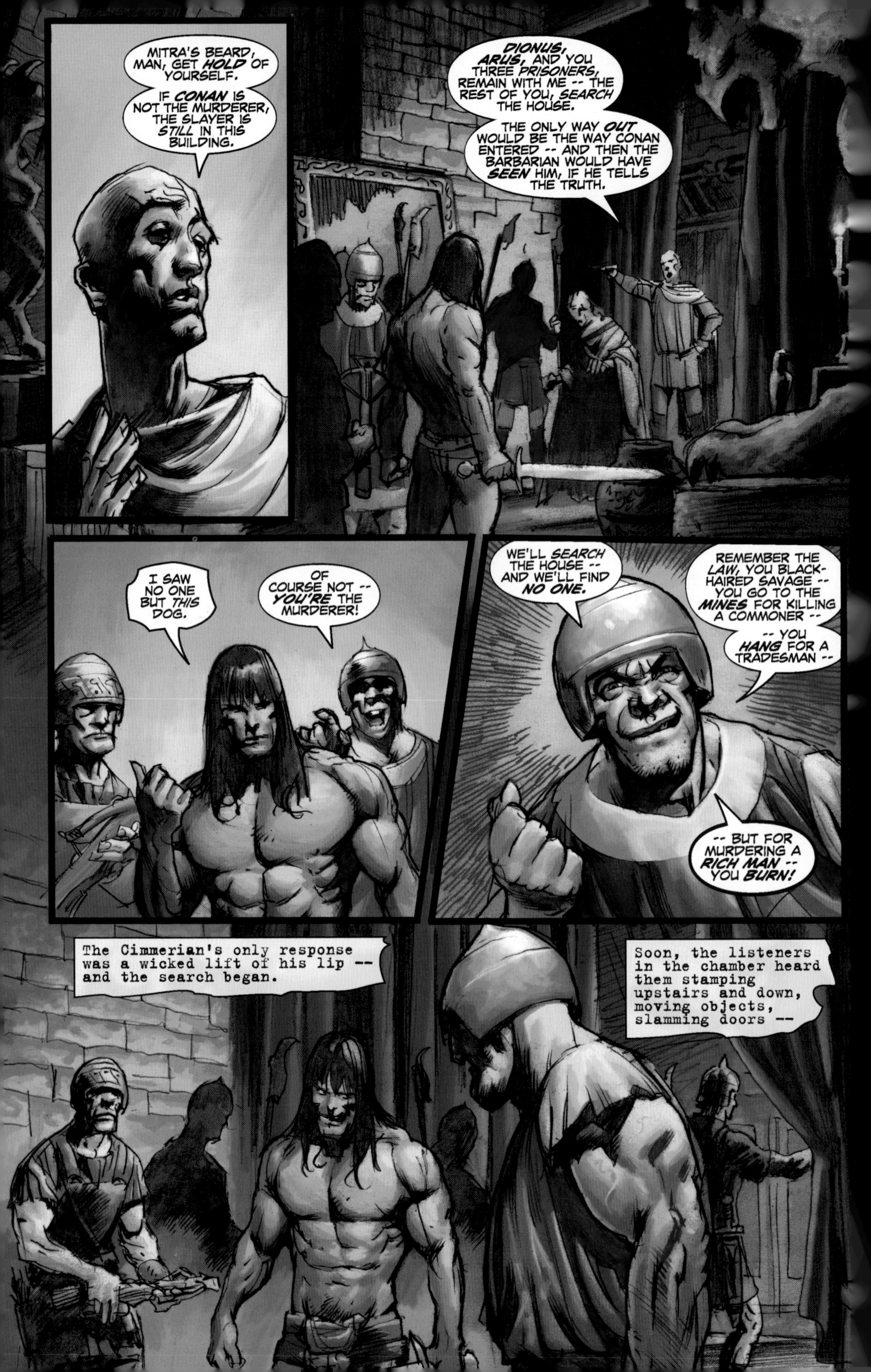
MITRA'S BEARD, MAN, GET HOLD OF YOURSELF.
IF CONAN IS NOT THE MURDERER, THE SLAYER IS STILL IN THIS BUILDING.
DIONUS, ARUS, AND YOU THREE PRISONERS, REMAIN WITH ME -- THE REST OF YOU, SEARCH THE HOUSE.
THE ONLY WAY OUT WOULD BE THE WAY CONAN ENTERED -- AND THEN THE BARBARIAN WOULD HAVE SEEN HIM, IF HE TELLS THE TRUTH.
I SAW NO ONE BUT THIS DOG.
OF COURSE NOT -- YOU'RE THE MURDERER!
WE'LL SEARCH THE HOUSE -- AND WE'LL FIND NO ONE.
REMEMBER THE LAW, YOU BLACK-HAIRED SAVAGE -- YOU GO TO THE MINES FOR KILLING A COMMONER --
-- YOU HANG FOR A TRADESMAN --
-- BUT FOR MURDERING A RICH MAN -- YOU BURN!
The Cimmerian's only response was a wicked lift of his lip -- and the search began.
Soon, the listeners in the chamber heard them stamping upstairs and down, moving objects, slamming doors --

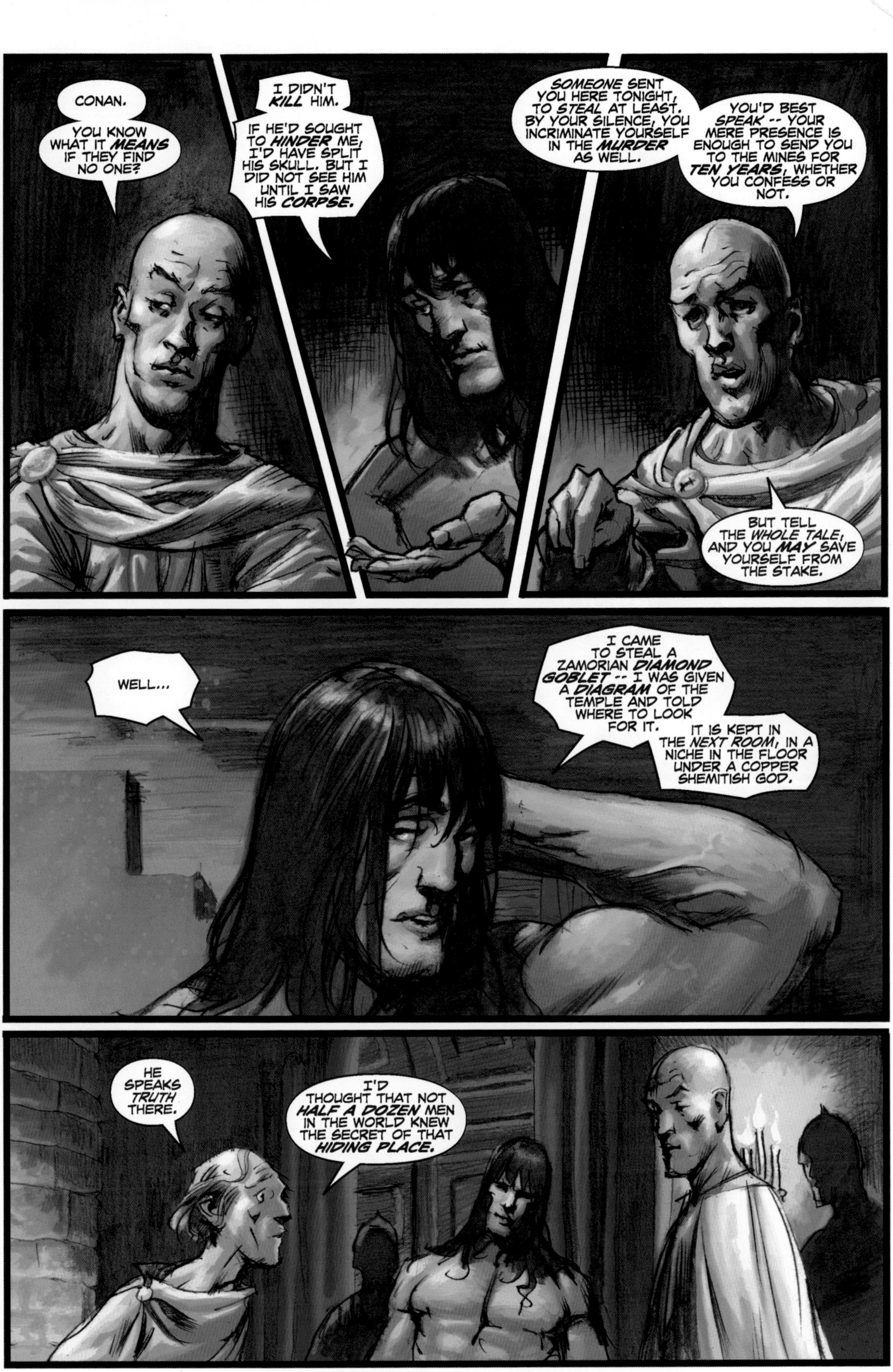
CONAN.
YOU KNOW WHAT IT MEANS IF THEY FIND NO ONE?
I DIDN'T KILL HIM.
IF HE'D SOUGHT TO HINDER ME, I'D HAVE SPLIT HIS SKULL. BUT I DID NOT SEE HIM UNTIL I SAW HIS CORPSE.
SOMEONE SENT YOU HERE TONIGHT, TO STEAL AT LEAST. BY YOUR SILENCE, YOU INCRIMINATE YOURSELF IN THE MURDER AS WELL.
YOU'D BEST SPEAK -- YOUR MERE PRESENCE IS ENOUGH TO SEND YOU TO THE MINES FOR TEN YEARS, WHETHER YOU CONFESS OR NOT.
BUT TELL THE WHOLE TALE, AND YOU MAY SAVE YOURSELF FROM THE STAKE.
WELL...
I CAME TO STEAL A ZAMORIAN DIAMOND GOBLET -- I WAS GIVEN A DIAGRAM OF THE TEMPLE AND TOLD WHERE TO LOOK FOR IT.
IT IS KEPT IN THE NEXT ROOM, IN A NICHE IN THE FLOOR UNDER A COPPER SHEMITISH GOD.
HE SPEAKS TRUTH THERE.
I'D THOUGHT THAT NOT HALF A DOZEN MEN IN THE WORLD KNEW THE SECRET OF THAT HIDING PLACE.

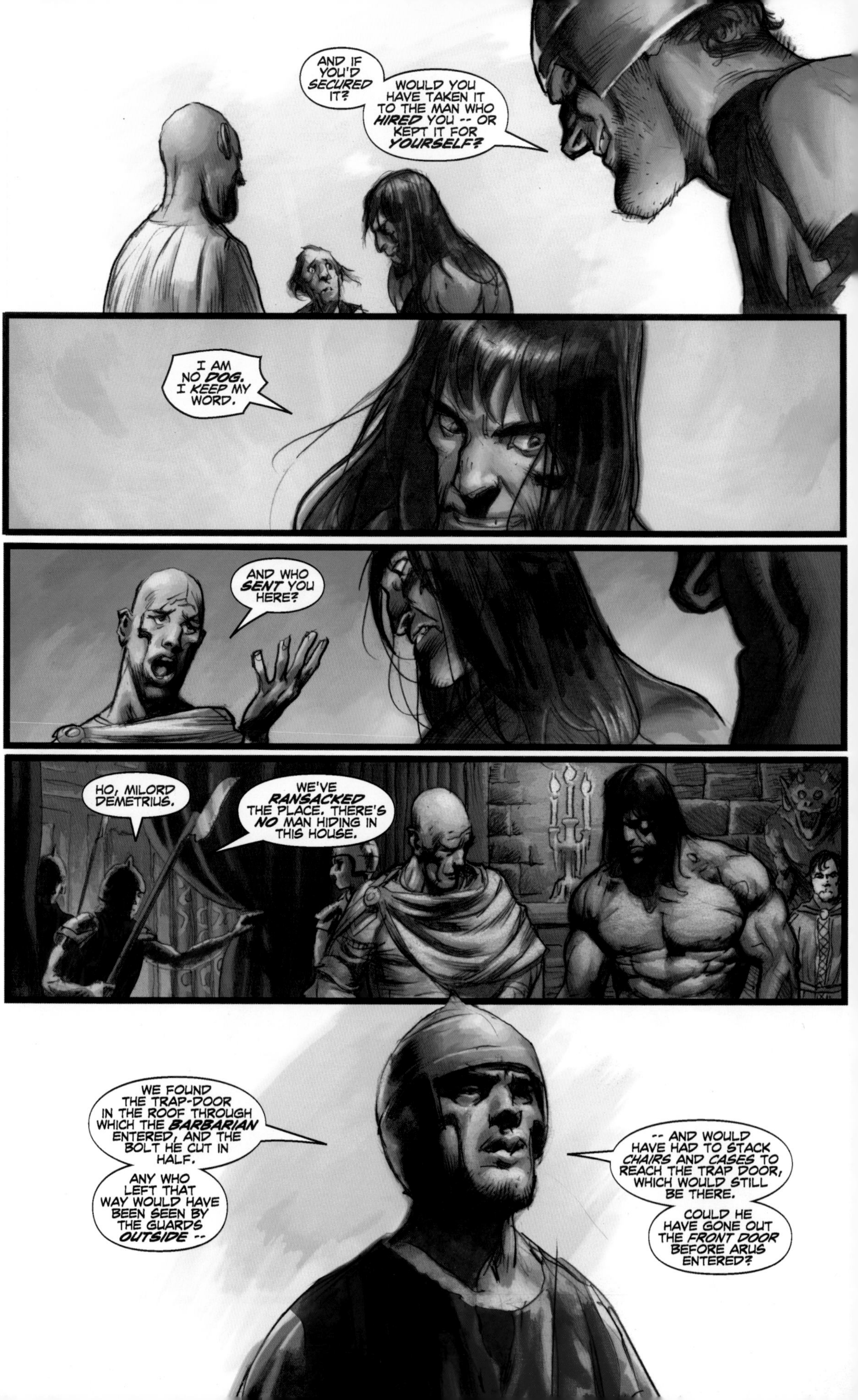
AND IF YOU'D SECURED IT?
WOULD YOU HAVE TAKEN IT TO THE MAN WHO HIRED YOU -- OR KEPT IT FOR YOURSELF?
I AM NO DOG. I KEEP MY WORD.
AND WHO SENT YOU HERE?
HO, MILORD DEMETRIUS.
WE'VE RANSACKED THE PLACE. THERE'S NO MAN HIDING IN THIS HOUSE.
WE FOUND THE TRAP-DOOR IN THE ROOF THROUGH WHICH THE BARBARIAN ENTERED, AND THE BOLT HE CUT IN HALF.
ANY WHO LEFT THAT WAY WOULD HAVE BEEN SEEN BY THE GUARDS OUTSIDE --
-- AND WOULD HAVE HAD TO STACK CHAIRS AND CASES TO REACH THE TRAP DOOR, WHICH WOULD STILL BE THERE.
COULD HE HAVE GONE OUT THE FRONT DOOR BEFORE ARUS ENTERED?

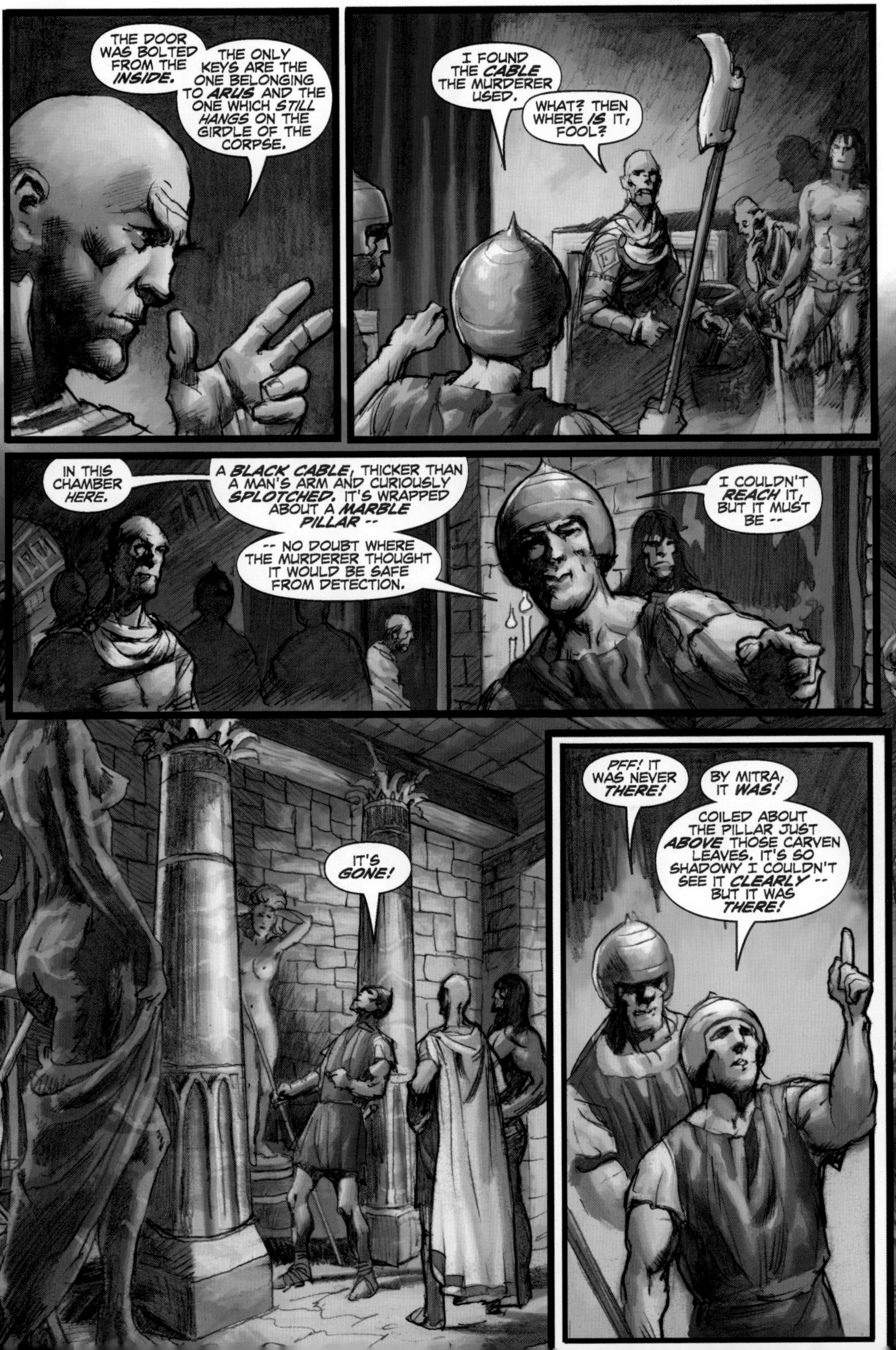
THE DOOR WAS BOLTED FROM THE INSIDE.
THE ONLY KEYS ARE THE ONE BELONGING TO ARUS AND THE ONE WHICH STILL HANGS ON THE GIRDLE OF THE CORPSE.
I FOUND THE CABLE THE MURDERER USED.
WHAT? THEN WHERE IS IT, FOOL?
IN THIS CHAMBER HERE.
A BLACK CABLE, THICKER THAN A MAN'S ARM AND CURIOUSLY SPLOTCHED. IT'S WRAPPED ABOUT A MARBLE PILLAR --
-- NO DOUBT WHERE THE MURDERER THOUGHT IT WOULD BE SAFE FROM DETECTION.
I COULDN'T REACH IT, BUT IT MUST BE --
IT'S GONE!
PFF! IT WAS NEVER THERE!
BY MITRA, IT WAS!
COILED ABOUT THE PILLAR JUST ABOVE THOSE CARVEN LEAVES. IT'S SO SHADOWY I COULDN'T SEE IT CLEARLY -- BUT IT WAS THERE!

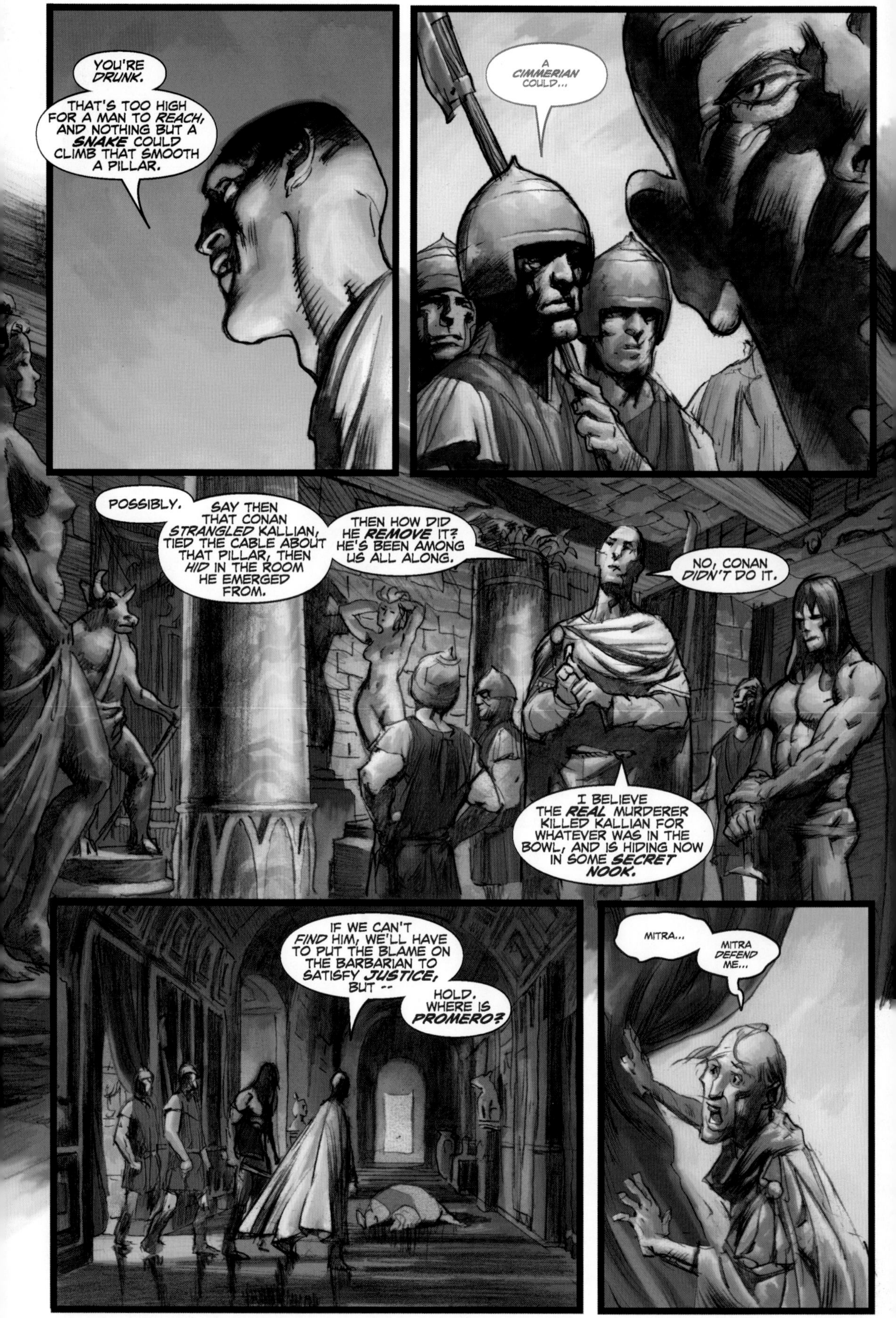
YOU'RE DRUNK.
THAT'S TOO HIGH FOR A MAN TO REACH, AND NOTHING BUT A SNAKE COULD CLIMB THAT SMOOTH A PILLAR.
A CIMMERIAN COULD...
POSSIBLY.
SAY THEN THAT CONAN STRANGLED KALLIAN, TIED THE CABLE ABOUT THAT PILLAR, THEN HID IN THE ROOM HE EMERGED FROM.
THEN HOW DID HE REMOVE IT? HE'S BEEN AMONG US ALL ALONG.
NO, CONAN DIDN'T DO IT.
I BELIEVE THE REAL MURDERER KILLED KALLIAN FOR WHATEVER WAS IN THE BOWL, AND IS HIDING NOW IN SOME SECRET NOOK.
IF WE CAN'T FIND HIM, WE'LL HAVE TO PUT THE BLAME ON THE BARBARIAN TO SATISFY JUSTICE, BUT --
HOLD. WHERE IS PROMERO?
MITRA...
MITRA DEFEND ME...

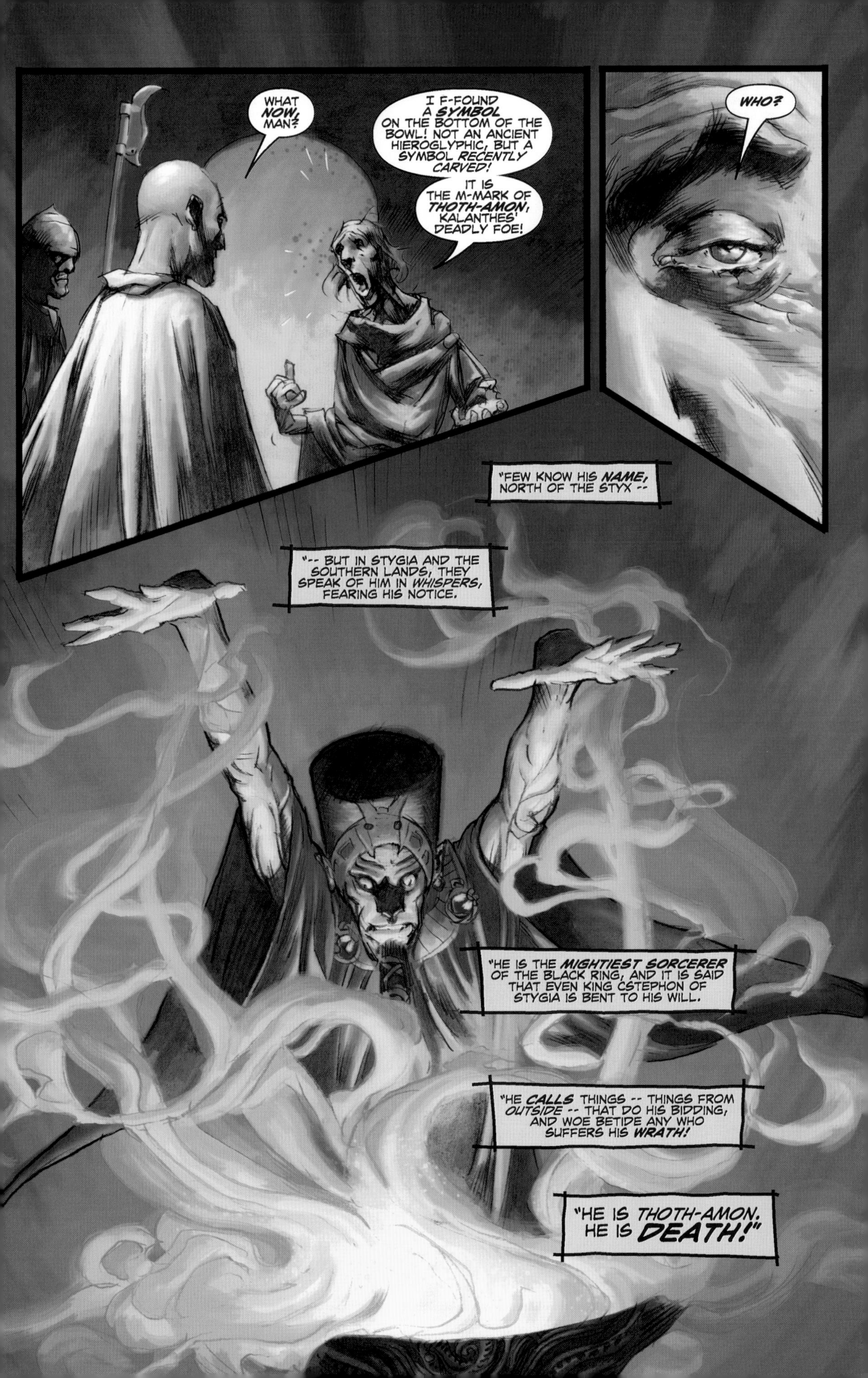
WHAT NOW, MAN?
I F-FOUND A SYMBOL ON THE BOTTOM OF THE BOWL! NOT AN ANCIENT HIEROGLYPHIC, BUT A SYMBOL RECENTLY CARVED!
IT IS THE M-MARK OF THOTH-AMON, KALANTHES' DEADLY FOE!
WHO?
"FEW KNOW HIS NAME, NORTH OF THE STYX --
"-- BUT IN STYGIA AND THE SOUTHERN LANDS, THEY SPEAK OF HIM IN WHISPERS, FEARING HIS NOTICE.
"HE IS THE MIGHTIEST SORCERER OF THE BLACK RING, AND IT IS SAID THAT EVEN KING CSTEPHON OF STYGIA IS BENT TO HIS WILL.
"HE CALLS THINGS -- THINGS FROM OUTSIDE -- THAT DO HIS BIDDING, AND WOE BETIDE ANY WHO SUFFERS HIS WRATH!
"HE IS THOTH-AMON. HE IS DEATH!"

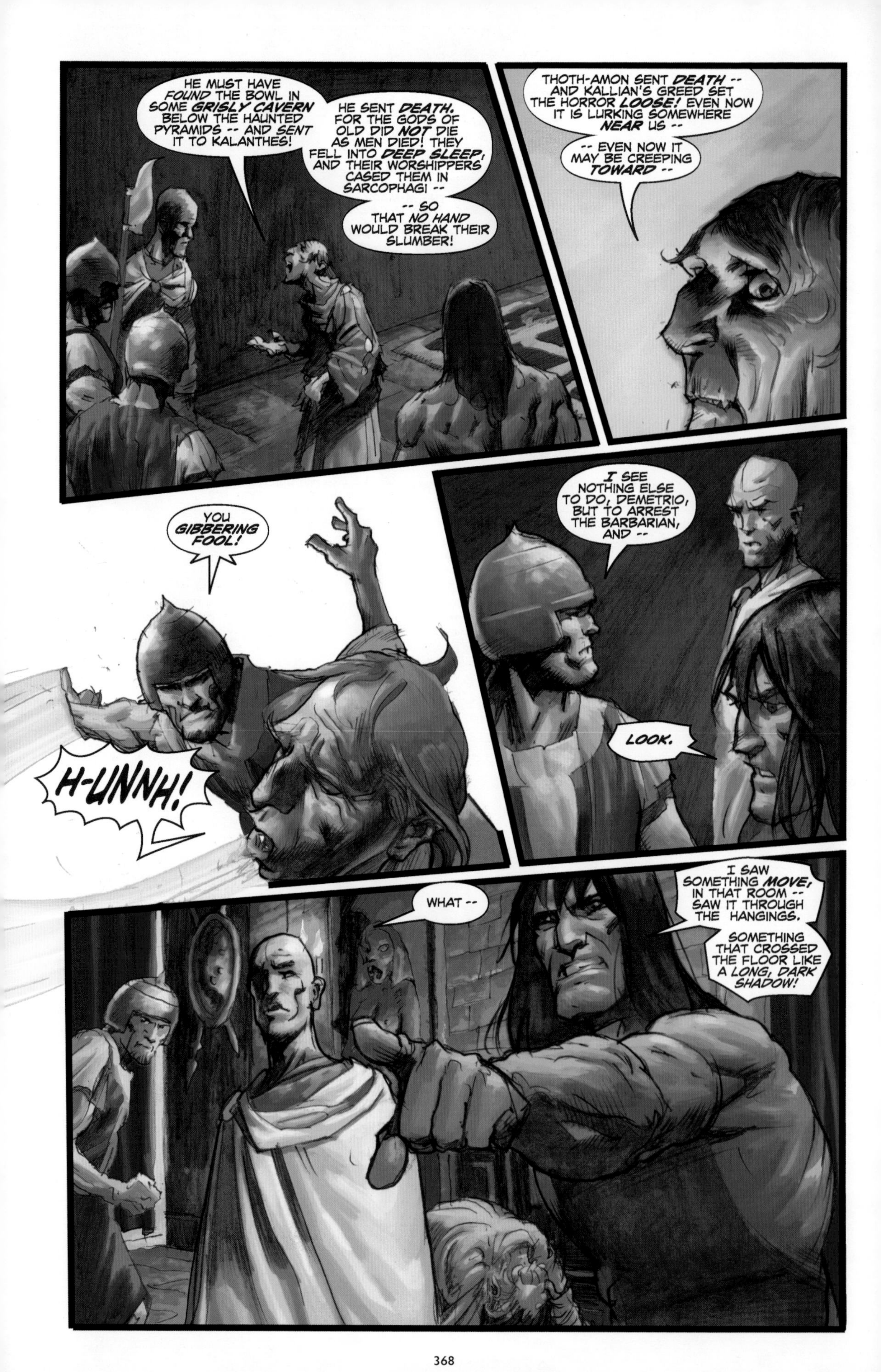
HE MUST HAVE FOUND THE BOWL IN SOME GRISLY CAVERN BELOW THE HAUNTED PYRAMIDS -- AND SENT IT TO KALANTHES!
HE SENT DEATH. FOR THE GODS OF OLD DID NOT DIE AS MEN DIED! THEY FELL INTO DEEP SLEEP, AND THEIR WORSHIPPERS CASED THEM IN SARCOPHAGI --
-- SO THAT NO HAND WOULD BREAK THEIR SLUMBER!
THOTH-AMON SENT DEATH -- AND KALLIAN'S GREED SET THE HORROR LOOSE! EVEN NOW IT IS LURKING SOMEWHERE NEAR US --
-- EVEN NOW IT MAY BE CREEPING TOWARD --
YOU GIBBERING FOOL!
H-UNNH!
I SEE NOTHING ELSE TO DO, DEMETRIO, BUT TO ARREST THE BARBARIAN, AND --
LOOK.
WHAT --
I SAW SOMETHING MOVE, IN THAT ROOM -- SAW IT THROUGH THE HANGINGS.
SOMETHING THAT CROSSED THE FLOOR LIKE A LONG, DARK SHADOW!

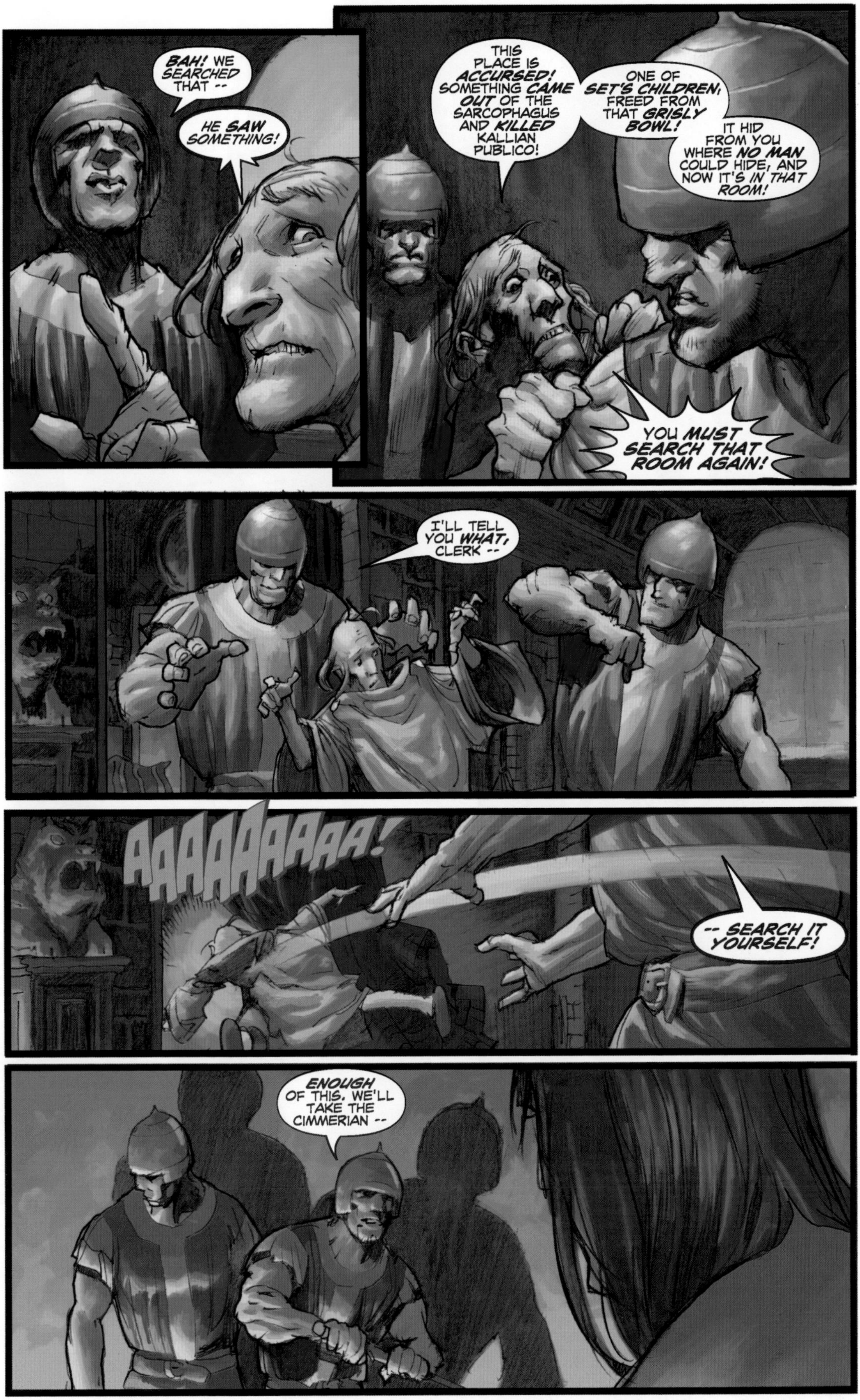
BAH! WE SEARCHED THAT --
HE SAW SOMETHING!
THIS PLACE IS ACCURSED! SOMETHING CAME OUT OF THE SARCOPHAGUS AND KILLED KALLIAN PUBLICO!
ONE OF SET'S CHILDREN, FREED FROM THAT GRISLY BOWL!
IT HID FROM YOU WHERE NO MAN COULD HIDE, AND NOW IT'S IN THAT ROOM!
YOU MUST SEARCH THAT ROOM AGAIN!
I'LL TELL YOU WHAT, CLERK --
AAAAAAAAA!
-- SEARCH IT YOURSELF!
ENOUGH OF THIS. WE'LL TAKE THE CIMMERIAN --

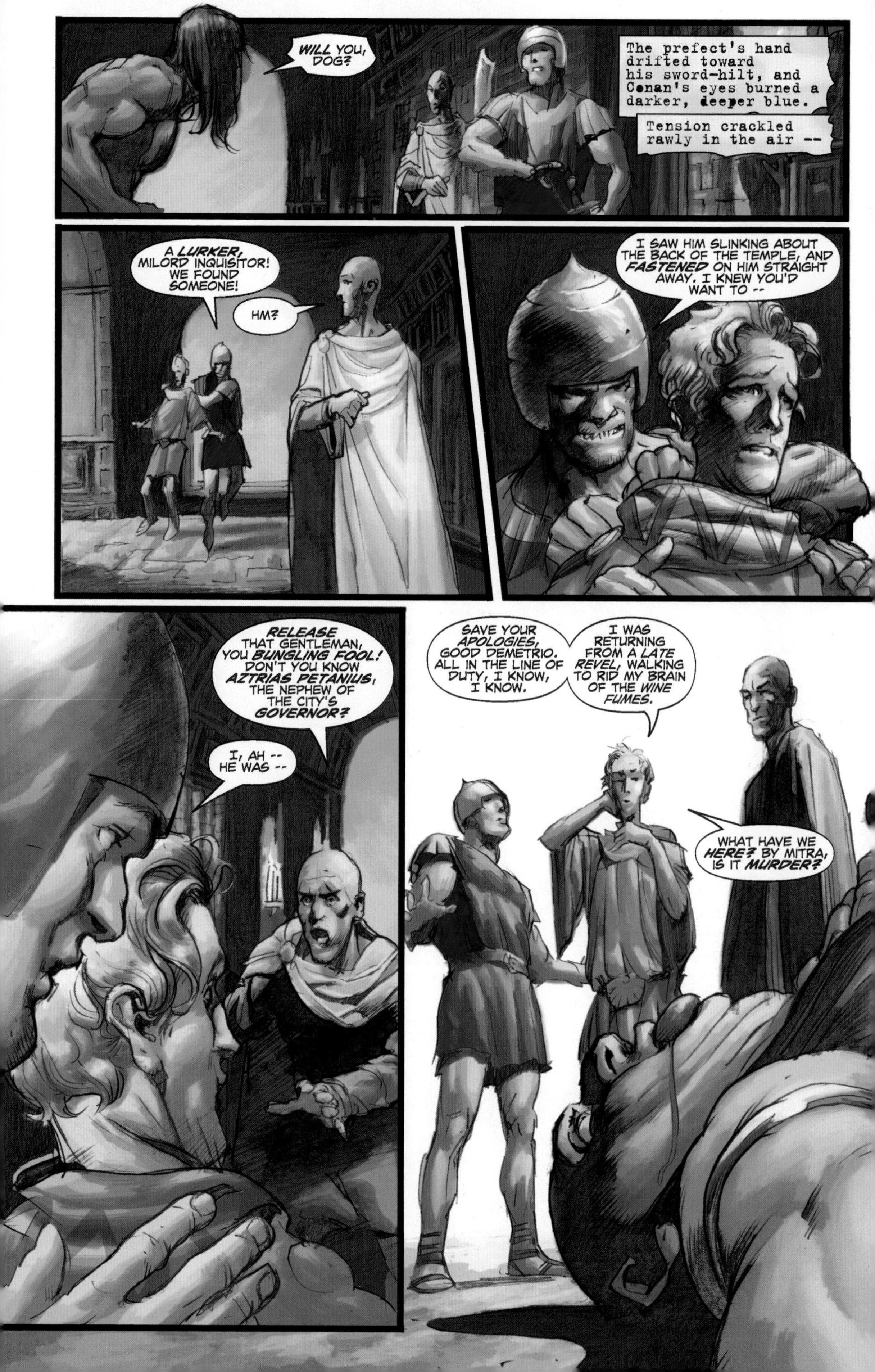
WILL YOU, DOG?
The prefect's hand drifted toward his sword-hilt, and Conan's eyes burned a darker, deeper blue.
Tension crackled rawly in the air --
A LURKER, MILORD INQUISITOR! WE FOUND SOMEONE!
HM?
I SAW HIM SLINKING ABOUT THE BACK OF THE TEMPLE, AND FASTENED ON HIM STRAIGHT AWAY. I KNEW YOU'D WANT TO --
RELEASE THAT GENTLEMAN, YOU BUNGLING FOOL! DON'T YOU KNOW AZTRIAS PETANIUS, THE NEPHEW OF THE CITY'S GOVERNOR?
I, AH -- HE WAS --
SAVE YOUR APOLOGIES, GOOD DEMETRIO. ALL IN THE LINE OF DUTY, I KNOW, I KNOW.
I WAS RETURNING FROM A LATE REVEL, WALKING TO RID MY BRAIN OF THE WINE FUMES.
WHAT HAVE WE HERE? BY MITRA, IS IT MURDER?

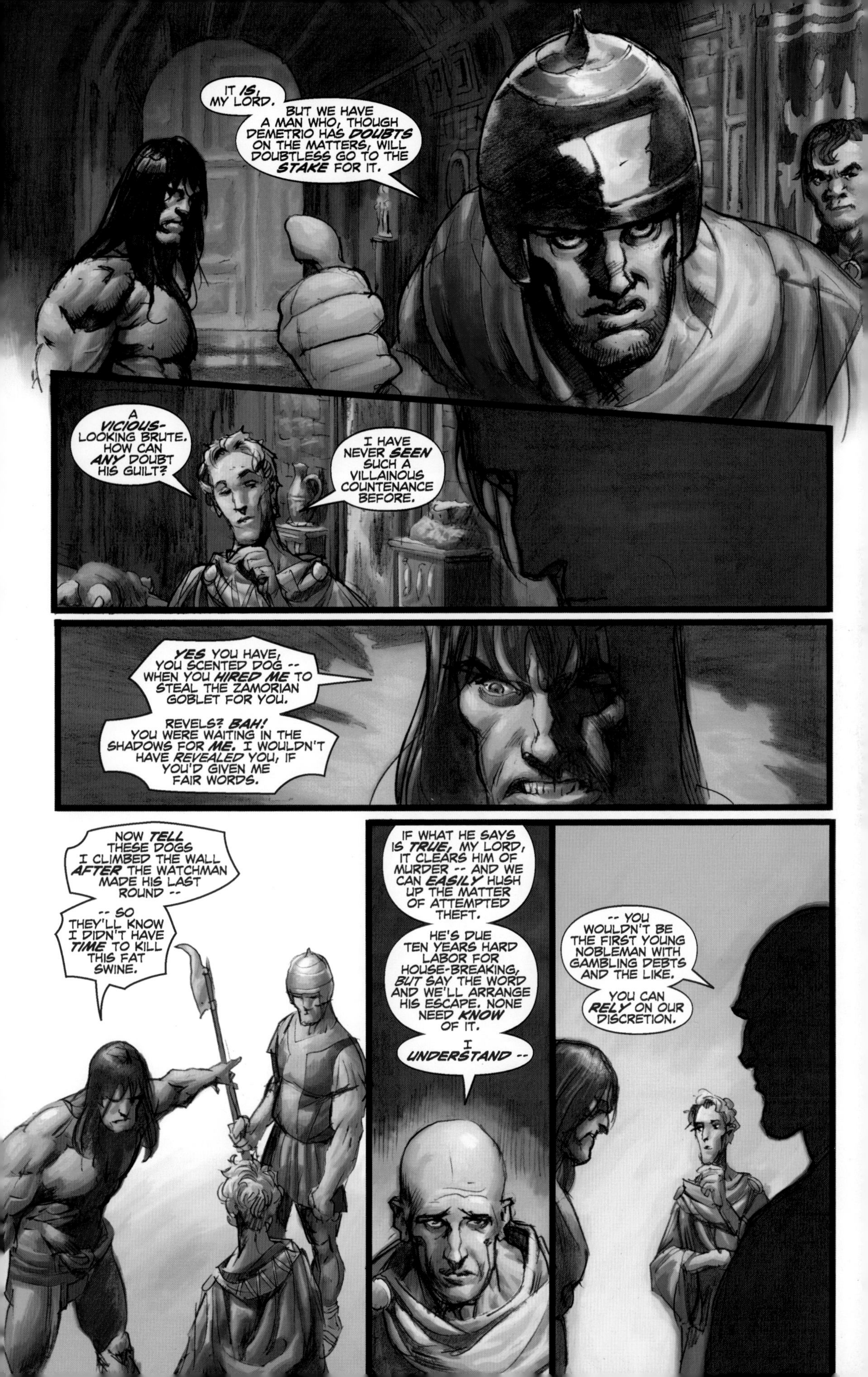
IT IS, MY LORD.
BUT WE HAVE A MAN WHO, THOUGH DEMETRIO HAS DOUBTS ON THE MATTERS, WILL DOUBTLESS GO TO THE STAKE FOR IT.
A VICIOUS-LOOKING BRUTE. HOW CAN ANY DOUBT HIS GUILT?
I HAVE NEVER SEEN SUCH A VILLAINOUS COUNTENANCE BEFORE.
YES YOU HAVE, YOU SCENTED DOG -- WHEN YOU HIRED ME TO STEAL THE ZAMORIAN GOBLET FOR YOU.
REVELS? BAH! YOU WERE WAITING IN THE SHADOWS FOR ME. I WOULDN'T HAVE REVEALED YOU, IF YOU'D GIVEN ME FAIR WORDS.
NOW TELL THESE DOGS I CLIMBED THE WALL AFTER THE WATCHMAN MADE HIS LAST ROUND --
-- SO THEY'LL KNOW I DIDN'T HAVE TIME TO KILL THIS FAT SWINE.
IF WHAT HE SAYS IS TRUE, MY LORD, IT CLEARS HIM OF MURDER -- AND WE CAN EASILY HUSH UP THE MATTER OF ATTEMPTED THEFT.
HE'S DUE TEN YEARS HARD LABOR FOR HOUSE-BREAKING, BUT SAY THE WORD AND WE'LL ARRANGE HIS ESCAPE. NONE NEED KNOW OF IT.
I UNDERSTAND --
-- YOU WOULDN'T BE THE FIRST YOUNG NOBLEMAN WITH GAMBLING DEBTS AND THE LIKE.
YOU CAN RELY ON OUR DISCRETION.

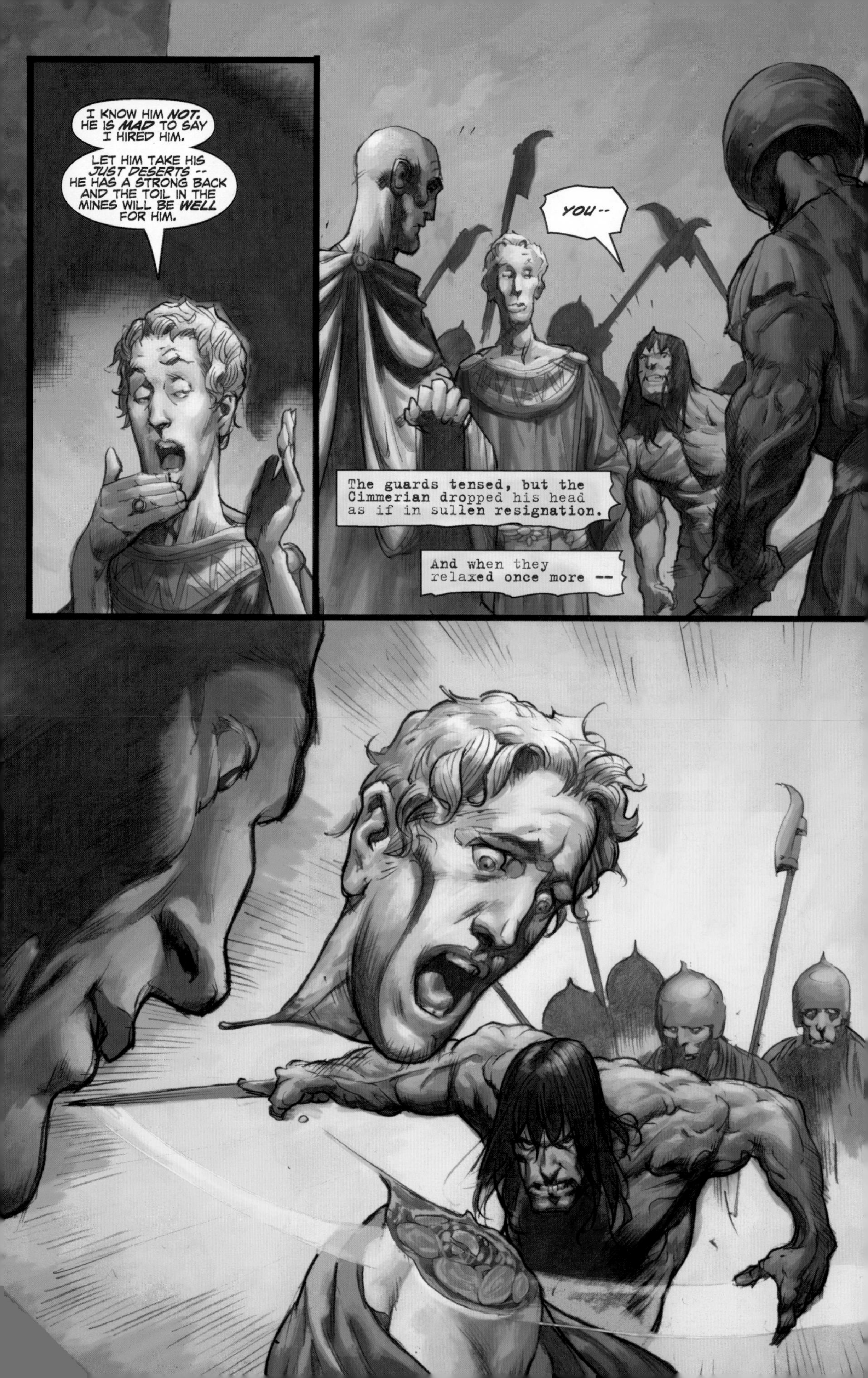
I KNOW HIM NOT. HE IS MAD TO SAY I HIRED HIM.
LET HIM TAKE HIS JUST DESERTS -- HE HAS A STRONG BACK AND THE TOIL IN THE MINES WILL BE WELL FOR HIM.
YOU --
The guards tensed, but the Cimmerian dropped his head as if in sullen resignation.
And when they relaxed once more --

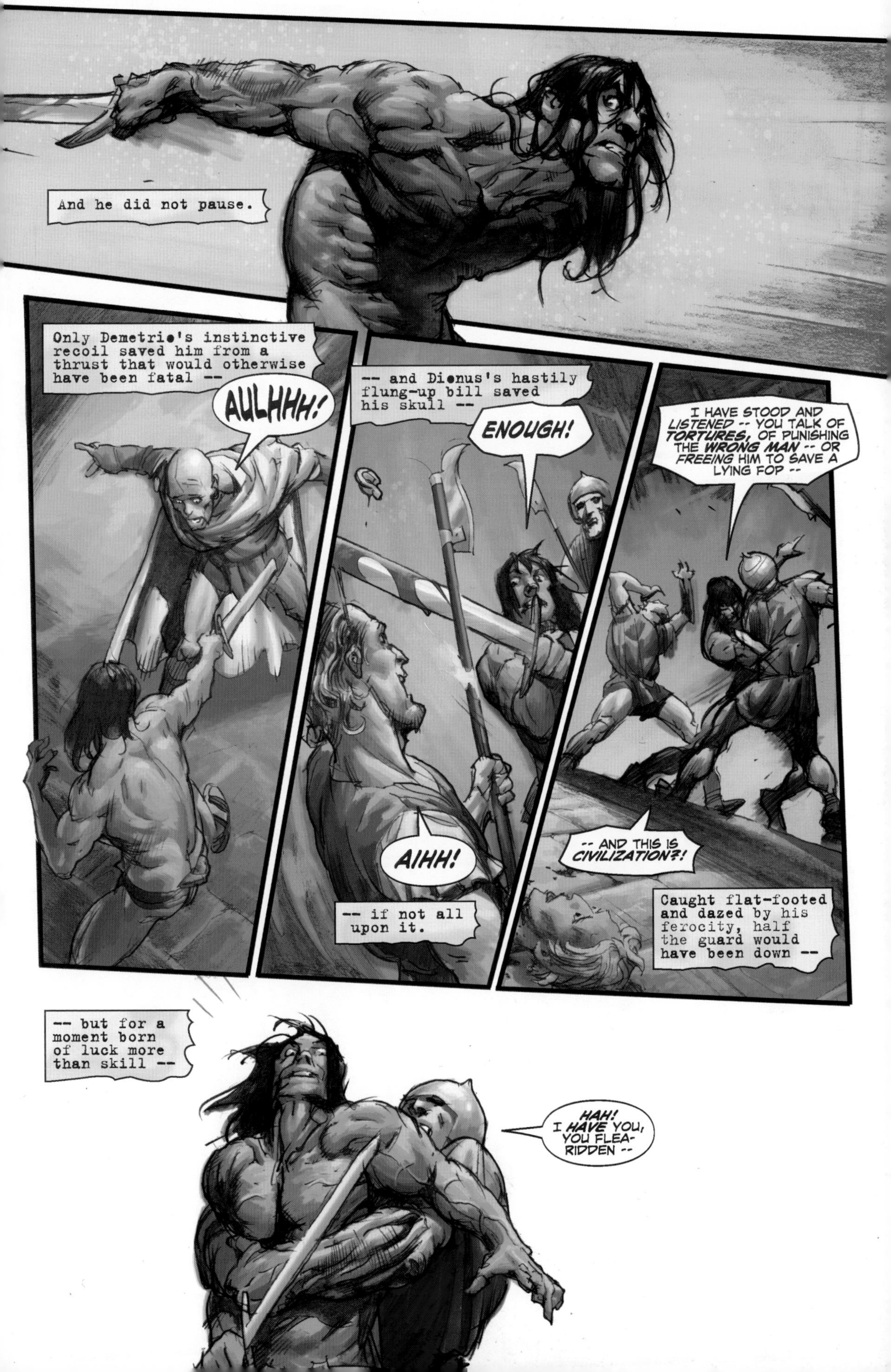
And he did not pause.
Only Demetrio's instinctive recoil saved him from a thrust that would otherwise have been fatal --
AULHHH!
-- and Dionus's hastily flung-up bill saved his skull --
ENOUGH!
AIHH!
-- if not all upon it.
I HAVE STOOD AND LISTENED -- YOU TALK OF TORTURES, OF PUNISHING THE WRONG MAN -- OR FREEING HIM TO SAVE A LYING FOP --
-- AND THIS IS CIVILIZATION?!
Caught flat-footed and dazed by his ferocity, half the guard would have been down --
-- but for a moment born of luck more than skill --
HAH! I HAVE YOU, YOU FLEA-RIDDEN --

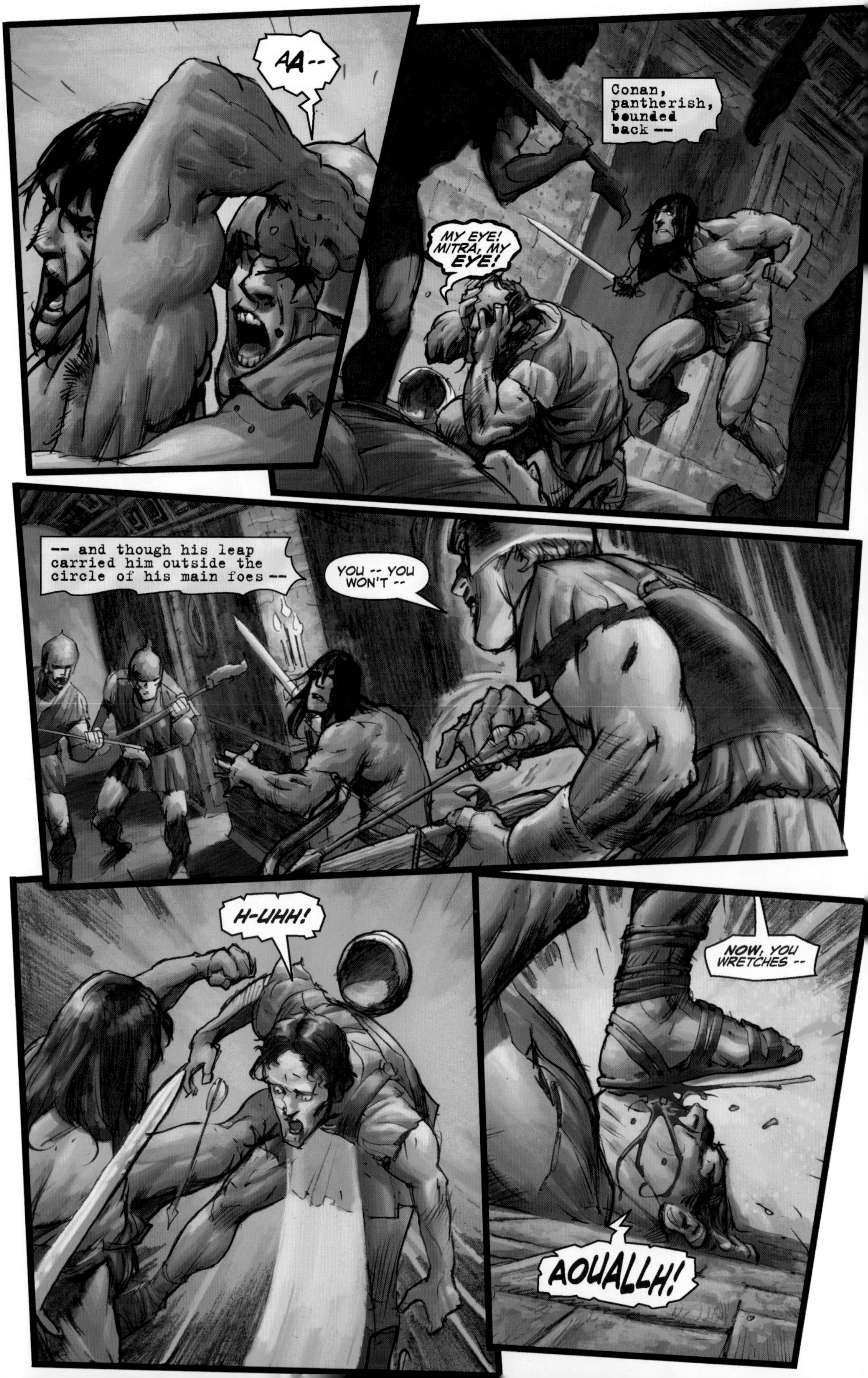
AA--
Conan, pantherish, bounded back --
MY EYE! MITRA, MY EYE!
-- and though his leap carried him outside the circle of his main foes --
YOU -- YOU WON'T --
H-UHH!
NOW, YOU WRETCHES --
AOUALLH!

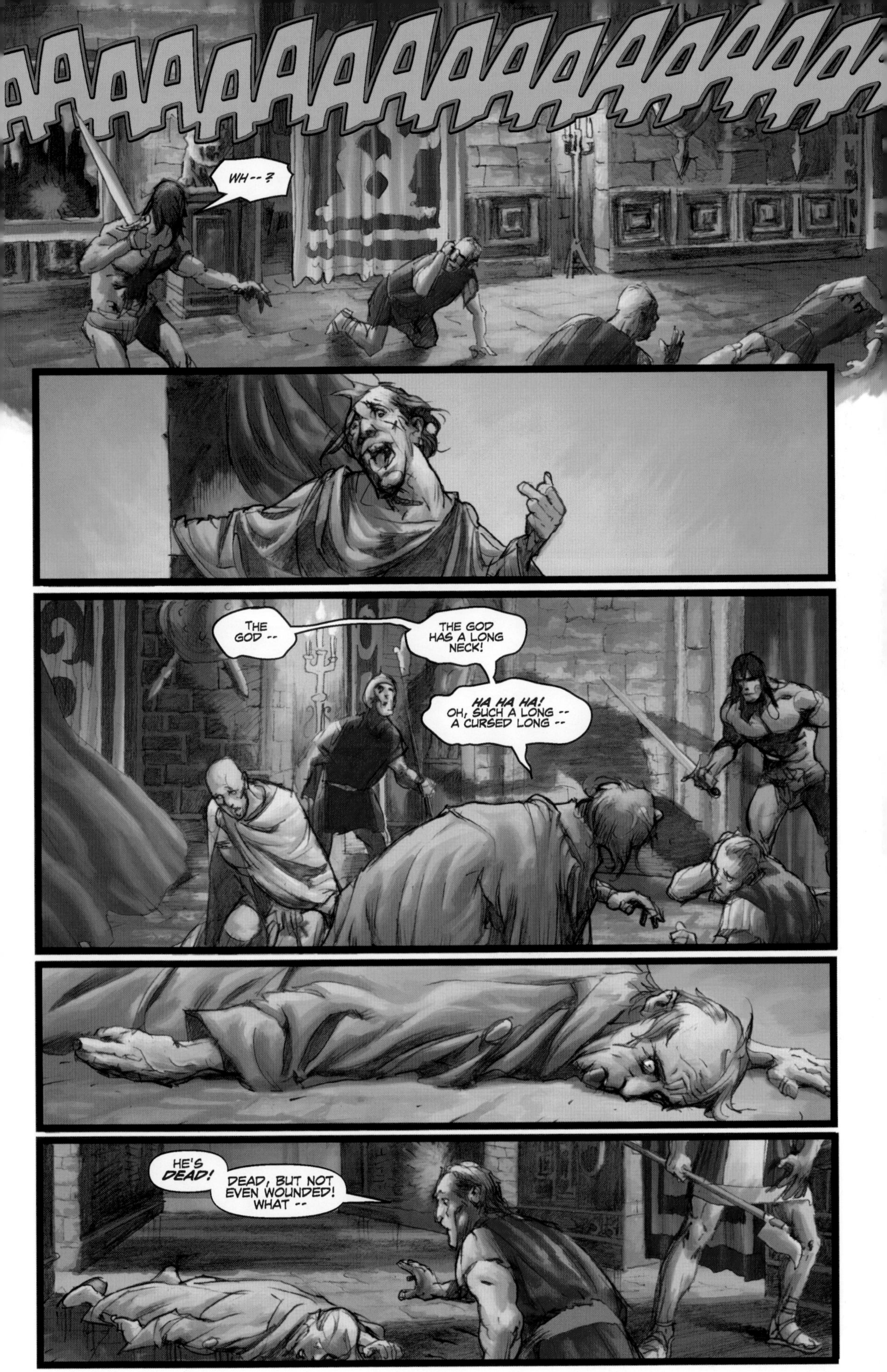
AAAAAAAAAAAAAAAA!
WH-- ?
THE GOD --
THE GOD HAS A LONG NECK!
HA HA HA! OH, SUCH A LONG -- A CURSED LONG --
HE'S DEAD!
DEAD, BUT NOT EVEN WOUNDED! WHAT --

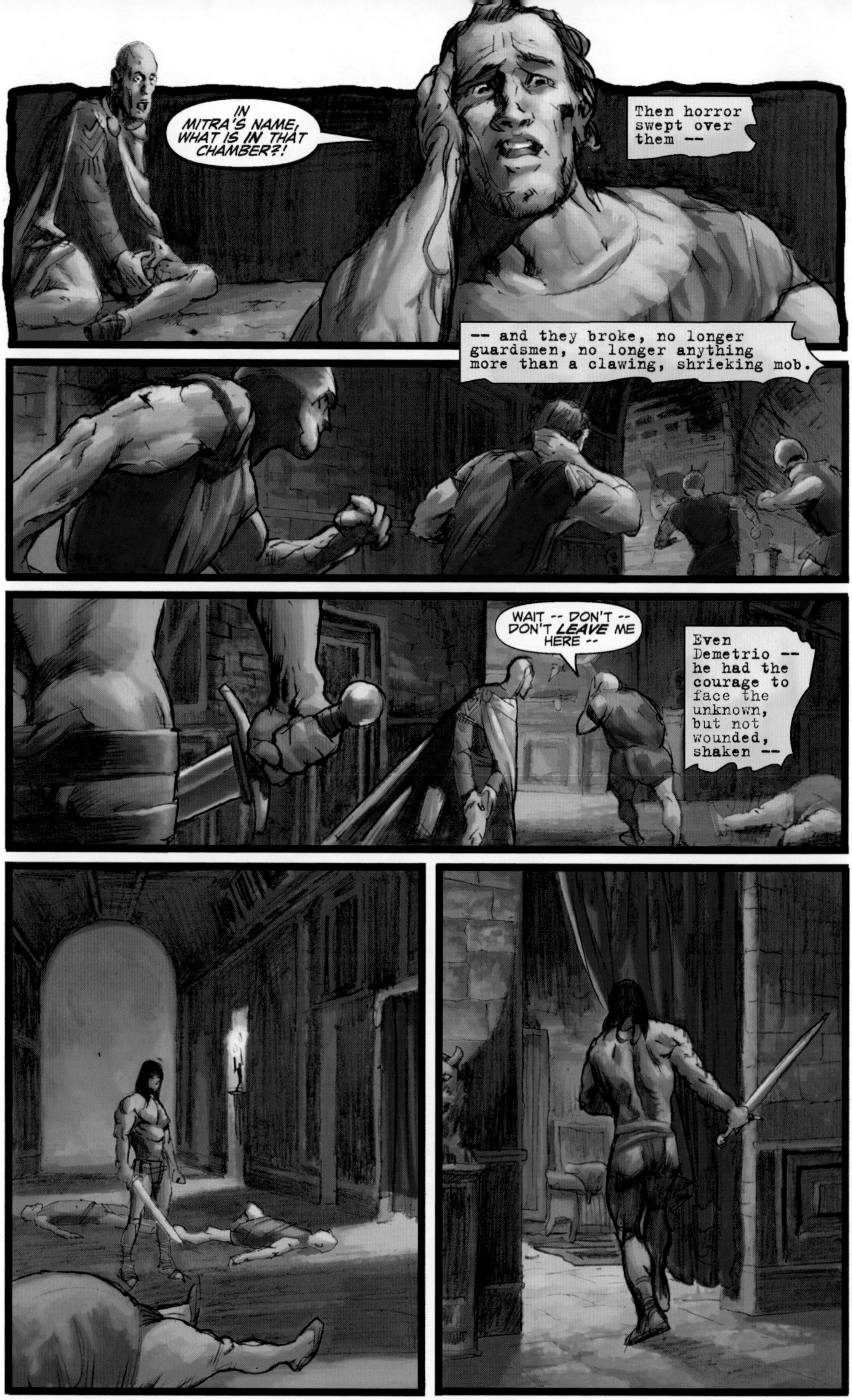
IN MITRA'S NAME, WHAT IS IN THAT CHAMBER?!
Then horror swept over them --
-- and they broke, no longer guardsmen, no longer anything more than a clawing, shrieking mob.
WAIT -- DON'T -- DON'T LEAVE ME HERE --
Even Demetrio -- he had the courage to face the unknown, but not wounded, shaken --

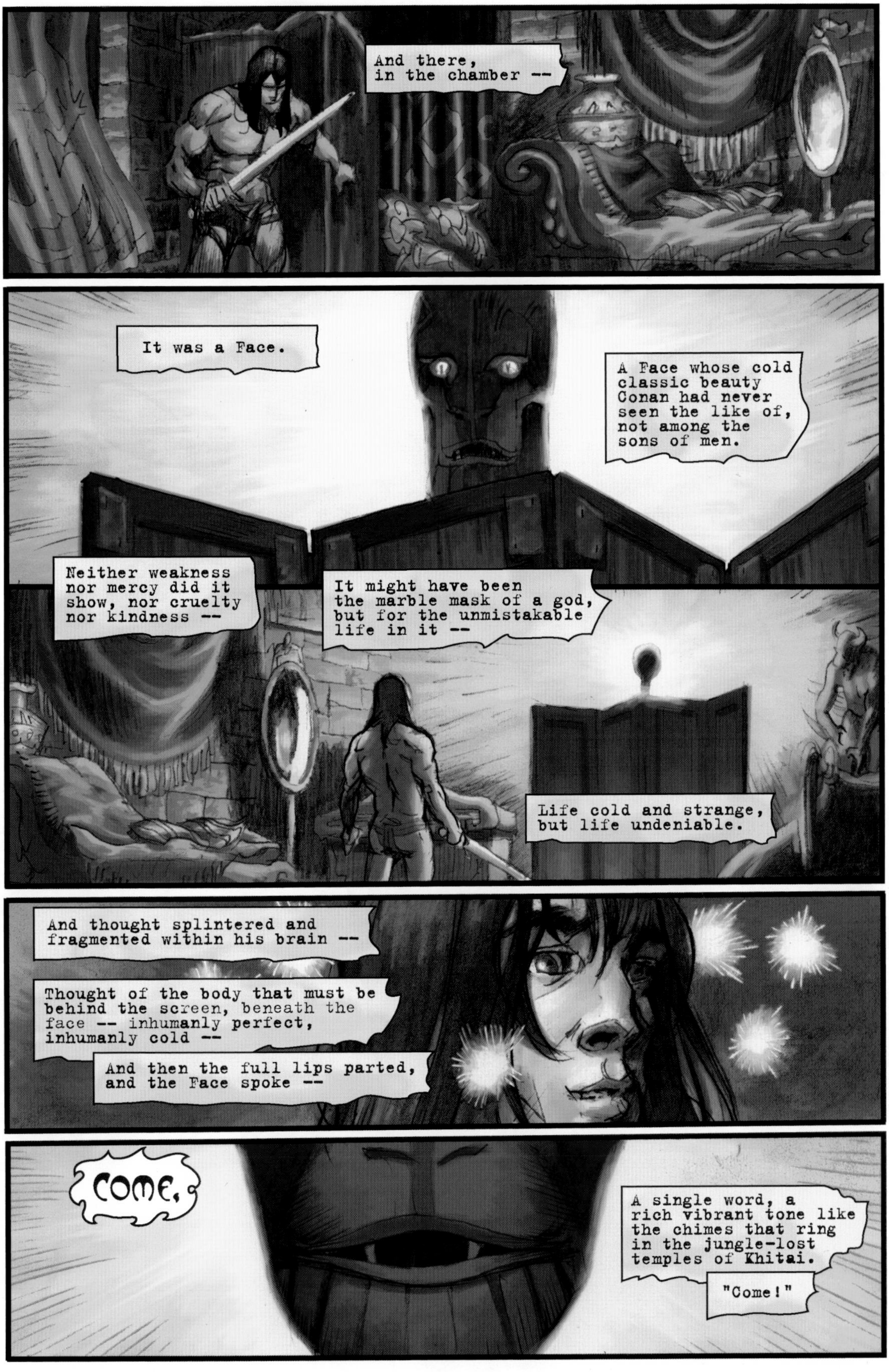
And there, in the chamber --
It was a Face.
A Face whose cold classic beauty Conan had never seen the like of, not among the sons of men.
Neither weakness nor mercy did it show, nor cruelty nor kindness --
It might have been the marble mask of a god, but for the unmistakable life in it --
Life cold and strange, but life undeniable.
And thought splintered and fragmented within his brain --
Thought of the body that must be behind the screen, beneath the face -- inhumanly perfect, inhumanly cold --
And then the full lips parted, and the Face spoke --
COME,
A single word, a rich vibrant tone like the chimes that ring in the jungle-lost temples of Khitai.
"Come!"

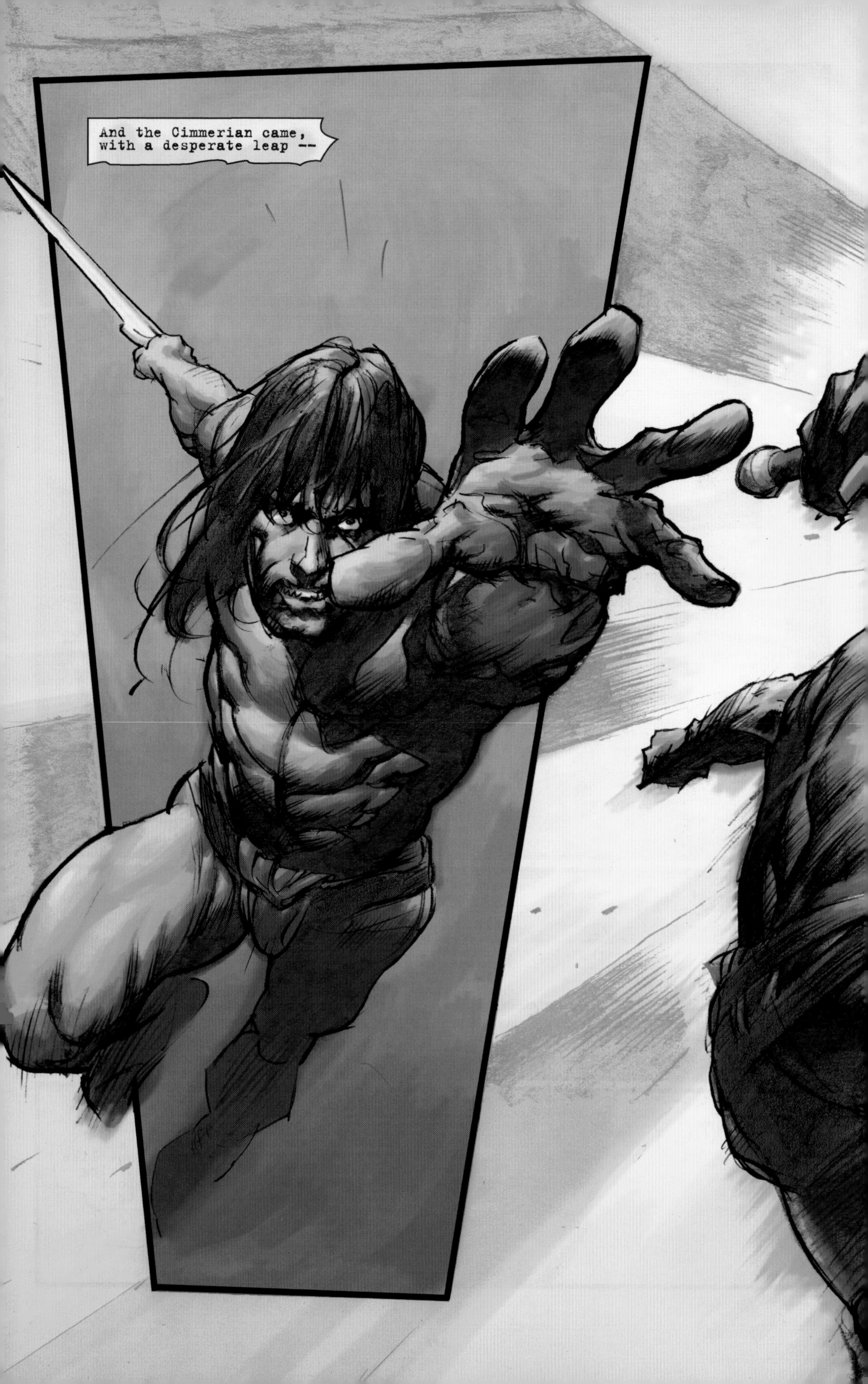
And the Cimmerian came, with a desperate leap --

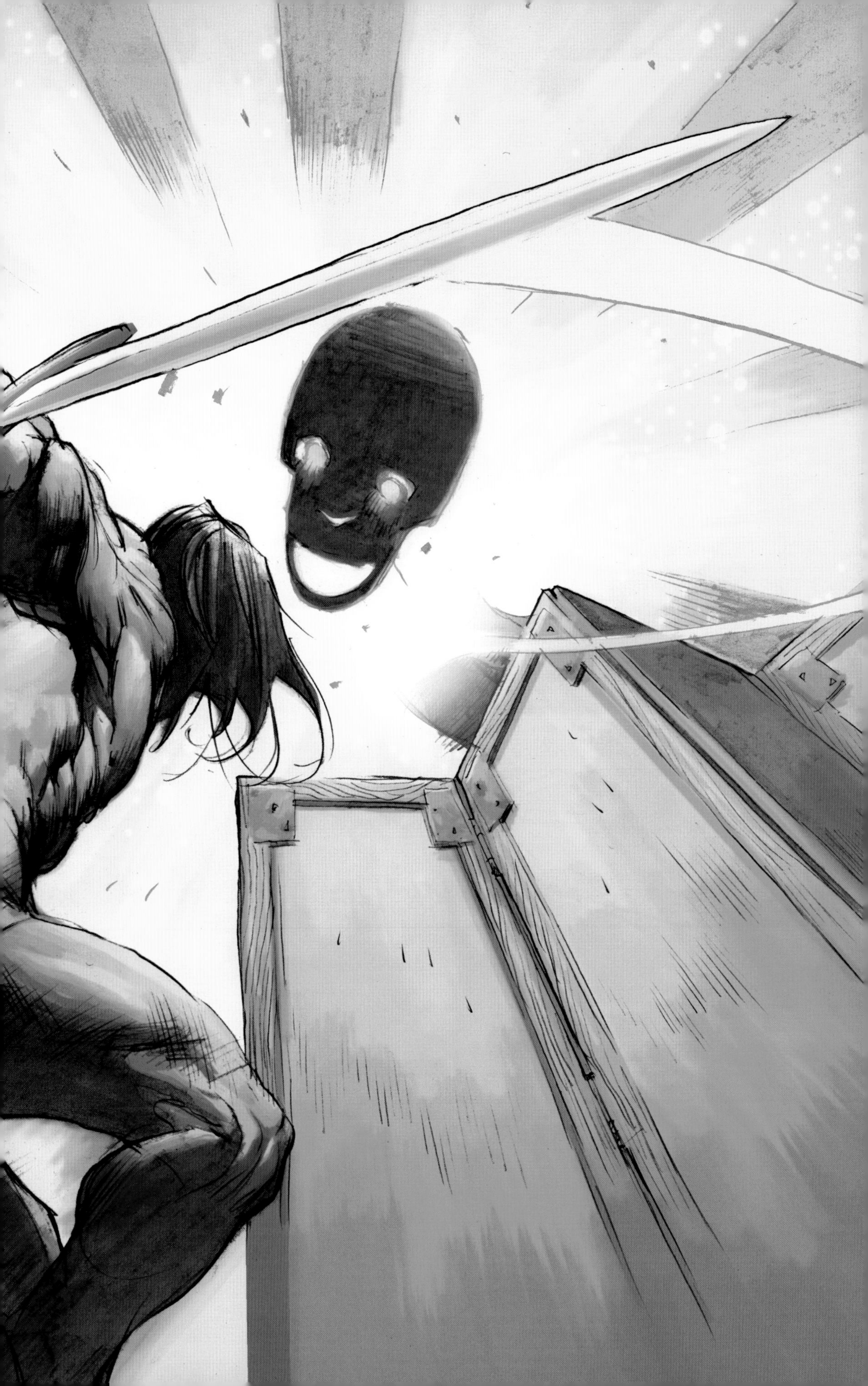

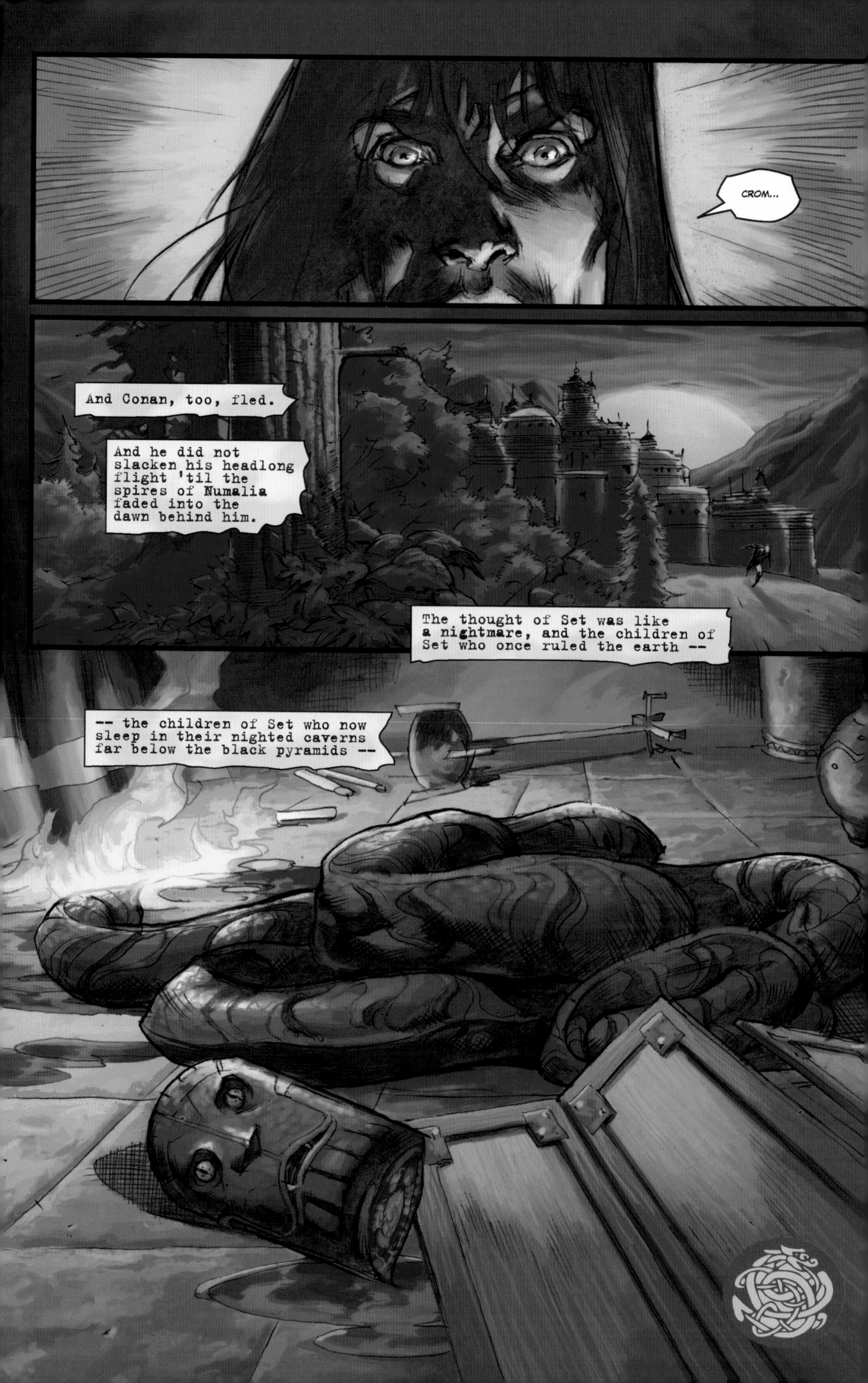
CROM...
And Conan, too, fled.
And he did not slacken his headlong flight 'til the spires of Numalia faded into the dawn behind him.
The thought of Set was like a nightmare, and the children of Set who once ruled the earth --
-- the children of Set who now sleep in their nighted caverns far below the black pyramids --

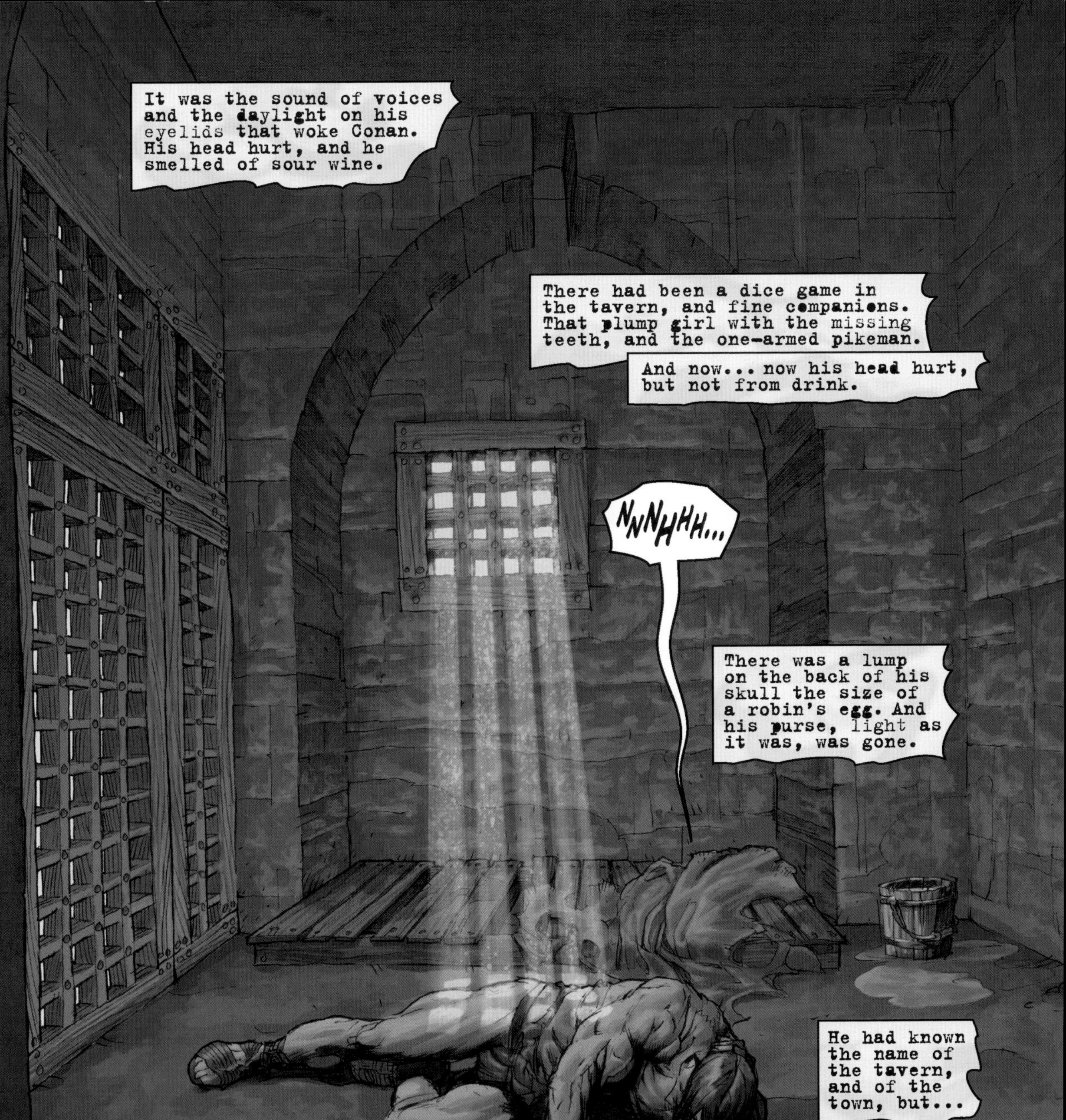

It was the sound of voices and the daylight on his eyelids that woke Conan. His head hurt, and he smelled of sour wine.
There had been a dice game in the tavern, and fine companions. That plump girl with the missing teeth, and the one-armed pikeman.
And now... now his head hurt, but not from drink.
NNNHHH...
There was a lump on the back of his skull the size of a robin's egg. And his purse, light as it was, was gone.
He had known the name of the tavern, and of the town, but...

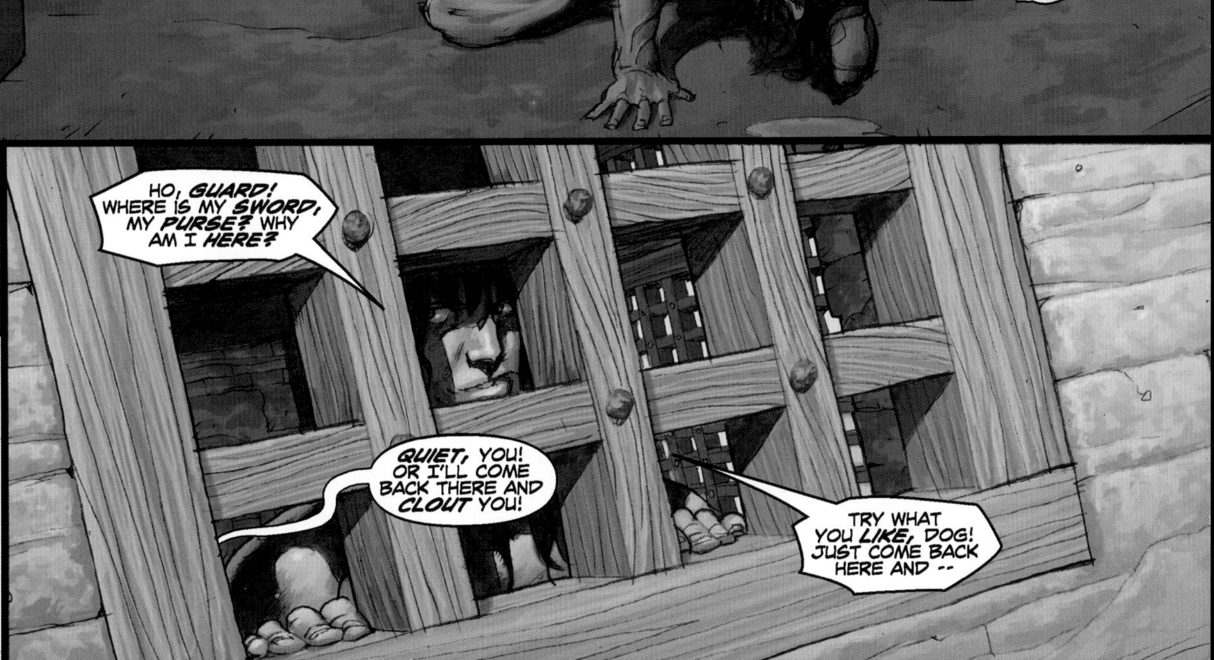

HO, GUARD! WHERE IS MY SWORD, MY PURSE? WHY AM I HERE?
QUIET, YOU! OR I'LL COME BACK THERE AND CLOUT YOU!
TRY WHAT YOU LIKE, DOG! JUST COME BACK HERE AND --

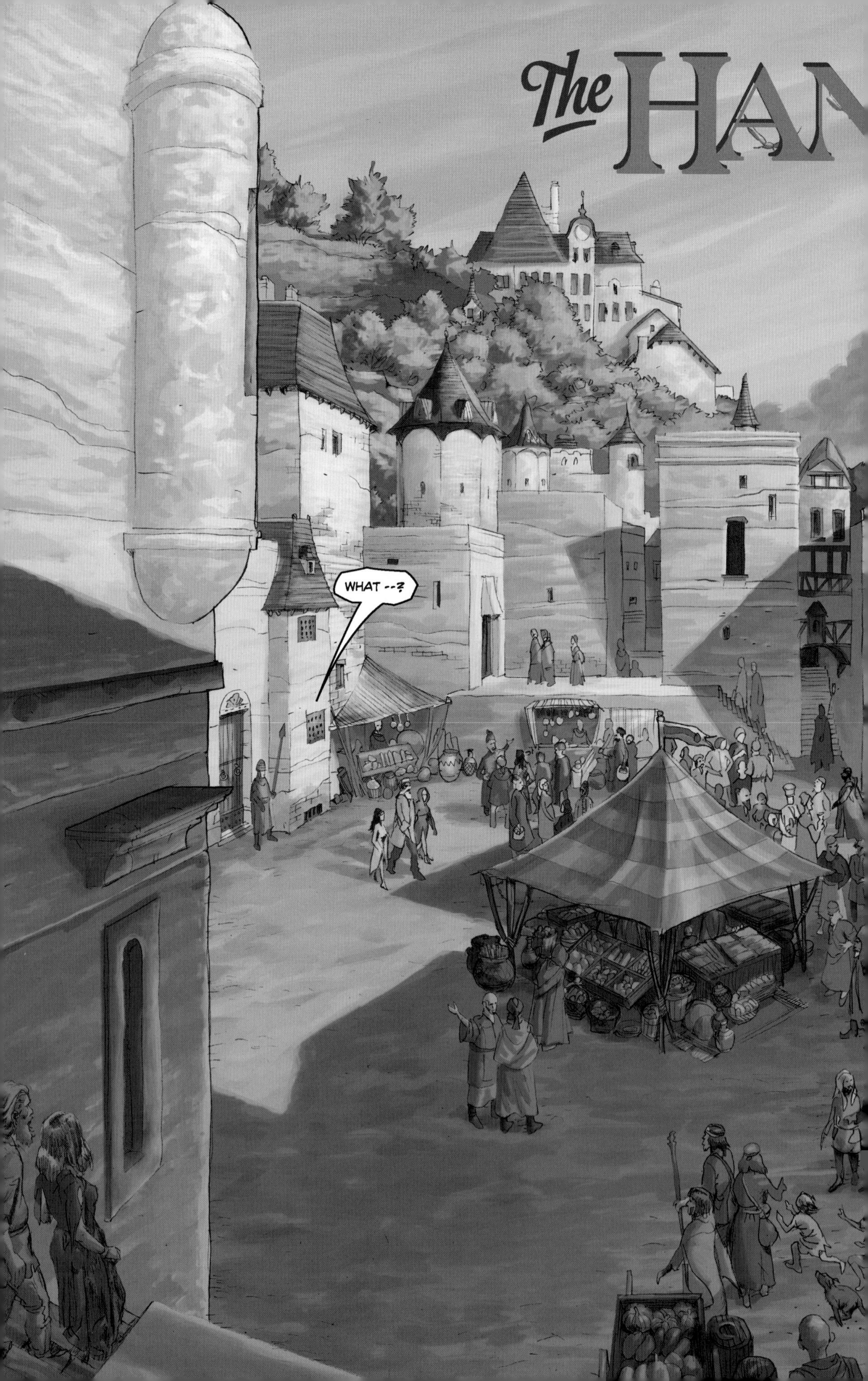
The HAN
WHAT --?

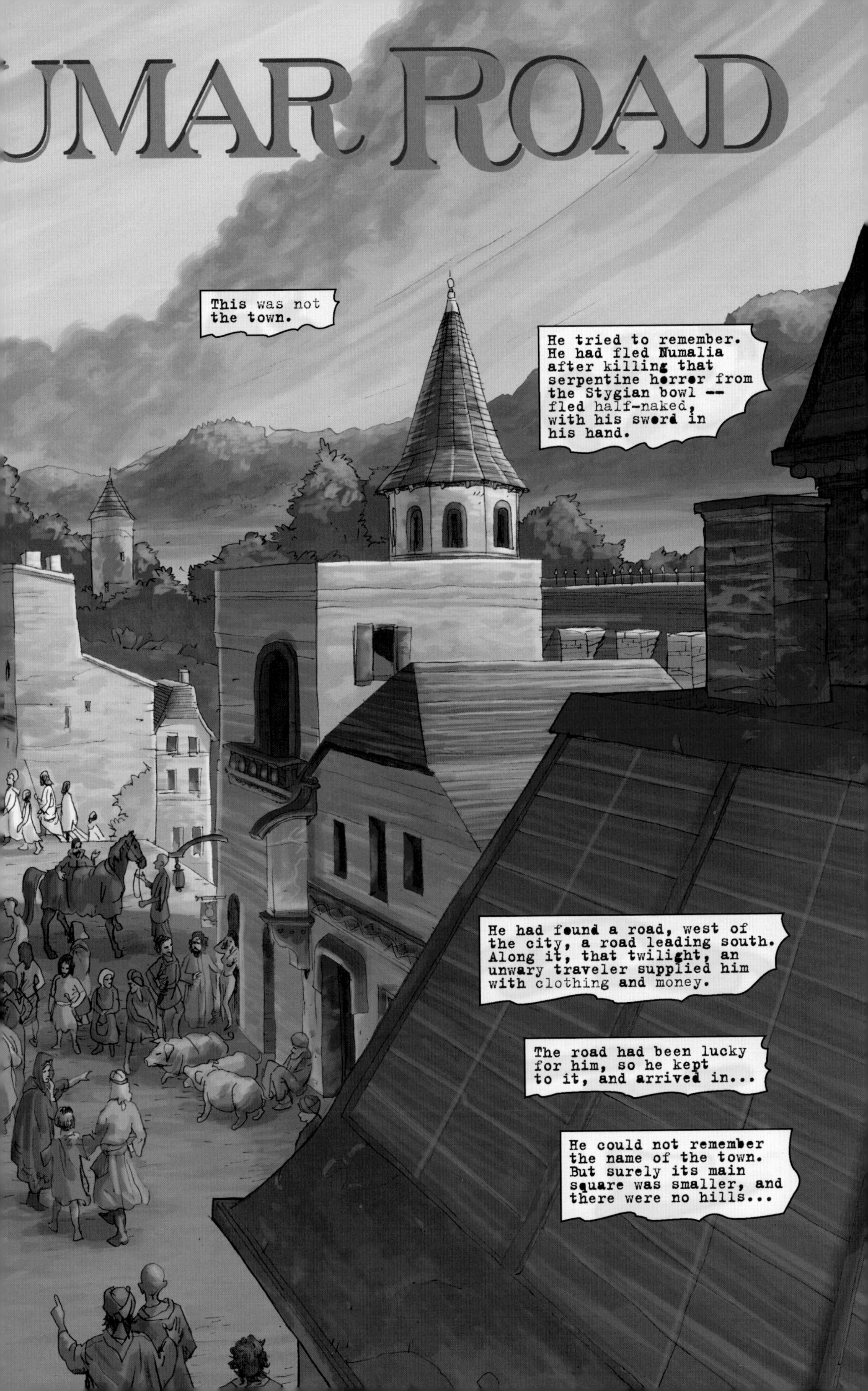
UMAR ROAD
This was not the town.
He tried to remember. He had fled Numalia after killing that serpentine horror from the Stygian bowl — fled half-naked, with his sword in his hand.
He had found a road, west of the city, a road leading south. Along it, that twilight, an unwary traveler supplied him with clothing and money.
The road had been lucky for him, so he kept to it, and arrived in...
He could not remember the name of the town. But surely its main square was smaller, and there were no hills...

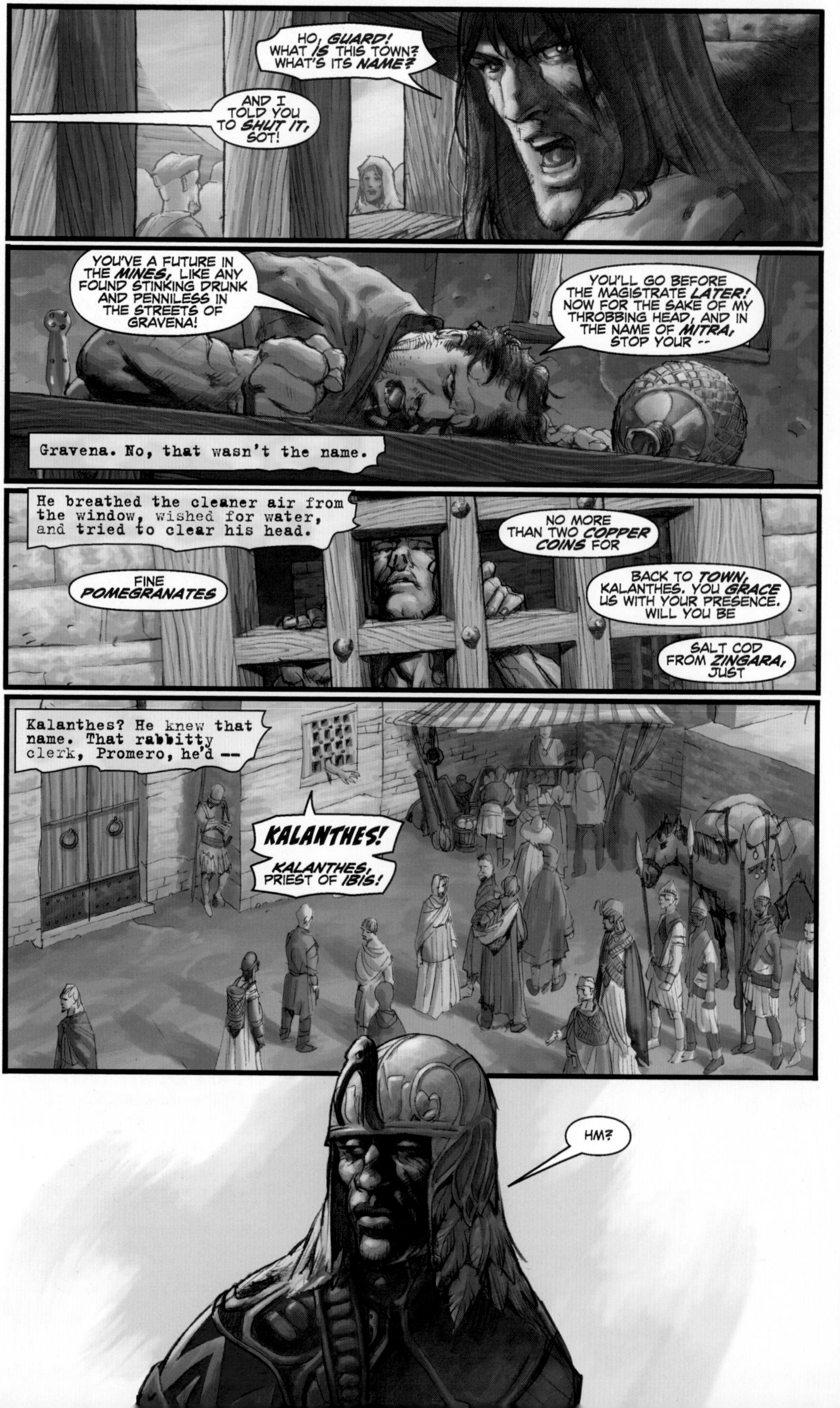
HO, GUARD! WHAT IS THIS TOWN? WHAT'S ITS NAME?
AND I TOLD YOU TO SHUT IT, SOT!
YOU'VE A FUTURE IN THE MINES, LIKE ANY FOUND STINKING DRUNK AND PENNILESS IN THE STREETS OF GRAVENA!
YOU'LL GO BEFORE THE MAGISTRATE LATER! NOW FOR THE SAKE OF MY THROBBING HEAD, AND IN THE NAME OF MITRA, STOP YOUR --
Gravena. No, that wasn't the name.
He breathed the cleaner air from the window, wished for water, and tried to clear his head.
NO MORE THAN TWO COPPER COINS FOR
FINE POMEGRANATES
BACK TO TOWN, KALANTHES. YOU GRACE US WITH YOUR PRESENCE. WILL YOU BE
SALT COD FROM ZINGARA, JUST
Kalanthes? He knew that name. That rabbitty clerk, Promero, he'd --
KALANTHES!
KALANTHES, PRIEST OF IBIS!
HM?

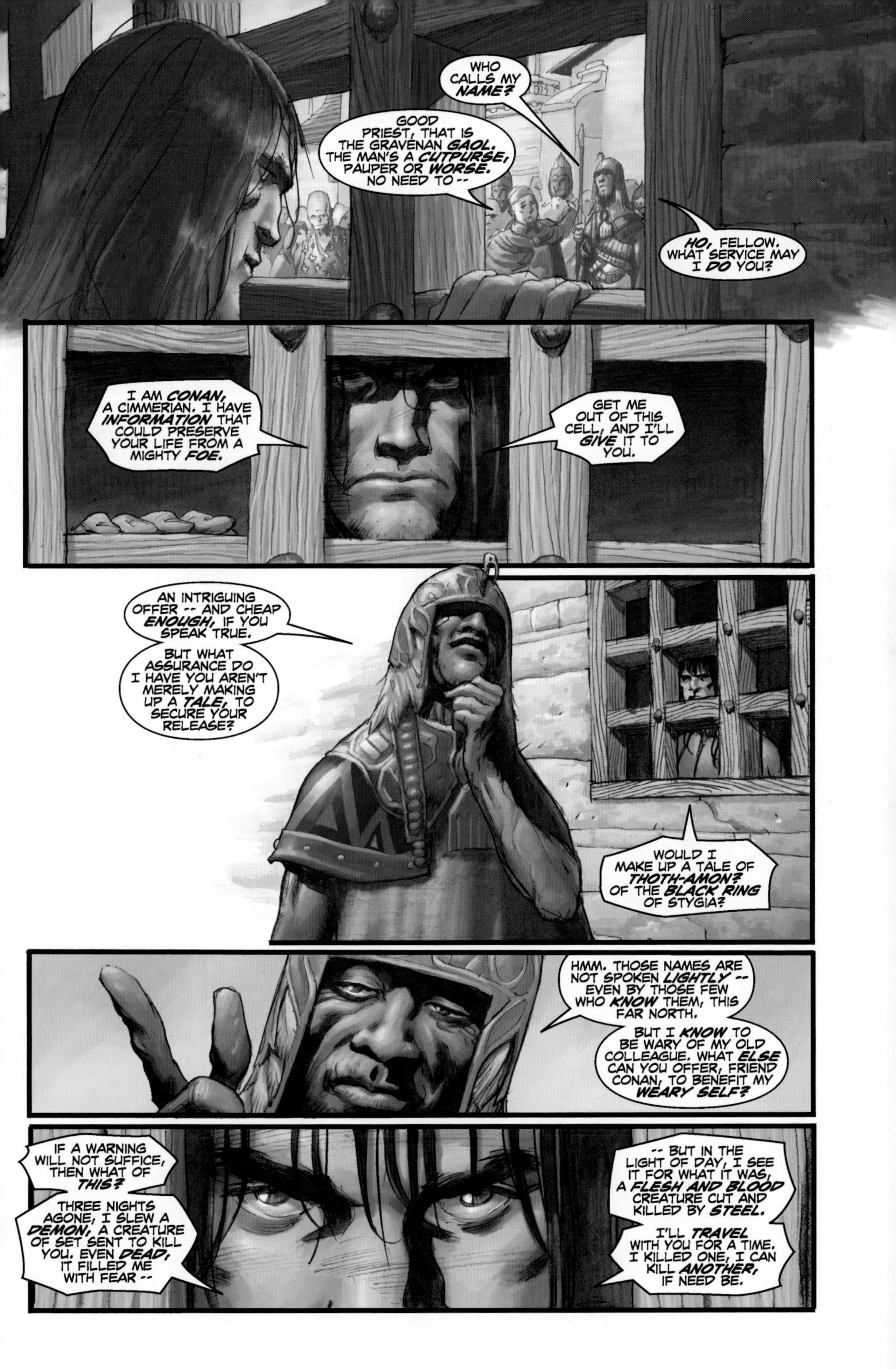
WHO CALLS MY NAME?
GOOD PRIEST, THAT IS THE GRAVENAN GAOL. THE MAN'S A CUTPURSE, PAUPER OR WORSE. NO NEED TO --
HO, FELLOW. WHAT SERVICE MAY I DO YOU?
I AM CONAN, A CIMMERIAN. I HAVE INFORMATION THAT COULD PRESERVE YOUR LIFE FROM A MIGHTY FOE.
GET ME OUT OF THIS CELL, AND I'LL GIVE IT TO YOU.
AN INTRIGUING OFFER -- AND CHEAP ENOUGH, IF YOU SPEAK TRUE.
BUT WHAT ASSURANCE DO I HAVE YOU AREN'T MERELY MAKING UP A TALE, TO SECURE YOUR RELEASE?
WOULD I MAKE UP A TALE OF THOTH-AMON? OF THE BLACK RING OF STYGIA?
HMM. THOSE NAMES ARE NOT SPOKEN LIGHTLY -- EVEN BY THOSE FEW WHO KNOW THEM, THIS FAR NORTH.
BUT I KNOW TO BE WARY OF MY OLD COLLEAGUE. WHAT ELSE CAN YOU OFFER, FRIEND CONAN, TO BENEFIT MY WEARY SELF?
IF A WARNING WILL NOT SUFFICE, THEN WHAT OF THIS?
THREE NIGHTS AGONE, I SLEW A DEMON, A CREATURE OF SET SENT TO KILL YOU. EVEN DEAD, IT FILLED ME WITH FEAR --
-- BUT IN THE LIGHT OF DAY, I SEE IT FOR WHAT IT WAS, A FLESH AND BLOOD CREATURE CUT AND KILLED BY STEEL.
I'LL TRAVEL WITH YOU FOR A TIME. I KILLED ONE, I CAN KILL ANOTHER, IF NEED BE.

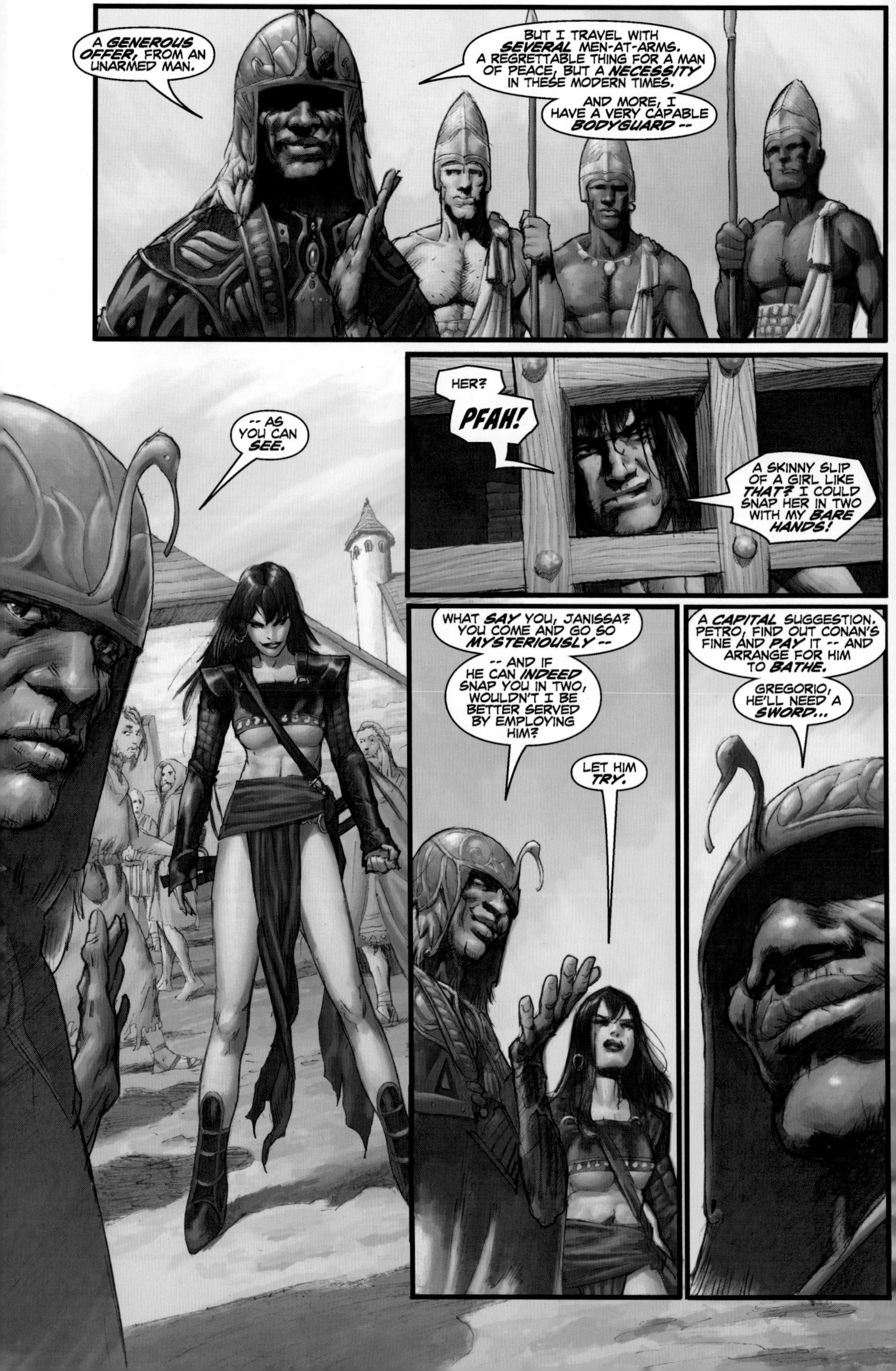
A GENEROUS OFFER, FROM AN UNARMED MAN.
BUT I TRAVEL WITH SEVERAL MEN-AT-ARMS. A REGRETTABLE THING FOR A MAN OF PEACE, BUT A NECESSITY IN THESE MODERN TIMES.
AND MORE, I HAVE A VERY CAPABLE BODYGUARD --
HER? PFAH!
A SKINNY SLIP OF A GIRL LIKE THAT? I COULD SNAP HER IN TWO WITH MY BARE HANDS!
-- AS YOU CAN SEE.
WHAT SAY YOU, JANISSA? YOU COME AND GO SO MYSTERIOUSLY --
-- AND IF HE CAN INDEED SNAP YOU IN TWO, WOULDN'T I BE BETTER SERVED BY EMPLOYING HIM?
LET HIM TRY.
A CAPITAL SUGGESTION. PETRO, FIND OUT CONAN'S FINE AND PAY IT -- AND ARRANGE FOR HIM TO BATHE.
GREGORIO, HE'LL NEED A SWORD...

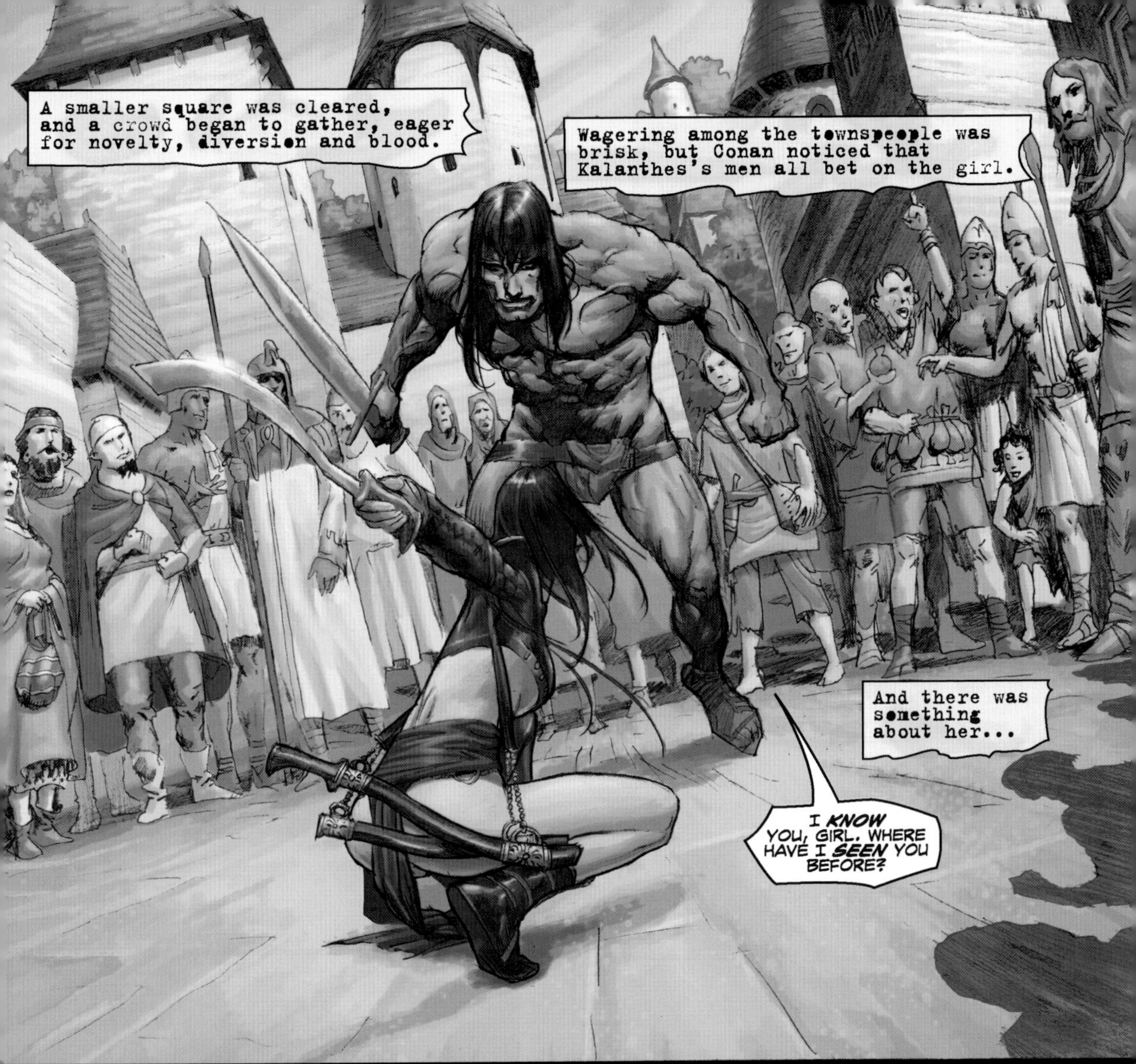
A smaller square was cleared, and a crowd began to gather, eager for novelty, diversion and blood.
Wagering among the townspeople was brisk, but Conan noticed that Kalanthes's men all bet on the girl.
And there was something about her...
I KNOW YOU, GIRL. WHERE HAVE I SEEN YOU BEFORE?
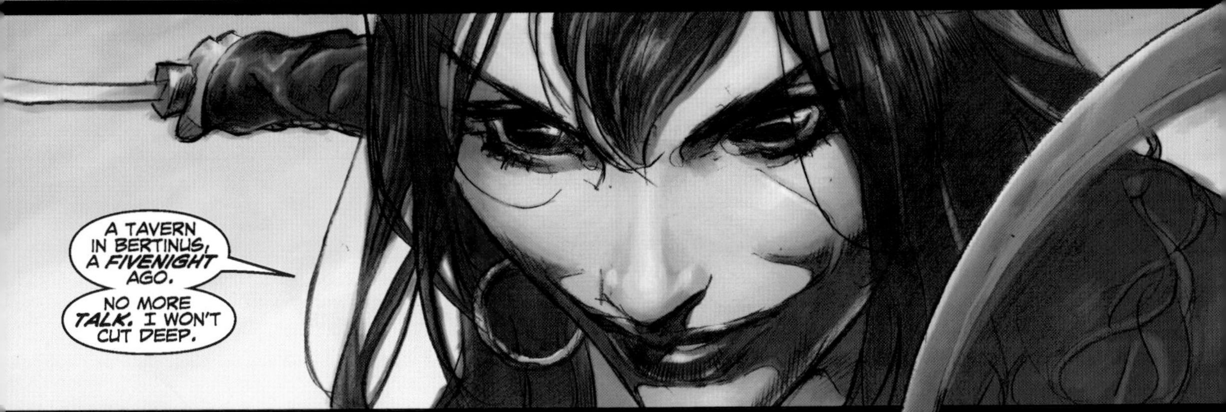
A TAVERN IN BERTINUS, A FIVENIGHT AGO.
NO MORE TALK. I WON'T CUT DEEP.
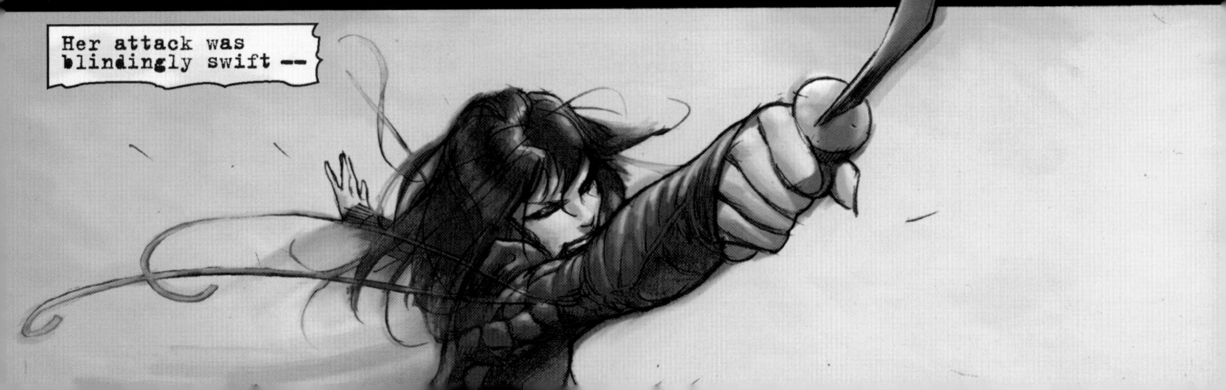
Her attack was blindingly swift --

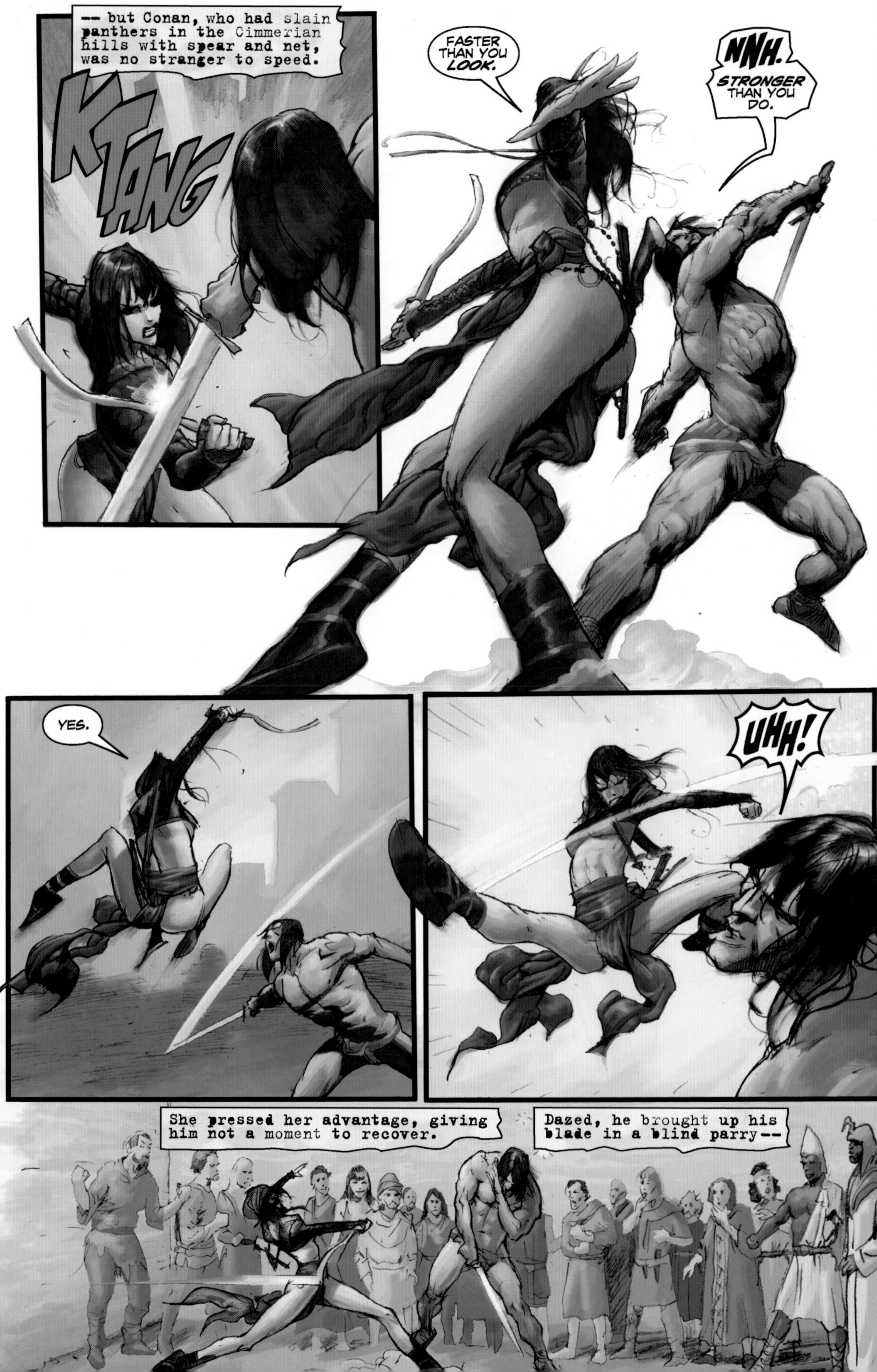
-- but Conan, who had slain panthers in the Cimmerian hills with spear and net, was no stranger to speed.
K'TANG
FASTER THAN YOU LOOK.
NNH. STRONGER THAN YOU DO.
YES.
UHH!
She pressed her advantage, giving him not a moment to recover.
Dazed, he brought up his blade in a blind parry --

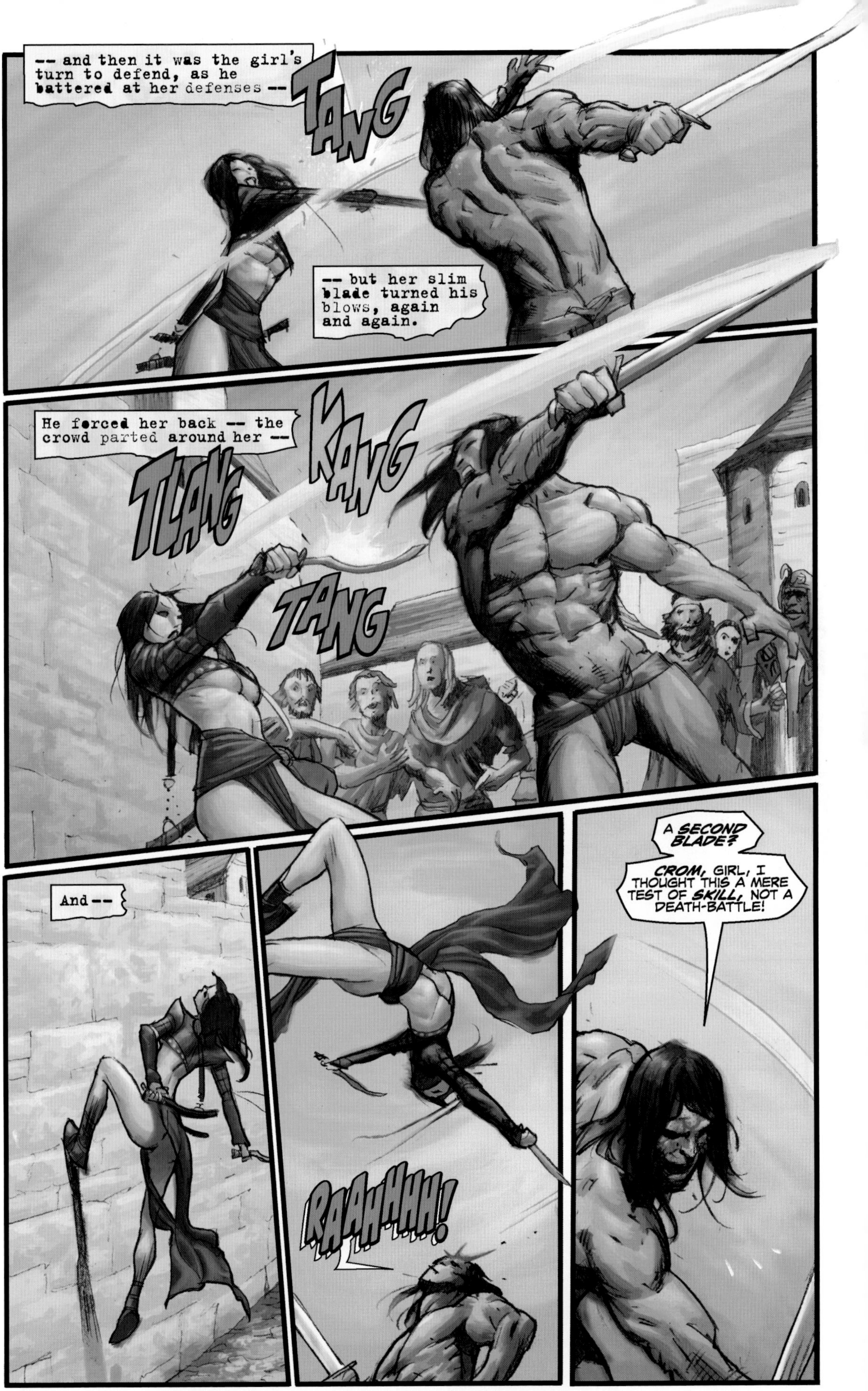

-- and then it was the girl's turn to defend, as he battered at her defenses --
TANG
-- but her slim blade turned his blows, again and again.
He forced her back -- the crowd parted around her --
KANG
TLANG
TANG
And --
RAAHHHH!
A SECOND BLADE?
CROM, GIRL, I THOUGHT THIS A MERE TEST OF SKILL, NOT A DEATH-BATTLE!

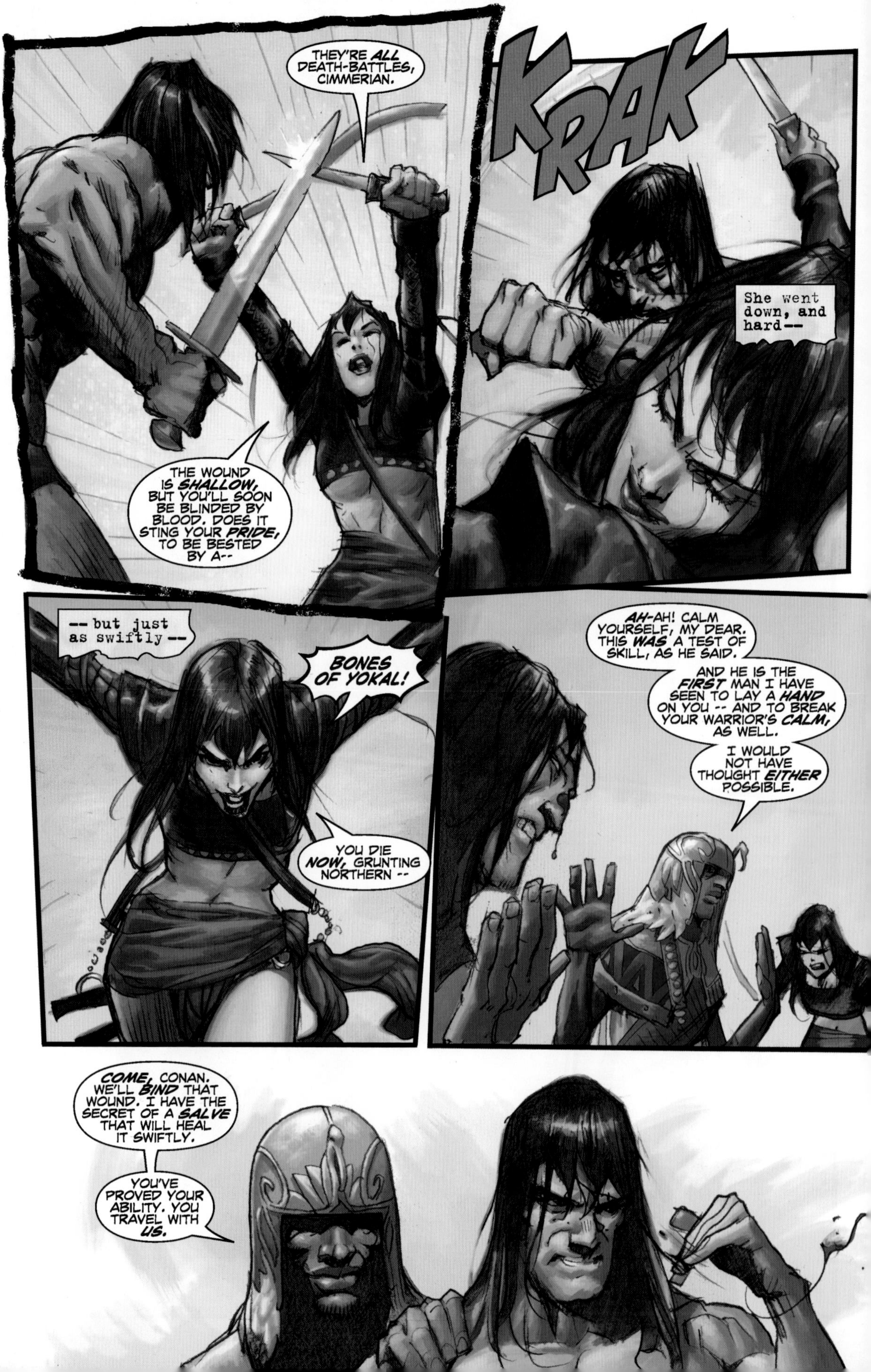

THEY'RE ALL DEATH-BATTLES, CIMMERIAN.
THE WOUND IS SHALLOW, BUT YOU'LL SOON BE BLINDED BY BLOOD. DOES IT STING YOUR PRIDE, TO BE BESTED BY A--
KRAK
She went down, and hard--
-- but just as swiftly --
BONES OF YOKAL!
YOU DIE NOW, GRUNTING NORTHERN --
AH-AH! CALM YOURSELF, MY DEAR. THIS WAS A TEST OF SKILL, AS HE SAID.
AND HE IS THE FIRST MAN I HAVE SEEN TO LAY A HAND ON YOU -- AND TO BREAK YOUR WARRIOR'S CALM, AS WELL.
I WOULD NOT HAVE THOUGHT EITHER POSSIBLE.
COME, CONAN. WE'LL BIND THAT WOUND. I HAVE THE SECRET OF A SALVE THAT WILL HEAL IT SWIFTLY.
YOU'VE PROVED YOUR ABILITY. YOU TRAVEL WITH US.

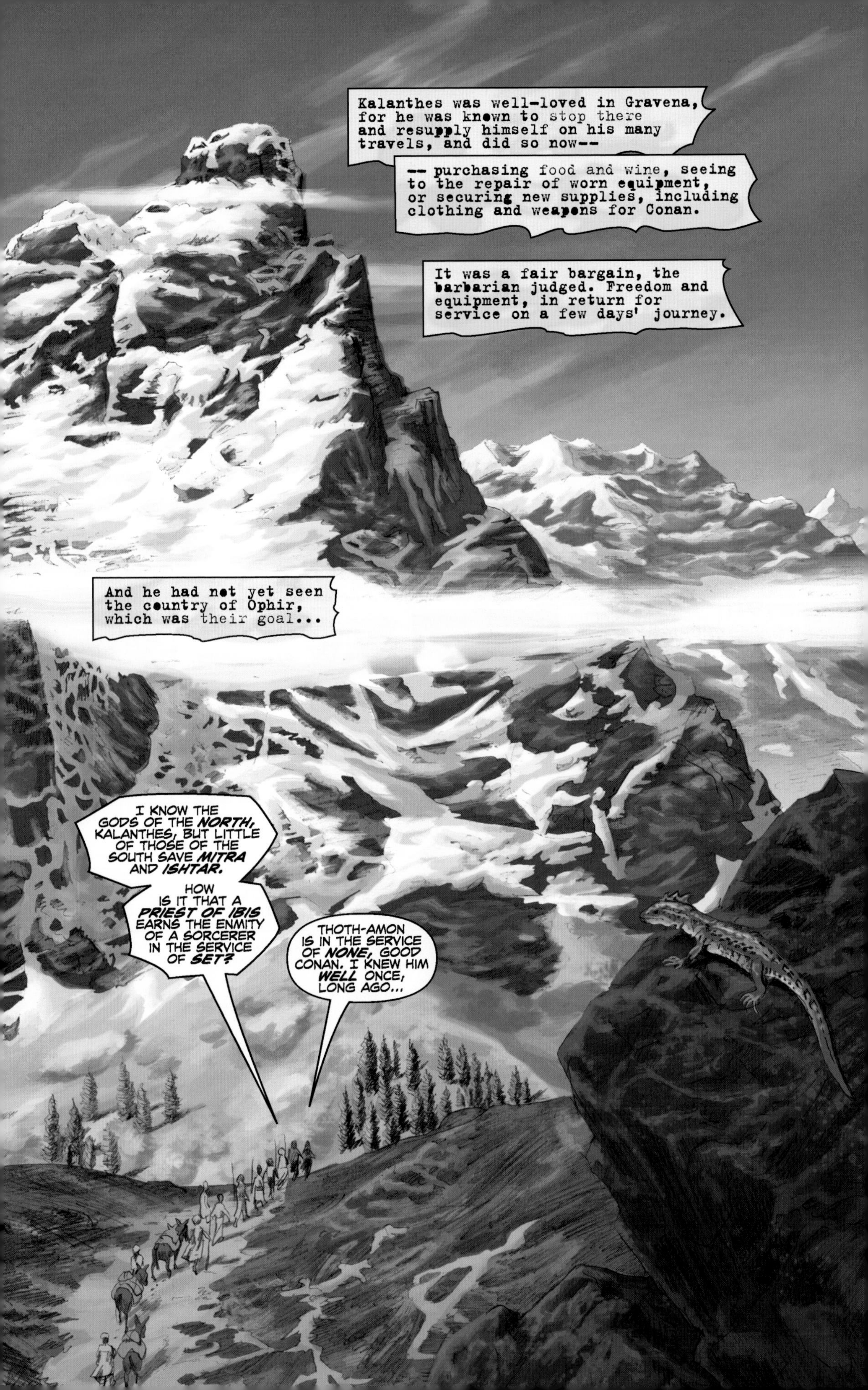
Kalanthes was well-loved in Gravena, for he was known to stop there and resupply himself on his many travels, and did so now--
-- purchasing food and wine, seeing to the repair of worn equipment, or securing new supplies, including clothing and weapons for Conan.
It was a fair bargain, the barbarian judged. Freedom and equipment, in return for service on a few days' journey.
And he had not yet seen the country of Ophir, which was their goal...
I KNOW THE GODS OF THE NORTH, KALANTHES, BUT LITTLE OF THOSE OF THE SOUTH SAVE MITRA AND ISHTAR.
HOW IS IT THAT A PRIEST OF IBIS EARNS THE ENMITY OF A SORCERER IN THE SERVICE OF SET?
THOTH-AMON IS IN THE SERVICE OF NONE, GOOD CONAN. I KNEW HIM WELL ONCE, LONG AGO...

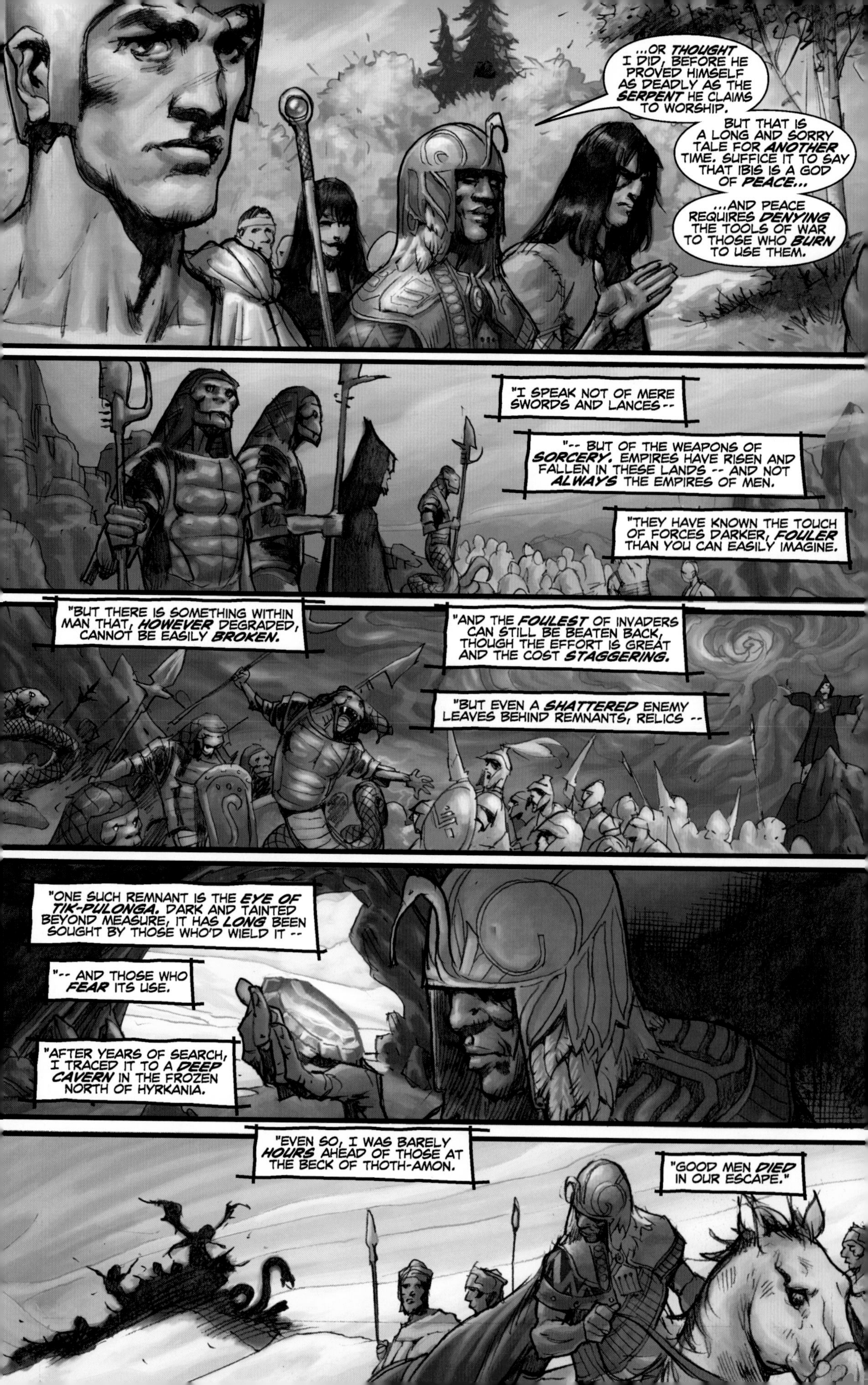
...OR THOUGHT I DID, BEFORE HE PROVED HIMSELF AS DEADLY AS THE SERPENT HE CLAIMS TO WORSHIP.
BUT THAT IS A LONG AND SORRY TALE FOR ANOTHER TIME. SUFFICE IT TO SAY THAT IBIS IS A GOD OF PEACE...
...AND PEACE REQUIRES DENYING THE TOOLS OF WAR TO THOSE WHO BURN TO USE THEM.
"I SPEAK NOT OF MERE SWORDS AND LANCES --
"-- BUT OF THE WEAPONS OF SORCERY. EMPIRES HAVE RISEN AND FALLEN IN THESE LANDS -- AND NOT ALWAYS THE EMPIRES OF MEN.
"THEY HAVE KNOWN THE TOUCH OF FORCES DARKER, FOULER THAN YOU CAN EASILY IMAGINE.
"BUT THERE IS SOMETHING WITHIN MAN THAT, HOWEVER DEGRADED, CANNOT BE EASILY BROKEN.
"AND THE FOULEST OF INVADERS CAN STILL BE BEATEN BACK, THOUGH THE EFFORT IS GREAT AND THE COST STAGGERING.
"BUT EVEN A SHATTERED ENEMY LEAVES BEHIND REMNANTS, RELICS --
"ONE SUCH REMNANT IS THE EYE OF TIK-PULONGA. DARK AND TAINTED BEYOND MEASURE, IT HAS LONG BEEN SOUGHT BY THOSE WHO'D WIELD IT --
"-- AND THOSE WHO FEAR ITS USE.
"AFTER YEARS OF SEARCH, I TRACED IT TO A DEEP CAVERN IN THE FROZEN NORTH OF HYRKANIA.
"EVEN SO, I WAS BARELY HOURS AHEAD OF THOSE AT THE BECK OF THOTH-AMON.
"GOOD MEN DIED IN OUR ESCAPE."

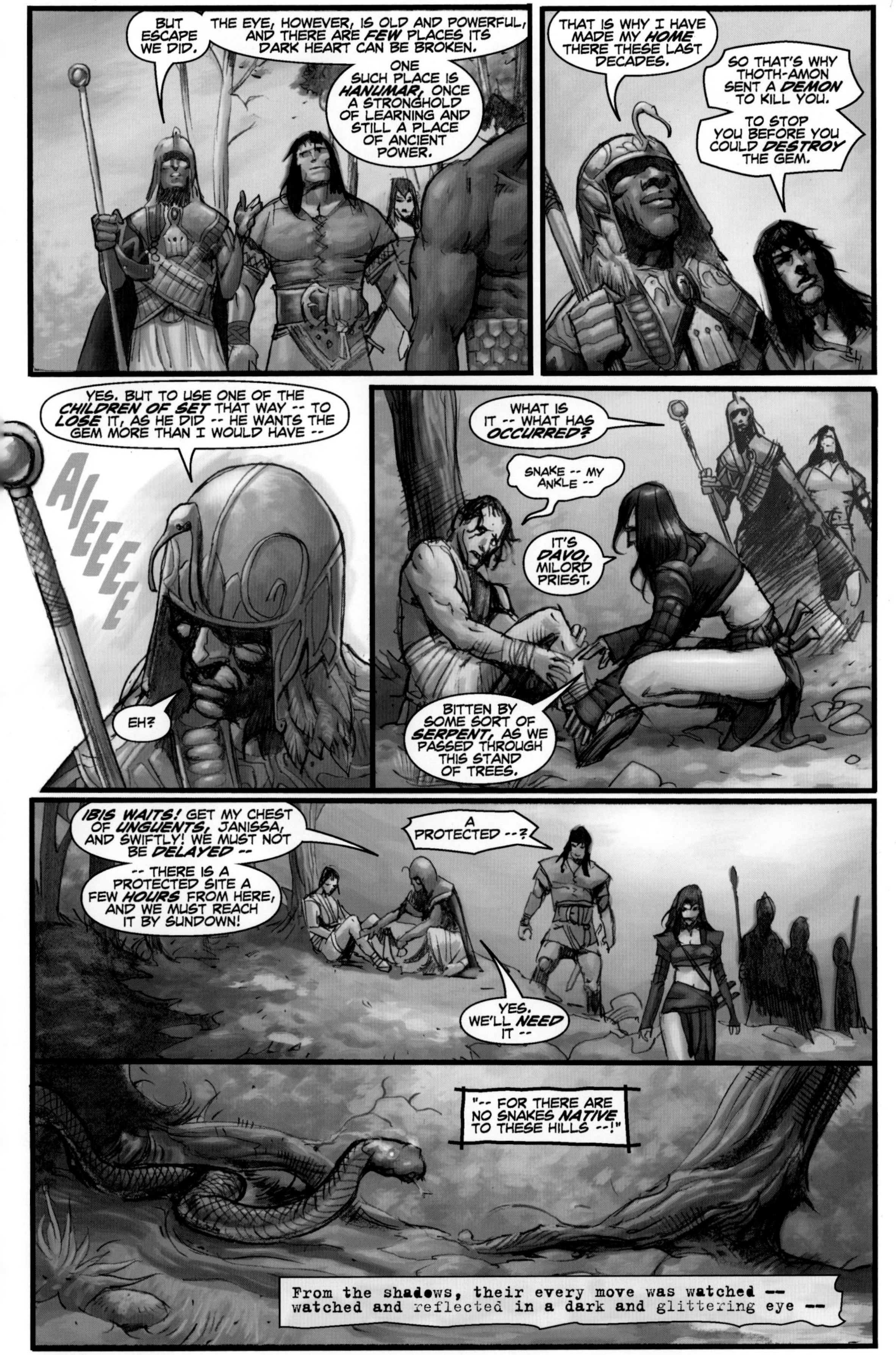

BUT ESCAPE WE DID.
THE EYE, HOWEVER, IS OLD AND POWERFUL, AND THERE ARE FEW PLACES ITS DARK HEART CAN BE BROKEN.
ONE SUCH PLACE IS HANUMAR, ONCE A STRONGHOLD OF LEARNING AND STILL A PLACE OF ANCIENT POWER.
THAT IS WHY I HAVE MADE MY HOME THERE THESE LAST DECADES.
SO THAT'S WHY THOTH-AMON SENT A DEMON TO KILL YOU.
TO STOP YOU BEFORE YOU COULD DESTROY THE GEM.
YES. BUT TO USE ONE OF THE CHILDREN OF SET THAT WAY -- TO LOSE IT, AS HE DID -- HE WANTS THE GEM MORE THAN I WOULD HAVE --
AIEEEE
EH?
WHAT IS IT -- WHAT HAS OCCURRED?
SNAKE -- MY ANKLE --
IT'S DAVO, MILORD PRIEST.
BITTEN BY SOME SORT OF SERPENT, AS WE PASSED THROUGH THIS STAND OF TREES.
IBIS WAITS! GET MY CHEST OF UNGUENTS, JANISSA, AND SWIFTLY! WE MUST NOT BE DELAYED --
-- THERE IS A PROTECTED SITE A FEW HOURS FROM HERE, AND WE MUST REACH IT BY SUNDOWN!
A PROTECTED --?
YES. WE'LL NEED IT --
"-- FOR THERE ARE NO SNAKES NATIVE TO THESE HILLS --!"
From the shadows, their every move was watched -- watched and reflected in a dark and glittering eye --

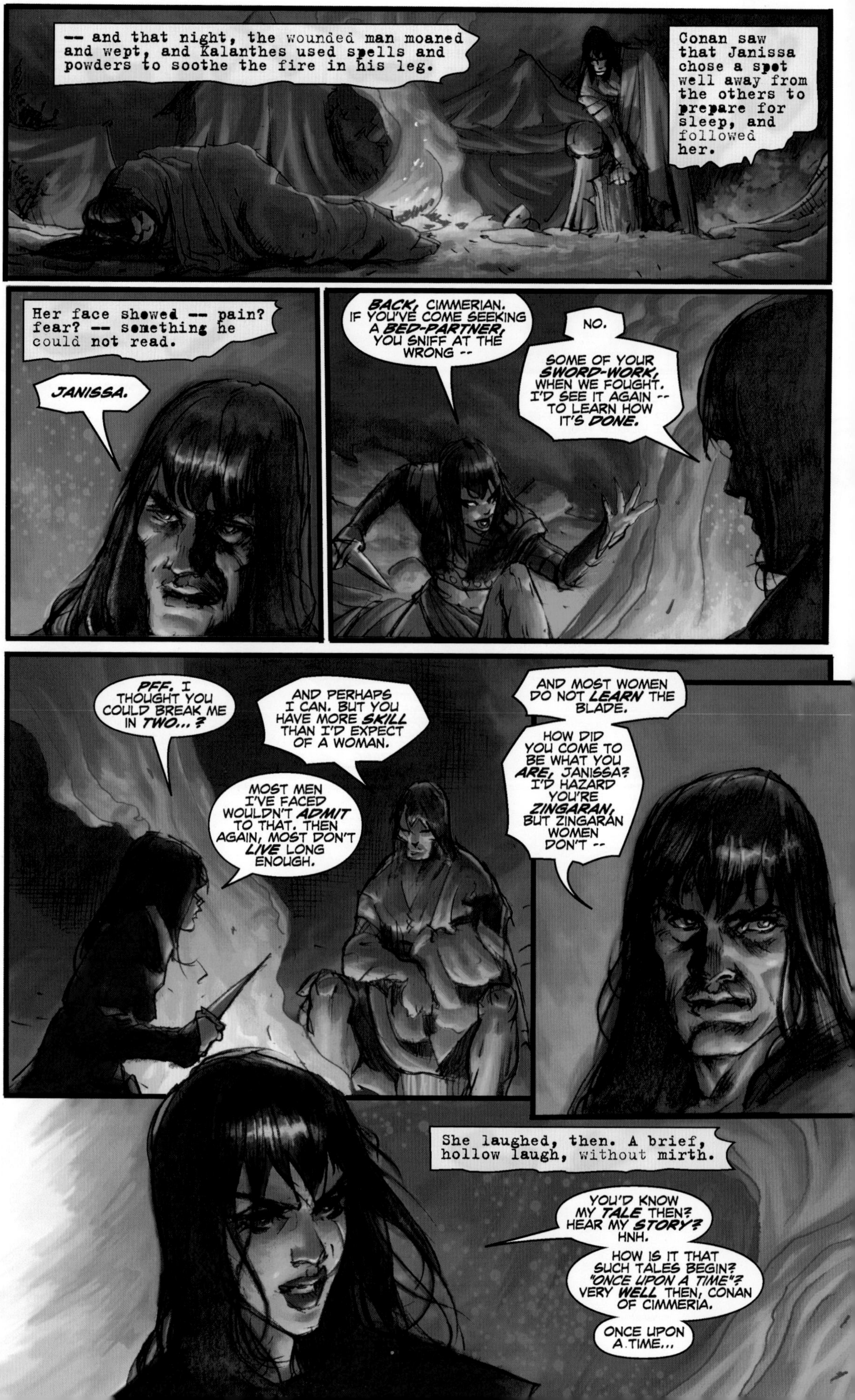
-- and that night, the wounded man moaned and wept, and Kalanthes used spells and powders to soothe the fire in his leg.
Conan saw that Janissa chose a spot well away from the others to prepare for sleep, and followed her.
Her face showed -- pain? fear? -- something he could not read.
JANISSA.
BACK, CIMMERIAN. IF YOU'VE COME SEEKING A BED-PARTNER, YOU SNIFF AT THE WRONG --
NO.
SOME OF YOUR SWORD-WORK, WHEN WE FOUGHT. I'D SEE IT AGAIN -- TO LEARN HOW IT'S DONE.
PFF. I THOUGHT YOU COULD BREAK ME IN TWO...?
AND PERHAPS I CAN. BUT YOU HAVE MORE SKILL THAN I'D EXPECT OF A WOMAN.
MOST MEN I'VE FACED WOULDN'T ADMIT TO THAT. THEN AGAIN, MOST DON'T LIVE LONG ENOUGH.
AND MOST WOMEN DO NOT LEARN THE BLADE.
HOW DID YOU COME TO BE WHAT YOU ARE, JANISSA? I'D HAZARD YOU'RE ZINGARAN, BUT ZINGARAN WOMEN DON'T --
She laughed, then. A brief, hollow laugh, without mirth.
YOU'D KNOW MY TALE THEN? HEAR MY STORY? HNH.
HOW IS IT THAT SUCH TALES BEGIN? "ONCE UPON A TIME"? VERY WELL THEN, CONAN OF CIMMERIA.
ONCE UPON A TIME...

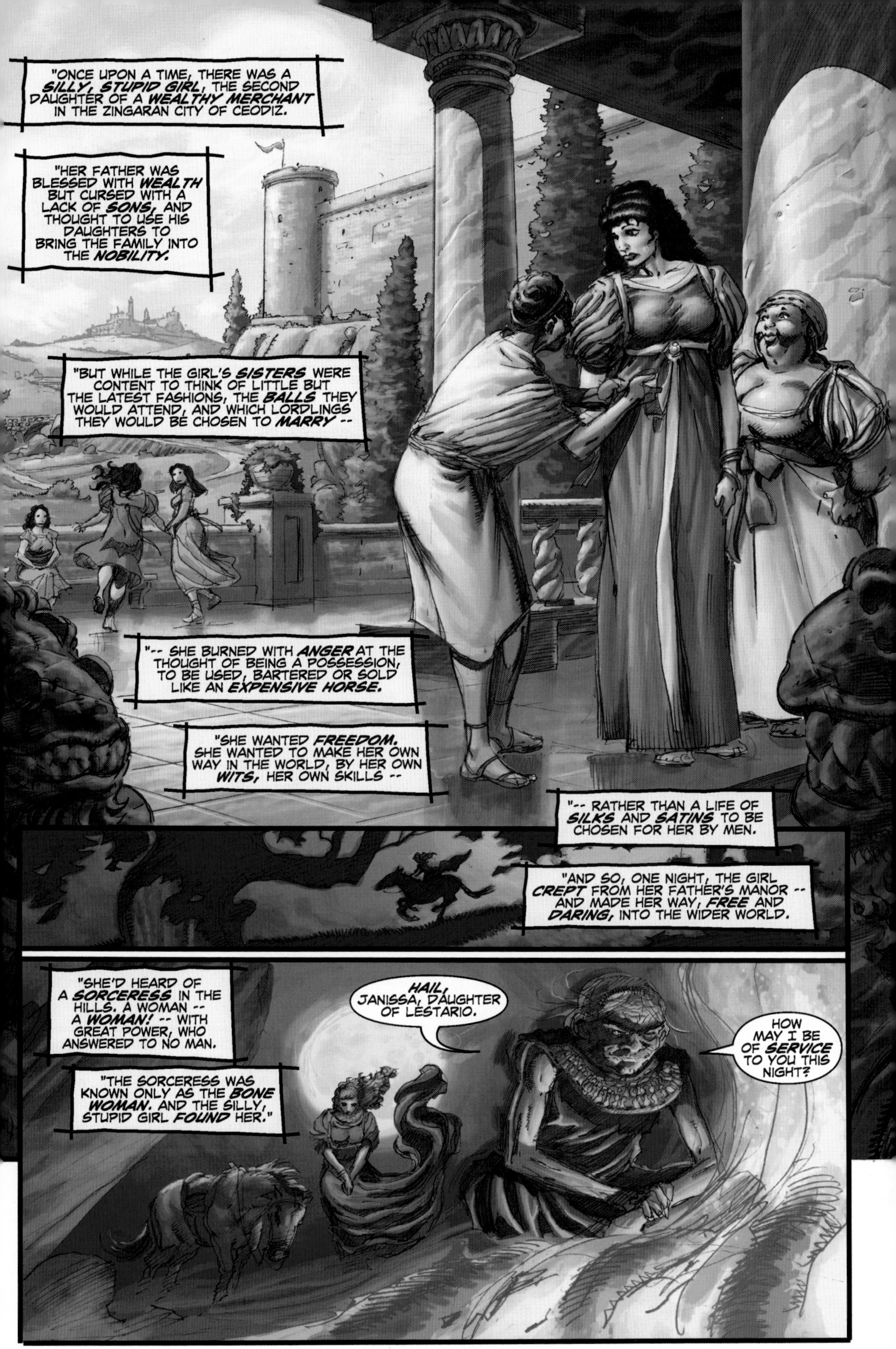
"ONCE UPON A TIME, THERE WAS A SILLY, STUPID GIRL, THE SECOND DAUGHTER OF A WEALTHY MERCHANT IN THE ZINGARAN CITY OF CEODIZ.
"HER FATHER WAS BLESSED WITH WEALTH BUT CURSED WITH A LACK OF SONS, AND THOUGHT TO USE HIS DAUGHTERS TO BRING THE FAMILY INTO THE NOBILITY.
"BUT WHILE THE GIRL'S SISTERS WERE CONTENT TO THINK OF LITTLE BUT THE LATEST FASHIONS, THE BALLS THEY WOULD ATTEND, AND WHICH LORDLINGS THEY WOULD BE CHOSEN TO MARRY --
"-- SHE BURNED WITH ANGER AT THE THOUGHT OF BEING A POSSESSION, TO BE USED, BARTERED OR SOLD LIKE AN EXPENSIVE HORSE.
"SHE WANTED FREEDOM. SHE WANTED TO MAKE HER OWN WAY IN THE WORLD, BY HER OWN WITS, HER OWN SKILLS --
"-- RATHER THAN A LIFE OF SILKS AND SATINS TO BE CHOSEN FOR HER BY MEN.
"AND SO, ONE NIGHT, THE GIRL CREPT FROM HER FATHER'S MANOR -- AND MADE HER WAY, FREE AND DARING, INTO THE WIDER WORLD.
"SHE'D HEARD OF A SORCERESS IN THE HILLS. A WOMAN -- A WOMAN! -- WITH GREAT POWER, WHO ANSWERED TO NO MAN.
"THE SORCERESS WAS KNOWN ONLY AS THE BONE WOMAN. AND THE SILLY, STUPID GIRL FOUND HER."
HAIL, JANISSA, DAUGHTER OF LESTARIO.
HOW MAY I BE OF SERVICE TO YOU THIS NIGHT?

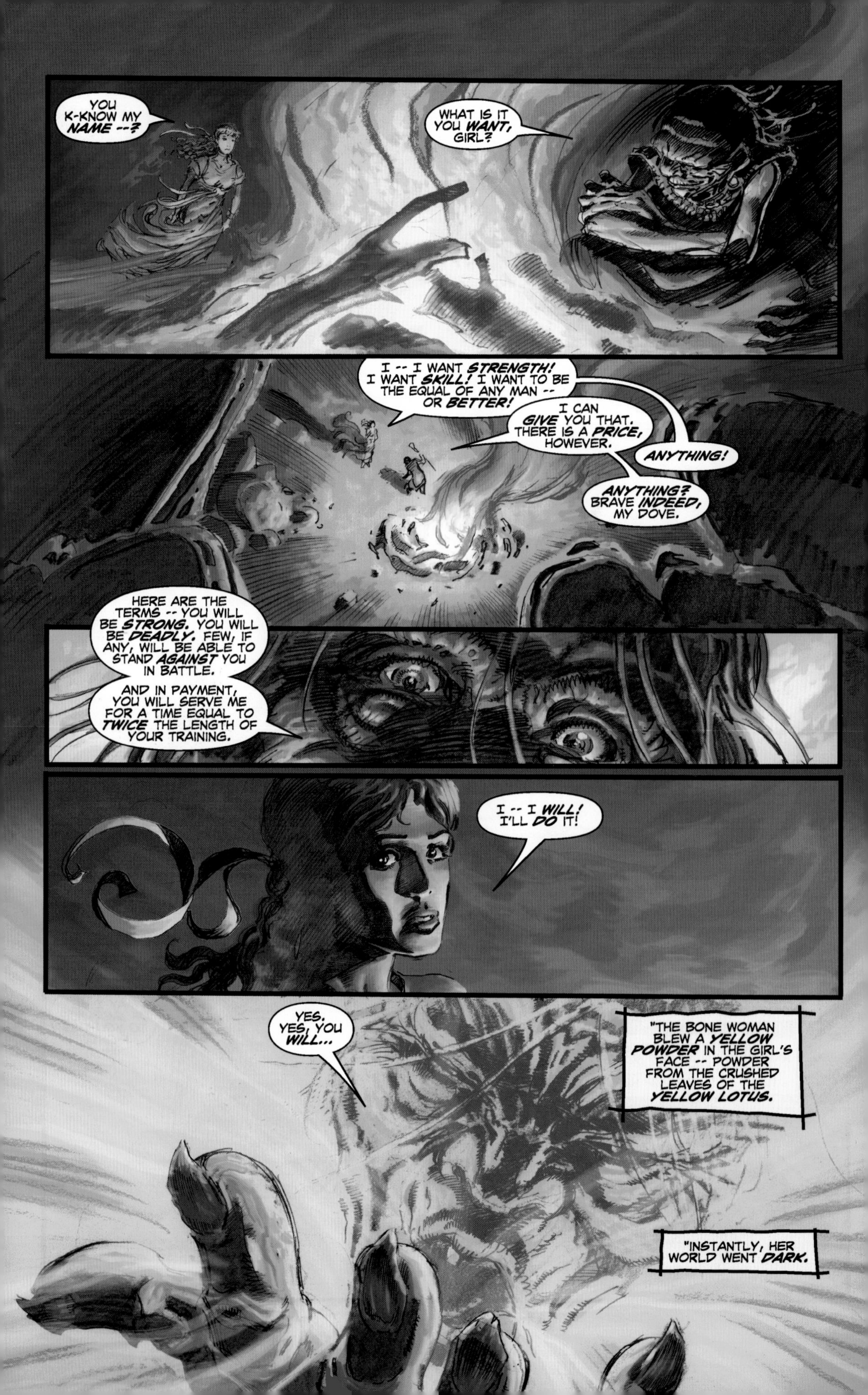
YOU K-KNOW MY NAME --?
WHAT IS IT YOU WANT, GIRL?
I -- I WANT STRENGTH! I WANT SKILL! I WANT TO BE THE EQUAL OF ANY MAN -- OR BETTER!
I CAN GIVE YOU THAT. THERE IS A PRICE, HOWEVER.
ANYTHING!
ANYTHING? BRAVE INDEED, MY DOVE.
HERE ARE THE TERMS -- YOU WILL BE STRONG. YOU WILL BE DEADLY. FEW, IF ANY, WILL BE ABLE TO STAND AGAINST YOU IN BATTLE.
AND IN PAYMENT, YOU WILL SERVE ME FOR A TIME EQUAL TO TWICE THE LENGTH OF YOUR TRAINING.
I -- I WILL! I'LL DO IT!
YES. YES, YOU WILL...
"THE BONE WOMAN BLEW A YELLOW POWDER IN THE GIRL'S FACE -- POWDER FROM THE CRUSHED LEAVES OF THE YELLOW LOTUS.
"INSTANTLY, HER WORLD WENT DARK.

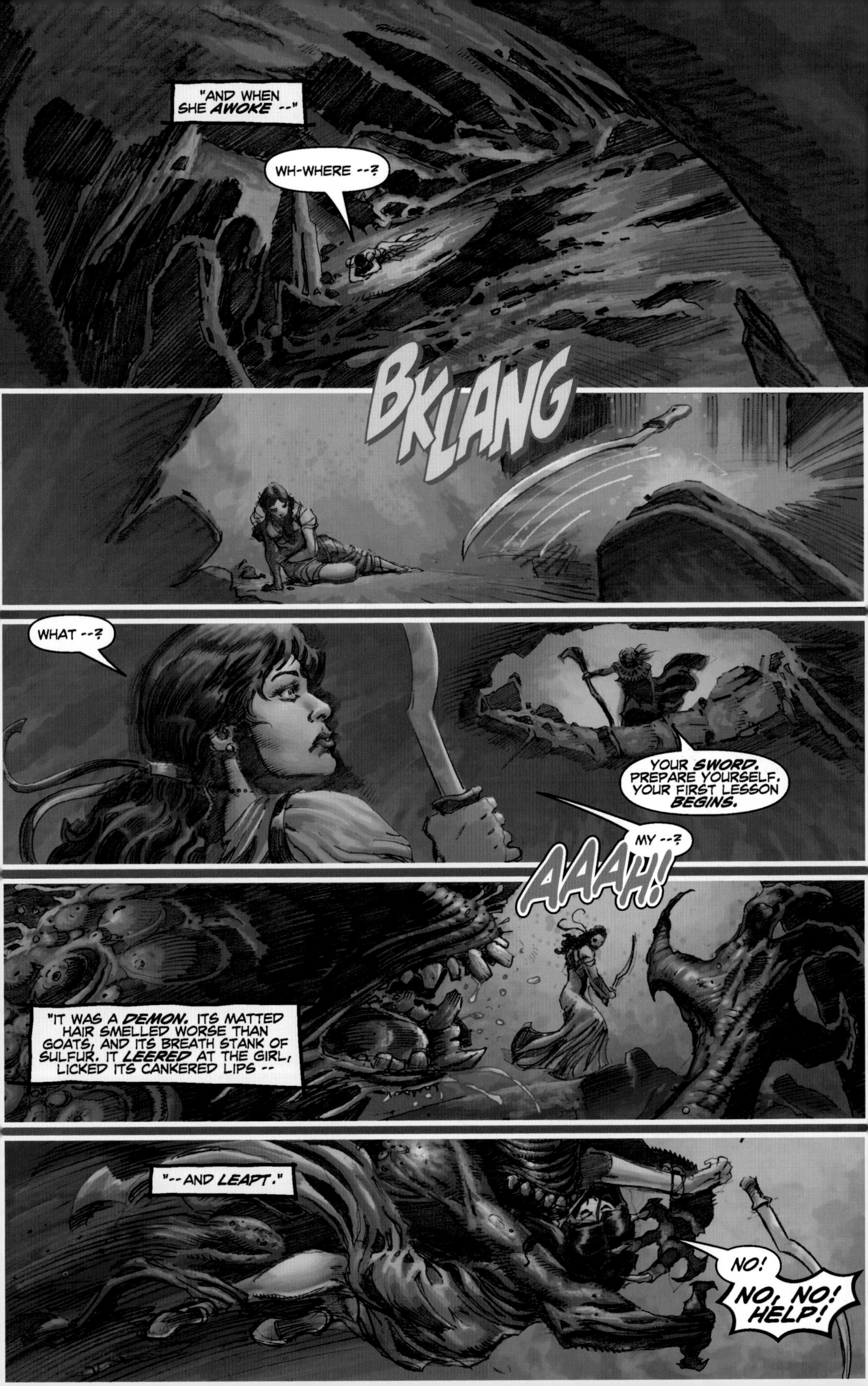
"AND WHEN SHE AWOKE --"
WH-WHERE --?
BKLANG
WHAT --?
YOUR SWORD. PREPARE YOURSELF. YOUR FIRST LESSON BEGINS.
MY --?
AAAH!
"IT WAS A DEMON. ITS MATTED HAIR SMELLED WORSE THAN GOATS, AND ITS BREATH STANK OF SULFUR. IT LEERED AT THE GIRL, LICKED ITS CANKERED LIPS --
"-- AND LEAPT."
NO!
NO, NO! HELP!

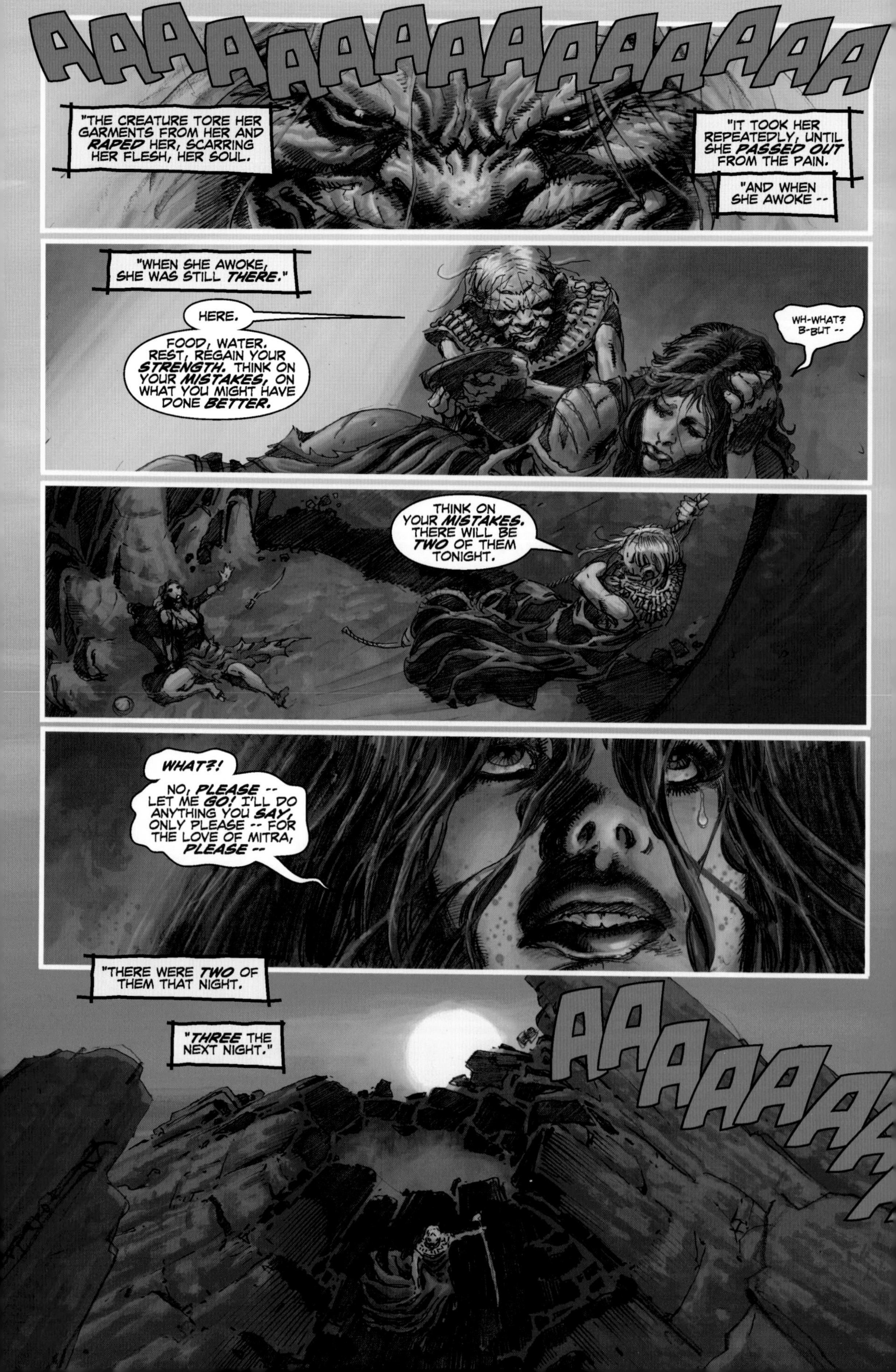
AAAAAAAAAAAAAAAA
"THE CREATURE TORE HER GARMENTS FROM HER AND RAPED HER, SCARRING HER FLESH, HER SOUL.
"IT TOOK HER REPEATEDLY, UNTIL SHE PASSED OUT FROM THE PAIN.
"AND WHEN SHE AWOKE --
"WHEN SHE AWOKE, SHE WAS STILL THERE."
HERE.
FOOD, WATER. REST, REGAIN YOUR STRENGTH. THINK ON YOUR MISTAKES, ON WHAT YOU MIGHT HAVE DONE BETTER.
WH-WHAT? B-BUT --
THINK ON YOUR MISTAKES. THERE WILL BE TWO OF THEM TONIGHT.
WHAT?!
NO, PLEASE -- LET ME GO! I'LL DO ANYTHING YOU SAY, ONLY PLEASE -- FOR THE LOVE OF MITRA, PLEASE --
"THERE WERE TWO OF THEM THAT NIGHT.
"THREE THE NEXT NIGHT."
AAAAAAAA

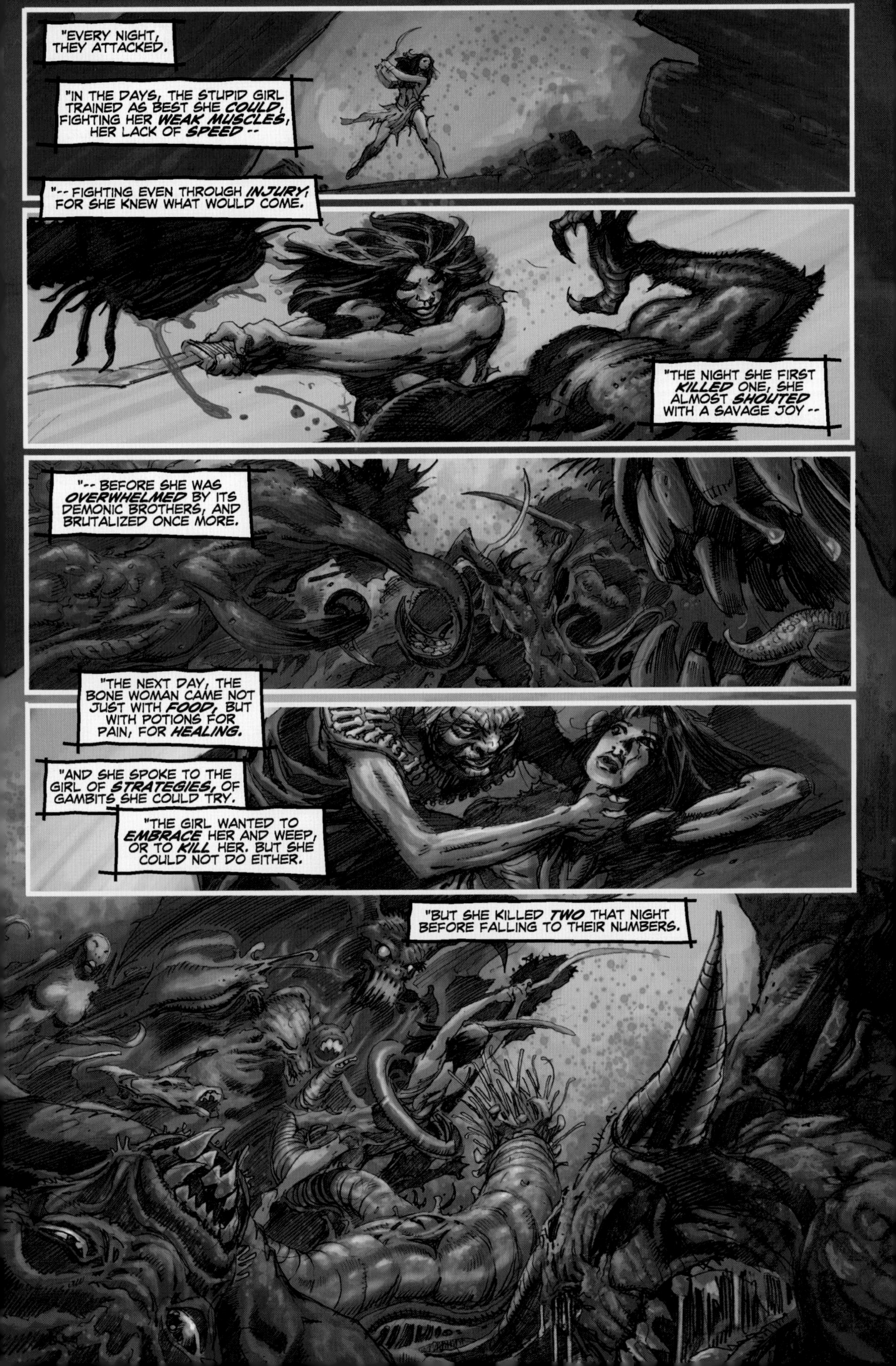

"EVERY NIGHT, THEY ATTACKED.
"IN THE DAYS, THE STUPID GIRL TRAINED AS BEST SHE COULD, FIGHTING HER WEAK MUSCLES, HER LACK OF SPEED --
"-- FIGHTING EVEN THROUGH INJURY, FOR SHE KNEW WHAT WOULD COME.
"THE NIGHT SHE FIRST KILLED ONE, SHE ALMOST SHOUTED WITH A SAVAGE JOY --
"-- BEFORE SHE WAS OVERWHELMED BY ITS DEMONIC BROTHERS, AND BRUTALIZED ONCE MORE.
"THE NEXT DAY, THE BONE WOMAN CAME NOT JUST WITH FOOD, BUT WITH POTIONS FOR PAIN, FOR HEALING.
"AND SHE SPOKE TO THE GIRL OF STRATEGIES, OF GAMBITS SHE COULD TRY.
"THE GIRL WANTED TO EMBRACE HER AND WEEP, OR TO KILL HER. BUT SHE COULD NOT DO EITHER.
"BUT SHE KILLED TWO THAT NIGHT BEFORE FALLING TO THEIR NUMBERS.

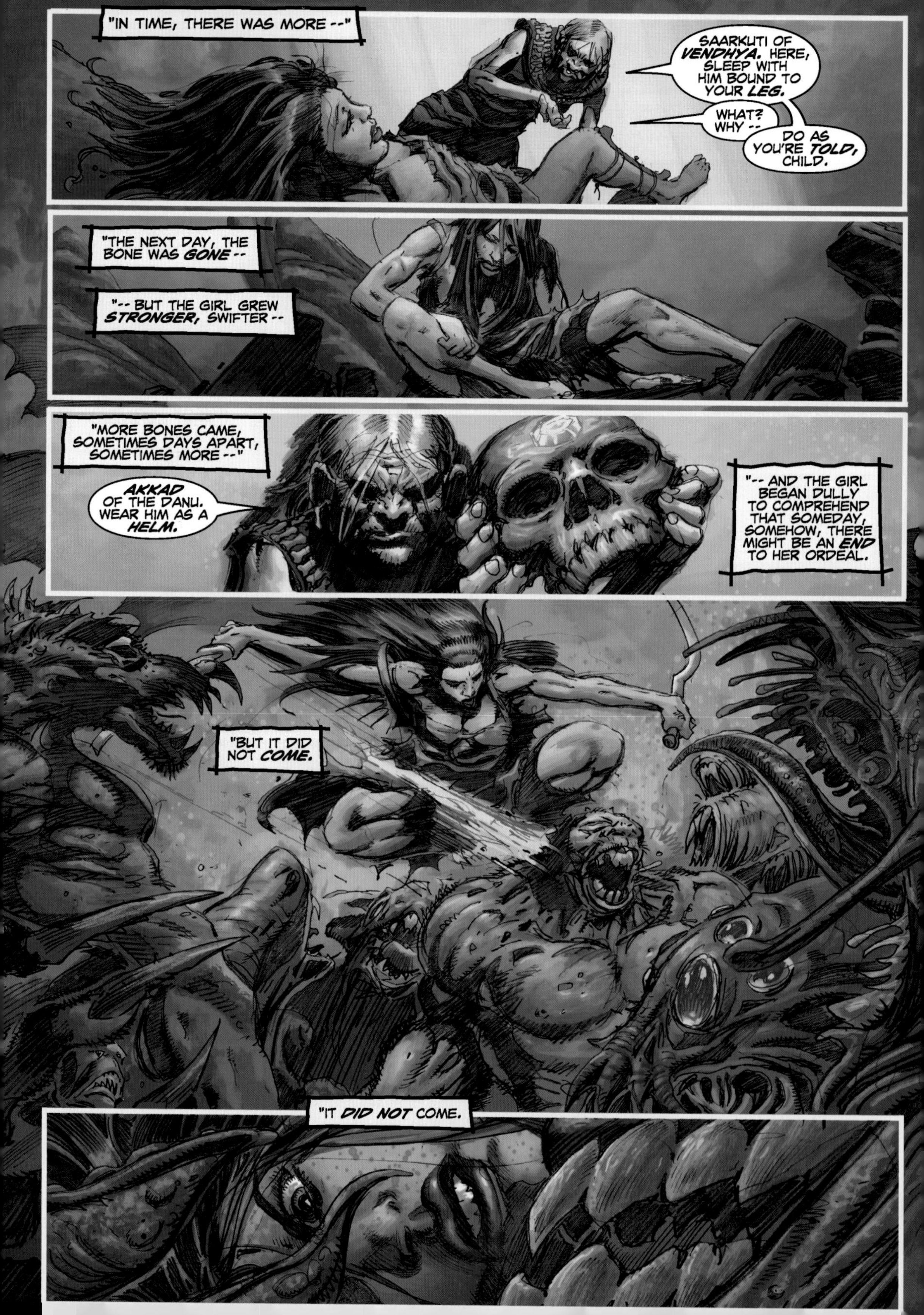
"IN TIME, THERE WAS MORE --"
SAARKUTI OF VENDHYA. HERE, SLEEP WITH HIM BOUND TO YOUR LEG.
WHAT? WHY --
DO AS YOU'RE TOLD, CHILD.
"THE NEXT DAY, THE BONE WAS GONE --
"-- BUT THE GIRL GREW STRONGER, SWIFTER --
"MORE BONES CAME, SOMETIMES DAYS APART, SOMETIMES MORE --"
AKKAD OF THE DANU. WEAR HIM AS A HELM.
"-- AND THE GIRL BEGAN DULLY TO COMPREHEND THAT SOMEDAY, SOMEHOW, THERE MIGHT BE AN END TO HER ORDEAL.
"BUT IT DID NOT COME.
"IT DID NOT COME.

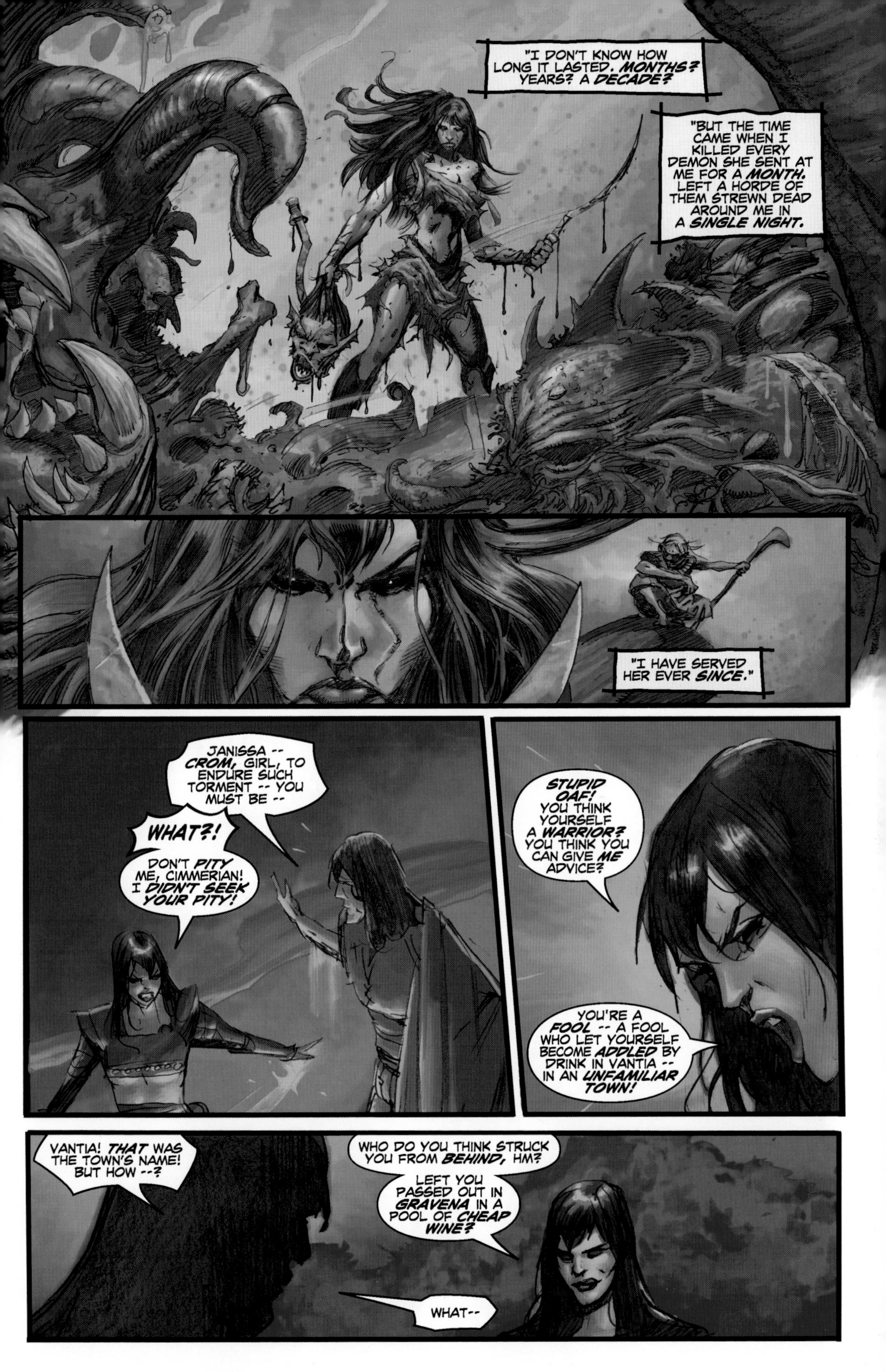
"I DON'T KNOW HOW LONG IT LASTED. MONTHS? YEARS? A DECADE?
"BUT THE TIME CAME WHEN I KILLED EVERY DEMON SHE SENT AT ME FOR A MONTH. LEFT A HORDE OF THEM STREWN DEAD AROUND ME IN A SINGLE NIGHT.
"I HAVE SERVED HER EVER SINCE."
JANISSA -- CROM, GIRL, TO ENDURE SUCH TORMENT -- YOU MUST BE --
WHAT?!
DON'T PITY ME, CIMMERIAN! I DIDN'T SEEK YOUR PITY!
STUPID OAF! YOU THINK YOURSELF A WARRIOR? YOU THINK YOU CAN GIVE ME ADVICE?
YOU'RE A FOOL -- A FOOL WHO LET YOURSELF BECOME ADDLED BY DRINK IN VANTIA -- IN AN UNFAMILIAR TOWN!
VANTIA! THAT WAS THE TOWN'S NAME! BUT HOW --?
WHO DO YOU THINK STRUCK YOU FROM BEHIND, HM?
LEFT YOU PASSED OUT IN GRAVENA IN A POOL OF CHEAP WINE?
WHAT--

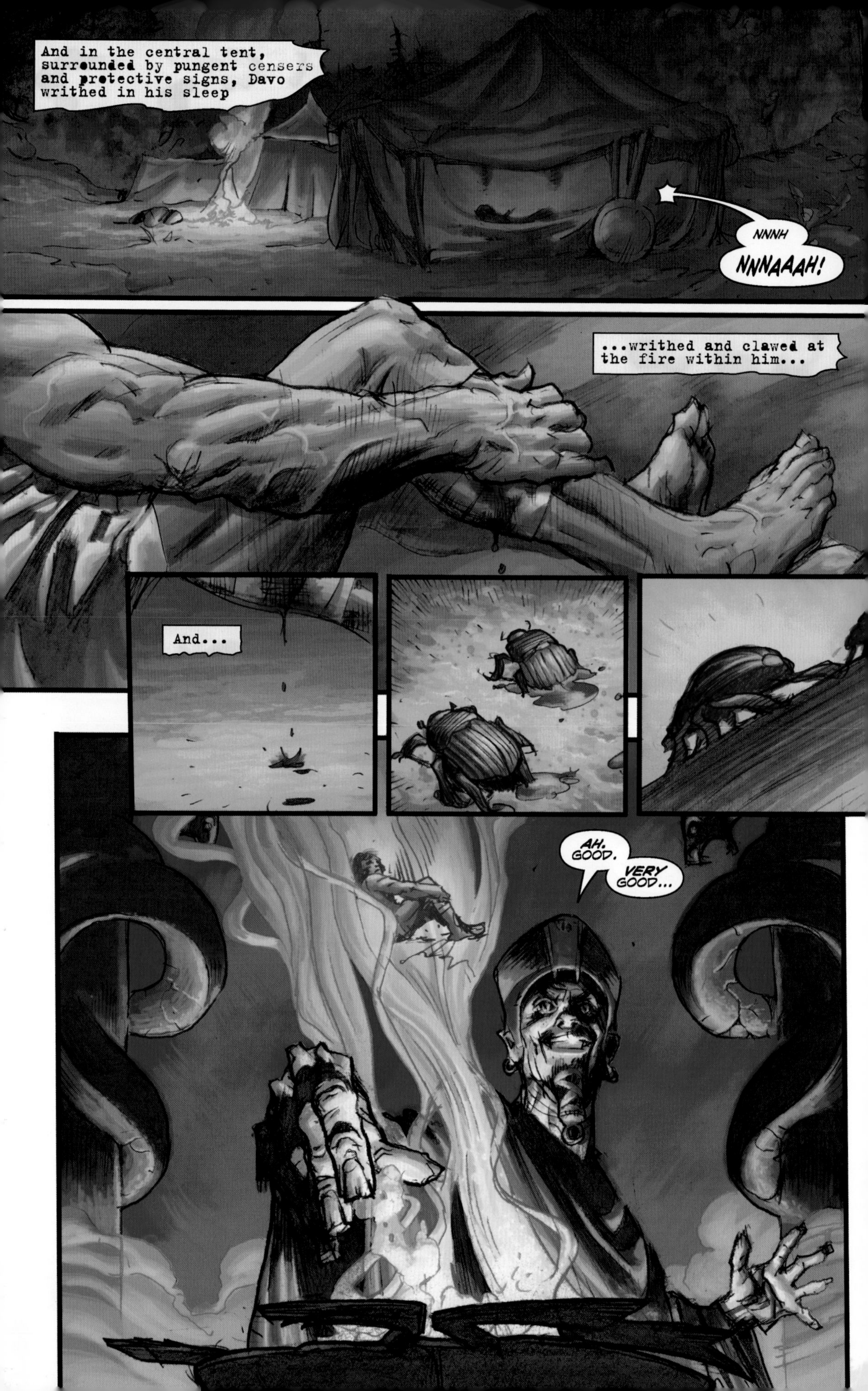

And in the central tent, surrounded by pungent censers and protective signs, Davo writhed in his sleep
NNNH
NNNAAAH!
...writhed and clawed at the fire within him...
And...
AH. GOOD.
VERY GOOD...

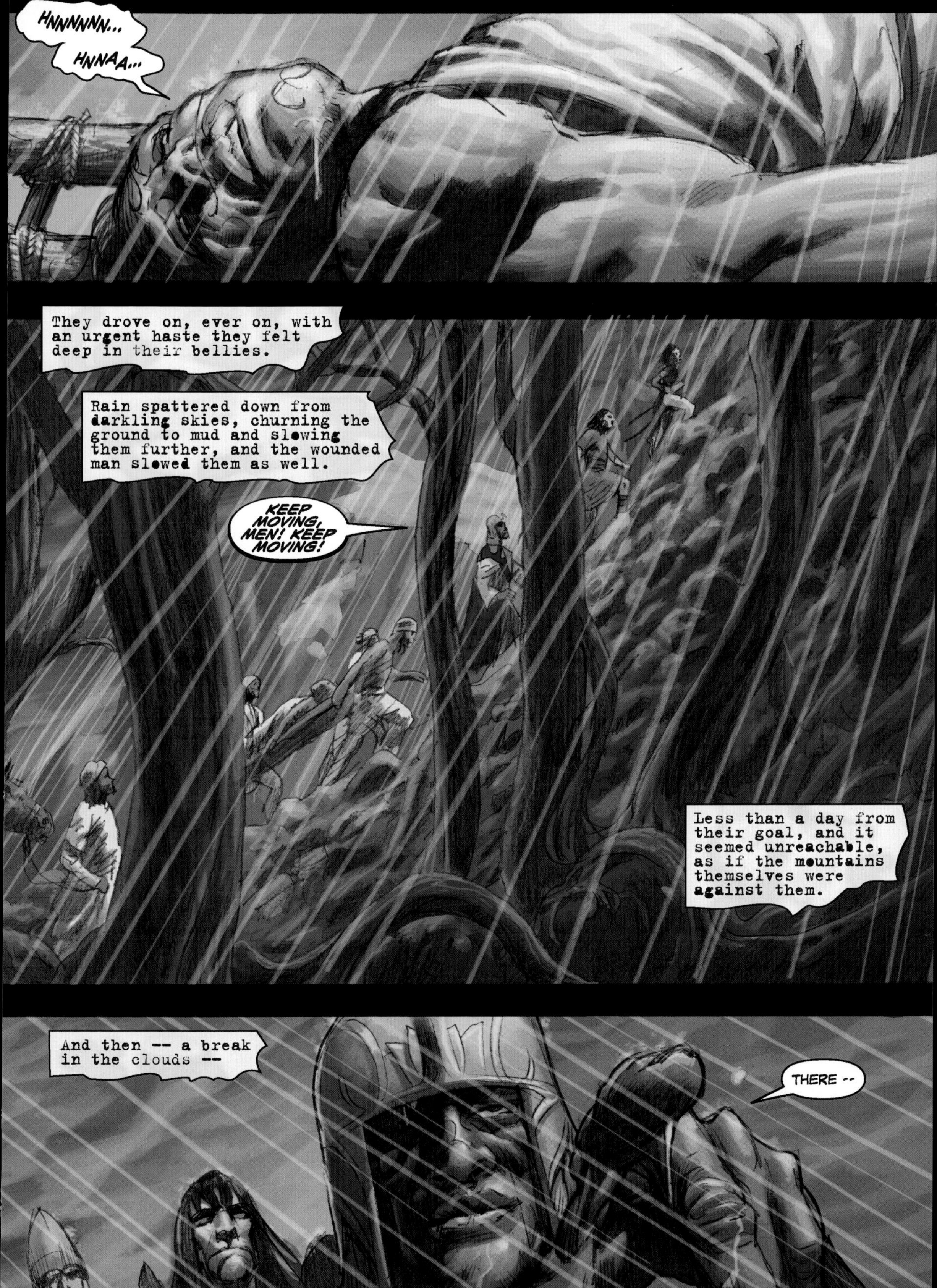
HNNNNNN...
HNNAA...
They drove on, ever on, with an urgent haste they felt deep in their bellies.
Rain spattered down from darkling skies, churning the ground to mud and slowing them further, and the wounded man slowed them as well.
KEEP MOVING, MEN! KEEP MOVING!
Less than a day from their goal, and it seemed unreachable, as if the mountains themselves were against them.
And then -- a break in the clouds --
THERE --

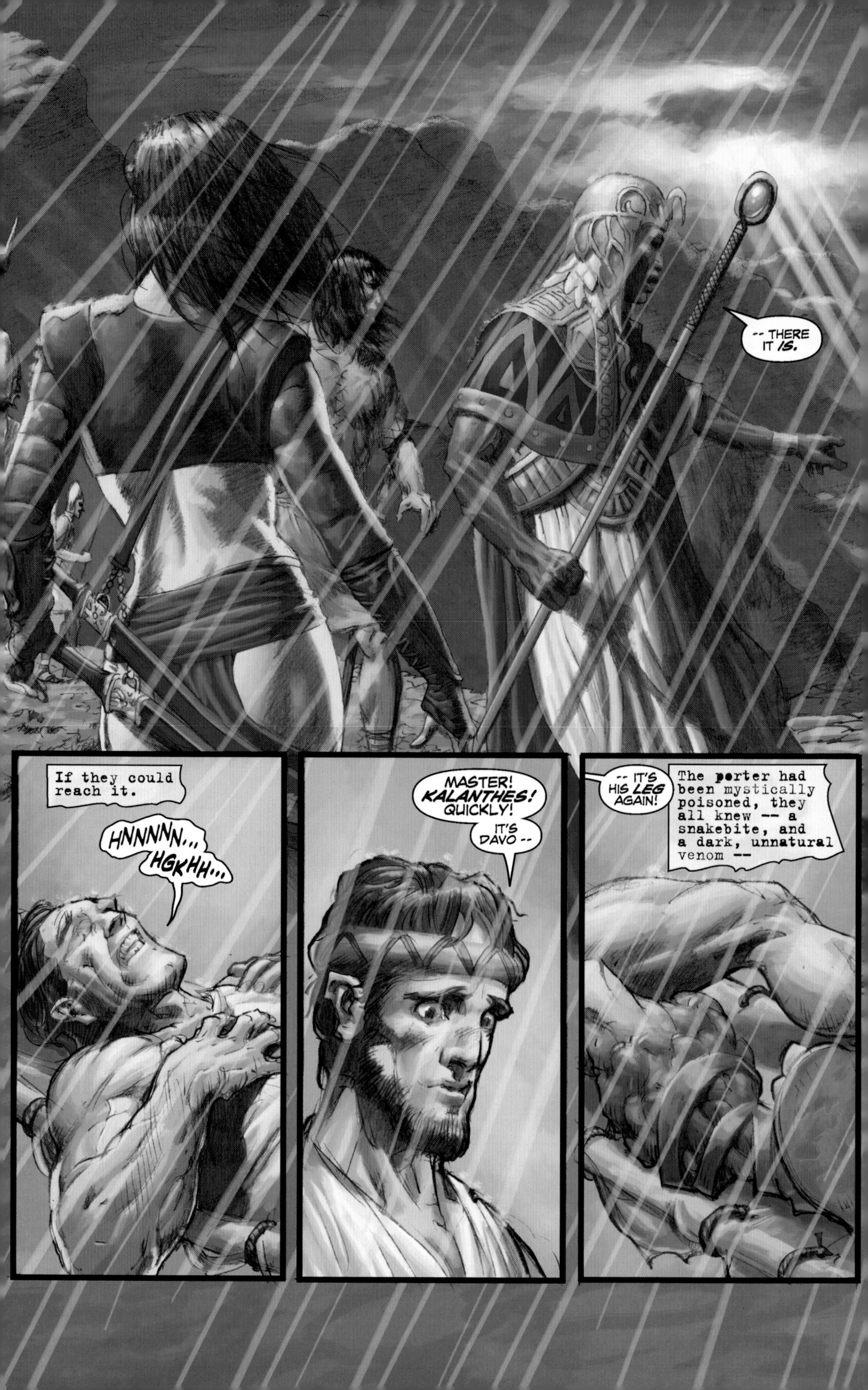
-- THERE IT IS.
If they could reach it.
HNNNNN... HGKHH...
MASTER! KALANTHES! QUICKLY!
IT'S DAVO --
-- IT'S HIS LEG AGAIN!
The porter had been mystically poisoned, they all knew -- a snakebite, and a dark, unnatural venom --

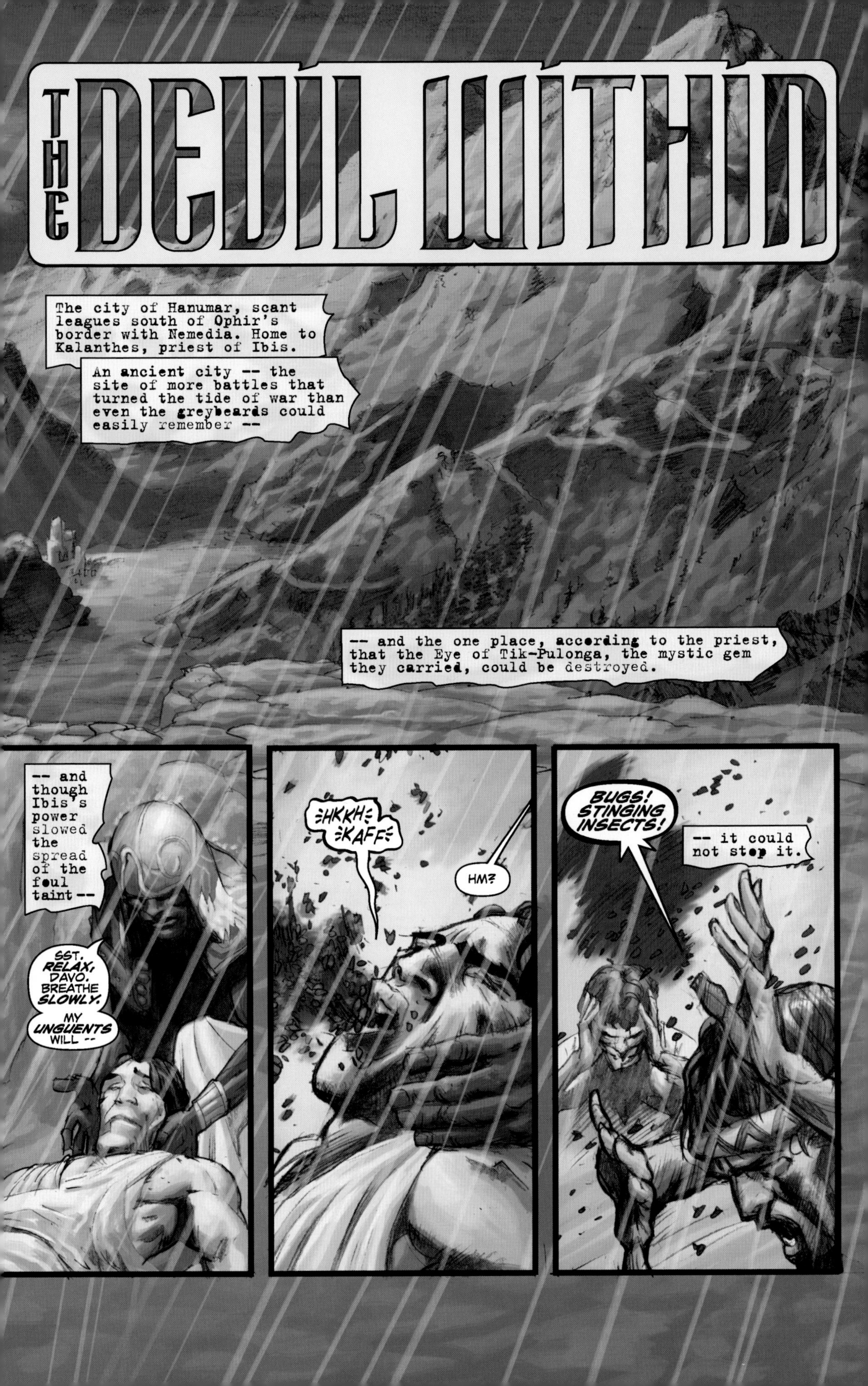
THE DEVIL WITHIN
The city of Hanumar, scant leagues south of Ophir's border with Nemedia. Home to Kalanthes, priest of Ibis.
An ancient city -- the site of more battles that turned the tide of war than even the greybeards could easily remember --
-- and the one place, according to the priest, that the Eye of Tik-Pulonga, the mystic gem they carried, could be destroyed.
-- and though Ibis's power slowed the spread of the foul taint --
SST. RELAX, DAVO. BREATHE SLOWLY. MY UNGUENTS WILL --
HKKH KAFF
HM?
BUGS! STINGING INSECTS!
-- it could not stop it.

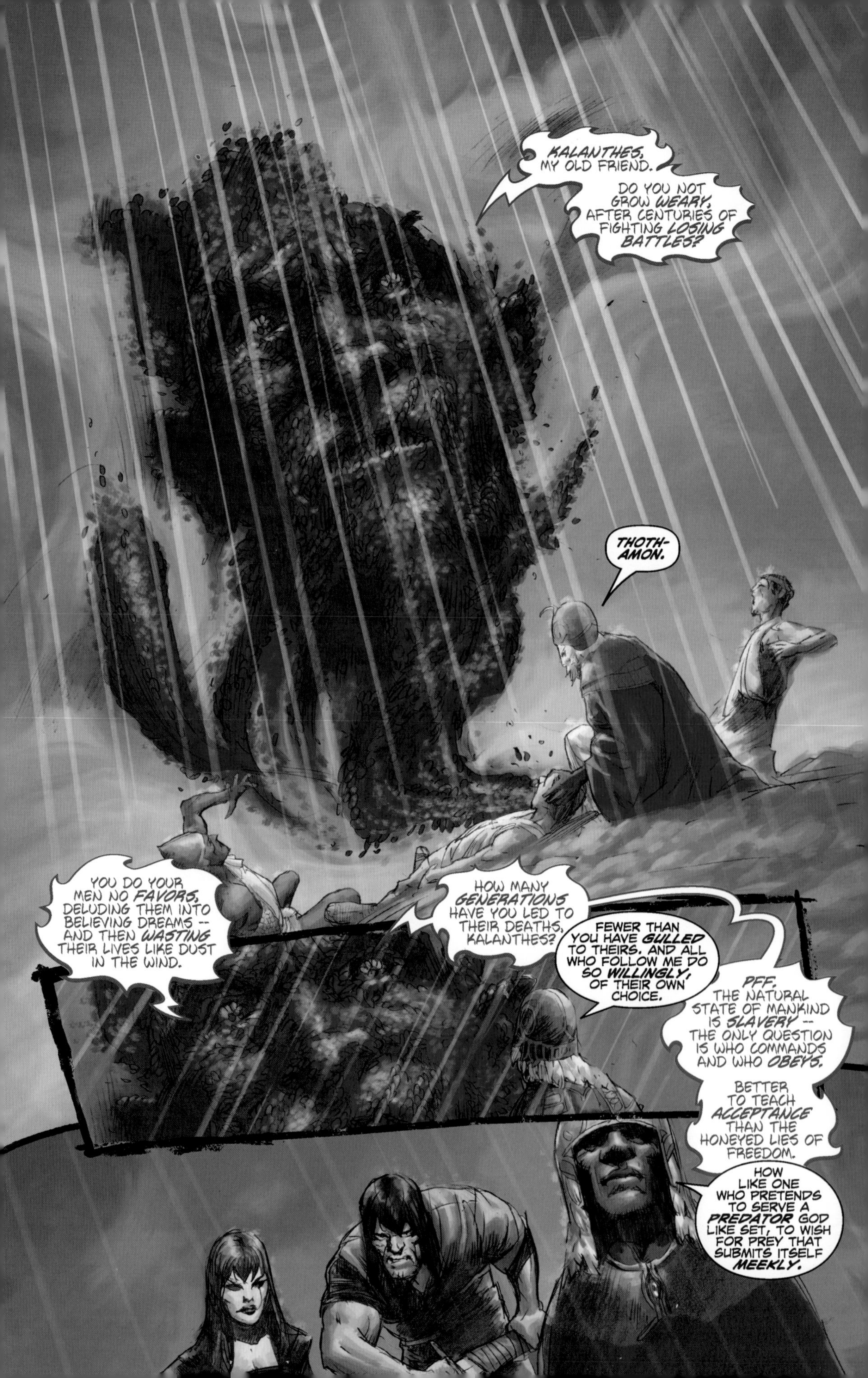
KALANTHES, MY OLD FRIEND.
DO YOU NOT GROW WEARY, AFTER CENTURIES OF FIGHTING LOSING BATTLES?
THOTH-AMON.
YOU DO YOUR MEN NO FAVORS, DELUDING THEM INTO BELIEVING DREAMS -- AND THEN WASTING THEIR LIVES LIKE DUST IN THE WIND.
HOW MANY GENERATIONS HAVE YOU LED TO THEIR DEATHS, KALANTHES?
FEWER THAN YOU HAVE GULLED TO THEIRS. AND ALL WHO FOLLOW ME DO SO WILLINGLY, OF THEIR OWN CHOICE.
PFF. THE NATURAL STATE OF MANKIND IS SLAVERY -- THE ONLY QUESTION IS WHO COMMANDS AND WHO OBEYS.
BETTER TO TEACH ACCEPTANCE THAN THE HONEYED LIES OF FREEDOM.
HOW LIKE ONE WHO PRETENDS TO SERVE A PREDATOR GOD LIKE SET, TO WISH FOR PREY THAT SUBMITS ITSELF MEEKLY.

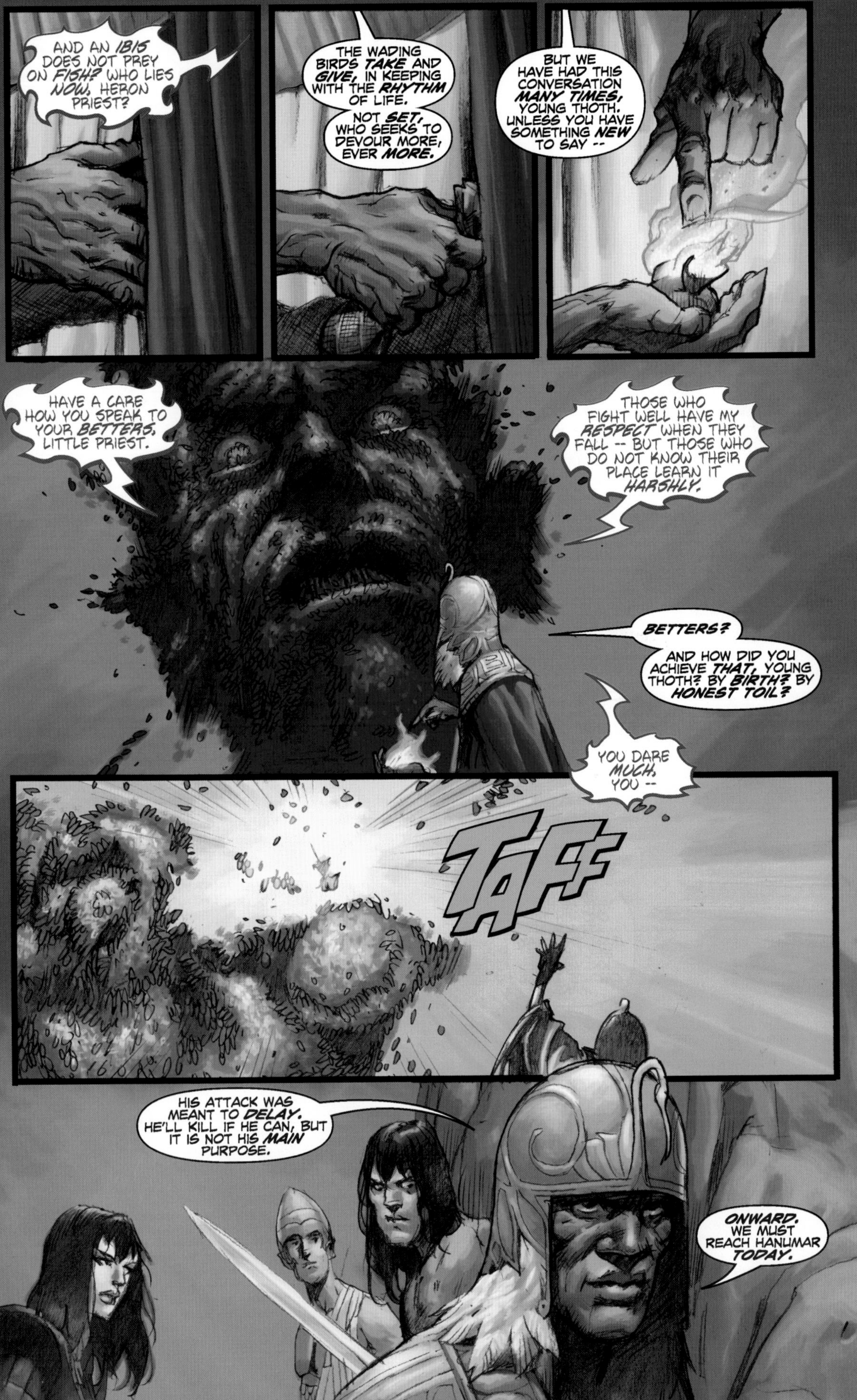
AND AN IBIS DOES NOT PREY ON FISH? WHO LIES NOW, HERON PRIEST?
THE WADING BIRDS TAKE AND GIVE, IN KEEPING WITH THE RHYTHM OF LIFE.
NOT SET, WHO SEEKS TO DEVOUR MORE, EVER MORE.
BUT WE HAVE HAD THIS CONVERSATION MANY TIMES, YOUNG THOTH. UNLESS YOU HAVE SOMETHING NEW TO SAY --
HAVE A CARE HOW YOU SPEAK TO YOUR BETTERS, LITTLE PRIEST.
THOSE WHO FIGHT WELL HAVE MY RESPECT WHEN THEY FALL -- BUT THOSE WHO DO NOT KNOW THEIR PLACE LEARN IT HARSHLY.
BETTERS?
AND HOW DID YOU ACHIEVE THAT, YOUNG THOTH? BY BIRTH? BY HONEST TOIL?
YOU DARE MUCH, YOU --
TAFF
HIS ATTACK WAS MEANT TO DELAY. HE'LL KILL IF HE CAN, BUT IT IS NOT HIS MAIN PURPOSE.
ONWARD. WE MUST REACH HANUMAR TODAY.

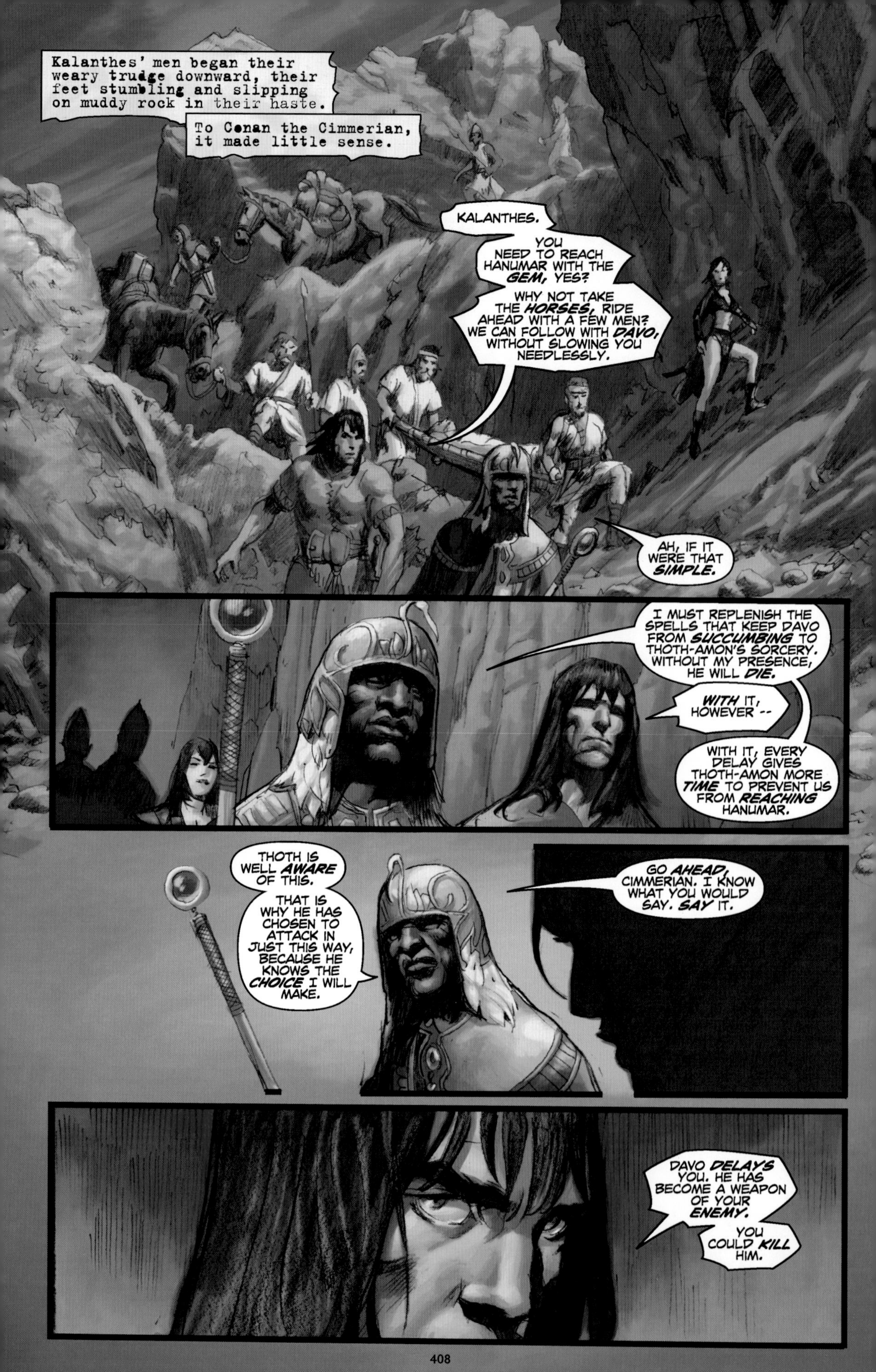
Kalanthes' men began their weary trudge downward, their feet stumbling and slipping on muddy rock in their haste.
To Conan the Cimmerian, it made little sense.
KALANTHES.
YOU NEED TO REACH HANUMAR WITH THE GEM, YES?
WHY NOT TAKE THE HORSES, RIDE AHEAD WITH A FEW MEN? WE CAN FOLLOW WITH DAVO, WITHOUT SLOWING YOU NEEDLESSLY.
AH, IF IT WERE THAT SIMPLE.
I MUST REPLENISH THE SPELLS THAT KEEP DAVO FROM SUCCUMBING TO THOTH-AMON'S SORCERY. WITHOUT MY PRESENCE, HE WILL DIE.
WITH IT, HOWEVER --
WITH IT, EVERY DELAY GIVES THOTH-AMON MORE TIME TO PREVENT US FROM REACHING HANUMAR.
THOTH IS WELL AWARE OF THIS.
THAT IS WHY HE HAS CHOSEN TO ATTACK IN JUST THIS WAY, BECAUSE HE KNOWS THE CHOICE I WILL MAKE.
GO AHEAD, CIMMERIAN. I KNOW WHAT YOU WOULD SAY. SAY IT.
DAVO DELAYS YOU. HE HAS BECOME A WEAPON OF YOUR ENEMY.
YOU COULD KILL HIM.

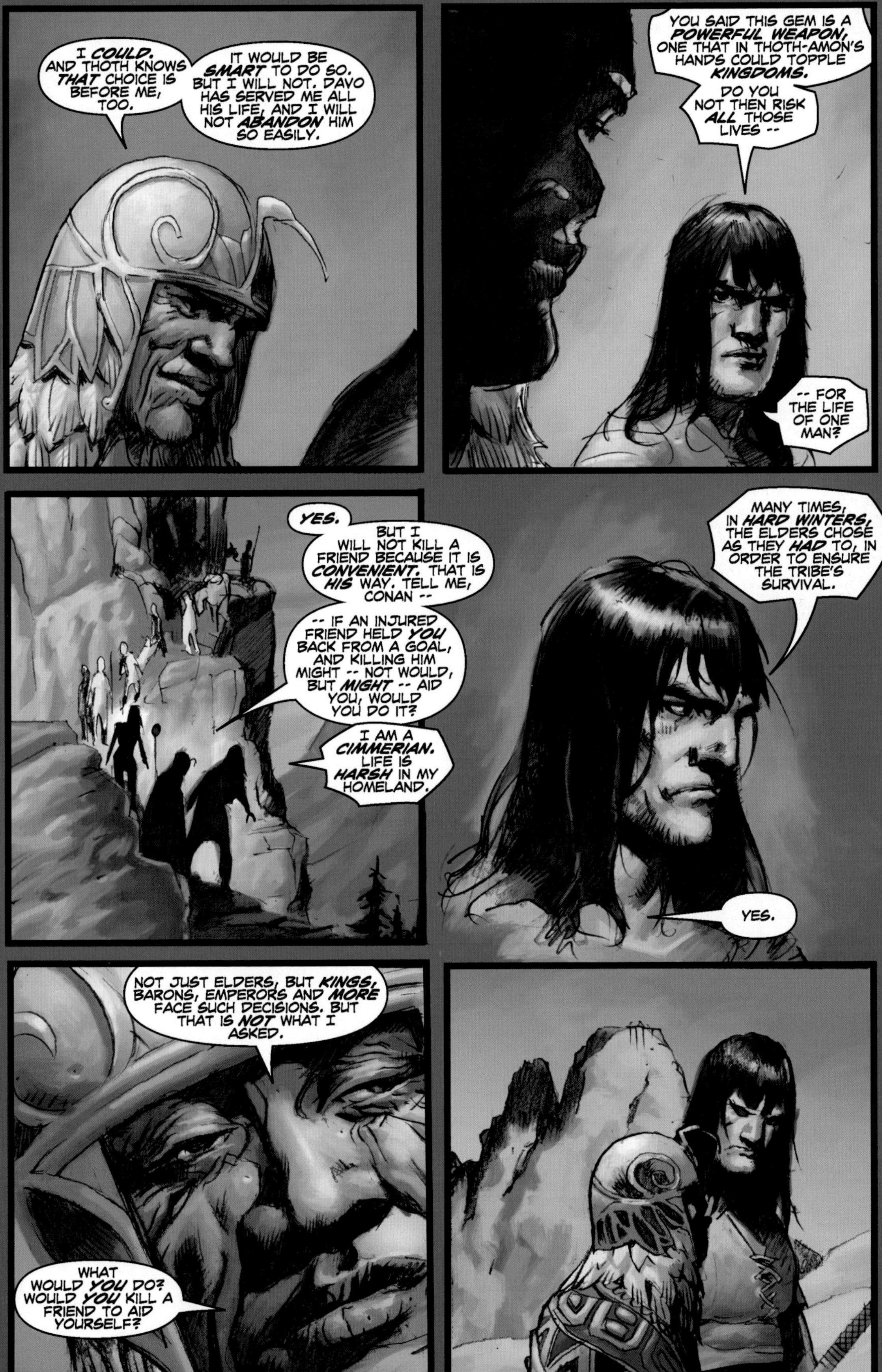
I COULD. AND THOTH KNOWS THAT CHOICE IS BEFORE ME, TOO.
IT WOULD BE SMART TO DO SO. BUT I WILL NOT. DAVO HAS SERVED ME ALL HIS LIFE, AND I WILL NOT ABANDON HIM SO EASILY.
YOU SAID THIS GEM IS A POWERFUL WEAPON, ONE THAT IN THOTH-AMON'S HANDS COULD TOPPLE KINGDOMS.
DO YOU NOT THEN RISK ALL THOSE LIVES --
-- FOR THE LIFE OF ONE MAN?
YES.
BUT I WILL NOT KILL A FRIEND BECAUSE IT IS CONVENIENT. THAT IS HIS WAY. TELL ME, CONAN --
-- IF AN INJURED FRIEND HELD YOU BACK FROM A GOAL, AND KILLING HIM MIGHT -- NOT WOULD, BUT MIGHT -- AID YOU, WOULD YOU DO IT?
I AM A CIMMERIAN. LIFE IS HARSH IN MY HOMELAND.
MANY TIMES, IN HARD WINTERS, THE ELDERS CHOSE AS THEY HAD TO, IN ORDER TO ENSURE THE TRIBE'S SURVIVAL.
YES.
NOT JUST ELDERS, BUT KINGS, BARONS, EMPERORS AND MORE FACE SUCH DECISIONS. BUT THAT IS NOT WHAT I ASKED.
WHAT WOULD YOU DO? WOULD YOU KILL A FRIEND TO AID YOURSELF?

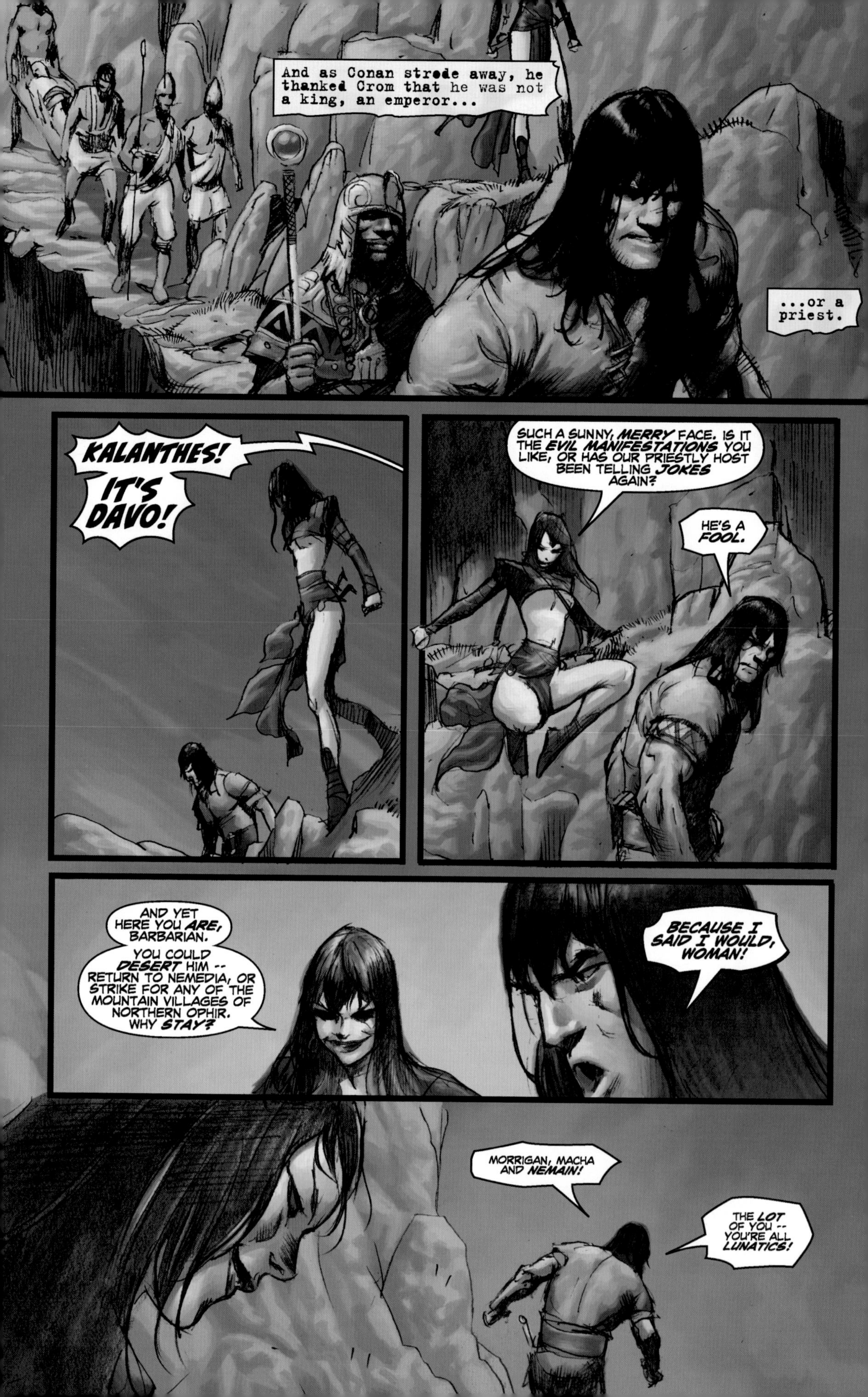
And as Conan strode away, he thanked Crom that he was not a king, an emperor...
...or a priest.
KALANTHES!
IT'S DAVO!
SUCH A SUNNY, MERRY FACE. IS IT THE EVIL MANIFESTATIONS YOU LIKE, OR HAS OUR PRIESTLY HOST BEEN TELLING JOKES AGAIN?
HE'S A FOOL.
AND YET HERE YOU ARE, BARBARIAN.
YOU COULD DESERT HIM -- RETURN TO NEMEDIA, OR STRIKE FOR ANY OF THE MOUNTAIN VILLAGES OF NORTHERN OPHIR. WHY STAY?
BECAUSE I SAID I WOULD, WOMAN!
MORRIGAN, MACHA AND NEMAIN!
THE LOT OF YOU -- YOU'RE ALL LUNATICS!

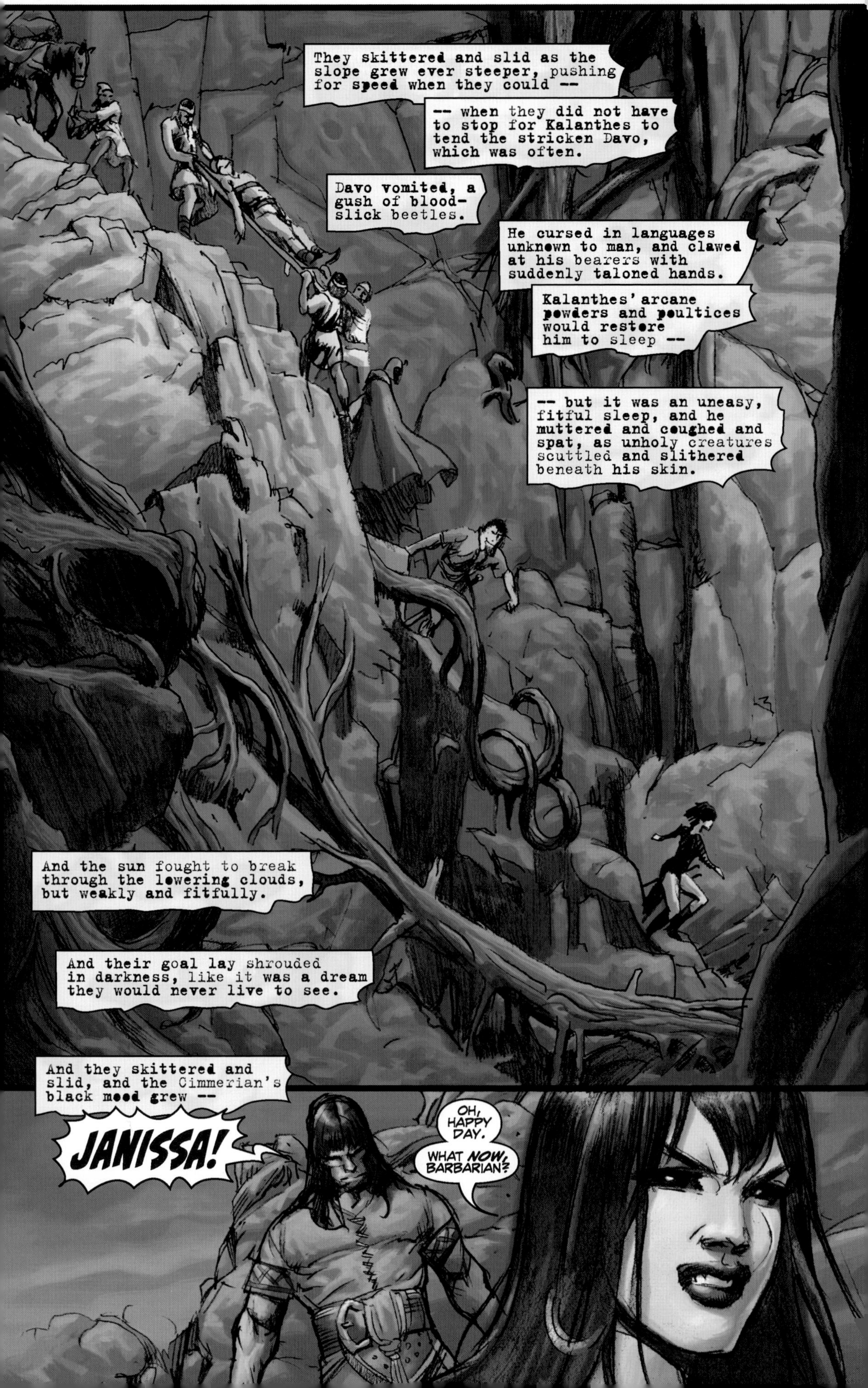
They skittered and slid as the slope grew ever steeper, pushing for speed when they could --
-- when they did not have to stop for Kalanthes to tend the stricken Davo, which was often.
Davo vomited, a gush of blood-slick beetles.
He cursed in languages unknown to man, and clawed at his bearers with suddenly taloned hands.
Kalanthes' arcane powders and poultices would restore him to sleep --
-- but it was an uneasy, fitful sleep, and he muttered and coughed and spat, as unholy creatures scuttled and slithered beneath his skin.
And the sun fought to break through the lowering clouds, but weakly and fitfully.
And their goal lay shrouded in darkness, like it was a dream they would never live to see.
And they skittered and slid, and the Cimmerian's black mood grew --
JANISSA!
OH, HAPPY DAY.
WHAT NOW, BARBARIAN?

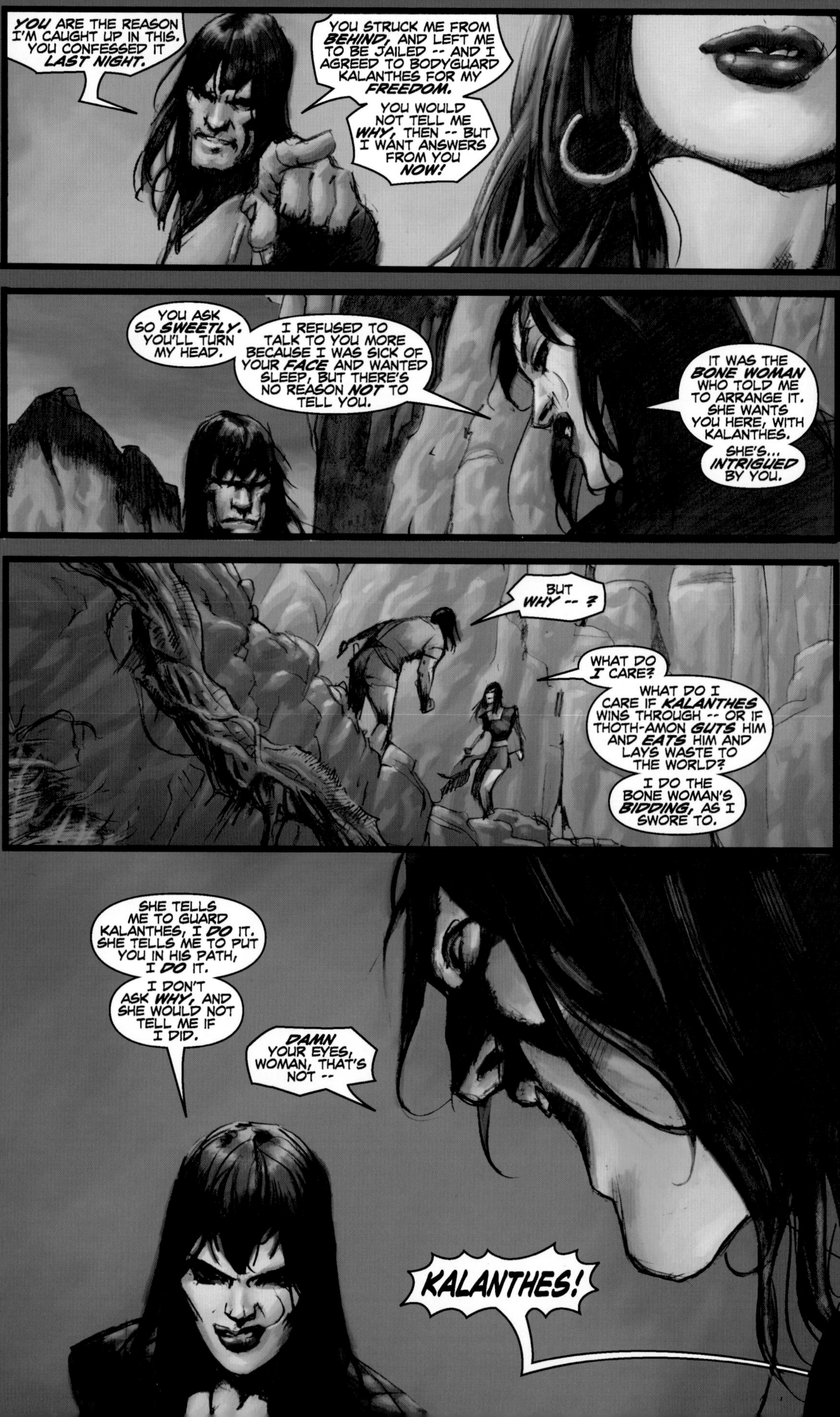
YOU ARE THE REASON I'M CAUGHT UP IN THIS. YOU CONFESSED IT LAST NIGHT.
YOU STRUCK ME FROM BEHIND, AND LEFT ME TO BE JAILED -- AND I AGREED TO BODYGUARD KALANTHES FOR MY FREEDOM.
YOU WOULD NOT TELL ME WHY, THEN -- BUT I WANT ANSWERS FROM YOU NOW!
YOU ASK SO SWEETLY. YOU'LL TURN MY HEAD.
I REFUSED TO TALK TO YOU MORE BECAUSE I WAS SICK OF YOUR FACE AND WANTED SLEEP, BUT THERE'S NO REASON NOT TO TELL YOU.
IT WAS THE BONE WOMAN WHO TOLD ME TO ARRANGE IT. SHE WANTS YOU HERE, WITH KALANTHES.
SHE'S... INTRIGUED BY YOU.
BUT WHY -- ?
WHAT DO I CARE?
WHAT DO I CARE IF KALANTHES WINS THROUGH -- OR IF THOTH-AMON GUTS HIM AND EATS HIM AND LAYS WASTE TO THE WORLD?
I DO THE BONE WOMAN'S BIDDING, AS I SWORE TO.
SHE TELLS ME TO GUARD KALANTHES, I DO IT. SHE TELLS ME TO PUT YOU IN HIS PATH, I DO IT.
I DON'T ASK WHY, AND SHE WOULD NOT TELL ME IF I DID.
DAMN YOUR EYES, WOMAN, THAT'S NOT --
KALANTHES!

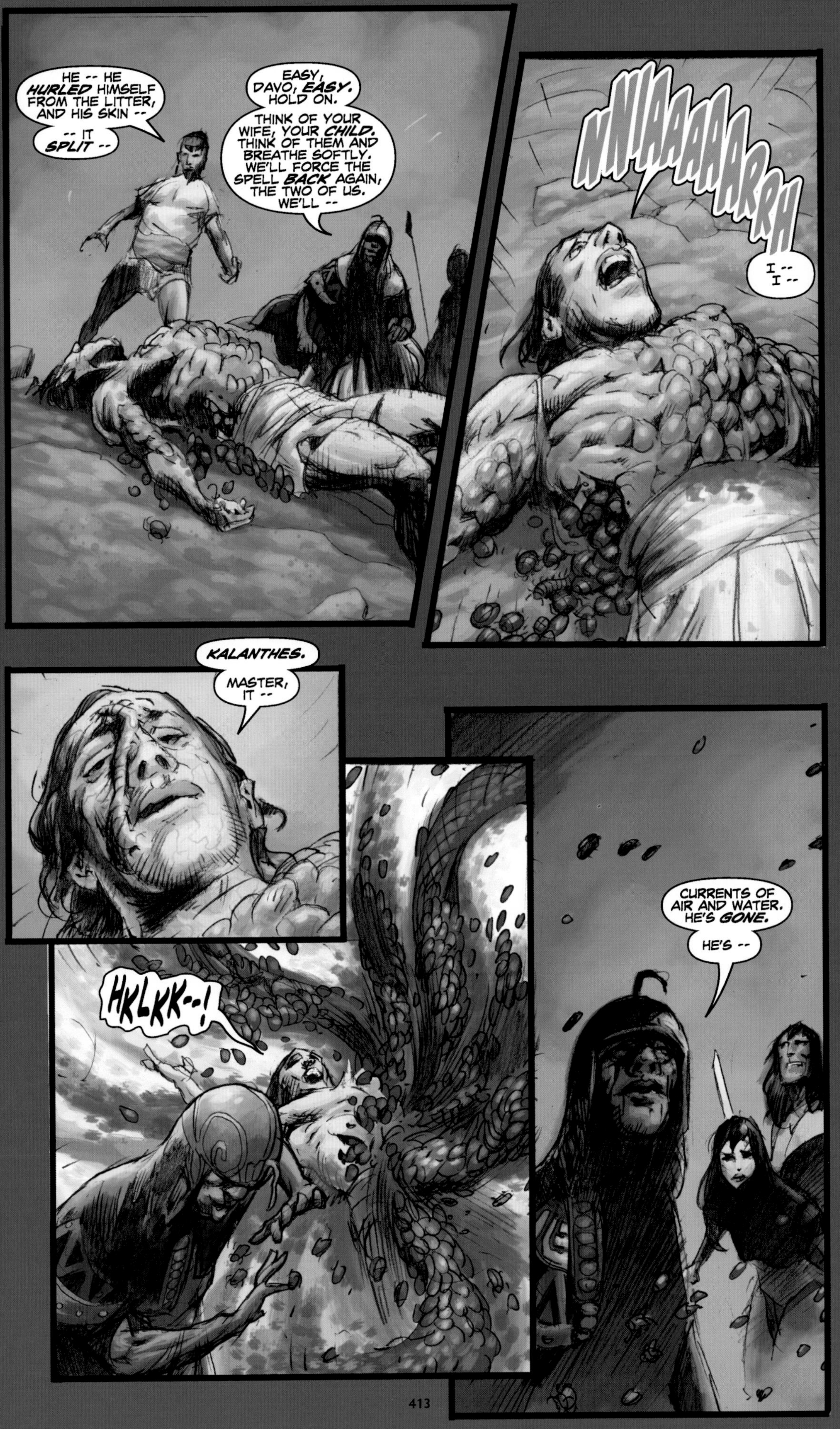
HE -- HE HURLED HIMSELF FROM THE LITTER, AND HIS SKIN --
-- IT SPLIT --
EASY, DAVO, EASY. HOLD ON.
THINK OF YOUR WIFE, YOUR CHILD. THINK OF THEM AND BREATHE SOFTLY. WE'LL FORCE THE SPELL BACK AGAIN, THE TWO OF US. WE'LL --
NNIAAAAAARRH
I -- I --
KALANTHES.
MASTER, IT --
HKLKK--!
CURRENTS OF AIR AND WATER. HE'S GONE.
HE'S --

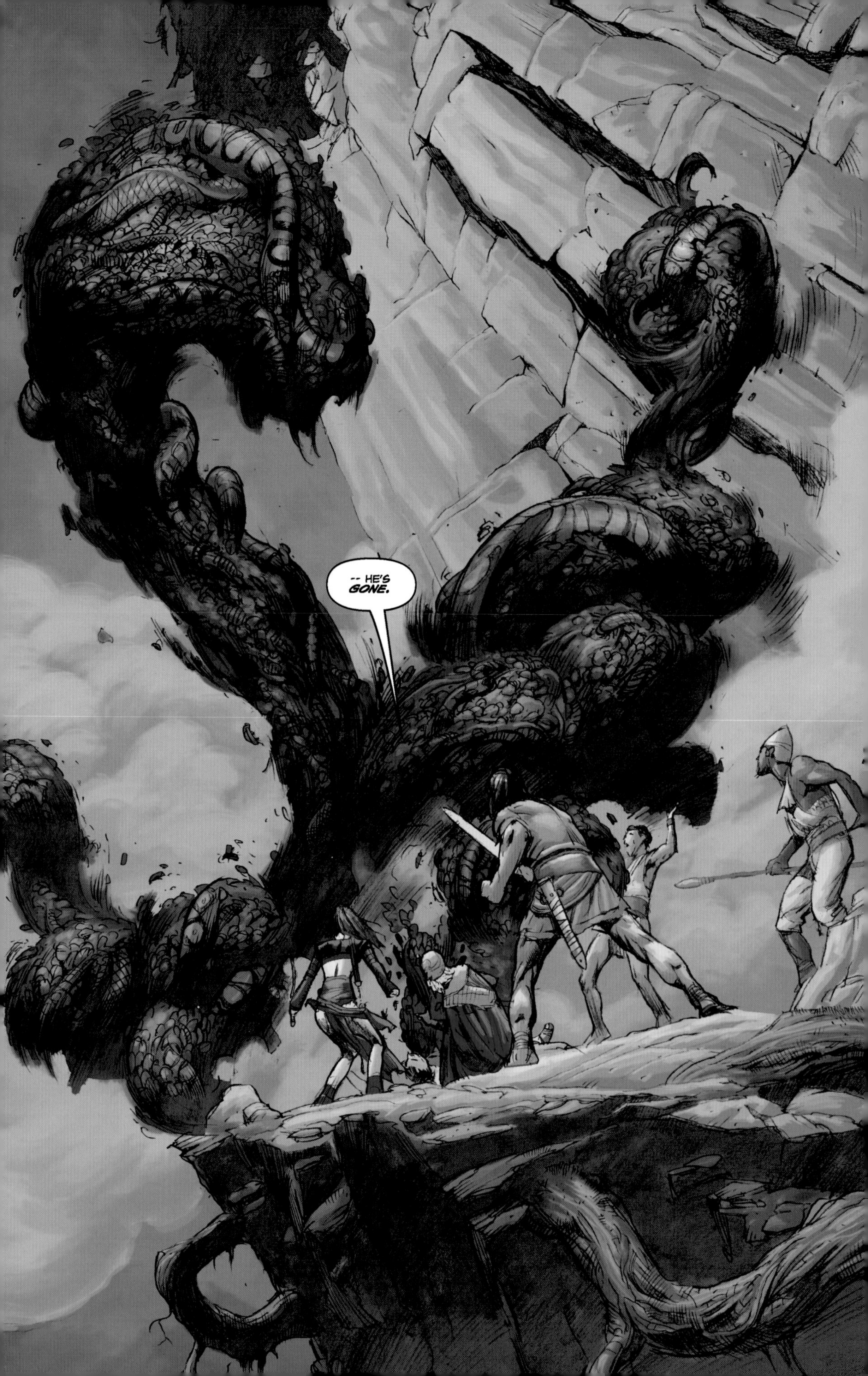
-- HE'S GONE.

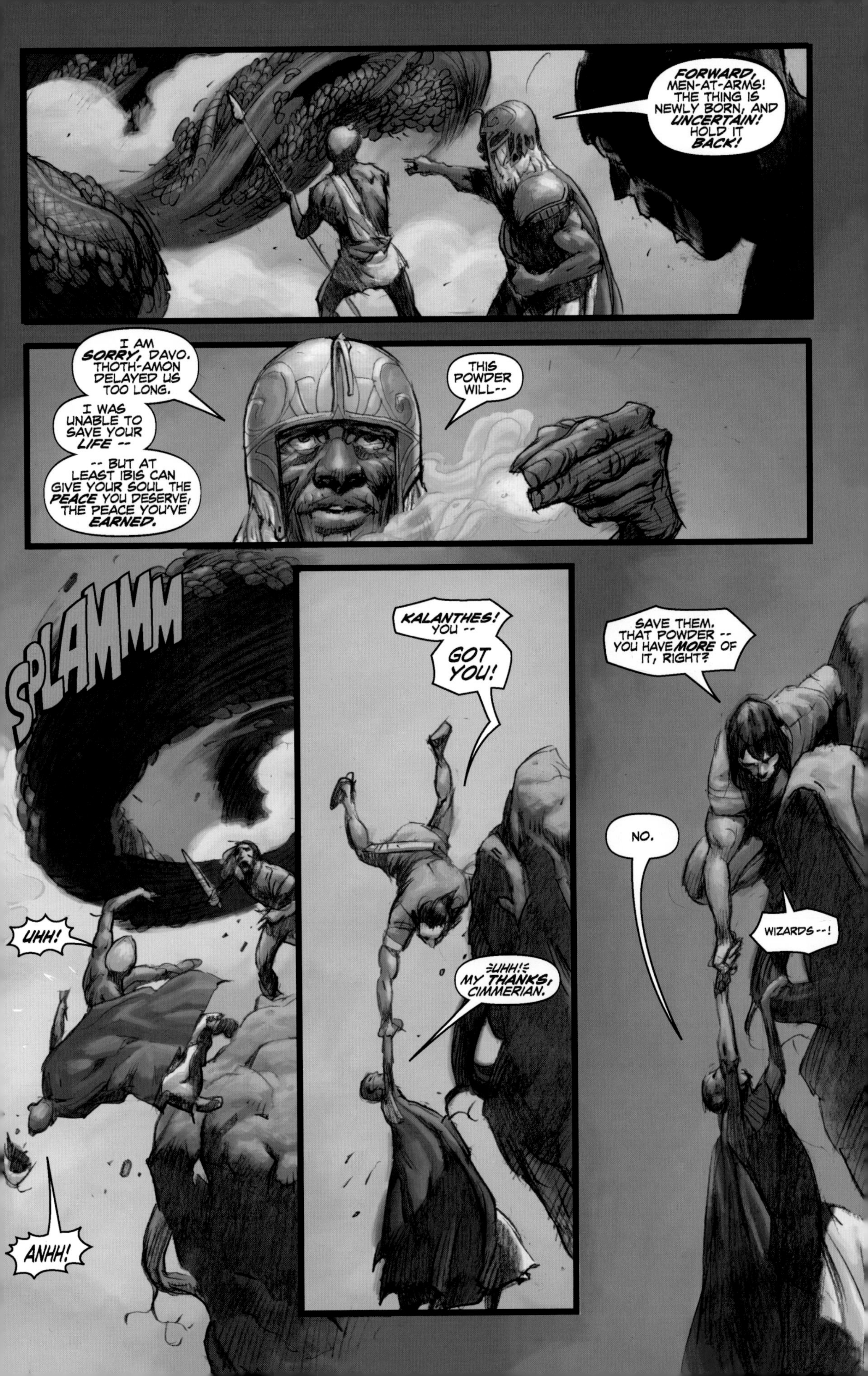
FORWARD, MEN-AT-ARMS! THE THING IS NEWLY BORN, AND UNCERTAIN! HOLD IT BACK!
I AM SORRY, DAVO. THOTH-AMON DELAYED US TOO LONG.
I WAS UNABLE TO SAVE YOUR LIFE --
-- BUT AT LEAST IBIS CAN GIVE YOUR SOUL THE PEACE YOU DESERVE, THE PEACE YOU'VE EARNED.
THIS POWDER WILL--
SPLAMMM
UHH!
ANHH!
KALANTHES! YOU --
GOT YOU!
UHH! MY THANKS, CIMMERIAN.
SAVE THEM. THAT POWDER -- YOU HAVE MORE OF IT, RIGHT?
NO.
WIZARDS--!

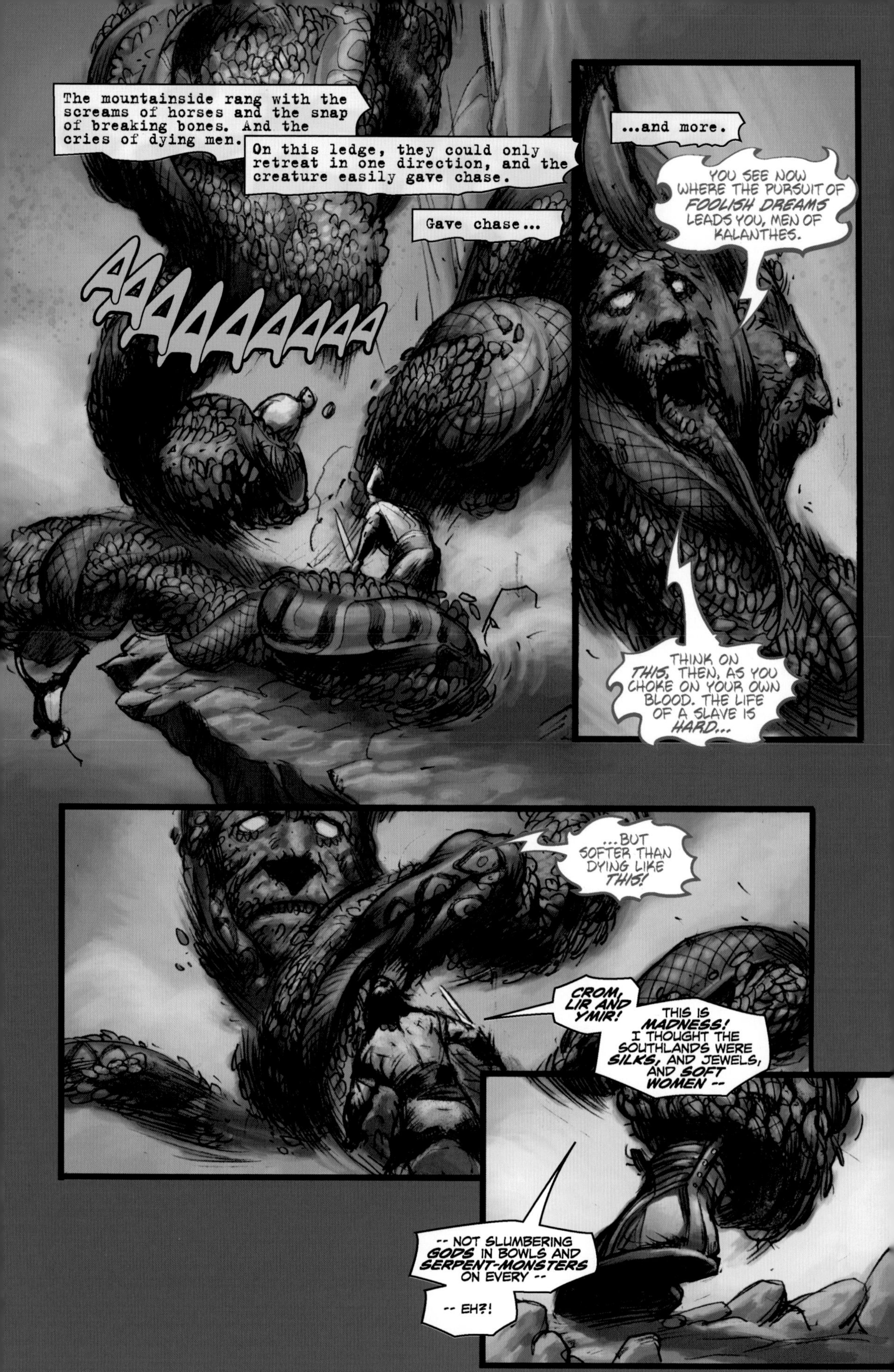

The mountainside rang with the screams of horses and the snap of breaking bones. And the cries of dying men.
On this ledge, they could only retreat in one direction, and the creature easily gave chase.
Gave chase...
AAAAAAAAAA
...and more.
YOU SEE NOW WHERE THE PURSUIT OF FOOLISH DREAMS LEADS YOU, MEN OF KALANTHES.
THINK ON THIS, THEN, AS YOU CHOKE ON YOUR OWN BLOOD. THE LIFE OF A SLAVE IS HARD...
...BUT SOFTER THAN DYING LIKE THIS!
CROM, LIR AND YMIR!
THIS IS MADNESS! I THOUGHT THE SOUTHLANDS WERE SILKS, AND JEWELS, AND SOFT WOMEN --
-- NOT SLUMBERING GODS IN BOWLS AND SERPENT-MONSTERS ON EVERY --
-- EH?!

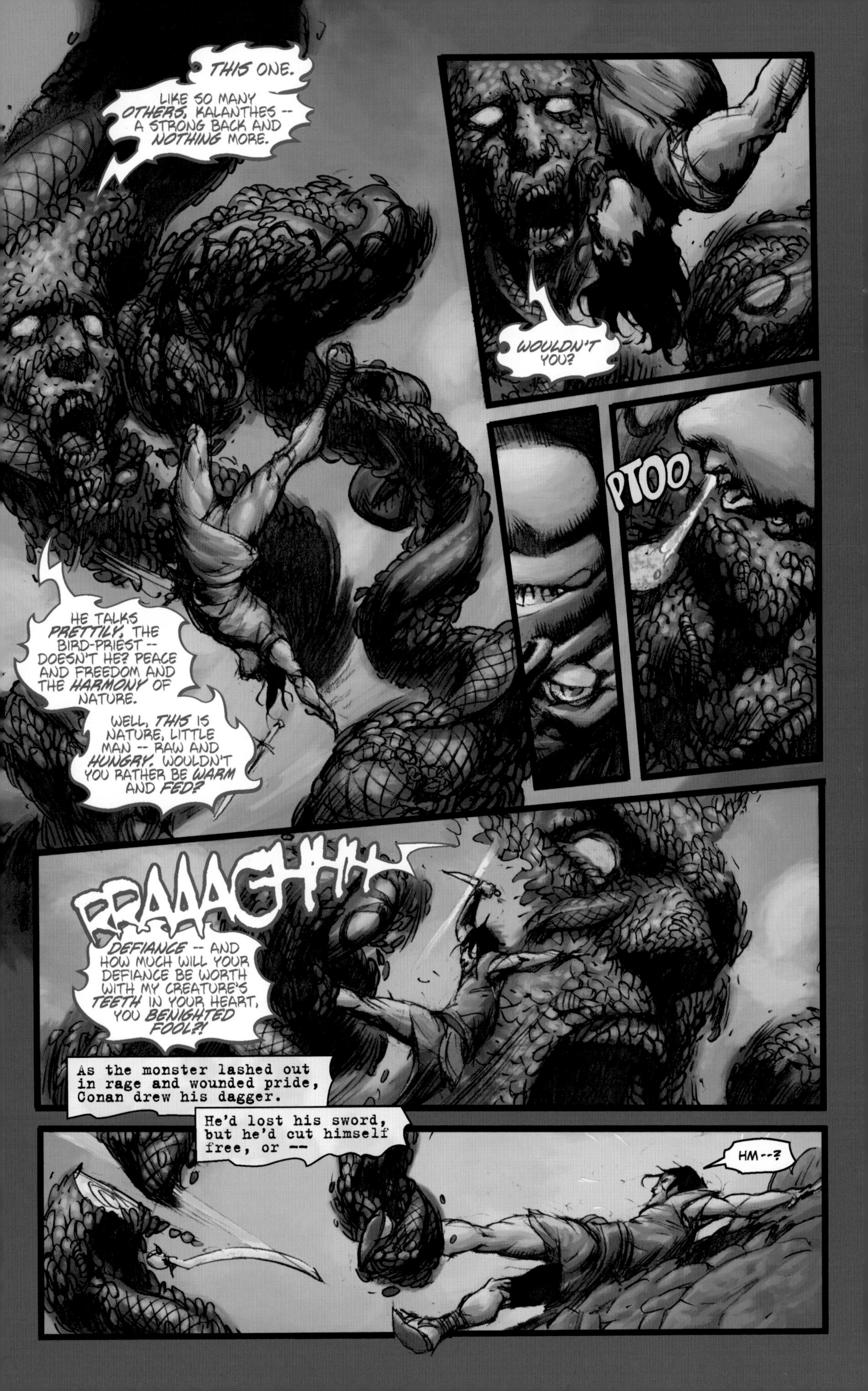
THIS ONE.
LIKE SO MANY OTHERS, KALANTHES -- A STRONG BACK AND NOTHING MORE.
WOULDN'T YOU?
HE TALKS PRETTILY, THE BIRD-PRIEST -- DOESN'T HE? PEACE AND FREEDOM AND THE HARMONY OF NATURE.
WELL, THIS IS NATURE, LITTLE MAN -- RAW AND HUNGRY. WOULDN'T YOU RATHER BE WARM AND FED?
PTOO
BRAAAGHHH
DEFIANCE -- AND HOW MUCH WILL YOUR DEFIANCE BE WORTH WITH MY CREATURE'S TEETH IN YOUR HEART, YOU BENIGHTED FOOL?!
As the monster lashed out in rage and wounded pride, Conan drew his dagger.
He'd lost his sword, but he'd cut himself free, or --
HM --?

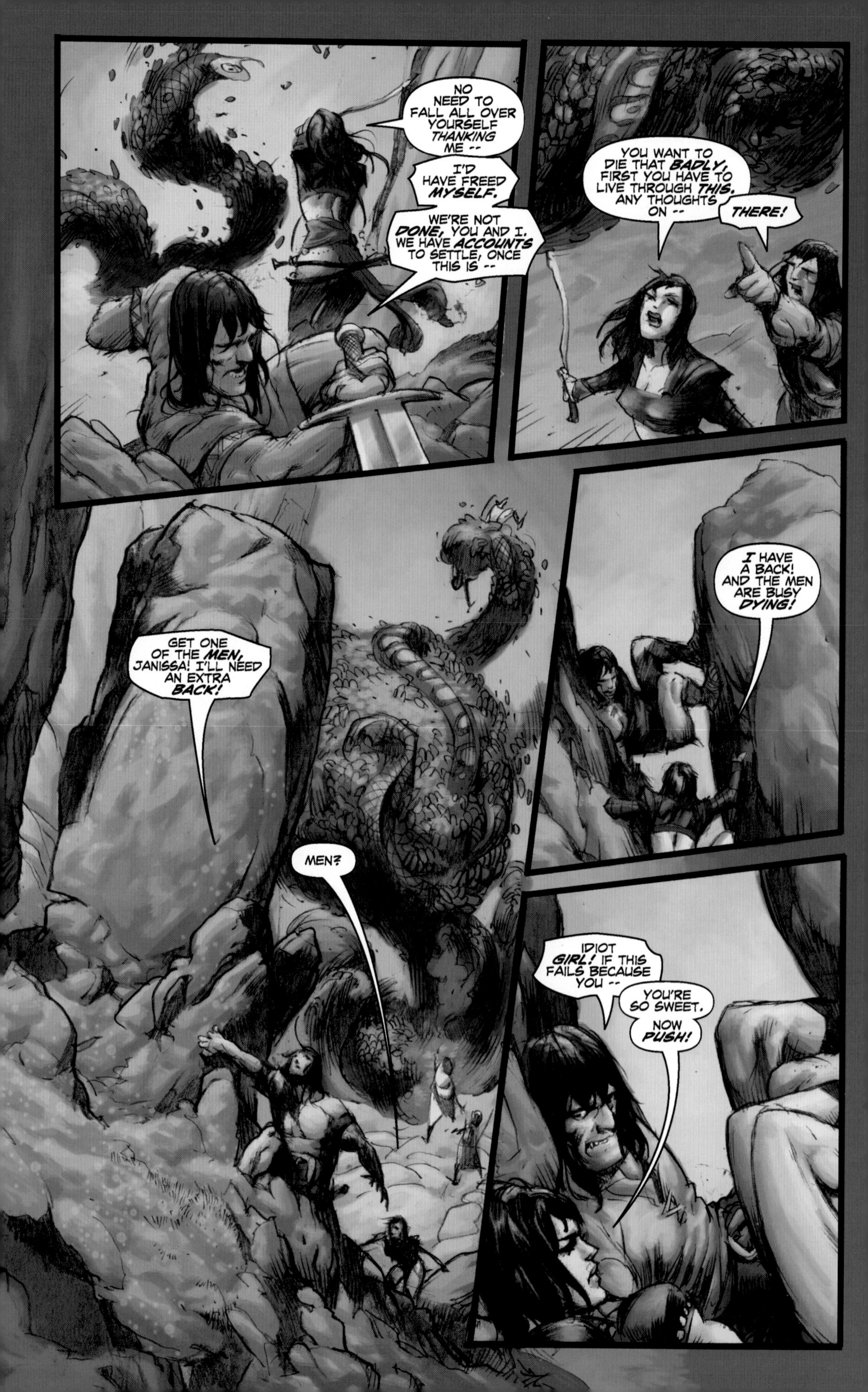
NO NEED TO FALL ALL OVER YOURSELF *THANKING* ME --
I'D HAVE FREED ***MYSELF.***
WE'RE NOT ***DONE,*** YOU AND I. WE HAVE ***ACCOUNTS*** TO SETTLE, ONCE THIS IS --
YOU WANT TO DIE THAT ***BADLY,*** FIRST YOU HAVE TO LIVE THROUGH ***THIS.*** ANY THOUGHTS ON --
THERE!
GET ONE OF THE ***MEN,*** JANISSA! I'LL NEED AN EXTRA ***BACK!***
MEN?
I HAVE A BACK! AND THE MEN ARE BUSY ***DYING!***
IDIOT ***GIRL!*** IF THIS FAILS BECAUSE YOU --
YOU'RE SO SWEET.
NOW ***PUSH!***

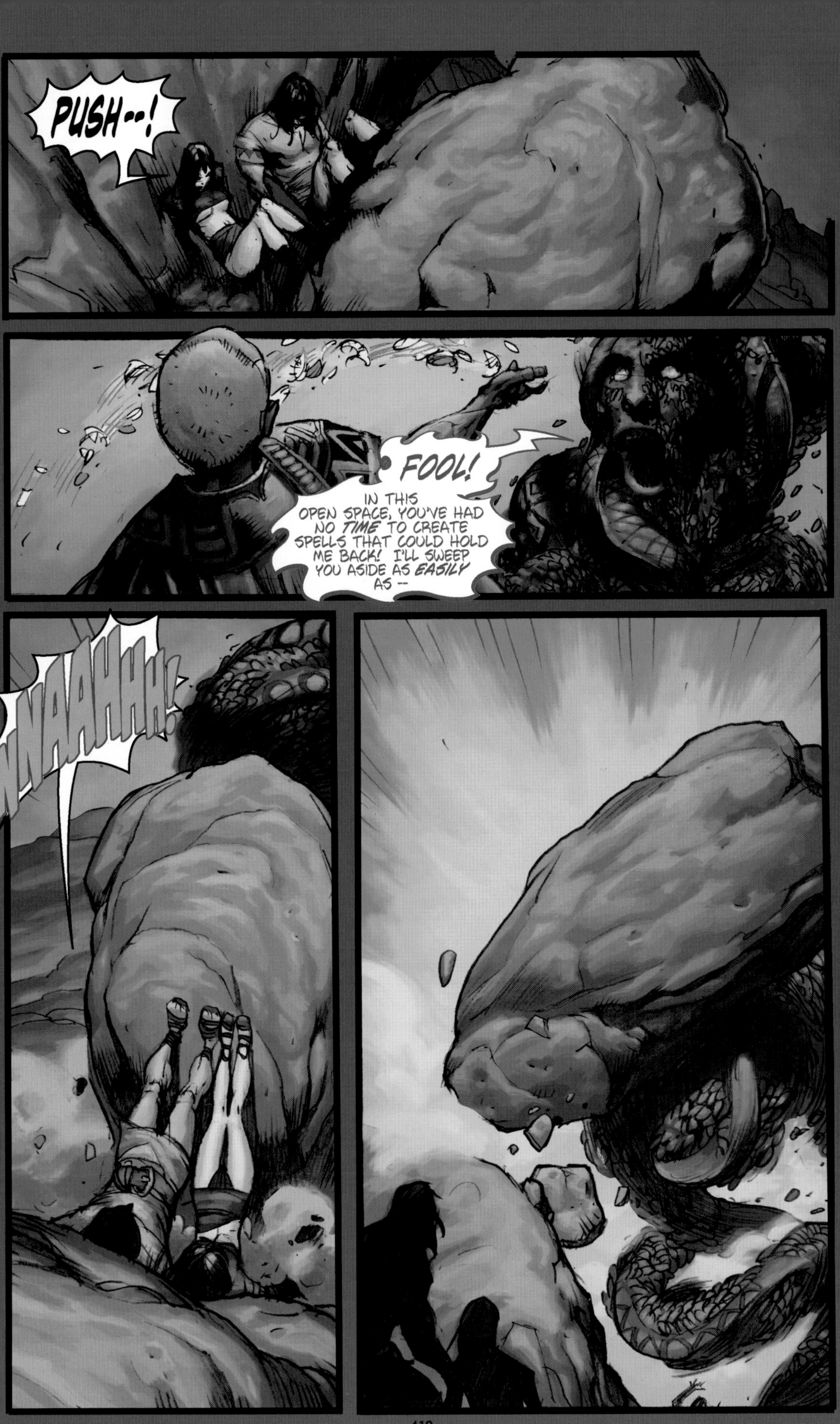
PUSH--!
FOOL! IN THIS OPEN SPACE, YOU'VE HAD NO TIME TO CREATE SPELLS THAT COULD HOLD ME BACK! I'LL SWEEP YOU ASIDE AS EASILY AS --
NNAAHHH!

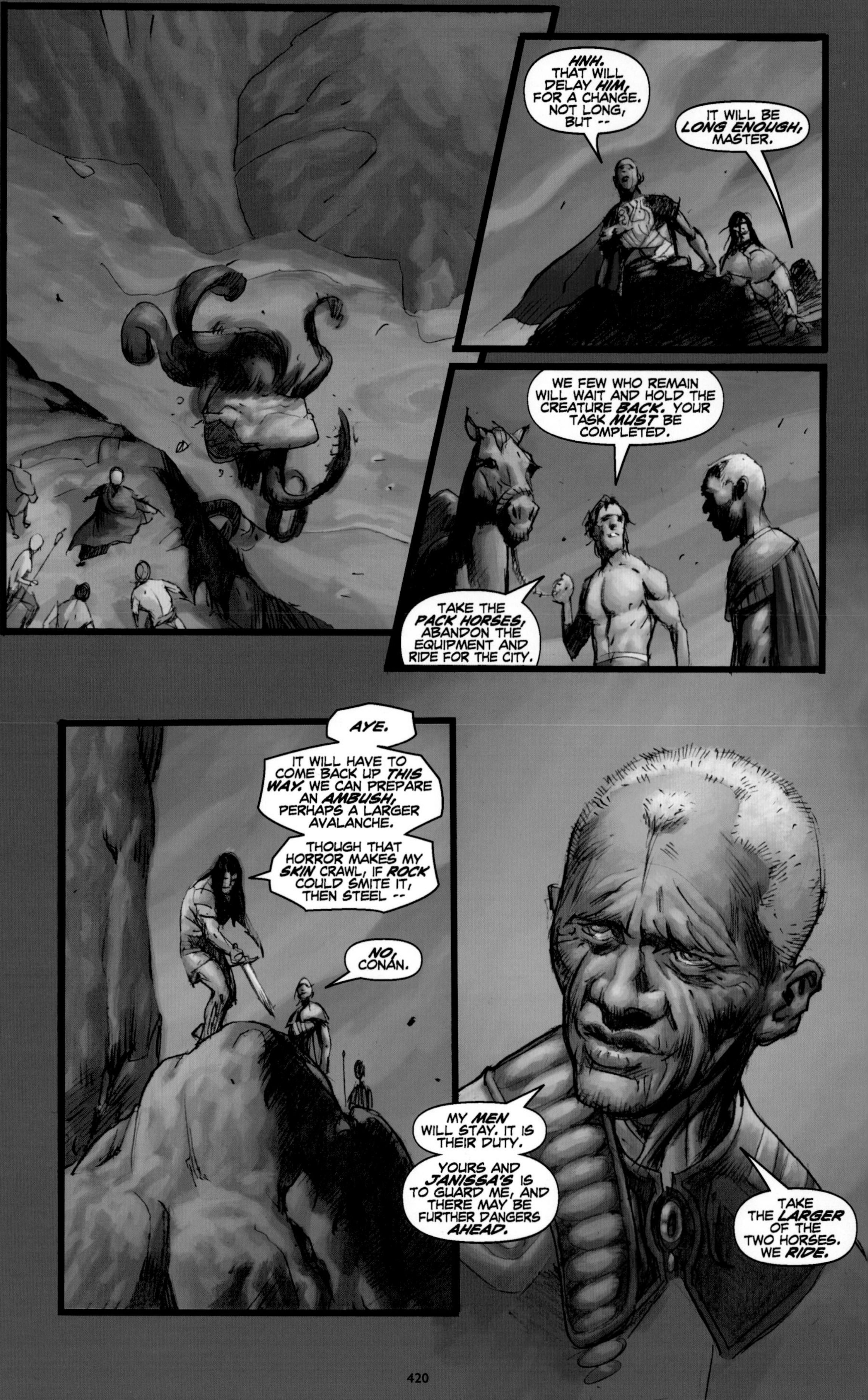
HNH. THAT WILL DELAY HIM, FOR A CHANGE. NOT LONG, BUT --
IT WILL BE LONG ENOUGH, MASTER.
WE FEW WHO REMAIN WILL WAIT AND HOLD THE CREATURE BACK. YOUR TASK MUST BE COMPLETED.
TAKE THE PACK HORSES, ABANDON THE EQUIPMENT AND RIDE FOR THE CITY.
AYE.
IT WILL HAVE TO COME BACK UP THIS WAY. WE CAN PREPARE AN AMBUSH, PERHAPS A LARGER AVALANCHE.
THOUGH THAT HORROR MAKES MY SKIN CRAWL, IF ROCK COULD SMITE IT, THEN STEEL --
NO, CONAN.
MY MEN WILL STAY. IT IS THEIR DUTY.
YOURS AND JANISSA'S IS TO GUARD ME, AND THERE MAY BE FURTHER DANGERS AHEAD.
TAKE THE LARGER OF THE TWO HORSES. WE RIDE.

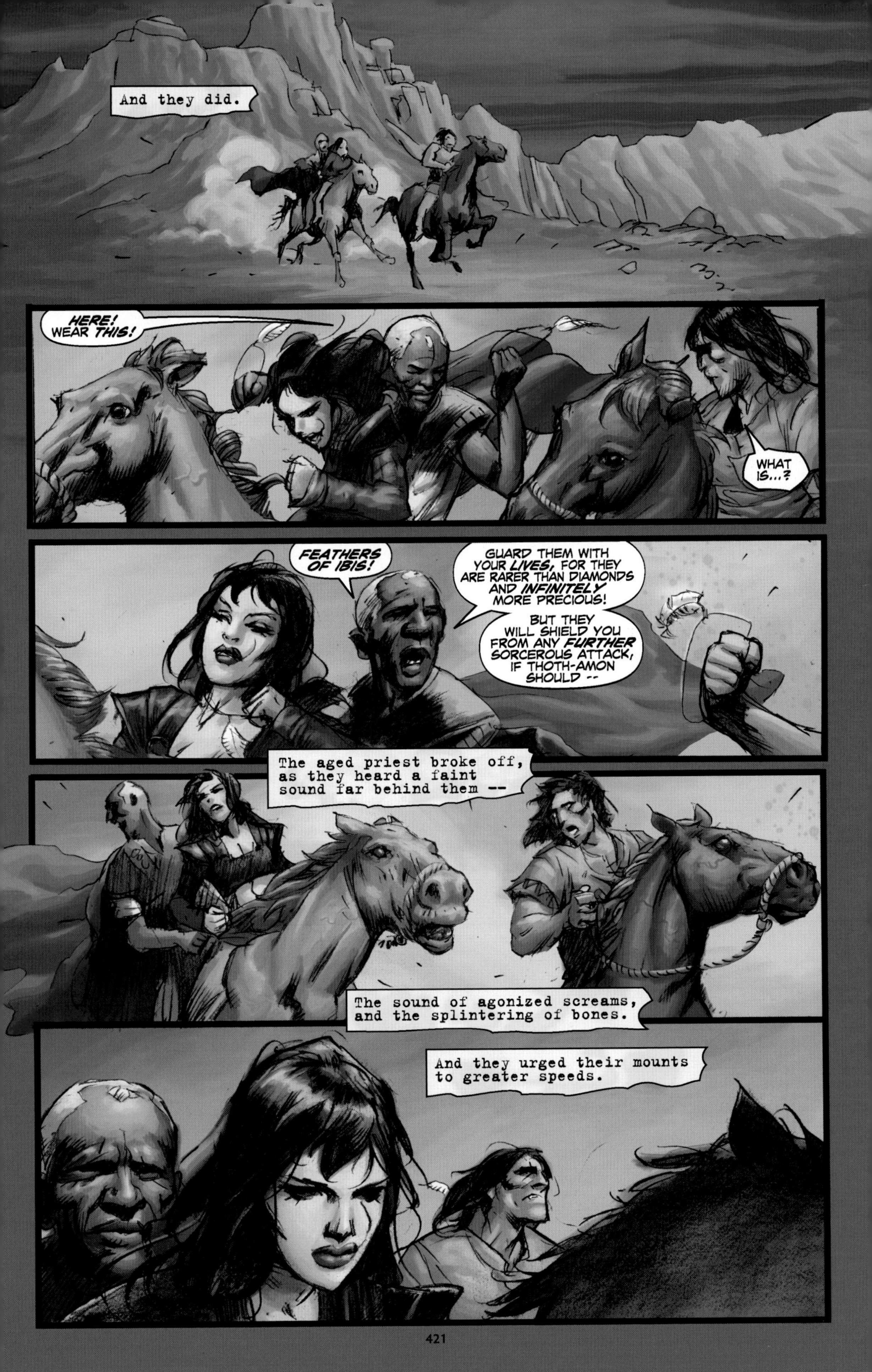

And they did.
HERE! WEAR THIS!
WHAT IS...?
FEATHERS OF IBIS!
GUARD THEM WITH YOUR LIVES, FOR THEY ARE RARER THAN DIAMONDS AND INFINITELY MORE PRECIOUS!
BUT THEY WILL SHIELD YOU FROM ANY FURTHER SORCEROUS ATTACK, IF THOTH-AMON SHOULD --
The aged priest broke off, as they heard a faint sound far behind them --
The sound of agonized screams, and the splintering of bones.
And they urged their mounts to greater speeds.

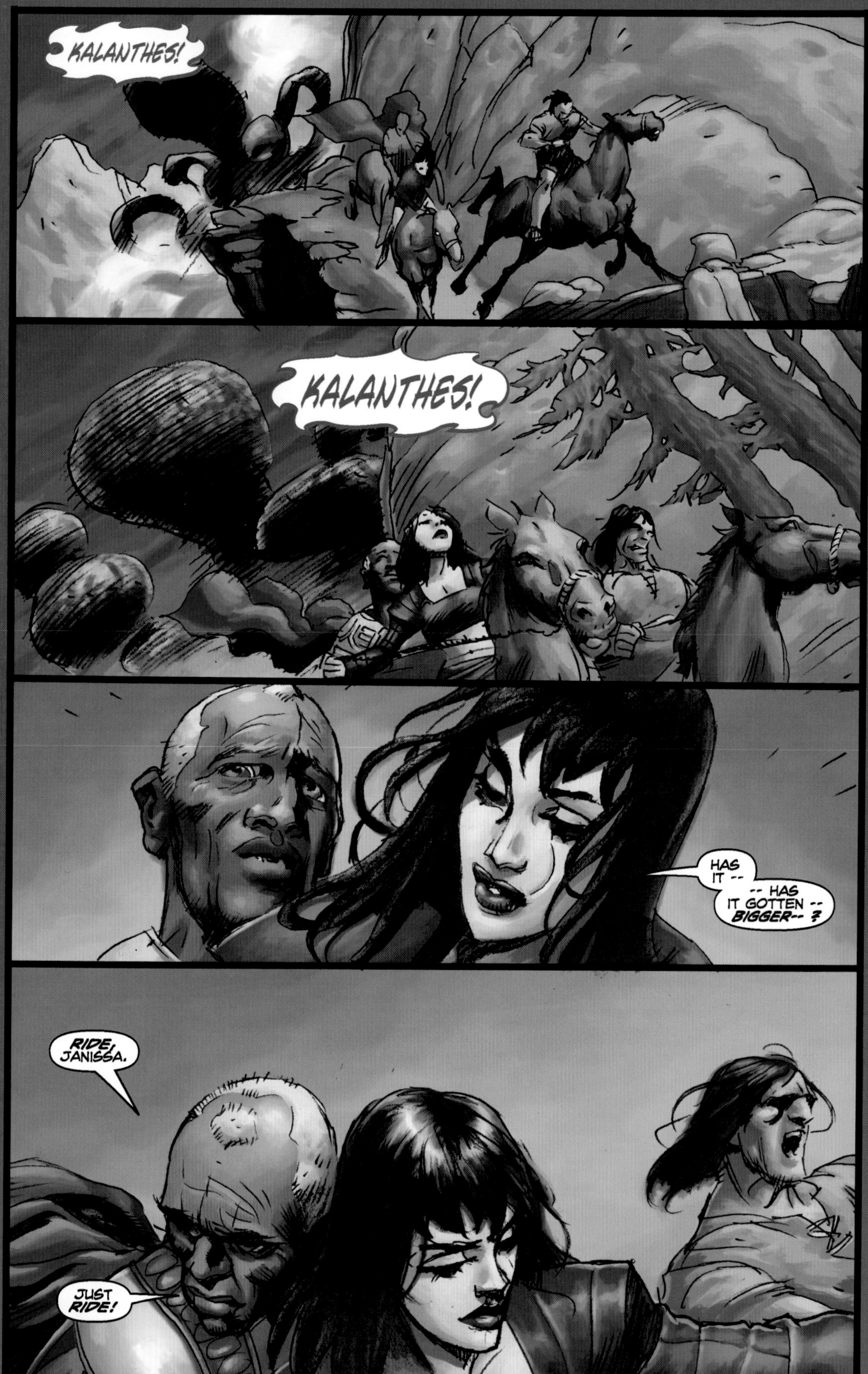
KALANTHES!
KALANTHES!
HAS IT --
-- HAS IT GOTTEN -- BIGGER-- ?
RIDE, JANISSA.
JUST RIDE!

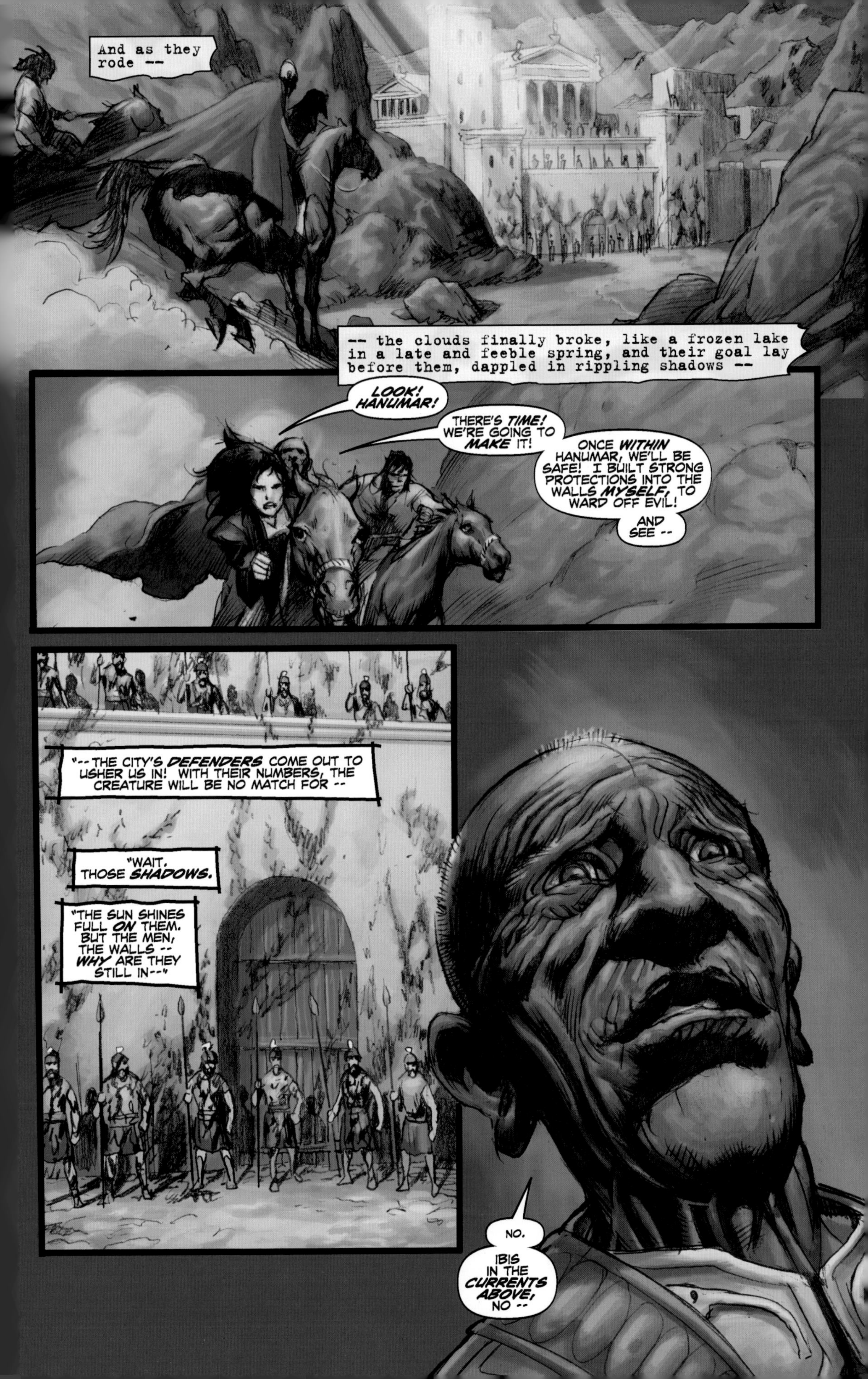

And as they rode --
-- the clouds finally broke, like a frozen lake in a late and feeble spring, and their goal lay before them, dappled in rippling shadows --
LOOK! HANUMAR!
THERE'S TIME! WE'RE GOING TO MAKE IT!
ONCE WITHIN HANUMAR, WE'LL BE SAFE! I BUILT STRONG PROTECTIONS INTO THE WALLS MYSELF, TO WARD OFF EVIL!
AND SEE --
"-- THE CITY'S DEFENDERS COME OUT TO USHER US IN! WITH THEIR NUMBERS, THE CREATURE WILL BE NO MATCH FOR --
"WAIT. THOSE SHADOWS.
"THE SUN SHINES FULL ON THEM. BUT THE MEN, THE WALLS -- WHY ARE THEY STILL IN--"
NO.
IBIS IN THE CURRENTS ABOVE, NO --

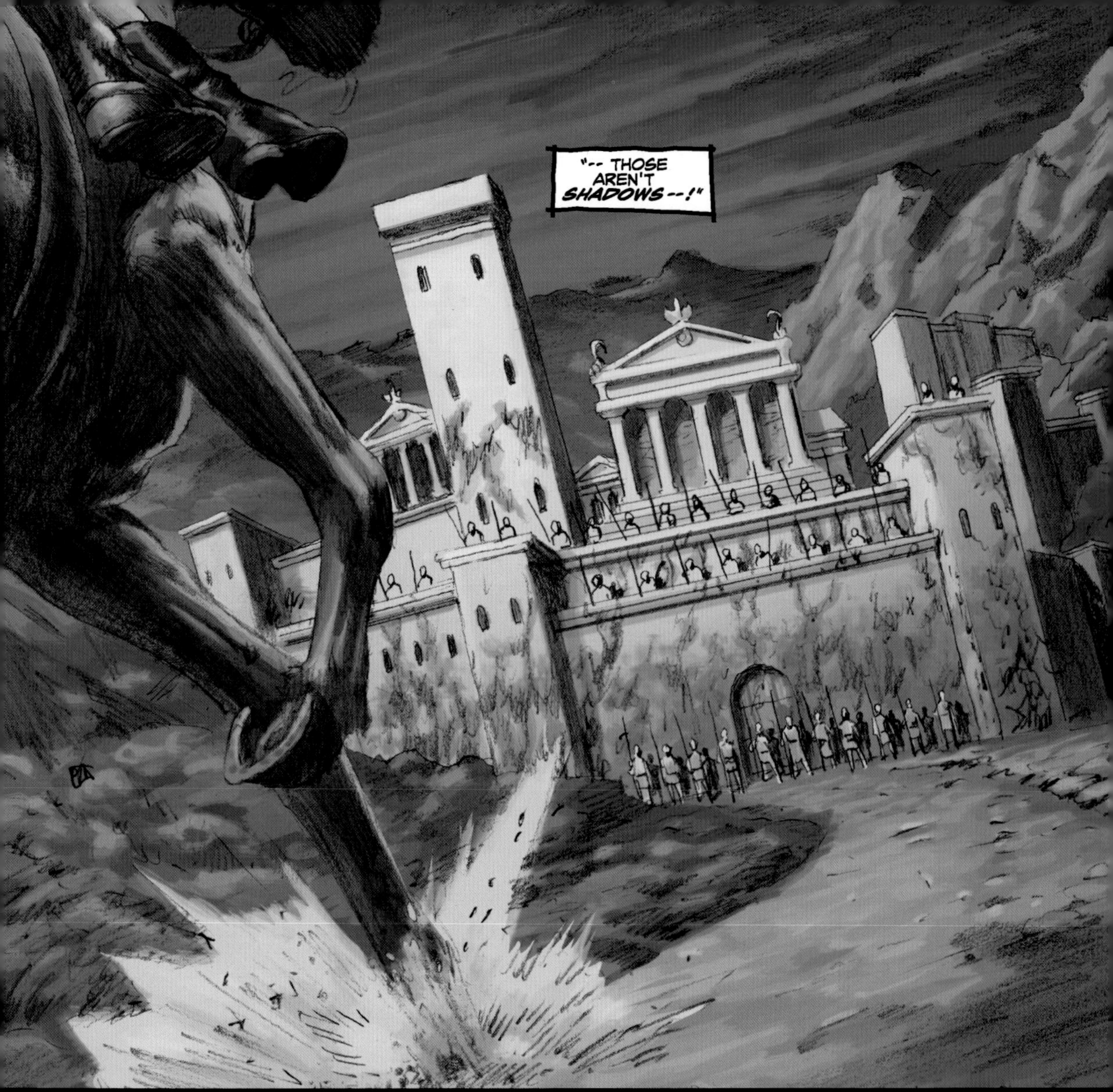
"-- THOSE AREN'T SHADOWS --!"
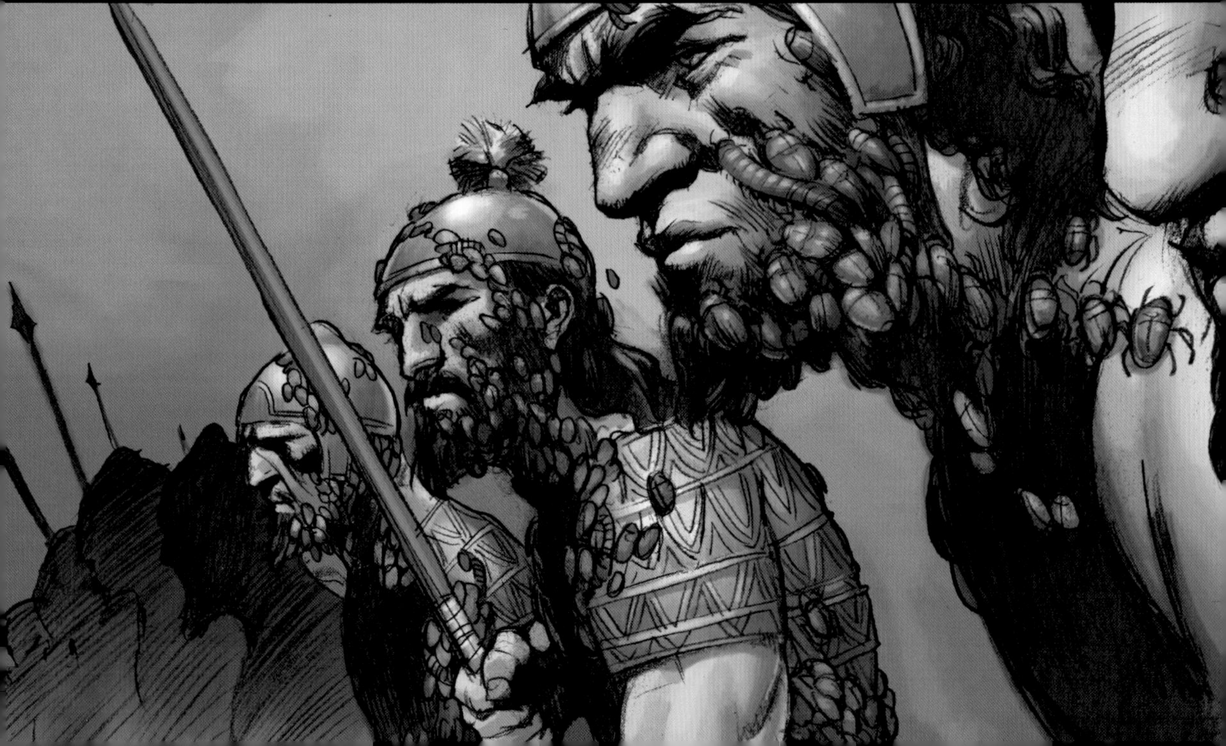

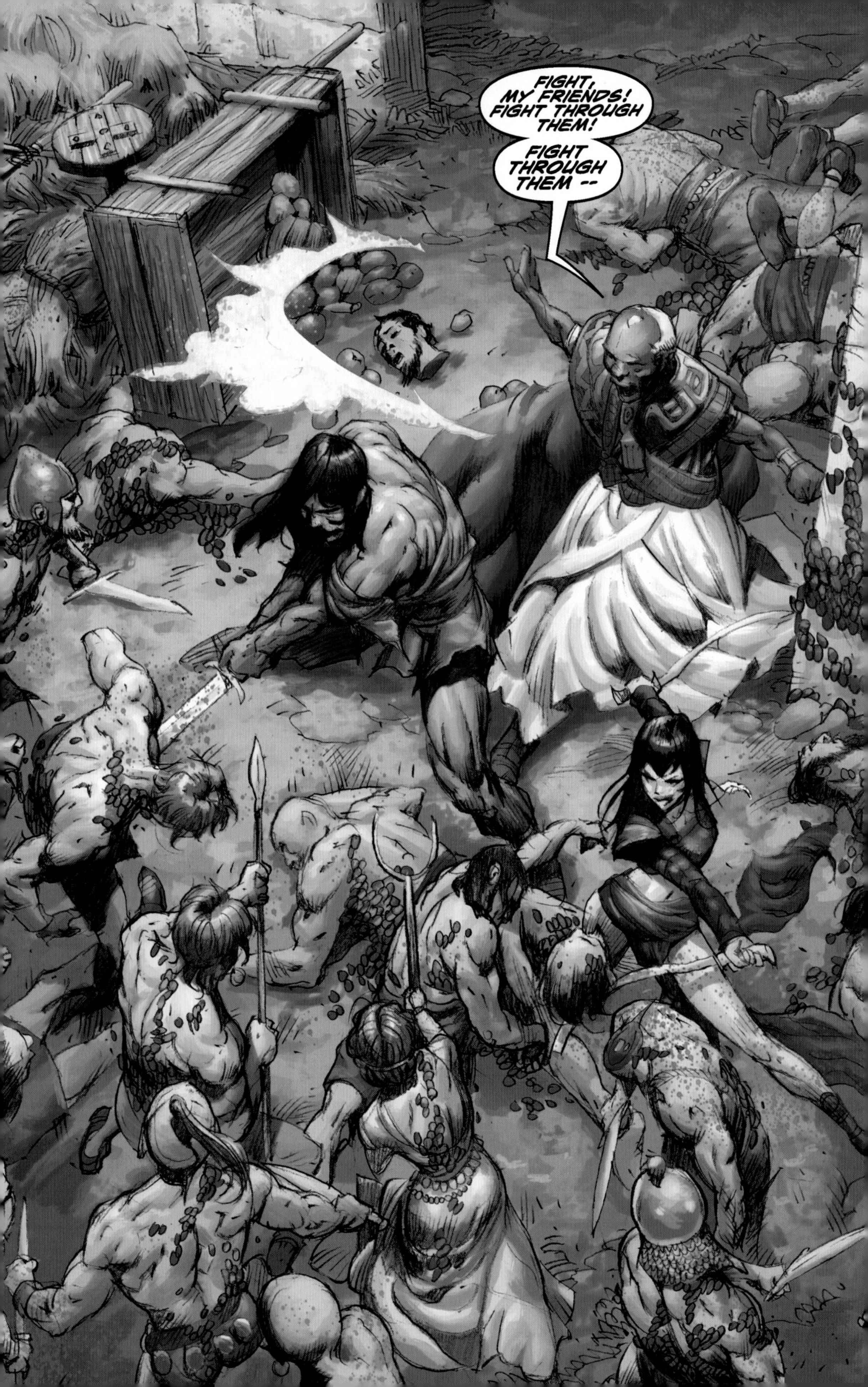
FIGHT, MY FRIENDS! FIGHT THROUGH THEM!
FIGHT THROUGH THEM --

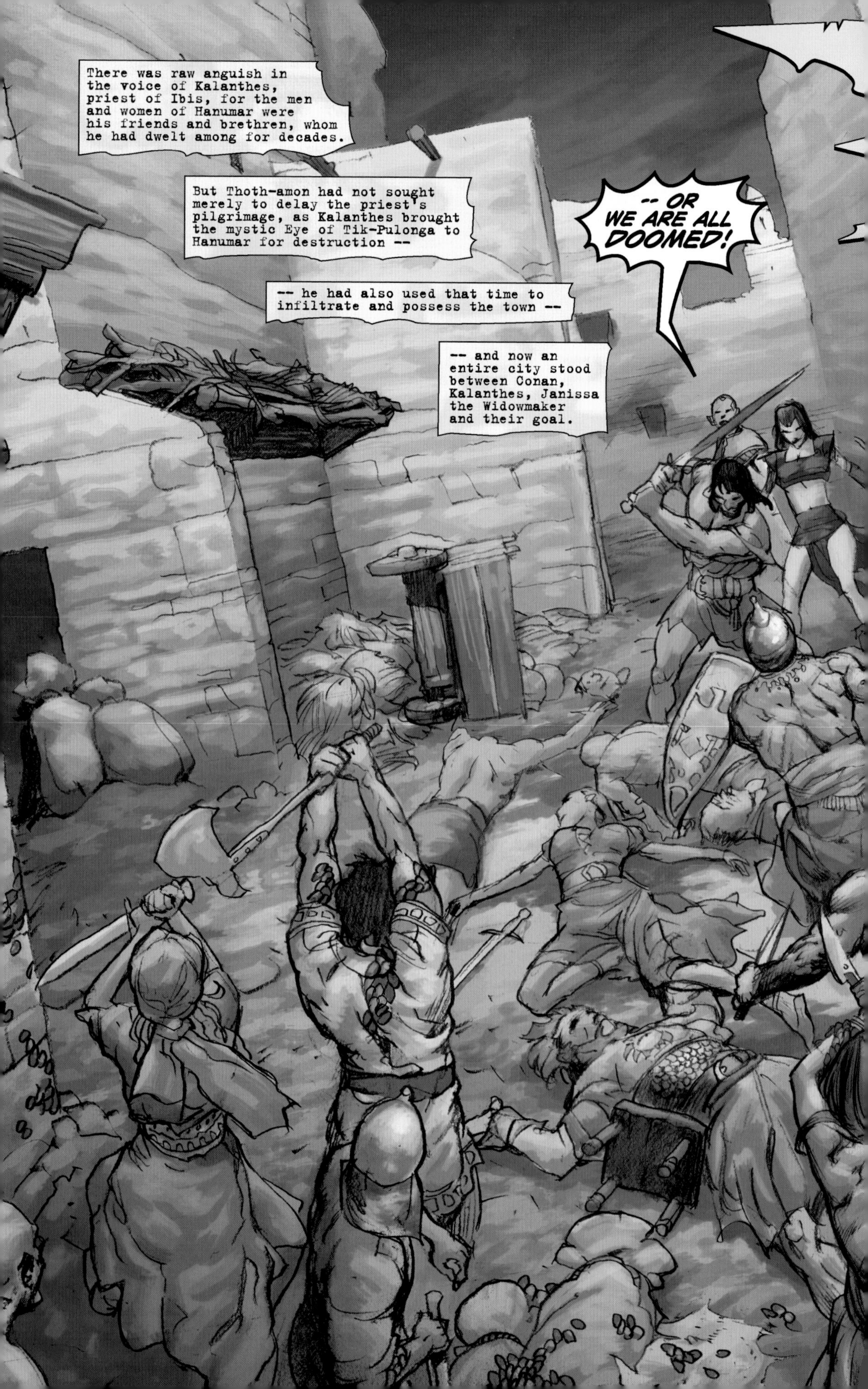
There was raw anguish in the voice of Kalanthes, priest of Ibis, for the men and women of Hanumar were his friends and brethren, whom he had dwelt among for decades.
But Thoth-amon had not sought merely to delay the priest's pilgrimage, as Kalanthes brought the mystic Eye of Tik-Pulonga to Hanumar for destruction --
-- he had also used that time to infiltrate and possess the town --
-- and now an entire city stood between Conan, Kalanthes, Janissa the Widowmaker and their goal.
-- OR WE ARE ALL DOOMED!

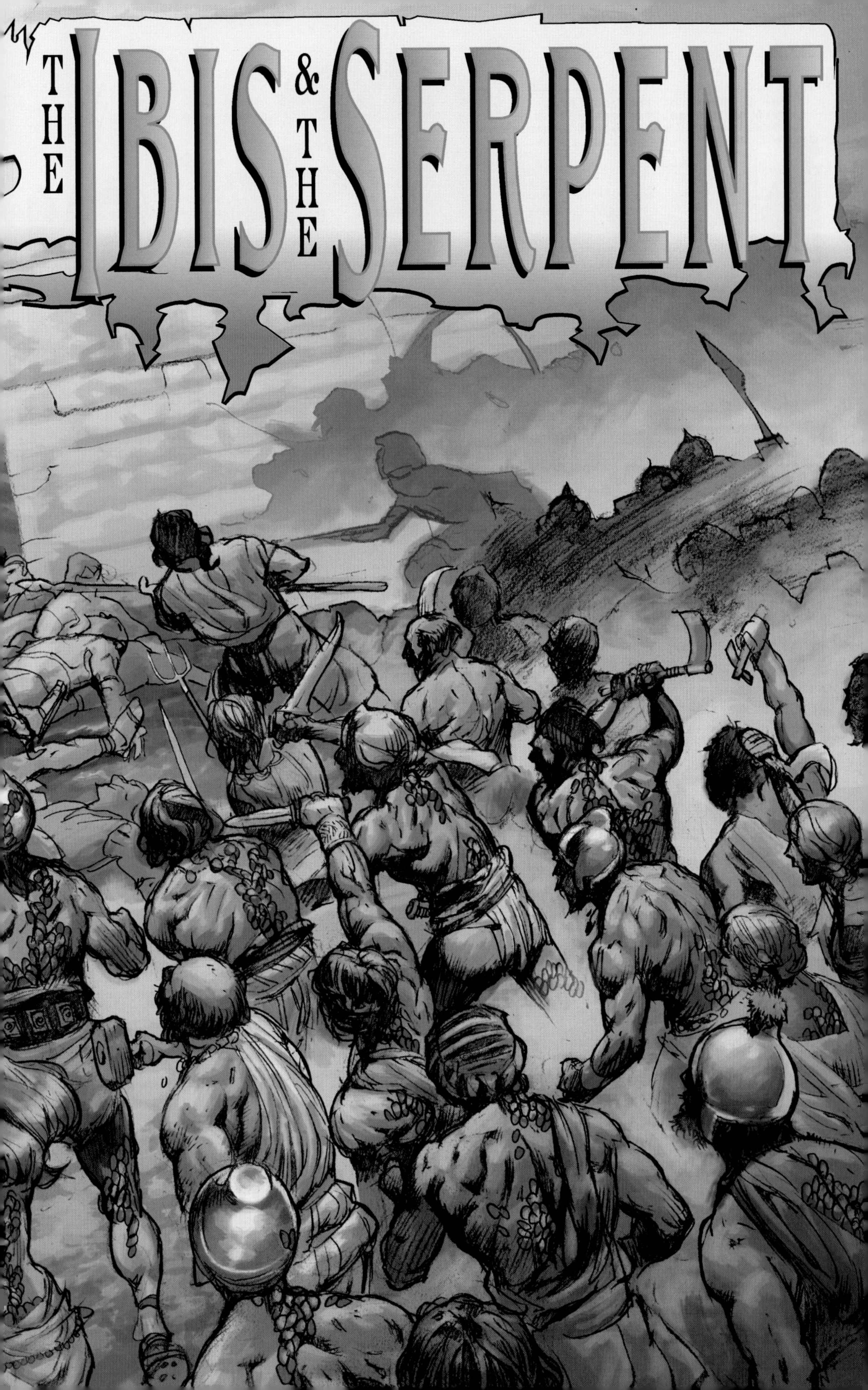
THE IBIS & THE SERPENT

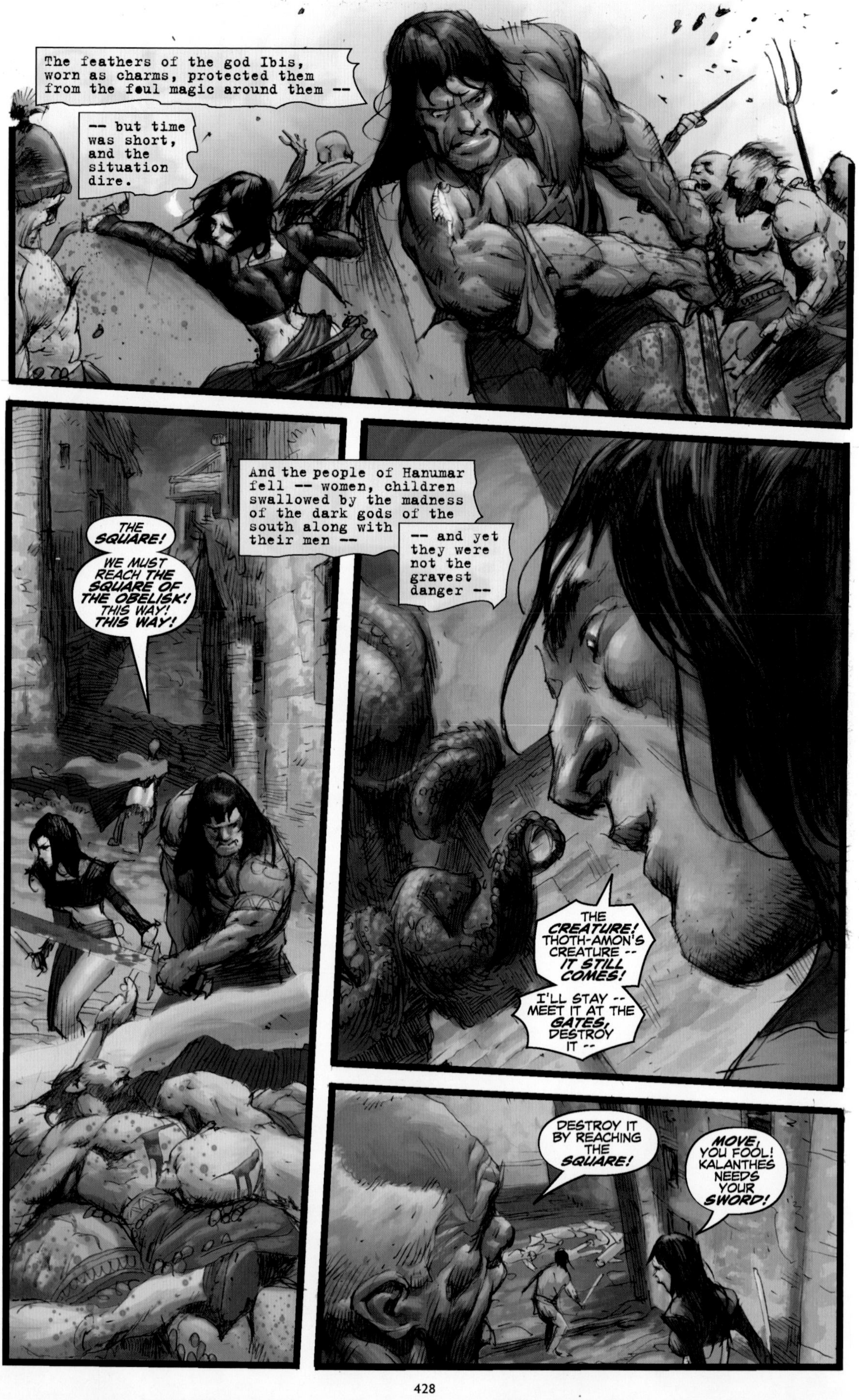
The feathers of the god Ibis, worn as charms, protected them from the foul magic around them --
-- but time was short, and the situation dire.
And the people of Hanumar fell -- women, children swallowed by the madness of the dark gods of the south along with their men --
THE SQUARE! WE MUST REACH THE SQUARE OF THE OBELISK! THIS WAY! THIS WAY!
-- and yet they were not the gravest danger --
THE CREATURE! THOTH-AMON'S CREATURE -- IT STILL COMES!
I'LL STAY -- MEET IT AT THE GATES, DESTROY IT --
DESTROY IT BY REACHING THE SQUARE!
MOVE, YOU FOOL! KALANTHES NEEDS YOUR SWORD!

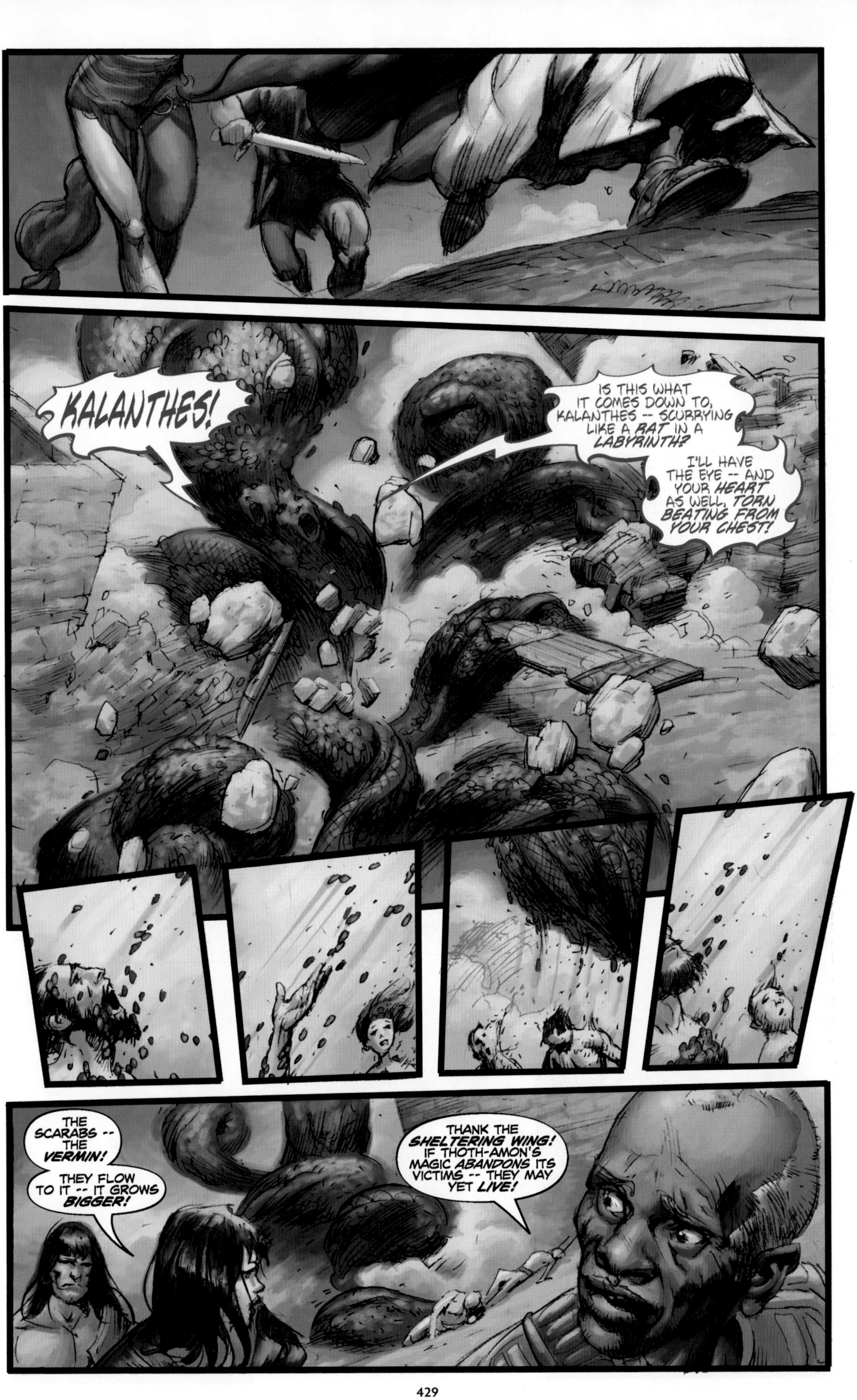
KALANTHES!
IS THIS WHAT IT COMES DOWN TO, KALANTHES -- SCURRYING LIKE A RAT IN A LABYRINTH?
I'LL HAVE THE EYE -- AND YOUR HEART AS WELL, TORN BEATING FROM YOUR CHEST!
THE SCARABS -- THE VERMIN!
THEY FLOW TO IT -- IT GROWS BIGGER!
THANK THE SHELTERING WING! IF THOTH-AMON'S MAGIC ABANDONS ITS VICTIMS -- THEY MAY YET LIVE!

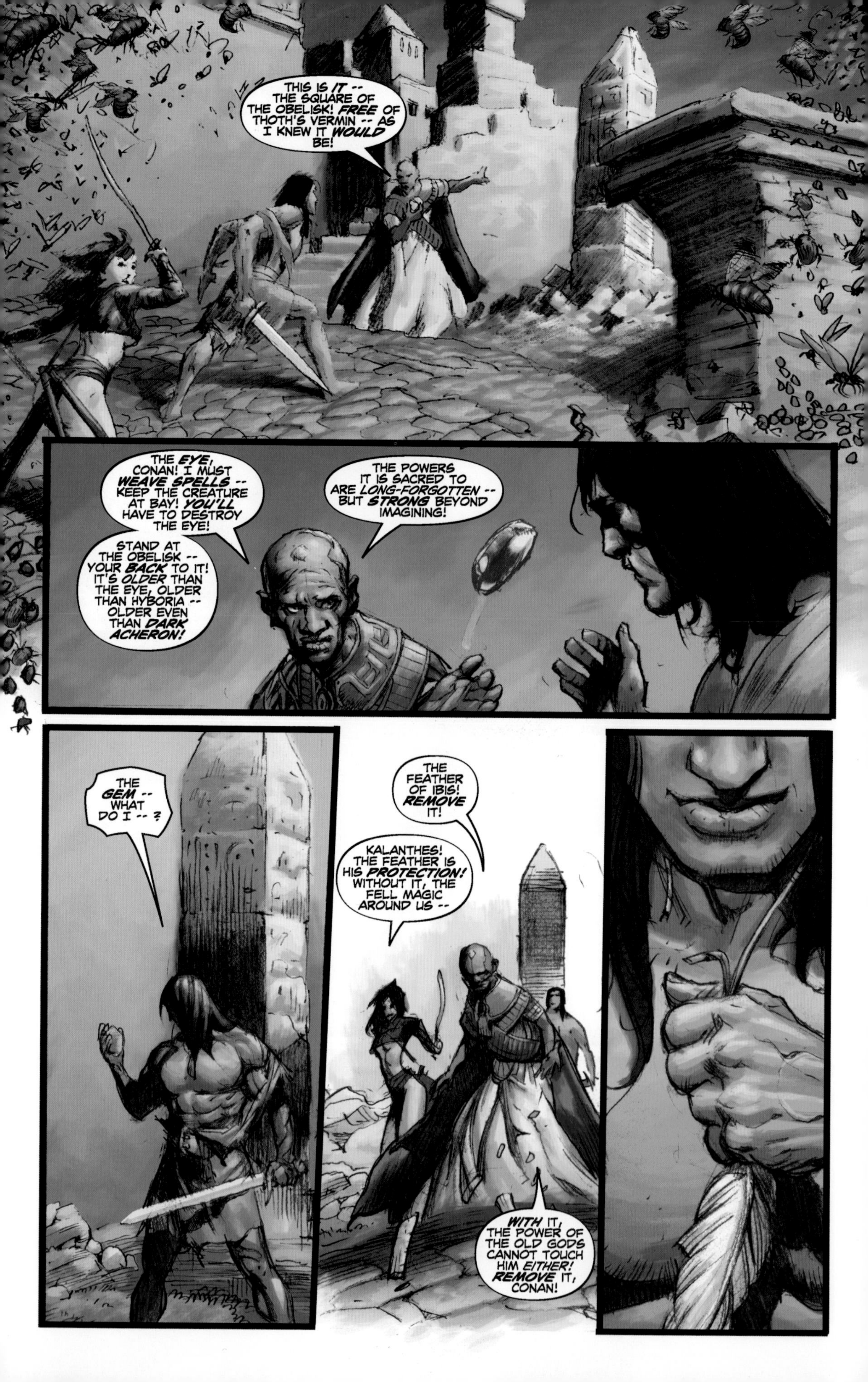
THIS IS *IT* -- THE SQUARE OF THE OBELISK! *FREE* OF THOTH'S VERMIN -- AS I KNEW IT *WOULD* BE!
THE *EYE*, CONAN! I MUST *WEAVE SPELLS* -- KEEP THE CREATURE AT BAY! *YOU'LL* HAVE TO DESTROY THE EYE!
STAND AT THE OBELISK -- YOUR *BACK* TO IT! IT'S *OLDER* THAN THE EYE, OLDER THAN HYBORIA -- OLDER EVEN THAN *DARK ACHERON!*
THE POWERS IT IS SACRED TO ARE *LONG-FORGOTTEN* -- BUT *STRONG* BEYOND IMAGINING!
THE *GEM* -- WHAT DO I -- ?
THE FEATHER OF IBIS! *REMOVE* IT!
KALANTHES! THE FEATHER IS HIS *PROTECTION!* WITHOUT IT, THE FELL MAGIC AROUND US --
WITH IT, THE POWER OF THE OLD GODS CANNOT TOUCH HIM *EITHER!* *REMOVE* IT, CONAN!

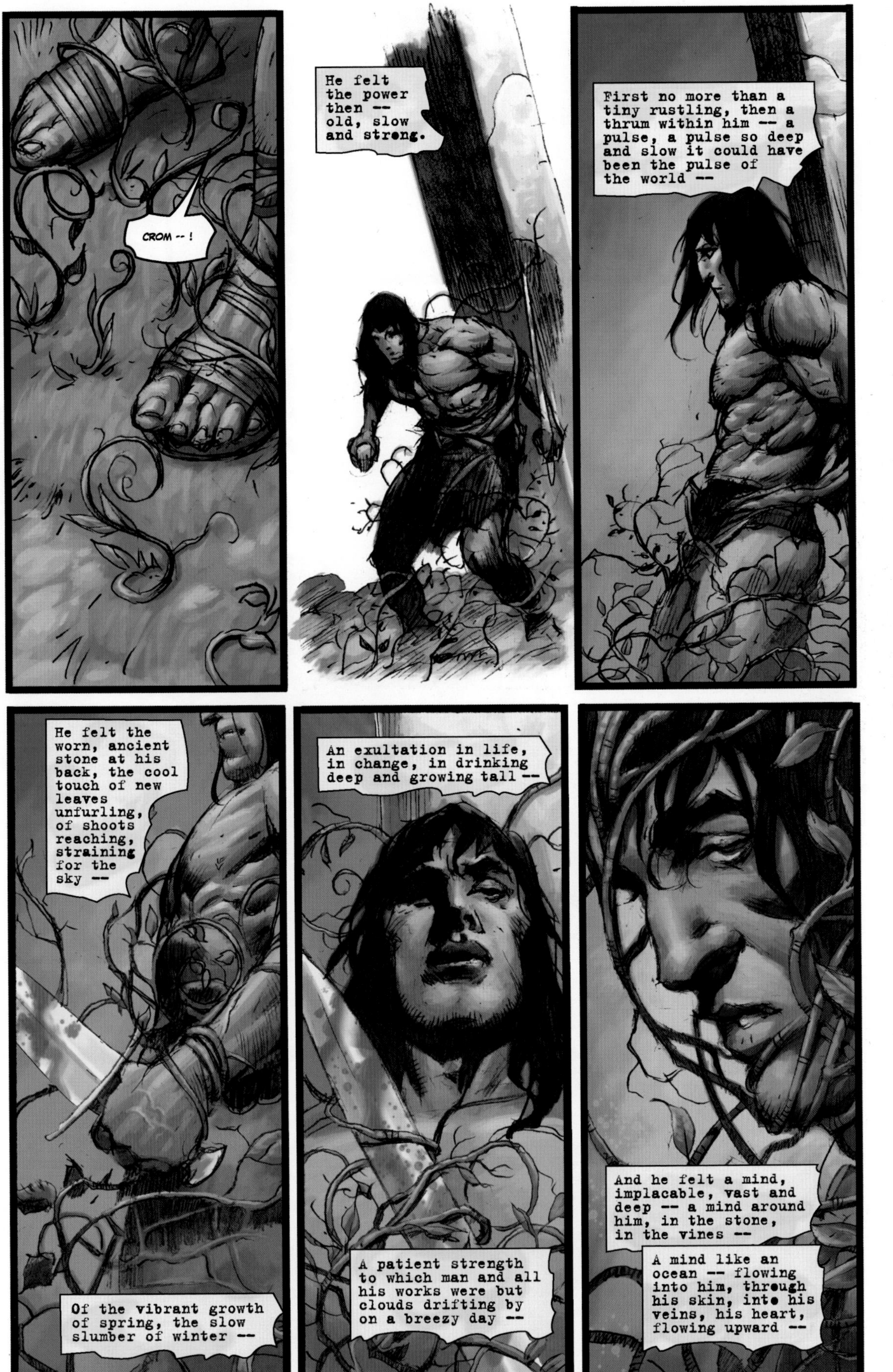
CROM -- !
He felt the power then -- old, slow and strong.
First no more than a tiny rustling, then a thrum within him -- a pulse, a pulse so deep and slow it could have been the pulse of the world --
He felt the worn, ancient stone at his back, the cool touch of new leaves unfurling, of shoots reaching, straining for the sky --
Of the vibrant growth of spring, the slow slumber of winter --
An exultation in life, in change, in drinking deep and growing tall --
A patient strength to which man and all his works were but clouds drifting by on a breezy day --
And he felt a mind, implacable, vast and deep -- a mind around him, in the stone, in the vines --
A mind like an ocean -- flowing into him, through his skin, into his veins, his heart, flowing upward --

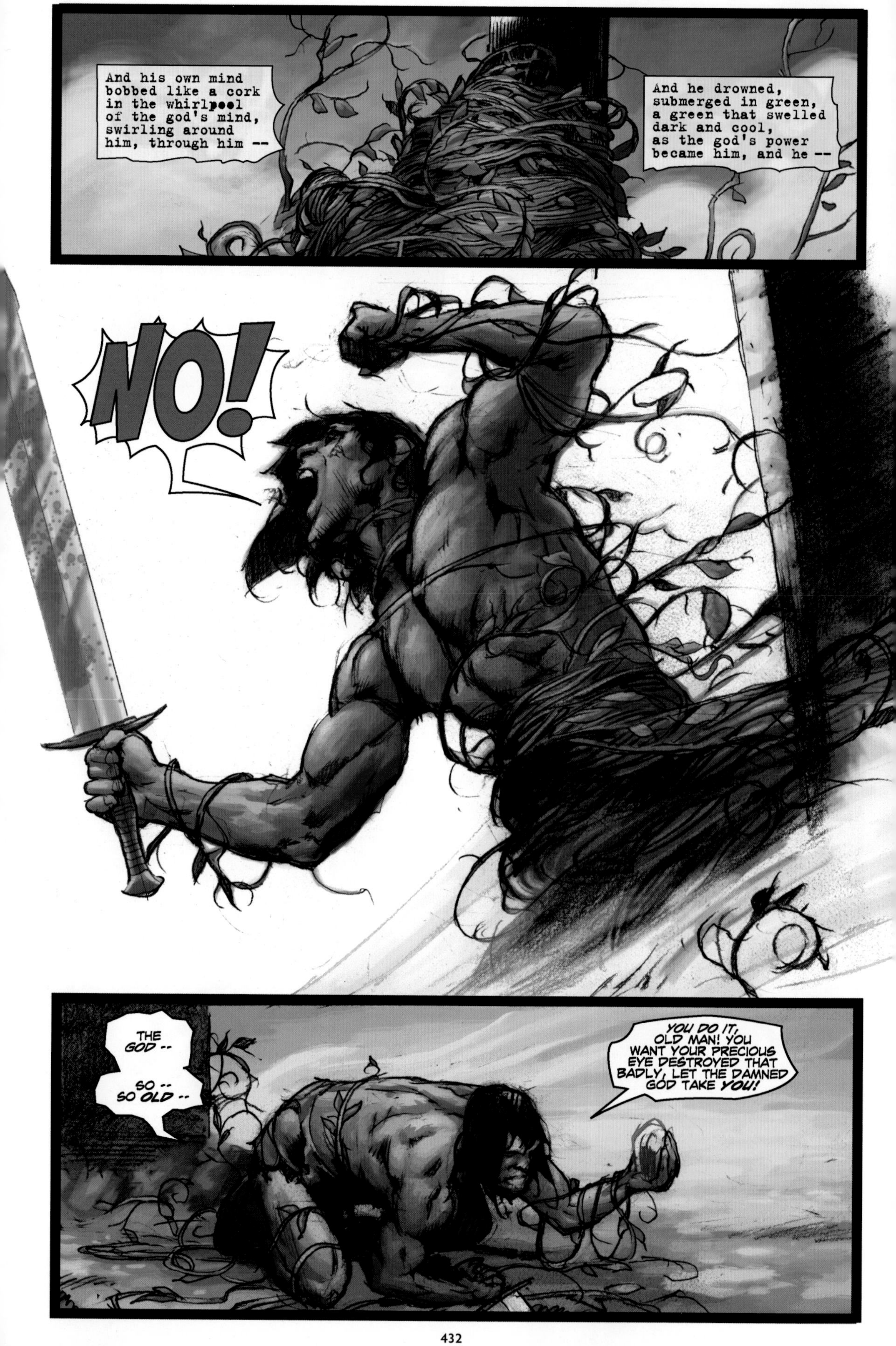

And his own mind bobbed like a cork in the whirlpool of the god's mind, swirling around him, through him --
And he drowned, submerged in green, a green that swelled dark and cool, as the god's power became him, and he --
NO!
THE GOD --
SO -- SO OLD --
YOU DO IT, OLD MAN! YOU WANT YOUR PRECIOUS EYE DESTROYED THAT BADLY, LET THE DAMNED GOD TAKE YOU!

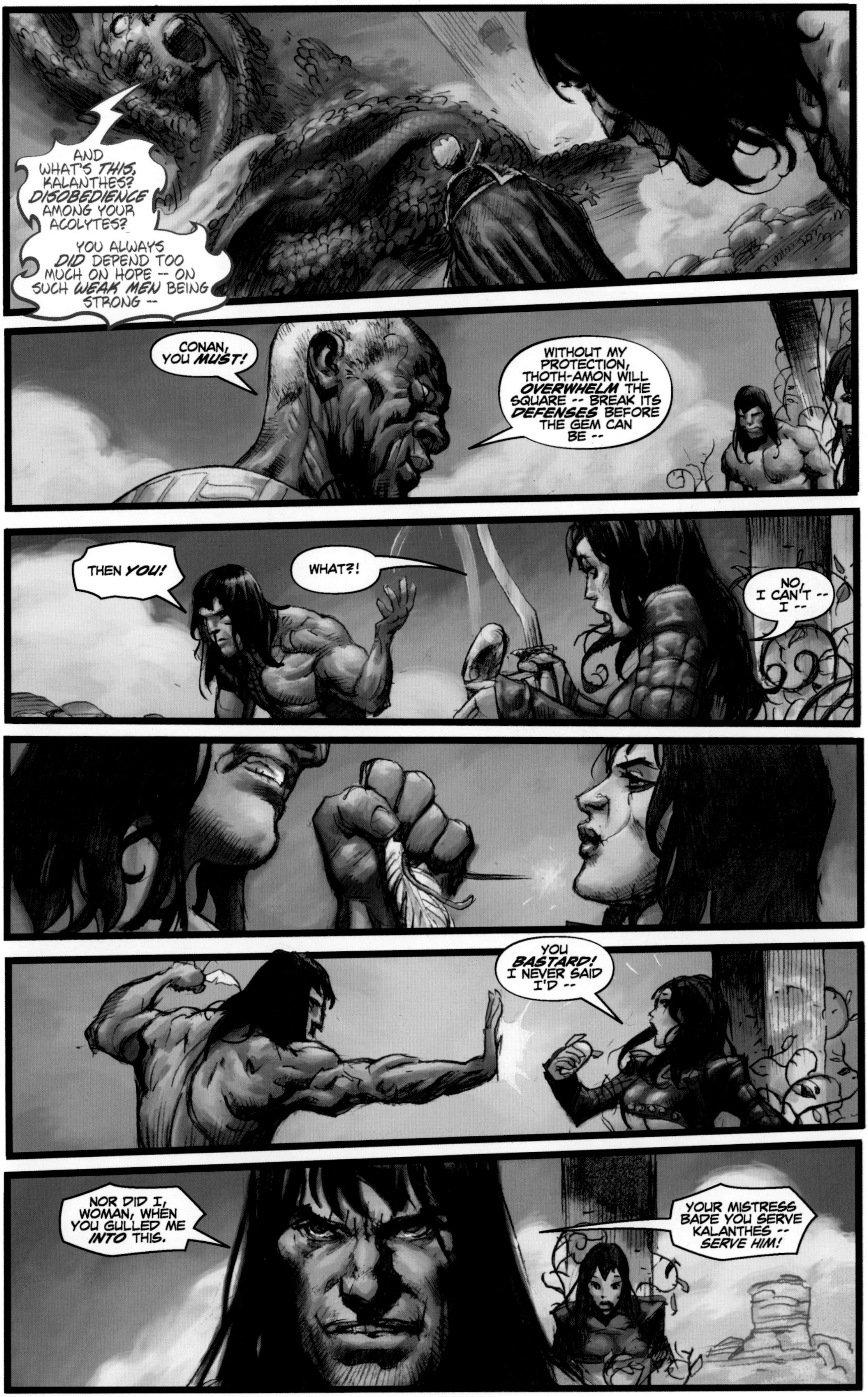
AND WHAT'S *THIS,* KALANTHES? *DISOBEDIENCE* AMONG YOUR ACOLYTES?
YOU ALWAYS *DID* DEPEND TOO MUCH ON HOPE -- ON SUCH *WEAK MEN* BEING STRONG --
CONAN, YOU *MUST!*
WITHOUT MY PROTECTION, THOTH-AMON WILL *OVERWHELM* THE SQUARE -- BREAK ITS *DEFENSES* BEFORE THE GEM CAN BE --
THEN *YOU!*
WHAT?!
NO, I CAN'T -- I --
YOU *BASTARD!* I NEVER SAID I'D --
NOR DID I, WOMAN, WHEN YOU GULLED ME *INTO* THIS.
YOUR MISTRESS BADE YOU SERVE KALANTHES -- *SERVE HIM!*

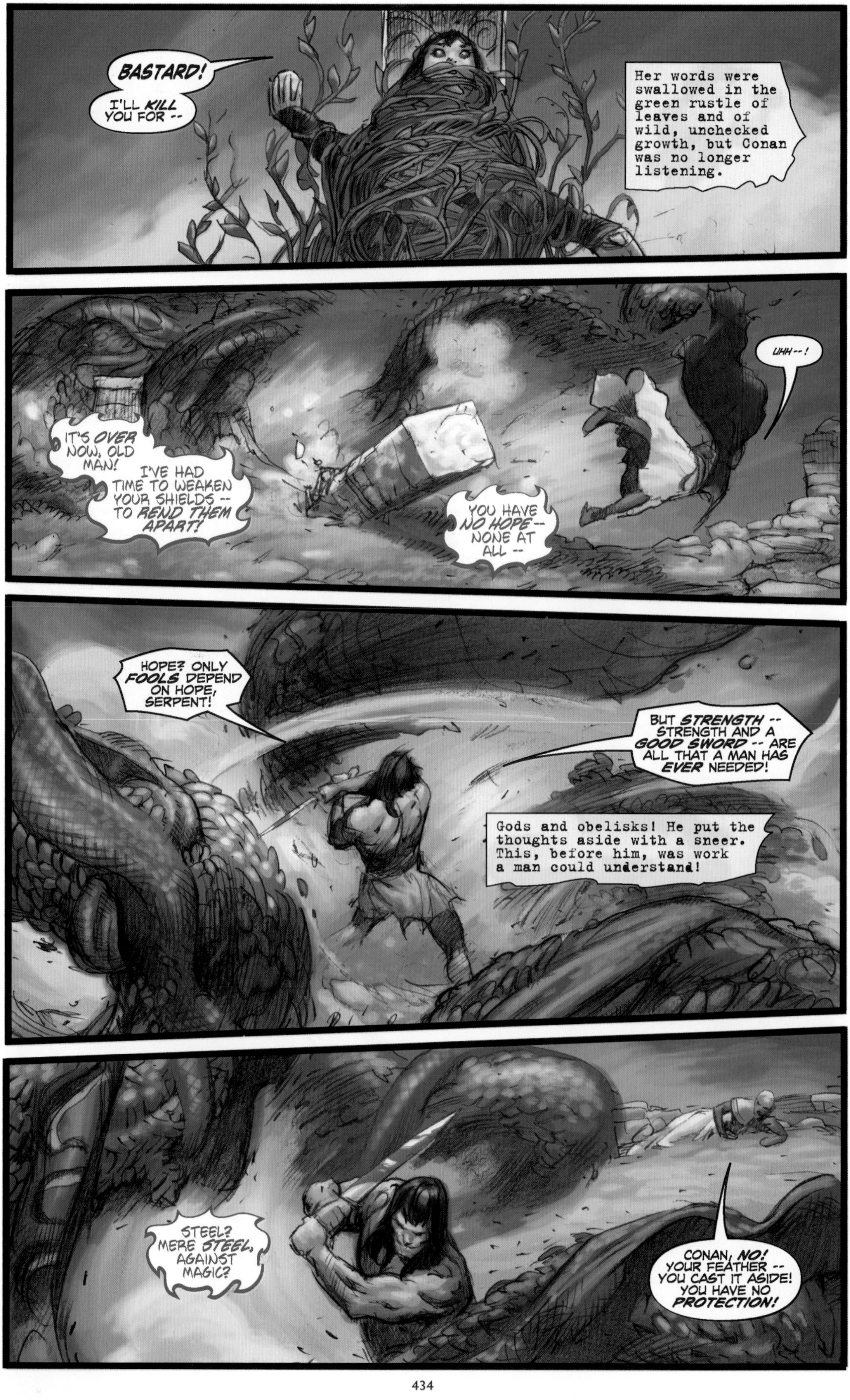
BASTARD!
I'LL KILL YOU FOR --
Her words were swallowed in the green rustle of leaves and of wild, unchecked growth, but Conan was no longer listening.
UHH -- !
IT'S OVER NOW, OLD MAN!
I'VE HAD TIME TO WEAKEN YOUR SHIELDS -- TO REND THEM APART!
YOU HAVE NO HOPE -- NONE AT ALL --
HOPE? ONLY FOOLS DEPEND ON HOPE, SERPENT!
BUT STRENGTH -- STRENGTH AND A GOOD SWORD -- ARE ALL THAT A MAN HAS EVER NEEDED!
Gods and obelisks! He put the thoughts aside with a sneer. This, before him, was work a man could understand!
STEEL? MERE STEEL, AGAINST MAGIC?
CONAN, NO! YOUR FEATHER -- YOU CAST IT ASIDE! YOU HAVE NO PROTECTION!

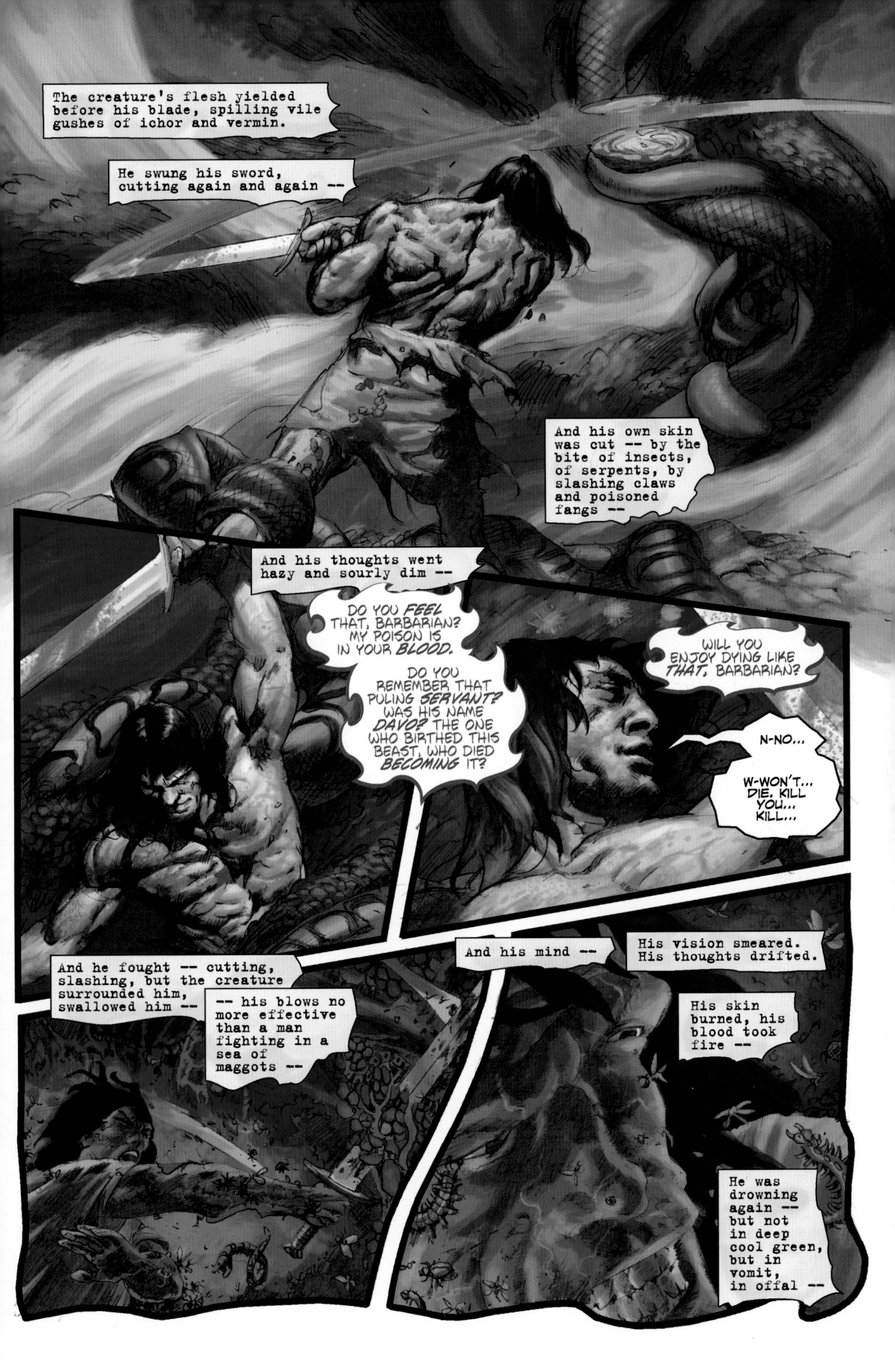

The creature's flesh yielded before his blade, spilling vile gushes of ichor and vermin.
He swung his sword, cutting again and again --
And his own skin was cut -- by the bite of insects, of serpents, by slashing claws and poisoned fangs --
And his thoughts went hazy and sourly dim --
DO YOU FEEL THAT, BARBARIAN? MY POISON IS IN YOUR BLOOD.
DO YOU REMEMBER THAT PULING SERVANT? WAS HIS NAME DAVO? THE ONE WHO BIRTHED THIS BEAST, WHO DIED BECOMING IT?
WILL YOU ENJOY DYING LIKE THAT, BARBARIAN?
N-NO...
W-WON'T... DIE. KILL YOU... KILL...
And he fought -- cutting, slashing, but the creature surrounded him, swallowed him --
-- his blows no more effective than a man fighting in a sea of maggots --
And his mind --
His vision smeared. His thoughts drifted.
His skin burned, his blood took fire --
He was drowning again -- but not in deep cool green, but in vomit, in offal --

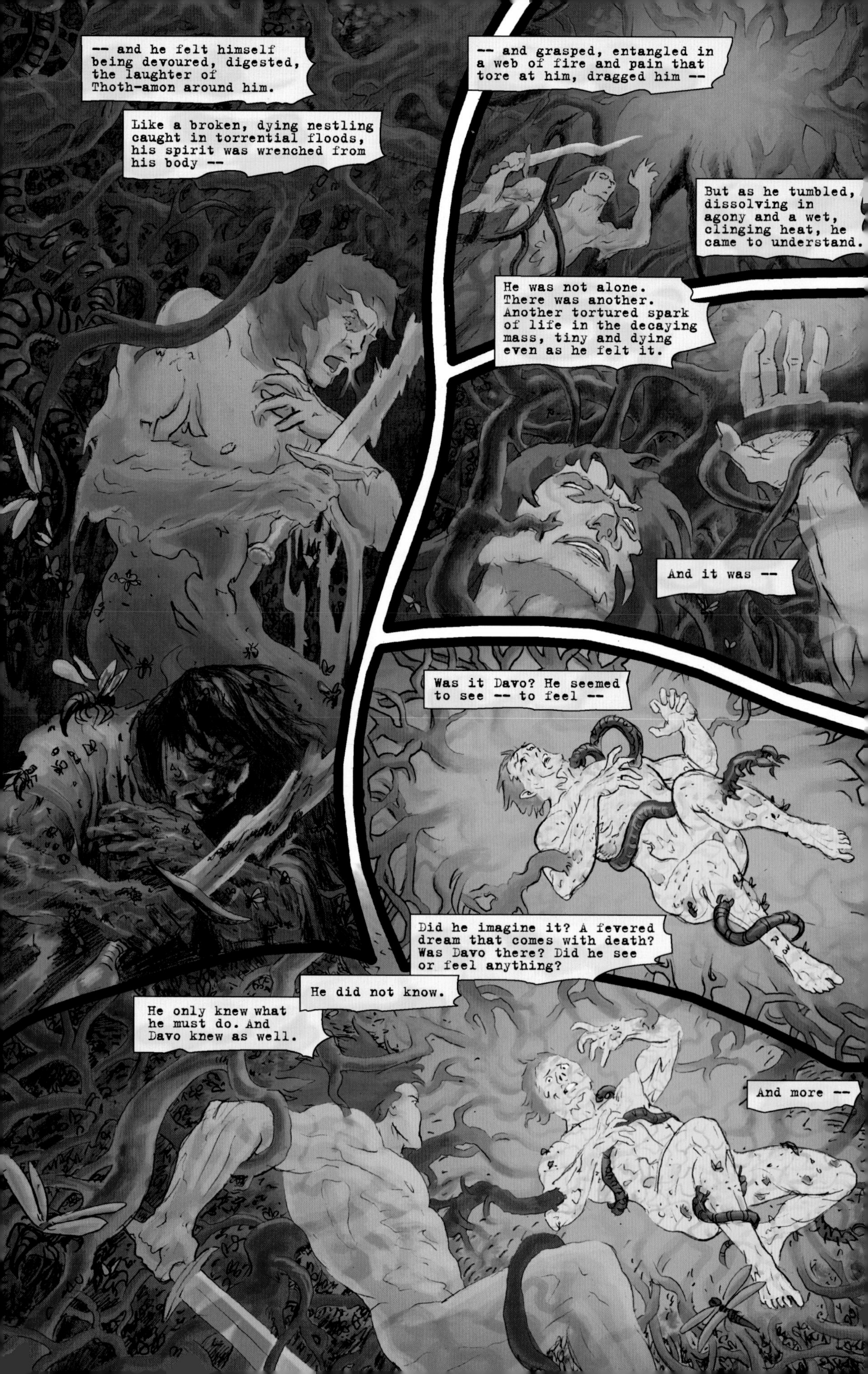
-- and he felt himself being devoured, digested, the laughter of Thoth-amon around him.
Like a broken, dying nestling caught in torrential floods, his spirit was wrenched from his body --
-- and grasped, entangled in a web of fire and pain that tore at him, dragged him --
But as he tumbled, dissolving in agony and a wet, clinging heat, he came to understand.
He was not alone. There was another. Another tortured spark of life in the decaying mass, tiny and dying even as he felt it.
And it was --
Was it Davo? He seemed to see -- to feel --
Did he imagine it? A fevered dream that comes with death? Was Davo there? Did he see or feel anything?
He did not know.
He only knew what he must do. And Davo knew as well.
And more --

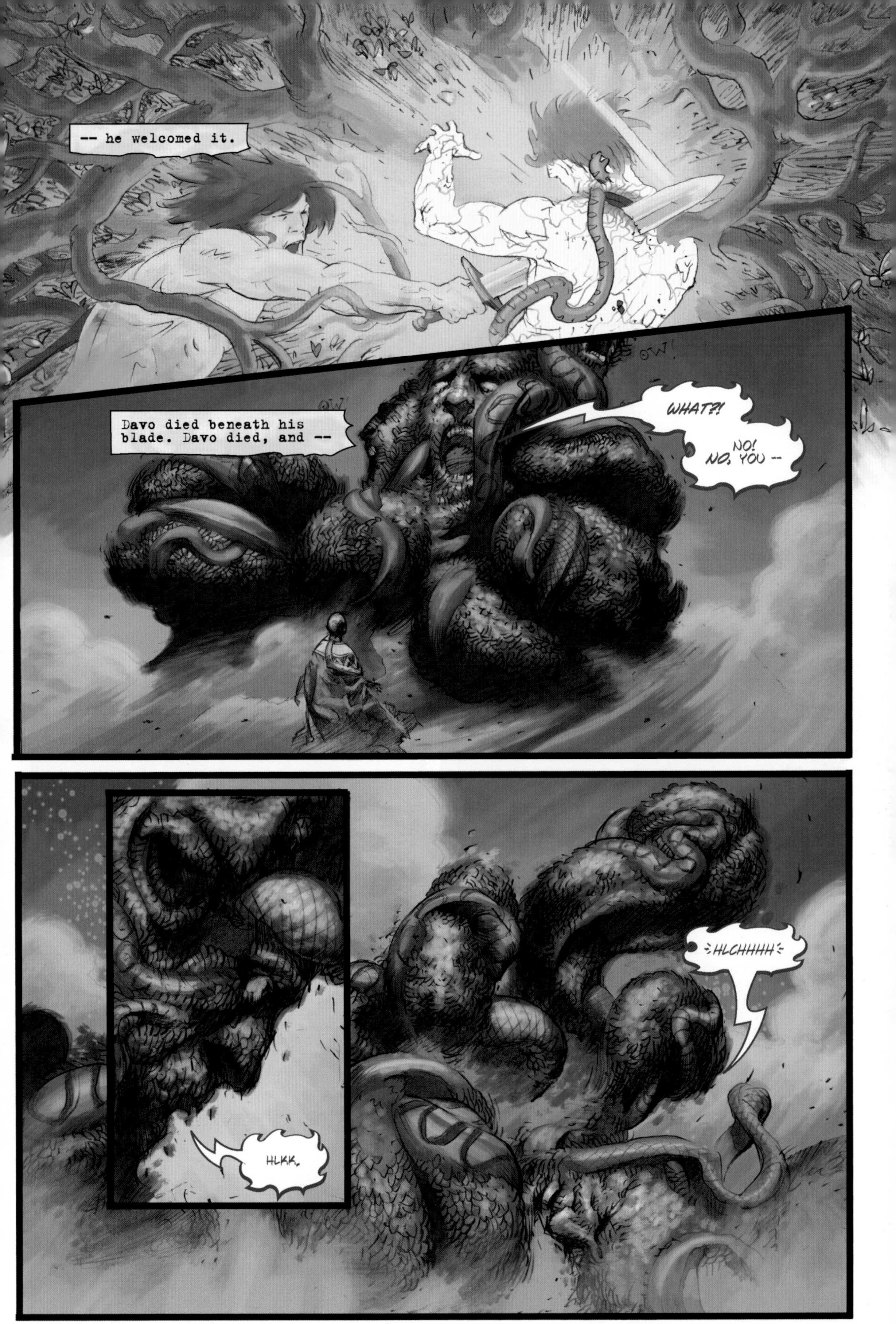
-- he welcomed it.
OW!
OW!
Davo died beneath his blade. Davo died, and --
WHAT?!
NO! NO, YOU --
HLKK.
HLCHHHH

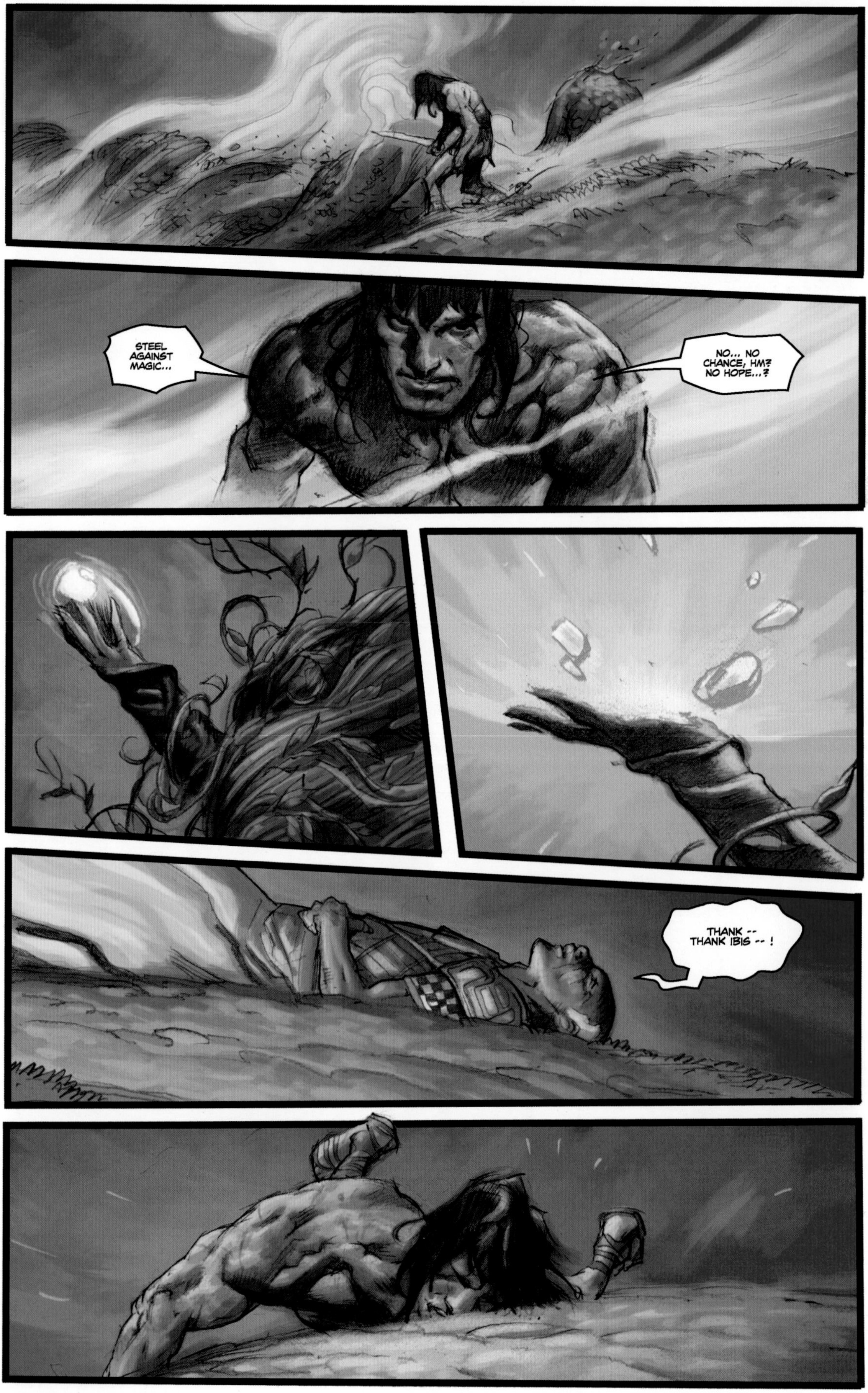
STEEL AGAINST MAGIC...
NO... NO CHANCE, HM? NO HOPE...?
THANK -- THANK IBIS -- !

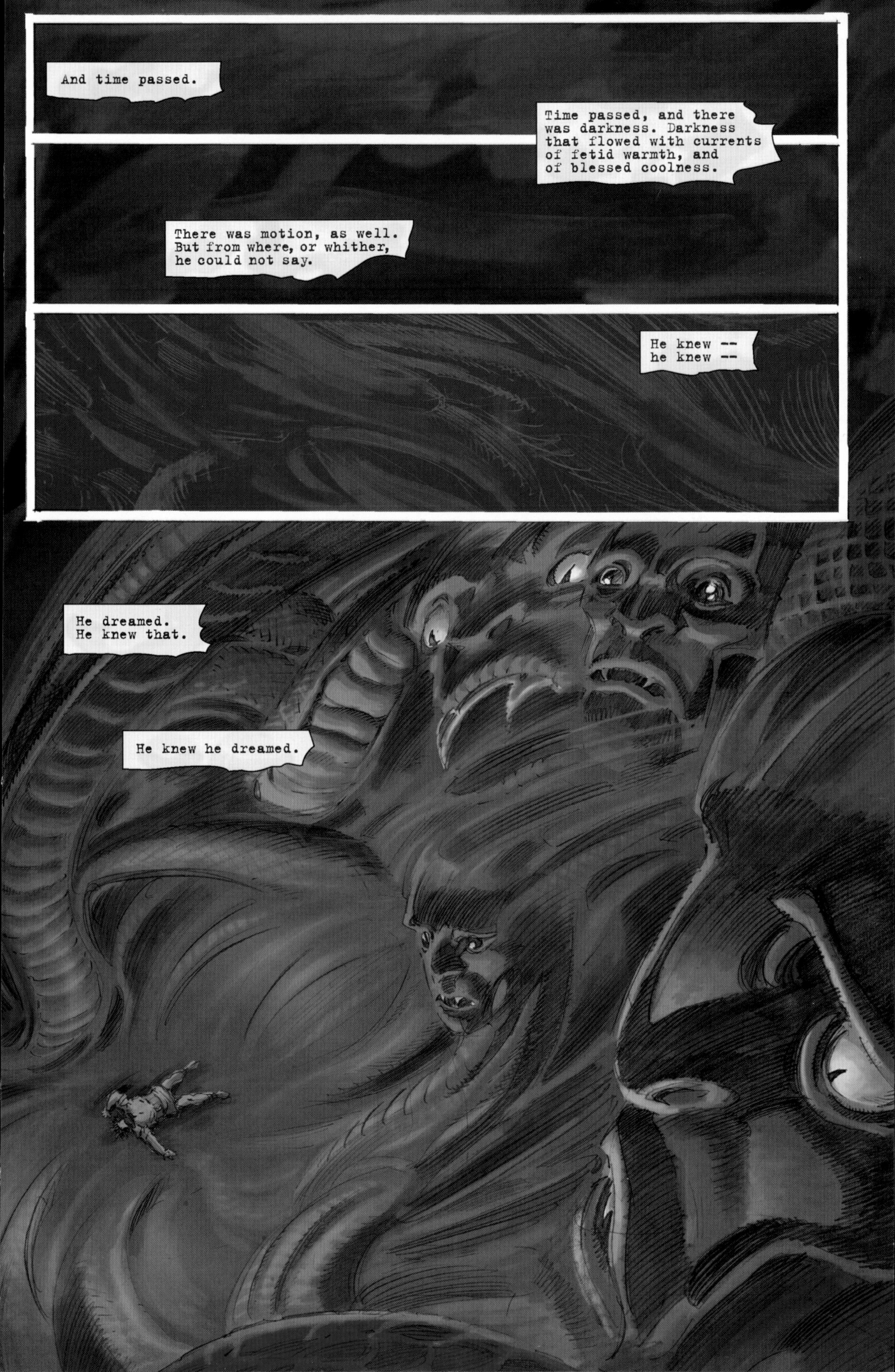
And time passed.
Time passed, and there was darkness. Darkness that flowed with currents of fetid warmth, and of blessed coolness.
There was motion, as well. But from where, or whither, he could not say.
He knew -- he knew --
He dreamed. He knew that.
He knew he dreamed.

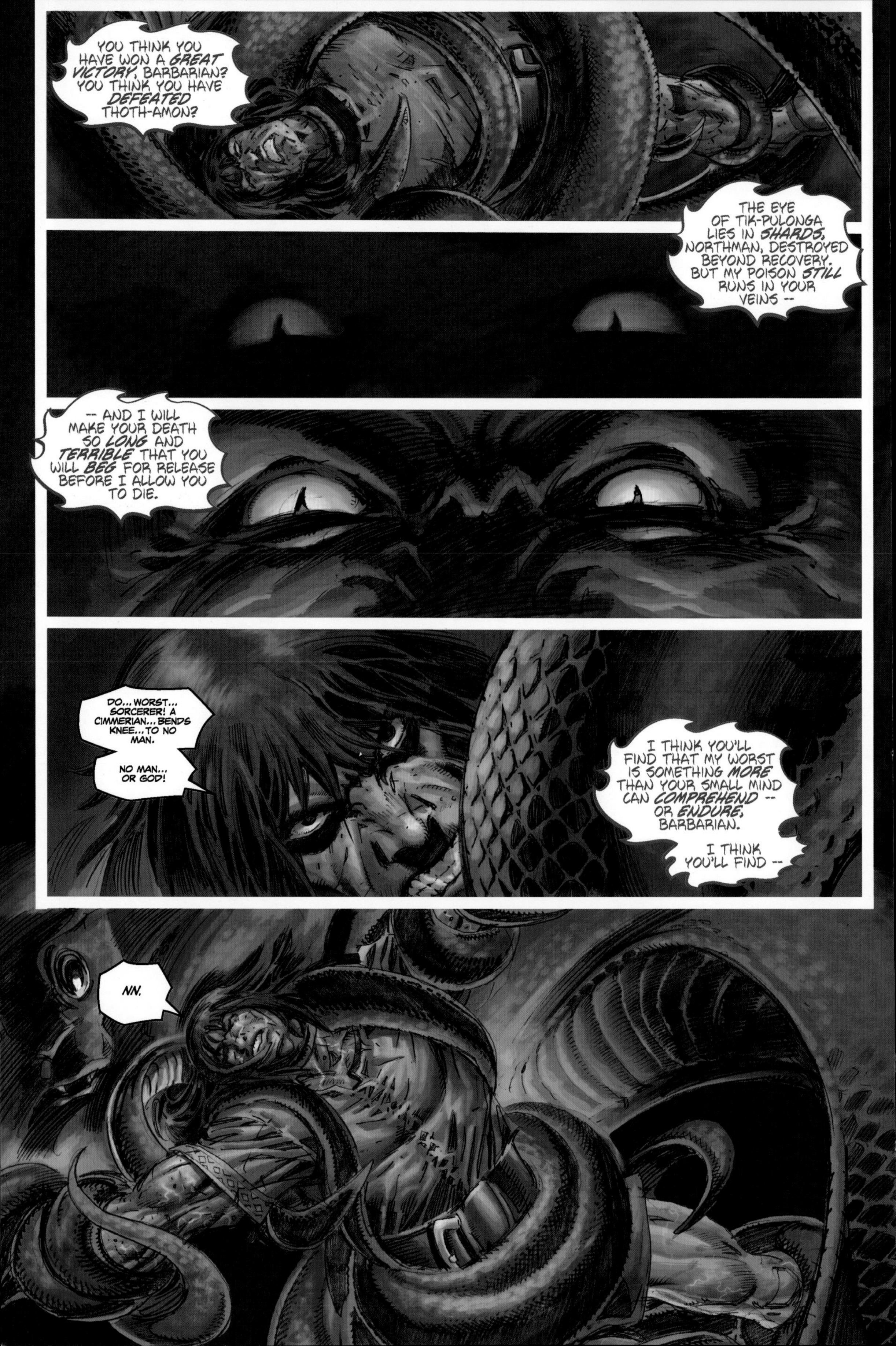
YOU THINK YOU HAVE WON A GREAT VICTORY, BARBARIAN? YOU THINK YOU HAVE DEFEATED THOTH-AMON?
THE EYE OF TIK-PULONGA LIES IN SHARDS, NORTHMAN, DESTROYED BEYOND RECOVERY. BUT MY POISON STILL RUNS IN YOUR VEINS --
-- AND I WILL MAKE YOUR DEATH SO LONG AND TERRIBLE THAT YOU WILL BEG FOR RELEASE BEFORE I ALLOW YOU TO DIE.
DO... WORST... SORCERER! A CIMMERIAN... BENDS KNEE... TO NO MAN.
NO MAN... OR GOD!
I THINK YOU'LL FIND THAT MY WORST IS SOMETHING MORE THAN YOUR SMALL MIND CAN COMPREHEND -- OR ENDURE, BARBARIAN.
I THINK YOU'LL FIND --
NN.

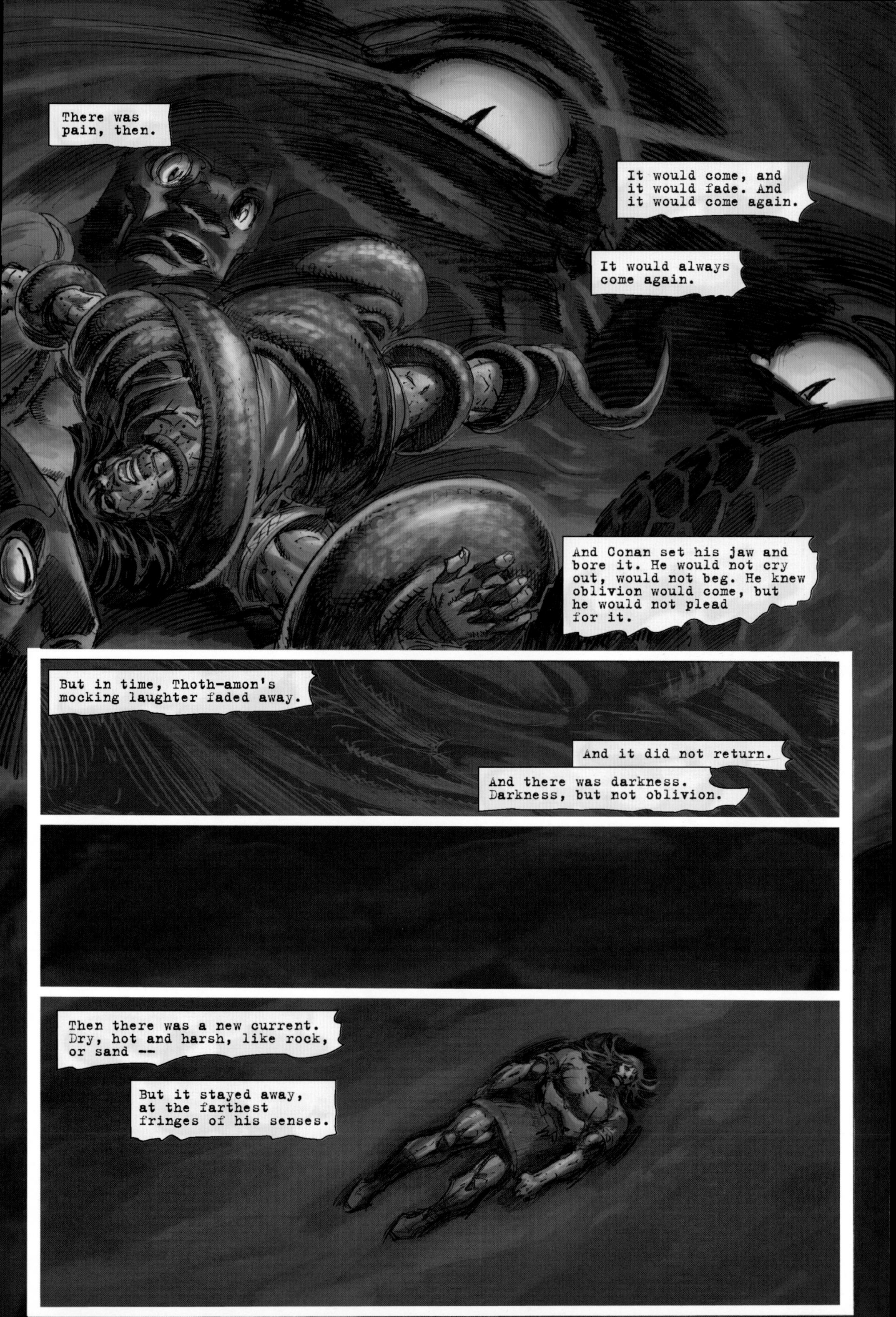
There was pain, then.
It would come, and it would fade. And it would come again.
It would always come again.
And Conan set his jaw and bore it. He would not cry out, would not beg. He knew oblivion would come, but he would not plead for it.
But in time, Thoth-amon's mocking laughter faded away.
And it did not return.
And there was darkness. Darkness, but not oblivion.
Then there was a new current. Dry, hot and harsh, like rock, or sand --
But it stayed away, at the farthest fringes of his senses.

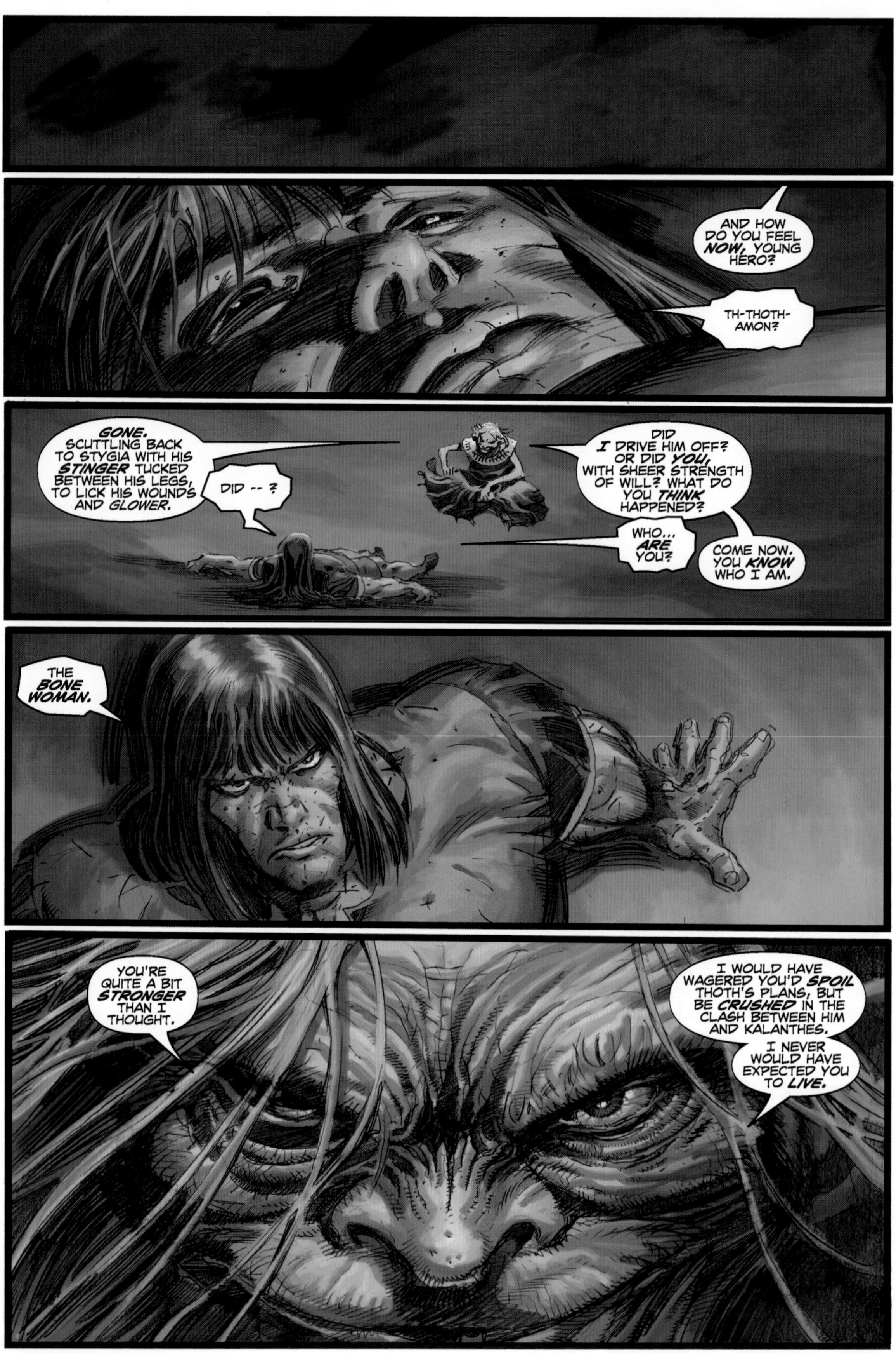
AND HOW DO YOU FEEL NOW, YOUNG HERO?
TH-THOTH-AMON?
GONE. SCUTTLING BACK TO STYGIA WITH HIS STINGER TUCKED BETWEEN HIS LEGS, TO LICK HIS WOUNDS AND GLOWER.
DID -- ?
DID I DRIVE HIM OFF? OR DID YOU, WITH SHEER STRENGTH OF WILL? WHAT DO YOU THINK HAPPENED?
WHO... ARE YOU?
COME NOW. YOU KNOW WHO I AM.
THE BONE WOMAN.
YOU'RE QUITE A BIT STRONGER THAN I THOUGHT.
I WOULD HAVE WAGERED YOU'D SPOIL THOTH'S PLANS, BUT BE CRUSHED IN THE CLASH BETWEEN HIM AND KALANTHES.
I NEVER WOULD HAVE EXPECTED YOU TO LIVE.

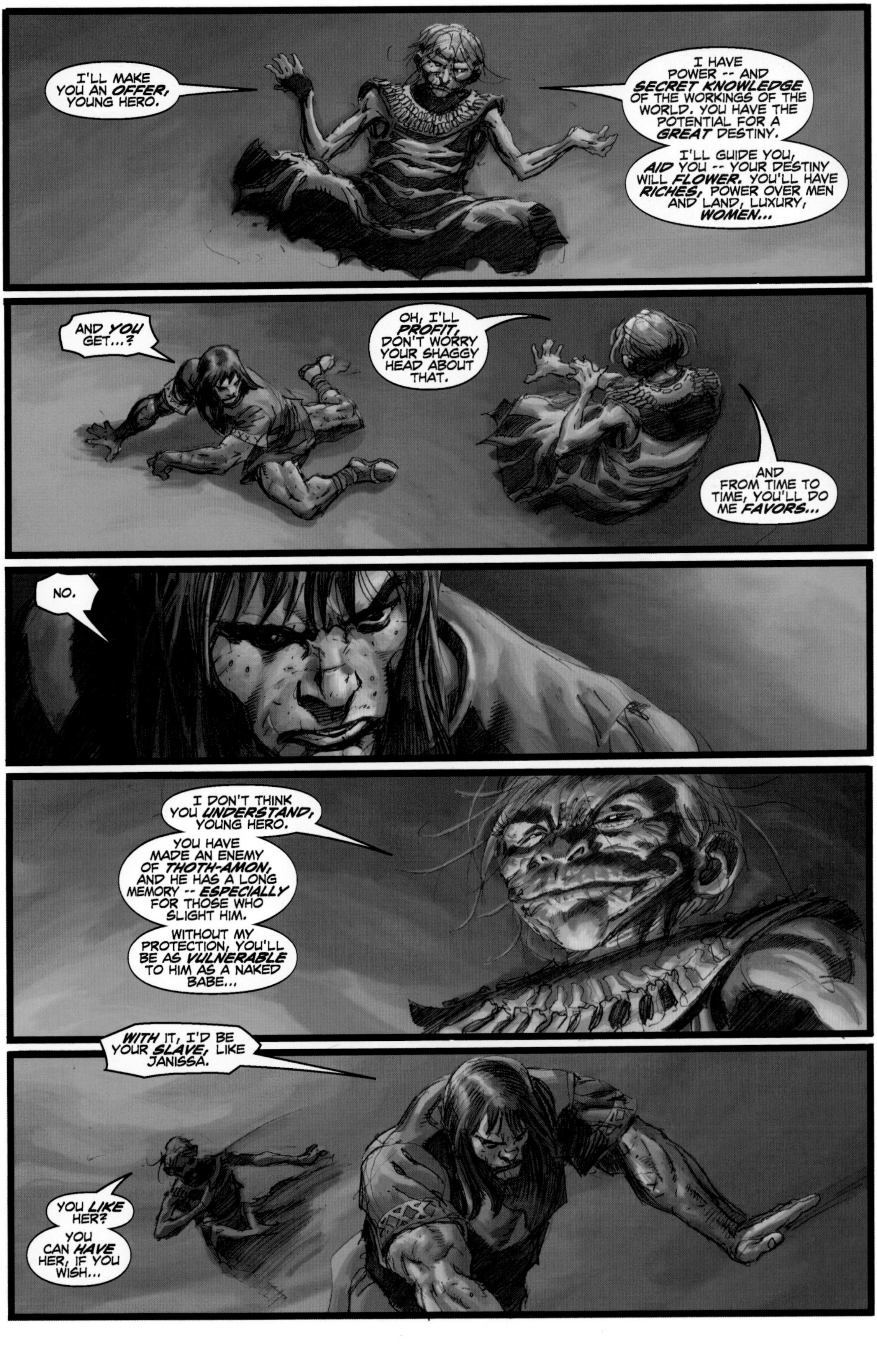
I'LL MAKE YOU AN OFFER, YOUNG HERO.
I HAVE POWER -- AND SECRET KNOWLEDGE OF THE WORKINGS OF THE WORLD. YOU HAVE THE POTENTIAL FOR A GREAT DESTINY.
I'LL GUIDE YOU, AID YOU -- YOUR DESTINY WILL FLOWER. YOU'LL HAVE RICHES, POWER OVER MEN AND LAND, LUXURY, WOMEN...
AND YOU GET...?
OH, I'LL PROFIT, DON'T WORRY YOUR SHAGGY HEAD ABOUT THAT.
AND FROM TIME TO TIME, YOU'LL DO ME FAVORS...
NO.
I DON'T THINK YOU UNDERSTAND, YOUNG HERO.
YOU HAVE MADE AN ENEMY OF THOTH-AMON, AND HE HAS A LONG MEMORY -- ESPECIALLY FOR THOSE WHO SLIGHT HIM.
WITHOUT MY PROTECTION, YOU'LL BE AS VULNERABLE TO HIM AS A NAKED BABE...
WITH IT, I'D BE YOUR SLAVE, LIKE JANISSA.
YOU LIKE HER? YOU CAN HAVE HER, IF YOU WISH...

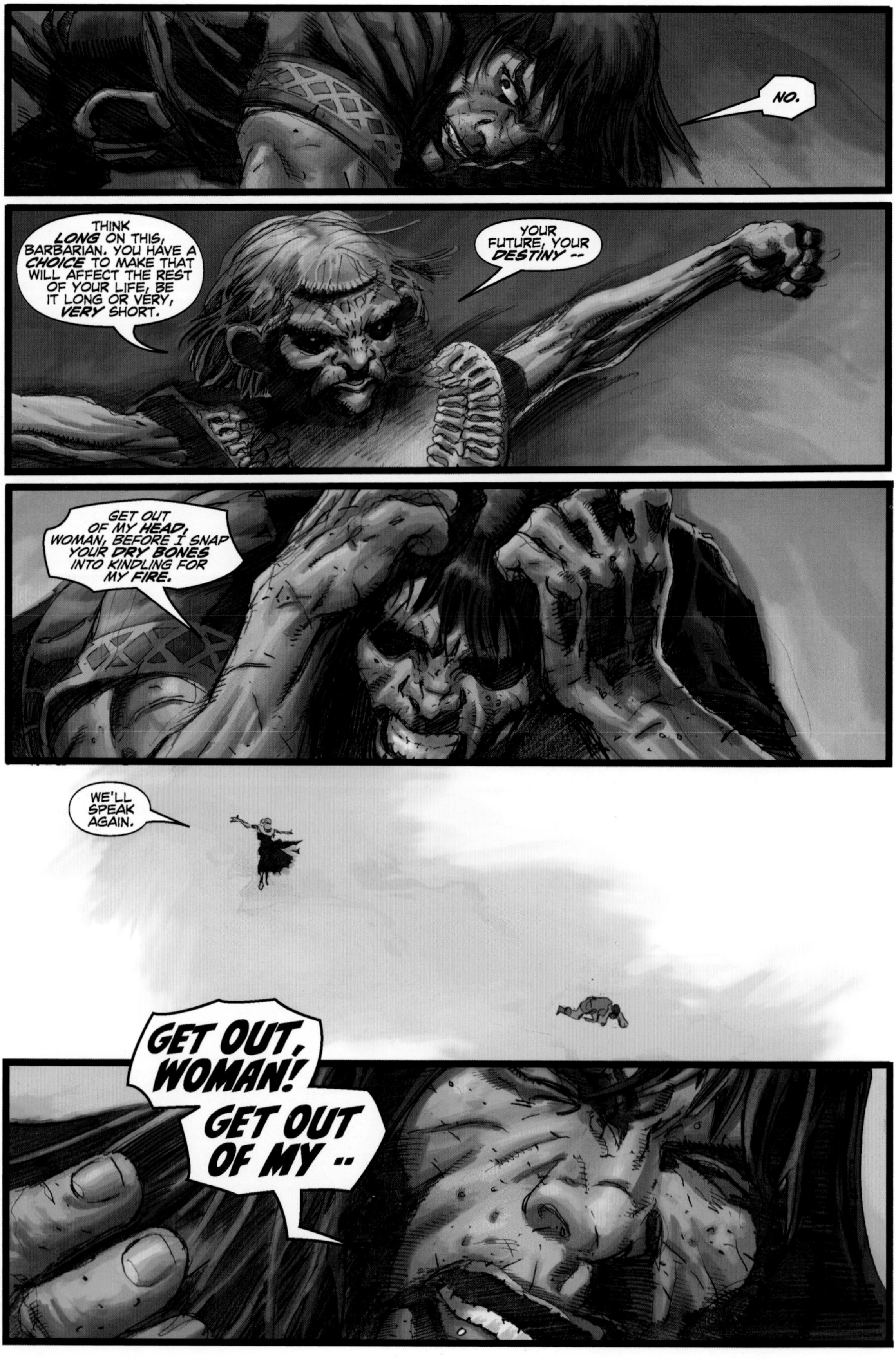
NO.
THINK LONG ON THIS, BARBARIAN. YOU HAVE A CHOICE TO MAKE THAT WILL AFFECT THE REST OF YOUR LIFE, BE IT LONG OR VERY, VERY SHORT.
YOUR FUTURE, YOUR DESTINY --
GET OUT OF MY HEAD, WOMAN, BEFORE I SNAP YOUR DRY BONES INTO KINDLING FOR MY FIRE.
WE'LL SPEAK AGAIN.
GET OUT, WOMAN! GET OUT OF MY --

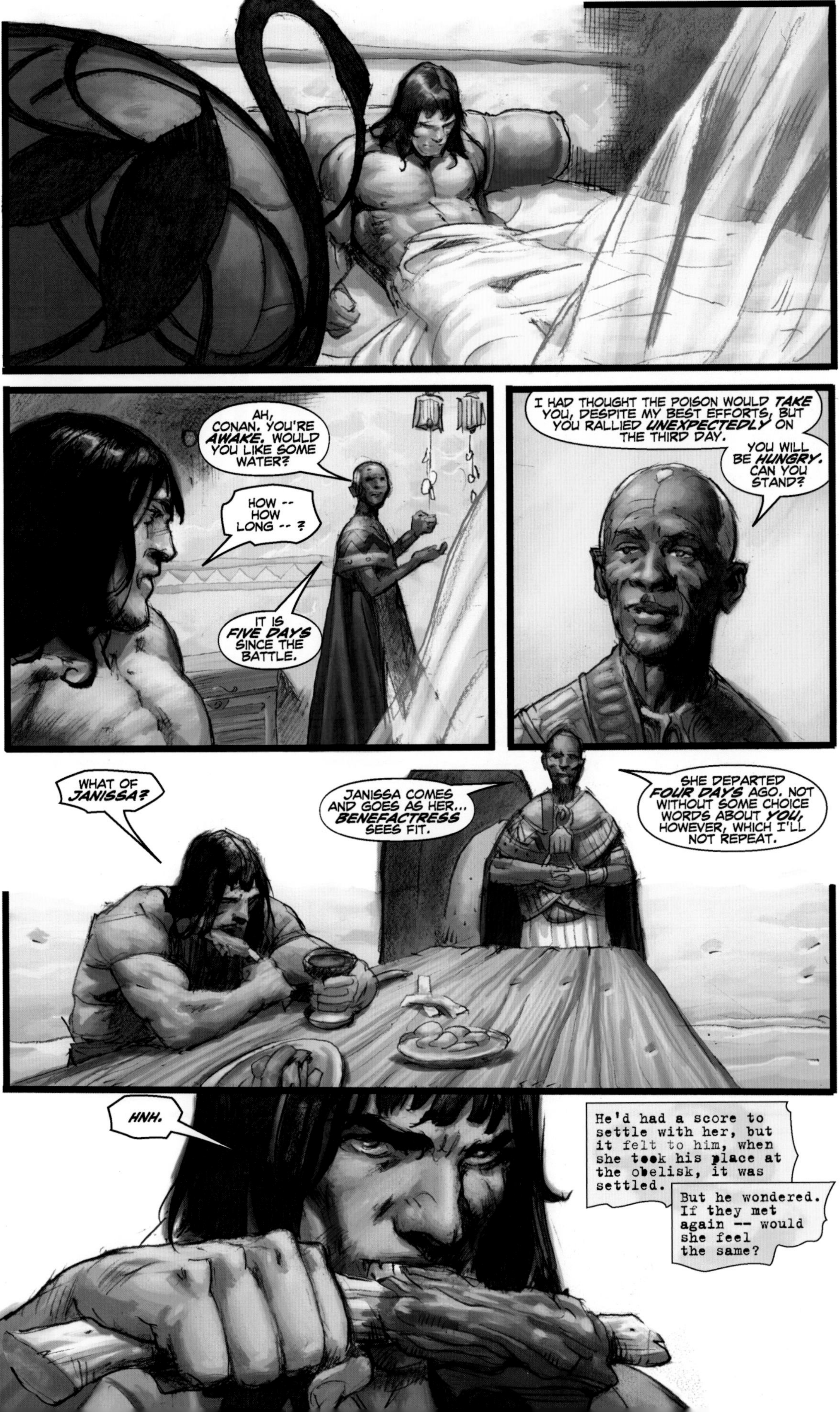

AH, CONAN. YOU'RE AWAKE. WOULD YOU LIKE SOME WATER?
HOW -- HOW LONG -- ?
IT IS FIVE DAYS SINCE THE BATTLE.
I HAD THOUGHT THE POISON WOULD TAKE YOU, DESPITE MY BEST EFFORTS, BUT YOU RALLIED UNEXPECTEDLY ON THE THIRD DAY.
YOU WILL BE HUNGRY. CAN YOU STAND?
WHAT OF JANISSA?
JANISSA COMES AND GOES AS HER... BENEFACTRESS SEES FIT.
SHE DEPARTED FOUR DAYS AGO. NOT WITHOUT SOME CHOICE WORDS ABOUT YOU, HOWEVER, WHICH I'LL NOT REPEAT.
HNH.
He'd had a score to settle with her, but it felt to him, when she took his place at the obelisk, it was settled.
But he wondered. If they met again -- would she feel the same?

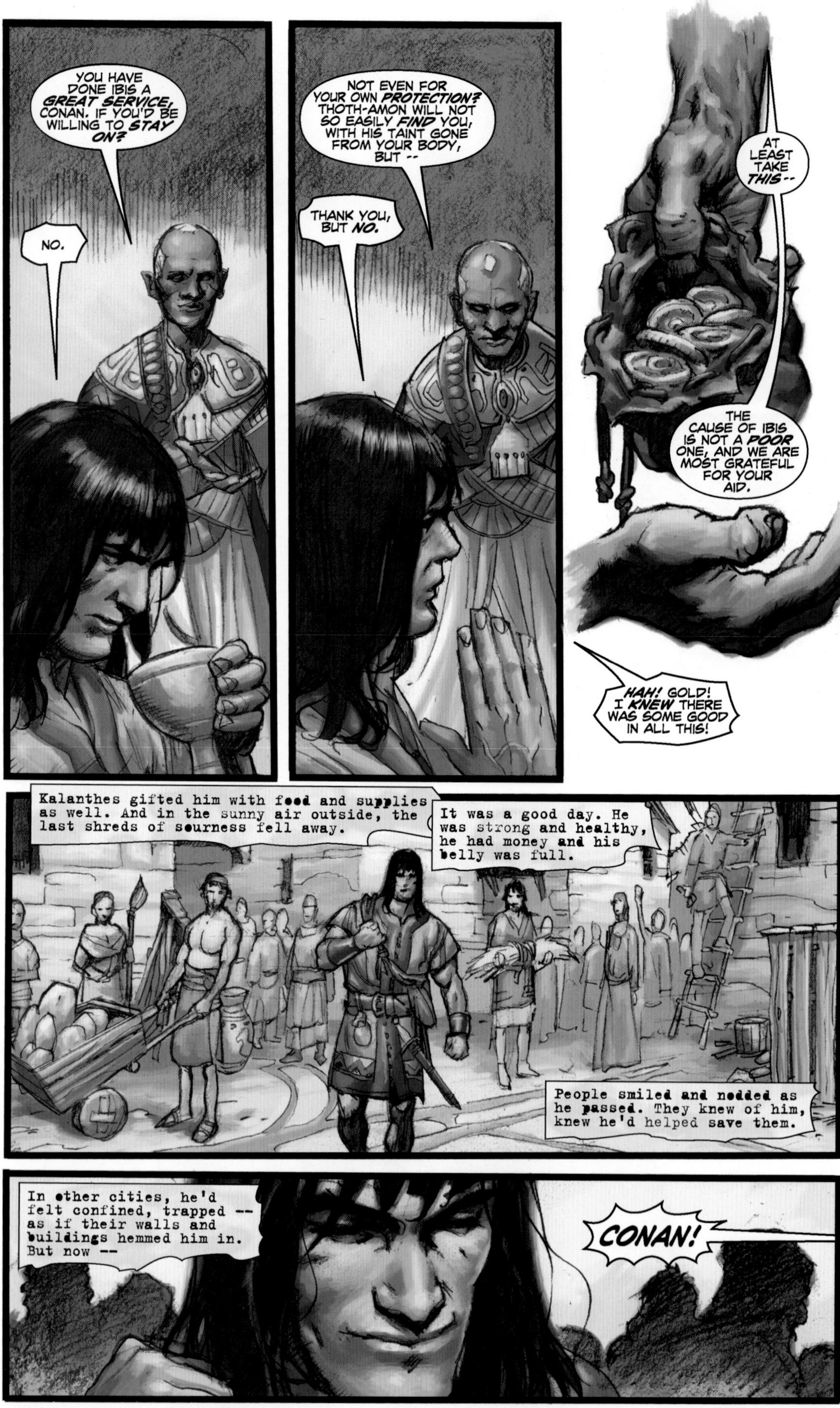
YOU HAVE DONE IBIS A GREAT SERVICE, CONAN. IF YOU'D BE WILLING TO STAY ON?
NO.
NOT EVEN FOR YOUR OWN PROTECTION? THOTH-AMON WILL NOT SO EASILY FIND YOU, WITH HIS TAINT GONE FROM YOUR BODY, BUT --
THANK YOU, BUT NO.
AT LEAST TAKE THIS --
THE CAUSE OF IBIS IS NOT A POOR ONE, AND WE ARE MOST GRATEFUL FOR YOUR AID.
HAH! GOLD! I KNEW THERE WAS SOME GOOD IN ALL THIS!
Kalanthes gifted him with food and supplies as well. And in the sunny air outside, the last shreds of sourness fell away.
It was a good day. He was strong and healthy, he had money and his belly was full.
People smiled and nodded as he passed. They knew of him, knew he'd helped save them.
In other cities, he'd felt confined, trapped -- as if their walls and buildings hemmed him in. But now --
CONAN!

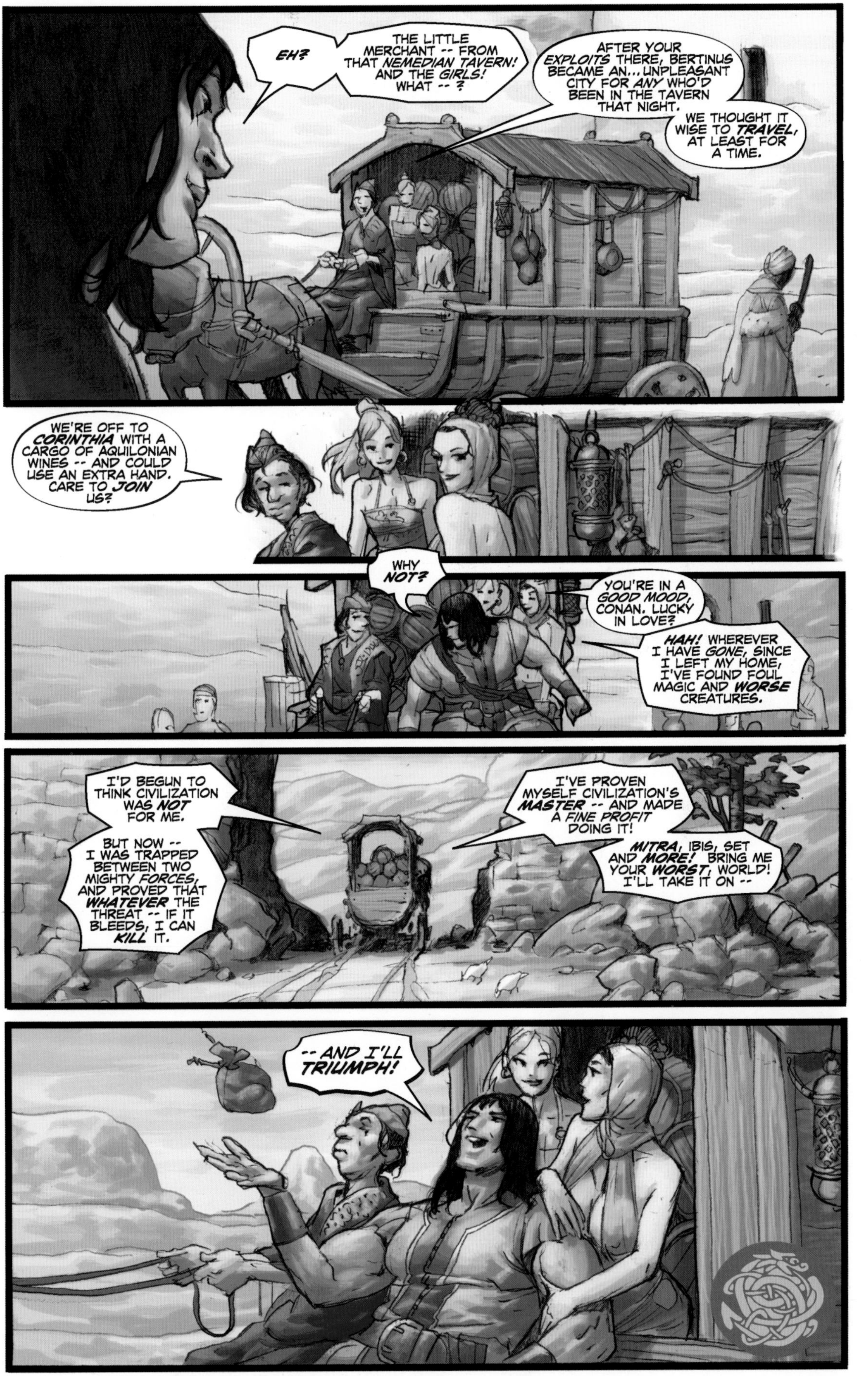
EH?
THE LITTLE MERCHANT -- FROM THAT NEMEDIAN TAVERN! AND THE GIRLS! WHAT -- ?
AFTER YOUR EXPLOITS THERE, BERTINUS BECAME AN... UNPLEASANT CITY FOR ANY WHO'D BEEN IN THE TAVERN THAT NIGHT.
WE THOUGHT IT WISE TO TRAVEL, AT LEAST FOR A TIME.
WE'RE OFF TO CORINTHIA WITH A CARGO OF AQUILONIAN WINES -- AND COULD USE AN EXTRA HAND. CARE TO JOIN US?
WHY NOT?
YOU'RE IN A GOOD MOOD, CONAN. LUCKY IN LOVE?
HAH! WHEREVER I HAVE GONE, SINCE I LEFT MY HOME, I'VE FOUND FOUL MAGIC AND WORSE CREATURES.
I'D BEGUN TO THINK CIVILIZATION WAS NOT FOR ME.
BUT NOW -- I WAS TRAPPED BETWEEN TWO MIGHTY FORCES, AND PROVED THAT WHATEVER THE THREAT -- IF IT BLEEDS, I CAN KILL IT.
I'VE PROVEN MYSELF CIVILIZATION'S MASTER -- AND MADE A FINE PROFIT DOING IT!
MITRA, IBIS, SET AND MORE! BRING ME YOUR WORST, WORLD! I'LL TAKE IT ON --
-- AND I'LL TRIUMPH!

GALLERY

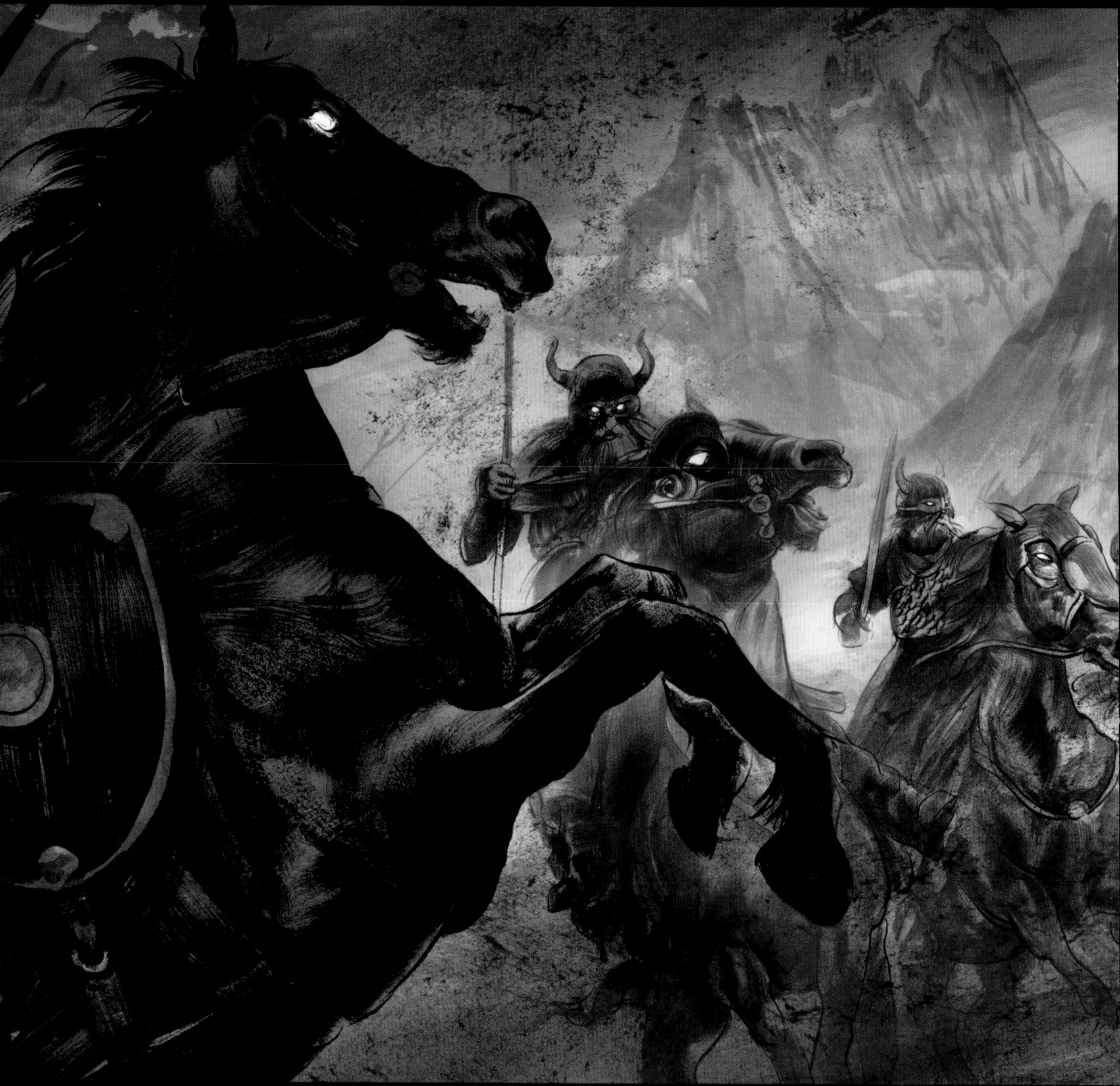

Illustration by **GREG RUTH**

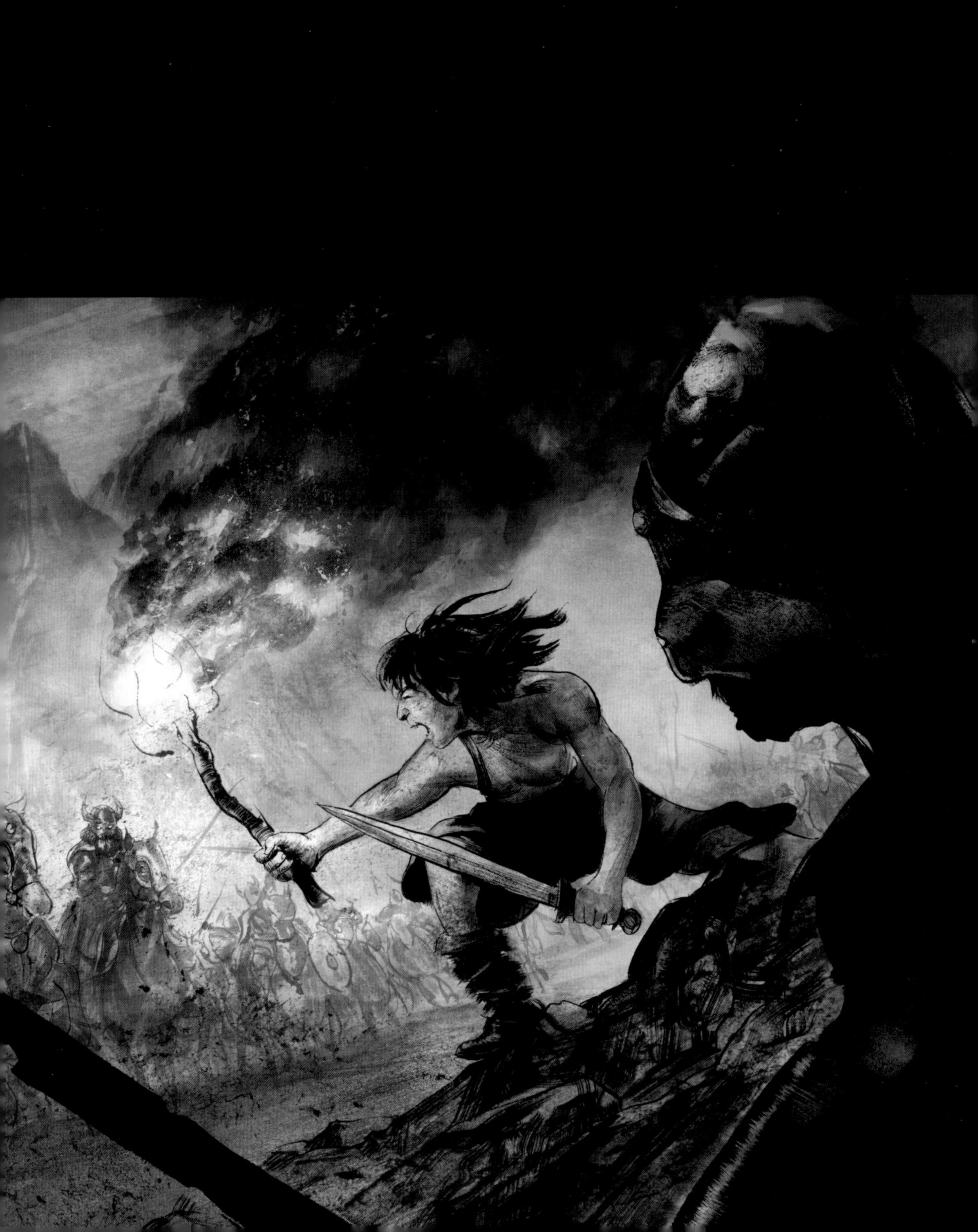

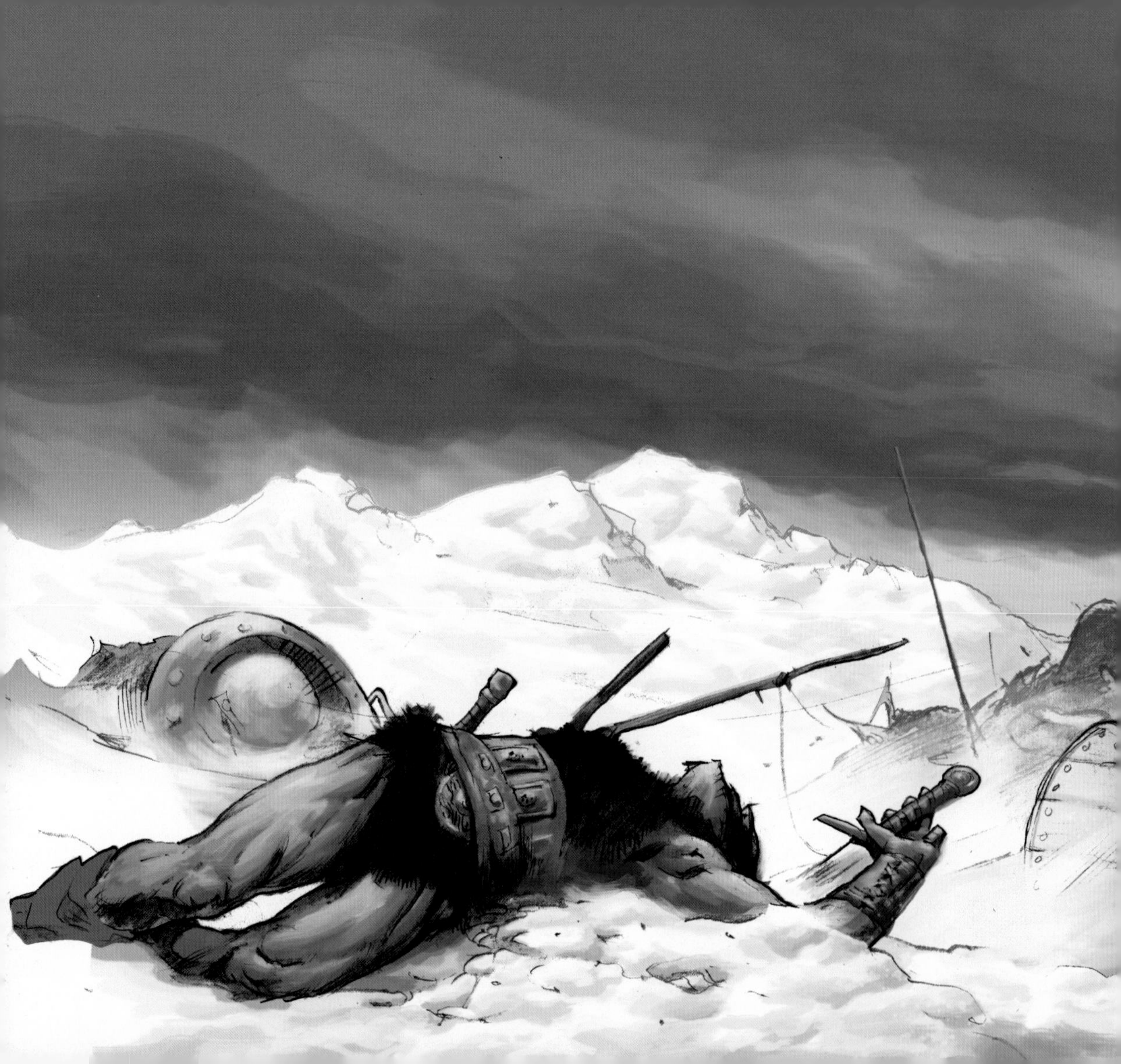

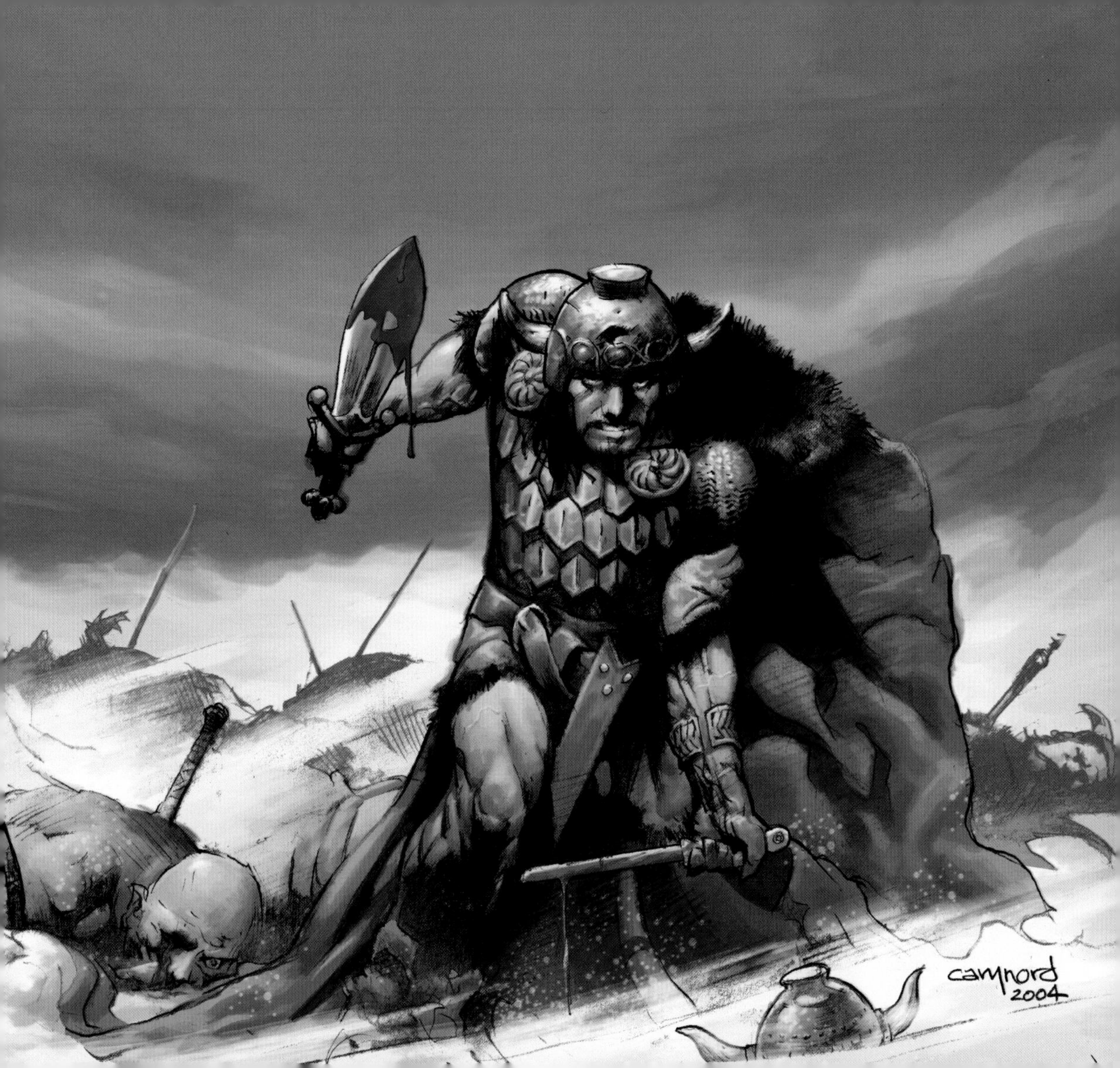
camnord
2004

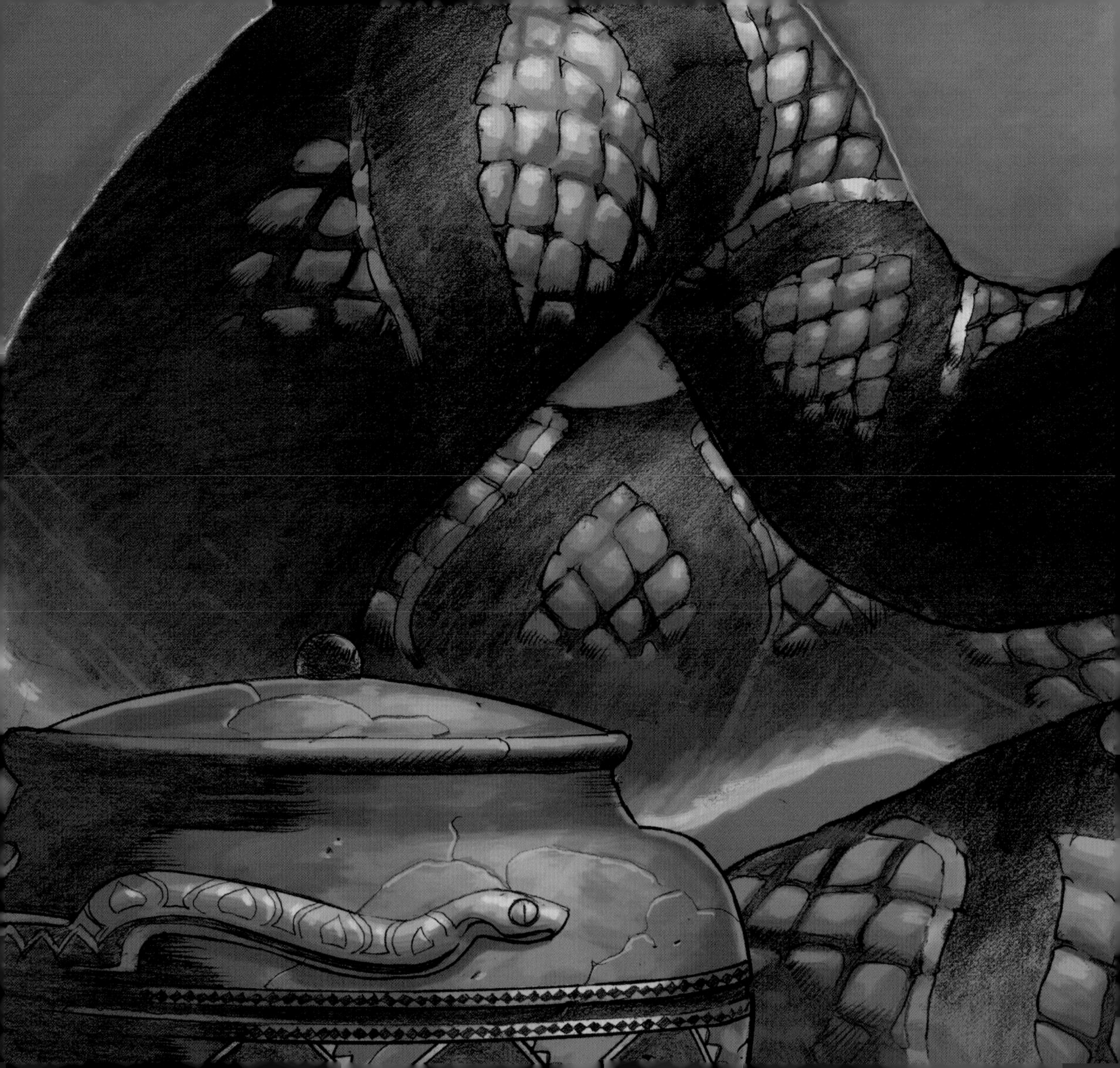

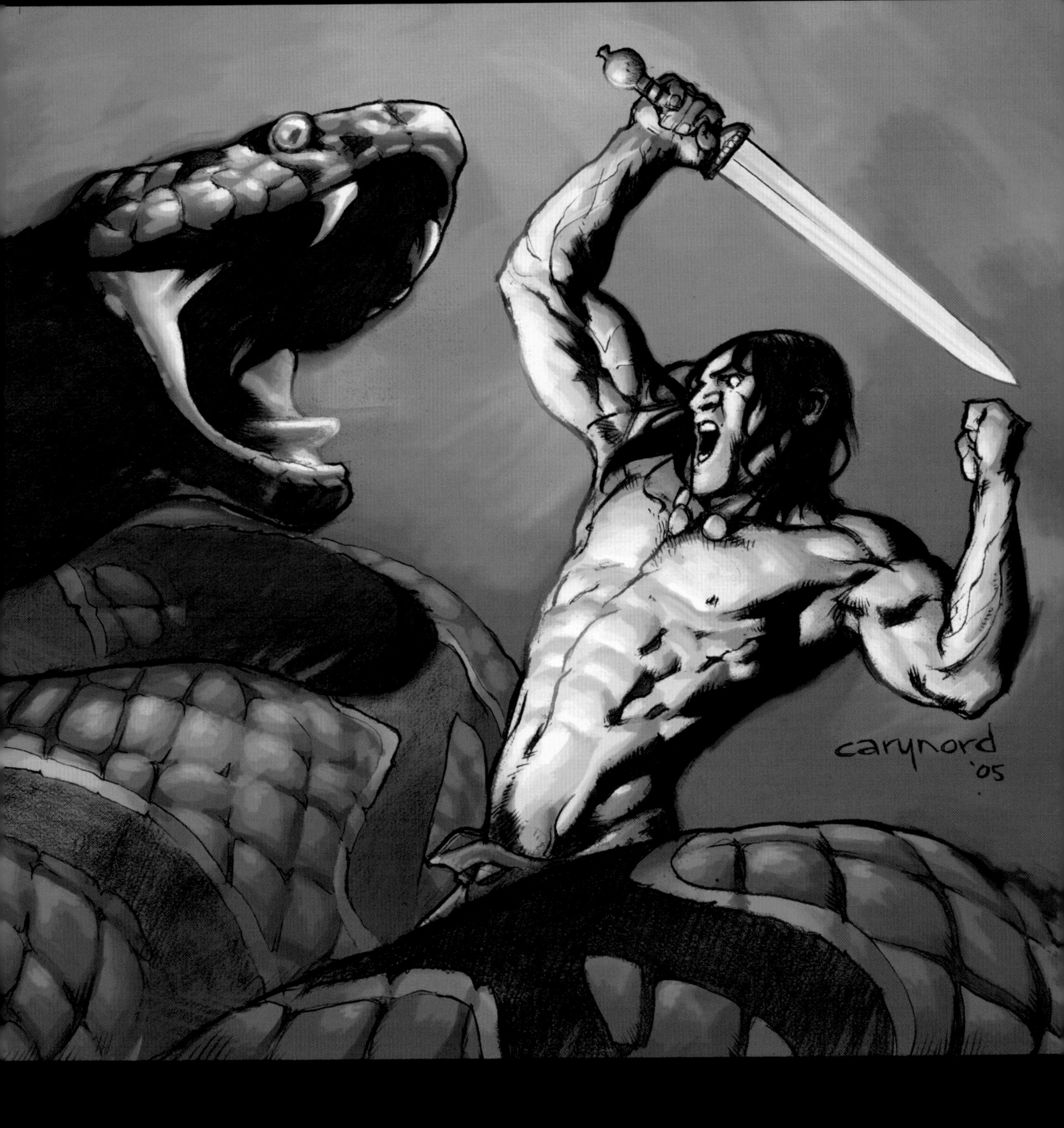
carynord
'05

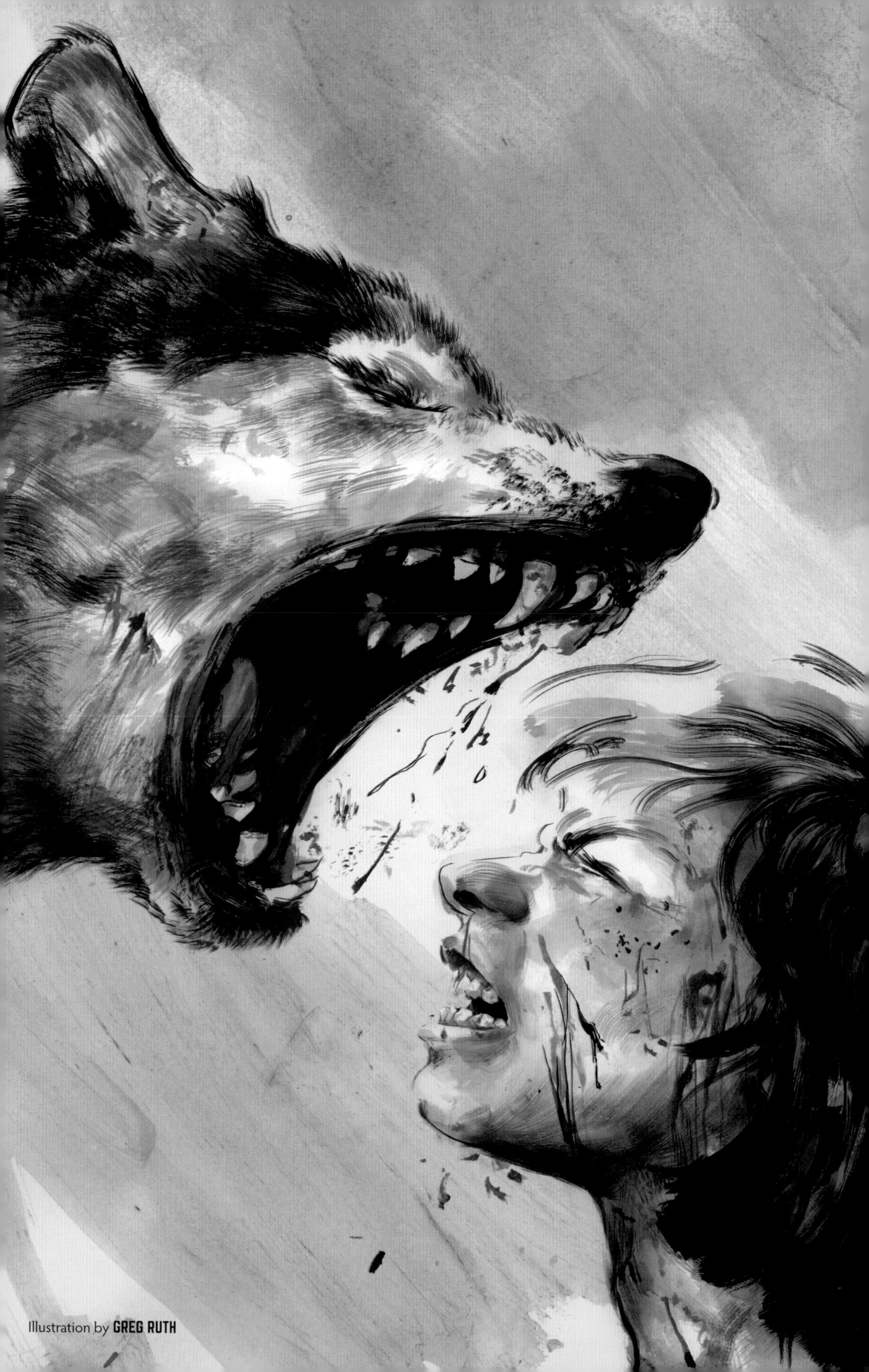

Illustration by **GREG RUTH**

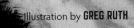
Illustration by GREG RUTH

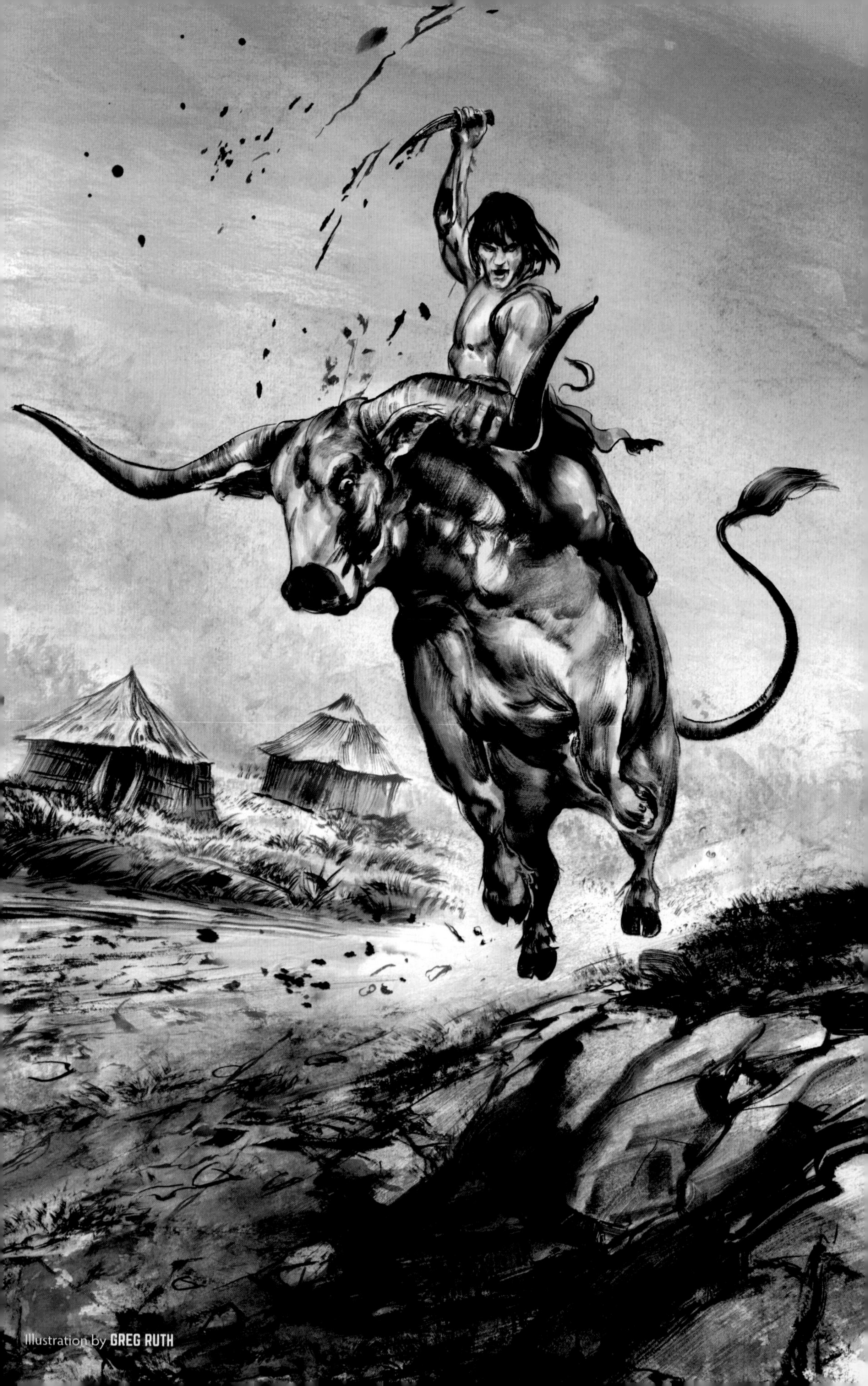

Illustration by GREG RUTH

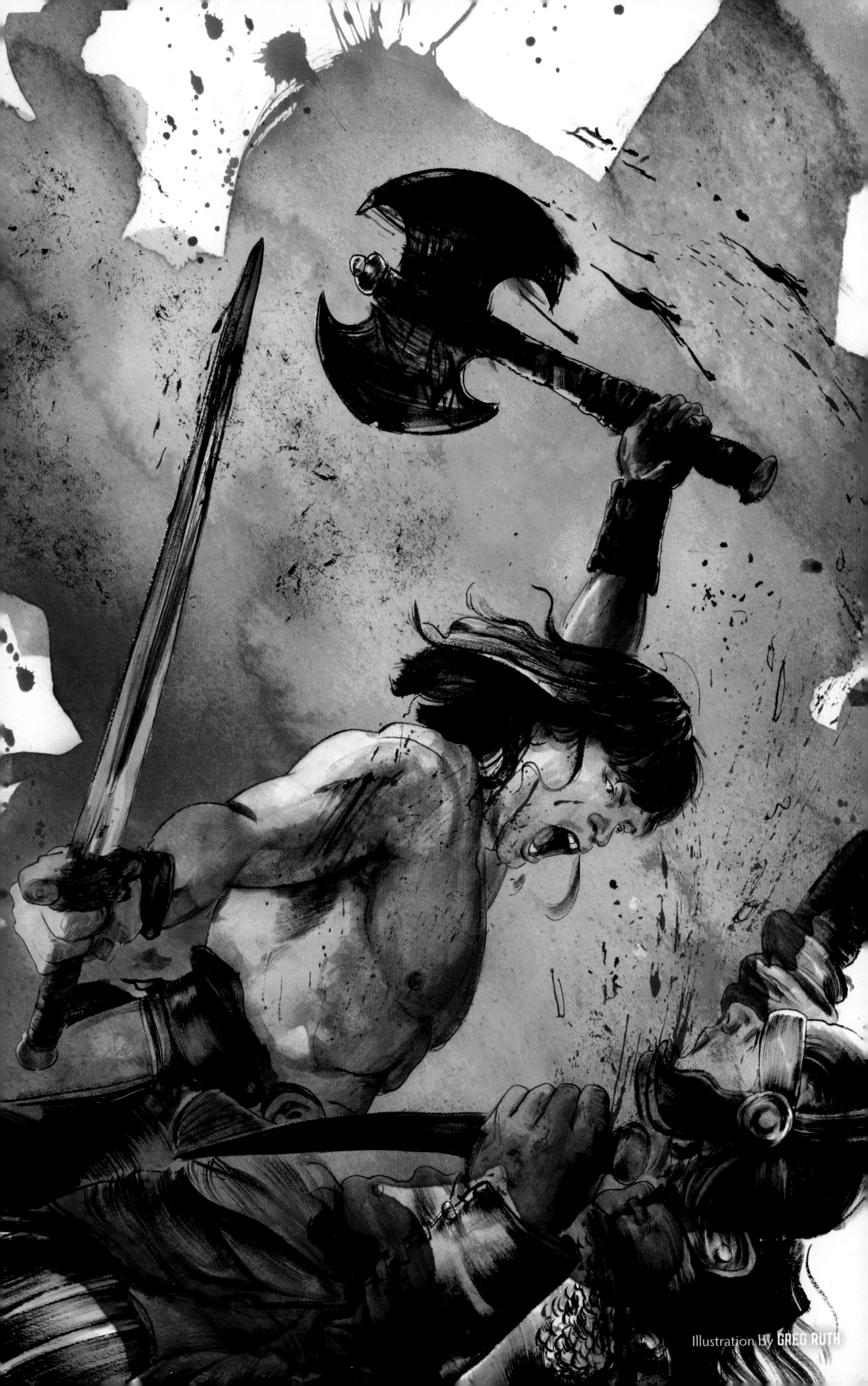

Illustration by GREG RUTH

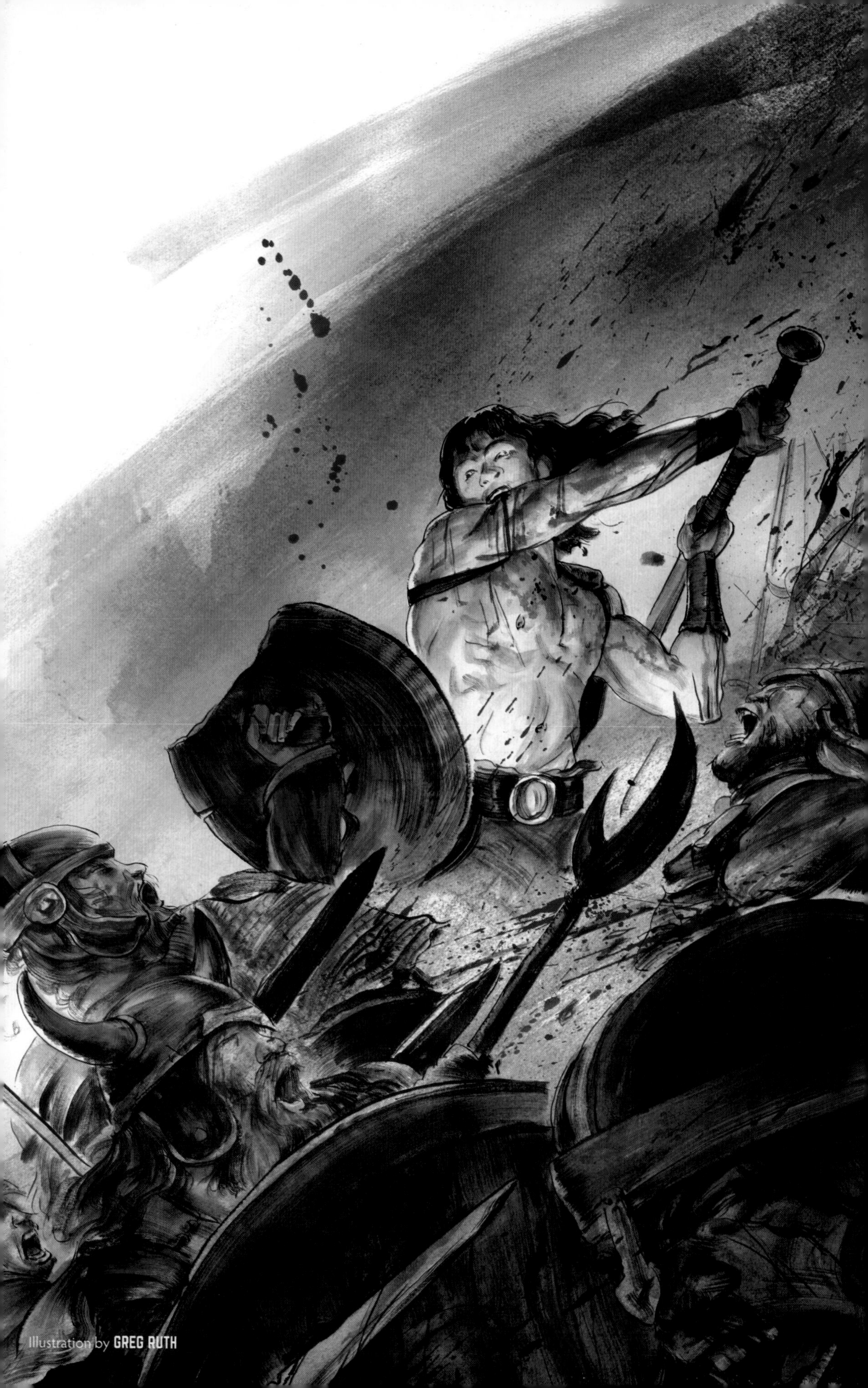

Illustration by **GREG RUTH**

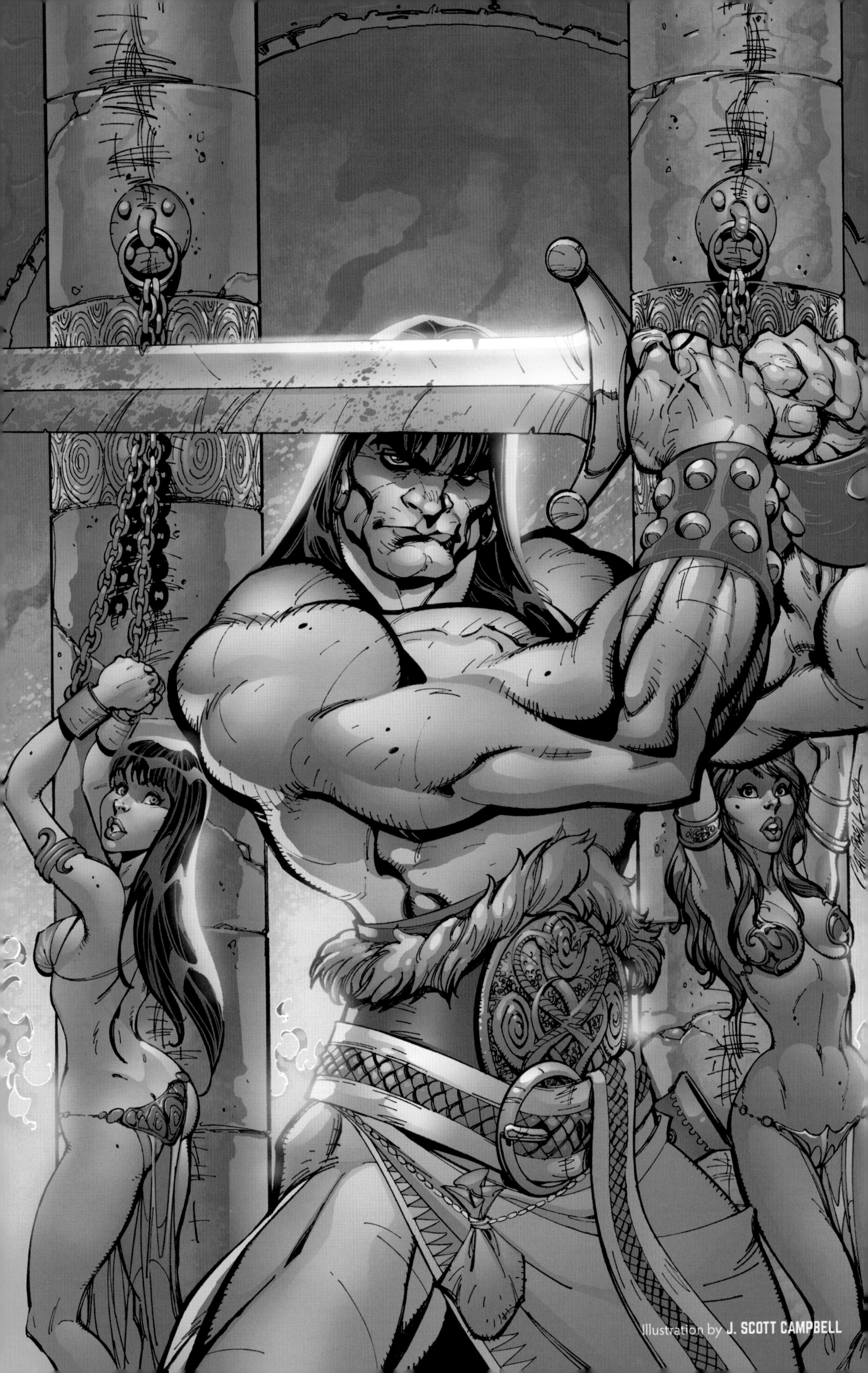

Illustration by J. SCOTT CAMPBELL

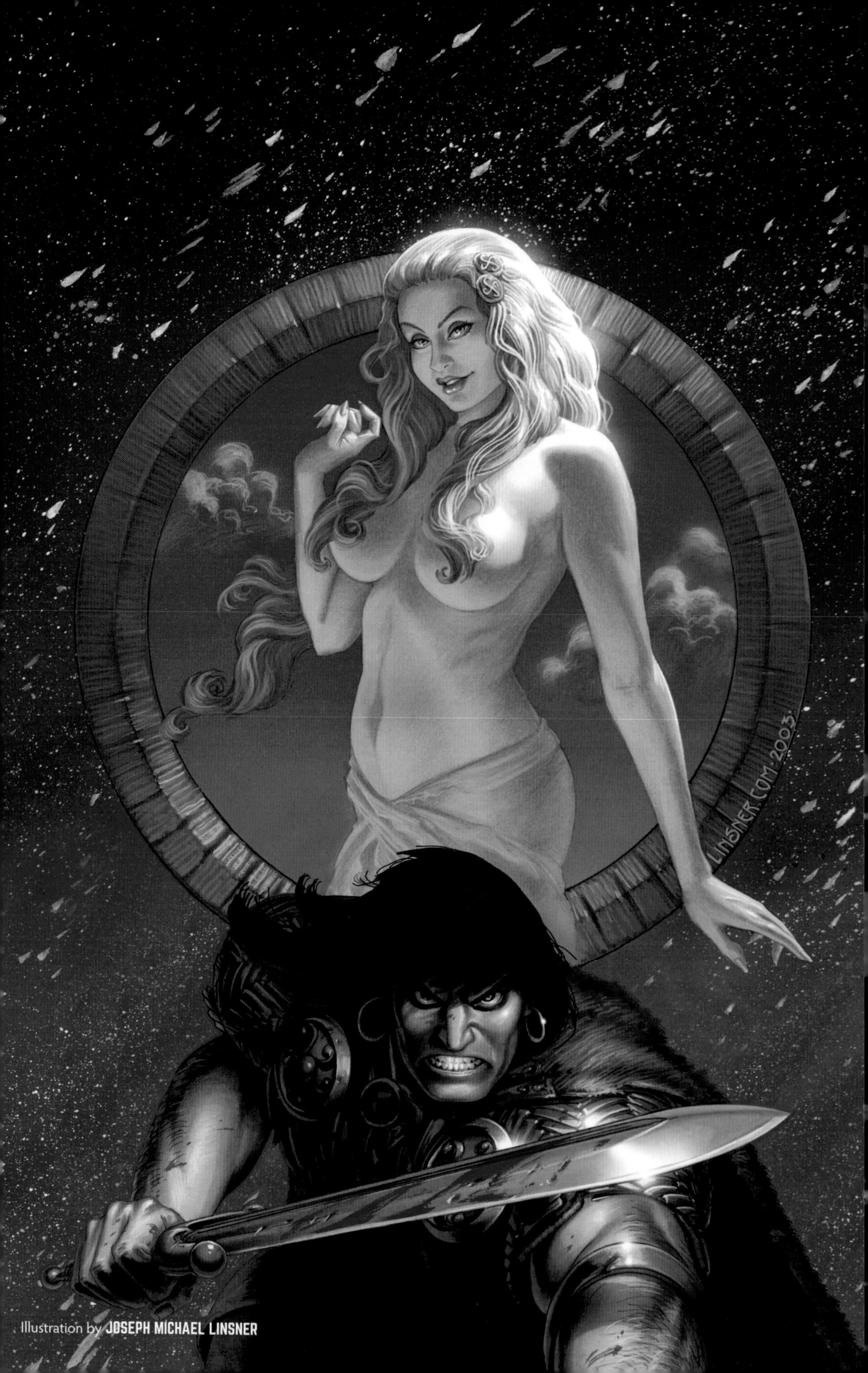
LINSNER.COM 2003

Illustration by **JOSEPH MICHAEL LINSNER**

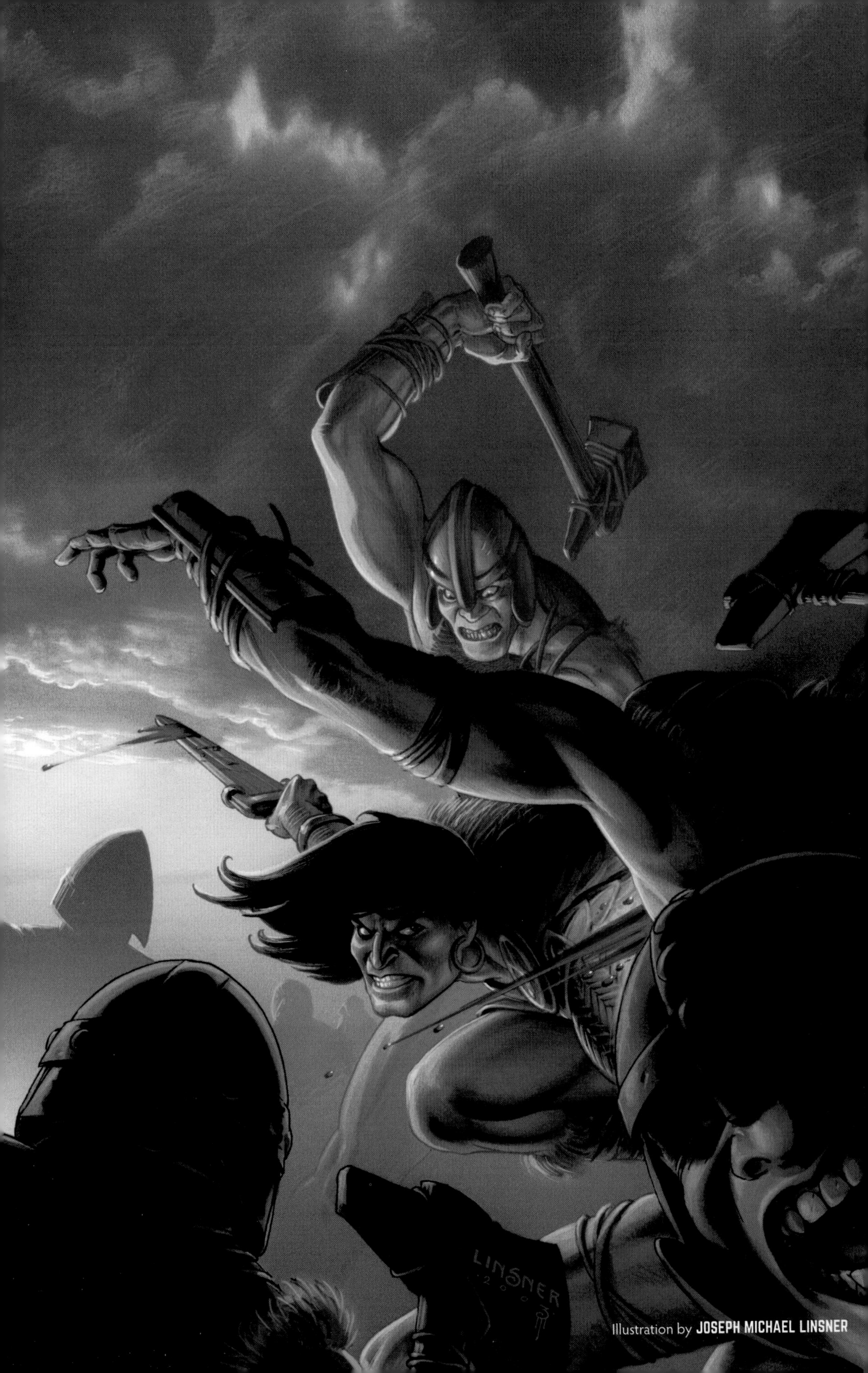
LINSNER
2003

Illustration by **JOSEPH MICHAEL LINSNER**

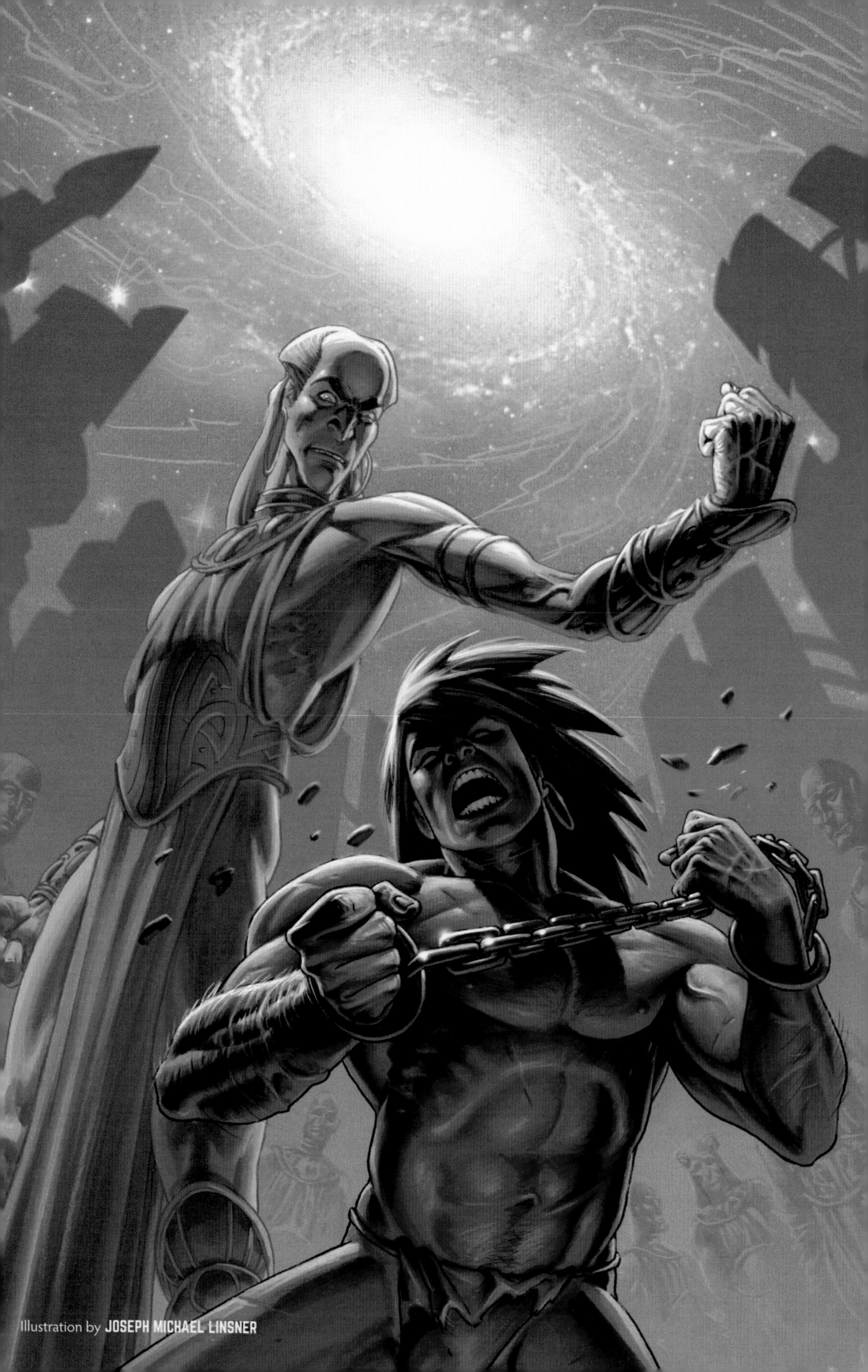

Illustration by **JOSEPH MICHAEL LINSNER**

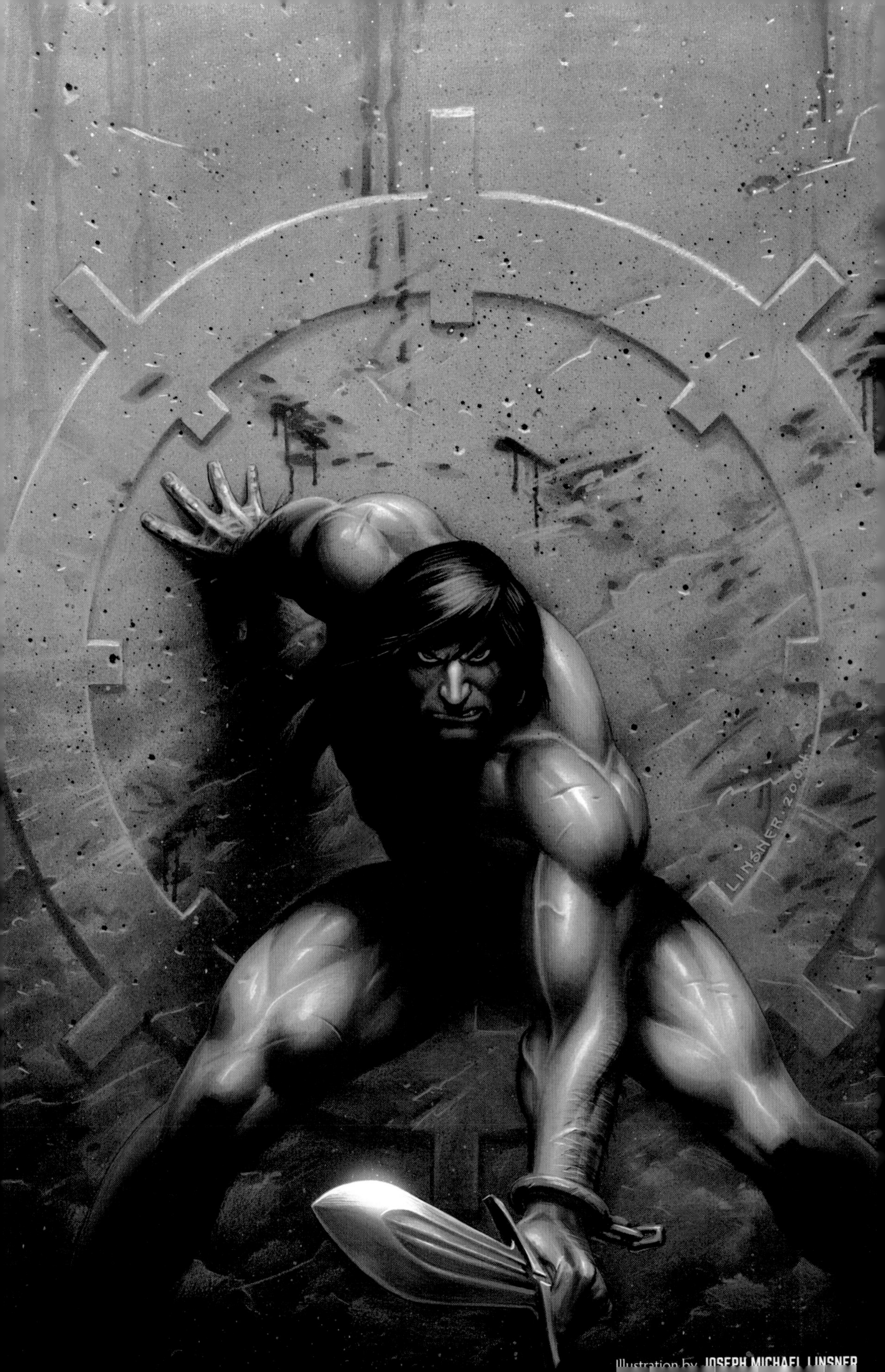
LINSNER 2004

Illustration by: JOSEPH MICHAEL LINSNER

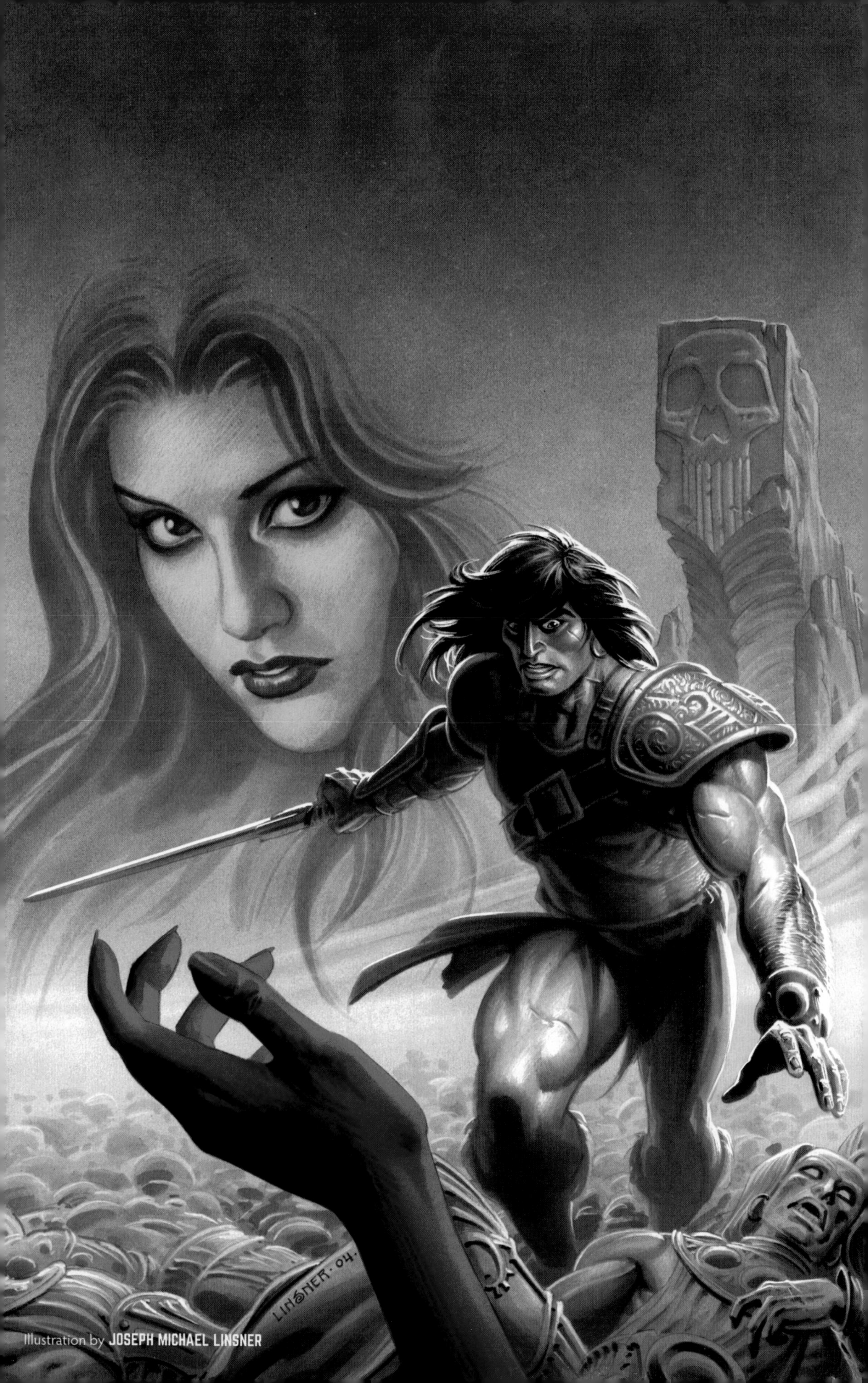
LINSNER·04.

Illustration by **JOSEPH MICHAEL LINSNER**

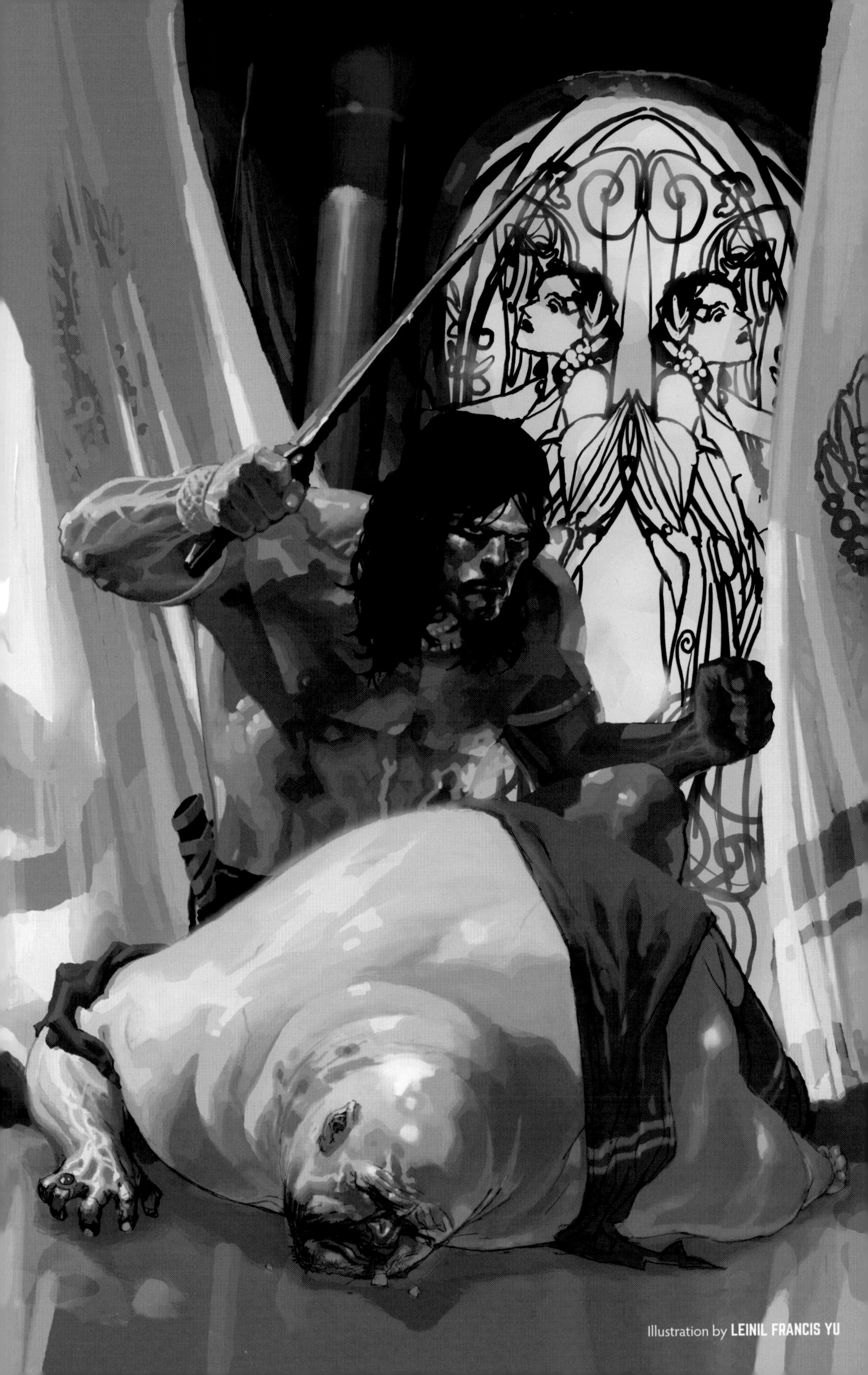

Illustration by **LEINIL FRANCIS YU**

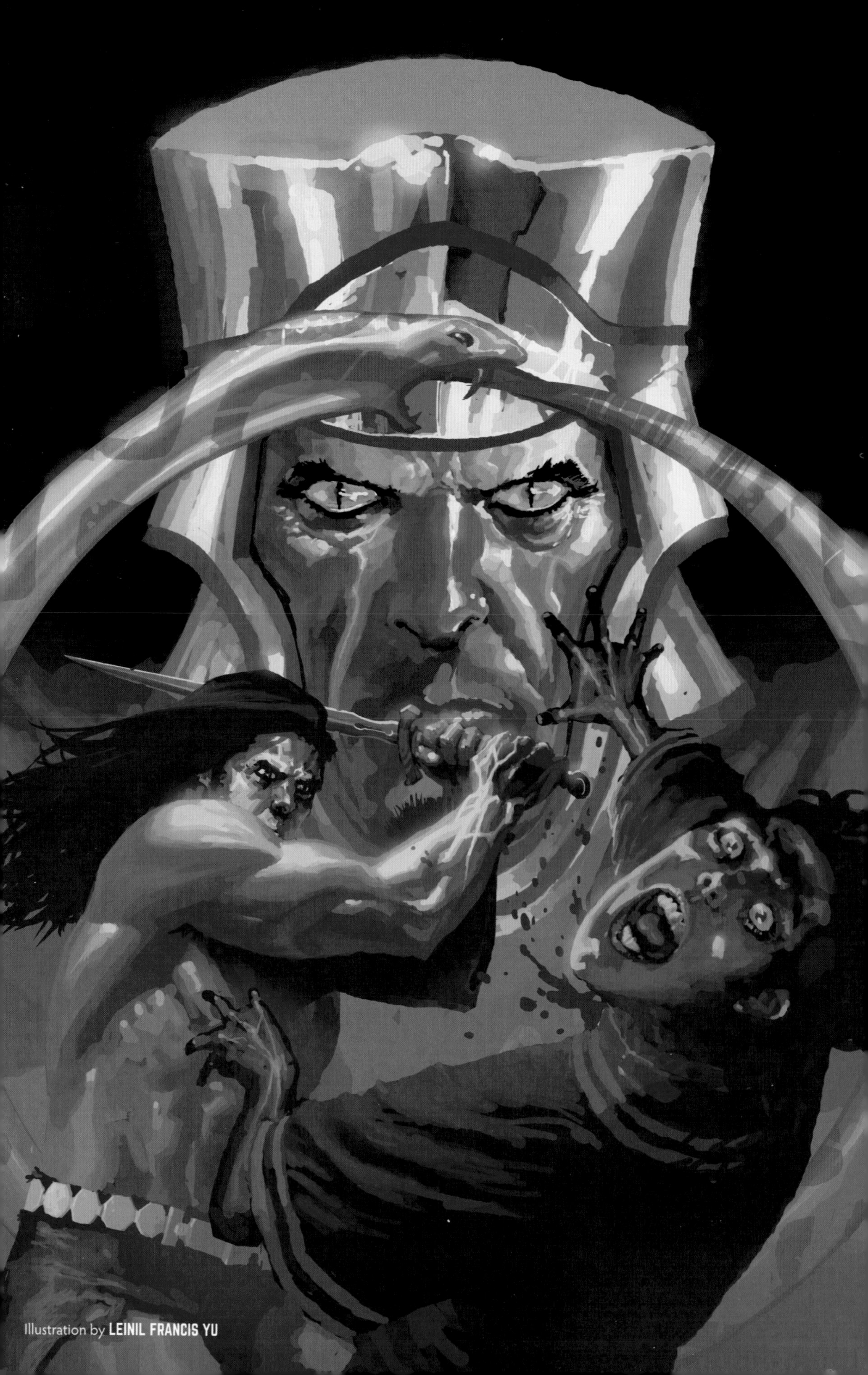

Illustration by **LEINIL FRANCIS YU**

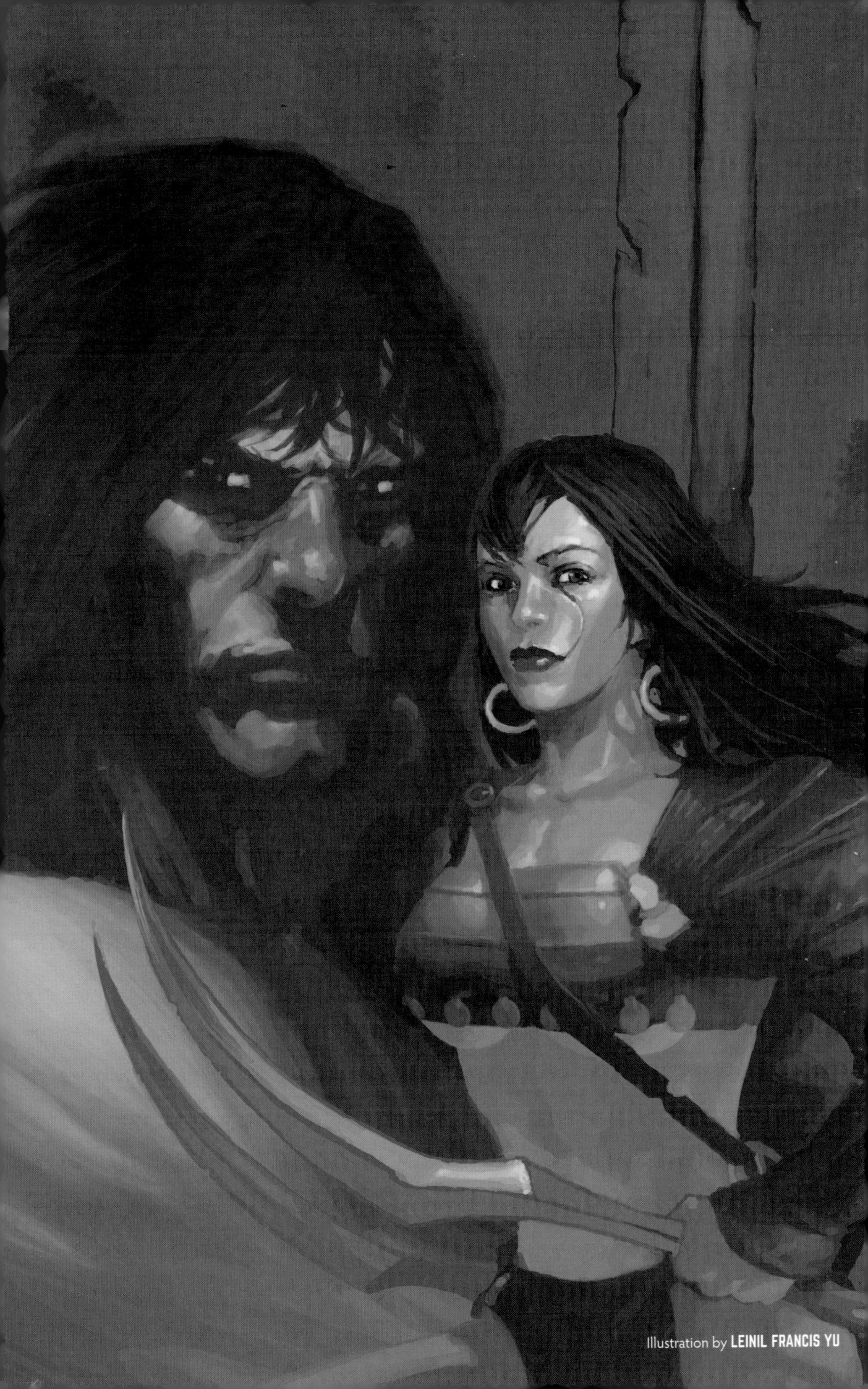

Illustration by **LEINIL FRANCIS YU**

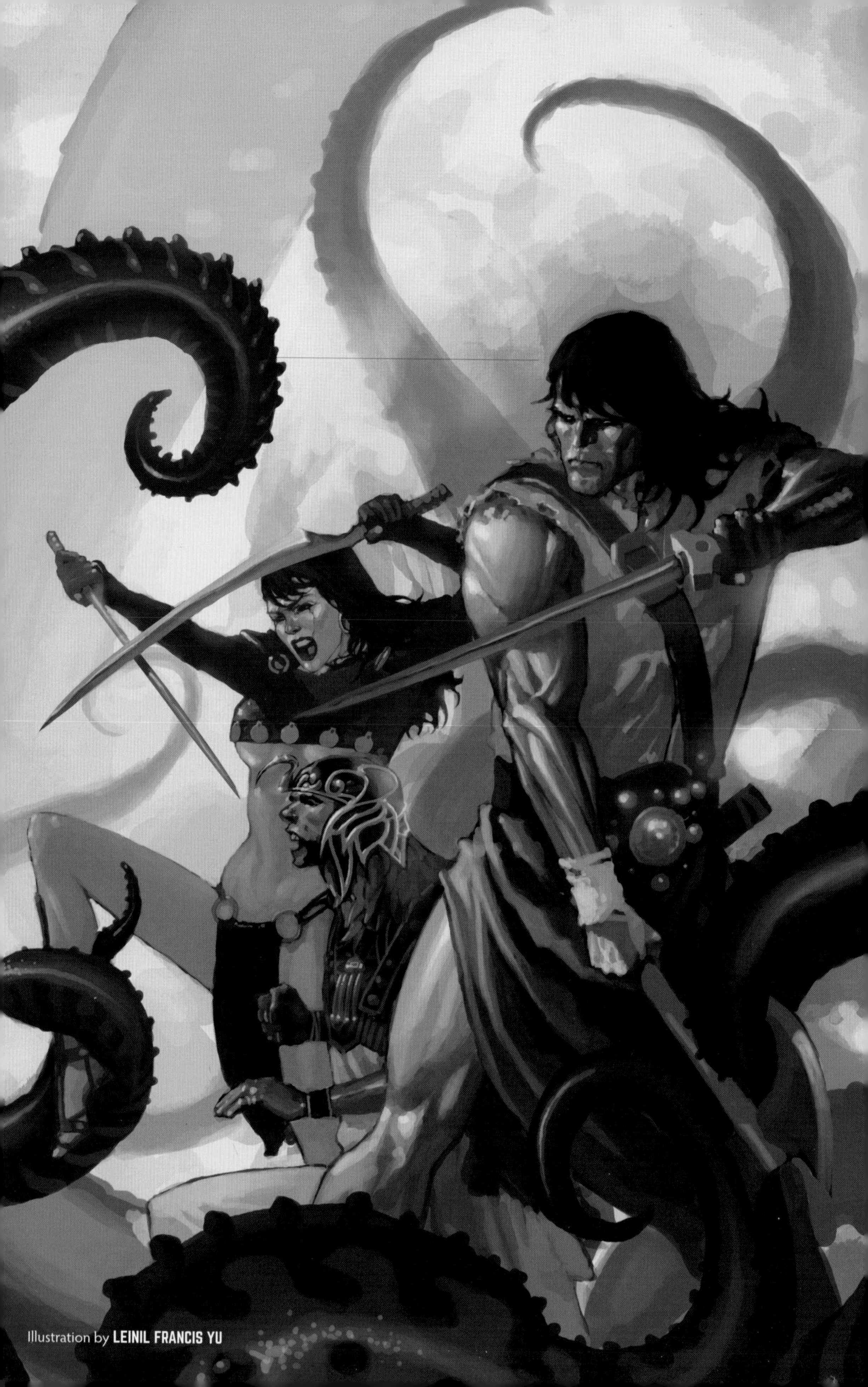

Illustration by **LEINIL FRANCIS YU**

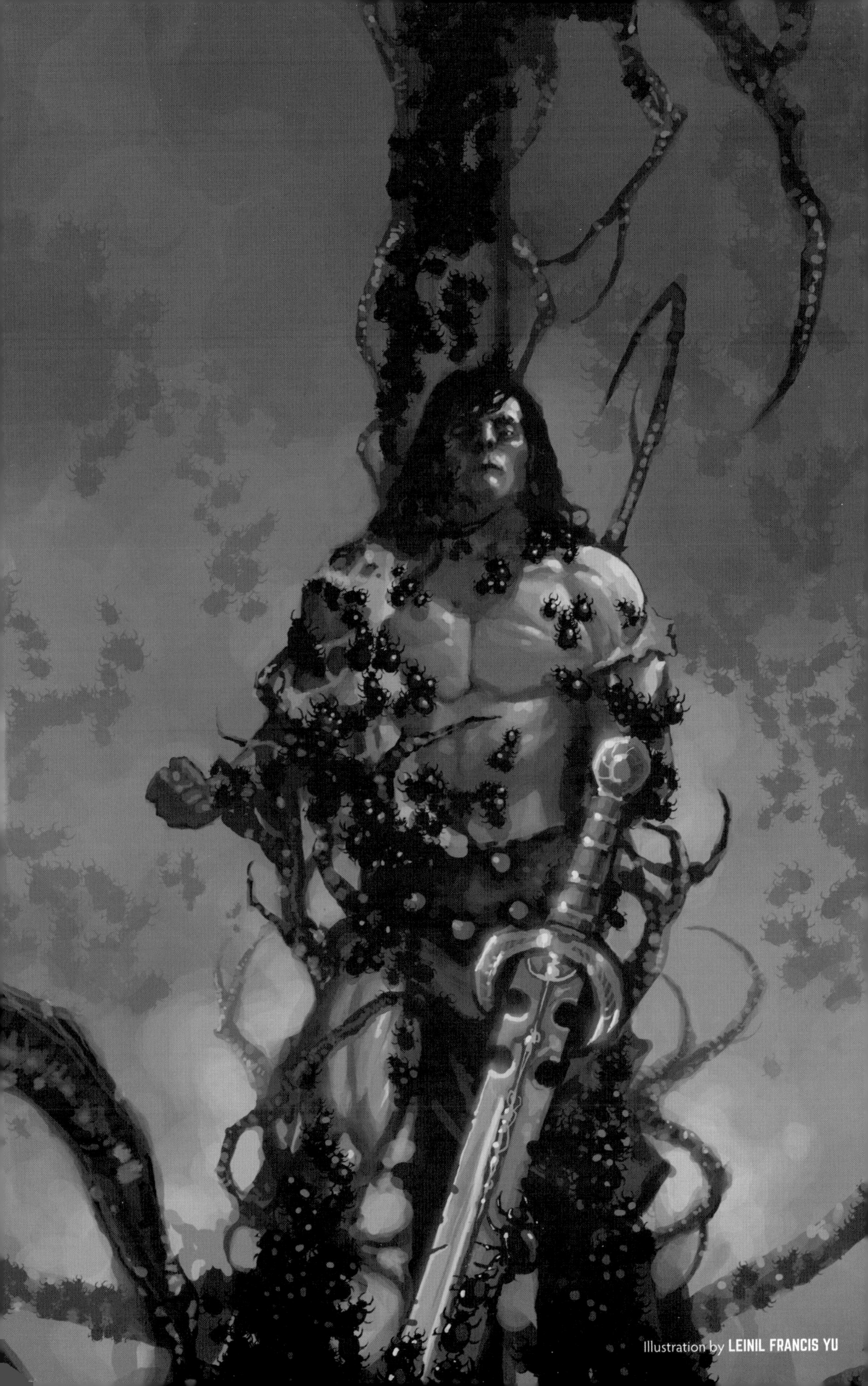

Illustration by **LEINIL FRANCIS YU**

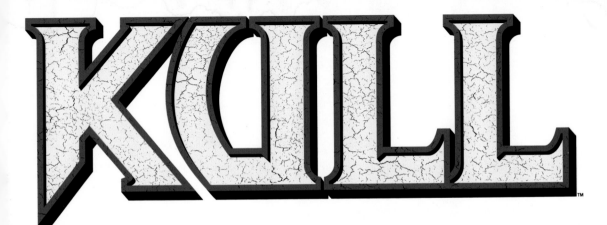

KULL

**THE CHRONICLES OF KULL
VOLUME 1: A KING COMES RIDING**
*Written by Roy Thomas,
Gerry Conway, and Len Wein
Art by Wallace Wood,
Bernie Wrightson, and others*
ISBN 978-1-59582-413-4 | $18.99

**THE CHRONICLES OF KULL
VOLUME 2: THE HELL BENEATH
ATLANTIS AND OTHER STORIES**
*Written by Roy Thomas,
Gerry Conway, and Len Wein
Art by Wallace Wood,
Bernie Wrightson, and others*
ISBN 978-1-59582-413-4 | $18.99

**THE CHRONICLES OF KULL
VOLUME 3: SCREAMS IN THE
DARK AND OTHER STORIES**
*Written by Roy Thomas,
Don Glut, and Steve Englehart
Art by John Buscema, Ernie Chan,
and Howard Chaykin*
ISBN 978-1-59582-585-8 | $18.99

**THE CHRONICLES OF KULL
VOLUME 4: THE BLOOD OF
KINGS AND OTHER STORIES**
*Written by Doug Moench
and Bruce Jones
Art by John Buscema and John Bolton*
ISBN 978-1-59582-684-8 | $18.99

**THE CHRONICLES OF KULL
VOLUME 5: DEAD MEN OF THE
DEEP AND OTHER STORIES**
*Written by Alan Zelenetz
Art by John Buscema, Charles Vess,
Klaus Janson, Bill Sienkiewicz, and
others*
ISBN 978-1-59582-906-1 | $18.99

**KULL VOLUME 1: THE SHADOW
KINGDOM**
*Written by Arvid Nelson
Art by Will Conrad and José Villarrubia*
ISBN 978-1-59582-385-4 | $18.99

**KULL VOLUME 2: THE HATE
WITCH**
*Written by David Lapham
Art by Gabriel Guzman, Tom Fleming, and
Mariano Taibo*
ISBN 978-1-59582-730-2 | $15.99

**KULL VOLUME 3: THE CAT AND
THE SKULL**
*Written by David Lapham
Art by Gabriel Guzman*
ISBN 978-1-59582-899-6 | $15.99

**THE SAVAGE SWORD OF KULL
VOLUME 1**
ISBN 978-1-59582-593-3 | $19.99
VOLUME 2
ISBN 978-1-59582-788-3 | $19.99

DarkHorse.com

AVAILABLE AT YOUR LOCAL COMICS SHOP OR BOOKSTORE
TO FIND A COMICS SHOP IN YOUR AREA, CALL 1-888-266-4226

For more information or to order direct:
• On the web: DarkHorse.com
• E-mail: mailorder@darkhorse.com
• Phone: 1-800-862-0052 Mon.–Fri. 9AM to 5PM Pacific Time.

MIKE RICHARDSON President and Publisher • **NEIL HANKERSON** Executive Vice President • **TOM WEDDLE** Chief Financial Officer • **RANDY STRADLEY** Vice President of Publishing • **MICHAEL MARTENS** Vice President of Book Trade Sales • **MATT PARKINSON** Vice President of Marketing • **DAVID SCROGGY** Vice President of Product Development • **DALE LaFOUNTAIN** Vice President of Information Technology • **CARA NIECE** Vice President of Production and Scheduling • **NICK McWHORTER** Vice President of Media Licensing • **KEN LIZZI** General Counsel • **DAVE MARSHALL** Editor in Chief • **DAVEY ESTRADA** Editorial Director • **SCOTT ALLIE** Executive Senior Editor • **CHRIS WARNER** Senior Books Editor • **CARY GRAZZINI** Director of Specialty Projects • **LIA RIBACCHI** Art Director • **VANESSA TODD** Director of Print Purchasing • **MATT DRYER** Director of Digital Art and Prepress • **MARK BERNARDI** Director of Digital Publishing • **SARAH ROBERTSON** Director of Product Sales • **MICHAEL GOMBOS** Director of International Publishing and Licensing